HANDBOOK
OF
INTERPERSONAL
COMMUNICATION

SECOND EDITION

HANDBOOK
OF
INTERPERSONAL
COMMUNICATION

SECOND EDITION

edited by

Mark L. Knapp
Gerald R. Miller

SAGE Publications
International Educational and Professional Publisher
Thousand Oaks   London   New Delhi

For information address:

 SAGE Publications, Inc.
2455 Teller Road
Thousand Oaks, California 91320

SAGE Publications Ltd.
6 Bonhill Street
London EC2A 4PU
United Kingdom

SAGE Publications India Pvt. Ltd.
M-32 Market
Greater Kailash I
New Delhi 110 048 India

Printed in the United States of America

Library of Congress Cataloging-in-Publication Data

Main entry under title:

Handbook of interpersonal communication / edited by Mark L. Knapp,
Gerald R. Miller.—2nd ed.
    p.   cm.
  Includes bibliographical references and indexes.
  ISBN 0-8039-4806-9
  1. Interpersonal communication. I. Knapp, Mark L. II. Miller,
Gerald R.
  BF637.C45H287 1994
  302.2—dc20   94-1177

94 95 96 97 98 10 9 8 7 6 5 4 3 2 1

Sage Production Editor: Astrid Virding

Gerald R. Miller
1932-1993

For your passion as a scholar,
your devotion to the field of communication,
your inspiration as a teacher,
your conversational wit and wisdom,
and the sheer joy of having known you

This book is lovingly dedicated to you

*Mark, Kelly, Art, Scott, Bob, Mac, Howie, Rick, Mike, Scott,
Judee, Jürgen, Leslie, Carol, Joe, Teri, Garth, Steve, Mary Anne,
Diane, Dave, Jim, Renee, Sandra, John, Brant, Chuck, Fred,
Teri, Kathy, Daena, Peggy, Lynn*

Contents

PART I

Basic Issues
and Approaches

1

Background and Current Trends
in the Study of Interpersonal Communication

Mark L. Knapp

Gerald R. Miller

Kelly Fudge

THE FIRST EDITION of the *Handbook of Interpersonal Communication* was published in the mid-1980s. It was a time when the number of scholars studying interpersonal communication and the volume of research on the topic were mounting rapidly. It was also a time when the literature on any topic related to interpersonal communication was spread across journals from a wide variety of academic disciplines. It seemed to be the right time to bring together under one cover the major theories and findings. Each chapter, written by an expert in that area, assessed where we had been, what we knew, what we didn't know, what we needed to know, and where we should be going. Like any major undertaking of this sort, it was not without flaws. Nevertheless, it became an important reference work for graduate students and faculty interested in the study of interpersonal communication.

Now, 9 years later, the authors are reassembled to reexamine their earlier writing and assess what theory and research from the first edition stood the test of time and what didn't, what new work needed to be included, and what constituted the new agenda for future work in their particular area of study in interpersonal communication. In addition to this "updating" of chapters from the previous edition, three new chapters are included: Chapter 8, "Culture, Meaning, and Interpersonal Communication," Chapter 11, "Supportive Communication," and Chapter 18, "Interpersonal Communication and Health Care." These chapters represent areas of central concern for understanding interpersonal processes and areas that have experienced rapid growth during the years since the first edition. Ideally, we might have included a chapter on technologically mediated interpersonal communication and one that examined the varieties of interpersonal communication throughout the life span. Certainly, both of these areas are of increasing interest to interpersonal scholars.

The organization of this *Handbook* is similar to that of the first edition. The first three chapters open up some of the key theoretical and methodological issues facing those who study interpersonal communication. The next five chapters focus on component parts of the process—verbal and nonverbal behavior, situational and cultural influence, and the characteristics each communicator brings to the encounter. The seven chapters in Part III focus on mutual influence and temporal processes as well as several functions of interpersonal processes such as social support, affect, influence, and power. Following these chapters, it seems appropriate to ask the question: What is interpersonal competence? Chapter 15 tackles that difficult issue. The final chapters examine interpersonal processes in four important and familiar relational contexts—coworkers, physicians and their patients, family members, and other social/personal relationships.

The rest of this introductory chapter is designed to set the stage for the book by (a) giving a brief historical perspective to the current study of interpersonal communication, (b) speculating on the trends that may have a strong influence on future studies of interpersonal communication, (c) looking at the term *interpersonal communication* itself, and (d) setting forth in capsule form the conceptual themes we see represented throughout the book.

Historical Highlights

In far more extensive historical accounts, other communication scholars have situated the study of interpersonal communication within the larger field of communication (Delia, 1987) and as a focus of study within speech communication (Rawlins, 1985). The history sketched here makes no pretense of documenting all the important authors and streams of thought that are in some way tied to current approaches to interpersonal communication. Instead, we have selected what we think are important contributions from the wide variety of disciplines and interdisciplinary thinkers in this area. As we will note later, it was not until the 1960s that interpersonal communication per se began to bloom profusely in the United States. As the following shows, there was a great deal of pioneering work that preceded that period.

Early twentieth century. In the early 1900s, Georg Simmel was making astute observations about interpersonal communication that are still debated today—such as "reciprocal knowledge," "characteristics of the dyad," interaction "rituals," "secrecy," "lies and truth," and "types of social relationships" (Simmel, 1950).

The 1920s and 1930s. Many intellectual seeds for the study of interpersonal communication were sown during this period. Elton Mayo and his colleagues at the Harvard Business School were uncovering the potential power of social interaction and social relationships in the work setting. These studies at the Western Electric Hawthorne plant raised important questions about supervisor-employee interaction as well as the role of peer interactions on productivity. This "human relations" movement set in motion subsequent thinking about the nature of supportive communication, openness, and the effects of showing concern for another's needs during interaction (Roethlisberger & Dickson, 1939).

The origins of "group dynamics" are recounted elsewhere (Cartwright & Zander, 1960; Hare, Borgatta, & Bales, 1955), but interpersonal studies owe much to this line of work that was in its infancy in the 1930s. Topics such as cooperation/competition, feedback, conflict, interaction sequences, methods for coding responses, sociometric choices, and social networks are all areas of shared interest for group and interpersonal scholars. The study of children's interaction during the 1930s also provided insights into systematic observation methods as well as identifying patterns of interaction such as cooperation and dominance (Murphy, Murphy, & Newcomb, 1937). It was the analysis of children's interaction during this period that also revealed the crucial process of role-taking (Piaget, 1926).

The belief that the self emerges out of one's interaction with significant others provided the foundation for the intellectual movement known as "symbolic interactionism" (Blumer, 1969; Mead, 1934). With the recognition that the way we respond to symbols affects the development of our selves and the nature of the society we live in, the 1930s also spawned the general semantics movement, which asked us to scrutinize closely our responses to symbols. Korzybski's *Science and Sanity* (1933) put forth the principles of general semantics, but books like Hayakawa's *Language in Action* (1939) were responsible for disseminating such ideas to the general public. Through examples of everyday experiences, the principles of general semantics continue to play an important role in textbooks devoted to improving one's interpersonal communication skills.

The 1940s and 1950s. Eliot Chapple (1953, 1970) believed that the matching of interaction rhythms led to an impression of harmony whereas mismatching signaled discord—regardless of the content. Intensity, timing, and patterns of temporal organization were all elements elicited through the use of his "standardized interview" (meaning one interviewer's behavior was predictable) and recorded by his "interaction chronograph." Interaction rhythm was, according to Chapple, central to understanding everyday competence in interpersonal communication as well as psychopathology.

In the field of psychiatry, the shift from an intrapersonal orientation to an interpersonal one was largely due to the lectures and writing of psychiatrist Harry Stack Sullivan (Chapman, 1976). Adult schizophrenia, Sullivan believed, was rooted in problematic interpersonal relations during childhood and adolescence. Another psychiatrist, Jurgen Ruesch, teamed up with anthropologist Gregory Bateson on a book that also explicated the role of communication in mental illness as well as issues of cultural organization (1951). Ruesch later cowrote the first book to use the term *nonverbal communication* in its title (Ruesch & Kees, 1956). Bateson's work was later to be the foundation for one of the most influential works to interpersonal scholars of the 1960s, *Pragmatics of Human Communication* (Watzlawick, Beavin, & Jackson, 1967).

Anthropologists Ray Birdwhistell (1952) and Edward T. Hall (1959) were interested in the total process of communication, but their pioneering efforts and observations of body movement, gestures, postures, and the use of space laid the groundwork for the area of study called "nonverbal communication"—predominantly examined as interpersonal behavior.

In the late 1950s, psychologist Fritz Heider's book, *The Psychology of Interpersonal Relations* (1958), helped launch a line of research on attribution theory that is integral to the study of interpersonal communication today. The 1950s concluded with the first of many influential books by sociologist Erving Goffman (1959,

1963), whose influence on the study of interpersonal communication has been enormous. Goffman's in-depth and provocative insights about the organization of social behavior and the important role played by seemingly mundane behaviors stimulated an interest in interpersonal life across the social sciences.

The 1960s, 1970s, and 1980s. Despite the wealth of ideas and writings during the decades preceding the 1960s, the blossoming of interpersonal communication as an academically identifiable area of study was primarily the result of societal forces. The social turmoil accompanying the civil rights movement and our subsequent involvement in Vietnam triggered in many citizens, particularly the young and idealistic, a deep-seated aversion to the manipulative and deceitful aspects of many mass media messages. An emerging concern for self-development and personal awareness gave rise to such face-to-face communicative activities as sensitivity training and consciousness-raising groups. Attacks on the traditional public and mass communication orientations of most communication scholars emphasized the importance of interpersonal communication to personal authentication. The integrity of our personal relationships, proclaimed the critics, rather than the persuasive wiles of media messages crafted by Madison Avenue hucksters and political consultants, shapes the daily quality of our lives. Referring to the field of speech communication, Delia (1987) contends that the events that transpired in the 1960s made interpersonal communication "the field's core research area" (p. 84) and that this has significantly influenced the field since. Buley, Petronio, Hecht, and Alberts (1993) underscore and extend this observation by stating, "Today, interpersonal communication is one of the largest areas within the field of communication" (p. 3).

Given the prevailing climate in the 1960s, it is hardly surprising that a book such as *Pragmatics of Human Communication* (Watzlawick et al., 1967), which exerted a profound effect on the subsequent study of interpersonal communication, had nothing to say about the ways communication can be used to extract money or concessions from others but offered considerable advice about the ways people can think about and perform their communicative activities so as to improve their personal relationships with marital partners and close friends. In a similar vein, Barnlund's (1968) anthology of theoretical and empirical papers, which stimulated interest in interpersonal communication among persons in speech communication and communication departments, focused on factors influencing the origination, development, and maintenance of interpersonal relationships. Argyle's (1969) review of research on "social interaction" and his resulting "social skills model" maintained a similar orientation.

Other manifestations of this heightened interest in interpersonal communication are readily identifiable. The burgeoning number of college and university courses covering aspects of interpersonal communication and interpersonal relations was accompanied by a spate of textbooks dealing with these topics—for example, Giffin and Patton (1971), Keltner (1970), and McCroskey, Larson, and Knapp (1971). Formal establishment of areas of emphasis in scholarly and professional associations of the communication disciplines, such as the Interpersonal and Small Group Interaction Interest Group of the Speech Communication Association and the Interpersonal Communication Division in the International Communication Association, signaled accelerating interest in the teaching and study of interpersonal communication processes. Convention programs dealing with aspects of interpersonal communication became the rule rather than the exception. One of these programs, held at the 1976 meeting of the International Communication Association in West

Berlin, Germany, spawned two state-of-the-art papers later published in the association's journal, *Human Communication Research* (Bochner, 1978; Miller, 1978). Evidence that interpersonal communication had become an important dimension of graduate education was provided by the convening of two national Doctoral Honors Seminars sponsored by the Speech Communication Association, one at Michigan State University and the other at Northwestern University.

Thus, by the late 1970s, the study of interpersonal communication had established itself as a major area of study along with mass communication in the United States. This was not the case in Europe, Asia, and South America. Even today, interpersonal communication outside the United States is likely to be housed within psychology, sociology, or anthropology and to have a different identifying label.

Interpersonal communication during the 1980s was characterized by a number of fresh theoretical perspectives. The coordinated management of meaning (Cronen, Pearce, & Harris, 1982; Pearce, 1976), uncertainty reduction (Berger & Bradac, 1982); contructivism (Delia, O'Keefe, & O'Keefe, 1982), dialectical theory (Baxter, 1988; Rawlins, 1983), and expectancy violations (Burgoon, 1983) were some theories that exerted an important influence during this time.

The bywords of the 1980s were *relationships* and *messages*. For some, the term *relationship* was a synonym for the *process* designated by the phrase *interpersonal communication*; for others, a relationship was one context (usually personal relationships) for studying interpersonal communication. The focus on messages (which included the cognitive processes *and* the spoken or written products) assumed a special importance for those who believed this was where communication scholars could make a special contribution to an understanding of interpersonal transactions.

The late 1980s and early 1990s seemed to be characterized by a tendency to embrace a variety of approaches to the study of interpersonal communication (e.g., quantitative and qualitative, micro and macro) and to face difficult questions about what we know and how we know it.

The Future

There are at least four well-established social and/or academic trends that are likely to have a distinct impact on future studies of interpersonal communication. These include an increasing attention to technology, culture, and biology. They also encompass a continuing concern for an "applied" perspective.

The widespread availability of technology for communicating is bound to play an important role in the way interpersonal transactions are thought of and manifested. Interactive video, virtual reality, computer bulletin boards, portable and video phones (among other technological changes) forecast an interpersonal world that is potentially very different than the current one. Interpersonal studies also have a history of being by and large culture and socioeconomic-class specific. In the future, it is reasonable to expect more interpersonal research questions that cut across cultural, class, and international boundaries. With some isolated exceptions, interpersonal studies have not explored the biological foundations of behavior. The central and guiding premise has been almost exclusively a "learned" perspective. We are not likely to see the study of interpersonal communication handed over to the geneticists. We may, however, find social scientists and humanists paying more attention to the growing body of work by geneticists that addresses issues of behavior and exploring avenues for possible integration.

Applied scholarship in interpersonal communication has a long tradition, but the resurgence of interest in the 1980s remains strong enough to suggest this trend may continue. The central question seems to be this: What do we/can we/should we take from our knowledge of interpersonal communication for application to the problems of everyday life? Assessment, accountability, and policy—long the practical province of larger and more formal systems—may become increasingly a concern for those who study interpersonal communication as well.

The Handbook of What?

What is interpersonal communication? Obviously, a large number of scholars collectively identify with and use the term *interpersonal communication* to describe their own work. These scholars also recognize, though, that there is considerable variety in how their colleagues conceptually and operationally define this area of study. In some respects, the construct of interpersonal communication is like the phenomenon it represents—that is, dynamic and changing. Thus attempts at specifying exactly what interpersonal communication *is* and *isn't* are often frustrating and fall short of consensus.

Bochner (1989) is probably correct in suggesting that the most we can expect interpersonal scholars to agree to is that they're studying "at least two communicators; intentionally orienting toward each other; as both subject and object; whose actions embody each other's perspectives both toward self and toward other" (p. 336). Cappella (1987), employing what he called definitional minimalism, said: "If interpersonal communication has any essential feature, it is that persons influence one another's behavior over and above that attributed to normal baselines of action" (p. 228).

Some of the key definitional issues that garner less consensus include the number of communicators involved, the physical proximity of the communicators, the nature of the interaction units used to explain an encounter, and the degree of formality and structure attending the interactants' relationship. In an effort to distinguish interpersonal studies from group, organizational, or mass communication, the number of communicators was commonly designated as two. However, two-person interactions may be extensions of larger networks; the parties may have membership in a larger group and their conversation is subject to the structures and norms of that group. In short, the assumption that the influence taking place in two-person transactions is entirely due to the behavior of those two persons is open to question. Another common practice, also open to question, is the practice of gathering data about a particular two-person interaction or two-person interactions in general by asking *individuals* to provide the data. Another assumption, made by some, is that interpersonal communication involves "face-to-face" interaction in which the communicators are in close physical proximity. Nevertheless, interactions mediated by telephones, computers, and other technology are also a part of the literature on interpersonal communication. There are interpersonal scholars, for example, whose research focuses on "long distance relationships."

The nature of the interaction units used as a basis for describing and explaining interpersonal transactions varies considerably among those who study interpersonal communication. Miller and Steinberg (1975) argued that the degree of "interpersonalness" in a relationship is determined by the kind of information participants use to make predictions about message exchanges. The more idiosyncratic, personal, and psychological information is considered "more interpersonal," and sociological or cultural information is considered "less interpersonal" or even "impersonal." Interactions where communicator roles are key and where sociological and cultural information is central are, however, very much a part of the literature of interpersonal communication. Furthermore, there are those who limit themselves to what are observable units while others do not; single message units satisfy some while others require sequences of messages; naturally occurring talk is crucial to some while anticipated behavior or imagined interactions are good enough for others to analyze. Using published research as an indicator, we still do not agree on whether it is important to examine nonverbal as well as verbal behavior or whether both parties to the interaction have to speak. Finally, it has been customary for interpersonal communication studies to focus on informal and unstructured interactions. But physician-patient interactions (Chapter 18) and supervisor-employee interactions (Chapter 16), job interviews, and other role-oriented exchanges are clearly a part of this literature.

The remaining part of this chapter deals with the conceptual perspectives and themes that seem to crop up repeatedly in these chapters. In addition, each issue is characterized by multiple conceptualizations, thereby creating a corpus of issues that are likely to be constant concerns to those who study interpersonal communication.

Conceptual Perspectives and Themes

The Interaction Process

Most students of interpersonal communication believe it is accurately thought of as a process—an ongoing, ever-changing event. Understanding the communication process, then, is largely a matter of understanding what happens over a given period of time.

Despite the belief that interpersonal communication is best studied as a process, it is not a consistent perspective manifested in our research. Philosophically, one might argue that process, by definition, is not something we can ever "capture" in our studies. Once we have identified a unit of interaction for study, the argument goes, we no longer "have" process. A less extreme position assumes we can learn about process by making multiple observations at multiple points in time over a given time span. In this view, an understanding of mutual adaptation in interpersonal communication can be achieved by observing moment-to-moment changes during interactive events. Kendon (1970), for example, using a filmed record, described moment-to-moment changes in movement, eye gaze, and speech during the flow of interaction; Gottman (1979) made some important discoveries about marital interaction from analyses of sequential exchanges between happy and unhappy couples; Cappella and Planalp (1981) analyzed a continuous audio record of informal conversation for moment-to-moment changes in vocalizations and pauses produced by both interactants; and Jacobs (Chapter 6) describes the work of several scholars who have examined the sequential nature and effects of dialogue in conversation.

Our studies of process, as Werner and Baxter point out in Chapter 9, will have to account for a variety of temporal characteristics. From both speaker and listener perspectives, it will be important to know how often a behavior occurs during a given period of time, what order or sequence characterizes the behavior under study, how long the behavior lasts when it occurs, and the rhythm, pacing, or "timing" of the behavior relative to co-occurring behaviors. Each of these temporal qualities occurs and can be analyzed at four levels: a specific utterance, a specific conversation (see Chapter 6), during the course of a relationship (see Chapter 17), during the course of a lifetime (see Chapter 16). The study of time and timing in interpersonal transactions should also provide us with a much better understanding of how to behaviorally distinguish developmental phases common to many experiences, such as accomplishing a goal for the first time, reestablishing the goal state, maintaining the goal state in the absence of threat, or maintaining the goal state in the presence of threat.

Persistent and guiding questions for any efforts directed at studying interaction as a process include the following: (a) If change is a constant, how should we conceptualize and operationalize periods of stability and periods of transition? (b) How much change is change and from whose perspective? (c) If we can't examine all aspects of the interaction process, how do we explain the potential changes in the system brought about by the units we choose not to examine?

A Focus on Behavior

A strong and persistent theme throughout this volume concerns the value of describing and analyzing naturally occurring overt verbal and nonverbal behavior. Our current focus represents a return to the rich tradition of systematic observations of behavior represented by scholars such as Birdwhistell, Goffman, Scheflen, Ruesch, and Bateson. This is in contrast to the once predominant method of gathering data about interpersonal communication, which was the self-report questionnaire and/or scale. These inventories were easily administered to large numbers of respondents and were intended to provide a foundation for broad-based generalizations about interpersonal communication.

Although some research programs continue to rely heavily on self-report data, more and more researchers are questioning the adequacy of knowledge about communication behavior based solely on self-report data. Can people accurately recall or predict some aspects of their interpersonal communication behavior, for example, their touching behavior? Have we developed a body of knowledge that is limited to what people *think* they would do? Isn't there a need to supplement or seek validation of self-reports with observations of actual interaction behavior? Is it enough to know the attitudes, opinions, and perceptions of *one* interaction partner often removed from any interaction context? How will the preferences expressed on the questionnaire manifest themselves in the presence of another person or persons governed by various situational constraints?

To address such questions, an expanding cadre of communication scholars has chosen to focus on manifest behavior. Of interest, these efforts both have provided an important supplement to our understanding of interpersonal communication and have pointed out some inadequacies when we focus *exclusively* on overt behavior. Even though we still have much to learn from the study of overt behavior, it is already clear that, first, what transpires during interpersonal transactions is more than mere responses to manifest signals. Communicator expectations, fantasies, plans, and the like may provide the basis for response; behaviors *not* shown by the interaction partner may provide the basis for response; behaviors shown in previous interactions (with and not with the current partner) may guide and direct subsequent reactions. Ironically, then, our examination of overt behavior has shown us the necessity of obtaining self-report data. Unlike many past efforts, however, these self-descriptions are much more likely to be anchored by a specific context. In like manner, the study of behavior within the confines of a two-person transaction has made it clear that, to understand dyadic behavior, we need to extend our analyses beyond the dyad. Interpersonal behavior will be more fully understood as we extend the boundaries of analysis to include the social networks impinging on the two communicators, rules and constraints imposed by social and institutional cultures, interaction history, and so forth. Second, what transpires behaviorally during interpersonal transactions is often extremely subtle and complex—involving behavioral configurations amenable to multiple interpretations, multiple intensities, and multiple degrees of consistency.

Another perspective associated with the focus on behavior is the gradual merging of verbal and nonverbal observations. Interpersonal communication scholars probably recognized the vital contributions of proxemic, kinesic, olfactory, vocal, and verbal signals for understanding interpersonal communication, but the early emphasis was clearly on verbal behavior.

As the number of scholars studying nonverbal behavior increased, a separate area of study developed. The study of verbal behavior and the study of nonverbal behavior appeared, for practical purposes, to be independent of one another. Researchers who studied facial expressions, eye gaze, or proxemics commonly did not spend much time analyzing co-occurring verbal behavior, and researchers who describe themselves as discourse or conversation analysts commonly did not claim expertise with nonverbal phenomena. We can learn much by tapping the depths of verbal and nonverbal behaviors separately, but we will learn more about interpersonal communication when the interaction of both systems forms the basis for analysis, as is the case with some analyses of turn-taking and lying behavior.

As we learn more about analyzing verbal and nonverbal signals, there will probably be fewer studies that simply sum the frequency of several behaviors and more that address the interdependence and coordination of behavior. When we have reached that point, our current preoccupation with the question of whether verbal or nonverbal behavior is more important should be moot. Studying the interrelationships of verbal and nonverbal behavior in social interaction will also demand more attention to how these signals are perceived. We do not observe all those signals made available to us, nor do we process all that we do perceive in the same way. Some of these questions about the perception of signals require an understanding of the perceiver and the signal interpretation process, but describing the nature of the signals themselves is also an integral part of understanding the process. There is much to learn about the impact of signals and combinations of signals that is related to their intensity, relevance, and location.

Our focus on behavior has also shifted from laboratory settings for observation to naturally occurring contexts. Once more popular than today, the study of communicative behavior in controlled laboratory settings attempted to discover the bases for predicting interpersonal behavior. Although behavior was the focus in the early experimental studies, the validity of the findings for naturally occurring interactive events was often challenged. For instance, some charged that we did not have enough descriptive information about how normal interaction proceeded to manipulate it realistically. As a result, it was argued, research participants were asked to react to unusual and sometimes extreme stimuli. Further, critics believed that a person's responses to an interaction partner who was unable to respond (presented in slides or on audiotape), who was unwilling to respond (a "neutral" confederate), or who inflexibly responded (programmed to respond only in certain ways) did not elicit typical interaction behavior from the research participants. Even a fundamental tenet of experimental research requiring some components of the interaction situation to be "kept constant" while others are manipulated seemed to run counter to the prevailing theoretical belief that constancy is not characteristic of ongoing interaction. As a result of these and other challenges, it became increasingly apparent that it was necessary to find out more about the structure and operation of interpersonal behavior in naturally occurring situations. Data from these observations could, if desired, be used to construct laboratory conditions that more closely approximate naturally occurring interactions.

The observation of behavior outside the laboratory context seems to have underlined the importance and the impact of context on behavior and to have given us a renewed appreciation for the difficulty in predicting behavior across different contexts. We also seem more aware of the need to measure the sequencing and quality of responses as well as the quantity.

Context

Bateson (1978) said, "Without context, words and actions have no meaning at all" (p. 15). This assertion about the critical dependence of communication on context for the generation of meanings is likely to garner substantial agreement among interpersonal scholars and practitioners. Contextual information is considered crucial for "thick descriptions" (Geertz, 1973) of communication events. An examination of retrospective contexts (all actions that precede a particular behavior that might help interpret that behavior) and emergent contexts (all events that follow the behavior that might help in interpreting the behavior) adds further depth of understanding to the interpersonal episodes.

Context has been considered in many diverse ways: (a) as broad areas defining the field of communication (interpersonal communication and so on); (b) as social settings (e.g., cocktail parties) and institutional settings (e.g., schools, prisons); (c) as types of relationships and roles (e.g., task, social, and family); (d) as objects or characteristics of the environment; and (e) as message variables (e.g., language style, affect displays preceding and subsequent to text). Therefore context may encompass psychological, behavioral, and environmental perspectives.

Given the diversity of perspectives on the nature of context, the multiplicity of methods for studying context is not surprising. For contemporary schema theorists (Brown & Yule, 1983), general contextual information leads the investigator to examine patterns in linguistic organization, while linguistic and other contextual cues mobilize the search for particular schematic patterns. Ethnomethodologists describe context in terms of the reflexivity of language understanding (Leiter, 1980). Linguistic utterances are taken as prompts to the overall pattern of meaning, and that pattern operates as a context within which the utterances make sense (see Chapter 6). Yet, for uncertainty reduction theorists, context is a source of information (Berger, 1987) and an object of uncertainty. Likewise, attribution theorists and expectancy violation theorists consider context to be a source of information for evaluating the other's behavior (see Chapters 7 and 15). A key source of difference in these perspectives concerns the interrelationship of context and communication. Is context so much a part of the communication process that it is distorted when considered apart from the process? As Duck and Pittman state (Chapter 17), communication is embedded in context. Or is it one of the many external and isolated sources of influence on message selection and interpretation?

Minimally, we need to consider the extent to which our research contexts (however conceptualized) match the contexts to which we apply our findings and the extent to which we can learn more about contexts (however conceptualized) by studying them directly. Furthermore, interpersonal researchers need to specify how and why context affects communication, for, as Rawlins (1987) states, people and messages both transform and are transformed by context.

Social Cognition

In one way or another, each chapter in this book addresses the role of human thought processes as they interface with interpersonal transactions. The study of interpersonal communication has, from the beginning, recognized the important reciprocal relationship between thought and overt behavior; but in recent years we have greatly advanced our understanding of this area—largely because some scholars in communication and social psychology have made this their sole focus of investigation. The work in this area can be subdivided into two nonexclusive categories: understanding the interrelationships of social cognition and social behavior and understanding the formation and organization of social cognition.

Virtually any thought about any aspect of our experience has the potential to affect behavior in any given encounter. However, the thoughts that are likely to have the most relevance for communicative events are thoughts about the nature of human interaction itself. Usually the thoughts about self, other, and situation are the designated units for investigation. Information representing thought is usually gathered before and/or after encounters, rarely during them. In the past, some researchers ignored perceptual information from actual interactants, relying instead on the reactions of large groups of uninvolved observers as a basis for understanding the overt and covert behavior of interactants.

Thoughts that influence behavior may be relatively abstract ("Friends are people who stick by you when the going gets tough") or concrete ("Mary is a person who would probably turn me in for taking a pencil home from the office"). Similarly, more abstract thoughts of what kind of people we are and more concrete thoughts about what kind of people we are as communicators or as a communicator with *this* person in *this* situation may influence the manifested behavior. Situations, too, are thought of in general ways and as a specific communication context. Researchers often focus on a single unit of analysis; for example, studies of others include impression formation, attribution theory, or perspective-taking; studies of communicator cognition include work on self-consciousness, self-awareness, self-monitoring, and communicative apprehension; situational cognitions are fully reviewed in Chapter 5. We are just beginning to undertake the more complex job of studying the influence of combined self/other/situation thoughts on behavior. If it were merely a matter of determining how thoughts influence behavior, the task would be easier but less representative of what seems to actually happen. Thoughts affect behavior, and behavior, in turn, reshapes the memory of the original thought(s) as well as ensuing thoughts. If the process of gathering information for research purposes is thought of as a communicative process, our understanding of social cognition will continue to affect our methods of research too—as it already has (see Chapters 2 and 3).

As part of the effort to understand how social thoughts and social behavior were interrelated, it became clear that we needed to know more about how people form, organize, and interpret information germane to human interaction. These processes are discussed throughout this volume as attitudes, expectations, inferences, scripts, schemas, fantasies, rules, and wishful thinking. The study of how we form and organize our social thoughts has reemphasized the multilevel process involved in interpreting and/or assigning meaning to behavioral signals. Any given signal or sequence of signals may be taken at any one or combination of at least five levels: (a) the literal message content, (b) a response to how the partner's preceding response was interpreted, (c) an indicator of how the partner should respond to a message, (d) an indicator of how one feels about oneself or partner as a person, and/or (e) whether further interaction (now or later) is desired.

Consciousness and Intent

Throughout this book, readers repeatedly will be confronted with issues bearing on consciousness and intent. Communication scholars periodically acknowledge the importance of those issues, but a variety of perspectives continue to permeate the literature. For many, intentionality is criterial for defining communication (Bowers & Bradac, 1984).

From one perspective, the central question is the extent to which communicators "know what they're doing" or, in the case of recalled experiences, the extent to which they "know what they did." Consciousness is a prerequisite for communicating. Much of the work on persuasion and compliance gaining, for example, rests on the belief that communicators identify their goals, analyze their targets and situations, and select strategies calculated to maximize their desired outcomes. Research programs reported in a number of chapters in this book highlight this focus on control and planned social influence with the treatment in Chapters 14 and 15 being lengthy and explicit. In contrast, ritualistic communication acts, spontaneous displays of emotion, various actions related to the management and structure of conversation, and habitual patterns of interaction occurring in long-term relationships suggest a very low (or absent) level of awareness and planning. Again, this perspective is implicitly or explicitly manifested in a number of different chapters with Chapter 10 providing an extended discussion.

Theoretically, there seems to be agreement on some fundamental issues concerning consciousness and intent, such as (a) that there are multiple levels and degrees of consciousness involved in communicating, (b) that more than one intention can occur during a communicative act, (c) that consciousness and intent can change during the act of communicating, and (d) that communicators may be aware of a general goal and unaware of some specific intentions for reaching that goal (Stamp & Knapp, 1990). Nevertheless, the assumptions underlying our research often seem to assume a far less complex process. For example, the truism that we don't always "say what we mean or mean what we say" has not been much of a driving force for research in interpersonal communication to date.

The question of what is going on in the mind of a communicator is of little relevance to those who believe attributions of intent are what really matter in human transactions. In this view, observable behavior is what counts. Planning and consciousness are assessed behaviorally and perceptions of effort, persistence, emphasis, and situational expectations are used as representative criteria for assessing intent.

Despite the long-standing interest in the subject of intentions and the widespread belief that interaction is best conceived of as a process, relatively little work has been directed at how communicators negotiate intentions. From this perspective, neither the nature of the cognitive activity nor the perceptions of a person's behavior gives us the information necessary for understanding intentions in everyday communicative life. Intent from this perspective is a jointly constructed product.

Meaning

How do we conceptualize meaning in interpersonal transactions? How is meaning created? Is meaning something that can be "located" in a particular place? Answers to these questions permeate our research—usually as undiscussed but guiding assumptions. In theory development, though, the centrality and importance of meaning requires more explicit treatment. Symbolic interactionists, among others, believe things have no meaning apart from our interaction with others. In this sense, then, the way we think about meaning in interaction is inseparable from the way we view human understanding and action.

The meanings of meaning among scholars concerned with human interaction, while diverse, are not wholly incompatible. Grossberg (1982) uncovered three predominant perspectives among communication scholars: (a) those who viewed meanings as entities that can be exchanged, (b) those who viewed meanings as emergent products shared by the interactants, and (c) those who viewed meanings as the environment through which life is experienced. Littlejohn (1989) concluded his review of various theoretical contributions to communication study by identifying three major approaches to meaning: structural, interactional, and cognitive. The attempt to "locate" meaning in space and time and the attempt to specify how meaning emerges seem to be the goals shared among these different approaches.

To those who think of meaning as infused in the totality of the environment through which life is experienced, the idea of "locating" the site of meaning must seem like a strange task indeed. Nevertheless, there are those who locate meaning in the text or message itself, those who subscribe to "finding" meaning in the process of interaction, and those who pinpoint meaning in the confines of the brain. Beliefs about how meaning emerges are—not surprising—dependent on how one thinks about the site of meaning. For some, it is important to focus on the supposed inherent properties associated with signs and their referents; for others, it is the structure and sequencing of messages that trumpet meaning; still others combine various textual aspects with interpreter decisions; cultural and interactional rules pave the way to meaning for some; others believe the key to unlocking meaning is found in the negotiated process involved in developing shared interpretations; but it is the way information is mentally processed that brings meaning to life for others. Littlejohn (1989) offers the following as a way of bridging some of these divergent perspectives. Meaning, he says, is probably best thought of as "an outcome of the interplay between the structure of the message, the use of the message in actual situated interaction, and the mental process necessary to manage information and make interpretation" (p. 381).

As the interpersonal communication literature is not shy about praising the value of shared experiences and shared understandings, we would like to underline what others have said: that the concept of "sharing" itself is a construct that is subject to considerable variation. Daily discourse is replete with incongruent, ambiguous, and incomplete messages. And it is quite likely that interactants are able to effectively coordinate their behavior without much shared meaning (Cronen et al., 1982; Pearce, 1976). Bochner (1989) hints that, when sharing does occur, it may not be so much a sharing of meanings associated with a specific interaction as it is a sharing of beliefs about interactions in general and our mutual contributions thereto: "The 'real' world of interpersonal communication is only partially a shared one in which a sense of sharing is the product of mechanisms of control over meanings as well as the mutual faith in a shared social world" (p. 338).

Individual Differences

Contemporary students of communication differ on the explanatory value of individual difference variables. Whereas some researchers believe these variables contribute vitally to our understanding of communication processes, others view their contribution as relatively trivial. Despite this lack of consensus, individual difference variables continue to strongly influence our thinking about interpersonal communication, as these *Handbook* chapters amply illustrate.

Particularly appealing are those individual difference variables that seem to be logically yoked to a specific conception of interpersonal communication or to a set of theoretical propositions about interpersonal communication processes. To illustrate, consider the personality or trait characteristic of *self-monitoring* (Snyder, 1974, 1979). High and low self-monitors differ in their sensitivity to social cues as well as their ability to adjust their behaviors to conform with situational exigencies and expectations. More specifically, high self-monitors are sensitive to variations in situations and adjust their behavior accordingly. Conversely, low self-monitors approach situations consistently and project a relatively consistent "self" from one situation to the next. Thus Elliott (1979) found that high self-monitors were more highly motivated to obtain information that might aid them in communicating effectively with another. In addition, when compared with their low self-monitoring counterparts, high self-monitors were more successful in convincing others that they subscribed to a particular attitudinal position, whether or not their espoused attitudes accurately mirrored their actual ones. Stated differently, high self-monitors both told the truth and deceived more persuasively than did low self-monitors.

Clearly, these differences are relevant to many of the issues examined in the following chapters. Miller, Cody, and McLaughlin (Chapter 5) consider how self-monitoring influences situational preferences, citing research that demonstrates sharply varying views concerning desirable situational characteristics. Given their sensitivity to cues, high self-monitors would be expected to excel at selecting appropriate control strategies and at communicating control-oriented messages effectively (Chapter 14), an expectation confirmed by the Elliott study cited above. Finally, though not explored extensively by Parks, relationships between level of self-monitoring and the conception of communicative competence he develops in Chapter 15 are readily apparent.

Similar analyses can be offered for such personality variables as *communication apprehension* (Daly & McCroskey, 1984) and *Machiavellianism* (Christie & Geis, 1970). Parks (Chapter 15) devotes considerable attention to the theoretical and empirical links between communication apprehension, learned helplessness, and perceptions of interpersonal competence. Machiavellianism is particularly relevant to issues of interpersonal control because high Machiavellians are prone to treat people as objects and are likely to see successful control as an end in itself. They are relatively unconstrained in their selection of control strategies (Chapter 14). By contrast, low Machiavellians would be expected to be more sensitive to the ethical implications of using antisocial or deceptive strategies.

The three traits we have alluded to thus far are best thought of as organismic variables, that is, they signify dispositional states existing (or at least postulated as existing) within communicators and *mediating* symbolic and nonsymbolic responses to symbolic and nonsymbolic stimuli. In addition, individual behavioral differences exert an impact on many of the interpersonal processes discussed in these chapters. To mention but one example, Giles and Street (Chapter 4) detail numerous speech behaviors, such as dialect, rate, and fluency, that influence perceptions of such communicator characteristics as competence and sociability. Although most of the research dealing with these communicative behaviors has involved judgments of relative strangers, the findings have the potential to contribute to our understanding of the development of interpersonal relationships.

We conclude our discussion of this theme by reemphasizing the fact that most individual difference variables discussed in these chapters are linked logically to other constructs and propositions of interest to the authors. In general, indiscriminate correlation of large batteries of individual difference measures with other communication variables, without reasonable a priori grounds for anticipating particular relationships, has proved to be a scientific dead end. Students of interpersonal communication can probably employ individual difference variables to increase explanatory and predictive power, but only if such variables fit conceptually into a broader theoretical context.

A Perspective on Perspectives

Interpersonal scholarship contains both the manifest content of its research findings and a latent content of ideological assumptions (Lannamann, 1991). While we have spent considerable time performing self-critiques of our methodology and our research findings, we have focused far less attention on an examination of our ideological assumptions. Some have argued that interpersonal scholars have been slower to engage in this process of questioning our ideological assumptions than have scholars in other subareas of communication (Leeds-Hurwitz, 1992). In fact, Bochner (Chapter 2) asserts that interpersonal communication scholars have generally ignored the moral, ideological, and narrative knowledge attendant to their subject matter.

Lannamann (1991) believes that an understanding of the role of ideology in interpersonal communication is necessary to avoid the perils of reifying cultural practices and legitimizing current social orders through our research findings. "Ideology," says Lannamann, "is effective; it frames the struggle over which meanings are naturalized as common sense" (p. 182). Fitzpatrick (1993) concurs that an examination of our ideologies is called for and that much insight into personal and social relationships may be gained by incorporating interpretive and cultural perspectives. Further, an examination of our ideological assumptions helps protect interpersonal studies from a single, orthodox position that constrains or stifles new ideas and innovative approaches (Bochner, Chapter 2).

Parks (1982) addresses this issue directly and demonstrates how the ideology of intimacy (individuals are on an unending quest for closeness) defined the research agenda for many interpersonal scholars, thus resulting in the devaluation of other phenomena for study. Other ideologies, many of which are only implicit in the research, also frame our research endeavors. For instance, the ideology of control (persons desire and are driven to regulate others and their environment) steers researchers to search for and label communicative behaviors as manipulative, influencing, compliance gaining, or persuading (Miller & Knapp, 1985). Perhaps less common historically but no less influenced by ideological assumptions, feminist studies are directed by the beliefs that gender is a pervasive category for understanding human experience in general and interpersonal communication in particular and that the prevailing gender assumptions of society should be challenged.

Ultimately, questions directed at our ideological assumptions will also prompt us to reflect on our assumptions about how we go about determining what we know and don't know and how we search for answers to puzzling aspects of interpersonal communication. Currently, poststructuralists and postmodernists are challenging the core ideological assumptions of social science (Bochner, Chapter 2). The critics maintain that the dominance of facts over meanings and values is a practical issue rather than an ontological one; research need not be restricted to prediction and control. Accordingly, a meaning-centered approach to interpersonal studies calls for a breaking of the norms that have equated distance and disengagement with objectivity, that have favored universals over particulars, that have made standardized criteria for making judgments the sole province of rationality, and that have relegated history and context to factors which need to be "controlled." Fitzpatrick (1993) believes in a discovery process that maintains a social dimension and simultaneously maintains a "scientific" foundation. By rejecting a scientific approach completely, she argues, scholars are unable to specify how to judge among competing claims; however, by rejecting a more interpretive approach, the broader social issues of theory may be missed and social structures perpetuated (Fitzpatrick, 1993). Bochner (Chapter 2) suggests that other research practices—whether they aim to predict, interpret, criticize, change, or create—represent different discursive strategies that are useful modes of description for certain purposes. Thus a singularly "correct" perspective, he argues, does not exist because natural events and processes lend themselves to a multiplicity of descriptions depending on one's point of view.

References

Argyle, M. (1969). *Social interaction*. New York: Lieber-Atherton.

Barnlund, D. C. (1968). *Interpersonal communication: Survey and studies*. Boston: Houghton Mifflin.

Bateson, G. (1978). *Mind and nature: A necessary unity*. New York: E. P. Dutton.

Baxter, L. A. (1988). A dialectic perspective on communication strategies in relationship development. In S. W. Duck (Ed.), *A handbook of personal relationships* (pp. 257-273). New York: Wiley.

Berger, C. R. (1987). Communicating under uncertainty. In M. E. Roloff & C. R. Berger (Eds.), *Interpersonal processes: New directions in communication research*. Newbury Park, CA: Sage.

Berger, C. R., & Bradac, J. J. (1982). *Language and social knowledge: Uncertainty in interpersonal relations*. London: Edward Arnold.

Birdwhistell, R. L. (1952). *Introduction to kinesics: An annotation system for analysis of body motion and gesture*. Washington, DC: Foreign Service Institute, U.S. Department of State/Ann Arbor, MI: University Microfilms.

Blumer, H. (1969). *Symbolic interactionism: Perspective and method*. Englewood Cliffs, NJ: Prentice-Hall.

Bochner, A. P. (1978). On taking ourselves seriously: An analysis of some persistent problems and promising directions in interpersonal research. *Human Communication Research, 4*, 179-191.

Bochner, A. P. (1989). Interpersonal communication. In E. Barnouw, G. Gerbner, W. Schramm, T. L. Worth, & L. Gross (Eds.), *International encyclopedia of communications* (pp. 336-340). New York: Oxford University Press.

Bowers, J. W., & Bradac, J. J. (1984). Contemporary problems in human communication theory. In C. C. Arnold & J. W. Bowers (Eds.), *Handbook of rhetorical and communication theory* (pp. 871-893). Boston: Allyn & Bacon.

Brown, G., & Yule, G. (1983). *Discourse analysis*. Cambridge, MA: Cambridge University Press.

Buley, J., Petronio, S., Hecht, M., & Alberts, J. K. (1993). Interpersonal communication theory. In S. Petronio, J. K. Alberts, M. L. Hecht, & J. Buley (Eds.), *Contemporary perspectives on interpersonal communication* (pp. 3-17). Dubuque, IA: William C. Brown/Benchmark.

Burgoon, J. K. (1983). Nonverbal violations of expectations. In J. M. Wiemann & R. P. Harrison (Eds.), *Nonverbal interaction* (pp. 77-111). Beverly Hills, CA: Sage.

Cappella, J. N. (1987). Interpersonal communication: Definitions and fundamental questions. In C. R. Berger & S. H. Chaffee (Eds.), *Handbook of communication science* (pp. 184-238). Newbury Park, CA: Sage.

Cappella, J. N., & Planalp, S. (1981). Talk and silence sequences in informal conversations III: Interspeaker influence. *Human Communication Research, 7*, 117-132.

Cartwright, D., & Zander, A. (Eds.). (1960). *Group dynamics: Research and theory*. Evanston, IL: Row, Peterson.

Chapman, A. H. (1976). *Harry Stack Sullivan: His life and his work*. New York: Putnam.

Chapple, E. D. (1953). The standard experimental (stress) interview as used in interaction chronograph investigations. *Human Organizations, 12*, 23-32.

Chapple, E. D. (1970). *Culture and biological man: Explorations in behavioral anthropology*. New York: Holt, Rinehart & Winston.

Christie, R., & Geis, F. L. (1970). *Studies in Machiavellianism*. New York: Academic Press.

Cronen, V., Pearce, W. B., & Harris, L. (1982). The coordinated management of meaning. In F. E. X. Dance (Ed.), *Human communication theory: Comparative essays* (pp. 61-89). New York: Harper & Row.

Daly, J. A., & McCroskey, J. C. (Eds.). (1984). *Avoiding communication: Shyness, reticence and communication apprehension*. Beverly Hills, CA: Sage.

Delia, J. G. (1987). Communication research: A history. In C. R. Berger & S. H. Chaffee (Eds.), *Handbook of communication science* (pp. 20-98). Newbury Park, CA: Sage.

Delia, J. G., O'Keefe, B. J., & O'Keefe, D. J. (1982). The constructivist approach to communication. In F. E. X. Dance (Ed.), *Human communication theory: Comparative essays* (pp. 147-191). New York: Harper & Row.

Elliott, G. C. (1979). Some effects of deception and level of self-monitoring on planning and reaction to a self-presentation. *Journal of Personality and Social Psychology, 37*, 1282-1292.

Fitzpatrick, M. A. (1993). Communication in the new world of relationships. *Journal of Communication, 43*(3), 119-126.

Geertz, C. (1973). *The interpretation of cultures*. New York: Basic Books.

Giffin, K., & Patton, B. R. (1971). *Fundamentals of interpersonal communication*. New York: Harper & Row.

Goffman, E. (1959). *The presentation of self in everyday life*. Garden City, NY: Anchor.

Goffman, E. (1963). *Behavior in public places*. New York: Free Press.

Gottman, J. M. (1979). *Marital interaction: Experimental investigations*. New York: Academic Press.

Grossberg, L. (1982). Does communication theory need intersubjectivity? Toward an immanent philosophy of interpersonal relations. In M. Burgoon (Ed.), *Communication yearbook 6* (pp. 171-205). Beverly Hills, CA: Sage.

Hall, E. T. (1959). *The silent language*. Garden City, NY: Doubleday.

Hare, A. P., Borgatta, E. F., & Bales, R. F. (Eds.). (1955). *Small groups: Studies in social interaction*. New York: Knopf.

Hayakawa, S. I. (1939). *Language in action*. New York: Harcourt Brace Jovanovich. (Published in 1941 as *Language in thought and action*)

Heider, F. (1958). *The psychology of interpersonal relations*. New York: Wiley.

Keltner, J. W. (1970). *Interpersonal speech-communication: Elements and structures*. Belmont, CA: Wadsworth.

Kendon, A. (1970). Movement coordination in social interaction: Some examples described. *Acta Psychologia, 32*, 100-125.

Korzybski, A. (1933). *Science and sanity: An introduction to non-Aristotelian systems and general semantics*. Lancaster, PA: Science Press Printing Co.

Lannamann, J. W. (1991). Interpersonal communication research as ideological practice. *Communication Theory, 1*(3), 179-203.

Leeds-Hurwitz, W. (1992). Forum introduction: Social approaches to interpersonal communication. *Communication Theory, 2*(3), 131-139.

Leiter, K. (1980). *A primer on ethnomethodology*. New York: Oxford University Press.

Littlejohn, S. (1989). *Theories of human communication* (3rd ed.). Belmont, CA: Wadsworth.

McCroskey, J. C., Larson, C., & Knapp, M. L. (1971). *An introduction to interpersonal communication*. Englewood Cliffs, NJ: Prentice-Hall.

Mead, G. H. (1934). *Mind, self, and society*. Chicago: University of Chicago Press.

Miller, G. R. (1978). The current status of theory and research in interpersonal communication. *Human Communication Research, 4,* 164-178.

Miller, G. R., & Knapp, M. L. (1985). Introduction: Background and current trends in the study of interpersonal communication. In M. L. Knapp & G. R. Miller (Eds.), *Handbook of interpersonal communication*. Beverly Hills, CA: Sage.

Miller, G. R., & Steinberg, M. (1975). *Between people: A new analysis of interpersonal communication*. Chicago: Science Research Associates.

Murphy, G., Murphy, L. B., & Newcomb, T. M. (1937). *Experimental social psychology*. New York: Harper & Row.

Parks, M. (1982). Ideology in interpersonal communication: Off the couch and into the world. In M. Burgoon (Ed.), *Communication yearbook 5* (pp. 78-108). New Brunswick, NJ: Transaction.

Pearce, W. B. (1976). The coordinated management of meaning: A rules-based theory of interpersonal communication. In G. R. Miller (Ed.), *Explorations in interpersonal communication* (pp. 17-35). Beverly Hills, CA: Sage.

Piaget, J. (1926). *Language and thought of the child* (M. Gabain, Trans.). London: Routledge & Kegan Paul.

Rawlins, W. K. (1983). Negotiating close friendships: The dialectic of conjunctive freedoms. *Human Communication Research, 9,* 255-266.

Rawlins, W. K. (1985). Stalking interpersonal communication effectiveness: Social, individual, or situational integration? In T. W. Benson (Ed.), *Speech communication in the 20th century* (pp. 109-129). Carbondale: Southern Illinois University Press.

Rawlins, W. K. (1987). Gregory Bateson and the composition of human communication. *Research in Language and Social Interaction, 20,* 53-77.

Roethlisberger, F. J., & Dickson, W. J. (1939). *Management and the worker*. Cambridge, MA: Harvard University Press.

Ruesch, J., & Bateson, G. (1951). *Communication: The social matrix of psychiatry*. New York: Norton.

Ruesch, J., & Kees, W. (1956). *Nonverbal communication: Notes on the visual perception of human relations*. Los Angeles: University of California Press.

Simmel, G. (1950). *The sociology of Georg Simmel* (K. H. Wolff, Trans. and Ed.). New York: Free Press.

Snyder, M. (1974). Self-monitoring of expressive behavior. *Journal of Personality and Social Psychology, 30,* 526-537.

Snyder, M. (1979). Self-monitoring processes. In L. Berkowitz (Ed.), *Advances in experimental social psychology* (Vol. 12, pp. 85-128). New York: Academic Press.

Stamp, G. H., & Knapp, M. L. (1990). The construct of intent in interpersonal communication. *Quarterly Journal of Speech, 76,* 282-299.

Watzlawick, P., Beavin, J. H., & Jackson, D. D. (1967). *Pragmatics of human communication*. New York: Norton.

2

Perspectives on Inquiry II: *Theories and Stories*

Arthur P. Bochner

THESE ARE TROUBLING TIMES for the social sciences. Postmodernist and poststructuralist writers have challenged and deconstructed some of our most venerable notions about scientific knowledge and truth (Denzin, 1992; Dickens & Fontana, 1991; Foucault, 1970; Lyotard, 1984; Rorty, 1979; Rosenau, 1992). Their ideas raise serious doubts about the appropriateness and usefulness of rigid disciplinary boundaries that separate the humanities, social sciences, natural sciences, and arts (B. Gregory, 1988; D. Gregory & Walford, 1989; Rorty, 1982); about the dismissal of intuition, emotion, and myth (Ellis, 1991; Graff, 1979; May, 1991); about uncritical commitment to the rhetoric of rigor and objectivity (Agger, 1989; K. Gergen, 1982); and about the core values and ideological commitments of the social sciences (Foucault, 1980; Sampson, 1978).

These also are exciting times for the social sciences. The "crisis of confidence" inspired by postmodernism introduced new and abundant opportunities to reform social science and reconceive the objectives and forms of our work. Triggered by a more critical attitude about the ways in which language mediates how people experience and explain the world they live in, scholars are beginning to consider what social sciences would become if they were closer to literature than to physics, if they privileged stories rather than theories, and if they were self-consciously value-centered rather than pretending to be value-free (Coles, 1989; Richardson, 1990; Rorty, 1982; Sarbin, 1986).

To see social science as continuous with literature is to grant the legitimacy of narrative modes of scholarship that show what it means to live in a world mediated by the contingencies of using language and fashioning an identity, making it possible for us to consider people who have been ignored, forgotten, neglected, or misunderstood as "one of us" (Rorty, 1982, p. 203). Social scientists committed to this endeavor understand their goal as the moral one of enlarging and deepening a sense of community, human solidarity replacing objective knowledge as the principal purpose of research (Rorty, 1991a). They echo Rorty's (1982) sentiments that "what we hope for from social scientists is that they will act as interpreters for those with whom we are not sure how to talk. This is the same thing we hope for from our poets and dramatists and novelists" (p. 202).

Traditionally, interpersonal communication as a field of study has ignored or scorned the notion that its subject matter includes moral, ideological, or narrative knowledge. Like other academic disciplines emerging in the twentieth century, communication wanted a place at the trough of academic respectability, and that meant being true to science was more important than being true to the phenomena of joint action (Shotter, 1987). Consequently, the research vocabulary of interpersonal communication became primarily a scientific jargon that emphasizes "facts," "regularities," "causal conditions," "impacts," "behavioral observations," "prediction," and "control." Indeed, "control" has been largely accepted as the basic problematic of interpersonal communication (Bochner, 1984; Bochner, Cissna, & Garko, 1991).

My goal in this chapter is to broaden the range and scope of research on interpersonal communication. I want to bring the study of local narratives that display how people do things together in the process of "making meanings" into a more central and legitimated position in this field. I believe these goals can be achieved by positioning interpersonal communication as a field of study that bridges sciences and humanities and by putting human sense-making on a par with data analysis.

To reach the goal of a wider understanding and deeper appreciation for "cases," "instances," and "stories" that focus on personal, emotional, and contingent lived experiences, students of interpersonal communication must begin to confront openly and self-critically some of the most deeply entrenched and taken-for-granted assumptions and conventions of the academy, such as the need for "theory" (Berger, 1992) and the exalted importance of concepts and categories. The move to a "meaning-centered" focus also will require us to break the hold of certain disciplinary norms in communication, social psychology, and sociology that equate distance and detachment with objectivity, rationality with standardized criteria for making judgments, and that idealize the importance of universals over particulars, stability over change, routines over improvisations, graphs over stories, and the ahistorical over the contingent.

I offer this chapter as a corrective to the domination of "facts" over "meanings" and "values." I want to protect the study of interpersonal communication against the danger of allowing a single, orthodox perspective to constrain or suppress opportunities to introduce new ideas and innovative approaches to research. Beginning in graduate school, our conception of what to study, how to do research, and what forms of writing and reporting research will be acceptable are regulated by orthodox professional standards. Our careers depend to a large degree on how well our socialization takes, which means, operationally, how well we have been groomed to engage in the expected research experiences and to compose the expected texts (Rose, 1990). What we teach and what we learn is, to put it bluntly, a great deal of conformity (Krieger, 1991). Success in an academic career hinges on the ability to publish articles, books, or monographs in genres that, as Dan Rose says (1990), "resemble, or at least address in a conforming way, the literature cited in the ones that preceded them. If you write a nonconforming text, then the rewards of the discipline may be withheld because the book does not read as a legitimated contribution to knowledge" (p. 14).

Whither Meanings and Values

In the first edition of the *Handbook of Interpersonal Communication* (Knapp & Miller, 1985), I discussed the advantages of a pragmatist orientation to inquiry that replaces the concept of "truth" with the concept of "usefulness." In light of the deconstruction and decline of the theory of knowledge underlying scientific method—objectivity, falsification, separation of fact from theory, and linear progress (Davidson, 1984; Feyerabend, 1976; K. Gergen, 1982; Kuhn, 1962, 1977; Lyotard, 1984; Polanyi, 1962, 1966; Rorty, 1979), I suggested that researchers could now be liberated to shape their work in terms of its necessities instead of "received" ideas about what we must do to be upstanding scientists (Geertz, 1980). Following Richard Rorty's version of pragmatism (1982), I argued that research on interpersonal communication should be judged according to its practical value rather than its correspondence with reality (Bochner, 1985).

Pragmatism offers a perspective that focuses on the connection between purpose and mode of description. It starts with the question, "What do we want to do (with human beings)?" and then considers the modes of description that are useful for our purposes. Interpersonal communication is a domain of inquiry that must deal not only with "facts" but also with "meanings" and "values." On many occasions and under many different circumstances, we find it useful to be able to predict and control the outcome of prospective actions we may enact, but that is not the only thing we want to accomplish. Often we want to make sense of our communicative encounters and episodes with other people, to make them part of a coherent story of our lives, to understand and interpret what has or is happening, and to attach meanings to our actions and the actions of others (Ellis & Bochner, 1992). Moreover, at times we want to contest, engage, and/or change the ideals, rules, or values that are taken for granted when we enact routines of interpersonal interaction (Lannamann, 1991). All three of these goals—*prediction, interpretation*, and *criticism*—fall within the boundaries of a human science of interpersonal communication. They should not be construed, however, as competing modes of research that match objectivity against subjectivity, quantitative against qualitative methods, rationality against emotivism, or science against humanities. They simply reflect preferences for taking different points of view toward our subject matter: interpersonal communication.

The first edition of this book showed, however, that most research programs in the field promote a monolithic perspective on interpersonal communication. With the exception of one chapter that specifically compared perspectives on inquiry (Bochner, 1985), the volume contained only one reference to interpretive approaches to research and none to critical perspectives. Moreover, the only discussion of qualitative methods focused primarily on the scientific inadequacies of such methods with special attention given to the "limited," "subjective," and "naive[ly] depictive stance" of qualitative techniques (Poole & McPhee, 1985). Indeed, the impression given by the vast array of topics, themes, and research programs reviewed in the *Handbook* is that there really is only one point of view to be taken toward the study of interpersonal communication—a scientific perspective. On the whole, the *Handbook* characterizes interpersonal communication as a domain of research that seeks prediction and control by applying the conventional practices of scientific research and embodying the lofty virtues of objectivity, detachment, theory building, and generalization.

The dominance of "facts" over "meanings" and "values" is a practical, not an ontological, issue. There is nothing about the "nature" of interpersonal communication that makes it necessary to confine research to the goals of prediction and control. Nor is there any reason to believe that putting the tag "science" on research somehow makes it more significant, important, or useful. Human beings as communicators are not more authentically or realistically described in a neutral, detached, and "objective" scientific vocabulary than in any other vocabulary. One can only say that a vocabulary useful for the purposes of predicting may not be useful for other purposes, such as deciding what to do (Rorty, 1982). Often we face situations in which we need to decide what to do or say in order to live a life in which we "do the right thing" (Coles, 1989). These practical concerns provoke our interest in understanding the intricate challenges of interpersonal communication. In human sciences like interpersonal communication, knowledge that is worth having often is knowledge that widens our sense of community, deepens our capacity to empathize with people who are different than we are, and enlarges our capacity to cope with complicated contingencies of lived interpersonal experience. If we were able to see these as appropriate goals for academic research, we would not find a narrative and anecdotal style of writing and representing interactive experiences— a focus on meanings and values—so objectionable or threatening (Bostrom & Donohew, 1992).

Indeed, it may be instructive to ask why research on interpersonal communication should conform to a model of theory (Berger, 1991, 1992) or a "philosophy of science" (Burleson, 1992) that makes its task the "description" of objects when communication is not an object, nor a discipline studying objects, but consists of sequences of interactions and the activity of studying them (Bochner & Waugh, in press). Most orthodox empiricist research has been based on conceptions of messages that do not take into account interactive practices by which humans communicate by speech. Many years ago, Gregory Bateson (1972) showed that multiple levels of abstraction are involved even in the simplest communicative acts, and thus there is no such thing as a simple message. To interpret one message, we must rely on other messages that qualify, modify, or frame its meaning(s)—"without context there is no communication" (Bateson, 1972, p. 402). Yet it is just these metacommunicative aspects of the communication situation that orthodox conceptions of "theory" render unimportant or irrelevant.

Obstacles

Two obstacles stand in the way of reforming traditional research practices and legitimating optional modes of scholarship on interpersonal communication. The first obstacle is the reluctance to change the way we think about reality. On the whole, social scientists still tend to think of reality as something to get in touch with. Social science has not yet rid itself of traditional conceptions of reality that make the purpose of inquiry to know the world as it is, independent of human participation in it. Most research on interpersonal communication has been premised on the assumption that scientific method provides a means for "receiving knowledge," that is, procedures for objectively describing the "real" world in a manner that removes the knower or experiencer (see especially Bostrom & Donohew, 1992). This goal is thought to be accomplished by mandating that the investigator be positioned as morally neutral, detached, and disinterested, a spectator in the game of knowledge (Dewey, 1960). These "objectifying" procedures are buttressed by a traditional idea of theory, where theory attempts to describe in neutral and value-free terms what is already inscribed in mind or nature—what the world necessarily causes us to believe (if only we can apply the right methods)—and largely neglects the question of how meaning is performed and negotiated by speakers and interpreters (including interactions between investigators and "subjects").

As philosophers of history, language, and science from Thomas Kuhn to Donald Davidson have emphasized (Davidson, 1984, 1986; Derrida, 1981; Kuhn, 1962, 1977; Rorty, 1979; Sellars, 1963), however, "language does not give form or structure to the world, nor is it a medium linking nature to the mind; rather it is a part of actions and events in the world, a part of our actions and behavior, a matter of getting around in the world" (Bochner & Waugh, in press). The rub is that language activity mediates all attempts to represent reality; the world does not exist in the shape of the sentences we write when we theorize about it. What we come to say about the world involves the indistinguishable provocations of the world—what is out there—and the mediations of language by which we make claims about it. The notion of a "neutral language" that results from the observer's independence from what is being described—he or she is an observer of, not a participant in it—cannot be sustained. As Maturana (1991) writes:

> Since the observer cannot make any cognitive statement about anything independent of his or her operation as a living system, the notion of nature constitutively can refer only to what the observer does (in language) as a human being explaining his or her experiences as such, and, hence, it cannot refer to anything deemed independent of what the observer does. (p. 44)

As it turns out, science is positioned within, not above, historical and linguistic processes (Clifford & Marcus, 1986). And, as Rorty concludes (1982), "Objects are not 'more objectively' described in any vocabulary than in any other" (p. 203).

When Thomas Kuhn (1962, 1977) showed that the match between the ontology of a theory and its correspondence to a reality in nature was "illusive in principle," he was saying that the history of science could offer no warrant for thinking it is possible to distinguish unequivocally between what is in our minds and what is "out there" in the world (Kuhn, 1977). One of the lessons we should have learned from Kuhn was not to expect so much from science and to guard against being smug about pushing the rhetoric of objectivity and value neutrality. *The problem is not with science* but with a reverent and idealized view of science that elevates it above the contingencies of language and outside the circle of historical and cultural interests. Scientific method, per se, does not make it possible for the mind to transcend the skin (Shweder, 1986). What we are left with, then, is ourselves, the institutions we have constructed and developed, one of which is science. Science as an institution cannot achieve the ideal of objectivity but, as an institution, science has and can continue to exhibit the solidarity that makes it useful (Bochner & Waugh, in press; Rorty, 1991a).

If accounts and descriptions of objects are never completely independent of the accounter or describer, then writing and reading scientific (and literary) texts are activities contingent on language, rhetoric, power, gender, and history (Richardson, 1990). No set of procedures can remove the intrusions of the individual knower in order to "reflect" or "mirror" nature in some unmediated manner. Knowledge inevitably involves "attaching significance" by interpreting (Steedman, 1991).

The resistance of mainstream social science to reconstituting the traditional concept of "reality" is not hard to understand. To move away from the idea of a detached observer using neutral language to produce an unmediated mirroring of reality and toward the idea that all attempts to speak for, write about, or represent other people's lives are partial, situated, and mediated would radically reframe the issues about which research on interpersonal communication is concerned and the projects to which we are committed. Our research practices, then, would have to be understood as activities that inevitably create value and inscribe meanings and we would not hesitate to acknowledge that the texts we craft are "a site of moral responsibility" (Richardson, 1990, p. 36).

One of the main reasons for this resistance is the desire to cling to traditional distinctions between the objectivity of methods and the utility of narratives. "Telling" as a scholarly activity and mode of description has remained secondary to "knowing" (Rorty, 1989). As a result, the questions "How do you know?" or "What methods do you use?" have been regarded, in principle, as the first questions to ask about inquiry. When descriptions of the social world are viewed necessarily as involving a translation of knowing about something into telling about it, then the question that needs to be asked is not "How do you know?" but "Why do you talk that way?" Because the world of communication is not a world that speaks for itself, all attempts to represent this world must involve transforming a speechless reality into a discursive form that makes sense. We speak for the world; it does not speak for itself. And "where there are no sentences, there is no truth" (Rorty, 1989, p. 5). To the extent that descriptions of the social world thus involve translating *"knowing* into *telling,"* they may be viewed as narratives (White, 1980).

No matter how scientific we think we are being, our "descriptions" of interpersonal life end up as stories that interpret, construct, or assign meaning and value to the patterns of relating we have "observed." As Maines (1993) suggests, "All social science data are already interpreted data; the uninterpreted datum does not exist" (p. 22). Social scientists thus may be viewed principally as narrators, "spinners of professional tales we call 'theories' " (Maines, 1992, p. 32; also see Davis, 1974).

Inquiry aimed at prediction and control thus becomes only *one* among several optional ways of talking about reality and helping people cope with the mysteries, ambiguities, and strangeness of lived experiences. Research practices, whether they are aimed at predicting, interpreting, criticizing, changing, or creating, should be seen simply as different discursive strategies that are potentially useful modes of description *for certain purposes.*

The second obstacle to transforming orthodoxies of social science is the insistence on establishing enduring criteria to arbitrate or eliminate conflicting judgments. Faced with making judgments about the "significance" of interpretive scholarship, mainstream journal editors and referees often find themselves in a quandary. Do they use the standards of "rigor," "falsifiability," and "hypothesis-testing" that have been established to judge the merits of a "scientific" argument, though the purposes of interpretive research are directed toward "meanings" rather than "facts," "readings" rather than "observations," and "interpretations" rather than "findings"? If some other standards must be applied, what are those standards? Are such standards arbitrary or capricious? Can we specify what will count as a rigorous argument or a significant contribution to "knowledge"? The issue of criteria becomes especially complicated when it is assumed: First, there are always alternate and multiple interpretations of "meanings"; second, the researcher is not positioned as detached, neutral, and uninvolved; and, third, an author's authority over the "meaning" of a research text is secondary to a reader's, whose subjectively constructed meanings contribute significantly to a two-sided process of communication by which meanings of a text are created (Ellis, in press; Suleiman & Crosman, 1980).

Critics of interpretive social science worry that serious, rational, and objective scientific inquiry will be turned into relativism, solipsism, or cynicism unless a rigorous algorithm exists for deciding how to judge the significance of a case or a narrative (e.g., Bostrom & Donohew, 1992). They appeal to fears aroused by notions that in the absence of stringent criteria "anything will go" or "every interpretation will be as good as every other." On the surface, interpretive approaches seem to resist or elude systematic modes of evaluation. As Geertz (1973) observed, "You either grasp an interpretation or you do not, see the point of it or you do not, accept it or you do not" (p. 24). But those championing the cause of interpretive social science, including Geertz, do not hold the view that any interpretation is, in principle, as good as any other, or that an interpreter is free to make any claim without concern for what is reasonable to say or what will count as convincing. Fish (1982) argues that the persuasiveness of any interpretation rests ultimately on the degree to which it falls within the boundaries of a professional community's rules of argument or evidence:

> It is neither the case that interpretation is constrained by what is obviously and unproblematically "there," nor the case that interpreters, in the absence of such constraints, are free to read into a text whatever they like. . . . Interpreters are constrained by their tacit awareness of what is possible and not possible to do, what is and is not a reasonable thing to say, and what will and will not be heard as evidence in a given enterprise; and it is within those same constraints that they see and bring others to see the shape of the documents to whose interpretations they are committed. (p. 281)

If what we want to insist upon is agreement on propositions—the essence of a Galilean-based, predictive social science—then it makes sense to insist on reaching agreement beforehand on the criteria to which *all* arguments must appeal. But in a post-positivist community of social scientists, one in which the goal of inquiry becomes coping with reality rather than describing it accurately, where we understand that language cannot do the work of the eyes (Tyler, 1986), criteria are reconstrued in Rorty's (1982) terms "as temporary resting places constructed for specific utilitarian ends . . . a criterion . . . *is* a criterion because some social practice needs to block the road of inquiry, halt the regress of interpretations, in order to get something done" (p. xli).

The point is that all criteria—sample sizes, significance tests, statistical power estimates, and so on—refer to something we have established ourselves. No matter how "real" or "objective" they may seem to be, criteria are created by human beings in the course of evolving a set of practices to which we subsequently conform. Thus there is no standard of rationality or mode of rigorous argumentation that does not boil down to compliance with our own conventions (Rorty, 1982). Moreover, the whole issue of criteria ends up as little more than an attempt to reach for some source outside ourselves to arbitrate differences of opinion, protect against subjectivity, and ensure rationality. If we can see rationality as a process of achieving consensus and sustaining a conversation, rather than applying criteria and thwarting subjectivity—solidarity over objectivity—then we can dispose of the notion that we must judge new ideas and practices according to some preexisting, formally stipulated criteria and be content with saying "that the best way to find out what to believe is to listen to as many suggestions and arguments as you can" (Rorty, 1991a, p. 39).

Differences: Valid Theories/Lifelike Stories

In *The Call of Stories*, Robert Coles (1989) shares the tale of his tense and uncomfortable apprenticeship as a psychiatric resident at the Massachusetts General Hospital more than 30 years ago. Frightened by an awareness of his ignorance and inexperience in psychiatric practice, Coles recalls his nervousness as he contemplated what he would tell his supervisors, two senior psychoanalysts, about his feelings of "stupidity" and "inadequacy" in dealing with a "phobic patient." At their first meeting, one of his supervisors, Dr. Binger, suggested that Coles read more of the literature so that he would better understand "the nature of phobias," a teaching strategy that Coles retrospectively understood as an effort to build his confidence and mobilize his authority by putting him in possession of theoretical distinctions and conceptual knowledge. Dr. Binger was "a brilliant theorist," says Coles (1989, p. 5) and, whenever we were together, "I was ever fast to offer conceptualizations" that would help us formulate the case.

Coles's other supervisor, Dr. Ludwig, did more listening than talking. Compared with the other supervisor, Dr. Ludwig was "slow on the draw, perhaps over the hill," though as Coles put it, he did "get me going." Cupping his right ear with his right hand, Ludwig was determined to hear his young student out and urged Coles to speak up and talk louder. Coles initially sized him up as an affable old gent, a nice guy who became increasingly easy to converse with.

As time passed, Coles became aware that he wasn't getting very far with his "phobic" patient, but he did feel consoled by Dr. Binger, who would remind him that "phobics are hard to treat," though they could be a powerful source of knowledge about psychodynamics. Much to Coles's surprise, the low-keyed Dr. Ludwig was the one who inspired a turning point in his relationship with the "phobic" patient. Sensing his young student's disappointment and apprehension, Ludwig decided, on this day, to do more talking than listening. He told Coles a detailed and suspenseful story about a particular female patient of his who had been paralyzed by stifling worries and fears. Coles (1989) recalls being "quite taken up by listening, even forgetting for a long spell that this was a patient's 'clinical history' I was hearing . . . as I pictured her in my mind" (p. 6). The brief lecture that the elder Dr. Ludwig gave after his story stuck in Coles's mind for the rest of his psychiatric career: "The people who come to us bring us their stories. They hope they tell them well enough so that we understand the truth of their lives. They hope we know how to interpret their stories correctly. We have to remember that what we hear is *their story* (Coles, 1989, p. 7).

Coles had never thought of his patients as storytellers. He had learned that diagnosis was the really important activity of psychiatry. He had been taught to "get a fix" on the patient, determine what "factors" or "variables" were at work, and plan an intervention strategy accordingly. Professional maturity and competence had meant an ability to form abstractions, meticulously fitting a patient's symptoms to psychiatric theory, and not getting too involved. Conversely, Dr. Ludwig was saying: Understand, don't formulate; take an interest in the concrete details of life; don't bury them under psychiatric jargon; think of the life being expressed as a story to be respected not just data to be analyzed.

The lesson that Coles learned from Ludwig was not so much a criticism of diagnostic or evaluative procedures as it was a warning against the pitfalls of turning life mainly into categories and theories. He was being taught to ask what purposes theories serve and for whom. For many of us in the social sciences, Coles (1989, p. 20) concludes, all too often theory is used "as a badge of membership" or as "tokens of loyalty in the company of our colleagues." When Ludwig urged "more stories, less theory," he was trying to say that we shouldn't prematurely brush aside the particulars to get to the general. "What ought to be interesting, Dr. Ludwig kept insisting, is the unfolding of a lived life, rather than the confirmation such a chronicle provides for some theory" (p. 22).

As academics, most of us have developed a taste for theory as opposed to narrative. We think of theorizing about lives as our intellectual responsibility. We don't see storytelling as a viable option to theorizing. On the contrary, we tend to assume that theory substitutes for narrative, though, as Rorty (1991b) points out, "The attempt to find laws of history or essences of cultures—to substitute theory for narrative as an aid to understanding ourselves, others, and the options which we represent to one another—has been notoriously unfruitful" (p. 66).

Differences between a theory-directed and a story-centered field of inquiry correspond to differences between causal and interpretive approaches to research. On the whole, the causal orientation to the study of interpersonal communication is a restless search for enduring truths and universal generalizations (Berger & Calabrese, 1975; Berger & Chaffee, 1987; Cappella, 1987; Hewes & Planalp, 1987). Conversely, interpretive social science embraces the power of language to create and change the world, to make new and different things possible (Rabinow & Sullivan, 1987; Rorty, 1989; Taylor, 1971).

Causal social science emphasizes how we know about the world and tries to explain it; interpretive social science emphasizes how we talk about the world and tries to deal with it. The causal disposition champions a fixed external reality; the interpretive sees triumph over inherited or "received" versions of the world and its meanings as heroic. The causal vocabulary is a language of order, stability, routine, control, and destiny; the interpretive vocabulary emphasizes ambiguity, change, adventure, improvisation, and chance. The causal worldview fuels an appetite for abstraction, facts, and rigor. The interpretive worldview feeds a hunger for details, meanings, and peace of mind. The differences between causal and interpretive perspectives are real enough, but that is all they are—*differences*; as Rorty says (1982), only differences to be lived with, not issues to be resolved.

Can we live with these differences or must we vilify "the other" to validate and universalize our own preferences for the way to approach research? The main consequence of the philosophical change I have been promoting (Bochner, 1985) is to see ourselves as "intellectuals [who] tell enlightening stories to one another in an atmosphere of harmonious tolerance, instead of clobbering one another with arguments in a bombastic crusade for truth" (Gottlieb, 1991, p. 30). The causal and interpretive approaches do not compete with each other and should not be judged against the same standards of quality or significance. They merely express preferences to take a different point of view toward the subject matter of interpersonal communication. They seek different ends and employ different means to achieve them. Prediction and control do not compete against interpretation and understanding. Although I have used orthodox causal perspectives on the study of interpersonal communication as a reference point for justifying a broadened scope of inquiry, it has not been my intention to vilify the empiricist tradition.

J. Bruner (1986) considers narrative and logico-scientific "ways of knowing" to be two distinctively different but complementary ways of organizing experience and constructing reality. According to Bruner, the logico-scientific or "paradigmatic" mode emphasizes general causes, and uses standardized procedures to assure public verifiability and to reach empirical truths. The paradigmatic mode tests logically derived possibilities (hypotheses) against observables to reach formal conclusions about general causes, however tentative, that are warranted by the empirical evidence. Evidence is used to establish truthfulness.

Narratives also function as means of persuasion, but as Bruner (1986) observes, they are "fundamentally different: arguments convince one of their truth, stories of their lifelikeness" (p. 11). The storyteller is preoccupied with showing how lived experience is endowed with meaning. The result is not so much conclusive as it is believable. Stories invite us to enter horizons of the human condition where lived life is shown as comic, tragic, and absurd, and where endless opportunities exist to create a reality and live in it. "How to encompass in our minds the complexity of some lived moments in life?" asks Coles (1989, p. 128). "You don't do that with theories. You don't do that with a system of ideas. You do it with a story."

Narrative and Meaning

Interpretive social science refers to inquiry that attempts to move beyond objects to meanings and, in the process of grappling with meanings, to focus attention on values, thus affording an opportunity to recover and reclaim the moral importance and imagination of social science (Coles, 1989; Glassie, 1982). These reconfigured goals and assumptions of social inquiry move the study of human interaction to the borders of science and literature, where social science merges with humanities, where worn and unproductive distinctions between mind and body, reason and emotion, and object and subject can be dissolved (Rosaldo, 1989).

Narrative—the stories people tell about their lives—is both a means of "knowing" and a way of "telling" about the social world and communicative experience (Richardson, 1990). It is also a way of displaying the enactment of meanings—acts of self-creation. "The primary human mechanism for attaching meaning to human experiences," writes Brody (1987, p. 5), "is to tell stories about them." When we remember events that happened to us in our families or in our careers, and when we tell our colleagues, our children, lovers, or friends about them, we tell about the events in the form and language of stories: who did what to whom, where, when, and why. To have a self is to have a story and, usually, to want to tell your story to someone. As Richardson (1990) suggests, "Narrative is the best way to understand the human experience because it is the way humans understand their own lives" (p. 133). When we narrate our lives, we engage in what J. Bruner (1990) calls "acts of meaning."

Citing Dewey's (1948, p. 167) assertion that "action is always specific, concrete, individualized, unique," Kreiswirth (1992, p. 643) suggests that narrative draws attention to "the meaning of the daily detail." A concern with details of experience and the connections between narrative texts, the lives they represent, and a reader's participation in composing or co-constructing the meanings of a text are the features that most radically distinguish narrative social inquiry from more conventional approaches to social life (Ellis, in press). This is particularly the case when the narratives are autobiographies, life histories, diaries, memoirs, or biographies.

Rosenwald (1992) keenly observes that "life experience is larger and more ambiguous than any of its accounts . . . not only does the past live in the present, but it also appears different at every new turn that we take" (p. 275). Stories about lives are not to the point of being more or less "true" or "significant" than the living details to which they are responsive. Shaped by narrative practices, cultural understandings, and orientations to others, stories transform experience (Denzin, 1991; Derrida, 1978; Ellis, 1993b, in press; Ellis & Bochner, 1992). Rather, the point of a "storied life" is to pose a narrative "*challenge*" by confronting the record of a life, contemplating its possible meanings in order to extend them in an act of self-creation. "Satisfactory stories," Rosenwald (1992, p. 284) concludes, "excel through comprehensiveness" and coherence (Rosenwald, 1992, p. 284).

Thus we can judge a narrative, if judge we must, in terms of the consequences it produces—the new stories it arouses, the possibilities for reforming and reshaping a life it introduces. These consequences often precede rather than follow the story because they are enmeshed in the process of telling the life. Every narrator has a stake in her story; she is never indifferent. "The story of our lives becomes our lives," writes Adrienne Rich (1978, p. 34). Life stories are always "false," then, insofar as they contain both more and less than the life they depict. "Narrative truth" (Spence, 1982) thus should be seen as a developmental dialectic between the story and the life. It is the struggle to move life forward, "extinguishing the falseness" by becoming identical to the story, that consequently liberates the story's subject in an act of self-created meaning (Rosenwald, 1992). Anaïs Nin highlights this desire for self-created "narrative" meaning when she admits: "I could not live in any of the worlds offered to me. . . . I believe one writes because one has to create a world in which to live" (cited in Oakley, 1984; Ellis, in press).

In a narrative social science, the relationships among author, text, and reader are revised. The reader is repositioned away from being a passive "receiver" of knowledge and elevated to the status of coparticipant in the creation of meaning (Iser, 1978; Rosenau, 1992). The texts of narrative social science are more evocative than representational. An evocative text is a more demanding and interactive text because it assumes that readers will be active partners in dialogue with the text rather than "receivers" of unmediated knowledge. Recognizing the competing demands of communication and representation that can close down conversation and multiple interpretation (Tyler, 1986), a narrative social science drops the presumption of language as representation in order to forge a dialogue between writers and readers that emphasizes the collaborative dimensions of composing a life and its meanings (Ellis, 1993b, in press; Tyler, 1986). The participatory reality that narrative social science promotes is evocative and emergent, not representational and descriptive (Tyler, 1986). Coles (1989) captures the sense of evocation from a reader's point of view when he says, "The beauty of a good story is its openness—the way you or I or anyone reading can take it in, and use it for ourselves . . . there are many interpretations of a good story, and it isn't a question of which one is right or wrong but of what you do with what you've read" (p. 47).

Narrative Projects

In recent years, the interest in narrative among scholars in the human sciences has mushroomed. Several different disciplines have inaugurated new journals promoting the narrative study of lives (Josselson & Lieblich, 1993; McCabe, 1993) and an extensive corpus of books and monographs that reflect a shift from analytic to narrative modes of investigating and representing social life (e.g., Ellis, in press; Frank, 1991; Linden, 1993; Paget, 1993; Zola, 1982) have been published. Clearly, the turn toward narrative has a significant appeal to a wide audience across the human sciences. We can expect narrative approaches to research to increase their burgeoning role in the study of lives as investigators grapple with the importance of personal and emotional expression of lived experience, vanishing distinctions between subject and object and between data and interpretation, multiple and divergent layers of truth and rationalities, and lingering doubts about the rhetoric and reality of objective knowledge.

Space limitations preclude a comprehensive and thorough review of the literature on narrative and storytelling relevant to the study of interpersonal communication. A focus on social science as narratives has been advanced in sociology by Ellis (1993b, in press), Krieger (1984), Linden (1993), Maines (1992), Paget (1990, 1993), Richardson (1990, 1992), and Stone (1988); in psychology by J. Bruner (1986, 1990), Howard (1989, 1991), M. Gergen (1992), K. Gergen and M. Gergen (1983, 1986, 1988), M. Gergen and K. Gergen (1993), Josselson and Lieblich (1993), Mishler (1986), Parry (1991), Polkinghorne (1988), Rosenwald and Ochberg (1992), Sarbin (1986), Schafer (1992), Scheibe (1986), and Spence (1982); in anthropology by E. Bruner (1986), Clifford and Marcus (1986), Geertz (1973, 1980), Jackson (1989), Myerhoff (1978), Rosaldo (1989), Shweder (1986), Turner (1981), and Turner and Bruner (1986); in history by Carr (1986), De Certeau (1984), Hutcheon (1988), and White (1973, 1980); in economics by Klamer (1987) and McCloskey (1985, 1990); in medicine by Charon (1993), Coles (1989), and Kleinman (1989); and in communication by Bochner and Ellis (1992), Boje (1991), Conquergood (1991), Eisenberg and Goodall (1993), Fisher (1984), Goodall (1989), Neumann (1993), Norton (1989), Pacanowsky (1988), Rawlins (1991), and Secklin (1993), to name but a few. These and related works should be consulted for a more detailed introduction to narrative than can be provided here. As Maines (1993) suggests, this vast literature is highly interdisciplinary and promotes a tendency to blur genres that have traditionally divided sciences and humanities. Collectively, these works reveal that the human sciences have grown to "trust the tale" (Kreiswirth, 1992) and are now enmeshed in "narrative's moment" (Maines, 1993).

A narrative perspective focuses attention on the relationships between author and subject, on the expressive forms for making sense of lived experience and communicating it to others, on the entanglements that both separate and connect how interpersonal life is lived and how it is told to others, on the functions of stories and storytelling in creating and managing identity in a social world, and on the cultural narratives that circulate throughout our lives—the processes of "culture making" that silence minority voices and shape taken-for-granted assumptions that become scripted ways of acting. In this section I want to introduce five characteristics of a narrative perspective that should become central issues in the study of interpersonal communication.

(1) In a narrative perspective, writing about "others" is problematized and becomes a reflexive focal point for social research. How do the conventions and techniques of writing and doing research affect the products of the research process? In narrative research, one may assume a reflexive connection exists between the researcher's own life history and the stories of "subjects" or informants. The researcher's life history inevitably has an effect on the descriptions,

interpretations, and characterizations he or she tells about other persons and groups. Every depiction of an "other" necessarily implies a definition of self. As a result, in narrative studies, the researcher as a self is repositioned. Jackson (1989) claims that "our understanding of others can *only* proceed from within our own experience, and this experience involves our own personalities and histories as much as our field research" (p. 17). This means that the researcher is part of the "data." As Myerhoff (1978, p. 19) says, the others are "part of me, not *they*." Moreover, "when I judge these people," she writes (p. 28), "I judge myself." Neutrality thus gives way to what Victor Turner (1978, p. xvii) once called "compassionate objectivity," a commitment to enter a space where feelings merge with facts, and self *engages* others, in a quest to understand the forms through which we make our lives feel meaningful.

(2) In a narrative perspective, an autobiographical voice is encouraged and legitimated. Because the self is implicated in all narrative description, writing the "I" explicitly into research documents becomes acceptable—even necessary. The author's presence in the text should be seen, felt, and respected. Authorship is a responsibility fraught with moral and ethical dilemmas. If we are a part of our data, then we cannot ignore and should not hide the ways in which we precede from our own experiences, our own feelings and values, and our own life stories; and if, as von Foerster (1991) suggests, "we see ourselves through the eyes of the other," we ought to examine how we as researchers and as human beings are constructed by the others whose experiences we are trying to represent and by the cultural texts through which we are constructed as "others." This means that we should honor the first-person voice of others—our "subjects"—as well. Life histories, autobiographies, and first-person accounts often have as their purpose the humanizing objective of saying, in effect, "look what happened to me," instead of the orthodox, generalizing goal of suggesting "this will happen to you" (Frank, 1993). The power of autobiographical stories often rests on the degree to which they perform the dual function of being sufficiently unique to evoke comparisons and sufficiently universal to elicit identification. As Carolyn Ellis (in press) says in ending the tale of her intimate relationship with a significant other who was chronically ill:

> In writing my stories, I have not wanted to complain or call attention to the specialness of my personal disaster since I know from this experience, if from no other source, that there is nothing "exceptional" about my life or my tragedies. What I have hoped for is some companionship and comfort in my grief. . . . In return, I have wanted to offer comfort and "companionship in a common venture" (Mairs, 1993, p. 25) when your time for personal tragedy comes. (p. 348)

(3) In a narrative perspective, attention is focused on the ways in which narrative practices historically influence accounts of the past and future. Narrated experience is incomplete, situated, and partial. Conventions of writing, speaking, and performing our lives can function as a means to exclude optional voices and interpretations, and conceal ideological and moral commitments (Agger, 1989; White, 1980). The ways in which we narrate and perform our lives may also be subject to the significant influences of cultural forms of communication that circulate through life from birth to death. The images and meanings that flow through music, television, and cinema play a significant role in shaping the meanings and values we attach to romance, love, intimacy, and sexuality (Denzin,

1992). Some writers suggest that in our postmodern, video age we are voyeurs—watchers—adrift in a sea of visual and oral symbols that shape how we experience and talk about ourselves as men and women (Denzin, 1992; Poster, 1988). Our lives can become enactments of the soundtracks of our favorite music and the reels of our favorite films. Once we have received and integrated the meanings transmitted to us by these popular cultural forms, we begin to take them for granted. In this sense, many of the meanings we think we make and live may actually be chosen for us, not by us. Showing the ways in which the narrative forms of cinema, television, and popular music contribute to "culture making" (Carey, 1989) offers the critical possibilities of exposing the cultural plot and its narrative practices, and helping us understand how we learn to tell our lives in particular scripted ways that become woven into the fabric of our cognitive and emotional experience.

(4) In a narrative perspective, new and alternative forms for expressing and/or evoking lived experiences are explored. Investigators working from a narrative perspective are exploring alternative forms for representing experience in a "reader-" or "other-centered" way that encourages interactive and evocative participation. These forms include poetic representation (Kiesenger, 1992; Richardson, 1992); dramatic performance of personal narrative (Ellis & Bochner, 1992; Paget, 1993); first-person accounts (Broyard, 1992; Ellis, 1993b; Ernaux, 1991; Frank, 1991; Haskell, 1990; Lerner, 1978; Mairs, 1989; Murphy, 1987; Ronai, 1992, 1993; Zola, 1982); documentary, ethnographic, interactive film (Conquergood, 1985, 1990); photographic ethnography (Harper, 1982; Neumann, 1992); multivoiced, shared-narrative—twice-told tales (Butler & Rosenblum, 1991; Wolf, 1992; Yalom & Elkin, 1974); autobiographical short stories (Ellis, 1993a; Zola, 1982), true fiction (Roth, 1991), and co-constructed narrative (Bochner & Ellis, 1992; Ellis & Bochner, 1992).

(5) In a narrative perspective, the image we have of connections between writers and readers of social science texts is converted from neutral and distanced to participatory and involved. Texts of social science research are seen as necessarily selective, mediated, and open, encouraging dialogue, conversation, and inclusion of multiple voices. Narrative social science thus attempts to deepen an appreciation for evocative texts that concretize contingent lived experiences in a manner that encourages conversation among alternative voices and interpretations. The interactive, evocative, and participatory qualities of stories advance a narrative ethic that promotes the substitution of narrative and chance for contemplation and destiny (Rorty, 1991b).

Interpersonal Communication: Some Goals for Narrative Research

How can the study of interpersonal communication assimilate a narrative perspective? What would be the goals of narrative research on interpersonal communication? What would narrative research look like? First, narrative research on interpersonal communication would attempt to reproduce and highlight narrative practices of communication and joint action that are played out in the moment-to-moment contingencies of living *in* and *through* the open-ended processes of social life. One of the goals of narrative research is to construct multivoiced texts in which alternative voices and perspectives participate in expressing the meanings attached to the experiences being represented. Research attempts to simulate the narrative processes and procedures by which interactants co-construct the meanings of their experiences for themselves, as well as for others, and to show how these meanings may change as interactants or partners confront narrative constraints of negotiating "what things mean" with each other, and conveying meanings to relevant third parties. The research products highlight the force and relativity of different modes of description, conventions of writing and/or performing "social life," and styles of expression. This kind of research has been called "narrative co-construction" (Ellis & Bochner, 1992). The narrative texts produced in this research venture to show "meaning in the making" and also to provide an opportunity for the co-constructors themselves to produce a story that can provide coherence and sensibility to the experiences. A variant of this type of research is "twice-told tales" in which stories of the same event are presented from two different points of view, each written in the first person. Examples of twice-told tales include Butler and Rosenblum's *Cancer in Two Voices* (1991), Yalom and Elkin's *Every Day Gets a Little Closer: A Thrice-Told Therapy* (1974), Barnes and Berke's (1971) *Two Accounts of a Journey Through Madness* (1971), and Margery Wolf's (1992) *A Thrice-Told Tale: Feminism, Postmodernism, and Ethnographic Responsibility.*

Second, narrative research on interpersonal communication would seek to produce first-person, autobiographical accounts of epiphanies of lived interpersonal experience that display human actors coping with difficult circumstances. These accounts ordinarily employ a biographical method (Denzin, 1989) in which the investigator becomes an experimental subject who treats his or her experience as primary "data" (Jackson, 1989). First-person (autobiographical) accounts highlight the communicative practices through which a person's identity evolves and is put to use (J. Bruner, 1990). They show how interactants narrativize certain metaphors and meanings into their lives, as in Mukaia's (1989) gripping first-person account of "anorexia from within" in which she expresses the ways in which food and starvation were narrativized into her identity; the ways in which situated and multiple realities were enacted, as in Ronai's (1992) layered story about her ambivalence in assuming the dual identities of social science researcher and erotic dancer; and Ellis's (1993b) first-person account of the ambivalence of merging academic and family personas in coping with her brother's sudden death in an airplane crash.

These three examples are important for another reason. Each is a narrative account written by an academic about her own experience. In each case, the author considers her narrativized experience sufficient in itself, preferring to show rather than tell its meaning(s). The "research text" is a story, published as a story, complete (but open) in itself. The authors privilege stories over analysis, allowing and encouraging alternative "readings" and multiple interpretations.

Many individuals doing research on interpersonal communication were inspired to write about or study this subject through their own marriages, divorces, interpersonal conflicts, family experiences, emotional crises, and so on. Haven't many of us had the feeling at one time or another that we were writing about ourselves when we were reporting data about others? Yet we have not encouraged researchers to tell the stories of how their own relationships may have contributed to what they saw or may have wanted to see in the lived experiences of the persons whose relationships they were trying to represent. The work of Mukaia (1989), Ellis (1993b), and Ronai (1992, 1993) offers significant testimony for the claim that personal experiences of social scientists can contribute to our understanding of topics such as attraction, passion, sexuality, grief, loss, contradiction, ambivalence, commitment, pain, and humiliation.

Third, narrative research on interpersonal communication would aspire to produce texts that radically reframe the conventional sense we have of "self as observer" and "other as subject." By entering into an interactive relationship with the people we are studying, we would create an opportunity to focus on the ways in which our experience of ourselves is changed by them, as well as the ways in which we may be changing their experience (Jackson, 1989). Research on others thus would become an ardent exploration of a broadened self. As Rose (1987) explains, "It is another way to make ourselves more available to ourselves" (p. 6). Accordingly, research on interpersonal communication would be premised on the assumption that the researcher and the subjects are coparticipants and the ways in which "they" (the subjects) construct "us" (the observers) are as important as the ways in which we represent them (Jorgenson, 1991). This approach to research would fracture the boundaries between subject and object and detachment and involvement that have traditionally privileged what we have to say about them and what they can learn about themselves from us over what they have to say about us and what we can learn about ourselves from them. The research products would be multivocal and dialogic; we would be getting to know (and thereby acquiring knowledge of) the others by being with them in a way that would inspire conversations in which we exchanged views and experiences with them, challenged each other's perspectives, and placed their ideas on a par with ours. The texts produced by this form of research would include their voices and intelligibilities as well as our own. Gaining knowledge about interpersonal communication would thus become a process of being-together-with another person in the everyday world of lived experience, of actively exchanging and challenging points of view with each other, of testing these views against the experience of our own lives as well as our reflections and feelings about the "others," and of avoiding the temptation to subjugate mystery, doubt, and contradiction to the oppression of reason (Jackson, 1989).

Conclusion

To embrace the narrative study of lived experience in the ways I have suggested in this chapter is to open ourselves to the limits as well as the possibilities of our work, so that we don't merely analyze life but also live it. Some readers will no doubt find the type of work advocated above not to their liking, but resistance to a narrative perspective may stem from a nostalgia for certain conventional ideas about knowledge, rationality, and objectivity that are understandably difficult to relinquish. Nevertheless, the spirit and ideals of solidarity and community that have traditionally characterized social science as an institution offer hope that the differences that divide empiricist and interpretivist perspectives ultimately can be appreciated, understood, and lived with.

References

Agger, B. (1989). *Reading science: A literary, political, and sociological analysis.* Dix Hills, NY: General Hall.

Barnes, M., & Berke, J. (1971). *Two accounts of a journey through madness.* New York: Ballantine.

Bateson, G. (1972). *Steps to an ecology of mind.* New York: Ballantine.

Berger, C. (1991). Communication theories and other curios. *Communication Monographs, 58,* 101-113.

Berger, C. (1992). Curioser and curioser curios. *Communication Monographs, 59,* 101-107.

Berger, C., & Calabrese, R. (1975). Some explorations in initial interaction and beyond: Toward a developmental theory of interpersonal communication. *Human Communication Research, 1,* 99-112.

Berger, C., & Chaffee, S. (1987). The study of communication as a science. In C. Berger & S. Chaffee (Eds.), *Handbook of communication science* (pp. 15-19). Newbury Park, CA: Sage.

Bochner, A. (1984). The functions of communication in interpersonal bonding. In C. Arnold & J. Bowers (Eds.), *Handbook of rhetorical and communication theory* (pp. 544-621). Boston: Allyn & Bacon.

Bochner, A. (1985). Perspectives on inquiry: Representation, conversation, and reflection. In M. Knapp & G. R. Miller (Eds.), *The handbook of interpersonal communication* (pp. 27-58). Beverly Hills, CA: Sage.

Bochner, A., Cissna, K., & Garko, M. (1991). Optional metaphors for studying interaction. In B. Montgomery & S. Duck (Eds.), *Studying interpersonal interaction* (pp. 16-34). New York: Guilford.

Bochner, A., & Ellis, C. (1992). Personal narrative as a social approach to interpersonal communication. *Communication Theory, 2,* 65-72.

Bochner, A., & Waugh, J. (in press). Talking with as a model for writing about: Implications of Rortian pragmatism for communication theory. In L. Langsdorf & A. Smith (Eds.), *Recovering pragmatism's voice: The classical tradition and the philosophy of communication.* Albany: SUNY Press.

Boje, D. (1991). The storytelling organization: A study of story performance in an office-supply firm. *Administrative Science Quarterly, 36,* 106-126.

Bostrom, R., & Donohew, L. (1992). The case for empiricism: Clarifying fundamental issues in communication theory. *Communication Monographs, 59,* 109-129.

Brody, H. (1987). *Stories of sickness.* New Haven, CT: Yale University Press.

Broyard, A. (1992). *Intoxicated by my illness.* New York: Clarkson Potter.

Bruner, E. (1986). Ethnography as narrative. In V. Turner & E. Bruner (Eds.), *The anthropology of experience* (pp. 139-155). Urbana: University of Illinois Press.

Bruner, J. (1986). *Actual minds, possible worlds.* Cambridge, MA: Harvard University Press.

Bruner, J. (1990). *Acts of meaning.* Cambridge, MA: Harvard University Press.

Burleson, B. (1992). Taking communication seriously. *Communication Monographs, 59,* 79-86.

Butler, S., & Rosenblum, B. (1991). *Cancer in two voices.* San Francisco: Spinster.

Cappella, J. (1987). Interpersonal communication: Definitions and fundamental questions. In C. Berger & S. Chaffee (Eds.), *Handbook of communication science* (pp. 184-238). Newbury Park, CA: Sage.

Carey, J. (1989). *Communication as culture.* Boston: Unwin Hyman.

Carr, D. (1986). *Time, narrative, and history.* Bloomington: Indiana University Press.

Charon, R. (1993). Medical interpretation: Implications of literary theory of narrative for clinical work. *Journal of Narrative and Narrative History, 3,* 79-98.

Clifford, J., & Marcus, G. (1986). *Writing culture: The poetics and politics of ethnography.* Berkeley: University of California Press.

Coles, R. (1989). *The call of stories: Teaching and the moral imagination.* Boston: Houghton Mifflin.

Conquergood, D. (1985). *Between two worlds: The Hmong shaman in America* [Documentary film]. Chicago: Siegel Productions.

Conquergood, D. (1990). *The heart broken in half* [Documentary film]. Chicago: Siegel Productions.

Conquergood, D. (1991). Rethinking ethnography: Towards a critical cultural politics. *Communication Monographs, 58,* 179-194.

Davidson, D. (1984). *Inquiries into truth and interpretation.* Oxford: Clarendon.

Davidson, D. (1986). A nice derangement of epitaphs. In E. LePlore (Ed.), *Truth and interpretation: Perspectives on the philosophy of Donald Davidson* (pp. 433-446). New York: Basil Blackwell.

Davis, F. (1974). Stories and sociology. *Urban Life and Culture, 3,* 310-316.

De Certeau, M. (1984). *The practices of everyday life.* Los Angeles: University of California Press.

Denzin, N. (1989). *Interpretive biography.* Newbury Park, CA: Sage.

Denzin, N. (1991). *Images of postmodern society: Social theory and contemporary society.* London: Sage.

Denzin, N. (1992). *Symbolic interactionism and cultural studies: The politics of interpretation.* Oxford: Basil Blackwell.

Derrida, J. (1978). *Writing and difference.* London: Routledge & Kegan.

Derrida, J. (1981). *Positions.* Chicago: University of Chicago Press.

Dewey, J. (1948). *Reconstruction in philosophy.* Boston: Beacon.

Dewey, J. (1960). An empirical study of empiricisms. In R. Bernstein (Ed.), *John Dewey on experience, nature, and freedom: Representative selections.* New York: Liberal Arts.

Dickens, D., & Fontana, A. (Eds.). (1991). *Postmodernism and sociology*. Chicago: University of Chicago Press.

Eisenberg, E., & Goodall, H. (1993). *Organizational communication: Balancing creativity and constraint*. New York: St. Martin.

Ellis, C. (1991). Emotional sociology. *Studies in Symbolic Interaction, 12*, 123-145.

Ellis, C. (1993a). *Speaking of dying*. Unpublished manuscript.

Ellis, C. (1993b). There are survivors: Telling a story of sudden death. *The Sociological Quarterly, 34*, 711-713.

Ellis, C. (in press). *Final negotiations: Attachment, chronic illness and loss*. Philadelphia: Temple University Press.

Ellis, C., & Bochner, A. (1992). Telling and performing personal stories: The constraints of choice in abortion. In C. Ellis & M. Flaherty (Eds.), *Investigating subjectivity: Research on lived experience* (pp. 79-101). Newbury Park, CA: Sage.

Ernaux, A. (1991). *A woman's story* (T. Leslie, Trans.). New York: Ballantine.

Feyerabend, P. (1976). *Against method*. New York: Humanities.

Fish, S. (1982). Working on the chain gang: Interpretation in the law and literary criticism. In W. Mitchell (Ed.), *The politics of interpretation* (pp. 271-286). Chicago: University of Chicago Press.

Fisher, W. (1984). Narration as a human communication paradigm: The case of public moral argument. *Communication Monographs, 51*, 1-22.

Foucault, M. (1970). *The order of things: An archaeology of the human sciences*. New York: Random House.

Foucault, M. (1980). *Power/knowledge*. New York: Pantheon.

Frank, A. (1991). *At the will of the body: Reflections on illness*. Boston: Houghton Mifflin.

Frank, A. (1993). The rhetoric of self-change: Illness experience as narrative. *The Sociological Quarterly, 34*, 39-52.

Geertz, C. (1973). *The interpretation of cultures*. New York: Basic Books.

Geertz, C. (1980). Blurred genres: The refiguration of social thought. *The American Scholar, 49*, 165-182.

Gergen, K. (1982). *Toward transformation in social knowledge*. New York: Springer-Verlag.

Gergen, K., & Gergen, M. (1983). Narratives of the self. In T. Sarbin & K. Scheibe (Eds.), *Studies in social identity*. New York: Praeger.

Gergen, K., & Gergen, M. (1986). Narrative form and the construction of psychological science. In T. Sarbin (Ed.), *Narrative psychology: The storied nature of human conduct* (pp. 22-44). New York: Praeger.

Gergen, K., & Gergen, M. (1988). Narrative and the self as relationship. In L. Berkowitz (Ed.), *Advances in experimental social psychology* (Vol. 21). San Diego: Academic Press.

Gergen, M. (1992). Life stories: Pieces of a dream. In G. Rosenwald & R. Ochberg (Eds.), *Storied lives: The cultural politics of self-understanding* (pp. 127-144). New Haven, CT: Yale University Press.

Gergen, M., & Gergen, K. (1993). Narratives of the gendered body in popular autobiography. *The Narrative Study of Lives, 1*, 191-218.

Glassie, H. (1982). *Passing the time in Ballymenone: Culture and history of an Ulster community*. Philadelphia: University of Pennsylvania Press.

Goodall, H. (1989). *Casing a promised land*. Carbondale: Southern Illinois University Press.

Gottlieb, A. (1991, June 2). The most talked about philosopher. *New York Times Book Review*, p. 30.

Graff, G. (1979). *Literature against itself*. Chicago: University of Chicago Press.

Gregory, B. (1988). *Inventing reality: Physics as language*. New York: Wiley.

Gregory, D., & Walford, R. (Eds.). (1989). *Horizons in human geography*. London: Macmillan.

Harper, D. (1982). *Good company*. Chicago: University of Chicago Press.

Haskell, M. (1990). *Love and other infectious diseases*. New York: William Morrow.

Hewes, D., & Planalp, S. (1987). The individual's place in communication science. In C. Berger & S. Chaffee (Eds.), *Handbook of communication science* (pp. 146-183). Newbury Park, CA: Sage.

Howard, S. (1989). *A tale of two stories: Excursions into a narrative approach to psychology*. Notre Dame, IN: Academic Publications.

Howard, S. (1991). Culture tales: A narrative approach to thinking, cross-cultural psychology, and psychotherapy. *American Psychologist, 46*, 187-197.

Hutcheon, L. (1988). *A poetics of postmodernism: History, theory, fiction*. New York: Routledge.

Iser, W. (1978). *The act of reading: A theory of aesthetic response*. Baltimore: John Hopkins University Press.

Jackson, M. (1989). *Paths toward a clearing: Radical empiricism and ethnographic inquiry*. Bloomington: Indiana University Press.

Jorgenson, J. (1991). Co-constructing the interviewer/co-constructing "family." In F. Steier (Ed.), *Research and reflexivity* (pp. 210-225). London: Sage.

Josselson, R., & Lieblich, A. (Eds.). (1993). *The narrative study of lives*. (Annual published by Sage, Newbury Park, CA)

Kiesenger, C. (1992, November). *When our lives intersect: Poetic interpretation and the reflective stance*. Paper presented at the annual meeting of the Speech Communication Association, Chicago.

Klamer, A. (1987). As if economists and their subjects were rational. In J. Nelson, A. Megill, & D. McCloskey (Eds.), *The rhetoric of the human sciences* (pp. 163-183). Madison: University of Wisconsin Press.

Kleinman, A. (1988). *The illness narratives: Suffering, healing, and the human condition*. New York: Basic Books.

Knapp, M., & Miller, G. R. (Eds.). (1985). *Handbook of interpersonal communication*. Beverly Hills, CA: Sage.

Kreiswirth, M. (1992). Trusting the tale: The narrativist turn in the human sciences. *New Literary History, 23,* 629-657.

Krieger, S. (1984). Fiction and social science. *Studies in Symbolic Interaction, 5,* 269-286.

Krieger, S. (1991). *Social science and the self: Personal essays on an art form*. New Brunswick, NJ: Rutgers University Press.

Kuhn, T. (1962). *The structure of scientific revolutions*. Chicago: University of Chicago Press.

Kuhn, T. (1977). *The essential tension: Selected studies in scientific tradition and change*. Chicago: University of Chicago Press.

Lannamann, J. (1991). Interpersonal communication research as ideological practice. *Communication Theory, 1,* 179-203.

Lerner, G. (1978). *A death of one's own*. New York: Simon & Schuster.

Linden, R. (1993). *Making stories, making selves: Feminist reflections on the holocaust*. Columbus: Ohio State University Press.

Lyotard, J. (1984). *The postmodern condition: A report on knowledge*. Minneapolis: University of Minnesota Press.

Maines, D. (1993). Narrative's moment and sociology's phenomena: Toward a narrative sociology. *The Sociological Quarterly, 34,* 17-38.

Mairs, N. (1989). *Remembering the bone house: An erotics of place and space*. New York: Harper & Row.

Mairs, N. (1993, February 21). When bad things happen to good writers. *New York Times Book Review*, pp. 25-27.

Maturana, H. (1991). Science and daily life: The ontology of scientific explanations. In F. Steier (Ed.), *Research and reflexivity* (pp. 30-52). London: Sage.

May, R. (1991). *The cry for myth*. New York: Norton.

McCabe, A. (Ed.). (1993). *Journal of Narrative and Life History, 1993*(3) [entire issue]. (Journal published by Lawrence Erlbaum, Hillsdale, NJ)

McCloskey, D. (1985). *The rhetoric of economics*. Madison: University of Wisconsin Press.

McCloskey, D. (1990). *If you're so smart: The narrative of economic expertise*. Chicago: University of Chicago Press.

Mishler, E. (1986). The analysis of interview-narratives. In T. Sarbin (Ed.), *Narrative psychology: The storied nature of human conduct* (pp. 233-255). New York: Praeger.

Mukaia, T. (1989). A call for our language: Anorexia from within. *Women's Studies International Forum, 12,* 613-638.

Murphy, R. (1987). *The body silent*. New York: Holt.

Myerhoff, B. (1978). *Number our days*. New York: Simon & Schuster.

Neumann, M. (1992). The traveling eye: Photography, tourism, and ethnography. *Visual Sociology, 7,* 22-38.

Neumann, M. (1993). Living on tortoise time: Alternative travel as the pursuit of lifestyle. *Symbolic Interaction, 16,* 201-235.

Norton, C. (1989). *Life metaphors: Stories of ordinary survival*. Carbondale: University of Southern Illinois Press.

Oakley, A. (1984). *Taking it like a woman*. New York: Random House.

Pacanowsky, M. (1988). Communication in the empowering organization. In J. Anderson (Ed.), *Communication yearbook 11* (pp. 356-379). Newbury Park, CA: Sage.

Paget, M. (1990). Life mirrors work mirrors text mirrors life . . . *Social Problems, 37,* 137-148.

Paget, M. (1993). *A complex sorrow: Reflections on cancer and an abbreviated life*. Philadelphia: Temple University Press.

Parry, A. (1991). A universe of stories. *Family Process, 30,* 37-54.

Polanyi, M. (1962). Tacit knowing and its bearing on some problems of philosophy. *Review of Modern Physics, 34,* 601-616.

Polanyi, M. (1966). *The tacit dimension*. Garden City, NY: Doubleday.

Polkinghorne, D. (1988). *Narrative knowing and the human sciences*. Albany: SUNY Press.

Poole, M., & McPhee, R. (1985). Methodology in interpersonal communication research. In M. Knapp & G. R. Miller (Eds.), *Handbook of interpersonal communication* (pp. 171-201). Beverly Hills, CA: Sage.

Poster, M. (Ed.). (1988). *Jean Baudrillard: Selected writings*. Stanford, CA: Stanford University Press.

Rabinow, P., & Sullivan, W. (1987). *Interpretive social science: A second look*. Berkeley: University of California Press.

Rawlins, W. (1991). *Friendship matters: Communication, dialectics, and the life course*. New York: Aldine de Gruyter.

Rich, A. (1978). *On lies, secrets, and silence: Selected prose 1966-1978*. New York: Norton.

Richardson, L. (1990). Narrative and sociology. *Journal of Contemporary Ethnography, 19,* 116-135.

Richardson, L. (1992). The consequences of poetic representation: Writing the other, rewriting the self. In C. Ellis & M. Flaherty (Eds.), *Investigating subjectivity: Research on lived experience* (pp. 125-137). Newbury Park, CA: Sage.

Ronai, C. (1992). The reflexive self through narrative: A night in the life of an erotic dancer/researcher. In C. Ellis & M. Flaherty (Eds.), *Investigating subjectivity: Research on lived experience* (pp. 102-124). Newbury Park, CA: Sage.

Ronai, C. (1993, November). *Multiple reflections of child sex abuse: An argument for a layered account*. Paper presented at the annual meeting of the Speech Communication Association, Miami, FL.

Rorty, R. (1979). *Philosophy and the mirror of nature*. Princeton, NJ: Princeton University Press.

Rorty, R. (1982). *Consequences of pragmatism (essays 1972-1980)*. Minneapolis: University of Minnesota Press.

Rorty, R. (1989). *Contingency, irony, solidarity*. Cambridge: Cambridge University Press.

Rorty, R. (1991a). *Objectivity, relativism, truth: Philosophical papers* (Vol. 1). Cambridge: Cambridge University Press.

Rorty, R. (1991b). *Essays on Heidegger and others: Philosophical papers* (Vol. 2). Cambridge: Cambridge University Press.

Rosaldo, R. (1989). *Culture and truth: The remaking of social analysis*. Boston: Beacon.

Rose, D. (1987). *Black American street life: South Philadelphia, 1969-1971*. Philadelphia: University of Pennsylvania Press.

Rose, D. (1990). *Living the ethnographic life*. Newbury Park, CA: Sage.

Rosenau, P. (1992). *Postmodernism and the social sciences: Insights, inroads, and intrusions*. Princeton, NJ: Princeton University Press.

Rosenwald, G. (1992). Conclusion: Reflections on narrative understanding. In G. Rosenwald & R. Ochberg (Eds.), *Storied lives: The cultural politics of self-understanding* (pp. 265-289). New Haven, CT: Yale University Press.

Rosenwald, G., & Ochberg, R. (Eds.). (1992). *Storied lives: The cultural politics of self-understanding*. New Haven, CT: Yale University Press.

Roth, P. (1991). *Patrimony: A true story*. New York: Simon & Schuster.

Sampson, E. (1978). Scientific paradigms and social values: Wanted—a scientific revolution. *Journal of Personality and Social Psychology, 36,* 1332-1343.

Sarbin, T. (Ed.). (1986). *Narrative psychology: The storied nature of human conduct*. New York: Praeger.

Schafer, R. (1992). *Retelling a life: Narration and dialogue in psychoanalysis*. New York: Basic Books.

Scheibe, K. (1986). Self-narratives and adventure. In T. Sarbin (Ed.), *Narrative psychology: The storied nature of human conduct* (pp. 129-151). New York: Praeger.

Secklin, P. (1993). *Narratives from children of divorce*. Unpublished manuscript, Purdue University.

Sellars, W. (1963). *Science, perception and reality*. New York: Routledge.

Shotter, J. (1987). The social construction of an (us): Problems of accountability and narratology. In R. Burnett, P. McGee, & D. Clarke (Eds.), *Accounting for relationships: Explanation, representation, and knowledge* (pp. 225-247). London: Methuen.

Shweder, R. (1986). Divergent rationalities. In D. Fiske & R. Shweder (Eds.), *Metatheory in social science: Pluralisms and subjectivities* (pp. 163-196). Chicago: University of Chicago Press.

Spence, D. (1982). *Narrative truth and historical truth*. New York: Norton.

Steedman, P. (1991). On the relations between seeing, interpreting, and knowing. In F. Steier (Ed.), *Research and reflexivity* (pp. 53-62). London: Sage.

Stone, E. (1988). *Black sheep and kissing cousins: How our family stories shape us*. New York: Penguin.

Suleiman, S., & Crosman, I. (Eds.). (1980). *The reader in the text*. Princeton, NJ: Princeton University Press.

Taylor, C. (1971). Interpretation and the sciences of man. *Review of Metaphysics, 25,* 3-34, 45-51.

Turner, V. (1978). Foreword. In B. Myerhoff, *Number our days* (pp. xii-xvii). New York: Simon & Schuster.

Turner, V. (1981). Social dramas and stories about them. In W. Mitchell (Ed.), *On narrative* (pp. 141-168). Chicago: University of Chicago Press.

Turner, V., & Bruner, E. (1986). *The anthropology of experience.* Urbana: University of Illinois Press.

Tyler, S. (1986). Post-modern ethnography: From document of the occult to occult document. In J. Clifford & G. Marcus (Eds.), *Writing culture: The poetics and politics of ethnography* (pp. 122-140). Berkeley: University of California Press.

von Foerster, H. (1991). Through the eyes of the other. In F. Steier (Ed.), *Research and reflexivity* (pp. 63-75). London: Sage.

White, H. (1973). *Metahistory: The historical imagination in nineteenth-century Europe.* Baltimore: John Hopkins University Press.

White, H. (1980). The value of narrativity in the representation of reality. *Critical Inquiry, 7,* 5-27.

Wolf, M. (1992). *A thrice-told tale: Feminism, postmodernism, and ethnographic responsibility.* Stanford, CA: Stanford University Press.

Yalom, I., & Elkin, G. (1974). *Every day gets a little closer: A twice-told therapy.* New York: Basic Books.

Zola, I. (1982). *Missing pieces.* Philadelphia: Temple University Press.

3

Methodology in Interpersonal Communication Research

Marshall Scott Poole

Robert D. McPhee

THE HISTORY OF THOUGHT about social science is a history of metaphors. Social researchers have been likened to physicists, biologists, alchemists, and high priests. There is truth in most of these metaphors and a degree of irony in some, but they miss something essential. Most of all, we believe that social scientists resemble detectives in a murder mystery. Like a good detective, the researcher is confronted by a confusing pattern of clues meaningful in both an immediate and a deeper, sometimes hidden, sense. To unravel the mystery, the detective must probe and order this deeper "reality," relying on improvisation, inspiration, and luck. Once things fall into place, there is the possibility of true understanding and insight, but there is also the danger of misinterpreting the multitude of available signs. Some things, such as motives, can never be determined with certainty. Just as it is often unclear whether a crime has been committed, so many research problems are unclear or unformulated. As the detective deduces the crime, so must the researcher constitute and cast up the object of research. This requires a capacity to ask the right questions as well as a sense of what form the answer should take. Detective novels are replete with devices and strategies for attacking a mystery, and this is no less true of social scientific writing. Foremost among these is theory.

Theory, as Cappella (1977) has noted, is a "god-term" of social science. Theory is supposed to be a guiding light that orders observations and imposes pattern on an overwhelmingly complex world. Theory determines method: It indicates what

AUTHORS' NOTE: We would like to thank Kathryn Dindia, Mary Anne Fitzpatrick, Joe Folger, Dean Hewes, Ed Mabry, Lisa O'Dell, and Sally Planalp for their suggestions and comments. We have persisted in our errors despite their sound advice.

data are appropriate and places limits on how these data may best be obtained. In this view, an emphasis on method apart from theory is misguided and may be downright misleading.

The implication is that an emphasis on methodology is mindless technicianship, the resort of tinkerers steeped in "dust-bowl empiricist" philosophy. Of course, there is much justice in this position. Cappella (1977) argued that researchers tend to obey the "law of the hammer" with respect to methods; whatever methodologies are in vogue tend to be used over and over, even if they are ill-suited for the questions being asked. In 1991 Berger reiterated his point, bemoaning the "methodological fixation" of communication researchers. However, the sharp distinction between theory and method implied by many discussions is based on a vastly oversimplified picture of how research operates. While it is true that all observation is theory laden, it is also true—as the pragmatist philosophers realized—that what we can know is determined by the available methods for knowing. Like Agatha Christie's fictional detective Hercule Poirot, the social detective must have an effective method because method is one's point of contact with the world. The types of constructs and propositions in our theories, as well as the degree of certainty attached to them, are all dependent on our methodological repertoire. Rather than theory types, it is more accurate to think of *theory-method* complexes as the driving force in the research enterprise.

Consider the example of interpersonal attraction theory. Those research programs employing laboratory methods, such as Byrne's (1969) and N. A. Anderson's (1981), tend to focus on variables conducive to experimental control—reinforcement schedules, uncertainty, and balance of positive and negative remarks. Other programs, like Altman and Taylor's (1973), began with a focus on development of relational attraction over fairly long periods of time and thus tended to focus more on field-centered methods, which in turn supported the dynamism and complexity of their model of shared experience during relational development. Theoretical choices and methodological choices determine each other in a dialectical manner. Methodological preferences shape the types of theory that evolve, just as theories shape methods.

No discussion of methods can be separated from a consideration of how theory and methodology articulate, and the key joining point is where method ties into the process of scientific reasoning. To understand this tie, it is useful to distinguish four elements: substantive theoretical assumptions, modes of explanation, modes of inquiry, and methodological technique. *Substantive theoretical assumptions* are those aspects of a theory's content that are particular to the phenomena the theory covers. Substantive assumptions may be quite specific (for example, a definition of self-disclosure) or general, expressing some assumption about the way a phenomenon "is" (for example, the assumption that cognitive processes rather than social forces are the key to explaining self-disclosure). In addition to substantive assumptions, all theories take a characteristic approach to explaining or understanding phenomena, a characteristic *mode of explanation*. Some theories attempt to delineate causal forces determining a phenomenon; others explain them as a product of rule-governed action; still others employ a complex of the two modes. *Mode of inquiry* refers to the strategy the researcher employs in studying a phenomenon. In particular, it indexes the relationship between theory and observational practices: Does theory precede or follow from observation, or do the two develop simultaneously? Finally, *methodological technique* represents what have traditionally been referred to as "methods," procedures of design, data collection, and analysis used to investigate interpersonal phenomena.

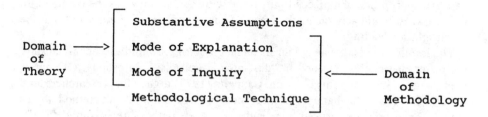

Figure 3.1. Four Elements of the Theory-Method Complex

Substantive assumptions clearly belong to the realm of "theory" and techniques clearly belong to "methods." Modes of explanation and modes of inquiry are sometimes treated as part of theory and sometimes as part of methodology; they constitute the linking pin of the theory-method complex. Together, substantive assumptions, modes of explanation, and modes of inquiry should dictate the range of appropriate techniques. In practice, choice of techniques is usually determined by the researcher's preferences in one of the three areas—for example, a commitment to grounded theory—but ideally all three elements should be considered. The relationship among substantive assumptions, modes of explanation, and modes of inquiry is complex. In combination, a mode of inquiry and a mode of explanation form a *template* that determines the form substantive theory can take, as shown in the previous example. At the same time, characteristics of the phenomenon under study make some templates more suitable than others. Clearly, the researcher must strike a balance among substantive assumptions, mode of inquiry, and mode of explanation, trading off one against the others to find a fruitful combination.

Having said this, we hasten to add that explicit theories do not always precede or guide research. Sometimes researchers do not grapple with their implicit theories until data are gathered, and many good ideas emerge after a study is done, when researchers speculate on and interpret their findings. However, establishing a clear sense of the relevant theory-method complex is also important in these cases. After-the-fact sense making and reformulation are just as critical as a priori planning. Being clear on where one's post hoc theorizing stands makes extensions and future work more systematic and useful.

In this chapter, we will define methodology in its broadest sense, encompassing modes of explanation, modes of inquiry, and techniques. The first section considers the modes of explanation and modes of inquiry applicable to the study of interpersonal communication. We will explore various templates implied by combinations of modes of inquiry and explanation, the techniques templates emphasize, and their untapped potential. The second and third sections are concerned with various techniques and how they relate to the theoretical templates. The second section covers data collection and measurement techniques, while the third discusses a broad spectrum of techniques for data analysis. In the conclusion, we consider new moves and likely directions in interpersonal methodology.

The primary concern of this chapter is not how to employ the techniques in question; full discussions are available in primary sources. Rather, we will focus on (a) what a given technique can do, (b) the crucial assumptions required to employ the technique properly, (c) the kinds of claims that can be made using the technique and which templates these apply to, and (d) common abuses and how they might be avoided. In short, this chapter is concerned with methods-in-use and their implications for theory development in interpersonal communication. It attempts to specify guidelines for technical choices that permit the most effective possible match between theory and technique. We hope it will equip the social sleuth with a "method" for detecting the patterns and determinations in the interpersonal communication.

Modes of Explanation, Modes of Inquiry, and Theoretical Templates

In the introduction, we defined modes of inquiry and modes of explanation in general terms. Here we will explore them in more detail, laying out three basic modes of explanation and three modes of inquiry. In combination, the modes of explanation and inquiry form nine theoretical templates. These templates, discussed below and portrayed in Figure 3.2, determine the form a research study can take. They constitute an array of possibilities for interpersonal communication research. The templates should be regarded as ideal types for research; although few studies exactly conform to the descriptions below, the templates constitute standards for selecting and planning research strategies and for making technical choices. To understand them, it is first necessary to consider the two sets of modes.

Modes of Explanation

The goals of social science are *explanation* and *understanding*. However, the meaning of these two terms is elusive. There have been many attempts to define explanation and understanding in the abstract, but they are better understood by considering the operations they involve. We can distinguish three types of explanation and understanding (generally called *explanation* here), each involving different operations and assumptions and a different sense of what scientific inquiry is: causal explanation, conventional explanation, and dialectical explanation. Causal, conventional, and dialectical explanations can be distinguished in terms of (a) the assumptions they make about the researcher's relation to the object of study; (b) the forms of explanation they advance and the criteria by which these explanations are evaluated; and (c) their assumptions about the proper reference point for inquiry.

Causal explanations assume the researcher is an independent observer of the phenomenon under study. The object of research is taken to exist in a real, objectifiable world that serves as the starting point of inquiry (even social phenomena are assumed to be objectifiable). Causal explanations consist of networks of propositions of the form "X causes Y, under conditions $C_1, \ldots C_n$," where X and Y are variables or constructs identified by the researcher and $C_1 \ldots C_n$ are statements of scope or qualifying conditions for the causal relation to hold. For example, Leary's (1957) "interpersonal reflex" can be explained by a law of the following form: *Hostile (affiliative) behavior from one party causes the other to respond in like manner, when (a) the two parties have nearly equal power, (b) the parties belong to the same culture.* The list of scope conditions would become unmanageably long if every possible qualifier were included, so most causal propositions include an "other things being equal" clause. The nature of causality is the subject of considerable debate, but there is general agreement that a valid causal law must (a) be general and (b) describe a necessary relationship between cause and effect

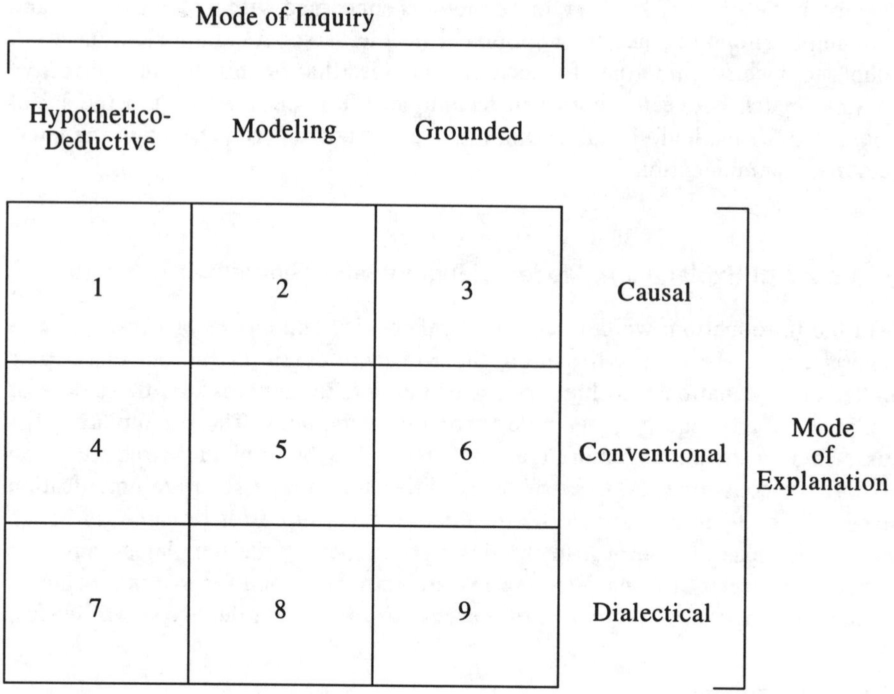

Mode of Inquiry

Hypothetico-Deductive	Modeling	Grounded	
1	2	3	Causal
4	5	6	Conventional
7	8	9	Dialectical

Mode of Explanation

Figure 3.2. Nine Research Templates

(Achinstein, 1971). The causal linkage in the law may be strictly deterministic, or it may state that effect follows cause only with a certain probability. In perhaps the most useful analysis of causality for social scientists, Harré and Madden (1975) argue that an adequate causal explanation specifies a generative mechanism that can account for the phenomenon and its effects. Such a generative mechanism consists of a "causal agent" that is the driving force behind the cause and a mechanism governing the action of that agent.

Causal explanation grants the researcher a privileged position with respect to defining constructs, discerning causal linkages, and testing or verifying causal hypotheses. The researcher's perspective by itself is assumed to give an adequate depiction of the world, with no need for cross-checking or verification from the subjects of study. Evaluation of causal explanations thus turns on tests of the adequacy of the researcher's reasoning and procedures: The researcher's explication of constructs is checked for internal logic and richness; measures are checked for construct validity with reference to the researcher's theoretical network (Cronbach & Meehl, 1955); and causal linkages are tested using designs and statistical procedures that permit control of intrusive factors and errors not allowed for in the researcher's formulation. In short, causal explanation privileges the researcher's perspective as an objective, legitimate viewpoint for scientific inquiry.

Like causal explanations, *conventional explanations* presume the independence of researcher and the subject of research. However, rather than assuming an objectifiable, natural world, conventional explanation assumes the world is a social product and takes the perspectives of subjects in that world as its starting point. Subjects are assumed to actively monitor and control their behavior with reference to conventions, variously conceived as rules, schemas, types, or structures, among other things. Conventional explanations consist in demonstrating how subjects— who could have done otherwise—acted or reacted in a fashion that is meaningful, understandable, or efficacious in the context of pertinent conventions. An adequate conventional explanation does not have to be necessary or general, nor does it have to show temporal ordering of cause to effect: A conventional explanation seeks to fit phenomena into a pattern meaningful to the active subject, and this pattern entails the possibility of events and the capability of actors rather than a necessary connection. For example, a conventional explanation of Leary's interpersonal reflex might explore what behaviors counted as hostile or affiliative to subjects and account for matching behavior in light of subjects' adherence to the norm of reciprocity. This explanation would not rest its claim to validity on its generality or on showing a necessary linkage between behavior and norm, but instead on its ability to show how the norm makes matching behavior meaningful and sensible to subjects. In form, conventional explanations range from the rather loose inter- pretive account implied above to deductive models like the practical syllogism (Cushman & Pearce, 1977; Von Wright, 1971). Regardless of their level of formal- ity, conventional explanations are grounded in the subjects' point of view. The researcher discovers conventions by probing the actor's phenomenology and cul- ture, and conventional explanations attempt to account for action in a manner that reflects subjects' experience. The researcher's formulation of conventions and his or her explanations may differ from the actor's own statements (as do those of conversational analysts), but even these second order formulations are presumed to be grounded in the actor's rules and meanings. Conventional schemes may be tested by assessing whether the behaviors or cognitions they entail are consistent with the actor's behaviors or cognitions (as is done with systems of linguistic rules), by determining whether the conventions enable an outsider to "pass" as a native, or by asking subjects directly whether the rules or schemes hold. Conventional explanation subordinates the researcher's point of view to the subject's but leaves the researcher independent, as knower and cataloger of the subject's schemes.

Like conventional explanation, *dialectical explanation* assumes its objects of study are socially constituted. However, in contrast to causal or conventional types, dialec- tical explanations do not presume the independence of researcher and the subject of research. Instead, scientific inquiry is taken to consist of mediation between two perspectives—the researcher's and the subject's—and neither is privileged. Because of this, dialectical explanations combine aspects of causal and conventional explana- tions; they specify how causal forces condition action while actors influence the operation of these same forces. Causality plays an important role in dialectical expla- nation, but it moves along a complex path. People act, but not in circumstances of their own choosing. Forces beyond actors' control determine the available rules, schemes, and structures, and how they can be applied. Within this determination, actors' conventions form the grounds for the operation of causal forces and shape the impact of those forces in the situation. Moreover, systems of action are themselves involved in the generation and movement of causal forces. So action is conditioned by causal forces, which are themselves shaped by action, which is conditioned by causal forces, which are shaped by action, and so forth.

A dialectical explanation of Leary's interpersonal reflex might emphasize a norm such as reciprocity, but it would also take into account the larger conventional and causal context that shapes how that norm operates in any specific instance. For instance, A's friendly gesture might be systematically misinterpreted (or strategically interpreted) as submissiveness in a situation where B thinks (or wants) status differences to be important and has (or wants) high status. If A anticipated this situation, A would have to be careful to design his or her gesture of simple friendliness to appear "friendly but not weak." The appropriateness of this strategy would depend on the larger conventional and causal context, and other conditions might render it ineffective. Such a gesture might be inappropriate in a more egalitarian situation; it might be impossible to avoid B's status consciousness; or showing friendliness might be possible only if causal factors like A's cultural experience and communicative competence permit.

Unlike conventional explanations, whose only requirement is the explanation of action in terms of rules or schemes, dialectical explanations must also specify causal forces that determine the types of conventions available and how actors can use these conventions. Hence the dialectical explanation must probe the nature of domination in our society and how this carries over into interpersonal relationships. The researcher cannot take rules as given (as a conventional explanation does) but must explore what gives the rules pattern and force. Historical evidence frequently plays an important role in this process because causes are embedded in previous, often long-established action systems. However, discovering causal forces does not complete a dialectical explanation. Causes operate through shaping the action system, and because of this, the mediation of causal forces by action must be explored. In this case, the impact of causal forces on matching behavior must be understood as actively "filtered" through schemes and structures associated with interpersonal relationships. This filtering does not represent "slippage" or "error" (as a purely causal explanation would assume) but is the mechanism through which the cause operates and is regarded as an integral aspect of any explanation. Causality does not entail a direct "$X \rightarrow Y$" relationship but instead something like "X influences conventions $Z_1, \ldots Z_n$, which lead to Y, in the context of the action system W." Causes and conventions interact in this explanation, and the ratio of determinism to action varies from case to case. In some instances, causal determination is so rigid that subjects have little latitude (though in principle, they always "could have done otherwise"), whereas in other cases, causal forces are largely attenuated by actors' control over conventions and contingencies.

This interpenetration of cause and action necessitates the double mediation of researcher's and subject's perspectives. The researcher is in a better position to identify causal forces but can only understand how these forces operate and how significant they are by taking the active role of the subject and the channeling influence of society into account. Hence evaluation of dialectical explanations is subject to two sets of criteria, those for causal explanations and those for conventions. Once the operation of causal forces has been established by statistical techniques, their impact on the action system must be spelled out. A successful dialectical explanation articulates causal forces and their impact on active subjects.

Causal explanations emphasize objectifiable forces; conventional explanations focus on subjectivity (or intersubjectivity); and dialectical explanations emphasize conditioned subjectivity (or intersubjectivity). In drawing these distinctions, it is not necessary to argue that one mode of explanation is better than any other. Each mode has its advocates, and each possesses strengths and weaknesses relative to the others. Judging by the programmatic statements of communication scholars, most researchers in our field would be aiming at explanations that account for action in complex systems, that is, at dialectical explanations. In practice, however, the great majority of communication researchers employ either causal or conventional explanations and do not consider their relationship. The dialectical mode will not necessarily work better than the others, but it does seem to aim at many of the goals put forth by interpersonal researchers and therefore deserves more explicit attention than it has previously received.

Modes of Inquiry

Even when a researcher is clear on his or her substantive assumptions and mode of explanation, there is still the question of how theory and data are related during the process of inquiry. Three modes of inquiry can be distinguished.

In the *hypothetico-deductive* mode of inquiry, the researcher generates hypotheses from theory, develops operational definitions of theoretical constructs, and sets up a study (experimental, field, or survey) to test the hypotheses. Theory is prior to data collection and hypothesis testing, and these steps are strictly separated. By far, the majority of interpersonal communication studies operate in this mode.

A second mode of inquiry is *modeling*, in which theory, operationalization, and data patterns are treated simultaneously (see Levine & Fitzgerald, 1991; McPhee & Poole, 1981). A model is a representation of a situated theory. It gives a direct depiction of how the theory generates the observed data in a specific context. For example, Newton's mechanics presents a general theory of motion; a model of the solar system would consist of equations consistent with Newtonian principles but would represent the forces exerted on each specific planet by others and by the sun. The behavior of the data (in this case, the paths of planets around the sun) is directly described by the equations of the model, which represent a situated case of the general theory. Models often use mathematical representations (for example, Hunter, Danes, & Cohen, 1984) but may also be cast in logical verbal or pictorial formalisms (for example, Pearce & Cronen's, 1980, model of rule following, or Brown & Levinson's, 1978, politeness hierarchy). Comparing model predictions with observed data enables the researcher not only to test the model but also to pinpoint those aspects of the model that are problematic. Treating theory, operationalization, and data simultaneously is obviously more demanding and difficult than the traditional mode of inquiry, but it has the advantages of greater precision and of clarifying assumptions behind the theory (Cappella, 1977; McPhee & Poole, 1981).

The third mode of inquiry is the development of *grounded theory* (Glaser & Strauss, 1967; Strauss, 1987). The researcher goes directly to the phenomenon itself and develops concepts, hypotheses, and theoretical propositions from direct experience with the data. Grounded theory takes a "bottom-up" approach, as opposed to the "top-down" move of the traditional mode; theory emerges from observation, rather than being prior to it. Once hypotheses or generalizations have been developed, they may be "tested" in the situation or in another context, but this is by no means equivalent to hypothesis testing in the traditional mode. Advocates of grounded theory argue that it makes the researcher more sensitive to particular nuances of the phenomenon and removes "blinders" imposed on the researcher by an a priori theory. Critics argue that the situated nature of grounded theory does not allow for generalization or for rigorous testing of its propositions.

Over the years, there has been considerable roiling of waters concerning which mode of inquiry is best for the study of interpersonal communication. There have been militant advocates of grounded theory (Fisher & Hawes, 1971) and of modeling (Cappella, 1977) and equally militant defenders of traditional hypothesis testing (Berger, 1975; Miller & Berger, 1978). Taken together, these show there is a good case for the employment of each mode of inquiry as well as disadvantages or problems with the employment of any mode. Rather than being correct or incorrect, we would submit that the three modes of inquiry are comparatively advantageous or disadvantageous, depending on the subject of study, and would encourage flexibility in choosing a mode of inquiry.

Templates and Tools

When modes of explanation and modes of inquiry are crossed, nine templates result, each of which represents a different methodological strategy. These templates form the grounds for methodological choice and function on at least two levels.

First, the templates are *descriptions* of the range of options open to interpersonal communication research. In addition to the many efforts that fall clearly in a single template, there are numerous "borderline" or mixed studies that seem to combine aspects of several templates. Some of these are misconceived projects that should be organized by a single template but are complicated by extraneous concerns or assumptions. Others are hybrids that employ different templates in different phases of research (for example, grounded inquiry at first, then modeling in later stages) or different templates side by side in parallel research efforts (for example, research into rules that poses some hypotheses but also uses grounded inquiry to look for other rules). The scheme presented here is useful in both cases.

The templates also serve a *normative* function. Each template embodies different assumptions and characteristic forms of inference and proof. Within these limits, some techniques are more appropriate than others. The scheme can be used to guide selection of techniques and evaluation of previous technical choices. Further, the templates also suggest how the results of applying techniques should be interpreted. Most techniques can be used in several different templates. Because each template involves different types of claims and makes different assumptions about the nature of the phenomenon under study, the same technique can yield quite different evidence and conclusions under different templates. For example, a contingency table analysis of the distributions of dominant and submissive acts by gender in marital interaction might be adduced to support a "law" of male dominance for a study conducted in Cell 1, which aims for causal explanations and uses the hypothetico-deductive mode of inquiry. The same result might be interpreted as supporting a set of inductively derived rules of male-female interaction when employed in Cell 6, which uses conventional explanations and grounded techniques to derive rules; the contingency table analysis would be post hoc evidence verifying researcher intuitions. The various uses for techniques will become apparent as each cell in Figure 3.2 is discussed, along with its strengths, weaknesses, and technical affinities.

Cell 1: Causal explanation, hypothetico-deductive inquiry. Traditionally, this template has been regarded as the norm for empirical research in interpersonal communication. As its name implies, the researcher first specifies causal hypotheses, then sets up a research design to test the hypotheses and rejects or fails to reject the hypotheses based on the data. Theory development precedes and is independent of data collection and analysis. Cell 1 is by far the most frequently employed strategy in interpersonal communication research; most attraction and self-disclosure research, for example, falls in Cell 1 (see, for example, Berger & Calabrese, 1974; Burleson & Denton, 1992; Sunnafrank & Miller, 1981). At present, the techniques most commonly employed in this cell include experimental designs, statistical model-testing methods (such as path analysis), and those developmental techniques designed to establish causality.

Causal, hypothetico-deductive research has several advantages: (a) It yields general, necessary explanations; (b) cast correctly, its hypotheses are clearly falsifiable; and (c) it can result in extremely powerful theories that permit precise prediction and control. Along with these strengths come weaknesses and biases as well. Cell 1 research tends to gloss over unique particular aspects of the phenomenon under study. It favors precise, tightly controlled conceptualization and measurement of constructs, and this may lead to a reification of variables and a dismissal of the subject's perspective when it should be taken into account. Moreover, there are some cases in which causal, hypothetico-deductive explanation is not adequate, notably instances with recursive layered effects and those in which phenomena are continually renegotiated and redefined by actors. Overemphasis on causal understanding can lead to distortion and oversimplification of cases in which determinations are not strong or play a secondary role. A new direction of particular interest is the role qualitative techniques could play in supporting claims of temporal ordering and causal influence.

Cell 2: Causal explanation, modeling inquiry. Cappella (1977) advocates this approach to communication research, which has been used increasingly in recent years. In this template, a causal theory is represented as a model directly depicting the pattern or "behavior" of data. For example, if disclosure of similarities is assumed to lead to liking, the amount of self-disclosure can be related to liking in a mathematical equation linking the two variables: for instance, $Y_1 + \alpha \sum_{i=1}^{n} V_i = Y_2$, where Y_1 is the initial attraction level to the other, V_i is the valence of the "ith" message received about the other, α is an "effect strength" constant for the sum of n messages received between times 1 and 2, and Y_2 is the resulting attraction level. This equation directly links theory and observables and can be tested by comparing its predictions against actual observations. Cappella has used this approach to study talk-silence sequences in conversations (Cappella, 1979, 1980; Cappella & Planalp, 1981). Other applications include studies of attitude change by Hunter et al. (1984) and research on awkward silences by McLaughlin and Cody (1982). In many cases, this template results in the development of nonlinear dynamic models, which can account for a number of complex phenomena, such as sudden shifts in behavior, self-sustaining periodic patterns, and apparently random change (Buder, 1991; Levine & Fitzgerald, 1991). The recent popularity of chaos theory and self-organizing systems theory accounts, in part, for the recent interest in this template. The causal, modeling template should not be confused with path analysis and structural equation modeling techniques, which are often termed causal modeling. These two are statistical techniques rather than research strategies and can be used with any cell based on causal or dialectical explanation forms.

There are notable advantages to the causal, modeling template. Modeling enables researchers to simulate the behavior of a complex network of several variables and determine which variables or parameter values are central to the causal process as well as the general qualitative behavior of dependent variables. The results of these simulations can then be translated into testable predictions. As Pavitt and Cappella (1979) stated, simulation modeling enables researchers to identify "discriminable features" of the process being modeled, features whose presence or absence can enable falsification of the model. Modeling also forces the researcher to specify precisely and completely the theoretical assumptions, constructs, and connections between variables (see Cappella, 1977). Without specification much more precise than that underlying verbal theory, building the model is impossible. One particularly interesting feature of this and the other modeling cells is that the researcher often learns more when the model fails than when it succeeds. Tracing a failure can make us aware of previously unnoticed aspects of the phenomenon and permit modification of basic theoretical assumptions (McPhee & Poole, 1981). The methods generally used to test causally based models include statistical model-testing methods, techniques for evaluating descriptive models, time-series techniques, and developmental techniques (see Levine & Fitzgerald, 1991, for an excellent introduction).

There are several shortcomings of this template. Causal theories based on models are often less generalizable than Cell 1 theories because models are tied to particular cases and particular instantiations of variables. Then, too, some theoretical statements cannot be represented in a model (especially a mathematical model) without distorting or impoverishing them (see McPhee & Poole, 1981, for examples). Finally, data are often so unreliable and "fuzzy" that they do not permit us to select among competing models. With subjective expected utility models, for example, a model with multiplicative combinations of attributes cannot be distinguished empirically from an additive model (Behling & Dillard, 1984).

Cell 3: Causal explanation, grounded theory. The grounded theory approach modifies the causal explanatory pattern considerably. In Cell 3, the researcher looks for causal linkages embedded *in a particular situation.* These may be generalized to other situations but they do not have to be; grounded theories may cover only a single case. Because Cell 3 research is tied to a particular context and because it does not employ classical hypothesis testing, it is not possible to determine with certainty what feature of an action or context is responsible for an effect, though certain possibilities may be excluded by the nature of the situational description (Menzies, 1982). Causal linkages in Cell 3 do not have the abstract, necessary entailments implied in Cells 1 and 2, though they can claim sufficiency. For example, Izraeli (1977, example from Menzies, 1982) mentions a manager promoting a deputy to gain a supporter. That this is causally effective depends on the unspecified context: the character of the deputy, norms in the plant, the plant's institutional arrangements, and so forth—all things that are not controlled to see if the obtained effects are the direct result of the action. Instead, the researcher relies on common sense and his or her knowledge of the social world to deduce causality. To generate causal, grounded theory, the researcher engages the phenomenon, derives sensitizing concepts and key linkages, and uses these to put together an account of causal determinations in the situation. Although most studies employing ethnographic and symbolic interactionist approaches make causal claims, we have found no interpersonal communication studies that use this approach self-consciously. A good example relevant to interpersonal communication is Bott's (1971) book, *Family and Social Network,* which induces from interviews of 20 families a set of variables and a causal hypothesis that is used to explain differences in conjugal relations.

Compared with Cells 1 and 2, Cell 3 has the disadvantages of being less general and having weaker necessity. Further, although Cell 1 and Cell 2 hypotheses are falsifiable if properly set up, the situation is more ambiguous for Cell 3 propositions. Because they are derived by grounded methods, no a priori test of Cell 3 propositions is possible; however, once a causal linkage has been isolated, it is possible to test it in other contexts. The advantages of Cell 3 vis-à-vis Cells 1 and 2 include its ability to generate a much more detailed account of causality than a general theory allows and much greater sensitivity to particular features of the phenomenon. Vis-à-vis templates based on conventional explanation (which it is commonly combined with), Cell 3 has two advantages: (a) It provides an account that orders determinants and consequences, rather than simply fitting things into a pattern, and (b) it permits the researcher to focus on causality, a crucial part of subjects' interpretive schemes and, arguably, the key scheme employed by acting subjects.

Cell 3 is underused in interpersonal communication research. Probably the reason for this is the long-standing suspicion of causal researchers toward any particularized inquiry and the equally well-established leeriness of conventionalists toward causal-based accounts. Certainly most "qualitative" research reports contain causal reasoning. There is no reason this could not benefit from greater formalization.

Cell 4: Conventional explanation, hypothetico-deductive inquiry. In this template, a set of rules or an interpretive scheme is specified and then tested empirically. The rules or schemes serve as a hypothesis that is tested by comparing subjects' behavior in a particular situation to patterns that would be expected if the rules held. Interpersonal communication studies employing this template include Planalp and Tracy's (1980) research on rules governing topic changes and Wilson's (1990) study of rules governing selection of interaction goals.

The advantages of this cell include those of conventionalist inquiry in general; it is sensitive to the active role of subjects and does not require strict assumptions about cause and effect (which may not reflect the nature of human action) but allows for loose, multiple linkages between "inputs" and action. Vis-à-vis Cell 6—grounded explanation, conventional inquiry—it has the advantage of systematically testing whether rules hold rather than allowing the validity of rules to rest wholly on the researcher's "discovery techniques." The disadvantages of this template include the following: (a) It has weaker generality than the causal cells; (b) its explanations are not necessary in the way causal explanations are (Cushman & Pearce, 1977, have argued that conventional explanations possess a form of necessity based on normative force, that is, practical necessity); and (c) emphasis on testing can also create a tendency to stress the researcher's perspective over the subject's, thus violating a basic premise of conventionalist inquiry. The techniques normally used in Cell 4 research are experimental design and statistical model-testing techniques, although in principle descriptive quantitative techniques, developmental techniques, and some qualitative techniques could also be applied (see below).

Cell 5: Conventional explanation, modeling inquiry. This template is similar to Cell 4, but rather than a convention or set of conventions, the researcher posits a model of convention use or a hierarchical model of conventions. In Cell 5, the researcher is explicit about the process by which conventions enter into behavior and the relationships among conventions. Unlike models in Cell 2, Cell 5 models are usually verbal or logical in form. Once a model is developed, it is tested against actual behavior, as in Cell 4. Further, as in Cell 4, the test should involve checking to see whether subjects actually hold the conventions in question. Examples of Cell 5 research include Sacks, Schegloff, and Jefferson's (1974) model of turn-taking in conversation, the rule models described in Pearce and Cronen (1980), and Donohue's (1981) model of negotiation rules. Vroom and Jago's (1974) model of leadership behavior presents a paradigmatic example of rule modeling and testing.

The advantages of Cell 5 include all those for Cell 4, plus the benefits of modeling over hypothetico-deductive inquiry discussed under Cell 2. Like other modeling templates, this one may require more precision than the phenomenon allows. Moreover, a large number of models involving different conventions may fit a single phenomenon, and it may be impossible to determine which model works the best. The techniques commonly used in this cell include experimental designs, statistical model testing, and quantitative descriptive techniques such as Markov modeling. Both Cells 4 and 5 are too seldom used. They provide the critical step of falsification or verification needed to supplement the discovery stage, which represents the extent of most conventionalist research (see Tudor, 1976).

Cell 6: Conventional explanations, grounded theory. Studies in this cell are by far the most common among conventionalist research in interpersonal communication. Indeed, for many, conventionalist research and grounded theory are synonymous. In Cell 6 research, the investigator uses qualitative techniques of discovery and analysis to uncover conventions and how they are used (see below). Although there is room for informal testing of conventions by cross-checking and testing expectations in the situation, the burden of validity rests primarily on the strength of the researcher's insight and his or her discovery techniques. There is no hypothesis testing. Examples of research in this template include Philipsen's (1975) study, "Speaking 'Like a Man' in Teamsterville," and B. J. Hall's (1991) study of alignment rules.

The advantages of this template compared with Cells 1 through 3 have been covered in the discussions of Cells 4 and 5. Compared with Cells 4 and 5, the conventional, grounded theory template has the advantage of emphasizing discovery procedures, thereby sensitizing the researcher to particularities of the phenomenon. Indeed, of all the templates, Cell 6 brings the researcher into the most intimate contact with his or her subject. It is certainly the template with the least systematic approach and therefore is not as likely to impose formalisms that disguise or distort. In terms of disadvantages, its general lack of systematic evaluation can reduce confidence in the representativeness and generality of Cell 6 findings. In particular, there is no test of a basic assumption of conventionalist explanation—that the conventions reflect subjects' rules or schemes accurately. Rather, the researcher's techniques of contact, observation, and analysis are supposed to guarantee adequate penetration of the subjects' perspective. However, there is often no way of determining whether it has been or not. Some means of avoiding this and other problems with Cell 6 research are considered below.

Cell 7: Dialectical explanation, hypothetico-deductive inquiry. This is the most common of the three dialectical templates. The researcher generates hypotheses about how conventions and the causal factors that influence them and give them force will function in action systems. The researcher must test hypotheses about how the subject behaves in the given action system as well as several hypotheses about the action system itself. These system tests include (a) whether the hypothesized conventions are held and used by subjects; (b) whether causal factors hold and operate as hypothesized; and (c) whether subjects are conscious of the causal factors and, if so, how this consciousness influences the system. Generation of the insights needed to produce a dialectical theory suggests the need for powerful discovery techniques, which are then complemented by hypothesis-testing techniques. A study of group decision making by Poole and DeSanctis (1992) provides one example of Cell 7. They analyzed the use of rules in decision-making interaction and determined the influence of two types of procedural agendas on the structuration of rules. They also explored the relationships of various types of rule use to decision outcomes.

Cell 7 studies combine many of the advantages of Cells 1 and 4. They have a degree of sensitivity to the phenomenon characteristic of conventional studies but also incorporate strong tests in the tradition of causal, hypothetico-deductive studies. Moreover, dialectical studies are more powerful than conventional research because they also focus on the forces that shape conventions and condition their operation. However, the same features that give Cell 7 studies their unique advantages can also generate problems. For one thing, Cell 7 studies are quite complex and require considerable time and resources; the payoff in terms of insight may not justify the investment for many projects. Compared with the straightforward, powerful accounts provided by the causal cells, dialectical theories may sometimes seem overly complex and convoluted. Second, because dialectical theories posit a recursive spiral of dependencies among causal and conventional features, their constructs may sometimes lack integrity. It is all well and good to argue, as we did above, that matching in interpersonal systems is based on interpretations shaped by systems of domination in our culture, which are themselves shaped by interpretations and actions within the systems of domination and so forth. In this argument, the interpretive scheme is conditioned by causal forces that are themselves dependent on action, which is further conditioned and so forth—all of which makes the stability, and therefore the scientific usefulness, of explanatory constructs problematic. Unless these interweaving influences are carefully specified and traced out, the resulting account may be too fluid to be useful.

Cell 8: Dialectical explanation, modeling inquiry. Studies in Cell 8 bear the same relation to those in Cell 7 as Cell 2 studies bear to those in Cell 1. Much the same reasoning and relations are involved in Cell 7 and Cell 8, but instead of hypotheses and corresponding observables, the researcher posits a model that directly depicts the pattern of observable behavior in the system. The model—which may be mathematical, logical, or verbal—specifies the causal forces and conventions operating in the system and uses these to derive predicted behavioral patterns. These are then compared with observed patterns to test the model. In addition, independent tests for the existence of causal forces and conventions also must be conducted. Once again, evidence for the model is accumulated through multiple, layered studies and tests. We could find no examples of such models in the interpersonal literature, though the Pearce and Cronen (1980) model discussed under Cell 5 could be a Cell 8 model if it were supplemented by an analysis of causal forces conditioning their rules and the rule-following process and of how the operation of causal forces depended on actors' use of conventions.

The advantages and disadvantages of Cell 8 compared with Cells 1 through 6 were discussed under Cell 7. Vis-à-vis Cell 7, Cell 8 studies have the advantages and disadvantages of modeling in relation to hypothetico-deductive inquiry, as discussed under Cell 2.

Cell 9: Dialectical explanation, grounded inquiry. In this template, the researcher develops a dialectical account through immediate observation and grounded induction. Theories in this template are similar to those in Cells 7 and 8 except for their notion of causality, which is the embedded causality discussed under Cell 3 above. As with the other dialectical templates, multiple studies are usually required to pin down the different aspects of the theory, and both immediate and historical data are used. In common with all grounded theories, Cell 9 research is tied to the limited context of its induction. R. D. Laing's (1962) observations in *The Self and Others* and Willis's (1977) study of how working-class boys are socialized to become laborers are examples of Cell 9 research.

Advantages and disadvantages of Cell 9 versus the first six cells have been discussed under Cell 7. In comparison with Cells 7 and 8, Cell 9 has the advantages and disadvantages of grounded theories mentioned under Cells 3 and 6. A particular problem with Cell 9 is the difficulty of developing embedded causal claims. A key move in dialectical explanation is to explore historical connections in the larger society. It is difficult to do this in a purely grounded theory because such connections suggest that general causes and a priori assumptions be brought to bear. Any theory that does this has a tendency to become a hybrid of Cells 7 or 8 and Cell 9. Notwithstanding, its capacity to incorporate both causal and conventional features in grounded theory makes this template an unexploited resource for interpersonal communication research.

Summary. There has been a tendency for research to confine itself to only a few of the nine templates. Social science is ideological, and arguments about the "right" way to conduct inquiry tend to create the assumption that only certain templates are valid. For example, causal explanation is generally associated with the traditional hypothetico-deductive mode of inquiry, and conventional explanation with development of grounded theory. There is no reason that either causal or conventional explanations cannot be associated with another mode of inquiry, but their uses with the other templates are not widely advertised. Arguments in favor of particular templates are often cast as critiques of other positions, and, unfortunately, defending a particular mode of inquiry or explanation sometimes assumes more importance than addressing substantive questions. We would suggest that, although debate is valuable, generalized attacks often hide other possibilities and blind us to the fact that all research involves choice from a range of potential approaches, each of which should be considered on its own merits for the question at hand. Advocacy of one "correct" template flies in the face of effective, creative research. But beyond innovation, effective research is grounded in the capacity to match investigative strategies to the object of research. The matching process not only creates a happy marriage of theory and technique but also serves as an important means of exploring the nature of the phenomenon by finding out how it can be conceptualized, measured, and analyzed.

The template adopted by a researcher influences his or her technical choices and also how a chosen technique is employed. It is, however, important to reemphasize that the templates are not the only consideration in choosing methods. Selection of techniques depends also on the substantive nature of the phenomenon and the researcher's substantive theoretical assumptions. There are many ways to match projects and templates, and the process defies codification into a set of rules and guidelines that state in definitive terms the connection between templates and techniques. Each template places different demands on the researcher and thereby creates certain technical preferences and affinities, but many of the techniques discussed below can be applied to numerous templates in one form or another.

The matrix of templates is designed to serve as a unifying scheme for practical choice, to indicate how the techniques in the next two sections could be used, and to suggest the various sorts of claims that could be made with them. Although it is not always explicitly present, this scheme forms the backdrop for the discussion to follow.

Data Gathering and Measurement Techniques

Interpersonal communication research has always been eclectic in its choice of observational methods. They span the entire range, from psychometric instruments to participant observation, with considerable distance covered in between. This section considers key issues relevant to these methods, in particular, problems of validity and reliability in measurement and observation. Validity is the most important issue in any consideration of data collection procedures. Research is fruitless without valid data, and it is not sufficient simply to assume our data are good. In the case of quantitative instruments, we must ask whether our measures do indeed tap the variables or constructs they are designed to assess. For direct observational methods, we must inquire whether our observational strategies contaminate the phenomenon and whether the interpretations and inferences drawn from observations are sound or biased. Reliability is a necessary condition for validity. In a technical sense, it is defined only for quantitative measures; but in a broader sense, as an assessment of how much error is in an observation or measurement, reliability is also meaningful for qualitative techniques.

This section has five parts. First, we will consider the construction and validation of tests and questionnaire instruments, the most commonly employed quantitative tools in interpersonal communication research. In this section we will also consider three techniques for observation. Part two will focus on interaction analysis, part three on discourse analysis, and part four on ethnography. Finally, we will consider some additional measurement issues.

Tests and Questionnaire Instruments

Much interpersonal communication research uses questionnaires, interviews, and other instruments to elicit subject reports of attitudes, beliefs, behavior, attributes, communication, others' behavior, recall of cognitive processes, rehearsal of messages, and so forth. A number of these are compiled in a recent book edited by Rubin, Palmgreen, and Sypher (in press). Too often, communication researchers construct their instruments in an ad hoc fashion, giving a nod to the gods of psychometrics by calculating a reliability coefficient and perhaps running a factor analysis. It is true that many statistical methods are fairly robust to violations of scale assumptions. It is also true that face validity of an instrument often signals other forms of validity. So perhaps there is not much wrong with many improvised instruments. However, researchers can never be sure their instruments are good without following systematic and careful procedures to construct and evaluate them. Because any data analysis is only as good as the data, it seems only sensible to devote some time and care to ensuring that our instruments are as good as possible.

Comprehensive treatments of the development and design of instruments can be found in the psychometric and survey research literature (e.g., Crocker & Algina, 1986; Cronbach, 1990; Fink & Kosecoff, 1985; Sudman & Bradburn, 1983). We will focus on issues useful for communication researchers and on some problems in current interpersonal communication research.

Conceptualization and design is the first step in the development of instruments. Construct definition is closely related to the theory-building process, because constructs acquire meaning by virtue of their place in theory. Ideally, instrument design should start with a clear construct definition before any items are written or questions tested. However, definition does not stop once the researcher has begun to construct the measure. It continues throughout the process, because writing items often forces the researcher to clarify definitional issues such as whether a construct is a state or a trait, an externally verifiable report or a description of a private subjective state, a uni- or multidimensional construct.

Ideally, conceptual analysis and construct definition directly guide the generation of items or questions. One useful way to use construct definitions to guide item construction is to specify *facets*, a set of independent item properties that stake out the universe of possible items that could be included in the measure (Borg, 1979; Foa, 1965; see Bell, 1986, for an application of facet analysis to interpersonal communication). Some facets vary between items, but others represent properties that must be present for item validity. For instance, the following could be a network-related question about amount of communication: "How often per week do you talk with your best friend (name previously supplied)?" Facets characterizing such an item might include (a) focus, in this case, own communication behavior; (b) object, own best friend; (c) behavior specification, "talk with"; (d) time period, week; and so on. Some of those facets might be varied to generate items (for example, "talk with" might be changed to "influence" to generate another item), whereas others would remain stable. Ideally, the facet list enables us to specify precisely the universe of possible items by stating which facets are important.

Instrument design requires sampling from the universe of possible items in order to meet certain specifications. Some specifications refer to practical limitations, such as the number and length of items. Others are methodological in that items must be designed to "fit" the researcher's method of analysis. A good source of guidance in writing items and constructing tests is the rapidly growing empirical base of knowledge about instrumentation effects. This work covers question design and also questionnaire package design and interviewer conduct. Some representative reviews include Dillman (1978), Fink and Kosecoff (1985), Rossi, Wright, and Anderson (1983), and Sudman and Bradburn (1983).

At the conceptual level, all tests should explicitly refer to some model of the relationship between responses and the underlying construct. The most common and robust model is classical true-score theory (Crocker & Algina, 1986; Lord & Novick, 1968). This model assumes responses are distributed normally about the value of the measured trait or construct. The use of factor analysis and confirmatory factor analysis to construct and evaluate tests assumes the classical true-score model. A second test theory, item response theory or latent trait theory, has developed in recent years (Hambleton & Swaminathan, 1985; Jones & Appelbaum, 1989; Lord & Novick, 1968). It assumes that different nonlinear curves (normal ogive, logistic, Poisson) relate item responses to levels of underlying traits or constructs. Although item response models require more restrictive assumptions than classical test theory, tests that include these assumptions have certain advantages, including the following: (a) An item response model enables precise estimation of the examinee's latent trait value from any subset of items that fits the model, thus reducing testing time and permitting easy development of alternative questionnaire forms, and (b) the measured trait is invariant over groups, provided the test is unidimensional.

Once the instrument has been defined and constructed, the second step is empirical evaluation. At least two questions should be addressed in this evaluation: (a) Does the instrument meet the assumptions of its measurement model and scale type? and (b) Is the instrument reliable and valid?

Methods to assess whether an instrument satisfies the assumptions of its measurement model and scale type are described in most psychometric texts. The best way to ensure that an instrument meets measurement model assumptions is careful application of empirical test construction methods. Good examples of the application of classical test theory to interpersonal communication constructs are the development of the verbal aggressiveness and argumentiveness scale (Infante & Rancer, 1982; Infante & Wigley, 1986) and the evaluation of rival measurement models for communication apprehension (Levine & McCroskey, 1990). The classical model of test theory underlies nearly every communication scale we reviewed. The field has not yet taken advantage of item response theory, even for constructs that seem to fit it well, such as communication competence.

Little interpersonal communication research has evaluated scaling assumptions. However, this is an important issue. If what we think is an interval or ratio scale can only satisfy the assumptions of an ordinal scale, then we may inadvertently use the wrong statistical methods. The debate over which question and response format should be used to assess compliance-gaining strategies illustrates the importance of scale development (see Burleson et al., 1988, and the responses to this article in *Human Communication Research, 15*; see also Dillard, 1988; Hunter & Boster, 1987). Another interesting study is Rothenbuhler's (1991) use of a log-linear latent class model to test a Guttman scale of community involvement. An interesting and unique approach to scaling that does not fit any current test theory is presented in Woelfel & Fink (1980; see Craig, 1983, for a critique of this approach).

The second empirical question concerns reliability and validity assessment (Crocker & Algina, 1986). The assessment of reliability depends on the underlying measurement model and type of scale used. For instance, use of coefficient alpha is appropriate for measures composed of multiple-item Likert scales, but it would not be appropriate for assessing reliability of a Guttman scale because items low and high in difficulty on a Guttman scale are not expected to have very high correlations.

The most widely used methods of assessing reliability (test-retest, split-half, coefficient alpha) are designed for the assessment of reliability between two sets of measures—such as a test and a retest, or ratings by two different judges—or internal consistency of a single test. But these severely limit the range of measurement possibilities researchers can evaluate. Cases not covered by traditional reliability methods occur when three or more judges rate the same behaviors, when two or more different (but nonparallel) forms of the same test are used, or when two or more raters score events on more than one occasion, to name just a few. Generalizability theory (Crocker & Algina, 1986; Cronbach, Gleser, Nanda, &

Rajaratnam, 1972; Jones & Appelbaum, 1989) is a general approach to reliability assessment that covers most cases.

The theory of generalizability posits that a measure is useful insofar as its findings generalize to a broader set of measurements. For instance, from a given observation, we might wish to generalize to observations made using other tests constructed in an identical way (the idea behind internal-consistency reliability), observations made at a later time (time one-time two reliability or stability), observations by other raters (interrater reliability), or observations using different but valid measures of the same construct. Because error is what prevents this generalization, conducting a generalizability study involves distinguishing the sources of error any type of measurement might have and determining how large each error component is. For example, assume we have three raters score children's role-taking ability after seeing them for 15 minutes in each of three play situations—in the sandbox, on playground equipment, and at their juice breaks—over three different days. Variation in ratings might be due to observer, to situation, and to day. The generalizability study would determine how serious each error component is and the degree to which we could generalize over observers, situations, and days. For many years, the use of generalizability theory was limited by lack of estimators of some of the generalization coefficients, but in recent years, methods have been developed that can be implemented with most common statistical packages (Jones & Appelbaum, 1989).

Validity assessment is described in numerous sources (e.g., Allen & Yen, 1979; Crocker & Algina, 1985; Cronbach, 1990). One of the most common methods for validation in interpersonal communication research has been the multitrait, multimethod (MTMM) approach described originally by Campbell and Fiske (Crocker & Algina, 1986). Several problems with the original approach have been considered. First, any study is limited by the particular set of methods and traits used. Second, visual inspection of the matrix often can be misleading due to sampling error. To counteract this problem, formal methods of interpreting MTMM matrices using ANOVA, nonparametric methods, and confirmatory factor analysis have been developed (Schmitt & Stults, 1986). Third, halo or leniency effects can further cloud interpretation of MTMM matrices. Several researchers have described methods to correct for these effects by identifying and partialing out "general bias" factors from the analysis of the MTMM correlations (Schmitt & Stults, 1986). Schmitt and Stults (1986) reviewed studies that compared the various methods for analysis of MTMM matrices just mentioned and concluded that they led to similar results only in cases where the test met either all or none of Campbell and Fiske's original four criteria for validity. In cases where only some of the criteria were met, no clear conclusions could be drawn, and different methods led to different conclusions. Schmitt and Stults make a strong argument that confirmatory factor analysis is the most comprehensive method for validity analysis.

Structural equation modeling, the general methodology that includes confirmatory factor analysis, also has great potential for validity studies (Bollen, 1989; Kenny, 1979). It enables researchers to separate reliability from validity and to isolate validity components from other error components that cloud the interpretation of traditional validity coefficients.

Ideally, we should not stop once a test has been empirically evaluated; evaluation of a measurement instrument should continue during its use in research. In particular, it is often wise to dry-run several subjects through the whole study procedure, then interview them about their understanding of and reasons for responses to the measurement instrument to make sure the research context does not invalidate it. Furthermore, accumulation of validity evidence is an ongoing process, and it is often a good idea to reassess measures in light of emerging results (e.g., Burleson et al., 1988). Also, during the process of data analysis, a number of statistical techniques allow us to identify and adjust for discrepancies in measurement instruments that do not perform as intended (see McPhee & Babrow, 1987).

We believe that two practices common in instrument development by interpersonal communication researchers should be reconsidered. First, communication researchers seem to rely too much on exploratory factor analysis as a basis for understanding and evaluating questionnaire instruments. Exploratory factor analysis is very broad and flexible, but the information it gives about a test is also complex. Any simple approach to test evaluation using factor-analytic results could be either misleading or inappropriate because the factor-analytic model is simply not designed to supply all the information needed to validate instruments. Moreover, the results of exploratory factor analysis may not replicate because of error due to the particular sample and situation utilized. Cronkhite (1976) reports some very interesting findings on the interaction effects of rater, concept rated, and scale identity on the factor structure of multi-item evaluative semantic differential scales. Confirmatory factor analysis, which tests hypotheses about factor structures, is a more powerful and comprehensive method (see also the discussion of factor analysis below).

A second problem in some communication test development procedures is that important properties of the measure or underlying construct are not adequately articulated and evaluated. Hewes and Haight (1979) examined the "cross-situational consistency" of several supposed communication "traits" that were thought to characterize subjects. The relatively low correlations they found seem to indicate that the measured behaviors displayed much less consistency than the term *trait* suggests. They traced these failings in part to inadequate conceptualization of constructs. (See Hewes & Haight, 1980; Jaccard & Daly, 1980, for discussion of the specific application of this problem to questionnaire measures.)

As described here, the instrument development process seems to be associated most strongly with the causal templates. However, it is also appropriate for the conventional or dialectical templates, if item generation and test design and validation take into account subject understandings and concepts. A measurement model for these templates must be discovered, not imposed a priori, probably through an initial phase of grounded research, and the final test should possess representational validity (see the next section).

Interaction Analysis

In our discussion of this method and also discourse analysis and participant observation, we have avoided lengthy "how-to" discussions, because they are well described in referenced sources. Instead, we have chosen to focus on the interlocking problems of validity and proof because these are the main sources of difficulty for observational methods at present.

Interaction analysis refers to any systematic method of *classifying* verbal and nonverbal behavior, ranging from formal category systems such as Bales's (1970) IPA and Fisher's (1970) Decision Proposal Coding System to systems for classifying speech acts (e.g., J. R. Searle, 1976). These methods have in common the interpretation of utterances according to a standard set of rules developed by the researchers. Four key issues facing interaction analysis are category construction, reliability, validity, and the adaptation of coding systems to different contexts.

There are several discussions of how to construct interaction analysis systems (Folger, Hewes, & Poole, 1984; Lazarsfeld & Barton, 1969; Poole, Folger, & Hewes, 1987; Trujillo, 1986). Construction of systems can follow two routes. In one, a logically complete system is elucidated. The internal logic of such a system yields an exhaustive classification, usually according to a logical choice tree that rigidly specifies coding choices (see, for example, P. A. Anderson, 1983). Such an approach makes classification straightforward, but the logical demands of constructing the decision tree may distort the meaning of the discourse to its speakers. It is easy to replace speaker's sense of the language with the classifier's "neater" and "more logical" interpretations. The second, more common approach involves compiling categories that index relevant functions in the discourse being studied. These functions are often specified by the researcher's theory, as in the case of the Rogers-Farace (1975) relational coding system; and they may also have considerable internal structure, as does Bales's IPA system. Alternatively, the system may be developed with a grounded approach to reflect the functions the observer sees in the situation. Hawes's (1972) interview coding system is based on this approach. As opposed to the logically complete approach, this second strategy relies more on the observer's natural interpretive abilities to determine classifications. The second approach to designing classification systems is advantageous because it is more responsive to the particular nature of the discourse than the first, but it is correspondingly less "clean" and its rules harder to apply consistently. Regardless of how the system is designed, researchers also face other crucial choices, as outlined in an excellent article by Hewes (1979).

Coding reliability, a necessary condition for classificatory validity, can be separated into two components: (a) *unitizing reliability*, which refers to the coder's ability to agree on how the discourse should be parsed into units, and (b) *classificatory reliability*, which refers to the level of agreement on how units should be classified. Folger et al. (1984) provide an extensive discussion of different means of assessing reliability and of special cases in which reliability is particularly critical. Zwick (1988) compares different interrater reliability coefficients. It is important to assess reliability both at the level of the overall coding system and at the level of the individual categories. As Hewes (1985; Folger et al., 1984) have noted, even for coding systems with high overall reliability, there may be particular categories with low reliability, and this can seriously disrupt certain types of data analysis methods.

In abstract terms, the validity of interaction analysis systems is the degree to which they actually yield the types of information they are designed to obtain. Exactly what constitutes validity and how validity is assessed depends on what types of claims the researcher is attempting to make about interaction (Folger et al., 1984; Poole et al., 1987). At least three types of claims might be made about observations of interaction. First, a researcher may only want to identify acts theoretically interesting to him or her, regardless of how the actors themselves interpret the acts. In this mode of observation, which Poole et al. (1987) term *observer-privileged,* the researcher aspires to explain interaction from the outside without reference to subjects' perspectives. Much research with interaction analysis, particularly in the causal templates, works under this assumption. But a researcher may also want to use a coding system to identify how subjects interpret interaction. The researcher may seek to develop categories that identify the shared meaning utterances have for members of a culture. This observational mode, called the *generalized subject-privileged* mode by Poole et al. (1987), is the aspiration of many coding systems, including those based on the identification of speech acts. But the researcher may try to go even further and use a coding system to identify the idiosyncratic meanings of utterances for people in a particular relationship, in *restricted subject-privileged mode*. Labov and Fanshel (1977) use this mode of observation in their book *Therapeutic Discourse*.

It is easy to aspire to one of the three modes of observation, but the researcher's claims about his or her classifications must be backed up by evidence for their validity. Each mode of observation requires different types of evidence. For observer-privileged systems, which code according to the researcher's point of view, the classic techniques of assessing construct validity are sufficient. However, for subject-privileged systems, which attempt to get at subjects' meanings, the researcher also must provide evidence that they actually represent subjects' interpretations. Several methods for assessing the *representational validity* of coding systems have been developed (see Folger et al., 1984, for a review of these methods; see also Poole & Folger, 1981). The importance of formally establishing the validity of coding systems is illustrated by O'Donnell-Trujillo's (1982) comparison of two relational coding systems that purported to code the same constructs. He found a very low degree of overlap in codings, suggesting that one or both were "off base." But which one is? Without validity assessment, it is impossible to establish.

Finally, even coding systems designed for general use must be adapted to specific cases. This generally involves making special assumptions about what rules mean and how they are applied. Cicourel (1980) has argued that these adaptations should be reported in a methodological appendix, along with more detail on coder background and training than is normally supplied.

Discourse Analysis

Rather than coding interaction explicitly, many interpersonal communication researchers use texts, recordings, or transcriptions of discourse as a base from which they directly formulate categories and generalize to knowledge claims. Tracy (1991) distinguishes five approaches to discourse analysis: conversational analysis, formal/structural analysis, culturally focused analysis, discourse processing, and discourse and identity. These differ in their assumptions as to whether researchers should use only naturally occurring discourse or may construct discursive examples to illustrate points, whether and how discourse data should be supplemented by other forms of data (e.g., information about context), and what are the most appropriate systems for recording and transcription of discourse. The best known of these methods is conversational analysis (CA), which has the largest literature base and the longest tradition. In this section, we will focus on CA, while commenting on issues of concern to all the approaches.

Based on a number of accounts (especially Hopper, Koch, & Mandelbaum, 1986; Psathas, 1990), there are at least five stages in the progression from interaction itself to a CA reading: accumulation of data, transcription, identification of a focal phenomenon, interpretation of the phenomenon, and building arguments for the analysis. These stages routinely overlap and cycle back, and we array them in this order mainly to organize distinctive issues related to each stage. The last two stages are more akin to what we call data analysis than to data gathering, so we shall delay their discussion until the section on qualitative analysis methods.

Conversational analysis is famous for emphasizing its empirical reliance on publicly available records of actual interaction based on the contentions that conversation creates its own order by displaying it (Attewell, 1972), that intuitions about conversation are often incorrect, and that precision timing is important for much of the coordination in interaction. CA argues that research should begin with accumulation of a data stock, which analysts use both to find phenomena to do research on and to supply examples supporting or challenging their analysis of the phenomena. While CA may accept snippets of conversation written down by an interested researcher, audiotaped or videotaped records are preferred. CA typically uses both verbal and nonverbal information available on a tape, because a number of its practitioners have shown the importance of gaze, gestures, and so on, for adequate analysis even of such basic CA topics as turn-taking (Frankel, 1983; Psathas, 1990). The other schools reviewed by Tracy (1991) are more flexible about the range of acceptable data, allowing created or recalled examples and descriptions, among other data types. They argue that such data are permissible because they shed light on theorized processes of discourse generation. Certainly analyses such as Wiemann's (1981) suggest that there is nothing particularly objective about video- and audiotapes. They are not "transparent" records of events but introduce biases, depending on the researcher's perspective when arranging the taping and analyzing the tapes.

Once interaction has been recorded, it must be transcribed. CA demands painstaking and detailed transcriptions that put extra effort into describing pauses, nonverbal vocalizations, and relative timing of overlaps and interruptions, almost always using conventions and notation devised by Gail Jefferson (Schenkein, 1978). Transcription by the researcher, not by assistants, is seen as crucial to concept formation and even understanding of the data. In many cases, deciphering just what is going on in an audiotaped record is very difficult, and sometimes it takes a group to produce a high-quality transcript (Hopper et al., 1986). Reliability, of signal concern for quantitative data, is also important for transcripts, but it is rarely addressed by discourse analysts. As Tracy indicates, many discourse analysts not adhering so closely to CA use transcripts that seem much more like normal texts, partly because testing their theoretical points does not require the detail (and consequent difficulty) of CA conventions. On the other hand, Hopper et al. (1986) note that a number of CA-aligned researchers have developed supplemental notations to augment the usual notation with information about gaze, intonation, and so on. Moreover, Edelsky (1982) and Ochs (1979) demonstrate that transcription patterns of any sort are not theoretically neutral—different approaches to transcription reveal some facts but obscure others. These authors argue persuasively that important theoretical insights are obscured by the CA transcription conventions.

During or after the initial transcription process, researchers begin to look for and conceptualize a phenomenon of interest. CA emphasizes that finding and adequately describing a phenomenon is far from easy, demanding repeated trials and critical assessments. Hopper et al. (1986) and Psathas (1990) recommend methods such as repeating a section of tape or transcript over and over, focusing on very small segments, limiting oneself to details that another party to the conversation could register, remaining open to new insights or features, and trying out initial descriptions in groups for critical emendation. Even scholars who bring theoretical concerns in with them can profit by remaining open to unexpected relevances in the discourse.

Fieldwork and Participant Observation

Several interpersonal communication studies based on qualitative analysis of fieldwork have appeared in the past two decades (e.g., Jones & Yarbrough, 1985; Philipsen, 1975). These studies generally use participant observation to gather primary data. Participant observation has great potential, because it gives the researcher detailed knowledge of communication processes in context. It can also give the researcher something laboratory studies can never yield, namely, an idea of whether the object of study really is important in the social world and of how it fits in with other social forces.

Many good treatments of field research and participant observation give extensive suggestions on how to conduct good research (e.g., Cicourel, 1964; Denzin, 1989; Schwartz & Jacobs, 1979; Strauss, 1987). Here, we will concern ourselves with three important issues related to the adequacy of observational data: the role of the researcher, how the researcher interacts with and "interprets" subjects, and the reliability and validity of observations.

The participant observer can take a number of different roles, which differ in terms of "distance" from the subject of study. The role the observer takes determines the types of data she or he obtains and the aspects of subjects' meanings this data can illuminate. In one of the earliest and best discussions, Gold (1958) distinguishes four roles: the complete observer, the observer-as-participant, the participant-as-observer, and the complete participant. Generally, it seems that the researcher's theoretical perspective guides the selection of one or the other role.

This observation seems to go against the common notion that participant observation research is open-ended or dedicated to the development of "grounded" theory. Although it is true that the particular explanatory concepts or mechanisms are drawn out "inductively" or "retroductively" or by means of "situationally guided hypotheses," most researchers have at least an implicit theory of what is important to look for. Consider, for example, Philipsen's (1975) study of the ethnography of communication in "Teamsterville." Philipsen took the role of participant-as-observer and found a set of communicative rules, because these are the things to which his ethnographic perspective sensitized him. Had Philipsen been operating from Garfinkel's or Cicourel's ethnomethodologies, he would have focused on practical reasoning and accounting behaviors. Had he been using Goffman's frame, he would likely have found self-presentation and strategic behavior to play a critical role in being a "Man" in "Teamsterville." Each perspective sensitizes the researcher to some concepts or phenomena and deemphasizes others, determining the role he or she adopts, what can be discovered, and the form the findings can take.

These considerations underscore the need for the researcher to work out his or her theoretical commitments prior to going out in the field (Cicourel, 1964). It is certainly a mistake to form strong hypotheses; too easily, they turn into self-fulfilling prophecies. However, it is also a mistake to go in without clear ideas on the types of concepts we are looking for; without these it is difficult, if not impossible, to carry out meaningful observation, distill concepts from observations, and write a coherent account.

While selecting a role is an important first step, it does not totally determine the participant observer's data. What the participant-observer finds out is, in a very real sense, dependent on how he or she interacts with subjects and enters into their worlds (Whyte, 1955). The observer can only observe and perhaps ask questions; he or she cannot experience social practices firsthand. The participant-as-observer experiences them firsthand, but his or her experience is conditioned and limited by the degree of access gained under study. If the participant-as-observer never advances beyond novitiate training in a religion, he or she cannot know the "inner" workings of the religion for those who are full-fledged members. For this reason, the way in which the participant-observer gains access to the field setting, the problems and refusals, and the shifts in his or her interpretations as time goes by and he or she becomes more "experienced" are important to understanding the researcher's account. They specify the relationships that underlie and "contextualize" the researcher's findings.

Several strategies are available for dealing with this problem. One suggestion is that research reports should be written as "natural histories" that recount the entire research process from beginning to end, emphasizing the researcher's interpretations (and changes in them) at each point along the way. Such an account enables the reader to identify shifts in the researcher's attitude and interpretations as the project unfolded and gives the reader hints about mistakes or narrowness in the researcher's interpretations. Second, Cicourel (1964) suggests that details such as making contacts and problems with interviews or encounters should be reported alongside relevant findings to give them perspective. Alternatively, he suggests a methodological appendix for reporting these details. Third, participant-observers can try to work out the practical reasoning behind their interpretations. Just like quantitative researchers, they should consider likely alternative interpretations and adduce evidence in their reports to rule these out. By exhausting at least the most plausible alternatives, they can pin down their points more definitely and tighten them considerably.

A third concern for participant-observers is the *reliability* and *validity* of their "data." These terms have traditionally been associated with quantitative measurement techniques; however, they have clear analogues in observational procedures and qualitative researchers are becoming increasingly concerned with reliability and validity (Kirk & Miller, 1986; LeCompte & Goetz, 1982). Kirk and Miller (1986) argue that, in both quantitative and qualitative research, reliability and validity refer to the process of gaining some degree of objectivity vis-à-vis subject matter. Validity consists of finding some way to "call things by their right names," and in qualitative research it depends on refinement of ethnographic methods and on never-ending exploration and checking of interpretations. Kirk and Miller argue that reliability assessment in qualitative research depends on comparison of observations over time and across different sites. They believe that discovery of unreliability often advances understanding, because researchers must reconcile competing accounts and uncover whether the unreliability is due to some important underlying factor or to researcher errors. Field notes are crucial in the analysis of reliability, and Kirk and Miller recommend some methods for increasing uniformity in notes made by different researchers and by the same researcher on different occasions. LeCompte and Goetz (1982), discussed below, also suggest a number of ways to enhance the reliability and validity of ethnographic data.

Other Issues

An increasingly common method of measuring communication is the use of subjects' *reports or recollections* of their interactions. These are collected by methods including (a) having subjects or observers make retrospective global ratings of interaction episodes (Metts, Sprecher, & Cupach, 1991; Poole et al., 1987); (b) collecting retrospective subject accounts or narratives of interaction (Burnett, 1991; see also Bochner, this volume); (c) having subjects keep interaction diaries or logs (Duck, 1991); and (d) stimulated recall, in which subjects comment on videotapes of their own interaction (Frankel & Beckman, 1982). Advantages of these methods include the ability to capture the subjects' interpretations of inter-action (often in their own words), the generation of meaningful summary data for complex events, and access to otherwise inaccessible interactions such as intimate encounters. These approaches seem quite promising, and guidelines for using them are growing more sophisticated. However, these methods, too, must shoulder the burden of proving their validity and reliability in the face of several possible problems. As Poole et al. (1987) note, global ratings of interaction often do not correlate highly with direct coding on similar dimensions and may be subject to bias due to rater's implicit theories of interaction. All four methods are vulnerable to various cognitive biases (Metts et al., 1991, pp. 168-169) and limitations on what can be recalled (Duck, 1991; Ericsson & Simon, 1980; Nisbett & Wilson, 1977). Accounts and stimulated recall data may also be problematic due to subjects' language deficiencies and lack of insight. The various sources cited here discuss other limitations as well as means for mitigating the various problems.

Another important issue is the measurement of *change.* It has become more pressing with the development of increasingly sophisticated methods for analysis of communication processes and longitudinal data. At first, calculating change scores seems to be simply a matter of subtraction; however, change scores suffer from several problems including low reliability, "regression toward the mean," and a tendency for measures to change in meaning to subjects over time (Collins & Horn, 1991; Cronbach & Furby, 1970). Hence simple change scores should be used very carefully or alternative methods such as analysis of covariance with pretest scores as covariates should be used (Cook & Campbell, 1979). Several chapters in an excellent book edited by Collins and Horn (1991) discuss the measurement of change.

Another important measurement issue centers on whether quantitative variables are *meaningful.* To this point such variables have been regarded as nonproblematic. However, several researchers, including Blumer (1956), Churchill (1963), Cicourel (1964), Garfinkel (1967), and Schutz (1964), have raised powerful objections to quantitative measurement as traditionally practiced. One problem stems from the fact that, once a variable or construct is defined, it often becomes a taken-for-granted feature of the world. For researchers, constructs like attitude, norm, or attraction become second nature, and it is easy to confuse the construct measured by a set of technical rules with the phenomenon itself. Several writers have commented on this tendency to reify variables and its attendant dangers. One problem with this interpretation of variables is that it may "freeze" or present too static a picture of a construct that is negotiated or "in process" (Cicourel, 1972). Also, it may hide cases where a concept is forced into a measurement scale that oversimplifies or distorts it (Churchill, 1963).

Related to this is Schutz's dictum that scientific constructs should be rooted in actors' meanings. This concern seems particularly appropriate for interpersonal communication research because many theories explicitly try to explain interpersonal behavior from the subjects' point of view. Despite this goal, it is easy for researchers to impose their own constructs and models on subjects, substituting observers' insights for actors' processes and understandings. This often occurs out of the awareness of the researchers, because they take social scientific constructs for granted and do not consider that they may only reflect professional discourse and not subjects' perspectives. Taking this point of view seriously means that researchers should ask hard questions about their constructs: For example, is the way we conceptualize relational control consistent with how subjects see control issues? Are the statements we call dominant actually seen as such by subjects? Are subjects even concerned with control in day-to-day interaction? At least for those theories that purport to capture subjects' perspectives (to use the terms mentioned above, those working in the subject-privileged perspectives), continuous attention to the representativeness of their constructs and measures is the price of their greater immediacy.

These arguments can be taken as indictments of quantitative research. However, we believe it is more profitable to consider them as *topoi* for critiquing and gaining insight into our constructs and measures. Raising these questions does take considerable time and could throw a monkey wrench into fast-burgeoning theoretical machinery, but the increased sensitivity this endeavor lends to our constructs will more than repay the effort. Studies like Rawlins's (1983) research on openness clearly illustrate the power of scrutinizing traditional concepts.

Summary

Figure 3.3 presents a summary of some measurement and observational techniques discussed in this section and their relationship to the templates. The symbol in each box represents our estimation of the degree to which the technique is currently used by interpersonal communication researchers working in the various templates and our judgment of the potential usefulness of the technique in each template. Although somewhat impressionistic, this figure illustrates current practice and promising applications of these techniques.

Analytical Techniques

This section focuses on patterns of analytical reasoning in statistical techniques and qualitative analysis. Patterns of reasoning are the most important aspect of analysis, though more attention is often devoted to technical aspects and details of application. Although the patterns discussed here are usually associated with either quantitative or qualitative techniques, most can be employed in both areas. Despite the supposed rift between quantitative and qualitative methods, both are subject to the same requirements of inference and proof, and both can employ similar canons of reasoning.

We have grouped analytical techniques into seven families: experimental design, statistical model testing, descriptive techniques, time-series techniques, developmental techniques, qualitative techniques. For each genre, we discuss its core assumptions and range of applications, predominant techniques, its affinities to the templates, its strengths and weaknesses, and new methodological opportunities.

Experimental Design

When social scientists discuss methods, their most general concerns are with matters of measurement, design, and analysis. The middle term, design of research

TEMPLATE

TECHNIQUE	1	2	3	4	5	6	7	8	9
Questionnaires	★	★	◆	★	◆	Ø	◆	◆	☺
Facet Analysis	☺	☺	☺	☺	☺	☺	☺	☺	☺
Scale Analysis	◆	◆	Ø	☺	☺	Ø	☺	☺	Ø
Reliability Assessment	★	★	Ø	◆	◆	Ø	◆	◆	Ø
Formal Validity Assessment	★	★	☺	☺	☺	Ø	☺	☺	Ø
Generalizability Study	☺	☺	☺	☺	☺	Ø	☺	☺	Ø
Interaction Coding	★	★	Ø	◆	◆	Ø	☺	☺	Ø
Representational Validity Assessment	◆	☺	☺	◆	◆	☺	☺	☺	☺
Discourse Analysis	Ø	Ø	Ø	◆	☺	★	☺	◆	★
Participant Observation	☺	☺	★	☺	☺	★	◆	◆	★
Reports or Recollection Measures	◆	◆	★	◆	◆	★	◆	◆	★
Critique of Construct Meaning	☺	☺	★	☺	☺	★	★	★	★

Key: ★ = Used very much with success
◆ = Used somewhat and has more potential
☺ = Used little but has potential
Ø = Not useful

Figure 3.3. Selected Measurement and Observational Techniques and Their Potential and Actual Use in the Templates

procedures, is at least as broad as the other two, yet we will devote little space to it in part because it is the area in which the least fundamental change and debate has occurred and in part because it has been covered in the discussion of the nine templates (see Keppel, 1973; Kirk, 1982; Winer, Brown, & Michels, 1990, for extensive treatments of experimental design).

The design of studies is generally concerned with three goals: uncovering or bringing into focus the effects of interest, avoiding or controlling threats to the validity of inferences, and generalizing the conclusions to some universe of interest. Influenced by critiques of positivism to disregard the natural science model, social scientific researchers sometimes underemphasize the ingenuity required to strip away distracting or deceptive elements in order to isolate and analyze the effects of interest. Yet much of the best social scientific research turns on precisely this, and design is the critical factor in such cases. Interpersonal communication researchers tend to use simple, traditional designs (for example, two- and three-way completely crossed ANOVAs or analysis of covariance). More complex and "exotic" designs, such as Latin square or blocked designs, have advantages over the simple designs in terms of efficiency and power. A study of second-guessing by Hewes, Graham, Doelger, and Pavitt (1985) provides a good example of this.

The second goal, that of dealing with validity threats, has been articulated by Campbell and Stanley (1966). In their extension of this theme, Cook and Campbell (1979) note four major types of validity: the construct validity of causes and effects, statistical conclusion validity, internal validity, and external validity. These refer to our confidence in our ability to answer four questions about a study: (a) Do the manipulations and measurements correspond to the variables we intend to study? (b) Do the data indicate a relationship between these variables? (c) Given the relationship, is it causal in this study? (d) Can we generalize the presence of causation to a wider context than this sample? Cook and Campbell argue that internal validity is primary, although they note disagreements and strong necessary qualifications on this primacy (pp. 83-91). Therefore much of their analysis is concentrated on designs that can remove the threats to internal validity.

Randomization and controlled manipulation are important methods to guard against validity threats. The classic experimental design with random assignment to treatments and controlled manipulation is the most rigorous protection. It enables unambiguous identification of causal effects and partitioning of variance among effects. Neither nonexperimental designs, which do not control manipulations, nor quasi-experimental designs, which do not have random assignment, permit this degree of protection or inferential rigor. Numerous analytical adjustments are available for improving the rigor of these designs. Cook and Campbell (1979) describe a number of quasi-experimental designs, some of which are tailored to solve troublesome inferential problems. Path analysis and structural equation modeling (see below) permit causal analysis in nonexperimental designs. There are also methods for achieving approximate variance partitions for factors in nonexperimental designs (McPhee & Seibold, 1979). Experimental designs are the surest guarantee of validity, but other designs can be made strong as well.

Our third goal, generalization of conclusions to a broader context, is the one on which most controversy in interpersonal communication research has centered. Interest in this issue has been raised by Jackson and Jacobs's (1983) article on messages as variables. Jackson and Jacobs note that studies often use a single message to represent a communication variable category or level. And when multiple messages are employed, an incorrect statistical tool (fixed-effects rather than random-effects ANOVA) is almost always employed. Neither procedure supports conclusions that generalize to messages in general, and Jackson and Jacobs show that general conclusions drawn in the past are subject to error. They recommend developing multiple messages, despite the difficulty of that enterprise, and the use of random-effects ANOVA procedures.

This essay has produced considerable controversy and reflection, and several qualifications and counterarguments have been raised (Burgoon, Hall, & Pfau, 1991; Hunter, Hamilton, & Allen, 1989; Jackson, O'Keefe, Jacobs, & Brashers, 1989; Morley, 1988). Morley (1988) and others have noted that the use of fixed-effects designs is appropriate when the levels chosen exhaust all possible levels of the message phenomenon (e.g., the speaker is male or female) or when generalizing only to the fixed levels is conceptually important. Morley also notes some problems with the quasi-F statistic typically used to analyze random-effects designs, including low power and lack of a reference distribution.

Hunter et al. (1989) argue that individual studies using single messages have definite advantages over the suggestions of Jackson and Jacobs, because a variety of rigorously controlled studies can be examined for differential message impacts using meta-analysis. We believe this response stems from a profound difference in the conception of communication between the two sides. The random-effects camp includes researchers influenced by qualitative techniques such as conversational analysis. The evidence such perspectives offer for people's sensitivity to complexities of message structure and context is striking. This view of the complexity and sensitivity of communication naturally leads to an emphasis on the variety of ways any typical message variable can work in context. The single-message camp focuses instead on experimental rigor and statistical power. For them, the impact of a message is presumed to be a fairly simple function of a few features (amount of evidence, language intensity, and so on), and research should be designed to demonstrate that with maximum efficiency. Using multiple messages necessarily reduces power and control.

The controversy is not resolved at the time of this writing. Both strategies have, in the long run, the capacity to detect general treatment effects and treatment-by-replication interactions that indicate that the treatment varies in its effects across different message contexts. And meta-analysis of multiple studies does permit the attainment of large sample sizes and diversity of experimental contexts, which will enhance generalizability of conclusions.

Nonetheless, we think the multiple-message, random-effects strategy is preferable. First, single-message studies are unable to detect treatment-by-message interactions or to distinguish their effects from those of a main treatment effect of theoretical interest. They are thus liable to find invalid significant results (that is, have an inflated Type 1 error rate); and even if multiple messages are used, fixed-effect statistics incur this inflated error rate (Jackson & Brashers, in press). Second, the random-effects approach seems to possess the advantages of "face validity" and caution. We do typically seek to generalize ideas about message variables to an infinite population of messages characterized by those variables, and the random-effects strategy registers that intent. And, if the message context in which a treatment is embedded does make a difference, the random-effects strategy has protected us.

The cornerstone of experimental statistics, ANOVA, continues to be preeminent in interpersonal communication research. Because it is so well established, it is easy to overlook new developments in ANOVA methodology. Wilcox (1987) has questioned the wisdom of disregarding violations of the assumption of homogeneity of variance across cells in ANOVA designs. He marshals convincing evidence that heterogeneous variance can be much more damaging than is commonly assumed, inflating Type I error rates as much as fourfold and seriously reducing statistical power. He suggests several alternatives to the traditional F-test that may be more appropriate when heteroscedasticity occurs. On a different note, Rosenthal and Rosnow (1985) have argued that, when the researcher has definite expectations regarding the pattern of results across cells, omnibus F-tests may be inappropriate and may actually miss real differences. Instead, they recommend the use of planned contrasts that test the predicted pattern of means. Theory and methodology for ANOVA continues to be a very active area of research, with improvements and refinements coming regularly.

Statistical Model-Testing Techniques

Many statistical approaches have been advanced to test correlational or causal relationships among variables. The mainstream of statistical analysis in social science involves (a) developing a hypothesis that one or more (independent) variables are unidirectionally related to another (dependent) variable, (b) working out a statistical model that reflects this hypothesis, and (c) testing the model. This approach is consistent with the hypothetico-deductive mode of inquiry. A statistical model is clearly subordinate and subsequent to the conceptual hypothesis and thus is not related to the modeling mode of inquiry. The decision about data-model conformity can be highly complex, but usually it simply consists of rejecting a general null hypothesis of no relationship between dependent and independent variables in favor of the hypothesis of relationship. Often the statistical models are special versions of the "General Linear Model," a relatively simple and flexible functional form that is very well understood by statisticians and is easy to use in most cases of interest to social scientists (S. R. Searle, 1971).

The array of techniques for statistical hypothesis testing include correlation, ANOVA, regression, multivariate analysis of variance (MANOVA), canonical correlation, path analysis, structural equation modeling, and multivariate categorical analysis (log-linear analysis, logit analysis, and their relatives). This literature is so large that it is impractical to attempt a summary. Instead, we will focus on developing trends and problems in our field. A short list of good sources includes: Pedhazur (1982), Weisberg (1985), and Wonnacott and Wonnacott (1979) for regression and its variants; Morrison (1990) and Tatsuoka (1988) for multivariate techniques in general; Bollen (1989), Jöreskog and Sörbom (1989), and McPhee and Babrow (1987) for structural equation modeling and path analysis; Bishop, Feinberg, and Holland (1975), Christensen (1990), Everitt (1977), and Feinberg (1989) for multivariate categorical analysis.

Several trends in the use of multivariate techniques in interpersonal communication research are noteworthy. First, it has become commonplace to conduct simultaneous analysis of *multiple dependent variables* with canonical correlation, multivariate analysis of variance and covariance, and tests of equality of vectors of means or covariance matrices (e.g., Gudykunst, 1985; Mulac, Weimann, Widenmann, & Gibson, 1988; for general treatments, see, e.g., Morrison, 1990; Tatsuoka, 1988). This is appropriate if the dependent variables are conceptually related and their combination is meaningful, because the test is more efficient and may be more powerful. Also, problems with alpha-level inflation due to multiple statistical tests are avoided. But there is also a catch: A multivariate statistical test is designed for hypotheses involving a *linear combination* of variables, not a set of discrete variables. If one is really interested in variables on their own, not their weighted sums, then the gains may be illusory (Morrison, 1990).

The use of *structural equation modeling*, which subsumes causal analysis and path analysis, has grown rapidly in interpersonal research (see, e.g., Stiff, Dillard, Somera, Kim, & Sleight, 1988; for general sources, see Bollen, 1989; E. L. Fink, 1980). This growth stems in part from the availability of easy-to-use programs such as LISREL (Jöreskog & Sörbom, 1989) and EQS (Bentler, 1989). Structural equation modeling can be used to test traditional path models, causal models with unobserved latent variables with multiple indicators, causal models with feedback loops, and longitudinal models that incorporate correlated errors and unreliability of measurement, and it can also be used to conduct confirmatory factor analysis (Bollen, 1989; Bollen & Long, 1993; Collins & Horn, 1991). It has grown into a general data analytic model that rivals the general linear model. However, there are also problems. Methods for assessing fit of structural equation models are far from foolproof (though there have been advances in recent years; see Bollen & Long,

1993). Further, the computer programs make fitting many alternative models so easy that modeling may become a "dust-bowl" enterprise, unguided by theory.

McPhee and Babrow (1987) surveyed six years of communication research and found that methodological errors could have been avoided in many studies if causal modeling methods had been used; but in research using causal modeling, the methods were quite often misused and misreported. They list standards for using and reporting this clearly valuable technique.

A third trend in interpersonal research is the use of *categorical data analysis methods*, most notably *log-linear analysis* of multiway contingency tables (e.g., Burggraf & Sillars, 1987). Different approaches to log-linear analysis have been developed by Goodman (e.g., 1978) and by Bishop et al. (1975; Feinberg, 1989). For the analysis of binary data, these methods are both logically and empirically superior to regression analysis of dummy variables (Knoke, 1975). Methods have been developed for the analysis of causal relationships among categorical variables (Goodman, 1978), testing Markov chain assumptions (Bishop et al., 1975), and analyzing social interaction (Bakeman & Gottman, 1986). It is also possible to analyze the effects of continuous independent variables on categorical dependent variables through probit or logit analysis (Hosmer & Lemeshow, 1989; Maddala, 1983). Users of these methods must deal with several problems. Testing even a relatively simple hypothesis using log-linear analysis often involves a complex hierarchical model that is hard to interpret relative to other available techniques. Coefficients from log-linear, logit, and probit models, the analogues of beta weights in regression or effects in ANOVA, are often difficult to interpret. Moreover, finding an adequate model requires extensive reliance on statistical tests that may be overly sensitive to sample size, as available measures of "effect size" are open to serious question (Rosenthal, 1980).

A fourth class of statistical models with high potential for interpersonal communication research are *multilevel models*, which are designed to distinguish effects due to individuals from effects due to relations between those individuals or to larger social units the individuals are members of (family, school, organization). These models enable researchers to sort out effects due to individual characteristics or psychological processes from those due to social processes and interaction. One useful model is the "social relations model" (Kenny & Kashy, 1991; Kenny & La Voie, 1984). This approach (basically a variant of ANOVA) uses data from cases in which each person in a group interacts with everyone else to isolate effects on each person's behavior due to (a) the person's own general tendencies, (b) the general tendencies of the other with whom he or she is interacting, (c) the specific relationship of the two, and (d) occasion-specific error variance. The method also allows us to study a number of different kinds of reciprocity between partners. However, the social relations model suffers from an important drawback as well; it only allows for dyadic influence and omits triadic, tetradic, and higher-order influences. Multilevel analysis (Bryk & Raudenbush, 1992; Goldstein, 1987), which fits hierarchical linear models for the effects of individuals and higher level social units, is more flexible. For example, a multilevel analysis could determine the relative effects of individual and of family on the relationship between conflict style and relational satisfaction. Multilevel analysis also enables researchers to determine if there are individual differences within social units. The method can be applied to repeated measures data, longitudinal time series, and meta-analysis.

Though it has received relatively little attention in interpersonal communication research, *exploratory data analysis* (Mosteller & Tukey, 1977; Tukey, 1977) continues to have great potential. Rather than simply applying a prefabricated model to data and interpreting prefabricated results, techniques have been developed to look "inside" data sets, discovering relationships as well as testing them. In this case the researcher becomes more of a "detective" and less of a "sanctifier." Since the original two books, the methods have been refined considerably.

An important concern applies to all procedures employing statistical tests in this and other sections—*statistical power*. Power analysis is important because it permits researchers to calculate sample sizes and alpha levels needed to avoid Type II errors. Although it is generally recommended that estimates of power of statistical tests be reported, this is seldom done in practice. In a review of communication studies, Chase and Tucker (1975) found that few assessed power and that actual power was low for small or medium effect sizes and interaction effects, making Type II errors extremely likely. Reporting of power has improved somewhat in recent years, but it still seems to be a secondary concern at best. Cohen's (1988) well-known book gives power levels for many statistics, and Kraemer and Thiemann (1987) provide formulas for easy calculation of power levels. Walster and Cleary (1970) report a method of jointly setting power and alpha level for a given sample size so as to minimize both Type I and Type II errors.

Descriptive Techniques

A number of techniques have been developed to simply describe or dimensionalize data. This review will consider two genres of methods: (a) techniques for clustering or dimensionalizing items or persons, including factor analysis, multidimensional scaling (MDS), and cluster analysis; and (b) techniques for displaying dependencies among observations, notably Markov modeling.

(1) Clustering techniques. Factor analysis, MDS, and cluster analysis are similar in many respects, but there are critical differences. All three methods permit the researcher to identify clusters of items or persons. However, factor analysis and MDS are more complex than cluster analysis because they also identify dimensions along which items or persons vary. In turn, factor analysis is more complex than MDS procedures because it assumes that the dimensions reflect variables or constructs underlying the items or persons, whereas MDS makes no such assumption. This discussion will focus not so much on full discussions of the three techniques as on strengths and weaknesses of the various techniques and on problems in their use and possible solutions.

Factor analysis is still the most common clustering technique in interpersonal communication research (for example, Infante & Wigley, 1986; McCroskey, 1978). As noted above, the factor-analytic model posits one or more factors underlying a set of items (see Cureton & D'Agostino, 1983, and McDonald, 1985, for good recent treatments of factor analysis). The factors may be a personality variable, such as communication apprehension, or variables that allow discrimination among or ordering of a number of stimuli, such as the compliance-gaining situations studied by Cody, Woelfel, and Jordan (1983). In each case, subjects respond to a number of items designed to be representative of the underlying constructs, and the analysis derives the factors basic to the items. Compared with the other two clustering methods, factor analysis is advantageous because it attempts to allow for measurement error through the use of communalities. It also permits a clear determination of the amount of variance in the items accounted for by the factor solution.

Among the problems in using factor analysis is that the solution is not unique. Hence interpretation of factors has a large subjective component and is influenced by the researcher's theories or preconceptions. This can be problematic because researchers often label factors with names drawn from previous factor analyses, even though different items may load on them (Cronkhite & Liska, 1976). Second, as Cronkhite and Liska (1976) note, a factor analysis is only as good as the item pool. They recommend having subjects generate items to replace the common practice of using researcher-generated items, which may artificially restrict the scope of the analysis. Cronkhite (1976) also found instability in evaluative-factor solutions based on rater-concept-scale interactions, suggesting that much more care must be taken with factor-analytic designs than is often recognized.

There are at least two problems with current uses of factor analysis in interpersonal communication research. First, interpersonal communication research has placed too much emphasis on orthogonal factor rotations. Although orthogonality guarantees that dimensions are independent, it is unclear why this is always a desirable property. Often subjects' judgmental criteria are correlated (for example, Hayes & Sievers, 1972), and forcing a solution into orthogonality may distort the representation. Using an oblique rotation may better represent underlying dimensions and certainly facilitates identification of clusters of variables.

Second, exploratory factor-analytic procedures are sometimes used to assess hypotheses about factor structures. However, factor indeterminacy makes assessments suspect. A better approach is to use confirmatory factor analysis (Bollen, 1989; McDonald, 1985). With this technique, a hypothesized factor structure is tested against the data (see, e.g., Burgoon & Hale, 1987; Seibold & McPhee, 1980).

MDS derives a multidimensional representation of a set of items (persons) based on a measure of distance between each pair of items (see Davison, 1983; Lingoes, Roskam, & Borg, 1979; Young, 1987). The nature of this measure can vary widely, from correlations (smaller correlations signaling greater distances) to subjects' judgments of similarity for each pair of items. Varieties of MDS can be distinguished along two dimensions. First, we can distinguish metric procedures, which assume distance measures are continuous, from nonmetric procedures, which assume only that distance measures reflect a rank order of distances among points (see Bell, 1986, and Kellerman, Reynolds, & Chen, 1991, for examples of nonmetric MDS; Poole & Folger, 1981, and Woelfel & Fink, 1980, for metric MDS applications; and Craig, 1983, for a critique of metric methods). Nonmetric MDS techniques obviously make less rigorous demands on the data than metric methods, but they do not yield unique solutions, whereas most metric techniques do. This latter property represents a clear advantage of metric techniques over factor analysis. A disadvantage of nonmetric techniques lies in the difficulty of determining the correct dimensionality of the solutions, which is normally done by comparing a stress (or alienation) coefficient for various solutions. Distributions of stress values derived via Monte Carlo techniques make this judgment somewhat easier (Spence & Ogilvie, 1973). Weeks and Bentler (1979) compared metric and nonmetric techniques and found that metric methods gave better results than nonmetric techniques, even with rank distance data.

Second, MDS procedures that collapse individual responses can be distinguished from those that do not. Most traditional MDS models take averages or weighted averages of distances across subjects as their distance measures. This makes it impossible to determine whether there are differences among respondents or whether the representation maps common perceptions. However, determining whether a representation is common is an important problem for several areas of interpersonal communication research. For researchers interested in rules or interpretive schemes, testing for a common representation is one way of establishing whether rules or schemes are shared or whether there are interpretive subcommunities. For researchers interested in communication-related traits, it is a way to identify subgroups with different reactions to messages. Several MDS techniques take intersubject differences into account. The most famous individual difference MDS model, INDSCAL (Carroll & Chang, 1970), finds a common space and determines the weights subjects attach to different dimensions. Although this model permits identification of subsets of subjects, there is some question as to whether these weights really improve fit over a common solution. A second method, PINDIS, allows this to be determined (Lingoes & Borg, 1978). PINDIS fits a common solution and then several solutions with additional constraints, including (a) individual weights for dimensions, like INDSCAL; (b) unique perspectives (origins) for each subject; and (c) shifts in certain items for subsets of subjects. Each of these solutions has a unique psychological interpretation, and PINDIS estimates the amount of variance accounted for by each, permitting determination of which solution, if any, is better than a common solution for all subjects. Three-mode factor analysis (Tucker, 1972) can allow determination of individual differences within the factor-analytic model.

Cluster analysis groups items on the basis of some measure of association (Arabie & Hubert, 1992; Cormak, 1971; Milligan & Cooper, 1987). These techniques operate through iteratively combining (or dividing) items and clusters one pair at a time. Four major types of clustering methods were identified by Milligan and Cooper: (a) hierarchical methods, which start by combining entities and successively generating larger clusters (these include the most common methods used in interpersonal communication research, including single link, complete link, and group average methods); (b) partitioning methods, which start with the entire group and partition it into subsets; (c) overlapping methods, which create overlapping clusters (these include clique identification or clumping methods); and (d) ordination methods (including MDS and other scaling methods). Of the hierarchical methods, Ward's and other group average methods generally turn out to provide the best results in Monte Carlo and other validation studies (Milligan & Cooper, 1987; Morey, Blashfield, & Skinner, 1983). For the partitioning methods, convergent K-means procedures tend to provide the best results (Milligan & Cooper, 1987). Milligan and Cooper reported that no definite comparisons could be drawn between overlapping methods or seriation methods. Several tests have been developed to aid researchers to determine the number of clusters and to test hypotheses about clusters (Arabie & Hubert, 1992; Milligan & Cooper, 1987).

(2) Markov analysis. Markov analysis could also be discussed under time-series methods, but its use as a method for display and analysis of sequential data is well known in our field (see Hewes, 1975, 1979, for good introductions to sequential analysis).

Basically, Markov analysis tests how well we can predict acts on the basis of preceding acts. A first-order Markov process would predict the occurrence of acts from the immediately preceding act, a second-order process from the two immediately preceding acts, a third-order process from three, and so on. The core of the model is a transition matrix displaying the probability that an act (or two acts, or three acts, and so forth) will be followed by various other acts. This transition matrix can be interpreted for ideas about the sequential structure in the observed interaction. For example, Williamson and Fitzpatrick (1985) used Markov models to describe relational control patterns in marital types.

The use of Markov analysis to describe sequential structure can be justified on two grounds. First, interaction is responsive, and the Markov model describes this responsiveness well. Second, researchers have had considerable success with such models; they fit well and have generated insights. However, several critiques suggest that these reasons may be contestable (Hewes, 1979; McPhee & Poole, 1981; O'Keefe, Delia, & O'Keefe, 1980). At base, the use of Markov models as descriptions assumes interaction unfolds in an orderly, sequential manner and can be described in terms of categorical state changes. O'Keefe et al. (1980) note that interaction is seldom this orderly, with responses often coming several statements after an act. Second, as McPhee and Poole (1981) observe, merely establishing that a Markov model fits does not necessarily yield meaningful information; only in the context of theoretical assumptions not implicit in descriptive attempts are these conditions interpretable. Hewes (1979) discusses several techniques that incorporate theoretical assumptions into Markov models. A particularly interesting method takes the values in the Markov transition matrix as dependent variables in a causal model specifying factors that determine transition probabilities. This approach, employed by Cappella (1979, 1980), permits direct inclusion of theoretical factors in the model. For other examples of theoretical uses of Markov models, see Hewes (1980) and McLaughlin and Cody (1982).

Lag sequential analysis (Sackett, 1979), another sequential probability model, has met with increasing acceptance in interpersonal communication research (see, e.g., Dindia, 1986; McLaughlin & Cody, 1982). It has allowed researchers to characterize frequently occurring act sequences, for instance, chains of interaction leading to or following some criterial event, such as awkward silences. Since its original formulation, several corrections and additions to the technique have been proposed, including corrections of the test statistic and adjustment of the null hypothesis for bias in the sampling method (Allison & Liker, 1982; Kellerman, 1988; Morley, 1987). Indeed, these and other corrections led a number of communication researchers to report revisions to the results of previous studies in a 1984 issue of *Human Communication Research*. Kellerman (1988) provides a rigorous critique of lag sequential analysis, showing that by itself it provides "(1) an incomplete description of the pattern of dependencies in sequentially ordered categorical data, and (2) a potential for inaccurate description of the pattern of dependencies" (p. 2). While lag sequential analysis is still useful for the investigation of prototypical sequences of acts, Kellerman recommends that it be used in conjunction with a Markov analysis of the same data. The Markov analysis would establish the order of the process generating the data, and the lag sequential analysis could be used to characterize and analyze specific sequences of interest.

In general, the techniques discussed in this section have been employed by researchers using hypothetico-deductive templates (Cells 1, 4, and 7). Markov analysis and confirmatory clustering techniques have also been used by those working in the modeling templates. These techniques, particularly clustering and typological methods, represent an untapped resource for grounded theory research. For example, once a Markov transition matrix is computed, the grounded researcher might look at examples of both frequent and rare interacts to see if the interact categories have a homogeneous meaning that goes beyond the act category definitions or that might be correlated with some contextual or other variable (see Fisher

& Hawes, 1971). Clustering and typological methods could be employed by grounded theory research to identify groups of similar subjects; once groups have been isolated, researchers could use grounded strategies to identify features or processes that account for this differentiation. Factor-analytic and MDS methods also can be employed to map subjects' interpretive schemes (for example, Poole & Folger, 1981). This is not only useful for grounded research but also for conventional and dialectical approaches.

Time-Series Analysis

There has been some interest in time-series analysis in interpersonal communication research (Cappella, 1980; Cappella & Planalp, 1981; Gottman, 1981; Van Lear, 1991). A number of texts outlining time-series procedures for social scientists are available (Chatfield, 1975; Gottman, 1981; Gregson, 1983; for experiment-related time series, see Cook & Campbell, 1979; a good article-length summary of current practice is Catalano, Dooley, & Jackson, 1983).

Time-series analysis usually involves one or more continuous variables, measured for one or more "subjects" (which may be people, families, groups, and so on) at several regularly spaced points in time (40 observations is often mentioned as the minimum number of observations for a time-series analysis). Arundale (1980) provides detailed information on the importance of the length of the interval between data points. Methods are also available for the analysis of nominal level time series, though Markov or other stochastic models are usually used instead.

Time-series analysis involves filtering out the random error associated with a series of data and then identifying two types of temporal dependence in observations: *autoregression* (dependence of each observation on past observations) and *moving average processes* (dependence of each observation on some of the "shocks" that caused change in past observations). Based on time-series analysis, one can answer several questions, including the following: (a) Is there order in the longitudinal process or is it random? (b) Is there a general trend in development? and (c) Are there cycles in the data that suggest regular social processes. It is also possible to study the impacts of causal factors on time series using time-series regression and vector autoregression, and to identify relationships between time series (Chatfield, 1975; Freeman, Williams, & Lin, 1988).

Time-series methods have great potential for interpersonal communication research. They provide rigorous descriptions of the nature and constitution of temporal processes, along with clear accounts of the complexities of temporal data. Time-series methods enable us to disentangle relationships and causal effects from correlated errors common in longitudinal data (Catalano et al., 1983, lists a hierarchy of strategies). Also, knowledge of time-series methods aids one in recognizing, describing, and analyzing rather unique effects, such as hysteresis—a series that follows two different paths depending on whether it runs forward or backward (Gregson, 1983).

A problem with time-series techniques is that it is hard to specify the model of temporal dependence a priori. The inductive process involved in the identification of the time-series model should not extend to substantive relationships among variables. The best protection against this is to have a clear theory. Second, when temporal dependencies are more complex than the two types of dependencies identified by normal time-series analysis, these methods are liable to fail or mislead (McCleary & Hays, 1980).

The importance of theory in time-series analysis suggests that it is most often used in the hypothetico-deductive, causal template. However, it is also possible to develop models of longitudinal data more complex than typical time-series models. Nonlinear models such as those discussed in McPhee and Poole (1981), Buder (1991), and Levine and Fitzgerald (1991) are one class of models that could be used for this purpose. They can capture very complex, even chaotic, temporal patterns. Another alternative is event history analysis, which enables researchers to trace when critical events or turning points occur (Snyder, 1991).

Techniques for the Analysis of Development

The use of a developmental framework is important because it allows for the effects of previous experience and of progress or decay on interpersonal communication. Areas to which developmental perspectives have been applied include interpersonal communication among children (for example, Delia, Kline, & Burleson, 1979) and relationship development (for example, Huston, Surra, Fitzgerald, & Cate, 1981; Van Lear, 1991). The study of development requires research strategies and techniques different than those discussed to this point.

First, development should be distinguished from both change and growth. By definition, development involves more than simple change. It implies continuous and patterned change, with a clear sense of directionality, either progress or decay. Development also implies more than simple growth because it involves the interrelationship of several variables over time, whereas growth can refer simply to increase in a single variable. The study of development is generally presumed to require longitudinal data from the same subjects, though cross-sectional designs have also been used (for example, a cross-sectional study of relational development might sample couples who have been together for 1, 3, and 6 months in a single administration, as opposed to a longitudinal study tracking the couples through 6 months).

Schaie (1970; Schaie & Baltes, 1975) has developed a comprehensive analysis of the components underlying developmental change. According to Schaie, three classes of independent variables can account for developmental changes:

1. *Age,* that is, variables associated with the aging process in the subject at the time of measurement: This component indexes effects tied to "purely" developmental processes.
2. *Cohort,* that is, variables that influence all subjects born or initiated at the same time: This class includes general environmental and historical effects that the set of subjects of a given age or length of participation may have experienced in common. For example, in a study conducted in 1984, middle-class couples who have been together 2 years would have gone through a recession together, whereas couples together 3 months would likely have a relationship not touched by serious economic fears.
3. *Time of measurement,* that is, variables affecting subjects at the time they are measured but that are noncumulative: These have only an immediate or transient effect, though their effects may be important.

Schaie and his colleagues lay out several designs for sorting out which of the three effects is responsible for observed developmental changes. Clearly, only *age* effects index developmental influences in the "pure," internally driven sense. *Cohort* effects index influences of exogenous forces on development and are therefore also important. *Time of measurement* effects are accidental and do not index developmental processes.

Schaie's model has provoked critical debate (Adam, 1978), but his distinctions seem to be quite useful. They point out possible problems with cross-sectional data; in particular, it is difficult to separate time and cohort effects from age effects. Schaie's model also indicates the different classes of determinants that could be operating in developmental data. Researchers interested in establishing a true developmental effect should show that observed effects are not the result of accidental factors, something few interpersonal researchers interested in development have done. Greater attention to Schaie's components and their interrelations would pay off in enhanced understanding of interpersonal processes and greater confidence in the reliability of research results.

Within this theoretical frame, two classes of techniques for studying development can be distinguished: techniques for describing and testing whether a given developmental pattern occurs and techniques for assessing correlational or causal relationships among developmental variables (Wohlwill, 1973, presents an excellent introduction to developmental methods).

Establishing developmental patterns. Techniques for describing and testing developmental patterns can use either nominal or continuous data. Nominal data generally consist of a series of longitudinal observations indicating whether or not a particular stage or indicator of stage is present at each point in time. In this case, a developmental description can best be derived and tested through the analysis of the observed pattern as a Guttman scale or some variation thereof. This is equivalent to testing whether a single series of stages can describe the developmental process. Various methods are available for developmental patterns in nominal data. For fairly simple patterns, a test of Guttman scalability can be applied (TenHouten, 1969). The existence of more complex patterns can be tested by comparing a hypothesized pattern matrix to the observed matrix; Leik and Matthews (1968), Wohlwill (1973), and Hubert and Schultz (1976) report tests for this.

Holmes and Poole (1991) describe a flexible phase mapping method that can derive a phase sequence from categorical indicators of phases. One advantage of this method is that it does not require researchers to posit a set number of phases prior to analysis; it can adapt to the number of phases in the case at hand. The method also can identify phases of varying lengths. Hence it makes it possible to identify multiple sequences of development that qualitatively differ from one another rather than simply assessing whether, on average, observed sequences conform to a model. Once a set of sequences has been identified, typologies of developmental paths can be identified using sequence comparison methods such as optimal matching and clustering (Abbott, 1990; Holmes & Poole, 1991).

Methods are also available for describing and testing hypotheses about developmental curves based on continuous measures. The most well known is trend analysis, which permits tests for nonlinear components of curves (quadratic, cubic, quartic, and so forth; see Keppel, 1973; Wohlwill, 1973). Van Lear (1991) used Fourier analysis of time series to study relationship development. In addition, Tucker (1966) has developed a procedure that takes a set of curves for a sample of subjects and groups the subjects together based on similarity in development. Huston et al. (1981) have used this procedure to identify distinct types of relational development patterns during courtship.

Relationships among variables. Two types of relationships among variables can be considered in developmental studies. First, researchers may be interested in whether two or more ordered variables are linked together in developmental processes, that is, whether they codevelop or one leads another. For example, this issue is very important in studies of the development of communicative skills. Are certain skills correlated and therefore related to an underlying developmental process, or does one skill presuppose (or prefigure) another? It is also important for phenomena that involve parallel development on two or more variables. For example, relational development might involve parallel evolution of intimacy and life aspirations, and it would be useful to know if these progress through the same stages. Wohlwill (1973) discusses several ways of teasing out codeveloping relationships with contingency tables. It is also possible to use factor analysis to determine whether a single dimension underlies diverse developmental phenomena (Bentler, 1973). For example, Rubin (1973) factored measures of four types of egocentrism—communicative egocentrism, cognitive egocentrism, spatial egocentrism, and role-taking egocentrism—for children from ages 2 to 8. He found all measures loaded on a single factor and argued all four measures were manifestations of a unitary construct. Factor analysis also can be used to find changes in the factor structure through the course of development.

Researchers also may be interested in causal relationships among developmental variables. Most often, this refers to linear causality, which can be assessed via the panel designs and structural equation modeling discussed above. However, as Overton and Reese (1973) note, linear causality may hold unambiguously only for mechanistic developmental models. Another class of models, organismic models, posit reciprocal and dialectical causation, governed by a teleological relationship implicit in the evolving whole (Werner's theory of development is one example of an organismic model). Because it is difficult to sort out reciprocal causation (particularly in cases with uneven development), codevelopment may be the only relationship researchers can establish for many organismic models.

Our review of interpersonal communication research uncovered little attention to the issues raised in this section. Most research concerned with development simply compares correlations for different ages or cohorts or simply uses ANOVA designs, without regard to possible confounding factors or problems of proof. The methods considered here are clearly applicable to hypothetico-deductive and modeling modes of inquiry. The mechanistic model is appropriate for causal research, whereas the organismic model may be more useful for conventional or dialectical modes of explanation.

Qualitative Techniques

In this section, we will cover issues relevant to a variety of techniques ranging from microanalysis of interaction, as in some discourse analysis, to broad-ranging reconstructive analysis of communication practices, as in communication ethnography. Interest in qualitative techniques is growing in interpersonal communication, as is evident from recent symposia in the *Western Journal of Speech Communication* (*53*, Spring, 1989) and in *Communication Theory* (2, May and November, 1992). In part, this is due to increased interest in the conventional and dialectical modes of explanation. Communication researchers have explicitly claimed the advantages of such methods. They seem to treat directly the meaningful "stuff" of communication in a way adequate to the phenomenon and pay attention to history and context, which clearly influence interaction, yet are neglected in typical quantitative analysis.

Qualitative analysis is usually associated with the grounded mode of inquiry; however, this is by no means a necessary connection. Indeed, early qualitative work in sociology and anthropology often emphasized its compatibility with causal and hypothetico-deductive modes of inquiry and explanation. And qualitative analysis of large numbers of cases, for instance, can generate a database for statistics that allows hypothesis testing or model construction (e.g., Mintzberg, Raisinghani, & Theoret, 1976).

However, with interpretive modes of inquiry often come subjective and relativistic views of method; it is important to draw some distinctions here. "Interpretive" theory (whether conventional or dialectical) typically rests on two premises that seem to challenge the grounds of social scientific method. First, it promotes the idea that knowledge is a constitutive relation of knowledgeable community and known. Knowledge is never a neutral representation of an independently given reality, never beyond supplement or critique. This can be taken to imply that all accounts—method based or not—are merely relative to the particular standpoint of the subjective observer, and so of little certifying value. Second, the communication studied by interpretive scholars is often described as situationally emergent, socially constructed reality. Some interpretive researchers have argued that scientific study does not suit such variable and idiosyncratic phenomena.

Such relativist and idiographic assumptions deserve serious consideration. However, we assume throughout this discussion that valid generalization—about the phenomenon studied if not about how a given individual will manifest it—is a reasonable and broadly shared goal for most qualitative researchers. Knowledge, while subjective, can be derived using methods that have proven themselves in practice and critique in the judgment of a scientific community (Bernstein, 1983). And communication, while often of a depth and complexity that challenges scientific theories, can still exhibit general and regular patterns.

Two issues are immediately relevant when we seek to use qualitative techniques to draw general conclusions. First, what about the reliability and validity both of the data and of its application as evidence? Second, how can qualitative accounts be chosen and interpreted to certify general conclusions without incurring self-serving biases?

Reliability and validity have been discussed extensively above, especially as relevant to coding systems. Much of that discussion is relevant here, given that qualitative analysis often involves the categorization of records of communication. A good review of the relevance of reliability and validity specifically to ethnographic data is provided by LeCompte and Goetz (1982). They make two general points about the reliability and validity of qualitative data. First, because qualitative inquiry is generally grounded and processual, the qualities of reliability and validity, and factors that affect these properties, are somewhat transformed. For instance, in quantitative contexts, reliability means that another researcher studying the same phenomena will come to the same or parallel descriptive results. But in grounded inquiry, the cultural description will rest in large part on the process of concept formation and linkage, that is, on pattern recognition and creative but theoretically guided inference by the researcher. So differences in theoretical position or inference style may be considered as reliability threats, just as differences in coder interpretation of categories. And, more important, reliability in his interpretation is related not just to particular variables but to the whole conceptual frame resulting from research.

Central to reliability in qualitative research is social structural position of researcher and informants or interviewees. LeCompte and Goetz (1982) mention several cases in which researchers have offered very different descriptions of the same culture or interaction system because they and their informants have different social roles within the research site. Related to this is the problem of bias in informant selection—the subjects who are willing and able to talk to an outside researcher may be systematically different than other "natives," especially in their attitude toward and access to the researcher's perspective.

A third important reliability/validity issue has been raised in discussions of qualitative microanalyses. Grimshaw (1982) has emphasized the "paradox of microanalysis," also discussed by Pittenger, Hockett, and Daheny (1960) and Labov and Fanshel (1977). Minute and repeated analysis of recordings and transcripts may expose and highlight features that are not important in practice. For example, microanalysis may find incoherence or conflict in interaction without equally exposing the inattention and work that neutralize such disharmony in practice. "Lengthy concentration of attention on the one event can easily blow up its significance far out of proportion to its original duration and its actual setting. One must not mistake the five-inch scale model for the fly itself" (Pittenger et al., 1960, cited in Labov & Fanshel, 1977, p. 22).

These factors, and others, have awakened researchers from the dream of direct contact with reality that the density and meaningfulness of qualitative data sometimes arouses; recent work has explicitly emphasized some of the resources by which qualitative method can guard against threats to reliability and validity. One such resource is replication. Research involving inference from a number of qualitative case studies is becoming more common. Jules Henry (1975) and Ralph Larossa (1977) have reported in-depth analyses of interaction patterns of a number of families to support general conclusions. Another resource is triangulation— reliance on data from a number of sources and observers, often with the capacity to ask for further information or explanations to resolve inconsistencies or unclear data.

A third resource for research with large-scale focus is supplemental microanalysis (provided the paradox of microanalysis can be counteracted). Agar and Hobbs (1982), for instance, use knowledge of coherence strategies drawn from discourse analysis and artificial intelligence work to separate and identify themes and norms of a drug user's subculture from communicative adaptations by the user to the interviewers.

At this point, normal concerns of reliability and validity begin to merge with the concern for *certification*—for using qualitative data as systematic support for a general conclusion. Theorists have dealt with four related questions about certification. First, they have devoted systematic attention to the process of constructing *arguments* using qualitative examples as evidence. Second, they have developed standards for testing *formal models* using qualitative data. Third, they have dealt with the problem of *comparing* qualitative data sets from different research sites or different studies in pursuit of general conclusions. Finally, they have noted a variety of ways qualitative data can be *related* to quantitative data.

Qualitative research often attempts to use situated data to warrant general conclusions (Glaser & Strauss, 1967). In recent years, conversation-analytic and related methods of using discourse data to ground arguments for general conclusions have been the object of special attention and controversy (Cappella, 1990; Hopper et al., 1986; Jackson, 1986; Jacobs, 1986, 1990; Pomerantz, 1990). An initial concern for all these parties seems to be the possibility of a bias that might be called "suggestivity"—finding one or several examples that "make sense" on a certain reading and then being influenced by that reading to look for other examples that agree with it, without noticing the counterevidence. Cappella (1990) emphasizes that traditional empirical methods of objective sampling from a clearly specified population, followed by testing for departures from randomness, remain the best way of guarding against this sort of bias. Conversation analysts have responded partly by noting that their method of proof—labeled "analytic induction" by Jackson, based on its analogy to a pragmatist method—does employ some traditional empiricist strategies. For instance, it uses Mills's "method of difference" by seeking to array contrasting examples, one with and one without a feature that is claimed to be crucial. Also, they seek examples that vary as widely as possible while still displaying the hypothesized pattern. But they argue that the normative framework of conversation also enables analysts to go beyond traditional methods; by presenting subjects with various examples and analyzing their reactions and interpretations, such as the recognition that a given statement is flawed, theories about rules underlying conversation can be tested and modified. We believe an additional strategy might also help assuage doubts raised by the suggestivity problem: Researchers could describe the methods they used to collect transcripts and to identify and select examples from a corpus of transcripts. After a clear statement of the empirical claim embodied in the research (Jackson, 1986), a study could include maximally explicit description of the features that guided the search through the corpus and the evolution of that search (Cicourel, 1980; Hopper et al., 1986). Such an account would both make evident the empirical testing accomplished by the search for examples and permit measured assessment of possible biases and flaws.

A step beyond general argument generation is the construction and certification of formal models derived to "explain" qualitative findings. Well-known examples are the structuralism of Piaget, Lévi-Strauss, and Chomsky, and the systems of rules offered by Sacks et al. (1974) and by Brown and Levinson (1978). In communication, examples include the rules approaches offered by Pearce and Cronen (1980) and by Cushman and Cahn (1984), and the language-action hierarchy of Frentz and Farrell (1976). Research related to this formal modeling approach has had either (or both) of two goals: to support some specific formal model underlying interaction or to explain more abstract properties of the model. The latter aim is often adopted because of presumed individual differences, instability, or cross-model consistency in properties.

Theorists have articulated standards for validation of formal models; such standards affect both the type of models developed and the procedures and data that must be used in validation. For instance, Cushman and Pearce (1977) suggest three standards for studies of communication rules based on practical force: (a) a task that is the generative mechanism for the rules must be located; (b) episodic sequences stipulated by the rules must be described and assessed for generality and necessity; and (c) the structure of rule-based inference leading to action must be stipulated. Pearce and Cushman argue that each of these three claims needs empirical support and develop this argument in a critique of four putative rules studies. Adler (1978) adds some additional detail on methods for falsifying rules models. Another set of standards has been articulated by Chomsky (1957): (a) observational adequacy (the rules generate all and only the appropriate behaviors), (b) descriptive adequacy (the rules assign correct "structural descriptions" to behaviors that indicate the similarities and differences among the meanings of different behaviors), and (c) explanatory adequacy (underlying the rules is a conception of behavior that shows how that set of rules comes to be learned or developed). Later writers (for example, Cicourel, 1981) have argued that this set of standards must be supplemented with two additional standards: (d) an adequate rules theory must explain the meaningful relations of rule violations to rule-consistent behavior and (e) it must explain process (for example, the cognitive operations involved in generating the behavior) as well as outcome facts. These standards are reflected in the range of data that might be required to adequately support a rules theory—data about the behaviors generated by the rules, data about how those behaviors are different or similar to one another in meaning and structure, data about the process of learning to perform the behaviors, data about the cognitive operations involved in behaving, and data about the relations of rule-governed behaviors to rule-violating behaviors.

Heightened awareness of the difficulty of adequately supporting a formal model with data has led to some demanding standards for data sets. An example is the set of criteria outlined by Grimshaw (1982) for conversational studies: more than two participants, with varying power, all involved in the interchange; a full (audio plus visual) recording, supplemented by extensive knowledge of historical and factual context; and rights to publish data and analysis. But even such a data set could not necessarily meet all the standards suggested by Chomsky above.

To this point, we have focused on issues related to reliability, validity, and generalization from a single study. More global is the problem of combining qualitative databases, perhaps created by multiple researchers, studying multiple sites, perhaps in multiple studies. McPhee (1990) raises a question: Given that studies often involve substantial reflexive adjustment to the people and situation of the research, can the studies be combined at all? He suggests three possible cases and suggests methods for seeking and assessing comparability.

If we assume the databases *are* comparable, techniques are available for working through the huge masses of data typical of qualitative research. It is not uncommon for an ethnographic study to run for months and generate hundreds of pages of field notes. Close analysis of interaction often involves reconciling thousands of data specimens at different levels of abstraction (see, for example, Labov & Fanshell, 1977). This problem is compounded for studies involving multiple sites and longitudinal data collection. With large data sets, it is often difficult for the research to maintain consistent standards of classification and evaluation; standards used on one day may shift the next, and human fatigue makes mistakes likely, if not unavoidable. For qualitative analysts, the problem is to achieve consistency but, at the same time, to preserve closeness to phenomena and fine judgmental capacities.

Miles and Huberman (1984) discuss several methods for display and reduction of qualitative data to ease the task of managing large databases but to preserve qualitative strengths. They argue that one key to qualitative analysis lies in methods of displaying data in graphic or matrix forms. These displays help researchers make sense of large data sets, which may be spread over hundreds of pages. These also can do the basic work of laying out main findings for the reader, leaving the text to provide illustrations and qualifications. Miles and Huberman discuss several varieties of displays, including checklist matrices, progressive matrices, causal matrices, predictor-outcomes matrices, event networks, and causal networks, as well as principles for coding and classifying qualitative data. These displays aid the researcher in moving from the identification of key constructs to specification of influences in the system. Other methods for grappling with large bodies of qualitative data are discussed in Van Maanen (1984) and in the series on qualitative methodology that Van Maanen edits for Sage Publications. Also of interest is the growing body of software to aid in the management and analysis of large bodies of qualitative data (e.g., Pfaffenberger, 1987).

So far, we have discussed qualitative techniques as the sole method used in a study. However, more researchers are combining quantitative and qualitative methods in a single study (e.g., Sillars, Burggraf, Yost, & Zietlow, 1992). Some ways of doing this are commonplace—for instance, to construct a category scheme, it is very common to begin with open-ended questions and content analyze their results. But there are also several more innovative ways of combining the two methods. First, qualitative data can suggest and support the chain of influences relating two quantitative variables. For instance, the interview results provided by Delia and Clark (1977) show not just differences in adaptive communication but differences in using interpretations of other people as a basis for adapting—a link between independent and dependent variables in their study. Second, within a large-scale qualitative study, a recurrent quantitative variable may be useful in predicting differences arising within the study. For instance, Barley (1986) uses the frequency of certain script types in interaction to predict the emergence of specific role relations, a process that is focal for his larger-scale ethnography. Qualitative study also seems suitable to the examination of outliers (cases not fitting a quantitative relationship) in a statistical analysis as well as for the critical analysis of variables (described above). Bryman (1988) gives more examples of these possibilities.

Another direction for qualitative analysis, away from a naive depictive stance, is toward a more critical, redescriptive focus. Examples here include Henry's (1963) examination of culture against man and Katriel and Philipsen's (1981) examination of "communication" as an American cultural category. Such studies rest on qualitative analyses and draw on the resources listed above. Both studies just referred to, for instance, use information from multiple sources and about multiple cases. These studies reflect a relative awareness of their limits and use their data and analysis not as verification of general patterns or hypotheses but as evidence drawn on to develop as well as to support an argument. The argument itself in such studies tends to be either critical—oriented to expose an underlying structure of social phenomena in conflict with general values—or dialectical, in the sense of Wittgenstein's *Tractatus* or Stanley Fish's *Self-Consuming Artifacts*—oriented to "raise" our consciousness using ethnographic evidence in a way that carries us beyond the evidence itself.

Meta-Analysis

Meta-analysis (Hunter & Schmidt, 1990; Rosenthal, 1991) developed in response to two problems with traditional literature reviews: their lack of attention to sampling error and their inability to combine results of various studies with statistical rigor. The first problem can be quite serious. For instance, Hunter and Schmidt (1990) describe a simulation that sampled a population in which two variables were correlated at a constant level; sample correlations ranged from $-.10$ to $.76$ and seemed to be influenced by third variables even though they had no relation to them. Meta-analysis tries to take the complex and counterintuitive factor of sampling error into account in drawing conclusions from arrays of studies.

The goal of meta-analysis is to find a maximally simple statistical model that can integrate and explain the results of multiple data sets. If, for example, the correlation of two variables is of interest, meta-analysis can take all studies done relating those two variables, generate a statistically optimal estimate of the correlation based on all the data, and test the hypothesis that correlational value was the true population value underlying all the studies, even if they came to very diverse conclusions. If the hypothesis that all the studies reflected one correlational value fails, meta-analysis enables researchers to identify moderator variables to explain why the correlation varied from study to study.

Hunter and Schmidt (1990) suggest the following steps for meta-analysis: (a) Assimilate as much of the entire corpus of studies as possible. This involves searching computer databases for publications in a wide range of fields, locating dissertations, theses, and government reports, and including unpublished studies as well. These latter two sources are important because null results often do not make it into publication. (b) Correct the study statistics for various biases that can impede statistical combination. Hunter and Schmidt (1990) offer an extensive list of such biases and how to correct them. (c) Calculate a mean effect size across studies. (d) Test the hypothesis that there is no difference in effect sizes across studies. If this hypothesis cannot be rejected, the analysis stops at this point, and the mean effect size is reported and explicated. (e) If there is a difference in effect sizes across studies, the influence of various moderators on effect sizes can be tested (see also Hall & Rosenthal, 1991). Only those moderator variables for which there is a substantive theoretical justification can be included. One should not code every possible moderator, because the resulting tests are difficult to interpret without theory.

Meta-analysis is used with increasing frequency in interpersonal communication research and has already had a substantial impact upon our knowledge (see Hale & Dillard, 1991). However, several issues must be kept in mind when contemplating a meta-analysis. First, the technique is still relatively new, and there are differing views about validity of procedures. Second, valid meta-analysis depends on availability of data, both about the whole range of study results that are relevant and about the studies themselves. Relatively weak and insignificant findings are more likely to go unpublished and be unavailable for analysis, biasing estimates and significance tests. And the studies that are published may not include enough information to allow correction of biases as mentioned in step two. The good news about this issue is that meta-analysts are often open and systematic about reporting these weaknesses and estimating their effects (D. J. O'Keefe, 1991, presents some excellent recommendations for meta-analysis in communication research).

Two issues pertain to the employment of meta-analysis to find moderator variables that explain differences in correlations. One problem here is that the search for such variables is nearly always post hoc and risks capitalizing on chance. A moderator "uncovered" by a meta-analyst searching through study descriptions may "explain" study differences purely by chance, or it may be correlated with a true moderator that goes unnoticed. Every alleged moderator should be supported in a new study before acceptance. Another problem is that such moderators can be found only if different studies vary enough on the moderator variable for the difference to register in the meta-analysis. If studies conform to the pattern of an early study, they may conceal a significant moderator.

Finally, there has been a controversy related to the message design issue discussed above in the section on experimental design. Several researchers (Allen et al., 1990; Hunter et al., 1989; Morley, 1988) have argued that meta-analysis of individual message studies are actually better than designs that incorporate multiple messages. Following this approach, Allen et al. (1990) use meta-analysis to combine the results of numerous replications with single-message manipulations. Jackson (1991) shows that many of the statistics employed in meta-analysis are equivalent to those used in ANOVA and argues that ANOVA has certain advantages over meta-analytic statistics.

Meta-analysis is most applicable to studies done in the causal, hypothetico-deductive cell, but it could be applied to studies from other cells where statistical tests had been performed. In addition, the reasoning behind meta-analysis can be extended to other areas, as shown by the techniques for meta-analysis of qualitative studies (Noblit & Hare, 1991).

New Directions

A review of methods for studying interpersonal communication cannot end without mentioning additional methods that have high potential but have not been widely used.

Network analysis. This approach has seen explosive growth in recent years in sociology, organizational communication, and related fields. Though most commonly associated with organizational communication, the network approach has been applied to interpersonal relations by a number of researchers (Boissevain, 1974; Bott, 1971; Fischer, 1982; Newcomb, 1961). A common finding in this work is that interpersonal relationships and behavior can be affected significantly by the networks in which they are embedded. As promising as the approach is, study of networks in interpersonal communication research is sparse (Eggert & Parks, 1986; Healey & Bell, 1990; Milardo, 1987). Several widely accessible packages have made network analysis accessible to researchers, including NEGOPY, UCINET (Borgatti, Everett, & Freeman, 1992), and STRUCTURE (Burt, 1989). It is unfortunate that the study of interpersonal communication has not used this approach more extensively.

Historical-critical research. Another promising approach is the historical-critical study of interpersonal interaction patterns. This perspective assumes that patterns of interpersonal communication are constituted and influenced by larger social, economic, and cultural contexts. For instance, the influence of capitalism on aspects of interpersonal relationships has been analyzed by Sennett (1974), Zaretsky (1976), Willis (1977), and Poster (1980). Several of these studies argue that the capitalist sociopolitical context distorts interpersonal relationships by causing them to be part of the process by which people learn to take their place in the capitalist economy (e.g., Poster, 1980; Willis, 1977). This perspective also implies that the background norms that we use to define what is appropriate or effective interpersonal communication are historically bound: Interpersonal communication is different now than it was and will be different still in the future. Our studies of interpersonal communication should, but rarely do, take these contextual effects into account. This would require them to use analytic methods and information sources that allow separation of context effects from cross-context regularities. Historical-critical methods are clearly related to more traditional qualitative methods.

Figure 3.4 presents a summary of selected techniques discussed in this section and their actual and potential use in interpersonal communication research.

TEMPLATE

TECHNIQUE	1	2	3	4	5	6	7	8	9
Experimental Design	★	◆	☺	★	◆	Ø	☺	☺	Ø
MANOVA and relatives	★	Ø	☺	☺	Ø	Ø	☺	Ø	Ø
Structural Equation Modeling	★	◆	☺	☺	☺	Ø	☺	☺	Ø
Categorical Analysis	★	◆	☺	◆	◆	Ø	◆	☺	Ø
Multilevel Models	☺	☺	Ø	☺	☺	Ø	☺	☺	Ø
Exploratory Data Analysis	☺	Ø	☺	☺	Ø	Ø	☺	☺	Ø
Factor Analysis	★	★	◆	◆	☺	Ø	☺	☺	Ø
MDS	★	◆	☺	◆	☺	☺	☺	☺	☺
Cluster Analysis	◆	☺	☺	◆	☺	☺	☺	☺	☺
Markov Analysis	◆	★	◆	◆	◆	Ø	☺	☺	Ø
Lag Sequential Analysis	◆	☺	◆	☺	☺	Ø	☺	☺	Ø
Time-Series Methods	◆	☺	☺	Ø	Ø	Ø	☺	☺	☺
Developmental Methods	◆	◆	☺	☺	☺	☺	☺	☺	☺
Qualitative Approaches	Ø	Ø	Ø	☺	◆	★	◆	◆	★
Tabular Analysis of Qualitative Data	☺	☺	☺	☺	☺	☺	☺	☺	☺
Formal Models of Qualitative Data	☺	☺	◆	◆	◆	◆	◆	◆	◆
Meta-Analysis	★	☺	☺	☺	☺	☺	☺	☺	☺
Network Analysis	◆	◆	☺	☺	☺	☺	☺	☺	☺
Historical-Critical Analysis	☺	☺	☺	☺	☺	◆	◆	◆	◆

Key: ★ = Used very much with success
      ◆ = Used somewhat and has more potential
      ☺ = Used little but has potential
      Ø = Not useful

Figure 3.4. Selected Analytical Techniques and Their Potential and Actual Use in the Templates

Conclusion

This review has been guided by our conviction that interpersonal communication research should pay greater attention to the theory-technique linkage. The need for researchers to justify methodological choices in terms of their adequacy for answering research questions is one of the foundations of social science. Yet, these justifications are too often missing or sorely inadequate in reports of interpersonal communication research. Our investigative reasoning needs to convey a greater sense of continuity between theory and technique. This requires increased precision in linking theory and method and an awareness of how theory, template, and technique mesh to create knowledge of interpersonal communication. It is especially important to notice how templates and techniques shape theory; this influence is often ignored and being aware of it enables us to make conscious choices regarding our modes of knowing. Cappella's (1977) review emphasized the need to spell out theory-method linkages and advocated modeling as the means of doing this. We would build on his insights by recognizing that modeling is not the only form of inquiry suited for this clarification. All nine templates can be used to bridge the gap between abstract theory and technique and each has its own strengths and weaknesses.

In the second and third sections, we attempted to spell out some actual and possible links between templates and techniques, but the range of these relationships is so extensive that it defies complete enumeration. Following the pattern set forth in those sections should enable the reader to generate many others. The key is to use the intersection of inquiry mode and explanation as a criterion for selecting or eliminating techniques. The selection process also may differ, depending on the stage of inquiry. For example, in the conventional, grounded template, the use of clustering or hypothesis-testing techniques is not appropriate early on, when the researcher is searching for insights, but may be during later stages after interesting constructs and relationships have been uncovered.

It is important to break the tyranny of certain theory-technique links, in particular the marriage of causal explanation to hypothetico-deductive inquiry and conventional explanation to grounded inquiry. These templates represent valuable approaches, but they often discourage researchers from trying other approaches. Greater use of the other seven templates could greatly enhance the power and sensitivity of communication research. Truly important and robust discoveries should hold across investigative domains, and exploring them with several distinct approaches should make their implications much clearer than a one-sided strategy.

It is also important to bridge the greatly overestimated gap between "qualitative" and "quantitative" approaches. Close examination of the patterns of reasoning underlying the various techniques clearly shows affinities in both "camps." Canons of causal analysis such as the necessity to assess or control for competing causes, to establish necessary connections, to control for factors introducing errors, and to employ systematic sampling are also exhibited in qualitative reasoning. Conversely, premises of interpretive research—for example, going below surface phenomena to uncover underlying meanings, focusing on the significance or meaning of phenomena rather than objectifying them, and strategies for avoiding reification of the researcher's constructs—can be important correctives for quantitative investigations. Greater penetration of each domain by the other increases the validity of interpersonal communication research substantially.

Finally, there is a need to fight against the narcissism of technique. Communication research, and social science generally, has witnessed an ever-increasing emphasis on the importance of method. The huge market for texts on both quantitative and qualitative methodology attests to this trend. This is a healthy development in many respects because it contributes to more deliberate and discriminating technical choices. However, problems lurk beneath the shimmering surface of this technical emphasis. Researchers without extensive background in statistics and mathematics must take the operations of complex procedures on faith. Techniques such as time-series analysis, LISREL, and complex factor-analytic or clustering procedures involve sophisticated algorithms and restrictive assumptions that can easily be misunderstood and misapplied by even the wariest investigator. The statistical properties of many procedures are not well understood, and even their creators acknowledge ambiguous areas.

These considerations recommend great care in interpreting the results of these procedures; the path from raw data to output is often torturous and unclear. However, the ethos of technique can cause us to adopt an uncritical attitude and to assume that results from these methods are valid and meaningful, simply because they are on the "cutting edge" of the methodological advance and because we are accustomed to trusting statistics. We transfer our faith in means and variances to the parameters of a LISREL solution. This can lead to an unjustified overestimation of the validity and generalizability of our results. The only corrective is careful testing of assumptions underlying the methods and attention to features that might qualify results, such as standard errors of estimates, as well as a healthy dose of skepticism. Nor are qualitative methods immune from this problem. Qualitative discussions are filled with invocations of the magic term *triangulation,* without much attention to the validity of data being triangulated or how contradictory findings can be reconciled.

The narcissism of technique also supports another dangerous tendency—the substitution of method for thought. In the introduction, we argued that theory and method interpenetrate and advocated greater attention to their interrelationship. This was not meant to deny that insight and creativity are the wellsprings of good research. Without good, solid ideas, the most sophisticated and careful research strategy is fruitless. The complexities of analytical reasoning encourage greater attention to method than to ideas, and this can result in sophisticated studies that advance the field a little. The social detective, like his or her novelistic counterpart, must constantly push toward a truer picture until all pieces of the mystery fall into place. Significant progress depends both on substance and on method, and neither can be slighted without harming the whole.

References

Abbott, A. (1990). A primer on sequence methods. *Organization Science, 1,* 375-392.

Achinstein, P. (1971). *Laws and explanation.* Oxford: Oxford University Press.

Adam, J. (1978). Sequential strategies and the separation of age, cohort, and time-of-measurement contributions to developmental data. *Psychological Bulletin, 85,* 1309-1316.

Adler, K. (1978). On the falsification of rules theories. *Quarterly Journal of Speech, 64,* 427-438.

Agar, M., & Hobbs, J. R. (1982). Interpreting discourse: Coherence and the analysis of ethnographic interviews. *Discourse Processes, 5,* 1-32.

Allen, M., Hale, J., Mongeau, P., Berkowitz-Stafford, S., Stafford, S., Shanahan, W., Agee, P., Dillon, K., Jackson, R., & Ray, C. (1990). Testing a model of message sidedness: Three replications. *Communication Monographs, 57,* 275-291.

Allen, M., & Yen, W. (1979). *Introduction to measurement theory.* Monterey, CA: Brooks/Cole.

Allison, P. D., & Liker, J. K. (1982). Analyzing sequential categorical data on dyadic interaction: A comment on Gottman. *Psychological Bulletin, 91,* 393-403.

Altman, I., & Taylor, D. A. (1973). *Social penetration.* New York: Holt, Rinehart & Winston.

Anderson, N. A. (1981). *Foundations of information integration theory.* New York: Academic Press.

Anderson, P. A. (1983). Decision making by objective and the Cuban missile crisis. *Administrative Science Quarterly, 28,* 201-222.

Arabie, P., & Hubert, L. J. (1992). Combinatorial data analysis. In L. Porter & M. Rosenzweig (Eds.), *Annual review of psychology* (Vol. 43, pp. 169-203). Palo Alto, CA: Annual Reviews.

Arundale, R. B. (1980). Studying change over time: Criteria for sampling from continuous variables. *Communication Research, 7,* 227-263.

Attewell, P. (1972). Ethnomethodology since Garfinkel. *Theory and Society, 1,* 179-210.

Bakeman, R., & Gottman, J. (1986). *Observing interaction: An introduction to sequential analysis.* Cambridge: Cambridge University Press.

Bales, R. F. (1970). *Personality and interpersonal behavior.* New York: Holt, Rinehart & Winston.

Barley, S. (1986). Technology as the occasion for structuring: Evidence from observations of CT scanners and the social ordering of radiology departments. *Administrative Science Quarterly, 31,* 78-108.

Behling, O., & Dillard, J. F. (1984). A problem in data analysis: Implications for organizational behavior research. *Academy of Management Review, 9,* 37-46.

Bell, R. A. (1986). The multivariate structure of communication avoidance. *Communication Monographs, 53,* 265-375.

Bentler, P. M. (1973). Assessment of developmental factor change at the individual and group level. In J. R. Nessleroade & H. W. Reese (Eds.), *Life-span developmental psychology: Methodological issues.* New York: Academic Press.

Bentler, P. M. (1989). *EQS structural equations program manual.* Los Angeles: BMDP Statistical Software.

Berger, C. R. (1975). The covering law perspective as a basis for the study of human communication. *Communication Quarterly, 25,* 7-18.

Berger, C. R., & Calabrese, R. J. (1974). Some explorations in initial interaction and beyond: Toward a developmental theory of interpersonal communication. *Human Communication Research, 1,* 99-112.

Bernstein, R. (1983). *Beyond objectivism and relativism: Science, hermeneutics, and praxis.* Philadelphia: University of Pennsylvania Press.

Bishop, Y. M., Feinberg, S., & Holland, P. W. (1975). *Discrete multivariate analysis: Theory and practice.* Cambridge: MIT Press.

Blumer, H. (1956). Sociological analysis and the "variable." *American Sociological Review, 21,* 683-690.

Boissevain, J. (1974). *Friends of friends.* New York: St. Martin's Press.

Bollen, K. A. (1989). *Structural equation models with latent variables.* New York: Wiley.

Bollen, K. A., & Long, J. S. (1993). *Testing structural equation models.* Newbury Park, CA: Sage.

Borg, I. (1979). Some basic concepts of facet theory. In J. C. Lingoes, E. E. Roskam, & I. Borg (Eds.), *Geometric representations of relational data: Readings in multidimensional scaling* (pp. 65-102). Ann Arbor, MI: Mathesis.

Borgatti, S. P., Everett, M. G., & Freeman, L. C. (1992). *UCINET IV version 1.0 reference manual.* Columbia, SC: Analytic Technologies.

Bott, E. (1971). *Family and social network.* New York: Free Press.

Brown, P., & Levinson, S. (1978). Universals in language usage: Politeness phenomena. In E. N. Goody (Ed.), *Questions and politeness: Strategies in social interaction* (pp. 56-289). Cambridge: Cambridge University Press.

Bryk, A. S., & Raudenbush, S. W. (1992). *Hierarchical linear models.* Newbury Park, CA: Sage.

Bryman, A. (1988). *Quantity and quality in social research.* London: Unwin-Hyman.

Buder, E. H. (1991). A nonlinear dynamic model of social interaction. *Communication Research, 18,* 174-198.

Burggraf, C. S., & Sillars, A. L. (1987). A critical examination of sex differences in marital communication. *Communication Monographs, 54,* 276-294.

Burgoon, J. K., & Hale, J. C. (1987). Validation and measurement of fundamental themes of relational communication. *Communication Monographs, 54,* 19-41.

Burgoon, M., Hall, J., & Pfau, M. (1991). A test of the "messages-as-fixed-effect fallacy" argument: Empirical and theoretical implications of design choices. *Communication Quarterly, 39,* 18-34.

Burleson, B. R., & Denton, W. H. (1992). A new look at similarity and attraction in marriage: Similarities in social-cognitive and communication skills as predictors of attraction and satisfaction. *Communication Monographs, 59,* 268-287.

Burleson, B. R., Wilson, S. R., Waltman, M. S., Goering, E. M., Ely, T. K., & Whaley, B. B. (1988). Item desirability effects in compliance-gaining research: Seven studies documenting artifacts in the strategy selection procedure. *Human Communication Research, 14,* 429-486.

Burnett, R. (1991). Accounts and narratives. In B. M. Montgomery & S. Duck (Eds.), *Studying interpersonal interaction* (pp. 121-140). New York: Guilford.

Burt, R. S. (1989). *Structure version 4.0.* New York: Columbia University.

Byrne, D. (1969). Attitudes and attraction. In L. Berkowitz (Ed.), *Advances in experimental social psychology* (Vol. 4, pp. 35-89). New York: Academic Press.

Campbell, D. T., & Stanley, J. C. (1966). *Experimental and quasi-experimental designs for research.* Skokie, IL: Rand McNally.

Cappella, J. N. (1977). Research methodology in communication: Review and commentary. In B. D. Ruben (Ed.), *Communication yearbook 1* (pp. 37-53). New Brunswick, NJ: Transaction.

Cappella, J. N. (1979). Talk-silence sequences in informal conversations I. *Human Communication Research, 6,* 3-17.

Cappella, J. N. (1980). Talk and silence sequences in informal conversations II. *Human Communication Research, 6,* 130-145.

Cappella, J. (1990). The method of proof by example in interaction analysis. *Communication Monographs, 57,* 236-242.

Cappella, J. N., & Planalp, S. (1981). Talk and silence sequences in informal conversations III: Interspeaker influence. *Human Communication Research, 7,* 117-132.

Carroll, J. D., & Chang, J. J. (1970). Analysis of individual differences in multidimensional scaling via an N-way generalization of Eckart-Young decomposition. *Psychometrika, 35,* 283-320.

Catalano, R. A., Dooley, D., & Jackson, R. (1983). Selecting a time-series strategy. *Psychological Bulletin, 94,* 506-523.

Chase, L. J., & Tucker, R. K. (1975). A power-analytic examination of contemporary communication research. *Communication Monographs, 42,* 29-41.

Chatfield, C. (1975). *The analysis of time-series: Theory and practice.* London: Chapman and Hill.

Chomsky, N. (1957). *Syntactic structure.* The Hague, the Netherlands: Mouton.

Christensen, R. (1990). *Log-linear models.* New York: Springer-Verlag.

Churchill, L. (1963). Types of formalization in small group research. *Sociometry, 26,* 373-390.

Cicourel, A. V. (1964). *Method and measurement in sociology.* New York: Free Press.

Cicourel, A. V. (1972). Basic and normative rules in the negotiation of status and role. In D. Sudnow (Ed.), *Studies in social interaction* (pp. 229-258). New York: Free Press.

Cicourel, A. V. (1980). Three models of discourse analysis: The role of social structure. *Discourse Processes, 3,* 101-132.

Cicourel, A. V. (1981). The role of cognitive-linguistic concepts in understanding everyday social interactions. *Annual Review of Sociology, 7,* 87-106.

Cody, M. J., Woelfel, M. L., & Jordan, W. J. (1983). Dimensions of compliance-gaining situations. *Human Communication Research, 9,* 99-113.

Cohen, J. (1988). *Statistical power analysis for the behavioral sciences* (2nd ed.). Hillsdale, NJ: Lawrence Erlbaum.

Collins, L. M., & Horn, J. L. (1991). *Best methods for the study of change.* Washington, DC: American Psychological Association.

Cook, T. D., & Campbell, D. T. (1979). *Quasi-experimentation: Design and analysis issues for field settings.* Chicago: Rand McNally.

Cormak, R. M. (1971). A review of classification. *Journal of the Royal Statistical Society, 143,* 321-367.

Craig, R. T. (1983). Galilean rhetoric and practical theory. *Communication Monographs, 50,* 395-412.

Crocker, L., & Algina, J. (1986). *Introduction to classical and modern test theory.* New York: Holt, Rinehart & Winston.

Cronbach, L. (1990). *Essentials of psychological testing* (5th ed.). New York: Harper-Collins.

Cronbach, L., & Furby, L. (1970). How should we measure "change"—or should we? *Psychological Bulletin, 74,* 68-80.

Cronbach, L. J., Gleser, G. C., Nanda, H., & Rajaratnam, N. (1972). *The dependability of behavioral measurements: Theory of generalizability for scores and profiles.* New York: Wiley.

Cronbach, L. J., & Meehl, P. E. (1955). Construct validity in psychological tests. *Psychological Bulletin, 52,* 281-302.

Cronkhite, G. (1976). Effects of rater-concept-scale interactions and use of different factoring procedures upon evaluative factor structure. *Human Communication Research, 2,* 316-329.

Cronkhite, G., & Liska, J. (1976). Critique of factor analytic approaches to the study of credibility. *Communication Monographs, 43,* 91-107.

Cureton, E. E., & D'Agostino, R. B. (1983). *Factor analysis: An applied approach.* Hillsdale, NJ: Lawrence Erlbaum.

Cushman, D. P., & Cahn, D. (1984). *Communication in interpersonal relationships.* Albany: SUNY Press.

Cushman, D. P., & Pearce, W. B. (1977). Generality and necessity in three types of human communication theory with special attention to rules theory. *Human Communication Research, 3,* 344-353.

Davison, M. L. (1983). *Multidimensional scaling.* New York: Wiley.

Delia, J., & Clark, R. (1977). Cognitive complexity, social perception, and the development of listener-adapted communication in six-, eight-, ten-, and twelve-year-old boys. *Communication Monographs, 44,* 326-345.

Delia, J. G., Kline, S. K., & Burleson, B. R. (1979). The development of persuasive communication strategies in kindergartners through twelfth-graders. *Communication Monographs, 46*, 241-256.

Denzin, N. K. (1989). *Interpretive interactionism.* Newbury Park, CA: Sage.

Dillard, J. P. (1988). Compliance-gaining message selection: What is our dependent variable? *Communication Monographs, 55*, 162-183.

Dillman, D. A. (1978). *Mail and telephone surveys: The total design method.* New York: Wiley.

Dindia, K. (1986). Antecedents and consequences of awkward silence: A replication using revised lag sequential analysis. *Human Communication Research, 13*, 108-125.

Donohue, W. A. (1981). Development of a model of rule use in negotiation interaction. *Communication Monographs, 48*, 106-120.

Duck, S. (1991). Diaries and logs. In B. M. Montgomery & S. Duck (Eds.), *Studying interpersonal interaction* (pp. 141-161). New York: Guilford.

Edelsky, C. (1982). Who's got the floor? *Language in Society, 10*, 383-421.

Eggert, L. L., & Parks, M. R. (1986). Communication network involvement in adolescents' friendships and romantic relationships. In M. McLaughlin (Ed.), *Communication yearbook 10* (pp. 283-322). Newbury Park, CA: Sage.

Ericsson, K. A., & Simon, H. A. (1980). Verbal reports as data. *Psychological Review, 87*, 215-251.

Everitt, B. (1977). *The analysis of contingency tables.* New York: Wiley.

Feinberg, S. (1989). *The analysis of cross-classified categorical data* (2nd ed.). Cambridge: MIT Press.

Fink, A., & Kosecoff, J. (1985). *How to conduct surveys: A step-by-step guide.* Beverly Hills, CA: Sage.

Fink, E. L. (1980). Unobserved variables within structural equation models. In P. R. Monge & J. N. Cappella (Eds.), *Multivariate techniques in human communication research* (pp. 111-142). New York: Academic Press.

Fischer, C. S. (1982). *To dwell among friends: Personal networks in town and city.* Chicago: University of Chicago Press.

Fisher, B. A. (1970). Decision emergence: Phases in group decision making. *Speech Monographs, 37*, 53-66.

Fisher, B. A., & Hawes, L. C. (1971). An interact system model: Generating a grounded theory of small groups. *Quarterly Journal of Speech, 57*, 444-453.

Foa, U. G. (1965). New developments in facet design and analysis. *Psychological Review, 72*, 262-274.

Folger, J. P., Hewes, D., & Poole, M. S. (1984). Coding social interaction. In B. Dervin & M. Voight (Eds.), *Progress in the communication sciences* (pp. 115-161). New York: Ablex.

Frankel, R. (1983). The laying on of hands: Aspects of the organization of gaze, touch, and talk in a medical encounter. In S. Fisher & A. D. Todd (Eds.), *The social organization of doctor-patient communication* (pp. 19-54). Washington, DC: Center for Applied Linguistics.

Frankel, R. M., & Beckman, H. B. (1982). Impact: An interaction-based method for preserving and analyzing clinical interactions. In L. S. Pettegrew, P. Arnston, D. Bush, & K. Zoppi (Eds.), *Explorations in provider and patient interaction* (pp. 71-86). Nashville, TN: Humana.

Freeman, J. R., Williams, J. T., & Lin, T. (1988). *Modeling political processes.* Unpublished manuscript, University of Minnesota, Department of Political Science.

Frentz, T. A., & Farrell, T. B. (1976). Language-action: A paradigm for communication. *Quarterly Journal of Speech, 62*, 333-349.

Garfinkel, H. (1967). *Studies in ethnomethodology.* Englewood Cliffs, NJ: Prentice-Hall.

Glaser, B. G., & Strauss, A. (1967). *The discovery of grounded theory: Strategies for qualitative research.* Chicago: Aldine.

Gold, R. L. (1958). Roles in sociological field observations. *Social Forces, 36*, 217-223.

Goldstein, H. (1987). *Multilevel models in educational and social research.* New York: Oxford University Press.

Goodman, L. A. (1978). *Analyzing qualitative/categorical data: Log-linear models and latent structure analysis.* Cambridge, MA: Abt.

Gottman, J. M. (1981). *Time-series analysis: A comprehensive introduction for social scientists.* New York: Cambridge University Press.

Gregson, R. A. M. (1983). *Time-series in psychology.* Hillsdale, NJ: Lawrence Erlbaum.

Grimshaw, A. (1982). Comprehensive discourse analysis: An instance of professional peer interaction. *Language in Society, 11*, 15-47.

Gudykunst, W. B. (1985). The influence of cultural similarity, type of relationship, and self-monitoring on uncertainty reduction processes. *Communication Monographs, 52*, 203-217.

Hale, J. L., & Dillard, J. P. (1991). The uses of meta-analysis: Making knowledge claims and setting research agendas. *Communication Monographs, 58*, 463-471.

Hall, B. J. (1991). An elaboration of the structural possibilities for engaging in alignment episodes. *Communication Monographs, 58*, 79-100.

Hall, J. A., & Rosenthal, R. (1991). Testing for moderator variables in meta-analysis: Issues and methods. *Communication Monographs, 58*, 437-448.

Hambleton, R. K., & Swaminathan, H. (1985). *Item response theory: Principles and applications.* Boston: Kluwer-Nijhoff.

Harré, R., & Madden, E. H. (1975). *Causal powers: A theory of natural necessity.* Oxford: Basil Blackwell.

Hawes, L. (1972). Development and application of an interview coding system. *Central States Speech Journal, 23*, 92-99.

Hayes, D., & Sievers, S. (1972). A sociolinguistic investigation of the "dimensions" of interpersonal behavior. *Journal of Personality and Social Psychology, 24*, 254-261.

Healey, J. G., & Bell, R. A. (1990). Effects of social networks on individual's responses to conflicts in friendship. In D. D. Cahn (Ed.), *Intimates in conflict: A communication perspective.* Hillsdale, NJ: Lawrence Erlbaum.

Henry, J. (1963). *Culture against man.* New York: Vintage.

Henry, J. (1975). *Pathways to madness.* New York: Vintage.

Hewes, D. E. (1975). Finite stochastic modelling of communication processes. *Human Communication Research, 1*, 217-283.

Hewes, D. E. (1979). The sequential analysis of social interaction. *Quarterly Journal of Speech, 65*, 56-73.

Hewes, D. E. (1980). An axiomatized stochastic process theory of the relationships among messages, mediating variables, and behaviors. In D. P. Cushman & R. D. McPhee (Eds.), *The message-article-behavior relationship* (pp. 43-88). New York: Academic Press.

Hewes, D. E. (1985). Systematic biases in coded social interaction data. *Human Communication Research, 11*, 554-574.

Hewes, D. E., Graham, M. L., Doelger, J., & Pavitt, C. (1985). "Second guessing": Message interpretation in social networks. *Human Communication Research, 11*, 299-335.

Hewes, D. E., & Haight, L. R. (1979). The cross-situational consistency of communication behaviors: A preliminary investigation. *Communication Research, 6*, 243-270.

Hewes, D. E., & Haight, L. R. (1980). Multiple-act criteria in the validation of communication traits: What do we gain and what do we lose? *Human Communication Research, 6*, 354-366.

Holmes, M. E., & Poole, M. S. (1991). Longitudinal analysis. In B. M. Montgomery & S. Duck (Eds.), *Studying interpersonal interaction* (pp. 286-302). New York: Guilford.

Hopper, R., Koch, S., & Mandelbaum, J. (1986). Conversation analysis methods. In D. Ellis & W. Donohue (Eds.), *Contemporary issues in language and discourse processes* (pp. 169-186). Hillsdale, NJ: Lawrence Erlbaum.

Hosmer, D. W., & Lemeshow, S. (1989). *Applied logistic regression.* New York: Wiley.

Hubert, L., & Schultz, J. (1976). Quadratic assignment as a general data analysis strategy. *British Journal of Mathematical and Statistical Psychology, 29*, 190-241.

Hunter, J. E., & Boster, F. J. (1987). A model of compliance-gaining message selection. *Communication Monographs, 54*, 63-84.

Hunter, J. E., Danes, J. E., & Cohen, S. H. (1984). *Mathematical models of attitude change.* New York: Academic Press.

Hunter, J. E., Hamilton, M. A., & Allen, M. (1989). The design and analysis of language experiments in communication. *Communication Monographs, 56*, 341-363.

Hunter, J. E., & Schmidt, F. L. (1990). *Meta-analysis: Cumulating research findings across studies* (2nd ed.). Newbury Park, CA: Sage.

Huston, T. L., Surra, C., Fitzgerald, N., & Cate, R. (1981). From courtship to marriage: Mate selection as an interpersonal process. In S. Duck & R. Gilmour (Eds.), *Personal relationships: Vol. 2. Developing personal relationships* (pp. 53-90). New York: Academic Press.

Infante, D. A., & Rancer, A. S. (1982). A conceptualization and measurement of argumentativeness. *Journal of Personality Assessment, 46*, 72-80.

Infante, D. A., & Wigley, C. J. (1986). Verbal aggressiveness: An interpersonal model and measure. *Communication Monographs, 53*, 61-69.

Izraeli, D. (1977). Settling in: An interactionist perspective on the entry of a new manager. *Pacific Sociological Review, 20*, 135-160.

Jaccard, J., & Daly, J. (1980). Personality traits and multiple act criteria. *Human Communication Research, 6*, 367-377.

Jackson, S. (1986). Building a case for claims about discourse structure. In D. Ellis & W. Donohue (Eds.), *Contemporary issues in language and discourse processes* (pp. 129-148). Hillsdale, NJ: Lawrence Erlbaum.

Jackson, S. (1991). Meta-analysis for primary and secondary data analysis: The super-experiment metaphor. *Communication Monographs, 58*, 449-462.

Jackson, S., & Brashers, D. E. (in press). M > 1: Analysis of treatment × replication designs. *Human Communication Research.*

Jackson, S., & Jacobs, S. (1983). Generalizing about messages: Suggestions for the design and analysis of experiments. *Human Communication Research, 9*, 169-191.

Jackson, S., O'Keefe, D., Jacobs, S., & Brashers, D. (1989). Messages as replications: Toward a message-centered design strategy. *Communication Monographs, 56*, 364-384.

Jacobs, S. (1986). How to make an argument from example in discourse analysis. In D. Ellis & W. Donohue (Eds.), *Contemporary issues in language and discourse processes* (pp. 149-168). Hillsdale, NJ: Lawrence Erlbaum.

Jacobs, S. (1990). On the especially nice fit between qualitative analysis and the known properties of conversation. *Communication Monographs, 57*, 243-249.

Jones, L. V., & Appelbaum, M. I. (1989). Psychometric methods. In L. Porter & M. Rosenzweig (Eds.), *Annual review of psychology* (Vol. 40, pp. 23-43). Palo Alto, CA: Annual Reviews.

Jones, S. E., & Yarbrough, A. E. (1985). A naturalistic study of the meanings of touch. *Communication Monographs, 52*, 19-56.

Jöreskog, K. G., & Sörbom, D. (1989). *LISREL 7: A guide to the program and applications* (2nd ed.). Chicago: SPSS.

Katriel, T., & Philipsen, J. (1981). "What we need is communication": "Communication" as a cultural category in some American speech. *Communication Monographs, 48*, 301-317.

Kellerman, K. (1988, May). *The limits of lag sequential analysis in the description of patterns of dependency: Incomplete, unbounded, and inaccurate descriptions of dependence.* Paper presented at the International Communication Association Convention, New Orleans.

Kellerman, K., Reynolds, R., & Chen, J. B. (1991). Strategies of conversational retreat: When parting is not sweet sorrow. *Communication Monographs, 58*, 362-383.

Kenny, D. A. (1979). *Correlation and causation.* New York: Wiley-Interscience.

Kenny, D. A., & Kashy, D. A. (1991). Analyzing interdependence in dyads. In B. M. Montgomery & S. Duck (Eds.), *Studying interpersonal interaction* (pp. 275-285). New York: Guilford.

Kenny, D. A., & La Voie, L. (1984). The social relations model. In L. Berkowitz (Ed.), *Advances in experimental social psychology* (Vol. 18, pp. 141-182). New York: Academic Press.

Keppel, G. (1973). *Design and analysis: A researcher's handbook.* Englewood Cliffs, NJ: Prentice-Hall.

Kirk, J., & Miller, M. L. (1986). *Reliability and validity in qualitative research.* Newbury Park, CA: Sage.

Kirk, R. E. (1982). *Experimental design: Procedures for the behavioral sciences* (2nd ed.). Belmont, CA: Brooks/Cole.

Knoke, D. (1975). A comparison of log-linear and regression models for systems of dichotomous variables. *Sociological Methods and Research, 3*, 416-434.

Kraemer, H. C., & Thiemann, S. (1987). *How many subjects? Statistical power analysis in research.* Newbury Park, CA: Sage.

Labov, W., & Fanshel, D. (1977). *Therapeutic discourse: Psychotherapy as conversation.* New York: Academic Press.

Laing, R. D. (1962). *The self and others.* Chicago: Quadrangle.

LaRossa, R. (1977). *Conflict and power in marriage.* Beverly Hills, CA: Sage.

Lazarsfeld, P., & Barton, A. (1969). Qualitative measurement: A codification of techniques for the social sciences. In L. Krimmerman (Ed.), *The nature and scope of the social sciences* (pp. 514-539). Englewood Cliffs, NJ: Prentice-Hall.

Leary, T. (1957). *Interpersonal diagnosis of personality.* New York: Ronald.

LeCompte, M. D., & Goetz, J. P. (1982). Problems of reliability and validity in ethnographic research. *Review of Educational Research, 52*, 31-60.

Leik, R., & Matthews, M. (1968). A scale for developmental processes. *American Sociological Review, 33*, 62-75.

Levine, R. L., & Fitzgerald, H. E. (Eds.). (1991). *Analysis of dynamic psychological systems* (Vols. 1-2). New York: Plenum.

Levine, T. R., & McCroskey, J. C. (1990). Measuring trait communication apprehension: A test of rival measurement models of the PRCA-24. *Communication Monographs, 57*, 62-72.

Lingoes, J. C., & Borg, I. (1978). A direct approach to individual differences scaling using increasingly complex transformations. *Psychometrika, 43*, 491-519.

Lingoes, J. C., Roskam, E. E., & Borg, I. (Eds.). (1979). *Geometric representations of relational data: Readings in multidimensional scaling.* Ann Arbor, MI: Mathesis.

Lord, F. M., & Novick, M. R. (1968). *Statistical theory of mental test scores*. Reading, MA: Addison-Wesley.

Maddala, G. S. (1983). *Limited-dependent and qualitative variables in econometrics*. Cambridge: Cambridge University Press.

McCleary, R., & Hays, R. L. (1980). *Applied time series analysis for the social sciences*. Beverly Hills, CA: Sage.

McCroskey, J. C. (1978). Validity of the PRCA as an index of oral communication apprehension. *Communication Monographs, 45*, 192-203.

McDonald, R. P. (1985). *Factor analysis and related methods*. Hillsdale, NJ: Lawrence Erlbaum.

McLaughlin, M., & Cody, M. (1982). Awkward silences: Behavioral antecedents and consequences of the conversational lapse. *Human Communication Research, 8*, 299-316.

McPhee, R. D. (1990). Alternate approaches to integrating longitudinal case studies. *Organization Science, 1*, 393-406.

McPhee, R. D., & Babrow, A. S. (1987). Causal modeling in speech communication research: Use, disuse and misuse. *Communication Monographs, 54*, 344-366.

McPhee, R. D., & Poole, M. S. (1981). Mathematical modeling in communication research: An overview. In M. Burgoon (Ed.), *Communication yearbook 5* (pp. 159-161). New Brunswick, NJ: Transaction.

McPhee, R. D., & Seibold, D. R. (1979). Rationale, procedures, and applications for decomposition of explained variance in multiple regression analysis. *Communication Research, 6*, 345-384.

Menzies, K. (1982). *Sociological theory in use*. London: Routledge & Kegan Paul.

Metts, S. R., Sprecher, S., & Cupach, W. R. (1991). Retrospective self-reports. In B. M. Montgomery & S. Duck (Eds.), *Studying interpersonal interaction* (pp. 162-178). New York: Guilford.

Milardo, R. M. (1987). Changes in social networks of males and females following divorce: A review. *Journal of Family Issues, 8*, 78-96.

Miles, M. B., & Huberman, A. M. (1984). *Qualitative data analysis: A sourcebook of new methods*. Beverly Hills, CA: Sage.

Miller, G. R., & Berger, C. (1978). On keeping the faith in matters scientific. *Western Journal of Speech Communication, 42*, 44-57.

Milligan, G. W., & Cooper, M. C. (1987). Methodology review: Clustering methods. *Applied Psychological Measurement, 11*, 329-354.

Mintzberg, H., Raisinghani, D., & Theoret, A. (1976). The structure of "unstructured" decision processes. *Administrative Science Quarterly, 21*, 246-275.

Morey, L. C., Blashfield, R. K., & Skinner, H. A. (1983). A comparison of cluster analysis techniques within a sequential validation framework. *Multivariate Behavioral Research, 18*, 309-329.

Morley, D. D. (1987). Revised lag sequential analysis. In M. L. McLaughlin (Ed.), *Communication yearbook 10* (pp. 172-182). Newbury Park, CA: Sage.

Morley, D. D. (1988). Meta-analytic techniques: When generalizing to message populations is not possible. *Human Communication Research, 15*, 112-126.

Morrison, D. F. (1990). *Multivariate statistical methods* (3rd ed.). New York: McGraw-Hill.

Mosteller, F., & Tukey, J. W. (1977). *Data analysis and regression*. Reading, MA: Addison-Wesley.

Mulac, A., Weimann, J. M., Widenmann, S. J., & Gibson, T. W. (1988). Male/female language differences and effects in same-sex and mixed-sex dyads: The gender linked language effect. *Communication Monographs, 55*, 315-355.

Newcomb, T. (1961). *The acquaintance process*. New York: Holt, Rinehart & Winston.

Nisbett, R. E., & Wilson, T. D. (1977). Telling more than we can know: Verbal reports on mental processes. *Psychological Review, 84*, 231-259.

Noblit, G. W., & Hare, R. D. (1991). *Meta-ethnography: Synthesizing qualitative studies*. Newbury Park, CA: Sage.

Ochs, E. (1979). Transcription as theory. In E. Ochs & B. Schieffelin (Eds.), *Developmental pragmatics* (pp. 43-72). New York: Academic Press.

O'Donnell-Trujillo, N. (1982). Relational communication: A comparison of coding systems. *Communication Monographs, 48*, 91-105.

O'Keefe, B., Delia, J., & O'Keefe, D. (1980). Interaction analysis and the analysis of interactional organization. In N. K. Denzin (Ed.), *Studies in symbolic interactionism* (Vol. 3, pp. 25-57). Greenwich, CT: JAI.

O'Keefe, D. J. (1991). Extracting dependable generalizations from the persuasion effects literature: Some issues in meta-analytic reviews. *Communication Monographs, 58*, 472-481.

Overton, W. F., & Reese, H. W. (1973). Models of development: Methodological implications. In J. R. Nesslroade & H. W. Reese (Eds.), *Life span developmental psychology: Methodological issues* (pp. 65-86). New York: Academic Press.

Pavitt, C., & Cappella, J. N. (1979). Coorientational accuracy in interpersonal and small group discussions: A literature review, model, and simulation. In D. Nimmo (Ed.), *Communication yearbook 3* (pp. 123-156). New Brunswick, NJ: Transaction.

Pearce, W. B., & Cronen, V. E. (1980). *Communication, action and meaning.* New York: Praeger.

Pedhazur, E. J. (1982). *Multiple regression in behavioral research: Explanation and prediction.* New York: Holt, Rinehart & Winston.

Pfaffenberger, B. (1987). *Microcomputer applications in qualitative research.* Newbury Park, CA: Sage.

Philipsen, G. (1975). Speaking "like a man" in Teamsterville: Cultural patterns of role enactment in an urban neighborhood. *Quarterly Journal of Speech, 61,* 13-22.

Pittenger, R. E., Hockett, C. F., & Daheny, J. J. (1960). *The first five minutes.* Ithaca, NY: Paul Martineau.

Planalp, S., & Tracy, K. (1980). Not to change the topic but . . .: A cognitive approach to the management of conversation. In D. Nimmo (Ed.), *Communication yearbook 4* (pp. 237-258). New Brunswick, NJ: Transaction.

Pomerantz, A. (1990). Conversation analytic claims. *Communication Monographs, 57,* 231-236.

Poole, M. S., & DeSanctis, G. (1992). Microlevel structuration in computer-supported group decision-making. *Human Communication Research, 19,* 5-49.

Poole, M. S., & Folger, J. P. (1981). A method for establishing the representational validity of interaction coding systems: Do we see what they see? *Human Communication Research, 8,* 26-42.

Poole, M. S., Folger, J. P., & Hewes, D. E. (1987). Analyzing interpersonal interaction. In M. E. Roloff & G. R. Miller (Eds.), *Interpersonal processes* (pp. 220-256). Newbury Park, CA: Sage.

Poster, M. (1980). *Critical theory of the family.* New York: Seabury.

Psathas, G. (1990). Introduction: Methodological issues and recent developments in the study of naturally occurring interaction. In G. Psathas (Ed.), *Interaction competence* (pp. 1-30). Lanham, MD: University Press.

Rawlins, W. K. (1983). Openness as problematic in ongoing friendships: Two conversational dilemmas. *Communication Monographs, 50,* 1-13.

Rogers, E., & Farace, R. (1975). Analysis of relational communication in dyads: New measurement procedures. *Human Communication Research, 1,* 222-239.

Rosenthal, H. (1980). Review of L. A. Goodman's *Analyzing qualitative/categorical data: Log-linear models and latent structure analysis. Contemporary Sociology, 9,* 207-211.

Rosenthal, R. (1991). *Meta-analytic procedures for social research* (rev. ed.). Newbury Park, CA: Sage.

Rosenthal, R., & Rosnow, R. L. (1985). *Contrast analysis: Focused comparisons in the analysis of variance.* Cambridge: Cambridge University Press.

Rossi, P. H., Wright, J. D., & Anderson, A. B. (Eds.). (1983). *Handbook of survey research.* New York: Academic Press.

Rothenbuhler, E. W. (1991). The process of community involvement. *Communication Monographs, 58,* 63-78.

Rubin, K. H. (1973). Egocentrism in childhood: A unitary construct. *Child Development, 14,* 102-110.

Rubin, R., Palmgreen, D., & Sypher, H. (in press). *Communication research measures.* New York: Guilford.

Sackett, G. P. (1979). The lag sequential analysis of contingency and cyclicity in behavioral interaction research. In J. Osfsky (Ed.), *Handbook of infant development* (pp. 623-649). New York: Wiley.

Sacks, H., Schegloff, E. A., & Jefferson, G. (1974). A simplest systematics for the organization of turn-taking in conversation. *Language, 50,* 696-735.

Schaie, K. W. (1970). A reinterpretation of age-related changes in cognitive functioning. In L. R. Goulet & P. B. Baltes (Eds.), *Life-span development: Research and theory* (pp. 485-507). New York: Academic Press.

Schaie, K. W., & Baltes, P. B. (1975). On sequential strategies in development: Description or explanation. *Human Development, 18,* 384-390.

Schenkein, J. N. (Ed.). (1978). *Studies in the organization of conversational interaction.* New York: Academic Press.

Schmitt, N., & Stults, D. M. (1986). Methodology review: Analysis of multitrait-multimethod matrices. *Applied Psychological Measurement, 10,* 1-22.

Schutz, A. (1964). *Collected papers II: Studies in social theory.* The Hague, the Netherlands: Martinus Nijhoff.

Schwartz, H., & Jacobs, J. (1979). *Qualitative sociology: A method to the madness.* New York: Free Press.

Searle, J. R. (1976). A classification of illocutionary acts. *Language in Society, 5,* 1-23.

Searle, S. R. (1971). *Linear models*. New York: Wiley.

Seibold, D., R., & McPhee, R. D. (1980). A new analysis of Daly's assessment of social communicative anxiety via self-reports: A comparison of measures. *Communication Monographs, 47*, 149-152.

Sennett, R. (1974). *The fall of public man*. New York: Random House.

Sillars, A. L., Burggraf, C. S., Yost, S., & Zietlow, P. H. (1992). Conversational themes and marital relationship definitions: Quantitative and qualitative investigations. *Human Communication Research, 19*, 124-154.

Snyder, L. B. (1991). Modeling dynamic communication processes with event history analysis. *Communication Research, 18*, 464-486.

Spence, I., & Ogilvie, J. (1973). A table of expected stress values for random nonmetric multidimensional scaling. *Multivariate Behavioral Research, 9*, 511-517.

Stiff, J. B., Dillard, J. P., Somera, L., Kim, H., & Sleight, C. (1988). Empathy, communication, and prosocial behavior. *Communication Monographs, 55*, 198-213.

Strauss, A. (1987). *Qualitative analysis for social scientists*. Cambridge: Cambridge University Press.

Sudman, S., & Bradburn, N. M. (1983). *Asking questions: A practical guide to design*. San Francisco: Jossey-Bass.

Sunnafrank, M. J., & Miller, G. R. (1981). The role of initial conversations in attraction to similar and dissimilar strangers. *Human Communication Research, 8*, 18-25.

Tatsuoka, M. (1988). *Multivariate analysis: Techniques for educational and psychological research* (2nd ed.). New York: Macmillan.

TenHouten, W. (1969). Scale gradient analysis. *Sociometry, 32*, 80-98.

Tracy, K. (1991). Discourse. In B. M. Montgomery & S. Duck (Eds.), *Studying interpersonal interaction* (pp. 179-196). New York: Guilford.

Trujillo, N. (1986). Toward a taxonomy of small group interaction coding systems. *Small Group Behavior, 17*, 371-394.

Tucker, L. R. (1966). Learning theory and multivariate experiment: Illustration of generalized learning curves. In R. B. Cattell (Ed.), *Handbook of multivariate psychology* (pp. 476-501). Chicago: Rand McNally.

Tucker, L. R. (1972). Relations between multidimensional scaling and three mode factor analysis. *Psychometrika, 37*, 3-27.

Tudor, A. (1976). Misunderstanding everyday life. *Sociological Review, 24*, 479-503.

Tukey, J. W. (1977). *Exploratory data analysis*. Reading, MA: Addison-Wesley.

Van Lear, C. A. (1991). Testing a cyclical model of communicative openness in relationship development: Two longitudinal studies. *Communication Monographs, 58*, 337-361.

Van Maanen, J. (1984). *Qualitative methodology*. Beverly Hills, CA: Sage.

Von Wright, G. H. (1971). *Explanation and understanding*. Ithaca, NY: Cornell University Press.

Vroom, V., & Jago, A. (1974). Decision making as a social process: Normative models of leader behavior. *Decision Sciences, 5*, 160-186.

Walster, G. W., & Cleary, T. A. (1970). Statistical significance as a decision rule. In E. F. Borgatta & G. W. Bohrnstedt (Eds.), *Sociological methodology, 1970* (pp. 246-256). San Francisco: Jossey-Bass.

Weeks, D. B., & Bentler, P. M. (1979). A comparison of linear and monotone multidimensional scaling models. *Psychological Bulletin, 8*, 349-354.

Weisberg, S. (1985). *Applied linear regression* (2nd ed.). New York: Wiley.

Whyte, W. F. (1955). *Street corner society* (2nd ed.). Chicago: University of Chicago Press.

Wiemann, J. M. (1981). Effects of laboratory videotaping procedures on selected conversational behaviors. *Human Communication Research, 7*, 302-311.

Wilcox, R. R. (1987). New designs in analysis of variance. In L. Porter & M. Rosenzweig (Eds.), *Annual review of psychology* (Vol. 38, pp. 29-60). Palo Alto, CA: Annual Reviews.

Williamson, R. N., & Fitzpatrick, M. A. (1985). Two approaches to marital interaction: Relational control patterns in marital types. *Communication Monographs, 52*, 236-252.

Willis, P. (1977). *Learning to labor*. New York: Columbia University Press.

Wilson, S. R. (1990). Development and test of a cognitive rules model of interaction goals. *Communication Monographs, 57*, 81-103.

Winer, B. J., Brown, D. R., & Michels, K. M. (1991). *Statistical principles in experimental design* (3rd ed.). New York: McGraw-Hill.

Woelfel, J., & Fink, E. L. (1980). *The measurement of communication processes: Galileo theory and method*. New York: Academic Press.

Wohlwill, J. (1973). *The study of behavior development*. New York: Academic Press.

Wonnacott, R. J., & Wonnacott, T. H. (1979). *Econometrics*. New York: Wiley.

Young, F. W. (1987). *Multidimensional scaling: History, theory, and applications*. Hillsdale, NJ: Lawrence Erlbaum.

Zaretsky, E. (1976). *Capitalism, the family, and social life*. New York: Harper & Row.

Zwick, R. (1988). Another look at interrater agreement. *Psychological Bulletin, 103*, 274-378.

PART II

Fundamental Units

4

Communicator Characteristics and Behavior

Howard Giles

Richard L. Street, Jr.

RESEARCHERS EXPLORING THE ROLE of communicator characteristics have usually fallen into one of two broad categories. First, investigators have examined how particular individual differences—such as personality, psychological, and sociodemographic variables—associated with the communicator have been marked in verbal and nonverbal behavior. Second, researchers who study language attitudes and speech style have been concerned with identifying beliefs about communicators who possess different linguistic and paralinguistic attributes. In the first part of this chapter, we consider representative research from each of these two approaches that are rarely overviewed at all (let alone in any sense of a systematic manner) alongside each other. We trust the catalogue format of the first part will be a valuable encyclopedic resource in its own right allowing easy access to extant knowledge in these domains. In the first section, we overview the effect of self-monitoring, extraversion-introversion, dominance-submissiveness, Machiavellianism, communication apprehensiveness, cognitive stress and anxiety, and field dependence-independence on communicative behaviors. Next, we review how communication is affected by one's gender, age, socioeconomic status, status and power, race/culture, and physical disabilities. Finally in the first part of the chapter, we overview how dialect/accent/language, speech rate, pausing, vocal intensity, pitch, vocal attractiveness, talk duration, self-disclosure, language intensity, and some other variables allow communicators to infer the social and psychological characteristics of others.

In the second part, we propose ways in which the above-mentioned traditional paradigms of communicator characteristics can be enriched. First, we set forth

AUTHORS' NOTE: We are grateful to Joseph Cappella and Mark Palmer for their constructive comments on an earlier draft, to James J. Bradac and Jake Harwood for their input into the review section of this chapter, and to Mark Knapp for his thorough and useful editorial suggestions.

some limitations of previous approaches. Then we focus on research and theory into involvement behaviors and impression management, which constitute the underpinnings to a (complex) speculative model of cognitive characteristics of communicators in the third section. This latter approach is proffered as a complement to the traditional paradigms reviewed in the first part. It is our belief that such a perspective is an important and necessary precursor to any theoretically substantive and pragmatically relevant advances that can be made in the communicator characteristics arena of interpersonal communication.

I: Traditional Paradigms of Empirical Research

Psychological Variables

Self-Monitoring

According to Snyder (1974, 1979), the high self-monitor (HSM) is sensitive to self-presentation and expression to relevant others due to a concern with the appropriateness of his or her social behavior. Thus HSM individuals carefully monitor their verbal and nonverbal behavior. The low self-monitor (LSM) is not as concerned about appropriate self-presentation, nor does he or she have a well-developed repertoire of social behavior skills. Research has indicated that HSMs are better able to express emotional states through facial and vocal channels (Snyder, 1974), have shorter turns and more interruptive simultaneous speech (Dabbs, Evans, Hopper, & Purvis, 1980), and are more likely to initiate conversations (Ickes & Barnes, 1977) than LSMs. HSMs are more likely to reciprocate the intimacy, emotionality, and descriptive content of a partner's self-disclosure than LSMs (Daly, Vangelisti, & Daughton, 1987; Shaffer, Smith, & Tomarelli, 1982). Dabbs et al. (1980), however, observed no differences between HSMs and LSMs regarding gaze patterns and matching of pause and turn length duration. DeBono and Harnish (1988) have extended self-monitoring research to the field of persuasion. Their research indicates that HSMs will tend to process persuasive messages from expert sources without attending to the strength of the argument, but are more "critical" of "attractive" sources. The authors found the inverse pattern for LSMs. Some research indicates that the relationship between self-monitoring and communicative behavior may vary depending on the speaker's culture (Gudykunst, Nishida, & Schmidt, 1989; Trubisky, Ting-Toomey, & Lin, 1991). Specifically, self-monitoring appears to have more influence on communication in individualistic cultures (e.g., the United States) than in collectivistic cultures (e.g., Japan), due to the lack of attention to group-based relationships in self-monitoring measures.

Extraversion-Introversion

Relative to introverts, extraverts spend less time pausing prior to assuming a speaking turn (Ramsay, 1966; Siegman & Pope, 1965a). Several studies have indicated that extraverts speak a greater proportion of the time than introverts (Scherer, 1979a; Smolensky, Carmody, & Halcomb, 1990), although extraverts appear not to self-disclose significantly more (Morris, 1979). On other speech dimensions, differences between extraverts and introverts are equivocal. Markel,

Phillis, Vargas, and Harvard (1972) reported that fast speakers were more extraverted than slow speakers, but Steer (1974) observed no differences in speech rate of extraverts and introverts when expressing emotions (see also Ramsay, 1968). Mallory and Miller (1958) reported a low positive correlation between extraversion and vocal intensity, whereas Trimboli's (1973) correlation was higher and significant.

Siegman (1978) has suggested that the greater amount of pausing and less time speaking among introverts results from higher cognitive activity and less impulsivity relative to extraverts. On the other hand, the research may indicate that extraverts are more "communicatively expressive" than introverts. For example, Thorne (1987) has indicated that introverts and extraverts have distinctive communicative styles. She showed that extraverts tend to show a wide range of topics and claims of common ground, whereas introverts engaged in more focused problem talk. Relatedly within the nonverbal domain, Morris (1979) reported that extraverts are more accurate than introverts in sending emotions, concluding that extraverts are more nonverbally responsive than introverts. Exline and Fehr (1978) suggested that extraverts may be more visually active and look at partners more than do introverts (see, for example, Mobbs, 1968), but only regarding frequency, and not duration, of looks (see, for example, Rutter, Morley, & Graham, 1972). In a related finding, Akert and Panter (1990) have demonstrated that extraverts are more accurate and more confident in their decoding of nonverbal behaviors. However, the relationship between extraversion and interaction distance remains unclear. Some research has revealed that extraverts prefer closer interaction distances than introverts (Cook, 1970; Pedersen, 1973; Williams, 1976), whereas other studies report no differences between the two groups (Patterson, 1973; Patterson & Holmes, 1966; Tolor, 1975). Knapp (1978) speculated that these conflicting findings may be due to contextual factors such as the intimacy of the encounter. In intimate settings, introverts may prefer more space between interactants. In less intimate settings, interaction distance preferences may not discriminate between extraverts and introverts.

Dominance-Submissiveness

Individuals having dominant personalities seem to employ a confident and assertive interaction style. Relative to their submissive counterparts, dominant communicators have been reported to hold the floor more, interrupt more (Martindale, 1971; Roger & Nesshoever, 1987; Rogers & Jones, 1975; Scherer, 1979b), participate more actively in groups (Weinstein & Hanson, 1975), use fewer silent pauses (Scherer, 1979b), and have more resonant voices (Mallory & Miller, 1958; Weaver & Anderson, 1973). In a study of jurors, Scherer (1979a) observed that dominance was related to the use of "certainty" words (for example, "obviously," "without any doubt"; see Scherer, 1979a) but only for American and not for German jurors.

For other speech behaviors, the findings are less clear. Some research has indicated that dominance is positively related to vocal intensity (Mallory & Miller, 1958; Weaver & Anderson, 1973), whereas other research found no relationship (Scherer, 1979a). The relationship between pitch and dominance is more confusing as dominance has been associated with high pitch (Scherer, 1979a), low pitch (Weaver & Anderson, 1973), and pitch range (Scherer, 1979b). The speech behavior of dominant personalities has been attributed to habitually elevated arousal levels (Scherer, 1979a) and to amount of muscle tension throughout the vocal system (Laver, 1975).

Machiavellianism

The high Machiavellian (Mach) individual manipulates others for personal objectives more than does the low Mach. The limited amount of research on Machiavellianism and communication has primarily focused on nonverbal behavior. During social interaction, high Machs tend to look at partners more than do low Machs (Knapp, 1978). For example, one study reported that, after being accused of cheating, high Machs gazed at the accuser to present an appearance of innocence whereas low Machs looked away (Exline, Thibaut, Hickey, & Gumpert, 1970). Geis and Moon (1981) observed that lying high Machs were more believable than were lying low Machs, although O'Hair, Cody, and McLaughlin (1981) could not distinguish between high and low Machs in terms of leakage of nonverbal cues of deception. These findings are particularly interesting given recent evidence that high Mach parents tend to raise high Mach children (Rai & Gupta, 1989). Knapp, Hart, and Dennis (1974) reported minimal behavioral differences among deceivers and nondeceivers as a function of Machiavellianism.

Reticence/Communication Apprehension/Unwillingness to Communicate

Under this general rubric, we consider research related to reticence (Phillips, 1968), communication apprehension (McCroskey, 1977), willingness to communicate (McCroskey & Daly, 1984; Mortensen & Arntson, 1974), and social anxiety. These constructs in some fashion tap into an individual's predilection to engage in communication or social activity with others. Some attempts have been made recently to examine the mutual relationships of these variables (Booth-Butterfield & Butterfield, 1986) and to uncover dimensions underlying them (Bell, 1986). Although much research has been conducted with these variables and with attention to intercultural issues (Gudykunst, 1988), surprisingly little has focused on actual communication behaviors (a notable exception is Burgoon & Koper, 1984).

For some communicative dimensions, the findings have been relatively consistent. Phillips (1968) reported that reticent speakers produced more hesitancies in speech than nonreticent speakers. McKinney (1982) observed that, although group interaction processes were not impeded by reticent group members, these individuals were less effective participants due to limited vocal activity and were less likely to emerge as leaders. Van Kleeck and Street's (1982) study of adult interaction with talkative and reticent 3-year-olds indicated that not only did the reticent children talk less but their speech was characterized by a lower mean length of utterance (MLU), less lexical diversity, a smaller proportion of complex sentences, a higher proportion of assertive statements, and a lower proportion of requestive remarks. In two studies, Burgoon and Koper (1984) found consistent behavioral patterns associated with communication reticence (as measured in the PRCA and UCS scales). As reticence increased, respondents nodded less, showed less facial pleasantness and animation, displayed more anxiety and tension, leaned away more, and communicated greater disinterest.

Hewes and his colleagues (Hewes & Haight, 1979, 1980; Hewes, Haight, Szalay, & Evans, 1977) have criticized the cross-situational validity of various measures of communication avoidance. Using a composite index of six situational behaviors (duration of an impromptu speech, duration of interaction in a small group, duration of responses in an interview, latency of responses, number of persons contacted, and choice of written versus oral assignments), Hewes and Haight (1979, 1980) found no support for the proposition that reticence and predisposition toward verbal behavior influenced these behaviors across situations. However, within specific domains, Hewes and Haight (1979) reported significant negative correlations between PVB and response durations in a free association task and in duration of interaction in small groups.

Other research also indicates that the relationship between one's attitudes toward communication and one's communicative behaviors varies for different situations and tasks. For example, McCroskey (1977) has noted that some research suggests that high communication apprehensives talk and disclose less than low apprehensives. On the other hand, Booth-Butterfield and Butterfield (1986) found that measures of reticence were not significantly related to any behavioral measures, a finding that they saw as cause for concern for those using the reticence measure (see also, Levine & McCroskey, 1990). Burgoon and Hale (1983) reported that, on essay tasks and prepared messages in which respondents filled in the blanks, high oral communication apprehensives displayed greater productivity, less intense language, more varied vocabulary, more complex language, and less comprehensible vocalizations. Jordan and Powers (1978) reported verbal behavior differences between the two groups but only as a function of context. In personal, informal settings, high communication apprehensives used shorter words, more adjectives and adverbs, and more phrase repetitions than low apprehensives. However, there were no differences between the two groups in a social, formal context. Miura (1985) demonstrates that bidialectal speakers experience different levels of apprehension depending on context. His sample experienced significantly more apprehension when speaking standard English than when using local Hawaiian dialect. Research regarding predisposition toward verbal behavior (PVB) and communication also has been mixed. Arntson, Mortensen, and Lustig (1980) observed high PVB respondents talking longer, interrupting less, and initiating more ideas than their low PVB counterparts. However, in a highly structured interview setting, no differences between high and low PVB persons were found for response durations (Arntson & Mortensen, 1976; Mortensen & Arntson, 1974).

Considered collectively, this research to some extent reveals that, compared with their counterparts, communicatively anxious and reticent communicators display less responsiveness, expressiveness, and involvement in their interactions with others. However, there is considerably more data indicating that the relationships between fears about communicating with others and actual communicative behaviors is quite complex and mediated by contextual factors and other individual difference variables.

Anxiety and Cognitive Stress

There appear to be curvilinear relationships between anxiety and speech tempo and productivity measures. Siegman (1978) has proposed that mild and moderate levels of anxiety tend to accelerate speech (faster rates and fewer pauses), whereas very low and very high anxiety levels produce slower speech and longer pauses. Other research indicates that anxious individuals maintain greater physical and psychological distance between themselves and interlocutors. For example, anxiety-prone individuals maintain greater distances than those not anxiety prone

(Knapp & Hall, 1992; Patterson, 1982a). Communicators experiencing higher cognitive stress, a construct related to anxiety, tend to exhibit less verbal immediacy (that is, the degree to which a subject's language reflects avoidance or approach toward a person or topic), language intensity, and lexical diversity than do individuals less stressed (Bradac, Bowers, & Courtright, 1979). Finally, Kimble and Seidel (1991) found that persons who were low in confidence about answers to questions posed by the researchers exhibited high response latencies and lower speech volume.

However, as with communication apprehension and reticence, the relationship between anxiety and communicative behavior appears to be mediated by the type of communicative exchange and whether the anxiety is a situational or a trait characteristic. For example, Helfrich and Dahme (1974, cited in Scherer, 1979a) showed that, relative to low anxious respondents, highly anxious individuals increased their number of pauses but only in threatening situations. No differences were observed between the two groups in positively valued situations. Also, anxiety arousal appears to facilitate performance of simple and familiar tasks (that is, tasks requiring minimal cognitive activity and habituated speech sequences) but interfere with complex and unfamiliar tasks. Following a comprehensive literature review, Murray (1971) concluded that verbal quantity (that is, amount or time of talk) was positively related to trait anxiety but negatively associated with situational anxiety. However, silence was negatively associated with trait anxiety but positively correlated with situational anxiety. Similarly, increases in situational anxiety appear to increase speech disturbances (for example, false starts, incomplete phrases, and so forth), though no relationship appears between trait anxiety and speech disturbances (Siegman, 1978). Gudykunst (1988) has presented a theoretical account of the relationships between uncertainty reduction (Berger & Bradac, 1982) and anxiety in intercultural communication.

In sum, there is no clear picture regarding the relationship between anxiety and communication behavior. This relationship appears to be mediated by a host of influences including situation, state versus trait anxiety, operationalization of anxiety, and nature of the task (Scherer, 1979a; Siegman, 1978).

Cognitive Complexity

Much of the research on cognitive complexity (that is, the extent of differentiation and/or abstractness of one's construct system for perceiving others) and communication has focused on the ability of communicators to adapt messages, given listener characteristics, to meet persuasive or other interpersonal needs (see Kline, 1991; McCroskey & Daly, 1984). O'Keefe and Sypher (1981) concluded that there is considerable evidence that positive relationships exist between cognitive complexity and indices of sophisticated communication such as the degree of listener-adaptedness among children's persuasive messages (Clark & Delia, 1977; however, null results were reported by Ritter, 1979), children's ability to adapt to conversational deviance (Reardon, 1982), adults' ability to modify the number and quality of persuasive messages toward targets (Applegate, 1982; O'Keefe & Delia, 1979), communication effectiveness in a password game and Tinkertoy building tasks (Hale, 1980), the development of person-centered regulative strategies (Applegate & Delia, 1980), and social perspective taking (Kline, Pelias, & Delia, 1991). Such measures have implications for the accommodative sensitivity of high/low cognitive complexity communicators (Applegate, Kline, & Delia, 1991).

Also, during informal conversation, high cognitively complex participants spent more time talking about themselves, whereas low cognitively complex individuals spent more time talking about external topics (Delia, Kline, & Burleson, 1979). Burleson and Samter (1990) indicate that level of complexity is also related to perceptions of the communicative skills important in peer relationships. High cognitive complexity participants saw affectively oriented communicative skills as important in a prospective friend, whereas noncomplex individuals rated nonaffectively oriented skills as important. High complexity individuals have also been shown to be better at decoding nonverbal behaviors, at least in situations of high arousal (Uhlemann, Lee, & Hasse, 1989), to display higher levels of lexical diversity (Powers, Jordan, Gurley, & Lindstrom, 1986), and to display higher levels of verbal (Hale, 1986) and written (Sypher, Witt, & Sypher, 1986) communication ability. Support for this assertion also emerges from the work of Neuliep and Hazleton (1985), who demonstrate a significant negative relationship between cognitive complexity and communication apprehension.

Although cognitive complexity appears positively related to sophisticated communication, the nature of "complexity" in this relationship changes with age. Communication effectiveness in childhood is related to construct differentiation (that is, the number of constructs). However, into adolescence and adulthood, communication effectiveness becomes a function of construct abstractness (that is, interrelationships among constructs; see Delia et al., 1979; O'Keefe & Sypher, 1981).

Field Dependence/Independence

Field dependence refers to differential responsiveness of individuals to external and internal cues (Feldstein & Welkowitz, 1978). Field dependent persons are more responsive to external cues, whereas field independent persons are responsive to internal cues. Doob (1958) observed no significant relationship between field independence (or psychological differentiation) and number of adverbs, noun qualifiers, pronouns, and action verbs in essays. However, Steingart, Freedmann, Grand, and Buchwald (1975) reported that for female respondents field independence was positively related to amount of talk but negatively correlated with words per sentence. Within families, field independence is related to use of "I" words, whereas field dependence is related to the use of "we" words (Dreyer, Dreyer, & Davis, 1987). These findings have implications for notions of separateness/connectedness to the family unit. Al-Nesir, Keenan, and Langer (1991) have demonstrated that among young children field independents are better at message evaluation skills, and it is argued that these children are more advanced in the development of referential communication. An advantage for field independent college students in learning a second language has also been shown (Carter, 1988). Sousa-Poza and Rohrberg (1977) found field dependents to produce more continuous body touching movements than field independents. Finally, relative to more differentiated (field independent) persons, individuals with less psychological differentiation (these persons are also more sensitive to interpersonal cues) matched partners' switching pauses to a greater extent (Feldstein & Welkowitz, 1978).

Need for Affiliation and Approval

Those that have a high need for affiliation tend to prefer closer distances and glance at partners more than those with lower affiliation needs (Knapp & Hall,

1992; Patterson, 1978). Duncan and Fiske (1977) reported no stable patterns among inclusion needs, turn length, number of turns, and turn time. Those that have a high need for approval matched partners' vocal intensity (Natale, 1975a) and pause durations (Natale, 1975b) more than did individuals with low approval needs. Those with high need for approval and esteem have been shown to produce shorter sentences in written communication than those with high esteem needs (Virk, Sharma, & Bhan, 1986). The proposition that persons with high approval needs look at interaction partners more has received mixed support (Efran, 1968).

Sociodemographic Variables

Gender

Of all sociodemographic difference variables in communication, gender has been the most predominantly studied. We discuss these effects under headings of noncontent speech, verbal, and nonverbal behavior.

Noncontent speech. The speech of men and women differs most in terms of vocal pitch. Adult women have higher pitch levels and greater pitch variability than do adult men because of the male's thicker vocal folds (P. M. Smith, 1979; Spencer, 1988). Other gender differences in speech appear due to socialization processes as opposed to biological factors. Across many cultures, men and women sometimes have discriminating pronunciation patterns (P. M. Smith, 1979). For example, in Montreal, females tend to pronounce the liquid "l" more often (Sankoff & Cedergren, 1971). In Scotland, Romaine and Reid (1976) observed girls articulating the dental "t" (for example, water, got) more often than boys. In the United States, a few studies have indicated that females pronounce postvocalic "r" and "ing" verb endings (as opposed to "in") more than males. Such differences led Lakoff (1975) and Kramarae (1982) to conclude that women use more standard and hypercorrect speech forms than men. However, several comprehensive reviews (Fisher, 1983; Haas, 1979; P. M. Smith, 1985) have demonstrated conflicting findings and give little credence to this proposition.

Males have been shown to speak louder than women but only in same-sex dyads. Both men and women increased vocal intensity with opposite-sex partners (Markel, Prebor, & Brandt, 1972). On the other hand, Kimble, Yoshikawa, and Zehr (1981) reported women spoke louder to women than to men, whereas men did not vary vocal intensity as a function of partner gender. During interaction, women may compensate for external noise more than men by adjusting vocal intensity (Von Raffler-Engel & Buckner, 1976), which supports the claim that women may be more sensitive to interpersonal cues than men. Miller, Reynolds, and Cambra (1987) indicate that white American males and females do not differ in level of language intensity, whereas Japanese American and Chinese American males used higher intensity than their counterpart females. Finally, research on gender and speaking time has generated mixed results. In mixed-sex dyads, men have talked longer (Argyle, Lalljee, & Cook, 1968; Hilpert, Kramer, & Clark, 1975; Wood, 1966); in same-sex dyads, women had longer vocalization durations (Ickes & Barnes, 1977; Markel, Lang, & Saine, 1976); in groups, men talked more (Eakins & Eakins, 1976; Strodtbeck & Mann, 1956); in groups, a responsive group leader received more responses from men, whereas an unresponsive group member received more talk from females (Wright, 1976); during picture description tasks, men spoke longer (Swacker, 1975); and among couples, feminist wives spoke for longer periods than their husbands, with the opposite being true for couples having a nonfeminist wife (Hershey & Werner, 1975).

Verbal behavior. No consistent relationship emerges regarding gender and conversational dominance. Two studies (Eakins & Eakins, 1976; Zimmerman & West, 1975) indicated that men interrupt more than do women, especially in mixed-sex interactions. However, Rogers and Jones (1975) found no gender effects for interruption and floor time. Similarly, Marche and Peterson (1993) demonstrated that males did not interrupt females with greater frequency and that females were not interrupted by their partners (whether male or female) more frequently than were males. Kimble et al. (1981) reported no clear pattern regarding verbal and vocal assertiveness among men and women in same- and mixed-sex dyads. Similarly, regardless of sex composition of groups, Fisher (1983) observed no significant sex effects on patterns of cooperativeness and competitiveness.

Women have self-reported more self-disclosure than men (Rosenfeld, 1979), although Morgan's (1976) study revealed greater disclosure by females for intimate but not for nonintimate topics. Regarding other conversational features, women have used more questions (Fishman, 1980), talked less about money, sex, sports, and news (Haas & Sherman, 1982), and used fewer obscene and profane expletives (Bailey & Timm, 1976; although see De Klerk, 1991) than did men. When storytelling, McLaughlin, Cody, Kane, and Robey (1981) reported that women make greater use of story sequencing services, suggesting that women were more likely to provide a warrant for introducing a story into ongoing talk. Andrews (1987) found that women reported less confidence than did men regarding the effectiveness of expressed arguments, although trained raters observed no difference between men and women in argument quality. Men were more likely than women to use criterion-based arguments. Finally, Garai and Scheinfeld (1968) indicated that women were more fluent than men, though other studies failed to substantiate this finding (Cherry, 1975; Silverman & Zimmer, 1976; P. M. Smith, 1979).

Within medical settings, female physicians appear to be more "patient centered" when interacting with patients. For example, Meeuwesen, Schaap, and van der Staak (1991) reported that female providers in their study were more attentive and less directive than male doctors. In a study of 537 consultations, Roter, Lipkin, and Korsgaard (1991) observed that women doctors conducted longer consultations and engaged in more partnership building, question asking, and information giving than did the male physicians. Of interest, Roter et al. (1991) also found that patients communicated differently to women practitioners than to male practitioners. Specifically, patients were more communicatively expressive (in terms of offering opinions and giving information) and asked more questions when visiting with women doctors.

For some verbal behaviors, gender differences appear to be a function of the gender of the interaction partners. Piliavin and Martin (1978) concluded that, in general, men tend to use more task-oriented remarks and women more socioemotional statements (using Bales's content categories). However, in mixed-sex groups, women became more task oriented and less socioemotional. Martin and Craig's (1983) findings included the following: (a) Unacquainted males and females produced about the same number of qualifying words (for example, "maybe," "sort of") when talking to males, but males produced more and females less when talking to females; (b) both men and women produced more false starts when speaking to someone of their own rather than opposite sex; and (c) inequality between dyad members in number of words spoken was greater in female than in male and mixed-gender dyads. Martin and Craig concluded that these results suggest a more relaxed pattern of talk within same-gender dyads, especially for women.

Aries (1967) reported that, in same-gender groups, a few men did most of the talking, and themes included competition, sports, and physical aggression. Women, however, directed comments to the entire group and discussed home, family, feelings, and self. In mixed-gender groups, men initiated and received more talk. Also, men spoke less of aggression and competition, and women talked less of home and family. Shimanoff (1983) observed men and women talking relatively equally about emotions. Women did not seem to vary emotional expressions as a function of partner's gender, but men used more affect words and talked more about emotions with women. Stimpson, Robinson, and Gregory (1987) show that on male-oriented tasks high competent men and low competent women talk the most. During a female-oriented task, the inverse pattern emerges, with high competent women and low competent men talking more.

Gender differences among verbal behaviors are also influenced by age. Girls apparently develop more mature conversational styles earlier than boys such as fewer interruptions and talk-overs (H. Smith, 1977), more adaptive and complex conversational strategies (Haslett, 1983a, 1983b), and more efficient communication during cooperative tasks (Stipek & Nelson, 1980). Staley (1982) reported that 4-year-old boys talked twice as much as girls, and Brounell and Smith (1973) observed the opposite in dyads and groups. Staley (1982) also found sex differences in the use of interpretive, reflexive, and descriptive language to diminish between the ages of 4 to 16. Cultural differences are also important. Singh and Lele (1990) point out that attention should be paid to the cultural differences in gender-power hierarchies, and, in doing so, they challenge Valentine's (1985) discussion of the relationships between gender and communication in India.

Nonverbal behaviors. Interaction distance preferences between men and women are influenced by gender of partner, the relationship between interactants, and other situational factors. In same-gender dyads and groups, females interact more closely than males (Patterson, 1978; Willis, 1966). In mixed-gender dyads, women's approaches toward men reflect greater distance than toward women, but men approach either gender at similar distances (Knapp, 1978; Patterson, 1978; Willis, 1966). White (1975) reported that respondents sat farther from a high status female confederate than from an equal status female, but sat closer to a high status rather than low status male. Finally, Marshall and Heslin (1975) observed that, under crowded conditions, women reacted more positively than men with same-sex others. However, when the task was long, men responded more favorably under the crowded conditions.

Several studies have indicated that women gaze more at cointeractants regardless of gender than do men (Dabbs et al., 1980; Duncan, 1983; Exline, 1963; Exline, Gray, & Schuette, 1965; Henley, 1977; Knapp & Hall, 1992). However, two studies found no sex effects for gaze (Coutts & Schneider, 1975; LaFrance & Mayo, 1976). However, in the Coutts and Schneider study, the persons present were not allowed to talk during an audio-discrimination task. Women have nonverbally demonstrated more interaction involvement and affiliation than men (Ickes & Barnes, 1977). On the other hand, Cegala, Savage, Brunner, and Conrad (1982) have proposed that interaction involvement is differentially manifested for men and women. For males, high interaction involvement is indexed by less body movement and more eye gaze during speaking. For females, high involvement is represented by object-focused gesturing and discrete movements during speaking. Women also have used fewer gestures than men (Ekman & Friesen, 1972). In interactions with disliked others, males have exhibited less sideways-leans (for male partners only), whereas females exhibited more sideways-leans (Mehrabian, 1969). Finally, some studies have indicated females display emotions better than do males (Buck, Miller, & Caul, 1974; Zaidel & Mehrabian, 1969; Zuckerman, Hall, DeFrank, & Rosenthal, 1977), but other investigations have reported null results (R. Buck, 1975; Dunhame & Herman, 1975).

In short, except for vocalic behaviors related to anatomical differences between men and women, few robust generalizations can be made regarding communicative behavior differences between men and women. P. M. Smith (1985) has posited that, when differences do exist, they likely reflect sex-preferential tendencies rather than sex-exclusive tendencies. In a similar vein, Brown and Levinson (1979; see also Kramarae, 1982) concluded that most gender speech markers result from the hierarchical status relationship between men and women or from divergent social networks. Holtgraves and Yang (1992) provide evidence for this assertion in a cross-cultural context. An additional factor may be that, though gender differences exist in language use, researchers have not identified them. For example, Mulac and his associates (Mulac & Lundell, 1980; Mulac & Rudd, 1977) found respondents rated transcripts of female talk higher on aesthetic quality, whereas male talk was viewed as more dynamic, aggressive, and strong. Shaw (1977, cited in Martin & Craig, 1983) reported the verbal behavior of male job applicants was rated more fluent, active, confident, and effective than female applicants'. In all three studies, the speech was presented in transcripts and all obvious cues of gender deleted. Thus these findings must represent actual differences, though the authors could not identify them at the time (Martin & Craig, 1983). Mulac, Lundell, and Bradac (1986) offer a first description of the nature of these differences. They found that 35 language features could account for 95% of the between-gender variability.

Of course, other factors may account for the failure of extant research to identify communication behavior differences solely as a function of gender. These include the use of perceptual measures, observing isolated behaviors, gender composition of interaction partners, and changes in men's and women's societal roles. As mentioned earlier, perhaps scholars should examine sex effects in communication as sex preferential rather than sex exclusive (P. M. Smith, 1985).

Age

Obviously children's communication skills improve and expand rapidly into adolescence (Anderson, 1992; Foster, 1990; Romaine, 1984) as their speech becomes more phonologically, grammatically, and semantically complex (for reviews, see Durkin, 1988; Foss & Hakes, 1978; Helfrich, 1979). Although little is known about such changes from young adulthood to middle age, old age is often characterized by decrements in cognitive, linguistic, and vocal prowess.

Regarding verbal behavior, initially 2- and 3-year-olds verbally master information about the environment (interpretation) and use speech to express needs and ideas (expressive and relational functions). However, conflict episodes with peers are still characterized by physical force and nonword vocal signals. From 4 to 5 years of age, a projective function emerges (messages concerned with exploring situations through imagination and past experiences). Also, 5-year-olds begin to manage conflict episodes by using adaptive strategies with sustained discourse focusing on triggering events (Haslett, 1983a, 1983b). Whereas syntax development progresses dramatically through the first 6 years (for example, increases in differentiated structure and embeddedness; see Hass & Wepman, 1974), syntactic differences between adults and children after age 6 are not obvious (Helfrich, 1979). We should note, however, that age alone is not a good predictor of syntactic development because of strong individual differences in the rate of development (Helfrich, 1979). In addition, it is worth pointing out the strong evidence for sophisticated preverbal social interaction even at very young ages (Camaioni & Laicardi, 1985; Rutter & Durkin, 1987).

As age increases from 3 to 7, there are accompanying increases in children's abilities to match the switching pause duration, turn length, utterance number, and speech rate of interactant partners (Garvey & BenDebba, 1974; Street, 1983; Street, Street, & Van Kleeck, 1983; Welkowitz, Cariffe, & Feldstein, 1976). Furthermore, younger children (3-year-olds) observe closer interaction distances than older children (7-year-olds; see Knapp, 1978).

The ability to adapt persuasive and other messages toward characteristics of targets progresses in a roughly linear fashion between the ages of 6 to 18 (Clark & Delia, 1976; Delia & Clark, 1977; Delia et al., 1979; Ritter, 1979). Dittmann (1972) reported that children in first through fifth grades used virtually no back-channel reinforcing remarks such as "yeah," "I see," and "mm-hmm." By the eighth grade, Dittmann observed a dramatic increase in these responses. Willis and his associates (Willis & Hoffman, 1975; Willis & Reeves, 1976) reported that, between kindergarten and adulthood, touching readily declines.

A few studies have examined speech development across the entire life span (see Nussbaum, 1989). From childhood into adulthood, pitch decreases, pitch range increases, speech rate increases, and number and duration of pauses decrease. Into middle and old age, these trends reverse themselves (Helfrich, 1979; Kowal, O'Connell, & Sabin, 1975; Mysak, 1959; Sabin, Clemmer, O'Connell, & Kowal, 1979; Yairi & Clifton, 1972). These dramatic changes in childhood and in old age are attributed to vocal and cognitive maturation and deterioration, respectively (Helfrich, 1979). The increase in pause behavior and slower speech rates in middle-aged relative to young adults may be due to the more reflective speech of the former (Sabin et al., 1979). Recently, some work has emerged on communicative phenomena in middle age. Harwood and Giles (1993) provide data relating to young individuals' experiences and stereotypes of communication with middle-aged individuals, together with a theoretically grounded model of communication in middle age.

Finally, research on the interaction styles of the elderly is still limited but is going through a growth period currently. One study examined crowding, task performance, and interactions of young (college) and old (over 60) females. Smith, Reinheimer, and Gabbard-Alley (1981) observed older women exhibiting positive communication behavior in response to close distances in a small room, whereas the younger women responded more negatively in the same condition.

A large body of work has emerged in recent years examining intergenerational communication between the elderly and younger individuals (Nussbaum, Thompson, & Robinson, 1989; Ryan, Giles, Bartolucci, & Henwood, 1986). For instance, Coupland and associates (Coupland, Coupland, & Giles, 1991; Coupland, Coupland,

Giles, & Henwood, 1988) have described a number of characteristics of intergenerational communication, such as elderly painful self-disclosure and disclosures of chronological age. Their work has consistently rejected "decremental" approaches to communication and aging (Coupland & Coupland, 1990) and has provided some new theoretically grounded understandings of communication across the life span. Clearly, justification exists for more research on variables influencing the behaviors and consequences of the social interaction of middle-aged and elderly adults.

Socioeconomic Status (SES)

Basil Bernstein (1962, 1964, 1972) was primarily responsible for the recent interest in communication differences among socioeconomic classes. Bernstein proposed that the middle and upper classes used "elaborated codes," speech characterized by verbal elaboration of meaning and the articulation of a speaker's intent through explicit verbal forms. The lower classes used a "restricted code," characterized by limited lexical and syntactic choices and thus highly predictable speech (Siegman, 1978). Relative to middle and high SES speakers in England and the United States, low SES communicators have been reported to be more likely to increase the proportion of high status phonological variants as situations become more formal (Labov, 1966; Trudgill, 1974); maintain greater conversational distance (Scherer, 1974); talk less (Jones & McMillan, 1973; Lawton, 1968); use less complex syntax; exhibit less lexical diversity of nouns, verbs, adjectives, and adverbs (W. P. Robinson, 1979); and communicate fewer descriptive attributions of stimulus pictures (Baldwin, McFarlane, & Garvey, 1971) or game rules (Pozner & Saltz, 1974). Such findings are observable even in fairly young children (Przetacznik-Gierowska, 1989). In addition, several studies have indicated that naive listeners are generally able to identify a speaker's social class given only vocal cues (Harms, 1963; Moe, 1972; Putman & O'Hern, 1955).

However, Bernstein's hypothesis has been widely criticized (see, for example, Arntson, 1982; Houston, 1970; W. P. Robinson, 1979; Stipek & Nelson, 1980; Taylor & Clément, 1974). First, contradictory findings are evident. Bernstein (1962) reported that a lower-class group of 16-year-olds spent less time pausing than a middle-class group. Siegman and Pope (1965b) found that, among female nursing students, lower-class students used more pauses on topics when an interviewer focused on family topics. No significant relationship emerged between social class and pause behavior on topics of school experiences. W. P. Robinson (1979) concluded that lower SES children and adults are less effective communicators of referential information. However, Stipek and Nelson (1980) observed no communication effectiveness differences between high and low SES children. Second, many studies of SES and speech are questionable on methodological grounds (W. P. Robinson, 1979). When one considers evidence across an array of speech measures, Arnston (1982) concludes that there is little support for elaborated and restricted codes (see also Haslett, 1990).

Finally, the relationship between SES and communicative behavior may be confounded by the power relationship between interacting partners. For example, in medical settings, doctors exhibit considerably more control over the encounter (e.g., talk more, give more directives, interrupt more) than do patients (Waitzkin, 1984). However, these differences are particularly noticeable with patients having a high school education or less. For example, Street (1991, 1992) reported that less educated patients (and parents of patients) generally talk less, ask fewer questions, and express fewer opinions than do patients who have attended college.

Status/Power Relationship

In high and low power dyads, low power participants have directed more eye contact toward high power partners when listening than when speaking (Efran, 1968). However, high power participants tended to look more when speaking than when listening (Exline, Ellyson, & Long, 1975). Knapp (1978) summarized findings suggesting that gazing is moderate toward very high status addressees, high toward moderately high status addressees, and minimal toward low status partners.

Regarding body orientation, shoulder orientation was reported as being more direct (when standing) with a high status rather than a low status listener (Mehrabian, 1969); superior position persons kept heads raised more (Knapp, 1978); and in psychiatric sessions, psychiatrists (high status) usually held relaxed postures, whereas clients (low status) were more rigid and formal (Goffman, 1961). Finally, high status persons seemed to initiate more touch than low status counterparts (Knapp & Hall, 1992).

Within the speech domain, Giles and Powesland (1975) have suggested that low status/power participants should converge more toward high status/power partners than vice versa because of the former's greater need for the latter's approval (for example, an employment interview). However, Thakerar, Giles, and Cheshire (1982), after observing high/low status dyads of staff nurses and nursing students, reported mutual speech rate and accent convergence. Presumably, the high status party converged to foster communicative effectiveness, while the low status party converged to earn approval. Richmond, Davis, Saylor, and McCroskey (1984) indicate that power within organizations is related to behavioral alteration techniques. Superiors and subordinates displayed some distinct patterns in the use of such techniques. For recent analyses of the complex roles of power in language and silence, see Ng and Bradac (1993) and Jaworski (1992), respectively.

Race/Culture

Obviously, members of various races and cultures have developed dialects differing on phonological, syntactic, and lexical levels. Ethnic speech markers are usually attenuated when an ethnic group (usually subordinate) has a desire to assimilate into a dominant culture. However, if the groups strive for psycholinguistic distinctiveness, ethnic markers are likely to be emphasized (Giles, 1979; Giles & Johnson, 1987).

Blacks in conversations have been reported to gaze more as speakers and less as auditors, whereas whites exhibited the opposite patterns (LaFrance & Mayo, 1976). Similarly, whites look more at authority figures when the figure is talking (Exline et al., 1975), but blacks usually do not look the speaking authority figure in the eye (K. R. Johnson, 1972). For a recent discussion of African American communication patterns, see Hecht, Ribeau, and Collier (1993).

Some have proposed that "high contact" cultures such as in Latin America, Italy, and the Middle East prefer closer interaction distances than "low contact" cultures such as in the United States and Northern Europe (see Patterson, 1978, for review). Watson and Graves (1966) reported that Italians and Arabs touch more and stand closer together than do Americans. However, one study observed no significant distance differences between Latin American students and American students (Forston & Larson, 1968). Bauer's (1973) study revealed that, among college students, blacks approach their partners more closely than do whites. However,

Aiello and Jones (1971; Jones & Aiello, 1973) reported that black children in the first and second grades interacted more closely than whites of the same age, but these differences began to reverse themselves by the time children were in the fifth grade. Comparing the conversational distance preferences of Japanese, Venezuelans, and Americans, Sussman and Rosenfeld (1982) found that preferred distance was a function of race and the language used in the interaction. When using their native languages, Japanese sat farther apart than did Americans, who in turn sat farther apart than did the Venezuelans. However, when speaking English, the Japanese and Venezuelans more closely approximated American conversational distance. As Knapp (1978) has observed, much of the research on culture and distance conflicts. One confounding variable in these studies appears to be SES (Patterson, 1978; Scherer, 1974).

Recent years have seen a growth in work examining cultural differences in verbal phenomena (Hewitt, 1986; Kim & Gudykunst, 1987; Ting-Toomey, 1986) and communicative competence (Kealey, 1989; Wiseman, Hammer, & Nishida, 1989). This work has illustrated the ways in which communication across cultures can be problematic (Hecht, Ribeau, & Alberts, 1989): the accommodation of individuals both to particular partners (Gallois, Franklyn-Stokes, Giles, & Coupland, 1988) and to a larger cultural milieu (Van den Berg, 1988); the relationship of intercultural communication to the AIDS crisis (Singer, 1991); and the problems of intercultural communication in the courtroom (De Jongh, 1991), the doctor's office (Erzinger, 1991), work settings (Dean & Popp, 1990), and the classroom (Sanders & Wiseman, 1990).

Physical Handicaps/Disability

Thompson (1981, 1982a) has found that, relative to their nonhandicapped counterparts, physically handicapped children were less able to adapt persuasive messages to various situations. Thompson (1982b) also observed both physically handicapped and nonhandicapped children had difficulty communicating to handicapped peers. Thompson concluded that mainstreaming helped children overcome these deficiencies. A focus of recent work on handicap has been the processes surrounding disclosure concerning a disability. Braithwaite (1991) discusses strategies used by people with physical disabilities to manage nondisabled individuals' (perceived) expectations of disclosure. These included regulating private boundaries and seeking to be acknowledged as "persons first." Royse and Edwards (1989) indicate that people with disabilities did not generally feel more at ease after disclosure concerning disabilities. Their respondents rarely sought such disclosure from other people with disabilities, although such seeking was fairly common among those people who had only recently become disabled (see also, Coleman & DePaulo, 1991). Little work to date has focused upon communicative disabilities, and this would seem a profitable direction for future studies (see Burley & Morley, 1987). Important theoretical developments have been suggested by Braithwaite (1990), who suggests a conceptualization of disability in cultural terms.

Speech Evaluation and Language Attitudes

In this section, we consider listeners' evaluative and personality judgments of speech style. We purposely excluded literature on nonverbal decoding studies because of space limitations and because other reviews of this literature were available (see Cappella, 1985). We initially focus on single behavior channels, followed by examination of multiple behaviors and perceptual/evaluative biases influencing speech judgments.

Dialect/Accent/Language

Following recent extensive literature reviews, Bradac (1990) and Giles, Hewstone, Ryan, and Johnson (1987) similarly concluded that receivers generally upgrade dominant or prestigious group accents and dialects on dimensions of perceived competence, status, intelligence, and success. These standard or dominant group speech varieties are usually preferred in formal contexts such as at businesses and schools. Regional or inferior group speech variants are usually perceived to be trustworthy and likable and are preferred by in-group members in informal contexts such as at bars and at home. Support for this kind of pattern has been found in the United States (Bradford, Ferror, & Bradford, 1974; J. Buck, 1968; de la Zerda & Hopper, 1979; Hopper, 1977), the United Kingdom (Cheyne, 1970; Elyan, Smith, Giles, & Bourhis, 1978; Giles, 1971a, 1971b; Giles & Powesland, 1975; Strongman & Woosley, 1967), Canada (Genesee & Holobow, 1989; Lambert, 1967; D. T. Miller, 1975; Taylor & Clément, 1974), Australia (Foon, 1986; Hogg, D'Agata, & Abrams, 1989; Nesdale & Rooney, 1990), Catalonia (Woolard, 1989), China (Kalmar, Zhong, & Xiao, 1987), Nigeria (Mgbo-Elue, 1987), and Peru (Wolck, 1973).

The consequences of these speech preferences are apparent in various contexts. In the United States, standard speech is favored for white-collar and supervisory positions, whereas nonstandard speech (black English or Spanish accented) is appropriate for manual labor positions (Hopper, 1977; Hopper & Williams, 1973). Seggie, Smith, and Hodgins (1986) performed a similar study in an Australian setting. They demonstrated that the evaluations given to different accents varied according to the group membership of those making the evaluations. In educational contexts, teachers' evaluations of students' language are good predictors of teachers' expectancies for performance (Williams, 1976). Students with standard or middle-class speech are likely to be perceived as more intelligent and ambitious as well as receive better grades in the United States (Hewett, 1971; Williams, 1976), Ireland (J. Edwards, 1979a, 1979b) and Canada (Frender, Brown, & Lambert, 1970). Persuasion studies in England have produced mixed results. Powesland and Giles (1975) reported a nonsignificant trend for the prestigious received-pronunciation accent (R-P) to elicit more attitude change than the Bristol variant. However, Giles (1973) reported that, although the more prestigious accents generated perceptions of better quality arguments, the more nonstandard speech forms were more persuasive. Prestigious speech styles also appear to be related to increased compliance with requests (Bourhis & Giles, 1977; Kristiansen & Giles, 1992). Finally, prospective doctors tended to diagnose R-P accented symptoms as psychosomatic-related and the same symptoms in a regional guise as physically related (Fielding & Evered, 1980).

The dialect/accent evaluation process is also mediated by speaker-listener similarity, contextual information, and message content. Both dominant and subordinate group members have upgraded standard speech on competence dimensions. However, in-group members have preferred their own speech in informal contexts and have evaluated it as more sociable and trustworthy than the speech of out-group members, especially if in-group members value their ethnic speech. Support for this claim has come from Wales (Bourhis & Giles, 1977), Mexican Americans in the United States (Carranza & Ryan, 1975; Flores & Hopper, 1975), England (Giles, 1971a, 1971b), and southern whites and blacks in the United States (Luhman, 1990; Tucker & Lambert, 1969). Likewise, some ethnic groups (for example, whites in the United States) have perceived some out-group speech (for example, German accented or black English) negatively on competence and sociability dimensions (Hewett, 1971; Naremore, 1971; Ryan & Bulik, 1982). Perceptions of accent similarity have led to beliefs of attitude similarity (Delia, 1972; Sebastian & Ryan, 1985). Similarly, there is evidence that ethnic group members will downgrade fellow in-group members who switch to the dominant language (Hogg et al., 1989), an "ethnolinguistic betrayal" effect. In addition, speakers with more restrictive norms of what is "appropriate" standard English tend to downgrade nonstandard forms (McKirnan & Hamayan, 1980). Finally, in bilingual contexts, interactants who used the dominant language of interlocutors were usually perceived more favorably than those who did not (Genesee & Bourhis, 1982; Giles, Taylor, & Bourhis, 1973; Simard, Taylor, & Giles, 1976).

Most dialect/accent evaluation studies probably reflect ethnic and speech stereotyping processes. However, stereotypic responses may be altered by other information contextualizing the speech stimulus (Delia, 1972). Aboud, Clément, and Taylor (1974) posited that persons with characteristics more socially desirable than expected (for example, standard speech forms) may overcome an initially negative cue (for example, race). Hopper (1977) reported that blacks using standard English received more positive evaluations than white standard English speakers in job interview settings. Ryan and Sebastian (1980) noted that Spanish-accented speech was viewed more favorably when the speaker was middle status rather than low status (see also Dowd & Bengtson, 1978; Sebastian & Ryan, 1985). On the other hand, negative or neutral information can diminish initially favorable impressions. Delia (1972) revealed that the relatively positive evaluations of General American dialect speakers (as opposed to Southern and New England dialects) were attenuated with the advent of neutral information. The impact of contextual information is likely to depend on the strength of the stereotype. For example, Williams, Whitehead, and Miller (1972) demonstrated that observers perceived black children's standard speech as more ethnic and nonstandard than the same speech from white children. Similarly, Giles and Sassoon (1983) reported that middle-class social standing did not overcome the negative attributions given to a Cockney-accented speaker. Abrams and Hogg (1987) have also drawn attention to the comparisons that people make when evaluating a particular accent. In their study, listeners from Dundee downgraded Glasgow speakers when comparing them with a Dundee accent. However, when the Glasgow accent was presented alongside a standard English accent, evaluations of the Glasgow accent rose to a level above ratings of the Dundee speakers in the first condition.

Message content can interact with vocal behavior to influence interpersonal judgments (Hart & Brown, 1974). Schenk-Hamlin (1978) reported the speech stereotyping process was most intense for listeners when Southern speakers spoke on an issue relevant to the stereotype (for example, desegregation) than when speaking on a less relevant issue (for example, grain reserves). Although finding an insignificant trend for R-P accents to be more persuasive, Powesland and Giles (1975) observed the greatest attitude change when the R-P-accented speaker delivered a left-wing message against the Industrial Relations Act. Presumably, this message was incompatible with what one would expect of R-P accented speakers.

Finally, Johnson and Buttny (1982) demonstrated that black speech was downgraded relative to white speech, but only when message content was abstract rather than experiential.

Speech Rate

Speech rate evaluation research has similarly focused on receivers' competence and sociability judgments of speakers. B. L. Brown's (1980) and Street and Brady's (1982; Street, Brady, & Putnam, 1983; see also Ray, 1986) research has consistently revealed denigration of slow speech on dimensions of competence and sociability and linear relationships between rate and competence, with faster rates being judged most competent. Woodall and Burgoon (1983) did not find rate to be related to competence, but this study reported very low statistical power. Speech rate appears to be a salient communicator characteristic, given research indicating that speech rate is judged accurately from masked stimuli (Bond, Feldstein, & Simpson, 1988) and purely visual information (Green, 1987). Indeed, Miller and Dexter (1988) provide evidence that individuals cannot ignore speaking rate entirely.

Using machine-manipulated speech, B. L. Brown (1980) has uniformly revealed a curvilinear relationship between rate and sociability (his measure was labeled "benevolence"). Street and Brady (1982; Street, Brady, & Lee, 1984; Street, Brady, & Putnam, 1983), however, have used speakers fluently and naturally manipulating rate and reported moderate to relatively faster rates to be most socially attractive. Similarly, Miller, Marayama, Beaber, and Valone (1976) observed that listeners perceived fast speech more trustworthy than moderate and slow rates. Siegman and Reynolds (1982) and Stewart and Ryan (1982) also reported favorable responses to fast speech. Street, Brady, and Putnam (1983) concluded that relatively fast, fluent speech (197-324 syllables per minute) can also be considered socially attractive, but rates toward fast extremes (e.g., 376 syllables per minute) diminish in attractiveness. These data suggest that receivers have speech rate stereotypes associating fast speech with competence and moderate to somewhat faster speech with sociability, although this can vary cross-culturally (Lee & Boster, 1992; Peng, Zebrowitz, & Lee, 1993). Although such stereotypes appear to exist (B. L. Brown, 1980; Street, Brady, & Putnam, 1983), speech rate evaluation is mediated by additional factors such as speaker-listener rate similarity, communication context, speaker age and sex, persuasive objectives, and mode of presentation.

From the speech accommodation perspective (see Giles & Powesland, 1975; Street & Giles, 1982), Giles and Smith (1979) proposed and supported the claim that adjusting one's speech rate level to that rate level characteristic of one's listeners enhances communicative effectiveness and favorable impression formation. Street (1982) and Putnam and Street (1984) also provided support for this proposition. Street and Brady (1982) suggested that moderate rates were judged most sociable because most listeners typically spoke at moderate rate levels. In two tests of these claims, Street and Brady (1982; Street, Brady, & Putnam, 1983) found speaker rate level and rate similarity to significantly influence both competence and social attractiveness judgments. Street, Brady, and Putnam (1983) concluded that interactants' speech rate preference regions encompass rates similar to somewhat faster than their own.

More recently, Buller and Aune (1988) demonstrated that persons with high nonverbal sensitivity spoke more rapidly than their low sensitivity counterparts. They attributed higher intimacy and immediacy to persons attempting to gain compliance when these persons spoke rapidly, and they were more likely to comply with the requests of fast-speaking compliance seekers. These outcomes were explained in terms of communication accommodation theory (Giles, Coupland, & Coupland, 1991). A later study by Buller, LePoire, Aune, and Eloy (1992) showed that perceptions of social attractiveness and status mediated the relationship between speech rate and compliance. Once again, speech rate similarity had an important effect, in this case enhancing judgments of social attractiveness.

Communication context also influences speech rate judgments. Brown, Giles, and Thakerar (1985) reported that the detrimental effects of slow speech may be nullified if listeners can favorably account for the slow speech (for example, helping an audience understand an unfamiliar topic). Also, for intimate topics (for example, how one can tell if becoming sexually aroused), slow speech is tolerated, if not preferred (Siegman & Reynolds, 1982). For formal contexts requiring careful and deliberate formulation of responses (such as employment interviews), slower speech may be more acceptable than in informal settings (such as casual conversation; see Street, Brady, & Putnam, 1983). Siegman (1978) has reviewed similar findings regarding stressful topics.

Most speech rate evaluation studies have employed male voices and have generalized findings to the entire population (see, for example, B. L. Brown, 1980; Street & Brady, 1982). For women speakers, faster rates are also associated with competence and status (Aronovitch, 1976; Ball et al., 1982; Street et al., 1984; Thakerar et al., 1982). However, speech rate appears unrelated to the perceived social attractiveness of women speakers (Aronovitch, 1976; Crown, 1980; Siegman & Reynolds, 1982; Street et al., 1984).

Generally, young adults negatively respond to the speech of the elderly (Ryan & Capadano, 1978). However, when exhibiting positive speech features (such as relatively fast speech), elderly speakers are upgraded on competence dimensions. Similar to the effects of speaker sex, young adult listeners appear to have differing speech criteria for evaluating the social attractiveness of young and old male speakers. On impressions of benevolence, young males with slow rates were downgraded. Speech rate did not influence similar impressions of elderly male speakers. Thus it appears that speech rate affects the perceived attractiveness of young males but not of women and older males. However, a more recent study by Giles, Henwood, Coupland, Harriman, and Coupland (1992) obtained cognitive response data that showed a pattern where listeners were generally very positive about fast-talking, older-sounding male speakers and were very negative about younger males who talked slowly. In contrast to stereotypes, Tomoeda, Bayles, Boone, and Kaszniak (1990) have demonstrated that slowing speech rate to Alzheimer's patients does not increase their comprehension of a message. In contrast, normal elderly listeners' comprehension was found to decline with markedly increased rate (Hyland & Weismer, 1988).

The relationship between speech rate and persuasive effectiveness remains unclear. Some have found persuasiveness to be enhanced by fast rates (Mehrabian & Williams, 1969; Miller et al., 1976) and moderate rates (Apple, Streeter, & Krauss, 1979). Woodall and Burgoon (1983) reported no significant relationship between rate and attitude change. It would appear that rate interacts with other features of the communication event in determining persuasiveness. With regard to persuasive objectives, fast speech rates have been found to inhibit rebuttal attempts to counterattitudinal messages and to inhibit favorable evaluation of a proattitudinal message (Smith & Shaffer, 1991). Buller et al. (1992) provide evidence that speech rate may influence persuasion through the mediating mechanism of social attractiveness. Speech rates that are viewed as socially attractive in a given context are seen as the most likely to elicit desired responses from the target.

Finally, one study observed differential speech rate effects as a function of presentational mode (Woodall & Burgoon, 1983). Subjects hearing audio-only messages were more influenced by speaker rate than those receiving the same message audiovisually. Perhaps when listeners are able to process only the speech signal, vocal behaviors such as rate have greater impact upon perceptual judgments.

Pauses

Two types of pauses in discourse are internal pauses (pauses within a speaker's turn) and response latencies (pauses between speaker turns). Several studies have revealed inverse relationships between favorable speaker evaluations and length of internal pauses (Lay & Burron, 1968; Newman, 1982; Scherer, 1979a; Siegman & Reynolds, 1982) and of response latencies (Baskett & Freedle, 1974; Street, 1982). However, Baskett and Freedle found that short latencies (less than 1 second) were perceived as the most competent, but moderate latencies (1-3 seconds) were considered the most trustworthy. Consistent with these findings, Williams (1976) suggested that, relative to standard speech, black nonstandard speech contained more pauses. This may be one reason this speech style has been downgraded. An important factor mediating these evaluative effects is the ease with which pauses are detected. Ulasevich, Leaton, Kramer, and Hiecke (1991) have indicated that pause detection is significantly more reliable when semantic cues are present. Stuckenberg and O'Connell (1988) have indicated that respondents overestimate occurrence but underestimate duration of pauses. In addition, they show some cultural differences—their German respondents detected pauses more reliably than American respondents.

Two factors mediating these evaluative processes are speaker-listener pause duration similarity and context. Street (1982) reported that, in fact-finding interview settings, the interviewee was perceived as most socially attractive and confident when adjusting his original response latency (3 seconds) to that of the interviewer (1 second) than when maintaining the original latency or making it more dissimilar (5 seconds). Of course, it is uncertain whether this finding is due to length of latencies or latency similarity. However, Street (1984) found that, during fact-finding interviews, response latency similarity was significantly related to the favorability of participants' evaluations of interlocutors. Regarding context, Newman (1982) reported that legitimized periods of silence (that is, participants were conversing while working on a sculpting assignment) did not elicit negative responses from observers.

Vocal Intensity

Up to a moderately high level, increments in perceived vocal intensity are positively related to impressions of extraversion, sociability, emotional stability, boldness, and dominance (Aronovitch, 1976; Hollien, Gelfer, & Carlson, 1991; Scherer, 1979a). However, excess loudness may inhibit speakers' effectiveness in public communication contexts (Pearce & Brommel, 1972). Speakers' gender may influence listeners' perception of communicators having varying loudness levels. Although increases in vocal intensity enhanced perception of logical abilities for both male and female speakers, male voices were rated as less nervous and emotional than female voices of the same intonation and vocal intensity characteristics (Robinson & McArthur, 1982). Hollien et al. (1991) appear to show that there are few age or gender differences in the evaluation of varying vocal intensities.

Vocal Pitch

Research on listeners' impressions of speakers' varying pitch levels is conflicting. Apple, Streeter, & Krauss (1979) reported negative attributions such as deceit and nervousness with increases in speaker pitch. However, Scherer (e.g., Scherer, London, & Wolf, 1973) noted that higher vocal pitch fostered impressions of competence, dominance, and assertiveness. Aronovitch (1976) reported that higher vocal pitch levels were characteristic of kind, humorous, emotional, and immature women but did not influence impressions of male speakers. Scherer (1979a) attributes these inconsistencies for male speakers to two factors. First, Apple et al. used machine-manipulated pitch, whereas Scherer employed voices naturally varying in pitch. Natural voices may be viewed more positively than synthetic speech. Second, Scherer proposes that, up to a certain threshold within the male pitch range (around 140 Hz), higher pitch is associated with extraversion, competence, confidence, and assertiveness. However, if male vocal pitch approaches the female pitch range, impressions quickly become unfavorable. Ekman, O'Sullivan, Friesen, and Scherer (1991) have shown that pitch can be a useful predictor variable in detecting deception. In addition, vocal pitch has been found to be characteristic of certain depressive syndromes (Stassen, Bomben, & Gunther, 1991). Finally, a raising of pitch has been noted as characteristic of both parents' talk to children ("motherese"; Shute, 1987) and the "baby talk" often addressed to elderly individuals (Caporael, Lukaszewski, & Culbertson, 1983).

The findings on pitch variability are consistent. Greater pitch variability has been linked to perceived speaker dynamism, potency, extraversion, and benevolence (Scherer, 1979a).

Vocal Attractiveness

Zuckerman and Driver (1989) provide some evidence that there is a stereotype for vocal attractiveness that functions similarly to the well-established stereotype for physical attractiveness. These researchers demonstrated that attractive voices were rated more favorably than unattractive voices on various personality dimensions. This was especially true in a voice-only condition compared with a voice-plus-face condition. A later study by Zuckerman, Hodgins, and Miyake (1990) obtained a vocal attractiveness by physical attractiveness interaction indicating that effects were strongest for persons who are attractive in both channels. The effects of attractiveness were weaker when judges were acquainted with the persons who served as stimuli in the experiment. A study by Buller and Burgoon (1986) suggests that nonverbal sensitivity may mediate reactions to vocal attractiveness: Persons low in nonverbal sensitivity complied more with hostile voices, whereas sensitive persons complied more with pleasant voices.

Talk Duration

Amount of talk in group contexts has correlated significantly with impressions of dominance, likability, extraversion, and emotional stability (Scherer, 1979a).

Interactants with long floor-holdings have high scores on dimensions of emotional stability, conscientiousness (Scherer, 1979a), and competence (Hayes & Meltzer, 1972). However, Stang (1973) indicated that medium-length turns elicited higher attractiveness ratings. Street (1982) reported that interviewees who maintained a consistent turn duration throughout the interview or who modified turn length concordantly with the interviewer were viewed as more socially attractive than interviewees adjusting turn durations opposite the interviewer's. Brooke and Ng (1986) measured influence rankings in small discussion groups and found that influence was correlated with number of speaking turns exclusively (not with polite forms or tag questions, for example). A later study by Ng, Bell, and Brooke (in press) determined that turns representing interruptions were primarily responsible for rankings of influence. A study by Mulac (1989) indicates that amount of talk and mean length of utterance are positively associated with ratings of speaker dynamism, a measure of perceived power. Finally, Palmer (1989) showed that, in naturalistic conversations, length of utterance was directly related to judgments of dominance, especially when utterances were unrelated to preceding utterances.

Whereas the above speech variables focused on vocalic and dialect behavior, the following concern verbal and linguistic dimensions of talk.

Self-Disclosure

Of the content dimensions of talk, self-disclosure has been most widely researched. Initially, researchers assumed that revealing intimate information about oneself was healthy, fostering favorable impressions and relationship development (see, for example, Jourard & Friedman, 1970; Worthy, Gary, & Kahn, 1969). Self-disclosures by one participant were likely to elicit disclosures of equal intimacy by that participant's partner (Cozby, 1972; Davis, 1977; Derlega, Harris, & Chaikin, 1973). Interactants not reciprocating partners' intimacy level of disclosures have been liked less than those matching disclosure levels (Chaikin & Derlega, 1974).

Later investigations have questioned the generality of these phenomena. The dynamics of self-disclosure processes appear to be influenced by a host of factors including norms, valence, topic, relationship among interactants, setting, and other language variables (Bradac, Hosman, & Tardy, 1978; Gilbert, 1976; Tardy, Hosman, & Bradac, 1981). Disclosing intimate information to strangers can be deemed inappropriate (Berger, Gardner, Clatterbuck, & Schulman, 1976) or may be viewed more acceptable if the information is positive rather than negative (Gilbert, 1976). For very intimate relationships, Gilbert (1976) proposed that positive revelations about self may not foster relational growth as well as negative information does. Socially deviant information appears inappropriate regardless of the intimacy level (Chaikin & Derlega, 1974). Yet, communication about a physical disability can make participants more comfortable and handicapped persons more acceptable as partners (Thompson, 1982a; although see Royse & Edwards, 1989). Rosenfeld (1979) indicated that disclosure deemed appropriate can increase love, liking, attraction, trust, and mental health.

Language intensity mediates responses to violations of the self-disclosure reciprocity norm. Bradac et al. (1978) reported that listeners favorably evaluated interactants who reciprocated highly intense and highly intimate messages from partners. However, interactants were liked more when responding to a low intensity-low intimacy message with a high intimate-low intense message rather than a reciprocal one. Apparently, the former response constitutes a move toward relationship escalation. Relatedly, Hosman (1987) hypothesized that topical reciprocity influences responses to reciprocity of intimacy level, specifically that messages reciprocating both topic and intimacy level would be evaluated more positively than would messages reciprocating either topic or intimacy level. Some support was obtained for this hypothesis, especially when initial messages were low in intimacy.

Although not dealing with evaluative processes per se, Dindia (1982, 1983, 1985) has reported little support for the reciprocity norm among strangers during their initial interaction, though their perceived disclosure rates were correlated. Dindia (1982) did indicate that second and third interactions among strangers were characterized by related amounts of disclosure but not on a reciprocal, act-by-act basis. Dindia (1983, 1985) posited that generalizing about reciprocal patterns of disclosure is hindered by inconsistencies between observational and experimental findings, incongruities between perceived versus actual disclosure, the questionable validity of self-reports, and the assumption that positively related disclosure is reciprocal. Hosman (1987) investigates the relationships between topic reciprocity and self-disclosure reciprocity. His results indicate that there may be flaws in Dindia's (1982) research because her analysis failed to control for topic reciprocity.

Work by Coupland, Coupland, Giles, Henwood, and Wiemann (1988) has examined the *process* of elderly self-disclosure in intergenerational interactions as well as young individuals' evaluations of this self-disclosure. This work is important in drawing attention to the multiple ways in which self-disclosure may be elicited and managed by interactants and hence moves away from a unidimensional notion of self-disclosure.

Language Intensity

As previously defined, *language intensity* refers to the degree to which language deviates from affective neutrality. *Love* is more intense than *like*; *utterly devastated* is more intense than *disappointed.* In their review, Bradac et al. (1979) concluded the following: (a) Language intensity enhances attitude reinforcement of attitudinally congruent messages but hinders attitude change and perceived competence when message content is discrepant to receivers' attitudes, and (b) obscenity (a form of intensity) is inversely related to attitude change and perceived competence. Hamilton, Hunter, and Burgoon (1990) have demonstrated that language intensity will enhance persuasiveness of a high credible source, while reducing the persuasiveness of a low credible source. Other studies (e.g., Miller, Reynolds, & Cambra, 1987) suggest that a variety of cultural and situational variables influence the production of, and response to, high or low intensity language. It appears to be the case that, in the United States at least, men are freer to use high intensity forms than are women if the criterion is attitude change or compliance gaining (Burgoon, Birk, & Hall, 1991).

Miscellaneous Verbal Behaviors

Powerless speech includes hedges, intensifiers, polite forms, and hesitations, whereas powerful speech omits these. In courtroom settings, powerful testimony was perceived as more competent, trustworthy, dynamic, and convincing than powerless testimony (Lind & O'Barr, 1979). However, Bradac, Hemphill, and

Tardy's (1981) study indicated that respondents attributed greater fault to defendants and plaintiffs using high power styles. In study two, though, respondents exposed to both styles did not differ between the two regarding fault ascription (see also Hosman, 1989). A recent study suggests that the power-of-style variable has a greater effect upon evaluations of communicators (specifically, communicator competence) than it does upon persuasive effectiveness (Gibbons, Busch, & Bradac, 1991).

Cantor (1979) noted that polite imperatives (for example, "Please contribute to our fund") were persuasive in soliciting funds relative to other grammatical forms. However, Bradley (1981) posited that impact of grammatical forms may vary as a function of speakers' gender. In mixed-gender groups, females who used arguments with more qualifying phrases (for example, tag questions and disclaimers) exerted less influence and were perceived not as intelligent and knowledgeable as women not using qualifiers. Evaluations of men did not tend to vary in accordance with the presence or absence of qualifiers. Bradley suggested certain linguistic devices by women may be more readily devalued due to the lower status of the female source. On the other hand, Robinson and Reis (1989) found that women were not downgraded compared with men for interrupting in conversations; generally, interrupters received negative judgments for sociability.

Verbal immediacy has been positively related to perceptions of "open communication" (Montgomery, 1981), competence, and character (Bradac et al., 1979). In their review, Bradac et al. (1979) proposed that lexical diversity is positively related to competence, socioeconomic status, message effectiveness, and similarity. Also, the effects of lexical diversity appear to be greater when the source is ascribed high status.

Speech evaluation research has primarily manipulated speech behaviors singularly (for example, speech rate or self-disclosure). Speech behavior, of course, is not produced singularly but concomitantly. Several speech behaviors can influence evaluative processes in a complex interactive fashion.

Multiple Speech Behaviors and Perceived Speech

Scherer (1979b) reported that influence among American jurors was related to number of utterances, number of repetitions and interruptions, loudness, number of silent pauses, and pitch range contours. Pearce and Brommel (1972) noted that speakers using a "conversational style" (that is, lower pitch, less volume, less use of pause, less pitch variety) were rated as more credible than those using a "dynamic" style. This finding is inconsistent with other studies that have reported denigration of lower pitch and loudness levels (Aronovitch, 1976; Scherer, 1979a). Apparently, consideration of these multiple speech behaviors in this public speaking context affected the gestalt view of the communicative event such that the evaluations were not in line with previous research on these behaviors individually.

Ray (1986) examined the interactions of speech rate, pitch variation, and vocal intensity on competence and benevolence. High pitch variation and fast speech rate were found to enhance competence ratings. High speech rate and low pitch were rated lowest on benevolence, whereas low loudness and high pitch variation led to the highest benevolence ratings.

Giles et al. (1992) examined the interactions of accent, speech rate, and age of voice on a group of British respondents. Their diverse findings indicate that the complex interactions of multiple speech behaviors deserve more thorough examination. Specifically, they found that certain speech behaviors (standard accent, fast speech rate) were sufficient to largely overcome the stereotypically negative evaluations of older sounding speech (although the voices were not judged as particularly old). Also, the results indicated that "too many" prestige elements (young, fast speech, standard accent) can result in negative evaluations. The authors caution that attention should be paid to the negative as well as positive consequences of using prestige forms.

Although speech convergence usually facilitates favorable impressions, Giles and Smith (1979) observed that an English speaker was most positively evaluated by a Canadian audience when he converged speech rate and message content but maintained his normal accent than when he converged all three behaviors. In a fact-finding interview setting, Street (1982) studied observers' reactions to an interviewee variously accommodating speech rate, response latency, and turn duration toward the interviewer. Two speech patterns emerged most favorably: (a) when the interviewee converged response latency and maintained a faster speech rate and longer turn duration and (b) when the interviewee converged speech rate and held the floor for a duration comparable to the interviewer's floor-holding. Street interpreted these results as observers' approval of two speech strategies. The second established a more egalitarian speech format to the interviewer, and the first maintained optimal sociolinguistic distance given the interviewee-interviewer role differences. Bradac and Wisegarver (1984) investigated the effects of lexical diversity, accent, and socioeconomic status on status evaluations. Their results appeared to show that these variables had an additive effect.

More recently, Hosman and Wright (1987) examined the combined effects of hedges and hesitations (two of the components of "powerless" speech) in a single experimental design. They found that the presence of a high level of hedging or hesitation was sufficient to depress ratings of authoritativeness; on the other hand, a low level of hedging and a low level of hesitation produced positive ratings. In a later study, Hosman (1989) compared the separate and combined effect of hedges, hesitations, and intensifiers with the effect of a prototypically powerless message (one containing all of the features of powerless speech described above). As in the previous study, hedges and hesitations individually negatively affected judgments of authoritativeness. Additionally, high intensifier/low hedge/low hesitation messages and low intensifier/low hedge/low hesitation messages differed from the prototypically powerless message, indicating that the effect of intensifiers is dependent on the level of hedging and hesitation. In another study that is arguably related to power, Mulac and Lundell (1986) examined the extent to which 31 linguistic variables could discriminate male and female speakers. They found that 17 of these variables in combination were discriminative, and, furthermore, these variables predicted ratings of speakers' sociointellectual status, aesthetic quality, and dynamism. Finally, Burgoon, Birk, and Pfau (1990) examined the combined effects of 22 vocalic, kinesic, and proxemic variables on judgments of credibility and persuasiveness. The results were complex, but among other things greater vocal and facial pleasantness were positively associated with judgments of communicator competence. Persuasiveness was positively associated with vocal pleasantness, physical immediacy, facial expressiveness, and kinesic relaxation.

Most speech evaluation research manipulates actual message features. Such an assumption may be suspect. Street and Hopper's (1982) review indicated that factors such as racial prejudices (Williams et al., 1972), prototypes (Cantor & Mischel, 1979; Scherer, 1979a), sex role expectations (Haas, 1979; Lowery, Snyder, & Denney, 1976), status (Ball et al., 1982; Thakerar & Giles, 1981; Thakerar et al.,

1982), and listeners' goals or motivations (Bourhis, Giles, Leyens, & Tajfel, 1979; Larsen, Martin, & Giles, 1977) can result in interactants' perceiving interlocutors' message characteristics that are not actually in the speech or in exaggerating the existence of certain speech features. Bond and Feldstein (1982) reported that perceived speech rate is positively related to vocal frequency and intensity. The authors proposed that these relationships are a function of repeated experience of almost always hearing such covariations in naturally occurring speech.

II: Future Directions

A Critical Appraisal of Traditional Paradigms Research

The foregoing has provided us with a somewhat unique documentation of research on the role of communicator characteristics in interpersonal communication. Yet, the net result of the first part of the chapter has been a noticeable empirical absence of compelling main effect findings for communicator characteristics. One of the issues here seems to be that psychological variables in themselves are not sufficient to account for the variance in communicator behaviors. Many of them interact with sociodemographic variables (for example, sex and age) as well as features of the context—anxiety being an archetypal case. In the light of the psychological literature on the person × situation (Argyle, Furnham, & Graham, 1981) and attitude/behavior (Ajzen & Fishbein, 1980) debates, perhaps this is all none too surprising. Indeed, where main effects have been reported, no doubt many of these would likewise dissipate if potent situational and sociodemographic variables were introduced into our experimental designs. Although the second section in part I of the chapter provides us with more concrete profiles regarding the communicator correlates of sociodemographic characteristics, here again few substantive main effects emerged. For instance, gender of communicator is heavily influenced by the gender of receiver and communicator role, socioeconomic status by contextual factors, race/ethnicity by the particular subgroups one is investigating, and even age by level of cognitive development and gender.

Rather than extol the virtues and considerable value of traditional research on communicator characteristics, we feel it incumbent upon us to critically assess our cumulative knowledge in a constructive manner that can lead to some priorities for future research directions. Different investigators have measured different communicative dependent measures according to their own predilections and intuitions, with a heterogeneity of interaction goals and situations reigning supreme. Indeed, research in the first and second sections in the first part of the chapter can be characterized, as it was in the first edition of this chapter published in 1985, as

1. being overly concerned with student populations and unfamiliar others;
2. affording negligible attention to how communicators themselves construe their identity and the dimensions of the situations they are in (too often communicators and communicatees are allocated objectively to membership in large-scale, social categories and social situations according to external criteria decided upon by investigators themselves);
3. studying communicative dependent measures largely in isolation from each other (that is, we look at speech rate; you examine fundamental frequency);
4. being largely either encoder or decoder biased;

5. giving negligible attention to the influence of extrasituational social forces such as the perceiver relevance of the social network to the interaction and the nature of the social structure;
6. proliferating "in-out" studies in which people are studied on one (usually exceptionally brief) static occasion in which the focus has been on relegating language behaviors to the status of passive, dependent variables of social processes; and
7. having little recourse to the functions of language or to the nature of the strategies employed.

The most robust findings emerge from the third section ("Speech Evaluation and Language Attitudes") in part I of the chapter. There is some consensus about the social meanings of verbal and vocal (as well as visual and nonverbal; see Cappella, 1985, 1989) behaviors. Use of a standard accent, high lexical diversity, fast speech rate, immediacy, certainty phrases, moderate loudness and talkativeness, and few pauses afford communicators attributions of high competence and assertiveness from observers. Yet, here again, cultural context, nature of setting, stage of relationship, topic, type of listener, interactive goals, and so forth can all interact to produce quite different and sometimes what might appear to be superficially "contradictory" evaluative patterns (self-disclosure is a prime case). Nevertheless, main effects for the social meanings of language behaviors have been abundant and found to have profound consequences in many applied (albeit simulated) settings (Kalin, 1982). At the same time, and despite recent theoretical advances in the language attitudes domain with respect to interethnic relations (Ryan, Giles, & Sebastian, 1982; Ryan, Hewstone, & Giles, 1984), studies in this genre have also not passed by uncriticized. Giles and Ryan (1982) and Street (1993) have characterized deficiencies in this area such as that independent speech variables are concocted in a social, psychological, and linguistic vacuum; listener-judges are featured almost as cognitive—as well as affective (Cargile, Giles, Bradac, & Ryan, in press)—nonentities; aspects of context are socially and subjectively sterile; individual message variables are assumed to have effects independent of other message features present; message evaluators tend to be observers of communicative events and not interacting partners; and message features are devised without recourse to their situational, functional, and behavioral implications.

The rest of this chapter is to argue for a complementary framework of cognitive characteristics of communicators that can guide our future work in a manner that not only extends the types of variables examined in the first and second sections of part I but also integrates the language attitudes research of the third section as well.

Influential Frameworks

The development of our own thinking has been influenced heavily by two recent perspectives, namely, Patterson's (1982a, 1982b, 1983) sequential model of nonverbal exchange and social psychological research into impression management (Arkin, 1981; Tedeschi, 1981; Tedeschi & Norman, 1985; Weary & Arkin, 1981). The nature of both can, of course, only be sketchily drawn in this context. As will become evident later, these ideas underscore the guiding principles (or generalizations) of our own approach. Let us overview briefly Patterson's model first.

Patterson's Model and a Critique

Although Patterson's behavioral focus is on involvement, he does make claims as to its utility for interactive behavior in general. Moreover, it is arguably one of the most comprehensive conceptual formulations in interpersonal communication to date. Among its attractive features, and ones that counter some of the deficiencies in the area outlined above, are that it attends explicitly to interactional functions as well as the sequential nature of cognitive processes, addresses (as do Cappella & Greene, 1982) the potential role of arousal, and highlights the salience of the other's behavior and subsequent behavioral adjustments to it. In overview, and largely in Patterson's own words, the model can be described as follows.

The sequential functional model assumes that each person brings to an interaction a specific set of personal characteristics (and these are articulated largely in such terms as personality traits and membership in large-scale social categories), past experiences, and relational-situational constraints. With respect to the last component, Patterson focuses mainly on an ecological psychological analysis of objective features of a situation, molding the behaviors appropriate to a given relationship. This group of so-called antecedent factors exercises its influence covertly at the "preinteractional stage" by determining behavioral dispositions with which communicators are comfortable, precipitating a potential arousal change, and developing cognitive and affective expectancies. The joint effect of these three mediators shapes the perception of the interaction's function and limits the range of involvement behaviors displayed. The combined influence of each person's preferred involvement level and five functional cognitions (namely, information exchange, regulation, intimacy, social control, and service task) in turn shapes expectancies about the other person's level of involvement. A stable exchange is defined as one in which the discrepancy between the expected and the actual involvement of the other person is minimal. When that discrepancy is large, instability results, inducing cognitive-affective assessments of it. This can lead to either adjustments in nonverbal involvement (see Cappella & Greene, 1982), a reassessment of the interaction's function, or perhaps a combination of both. Successful involvement adjustments and a more complementary functional reassessment (relative to the other person's functional assessment) should facilitate a more stable exchange.

We see a number of problems with adopting Patterson's extremely useful and insightful model wholesale for our own communicator characteristics framework. First, the model is overly ambitious in assigning mechanisms for the termination of an interaction. Although instabilities of the type espoused by Patterson in terms of differential perceived functions and involvement levels could conceivably facilitate swifter termination, on many occasions interaction rules (see McCann & Higgins, 1992) are so potent as to temper these effects, and in any case other factors such as misattributions of intent, differential knowledge, threat to identity, interpersonal justice, and so forth might assume more importance (Blakar, 1985; Dubé-Simard, 1983). A separate model for the determinants of communication termination in intergroup and interpersonal encounters is really required here.

Second, there is some lack of conceptual clarity in the model. For instance, the distinctions between antecedent, preinteractional, and interactional phases are difficult to conceptualize differentially, let alone to operationalize. One wonders why the situational-relational component is an antecedent, whereas the functional component appears to have some autonomous influence much later sequentially in the so-called interactional phase. Function is accorded an extremely important explanatory role in this model that may well be unwarranted. In any case, how the functional analysis defines level of involvement enacted is left rather vague. The role of "expectancies" is also rather confusing; sometimes it is articulated as being activated at the antecedent phase of relational-situational variables, other times in the preinteractional phase of cognitive assessment, and then also at the interactional phase itself. Finally, the "cognitive-affective" component appears as an unconvincing potpourri of "any kind of evaluative response . . . to more complex patterns of cognition" (Patterson, 1983, p. 24). In other words, here sit smoldering: preferences, automatic scripts, and complex decision-making mechanisms.

Third, the antecedent factors appear too simplistic and asocial for our tastes. As mentioned previously, personal factors are defined almost exclusively in objective terms. The important role of the communicator's subjective definition of personal and social identity is afforded no central role here. Work along the traditional lines of Tajfel (1982) has pointed to the fact that defining an interaction, albeit a dyadic encounter, can have a profound effect on encoding and decoding communicative behaviors (Giles & Coupland, 1992), as can one's cognitive representations of sociostructural forces (Bourhis & Giles, 1977; Harwood, Giles, & Bourhis, in press). Similarly, research on construals of the situation by Cody and McLaughlin (1980), Forgas (1981), and Wish (1978), on the one hand, and work on the development and dissolution of relationships by Berger and Bradac (1982), Duck (1992), Fitzpatrick (1987), and Noller and Fitzpatrick (1988), to name a few on the other hand, suggests not only a simplistic, underworked "relational-situational component" but that there is much heavy-duty cognitive processing of situations and relationships operating potentially in different interactions (see Semin & Fielder, 1992). Thus the way individuals define a situation in terms of Wish's dimensions; construe its specific goals (Argyle et al., 1981); perceive its macrosituational norms in terms of modesty, fairness, competitiveness, and so forth (Weary & Arkin, 1981); and define the components of the specific norms (McKirnan & Hamayan, 1980) and communication rules that are operating influences the nature of message output. Also, the way individuals define their relationships in terms of uncertainty levels (Berger & Bradac, 1982) and their perceived rules and norms, ideologize their relationships (Fitzpatrick, 1990), and cognize the importance of others present or even absent in the network (Milardo, 1982) has other important influences. As an illustrative example of the importance of just a few of the foregoing, Giles and Hewstone (1982, p. 198) proposed that objectively describing a social situation as a formal interview on a serious topic with a 90-year-old black woman may have little predictive value concerning her likely speech patterns if she herself defines the interview informally, considers the subject matter irrelevant and trivial, and feels "white" and 50 years of age.

Fourth, and relatedly, Patterson's model focuses upon sequential processing among the model's components although no such evidence exists clearly for it, let alone the precise nature of it. At the present time, we would prefer to consider the possibility of parallel processing of many of the cognitive elements until such a time as convincing arguments and data afford us reasonable levels of certainty as to how it operates (see Bock, 1982; Johnson-Laird, 1983). Of interest, however, Patterson (1983) does lend some credence to the notion of multiple functions being involved in an interaction at any one time, although no schematic status is afforded it in his model. Fifth, in Patterson's model and in others, there are presumed isomorphisms between actual own and actual other's message variables on the one hand and one's perceptions of these on the other (see Weary & Arkin, 1981). Street and Hopper (1982) reviewed the literature showing that one's identities, goals, and aspirations can dictate one's perceptions, evaluations of, and attributions about a message that can in no way correspond to the actual objective qualities of the message produced in some situations. This, together with the lack of explicit attention to actual versus perceived arousal, is a distinction that needs to be drawn theoretically in any further robust formulation; this is a cognitive issue much akin to the brunt of our argument in our third bone of contention above. Sixth, and finally, there is little social motivational force guiding individuals A and B in Patterson's model; one has the impression of the individual as a cognitive-physiological automaton. Although Patterson does have recourse to highlighting the importance of impression management and self-presentation in the context of his "social control" function, no attention is afforded the important work of Tedeschi, Arkin, and others (see below), which we believe to be fundamental in pointing to crucial social needs of interactants and the verbal strategies they use in this regard. As their analyses help provide a succinct motivational basis for our own approach, it is to this area of inquiry we now turn. At the same time, it is not our intent to belittle Patterson's important work and contribution to this area. It is possible that a number of the foregoing issues, with flexibility, could be implicated in the model as it stands or at least in a revision of it. As will be seen, we owe much to Patterson's initiative and advances. Our own contribution to communicator characteristics is proferred later as a modest elaboration of some of the variables, mechanisms, and processes perhaps underdeveloped in the context of a broader view of communicational features beyond involvement behaviors.

The Social Psychology of Impression Management

Tedeschi and Reiss (1981a) rightly point to the fact that current research in impression management obviously had its impetus from outside social psychology, including the dramaturgical perspective of Goffman (1959). They claim that it was likely to be a zeitgeist of the 1980s in social psychology owing to its avowed explanatory potential for dealing with a wide range of social psychological phenomena (Baumeister, 1982; Tedeschi, 1981). We have been excited by this prospect. Not only does it sidestep some of the dangers inherent in much, although obviously not in all (Higgins & McCann, 1984), current social cognition, but it also resurrects the study of verbal activity as a valued resource of social behavior to its rightful status as a core interest of social psychologists (Farr, 1980). Furthermore, Baumeister (1982) points not only to humans needing to cognitively process informational input but also to their needing to communicate with their social environment in order to organize, simplify, and control it.

As Tedeschi and Norman (1985) state:

> People have few goals which do not require the aid or mediation of others. . . . If people want love, respect, status or esteem, they must do something to get others to react to them in these ways. . . . Since these others are not simply waiting to provide what we want, it is necessary to assert ourselves and try to be effective in influencing others to do what we need them to do, so we can have what we want. If actors have those characteristics, attributes, or identities that facilitate various forms of influence, they should experience greater success and obtain more rewards than people who do not possess them. (p. 301)

In this vein, Tedeschi and his colleagues, since the early 1970s (Tedeschi, 1972, 1974), have characterized individuals as possessing a primary motive of wishing to proliferate their sphere of social influence and power. Tedeschi and Reiss (1981a) argue that it is little wonder people try to achieve the power resource of inducing others to like them as this increases the probabilities that the target will (a) trust them more; (b) accept and believe more readily their accounts, communications, and claims; (c) harm them less; and (d) reward them more.

Tedeschi and Norman (1985) have speculated on the relationship between self-esteem and social influence. The idea here is, as elsewhere, that individuals possess more self-esteem the more they believe their real self corresponds to their ideal self. The latter is envisaged as that cognitive construction that has been provided us by those whom we value positively and model as being socially influential. Many of our self-presentations are therefore aimed at instilling in others feelings and attributions that accept us as being akin to our own particular, ideal identities. From social comparison (Festinger, 1954) and symbolic interactionist (Mead, 1934) traditions, it is argued that much of our self-perception is molded by our views of how others construe us. It follows therefore, as Weary and Arkin's (1981) model of attributional self-presentation highlights, that we monitor very carefully our own impression management behaviors and significant others' reactions to them not infrequently. (This is not, however, to suggest that such self-presentations are always, or even usually, deliberate and at the level of conscious awareness; oftentimes they could be conceived of in terms of scripts; see Abelson, 1981; Patterson, 1983.) In this vein, then, increases in self-esteem are barometers of how much social influence we are enjoying. The more discrepancy that is perceived to exist between our real and ideal selves, the more negative self-esteem we feel and, by implication, the less social influence we feel we can espouse. Situations, or predicaments, that provide us with so-called spoiled identities require us to initiate "defensive" impression management behaviors to "save face" (Goffman, 1959), eliminate our loss of self-esteem, and restore our own sphere of social influence (Schlenker, 1980). Arkin (1981) introduces a particular form of this mechanism in terms of "protective" self-presentation. This author argues that such behaviors are enacted when the individual construes a high subjective probability of a particular assertive presentation failing. This is likely particularly when (a) the other is capricious or ambiguous in terms of beliefs, qualifications, and so forth (see Berger & Bradac, 1982); (b) significant others are likely suddenly to present themselves; (c) the relationship is likely to be a lasting one, socially, occupationally, and so forth; and (d) the speaker may not be able to enact or monitor influence behaviors effectively. In such situations, individuals might manifest protective presentations by adopting an innocuous or attentive communication style (Norton, 1983) aimed at avoiding social disapproval until such a time as cognitive uncertainty about the other(s) and the situation are decreased or the opportunity for adopting appropriate assertive presentational behaviors occurs.

Tedeschi, Lindskold, and Rosenfeld (1985, chap. 3, pp. 65-96) proffered a distinction between assertive and defensive tactical and strategic self-presentations. Assertive tactics (e.g., ingratiation, self-promotion, enhancements) are undertaken from moment to moment to achieve short-term goals of asserting one's social power given expediencies of the immediate situation. Assertive strategies, on the other hand, are those longer term, transsituational presentations (e.g., credibility, status, esteem) that are aimed at fostering a reputation for oneself as close to the ideal self as possible. Baumeister (1982) terms these *self-constructive* presentations. After all, it is rare that individuals will accrue enduring reputational benefit from single, isolated tactics. If, however, a person has had a history of

needing perpetually to activate defensive tactics (e.g., accounts, disclaimers, resti-
tution, prosocial behavior), it is possible that such adaptive presentations will
habituate into a defensive strategy (e.g., phobias, learned helplessness, drug abuse).
As Tedeschi and Norman (1985) claim, these "behaviors tend to lock the person
into a life style characterized by defensive, avoidance and escape reactions at the
expense of assertive, approach, and acquisitive patterns of behavior" (p. 320).

In this light, self-presentation theorists have begun to explore the ramifications
of their analysis for understanding individual differences in personality (Arkin,
1981; Tedeschi & Norman, 1985; Weary & Arkin, 1981). It does not seem unrea-
sonable to conceive of self-monitoring, needs for approval and affiliation, extraversion, Machiavellianism, internal locus of control, and exhibitionism as specific
strategies of assertive impression management, whereas those of reticence/appre-
hensiveness/social anxiety, submission, introversion, and external locus of control
could be more defensive strategies. Such an approach, in and of itself, might imply
a radical reappraisal of research orientations of the type depicted in the first section
of part I of this chapter in terms of performance styles.

Research has been concerned with documenting and providing a taxonomy of
the different forms of self-presentation that exist. Unfortunately, space precludes
any actual description of these tactics and strategies (see, for example, Jones &
Wortman, 1973; Kolditz & Arkin, 1982; Schlenker, 1980; Tedeschi & Reiss,
1981b), yet suffice to say that a mere superficial perusal of them suggests that the
majority are manifested behaviorally by nonverbal, vocal, and linguistic means.
Although self-presentation theorists have not yet had recourse to the relevant
literatures in communication science, social psychology of language, or sociolinguistics, it is obvious that a symbiotic relationship would prove theoretically
important. For instance, tactics of speech convergence (Street & Giles, 1982) and
compensatory warmth (Ickes, Patterson, Rajecki, & Tanford, 1982) can be understood as tactics of assertive self-presentation; accent and speech rate divergence
might profitably be considered a defensive tactic; and the oft-quoted case of the
"nonverbal" lower-class, ethnic minority child (Edwards, 1979a, 1979b) might on
some occasions be construed as a protective, self-presentational tactic (Kochman,
1982). Cappella (1984) has been investigating the role of communicator style as a
mediator of interpersonal attraction with a view to determining whether a meshing
of interpersonal styles (whether similarity or complementarity) is as good, if not
better, an indicator of mutual liking than the ubiquitous, belief congruity construct
(see also Norton, 1983). If such a perspective is shown to have merit, it may well
be that the other's actual and/or perceived style has such potency in different situations
owing to its value in facilitating the actor's own self-constructive presentational
tactics and hence social power. Furthermore, strategies of assertive impression
management, whether in terms of reputational trustworthiness, attractiveness, or
status, are all manifest importantly by nonverbal, vocal, and verbal behaviors and
styles (see the third section in part I of the chapter).

Cognitive Communicator Characteristics: A Model

Having overviewed Patterson's model, highlighted some problems with it for
developing our own communicator characteristics approach, and outlined self-presentation theory, let us now build on these foundations. The guiding principles
forming the core of our complementary framework for future research into com-

municator characteristics are enumerated below. Although we have not highlighted all aspects of the approach, such as the roles of behavioral repertoire, measured arousal, scripts, and so forth, we feel the following principles encapsulate the essence of our position:

1. Communicative behavior can be a function of the self-presentational tactics or strategies employed by interactants in asserting or defending their spheres of social influence.
2. Language attitudes can function as important mediators in shaping such self-presentations.
3. Communicative behavior can be a function of interactants' changing cognitive representations of their (a) identities, (b) situational and relationship definitions and goals, and (c) levels of arousal.
4. Communicative behavior can be a function of (a) monitored own and partner's perceived behaviors and (b) the evaluations and attributions accorded these.

With due regard to the valued law of parsimony in scientific inquiry, we could have concluded this chapter by means of an elaboration of these guiding principles. Instead, we have opted to formulate our discussion in terms of a highly speculative model that, although it cannot be derived from current empirical research, attempts to generate some specific relationships between elements inherent in the generalizations. For some tastes, no doubt, the scheme will appear overly complex. Nevertheless, it is our belief that current models of interpersonal communication only scratch the surface of the cognitive variables, mechanisms, and processes involved. Although we are fully aware of the dangers inherent in proliferating models ad infinitum, we do see the necessity for a new, more complex heuristic to emerge of the type we are to espouse. Accordingly, the following has the aim of alleviating limitations in the sequential model of nonverbal exchange by highlighting the wealth of cognitive characteristics potentially available to communicators in such a way that is informed by self-presentation theory. Let us therefore briefly weave the gist of our principles above within the context of our model schematized as in Figure 4.1.

"Personal factors" in Figure 4.1 refer to those objective features of oneself and one's socialization, such as physical states and sociodemographic characteristics (for example, age, sex, SES, ethnicity) that affect "experiential knowledge" (memory) on the one hand and "behavioral repertoire" possibilities on the other. Our experiential knowledge component contains at least four important, interrelated elements: (a) the cultural content of appropriate behaviors suited to specific social contexts; (b) the content of our social stereotypes for various social groupings considered hierarchically in terms of superordinate categories (for example, the elderly) and basic categories (for example, senior citizen, grandmother) and their prototypes (Brewer, Dull, & Lui, 1981); (c) the content of our linguistic and communicative expectancies (Burgoon, 1993; Burgoon & Miller, 1985; Kramer, 1977) of these social categories (this component allies well with the third section in the first part of this chapter on language attitudes, albeit more or less detailed in specific ways depending upon our personal factors and self-concept); and (d) our knowledge about our own communicative capabilities and social skills, that is, our subjective behavior repertoire. This font of experiential knowledge, like the aforementioned behavioral repertoire, can be selected from according to our own functional needs (Tajfel, 1981) and mediates our self-presentational tactics and behavioral dispositions. This socially dynamic, experiential knowledge constantly shapes our real and ideal self-concepts that form the motivational driving force

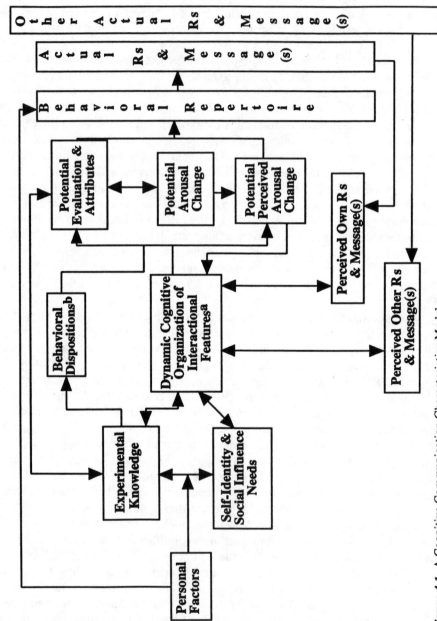

Figure 4.1. A Cognitive Communication Characteristics Model
a. See Tables 4.1 and 4.2.
b. See Table 4.2.

136

Table 4.1 Communicator Characteristics in Terms of Cognitive Representations

1. Personal Identity (Suls, 1982)
2. Social Identity (Giles & Johnson, 1981)
3. Self-Presentational Immediate Goals (Arkin, 1981)
4. Self-Constructive Presentational Goals (Baumeister, 1982)
5. Social Network (Milardo, 1982)
6. Sociostructural Forces (Johnson et al., 1983)
7. Prior Experiences
8. Temporal Constraints
9. Situational Construals (Forgas, 1983)
10. Situational Norms of Language (McKirnan & Hamayan, 1980)
11. Social Norms (Weary & Arkin, 1981)
12. Rules of Communication (Higgins, 1980)
13. Relational Identity (Fitzpatrick, 1987)
14. Relationship Rules/Norms (Rand & Levinger, 1979)
15. Relationship Construals (Forgas & Dubosz, 1980)
16. Relationship/Other Knowledge (Berger & Bradac, 1982)
17. Expectations About Other(s) (Caporael et al., 1983)
18. Anticipations of Other's Expectations About Self (Burgoon & Miller, 1985)
19. Topic Construals (Maynard, 1980)
20. Information Exchange Function (R. Brown, 1977)
21. Interactional Regulation Function (Street et al., 1983)
22. Intimacy Function (Duck, 1992)
23. Service-Task Function (Abelson, 1981)
24. Control Function (G. R. Miller, 1983)
25. Mode (Rimé, 1984)
26. Cognitive Planning/Behavioral Rehearsal (M. Burgoon, 1983)
27. Role Requirements (Brown & Levinson, 1979)

behind our needs for social power and influence (à la the self-presentationists). In Figure 4.1, the latter constitute our "self-identity and social influence needs" component.

Self-identity/needs and experiential knowledge influence our ongoing "cognitive organization of interactional features" (see Figure 4.1). Table 4.1 presents an array of the cognitive representations that can be potentially activated in ongoing situations. We believe that items 3 and 4 in Table 4.1 are activated perpetually at least at a minimal level. As with Lugarski's Law of Cybernetic Entomology, which claims there is always yet one more bug to discover (see Boster, Stiff, & Reynolds, 1983), the list is historically representative but not exhaustive. We also do not consider these cognitive representations to be mutually exclusive; many are interdependent. For instance, activation of item 2 (Table 4.1) is likely to coactivate item 6, or vice versa; item 9 is likely to coactivate items 10, 12, 14, 22, and so forth. Indeed, it is just possible to provide a speculative, implicational analysis of such cognitive representational interdependencies, although future empirical research along these lines would likely prove this exercise presently less than worthwhile. It should be noted that this scheme, unlike Patterson's model, affords no autonomous status to interactional function(s). The perspective at this stage of model building is on the parallel processing of those cognitive presentations in Table 4.1 and relies upon the multilevel simultaneous capacity of the human mind (Bock, 1982; Johnson-Laird, 1983).

For the moment, let us take the very simplest of cases in which very little is activated in Table 4.1, just item 4, a self-constructive, presentational goal. The actual content of this habitual goal (for example, to appear friendly and sociable) is not likely to induce arousal or evaluative changes in its own right (see the latter components in Figure 4.1). The "behavioral disposition" in this case, perhaps a self-presentation strategy of an open and dramatic style (see Norton, 1983), also itself is not likely to cause arousal or affective changes (see Figure 4.1). It will simply be selected scriptually from the behavioral repertoire as it very often has been. In this instance, perceptions of one's own communication, the perception of the other's reactions to it, as well as perceptions of the other's message subsequently are probably going to be monitored by the communicator at a minimal level of awareness. This assumes, of course, that the self-presentation appears effective and the partner does not produce counterstereotypical or unexpected communicative patterns. We have thus moved through the model in Figure 4.1 rather swiftly when few cognitive representations of identity, situation, interactional goals, and the relationship are activated (see for example, Tracy & Coupland, 1991).

Probably the more general case is that in which a number of, and even many, cognitive representations assume subjective salience. Obviously, there is some processing limit to the number and type of cognitive representations possible at any given time (Norman, 1981). Future research might well be able to discover the manner in which different individuals and groups, perhaps, cognitively factor-analyze the items in Table 4.1 into coherent, manageable proportions. Indeed, models of speech perception and word processing may guide our research in this direction (for example, Morton, 1969; Repp, 1977). Our own preference (after Palmer, 1984) would be exploring the valuable ideas of Oden and Massaro's (1978) fuzzy logical model of sound perception for the identification of situational and identity patterns. This perspective could be extended to allow for communicators scanning and extracting features from the situation, self, and behavior of others, which are combined in a composite abstract pattern and then matched to prototypes stored in memory (our "experiential knowledge" component). In any case, the more cognitively complex and field independent the speaker, the more likely more cognitive representations and their resultant identification patterns will assume salience and, perhaps, the more they will change from moment to moment as one's own output and one's partner's input are perceived and evaluated. Obviously, the specific contents of each of these representations are crucial. Separate illustrations of such cognitive representational contents are provided in a compact manner in the left-hand column of Table 4.2. Needless to say, the actual nature of these cognitive representational contents in any instance will be mediated by self-identity/needs and experiential knowledge. Cognitive contents can of course vary in their idealized specificity. For instance, sometimes we are not that certain about the precise norms of the situation we are in or the strength of the "grapevine" operating between our friends and acquaintances. Of interest, message output can sometimes be a function of influential people who are actually not physically present yet who will subsequently and predictably hear details about the encounter from those who were there. Given that cognitive representational contents influence our behavioral dispositions (see Figure 4.1), the less ambiguous they are, the stronger the tendency will be.

As the model suggests, the actual resultant behavioral dispositions are mediated by experiential knowledge, and this occurs on two important counts. First, our experiential knowledge—and particularly the language attitudes element of that—will shape the appropriate behavioral disposition. Based on findings from the sociolinguistics and communication literatures, the right-hand column of Table 4.2

Table 4.2 Illustrative Contents of Cognitive Representations Having High Subjective Salience and Their Exemplified Potential Behavioral Dispositions

Cognitive Representations	Contents	Behavioral Dispositions
1	Self-focus	Self-referencing
2	Ethnic and class identifications	(Downward) accent divergence
3	Gain other's liking	Ingratiation, enhancements, blasting
4	Appear friendly, intriguing, having sense of humor	Open, dramatic style, self-disclosures, jokes
5	Partner likely to divulge to significant others	Avoid negative self-disclosures, jokes
6	Highly iniquitous institutional support for in-group	Downward accent convergence
7	Bad news	No pitch variety, slow rate
8	Brief, once-only encounter, opportunity	Concise, precise language
9	Cooperative, relaxed, equal	Informal verbal style
10	Wide range of informality felt appropriate	Use of slang, colloquialisms, obscenities
11	Altruism	Attentive, other-focused, negotiative
12	Take the role of the other	Speech rate and content convergences
13	"Separate" ideology	Interpersonal distance, avoid conflict
14	Affective interdependence	Agree, in-group terms, looking
15	Sexuality	Touching, taken-for-granteds
16	Very uncertain about state relationship is in	Interrogation, knowledge-gaining tactics
17	Aged, cold	Accommodate to aged stereotype, compensatory warmth
18	Very British	Refined, metaphoric usage
19	Important, expertise available	Talkative, assertive style, certainty phrases
20	Providing instructions	Nominal style, gesture
21	Maintain floor as long as possible	Few pauses, counterinterruptions
22	Become more friendly with	Involvement behaviors
23	Delivering a colloquium	Technical language, nominal style
24	Persuade person to donate money	Altruistic compliance-gaining strategy
25	Unfamiliarity with television conferencing	Attentive to facial expressions, self-monitor
26	Practiced one's testimony	Fluent, discourse sequenced
27	Good interviewee	Deferent, polite

provides examples of potential behavioral dispositions arising from the corresponding contents on the left-hand side of that table. For instance, in the case of item 18, such a content will dictate the nature of the refinements and the metaphoric usage employed. In the case of item 17 (Table 4.2), the contents define the communicative behaviors that correspond best to our stereotype of the elderly or some basic subcategory of it. Most certainly our experiential knowledge elements will define the nature of the ingratiation tactics employed as well as perhaps their sequential occurrence in item 3 (Table 4.2). Second, however, experiential knowledge will render the behavioral dispositions more or less realistic for the actor. For instance, a presumed inability (whether it is correct or false, objectively) to tell jokes would eliminate such a behavioral disposition arising in the case of the cognitive representation Content 5. In other words, having the social knowledge and will is one thing; believing you have the necessary communicative skills is another. The resultant dispositions will manifest only those behaviors considered feasible by the self.

Both the cognitive representational contents and the ultimate behavioral dispositions are subject to potential evaluative and arousal analyses as depicted in Figure 4.1. For instance, activation of Contents 8, 17, 21, and 23 (see Table 4.2 again) and/or dissatisfaction with one's behavioral dispositions (as in the case in which there is a perceived discrepancy between what is situationally appropriate and what is actually possible) could well lead to a potential negative affective state. This could induce increased arousal, which may or may not be perceived as such by the sender. If such an arousal change is perceived in this particular case, it could cause cognitive representational reactivation affecting self, other, and situational attributional processes and perhaps accentuate the aforementioned negative feelings. Alternatively, other routings could take place (see Figure 4.1). The cognitive representational contents and behavioral dispositions could lead directly to arousal changes. These again may or may not be perceived by the sender (as in the case of a jogger who is still physiologically aroused unbeknownst to him- or herself some time after apparent recovery). If they are inwardly detected, they could (in line with Patterson's, 1976, arousal-labeling model) stimulate cognitive representational reactivity and/or affective-attributional processing. Herein, potential negative feelings might then accompany this increased and felt arousal. In sum, then, whether or not the actual behavioral dispositions are isomorphic with actual message outcomes selected from the behavioral repertoire depends on evaluative/arousal processing, itself potentially mediated by cognitive representational reactivation (see Figure 4.1).

We are now in a position to propose some initial, and admittedly highly speculative, hypotheses about the nature of the sender's message outcome and its implications for self- and other-monitoring:

Hypothesis 1: Behavioral dispositions will be selected from the behavioral repertoire when (a) no or only moderate arousal change occurs, and the arousal is not perceived by the individual, and (b) moderate to high arousal is perceived and labeled positively (for example, happiness, pride).

Hypothesis 2: Behavioral dispositions will not be manifested in performance when (a) arousal change is not perceived by the sender, but is actually high, and (b) moderate to high arousal is perceived and labeled negatively (for example, anger, irritation, threat).

The performances subsequent to Hypothesis 2 above would be characterized by disruptions such as disfluencies, ill-conceived taken-for-granteds, redundancies, and overabstractions, among others. The extent of these disruptions would be a direct function of negative affect and/or arousal. In addition, we would propose that those high in social self-esteem would select self-protective presentational tactics from their behavioral repertoires until negative affect and/or arousal had dissipated, whereas those low in social self-esteem would select self-defensive strategic scripts.

Following Weary and Arkin's (1981) attributional self-presentational model, we would propose that the monitoring of one's own message, and others' feedback cues to it, is an important process in our model. Self- and situational-monitoring are crucial to guiding our self-identity needs for gaining and affecting social influence. However, following Street and Hopper's (1982) model of speech style evaluation, we would also wish to make a distinction (often not explicit in many other models) concerning actual versus perceived message outcomes from self and partner(s). After all, our self-identity and cognitive representational activity will influence, oftentimes dramatically, what we think we and others are doing as schematized in Figure 4.1. We propose further tentative hypotheses based mostly on potential attributional outcomes (see Langer & Newman, 1979) of felt arousal:

Hypothesis 3: If no arousal is felt, then self- and other-monitoring will both be moderately high.

Hypothesis 4: Monitoring of own message will be especially high when felt arousal (positive or negative) is attributed to own dispositions and attributes. Under these conditions, blame for poor self-presentation can be laid at the door of the sender.

Hypothesis 5: Monitoring of other's reactions to own messages will be especially high when felt arousal (again positive or negative) is attributed to sources external to self (that is, formal situation, novel task, unexpected behaviors from other). Under these circumstances (see Roloff & Berger, 1982), the most important cues guiding social influence attempts are considered somewhat outside the self's control.

Obviously, perceived negative or ambiguous cues from either self or the other will reactivate perhaps different cognitive representational contents beyond, but including, those interactional functions mentioned by Patterson (for example, change in situational definition, perceived norms, relationship, identity of the other). This may cause a potential modification of behavioral dispositions (see Figure 4.1). These communicative tendencies are then potentially subject to evaluative-arousal analyses, which accordingly may determine the actual adjustments made. Positively perceived self-presentations and other's reactions to them are likely to bolster self-esteem (Weary & Arkin, 1981). Indeed, this is likely to influence the nature of further self-presentational tactics and especially self-constructive strategies. The perception of negative outcomes, on the other hand, has the potential for decreasing self-esteem and inculcating self-protective or defensive tactics. Following the work of Higgins and colleagues (see Higgins & McCann, 1984), the manner in which one accommodates a message according to the characteristics of the audience has a crucial impact on the ways in which the actual events and information one is transmitting to another are stored in memory or experiential knowledge; "saying is believing." All the previous feedback loops are depicted in Figure 4.1.

Naturally enough, the other's subsequent and reactive message (rather than listener cues) is a substantive component of this and other models (see Cappella & Greene, 1982; Patterson, 1982b). However, an important component lacking in many theoretical systems is the fact that individuals monitor not only their own listening reactions to others' messages but the others' perceptions of those very same decoding reactions. In other words, self-presentation is affected potentially just as much by listening behaviors as by speaking. In any case, the self's perception of the other's message (again mediated by cognitive representational forces) acts as an independent variable (rather than the typical dependent status afforded it in studies), partly defining social reality for the self (Giles & Hewstone, 1982). For instance, a high status other's message may well provide us with the cognitive representational material we have been awaiting, as lower status persons ourselves, in order to increase content specificity and guide our behavior effectively (see Berger & Bradac, 1982). Also, and in line with discrepancy-arousal theory (Cappella & Greene, 1982), unexpected involvement and perceived radicalism, modernism, and competence from an elderly other (see item 17, Table 4.2) could lead directly to arousal, negative affect, and compensatory performance. However, it is our contention that other potential cognitive representational contents, coactivated together with their own behavioral dispositions and attending evaluative-attributional analyses (let alone self-identity), can be important mediating mechanisms determining the actual subsequent responses and messages from the self.

In a recent model of language attitudes in intergroup settings, Ryan et al. (1984) discussed the ways in which perceived sociohistorical relationships between groups affect perceptions of each other's language behaviors. Indeed, the precise nature of these cognitive representations is argued as influencing the nature of the evaluative traits brought into affective salience. Hence it is likely that the evaluative component of our model is a bubbling reservoir of affective criteria brought to life (and perhaps having feedback potential) according to the dictates of cognitive representational contents. Such a perspective offers much hope for understanding the tremendous heterogeneity that underlies different language attitudes toward similar stimulus material depending on context, historical time, and subgroup involved (Ryan & Giles, 1982).

Our model, like Patterson's, is a self-perpetuating one with cognitive representations being activated, eliminated, and reactivated in different combinations much like a departure board at a busy international airport with its flashing lights and destination signs. Although the aforementioned components and processes have their input in determining the termination of an encounter, we believe a further theoretical system is necessary as a heuristic to do justice to the many variables involved (Blakar, 1985).

Before closing this section, it is worth noting that a preliminary test of a part of the Cognitive Communicator Characteristics Model was conducted by Comstock and Buller (1991). These researchers examined self-identity and situational predictors of adolescents' strategic choices while engaging in (imagined) conflict with their parents. The researchers reasoned on the basis of the model that adolescents with high social self-esteem would use integrative conflict strategies under conditions of low salience (and accordingly low arousal), whereas adolescents with low social self-esteem would use distributive conflict strategies. Further, they predicted that under conditions of high salience (and high arousal) self-identity dispositions would lose their force, and, instead, the adolescents would choose conflict strategies reflecting parental strategic choices (a situational influence). Support was not obtained for the self-identity prediction; on the other hand, under the condition of high salience, adolescents chose strategies that corresponded to those that they imagined their parents would choose. The researchers suggest that a different measure of self-esteem might yield results more consistent with the predictions of the model. It is also the case that an examination of actual behaviors in adolescent-parent conflict (as opposed to imagined behaviors) could yield a different set of outcomes—whether these would be consistent with the model is an open question.

III: Conclusions

We have, then, a dynamic model that has some important advantages over its forefathers. Indeed, as we have seen, it has modest predictive value and potential. It is truly cognitive in its effort after reflecting the enormous capacity we, as humans, have for processing, evaluating, and attributing cognitive representations. Perhaps its strongest feature, however, is its social character. This can be gleaned from the model's allusion to relational knowledge and the social network implications of the actual interaction in the context of the macrostructure, by focusing upon perceived output and input from a speaker-hearer perspective (see McGregor, 1983) and by highlighting social influence needs allied to self-identity. Another important strength is its heuristic potential for being able to integrate conceptually (in ways space precludes us from enumerating) important features of other models such as communication-game (Higgins, 1980), cognitive-motor (Rimé, 1984), arousal-labeling and nonverbal functional exchange (Patterson, 1976, 1983), cognitive uncertainty (Berger & Bradac, 1982), arousal-discrepancy (Cappella & Greene, 1982), and language attitude (Ryan et al., 1984) theories. Presentation of this model does not mean we advocate all work at this global, heuristic level. Yet it does, in line with Table 4.2 and Street and Cappella's research (1985), suggest that we should pursue multiple levels of communicative analysis. Researchers obviously must pursue their own particular quirks and interests, but it seems eminently possible for us to look to ways in which we can all articulate our concerns in a macroconceptual scheme, whether this one or another. Models such as Patterson's and our Cognitive Communicator Characteristics Model allow us to fight our way out of a general theoretical vacuum and enable us to construct more specific, detailed models of behavioral sequencing, interpersonal relationship development, intergroup communication, and so forth. As important, our model stresses the need for self-presentation theory and the communication-game approach to consider more explicitly intergroup processes, rules, and strategies. It also nudges speech accommodation theory, on the one hand, to contemplate the value of arousal mechanisms and discrepancy arousal and, on the other hand, to assess the value of self-identity processes.

Obviously, we would echo Patterson's sentiments regarding his own model in that the one we have presented herein will be replaced somewhat quickly. There are of course many fuzzy edges and enormous chasms as well as a dearth of empirical data, all of which could benefit from cognitive science and psychophysiological inputs. Among the most compelling of problems revolve around the manner in which communicators come to process the cognitive representations apparent in Table 4.1 and the implied sequential primacy of this over the evaluative and arousal components of the model. Nevertheless, the precise relationships in the model are to our mind ultimately less important than the components themselves as highlighted in our four principles. In other words, the sum of the parts is greater than the whole. But if we persist in following only the "old" paradigms of the first part of this chapter, continue to measure social categories objectively and to analyze solely communication variables in isolation from each other, deny the importance of self-identity processes, and construct our studies in a social vacuum without due respect to theory building, the empirical status of "communicator characteristics" research will suffer as a result. Indeed, until we investigate the ways in which interpersonal communication is influenced by, and itself shapes, the cognitive characteristics of interactants, many apparently contradictory findings will continue to emerge. Our four principles suggest that interactants' cognitive characteristics of themselves, their relationships, situational definitions, and so forth—as well as the affect associated with these (see Cargile et al., in press; Gallois, 1993)—mediate communicative behaviors in ways thus far unexplored empirically. Table 4.1, for example, affords us a concrete handle methodologically and theoretically on some of the literature sources that should prove helpful in that direction. As emphasized at the outset of the second part of this chapter, we do not advocate the abandonment of studies allocating people to objective social categories or personality variables, yet we do recommend understanding fully the dynamics and processes of interpersonal communication. These are just a set of starting blocks available to us.

References

Abelson, R. P. (1981). Psychological status of the script concept. *American Psychologist, 36,* 715-729.

Aboud, F. D., Clément, R., & Taylor, D. M. (1974). Evaluative reactions to discrepancies between social class and language. *Sociometry, 37,* 239-250.

Abrams, D., & Hogg, M. A. (1987). Language attitudes, frames of reference, and social identity: A Scottish dimension. *Journal of Language and Social Psychology, 6,* 201-214.

Aiello, J. R., & Jones, S. E. (1971). Field study of the proxemic behavior of young school children in three subcultural groups. *Journal of Personality and Social Psychology, 19,* 351-356.

Ajzen, I., & Fishbein, M. (1980). *Understanding attitudes and predicting social behavior.* Englewood Cliffs, NJ: Prentice-Hall.

Akert, R. M., & Panter, A. T. (1990). Extraversion and the ability to decode nonverbal communication. *Personality and Individual Differences, 9,* 965-972.

Al-Nesir, R., Keenan, V., & Langer, P. (1991). Field dependence-independence in the development of referential communication. *Bulletin of the Psychonomic Society, 29,* 17-18.

Anderson, E. S. (1992). *Speaking with style: The sociolinguistic skills of children.* London: Routledge.

Andrews, P. H. (1987). Gender differences in persuasive communication and attribution of success and failure. *Human Communication Research, 13,* 372-385.

Apple, W., Streeter, L. A., & Krauss, R. M. (1979). Effects of pitch and speech rate on personal attributions. *Journal of Personality and Social Psychology, 37,* 715-727.

Applegate, J. L. (1982). The impact of construct system development on communication and impression formation in persuasive context. *Communication Monographs, 49,* 277-289.

Applegate, J. L., & Delia, J. G. (1980). Person-centered speech, psychological development, and the contexts of language usage. In R. N. St. Clair & H. Giles (Eds.), *The social and psychological contexts of language* (pp. 245-282). Hillsdale, NJ: Lawrence Erlbaum.

Applegate, J. L., Kline, S. L., & Delia, J. G. (1991). Alternative measures of cognitive complexity as predictors of communication performance. *International Journal of Personal Construct Psychology, 4,* 193-213.

Argyle, M., Furnham, A., & Graham, J. (1981). *Social situations.* Cambridge: Cambridge University Press.

Argyle, M., Lalljee, M., & Cook, M. (1968). The effects of visibility on interaction in a dyad. *Human Relations, 21,* 3-17.

Aries, E. (1967). Interaction patterns and themes of male, female, and mixed groups. *Small Group Behavior, 7,* 7-18.

Arkin, R. M. (1981). Self-presentation styles. In J. T. Tedeschi (Ed.), *Impression management theory and social psychological research* (pp. 311-333). New York: Academic Press.

Arntson, P. (1982). Testing Basil Bernstein's sociolinguistic theories. *Human Communication Research, 9,* 33-48.

Arntson, P., & Mortensen, C. D. (1976, December). *Predispositions toward verbal behavior: Replication and extension.* Paper presented at the annual meeting of the Speech Communication Association, San Francisco.

Arntson, P., Mortensen, C. D., & Lustig, M. W. (1980). Predispositions toward verbal behavior in task-oriented interaction. *Human Communication Research, 6,* 239-252.

Aronovitch, C. D. (1976). The voice of personality: Stereotyped judgments and their relation to voice quality and sex of speaker. *Journal of Social Psychology, 99,* 255-270.

Bailey, L. A., & Timm, L. A. (1976). More on women's- and men's-expletive. *Anthropological Linguistics, 18,* 438-449.

Baldwin, T. L., McFarlane, P. T., & Garvey, C. J. (1971). Children's communication accuracy related to race and socioeconomic status. *Child Development, 42,* 345-357.

Ball, P., Byrne, J., Giles, H., Berechree, P., Griffiths, J., MacDonald, H., & McKendrick, I. (1982). The retrospective speech halo effect: Some Australian data. *Language and Communication, 2,* 277-284.

Baskett, G. D., & Freedle, R. O. (1974). Aspects of language and the social perception of lying. *Journal of Psycholinguistic Research, 3,* 117-130.

Bauer, E. A. (1973). Personal space: A study of blacks and whites. *Sociometry, 36,* 402-408.

Baumeister, R. F. (1982). A self-presentation view of social phenomena. *Psychological Bulletin, 91,* 3-26.

Bell, R. A. (1986). The multivariate structure of communication avoidance. *Communication Monographs, 53,* 365-375.

Berger, C. R., & Bradac, J. J. (1982). *Language and social knowledge.* London: Edward Arnold.

Berger, C. R., Gardner, R. R., Clatterbuck, G. W., & Schulman, L. S. (1976). Perceptions of information sequencing in relationship development. *Human Communication Research, 3,* 29-46.

Bernstein, B. (1962). Linguistic codes, hesitation phenomena, and intelligence. *Language and Speech, 5,* 31-46.

Bernstein, B. (1964). Elaborated and restricted codes: Their social origins and some consequences. *American Anthropologist, 66,* 55-64.

Bernstein, B. (1972). Social class, language, and socialization. In S. Moscovici (Ed.), *The psychology of language* (pp. 222-242). Chicago: Markham.

Blakar, R. (1985). Towards a theory of communication in terms of preconditions: A conceptual framework and some empirical explorations. In H. Giles & R. St. Clair (Eds.), *Recent advances in language, communication and social psychology* (pp. 10-40). London: Lawrence Erlbaum.

Bock, J. K. (1982). Toward a cognitive psychology of syntax: Information processing contributions to sentence formulation. *Psychological Review, 89,* 1-47.

Bond, R. N., & Feldstein, S. (1982). Acoustical correlates of the perception of speech rate: An experimental investigation. *Journal of Psycholinguistic Research, 11,* 539-557.

Bond, R. N., Feldstein, S., & Simpson, S. (1988). Relative and absolute judgments of speech rate from masked and content-standard stimuli: The influence of vocal frequency and intensity. *Human Communication Research, 14,* 548-568.

Booth-Butterfield, M., & Butterfield, S. (1986). Effects of evaluation, task structure, trait-CA, and reticence on state-CA and behavioral disruption in dyadic settings. *Communication Monographs, 53,* 144-159.

Boster, F., Stiff, J. B., & Reynolds, R. A. (1983, May). *Do persons respond differently to inductively-derived lists of compliance-gaining messages?* Paper presented at the annual meeting of the International Communication Association, Dallas, TX.

Bourhis, R. Y., & Giles, H. (1977). The language of intergroup distinctiveness. In H. Giles (Ed.), *Language, ethnicity, and intergroup relations* (pp. 119-135). London: Academic Press.

Bourhis, R. Y., Giles, H., Leyens, J., & Tajfel, H. (1979). Psycholinguistic distinctiveness: Language divergence in Belgium. In H. Giles & R. St. Clair (Eds.), *Language and social psychology* (pp. 158-185). Oxford: Basil Blackwell.

Bradac, J. J. (1990). Language attitudes and impression formation. In H. Giles & W. P. Robinson (Eds.), *Handbook of language and social psychology* (pp. 387-412). Chichester, England: Wiley.

Bradac, J. J., Bowers, J. W., & Courtright, J. A. (1979). Three language variables in communication research: Intensity, immediacy, and diversity. *Human Communication Research, 5,* 257-269.

Bradac, J. J., Hemphill, M. R., & Tardy, C. H. (1981). Language style on trial: Effects of "powerful" and "powerless" speech upon judgments of victims and villains. *Western Journal of Speech Communication, 45,* 327-341.

Bradac, J. J., Hosman, L. A., & Tardy, C. H. (1978). Reciprocal disclosures and language intensity: Attributional consequences. *Communication Monographs, 45,* 1-17.

Bradac, J. J., & Wisegarver, R. (1984). Ascribed status, lexical diversity, and accent: Determinants of perceived status solidarity and control of speech style. *Journal of Language and Social Psychology, 3,* 239-256.

Bradford, A., Ferror, D., & Bradford, G. (1974). Evaluative reactions of college students to dialect differences in the English of Mexican-Americans. *Language and Speech, 17,* 255-270.

Bradley, P. H. (1981). The folk-linguistics of women's speech: An empirical examination. *Communication Monographs, 48,* 73-90.

Braithwaite, D. O. (1990). From majority to minority: An analysis of cultural change from ablebodies to disabled. *International Journal of Intercultural Relations, 14,* 465-483.

Braithwaite, D. O. (1991). "Just how much did that wheelchair cost?" Management of privacy boundaries by persons with disabilities. *Western Journal of Speech Communication, 55,* 254-274.

Brewer, M. B., Dull, V., & Lui, L. (1981). Perceptions of the elderly: Stereotypes as prototypes. *Journal of Personality and Social Psychology, 41,* 656-670.

Brooke, M. E., & Ng, S. H. (1986). Language and social influence in small conversational groups. *Journal of Language and Social Psychology, 5,* 201-210.

Brounell, W., & Smith, D. R. (1973). Communication patterns, sex, and length of verbalization in the speech of four-year-old children. *Speech Monographs, 40,* 310-316.

Brown, B. L. (1980). Effects of speech rate on personality attributions and competing ratings. In H. Giles, W. P. Robinson, & P. M. Smith (Eds.), *Language: Social psychological perspectives* (pp. 293-300). Oxford: Pergamon.

Brown, B. L., Giles, H., & Thakerar, J. N. (1985). Speaker evaluations as a function of speech rate, accent and context. *Language and Communication, 5,* 207-222.

Brown, P., & Levinson, S. (1979). Social structure, groups, and interaction. In K. R. Scherer & H. Giles (Eds.), *Social markers in speech* (pp. 291-342). Cambridge: Cambridge University Press.

Brown, R. (1977). Introduction. In C. E. Ferguson & C. A. Ferguson (Eds.), *Talking to children: Language input and acquisition* (pp. 1-27). New York: Cambridge University Press.

Buck, J. (1968). The effects of Negro and white dialectical variations upon attitudes of college students. *Speech Monographs, 35,* 181-186.

Buck, R. (1975). Nonverbal communication of affect in children. *Journal of Personality and Social Psychology, 31,* 644-653.

Buck, R., Miller, R. E., & Caul, W. F. (1974). Sex, personality, and physiological variables in the communication of affect via facial expression. *Journal of Personality and Social Psychology, 30,* 587-596.

Buller, D. B., & Aune, R. K. (1988). The effects of vocalics and nonverbal sensitivity on compliance: A speech accommodation explanation. *Human Communication Research, 14,* 301-332.

Buller, D. B., & Burgoon, J. K. (1986). The effects of vocalics and nonverbal sensitivity on compliance: A replication and extension. *Human Communication Research, 13,* 126-144.

Buller, D. B., LePoire, B. A., Aune, R. K., & Eloy, S. V. (1992). Social perceptions as mediators of the effect of speech rate similarity on compliance. *Human Communication Research, 19,* 286-311.

Burgoon, J. (1993). Interpersonal expectations, expectancy violations, and emotional communication. *Journal of Language and Social Psychology, 12,* 30-48.

Burgoon, J. K., Birk, T. S., & Pfau, M. (1990). Nonverbal behaviors, persuasion, and credibility. *Human Communication Research, 17,* 140-169.

Burgoon, J. K., & Hale, J. L. (1983). Dimensions of communication reticence and their impact on verbal encoding. *Communication Quarterly, 31,* 302-312.

Burgoon, J. K., & Koper, R. J. (1984). Nonverbal and relational communication associated with reticence. *Human Communication Research, 10,* 601-626.

Burgoon, M. (1983). Argument from Aristotle to analysis of variance: A modest reinterpretation. *Journal of Language and Social Psychology, 2,* 105-121.

Burgoon, M., Birk, T. S., & Hall, J. R. (1991). Compliance and satisfaction with physician-patient communication: An expectancy theory interpretation of gender differences. *Human Communication Research, 18,* 177-208.

Burgoon, M., & Miller, G. R. (1985). An expectancy theory interpretation of language and persuasion. In H. Giles & R. N. St. Clair (Eds.), *Recent advances in language, communication and social psychology* (pp. 199-229). London: LEA.

Burleson, B. R., & Samter, W. (1990). Effects of cognitive complexity on the perceived importance of communication skills in friends. *Communication Research, 17,* 165-182.

Burley, P. M., & Morley, R. (1987). Self-monitoring processes in stutterers. *Journal of Fluency Disorders, 12,* 71-78.

Camaioni, L., & Laicardi, C. (1985). Early social games and the acquisition of language. *British Journal of Developmental Psychology, 3,* 31-39.

Cantor, J. R. (1979). Grammatical variations in persuasion: Effectiveness of four forms of request in door-to-door solicitations for funds. *Communication Monographs, 46,* 296-305.

Cantor, N., & Mischel, W. (1979). Prototypes in person perception. In L. Berkowitz (Ed.), *Advances in experimental social psychology* (Vol. 12, pp. 1-52). New York: Academic Press.

Caporael, L. R., Lukaszewski, M. P., & Culbertson, G. H. (1983). Secondary baby talk: Judgments by institutionalized elderly and their caregivers. *Journal of Personality and Social Psychology, 44,* 746-754.

Cappella, J. N. (1984). The relevance of the microstructure of interaction to relationship change. *Journal of Personal and Social Relationships, 1,* 239-264.

Cappella, J. N. (1985). Controlling the floor in conversations. In A. W. Siegman & S. Feldstein (Eds.), *Multichannel integrations of nonverbal behavior.* Hillsdale, NJ: Lawrence Erlbaum.

Cappella, J. N. (Ed.). (1989). Linking the verbal and nonverbal channels [Special double issue]. *Journal of Language and Social Psychology, 8*(3, 4).

Cappella, J. N., & Greene, J. O. (1982). A discrepancy-arousal explanation of mutual influence in expressive behavior for adult-adult and infant-adult interaction. *Communication Monographs, 49,* 89-114.

Cargile, A., Giles, H., Bradac, J. J., & Ryan, E. B. (in press). Language attitudes as a social process. *Language and Communication.*

Carranza, M. A., & Ryan, E. B. (1975). Evaluative reactions of bilingual Anglo and Mexican American adolescents toward speakers of English and Spanish. *International Journal of the Sociology of Language, 6,* 83-104.

Carter, E. F. (1988). The relationship of field-dependent/independent cognitive style to Spanish language achievement and proficiency: A preliminary report. *Modern Language Journal, 72,* 21-30.

Cegala, D. J., Savage, G. T., Brunner, C. C., & Conrad, A. B. (1982). An elaboration of the meaning of interaction involvement: Toward the development of a theoretical concept. *Communication Monographs, 49,* 229-248.

Chaikin, A. L., & Derlega, V. J. (1974). Liking for the norm-breaker in self-disclosure. *Journal of Personality, 42,* 117-129.

Cherry, L. (1975). Teacher-child verbal interaction: An approach to the study of sex differences. In B. Thorne & N. Henley (Eds.), *Language and sex: Difference and dominance* (pp. 172-183). Rowley, MA: Newbury House.

Cheyne, W. (1970). Stereotyped reactions to speakers with Scottish and English regional accents. *British Journal of Social and Clinical Psychology, 9,* 77-79.

Clark, R. A., & Delia, J. G. (1976). The development of functional persuasive skills in childhood and early adolescence. *Child Development, 47,* 1008-1014.

Clark, R. A., & Delia, J. G. (1977). Cognitive complexity, social perspective-taking and functional persuasive skills in second- to ninth-grade children. *Human Communication Research, 3,* 128-134.

Cody, M., & McLaughlin, M. L. (1980). Perceptions of compliance-gaining situations: A dimensional analysis. *Communication Monographs, 47,* 132-148.

Coleman, L. M., & DePaulo, B. M. (1991). Uncovering the human spirit: Moving beyond disability and "missed" communication. In N. Coupland, H. Giles, & J. M. Wiemann (Eds.), *"Miscommunication" and problematic talk* (pp. 61-84). Newbury Park, CA: Sage.

Comstock, J., & Buller, D. B. (1991). Conflict strategies and adolescents' use with their parents: Testing the Cognitive Communicator Characteristics Model. *Journal of Language and Social Psychology, 10,* 47-59.

Cook, M. (1970). Experiments on orientation and proxemics. *Human Relations, 23,* 61-76.

Coupland, N., & Coupland, J. (1990). Language and later life. In H. Giles & W. P. Robinson (Eds.), *Handbook of language and social psychology* (pp. 451-470). Chichester, England: Wiley.

Coupland, N., Coupland, J., & Giles, H. (1991). *Language, society and the elderly: Discourse, identity and aging.* Oxford: Basil Blackwell.

Coupland, N., Coupland, J., Giles, H., & Henwood, K. (1988). Accommodating the elderly: Invoking and extending a theory. *Language in Society, 17,* 1-41.

Coupland, J., Coupland, N., Giles, H., Henwood, K., & Wiemann, J. M. (1988). Elderly self-disclosure: Interactional and intergroup issues. *Language and Communication, 8,* 109-133.

Coutts, L. M., & Schneider, F. W. (1975). Verbal behavior in an unfocused interaction as a function of sex and distance. *Journal of Experimental Social Psychology, 11,* 64-77.

Cozby, P. C. (1972). Self-disclosure, reciprocity, and liking. *Sociometry, 35,* 151-160.

Crown, C. L. (1980). Impression formation and the chronography of dyadic interactions. In M. Davis (Ed.), *Interaction rhythms: Periodicity in communicative behavior* (pp. 225-248). New York: Human Sciences.

Dabbs, J. M., Evans, M. S., Hopper, C. H., & Purvis, J. A. (1980). Self-monitors in conversation: What do they monitor? *Journal of Personality and Social Psychology, 39,* 278-284.

Daly, J. A., Vangelisti, A. L., & Daughton, S. M. (1987). The nature and correlates of conversational sensitivity. *Human Communication Research, 14,* 167-202.

Davis, J. (1977). Effects of communication about interpersonal process on the evolution of self-disclosure in dyads. *Journal of Personality and Social Psychology, 35,* 31-37.

Dean, O., & Popp, G. E. (1990). Intercultural communication effectiveness as perceived by American managers in Saudi Arabia and French managers in the US. *International Journal of Intercultural Relations, 14,* 405-424.

DeBono, K. G., & Harnish, R. J. (1988). Source expertise, source attractiveness, and the processing of persuasive information: A functional approach. *Journal of Personality and Social Psychology, 55,* 541-546.

De Jongh, E. M. (1991). Foreign language interpreters in the courtroom: The case for linguistic and cultural proficiency. *Modern Language Journal, 75,* 285-295.

De Klerk, V. (1991). Expletives: Men only? *Communication Monographs, 58,* 156-169.

de la Zerda, N., & Hopper, R. (1979). Employment interviewers' responses to Mexican-accented speech. *Communication Monographs, 46,* 126-134.

Delia, J. G. (1972). Dialects and the effects of stereotypes on interpersonal attraction and cognitive processes in impression formation. *Quarterly Journal of Speech, 58,* 285-297.

Delia, J. G., & Clark, R. A. (1977). Cognitive complexity, social perception, and the development of listener-adapted communication in six-, eight-, ten-, and twelve-year-old boys. *Communication Monographs, 44,* 326-345.

Delia, J. G., Kline, S. L., & Burleson, B. R. (1979). The development of persuasive communication strategies in kindergartners through twelfth-graders. *Communication Monographs, 46,* 241-256.

Derlega, V. J., Harris, M. S., & Chaikin, A. L. (1973). Self-disclosure, reciprocity, liking, and the deviant. *Journal of Experimental Social Psychology, 9,* 277-284.

Dindia, K. (1982). Reciprocity in self-disclosure: A sequential analysis. In M. Burgoon (Ed.), *Communication yearbook 6* (pp. 506-528). Beverly Hills, CA: Sage.

Dindia, K. (1983, May). *Reciprocity of self-disclosure: Limitations and illusions.* Paper presented at the annual meeting of the International Communication Association, Dallas, TX.

Dindia, K. (1985). A functional approach to self-disclosure. In R. L. Street, Jr., & J. N. Cappella (Eds.), *Sequence and pattern in communicative behavior* (pp. 142-160). London: Edward Arnold.

Dittmann, A. T. (1972). Development factors in conversational behavior. *Journal of Communication, 22,* 404-423.

Doob, L. W. (1958). Behavior and grammatical style. *Journal of Abnormal and Social Psychology, 56,* 398-401.

Dowd, J. J., & Bengtson, V. L. (1978). Aging in minority population: An examination of the double jeopardy hypothesis. *Journal of Gerontology, 33,* 427-436.

Dreyer, A. S., Dreyer, C. A., & Davis, J. E. (1987). Individuality and mutuality in the language of families of field-dependent and field-independent children. *Journal of Genetic Psychology, 148,* 105-117.

Dubé-Simard, L. (1983). Genesis of social categorization, threat to identity and perception of social injustice: Their role in intergroup communication. *Journal of Language and Social Psychology, 2,* 183-205.

Duck, S. (1992). *Human relationships* (2nd ed.). Newbury Park, CA: Sage.

Duncan, S. D., Jr. (1983). Speaking turns: Studies of structure and individual difference. In J. M. Wiemann & R. P. Harrison (Eds.), *Nonverbal interaction* (pp. 149-178). Beverly Hills, CA: Sage.

Duncan, S. D., Jr., & Fiske, D. W. (1977). *Face-to-face interaction: Research, methods, and theory.* Hillsdale, NJ: Lawrence Erlbaum.

Dunhame, R., & Herman, J. (1975). Development of a female faces scale for measuring job satisfaction. *Journal of Applied Psychology, 60,* 629-631.

Durkin, K. (1988). The social nature of social development. In M. Hewstone, W. Stroebe, J. Codol, & G. M. Stephenson (Eds.), *Introduction to social psychology: A European perspective* (pp. 39-59). Oxford: Basil Blackwell.

Eakins, B. W., & Eakins, C. (1976). Verbal turn-taking and exchanges in faculty dialogue. In B. Dubois & I. Crouch (Eds.), *The sociology of the languages of American women* (pp. 53-62). San Antonio, TX: Trinity University Press.

Edwards, J., Jr. (1979a). Judgments and confidence in reaction to disadvantaged speech. In H. Giles & R. St. Clair (Eds.), *Language and social psychology* (pp. 22-44). Oxford: Basil Blackwell.

Edwards, J., Jr. (1979b). *Language and disadvantage.* London: Edward Arnold.

Efran, J. S. (1968). Looking for approval: Effect on visual behavior of approbation from persons differing in importance. *Journal of Personality and Social Psychology, 10,* 21-25.

Ekman, O., O'Sullivan, M., Friesen, W. V., & Scherer, K. R. (1991). Invited article: Face, voice and body in detecting deceit. *Journal of Nonverbal Behavior, 15,* 125-135.

Ekman, P., & Friesen, W. V. (1972). Hand movements. *Journal of Communication, 22,* 353-374.

Elyan, O., Smith, P. M., Giles, H., & Bourhis, R. Y. (1978). R-P female-accented speech: The voice of perceived androgyny? In P. Trudgill (Ed.), *Sociolinguistic patterns in British English* (pp. 122-130). London: Edward Arnold.

Erzinger, S. (1991). Communication between Spanish-speaking patients and their doctors in medical encounters. *Culture, Medicine and Psychiatry, 15,* 91-110.

Exline, R. V. (1963). Explorations in the process of person perception: Visual interaction in relation to composition, sex, and need for affiliation. *Journal of Personality, 31,* 1-20.

Exline, R. V., Ellyson, S. L., & Long, B. (1975). Visual behavior as an aspect of power role relationships. In P. Pilner, L. Krames, & T. Holloway (Eds.), *Advances in the study of communication and affect* (Vol. 2, pp. 21-51). New York: Plenum.

Exline, R. V., & Fehr, B. J. (1978). Applications of semiosis to the study of visual interaction. In A. Siegman & S. Feldstein (Eds.), *Nonverbal behavior and communication* (pp. 117-158). Hillsdale, NJ: Lawrence Erlbaum.

Exline, R. V., Gray, D., & Schuette, D. (1965). Visual behavior in a dyad as affected by interview content and sex of respondent. *Journal of Personality and Social Psychology, 1,* 201-209.

Exline, R. V., Thibaut, J., Hickey, C. B., & Gumpert, P. (1970). Visual interaction in relation of Machiavellianism and an unethical act. In R. Christie & F. Geis (Eds.), *Studies in Machiavellianism* (pp. 53-75). New York: Academic Press.

Farr, R. M. (1980). Homo loquens in social psychological perspective. In H. Giles, W. P. Robinson, & P. M. Smith (Eds.), *Language: Social psychological perspectives* (pp. 409-413). Oxford: Pergamon.

Feldstein, S., & Welkowitz, J. (1978). A chronography of conversation: In defense of an objective approach. In A. Siegman & S. Feldstein (Eds.), *Nonverbal behavior and communication* (pp. 329-378). Hillsdale, NJ: Lawrence Erlbaum.

Festinger, L. (1954). A theory of social comparison processes. *Human Relations, 7,* 117-140.

Fielding, G., & Evered, C. (1980). The influence of patients' speech upon doctors: The diagnostic interview. In R. N. St. Clair & H. Giles (Eds.), *The social and psychological contexts of language* (pp. 51-72). Hillsdale, NJ: Lawrence Erlbaum.

Fisher, B. A. (1983). Differential effects of sexual composition and interactional context on interaction patterns in dyads. *Human Communication Research, 9,* 225-238.

Fishman, P. M. (1980). Conversational insecurity. In H. Giles, W. P. Robinson, & P. M. Smith (Eds.), *Language: Social psychological perspectives* (pp. 127-132). Oxford: Pergamon.

Fitzpatrick, M. A. (1987). *Between husbands and wives.* Newbury Park, CA: Sage.

Fitzpatrick, M. A. (1990). Models of marital interaction. In H. Giles & W. P. Robinson (Eds.), *Handbook of language and social psychology* (pp. 413-432). Chichester, England: Wiley.

Flores, N., & Hopper, R. (1975). Mexican-Americans' evaluations of spoken Spanish and English. *Speech Monographs, 42,* 91-98.

Foon, A. E. (1986). A social structural approach to speech evaluation. *Journal of Social Psychology, 126,* 521-530.

Forgas, J. (1981). *Social episodes: The study of interaction routines.* London: Academic Press.

Forgas, J. (1983). Language, goals, and situation. *Journal of Language and Social Psychology, 2,* 267-293.

Forgas, J., & Dubosz, B. (1980). Dimensions of romantic involvement: Towards a taxonomy of heterosexual relationships. *Social Psychology Quarterly, 43,* 290-300.

Forston, R. F., & Larson, C. U. (1968). The dynamics of space: An experimental study in proxemic behavior among Latin Americans and North Americans. *Journal of Communication, 18,* 109-116.

Foss, D. J., & Hakes, D. T. (1978). *Psycholinguistics.* Englewood Cliffs, NJ: Prentice-Hall.

Foster, S. H. (1990). *The communicative competence of young children.* London: Longman.

Frender, R., Brown, B., & Lambert, W. E. (1970). The role of speech characteristics in scholastic success. *Canadian Journal of Behavioral Sciences, 2,* 299-306.

Gallois, C. (1993). The language and communication of emotion. *American Behavioral Scientist, 36,* 309-338.

Gallois, C., Franklyn-Stokes, A., Giles, H., & Coupland, N. (1988). Communication accommodation in intercultural encounters. In Y. Y. Kim & W. B. Gudykunst (Eds.), *Theories in intercultural communication* (pp. 157-185). Newbury Park, CA: Sage.

Garai, J. E., & Scheinfeld, A. (1968). Sex differences in mental and behavioral traits. *Genetic Psychology Monographs, 77,* 169-299.

Garvey, C., & BenDebba, M. (1974). Effects of age, sex, and partner on children's dyadic speech. *Child Development, 45,* 1159-1161.

Geis, F. L., & Moon, T. H. (1981). Machiavellianism and deception. *Journal of Personality and Social Psychology, 41,* 766-775.

Genesee, F., & Bourhis, R. Y. (1982). The social psychological significance of code switching in cross-cultural communication. *Journal of Language and Social Psychology, 1,* 1-28.

Genesee, F., & Holobow, N. E. (1989). Change and stability in intergroup perceptions. *Journal of Language and Social Psychology, 8,* 17-38.

Gibbons, P., Busch, J., & Bradac, J. J. (1991). Powerful versus powerless language: Consequences for persuasion, impression formation, and cognitive response. *Journal of Language and Social Psychology, 10,* 115-133.

Gilbert, S. J. (1976). Empirical and theoretical extensions of self-disclosure. In G. R. Miller (Ed.), *Explorations in interpersonal communication* (pp. 197-216). Beverly Hills, CA: Sage.

Giles, H. (1971a). Ethnocentrism and evaluation of accented speech. *British Journal of Social and Clinical Psychology, 10,* 187-188.

Giles, H. (1971b). Patterns of evaluations to RP, South Welsh, and Somerset accented speech. *British Journal of Social and Clinical Psychology, 10,* 280-281.

Giles, H. (1973). Communicative effectiveness as a function of accented speech. *Speech Monographs, 40,* 330-331.

Giles, H. (1979). Ethnicity markers in speech. In K. R. Scherer & H. Giles (Eds.), *Social markers in speech* (pp. 251-290). Cambridge: Cambridge University Press.

Giles, H., Coupland, J., & Coupland, N. (Eds.). (1991). *The contexts of accommodation.* New York: Cambridge University Press.

Giles, H., & Coupland, N. (1992). *Language: Contexts and consequences.* Pacific Grove, CA: Brooks/ Cole.

Giles, H., Henwood, K., Coupland, N., Harriman, J., & Coupland, J. (1992). Language attitudes and cognitive mediation. *Human Communication Research, 18,* 500-527.

Giles, H., & Hewstone, M. (1982). Cognitive structures, speech and social situations: Two integrative models. *Language Sciences, 4,* 188-219.

Giles, H., Hewstone, M., Ryan, E. B., & Johnson, P. (1987). Research in language attitudes. In U. Ammon, N. Dittmar, & K. J. Mattheier (Eds.), *Sociolinguistics: An interdisciplinary handbook of the science of language* (Vol. 1, pp. 585-597). Berlin: de Gruyter.

Giles, H., & Johnson, P. (1981). The role of language in ethnic group relations. In J. C. Turner & H. Giles (Eds.), *Intergroup behavior* (pp. 199-243). Oxford: Blackwell and Chicago University Press.

Giles, H., & Johnson, P. (1987). Ethnolinguistic identity theory: A social psychological approach to language maintenance. *International Journal of the Sociology of Language, 68,* 66-99.

Giles, H., & Powesland, P. F. (1975). *Speech style and social evaluation.* London: Academic Press.

Giles, H., & Ryan, E. B. (1982). Prolegomena for developing a social psychological theory of language attitudes. In E. B. Ryan & H. Giles (Eds.), *Attitudes towards language variation* (pp. 208-223). London: Edward Arnold.

Giles, H., & Sassoon, C. (1983). The effect of speaker's accent, social class background, and message style on British listeners' social judgments. *Language and Communication, 3,* 305-313.

Giles, H., & Smith, P. M. (1979). Accommodation theory: Optimal levels of convergence. In H. Giles & R. N. St. Clair (Eds.), *Language and social psychology* (pp. 45-65). Baltimore: University Park Press.

Giles, H., Taylor, D. M., & Bourhis, R. Y. (1973). Towards a theory of interpersonal accommodation through language: Some Canadian data. *Language in Society, 2,* 177-192.

Goffman, E. (1959). *The presentation of self in everyday life.* New York: Doubleday.

Goffman, E. (1961). *Encounters: Two studies in the sociology of interaction.* Indianapolis: Bobbs-Merrill.

Green, K. P. (1987). The perception of speaking rate using visual information from a talker's face. *Perception and Psychophysics, 42,* 587-593.

Gudykunst, W. B. (1988). Uncertainty and anxiety. In Y. Y. Kim & W. B. Gudykunst (Eds.), *Theories in intercultural communication* (pp. 123-156). Newbury Park, CA: Sage.

Gudykunst, W. B., Nishida, T., & Schmidt, K. L. (1989). The influence of cultural, relational, and personality factors on uncertainty reduction processes. *Western Journal of Speech Communication, 53,* 13-29.

Haas, A. (1979). Male and female spoken language differences: Stereotypes and evidence. *Psychological Bulletin, 86,* 616-626.

Haas, A., & Sherman, M. A. (1982). Reported topics of conversation among same-sex adults. *Communication Quarterly, 30,* 332-342.

Hale, C. L. (1980). Cognitive complexity as a determinant of communication effectiveness. *Communication Monographs, 47,* 304-311.

Hale, C. L. (1986). Impact of cognitive complexity on message structure in a face-threatening context. *Journal of Language and Social Psychology, 5,* 135-143.

Hamilton, M. A., Hunter, J. E., & Burgoon, M. (1990). An empirical test of an axiomatic model of the relationship between language intensity and persuasion. *Journal of Language and Social Psychology, 9,* 235-255.

Harms, L. S. (1963). Status cues in speech: Extra-race and extra-region identification. *Lingua, 12,* 300-306.

Hart, R. J., & Brown, B. L. (1974). Interpersonal information conveyed by the content and vocal aspects of speech. *Speech Monographs, 41,* 371-380.

Harwood, J., & Giles, H. (1993). Creating intergenerational distance: Language, communication and middle-age. *Language Sciences, 15,* 1-24.

Harwood, J., Giles, H., & Bourhis, R. Y. (in press). The genesis of vitality theory: Historical patterns and discoursal dimensions. *International Journal of the Sociology of Language.*

Haslett, B. J. (1983a). Communication functions and strategies in children's conversations. *Human Communication Research, 9,* 114-129.

Haslett, B. J. (1983b). Preschoolers communicative strategies in gaining compliance from peers: A developmental study. *Quarterly Journal of Speech, 69,* 84-99.

Haslett, B. J. (1990). Social class, social status, and communicative behavior. In H. Giles & W. P. Robinson (Eds.), *Handbook of language and social psychology* (pp. 309-328). Chichester, England: Wiley.

Hass, W. A., & Wepman, J. M. (1974). Dimensions of individual difference in the spoken syntax of school children. *Journal of Speech and Hearing Research, 17,* 455-469.

Hayes, D. P., & Meltzer, L. (1972). Interpersonal factors based on talkativeness: Fact or artifact. *Sociometry, 35,* 538-561.

Hecht, M. L., Ribeau, S. A., & Alberts, J. K. (1989). An Afro-American perspective on interethnic communication. *Communication Monographs, 56,* 385-410.

Hecht, M. L., Ribeau, S. A., & Collier, M. J. (1993). *African American communication.* Newbury Park, CA: Sage.

Helfrich, H. (1979). Age markers in speech. In K. R. Scherer & H. Giles (Eds.), *Social markers in speech* (pp. 63-107). Cambridge: Cambridge University Press.

Henley, N. (1977). *Body politics: Power, sex, and nonverbal communication.* Englewood Cliffs, NJ: Prentice-Hall.

Hershey, S., & Werner, E. (1975). Dominance in marital decision making in women's liberation and non-women's liberation families. *Family Process, 14,* 223-233.

Hewes, D., & Haight, L. (1979). The cross-situational consistency of communicative behaviors. *Communication Research, 6,* 243-270.

Hewes, D., & Haight, L. (1980). Multiple-act criteria in the validation of communication traits: What do we gain and what do we lose? *Human Communication Research, 6,* 352-366.

Hewes, D., Haight, L., Szalay, S., & Evans, D. E. (1977, July). *On predicting none of the people none of the time: A test of two alternative relationships between personality and communicative choice.* Paper presented at the annual meeting of the International Communication Association, Berlin.

Hewett, N. (1971). Reactions of prospective English teachers toward speakers of a nonstandard dialect. *Language Learning, 21,* 205-212.

Hewitt, R. (1986). *White talk black talk: Inter-racial friendship and communication amongst adolescents.* Cambridge: Cambridge University Press.

Higgins, E. T. (1980). The "communication game": Implications for social cognition and persuasion. In E. T. Higgins, C. P. Herman, & M. P. Zanna (Eds.), *Social cognition: The Ontario Symposium* (pp. 343-392). Hillsdale, NJ: Lawrence Erlbaum.

Higgins, E. T., & McCann, C. D. (1984). Social encoding and subsequent attitudes, impressions and memory: "Context-driven" and motivational aspects of processing. *Journal of Personality and Social Psychology, 47,* 26-39.

Hilpert, F., Kramer, C., & Clark, R. A. (1975). Participants' perceptions of self and partner in mixed-sex dyads. *Central States Speech Journal, 26,* 52-56.

Hogg, M. A., D'Agata, P., & Abrams, D. (1989). Ethnolinguistic betrayal and speaker evaluation among Italian Australians. *Genetic, Social and General Psychology Monographs, 115,* 153-181.

Hollien, H., Gelfer, M. P., & Carlson, T. (1991). Listening preferences for voice types as a function of age. *Journal of Communication Disorders, 24,* 157-171.

Holtgraves, T., & Yang, J. (1992). Interpersonal underpinnings of request strategies: General principles and differences due to culture and gender. *Journal of Personality and Social Psychology, 62,* 246-256.

Hopper, R. (1977). Language attitudes in the employment interviews. *Communication Monographs, 44,* 346-351.

Hopper, R., & Williams, F. (1973). Speech characteristics and employability. *Speech Monographs, 40,* 296-302.

Hosman, L. A. (1987). The evaluational consequences of topic reciprocity and self-disclosure reciprocity. *Communication Monographs, 54,* 420-435.

Hosman, L. A. (1989). The evaluative consequences of hedges, hesitations, and intensifiers: Powerful and powerless speech styles. *Human Communication Research, 15,* 383-406.

Hosman, L. A., & Wright, J. W. (1987). The effects of hedges and hesitations on impression formation in a simulated courtroom context. *Western Journal of Speech Communication, 51,* 173-188.

Houston, S. (1970). A re-examination of some assumptions about the language of the disadvantaged child. *Child Development, 41,* 947-962.

Hyland, J. D., & Weismer, G. (1988). The effects of three feedback modes on the ability of normal geriatric individuals to match speaking rate. *Journal of Speech and Hearing Disorders, 53,* 271-279.

Ickes, W., & Barnes, R. D. (1977). The role of sex and self-monitoring in unstructured dyadic interactions. *Journal of Personality and Social Psychology, 35,* 315-330.

Ickes, W., Patterson, M. L., Rajecki, D. W., & Tanford, S. (1982). Behavioral and cognitive consequences of reciprocal versus compensatory responses to pre-interaction expectancies. *Social Cognition, 1,* 160-190.

Jaworski, A. (1992). *The power of silence.* Newbury Park, CA: Sage.

Johnson, F. L., & Buttny, R. (1982). White listeners' responses to "sounding black" and "sounding white": The effect of message content on judgments about language. *Communication Monographs, 49,* 33-49.

Johnson, K. R. (1972). Black kinesics: Some nonverbal communication patterns in the black culture. In L. A. Samovar & R. E. Porter (Eds.), *Intercultural communication: A reader* (pp. 259-268). Belmont, CA: Wadsworth.

Johnson, P., Giles, H., & Bourhis, R. Y. (1983). The viability of ethnolinguistic vitality: A reply to Husband and Khan. *Journal of Multilingual and Multicultural Development, 4,* 255-269.

Johnson-Laird, P. N. (1983). *Mental models: Toward a cognitive science of language, inference, and consciousness.* Cambridge, MA: Harvard University Press.

Jones, A. J., & McMillan, W. B. (1973). Speech characteristics as a function of social class and situational factors. *Child Development, 44,* 117-121.

Jones, E. E., & Wortman, C. (1973). *Ingratiation: An attributional approach.* Morristown, NJ: General Learning Press.

Jones, S. E., & Aiello, J. R. (1973). Proxemic behavior of black and white first-, third-, and fifth-grade children. *Journal of Personality and Social Psychology, 25,* 21-27.

Jordan, W. J., & Powers, W. G. (1978). Verbal behavior as a function of apprehension and social context. *Human Communication Research, 4,* 294-300.

Jourard, S. M., & Friedman, R. (1970). Experimenter-subject "distance" and self-disclosure. *Journal of Personality and Social Psychology, 15,* 278-282.

Kalin, R. (1982). The social significance of speech in medical, legal and occupational settings. In E. B. Ryan & H. Giles (Eds.), *Attitudes towards language variation* (pp. 148-163). London: Edward Arnold.

Kalmar, I., Zhong, Y., & Xiao, H. (1987). Language attitudes in Guangzhou, China. *Language in Society, 16,* 499-508.

Kealey, D. J. (1989). A study of cross-cultural effectiveness: Theoretical issues, practical application. *International Journal of Intercultural Relations, 13,* 387-428.

Kim, Y. Y., & Gudykunst, W. B. (Eds.). (1987). *Cross-cultural adaptations: Current theory and research.* Newbury Park, CA: Sage.

Kimble, C. E., & Seidel, S. D. (1991). Vocal signs of confidence. *Journal of Nonverbal Behavior, 15,* 99-106.

Kimble, C. E., Yoshikawa, J. C., & Zehr, H. D. (1981). Vocal and verbal assertiveness in same-sex and mixed-sex groups. *Journal of Personality and Social Psychology, 40,* 1047-1054.

Kline, S. L. (1991). Construct differentiation and person-centered regulative messages. *Journal of Language and Social Psychology, 10,* 1-28.

Kline, S. L., Pelias, R. J., & Delia, J. G. (1991). The predictive validity of cognitive complexity measures on social perspective taking and counseling communication. *International Journal of Personal Construct Psychology, 4,* 347-357.

Knapp, M. L. (1978). *Nonverbal communication in human interaction.* New York: Holt, Rinehart & Winston.

Knapp, M. L., & Hall, J. A. (1992). *Nonverbal communication in human interaction* (2nd ed.). New York: Holt, Rinehart & Winston.

Knapp, M. L., Hart, R., & Dennis, H. (1974). An exploration of deception as a communication construct. *Human Communication Research, 1,* 15-29.

Kochman, T. (1982). *Black and white styles in conflict.* Chicago: University of Chicago Press.

Kolditz, T. A., & Arkin, R. M. (1982). An impression management interpretation of the self-handicapping strategy. *Journal of Personality and Social Psychology, 43,* 492-502.

Kowal, S., O'Connell, D. C., & Sabin, E. J. (1975). Development of temporal patterning and vocal hesitations in spontaneous narratives. *Journal of Psycholinguistic Research, 4,* 195-207.

Kramarae, C. (1982). Gender: How she speaks. In E. B. Ryan & H. Giles (Eds.), *Attitudes towards language variation* (pp. 84-98). London: Edward Arnold.

Kramer, C. (1977). Perceptions of female and male speech. *Language and Speech, 20,* 151-161.

Kristiansen, T., & Giles, H. (1992). Compliance-gaining as a function of accent: Public requests in varieties of Danish. *International Journal of Applied Linguistics, 2,* 17-35.

Labov, W. (1966). *The social stratification of English in New York City.* Washington, DC: Center for Applied Linguistics.

LaFrance, M., & Mayo, C. (1976). Racial differences in gaze behavior during conversations: Two systematic observational studies. *Journal of Personality and Social Psychology, 33,* 547-552.

Lakoff, R. (1975). *Language and woman's place.* New York: Harper & Row.

Lambert, W. E. (1967). A social psychology of bilingualism. *Journal of Social Issues, 23,* 91-109.

Langer, E., & Newman, H. (1979). The role of mindlessness in a typical social psychological experiment. *Personality and Social Psychology Bulletin, 5,* 295-298.

Larsen, K. S., Martin, H. J., & Giles, H. (1977). Anticipated social cost and interpersonal accommodation. *Human Communication Research, 3,* 303-308.

Laver, J. D. M. (1975). *Individual features in voice quality.* Unpublished doctoral dissertation, University of Edinburgh, Scotland.

Lawton, D. (1968). *Social class, language, and education.* London: Routledge & Kegan Paul.

Lay, C. H., & Burron, B. F. (1968). Perception of the personality of the hesitant speaker. *Perceptual and Motor Skills, 26,* 951-956.

Lee, H. O., & Boster, F. J. (1992). Collectivism-individualism in perceptions of speech rate: A cross-cultural comparison. *Journal of Cross-Cultural Psychology, 23,* 377-388.

Levine, T. R., & McCroskey, J. C. (1990). Measuring trait communication apprehension: A test of rival measurement models of the PRCA-24. *Communication Monographs, 57,* 62-72.

Lind, E. A., & O'Barr, W. M. (1979). The social significance of speech in the courtroom. In H. Giles & R. N. St. Clair (Eds.), *Language and social psychology* (pp. 66-87). Baltimore: University Park Press.

Lowery, C. R., Snyder, C. R., & Denney, N. W. (1976). Perceived aggression and predicted counter aggression as a function of sex of dyad participants: When males and females exchange verbal blows. *Sex Roles, 2,* 339-346.

Luhman, R. (1990). Appalachian English stereotypes: Language attitudes in Kentucky. *Language in Society, 19,* 331-348.

Mallory, E., & Miller, V. A. (1958). A possible basis for the association of voice characteristics and personality traits. *Speech Monographs, 25,* 255-260.

Marche, T. A., & Peterson, C. (1993). The development and sex-related use of interruption behavior. *Human Communication Research, 19,* 388-408.

Markel, N. N., Lang, J. F., & Saine, T. J. (1976). Sex effects in conversational interaction: Another look at male dominance. *Human Communication Research, 2,* 356-364.

Markel, N. N., Phillis, J. A., Vargas, R., & Harvard, K. (1972). Personality traits associated with voice types. *Journal of Psycholinguistic Research, 1,* 249-255.

Markel, N. N., Prebor, L. D., & Brandt, J. F. (1972). Biosocial factors in dyadic communication. *Journal of Personality and Social Psychology, 23,* 11-13.

Marshall, J. E., & Heslin, R. (1975). Boys and girls together: Sexual composition and effect of density and group size on cohesiveness. *Journal of Personality and Social Psychology, 31,* 952-961.

Martin, J. N., & Craig, R. T. (1983). Selected linguistic sex differences during initial social interactions of same-sex and mixed-sex student dyads. *Western Journal of Speech Communication, 47,* 16-28.

Martindale, D. A. (1971). *Effects of environmental context in negotiating situations: Territorial dominance behavior in dyadic interactions.* Unpublished doctoral dissertation, City University of New York.

Maynard, D. W. (1980). Placement of topic changes in conversation. *Semiotica, 30,* 263-290.

McCann, C. D., & Higgins, E. T. (1992). Personal and contextual factors in communication: A review of the "communication game." In G. R. Semin & K. Fielder (Eds.), *Language, interaction and social cognition* (pp. 144-172). Newbury Park, CA: Sage.

McCroskey, J. C. (1977). Oral communication apprehension: A summary of recent theory and research. *Human Communication Research, 4,* 78-98.

McCroskey, J. C., & Daly, J. A. (1984). *Personality and interpersonal communication.* Beverly Hills, CA: Sage.

McGregor, G. (1983). Listener's comments on conversations. *Language and Communication, 3,* 271-304.

McKinney, B. C. (1982). The effects of reticence in group interaction. *Communication Quarterly, 30,* 124-128.

McKirnan, D., & Hamayan, E. (1980). Language norms and perceptions of ethnolinguistic group diversity. In H. Giles, W. P. Robinson, & P. M. Smith (Eds.), *Language: Social psychological perspectives* (pp. 161-170). Oxford: Pergamon.

McLaughlin, M. L., Cody, M. J., Kane, M. L., & Robey, C. S. (1981). Sex differences in story receipt and story sequencing variables. *Human Communication Research, 7,* 99-116.

Mead, G. H. (1934). *Mind, self and society.* Chicago: University of Chicago Press.

Meeuwesen, L., Schaap, C., & van der Staak, C. (1991). Verbal analysis of doctor-patient communication. *Social Science and Medicine, 32,* 1143-1150.

Mehrabian, A. (1969). Significance of posture and position in the communication of attitude and status relationships. *Psychological Bulletin, 71,* 359-373.

Mehrabian, A., & Williams, M. (1969). Nonverbal concomitants of perceived and intended persuasiveness. *Journal of Personality and Social Psychology, 13,* 37-58.

Mgbo-Elue, C. N. (1987). Social psychological and linguistic impediments to the acquisition of a second Nigerian language among Yoruba and Ibo. *Journal of Language and Social Psychology, 6,* 309-318.

Milardo, R. M. (1982). Friendship networks in developing relationships: Converging and diverging social environments. *Social Psychology Quarterly, 45,* 162-172.

Miller, D. T. (1975). The effect of dialect and ethnicity on communicator effectiveness. *Speech Monographs, 42,* 69-74.

Miller, G. R. (1983). On various ways of skinning symbolic cats: Recent research on persuasive message strategies. *Journal of Language and Social Psychology, 2,* 123-140.

Miller, J. L., & Dexter, E. R. (1988). Effects of speaking rate and lexical status on phonetic perception. *Journal of Experimental Psychology: Human Perception and Performance, 14,* 369-378.

Miller, M. D., Reynolds, R. A., & Cambra, R. E. (1987). The influence of gender and culture on language intensity. *Communication Monographs, 54,* 101-105.

Miller, N., Marayama, G., Beaber, R. J., & Valone, K. (1976). Speed of speech and persuasion. *Journal of Personality and Social Psychology, 34,* 615-624.

Miura, S. Y. (1985). Communication apprehension and bi-dialectal speakers: An exploratory investigation. *Communication Research Reports, 2,* 1-4.

Mobbs, N. A. (1968). Eye contact in relation to social introversion-extraversion. *British Journal of Social and Clinical Psychology, 7,* 305-306.

Moe, J. D. (1972). Listener judgments of status cues in speech: A replication and extension. *Speech Monographs, 39,* 144-147.

Montgomery, B. M. (1981). Verbal immediacy as an indicator of open communication content. *Communication Quarterly, 30,* 24-34.

Morgan, B. S. (1976). Intimacy of disclosure topics and sex differences in self-disclosure. *Sex Roles, 2,* 161-166.

Morris, L. W. (1979). *Extroversion and introversion.* New York: Wiley.

Mortensen, C. D., & Arntson, P. H. (1974). The effects of predispositions toward verbal behavior on interaction patterns in dyads. *Quarterly Journal of Speech, 61,* 421-430.

Morton, J. (1969). Interaction of information in word recognition. *Psychological Review, 76,* 165-178.

Mulac, A. (1989). Men's and women's talk in same-gender and mixed-gender dyads: Power or polemic? *Journal of Language and Social Psychology, 5,* 249-270.

Mulac, A., & Lundell, T. L. (1980). Differences in perception created by syntactic-semantic productions of male and female speakers. *Communication Monographs, 47,* 111-118.

Mulac, A., & Lundell, T. L. (1986). Linguistic contributors to the gender-linked language effect. *Journal of Language and Social Psychology, 5,* 81-101.

Mulac, A., Lundell, T. L., & Bradac, J. J. (1986). Male/female language differences and attributional consequences in a public speaking situation: Toward an explanation of the gender-linked language effect. *Communication Monographs, 53,* 115-129.

Mulac, A., & Rudd, M. J. (1977). Effects of selected American regional dialects upon regional audience members. *Communication Monographs, 44,* 185-195.

Murray, D. C. (1971). Talk, silence, and anxiety. *Psychological Bulletin, 75,* 224-260.

Mysak, E. D. (1959). Pitch and duration characteristics of older males. *Journal of Speech and Hearing Research, 2,* 46-54.

Naremore, R. C. (1971). Teachers' judgments of children's speech: A factor analytic study of attitudes. *Speech Monographs, 38,* 17-27.

Natale, M. (1975a). Convergence of mean vocal intensity in dyadic communications as a function of social desirability. *Journal of Personality and Social Psychology, 32,* 790-804.

Natale, M. (1975b). Social desirability as related to convergence of temporal speech patterns. *Perceptual and Motor Skills, 40,* 827-830.

Nesdale, A. R., & Rooney, R. (1990). Effect of children's ethnic accents on adults' evaluations and stereotyping. *Australian Journal of Psychology, 42,* 309-319.

Neuliep, J. W., & Hazleton, V. (1985). Cognitive complexity and apprehension about communication: A preliminary report. *Psychological Reports, 57,* 1224-1226.

Newman, H. M. (1982). The sounds of silence in communicative encounters. *Communication Quarterly, 30,* 142-149.

Ng, S. H., Bell, D., & Brooke, M. E. (in press). Gaining turns and achieving high influence in small conversational groups. *British Journal of Social Psychology.*

Ng, S. H., & Bradac, J. J. (1993). *Power in language.* Newbury Park, CA: Sage.

Noller, P., & Fitzpatrick, M. A. (Eds.). (1988). *Perspectives on marital interaction.* Clevedon, England: Multilingual Matters.

Norman, D. A. (1981). Categorization of action slips. *Psychological Review, 88,* 1-15.

Norton, R. (1983). *Communicator style.* Beverly Hills, CA: Sage.

Nussbaum, J. (Ed.). (1989). *Life-span communication: Normative processes.* Hillsdale, NJ: Lawrence Erlbaum.

Nussbaum, J., Thompson, T., & Robinson, J. D. (1989). *Communication and aging.* New York: Harper & Row.

Oden, G. C., & Massaro, D. W. (1978). Integration of featural information in speech perception. *Psychological Review, 85,* 172-191.

O'Hair, H. D., Cody, M. J., & McLaughlin, M. L. (1981). Prepared lies, spontaneous lies: Machiavellianism, and nonverbal communication. *Human Communication Research, 7,* 325-339.

O'Keefe, B. J., & Delia, J. G. (1979). Construct comprehensiveness and cognitive complexity as predictors of the number and strategic adaptation of arguments and appeals in a persuasive message. *Communication Monographs, 46,* 231-240.

O'Keefe, D. J., & Sypher, H. E. (1981). Cognitive complexity measures and the relationship of cognitive complexity to communication. *Human Communication Research, 7,* 72-92.

Palmer, M. T. (1984). *A fuzzy approach to comprehending nonverbal communication.* Unpublished paper, University of Wisconsin—Madison.

Palmer, M. T. (1989). Controlling conversations: Turns, topics and interpersonal control. *Communication Monographs, 56,* 1-18.

Patterson, M. L. (1973). Compensation in nonverbal immediacy behaviors: A review. *Sociometry, 36,* 237-252.

Patterson, M. L. (1976). An arousal model of interpersonal intimacy. *Psychological Review, 83,* 235-245.

Patterson, M. L. (1978). The role of space in social interaction. In A. W. Siegman & S. Feldstein (Eds.), *Nonverbal behavior and communication* (pp. 265-290). Hillsdale, NJ: Lawrence Erlbaum.

Patterson, M. L. (1982a). Personality and nonverbal involvement: A functional analysis. In W. Ickes & E. S. Knowles (Eds.), *Personality, roles, and social behavior* (pp. 141-164). New York: Springer-Verlag.

Patterson, M. L. (1982b). A sequential functional model of nonverbal exchange. *Psychological Review, 89,* 231-249.

Patterson, M. L. (1983). *Nonverbal behavior: A functional perspective.* New York: Springer-Verlag.

Patterson, M. L., & Holmes, D. S. (1966, August). *Social interaction correlates of the MPI extraversion introversion scale.* Paper presented at the annual meeting of the American Psychological Association, New York.

Pearce W. B., & Brommel, B. J. (1972). Vocalic communication in persuasion. *Quarterly Journal of Speech, 58,* 298-306.

Pedersen, D. M. (1973). Correlates of behavioral personal space. *Psychological Reports, 32,* 828-830.

Peng, Y., Zebrowitz, L. A., & Lee, H. K. (1993). The impact of cultural background and cross-cultural experience on impressions of American and Korean male speakers. *Journal of Cross-Cultural Psychology, 24,* 203-220.

Phillips, G. M. (1968). Reticence: Pathology of normal speakers. *Speech Monographs, 35,* 39-49.

Piliavin, J. A., & Martin, R. R. (1978). The effects of sex composition of groups on style of social interaction. *Sex Roles, 4,* 281-296.

Powers, W. G. (1978). The rhetorical interrogative: Anxiety or control? *Human Communication Research, 4,* 44-47.

Powers, W. G., Jordan, W. J., Gurley, K., & Lindstrom, E. (1986). Attributions toward cognitively complex sources based upon message samples. *Communication Research Reports, 3,* 110-114.

Powesland, P. F., & Giles, H. (1975). Persuasiveness and accent-message incompatibility. *Human Relations, 28,* 85-93.

Pozner, J., & Saltz, E. (1974). Social class, conditional communication, and egocentric speech. *Developmental Psychology, 10,* 764-771.

Przetacznik-Gierowska, M. (1989). Children's communicative skills expressed in story-telling. *Polish Psychological Bulletin, 20,* 103-111.

Putman, G. N., & O'Hern, E. (1955). The status significance of an isolated urban dialect. *Language, 31,* 1-32.

Putnam, W., & Street, R. L., Jr. (1984). The conception and perception of noncontent speech performance: Implications for speech accommodation theory. *International Journal of the Sociology of Language, 46,* 97-114.

Rai, S. N., & Gupta, M. D. (1989). Effects of parental Machiavellian behavior on children. *Psychological Studies, 34,* 175-180.

Ramsay, R. W. (1966). Personality and speech. *Journal of Personality and Social Psychology, 4,* 116-118.

Ramsay, R. W. (1968). Speech patterns and personality. *Language and Speech, 11,* 54-63.

Rand, M., & Levinger, G. (1979). Implicit theories of relationship: An intergenerational study. *Journal of Personality and Social Psychology, 37,* 645-661.

Ray, G. B. (1986). Vocally cued personality prototypes: An implicit personality theory approach. *Communication Monographs, 53,* 266-276.

Reardon, K. K. (1982). Conversational deviance: A structural model. *Human Communication Research, 9,* 59-74.

Repp, B. H. (1977). Dichotic competition of speech sounds: The role of acoustic stimulus structure. *Journal of Experimental Psychology: Perception and Performance, 3,* 37-50.

Richmond, V. P., Davis, L. M., Saylor, K., & McCroskey, J. C. (1984). Power strategies in organizations: Communication techniques and messages. *Human Communication Research, 11,* 85-108.

Rimé, B. (1984). Nonverbal communication: A cognitive-motor theory. In W. Doise & S. Moscovici (Eds.), *Current issues in European psychology.* Cambridge: Cambridge University Press.

Ritter, E. M. (1979). Social perspective-taking ability, cognitive complexity, and listener-adapted communication in early and late adolescence. *Communication Monographs, 46,* 40-51.

Robinson, J., & McArthur, L. Z. (1982). Impact of salient vocal qualities on causal attributions for a speaker's behavior. *Journal of Personality and Social Psychology, 43,* 236-247.

Robinson, L. F., & Reis, H. T. (1989). The effects of interruption, gender, and status on interpersonal perceptions. *Journal of Nonverbal Behavior, 13,* 141-154.

Robinson, W. P. (1979). Speech markers and social class. In K. R. Scherer & H. Giles (Eds.), *Social markers in speech* (pp. 211-249). Cambridge: Cambridge University Press.

Roger, D., & Nesshoever, W. (1987). Individual differences in dyadic conversational strategies: A further study. *British Journal of Social Psychology, 26,* 247-255.

Rogers, W. T., & Jones, S. E. (1975). Effects of dominance tendencies on floor-holding and interruption behavior in dyadic interaction. *Human Communication Research, 1,* 113-122.

Roloff, M. E., & Berger, C. R. (Eds.). (1982). *Social cognition and communication.* Beverly Hills, CA: Sage.

Romaine, S. (1984). *The language of children and adolescents.* Oxford: Basil Blackwell.

Romaine, S., & Reid, E. (1976). Glottal sloppiness? A sociolinguistic view of urban speech in Scotland. *CITE Journal "Teaching English," 9,* 12-16.

Rosenfeld, L. B. (1979). Self-disclosure avoidance: Why I am afraid to tell you who I am. *Communication Monographs, 46,* 63-74.

Roter, D., Lipkin, M., Jr., & Korsgaard, A. (1991). Sex difference in patients' and physicians' communication during primary visits. *Medical Care, 29,* 1083-1093.

Royse, D., & Edwards, T. (1989). Communicating about disability: Attitudes and preferences of persons with physical handicaps. *Rehabilitation Counseling Bulletin, 32,* 203-209.

Rutter, D. R., & Durkin, K. (1987). The development of turn-taking in mother-infant interaction: Longitudinal and cross-sectional studies of vocalizations and gaze. *Development Psychology, 23,* 54-61.

Rutter, D. R., Morley, I. E., & Graham, J. C. (1972). Visual interaction in a group of introverts and extraverts. *Journal of Social Psychology, 2,* 371-384.

Ryan, E. B., & Bulik, C. M. (1982). Evaluations of middle-class and lower-class speakers of standard American and German-accented English. *Journal of Language and Social Psychology, 1,* 51-61.

Ryan, E. B., & Capadano, H. L. (1978). Age perceptions and evaluative reactions toward adult speakers. *Journal of Gerontology, 33,* 98-102.

Ryan, E. B., & Giles, H. (Eds.). (1982). *Attitudes towards language variation.* London: Edward Arnold.

Ryan, E. B., Giles, H., Bartolucci, G., & Henwood, K. (1986). Psycholinguistic and social psychological components of communication by and with the elderly. *Language and Communication, 6,* 1-24.

Ryan, E. B., Giles, H., & Sebastian, R. J. (1982). An integrative perspective for the study of attitudes toward language variation. In E. B. Ryan & H. Giles (Eds.), *Attitudes towards language variation* (pp. 1-19). London: Edward Arnold.

Ryan, E. B., Hewstone, M., & Giles, H. (1984). Language and intergroup attitudes. In J. R. Eiser (Ed.), *Attitudinal judgment* (pp. 135-158). New York: Springer-Verlag.

Ryan, E. B., & Sebastian, R. (1980). The effects of speech style and social class background on social judgments of speakers. *British Journal of Social and Clinical Psychology, 19,* 229-233.

Sabin, E. J., Clemmer, E. J., O'Connell, D. C., & Kowal, S. (1979). A pausological approach to speech development. In A. W. Siegman & S. Feldstein (Eds.), *Of speech and time* (pp. 35-55). Hillsdale, NJ: Lawrence Erlbaum.

Sanders, J. A., & Wiseman, R. L. (1990). The effects of verbal and nonverbal teacher immediacy on perceived cognitive, affective, and behavioral learning in the multicultural classroom. *Communication Education, 39,* 341-353.

Sankoff, G., & Cedergren, H. (1971). Some results of a sociolinguistic study of Montreal French. In R. Darnell (Ed.), *Linguistic diversity in Canadian society* (pp. 61-87). Edmonton, Canada: Linguistic Research.

Schenk-Hamlin, W. J. (1978). The effects of dialectical similarity, stereotyping, and message agreement on interpersonal perception. *Human Communication Research, 5,* 15-26.

Scherer, K. R. (1974). Voice quality analysis of American and German speakers. *Journal of Psycholinguistic Research, 3,* 281-290.

Scherer, K. R. (1979a). Personality markers in speech. In K. R. Scherer & H. Giles (Eds.), *Social markers in speech* (pp. 147-209). Cambridge: Cambridge University Press.

Scherer, K. R. (1979b). Voice and speech correlates of perceived social influence in simulated juries. In H. Giles & R. St. Clair (Eds.), *Language and social psychology* (pp. 88-120). London: Basil Blackwell.

Scherer, K. R., London, H., & Wolf, J. J. (1973). The voice of confidence: Paralinguistic cues and audience evaluation. *Journal of Research in Personality, 7,* 31-44.

Schlenker, B. R. (1980). *Impression management: The self-concept, social identity and interpersonal relations.* Monterey, CA: Brooks/Cole.

Sebastian, R. J., & Ryan, E. B. (1985). Speech cues and social evaluation: Markers of ethnicity, social class, and age. In H. Giles & R. N. St. Clair (Eds.), *Recent advances in language, communication, and social psychology* (pp. 112-143). Hillsdale, NJ: Lawrence Erlbaum.

Seggie, I., Smith, N., & Hodgins, P. (1986). Evaluations of employment suitability based on accent alone: An Australian case study. *Language Sciences, 8,* 129-140.

Semin, G. R., & Fielder, K. (Eds.). (1992). *Language, interaction and social cognition.* Newbury Park, CA: Sage.

Shaffer, D. R., Smith, J. E., & Tomarelli, M. (1982). Self-monitoring as a determinant of self-disclosure reciprocity during the acquaintance process. *Journal of Personality and Social Psychology, 43,* 163-175.

Shimanoff, S. B. (1983). The role of gender in linguistic references to emotive states. *Communication Quarterly, 30,* 174-179.

Shute, H. B. (1987). Vocal pitch in motherese. *Educational Psychology, 7,* 187-205.

Siegman, A. W. (1978). The telltale voice: Nonverbal messages of verbal communication. In A. W. Siegman & S. Feldstein (Eds.), *Nonverbal behavior and communication* (pp. 183-244). Hillsdale, NJ: Lawrence Erlbaum.

Siegman, A. W., & Pope, B. (1965a). Personality variables associated with productivity and verbal fluency in the initial interview. In *Proceedings of the 73rd Annual Convention of the American Psychological Association* (pp. 273-274). Washington, DC: American Psychological Association.

Siegman, A. W., & Pope, B. (1965b). Effects of question specificity and anxiety producing messages on verbal fluency in the initial interview. *Journal of Personality and Social Psychology, 4,* 188-192.

Siegman, A. W., & Reynolds, M. (1982). Interviewee-interviewer nonverbal communications: An interactional approach. In M. Davis (Ed.), *Interaction rhythms: Periodicity in communicative behavior* (pp. 249-276). New York: Human Sciences.

Silverman, E. M., & Zimmer, C. H. (1976). The fluency of women's speech. In B. Dubois & I. Crouch (Eds.), *The sociology of the languages of American women* (pp. 131-136). San Antonio, TX: Trinity University Press.

Simard, L., Taylor, D. M., & Giles, H. (1976). Attribution processes and interpersonal accommodation in a bilingual setting. *Language and Speech, 19,* 374-387.

Singer, M. (1991). Confronting the AIDS epidemic among IV drug users: Does ethnic culture matter? *AIDS Education and Prevention, 3,* 258-283.

Singh, R., & Lele, J. K. (1990). Language, power, and cross-sex communication strategies in Hindi and Indian English revisited. *Language and Society, 19,* 541-546.

Smith, H. (1977). Small group interaction at various ages: Simultaneous talking and interruption of others. *Small Group Behavior, 8,* 65-74.

Smith, M. J., Reinheimer, R. E., & Gabbard-Alley, A. (1981). Crowding, task performance, and communicative interaction in youth and old age. *Human Communication Research, 7,* 259-272.

Smith, P. M. (1979). Sex markers in speech. In K. R. Scherer & H. Giles (Eds.), *Social markers in speech* (pp. 109-146). Cambridge: Cambridge University Press.

Smith, P. M. (1985). *Language, the sexes, and society*. Oxford: Basil Blackwell.

Smith, S. M., & Shaffer, D. R. (1991). Celerity and cajolery: Rapid speech may promote or inhibit persuasion through its impact on message elaboration. *Personality and Social Psychology Bulletin, 17*, 663-669.

Smolensky, M. W., Carmody, M. A., & Halcomb, C. C. (1990). The influence of task type, group structure and extraversion on uninhibited speech in computer-mediated communication. *Computers in Human Behavior, 6*, 261-272.

Snyder, M. (1974). Self-monitoring of expressive behavior. *Journal of Personality and Social Psychology, 30*, 526-537.

Snyder, M. (1979). Self-monitoring processes. In L. Berkowitz (Ed.), *Advances in experimental social psychology* (Vol. 12, pp. 85-128). New York: Academic Press.

Sousa-Poza, J. F., & Rohrberg, R. (1977). Body movement in relation to type of information (person- and nonperson-oriented) and cognitive style (field dependence). *Human Communication Research, 4*, 19-29.

Spencer, L. E. (1988). Speech characteristics of male-to-female transsexuals: A perceptual and acoustic study. *Folia Phoniatrica, 40*, 31-42.

Staley, C. M. (1982). Sex-related differences in the style of children's language. *Journal of Psycholinguistic Research, 11*, 141-158.

Stang, D. J. (1973). Effect of interaction rate on ratings of leadership and liking. *Journal of Personality and Social Psychology, 27*, 405-408.

Stassen, H. H., Bomben, G., & Gunther, E. (1991). Speech characteristics in depression. *Psychopathology, 24*, 88-105.

Steer, A. B. (1974). Sex differences, extraversion, and neuroticism in relation to speech rate during the expression of emotion. *Language and Speech, 17*, 80-86.

Steingart, I., Freedmann, N., Grand, S., & Buchwald, C. (1975). Personality organization and language behavior: The imprint of psychological differentiation on language behavior in varying communication conditions. *Journal of Psycholinguistic Research, 4*, 241-255.

Stewart, M. A., & Ryan, E. B. (1982). Attitudes toward younger and older adult speakers: Effects of varying speech rates. *Journal of Language and Social Psychology, 1*, 91-110.

Stimpson, D. V., Robinson, P., & Gregory, J. (1987). Self-monitoring and competence as determinants of sex differences in social interaction. *Journal of Personality and Social Psychology, 127*, 159-162.

Stipek, D., & Nelson, K. (1980). Communication efficiency in middle- and lower-SES dyads. *Human Communication Research, 6*, 168-177.

Street, R. L., Jr. (1982). Evaluation of noncontent speech accommodation. *Language and Communication, 2*, 13-31.

Street, R. L., Jr. (1983). Noncontent speech convergence and divergence in adult-child interactions. In R. N. Bostrom (Ed.), *Communication yearbook 7* (pp. 369-395). Beverly Hills, CA: Sage.

Street, R. L., Jr. (1984). Speech convergence and speech evaluation in fact-finding interviews. *Human Communication Research, 11*, 139-169.

Street, R. L., Jr. (1991). Information-giving in medical consultations: The influence of patients' communicative styles and personal characteristics. *Social Science and Medicine, 32*, 541-548.

Street, R. L., Jr. (1992). Communicative styles and adaptations in physician-parent consultations. *Social Science and Medicine, 34*, 1155-1163.

Street, R. L., Jr. (1993). Analyzing messages and their outcomes: Questionable assumptions, possible solutions. *Southern Communication Journal, 58*, 85-90.

Street, R. L., Jr., & Brady, R. M. (1982). Speech rate acceptance ranges as a function of evaluative domain, listener speech rate, and communication context. *Communication Monographs, 49*, 290-308.

Street, R. L., Jr., Brady, R. M., & Lee, R. (1984). Evaluative responses to communicators: The effects of speech rate, sex, and interaction context. *Western Journal of Speech Communication, 48*, 14-27.

Street, R. L., Jr., Brady, R. M., & Putnam, W. B. (1983). The influence of speech rate stereotypes and rate similarity on listeners' evaluations of speakers. *Journal of Language and Social Psychology, 2*, 37-56.

Street, R. L., Jr., & Cappella, J. N. (Eds.). (1985). *Sequence and pattern in communicative behavior*. London: Edward Arnold.

Street, R. L., Jr., & Giles, H. (1982). Speech accommodation theory: A social cognitive approach to language and speech behavior. In M. Roloff & C. Berger (Eds.), *Social cognition and communication*. Beverly Hills, CA: Sage.

Street, R. L., Jr., & Hopper, R. (1982). A model of speech style evaluation. In E. B. Ryan & H. Giles (Eds.), *Attitudes towards language variation* (pp. 175-188). London: Edward Arnold.

Street, R. L., Jr., Street, N. J., & Van Kleeck, A. (1983). Speech convergence among talkative and reticent three-year-olds. *Language Sciences, 5,* 79-96.

Strodtbeck, F. L., & Mann, R. D. (1956). Sex role differentiation in jury deliberations. *Sociometry, 19,* 3-11.

Strongman, K., & Woosley, J. (1967). Stereotyped reactions to regional accents. *British Journal of Social and Clinical Psychology, 6,* 154-162.

Stuckenberg, A., & O'Connell, D. G. (1988). The long and short of it: Reports of pause occurrence and duration in speech. *Journal of Psycholinguistic Research, 17,* 18-28.

Suls, J. (1982). *Psychological perspectives on the self.* Hillsdale, NJ: Lawrence Erlbaum.

Sussman, N. M., & Rosenfeld, H. M. (1982). Influence of culture, language, and sex on conversational distance. *Journal of Personality and Social Psychology, 42,* 66-74.

Swacker, M. (1975). The sex of the speaker as a sociolinguistic variable. In B. Thorne & N. Henley (Eds.), *Language and sex: Difference and dominance* (pp. 76-83). Rowley, MA: Newbury House.

Sypher, H. E., Witt, D. E., & Sypher, B. D. (1986). Interpersonal cognitive differentiation measures as predictors of written communication ability. *Communication Monographs, 53,* 376-382.

Tajfel, H. (1981). Social stereotypes and social groups. In J. C. Turner & H. Giles (Eds.), *Intergroup behavior* (pp. 144-167). Chicago: Chicago University Press.

Tajfel, H. (1982). *Social identity and intergroup relations.* Cambridge: Cambridge University Press.

Tardy, C. H., Hosman, L. A., & Bradac, J. J. (1981). Disclosing self to friends and family: A re-examination of initial questions. *Communication Quarterly, 29,* 263-268.

Taylor, D. M., & Clément, R. (1974). Normative reactions to styles of Quebec French. *Anthropological Linguistic, 16,* 212-217.

Tedeschi, J. T. (Ed.). (1972). *Social influence processes.* Chicago: Aldine.

Tedeschi, J. T. (Ed.). (1974). *Perspectives on social power.* Chicago: Aldine.

Tedeschi, J. T. (Ed.). (1981). *Impression management theory and social psychological research.* New York: Academic Press.

Tedeschi, J. T., Lindskold, S., & Rosenfeld, P. (1985). *Introduction to social psychology.* St Paul, MN: West.

Tedeschi, J. T., & Norman, N. (1985). Social power, self-presentation and the self. In B. R. Schlenker (Ed.), *Self and identity* (pp. 293-322). New York: McGraw-Hill.

Tedeschi, J. T., & Reiss, M. (1981a). Identities, the phenomenal self, and laboratory research. In J. T. Tedeschi (Ed.), *Impression management theory and social psychological research* (pp. 3-22). New York: Academic Press.

Tedeschi, J. T., & Reiss, M. (1981b). Verbal tactics of impression management. In C. Antaki (Ed.), *Ordinary language explanations of social behavior* (pp. 271-309). London: Academic Press.

Thakerar, J. N., & Giles, H. (1981). They are—so they speak: Noncontent speech stereotypes. *Language and Communication, 1,* 251-256.

Thakerar, J. N., Giles, H., & Cheshire, J. (1982). Psychological and linguistic parameters of speech accommodation theory. In C. Fraser & K. R. Scherer (Eds.), *Advances in the social psychology of language* (pp. 205-255). Cambridge: Cambridge University Press.

Thompson, T. L. (1981). The development of communication skills in physically handicapped children. *Human Communication Research, 7,* 312-324.

Thompson, T. L. (1982a). "You can't play marbles—you have a wooden hand": Communication with the handicapped. *Communication Quarterly, 30,* 108-115.

Thompson, T. L. (1982b). The development of listener-adapted communication on physically handicapped children: A cross-situational study. *Western Journal of Speech Communication, 46,* 32-44.

Thorne, A. (1987). The press of personality: A study of conversations between introverts and extraverts. *Journal of Personality and Social Psychology, 53,* 718-720.

Ting-Toomey, S. (1986). Conflict styles in black and white subjective cultures. In Y. Y. Kim (Ed.), *Current research in interethnic communication* (pp. 75-89). Newbury Park, CA: Sage.

Tolor, A. (1975). Effects of procedural variations in measuring interpersonal distance by means of representational space. *Psychological Reports, 36,* 475-491.

Tomoeda, C. K., Bayles, K. A., Boone, D. R., & Kaszniak, A. W. (1990). Speech rate and syntactic complexity effects on the auditory comprehension of Alzheimer patients. *Journal of Communication Disorders, 23,* 151-161.

Tracy, K., & Coupland, N. (Eds.). (1991). Multiple goals in discourse [Special double issue]. *Journal of Language and Social Psychology, 9* (1, 2).

Trimboli, F. (1973). Changes in voice characteristics as a function of trait and state personality variables. *Dissertation Abstracts International, 33,* 3965.

Trubisky, P., Ting-Toomey, S., & Lin, S. (1991). The influence of individualism-collectivism and self-monitoring on conflict styles. *International Journal of Intercultural Relations, 15,* 65-84.

Trudgill, P. (1974). *The social differentiation of English in Norwich.* Cambridge: Cambridge University Press.

Tucker, G. R., & Lambert, W. E. (1969). White and Negro listeners' reactions to various American-English dialects. *Social Forces, 47,* 463-458.

Uhlemann, M. R., Lee, D. Y., & Hasse, R. F. (1989). The effects of cognitive complexity and arousal on client perception of counselor nonverbal behavior. *Journal of Clinical Psychology, 45,* 661-665.

Ulasevich, A., Leaton, B., Kramer, D., & Hiecke, A. E. (1991). American and Japanese respondents' reports of pause occurrences and duration. *Language and Communication, 11,* 299-307.

Valentine, T. (1985). Sex, power, and linguistic strategies in the Hindi language. *Studies in the Linguistic Sciences, 15,* 195-211.

Van den Berg, M. E. (1988). Long term accommodation of (ethno)linguistic groups toward a societal language norm. *Language and Communication, 8,* 251-269.

Van Kleeck, A., & Street, R. L., Jr. (1982). Does reticence mean just talking less? Qualitative differences in the language of talkative and reticent preschoolers. *Journal of Psycholinguistic Research, 11,* 609-629.

Virk, J., Sharma, R. C., & Bhan, R. N. (1986). Socio-metric status, language style, and needs in adolescent cliques. *Psycho-Lingua, 16,* 53-60.

Von Raffler-Engel, W., & Buckner, J. (1976). A difference beyond inherent pitch. In B. Dubois & I. Crouch (Eds.), *The sociology of the languages of American women* (pp. 115-118). San Antonio, TX: Trinity University Press.

Waitzkin, H. (1984). Doctor-patient communication: Clinical implications for social scientific research. *JAMA, 252,* 2441-2446.

Watson, O. M., & Graves, T. D. (1966). Quantitative research in proxemic behavior. *American Anthropologist, 68,* 971-985.

Weary, G., & Arkin, R. M. (1981). Attitudinal self-presentation. In J. H. Harvey, M. J. Ickes, & R. Kidd (Eds.), *New directions in attribution theory and research* (Vol. 3). Hillsdale, NJ: Lawrence Erlbaum.

Weaver, J. C., & Anderson, R. J. (1973). Voice and personality interrelationships. *Southern Speech Communication Journal, 38,* 262-278.

Weinstein, M., & Hanson, R. G. (1975). Personality trait correlates of verbal interaction levels in an encounter group context. *Canadian Journal of Behavioral Sciences, 7,* 192-200.

Welkowitz, J., Cariffe, G., & Feldstein, S. (1976). Conversational congruence as a criterion for socialization in children. *Child Development, 47,* 269-272.

White, M. J. (1975). Interpersonal distance as affected by room size, status, and sex. *Journal of Social Psychology, 95,* 241-249.

Woolard, K. (1989). *Double talk: Bilingualism and the politics of ethnicity in Catalonia.* Stanford, CA: Stanford University Press.

Williams, F. (1976). *Exploration of the linguistic attitudes of teachers.* Rowley, MA: Newbury House.

Williams, F., Whitehead, J. L., & Miller, L. (1972). Relations between attitudes and teacher expectancy. *American Educational Research Journal, 9,* 263-277.

Willis, F. N. (1966). Initial speaking distance as a function of the speaker's relationship. *Psychonomic Science, 5,* 221-222.

Willis, F. N., & Hoffman, G. E. (1975). Development of tactile patterns in relation to age, sex, and race. *Developmental Psychology, 11,* 88-96.

Willis, F. N., & Reeves, D. L. (1976). Touch interactions in junior high students in relation to sex and race. *Developmental Psychology, 12,* 91-92.

Wiseman, R. L., Hammer, M. R., & Nishida, H. (1989). Predictors of intercultural communication competence. *International Journal of Intercultural Relations, 13,* 349-370.

Wish, M. (1978). Dimensions of dyadic communication. In S. Weitz (Ed.), *Nonverbal communication* (pp. 371-378). New York: Oxford University Press.

Wolck, W. (1973). Attitudes toward Spanish and Quechua in bilingual Peru. In R. W. Shay & R. W. Fasold (Eds.), *Language attitudes: Current trends and prospects* (pp. 148-173). Washington, DC: Georgetown University Press.

Wood, J. (1966). The influence of sex and knowledge of communication effectiveness on spontaneous speech. *Word, 22,* 112-137.

Woodall, G. W., & Burgoon, J. K. (1983). Talking fast and changing attitudes: A critique and clarification. *Journal of Nonverbal Behavior, 8,* 126-142.

Woolard, K. (1989). *Double talk: Bilingualism and the politics of ethnicity in Catalonia.* Stanford, CA: Stanford University Press.

Worthy, M. A., Gary, I., & Kahn, G. M. (1969). Self-disclosure as an exchange process. *Journal of Personality and Social Psychology, 13,* 59-63.

Wright, F. (1976). The effects of style and sex of consultants and sex of members in self-study groups. *Small Group Behavior, 7,* 433-456.

Yairi, E., & Clifton, N. F., Jr. (1972). Disfluent speech behavior of preschool children, high school seniors, and geriatric persons. *Journal of Speech and Hearing Research, 15,* 714-719.

Zaidel, S., & Mehrabian, A. (1969). The ability to communicate and infer positive and negative attitudes facially and vocally. *Journal of Experimental Research in Personality, 3,* 233-241.

Zimmerman, D. H., & West, C. (1975). Sex roles, interruptions, and silences in conversation. In B. Thorne & N. Henley (Eds.), *Language and sex: Difference and dominance* (pp. 105-129). Rowley, MA: Newbury House.

Zuckerman, M., & Driver, R. E. (1989). What sounds beautiful is good: The vocal attractiveness stereotype. *Journal of Nonverbal Behavior, 13,* 67-82.

Zuckerman, M., Hall, J. A., DeFrank, R. S., & Rosenthal, R. (1977). Encoding and decoding of spontaneous and posed facial expressions. *Journal of Personality and Social Psychology, 34,* 966-977.

Zuckerman, M., Hodgins, H., & Miyake, K. (1990). The vocal attractiveness stereotype: Replication and elaboration. *Journal of Nonverbal Behavior, 14,* 97-112.

5

Situations and Goals as Fundamental Constructs in Interpersonal Communication Research

Lynn Carol Miller

Michael J. Cody

Margaret L. McLaughlin

IN THE LATE 1970s and early 1980s, there was a flurry of research and theory focused on the perception and categorization of situations. Much of this interest was in response to a growing dissatisfaction with oversimplistic and mechanistic models that tried to link personality traits and attitudes to behavior. In personality-social psychology, Mischel (1979, p. 740) argued against models of behavior in which prediction is based on a "few behavioral signs" and called attention to the necessity of studying the reciprocal interaction between person and context in fine-grained detail. Similarly, "interactionists" (Endler, 1982; Endler & Edwards, 1978) advocated that research focus on "modern interactionism," which holds that overt behavior is a function of the continuous feedback between the person and the situation, that the person is an intentional and active agent in the interaction process, that cognitive factors are the essential determinants of behavior, and that the psychological meaning assigned to the situation is a major determinant of behavior. In addition, the rise in attribution theories and cognitive heuristics, and evidence that individuals view the world through cognitive filters, led scholars increasingly to borrow constructs and processes from cognitive psychology in the hope that the integration of cognition, memory, social learning, and person-variables would provide direction in the understanding of naturally occurring behavior (see Taylor, 1981). These trends necessitated the rejection of the view of individuals as organisms that simply (or that only) react to external environmental cues and have raised the status of individuals to that of cognitive information processors, who, in order to act effectively, "must define situations, perceive other people, plan strategically, construct performance patterns, satisfy role demands and enforce them on others, and so on" (Athay & Darley, 1981, p. 282). Over the past decade, there has been an increased focus on goals and strategies, and how a variety of knowledge structures may influence social interaction and communication processes. It has been suggested that such goal-based units may provide a "common language" for thinking about persons, situations, and relationships (Miller & Read, 1987, 1991; Read & Miller, 1989). In the current work, we suggest that such units provide a useful framework for a more dynamic conceptualization of situations.

As communication scholars, our purpose is to advance an ecologically sound understanding and prediction of naturally occurring communicative behavior. To pursue such lofty goals requires an integration of the various ways in which individuals interact with the external environment, how they construe and update the meanings of their own and others' behaviors, and how these may be linked to their attempts to achieve their current and changing goals. Below, after discussing a variety of definitions and taxonomies regarding the concept "situation," we consider a variety of knowledge structures useful for understanding how situations are represented and the links among situation perception factors, goals, and strategies. Then, using connectionist models, we explore the dynamics of situational representation and enactment, considering the role of individual and cultural factors.

Situations: Definitions and Taxonomies of Situations

Definition of "Situation"

Argyle, Furnham, and Graham (1981) describe a situation as "the sum of features of the behavior system, for the duration of a social encounter" (p. 30). Goffman (1961) uses the term *social situation* to "refer to the full spatial environment anywhere within which an entering person becomes a member of the gathering that is (or does then become) present. Situations begin when mutual monitoring occurs and lapse when the next to last person has left" (p. 144). Such definitions place important limitations on how researchers typically have construed and treated "situations" in research. Below, we explicitly reevaluate these assumptions and argue for a more dynamic definition and conceptualization of a "situation."

First, previous definitions of situations assume that a "situation" exists only when *two or more individuals are physically present in a particular setting.* But couldn't a situation "exist" with only one person present; wouldn't a woman facing a storm in her leaking boat be in a "crisis situation"? Or wouldn't businesswomen be in a conflict situation if each of the parties believed that the other was sabotaging her sales efforts—even if these women were not physically in each other's presence.

Second, such definitions *mark situational start and end points in terms of the physical arrival and departure of participants.* But it seems likely that for some communicators situations may begin before the interaction begins and may not be "over" until long after the physical interaction ceases. For example, a communicator may anticipate a relational breakup and attempt to "set the stage" to let the partner down as easily as possible. For the communicator, the situation may start long before an actual "disengagement event" occurs with a series of events set in place by the individual's goals, including plan making, attending to cues as the event unfolds, experiencing emotions, and so forth (Canary & Cody, 1994). The "situation" may continue for hours, days, months, or even years after the two individuals talk and agree to "disengage," as disengagers reflect on the relationship, reexperience emotions, and assess causes for relational decay. During this time, the construction of the "situation" may be altered as the individual reflects back on previous events in order to decide which interpretation or narrative most coherently explains the evidence or fits with one's goals (e.g., to garner social support or to be viewed as "the good guy"; see Harvey, Orbuch, & Weber, 1990; Harvey, Orbuch, Weber, Merbach, & Alt, 1992). In the process, the grieving partner will no doubt think back to many events preceding the disengagement event to rethink and reevaluate the meaning of various situations.

Third, older definitions assumed that "mutual monitoring" is necessary for a "situation" to be perceived. But if we hear on the news that our country is at war and our troops are "under fire," this is highly apt to be an anxiety-provoking situation for many, but with whom are we engaging in "mutual monitoring"? And even when *mutual monitoring* occurs, it *cannot guarantee similar situational constructions* by the participants.

Furthermore, such definitions seem not to fully grapple with several additional issues. First, there is a problem with *meaning and perspective*. Clearly, the meaning of the situation depends upon each individual's perspective, activated cognitions, and knowledge structures. For instance, an employer may perceive that she is being friendly and sociable, and that this is a "social-friendly situation," while various workers perceive the same behaviors as reflecting (a) a good-natured sense of humor, (b) a childish, immature, or insensitive person, or (c) demeaning sexual harassment (see Pryor, 1987; Pryor, LaVite, & Stoller, 1993, for an overview of this area). Furthermore, it may take hours, days, or months to reflect back on previous events in order to decide which interpretation is "best" (or which alternative explanation most coherently explains the evidence).

Second, it is unclear what the most useful level of analysis regarding situations may be. Situations may be the same or similar at a superficial level and quite different at a psychological level: This is perhaps nowhere clearer than in exploring the meaning of varying "situations" across cultures. For example, "bars" may have very different meanings in different cultures; on the other hand, romantic situations (i.e., situations in which one might be more likely to pursue amorous goals) may provide a more useful universal level of abstraction. Although the particulars leading members to conclude that a situation is a "romantic situation" may differ, activating the same abstract concept may be crucial to developing a shared understanding of a psychologically meaningful analogous "situation."

Third, older definitions do not grapple with the issue of change. Psychological "situations" are apt to shift and change during the very course of the interaction— even for the same individual. Situations appear more dynamic than these more static and concrete definitions seem to allow. How can we construe situations that allow us to capture such dynamics? For example, we could be in a "frustrating situation" because the podium, which is needed for a presentation, is unavailable. If one of those present improvises to provide a suitable podium, the situation ceases to be a frustrating one. It may, depending upon the particulars involved, turn into a cooperative and rewarding one, involving mixtures of relief, pride, and liking for various participants. Not only may the psychological "situation" change during the course of the interaction from the vantage point of a particular interactant, but at any point in time different interactants and observers may construe the situation to be quite different. Furthermore, "situations" for communicators may overlap:

Communicators may frequently need to grapple with multiple "situations" and their interfaces concurrently. Only a few interpersonal theories focus on anything remotely related to processes of change in behavior and inferences regarding communicative behaviors over time (e.g., speech accommodation theory—Giles, Coupland, & Coupland, 1991; Giles, Mulac, Bradac, & Johnson, 1987).

Thus we would argue that past definitions of situations were too static and concrete in nature. A situation does not require two individuals; one person would seem to suffice. Temporal start and end points need to be reconsidered; a more flexible time frame for understanding the situation should be considered. Perhaps we should also rethink the necessity of "mutual monitoring" and take into account in any definition of the situation the problem of meaning and perspective as well as the issue of change. Finally, we need to consider whether construing situations at a more abstract psychological level might prove more useful in understanding analogous situations across individuals and across cultures.

What then are the underlying structures that make a situation a situation? How can we study situations more dynamically? We concede that these questions are challenging ones and that we certainly will not be providing easy answers in this chapter. We also concede that the challenge of studying dynamic systems of persons and situations may require substantially more thought, effort, and analyses than the vast majority of studies so far published. Our goal, however, throughout this chapter is to summarize research on the various components that will facilitate a more dynamic assessment of situations, culminating with a modest proposal for how "situations" can be studied as dynamic constructions. First, however, we will review studies that examined how people perceive and categorize situations. Later, we will attempt to suggest how this work may be integrated into a more dynamic framework.

Taxonomies and Dimensional Analyses of Settings and Goals

Situation Perception and Categorization

Pervin (1978, pp. 79-80) has proposed that the "situation," as a source of influence on behavior, can be decomposed into three components: who is involved, where the action takes place, and what activities are involved. Pervin's three-component account of a "situation" provides a convenient point of departure for our review of taxonomic studies: (a) research on the classification of role relationships, that is, the "who" component; (b) studies of the settings of interaction, that is, the "where" component; (c) research on the nature of the situated activity, that is, the "what" component. Finally, we will discuss research on the global dimensions of situation perception, especially on the affective factors of situation perception.

Role relationships. Marwell and Hage (1970) took as their initial goal the elaboration of the underlying dimensions that lead to distinctions among categories of role relationships. They created a stimulus set of role relationships by consulting a dictionary and compiling a list of nouns referring to positions or roles—for example, *priest, son, social worker*. Then they generated a focal counterrole: altar boy, mother, unwed mother, and so on. Marwell and Hage then generated a set of 16 variables by crossing four relational elements (occupants, activities, locations, and occurrences) with four relational quantities (scope, intensity, integration, and independence). The results yielded a three-dimensional factor structure. The factors were labeled intimacy, visibility, and regulation.

Wish, Deutsch, and Kaplan (1976; Wish & Kaplan, 1977) conducted an INDSCAL analysis of similarity ratings of pairs of role relationships (husband-wife, lawyer-client, and so forth) and obtained a four-factor solution whose dimensions were interpreted as (a) competitive and hostile versus cooperative and friendly, (b) equal versus unequal power, (c) intense versus superficial, and (d) social-emotional and informal versus task oriented and formal. Wish et al. reported substantial differences in the person's emphasis with respect to the four dimensions. Subjects who were married, older, and more conservative tended to place greater importance on the first dimension (competitive and hostile versus cooperative and friendly), whereas the younger, unmarried, less conservative individual was apt to place greater weight on the last factor (social-emotional and informal versus task oriented and formal). Wish and Kaplan (1977) were able to replicate these four dimensions, at least in part, in a follow-up study; however, they found that the Wish et al. fourth dimension split into two distinct dimensions: (a) formal and cautious versus informal and open and (b) task oriented versus non-task oriented.

Synthesizing the work on the "who" component leaves us with eight candidate dimensions of role relationships: relational intimacy, visibility, regulation, cooperative-competitive orientation, formal orientation, equality, intensity, and task orientation.

Settings. Several projects have focused on fairly global assessments of settings (Craik, 1970, 1973; Russell & Ward, 1982; Stokols, 1978), but it is uncertain how macro-level assessments of physical settings affect interpersonal communication. For example, Ward's (1977) proposed dimensions of "man-made versus enclosed" and "land versus water" may be of interest to some on the basis of the activities occurring at such sites or in terms of eliciting emotions. However, scholars investigating situational prototypes generate information that may be more useful to interpersonal communication scholars (Cantor, Mischel, & Schwartz, 1982a, 1982b; Tversky & Hemenway, 1983).

Cantor et al. (1982b) assume that an actor's knowledge of a social setting is organized around and stored in long-term memory as a prototype that takes the form of a set of distinctive features usually associated with membership in the setting category. Cantor et al. proposed a four-category taxonomy of settings or situations, each of which is hierarchically structured so that settings of less generality (for example, "being at a bar mitzvah") are nested under a setting or situation of greater generality (such as "being at a religious ceremony"), which is in turn nested under a setting of still greater generality (for example, "being in an ideological situation"). The Cantor et al. taxonomy, which was constructed to be consonant with taxonomies of personality traits, such as Norman's (1963) conscientiousness, extroversion, emotional stability, and culture factors, contained four broad categories: (a) being in an ideological situation, (b) being in a social situation, (c) being in a stressful situation, and (d) being in a cultural situation. Cantor et al. had their subjects list properties characteristic of each of the setting categories, at each of the three levels of generality. One of their findings was that the subject prototypes did not exhibit the perfect nesting of attributes implied by their model. For example, a given trait might be ascribed to both the highest (being in a social situation) and the lowest (being at a cocktail party) levels of a category, but not to the middle level (being at a party).

Tversky and Hemenway (1983) were interested in generating a taxonomy of environmental scenes, which they describe as the "setting or context for objects, the background where objects are figural" (p. 125). Like Cantor et al. (1982b), Tversky and Hemenway adopt a hierarchical approach to the categorization of scenes. Beginning with the superordinate, a priori categories "indoors" and "outdoors," Tversky and Hemenway had individuals generate categories and subcategories of either indoor or outdoor scenes. Selecting the most frequently mentioned scenes, the authors constructed a three-tiered, double-pronged taxonomy as follows: Under category (1), indoor scenes, were nested (a) home ([1] single-family, [2] apartment); (b) school ([1] elementary, [2] high school); (c) store ([1] grocery, [2] department); and (d) restaurant ([1] fast-food, [2] fancy). Under category (2), outdoor scenes, were nested (a) park ([1] city, [2] neighborhood); (b) city ([1] midwestern, [2] industrial); (c) beach ([1] lake, [2] ocean), and (d) mountains ([1] Sierra, [2] Rocky). A second set of 210 individuals supplied setting attributes or features at different levels of generality. Results indicated that 95% of the attributes listed were "parts": For example, parks have parts such as trees, equipment, and so forth. Tversky and Hemenway also found that most of the parts supplied were neither at the superordinate (for example, indoor) or the subordinate (for example, single home) levels but at the intermediate, or what they term the *basic*, level (home, school, store, and so forth). Further, the authors found that the basic level of categorization was preferred in communication tasks such as describing scenes. Tversky and Hemenway concluded that the intermediate or basic level of taxonomic classification corresponds to the level in which scene schemas are likely to be organized and stored in memory.

What is useful about this work is that the knowledge of settings that communicators bring to their everyday interactions appears to be hierarchically structured at different levels of generality but retrieved and put to use primarily at intermediate levels of abstraction. This suggests that, if we are interested in predicting interpersonal behavior from features of settings, the success of our efforts may vary considerably depending upon the level of abstraction of our questioning. Thus, for example, if we want to know how a person will behave at a staff Christmas party, we might have the most success by trying to unearth the rules for appropriate behavior at an office party in general. The second useful idea that we can derive from these cognitive approaches to settings is the notion that setting knowledge is not just knowledge of the "where" component of an action sequence. According to which set of scholars you believe, setting knowledge consists of knowledge of persons and their proper activities in settings or knowledge of settings and their parts. In any event, the two studies make it clear that invoking a setting implies a good deal more than simply supplying a backdrop.

Activities. In an early study on the "activity" component, Krause (1970) distinguished among seven categories of behavior settings or situations: (a) joint working, (b) trading, (c) fighting, (d) sponsored teaching, (e) serving, (f) self-disclosing, and (g) playing. Magnusson (1971) also uncovered some dimensions of situation categorization, labeled as rewarding, negative, passiveness, social interaction, and active (working). These studies indicate that the nature of "activities" is an important determinant of how a situation is perceived (also see Ekehammar, Schalling, & Magnusson, 1975; Magnusson & Ekehammar, 1973; see below for typologies of goals).

Global perceptions of situations. A number of research efforts have been directed to recovering the global structure underlying perceptions of situations. Pervin

(1976) had subjects recall and evaluate everyday situations that they had experienced and regarded as important, and he concluded that people were remarkably consistent in using only the following four dimensions to perceive situations: friendly-unfriendly, tense-calm, dull-interesting, and constrained-free.

Forgas (1976, 1978, 1979, 1982) focused study on what he called "social episodes." Forgas used essentially the same research strategy on a number of different subject populations. In Forgas's (1976) study, housewives sorted events such as "playing with your children" and "having dinner with your family," while undergraduates assessed events relevant to their social environments (i.e., "going to the pictures with some friends" and "having an intimate conversation with your boy/girlfriend"). Two dimensions were recovered from the housewife data set: intimacy and subjective self-confidence (or "knowing/not knowing how to behave"). From the student data, three dimensions were recovered: involvement ("having an intimate conversation with your boy/girlfriend"), pleasantness ("going out for a walk with an acquaintance"), and subjective self-confidence. Forgas found that students had least confidence when in events requiring prolonged interaction with comparative strangers.

In a study of the perception of social episodes by members of two rugby teams, Forgas found that perceptual dimensions were consistent with known characteristics of the teams. For the highly cohesive Team 1, the obtained dimensions were friendliness, intimacy, and activity (Forgas, 1979, p. 189), whereas for the less cohesive Team 2, the primary dimension along which social episodes were perceived was evaluativeness, corroborating the fact that members of the team judged and ranked members on the basis of playing skill (or lack of skill). Forgas (1978) found that faculty/staff members perceive their social environments on the basis of four dimensions: involvement, evaluation (pleasant-unpleasant), anxiety, and social-emotional versus task.

Cody and McLaughlin (1980) had subjects rate scenarios against a set of scales measuring six proposed factors of situation perception: intimacy, dominance, resistance, personal benefits, relational consequences, and rights, the first five of the factors having emerged as significant in multidimensional scaling analyses. Factor analysis of the ratings of situations yielded a six-factor solution: personal benefits, dominance, rights, intimacy, consequences, and resistance. All of the factors but rights had been obtained in the MDS study; but if "rights" are construed to mean legitimacy of request, then perceived "right" to influence others is an important situational feature one must include in a typology of situational features (see below). Cody, Woelfel, and Jordan (1983) used confirmatory factor analysis to test the fit of a seven-factor model of situation perception that included the six factors obtained in Cody and McLaughlin plus a seventh factor, apprehension. The seven-factor (nonorthogonal) model was a good-fitting account of the structure underlying subjects' perceptions of selected hypothetical situations and was superior to alternative models.

Biggers and Masterson (1983) were interested in recovering the broad categories of "emotional responses" that different situations might evoke. A pool of 48 interpersonal situations was created, and subjects rated each of the situations against a set of scales measuring the proposed factors of emotional response: pleasure, arousal, and dominance. Biggers and Masterson found that approach of and avoidance of situations could be accounted for by the three factors, primarily involving perceived pleasure.

A synthesis suggests that there are at least six distinct factors involved in the global perception of situations. These factors have the property that they have been "discovered" by at least two different researchers or research teams. They include (a) intimacy, (b) friendliness, (c) pleasantness, (d) apprehension (obtained in Pervin, 1976, as "tense-calm"; in Forgas, 1976, as "subjective self-confidence"; in Cody et al., 1983, as "situation apprehension"), (e) involvement, and (f) dominance. These six factors taken together should provide a minimally adequate account of the structure of situation perception generally, although for specific situations like persuasive encounters, or relational disengagement, there are probably additional pertinent factors. A recurrent theme in the above analysis of situations, highlighted by Biggers and Masterson (1983), is the importance of emotion in situational analysis. Let us take a more detailed look at the links among situations, emotions, and goals.

Emotions and situations. As suggested above, many—if not most—of the situations we encounter in day-to-day experience may differ in terms of their affective features (e.g., pleasure, apprehension), and certain affective components may be related to approaching or avoiding situations (Biggers & Masterson, 1983). However, research scholars studying emotions have developed a fuller, more exhaustive view of how situations and goals are linked to emotions (see de Rivera, 1977; Frijda, 1987; Lazarus & Smith, 1988; Ortony, Clore, & Collins, 1988; Roseman, 1984; Roseman, Spindel, & Jose, 1990; Scherer, 1984, 1988). Roseman et al. (1990), for example, argue that six basic situational features elicit emotions. First, *situational state* deals with the extent to which outcomes or experiences were consistent with one's goals and reflected what the communicator wanted (versus unexpected, inconsistent, and undesirable outcomes and experiences). Second, *motivational state* deals with the extent to which outcomes or experiences were pleasurable, positive, and beneficial (versus painful, negative, and costly). Third, *probability* deals with the extent to which outcomes or experiences were predictable, certain, and void of doubt (versus unpredictable, uncertain, and doubtful). Fourth, *power* deals with the extent to which the individual felt powerful, strong, and able to cope with the situation (versus feeling powerless, weak, and unable to cope). Fifth, *legitimacy* deals with the levels of rights a person perceives—that what happened was just, that he or she deserved something good (versus an injustice and she or he deserved something bad to happen). Finally, *agency* deals with the extent to which events were caused by circumstances, by other people, or by the communicator. It should be obvious that Roseman's theory uses a number of situational features already described: pleasantness, probability (uncertainty, apprehension), power (or dominant role relationships), rights or legitimacy, and focus of activities/benefits.

Roseman et al. (1990) found that these situational features predictably had an impact on eliciting 16 discrete emotions. For example, positive emotions (joy, relief, hope, affection, and pride) were elicited when situational state was motive consistent, while inconsistent-motive situations resulted in negative emotions (disgust, distress, sadness, fear, frustration, anger, shame, guilt, regret, and unfriendliness). Surprise was the only emotion to be elicited when situational state was either motive consistent or inconsistent. Motivation to attain rewards elicited feelings of joy, while motivation to avoid punishments elicited feelings of relief. Certainty (the probability situational feature) was associated with feelings of joy (and in some situations with feelings of distress and sadness), while uncertainty was associated with relief, hope, and surprise. Subjects who believed they deserved a positive outcome (i.e., their rights were not fulfilled—this is the legitimacy distinction) naturally experienced frustration, anger, and regret (communication scholars also found similar emotions and conflict to follow when partners failed to uphold legitimate rights and obligations; see Canary & Cody, 1994). The agency distinction was related to a plethora of emotions; other people were seen as causes of affection, anger, and unfriendliness, while the self was seen as the causal agent in events eliciting pride, shame, guilt, and regret.

Finally, Roseman (1984) predicted that appraising oneself as strong in the presence of a negative outcome would result in particular emotions (i.e., frustration instead of sadness, distress, or fear; anger, instead of dislike; regret instead of guilt). While this hypothesis was not supported, possessing low power was generally associated with negative feelings. Roseman et al. (1990) argue, however, that assessments of power—as they measured them—may have resulted in assessments based on the outcome itself (e.g., I'm powerless if I couldn't prevent a negative event) rather than assessments of how effectively one might deal with the negative outcome in the future. Thus the role of power in appraisals of emotions in this latter sense is unclear. Nonetheless, there is fairly convincing evidence that a finite number of salient situational features (similar or isomorphic to the ones obtained in situation perception research) are strongly related to emotional states, most of which (e.g., friendliness, anger, affection, guilt) no doubt have pronounced effects on communicative behaviors.

Roseman's task was to ascertain the deep structures and dimensions that lead up to particular emotions. Our task, analogously, may be to ascertain what "deep structures" tend to elicit the inferences that this is an "x" and not a "y" situation. Let us suggest what we might need to know to approach situations in a similar way.

First, for emotions, there is a good vocabulary; we know what emotions (e.g., frustration versus anger) we are trying to understand and differentiate. Are there analogous "psychological situational" terms? Perhaps. In everyday language use, people do refer to particular situations. For example, they might say, "That was a challenging situation," "a frustrating situation," "a stressful situation," "a no-win situation," "a romantic situation," "a cooperative situation," or "a helpful situation." Many emotion terms (e.g., *sadness, disgusting, guilt, anger, fear*) suggest corresponding psychological situations (e.g., sad situation, disgusting situation, guilt-provoking situation, conflict situation, threatening situation). In fact, mapping situations onto Roseman's emotions might be a useful step. For example, threatening situations may map onto fear (uncertain, circumstance caused appraisal involving not achieving what one wants to achieve or not avoiding what one wants to avoid, and feeling that one may be relatively powerless to bring about the goals desired). Challenging situations, on the other hand, may map onto "hope" or "frustration." Challenging situations may result when the individual perceives that he or she may be able to bring to bear resources (e.g., is powerful) to respond effectively to the current circumstances.

Still, many situations may map onto a single "emotion." For example, in Roseman's theory, "liking" or "affection" is a positive emotion, elicited when one achieves that which one wishes to achieve or avoids that which one wishes to avoid and attributes this outcome to another. Situations that may fall within this liking emotion category may include a variety of situations (e.g., helpful situations, friendly situations, romantic situations, endearing situations, cooperative situations, intimate situations, supportive situations, and so forth). This suggests that emotions alone do not provide a complete basis for differentiating situations. To understand situations and differentiate among them seems to require a more complete understanding of persons, relationships, sequences of actions, and settings. This is a tall order indeed! Our task, however, might be easier if there were a common set of units for understanding the interfaces among persons, emotions, settings, relationships, actions, and so forth. Below, we consider how knowledge structures may provide for such a common set of units.

Knowledge Structures and Situations

Miller and Read (1987, 1991; Read & Miller, 1989) have argued for a common set of units—goals, plans, resources, and beliefs—that are useful for understanding persons, situations, relationships, and social interactions and the links among these. In addition, these concepts are useful for understanding other concepts that are important for understanding situations: emotions (Roseman, 1984; Roseman et al., 1990) and differences within and between cultures (D'Andrade & Strauss, 1992; Forgas, 1988).

Goals and Other Knowledge Structures

There is a long tradition in a variety of disciplines and domains suggesting that some knowledge structures—such as goals, plans, resources, and beliefs—might be particularly useful units for understanding persons (Adler, 1964; Allport, 1937; Cantor & Kihlstrom, 1987; Miller & Read, 1987, 1991; Mischel, 1973, 1979; Murray, 1938; Pervin, 1989; Read & Miller, 1989, 1993a, 1993b; Wilensky, 1983), situations and cultures (Argyle et al., 1981; Cody, Canary, & Smith, 1994; Cody & McLaughlin, 1985; D'Andrade & Strauss, 1992; Mischel, 1973, 1979; Pervin, 1989; Read & Miller, 1989), interactions (Dillard, 1990a, 1990b; Miller & Read, 1987, 1991; Read & Miller, 1989; Schank & Abelson, 1977), emotions (Lazarus, 1991; Roseman, 1984; Roseman et al., 1990), and relationships (Miller & Read, 1987; Planalp, 1985). Miller and Read (1987, 1991; Read & Miller, 1989) have argued, as we will see below, that goals (along with plans, resources, and beliefs) are such useful units of analysis because they may underlie so many different but interwoven and related concepts. Below, we provide a bit more detail regarding each of these units and then detail some of the links between situations and goals.

Goals. For our purposes, a goal is, simply, something that an individual wants or desires to attain because it is rewarding in its own right. Goals may be activated and made salient by the situation or the behaviors or appearance of others, or they may be chronically salient for individuals. Some researchers have focused on particular social goals common in relationships involving influence, compliance, or persuasion (Bisanz & Rule, 1990; Cody et al., 1994; Dillard, 1990a, 1990b). Others have focused on the goals specific to particular types of close relationships, such as sexual relationships (De Bro, 1993). Still others have sought to identify those goals that are prominent in interpersonal communication such as to seek pleasure, to show affection, to seek inclusion or attention, to escape, to relax, and to control others or the situation (Rubin, Perse, & Barbato, 1988). A recent hierarchical taxonomy of human goals (Chulef, 1993) suggests that goals tend to cluster into three higher-order clusters: personal, social, and family goals. The personal goal cluster includes goals related to intellectual and spiritual growth, ethics and happiness, enjoyment, and desires to experience life in new and exciting ways. The social cluster includes goals relevant to social interactions (e.g., to be friendly, competitive, cooperative, supportive, or approval seeking). The family goals cluster relates to family, marriage, romance, and sex.

Obviously, multiple goals may be activated at the same time. Exactly how one decides among these goals, or integrates them, is an important area of continuing theoretical and research activity (Berger & Jordon, 1992; Dillard, 1990a, 1990b; Greene & Lindsey, 1989; Miller & Read, 1987, 1991; Miller, Bettencourt, De Bro, & Hoffman, 1993; Wilson, 1990).

Plans and strategies. These are organized sequences of behaviors, often composed of sequences or subplans linked together, that are aimed at achieving one or more goals. Plans may contain considerable detail and can be relatively "automatic" or relatively "unconscious" (Bargh, 1990; Berscheid, 1983; Kellermann, 1992; Mandler, 1975; Miller & Read, 1987). Individuals are apt to have hierarchies of plans and strategies; which one is employed is apt to depend upon a host of factors such as one's perception of the context, the rapidity with which the choice must be made, prior experiences and expectations, and probable success of the strategy for achieving this goal and not adversely affecting other important goals. Although too voluminous a literature to review here (for recent reviews, see Canary & Cody, 1994; Daly & Wiemann, 1994), a number of communication scholars have examined strategies and plans for how to initiate a date (Berger & Bell, 1988), how to acquire resources from intimates (Roloff, Janiszewski, McGrath, Burns, & Manrai, 1988), how to maintain a marriage (Baxter & Dindia, 1990; Canary & Stafford, 1992), how to overcome obstacles to interpersonal compliance (Roloff & Janiszewski, 1989), or how to acquire information about the state of a relationship (Baxter & Wilmot, 1984). Some communication scholars have even argued that "communication, by its very nature, can not *not* be strategic" (Kellermann, 1992, p. 288).

Related to the idea of a plan or strategy is the concept of a script (Schank & Abelson, 1977). A script is a much more specific and stereotyped sequence of actions than a plan or strategy, which is more general and abstract. A variety of social interaction scripts (Pryor & Merluzzi, 1985), relational scripts (Honeycutt, Cantrill, & Greene, 1989), and sexual scripts (Burns, Mohnihan, & Miller, 1993; L. C. Miller et al., 1993) have been examined. Activating one portion of a sexual script, such as leaving with a man from a bar to go to "his place," may activate particular sexual scripts such as "one night stand" or "pickup" scripts (Read & Miller, 1993a). In early work on scripts, Bower, Black, and Turner (1979) discovered that confusion between different portions of medical scripts (e.g., going to see a dentist or doctor) occurred, which suggested that at least portions of scripts (e.g., waiting room scene) were general to all medical—and perhaps professional—scripts, and not specific to a particular medical interaction, while other portions of the scripts were specific to the particular medical interaction (e.g., seeing the drill in the dentist's office and climbing into the dentist's chair; opening one's month and saying "ah" when seeing a tongue depressor). A structure that was more general and flexible than scripts, but not so general and abstract as plans, was needed. To fill this void, Schank (1982) coined the phrase *MOPs*, or memory organizational packets that serve to organize scenes. MOPs have proven to be useful devices for understanding communication partners in social interactions (see Kellermann, 1991).

Beliefs. Which goals and strategies are chosen may also be influenced by one's beliefs about the world. One's beliefs may affect which goals and plans are implemented and what inferences are made about behavior (one's own as well as that of others). End beliefs relate to goals, per se, such as "having people like me is rewarding"; means beliefs, such as "disclosing about myself is a good way to get others to like and pay attention to me," are beliefs about the plans or strategies an individual would adopt to reach his or her goals. Beliefs may involve evaluations about morality and effectiveness of plans, and inferences about the characteristics and likely behavior of others generally (e.g., "People are basically out to get what they can"). Beliefs may also be specific to particular relationships (e.g., "If I tell her this, she'll continue talking to me"). These beliefs in particular relationships may guide future interpretations (Planalp, 1985). Individuals may have beliefs that are fairly idiosyncratic and other beliefs regarding appropriate behavior and how and what one should and shouldn't do that are shared with most members of a given culture or subculture (e.g., rules, norms).

Resources. Most of the time, to enact and carry out plans successfully, resources are needed. Surprisingly little is known about the role and nature of perceived and actual resources in influencing the successful completion and coordination of plans (Miller & Berg, 1984; Wilensky, 1983). Miller and Read (1987; Read & Miller, 1989) argue that resources could be broken down into personal resources that the individual had access to chronically such as cognitive resources, knowledge, specialized talents and abilities, social, expressive, and communicative skills, physical attributes, coping skills, status, possessions, and time; resources afforded by the nature of the situation, including access to others, objects, and experiences; and relational resources such as transactional memories (Wegner, Guiliano, & Hertel, 1985), material resources, affective, physical and psychological resources, and support.

Complex Structures Useful for Understanding Situations

As we argued earlier, goals, plans, resources, and beliefs may be important components of various higher-order structures important for understanding situations. Earlier, in describing work on emotions (Roseman, 1984; Roseman et al., 1990), it was apparent that perceptions regarding whether one's goals were achieved or not played a major role in appraisals of various emotional states in situations. Similarly, others have argued that goals, as well as plans, resources, and beliefs, are useful structures for thinking about traits and relationships. In fact, Miller and Read (1987, 1991; Read & Miller, 1989) have argued that some of these higher-order concepts, such as traits, are summaries of underlying configurations of knowledge structures.

Person structures. Miller and Read (1987; Read & Miller, 1989) have argued that a typical unit in personality—traits—could be usefully construed in terms of chronic configurations of goals, plans, resources, and beliefs. For example, Miller and Read (1987; Read & Miller, 1989) argued that traits such as loneliness and sociability and traits involving "self-presentation" could be thought of as having one or more components in common. For example, sociable and lonely individuals may want to make friends and please others; those interested in self-presentation, in contrast, may want to make a good impression. Sociable and lonely people, however, may differ in their chronic plans, resources, and beliefs—differences that may affect goal achievement over time. Sociable individuals and those chronically concerned with self-presentation—while having very different goals—might have considerable overlap in plans, resources, and beliefs. Support for this conceptualization of traits—especially the centrality of goals in making trait inferences—suggests its viability (Borkenau, 1990; Read, Jones, & Miller, 1990).

In addition, Miller and Read have been attempting to understand the deep structures—such as goals and other knowledge structures—that result in particular inferences about others involving traits and roles, such as whether someone is a "rapist" or a "regular guy" or whether the woman in a "rape trial" is a "slut" or a "diligent mother" and "innocent victim" (Miller & Read, 1991; Read & Miller, 1993a). Such units— goals, plans, resources, and beliefs—we would argue are useful not only for thinking about and making inferences about persons and situations but also useful for understanding and predicting how configurations of these units predict ongoing behavior.

Relationships. Goals, and their relationship to plans, resources, and beliefs, are apt to play a major role in differentiating various relationships from one another. As mentioned earlier, plans, resources, and beliefs may affect the successful completion of one's own goals; they may also affect the successful completion of a relationship partner's goals. And both intrapersonal goals and interpersonal goals may be complementary or they may conflict (for additional detail regarding the nature of these associations, see Miller & Read, 1987; Read & Miller, 1989; Wilensky, 1983). Early work by Abelson (1973) defined a number of *interpersonal themes* in terms of the interrelated plans of two individuals. In that framework, each actor's plan involved subgoals that could be facilitated or inhibited by the other. The interpersonal relations among these goals could be thought of in terms of the *role* of the agent, relative to the other (e.g., as an agent of the other's plan), the approval or disapproval of the other's plan (e.g., *an attitude*), and the resources of the other to facilitate or hinder that goal (e.g., *facilitative ability*). Defining a conceptual space, various interpersonal themes could be defined in terms of these dimensions. For example, betrayal can be viewed in the following way: One actor, having previously agreed to serve as an agent, instead hinders the other's goal, preventing that other from attaining it. Similarly, Miller and Read (1991) have argued that some terms, like *revenge,* have a storylike structure, regarding the relationships among the characters and the goals that were activated and achieved. Thus to say that someone sought revenge means that an actor had reason to think that another did her a wrong (blocked her goals), that she is in a position (e.g., has the resources) to keep the other from reaching his or her goals, and that she has attempted to achieve this outcome on one or more occasions.

There are several points of note here. First, goals, plans, resources, and beliefs of the parties of a relationship may interact to facilitate or hinder each partner's goal achievement. Such interpersonal themes and resultant affective reactions are apt to greatly affect the salience of various features of the situation and the nature of the "situation" that is construed by the interactants and by observers. Second, some personality and relationship terms in our language seem to be summaries that capture the richness of individuals' goals, resources, plans, and beliefs in their relationships with one another.

Understanding Situations

Situations and goals. Our meaning of "situations" is intimately interwoven with various types of "goals." For example, Cody et al. (1994) found that 42 situations commonly studied in "compliance-gaining" work can be more parsimoniously classified into 12 basic types of goals, with each goal defined or characterized in terms of a few salient situational features. For instance, a goal to *initiate a relationship* possesses salient characteristics involving potential long-term relational consequences, high levels of apprehension, high levels of personal benefits, and high levels of intimacy and homophily (similarity). The goal of *giving advice* can be characterized as involving low levels of situation apprehension, low levels of personal benefits (the relational partner is usually the one who benefits), and typically involves a close friend or relative (see Cody et al., 1994; Dillard, 1990a, for a discussion of goals and situational features that can be used to characterize goals).

The particular configuration of goals activated, whether we have achieved them or believe we can achieve them, and the role of others in facilitating or inhibiting goal achievement are apt to play an important role in our constructions that this is an "x" and not a "y" situation. Furthermore, the particular goal structures that are activated for a given individual are apt to play a role in the enactment of his or her behaviors that will in turn define the "situation" in the ongoing social interaction. *Goals* are a more dynamic unit than the larger and more abstract concept "situation." While situational features largely *describe* communicators' perceptions and summarize the anticipated or actual emotions that are elicited (see Cody et al., 1994, and Dillard, 1990a, 1990b, for more specific details on this matter), goals are apt to play a central role not only in defining the "situation" but in directing subsequent communicative behaviors, such as devising plans, implementing plans, and employing multiple tactics over time.

One of the advantages of studying goals deals with the basic fact that there are probably a finite, parsimonious set of goals (perhaps 12 to 30 goals), while there may exist hundreds of situations available for study. In addition, goals, as suggested above, can be construed as a common unit across a number of different domains that are relevant to situational constructions such as emotions, inferences about others' traits and characteristics, inferences about relationships, and so forth. This is crucial because these components are interwoven. A number of projects assessing the nature of goals (Bisanz & Rule, 1990; Cody et al., 1994; Dillard, 1990a, 1990b) indicate that the "who" component strongly affects the "what" or activities component; the goals communicators pursue are strongly interwoven with the relationships of the people involved in the situations. For example, most goals involving *obtaining permission* from others deal with parents and with others in positions of authority, while most *gain assistance* goals involve brothers/sisters or peers (i.e., friends, roommates, dates) (see Cody et al., 1994; Rule & Bisanz, 1987; Rule, Bisanz, & Kohn, 1985). Thus goals also provide a more dynamic approach to the study of communicative behaviors.

Situations as configurations. Others have argued that situations could be thought of not only in terms of goals but also in terms of structures analogous to plans, resources, and beliefs. For example, Argyle et al.'s (1981) analysis of situations argues for the importance of goals whose satisfaction a particular situation affords. In addition, associated with these situations are rules governing appropriate behaviors in these situations and roles people can fill: These make certain plans more salient and restrict others. Situations often afford resources important for successful goal enactment. More recently, others (e.g., Woods, 1993) have argued that the "effective stimuli in a multifaceted situation can be characterized, and the means is a semantic and pragmatic analysis of environment-cognitive agent relationships with respect to the goals/resources of the agent and the demands/constraints in the environment" (p. 231). Similarly, goals, and the plans and strategies necessary to achieve those goals, have been central concepts in understanding social interaction (e.g., Miller, Galanter, & Pribram, 1960; Schank & Abelson, 1977; Wilensky, 1983) and as reviewed earlier—what are apt to be important components of situations—emotions (Roseman, 1984; Roseman et al., 1990), traits (Miller & Read, 1987; Read & Miller, 1989), and relationships (Abelson, 1973; Miller & Read, 1987; Read & Miller, 1989).

What, then, makes a situation a situation? Perhaps it would be useful to rethink dimensions associated with situations in terms of configurations of goals, plans, resources, and beliefs. Whether a situation is positive or negative (pleasurable or not) would seem to greatly depend upon whether we are likely to achieve our goals or not (and whether we in fact succeed or not). Whether others are facilitating or inhibiting our goal achievement should play a major role in construing the situation as friendly or not, or cooperative or competitive. The greater the uncertainty—or the more our actions seem unable to bring about the desired goals or avoid undesired goals—the more anxious we may become. Resources of the individual and whether others can influence the outcome or not (as well as whether individuals have the right to influence and choose to influence others as well as whether the influence is desired or not, one way or two way, able to be resisted or not) are apt to play a major role in defining other important features of the situation (e.g., dominance). We would argue, then, that at any point in time the "situation," from the vantage point of the construer, is defined by the configuration of and relationships among activated evaluations of individuals' goals, whether these goals can (or should) be achieved or not and why or why not (e.g., an assessment of whether that which is needed to achieve these goals is available due to resources in the setting, through others or oneself, and whether others will move to block or facilitate goals—and why), and the current status and likelihood of the achievement of these goals.

Goals, plans, resources, and beliefs are useful concepts not only in thinking about making sense out of others' behaviors—but also in construing situations. They are also useful units for considering—once our goals have been activated by such a construction process—how our goals activate communicative behaviors.

"Situations" as Dynamic Constructions

When we enter into any situation, we are often confronted with a vast array of information about the persons in the context, their roles, the setting itself, and so forth. The work reviewed earlier suggests that different situations may be differentiated in terms of a variety of dimensions. For example, when considering the "who" of the situation, we use dimensions involving relational intimacy, visibility, regulation, the cooperative-competitive dimension, a future orientation, equality, and so forth. In considering global perceptions of situations, concepts such as intimacy, pleasantness, apprehension, involvement, and dominance may be important for differentiating one situation from the next, at least from the vantage point of each of the participants or audience members. And we have argued that many if not all of these dimensions might be rethought in terms of underlying goal structures. By doing so, we would argue, it becomes easier to think about the richness of the process of understanding situations and the dynamics by which our constructions of situations may change. To explore this process and make it more concrete, we rely on the following example of the William Smith Kennedy rape trial taken from Read and Miller (1993a).

> William Kennedy Smith met Patricia Bowman at AuBar, a West Palm Beach night spot. They talked, danced, and then left for the Kennedy family's oceanside compound. What followed, Patricia claimed, was a brutal rape; William claimed it was consensual sex. Was William—as argued by the defense attorney at his rape trial—a gregarious, "regular guy" besieged by a "woman scorned." Or, was he—as the prosecution argued—a "Dr. Jekyll" who turned into a "Mr. Hyde" and attacked an unsuspecting, diligent mother. Throughout the nationally televised trial, viewers' perceptions often shifted as new witnesses and testimony were introduced. (p. 526)

Relying on a model of social explanation (Miller & Read, 1991) that integrates work on a knowledge structure approach to understanding (e.g., Galambos, Abelson, & Black, 1986; Schank & Abelson, 1977; Wilensky, 1983), with Kintsch's (1988) construction-integration model of discourse comprehension and Thagard's (1989, 1992, 1993) model of explanatory coherence, Read and Miller (1993a) argue that individuals "understand" a situation at any point in time in the following way. Throughout the interaction, input (e.g., behavior, speech acts, appearance, events) activates related concepts (e.g., goals, plans, scripts, themes, traits, roles, resource availability) via a spreading activation process (e.g., Collins & Loftus, 1975). Initially, concepts are activated somewhat "promiscuously" (Kintsch, 1988) with little regard to their internal consistency. Thus alternative or contradictory explanations of the same event may be activated at the same time. These concepts are linked into a heterogeneous network. In contrast to Kintsch (1988), others have argued that there is a strong bias for linking concepts that have causal and goal-based relations to each other (Miller & Read, 1991, 1993a; see also Thagard, 1992, 1993). Possible plans may generate expectations and aid in interpreting subsequent input. Throughout, when we identify an action as part of a plan, we search for the goal that it is a part of and assess whether the goal is an end goal or part of a larger plan. If the latter, we try to identify the source of the plan, such as interpersonal roles, personal relationships, or other sources. And we assess whether this developing "model" jibes with other information available regarding the person, relationship, setting, and so forth. At this point the network consists of concepts that are relevant, irrelevant, or even inconsistent with the eventual representation and explanation of the event.

Because a more complete discussion of this process is available elsewhere (Miller & Read, 1991), it is sufficient to note here that concepts may be positively linked (e.g., where the activation of one concept increases the activation of another, such as a goal or causally related concepts), negatively linked (e.g., when two concepts contradict or are inconsistent with one another), or not linked at all. In Figure 5.1, we illustrate part of the Kennedy Smith rape trial. The concept or "node" represented in the upper-left-hand corner is as follows: "She was a caring and concerned single mother." The arrow to the node, "She wanted to get medical advice regarding her daughter," indicates a positive link such that the former explains why she engaged in the later behavior. The concept "she didn't want sex" is negatively associated with "she wanted sex" because these concepts contradict one another; the activation of one concept decreases the activation of another.

In a second step, the explanatory coherence of alternative representations of the network are evaluated. To do this, a parallel constraint satisfaction process

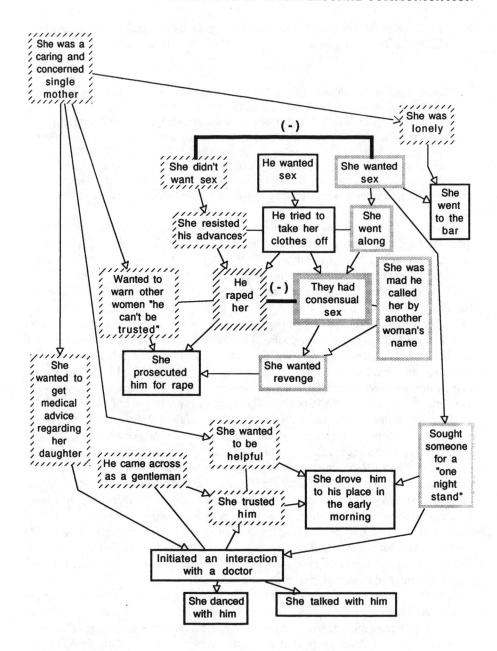

Figure 5.1. Nodes and Links Among Nodes in a Connectionist Network

(Rumelhart & McClelland, 1986), that implements Thagard's (1989) model of explanatory coherence, is applied to the network. These principles include, for example, *breadth*—that is, an explanation that explains more of the facts will be coherent. "William went with his uncle and cousin to the AuBar" and "William danced and talked to strangers" are both behaviors to be explained. The former could be explained by William's being "shy" (e.g., needing other males around to go to a bar); the second behavior could be explained by "being flirtatious."

However, because both behaviors could be explained by being gregarious, this trait receives activation from both behaviors and therefore receives the highest activation of the explanatory hypotheses. This is an example of how the principle of breadth is implemented by summing the activation of all the things that are explained. Other principles are also implemented in the simulation, including *parsimony or simplicity* (i.e., the explanation requiring the fewest assumptions will be more coherent); *being explained* (explanations are more acceptable if they are explained by further explanations); *unexplained data* (the goodness of a concept as an explanation for an individual's behavior should be reduced to the extent that some of the behavior is unexplained); *unification* (a set of explanatory hypotheses are more coherent if they *jointly* explain *all* the evidence rather than requiring unique explanatory hypotheses to explain pieces of evidence); and *analogy* (explanations are more coherent if they are supported by an *analogy* to another system with the same causal structure). In addition, Thagard (1992) argues that the evaluation of explanations is comparative; the coherence of an explanation is a function of the coherence of alternatives. The goodness of a mediocre explanation will decrease when a more coherent alternative explanation is available. This follows because conflicting explanations have inhibitory links to each other. Read and his colleagues (Read & Cesa, 1991; Read & Marcus-Newhall, 1993) have provided experimental evidence for most of these principles in the construction of social explanations.

In Figure 5.1, one set of nodes, marked with solid borders, are those that involve "facts" that are not in contention and that need to be explained in a simplified model of the sexual interaction between William Kennedy Smith and Patricia Bowman. Nodes supporting William Smith raping Patricia Bowman are marked with a diagonal-line border while nodes supporting Smith's not raping her are marked with a dense-dot border. If these were the only nodes activated, the conclusion that they had had consensual sex would be more activated than the conclusion that William had raped Patricia, and much more likely to provide the salient interpretation of the situation.[1] While our conclusion regarding rape may hinge on whether we believe the woman wanted sex or did not, these crucial nodes in the network may receive additional activation from other nodes not directly related to this issue (for example, whether the woman was seeking revenge or not).

This process iteratively converges on a pattern of node activations that is the best "compromise" among the constraints imposed by the positive and negative links among the nodes. The activation of each node is updated in parallel, based on its current activation, the activation of other nodes to which it is linked, and the strength of those links. This updating process continues until the activation of the nodes' asymptotes. Activation of a concept increases with more and stronger excitatory links and decreases with more and stronger inhibitory links. By this process, concepts that are not supported by other concepts "die out" and concepts that are supported are strengthened. Highly activated concepts are the representation of the interaction up to that point. As in most symbolic connectionist systems, the activation of a proposition indicates its degree of acceptability—the degree to which the individual believes that the proposition describes the world.

Miller and Read (1991) argue that the meanings of behaviors in social interactions are dynamic; that is, they are the continuing changing product of mutually influencing elements in the system (Miller et al., 1993). How does this analysis help us to understand "situations"? For any individual, at any point in time, the activated goals, plans, resources, and beliefs will be more or less likely to activate higher-order "situational" structures. (For example, "This is a challenging situation versus a threatening one." "This is a demeaning situation versus this is a 'stand up' no matter what the consequences situation." "This is a rape versus this is consensual sex." "This is a situation involving revenge or a 'wake-up' call to other women regarding sexual predators." And so on.)

Read and Miller (1993a) have argued that many of Patricia's behaviors such as dancing and talking to William in a bar in the early morning and driving home with him may have activated for many jurors the components of a one night stand sexual script (Miller et al., 1993); this would tend to enhance the activation of the consensual sex interpretation. The goals of wanting revenge versus wanting to warn other women are probably crucial ones, influencing rape versus consensual sex activation. Revenge here may be construed as an event script, or general "frame," possessing a number of slots that need to be filled. According to Read and Miller (1993),

> the slots are (1) a behavior, which consisted of bringing charges against William, (2) consequences of the behavior which consist of hurting William's reputation, possibly sending him to jail or hurting him professionally, (3) the roles (Patricia was a "woman scorned"; William was a "regular guy" who acted out a typical sexual script for a "one night stand") and the characteristics of the participants in the act (Patricia was emotionally unstable; because of that it only took being angry with William for using Patricia's wrong name after sex to provoke Patricia to try to hurt William; she was manipulative; William was gregarious, although sleazy), (4) resources involved (she gathered evidence such as goods from the compound to make a case that she was there that night; she provided enough evidence to the prosecution that they pursued the case in court; access to the media could also service to make a case against William), and (5) the goals and intentions of the participants (Patricia's goal was to hurt William to make him pay for having hurt her). To the extent these components are all activated by the set of behaviors and other inferences in the representation (and more so than an alternative representation), that trait, "revengeful" should be most activated as the most coherent explanation. Thus, the defense needed to activate such "slots" in building this case: the prosecution needed to deactivate them and activate an alternative trait frame (e.g., Patricia as a caring woman). (p. 532)

Note here that the trait frame being built may have many of the same slots as a "situation" frame for revenge. In any event, those structures or "nodes" that are most activated will be likely to define "the current situation."

Some situations may have many "slots" in common with one another. Consider threatening and challenging situations. In both, actors want to avoid something or achieve something but there are obstacles (e.g., intrapersonal, interpersonal, circumstantial) in the path of achieving the goal or goals. One is apt to construe a situation as "challenging" when one believes one has a good chance (i.e., because of resources and plans available) of overcoming those obstacles. If we view a situation as "threatening," the expectation for goal achievement is apt to be much lower and the consequences for failing to achieve the goal may be much greater. If differentiating components are more activated than the alternatives, one situational inference will be more activated than another. As the particulars underlying these constructions change, so too will the likely activation of the most activated construction. Situations that differ from one another in terms of one or two underlying components are more likely to be "transformed into" or "confused with" one another than situations differing in terms of many underlying components.

Given a current model of the situation—including a model of the goals of the other—higher-order structures, including our own currently activated goals, and perceptions of possible plans and resources to bring to bear to achieve these goals, may be activated and guide subsequent action. In the section below, we discuss the connection between situation perception and strategy enactment that will influence, in turn, how the next behavioral sequence will be incorporated into our representation of the next "situation."

On the Dynamics of Situations and Behavioral Enactment

Links Among Situation Perception Factors, Goals, and Message Strategies

The knowledge base concerning situations enables the individual to plan behavior that may effectively produce a desired outcome. A number of models of persuasion behaviors have been proposed over the years (Dillard, 1990a, 1990b; Hunter & Boster, 1978, 1979, 1984; Smith, 1984). Clark (1979; Clark & Delia, 1979), for instance, argued that strategies are selected on the basis of the importance of three goals: instrumental, relational, and identity management. A number of studies have shown that people select strategies on the basis of the costs or risks associated with the implementation of the strategies (for example, Cody, McLaughlin, & Schneider, 1981; Fitzpatrick & Winke, 1979; McLaughlin, Cody, & Robey, 1980; Sillars, 1980b). Nearly all of these models assume that there are strategies that are appropriate or normative for certain situations and that situation perception influences both the amount of pressure the agent will employ and the amount of cost associated with strategy selection.

Much of what we currently know about situational influences supports two general, yet parsimonious, propositions. First, a person employs a message strategy based on his or her perceptions of how effective the message will be in influencing the target's attitudes and/or behavior. Underlying this proposition is the assumption that, as individuals experience a sufficient number of situations to learn how to differentiate one situation from another, they also learn what tactics do not work in various situations and which tactics may lead to success. As Schlenker (1980) has noted, people will attempt to be successful by selecting messages that they believe are fitted to the situation as it appears to the audience. Hence, to be forgiven, increased penitence is required as the severity of the offense increases (Darby & Schlenker, 1982; Schlenker & Darby, 1981); to be persuasive, increased supporting evidence is required to overcome resistance; and so forth (for recent reviews of work on accounts and the consequences of accounts, see McLaughlin, Cody, & Read, 1993).

Second, when selecting an effective strategy, a person's choice of strategy is further refined by the desire to maximize his or her expected gains while minimizing costs—the "general hedonic proposition" (Schlenker, 1980, p. 17), or what is referred to as the "minimax principle" in bargaining. Many of the recently proposed models argue that cost or risk is fundamental to understanding why people select the strategies they select and implement. Costs, paralleling Clark and Delia's (1979) goals, can stem from an instrumental nature, a relational loss, or a discrediting of one's image. If a person used coercive power, for example, he or she may not only fail to change behavior but can prompt retaliation by the target, a coalition formed by the target, the target's union, and so forth; aggressive, or hostile, acts are often reciprocated (Cody & Braaten, 1992; Schonbach, 1990; Schonbach & Kleibaumhuter, 1990).

Unfortunately, we know remarkably little about links between situation perception and communicative behaviors for five reasons:

1. Relatively few studies have explored situational influences beyond the paper-pencil surveys that produced so many inconsistent findings in the 1970s and 1980s. Indeed, a number of studies have relied on paper-pencil surveys of "compliance-gaining messages" and have summed all of the "likelihood-of-use" evaluations into a single index of "message strategy selection" and failed to study basic theoretical bases of power (Raven & Kruglanski, 1970) or subtle forms of influence (i.e., Cialdini, 1993). Subsequently, we know that a number of situational features may not be related to increased pressure (Dillard & Burgoon, 1985), but results are far too limiting to warrant any other conclusion.

2. Relatively few studies have precalibrated perceptions of situations from the point of view of the respondents. We cannot assume that respondents share the same perceptions of situations as do experimenters, or that respondents' perceptions are homogeneous, or that the respondents' share identical motivations (see comments above concerning individual differences).

3. Relatively few studies have selected more than one situation to represent a general type of event in a factorial design (see, for instance, the chapter on interpersonal influence in O'Keefe, 1990).

4. Relatively few unflawed studies have explored the impact of more than two or three factors at a time.

5. Little research has truly reflected the interactional nature of communication.

For these reasons, we will very briefly overview some of the results that are available.

Intimacy. An increase in emotional attachment or in knowledge about one's partner affects whether certain strategies are functional or not and generally increases the importance of relational and image goals (see Fitzpatrick & Winke, 1979). Further, it is obvious that referent influence (appeals to love, empathic understanding, and so forth) can rarely be used effectively in less intimate relationships (Raven, Centers, & Rodrigues, 1975; Raven & Kruglanski, 1970). Generally, intimacy is associated with more integrative or "prosocial" tactics than with tactics destructive to the relationship, although research supporting both effects has been reported. "Liking" the target (Michener & Schwertfeger, 1972) and "desired liking from the target" (Clark, 1979) parallel the intimacy variable. Liking results in withdrawal from persuasion, the use of demand creation (requiring "that the influencer increase the target's desire for whatever outcomes the influencer mediates"), and avoidance of both outcome blockage and extension of the power network (Michener & Schwertfeger, 1972, p. 192). Generally, desire for liking results in strategies more conciliatory in nature than destructive (Baxter, 1984; Clark, 1979). More recently, De Bro (1993) has examined how various types of sexual relationships may be differentiated from one another in terms of their underlying goal configurations. For example, individuals in long-term relationships versus those in one night stands are more concerned with having positive feelings and less concerned with having control in the relationship; perhaps, not surprising, they are less likely to use deception as a strategy for negotiating safer sex.

On the other hand, some writers have argued that, when intimacy is significantly associated with prosocial strategies, the size of the effect is small when employing the Marwell and Schmitt (1967) strategies (see Boster & Stiff, 1984; Dillard & Burgoon, 1985). Further, Fitzpatrick and Winke (1979) found that, when engaging in a conflict, married persons employed more emotionally charged tactics than individuals who were exclusively dating.

How do we reconcile these results? As Dillard and Burgoon (1985) suggest, it is very likely that high intimacy not only reflects a particular set of qualities of the relationship (emotional attachment and so on) but also reflects a greater number of shared situations; nonintimates communicate in a limited range of events while intimates experience more situations together as well as a wider range of them. As a consequence, then, because most situations are positive (or else the relationship won't stay intimate for long), there is a significant but weak correlation between intimacy and prosocial strategies. When married couples recall "conflict" events, they recall qualitatively different types of conflicts than do couples who are only dating. Thus intimacy is linked to the functional utility of both empathic understanding/referent power and manipulation tactics but only moderately influences the use of conciliatory tactics. In the latter, the actual use of the tactics depends on whether an intimate other is contrasted with a disliked other (Clark, 1979; Michener & Schwertfeger, 1972) or depends on the operation of other characteristics of the situation (goals and so on), not merely the nature of the relationship. Additionally, Cody et al. (1994) found that goals college students pursued differed substantially from one type of relationship (parent, friend, roommate, and so on) to another (stranger, bureaucrat, and so on).

Dominance. Dominant, higher status communicators have a wider range of potential strategies available for use than do others (Kipnis & Cohen, 1980; Kipnis & Schmidt, 1980, 1983)—including assertiveness, negative administrative sanctions, making demands—as well as political strategies for further increasing power (see Bettinghaus & Cody, 1994, chap. 12; Putnam & Wilson, 1982; Wilkinson & Kipnis, 1978).

Rights to persuade. Dillard and Burgoon (1985) found that rights were significantly related to increased pressure, while Kipnis and Cohen (1980) found that, when assigning work to another (a context in which the agent has high rights), workers used more "assertiveness." McLaughlin et al. (1980), in a study of compliance resisting, found that high rights to resist were associated with justification and nonnegotiation tactics and with less negotiation (especially in nonintimate contexts) than when rights were limited. Legitimacy of request, or rights, plays an important role in organizational settings (see Hirokawa, Mickey, & Miura, 1991; also see Bettinghaus & Cody, 1994, chap. 12).

Personal benefits. The use of pressure in a message has been associated with the level of personal benefit to be derived for the communicator (Clark, 1979). Kipnis and Cohen (1980) found that, when the communicator desired a benefit from a superior, the agent used exchange and ingratiation. When the communicator desired a benefit from a coworker, the agent employed exchange, ingratiation, and also relied on outside agencies to block the actions of the target. When the agent desired to obtain a benefit from a subordinate, the agent used assertiveness and coalitions. Thus, when one seeks personal benefits, there is an increase in distributive tactics (and a decrease in ingratiation) as the status of the communicator (relative to the target) decreases. Dillard and Burgoon (1985) found that self-benefit was associated with pressure (when subjects responded to a hypothetical situation) and both self-benefit and other-benefit were associated (weakly) with increased pressure (when respondents recalled an event they had experienced personally).

Perceived resistance. Sillars (1980a) found that perceived cooperativeness (paralleling the resistance/unfriendly factor) was associated with the use of integrative strategies and the avoidance of both passive-indirect and distributive strategies. Similarly, Kipnis and Cohen (1980) found that, when targets demonstrated resistance by refusing to comply with an agent's first request, communicators were persistent and increased the use of personal negative sanctions (negative relational tactics similar to Sillars's distributive strategies; see also Kipnis & Schmidt, 1980; Wilkinson & Kipnis, 1978).

Relational consequences. Perception of the relational consequences of persuasive attempts has been the topic of a limited amount of research, with few consistent results (Cody et al., 1981; Lustig & King, 1980; McLaughlin et al., 1980; Miller, Boster, Roloff, & Seibold, 1977). Clark (1979; also Dillard & Burgoon, 1985) questioned both the validity of the construct and its function. However, there is no doubt that communication behaviors change and that different tactics are employed when involved with relational growth, relational maintenance, and relational disengagement and termination. Canary and Cody (1994), in fact, devote an entire chapter to each of these types of relational consequences.

Situation apprehension. "Situation apprehension" refers to the extent to which the agent feels he or she will experience tension or nervousness in the situation and no doubt reflects the extent to which the agent feels confident in managing the situation so that a desirable outcome is achieved (Greene & Sparks, 1983). Generally speaking, high situation apprehension (a) should reflect a desire to monitor one's image and (b) should emerge in the individual's social environment as an additional cost of attempting to persuade others. In the former case, then, it is not surprising to find that persons use more face-maintenance tactics and are more likely to attempt exchange arrangements when apprehension is high, and employ greater effort and pressure when situation apprehension is low (Cody et al., 1985).

Goal Activation and Behavioral Enactment

While situations, we would argue, are constructions, as suggested above, at any given time these constructions may play a tremendous role in activating goals. That, in turn, activates plans and strategies for behavioral enactment (Miller & Read, 1991; Miller et al., 1993). Is there a way, analogous to understanding how individuals may represent sequences of actions and situations, to model the process by which goals lead to strategic choices?

As Thagard (1993) argues,

Decision making is inference to the best plan. When people make decisions, they do not simply choose an action to perform, but rather adopt complex plans on the basis of a holistic assessment of various competing actions and goals. Choosing a plan is in part a matter of evaluating goals as well as actions. Choice is made by arriving at a plan or plans that involves actions and goals that are coherent with other actions and goals to which one is committed. (p. 2)

Thagard (1993) argues for a set of principles of "deliberative coherence" governing these relations among goals and actions and that specifies how decisions arise from them; he also implements these principles in a connectionist model. These include the following principles: *symmetry* (if one factor, action or goal x coheres with another y, then y coheres with x); *facilitation* (if some number of actions together facilitate goal x's achievement, those actions will each cohere with G and with one another, but, the more actions required, the lower the coherence among actions); *incompatibility* (when two or more factors cannot both be performed [strongly incoherent] or when they are difficult to achieve together [weakly incoherent]); *goal priority* (some goals are more intrinsically desirable above and beyond reasons of coherence); *judgment* (judgments regarding the acceptability of factual beliefs affect facilitation and competition relations); and *decision* (decisions depend upon the overall coherence of actions and goals). Thagard's model provides a bridge between representation, goal activation, and how enactment of a particular strategy may occur following the perception of a given "situation." The implementation of Thagard's principles (in a program called DECO) also allows for the fact that some goals may be chronically activated and goals can receive more or less activation given the particulars of the "situation." Thus both situational and person structures may make particular knowledge structures more or less salient and together they may affect which structures are more likely to play a guiding role in action—and subsequent representations of the new "situation."

Individual and Cultural Differences That Affect Which Goals Are Activated, Which Situations Are Entered, and How Situations Are Construed

We expect that across individuals and across cultures, communicators—by their very nature—are apt to process information in a similar way, with goal concepts being central to causal analysis and playing a crucial role in behavioral enactment. We, along with some anthropologists (D'Andrade, 1992), further suspect that communicators, across cultures, may grapple with many of the same goals. The differences may be shaped by the relative salience of those goals and how they play out and interact with differing experiences and expectations within cultures (see Spence, 1985). As Spence (1985) pointed out, Bakan (1966) in his book *The Duality of Human Existence* made a similar point when he argued that all human beings are guided by two opposing senses: a sense of self (or agency), involving the desire to assert and protect one's self, and a sense of selflessness (or communion), involving the desire to join with others. Bakan argued that individual and cultural differences emerge from our differential response to the challenges we all face in confronting and balancing these opposing forces. For example, there may be general gender and individual differences in responding to this challenge: Women (and "expressive" individuals; Spence & Helmreich, 1978) may emphasize the latter; men (and "instrumental" individuals; Spence & Helmreich, 1978), the former (Gilligan, 1982; Spence, 1985; Spence & Helmreich, 1978).

Gender

Consistent with such hypothesized gender differences, Cody et al. (1994) found that females, relative to males, (a) pursued more activities with brothers/sisters, roommates, and friends; (b) asked for more assistance from parents, brothers/sisters, and roommates; (c) gave more advice to parents and to brothers/sisters; (d) volunteered for more charity work; (e) performed more work on relationships; and (f) enforced more rules concerning rights and obligations with their roommates. This work suggests that relational maintenance with dating partners, roommates, and friends may be more important for women than it is for men.

Furthermore, to the extent that different goals are chronically more salient for women and men, they may guide how men and women construe the communicative behaviors of others. For example, Miller, Cooke, Tsang, and Morgan (1992) argued that, if concepts related to success-competition are more activated for men, then male perceivers in evaluating male targets engaging in a "masculine" behavior (such as bragging) would provide more polarized evaluations of those men regarding attributions of success. Women, on the other hand, would provide more polarized attributions of women on communal dimensions (e.g., expressive characteristics) in evaluating women who engage in more "feminine" communicative behaviors (e.g., disclosing positively rather than bragging). Their pattern of findings was consistent with such polarization effects. Thus differences in chronically activated goals may affect not only what situations we seek but also the meanings we construe regarding others' behaviors.

Traits

While numerous personality dimensions involve individual differences in underlying goals, historically, traits—and not goals—have been the unit of analysis in personality. Unfortunately, trait measures predict behavior only within a limited range of events. Trait measures predict some behaviors better than others for some people (especially when one averages over a set of events) and predict behavior over time better across "similar situations"; although what constitutes a "similar situation" is unclear (Bem & Allen, 1974; Block, 1971, 1977; Endler, 1982; Endler & Edwards, 1978; Epstein, 1979, 1983; Jaccard & Daly, 1980; Mischel, 1968; Mischel & Peake, 1982a, 1982b). Miller and Read (1987; Read & Miller, 1989) have argued that traits are culturally defined economical labels that help individuals "summarize" and make sense of observed regularities in configurations of commonly occurring goals, plans, resources, and beliefs. In fact, recent work by J. G. Miller (in press) suggests that trait concepts may not be universally useful for understanding persons. Thus understanding the emergent interactions among persons and situations may require a basic unit of analysis that is less static and culture specific than traits.

Still, most personality work has been conducted on traits. Even so, many traditional trait measures seem to address the resolution of a variety of goals and goal system tensions (Thorne & Miller, 1993; also see Markus & Kitayama, 1991, for a discussion of traits that may map onto cross-cultural differences). For example, contemporary personality dimensions such as "self-monitoring" may involve differences in how individuals chronically resolve a tension between wanting to "fit in" and be sensitive to contextual changes compared with wanting to maintain one's own sense of individuality and uniqueness. Such goal differences may affect behavioral choices or how situations are construed. Thus high self-monitoring individuals prefer entering into situations that provide them with clearly defined cues as to how to behave, whereas low self-monitoring individuals prefer entering into situations in which they can exhibit their own underlying predispositions (Snyder, 1979, 1987; Snyder & Cantor, 1980; see also Snyder & Gangestad, 1982; Snyder & Kendzierski, 1982).

Similarly, introversion-extraversion may be a dimension that captures two naturally occurring goal tendencies in individuals: a desire to be with others, on the one hand, and seek social stimulation involving assertiveness, competitiveness, and intimacy (Argyle et al., 1981; Furnham, 1981), versus a desire to be alone and avoid it. In many respects, most of us are in the middle on this dimension and our goals may vacillate over time. Consider our behavior at professional conferences. Initially, we find ourselves happily stimulated by others, then, after a while, feeling overstimulated, we seek the comfort of some less socially stimulating distraction or even the quiet of our hotel room.

And, along similar lines, forms of social anxiety, such as communication apprehension and loneliness, may involve a tension between wanting social attention and acceptance on the one hand and wanting to avoid rejection on the other. Lonely individuals who attribute their loneliness to personal shortcomings are less active in meeting other people (Peplau, Russell, & Heim, 1979). Further, the negative view of self, lack of social skills, and low trust in others appear to place lonely individuals in positions that perpetuate loneliness (Jones, Freeman, & Goswick, 1981; Solano, Batten, & Parish, 1982). Communication apprehension, shyness, and unwillingness to communicate are similarly related to avoidance of selected situations (Burgoon, 1976; McCroskey, 1982; Pilkonis, Heape, & Klein, 1980).

Some individuals (those who have an internal "locus of control") may have more proactive goals and believe that they can achieve those goals by enacting their plans, compared with those who believe that outcomes are dictated by chance (Rotter, 1966). Internal/external control is related to cognitive processes and to behaviors congruent with self-perceptions (Rotter, 1966; Rotter & Mulry, 1965). Internals value positive reinforcement more highly when they think that reinforcement is conditional on their own actions rather than on the basis of luck or chance and thus feel a greater sense of motivation to achieve when they perceive task accomplishment is due to their own efforts. On the other hand, a salient consideration for externals is the basic question of whether or not they are lucky; consequently, they derive little value from being attentive in a "skills-determined" task "since success or failure cannot necessarily be attributed to luck in such a situation" (Brownell, 1982, p. 759). A number of studies have found that internals perform better in a "skills" type of task than in a "chance" type of task, whereas externals perform better in a "chance" task (Baron, Cowan, Ganz, & McDonald, 1974; Baron & Ganz, 1972; Houston, 1972; Kahle, 1980; Lefcourt, 1972; Lefcourt & Wine, 1969; for additional information concerning locus of control, see Canary & Cody, 1994; Canary, Cody, & Marston, 1986; Canary, Cunningham, & Cody, 1988).

Clearly, however, individuals do not enter into new "situations" with simply a set of activated goals. Rather, individuals also enter into situations with preexisting experiences, beliefs and knowledge, resources, emotional tendencies, and so forth, all of which may not only affect what situations we enter but how we color and construe the current situation and make subsequent behavioral choices. While the particular array and configuration of preexisting structures is apt to be unique to each individual, as suggested above, patterns of similarities are apt to result in identifiable personality and gender differences. Such differences are also apt to result in marked cultural differences.

Cultural Differences in Situational Analysis and Goal Enactment

Bakan also argued that cultures would differ in how they responded to communal and agentic challenges. Eastern cultures appear to respond to this challenge by emphasizing communal goals; Western cultures appear to emphasize agentic goals (Bakan, 1966; Hui, 1988; Markus & Kitayama, 1991; J. G. Miller, in press; Triandis, 1989). Such shared understandings of cultural goals, "values, norms, expectations, and emphases" in a culture and language, Forgas (1988) argued, "cannot but shape the way we implicitly represent our social environment" (p. 191). Such structures are apt to play an important role in activating concepts and interpreting behavior during ongoing social interaction (also see Read, 1987, for a detailed discussion of these issues).

Research from a variety of domains (Wierzbicka, 1992) suggests that the way situations and persons are perceived may be dependent on particular language codes that may be tightly tied to the goals and beliefs salient in that code. For example, in Russian literature and speech, the use of the passive is common, with the suggestion that individuals have little control over what happens to them (Wierzbicka, 1992). In contrast, in the United States, the emphasis is on what the individual can do to control his or her own fate or destiny. This contrast between Russians and Americans seems to mirror the locus of control dimension mentioned earlier.

We have suspected for some time that in different cultures, on average, different goals may be more or less salient or activated. For example, Murphy and Murphy (1968), based on Hsu's (1963) comparative analysis of Chinese, Hindu, and American ways of life, argued that, in Chinese society historically, mutual dependence and having and maintaining strong kinship relationships were predominant goals; related to this, they argued that there was a prevailing strong "situational determinism" in which the "self is deeply rooted in close human relations" (p. 175). Such beliefs about self led, in this analysis, to such things as "fear of not living up to ancestral name" (wanting to avoid such an outcome), which results, according to their analysis, in conformity behaviors (e.g., strategies such as making proper funerals for parents, large clan temples and graveyards, and so forth). Increasing status for ambitious individuals was achieved by competitive action to gain resources to "dispense largesse in the kinship group" (p. 175). This contrasts with an American orientation in which the focus is on "self-reliance." In an ideal life, it was argued, the self is viewed as "distinct from all others . . . [with] a lack of permanent human relations . . . [leading to] . . . complete freedom of the individual" (p. 177). In "actual life in society," a focus on self-reliance leads to a focus on contractual relationships with more ambitious individuals trying "to get bigger rewards for lesser efforts, known as success" (p. 177). Fear of inferiority and desire to compete tend to make conformity salient; conformity in U.S. culture takes the form of prejudice against lower groups, keeping up with the Joneses, and so on. What is intriguing in this analysis is that, even when some of the salient structures may be similar (e.g., desire to conform and wanting to be successful, that is, ambitious), the strategies for their achievement and the beliefs relevant to these strategies and how they achieve goals are strikingly different. More recent work suggests that the goals and ways of construing meaning in Eastern cultures (Bond, 1986; J. G. Miller, in press) are more consistent with a communal orientation (Markus & Kitayama, 1991).

The salient goals, plans for achieving those goals, and beliefs of individuals in different cultures may differ along with the meanings of particular behaviors. Still, there may be a core of goals that are universally frequent or common across most cultures and which most humans can relate to, even when their means of achieving those goals may be quite different (D'Andrade, 1992). Understanding cross-cultural "translations" of situations may aid us in finding more universal situational "deep structures."

Analogous situations across cultures. Perhaps one potential way to gain insight into the "deep structure" of situations is to consider situations that—while different in their specific content—share a similar psychological meaning for members of different cultures. How can we explore that? Lee (in press) provides an exciting possibility in her exploration of humor and why jokes often do not "translate" across cultures. She starts with a "Far Side cartoon," labeled "Scientific Meat Market" in which male and female scientists are seen in a bar "sizing up" potential dating partners in terms of their scientific accomplishments, and bragging about their own. While this is funny for Americans, Lee points out that Taiwanese speakers may not "get it."

In the United States, a "bar" is a setting that is apt to activate a host of associations. Among these will be the possibility of a "dating scene" or "pickup place," or a place to meet friends after work and relax, or a place to take a date before dinner. It is clear that "a bar," however, may activate very different structures for Taiwanese. Lee (in press) points out that, in Taiwan, a "bar" is where businessmen (not businesswomen, wives, or potential dates) go to seek pleasure, "wild food," and seal business deals. At a psychological level, a "bar" scene in the United States is not analogous to a "bar" scene in Taiwan. What would be an analogous "situation" for the Taiwanese within their culture? To address this question, one approach is to move beyond the surface similarities of the settings and ask questions about the goals that are served in these different settings. If the goal of going to a bar in the United States is to find a date, what setting in Taiwan would serve that goal? Lee (in press) provides an intriguing analysis of an attempt to explore such analogous situations. She argues that humor is a syllogism (with major and minor premises and a conclusion) except that there are missing pieces. The joke teller gives only the minor premises (e.g., these are scientists, this is a bar) and relies on the audience's concrete knowledge of the culture to fill in missing pieces (e.g., scientists are nerdy; bars are where you meet people to date; you try to impress a potential date with your wealth, status, and good looks) and reach the conclusion, which, with humor, is laughter.

Unfortunately, members of different cultures may not share the major premises and thus may not laugh. For Taiwanese, scientists are esteemed and not nerdy; bars are not where you meet appropriate people to date—thus this is not a joke. What, Lee asks, would make for an analogous situation, that would make this a joke for the Taiwanese? She suggests that the essence of the underlying "situation" is one in which a given culture's "nerds" are trying to initiate a relationship with opposite sex "nerds" (in the typical setting where one finds a date in that culture), by trying to brag about that which the "nerds" would view as "accomplishments" to brag about. Substituting Taiwanese variants that fill these categories for the Taiwanese, she argues, will result in laughter, suggesting that the analogous "situation" has been successfully constructed. Lee's analysis makes several things clear. First, humor and jokes may be an intriguing way to explore cultural differences in understandings of concrete episodes and suggest ways to create analogous situations (that differ in their particulars). Second, this analysis suggests that the same sequence of actions may activate very different higher-order structures. To activate the same higher-order structures may require very different sequences of actions. And, third, for "situations" to be more cross-culturally meaningful, perhaps we should focus on this higher order of abstraction, where similarities in concepts needed to activate analogous situations may be found.

Summary and Directions for Future Research

What are the "fundamental units" for understanding situations? Although the answer to this question is still far from clear, we have argued that in many respects understanding "situations" requires a fundamental understanding of persons, emotions, settings, the meaning of sequences of actions, and relationships. It seems likely that understanding "situations" will require some "common units" for understanding not only situations but persons, relationships, emotions, and sequences of actions. We have argued that such units are apt to include goals, plans and strategies, "norms" (or beliefs), and resources. But how are these units and concepts combined and related to one another, once they are activated? Connectionist modeling approaches from cognitive science provide an intriguing way of thinking about situations in a more dynamic and "gestalt-like" framework. This more dynamic framework allows us to examine not only how communicators make sense and interpret events in ongoing interaction but how, in response to their changing constructions over time, communicators' enact and modify their own behavioral responses.

Connectionist models may also help to capture the interwoven nature of these concepts. The very same underlying structures that play a role in a trait attribution may play a fundamental role in a situational or emotional attribution as well. These underlying concepts and their links are apt to be part of a complex and richly textured web of understandings. If we are forced to make a person or a situation attribution, we may focus our attention on those—most highly activated—concepts that fall into that particular category within this web. Which attributions are made are apt to depend on which are more heavily activated, a function of a variety of factors including individual and cultural differences (J. G. Miller, in press). That is, Western cultures may have a richer vocabulary for trait terms and use these more frequently in making inferences about others (J. G. Miller, in press); Eastern cultures, which emphasize the contextualization of everyday behavior in their explanations of behavior, may have a richer natural language vocabulary for situations. Curiously, our very questions may force sharp boundaries between persons and situations that may not be apparent for the subjects in our research projects, and we may overlook the interconnectedness and fluidity of naturally occurring models of persons and situations in ongoing behavior in social interaction.

Needless to say, however, a great deal of work needs to be done in the years ahead. We shouldn't perceive situations as simply a "laundry list" of important factors; we need to think about how these factors combine to create emergent "wholes." Understanding "situations" will require not only understanding the component parts that make a particular situation "that particular situation" for a particular person in a given point in time, it will require that we understand how events and inferences about a variety of structures create particular situational "gestalts." If the overall situational "gestalt" is a function of what is apt to be activated at any given point in time, then we need to have a better understanding and assessment of "prior knowledge structures" influencing the ongoing construction and how these may be weighted in the ongoing construction process. How do such prior knowledge structures and previous learning experiences play a role in thinking about and making inferences about the current situation? Are some individuals and some members of particular cultures more likely to experience particular classes of situations (e.g., a competitive versus a cooperative situation; a controllable versus a hopeless situation) because different situational subcomponents are chronically salient or available? Do some cultures (e.g., Eastern) have a better natural vocabulary for construing "situations"? Can we come up with a vocabulary for "situations" analogous to our vocabulary for emotions? How do children come to make categorical distinctions between various situations? Do newcomers "learn" such distinctions following a similar developmental trajectory? Or do they learn a type of "reasoning by analogy" in which they transform—in some way—their native understanding of situations to map onto the new culture? Are there—perhaps at a more abstract level—situational "universals"? In addressing such questions, we will need to begin to look at the relative importance of subcomponents in the overall situational construction. For example, which subcomponents are more central to a particular overall situational categorization, and more apt—by their change—to affect a change in the overall situational classification? How do varying and shared perceptions of situations by different interactants affect the stability or volatility of the current situation? Do people move to a "common" interpretation of the situation under some conditions and not others? These are intriguing, dynamic questions that await the energy and imagination of future researchers.

Note

1. There are several versions of the Echo program. Here we employ the Echo2 version that assumes not only explicit contradictions (specified by the [(-)] bold lines on the diagram) but also implicit contradictions. For example, the nodes, "She wanted to be helpful," and "She trusted him," are treated as cohypotheses (indicated by the solid line between them) in explaining the node, "She drove him to his place in the early morning"; these cohypotheses are part of the prosecution's argument. Another node, "Sought someone for 'a one night stand' " (part of the defense's argument) also explains, "She drove him to his place in the early morning." These explanations (one consistent with the defense's story, one consistent with the prosecution's story) are treated in Echo2 as implicitly contradictory; thus, in Echo2, negative activation is sent between these contradictory links. Echo1 does not make these assumptions, and the difference, in this case, is crucial: Echo1 results in the more heavily activated explanation being the node, "He raped her," rather than the node, "They had consensual sex."

References

Abelson, R. P. (1973). The structure of belief systems. In R. C. Schank & K. M. Colby (Eds.), *Computer models of thought and language* (pp. 287-340). San Francisco: Freeman.

Adler, A. (1964). Individual psychology, its assumptions and its results. In H. M. Ruitenbeek (Ed.), *Varieties of personality theory* (pp. 65-79). New York: E. P. Dutton.

Allport, G. W. (1937). *Personality: A psychological interpretation.* New York: Holt.

Argyle, M., Furnham, A., & Graham, J. A. (1981). *Social situations.* Cambridge, MA: Cambridge University Press.

Athay, M., & Darley, J. M. (1981). Toward an interaction-centered theory of personality. In N. Cantor & J. Kihlstrom (Eds.), *Personality, cognition and social interaction* (pp. 281-308). Hillsdale, NJ: Lawrence Erlbaum.

Bakan, D. (1966). *The duality of human existence.* Chicago: Rand McNally.

Bargh, J. A. (1990). Auto-motives: Preconscious determinants of social interaction. In E. T. Higgins & P. M. Sorrentino (Eds.), *Handbook of motivation and cognition: Foundations of social behavior* (Vol. 2, pp. 93-130). New York: Guilford.

Baron, R. M., Cowan, G., Ganz, R. L., & McDonald, M. (1974). Interaction of locus of control and type of performance feedback: Considerations of external validity. *Journal of Personality and Social Psychology, 23,* 285-292.

Baron, R. M., & Ganz, R. L. (1972). Effects of locus of control and type of feedback on the task performance of lower-class black children. *Journal of Personality and Social Psychology, 21,* 124-130.

Baxter, L. A. (1984). An investigation of compliance-gaining as politeness. *Human Communication Research, 10,* 427-456.

Baxter, L. A., & Dindia, K. (1990). Marital partners' perceptions of marital maintenance strategies. *Journal of Social and Personal Relationships, 7,* 187-208.

Baxter, L. A., & Wilmot, W. W. (1984). "Secret tests": Social strategies for acquiring information about the state of the relationship. *Human Communication Research, 11,* 171-201.

Bem, D. J., & Allen, A. (1974). On predicting some of the people some of the time: The search for cross-situational consistencies in behavior. *Psychological Review, 81,* 506-520.

Berger, C. R., & Bell, R. A. (1988). Plans and the initiation of social relationships. *Human Communication Research, 15,* 217-235.

Berger, C. R., & Jordon, J. (1992). Planning sources, planning difficulty and verbal fluency. *Communication Monographs, 59,* 130-149.

Berscheid, E. (1983). Emotion. In H. H. Kelley et al. (Eds.), *Close relationships* (pp. 110-168). New York: Freeman.

Bettinghaus, E. P., & Cody, M. J. (1994). *Persuasive communication* (5th ed.). Fort Worth, TX: Harcourt Brace Jovanovich.

Biggers, T., & Masterson, J. T. (1983). *Emotion-eliciting qualities of interpersonal situations as the basis for a typology.* Unpublished manuscript, University of Miami.

Bisanz, G. L., & Rule, B. G. (1990). Children's and adult's comprehension of narratives about persuasion. In M. J. Cody & M. L. McLaughlin (Eds.), *The psychology of tactical communication* (pp. 48-69). Clevedon, England: Multilingual Matters.

Block, J. (1971). *Lives through time.* Berkeley, CA: Bancroft.

Block, J. (1977). Advancing the psychology of personality: Paradigmatic shift or improving the quality of research. In D. Magnusson & N. S. Endler (Eds.), *Personality at the crossroads: Current issues in interactional psychology* (pp. 37-63). Hillsdale, NJ: Lawrence Erlbaum.

Bond, M. H. (1986). *The psychology of the Chinese people.* New York: Oxford University Press.

Borkenau, P. (1990). Traits as ideal-based and goal-derived social categories. *Journal of Personality and Social Psychology, 58,* 381-408.

Boster, F. J., & Stiff, J. B. (1984). Compliance-gaining message selection behavior. *Human Communication Research, 10,* 539-556.

Bower, G. H., Black, J. B., & Turner, T. J. (1979). Scripts in memory for text. *Cognitive Psychology, 11,* 177-220.

Brownell, P. (1982). The effects of personality-situation congruence in a managerial context: Locus of control and budgetary participation. *Journal of Personality and Social Psychology, 42,* 753-763.

Burgoon, J. K. (1976). The unwillingness-to-communicate scale: Development and validation. *Communication Monographs, 43,* 60-69.

Burns, D. M., & Miller, L. C. (in press). Negotiating safer sex: The dynamics of African-American relationships. In P. J. Kalbfleisch & M. J. Cody (Eds.), *Gender, power, and communication in human relationships.* Hillsdale, NJ: Lawrence Erlbaum.

Burns, D., Monihan, J., & Miller, L. C. (1993). *Scripts in different types of sexual relationships for men and women.* Unpublished manuscript, University of Southern California, Los Angeles.

Canary, D. J., & Cody, M. J. (1994). *Interpersonal communication: A goal-based approach.* New York: St. Martin's Press.

Canary, D. J., Cody, M. J., & Marston, P. J. (1986). Goal types, compliance-gaining and locus of control. *Journal of Language and Social Psychology, 5,* 249-303.

Canary, D. J., Cunningham, E. M., & Cody, M. J. (1988). Goal types, gender, and locus of control in managing interpersonal conflict. *Communication Research, 15,* 426-446.

Canary, D. J., & Stafford, L. (1992). Relational maintenance strategies and equity in marriage. *Communication Monographs, 59,* 243-268.

Cantor, N., & Kihlstrom, J. K. (1987). *Personality and social intelligence.* Englewood Cliffs, NJ: Prentice-Hall.

Cantor, N., Mischel, W., & Schwartz, J. C. (1982a). Social knowledge: Structure, content, use and abuse. In A. H. Hastorf & A. M. Isen (Eds.), *Cognitive social psychology* (pp. 33-72). New York: Elsevier/North-Holland.

Cantor, N., Mischel, W., & Schwartz, J. (1982b). A prototype analysis of psychological situations. *Cognitive Psychology, 14,* 45-77.

Chulef, A. (1993). *Toward a hierarchical taxonomy of human goals.* Unpublished doctoral dissertation, University of Southern California, Los Angeles.

Cialdini, R. B. (1993). *Influence: Science and practice* (3rd ed.). New York: HarperCollins.

Clark, R. A. (1979). The impact on selection of persuasive strategies of self-interest and desired liking. *Communication Monographs, 46,* 257-273.

Clark, R. A., & Delia, J. G. (1979). Topoi and rhetorical competence. *Quarterly Journal of Speech, 65,* 187-206.

Cody, M. J., & Braaten, D. O. (1992). The social-interactive aspects of account-giving. In M. L. McLaughlin, M. J. Cody, & S. Read (Eds.), *Explaining the self to others* (pp. 225-244). Hillsdale, NJ: Lawrence Erlbaum.

Cody, M. J., Canary, D. J., & Smith, S. W. (1994). Compliance-gaining goals: An inductive analysis of actor's goal types, strategies, and successes. In J. A. Daley & J. Wiemann (Eds.), *Strategic interpersonal commununciation* (pp. 33-90). Hillsdale, NJ: Lawrence Erlbaum.

Cody, M. J., Greene, J. O., Marston, P., Baaske, E., O'Hair, H. D., & Schneider, M. J. (1985). Situation-perception and the selection of message strategies. In M. L. McLaughlin (Ed.), *Communication yearbook 9* (pp. 390-420). Beverly Hills, CA: Sage.

Cody, M. J., & McLaughlin, M. L. (1980). Perceptions of compliance-gaining situations: A dimensional analysis. *Communication Monographs, 47,* 132-148.

Cody, M. J., & McLaughlin, M. L. (1985). Models for the sequential construction of accounting episodes. In R. Street & J. Cappella (Eds.), *The sequential nature of social interaction: A functional approach* (pp. 50-69). London: Edward Arnold.

Cody, M. J., McLaughlin, M. L., & Schneider, M. J. (1981). The impact of intimacy and relational consequences on the selection of interpersonal persuasion strategies: A reanalysis. *Communication Quarterly, 29,* 91-106.

Cody, M. J., Woelfel, M. L., & Jordan, W. J. (1983). Dimensions of compliance-gaining situations. *Human Communication Research, 9,* 99-113.

Collins, A. M., & Loftus, E. F. (1975). A spreading activation theory of semantic processing. *Psychological Review, 82,* 407-428.

Craik, K. H. (1970). Environmental psychology. In K. H. Craik, B. Kleinmutz, R. L. Rosnow, R. Rosenthal, J. A. Cheyne, & R. H. Walters (Eds.), *New directions in psychology* (Vol. 4, pp. 1-22). New York: Holt, Rinehart & Winston.

Craik, K. H. (1973). Environmental psychology. *Annual Review of Psychology, 24,* 403-421.

Daly, J., & Wiemann, J. (1994). *Strategic interpersonal communication.* Hillsdale, NJ: Lawrence Erlbaum.

D'Andrade, R. G. (1992). Schemas and motivation. In R. D'Andrade & C. Strauss (Eds.), *Human motives and cultural models.* Cambridge: Cambridge University Press.

D'Andrade, R. G., & Strauss, C. (Eds.). (1992). *Human motives and cultural models.* Cambridge: Cambridge University Press.

Darby, B. W., & Schlenker, B. R. (1982). Children's reactions to apologies. *Journal of Personality and Social Psychology, 43,* 742-753.

De Bro, S. C. (1993). *Men's and women's dating goals in different types of sexual relationships as predictors of condom influence strategies.* Unpublished doctoral dissertation, University of Southern California, Los Angeles, Psychology Department.

de Rivera, J. (1977). *A structural theory of the emotions.* New York: International Universities Press.

Dillard, J. P. (1990a). The nature and substance of goals in tactical communication. In M. J. Cody & M. L. McLaughlin (Eds.), *The psychology of tactical communication* (pp. 70-90). Clevedon, England: Multilingual Matters.

Dillard, J. P. (Ed.). (1990b). *Seeking compliance.* Scottsdale, AZ: Gorsuch Scarisbrick.

Dillard, J. P., & Burgoon, M. (1985). Situational influences on the selection of compliance-gaining messages: Two tests of the predictive utility of the Cody-McLaughlin typology. *Communication Monographs, 52,* 289-304.

Ekehammar, B., Schalling, D., & Magnusson, D. (1975). Dimensions of stressful situations: A comparison between response analytic and stimulus analytic approaches. *Multivariate Behavioral Research, 10,* 155-164.

Endler, N. S. (1982). Interactionism comes of age. In M. P. Zanna, E. T. Higgins, & C. P. Herman (Eds.), *Consistency in social behavior: The Ontario Symposium* (Vol. 2, pp. 209-250). Hillsdale, NJ: Lawrence Erlbaum.

Endler, N. S., & Edwards, J. (1978). Person by treatment interactions in personality research. In L. A. Pervin & M. Lewis (Eds.), *Perspectives in interactional psychology* (pp. 141-169). New York: Plenum.

Epstein, S. (1979). The stability of behavior. I. On predicting most of the people much of the time. *Journal of Personality and Social Psychology, 39,* 1097-1126.

Epstein, S. (1983). Aggregation and beyond: Some basic issues on the prediction of behavior. *Journal of Personality, 51,* 310-392.

Fitzpatrick, M. A., & Winke, J. (1979). You always hurt the one you love: Strategies and tactics in interpersonal conflict. *Communication Quarterly, 27,* 3-11.

Forgas, J. P. (1976). The perception of social episodes: Categorical and dimensional representations of two different social milieus. *Journal of Personality and Social Psychology, 34,* 199-209.

Forgas, J. P. (1978). Social episodes and social structure in an academic setting: The social environment of an intact group. *Journal of Experimental Social Psychology, 14,* 434-448.

Forgas, J. P. (1979). *Social episodes: The study of interaction routines.* London: Academic Press.

Forgas, J. P. (1982). Episode cognition: Internal representations of interaction routines. In L. Berkowitz (Ed.), *Advances in experimental social psychology* (Vol. 15, pp. 59-101). New York: Academic Press.

Forgas, J. P. (1988). Episode representations in intercultural communication. In Y. Y. Kim & W. B. Gudykunst (Eds.), *Theories in intercultural communication* (pp. 186-212). Newbury Park, CA: Sage.

Frijda, N. H. (1987). Emotion, cognitive structure, and action tendency. *Cognition and Emotion, 1,* 115-143.

Furnham, A. (1981). Personality and activity preferences. *British Journal of Social and Clinical Psychology, 20,* 57-68.

Galambos, J. A., Abelson, R. P., & Black, J. B. (1986). *Knowledge structures.* Hillsdale, NJ: Lawrence Erlbaum.

Giles, H., Coupland, J., & Coupland, N. (1991). *Contexts of accommodation.* Cambridge: Cambridge University Press.

Giles, H., Mulac, A., Bradac, J. J., & Johnson, P. (1987). Speech accommodation theory: The first decade and beyond. In M. L. McLaughlin (Ed.), *Communication yearbook 10* (pp. 13-48). Newbury Park, CA: Sage.

Gilligan, C. (1982). *In a different voice: Psychological theory and women's development.* Cambridge, MA: Harvard University Press.

Goffman, E. (1961). *Encounters.* Indianapolis: Bobbs-Merrill.

Greene, J. O., & Lindsey, A. E. (1989). Encoding processes in the production of multiple-goal messages. *Human Communication Research, 16,* 120-140.

Greene, J. 0., & Sparks, G. G. (1983). The role of outcome expectations in the experience of a state of communication apprehension. *Communication Quarterly, 31,* 212-219.

Harvey, J. H., Orbuch, T. L., & Weber, A. L. (1990). A social psychological model of account-making in response to severe stress. *Journal of Language and Social Psychology, 9,* 191-207.

Harvey, J. H., Orbuch, T. L., Weber, A. L., Merbach, N., & Alt, R. (1992). House of pain and hope: Accounts of loss. *Death Studies, 16,* 99-124.

Hirokawa, R. Y., Mickey, J., & Miura, S. (1991). Effects of request legitimacy on the compliance-gaining tactics of male and female managers. *Communication Monographs, 58,* 421-436.

Honeycutt, J. M., Cantrill, J. G., & Greene, R. W. (1989). Memory structures for relationship escalation: A cognitive test of the sequencing of relational actions and stages. *Human Communication Research, 16,* 62-90.

Houston, B. K. (1972). Control over stress, locus of control and response to stress. *Journal of Personality and Social Psychology, 21,* 249-255.

Hsu, F. (1963). *Clan, caste, and club: A comparative study of Chinese, Hindu, and American ways of life.* Princeton, NJ: Van Nostrand.

Hui, C. H. (1988). Measurement of individualism-collectivism. *Journal of Research in Personality, 22,* 17-36.

Hunter, J., & Boster, F. J. (1978, November). *An empathy model of compliance-gaining message selection.* Paper presented at the annual meeting of the Speech Communication Association, Minneapolis, MN.

Hunter, J., & Boster, F. J. (1979, November). *Situational differences in the selection of compliance-gaining messages.* Paper presented at the annual meeting of the Speech Communication Association, San Antonio, TX.

Hunter, J., & Boster, F. J. (1984). *Message content and situational differences as determinants of compliance-gaining message selection.* Unpublished manuscript, Michigan State University.

Jaccard, J., & Daly, J. A. (1980). Personality traits and multiple-act criteria. *Human Communication Research, 6,* 367-377.

Jones, W. H., Freeman, J. E., & Goswick, R. A. (1981). The persistence of loneliness: Self and other determinants. *Journal of Personality, 49,* 27-48.

Kahle, L. R. (1980). Stimulus condition self-selection by males in the interaction of locus of control and skill-chance situations. *Journal of Personality and Social Psychology, 38,* 50-56.

Kellermann, K. (1991). The conversation MOP II: Progression through scenes in discourse. *Human Communication Research, 17,* 385-414.

Kellermann, K. (1992). Communication: Inherently strategic and primarily automatic. *Communication Monographs, 59,* 288-300.

Kintsch, W. (1988). The role of knowledge in discourse comprehension: A construction-integration model. *Pyschological Review, 95,* 163-182.

Kipnis, D., & Cohen, E. S. (1980, April). *Power tactics and affection.* Paper presented at the annual meeting of the Eastern Psychological Association, Philadelphia.

Kipnis, D., & Schmidt, S. M. (1980). Intraorganizational influence tactics: Explorations in getting one's way. *Journal of Applied Psychology, 65,* 440-452.

Kipnis, D., & Schmidt, S. M. (1983). An influence perspective on bargaining within organizations. In M. H. Bazerman & R. J. Lewicki (Eds.), *Bargaining inside organizations* (pp. 303-319). Beverly Hills, CA: Sage.

Krause, M. (1970). Use of social situations for research purposes. *American Psychologist, 25,* 748-753.

Lazarus, R. S. (1991). *Emotion and adaptation.* New York: Oxford University Press.

Lazarus, R. S., & Smith, C. A. (1988). Knowledge and appraisal in the cognition-emotion relationship. *Cognition and Emotion, 2,* 281-300.

Lee, W. S. (in press). Communication about humor as procedural competence in intercultural encounters. In L. A. Samovar & R. E. Porter (Eds.), *Intercultural communication: A reader* (7th ed.). Belmont, CA: Wadsworth.

Lefcourt, H. M. (1972). Recent developments in the study of locus of control. In B. A. Maher (Ed.), *Progress in experimental personality research* (pp. 1-41). New York: Academic Press.

Lefcourt, H. M., & Wine, J. (1969). Internal versus external control of reinforcement and the deployment of attention in experimental situations. *Canadian Journal of Behavioral Science, 1,* 167-181.

Lustig, M. W., & King, S. W. (1980). The effect of communication apprehension and situation on communication strategy choices. *Human Communication Research, 7,* 74-82.

Magnusson, D. (1971). An analysis of situational dimensions. *Perceptual and Motor Skills, 32,* 851-867.

Magnusson, D., & Ekehammar, B. (1973). An analysis of situational dimensions: A replication. *Multivariate Behavioral Research, 8,* 331-339.

Mandler, G. (1975). *Mind and emotion.* New York: Wiley.

Markus, H. R., & Kitayama, S. (1991). Culture and the self: Implications for cognition, emotion, and motivation. *Psychological Review, 98,* 224-253.

Marwell, G., & Hage, J. (1970). The organization of role-relationships: A systematic description. *American Sociological Review, 35,* 884-900.

Marwell, G., & Schmitt, D. R. (1967). Dimensions of compliance-gaining behavior: An empirical analysis. *Sociometry, 30,* 350-364.

McCroskey, J. C. (1982). Oral communication apprehension: A reconceptualization. In M. Burgoon (Ed.), *Communication yearbook 6* (pp. 136-170). Beverly Hills, CA: Sage.

McLaughlin, M. L., Cody, M. J., & Read, S. J. (1992). (Eds.). *Explaining one's self to others.* Hillsdale, NJ: Lawrence Erlbaum.

McLaughlin, M. L., Cody, M. J., & Robey, C. S. (1980). Situational influences on the selection of strategies to resist compliance-gaining attempts. *Human Communication Research, 7,* 14-36.

Michener, H. A., & Schwertfeger, M. (1972). Liking as a determinant of power tactic preference. *Sociometry, 35,* 190-202.

Miller, G. A., Galanter, E., & Pribram, K. H. (1960). *Plans and the structure of behavior.* New York: Holt, Rinehart & Winston.

Miller, G. R., Boster, F., Roloff, M. E., & Seibold, D. R. (1977). Compliance-gaining message strategies: A typology and some findings concerning effects of situational differences. *Communication Monographs, 44,* 37-51.

Miller, J. G. (in press). Taking culture into account in social cognitive development. In G. Misra (Ed.), *Socialization and social development in India.* Newbury Park, CA: Sage.

Miller, L. C., & Berg, J. H. (1984). Selectivity and urgency in interpersonal exchange. In V. Derlega (Ed.), *Communication, intimacy, and close relationships.* New York: Academic Press.

Miller, L. C., Bettencourt, A., De Bro, S., & Hoffman, V. (1993). Negotiating safer sex: Interpersonal dynamics. In J. Pryor & G. Reeder (Eds.), *The social psychology of HIV infection.* Hillsdale, NJ: Lawrence Erlbaum.

Miller, L. C., Cooke, L. L., Tsang, J., & Morgan, F. (1992). Should I brag? Nature and impact of positive and boastful disclosures for women and men. *Human Communication Research, 18,* 364-399.

Miller, L. C., & Read, S. J. (1987). Why am I telling you this? Self-disclosure in a goal-based model of personality. In V. Derlega & J. Berg (Eds.), *Self-disclosure: Theory, research, and therapy* (pp. 35-58). New York: Plenum.

Miller, L. C., & Read, S. J. (1991). A knowledge-structure approach to relationships. In G. Fletcher & F. Fincham (Eds.), *Cognition in close relationships*. Hillsdale, NJ: Lawrence Erlbaum.

Mischel, W. (1968). *Personality and assessments*. New York: Wiley.

Mischel, W. (1973). Toward a cognitive social learning reconceptualization of personality. *Psychological Review, 80,* 252-283.

Mischel, W. (1979). On the interface of cognition and personality: Beyond the person-situation debate. *American Psychologist, 34,* 740-754.

Mischel, W., & Peake, P. K. (1982a). In search of consistency: Measure for measure. In M. P. Zanna, E. T. Higgins, & C. P. Herman (Eds.), *Consistency in social behavior: The Ontario Symposium* (Vol. 2, pp. 187-208). Hillsdale, NJ: Lawrence Erlbaum.

Mischel, W., & Peake, P. K. (1982b). Beyond deja vu in the search for cross-situational consistency. *Psychological Review, 89,* 730-755.

Murphy, G., & Murphy, L. B. (1968). *Asian psychology*. New York: Basic Books.

Murray, H. (1938). *Explorations in personality*. New York: Oxford University Press.

Norman, W. T. (1963). Toward an adequate taxonomy of personality attributes: Replicated factor structure in peer nomination personality ratings. *Journal of Abnormal and Social Psychology, 66,* 574-583.

O'Keefe, D. J. (1990). *Persuasion: Theory and research*. Newbury Park, CA: Sage.

Ortony, A., Clore, G. L., & Collins, A. (1988). *The cognitive structure of emotions*. New York: Cambridge University Press.

Peplau, L. A., Russell, D., & Heim, M. (1979). The experience of loneliness. In I. Frieze, D. Bar-Tal, & J. Carrol (Eds.), *New approaches to social problems* (pp. 53-78). San Francisco: Jossey-Bass.

Pervin, L. A. (1976). A free-response description approach to the analysis of person-situation interaction. *Journal of Personality and Social Psychology, 34,* 465-474.

Pervin, L. A. (1978). Definitions, measurements and classifications of stimuli, situations and environments. *Human Ecology, 6,* 71-105.

Pervin, L. A. (Ed.). (1989). *Goal concepts in personality and social psychology*. Hillsdale, NJ: Lawrence Erlbaum.

Pilkonis, P. A., Heape, C., & Klein, R. H. (1980). Treating shyness and other relationship differences in psychiatric outpatients. *Communication Education, 29,* 250-255.

Planalp, S. (1985). Relational schemata: A test of alternative forms of relational knowledge as guides to communication. *Human Communication Research, 12,* 3-29.

Pryor, J. B. (1987). Sexual harassment proclivities in men. *Sex Roles, 17,* 269-290.

Pryor, J. B., LaVite, C. M., & Stoller, L. M. (1993). A social psychological analysis of sexual harassment: The person/situation interaction. *Journal of Vocational Behavior, 9,* 1-16.

Pryor, J. B., & Merluzzi, T. V. (1985). The role of expertise in processing social interaction scripts. *Journal of Experimental Social Psychology, 21,* 362-379.

Putnam, L. L., & Wilson, C. E. (1982). Communicative strategies in organizational conflicts: Reliability and validity of a measurement scale. In M. Burgoon (Ed.), *Communication yearbook 6* (pp. 629-652). Beverly Hills, CA: Sage.

Raven, B. H., Centers, R., & Rodrigues, A. (1975). The bases of conjugal power. In R. E. Cromwell & D. H. Olson (Eds.), *Power in families* (pp. 217-231). New York: Wiley.

Raven, B. H., & Kruglanski, A. W. (1970). Conflict and power. In P. Swingle (Ed.), *The structure of conflict* (pp. 69-109). New York: Academic Press.

Read, S. J. (1987). Constructing causal scenarios: A knowledge structure approach to causal reasoning. *Journal of Personality and Social Psychology, 52,* 288-302.

Read, S. J., & Cesa, I. L. (1991). This reminds me of the time when . . .: Reminding in explanation. *Journal of Experimental Social Psychology, 27,* 1-25.

Read, S. J., Jones, D. K., & Miller, L. C. (1990). Traits as goal-based categories: The role of goals in the coherence of dispositional categories. *Journal of Personality and Social Psychology, 58,* 1048-1061.

Read, S. J., & Miller, L. C. (1989). Inter-personalism: Toward a goal-based model of persons in relationships. In L. Pervin (Ed.), *Goal concepts in personality and social psychology* (pp. 413-473). Hillsdale, NJ: Lawrence Erlbaum.

Read, S. J., & Miller, L. C. (1993a). Rapist or "regular guy": Explanatory coherence in the construction of mental models of others. *Personality and Social Psychology Bulletin, 19,* 526-540.

Read, S. J., & Miller, L. C. (1993b). Dissonance and balance in belief systems: The promise of parallel constraint satisfaction processes and connectionist modeling approaches. In R. C. Schank & E. J. Langer (Eds.), *Volume in honor of Robert P. Abelson*. Hillsdale, NJ: Lawrence Erlbaum.

Read, S. J., & Newhall-Marcus, A. (1993). Explanatory coherence in social explanations: A parallel distributed processing account. *Journal of Personality and Social Psychology, 65,* 429-447.

Roloff, M. E., & Janiszewski, C. A. (1989). Overcoming obstacles to interpersonal compliance: A principle of message construction. *Human Communication Research, 16,* 33-61.

Roloff, M. E., Janiszewski, C. A., McGrath, M. A., Burns, C. S., & Manrai, L. A. (1988). Acquiring resources from intimates: When obligation substitutes for persuasion. *Human Communication Research, 14,* 364-396.

Roseman, I. J. (1984). Cognitive determinants of emotions: A structural theory. In P. Shaver (Ed.), *Review of personality and social psychology* (Vol. 5, pp. 11-36). Beverly Hills, CA: Sage.

Roseman, I. J., Spindel, M. S., & Jose, P. E. (1990). Appraisals of emotion-eliciting events: Testing a theory of discrete emotions. *Journal of Personality and Social Psychology, 59,* 899-915.

Rotter, J. B. (1966). Generalized expectancies for internal vs. external control of reinforcement. *Psychological Monographs, 80,* 1-28.

Rotter, J. B., & Mulry, R. C. (1965). Internal versus control of reinforcement and decision time. *Journal of Personality and Social Psychology, 2,* 598-604.

Rubin, R. B., Perse, E. M., & Barbato, C. A. (1988). Conceptualization and measurement of interpersonal communication motives. *Human Communication Research, 14,* 602-628.

Rule, B. G., & Bisanz, G. L. (1987). Goals and strategies of persuasion: A cognitive schema for understanding social events. In M. Zanna, P. Herman, & J. Olsen (Eds.), *Social influence: The Fifth Ontario Symposium on Personality and Social Psychology* (pp. 185-206). Hillsdale, NJ: Lawrence Erlbaum.

Rule, B. G., Bisanz, G. L., & Kohn, M. (1985). Anatomy of a persuasion schema: Targets, goals, and strategies. *Journal of Personality and Social Psychology, 48,* 1127-1140.

Rumelhart, D. E., & McClelland, J. L. (1986). *Parallel distributed processing: Explorations in the microstructure of cognition: Vol. 1. Foundations.* Cambridge: MIT Press.

Russell, J. A., & Ward, L. M. (1982). Environmental psychology. *Annual Review of Psychology, 33,* 651-688.

Schank, R. (1982). *Dynamic memory: A theory of reminding and learning in computers and people.* Cambridge: Cambridge University Press.

Schank, R., & Abelson, R. (1977). *Scripts, plans, goals, and understanding.* Hillsdale, NJ: Lawrence Erlbaum.

Scherer, K. R. (1984). On the nature and function of emotion: A component process approach. In K. R. Scherer & P. Ekman (Eds.), *Approaches to emotion* (pp. 293-317). Hillsdale, NJ: Lawrence Erlbaum.

Scherer, K. R. (1988). Criteria for emotion-antecedent appraisal: A review. In V. Hamilton, G. H. Bower, & N. H. Frijda (Eds.), *Cognitive perspectives on emotion and motivation* (pp. 89-126). Norwell, MA: Kluwer Academic.

Schlenker, B. R. (1980). *Impression management: The self-concept, social identity, and interpersonal relations.* Monterey, CA: Brooks/Cole.

Schlenker, B. R., & Darby, B. W. (1981). The use of apologies in social predicaments. *Social Psychology Quarterly, 44,* 271-278.

Schonbach, P. (1990). *Account episodes: The management or escalation of conflict.* New York: Cambridge University Press.

Schonbach, P., & Kleibaumhuter, P. (1990). Severity of reproach and defensiveness of accounts. In M. J. Cody & M. L. McLaughlin (Eds.), *The psychology of tactical communication* (pp. 229-243). Clevedon, England: Multilingual Matters.

Sillars, A. L. (1980a). Attributions and communication in roommate conflicts. *Communication Monographs, 47,* 180-200.

Sillars, A. L. (1980b). The stranger and the spouse as target persons for compliance-gaining strategies: A subjective expected utility model. *Human Communication Research, 6,* 265-279.

Smith, M. J. (1984). Contingency rules theory, context, and compliance behaviors. *Human Communication Research, 10,* 489-512.

Snyder, M. (1979). Self-monitoring processes. In L. Berkowitz (Ed.), *Advances in experimental social psychology* (Vol. 12, pp. 86-131). New York: Academic Press.

Snyder, M. (1987). *Public appearances, private realities: The psychology of self-monitoring.* New York: Freeman.

Snyder, M., & Cantor, N. (1980). Thinking about ourselves and others: Self-monitoring and social knowledge. *Journal of Personality and Social Psychology, 39,* 222-234.

Snyder, M., & Gangestad, S. (1982). Choosing social situations: Two investigations of self-monitoring processes. *Journal of Personality and Social Psychology, 43,* 123-135.

Snyder, M., & Kendzierski, D. (1982). Choosing social situations: Investigating the origins of correspondence between attitude and behavior. *Journal of Personality, 50,* 280-295.

Solano, C. H., Batten, P. G., & Parish, E. A. (1982). Loneliness and patterns of self-disclosure. *Journal of Personality and Social Psychology, 43,* 524-531.

Spence, J. T. (1985). Achievement American style: The rewards and costs of individualism. *American Psychologist, 40,* 1285-1295.

Spence, J. T., & Helmreich, R. L. (1978). *Masculinity and femininity: Their psychological dimensions, correlates and antecedents.* Austin: University of Texas Press.

Stokols, D. (1978). Environmental psychology. *Annual Review of Psychology, 29,* 253-295.

Taylor, S. E. (1981). The interface of cognition and social psychology. In J. H. Harvey (Ed.), *Cognition, social behavior and the environment* (pp. 189-212). Hillsdale, NJ: Lawrence Erlbaum.

Thagard, P. (1989). Explanatory coherence. *Behavioral and Brain Sciences, 12,* 435-467.

Thagard, P. (1992). Adversarial problem solving: Modeling an opponent using explanatory coherence. *Cognitive Science, 16,* 123-149.

Thagard, P. (1993). *Inference to the best plan: A coherence theory of decision.* Unpublished manuscript.

Thorne, A., & Miller, L. C. (1993). *Ebbs, flows, and other things we don't know about personality.* Unpublished manuscript.

Triandis, H. C. (1989). The self and social behavior in differing cultural contexts. *Psychological Review, 96,* 506-520.

Tversky, B., & Hemenway, K. (1983). Categories of environmental scenes. *Cognitive Psychology, 15,* 121-149.

Ward, L. M. (1977). Multidimensional scaling of the molar physical environment. *Multivariate Behavioral Research, 12,* 23-42.

Wegner, D. M., Guiliano, T., & Hertel, P. T. (1985). Cognitive interdependence in close relationships. In W. Ickes (Ed.), *Compatible and incompatible relationships* (pp. 253-276). New York: Springer-Verlag.

Wierzbicka, A. (1992). *Semantics, culture, and cognition: Universal human concepts in culture-specific configurations.* New York: Oxford University Press.

Wilensky, R. (1983). *Planning and understanding: A computational approach to human reasoning.* London: Addison-Wesley.

Wilkinson, I., & Kipnis, D. (1978). Interfirm use of power. *Journal of Applied Psychology, 63,* 315-320.

Wilson, S. R. (1990). Development and test of a cognitive rules model of interaction goals. *Communication Monographs, 57,* 81-103.

Wish, M., Deutsch, M., & Kaplan, S. (1976). Perceived dimensions of interpersonal relations. *Journal of Personality and Social Psychology, 33,* 409-420.

Wish, M., & Kaplan, S. (1977). Toward an implicit theory of interpersonal communication. *Sociometry, 40,* 234-246.

Woods, D. D. (1993). Process-tracing methods for the study of cognition outside of the experimental psychology laboratory. In G. A. Klein, J. Orasanu, R. Calderwood, & C. E. Zsambok (Eds.), *Decision making in action: Models and methods* (pp. 228-251). Norwood, NJ: Ablex.

6

Language and Interpersonal Communication

Scott Jacobs

THE CONCEPTS OF language and communication, although intimately related, have never really been happily married. Communication scholars will readily recognize that the use of language to formulate messages and to perform social actions is the paradigm case of communication. Almost all cases of communication that interest communication researchers involve talk or writing in some way. Still, efforts to ground notions of "message meaning" or "symbolic action" in a detailed account of the organization of linguistic forms and functions has always seemed to be so technical and tedious a task that it has been generally bypassed in the process of building communication theory. Likewise, students of language have often been reluctant to integrate their theories of language structure with what is manifestly the paradigm function of language, that of communication. Knowing what language does has commonly been thought to be superfluous to knowing what language is. While this attitude has begun to fade, the term *language* has been so thoroughly appropriated by the technical structural interests of sentence grammarians that any effort to study the uses of language or the structures of language beyond the sentence requires use of a whole new term: *discourse*.

Discourse analysis is an effort to close the gap between conceptions of communication process and language structure and function. Its research questions center on the role of language in constructing an "architecture of intersubjectivity" (Heritage, 1984; Rommetveit, 1974): How do you decide what to say when you talk? And how is it that when I speak words you understand me? How do we assemble linguistic units and place them into the interactional stream to produce fitting messages and sensible patterns of social interaction? It is generally assumed by discourse analysts that these sorts of questions will be answered by specifying the content and operational properties of a shared system of knowledge that informs linguistic choice and enables linguistic interpretation. Although well-developed, detailed models of this system of knowledge are beyond the reach of most areas of contemporary discourse analysis, there is a growing catalog of discursive forms and patterns that have become susceptible to systematic description. Analysis of these forms and patterns has led to an emerging consensus that any model of discourse must be compatible with certain fundamental properties. This chapter first summarizes those basic properties of discourse, then shows how they are manifested in the organization of conversational interaction. As we shall see, the effort to come to grips with these properties has led to a basic shift in the conceptual framework of discourse analysis from a "normative/code" model of discourse knowledge to a more "inferential/strategic" model.

Central Problems and Basic Properties

Language is systematically organized in a variety of ways beyond the units of word and sentence, all of which contribute to the information conveyed and the actions performed by a message. Linguistic organization can be described at various levels of conceptual structure that organize linguistic content (texts, stories, conversational topics, and so on), at various levels of pragmatic structure that organize linguistic action and interaction (speech acts, adjacency pairs, conversational episodes, and so on), or at levels of stylistic structure that integrate linguistic features with the characteristics of person and situation (for example, styles, codes, or message design logics). Discourse analysts are concerned with isolating these various structures and formulating principles for their construction and use. In analyzing these levels of organization, discourse analysts address three interrelated puzzles. From these puzzles have emerged some very general principles that operate across levels.

The Problem of Meaning

What sort of information is expressed by discourse structures, and what derivational operations enable people to express and interpret that information? How do we know facts about our language such as the following?

(1) "Is Sybil there?" can be used to request the addressee to call Sybil to the telephone.
(2) "You sure are hot" can literally refer to the addressee's body temperature or metaphorically refer to their streak of success or emotional state; and the utterance may also be used ironically to express just the opposite of the literal or metaphorical reference.
(3) Using *title plus last name* to address someone (for example, Dr. Welby) conveys that the addressee is someone of high power, status, and/or social distance.
(4) "John subscribes to *SPY*" ordinarily conveys that John reads *SPY*.

Somehow people are able to refer to events and to describe states of affairs. They can convey attitudes, beliefs, and desires. They express relationships to situation and addressee. They may speak plainly and explicitly or they may speak indirectly and figuratively. And they are very good at saying just enough for the hearer to be able to "fill in" what is left unsaid.

The Problem of Action

How do speakers and writers assemble messages? What kinds of choices and assessments enter into the decision of what to say, how to say it, and when? Why, for example, is it odd to introduce oneself just to ask for directions from a passerby on the sidewalk?

(5) Hi, my name is Scott Jacobs. Could you tell me where I could find a public telephone?

And what is it about sentence 6 that makes it a more fitting response than 7 or 8 when writing a thank you note to a friend for a gift that is awful (Bavelas, Black, Chovil, & Mullett, 1990)?

(6) I appreciate your thoughtfulness.
(7) The gift is perfect; I really love it.
(8) I don't like the gift and am going to exchange or return it.

Along another line, no one would think that uttering sentence 9 would ever fry the egg.

(9) I hereby fry this egg.

So, how is it that, given the right circumstances, uttering sentence 10 will marry Ralph and Linda, and uttering 11 will place the speaker under an obligation to be there Friday (Searle, 1989)?

(10) I hereby pronounce you husband and wife.
(11) I promise to be there Friday.

In producing a message, people decide what will make sense and what won't, what will work and what will not. They are more or less sensitive to the need to be polite. They know how to do things with words like *bet, beg,* and *complain.* There is a consequentiality to language use that speakers and writers more or less successfully take into account when constructing messages. And this consequentiality is intimately related to what any message means (Sanders, 1987).

The Problem of Coherence

The problems of meaning and action converge in the problem of coherence. What are the recognizably sensible and orderly patterns and relations among linguistic elements, and what principles govern the formation of those patterns? Clearly, all natural language users show great facility in finding the ways in which the elements of language "hang together" and in seeing to it that their own contributions do so. Such impressions are central to the sense of orderliness, meaningfulness, and appropriateness we find in language structure and use. But it is not at all clear how we construct coherent discourse. Why is it, for example, that we find it difficult to keep track of the topic in the following conversation (adapted from the musical comedy, *The Music Man*)?

(12) **A:** Mama, a man with a suitcase followed me home.

B: Did he say anything?

A: He tried.

B: Did you say anything?

A: Of course not, mama.

B: If you don't mind my saying so, it wouldn't have hurt to find out what the gentleman wanted.

A: I know what the gentleman wanted.

B: What, dear?

A: You'll find it in Balzac.

B: Well, excuse me for living, but I've never read it.

A: Neither has anyone else in this town.

B: There you go again with the same old comment about the low mentality of River City people, and taking it too much to heart.

A: Since the Madison County Library was entrusted to me for the purpose of improving River City's cultural level, you can't blame me for considering that the ladies of River City keep ignoring all my counsel and advice.

B: When a woman's got a husband and you've got none, why should she take advice from you, even if you can quote Balzac and Shakespeare, and all them other high-falutin' Greeks?

A: If you don't mind my saying so, you have a bad habit of changing every subject.

B: I haven't changed the subject. We were talking about that stranger.

A: What stranger?

B: With the suitcase. Who may be your very last chance.

We can recognize "topic drift," but it is not obvious how to define it (Hobbs, 1990a; Jacobs & Jackson, 1992). Alternatively, how is it that we are able to hear an utterance like that in example 13, but not an utterance like that in 14, as belonging in a conversational closing (Schegloff & Sacks, 1974, p. 249)?

(13) Well, I'll letchu go.

(14) What's up?

Somehow, natural language users can see in a string of sentences a story. They know how to make topically relevant contributions to conversations. They know how to reply to questions and offers, and they can organize arguments and lead up to invitations. They can open and close conversations. All of these skills involve the application of a system of knowledge for how discourse units fit together into well-formed wholes at higher levels of order.

Properties of Linguistic Communication

So, what kind of knowledge enables people to produce and understand discourse that is coherent, fitting, and meaningful? It is becoming increasingly apparent that any theory of language structure and use must be compatible with certain core facts, or basic principles.

(1) Linguistic communication requires shared principles for inference beyond information given by a "surface" reading. Whereas students of interpersonal communication have commonly emphasized the idiosyncratic and personal qualities of message interpretation, discourse analysts have started from the massive fact of the generally reliable and public quality of much interpretation. When people use language, they usually understand one another, and do so at an exceedingly intricate level of detail. And where there is ambiguity, vagueness, deception, confusion, and the like, this too results from public qualities of the discourse. Moreover, the message communicated may not be connected in any obvious way to what is directly and literally said. An adequate representation of the "message" conveyed may bear no obvious correspondence to the string of signs, or signals, that serve as the vehicle for that message. To see this, consider just some of the commonplace intuitions about what is being communicated in the following two-turn exchange.

(15) **Ruth Anne:** These are beautiful plants. The leaves are so waxy and green.

      Sally: Well, uh (.) actually Scott's the one who takes care of them. Hehhh. I don't do much of the housework.

Among the more obvious meanings that can be seen by any native language user are the following: Ruth Anne and Sally are having a casual conversation. Sally knows Scott and believes that Ruth Anne knows Scott—or at least knows who Scott is. Scott does not have any pertinent formal status over Ruth Anne or Sally.

The leaves mentioned by Ruth Anne are the leaves of the plants that are beautiful. Part of what makes the plants appear beautiful is the waxy and green appearance of their leaves. What Scott takes care of are the plants (and not the leaves, or the cats, or the old people next door), and taking care of the plants is the reason they are beautiful.

Ruth Anne is issuing a compliment to Sally. In doing so, Ruth Anne awards positive value to the plants appearing beautiful; Ruth Anne assumes that Sally is responsible for that appearance; and Ruth Anne thereby expresses approval of Sally.

Sally is not accepting Ruth Anne's compliment. Instead, Sally has deflected the compliment to Scott. The reason for the rejection is that Sally does not take care of the plants (as Ruth Anne seems to think) and so Sally cannot claim responsibility for their beauty. Sally also believes that Ruth Anne believes that Sally occupies the role of houseworker. Scott does most of the housework. Taking care of the plants is part of the housework.

Information like this is part of what we would want to call the meaning of the exchange. It is what gets communicated. Yet, strictly speaking, none of this information is literally and explicitly said. In effect, messages must be identified with the context that is constructed for a text, and not just with the meaning of the words themselves.

All of what is noted above is the product of inferences made in the process of constructing a sensible interpretation of what was said. That interpretation involves the construction of inferences based on finding the functional significance of what could have been said but wasn't (not saying "Thank you" or not saying "Mr. Jacobs" or "my husband" instead of "Scott"). It involves inferences guided by principles for designing coherent discourse. For example, Brown and Yule's *principle of local interpretation* (1983, p. 59) instructs hearers not to expand or change a context any more than is needed to arrive at an interpretation. Thus we ordinarily assume that Ruth Anne and Sally maintain the same topic, and so we infer that the leaves referred to are the leaves of the same plant that is beautiful and that taking care of the plants has something to do with the appearance of the plants.

Of course, these inferences are all defeasible. They can change given additional information. But the point is that these are the kinds of inferences that people make and these inferences are quite detailed, highly reliable, and far beyond the explanatory capacity of any correspondence theory of symbolic meaning. Any theory that equates message meaning with the literal meaning of what is said will miss how coherent and meaningful messages are produced and understood. Inference beyond the information given in the text is a characteristic process invited by all natural language use. A theory of linguistic communication needs to model the different types of inferences that people make and explain how people are able to derive such information from language. Most discourse analysts today take it for granted that the coherence of interactional patterns and the sense of messages must be explained in terms of a rich conceptual structure—a constructed context for the surface structure of what is actually said or written.

(2) Linguistic communication requires generative principles. The intricacy of our system for linguistic communication is made all the more remarkable when one considers the creative capacity for language use. Chomsky first drew widespread attention to this aspect of language (1959, 1972, pp. 11-12). He noted that any natural language user can spontaneously and effortlessly produce and understand a potentially infinite number of sentences that are completely novel—discourse that is not a repetition of anything we have ever heard before and is not in any obvious way similar in pattern to discourse we have spoken in the past.

Although Chomsky had in mind syntactic structures of sentences, similar observations could be made at a variety of levels of language organization. Theories that try to account for language production and understanding by appeal to sets of standardized patterns quickly exhaust themselves when they attempt to seriously model the flexibility of language use and the wide variety of possible structures. Consider as an example the variety of ways you might communicate to your spouse that you wish to leave a party.

(16) Let's go home.
(17) I want to leave.
(18) What time is it?
(19) This sure is boring.
(20) Don't you have to be up early tomorrow?
(21) Are you going to have another drink?
(22) Do you think the Millers would give you a ride home?
(23) You look ready to party all night.
(24) Did you get a chance to talk to everyone you wanted to?
(25) Is it starting to rain?
(26) It looks like it's stopped raining.

Although some ways to get your spouse to leave are more or less standardized and may be widely used, it would be seriously misleading to suggest that knowledge of such forms sufficiently characterizes the productive and interpretive capacities of a natural language user. The list could go on indefinitely. And the problem becomes even more unmanageable for patterns of interactional exchange and episodes. Certainly discourse is filled with standardized usages, recurrent patterns, and conventionalized forms of expression. And their occurrence is a matter of considerable interest (compare Hopper, 1992; Kellerman, Broetzmann, Lim, & Kitao, 1989).

But once the creative potential for language use is taken seriously, the basic problem confronted by the discourse analyst becomes one of explaining the massive fact of variability, innovation, and novelty in language patterning (compare Cappella, 1990; Jacobs, 1990). Discourse analysts today have begun to abandon the idea that discourse knowledge consists of some sort of behavioral repertoire or closed set of response types (see O'Keefe, 1990). If modeling discourse knowledge is to be a finite enterprise, standardized patterns alone cannot be the basis for its characterization. Such characterizations would be inherently incomplete. Rather than specifying a list of patterns that people are motivated to follow regularly, discourse models need to postulate a system of principles that enable people to generate an open-ended set of patterns, only some of which become what Cushman and Whiting (1972) term "standardized usages."

(3) Communicative meaning is context determined. If theories of action must somehow accommodate the generativity of language, then theories of meaning must acknowledge the contextualization of meaning. The meaning of any particular utterance is fixed with respect to a context of knowledge brought to bear in the process of interpretation. As Bransford and Johnson (1972) showed in very early studies, people must activate a relevant field of world knowledge in order to comprehend a text. Searle (1980) makes a similar point with sentences like the following:

(27) Bill cut the grass.
(28) The barber cut Tom's hair.
(29) Sally cut the cake.
(30) The tailor cut the cloth.

The word *cut* has the same literal meaning in all four sentences (Sanders, 1987). Nevertheless, the sense of the term changes depending upon what we know about the activity being indexed by the sentence. Cutting grass is not the same as cutting hair, cake, or cloth. And even the sense of "cut the grass" may change depending on whether Bill is understood to be, say, mowing a lawn or preparing a floral arrangement. And it is this need to activate a context of knowledge that makes it difficult to understand sentences 31-33.

(31) Mary cut the sand.
(32) Bill cut the mountain.
(33) Pat cut it.

We simply have no clear knowledge of what is involved in cutting mountains or sand. Likewise, even if we assume that "cut" in sentence 33 is meant literally, the lack of clear context leaves its sense incomplete and underdetermined.

A straightforward implication of context determination is that any particular utterance may mean multiple things depending upon its context of occurrence. There can be no simple assignment of meaning, given an utterance. Consider the following exchange overheard in a Mexican restaurant:

(34) **Customer:** Did you say sopapillas come with the chiles rellenos?
     Waitress: I'll get it right away sir.

Here, the customer's utterance occurred as the waitress was serving the orders for the table. His question called attention to the fact that no sopapillas had been delivered, served to check his expectation that his order would come with sopapillas, communicated that he wanted the sopapillas to be served at the same time as the chiles rellenos, and functioned to request the waitress to bring them. But the question would have been taken to mean something altogether different if the waitress had just placed sopapillas next to the customer's chiles rellenos. In that case, the customer could have been taken to communicate that he did *not* expect sopapillas and, perhaps, that he was concerned with whether they had been mistakenly served to him, whether he would be billed for them, and so on. And we can easily imagine an identical utterance being asked as the customer is ordering food. And here again the meaning would be quite different.

Once the importance of context in determining meaning is recognized, the idea that symbolic forms contain their own meanings quickly loses its attractiveness. It becomes impossible to sustain a project that tries to model inference by the kind of self-contained operations suggested below:

(35) "John is a bachelor" implies that John is not married.
(36) "Barbara is older than Carol. Carol is older than Mary" implies that Barbara is older than Mary.

There are meanings that are conventionally or logically determined in ways like this. But contextually inferred meanings are never logically or conventionally necessary in these ways because contextual inference requires hearers to assume premises in addition to what is said, and these premises are never necessarily relevant and are always to some degree uncertain. Rather than looking simply for ways to unpack meaning from symbolic containers, theories of discourse need to model the way in which meaning emerges by integrating text with context.

(4) Language structures are functional designs. The structures found in discourse are intimately related to the functional design of those structures. What "pattern" is found to exist in discourse depends on what functions are performed by that discourse. So, for example, the waiter's response in example 37 creates a meaningful and coherent exchange only by seeing how the customer's question is being used to gain information to decide on a possible order and how the waiter's utterance—while not an answer to the question—is being used as a reason for not being able to comply with that possible upcoming order.

(37) **Customer:** What's the chicken marsala like?
     Waiter: I'm sorry, we're all out of that tonight.

Any model of language use and structure must come to grips with a difficult problem: The functional design of language structure means that the principles of linguistic structuring are not just followed; they are used. The paradox this presents is that deviating from structural expectations and principles of order may make sense in a deeper functional representation of that order. Insult and humor often work precisely because natural language users recognize the existence of structural principles that are being apparently violated in the service of making some point (Ervin-Tripp, 1971). And language choice may reflect the demands of literal reference or the most obliquely metaphorical social meanings (Fitch, 1991). All this suggests that models of discourse knowledge must reflect how meaning and coherence emerge from the interplay of strategy and structure.

(5) Language use is multifunctional. What people say, how they say it, and where they say it in the stream of discourse all reflect the ways in which individuals manage multiple goals and situational demands to convey an assembly of information. In part, the multifunctionality of language use reflects the relevance of multiple levels of organization and order that apply to any utterance. All utterances, for example, participate in procedural and ritual orders, convey both topical and relational information, and contribute to varying aspects of discourse coherence (Clark & Delia, 1979; Ellis, 1992; Sigman, 1987). But functional organization also reflects communicators' ongoing assessments of locally emergent demands and possibilities in a situation (Mandelbaum & Pomerantz, 1991). What counts as a fitting contribution to a situation will depend upon the communicator's definition of it.

The important thing to see, however, is that the processes providing for multifunctionality may not simply be an additive organization of unifunctional processes. There is an *integrative* process that does not decompose into elementary functions. Thus an utterance like sentence 6 reflects one way of responding in a unified way to the demand to acknowledge a gift while avoiding telling a falsehood or making the friend feel bad. Utterances like sentences 7 and 8 are less successful in reconciling these goals. A great deal of what constitutes communicative "skill" in producing a message is the ability to formulate situational demands, to see the potential for pursuing goals, to imagine alternative definitions of a situation, and to construct messages so as to maximally satisfy those demands and goals (O'Keefe, 1991).

These properties of language structure and use exist at virtually all levels of discourse organization. How to model these properties is a recalcitrant puzzle that has shaped the direction of theory development.

The Normative Code Model

While discourse analysis owes a historical debt to early work in anthropology (Malinowski, 1923, 1935) and analytic philosophy (Austin, 1962; Wittgenstein, 1953), the major impetus for contemporary studies of discourse must be traced to the achievements and limitations of contemporary linguistics and Noam Chomsky's theory of transformational generative grammar. With the publication of *Syntactic Structures* (1957) from his dissertation, Chomsky started a revolution in linguistics (Newmeyer, 1980). It was largely through the philosophical and psychological controversies generated by his work that the analytic concepts and techniques of linguistics came to be disseminated throughout the social sciences and humanities (see Hook, 1969). Though the theory of transformational generative grammar applied strictly to certain formal properties of the syntax of sentences, the theory supplied a general paradigm for conceptualizing structure at any level of discourse and a motivation for expanding the initially narrow domain of "linguistic competence" to include aspects of communicative knowledge previously relegated to "performance" considerations.

Linguistics and Grammar

The goal of linguistic analysis is to specify those rules that constitute the grammar of a language. Put simply, a grammar describes the logical structure of relations between meanings and signals that are created by a code. The rules of a grammar are computational procedures that combine the elements of a language so as to specify the forms in which a "message" may acceptably appear. Linguists have generally analyzed the grammar of human languages into three components, or subsystems of rules. The rules governing the combinatorial relations among words in sentences are syntax. Semantics is the component of grammar that assigns meaning representations to the words and specifies the logical form of sentences. The rules that specify the sounds of a language and their permissible combinations is phonology.

Following de Saussure's (1916/1983) distinction between *langue* and *parole*, Chomsky (1965) argued that the subject matter of a theory of grammar was not language behavior per se but the linguistic competence of an idealized speaker-hearer of the language. That is, a grammar formally describes an isolatable system of knowledge restricted to the grammatical properties of sentences. Within this technical delimitation of the subject matter of "language," a theory of grammar would be capable of reproducing all the permissible sentences in a language (and none of the impermissible ones) and formally representing the distinctions and relations that natural language users can be brought to intuitively recognize within and among those sentences. So, for example, at the level of syntactic organization, any adequate theory of English grammar should be capable of distinguishing between examples 38 and 39.

(38) Colorless green ideas sleep furiously.

(39) Furiously sleep ideas green colorless.

Even though sentence 38 is nonsensical and bizarre, by comparing it with 39, any speaker of English can be brought to recognize that 38 has a kind of word order to it (i.e., it is grammatical)—a fact that demonstrates that speakers of a language seem to have a relatively autonomous knowledge of syntax (Chomsky, 1957, p. 15).

Such a system of knowledge is abstracted from actual performance considerations where restrictions on memory and attention, operation of extralinguistic beliefs about the speaker and the situation, and other aspects of knowledge and cognitive structure interact with the grammatical system in the process of actual discourse production and comprehension (Chomsky, 1972, pp. 115-116). The competence-performance distinction focuses attention on the principles of organization in the formation of sentences rather than on the factors influencing when and how people will actually recognize and exhibit behaviors of that type (Sanders, 1987). Johnson-Laird (1983) illustrates the distinction with a sentence from a book review:

(40) This book fills a much needed gap in the literature.

Many readers, at first glance, will take this sentence to be complimenting the book as being much needed. But that would be a mistaken reading. And the fact that we can recognize our mistake shows that we have a knowledge of language that is not always exhibited in practice.

While the "data" for much linguistic analysis are intuitions about hypothetical sentences, linguists recognize that not just any property can be directly intuited. Intuitions need to be clarified and disciplined through comparative analysis. It would probably be useless (even positively misleading) to directly ask a native speaker, for example, whether or not sentences 41 and 42 are syntactically identical.

(41) I left, for he made me nervous.

(42) I left, because he made me nervous.

Nevertheless, persons can see a grammatical and an ungrammatical sentence (marked by an asterisk) in the following pairs.

(43a) It was because I was nervous that I left.

(43b) *It was for I was nervous that I left.

(44a) Did you leave because he made you nervous?

(44b) *Did you leave for he made you nervous?

(45a) I left, because I was nervous and because I wanted to go.

(45b) *I left, for I was nervous and for I wanted to go.

On the basis of these asymmetries, one can reasonably conclude that a theory of English grammar should not treat *because* clauses and *for* clauses as syntactically identical, despite their similarity in semantic meaning (Smith & Wilson, 1990, p. 39).

Likewise, an adequate theory of English syntax should be able to represent that John is the object of sentence 46 but the subject of sentence 47, that sentences 48, 49, and 50 are structurally related, and that 51 is structurally ambiguous (between "flying a plane" and "a flying plane").

(46) John is easy to please.

(47) John is eager to please.

(48) John hit the ball.

(49) The ball was hit by John.

(50) Did John hit the ball?

(51) Flying planes can be dangerous.

Syntactic theory after Chomsky has produced exceedingly subtle and sophisticated formal analyses of the structure of language (compare with Soames & Perlmutter, 1979). The power of these analyses has led many to take them as exemplars for normative code modeling.

In advancing an exceedingly powerful theory of syntactic structure, Chomsky also called attention to three fundamental properties of syntax that demanded a wholesale reassessment of the complexity of the system. First, as mentioned earlier, Chomsky pointed out the infinite generativity of syntax. Just as with mathematical equations, natural language sentences are generated by a finite system of rules that can operate in combination with one another and recursively to produce an infinite range of possibilities. Consider, for example, the scope of the operation implied by sentences 52 and 53:

(52) The man runs the store on 59th Street.
(53) The man who took the cat that ate the mouse that ran down the stairs of the big white house that stands next to the church . . . runs the store on 59th Street.

Second, Chomsky called attention to the special way in which syntactic structures are hierarchically organized. As Lyons (1970, p. 60) points out, traditional grammarians had long recognized that the linear string of words in a sentence exhibits a hierarchial structure. For example, sentence 54 has a structural relation between a subject and a predicate.

(54) The girl reads the book.

The subject of the sentence (S) is a noun phrase (NP) that specifies a relation between a noun (N) and a definite article (T). The predicate is a verb phrase (VP) in which there is a relation between a verb (V) and its object, which is also a noun phrase consisting of a structural relation between a noun and a definite article. Such a hierarchial structure can be formally represented by means of the following rewrite rules (adapted from Chomsky, 1957, p. 28):

  (a) S → NP + VP
  (b) NP → T + N
  (c) VP → V + NP
  (d) T → the
  (e) N → girl, book, . . .
  (f) V → reads, eats, . . .

Each rule (X → Y) is to be interpreted as the instruction, "Rewrite X as Y," and provides the phrase structure representation of sentence 54 found in Figure 6.1.

The contribution that Chomsky made to understanding this hierarchial organization was to show that syntax consists of *structure-dependent* operations that cannot be modeled by any system that defines structural dependencies through linear relations between words (for example, "finite state grammar" of the sort illustrated by Shannon & Weaver's, 1949, information theory or by any Markov process). Chomsky argued that the syntactic rules operate on hierarchically defined units so that structural dependencies among units are maintained over an indefinitely large series of intervening elements. So, the relation between "The girl" and "reads" obtains at the level of structure defined by the main NP and VP in the sentence and is completely indifferent to the number of words and clauses that might be inserted between them. (Compare also sentences 52 and 53.) One striking possibility, which Chomsky (1957) argues, is that finite state grammars are in principle incapable of handling operations like those expressed in (g):

  (g) S → NP + S, VP

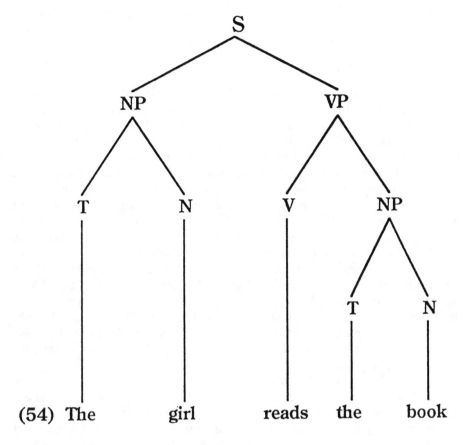

Figure 6.1. Tree Diagram

Because S is also a sentence, it too can have an embedded sentence and so on indefinitely, being restricted only by performance limitations of human memory. Thus we can generate the following:

(55) The girl reads the book.
(56) The girl the cat scratched reads the book.
(57) The girl the cat the dog ate scratched reads the book.

The third property of syntactic structure that Chomsky pointed out was its dual structure: Every sentence has a "surface structure" and a "deep structure." The surface structure consists of the words of the sentence in their order of occurrence in actual sentences. The deep structure corresponds to the level of representation on which a semantic mapping is made. The two levels are related through transformational rules. The postulation of some sort of "deep structure" appears necessary to explain the intuition that sentences 48, 49, and 50 all embody a common propositional structure, "John hit the ball." Likewise, the ambiguity of sentence 51 can be explained through generation of a common surface structure from two different deep structures. While Chomsky's particular version of deep structure has lost its widespread popularity (Sells, 1985), the concept was mainly taken metaphorically by discourse analysts to warrant a distinction between the linear structure of what is explicitly said and the conceptual structure of what is implicitly conveyed.

The General Model

By far the most popular approach to developing models of discourse has been to pick out from discourse some relatively manageable level of structural organization and, in Levinson's (1981, p. 93) phrase, "do a Chomsky" on it. "Doing a Chomsky" means showing how the organization of linguistic communication reflects a normatively regulated code for structuring and using linguistic categories. In this paradigm, discourse knowledge is taken to consist of a self-contained rule system that organizes the various levels of structure in a message in a way akin to a kind of "supergrammar." It amounts to a "rules and units" approach to modeling discourse (Taylor & Cameron, 1987).

Perhaps the real popularity of the Chomskyan vision of grammar is due to the way that it formalizes a commonsense model of communication. Reddy (1979) calls it the "conduit metaphor" and locates its principles in the very fabric of ordinary language usage. The intellectual foundations of a code model can be traced back to Locke (1690/1975; see Harris, 1987; Taylor, 1992). Akmajian, Demers, Farmer, and Harnish (1990, pp. 307-354) and Sperber and Wilson (1986, pp. 1-31) describe its appearance in information theory and linguistics in ways that bear a striking resemblance to Berlo's (1960) linear model. Wilson (1970) clearly articulates the normative aspects of code use.

The normative code model portrays linguistic communication as the transmission of a message in which a sender encodes meanings into a physical signal and a receiver decodes the message to derive a meaningful representation of it. Decoding and encoding occur through the application of a code. A code is a system of rules that specifies derivational relations between the elements at various structural levels (thus connecting meanings with public signs, or signals) and combinatorial relations among the elements at any given structural level (thus providing coherent configurations in the arrangement of signs). In encoding, senders consult the rules to determine what signal to transmit, given an intended meaning. In decoding, receivers consult the rules to determine the intended meaning, given a received signal.

Senders decide what message to send by consulting normative rules and conforming to their behavioral specifications. Norms are standing social expectations known and adhered to by members of a linguistic community, or internalized dispositions shared by members of that community. They can be stated in the form, "Given condition(s) C, act A is obligated (or permitted or prohibited)." The given conditions for action are contextual features that exist prior to the action. The act is any structural unit or combination of units defined by the language code. By recognizing relevant contextual features, actors call up the corresponding norms and decide what to do by following the behaviors associated with those conditions (Cushman & Whiting, 1972; Shimanoff, 1980).

Normative code models predict that communication will be successful just in case the receiver employs the same rules to decode the message that the sender employs to encode the message. Communication breakdowns will occur to the degree that the sender and receiver fail to share the same code rules. Indeed, one of the features of this model is that, in the absence of noise, proper application of code rules *guarantees* the meaning of a message, just as the rules of mathematics guarantee a determinate (or indeterminate) solution to an equation. Likewise, regularities in the production and patterning of messages will occur to the degree that normative rules are strongly internalized or sanctioned by members of a linguistic community and the relevant contextual features are clearly recognizable.

The following section examines the logic and prospects of this kind of model for the analysis of conversational interaction. Modeling the way in which the use of language creates and regulates interactional structure supplies a clear and obvious bridge between theories of language and theories of interpersonal communication. As will be shown, a normative code model runs into intractable problems—problems intimately connected to the properties of discourse discussed earlier. These problems have led discourse analysts to develop an alternative framework to be discussed in the concluding section of the chapter.

Extensions of the Normative Code Model to Conversational Interaction

By far the most influential approach to modeling meaning and coherence in conversation is one that assumes that coherent structural patterns consist of a series of moves or act types and that the functional meanings communicated by utterances can be typified in terms of these acts. It has been widely assumed that when analyzed in this way conversation will reveal a "grammar of natural conversation" (Schenkein, 1978, p. 3) or "social syntax" (Gumperz & Hymes, 1972, p. 348). The kinds of problems that cast doubt on the adequacy of such a conceptualization will be presented by first considering the ways in which discourse analysts have attempted to model conversational sequencing and then by turning to the ways in which they have attempted to model the expression and interpretation of conversational acts.

Sequencing rule approaches. In its simplest form, the orderliness of conversational sequencing might be modeled on the assumptions that (a) the units of conversational structure consist of utterances; (b) these utterances correspond to speech act types; and (c) the succession of utterances in conversation is regulated by rules that specify the range of speech act types that may appropriately follow any given speech act (Levinson, 1981; Mohan, 1974). In such a model, the assignment of speech act types is assumed to be essentially nonproblematic, the main problem being to account for their order of appearance. The advantage of such an assumption is that a model may be constructed by specifying irreducible conventions that operate directly on the surface structure of turns at talk.

The most familiar version of such a model grows out of the system of turn-taking rules proposed by Sacks, Schegloff, and Jefferson (1974). According to this rule system, one of the basic techniques for allocating turns is by initiating an adjacency pair. Adjacency pairs are action sequences such as question-answer, greeting-greeting, offer-acceptance/refusal, request-acceptance/rejection. Schegloff and Sacks (1974) argue that they are the basic constructional units for creating sequentially implicated turns at talk. Adjacency pairs are two turns long, having two parts said by different speakers in adjacent turns at talk. By using the first part of an adjacency pair (a "first pair part," or FPP), a speaker establishes a "next turn position" that casts the recipient into the role of respondent and structures the range of appropriate next moves to those second pair parts (SPPs) that are congruent with the FPP. Schegloff and Sacks (1974) suggest that this pairing is regulated by the following rule: "Given the recognizable production of a first pair part, on its first possible completion its speaker should stop and a next speaker should start and produce a second pair part from the pair type the first is recognizably a member of" (p. 239). Through such a rule, adjacency pairs create a sense of coherence in sequential structure that has been described by Schegloff (1972) in terms of conditional relevance: "By conditional relevance of one item on another we mean: Given the first, the second is expectable; upon its occurrence it can be seen to be a second item to the first; upon its nonoccurrence it can be seen to be officially absent" (p. 11).

Adjacency pairs are also regulated by a structural preference between the pair parts. Of the SPPs that can coherently combine with an FPP, there is usually one SPP that is preferred and one that is dispreferred. For example, Pomerantz (1978, 1984) has argued that evaluations are built to prefer an agreement with the evaluation ("Nice day today." "Yes, isn't it?"). And Atkinson and Drew (1979) argue that accusations prefer denials ("Who made this mess?" "It wasn't me").

Now, what is meant exactly by *structural preference* is not always clear. Bilmes (1988) has done the most careful exegesis, and his analysis suggests three more or less discrete senses that could be applied to adjacency pair structure. The first sense of preference follows from the notion of conditional relevance—if something is not done, it is noticeably absent so that the absence of a preferred SPP would imply the performance of a dispreferred SPP. Silence in response to an accusation, for example, would be taken as a tacit admission of guilt.

Another sense of preference often used by conversation analysts parallels the linguistic concept of "markedness" (Levinson, 1983, p. 333). In this sense, preferred SPPs are "unmarked" while dispreferred SPPs tend to be avoided by the discourse system and, when they occur, are "marked" in various ways as structurally irregular. Thus Levinson (1983) reviews literature suggesting that the components of adjacency pairs tend to be constructed in ways that avoid dispreferred SPPs and that dispreferred SPPs tend to be done in formats that are more complex than preferred SPPs. Dispreferred SPPs are characteristically indirect or mitigated, may be accompanied by accounts and explanations, and are often prefaced by various filler material and otherwise delayed.

A third sense of preference is similar to a functional principle of ordering and is related to a concept of repair. Certain SPPs, given an FPP, are normal and are what the FPP is designed to get while other SPPs are what the FPP is designed to avoid. This latter sense leads Jacobs and Jackson (1989) to postulate a general preference for agreement and to treat argument as a way of preparing for and repairing disagreements. Sacks (1987) also seems to point to this sense when suggesting that individuals phrase questions to get agreements (as in example 58) and answers to appear agreeable (as in example 59).

(58) **A:** They have a good cook there?
  ((pause))
  Nothing special?
 B: No, everybody takes their turns.

(59) **A:** 'N they haven't heard a *word* huh?
 B: Not a word, *uh*-uh. Not- Not a word. Not at all. *Except*- Neville's mother got a call . . .

It is also this sense that seems to lead Heritage (1984) to equate structural preference with a kind of principle of social solidarity. Regardless of particular sense, however, structural preference does not refer to the psychological desires or personal motivations of the participants but to institutional properties "built in" to the rule system itself.

The plausibility of a sequencing rule approach is further strengthened by the possibility for modeling broader stretches of conversation in the form of embedded or insertion sequences and presequences (Jefferson, 1972; Schegloff, 1972, 1980). Presequences are adjacency pairs whose component parts are interpreted relative to some adjacency pair yet to come. This prefatory character is part of their meaning (Jacobs & Jackson, 1983b; Sacks, 1967; Schegloff, 1980).

(60) **A:** You going to be finished soon?
     B: No, why?
     A: Well, it's getting pretty near the time we need to go pick up Curtie.
     B: OK. Well just give me a couple seconds to clean up and then we can go.

Insertion and embedded sequences are adjacency pairs that occur between an FPP and its SPP. These too are interpreted with respect to their position relative to the superordinate adjacency pair. Thus certain questions and statements can be understood as objections or contingent queries by virtue of their structural position between the FPP and SPP (Labov & Fanshel, 1977, p. 91).

(61) **A:** Can I have a pack of Merits?
     B: Regulars or hundreds?
     A: Regulars.
     B: Here you go.

These patterns of sequential expansion suggest rules permitting the repeated and recursive placement of subsidiary adjacency pairs before, within, and after any adjacency pair.

This analysis of adjacency pair relations and sequential expansion would appear to suggest, then, that the properties of conversational sequencing can be modeled on the basis of a three-component system of rules strikingly akin to that of a sentence grammar. Such a model requires (a) a turn-taking system for generating turn slots into which utterances may be placed, a procedure for assigning act meanings to utterances, and a set of rules for the "syntax" of conversation that can be formally expressed in terms of the basic adjacency pair relation where the subscripts designate pair parts drawn from the same type;

(A) $AP_i \rightarrow FPP_i + SPP_i$

(b) a specification of the types of adjacency pair parts where the subscripts indicate the adjacent pair type of which they can be a part; (c) an ordering of preference among the SPPs of each adjacency pair type in which dispreferred SPPs are lowest (as marked by asterisks);

(B) $FPP_i \rightarrow Greeting_A, Request_B, Question_C, Offer_D, \ldots$
(C) $SPP_i \rightarrow Greeting_A, Grant_B, *Refusal_{BD}, Answer_C, Acceptance_D, \ldots$

and (d) a rewriting rule that permits the optional expansion of adjacency pairs.

(D)   AP → (AP) + FPP + (AP) + SPP + (AP)

When applied as a system, these sorts of rules appear capable of representing many powerful intuitions natural language users have for sequential patterns as well as accommodating observable regularities in their use (Jose, 1988). By following such rules, the analyst can generate well-formed patterns and explain why the patterns in examples 62 and 63 appear ill-formed and why sequences like those in examples 64 and 65 appear to lack closure:

(62) A: How are you doing?
      B: No.
(63) A: How old are you?
      B: All right.
(64) A: Are you busy tonight?
      B: No, not really.
(65) A: Have you read this article?
      B: Which one is that?

Such rules can also represent the structural subordination of insertion sequences and presequences relative to some dominant adjacency pair by associating this with their derivative appearance through rewrite rules even though in the surface structure of talk they occur before the production and/or completion of the main adjacency pair. The rules can also represent hierarchical relations among utterances separated by indefinitely long stretches of conversation, and can generate indefinite embeddings analogous to those identified by Chomsky for sentence structures. Thus Schegloff (1972, p. 79) suggests that the following hypothetical exchange of questions and answers can be analyzed in the fashion of Figure 6.2.

(66) A: Are you coming tonight?
      B: Can I bring a guest?
      A: Male or female?
      B: What difference does that make?
      A: An issue of balance.
      B: Female.
      A: Sure.
      B: I'll be there.

So, a sequencing rule approach appears to offer a promising way to model conversational structure. Through a straightforward application of code rules and normative regulations, a variety of interesting structures and interpretations can be represented and explained. But numerous problems appear upon closer inspection.

First, there are a variety of ways to coherently fill the slot made for the appearance of an SPP that are not themselves SPPs to that FPP (Jacobs & Jackson, 1983a; Levinson, 1981; Sinclair & Coulthard, 1975). Consider what might coherently follow a straightforward question about time:

(67) FPP: What time is it?

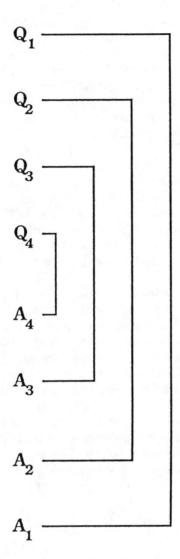

Figure 6.2. Recursive Embedding

??SPP: (i)   It's noon.
(ii) Ask Cal. He has a watch.
(iii) I'm sure it's still early.
(iv) Forget about the time and just do your work.
(v) Sorry, I don't have a watch.
(vi) It's just three minutes before class starts.

In addition to (i) direct answers, questions can also coherently receive (ii) passes that redirect the question, (iii) disagreeable responses that attempt to satisfy the demands of the question as well as possible, (iv) alternative proposals for action, (v) accounts for not answering, and (vi) indirect answers that primarily set up other information. And there are numerous other ways to coherently respond, including just showing the face of a wristwatch and saying nothing. To call all such acts "answers" reduces the sequencing rule to the empty claim that anything that is a coherent response is an answer. To drop back to the claim that "answers" are expected even if they do not occur does not explain what counts as an "answer" and still fails to explain what else can and cannot coherently follow a question. Either way, sequencing rules provide no obvious way to characterize the broad array of acts that can be a coherent reply. At best, the adjacency pair relation appears to be a normatively standardized pattern, not a general principle of sequential coherence.

Similar problems emerge in defining the constituents of structurally expanded sequences. Why, for example, are some sequences structurally subordinate expansions whereas others are digressions or wholly unrelated intrusions into an exchange (see Dascal & Katriel, 1979; Jacobs & Jackson, 1992)? What is it about some acts that places them within the structural environment of a dominant adjacency pair while excluding other temporally contiguous utterances? Sequential structure appears to be inextricably bound up in considerations of thematic content and topical continuity.

Difficulties also emerge when one tries to extend the analysis of sequential expansions to account for the full range of possible structural variations. For example, the presequential patterning of request-grant/refusal sequences may involve preemptive offers, hints, and counters, none of which is easily represented in terms of any surface structuring (Jacobs & Jackson, 1983b). Similarly, insertion sequences may exhibit complex structural relations that are not captured through rules of embedding. Notice that example 68 does not really contain an embedded sequence at all (Merritt, 1976, would argue the same for example 61). The "thanks" by B is directed at A's offer and not to the initial suggestion. So, accepting the offer as a solution to a potential objection obviates the need to produce an SPP to the initial suggestion. Contrast this with the hypothetical alternative in example 69, where "OK" would be heard to respond to the initial suggestion (because it is A's treat).

(68) **A:** Let's go eat.

  B: Well, it can't be anyplace very expensive.

  A: It's my treat today.

  B: Thanks.

(69) **A:** Let's go eat.

  B: Well, it can't be anyplace very expensive.

  A: It's my treat today.

  B: OK.

Both examples are coherent, but only example 69 can be represented by the sequential rules discussed so far.

The most immediate way out of these problems would be to postulate the existence of "transformational rules" that, like Chomskyan grammar, would provide a reading of "surface structure" utterances in terms of relations among act types represented in a kind of "deep structure." Such rules might permit operations of substitution, deletion, combination, and the like so that whatever appeared in actual utterances may be only indirectly related to the acts being performed at several hierarchically layered levels of functioning. Early efforts took this direction

(Churchill, 1978; Goffman, 1981; Labov, 1972; Merritt, 1976). But this approach has been generally abandoned. In part, this is because even this kind of representation exhausts itself in the face of the sequential complexities of actual interaction (Jacobs & Jackson, 1983b, pp. 293-295; Levinson, 1981). But it is also because such an approach, as we shall see, relies on a unifunctional and decontextualized notion of the acts as elements of those sequential structures.

At this point, it is worth noting a characteristic feature of all the reasoning about sequential structure so far: A sequencing rule approach uses act types as the labels for the structural units upon which relations of coherence are defined, but the functional properties of those acts do not enter into the characterization of why the relation should obtain. Strictly speaking, sequencing rules treat relations of coherence as essentially arbitrary and irreducible conventions of form. The meaning of an act is, at best, a derivative quality of the way it functions in grammatical relations with other acts. The sense and function of an utterance is determined by its sequential location. In other words, an answer is simply that class of utterances that can recognizably fill the slot of an SPP to a question and a question is simply that class of utterances that can recognizably combine with answers. A request is simply the class of utterances that takes grants and refusals as its SPP. A refusal is just that class of utterances that tends to occupy structurally dispreferred positions in relation to a request. As far as defining relations of coherence is concerned, question-answer or request-grant/refusal pairs might just as well be termed FPP_1-SPP_1 and FPP_2-SPP_{2p}/SPP_{2d} without any further specification of their meaning. Of course, there is nothing wrong with this sort of self-containment so long as there exists some independent procedure by which utterances can be assigned to, and generated from, act categories. The parallel here would be to a grammatical category such as definite article, which can be straightforwardly assigned to a word like *the*. The grammatical function of the category is defined relative to nouns within noun phrases (Ellis, 1992). Unfortunately, little clear progress has been made in identifying rules linking utterances to act types.

Utterances-act rules. The most straightforward approach to defining utterance-act linkages is to attempt to make the act type dependent upon the propositional content and syntactic form of the utterance. This corresponds to our intuitions that, for example, questions are characteristically associated with interrogative form, commands with imperative form, and statements with declarative form. Utterance content may also more or less explicitly contain information about the act being uttered.

(70) I promise not to talk with my mouth full.

(71) I bet it snows tonight.

(72) We find the defendant guilty as charged.

Such an approach does seem to be extendable to the description of a large class of standardized formulas and grammatical markers that are conventionally associated with the expression of a speech act (see Bach & Harnish, 1979, pp. 173-233, for an extensive review). For example, the formulas in 73 and 74 are conventionally associated with the performance of a request (Bach & Harnish, 1979) while the formulas in 75 and 76 are conventional ways to make a compliment (Knapp, Hopper, & Bell, 1984; Manes & Wolfson, 1981).

(73) Can/Will + (NEGATIVE) + (SUBJUNCTIVE) + You + IMPERATIVE? [Can you pass the salt? Would you open the door? Won't you come here? Can't you sit still? Couldn't you move?]

(74) How about VP-ing? [How about lending me a dime?]

(75) NP is/looks (really) POSITIVE ADJECTIVE [Your house looks really nice.]

(76) I (really) like/love NP [I like your haircut.]

Such an approach to identifying act-utterance linkages, however, quickly runs into insurmountable difficulties. One problem is the generativity in patterning. As the requests to leave the party in sentences 16 through 26 indicate, an indefinite range of nonstandardized forms may be employed to perform an act. Another problem is that none of these formulas can guarantee the meaning of the utterance as a matter of rule. "How about telling him yourself?" can be a suggestion, but in other contexts it can be a challenge, a criticism, a rhetorical answer, or a simple hypothetical question. "I like this shirt" can be a compliment, but it can justify wearing the shirt the speaker has on or it can be an act of selecting a shirt in a store.

Sensitive to these problems, a number of discourse analysts have suggested that utterance-act assignment rules must specify context so that utterance-act linkages are established only when certain contextual features are present. The contextual features most frequently appealed to are the felicity conditions associated with the valid performance of a speech act.

According to mainstream speech act theory (Austin, 1962; Searle, 1969), actions in language are regulated and defined by a set of rules that specify the necessary preconditions for validly performing those actions. Differences in these conditions will reflect differences in the kind of speech act being performed. In expressing a speech act, the speaker commits herself by rule to the wants and beliefs associated with the valid performance of the act. (See Searle, 1969, for an initial typology of these conditions and later revisions by Searle & Vanderveken, 1985, and Vanderveken, 1990.) So, for example, requests are subject to the requirement that the hearer is willing in principle to perform the requested act while orders require that the speaker have authority over the hearer. Information questions require that the speaker does not know the information asked for, while test questions require that the speaker does know the information but does not know whether the hearer knows the information. Or, again, promises commit the speaker to believing that the projected action is desired by the hearer; warnings commit the speaker to believing that the projected action is not desired by the hearer. And speech acts typically communicate some point or intent—what speech act the utterance "counts as" performing. For requesting, the utterance counts as an effort to get the hearer to do the desired action. For questioning, the utterance counts as an attempt to elicit the information from the hearer. The essential condition is satisfied just in those cases in which the other felicity conditions obtain.

The notion of felicity conditions has suggested to many speech act theorists that a speech act will be heard in those cases where it could be validly performed and not in those cases where its performance would be infelicitous. In other words, assuming that a speaker is encoding a message in accordance with the regulative constraints on linguistic action, a hearer can check whether or not a particular decoding would be consistent with a valid action. Along these lines, Gordon and Lakoff (1975) and Searle (1975) suggest that an utterance may trigger an indirect reading beyond its literal meaning in just those cases in which it is implausible that the speaker intends to be (simply) performing the act literally expressed in the utterance (that is, a simple statement, question, or imperative). The point that the speaker is really trying to make is cued by the fact that the propositional content of the utterance refers to a felicity condition for the indirect speech act, and this indirect reading is made if the other felicity conditions for that act are satisfied. Labov and Fanshel (1977) have proposed a similar rule for the specific case of requests. Under their rule, however, a request reading is an omnirelevant possibility. A request is searched for whenever reference is made to aspects of the proposed action or the preconditions for a request, regardless of whether or not the literal speech act is performed felicitously.

Neither of these rules is a fully satisfactory account of how act types get assigned to utterances. First, if we assume, like Searle (1975) and Gordon and Lakoff (1975), that a literal reading must be implausible in order to trigger an indirect reading of an utterance, how are we to handle cases in which a speaker means to perform both a direct and an indirect act? Consider example 77, where an instructor (me) asked an overtime student about his exam:

(77) How much longer will you be?

Not only did this utterance serve as an indirect request to finish up, it was also intended (and responded to) as an information question. Moreover, it also functioned as criticism. So, a "triggering" model based on the infelicitous performance of a literal act does not appear to be powerful enough, because it would never represent multiple acts. Alternatively, if we take Labov and Fanshel's (1977) proposal and presume the omnirelevant potential of any speech act (and not just requests), multiple act interpretations are possible, but we are faced with the problem that there is no clear way to stop the process of searching for additional indirect meanings. Talking to Labov and Fanshel's model natural language user would be like writing to a literary critic. Although natural language users do go beyond validly performed acts that are immediately apparent, they stop long before considering all possible interpretations (Clark, 1977).

A second, deeper problem for these models is that the determination of what is referred to by the propositional content of an utterance does not appear to be a rule-governed process at all. Both models assume that the propositional content of the utterance leads to an indirect reading by reference to a felicity condition for the indirect act. But, as Labov and Fanshel (1977, p. 84) note, this connection can be established only after the fact. Any propositional content can refer to any other proposition given a circuitous enough route. Because of this, they argue that a generative grammar connecting speech action to utterance forms cannot be written. One is left with the position that expectations and interpretations are guided by the context of activity. And while there is good evidence for this (Clark, 1979; Ervin-Tripp, 1976; Ervin-Tripp, Strage, Lampert, & Bell, 1987; Lecouteur, 1988; Levinson, 1979), at best this points to a jumble of cues for what is going on at any moment—a rather discouraging prospect for developing a grammar of conversation.

Toward an Inferential/Strategic Model

Problems like those discussed for a "grammar of conversational interaction" can be found at virtually all levels of discourse organization. The problem that repeatedly surfaces is that a normative code model is insufficient to explain the basic properties of language structure and use outlined at the beginning of this chapter—inference beyond the information given, generativity of patterning, contextual determination of meaning, functional design of structure, and multifunctionality. Extending a Chomskyan grammar for sentences to other domains of structure and use, which appeared to provide such a promising exemplar, has repeatedly run into a wall of resistance.

So, for example, the notion that topical coherence in texts and dialogue might be modeled by rules linking utterance form and content to the form and content of prior discourse (see Halliday & Hasan, 1976) has generally been given up by discourse analysts. Researchers in this area are instead turning to models assuming active constructive processes that bring to bear assumptions about speaker plans and strategies, general principles of rationality, and coherent representations of the world (Clark & Schaefer, 1989; Ellis, 1992; Grosz & Sidner, 1990; McLaughlin, 1984). From the very beginning, studies of stylistic code choice have encountered the phenomenon of blatant rule violation that is nevertheless meaningful and coherent (Brown & Gilman, 1960; Ervin-Tripp, 1971). These analysts are increasingly emphasizing the strategic basis for meaning in language choice (Brown & Levinson, 1987; Gumperz, 1982). Likewise, models of "story grammars" (Mandler & Johnson, 1977; Rumelhart, 1975) have given way to problem-solving approaches that integrate text with world knowledge and assumptions about speaker strategy (Hobbs, 1990b).

While current approaches take several directions, all share certain core assumptions that are at odds with those of a normative code model. Within an inferential/strategic model, messages are not understood to be transmitted through an encoding and decoding process that applies self-sufficient code rules to determine meaning. The process is viewed instead as a kind of problem-solving activity involving the assessment of mutual knowledge in the generation of speaker plans and hearer inferences as to the most plausible solution for what that speaker plan might be (Clark, 1992). In this view, apparent violations of normative expectations are "normalized" by the hearer seeing how those acts are rational solutions to the achievement of communicative ends and by the speaker assessing the likelihood that the hearer will find such a solution. Understanding a message is a matter of constructing a context of beliefs in which the speaker's utterance would make sense (Sperber & Wilson, 1986). And expressing a message is a matter of embodying through utterance that aspect of the intended context most likely to cue construction of that context for an addressee (Hermann, 1983; Lambert & O'Keefe, 1990). Rather than looking for messages in symbolic vehicles, for strategic/inferential models the context is the message (Sperber & Wilson, 1986).

How such a model might work can best be seen by illustrating its application to the problems of conversational interaction. Inferential/strategic models capitalize on the insight that utterances have points to them and preconditions for achieving those points (see Schank et al., 1982; Tracy, 1984). Conversations are coherent not because they conform to conventions of form defined across structural units of action but because they reflect a functionally sensible progression through joint activity. Rather than following rules of sequential form, people are assumed to reason from general principles of instrumental (i.e., means-ends) rationality (Jacobs & Jackson, 1983a; Levinson, 1981; Mohan, 1974; Pollack, 1990).

From an inferential/strategic perspective, it is this sort of functional design that underlies the structural coherence found by the sequencing rule approach. The adjacency pair is a standardized solution to the problem of communicating goals that an addressee must satisfy and then the addressee responding in a way that promotes or obstructs those goals. The properties of conditional relevance and structural preference find a general rationale in the functional design of the intended goal communicated by the FPP and in the way the SPP contributes to that goal. So, for example, questions have as part of their goal the intention to obtain information from the hearer, a goal achieved by supplying an answer. Requests have as their intended goal the performance of an action, a goal whose achievement is promised by a grant or denied by a refusal. (Notice that a refusal takes up the goal of the FPP, which is why it is conditionally relevant, but it obstructs that goal, which is why it is structurally dispreferred.) Such an analysis also accounts for the broad range of acts that are not SPPs but are still coherent replies (as in example 67). Such acts take up the point of the FPP in some way or another by trying to satisfy it by means other than an SPP, by supplying partial satisfaction, by renegotiating goals, by identifying the lack of relevant preconditions for achieving the goal, and so on.

The regularities and irregularities of sequential expansion can also be seen as the unfolding and interlocking of broader planlike structures. Presequences and insertion sequences are placed within the structural environment of a dominant adjacency pair in just those cases in which the acts are designed to establish or cancel a precondition necessary for the valid performance of an action (see Cohen & Perrault, 1979; Jacobs & Jackson, 1983a). Presequences and contingent queries are recognized as such just when their contribution to an underlying plan is recognized. Furthermore, the occurrence of a wide variety of irregular forms of expansion can be understood as coherent once it is seen how the conversationalists position their actions relative to the underlying goals of the conversation (Jacobs & Jackson, 1983b).

Similarly, an inferential/strategic account provides a promising way to model the communication of utterance meaning. The essential insight in the analyses of indirect speech acts discussed above is that the meaning of an utterance is discovered by constructing contexts in which an utterance can be found to have a rational functional design. One major line of analysis follows the direction charted by H. P. Grice (1989) and emphasizes how linguistic expression and interpretation are guided by very general background assumptions about rational communicative activity.

According to Grice, communication is guided by a *Cooperative Principle* (*CP*): "Make your contribution such as is required, at the stage in which it occurs, by the accepted purpose or direction of the talk exchange in which you are engaged" (p. 26). Speakers are expected to observe the CP in constructing messages and listeners assume speakers are doing so when interpreting those messages. Messages are sensible when it is understood how they pursue the accepted purpose of the talk exchange. Grice suggests that in addition to the CP messages are regulated by four classes of conversational maxims: quality (say what is true), quantity (be as informative as necessary, but not more so), relation (be relevant), and manner (be clear, efficient, orderly, and to the point). These maxims provide guides for constructing inferences (what Grice calls "implicatures") so that the message will be seen to satisfy the CP. According to Grice (1989), "to calculate a conversational implicature is to calculate what has to be supposed in order to preserve the supposition that the CP is being observed" (pp. 39-40). When the literal and direct meaning of what is said seems to violate the CP or one of its maxims, listeners do not simply conclude that the message is false, uninformative, irrelevant, unintelligible, or otherwise defective. Instead, listeners look beyond the face value of the message to construct plausible meanings that would satisfy the CP and its maxims.

This type of analysis of communicative meaning can be found in substance or form in a diverse set of models that apply to speech act inference and a variety of other discourse information (Bach & Harnish, 1979; Brown & Levinson, 1987; Clark & Haviland, 1977; Horn, 1984; Kasher, 1982; Leech, 1983; Levinson, 1983; Searle, 1975; Sperber & Wilson, 1986). While many of these approaches continue to privilege some notion of literal meaning as a first and simplest guess, many do not, and it is generally recognized in any case that contextual expectations interact with linguistic information to determine the meaning of the act performed.

The picture emerging, then, is one in which multiple sources of information are simultaneously weighed and assessed in relation to one another on the assumption that a rational solution to what is meant should be found. Rather than looking like a linear deductive process starting from linguistic input and ending, by rule, in a determinate meaning, the process of interpretation appears to look much more like a solution to an equation with several unknown values (Dascal, 1977). By juggling the unknowns in various ways, more than one solution may be obtained—a theoretically derived conclusion that accords well with the real-life uncertainties of human communication.

This framework also shows how conventional expectations about meaning may be deliberately exploited for communicative effect. As Levinson (1983) points out, theories like Grice's show

> a fundamental way in which a full account of the communicative power of language can never be reduced to a set of conventions for the use of language. The reason is that wherever some convention or expectation about the use of language arises, there will also therewith arise the possibility of the non-conventional exploitation of that convention or expectation. It follows that a purely conventional or rule-based account of natural language usage can never be complete, and that what can be communicated always exceeds the communicative power provided by the conventions of language and its use. (p. 112)

These models of conversational sequencing and utterance meaning also dovetail with recent calls to abandon speech acts as analytic categories altogether. Arguments by Levinson (1979), Jacobs (1989), and Schegloff (1988) all suggest that there is no principled way to restrict the functions served by utterances. A finite set of functions can be posited only by ignoring the situated distinctions in function drawn by ordinary language users. And for any speech act category that can be specified, there is no necessary and sufficient set of preconditions that define their valid performance. Analysts like Sanders (1987) and Sperber and Wilson (1986) question whether speech act categories have any representational role to play as participants interpret and respond to many kinds of utterances. Levinson (1981) and Jacobs and Jackson (1989) point to cases like the responses in examples 34 and 37 to suggest that what is represented are not speech acts per se but plans and goals pursued in the utterance. Indeed, if what participants attend to are the points of an utterance and the preconditions for achieving those points, this can be preserved in conversational models without taking on the conventional baggage of speech act categories. As Cohen and Levesque (1990) comment regarding their own model: "The view that illocutionary acts are not primitive and therefore need not be recognized explicitly is a liberating one" (p. 244).

Conclusion

This chapter has charted a general shift in the way discourse analysts think about the nature of language use and structure. Approaches to the problems of meaning and coherence were dominated by a normative code model of communication. That model cannot handle the manifest properties of linguistic communication and interaction, and promotes a misleading view of language meaning and language choice. Expression and interpretation are not matters of encoding and decoding meaning by determinate rules applied to signals, and language choice is not something dictated by normative regulations. In place of this model has emerged a view of linguistic communication as a process of strategic design and constructive inference. Messages are located in the interplay of text and context. Rather than a process mechanically played out by rule, discourse analysts have come to see linguistic communication as creative problem solving.

References

Akmajian, A., Demers, R. A., Farmer, A. K., & Harnish, R. M. (1990). *Linguistics* (3rd ed.). Cambridge: MIT Press.

Atkinson, J. M., & Drew, P. (1979). *Order in court*. London: Macmillan.

Austin, J. L. (1962). *How to do things with words*. Oxford: Clarendon.

Bach, K., & Harnish, R. M. (1979). *Linguistic communication and speech acts*. Cambridge: MIT Press.

Bavelas, J. B., Black, A., Chovil, N., & Mullett, J. (1990). *Equivocal communication*. Newbury Park, CA: Sage.

Berlo, D. K. (1960). *The process of communication*. New York: Holt, Rinehart & Winston.

Bilmes, J. (1988). The concept of preference in conversation analysis. *Language in Society, 17*, 161-181.

Bransford, J. D., & Johnson, M. K. (1972). Contextual prerequisites for understanding: Some investigations of comprehension and recall. *Journal of Verbal Learning and Verbal Behavior, 11*, 717-726.

Brown, G., & Yule, G. (1983). *Discourse analysis*. Cambridge: Cambridge University Press.

Brown, P., & Levinson, S. C. (1987). *Politeness*. Cambridge: Cambridge University Press.

Brown, R., & Gilman, A. (1960). The pronouns of power and solidarity. In T. A. Sebeok (Ed.), *Style in language* (pp. 253-276). Cambridge: MIT Press.

Cappella, J. N. (1990). The method of proof by example in interaction analysis. *Communication Monographs, 57*, 236-242.

Chomsky, N. (1957). *Syntactic structures*. The Hague, the Netherlands: Mouton.

Chomsky, N. (1959). Review of verbal behavior. *Language, 35*, 26-58.

Chomsky, N. (1965). *Aspects of the theory of syntax*. Cambridge: MIT Press.

Chomsky, N. (1972). *Language and mind*. New York: Harcourt Brace Jovanovich.

Churchill, L. (1978). *Questioning strategies in sociolinguistics*. Rowley, MA: Newbury House.

Clark, H. H. (1977). Bridging. In P. N. Johnson-Laird & P. C. Wason (Eds.), *Thinking: Readings in cognitive science* (pp. 411-420). Cambridge: Cambridge University Press.

Clark, H. H. (1979). Responding to indirect requests. *Cognitive Psychology, 11*, 430-477.

Clark, H. H. (1992). *Arenas of language use*. Chicago: University of Chicago.

Clark, H. H., & Haviland, S. E. (1977). Comprehension and the given-new contact. In R. O. Freedle (Ed.), *Discourse production and comprehension* (pp. 1-40). Norwood, NJ: Ablex.

Clark, H. H., & Schaefer, E. F. (1989). Contributing to discourse. *Cognitive Science, 13*, 259-294.

Clark, R. A., & Delia, J. G. (1979). Topoi and rhetorical competence. *Quarterly Journal of Speech, 65*, 187-206.

Cohen, P. R., & Levesque, H. J. (1990). Rational interaction as the basis for communication. In P. R. Cohen, J. Morgan, & M. E. Pollack (Eds.), *Intentions in communication* (pp. 221-255). Cambridge: MIT Press.

Cohen, P. R., & Perrault, C. R. (1979). Elements of a plan-based theory of speech acts. *Cognitive Science, 3*, 177-212.

Cushman, D., & Whiting, G. C. (1972). An approach to communication theory: Toward consensus on rules. *Journal of Communication, 22*, 217-238.

Dascal, M. (1977). Conversational relevance. *Journal of Pragmatics, 1*, 309-328.

Dascal, M., & Katriel, T. (1979). Digressions: A study in conversation coherence. *PTL, 4*, 203-232.

Ellis, D. G. (1992). *From language to communication*. Hillsdale, NJ: Lawrence Erlbaum.

Ervin-Tripp, S. M. (1971). Sociolinguistics. In J. A. Fishman (Ed.), *Advances in the sociology of language* (Vol. 1, pp. 15-91). The Hague, the Netherlands: Mouton.

Ervin-Tripp, S. (1976). Is Sybil there? The structure of some American English directives. *Language in Society, 5*, 25-66.

Ervin-Tripp, S. M., Strage, A., Lampert, M., & Bell, N. (1987). Understanding requests. *Linguistics, 25*, 107-143.

Fitch, K. L. (1991). The interplay of linguistic universals and cultural knowledge in personal address: Colombian *madre* terms. *Communication Monographs, 58*, 254-272.

Goffman, E. (1981). *Forms of talk*. Philadelphia: University of Pennsylvania.

Gordon, D., & Lakoff, G. (1975). Conversational postulates. In P. Cole & J. L. Morgan (Eds.), *Syntax and semantics: Vol. 3. Speech acts* (pp. 83-106). New York: Academic Press.

Grice, P. (1989). *Studies in the way of words*. Cambridge, MA: Harvard University Press.

Grosz, B. J., & Sidner, C. L. (1990). Plans for discourse. In P. R. Cohen, J. Morgan, & M. E. Pollack (Eds.), *Intentions in communication* (pp. 417-444). Cambridge: MIT Press.

Gumperz, J. J. (1982). *Discourse strategies*. Cambridge: Cambridge University Press.

Gumperz, J. J., & Hymes, D. (1972). [Editors' introduction to Sequencing in conversational openings, by E. A Schegloff, pp. 349-380]. In J. J. Gumperz & D. Hymes (Eds.), *Directions in sociolinguistics* (pp. 346-348). New York: Holt, Rinehart & Winston.

Halliday, M. A. K., & Hasan, R. (1976). *Cohesion in English*. London: Longman.

Harris, R. (1987). *The language machine*. London: Duckworth.

Heritage, J. (1984). *Garfinkel and ethnomethodology*. Cambridge, MA: Polity.

Hermann, T. (1983). *Speech and situation*. Berlin: Springer-Verlag.

Hobbs, J. (1990a). Topic drift. In B. Dorval (Ed.), *Conversational organization and its development* (pp. 3-22). Norwood, NJ: Ablex.

Hobbs, J. (1990b). *Literature and cognition*. Stanford, CA: Center for the Study of Language and Information.

Hook, S. (Ed.). (1969). *Language and philosophy*. New York: New York University.

Hopper, R. (1992). *Telephone conversation*. Bloomington: University of Indiana.

Horn, L. R. (1984). Toward a new taxonomy for pragmatic inference: Q-based and R-based implicature. In D. Schiffrin (Ed.), *Meaning, form, and use in context* (pp. 11-42). Washington, DC: Georgetown University Press.

Jacobs, S. (1989). Speech acts and arguments. *Argumentation, 3*, 23-43.

Jacobs, S. (1990). On the especially nice fit between qualitative analysis and the known properties of conversation. *Communication Monographs, 57*, 243-249.

Jacobs, S., & Jackson, S. (1983a). Speech act structure in conversation: Rational aspects of pragmatic coherence. In R. T. Craig & K. Tracy (Eds.), *Conversational coherence* (pp. 47-66). Beverly Hills, CA: Sage.

Jacobs, S., & Jackson, S. (1983b). Strategy and structure in conversational influence attempts. *Communication Monographs, 50*, 285-305.

Jacobs, S., & Jackson, S. (1989). Building a model of conversational argument. In B. Dervin, L. Grossberg, B. J. O'Keefe, & E. Wartella (Eds.), *Rethinking communication: Vol. 2. Paradigm exemplars* (pp. 153-171). Newbury Park, CA: Sage.

Jacobs, S., & Jackson, S. (1992). Relevance and digressions in argumentative discussion: A pragmatic approach. *Argumentation, 6*, 161-172.

Jefferson, G. (1972). Side sequences. In D. Sudnow (Ed.), *Studies in social interaction* (pp. 294-338). New York: Free Press.

Johnson-Laird, P. N. (1983). *Mental models*. Cambridge, MA: Harvard University Press.

Jose, P. E. (1988). Sequentiality of speech acts in conversational structure. *Journal of Psycholinguistic Research, 17*, 65-88.

Kasher, A. (1982). Gricean inference revisited. *Philosophica, 29*, 25-44.

Kellerman, K., Broetzmann, S., Lim, T., & Kitao, K. (1989). The conversation MOP: Scenes in the stream of discourse. *Discourse Processes, 12*, 27-62.

Knapp, M. L., Hopper, R., & Bell, R. A. (1984). Compliments: A descriptive taxonomy. *Journal of Communication, 34*, 12-31.

Labov, W. (1972). *Sociolinguistic patterns*. Philadelphia: University of Pennsylvania.

Labov, W., & Fanshel, D. (1977). *Therapeutic discourse*. New York: Academic Press.

Lambert, B. L., & O'Keefe, B. J. (1990, November). *Modelling message design*. Paper presented at the annual meeting of the Speech Communication Association, Chicago.

Lecouteur, A. J. (1988). Understanding unconventional requests. *Linguistics, 26*, 873-877.

Leech, G. (1983). *Principles of pragmatics*. London: Longman.

Levinson, S. C. (1979). Activity types and language. *Linguistics, 17*, 365-399.

Levinson, S. C. (1981). Some pre-observations on the modeling of dialogue. *Discourse Processes, 4*, 93-116.

Levinson, S. C. (1983). *Pragmatics*. Cambridge: Cambridge University Press.

Locke, J. (1975). *Essay concerning human understanding* (P. H. Nidditch, Ed.). Oxford: Clarendon. (Original work published 1690)

Lyons, J. (1970). *Noam Chomsky*. New York: Viking.

Malinowski, B. (1923). The problem of meaning in primitive languages. In C. K. Ogden & I. A. Richards (Eds.), *The meaning of meaning* (pp. 296-336). New York: Harcourt, Brace & World.

Malinowski, B. (1935). *Coral gardens and their magic* (2 vols.). New York: Dover.

Mandelbaum, J., & Pomerantz, A. (1991). What drives social action? In K. Tracy (Ed.), *Understanding face-to-face interaction* (pp. 151-166). Hillsdale, NJ: Lawrence Erlbaum.

Mandler, J. M., & Johnson, N. S. (1977). Remembrance of things parsed: Story structure and recall. *Cognitive Psychology, 9*, 111-151.

Manes, J., & Wolfson, N. (1981). The compliment formula. In F. Coulmas (Ed.), *Conversational routine* (pp. 115-132). The Hague, the Netherlands: Mouton.

McLaughlin, M. L. (1984). *Conversation*. Beverly Hills, CA: Sage.

Merritt, M. (1976). On questions following questions in service encounters. *Language in Society, 5*, 315-357.

Mohan, B. J. (1974). Do sequencing rules exist? *Semiotica, 12*, 75-96.

Newmeyer, F. J. (1980). *Linguistic theory in America*. New York: Academic Press.

O'Keefe, B. J. (1990). The logic of regulative communication: Understanding the rationality of message designs. In J. P. Dillard (Ed.), *Seeking compliance* (pp. 87-104). Scottsdale, AZ: Gorsuch Scarisbrick.

O'Keefe, B. J. (1991). Message design logic and the management of multiple goals. In K. Tracy (Ed.), *Understanding face-to-face interaction* (pp. 131-150). Hillsdale, NJ: Lawrence Erlbaum.

Pollack, M. E. (1990). Plans as complex mental attitudes. In P. R. Cohen, J. Morgan, & M. E. Pollack (Eds.), *Intentions in communication* (pp. 77-103). Cambridge: MIT Press.

Pomerantz, A. (1978). Compliment responses: Notes on the co-operation of multiple constraints. In J. Schenkein (Ed.), *Studies in the organization of conversational interaction* (pp. 79-112). New York: Academic Press.

Pomerantz, A. (1984). Agreeing and disagreeing with assessments: Some features of preferred/dispreferred turn shapes. In J. M. Atkinson & J. Heritage (Eds.), *Structures of social action* (pp. 57-101). Cambridge: Cambridge University Press.

Reddy, J. J. (1979). The conduit metaphor: A case of frame conflict in our language about language. In A. Ortony (Ed.), *Metaphor and thought* (pp. 284-324). Cambridge: Cambridge University Press.

Rommetveit, R. (1974). *On message structure*. London: Wiley.

Rumelhart, D. C. (1975). Notes on a schema for stories. In D. G. Bobrow & A. Collins (Eds.), *Representation and understanding* (pp. 211-236). New York: Academic Press.

Sacks, H. (1967). Unpublished lectures, University of California, Los Angeles.

Sacks, H. (1987). On the preferences for agreement and contiguity in sequences in conversation. In G. Button & J. R. E. Lee (Eds.), *Talk and social organization* (pp. 54-69). Clevedon, England: Multilingual Matters.

Sacks, H., Schegloff, E. A., & Jefferson, G. (1974). A simplest systematics for the organization of turn taking for conversation. *Language, 50*, 696-735.

Sanders, R. E. (1987). *Cognitive foundations of calculated speech*. Albany: SUNY Press.

Saussure, F. de (1983). *Cours de linguistique generale* (R. Harris, Trans). London: Duckworth. (Original work published 1916)

Schank, R. C., Collins, G. C., Davis, E., Johnson, P. N., Lytinen, S., & Reiser, B. J. (1982). What's the point? *Cognitive Science, 6*, 255-275.

Schegloff, E. A. (1972). Notes on a conversational practice: Formulating place. In D. Sudnow (Ed.), *Studies in social interaction* (pp. 75-119). New York: Free Press.

Schegloff, E. A. (1980). Preliminaries to preliminaries: "Can I ask you a question?" *Sociological Inquiry, 50*, 104-152.

Schegloff, E. A. (1988). Presequences and indirection. *Journal of Pragmatics, 12*, 55-62.

Schegloff, E. A., & Sacks, H. (1974). Opening up closings. In R. Turner (Ed.), *Ethnomethodology* (pp. 223-264). Harmondsworth, Middlesex, England: Penguin Education.

Schenkein, J. (1978). Sketch of an analytic mentality for the study of conversational interaction. In J. Schenkein (Ed.), *Studies in the organization of conversational interaction* (pp. 1-6). New York: Academic Press.

Searle, J. R. (1969). *Speech acts*. Cambridge: Cambridge University Press.

Searle, J. R. (1975). Indirect speech acts. In P. Cole & J. L. Morgan (Eds.) *Syntax and semantics: Vol. 3. Speech acts* (pp. 59-78). New York: Academic Press.

Searle, J. R. (1980). The background of meaning. In J. R. Searle, F. Kiefer, & M. Bierwisch (Eds.), *Speech act theory and pragmatics* (pp. 221-232). Dordrecht, Holland: D. Reidel.

Searle, J. R. (1989). How performatives work. *Linguistics and Philosophy, 12,* 535-558.

Searle, J. R., & Vanderveken, D. (1985). *Foundations of illocutionary logic*. Cambridge: Cambridge University Press.

Sells, P. (1985). *Lectures on contemporary syntactic theories*. Stanford, CA: Center for the Study of Language and Information.

Shannon, C. E., & Weaver, W. (1949). *The mathematical theory of communication*. Urbana: University of Illinois.

Shimanoff, S. B. (1980). *Communication rules*. Beverly Hills, CA: Sage.

Sigman, S. J. (1987). *A perspective on social communication*. Lexington, MA: Lexington.

Sinclair, J. M. C. H., & Coulthard, R. M. (1975). *Toward an analysis of discourse*. Oxford: Oxford University Press.

Smith, N., & Wilson, D. (1990). *Modern linguistics*. London: Penguin.

Soames, S., & Perlmutter, D. M. (1979). *Syntactic argumentation and the structure of English*. Berkeley: University of California.

Sperber, D., & Wilson, D. (1986). *Relevance*. Cambridge, MA: Harvard University Press.

Taylor, T. J. (1992). *Mutual misunderstanding*. Durham, NC: Duke University Press.

Taylor, T. J., & Cameron, D. (1987). *Analyzing conversation*. Oxford: Pergamon.

Tracy, K. (1984). Staying on topic: An explication of conversational relevance. *Discourse Processes, 7,* 447-464.

Vanderveken, D. (1990). *Meaning and speech acts* (2 vols.). Cambridge: Cambridge University Press.

Wilson, T. P. (1970). Normative and interpretive paradigms in sociology. In J. D. Douglas (Ed.), *Understanding everyday life* (pp. 57-79). Chicago: Aldine.

Wittgenstein, L. (1953). *Philosophical investigations* (G. E. M. Anscombe, Trans.). New York: Macmillan.

7

Nonverbal Signals

Judee K. Burgoon

POETS AND PUNDITS, SAGES AND SONGWRITERS, have all waxed lyrical about the powers of nonverbal communication, their sentiments captured in Edward Sapir's (1949) now famous quote: "We respond to gestures with an extreme alertness and, one might almost say, in accordance with an elaborate and secret code that is written nowhere, known to none, and understood by all" (p. 556). That the code is understood by all may be hyperbole, but it underscores the universality of nonverbal signals as a communication coding system. That the code may be known to none is a deficiency to be partly remedied in this chapter.

What Is Nonverbal Communication?

Most people have an intuitive sense about what nonverbal communication is. Often called "body language" in the popular vernacular, it is assumed to include gestures, facial expressions, body movement, gaze, dress, and the like to send messages. But this notion of body language is fairly vague and omits a number of important communicative nonverbal elements (such as use of the voice, touch, distancing, time, and physical objects as messages). Moreover, popularized books with such titles as *How to Read a Person Like a Book* and *Your Every Move Talks* promote (wrongly) the impression that all human behavior is communicative.

A corollary to this assumption is that "one cannot not communicate," a claim that has given rise to extended debate on what constitutes nonverbal communication. Originating in a classic work by Watzlawick, Beavin, and Jackson, the *Pragmatics of Human Communication* (1967), and now deeply entrenched in many basic communication texts, the claim, reinterpreted as "all nonverbal behavior is

AUTHOR'S NOTE: I am grateful to David Buller, Lesa Stern, Amy Ebesu, Laura Guerrero, Cindy White, and Mark Knapp for their helpful comments on this chapter.

communicative," reflects a *receiver (decoder) orientation* to nonverbal communication. The receiver orientation places the locus for deciding what is communication with the receiver. If a receiver thinks a behavior is a message, it is. This makes all human action potentially communicative. For example, an ear tug can be interpreted as discomfort or deception if an observer chooses to "read" it as that. Even the act of sleeping can be regarded as a "message" of inaccessibility to others. The only requirements are that the action occur in the presence of a receiver, who must be aware of it to form some interpretation of it.

Aside from the personal discomfort such a position may cause by putting everyone on the alert full time to the potential messages they and others are giving off, a serious pragmatic disadvantage of this position is that it becomes very difficult to arrive at any general principles about human communication if all human behavior counts as communication. It also places the locus of what constitutes communication strictly with the receiver, making the sender's role irrelevant. And it makes the term *communication* completely redundant with the term *behavior* and therefore dispensable.

At the other extreme is the *source (encoder) orientation*, which holds that only actions intended by a source qualify as communication. This narrows the domain of nonverbal communication considerably. The rub comes in the issue of intent. Apart from the practical obstacles to determining just which nonverbal behaviors are intentional and which are not, the issue of whether intentionality is a legitimate criterion for defining communication is a hotly contested one (see, e.g., Andersen, 1991; Bavelas, 1990; Clevenger, 1991; Kellermann, 1992; Knapp, 1984a; Motley, 1990a, 1990b, 1991; Stamp & Knapp, 1990). On one side of the issue is the argument that communication need not be intentional or even symbolic. In support of this position, Andersen (1991) has proposed a typology that distinguishes several types of nonverbal communication from incidental perceptions and nonreceived messages, including *intuitive communication* (incidentally received spontaneous communication, which purportedly covers much of nonverbal communication), *incidental communication* (intentionally sent symbolic messages that are received unconsciously), *informative communication* (symptomatic behaviors that are not intended as messages but are interpreted by receivers), and *interpretative communication* (spontaneous, analogic, and nonsymbolic messages that are consciously received and interpreted). These distinctions are reminiscent of earlier claims by Ekman and Friesen (1969b) and Knapp (1984b), among others, that informative or expressive behaviors—acts that produce similar interpretations in observers but are not intentional—are as relevant to understanding nonverbal exchanges as are purposive (intentional) behaviors.

On the other side of the issue are scholars like Motley (1990b) and Bavelas (1990), who argue for restricting communication to (a) *other-directed behavior* that is (b) *encoded* (i.e., transformed from a cognition into some code), (c) *symbolic* (including symptomatic behaviors that function as symbols), and (d) part of a *two-way, interactive process*. But the restrictiveness of this definition evaporates if one accepts Bavelas's (1990) contention that, in interactive situations, one cannot not communicate because one's behavior at minimum sends messages about availability for communication.

An alternative I have proposed that is sympathetic to Motley's and Bavelas's views while incorporating some of the preceding distinctions under a single umbrella is a *message orientation* (Burgoon, 1980). The message orientation shifts focus from senders and receivers to the behaviors themselves, specifically to what behaviors could reasonably function as messages within a given speech community. Thus I define *nonverbal communication* as *those behaviors other than words themselves that form a socially shared coding system; that is, they are typically sent with intent, typically interpreted as intentional, used with regularity among members of a speech community, and have consensually recognizable interpretations.* This approach is similar to that of Wiener, Devoe, Rubinow, and Geller (1972) in emphasizing socially shared rather than idiosyncratic behavior patterns. However, it is broader than their approach in that it includes habitual behaviors that have well-recognized meanings among members of the social system. The operative word is *typically.* If a behavior is often encoded deliberately and interpreted as meaningful by receivers or observers, it does not matter if, on a given occasion, it is performed unconsciously or unintentionally; it can still qualify as a message. For example, an "unintended" frown can be regarded as a message because the behavior is one that people typically encode as a signal of displeasure and typically decode as an intentional signal of displeasure. If we accept the notion that much of our daily nonverbal communication is well practiced and operates in a semiautomatic, unmonitored fashion (what some might call a "mindless" fashion), then it becomes more productive to identify the "vocabulary" of nonverbal communication than to divine intent on each occasion of a behavior's enactment. At the same time, the requirement that a behavior be used with regularity as part of a coding system implies that communicators frequently select it to convey a particular meaning and that recipients or observers treat it as a purposive and meaningful signal.

This approach does not ignore intent entirely. On any given occasion, both sender and receiver may recognize that a behavior was not deliberate or was not directed toward the other individual as a message. If a receiver recognizes that a frown was prompted by some external factor—such as stubbing one's toe—and was a spontaneous reaction not meant for an audience, neither sender nor receiver would regard it as a message on that occasion. Thus behaviors that both parties regard as unintentional or incidental are not communication. In this respect, the message orientation shares some commonality with Stamp and Knapp's (1990) *interaction perspective,* in which sender and receiver negotiate meanings within the context of a particular interaction. To the extent that an interactive perspective permits the concept of senders and receivers drawing upon a limited set of consensually based meanings associated with the behaviors in question, with the range of meanings being constrained by the contextual cues present in the interaction, the two perspectives would be compatible.

Although a distinction is often made between spontaneous and involuntary nonverbal expressions (variously labeled as signs, symptoms, indicative behavior, expressive behavior, rituals, or biologically shared signal systems) and symbolic or socially shared signal systems (e.g., Buck, 1988; Cronkhite, 1986; Ekman & Friesen, 1969b; Liska, 1986; Mahl, 1987), the message orientation does not exclude the former from the domain of nonverbal communication, unless it is so unfamiliar or unusual in form that others have no meaning for it. Rather, the focus on messages calls attention to the fact that much cathartic and expressive behavior takes the form of acts with shared meaning. When behaviors originating as "symptoms" or "signs" are used for communicative purposes, they in a sense become symbolic (see Motley, 1991).

Implicit in the message orientation is the assumption that nonverbal communication is rule governed. Just as a coding system must have semantic and syntactic rules, so must nonverbal signals as they are combined to form messages—if they are to be treated as a coding system. This assumption delimits the nonverbal domain to the extent that it excludes behaviors that lack consistent meanings and behaviors that fail to be combined in systematic, "grammatical" ways with other nonverbal signals.

Also implicit in the message orientation is the recognition that meanings are context dependent. As with our verbal lexicon, the possible interpretations for a given behavior or set of behaviors are constrained by the context in which it occurs and by the concurrent or preceding verbal and nonverbal behaviors. So, for example, a squint in the presence of bright sunlight might merely be regarded as an adaptive reaction to the environment (i.e., symptomatic) rather than as communicative; the same squint in the midst of a heated discussion about politics might be taken as a display of puzzlement or disagreement. If accompanied by head shaking and the statement, "Where do you get these crazy ideas?" the latter meaning would become increasingly probable.

Using this message-centered approach, some classes of nonverbal signals qualify as communication while others do not. For example, natural body odors, although a potential signal system (much as nonhuman species use them), do not meet the criteria of a coding system because they are not intentional, voluntarily encoded signals, nor do they typically evoke a consistent interpretation from receivers. Similarly, body type doesn't qualify as a message in itself because the individual is unable to manipulate it at will to encode a particular meaning (e.g., I can't decide to be tall today), although dieting, body building, and clothing choices emphasizing thinness or height might be seen as deliberate acts to modify the image one is projecting.

Guided by this orientation, my colleagues and I have identified seven classes of nonverbal signals as codes—vehicles for communication. These encompass most of the codes or channels traditionally regarded as part of nonverbal communication but omit some included by others (e.g., olfactics) and include some ignored by others. The seven are (a) *kinesics* (visual bodily movements, including gestures, facial expressions, trunk and limb movements, posture, gaze, and the like); (b) *vocalics or paralanguage* (use of vocal cues other than the words themselves, including such features as pitch, loudness, tempo, pauses, and inflection); (c) *physical appearance* (manipulable features such as clothing, hairstyle, cosmetics, fragrances, and adornments; nonmanipulable features such as physiognomy and height are excluded); (d) *haptics* (use of touch); (e) *proxemics* (use of interpersonal distance and spacing relationships); (f) *chronemics* (use of time as a message system, including such code elements as punctuality, waiting time, lead time, and amount of time spent with someone); and (g) *artifacts* (manipulable objects and environmental features that may convey messages from their designers or users).

The Importance of Nonverbal Behavior

In some respects, the importance of nonverbal communication should be patently obvious. After all, not only are nonverbal signals ubiquitous in interpersonal exchanges, they have always laid claim to communicative primacy—in our evolutionary development as a species, in our ontological development as individuals, and in our initial encounters with others. Notwithstanding, I wrote in the first edition of this volume that the designation . . . of nonverbal signals as "fundamental units" in interpersonal communication belies the recognition they have been given by the community of interpersonal communication scholars. . . . Too often, the nonverbal component of interpersonal interchanges has received only passing reference or has been ignored entirely. Such oversight can lead to some erroneous conclusions about the interpersonal communication process. (Burgoon, 1985a, p. 344)

My first thought in revising this version was that surely matters had changed considerably in the last decade. That hunch, however, proved to be overly optimistic. While it is true that some traditionally verbally oriented research has begun to recognize the importance of nonverbal communication in the total interpersonal communication enterprise, progress has been fairly slow. And so the case must still be made that nonverbal behavior is a fundamental and potent part of the interpersonal communication process.

Some Illustrations

Consider some popular lines of research and the risks involved in ignoring the nonverbal codes that accompany verbal behavior:

1. Reciprocity of intimate self-disclosure. An issue attracting substantial research attention is whether people reciprocate each other's level of intimacy in interpersonal interactions. A common format for studying this is to have a sender disclose intimate or nonintimate information about self on several topics and examine whether the receiver responds with equally intimate disclosures (see Dindia, 1982). A crucial assumption in these studies is that the sender's verbal behavior is what influences the receiver's verbal responses. A problem with this assumption is that it ignores the possibility of senders tempering their verbal behavior with accompanying nonverbal cues that intensify or deintensify the total intimacy level of the interaction. For example, people sometimes find highly intimate disclosures difficult to make and may tone them down with a nonintimate nonverbal style. Or if the disclosures are too impersonal, people may attempt to create an impression of intimacy by adding affiliative nonverbal cues. In either case, the "real" level of intimacy is different than the experimenter thinks, and it may be the nonverbal behaviors or the verbal-nonverbal combinations that are responsible for the receiver's response rather than the sender's verbal disclosure alone. Likewise, looking at only the receiver's verbal behavior as indicative of the receiver's intimacy level can be misleading. The receiver may also reciprocate or compensate for the verbal intimacy level, something demonstrated by Firestone (1977) and Hale and Burgoon (1984). The end result may be the false conclusion that reciprocity did not occur when in fact it did, or, conversely, that it did occur when in reality it did not.

2. Relational control strategies. As discussed in more detail in the Parks chapter in this volume, quantification of relational control has attracted extensive research attention. One coding system developed by Rogers and Farace (1975) is frequently used to identify who in an interaction is dominant or "in control." It defines one-up, one-cross, and one-down moves on the basis of people's verbal statements. A one-up move, such as a command, followed by a one-down move, such as a supportive reply, qualifies as an instance of dominance by the person engaging in the one-up behavior. The problems in relying strictly on verbal criteria to classify dominant and submissive (or symmetrical and complementary) behavior are two-fold. First, vocal (paralinguistic) behavior may alter significantly the function and meaning of an utterance. A reply that appears supportive on the surface—"I'll be happy to do it"—may actually not be supportive at all if said in a sarcastic voice. A question may actually be a command (instruction)—"Will you please stop bugging me?"—and so on. It becomes easy to misclassify specific utterances and draw faulty conclusions about who is controlling the interaction. Second, numerous other nonverbal behaviors have dominance-submission interpretations. When they accompany a verbal statement, they may neutralize or radically modify the total meaning of an utterance. For example, extreme physical proximity and a stare may turn an apparently mollifying statement into an aggressive one. Despite these shortcomings, much research has continued to use this coding system without taking accompanying nonverbal behavior into account (e.g., Courtright, Millar, Rogers, & Bagarozzi, 1990). One promising exception is a nonverbal coding system developed by Siegel, Friedlander, and Heatherington (1992), which includes 33 nonverbal behaviors that serve the same one-up and one-down functions as verbal behavior. Whether this system will gain acceptability remains to be seen.

3. Conflict and negotiation strategies. Several typologies and coding systems specify strategies or styles people use when managing disagreements or engaging in negotiation (see, e.g., Burggraf & Sillars, 1987; Donohue, 1981; J. B. Miller, 1989; Putnam & Wilson, 1982). The same problems apply here as for the relational control coding scheme. For example, an assertively expressed criticism can be transformed into a message of concern, liking, and nondominance when expressed in an unassertive nonverbal style (Stern, 1990). Or a regressive-appearing statement, such as this one: "Your point is well taken," can actually be a nonsupportive defending move if accompanied by such nonverbal behaviors as backward lean, indirect body orientation, gaze aversion, and facial impassivity. The failure to take account of the concomitant "nonverbal text" of a confrontation may lead to inaccurate conclusions about which tactics are successful or how confrontational a particular strategy is.

4. Compliance-gaining strategies. Much recent communication research has addressed the efficacy of Marwell and Schmitt's (1967) 16 strategies for gaining compliance (see the Seibold, Cantrill, & Meyers chapter, this volume). Although the strategies need not be defined exclusively in terms of verbal behavior, they have typically been studied only at the verbal level. For example, "personal expertise" is said to exist if a person makes an explicit claim of such, not if nonverbal credibility cues are presented. "Threats" are verbal ones, not nonverbal ones, and so forth. Narrow definitions of persuasive strategies not only lead to misestimates of how much influence is going on in actual face-to-face encounters but also direct research attention away from the significant interplay between verbal and nonverbal cues, which may be far more productive to study.

Nonverbal Impact

The examples above indirectly imply that nonverbal signals are integral to the total social meaning of an interaction. More direct substantiation is available. A much-repeated estimate in the popular literature is that 93% of the meaning in an exchange comes from nonverbal cues, leaving only 7% to be borne by the verbal utterance (Mehrabian & Wiener, 1967). Unfortunately, this estimate is based on faulty analysis (see Burgoon, Buller, & Woodall, 1989; Hegstrom, 1979), but its widespread citation has led many to believe that all estimates of nonverbal communication's importance are grossly exaggerated.

A more reasonable estimate comes from Birdwhistell (1955), who claimed that 60% to 65% of the meaning in a social situation is communicated nonverbally. Although he offered no empirical evidence for his assertion, it is squarely in line with an estimate derived from meta-analysis of 23 studies showing that approximately 31% of the variance in meaning can be attributed to the verbal channel, the remainder presumably accounted for by nonverbal cues or their interaction with verbal ones (Philpott, 1983).

The type of research reviewed in the meta-analysis compares verbal and nonverbal signals on their relative contributions to meaning. A series of studies by Argyle and associates (Argyle, Alkema, & Gilmour, 1971; Argyle, Salter, Nicholson, Williams, & Burgess, 1970) provide striking illustration of the potential impact of nonverbal elements. In those experiments, friendly, neutral, and unfriendly verbal passages were paired with friendly, neutral, and unfriendly nonverbal presentations; or superior, neutral, and inferior attitudinal statements were combined with parallel nonverbal behaviors. Even though the verbal and nonverbal presentations, when rated separately, were seen as relatively equal in strength, when combined the nonverbal cues accounted for as much as 12.5 times as much variance in meaning as did the verbal statements. An attempt to make the verbal presentation stronger in advance still produced more reliance on the nonverbal cues when both the verbal and the nonverbal were presented together.

Numerous other investigations have found that adults tend to place greater reliance on nonverbal than verbal cues in such varied circumstances as job interviews, assessments of leadership, therapeutic sessions, attitudinal expressions, and judgments of first impressions. The nonverbal cues are especially likely to be believed when they conflict with the verbal message. The research findings can be framed as a series of propositions regarding reliance on nonverbal as compared with verbal information (see Burgoon, 1985b; Burgoon, Buller, & Woodall, 1989, for summaries):

1. Adults generally rely more on nonverbal than verbal cues in determining social meaning. As a broad generalization, this principle holds but must be qualified by the propositions that follow.

2. Children rely more on verbal than nonverbal cues. As children acquire language, they become highly literal. For example, they do not interpret sarcasm well. Prior to puberty, however, they shift to greater belief in nonverbal signals.

3. Adult reliance on nonverbal cues is greatest when the verbal and nonverbal messages conflict; verbal cues become increasingly important as the messages become more congruent. Some research finds that, under congruent message conditions, verbal messages are believed over nonverbal ones. But more commonly, congruency among channels just makes the verbal and nonverbal coding systems more equal in their contribution to meaning.

4. Channel reliance depends on what communication function is operative. Verbal cues are more important for factual, abstract, and persuasive communications, whereas nonverbal cues are more important for relational, attributional, affective, and attitudinal messages. Not surprising, people rely on verbalizations for the denotative or "objective" meaning of a message. But for connotations, metamessages, emotional expressions, and meanings about the interpersonal relationship between speaker and auditor, people largely depend on nonverbal signals. This makes nonverbal behavior especially important in interpersonal contexts.

5. When content across channels is congruent, the information from all contributing channels tends to be averaged together equally; when content is incongruent, channels and cues may be weighted differentially. Sometimes a single cue or channel will be discounted if two or more other cues are consistent with each other. For example, forward lean and close proximity may be sufficient to convey conversational involvement even if a person leans backward. Sometimes people believe the most extreme or negative cue. But nonverbal cues still tend to be believed over verbal ones, even if the verbal message is more extreme.

6. Individuals have consistent biases in channel reliance. Some consistently depend on verbal information; some consistently depend on nonverbal information; and some are situationally adaptable. Although individuals have their personal predilections for which channels of information they attend to most often, the prevailing pattern is still one of relying more frequently and for more purposes on the nonverbal codes.

A variety of reasons have been offered for the significant dependence on nonverbal channels in interpreting and expressing interpersonal messages. These include possible innate origins for nonverbal attention and expression, phylogenetic and ontogenetic primacy of nonverbal cues as coding systems, belief in their veridicality and spontaneity, their ability to reveal psychological and emotional information about the interactants, their special suitability to handling interpersonal business while the verbal channel is simultaneously occupied with transmitting other information, and their substantial role in clarifying verbal content. Regardless of which reasons are most correct, it is clear that nonverbal signals are critical to understanding interpersonal communication.

Nonverbal Communication in Interpersonal Contexts

Just as the nonverbal side of interpersonal communication has often been neglected, so has the interpersonal side of nonverbal communication. A perusal of the extant nonverbal literature reveals that much of the work is not interpersonal in nature and therefore may not be directly generalizable to interpersonal communication. This raises the question of what would make this research "interpersonal."

Several criteria that my colleagues and I have forwarded for an interpersonal communication perspective on deception (Burgoon, Buller, Dillman, & Walther, 1993) are equally applicable to other functions of nonverbal behavior and coincide with many that Knapp (1985; Knapp, Cody, & Reardon, 1987) and Markman (1988) identified as increasingly salient when shifting from noninteractive to interactive situations and from perceptual to behavioral emphasis.

A first feature is investigating nonverbal signals in the context of actual interaction. This means that people do not simply judge another's nonverbal behavior via videotape, audiotape, or written transcript. Nor do they merely receive bogus information about the partner via an experimenter (common in attraction studies) or interact via some artificial note-passing system. Instead, they actually communicate with one another face-to-face or by telephone. Such interactions may be free-flowing conversations or may entail systematic changes in behavior by one or both participants (as in the case of experimentally manipulated behavior by a confederate).

When people interact with one another, numerous factors come into play that are absent in noninteractive situations. People become concerned with how they are presenting themselves to other participants, public norms for appropriate behavior become salient, and the demands of managing the conversation itself impinge upon the verbal and nonverbal behaviors that are displayed. Also, people may feel they have more at stake when they are confronted with a real person than when they respond, say, to a videotape. They may even have the sense that a fledgling relationship is in the making. Certainly, the perceived prospects for future interaction increase once people become acquainted. The sensory engagement and visceral reactions that occur in face-to-face interactions may also significantly alter behavior. A touch that seemed innocuous when viewed on videotape may elicit very different reactions when experienced personally.

Conversely, factors that are relevant when studied noninteractively may become inconsequential when studied interactively. Static preinteraction factors such as physical attractiveness may pale in comparison with dynamic qualities such as a person's engaging communication style or sense of humor that surface once a conversation begins. Sunnafrank (1992) has contended, for example, that attitude similarity prior to interaction evaporates as a predictor of attraction once people actually interact with one another. Burgoon, Manusov, Mineo, and Hale (1985) similarly found that initial differences in the qualifications of ostensive job applicants disappeared once the applicants were interviewed because their interview behavior made all of the confederate applicants appear credible.

A second feature of an interpersonal perspective is widening the lens beyond individuals to relationships. Senders and receivers each have goals, plans, expectations, preferences, behavioral routines, and interpretive processes that they bring to interpersonal encounters. The interplay among these factors and the extent to which one person's wants or behaviors are congruent or at cross-purposes with the other's add a new level of complexity to understanding nonverbal communication in interpersonal contexts because sender and receiver factors must be systematically linked to each other. Analyzing expectancy violations, for instance, requires connecting receiver expectations to sender-enacted behaviors. Often (but not always), this requires a shift from the individual to the dyad as the unit of analysis. Jointly defined behavioral patterns, sequences of moves and countermoves, and relationships between one person's behaviors and the other's interpretations become the typical bill of fare. Other relationship-level variables such as familiarity, liking, power, gender combination, credibility, and attraction also take on increasing prominence relative to individual characteristics such as personality, gender, authority, expertise, and physical attractiveness. And interaction *patterns* such as reciprocity, compensation, and dominance come to the fore.

A third feature is increasing emphasis on behavior. Behaviors are the currency through which interpersonal encounters and relationships are transacted. They are the concrete "goods" that are exchanged and form the basis for intangible, symbolic outcomes (such as love, concern) that come to define interpersonal relationships (see Kelley, 1986). Increased payoff comes from expanding the focus beyond psychological or cognitive variables to behavioral variables such as nonverbal communicator style, skills, and relational messages if we are to understand how people actually go about jointly managing interactions and constructing relationships.

As evidence of this shift toward a focus on actual performance, much communication and psychology literature has begun addressing what characteristics predispose individuals to be skilled, competent communicators. The result has been a proliferation of self-report measures related to communication skills and abilities. Although some neglect any mention of nonverbal behavior (e.g., Samter & Burleson's, 1990, Communication Functions Questionnaire), many measures now implicitly or explicitly acknowledge the role of nonverbal encoding and decoding abilities. Sample self-report measures include the Communication Competency Assessment Instrument (Rubin, 1982), the Communicator Style Measure (Norton, 1983), and the Interpersonal Orientation Measure (Swap & Rubin, 1983); others are noted later. Research has shown that nonverbal encoding and decoding skills are highly relevant predictors of interpersonal communication success and are featured prominently in all the interpersonal communication functions to be discussed.

A *fourth feature is emphasizing process and interaction dynamics.* A cardinal principle of interpersonal communication is that it is a dynamic, evolving process. Studying process typically involves examining temporal features and how nonverbal and verbal behaviors change longitudinally over the course of an interaction or relationship. Yet most interpersonal research has taken a static approach, tacitly treating behavior as constant rather than changeable and inspecting brief snippets of interaction that may be "shirttail cousins" to nonverbal dynamics in normal extended discourse.

A *fifth feature is acknowledging that most interpersonal communication occurs among familiar others.* Relational familiarity and anticipated future interaction are significant moderators of interaction behavior. Yet, most nonverbal research has been conducted among strangers. The result is that we know little about how patterns might differ among acquaintances, coworkers, friends, spouses, and family members, that is, in the kinds of interactions that make up the core of our everyday lives. In what follows, I will make special mention of research conducted among people who know one another.

A *sixth feature is treating interpersonal communication as "multi": multifunctional, multidimensional, and multivariate.* The call for treating nonverbal and interpersonal communication from a functional perspective has been sounded for more than two decades (see, e.g., Argyle, 1972; Burgoon & Saine, 1978; Ekman & Friesen, 1969b; Patterson, 1983, 1991). Dissecting nonverbal communication into its constituent parts is useful for studying communication structure. But the traditional decomposition into separate codes leads to a piecemeal and distorted understanding of the social and communicative role of nonverbal signals. Nonverbal behaviors operate as an integrated, coordinated system in achieving particular social functions, and their importance becomes more apparent when they are examined collectively. A multifunctional perspective also makes apparent that multiple behaviors, operating along multiple dimensions of meaning, are responsible for achieving any particular interpersonal objective.

The chief communicative functions accomplished by nonverbal behaviors include message production and processing, identification and identity management, impression formation and management, relational communication and relationship management, deception, emotion expression and management, conversation structuring and management, and social influence. The remainder of this chapter is devoted to reviewing major theories and pertinent research associated with each of these functions as they relate to interpersonal communication.

Message Production and Processing

If messages are the heart of the interpersonal communication enterprise, then nonverbal cues are the arteries through which the linguistic lifeblood courses. They connect, channel, and constrain the verbal constituents. In short, nonverbal cues are an inherent and essential part of message creation (production) and interpretation (processing).

In their seminal analysis of nonverbal behavior, Ekman and Friesen (1969b) recognized the interrelatedness of verbal and nonverbal cues by noting that nonverbal acts may repeat, augment, illustrate, accentuate, or contradict the words they accompany. They also observed that nonverbal acts can precede the words, substitute for them, or be unrelated to them. Most textbooks on nonverbal communication have emphasized the former relationships, thereby relegating nonverbal cues to a subordinate, collateral role. The empirical evidence is persuasive, however, that nonverbal cues not only are essential to verbal message encoding and decoding but are also "message bearers" in their own right. The ability to encode and decode nonverbal messages therefore becomes critically important to successful communication. What follows is a brief overview of the role of nonverbal cues and encoding and decoding skill in message production and processing.

Message Production

At the outset, certain nonverbal cues "set the stage" by indicating whether a context is to be understood as an interactional one or not and, consequently, what may count as a message. The mere presence of others does not create an "interpersonal communication" context; some level of "engagement" is necessary. Nonverbal cues perform this role. The "minimalist" hypothesis, as Bavelas (1990) calls it, is that people rely on nonverbal cues to signal, at minimum, their accessibility or inaccessibility to communication. Among the behaviors she cites (many taken from empirical studies) are gaze (whether one makes or avoids gaze, the latency before it occurs, and its duration), postural rigidity, vocal cues of concentration such as sighing or groaning, smiling, and looking at one's watch. A person who stares straight ahead, focuses intently on her work, or closes her eyes is communicating that she doesn't want to be bothered; if she smiles and makes eye contact, she is willing to interact. Other behaviors such as physical distance, indirect body orientation, crossed arms, and body blocks such as shielding one's eyes that create a *nonperson orientation* (see Burgoon, 1974) may likewise inhibit approach by others. In defining situations as interactional or noninteractional, nonverbal cues also determine whether other nonverbal behaviors should be regarded as messages. The importance of this framing function should not be underestimated. With verbal communication, the act of uttering words in another's presence is usually sufficient to signal an intent to communicate. With nonverbal communication, intent is not as obvious. Many nonverbal messages such as flirtations may occur in the absence of verbalizations. Yet, merely "behaving" in another's presence isn't sufficient to qualify as communication. Nonverbal cues of accessibility reduce ambiguity and help to distinguish potentially communicative behaviors from expressive or indicative ones.

This framing role is only the beginning. Nonverbal cues perform semantic, pragmatic, and syntactic functions (Ricci Bitti & Poggi, 1991; Scherer, 1980), conveying messages themselves or aiding the production of verbal messages. In their semantic and pragmatic roles, they may take the form of *emblems*, symbolic behaviors that have direct verbal translations; *illustrators*, gestures that accompany and clarify the verbal stream; *affect displays*, facial, postural, vocal, or tactile behaviors that convey primary emotional states; *regulators*, behaviors that manage conversational turn-taking; *adaptors*, autistic actions such as scratching or rubbing the self, picking at clothing, or manipulating objects that relieve private, personal needs but may be used to show disrespect (such as filing fingernails in a meeting); *relational messages* that define the nature of the interpersonal relationship; and other *rituals* that have clear meaning within a given culture and can stand alone (see Burgoon & Hale, 1984; Ekman & Friesen, 1969b; Liska, 1986). Syntactically, nonverbal cues may function to *segment* and *synchronize* the flow of speech (Scherer, 1980). We have all no doubt been amused at one time or another watching someone on the telephone gesturing dramatically and making exaggerated facial expressions, supposedly for the benefit of the unseeing listener. Although some of this nonverbal expressiveness is a matter of habit, it also may assist the speaker in punctuating and coordinating the verbal stream.

Consistent with the argument that nonverbal signals have linguisticlike functions, my colleagues and I have maintained that many nonverbal behaviors have well-recognized, consensual meanings and so fit a *social meaning model* (Burgoon, Coker, & Coker, 1986; Burgoon, Manusov, Mineo, & Hale, 1985; Burgoon & Newton, 1991). Bavelas and Chovil have proposed the same principle in their *integrated message model* (see Chovil, 1991). This view, adumbrated by Darwin's (1872/1965) observations a century ago, is bolstered by ethologists' claims that many nonverbal behaviors have a uniquely communicative purpose.

Based on evidence that nonverbal gestures closely parallel the temporal, semantic, and pragmatic properties of speech and are synchronized with verbal output, many scholars (e.g., Birdwhistell, 1970; Krauss, Morrel-Samuels, & Colasante, 1991; McNeill, 1985, 1992; Poyatos, 1983, 1992; Rimé & Schiaratura, 1991) have postulated that gestures and speech originate together as part of the same communicative intention, the resultant encoding process activating both a verbal-vocal utterance and a motoric (gestural) representation. Because gestures and words are inextricable parts of the total message, difficulties in finding the right word may be facilitated by first using the gesture that belongs with it; that is, they may "prime the pump" (Cohen, 1977). This is why gestures may often precede a verbalization. Even seemingly random gestures may also anticipate later utterances (Mahl, 1987). Thus nonverbal cues facilitate message production by (a) providing encoders an efficient mode in which to express content (such as spatial or visual information) and (b) facilitating the activation of words, concepts, ideas, and images used in utterance construction.

The interpersonal context serves to intensify some of this nonverbal activity and to suppress other behavior. Many gestures such as emphatic arm and hand movements, gestures depicting the train of thought, pointing, shrugging, and facial displays such as smiling and motor mimicry (expressions indicating empathy for another's plight) are more likely to occur when a receiver is visibly present or imagined; other gestures such as adaptors decrease (Bavelas, Black, Chovil, Lemery, & Mullett, 1988; Bavelas, Black, Lemery, & Mullett, 1986; Bull & Connelly, 1985; Chovil, 1991; Cohen & Harrison, 1973; Fridlund et al., 1990; Mahl, 1987). The fact that the former class of nonverbal cues often occurs in abbreviated fashion or not at all when other people are absent implies that they serve primarily a social or communicative function.

The interpersonal context also elicits another change in nonverbal behavior during message production: Nonverbal cues reveal encoding difficulty. When verbal utterances are complex, difficult to construct, or occur under stress (e.g., divulging highly personal information, expressing an abstract idea, responding during an embarrassing situation, giving complicated directions, delivering bad news, or making one's case during an argument), nonverbal performances suffer. Speech fluency is disrupted, adaptor use increases, and silent pauses become more numerous and lengthy (Barroso & Feld, 1986; Cappella, 1984; Goldman-Eisler, 1968; Mahl, 1987; Siegman, 1978). Thus nonverbal cues may signal difficulty in message production. Because these same cues may arise for other reasons—such as transitory emotional or mood states, anxiety, or restless disinterest—their significance is often ambiguous and "misread." Moreover, concurrent gestures and other nonverbal behaviors may be intended to compensate for encoding difficulties (Krauss et al., 1991). However, if cues fluctuate consistently with conditions that could reasonably be interpreted as cognitively demanding, they may be taken as legitimate signs of "heavy cognitive load."

Message Processing

On the receiving end, nonverbal cues play an equally important role in the attention, comprehension, recall, and interpretation of interpersonal messages. First, nonverbal cues may draw attention to a message. A primary function of gaze is to monitor and secure others' attention (Abele, 1986). Second, nonverbal cues may facilitate comprehension and recall by (a) reinforcing the underlying semantic content of a message, (b) clarifying syntactic relationships, and (c) supplying a context in which a message is embedded at the time of input (Folger & Woodall, 1982).

At the semantic level, emblems and certain kinds of illustrator gestures may add redundancy or semantic elaboration to specific utterances (Argyle, 1974; Birdwhistell, 1970; Cohen & Harrison, 1973; Kendon, 1980; Krauss et al., 1991; Riseborough, 1981) as well as depict and reflect the larger meanings of extended utterances (Kendon, 1983; McNeill & Levy, 1982). At the syntactic level, nonverbal cues may facilitate the "chunking" of linguistic content into phonemic clauses, which are probably the form in which linguistic information is processed (Boomer, 1965, 1978; Dittmann, 1972b). Paralinguistic suprasegmentals and parakinesic stress kinemes provide vocalic and kinesic punctuation so that words and clauses can be distinguished from one another (Birdwhistell, 1970). The synchronization of a speaker's nonverbal behaviors (self-synchrony) and the auditor's behaviors (interactional synchrony) to the rhythm of the speech stream may likewise aid comprehension of the incoming verbal input (Woodall & Burgoon, 1981).

At the contextual level, emblematic gestures and, to a lesser extent, emphasizing gestures serve as contextual retrieval cues, facilitating recall even of language not recognized on its own (Folger & Woodall, 1982; Woodall & Folger, 1981, 1985). Kinesic, physical appearance, and artifactual cues may also lend visual vividness to the stimulus cue complex, while haptic, proxemic, and vocalic cues may stimulate physiological arousal, thereby strengthening the associations between content and context in memory. Other nonverbal signals such as vocal nonfluencies, unpleasant voice qualities, extreme conversational distances, extreme physical (un)attractiveness, and excessive environmental stimulation may distract from, rather than center attention on, the verbal content of a message (Stacks & Burgoon, 1981). A meta-analysis showing that auditory and visual distractions reduce comprehension (Buller, 1986) implies that nonverbal behaviors may be unsuspected and intrinsic sources of distraction in interpersonal interchanges. However, anomalous and incongruent messages may also produce deeper cognitive processing (Woodall & Folger, 1982).

Finally, nonverbal cues may contribute to the inference-making process that is so central to initial comprehension (Woodall & Folger, 1982). In this respect, the role of nonverbal cues in social cognition processes becomes relevant. One particularly important factor is the strong visual bias of receivers. The tendency to orient to visual stimuli has long fascinated observers of the human situation. McLuhan and Fiore (1967) wrote, "The dominant organ of sensory and social orientation in pre-alphabet societies was the ear—hearing was believing. The phonetic alphabet forced the magic world of the eye. Man was given an eye for an ear" (p. 44). The "seeing is believing" visual cue primacy, which has been well documented in the literature (see Noller, 1985, for a summary), places a premium on nonverbal kinesic, proxemic, and physical appearance cues in interpersonal interactions. Speculations abound as to why this is the case. Apart from the aforementioned historical shifts from oral to written and electronically mediated cultures (see also Forsdale, 1981; Postman, 1985), four possible reasons related to interpersonal contexts are as follows: (a) Visual cues may be more semantically distinctive, especially in conveying emotional information, and therefore able to transmit information more efficiently per unit of time; (b) the face, because of its controllability, may offer more intentional information to a viewer; (c) visual cues can be scanned for a longer time than can more fleeting, sequentially presented vocal and verbal cues; and (d) vocal cues, which are automatically alerting, may be reserved as threat signals, leaving the visual channel as a primary information source during routine interchanges (Keeley-Dyreson, Burgoon, & Bailey, 1991).

Although visual primacy is often operative, there are several qualifications to this principle. In addition to the ones offered previously when comparing verbal channels with nonverbal ones, Burgoon, Buller, and Woodall (1989), Noller (1985), and Rosenthal, Hall, DiMatteo, Rogers, and Archer (1979) propose several factors that temper visual versus vocal channel reliance.

1. *Gender*: Females rely more on visual cues than do males; visual information from females is discounted more than that of males, especially by children.

2. *Message form*: Greater reliance shifts to vocal information when judging deception or discrepant messages.

3. *Dimension of judgment*: Visual information is more important for judging positivity-negativity; vocal information is more important for judging dominance, assertiveness, fearfulness, and sincerity.

4. *Culture*: Westernized, industrial cultures may be more visually oriented than non-Westernized ones, which may be auditorally oriented.

There are numerous other ways in which nonverbal cues contribute to biased or accurate information processing, often examined as part of person perception or social cognition. Some of these are considered below under "Impression Formation."

Nonverbal Encoding and Decoding Skill

Central to success in producing and interpreting messages are nonverbal encoding and decoding skills. Because sending ability is highly related to receiving ability, they are discussed together here. Friedman (1979) offers a justification for a shift in recent years away from traits as the basis for individual differences and toward skills: "The concept of nonverbal skills directs attention from what people are to what people can do interpersonally. Individual strengths and weaknesses are objectively tested and related to the outcomes of social interactions" (p. 16).

Typically, three techniques have been used in assessing nonverbal skills: standardized performance measures, individualized performance measures, and self-reports (Riggio, Widaman, & Friedman, 1985). Standardized measures include use of audio and video stimuli about which respondents must make judgments such as perceived emotional state, interpersonal relationship, and presence of deception. Examples include the Profile of Nonverbal Sensitivity (Rosenthal et al., 1979), FAST (Ekman, Friesen, & Tomkins, 1971), and the Interpersonal Perception Task (Archer & Costanzo, 1988; Costanzo & Archer, 1989). Individualized performance measures usually involve each respondent being videotaped while enacting various emotions, engaging in deceptions, or conducting live interaction; these samples are then assessed by other participants or judges. Sending accuracy scores are obtained for the senders; decoding accuracy scores are obtained for the judges. Finally, self-report measures entail individuals assessing their own nonverbal abilities. One such measure, the Social Skills Inventory (Riggio, 1986), measures skill in expressing, interpreting, and controlling nonverbal emotional expressions. Unfortunately, self-report measures do not show a high correspondence to standardized measures requiring actual encoding or decoding (see Riggio et al., 1985). Yet, both have been shown to predict communicative success (with some variability; see, e.g., Snodgrass & Rosenthal, 1985).

Numerous studies have been conducted on encoding and decoding skills. A meta-analysis of 75 quantitative studies by Hall (1979), coupled with findings from other contemporaneous or subsequent investigations (e.g., Buck, 1979; DePaulo & Rosenthal, 1979; Keeley-Dyreson et al., 1991; Kirouac & Dore, 1985; Lieberman, Rigo, & Campain, 1988; Manstead, Wagner, & MacDonald, 1986; Rosenthal & DePaulo, 1979; Rosenthal et al., 1979; Snodgrass & Rosenthal, 1985), warrant the following conclusions:

1. Encoding ability and decoding ability are correlated. Those who are better senders tend to be better receivers and vice versa, but the relationship is a modest one.

2. Encoding skills tend to be related to one another, as do decoding skills. Vocal encoding skill tends to correlate with visual encoding skill; the same is often, though not always, true of decoding skills. Those who are skilled at decoding messages of liking and disliking also tend to be skilled at judging ambivalent and deceptive messages.

3. Encoding ability and decoding ability correlate with personality. Encoding skill is greater among those who are expressive, extroverted, nonreticent, high in self-esteem, outgoing, high in self-monitoring, socially anxious, nondogmatic, persuasive, and physically attractive. Decoding skill is greater among those who are gregarious, sociable, nondogmatic, and low on Machiavellianism. Research specifically on self-reported expressivity reveals that expressives' nonverbal behaviors are easier to decode because they include a higher rate of "meaningful" gestural, head, and eye movements; are seen as more salient (novel, intense, complex, and changeable); and are more noticeable (Sullins, 1989). Thus expressive individuals are more animated and engaging.

4. Decoding ability increases with practice and training but is curvilinearly related to age. Maturation, increased social development, and practice all contribute to improved accuracy in interpreting nonverbal expressions (and can even eliminate the female advantage over several trials), up to a point. But elderly people lose some of their ability to detect emotions accurately, perhaps due to reductions in perceptual acuity, ability to concentrate, and memory. Thus the experiential gain due to longevity is offset by decrements in relevant cognitive and perceptual skills. Additionally, research in the deception arena suggests that highly experienced decoders (e.g., customs agents, police investigators, interrogators) are no better than novices and may actually do more poorly than novices, perhaps because experienced decoders become overly suspicious. Here again, experience isn't necessarily the best teacher.

5. Race, education, and intelligence do not appear to relate to encoding and decoding skill, but occupation does. People with better nonverbal skills tend to gravitate toward people-oriented occupations.

6. Women are generally better than men at encoding and decoding nonverbal messages. The encoding superiority exists regardless of age but may be limited to visual cues and to nondeceptive messages. Of the 21 relevant studies in Hall's analysis, 71% favored women as the better senders. (The only qualification was that results were too variable to support a consistent vocal effect.) The decoding superiority also exists regardless of age and gender of the stimulus person. Of the 61 relevant studies surveyed in Hall's analysis, 84% showed women to be more accurate interpreters than men. However, the magnitude of the encoding and decoding advantage is small.

Numerous conjectures have been offered for why women often exceed men in encoding and decoding ability. Two that Hall (1979) ruled out empirically are that women have greater empathic ability or greater alertness due to their relative social powerlessness. Other tentative hypotheses include greater practice adopting passive, submissive roles (and a resultant increase in interpretive skills); socialization to be more accommodating and to attend to intentional cues; innate differences; cognitive processing differences; differences in degree of linguistic involvement; and differences in hemispheric lateralization (with concomitant differences in processing skill). One alternative receiving empirical support is that men and women differ in degree of expressiveness. Women are more likely to externalize emotions, whereas men are more likely to internalize them (Buck, 1979). To the extent that women manifest their emotional states externally, their expressions are more readily understood, whereas men are more likely to experience high internal physiological arousal but outwardly to display less, making decoding of their expressions more difficult.

Identification and Identity Management

A core objective for communicators in interpersonal contexts is identification and identity management (Baumeister, 1982; Clark & Delia, 1979; Schlenker, 1985). Writings on self-image and identity increasingly acknowledge that our personal identities are partly a social construction; that is, they are shaped and negotiated through interactions with others (McCall, 1987). According to *social identity theory* (Tajfel, 1981), the "self" is defined by socio-cultural-demographic background—such as nationality, gender, age, education, occupation, religion—as well as by personality. Manifest indications of one's cultural, social, demographic, and personal characteristics serve as "identity badges," enabling individuals to project their own identification with various personal and social categories while simultaneously enabling observers to use the same cues as an instant means of classification. Thus, not only may individuals rely on their own nonverbal behaviors as affirmation or self-verification of their identities (see Swann, 1987), but others may also treat such information as outward reflections of the inner self.

Although the lines may blur between identity management and impression management, I am making a subtle distinction between the two. The former refers to presentation of the "phenomenological" self, that is, one's self-perceived "true" identity, while the latter refers to the strategic presentation of image for the benefit of an audience, a presentation that may depart from one's "inner self" (see Jones & Pittman, 1982). The former is typically reflected in fairly unconscious, highly internalized, and highly consistent patterns of verbal and nonverbal actions that reflect a person's own sense of self. Because such presentations may emanate from biological forces, acculturation, and learning processes, they may be more "indicative" than "communicative." Nevertheless, because individuals may also deliberately emphasize or deemphasize features of their identity (e.g., having plastic surgery, wearing native dress, or suppressing a dialect), it is useful to analyze how nonverbal cues convey social identities, especially as they are adapted in particular interpersonal relationships.

The available information on sociocultural, demographic, and personality differences far exceeds the space that can be devoted to it here. What follows is just a sampling of some major trends, all of which could be examined from the standpoint of individual difference variables but take on greater significance if recognized for their identification potential.

Cultural Differences

Cultures differ radically in their use of space, touch, time, and artifacts; in the symbolism of their attire; in their use of kinesic and vocalic cues; in short, in all the nonverbal codes (see, e.g., Gudykunst & Ting-Toomey, 1988; Hall, 1969, 1973, 1977; Leach, 1972; Morris, 1977; Morris, Collett, Marsh, & O'Shaughnessy, 1979; Ricci Bitti & Poggi, 1991). As one illustration, a distinction is often made between "contact cultures"—which prefer close interaction distances, frequent use of touch, higher rates of gaze, and more gestural animation—and their opposites, "noncontact cultures." Although this distinction has been criticized as overly simplistic, it reveals that people's habitual interpersonal interaction styles differ depending upon their cultural heritage. Even where cultures have similar behavior patterns, *cultural display rules* (Ekman, Friesen, & Ellsworth, 1972) may modify the exhibited pattern and the circumstances of a behavior's performance.

These culture differences become one vehicle for self-identification. By adhering to a culture's or a subgroup's norms, one may signal identification with it, thereby invoking all the characteristics and expectations stereotypically associated with members of that group (regardless of whether that is the sender's intent or not) and externalizing one's "collective self" (see Triandis, 1989). By violating a culture's norms (for example, wearing Western dress in a Moslem culture), one may likewise send a message distancing oneself from that culture and repudiating that identity. Mulac, Studley, Wiemann, and Bradac (1987) state:

> An extensive body of research has shown that social groups are distinguishable in terms of their communication style, whether verbal (syntax and semantics), para-linguistic (phonology and prosody), or nonverbal (for example, proximity, gestures, and facial expression). Functionally, it has been argued that a group's communication style helps members identify with one another while distinguishing themselves from outgroup members. (p. 324)

Prolific research on in-group/out-group relations (see, e.g., Fiske & Taylor, 1991) testifies to the importance of signaling one's in-group or out-group status. One theory that addresses this process explicitly is *communication accommodation theory* (Giles, Coupland, & Coupland, 1991; Giles, Mulac, Bradac, & Johnson, 1987; Giles & Smith, 1979; Giles, Taylor, & Bourhis, 1973), which postulates that people converge their speech patterns toward those of in-group members and diverge from those of out-group members. These outward manifestations of asso-ciation solidify identification with primary groups.

Gender Differences

A central ingredient of a person's self-image is her or his gender identity. The literature on nonverbal expression is rife with evidence of gender differences and possible explanations for these differences (see, e.g., Eagly, 1987; Gallaher, 1992; Hall, 1984; Hall & Halberstadt, 1986; Jones, 1986; Mayo & Henley, 1981; Mulac et al., 1987; Stewart, Cooper, & Friedley, 1986; Stier & Hall, 1984; Willis & Briggs, 1992). Some of these are rooted in primary (genetic) and secondary (physiological and anatomical) features associated with sexual functioning. Other biological differences between males and females likewise produce observable "nonverbal" differences in such physical characteristics as physical appearance and voice and may influence entire patterns of responding. Haviland and Malatesta (1981), citing male infants' greater emotional lability, propose that biobehavioral predispositions, in interaction with environmental influences and social learning processes, affect a whole range of nonverbal encoding and decoding patterns. When these sex-linked differences take behavioral form, they become part of what Birdwhistell (1970) labeled *tertiary gender displays*. Some feminine and masculine behavior patterns may stem from biological or cultural needs to distinguish the sexes and promote sexual attraction. Provocative walking and standing postures, grooming and adornment practices that emphasize female or male physical attributes, and vocal qualities that connote strength or weak-ness may fit this category. Other behavioral differences such as sitting with crossed ankles or crossed legs may be due to socially prescribed role expectations for masculine and feminine behavior.

One controversial aspect of these basic feminine and masculine display patterns is the extent to which they reflect differences in power. Henley (1977) theorized that men's nonverbal behavior is characterized by dominance, and women's, by submissiveness. Findings adduced to support this proposition include the following:

1. Men display more visual dominance (a higher ratio of looking while speaking to looking while listening) than women (Dovidio & Ellyson, 1985). Women also gaze more at conversational partners while speaking, while listening, and during pauses than do men. Although gaze is often cited as a submissive behavior, some research has shown it carries dominance connotations.

2. Women smile more and are more expressive facially and vocally than men. This expressivity typically takes positive and supportive rather than hostile forms and has been interpreted by some as a sign of appeasement.

3. Women are approached more closely, tolerate more spatial intrusion, give way to others more frequently, and take up less physical space than men. Men are more likely to dictate spacing and distancing patterns. These asymmetrical patterns of men controlling space and women accommodating parallel those between superiors and subordinates.

4. Women talk less, listen more, and are interrupted more often than men.

5. Women display more "submissive" postures and gestures such as the head tilt, open palm display, constricted arm and leg positions, and moderate postural tension.

6. Women use more rising vocal intonations (as in questions) and hesitations.

Several studies and meta-analyses have challenged these findings as well as whether the observed male-female differences should be attributed to dominance (see, e.g., Halberstadt & Saitta, 1987; Hall & Halberstadt, 1986; Marche & Peterson, 1993; Staley & Cohen, 1988; Stier & Hall, 1984). One alternative interpretation for any differences is that women are more affiliative and communal than men. Consistent with Bem's (1981) *gender schema theory* and Eagly's (1987) *gender role theory*, which assert that many gender differences are attributable to women and men conforming to culturally defined gender role expectations, women have been shown to have greater sensitivity and responsivity to the communication of others (Street & Murphy, 1987) and to engage in more socially oriented behavior in group situations (Eagly & Karau, 1991). The "dominance" findings above can be reinterpreted within this frame, inasmuch as all of them also convey supportiveness, nonaggressiveness, and positive affect. Other behaviors that fit an affiliation interpretation include the following:

7. Women adopt closer conversational distances with women as well as men, show preference for side-by-side seating, and respond more favorably than men to crowded situations.

8. Women accommodate to the interaction pattern of their partner; men do not.

9. Women are more animated and expressive than men facially and gesturally and are more inclined to express positive emotions; men are more inclined to express anger.

10. Women give as well as receive more touch than men and appear to seek physical contact to a greater extent than do men. (One exception is that men initiate more touch during courtship.) Women who talk more also initiate more touch, in keeping with an affiliativeness interpretation. Jones (1986) concludes that touch is feminine-appropriate and masculine-inappropriate.

To the extent that women's greater social sensitivity and supportiveness are partly a function of them often being in a subordinate role (Snodgrass, 1992), the two alternative interpretive frames are compatible rather than contradictory. Of course, other gender-linked differences do not neatly fit the above interpretations, and there are numerous ways in which men and women do not differ nonverbally (see, e.g., Staley & Cohen, 1988) either collectively or individually. This variability notwithstanding, a decision to adhere to or diverge from culturally prescribed masculine and feminine display patterns stands as a strong signal of gender identity.

Personality

Psychoanalytic, psychological, and communication literature has produced nonverbal profiles associated with personality traits such as extraversion-introversion, Machiavellianism, anxiety, authoritarianism, and need for affiliation; disorders such as schizophrenia, paranoia, depression, and hysteria; and communication predispositions such as communication apprehension, unwillingness to communicate, self-monitoring, social skills, and touch avoidance (regarding the latter, see, e.g., Andersen & Sull, 1985; Ayres, 1989; Burgoon & Koper, 1984; Burgoon, Pfau, Birk, & Manusov, 1987; Friedman & Miller-Herringer, 1991; Friedman, Prince, Riggio, & DiMatteo, 1980; Gallaher, 1992; Gifford, 1991; Remland & Jones, 1989; Street & Murphy, 1987). The relationships are sufficiently stable to conclude that nonverbal style "may be regarded as an aspect of personality rather than merely as a cue to it" (Gallaher, 1992, p. 143).

The nonverbal codes most often implicated in the manifestation of personality and psychological states are vocalics, kinesics, proxemics, haptics, and physical appearance. More specifically, talk time, loudness, speech errors, pitch, voice quality, vocal characterizers (such as crying or laughing), silences, interruptions, response latencies, amount of eye contact, head orientation and nods, leg movements, object adaptors, coordination of movement, amount of gesticulation, postural relaxation, amount of physical movement, conversational distance, amount of touch, personal grooming, and colorfulness of clothing have been implicated. Nonverbal behavior patterns such as gaze, loudness, speaking tempo, laughter, smiling, expressiveness, nervous mannerisms, conventionality of appearance, and general interpersonal style show impressive cross-situational consistency in interpersonal situations (Funder & Colvin, 1991; Gallaher, 1992). These therefore become reliable indicators of underlying psychological and emotional characteristics.

Other "identifying information" regarding age, race, education, occupation, and social status may also be revealed through nonverbal behavior. As Sherlock Holmes was quick to demonstrate, detectives often rely on combinations of seemingly inconsequential nonverbal cues to identify their quarry. This is because nonverbal demeanor is so often an "embodiment" of the person vis-à-vis his or her social relationships (Mahl, 1987).

Impression Formation and Management

Whereas the function of identification and identity management is grounded in an encoder perspective, examining how communicators manifest "who they are" through nonverbal signals, impression formation is grounded in a decoder perspective, examining how receivers use the same signals to form judgments of communicators. Impression management returns to an encoder perspective, examining the ways in which communicators strategically craft their nonverbal performances to create desired images, projecting "who they want to be."

Impression Formation

When people first meet or talk, they rapidly categorize one another on such characteristics as gender, age, socioeconomic status, political affiliation, nationality, and geographic residence. At the same time, they begin to draw inferences about political, social, and religious attitudes, personality traits, and global qualities such as attractiveness, likability, and credibility. This subconscious but instantaneous process of impression formation is highly stereotypical and fraught with misjudgments. But people rely on it nevertheless, perhaps because the pressure to reduce uncertainty is great (see Berger & Calabrese, 1975), because initially available information is accurate at some levels, and because, as Freud (1915-1917/1963) cautioned, even feeble indicators can reveal important information. Given that initial verbal exchanges are so often constrained by convention, the nonverbal cues, especially stable physical appearance, kinesic, and vocalic ones, take on particular importance in shaping interpersonal expectations and in generating a frame for interpreting subsequent behavior.

The extensive research on impression formation falls under such headings as social cognition, first impressions, and interpersonal perception. Early research is summarized and indexed elsewhere (Burgoon, 1980; Frye, 1980; Harper, Wiens, & Matarazzo, 1978; Kleinke, 1975; Knapp & Hall, 1992; Kramer, 1963; Siegman, 1978). Five key issues underlie the relationship between nonverbal cues and impression formation in interpersonal interaction: (a) How accurate and consensual are judgments made from nonverbal cues or channels (Kenny, 1991)? (b) What causes judgments to be biased? (c) Which nonverbal cues are most implicated in impression formation? (d) Do first impressions persist when people are allowed to interact? (e) What attributions are associated with nonverbal-based impressions?

The twin factors of accuracy and consensus in judgments relate to people's ability to make judgments of communicators that are, at minimum, consistent across multiple judges and, at maximum, accurate reflections of a person's "true" characteristics. Although it is possible to marshall considerable evidence of receiver agreement outstripping accuracy (i.e., observers share the same perceptions but those perceptions are often erroneous), recent research has begun to document that people's "hunches" can also be remarkably accurate (Smith, Archer, & Costanzo, 1991). Accuracy tends to be highest for judgments such as sex, age, occupation, and social status that are derivable from external and emblematic appearance and vocal cues (Burgoon, Buller, & Woodall, 1989). Judgments of attitudes, values, and personality traits are much more variable and subject to stereotyping; however, some personal and interpersonal characteristics can be judged accurately. For example, Berry (1991) found that enduring facial and vocal cues accurately predicted self-ratings of warmth and power; Kenny, Horner, Kashy, and Chu (1992) reported high accuracy as well as consensus on judgments of extraversion; Ambady and Rosenthal (in press) found that observations of nonverbal behavior as brief as 30 seconds or less predicted supervisor and student ratings of teacher effectiveness. Berry (1991) offers possible explanations for the high degree of accuracy in some judgments: (a) direct links between personality and behavior (as in "approachable" people using softer, warmer vocal patterns), (b) self-fulfilling prophecies (as in obese people being expected to be jolly, being treated as such, and internalizing that characteristic as part of their personality), and (c) repetitive expressions of affect becoming permanent appearance features (as in frequent scowling producing frown wrinkles or chronic depression producing a slumped posture). It should also be noted that many studies documenting inaccuracies examined single cues or codes rather than the multiple ones that interactants routinely have available. Impressions founded on combinations of cues, especially the dynamic ones available during interpersonal interaction, may be more accurate because the interrelationships among concurrent cues and their congruence with the context can be judged. Smith et al. (1991) concur:

> It now appears that multiple, redundant, interpretable cues are diffused throughout an interaction. . . . As a result, there are *many* paths to a correct inference, and perceivers will (quite correctly) cite as significant a disconcertingly wide variety of nonverbal cues. (p. 16)

Nevertheless, inaccuracies are commonplace. Sources of distortion in judgment are numerous and the topic of extensive social cognition research (see Fiske & Taylor, 1991; Zebrowitz, 1990). Relevant here is the extent to which the nature of the nonverbal behavior itself influences judgments. Two biases of special import are as follows:

1. The visual primacy effect. The previously noted strong orientation, at least in Western cultures, toward visual cues may cause overreliance on visual information and neglect of relevant auditory information.

2. "What is beautiful is good" stereotype. Attractive individuals are credited with more positive attributes such as intelligence, persuasiveness, poise, sociability, warmth, power, and employment success than unattractive individuals (Hatfield & Sprecher, 1986; Knapp, 1985).

These halo effects cause innumerable impressions to be influenced by attractiveness. Moreover, attractiveness in one channel "bleeds" into judgments in another channel. Zuckerman, Miyake, and Hodgins (1991) found that people's impressions of attractiveness in the visual channel influenced judgments in the auditory channel and vice versa; that is, there was cross-channel influence in judgments. Early research documented halo effects due to physical attractiveness; more recent research points to a vocal attractiveness stereotype being at least as potent—individuals with attractive voices evoke a wide range of positive impressions (Berry, 1990, 1991, 1992; Zuckerman & Driver, 1989; Zuckerman, Hodgins, & Miyake, 1990). Of interest, these effects are attenuated when people are familiar with one another or gain other relevant information (Berry, 1990; Morrow & McElroy, 1984), bolstering Knapp's (1985) contention that the potency of physical attractiveness biases should diminish once people begin to interact.

Most of the conclusions about physical attractiveness have been based on studies employing static stimuli judged once by strangers in noninteractive contexts. Multiple exposures, relational familiarity, personal knowledge, and opportunities to converse should make other dynamic factors such as kinesic and vocalic style increasingly important as relationships develop and people shift from category-based judgments to person-based ones (see Brewer, 1978; Fiske & Neuberg, 1990). Other sources of bias that have yet to be investigated but seem especially salient to ongoing interpersonal interactions are the relative importance of dynamic cues versus static ones and of frequently appearing behaviors versus rare ones.

Regarding the importance of specific nonverbal channels and cues in forming impressions, it is intuitively obvious that physical appearance, kinesic and vocalic demeanor, and proxemic patterns are the most immediately available sources of information. In keeping with the aforementioned visual primacy and beauty biases, the visual channel appears to be more important than the auditory channel in forming impressions of attractiveness (Raines, Hechtman, & Rosenthal, 1990; Zuckerman et al., 1991). Beyond static appearance cues, style factors such as expressivity, smiling, gaze, nonverbal immediacy and involvement, positivity of facial expressions, and apparent spontaneity contribute to perceived attractiveness (Burgoon & Hale, 1988; DePaulo, 1992; Gallaher, 1992; Kimble & Seidel, 1991; Manusov, 1991; Mueser, Grau, Sussman, & Rosen, 1984; Raines et al., 1990; Reis et al., 1990; Remland & Jones, 1989; Sabatelli & Rubin, 1986; Simpson, Gangestad, & Biek, 1992). For other judgments, facial and vocal cues related to maturity or babyishness, vocal loudness, pitch, pitch variety, tempo, delivery style, fluency, physical height and weight, gait, and self-touch have been shown to be reliable and consistent predictors of personality and social perceptions of power, warmth, and credibility (Barge, Schlueter, & Pritchard, 1989; Berry, 1990, 1991, 1992; Brownlow, 1992; Burgoon, Birk, & Pfau, 1990; Burgoon, Buller, & Woodall, 1989; Burgoon & Hale, 1988; Burgoon, Newton, Walther, & Baesler, 1989; Harrigan, Kues, Steffen, & Rosenthal, 1987; Ray, 1986; Remland & Jones, 1989; Siegman, 1978; Zebrowitz, 1990; Zuckerman & Driver, 1989).

The question of persistence of first impressions is especially relevant to interpersonal communication. If first impressions are transitory, then they should be of minimal importance once people begin to interact and become acquainted. If they have lasting impact, they may serve as a template through which all subsequent information is filtered and assimilated. The evidence tends to endorse the latter position. Kenny et al. (1992) found that consensus existing at "zero acquaintance" persisted after interacting, and Burgoon and Le Poire (1993) found that induced preinteraction expectancies about a target's communication style persisted, even when the target's actual nonverbal communication was contradictory. These findings match other evidence on the persistence of expectancy effects. But, cues differ in their persistence. As noted previously, in ongoing relationships, static or slow signals such as physical attractiveness diminish in importance, while dynamic cues rise in prominence. Cues that are novel, unexpected, or extreme may also have greater impact.

The final question of attributions associated with nonverbal impressions also has special import to interpersonal communication to the extent that the nonverbal behaviors are attributed to be intentional and to have message value. In a program of research addressing this question, Manusov (1990, 1991, 1992a, 1992b; Manusov & Rodriguez, 1991) found that many nonverbal behaviors such as immediacy changes, gaze, smiling, facial expressions, silences, tone of voice, and mirroring of another's behavior were interpreted as intentional. Negative behaviors were attributed to situational factors rather than target intent where such situational attributions could be made; otherwise, they were assumed to be purposeful acts and were evaluated more negatively on competence and social evaluation. Thus many of the dynamic nonverbal behaviors responsible for engendering impressions are assumed to be other-directed behaviors with intentional message value.

Impression Management

The flip side of impression formation is impression management: How can communicators use nonverbal cues to foster desired impressions? At the theory level, emphasis is on what macro-level strategies a communicator can use to project desired images along dimensions of believability, expertise, attraction, status, prestige, and the like. At the research level, emphasis is typically on what micro-level nonverbal cues actually encourage favorable impressions or are judged as appropriate or inappropriate in a particular context, the implication being that inappropriate or unacceptable behavior leads to failed performances. Thus much of the impression formation literature can be recast as revealing what nonverbal strategies enhance self-presentation.

Relevant theories in this area are Goffman's (1959, 1961, 1963, 1967, 1969, 1971, 1974) comprehensive dramaturgic analyses of self-presentation, which are replete with nonverbal illustrations and general principles for successful and unsuccessful role performances; Schlenker's (1980) and Tedeschi's (1982) impression management theories; E. E. Jones's (1964) ingratiation theory; Jones and Pittman's (1982) general theory of strategic self-presentation; and Burgoon and colleagues' expectancy violations theory. Because the latter two pertain most closely to empirical research on nonverbal impressions, they will be reviewed here. The reader is directed to Burgoon, Buller, and Woodall (1989) for reviews of the others.

Strategic Self-Presentation

Jones and Pittman (1982) define *strategic self-presentation* as "those features of behavior affected by power augmentation motives designed to elicit or shape others' attributions of the actor's dispositions" (p. 233). These presentations, which are typically intertwined with other social performances, need not be false, distorted, or discrepant from the phenomenal self but are motivated by a desire to secure or augment power. Gaining power is presumed to be facilitated by another holding a particular impression of the actor. Strategic self-presentation is less likely to occur (a) on purely expressive behavior, (b) during overlearned, highly ritualized social exchanges, (c) when there is high task orientation, or (d) when the overriding concern is for authenticity of one's disclosures (e.g., trying to get in touch with true feelings during therapy).

The five proposed strategies, which combine verbal content with nonverbal style, are highly reminiscent of the well-established dimensions of ethos or credibility and attraction in communication research (see McCroskey & McCain, 1974; McCroskey & Young, 1981). Much of the extant literature on nonverbal impressions can be incorporated under these strategies (see Burgoon, Birk, & Pfau, 1990; Burgoon, Buller, & Woodall, 1989; Harper, 1985; Henley, 1977; Kleinke, 1975; Knapp & Hall, 1992; and Mehrabian, 1981, for summaries).

1. Ingratiation. These attraction-seeking overtures, motivated by the desire to elicit an attribution of likability, dovetail with the communication-oriented credibility dimension of sociability and the attraction dimension of social attractiveness. Success depends on concealing ulterior motives. All the previously identified behaviors associated with perceived attraction, plus affinity-seeking behaviors such as smiling, may fit here.

2. Intimidation. Tactics in this category are intended to convince the target that the actor is dangerous, because the actor will either embarrass the target, cost the target in some way, cause self pain or embarrassment, behave unpredictably and irrationally, or be undeterred by compassion for others. Threat behaviors (e.g., stares and glares, physical intimidation), indicators of dynamism, and cues of dominance, power, and status may fit here. Cues proposed or confirmed as indicators of higher status and power include use or possession of larger, more private, and more luxuriously appointed spaces; greater access to other people's space, time, and possessions; initiation of conversational distance and touch patterns; asymmetrical use of touch and spatial intrusion (giving more, receiving less); indirect body orientation and backward lean; less frequent but more direct eye gaze and staring; less smiling and facial pleasantness and more frowning or scowling; greater postural relaxation and asymmetry; initiation of talk; more talk time; lower and more varied pitch; vocal cues of anger; use of vocal interruptions; more rapid speaking pace; and control of silences. Some research indicates that dominance strategies may be advisable for males but not for females (Camden & Kennedy, 1986; Raines et al., 1990; Sadalla, Kenrick, & Vershure, 1987).

3. Self-promotion. Tactics in this category, which are intended to stimulate attributions of competence, appear to incorporate elements of the task dimension of attraction and the competence and composure dimensions of credibility. Jones and Pittman (1982) suggest that this strategy may include some features of ingratiation and intimidation. Work on kinesic, proxemic, and vocal attributes fostering credibility and attraction indicates that vocal and facial pleasantness cues (fluency, pitch variety, smiling), kinesic/proxemic immediacy (physical closeness, frequent eye gaze, direct eye contact), conversational delivery style, and vocal and kinesic dominance cues (moderately rapid, loud, nonhesitant speech; facial expressiveness) are also relevant tactics.

4. Exemplification. Here the desire is to elicit attributions of integrity, sincerity, honesty, virtue, self-sacrifice, generosity, and so forth. This parallels the character dimension of credibility. Although tactics signaling political militancy (e.g., symbolic attire and gestures) fit here, vocal and kinesic pleasantness and expressiveness are also relevant. Voices rated as benevolent, for example, tend to be softer, slower paced, and varied.

5. Supplication. This strategy exploits one's own weakness and dependence, making the norm of obligation or social responsibility salient. Speculatively, physical appearance, vocal cues, and other behaviors that emphasize babyishness may belong here.

Expectancy Violations Theory

The strategic self-presentation theory offers a useful typology for classifying impression management strategies but does not explicate which strategies should be most effective under which circumstances. One theory that attempts to do so is expectancy violations theory (Burgoon, 1978, 1983, 1992; Burgoon & Hale, 1988; Burgoon & Jones, 1976). Originating as an attempt to explain effects of proxemic violations, the theory offers a series of assumptions and propositions predicting when nonverbal behaviors will produce positive outcomes, such as heightened credibility and attraction, or negative outcomes. A central premise of the theory is that nonverbal behaviors engender strong expectations that govern interaction patterns and outcomes. A second key premise is that nonverbal behaviors have message value. When meanings are unequivocal and/or congruent (in the case of multiple meanings), a social meaning model prevails such that interpretations and evaluations associated with the behaviors are predicted to influence outcomes directly. For example, high conversational involvement carries positive connotations, is evaluated positively (considered desirable), and should therefore evoke desirable evaluations of the communicator. When meanings are ambiguous or conflicting, *communicator reward valence* is posited to moderate the *cognitive-affective assessment* process. *Communicator valence* is a summary term for all the combined communicator characteristics that, on balance, cause the communicator to be regarded positively or negatively. For example, touch by a positive-valence communicator may be interpreted as a show of comfort or affiliation; the same touch by a negative-valence communicator may be interpreted as patronizing. And even if the same interpretation of affiliation is applied for both communicators, such an overture from a negative-valence communicator may be unwanted. The interpretation and evaluation process results in a net valence for the nonverbal act. Positively valenced acts are posited to produce positive outcomes and negatively valenced acts, negative outcomes. Violations of expectations are hypothesized to intensify this process by causing an attentional shift to the source of the violation and the behaviors themselves, thus making communicator and message characteristics more salient.

Research to date on this theory (Burgoon, 1978; Burgoon, Coker, & Coker, 1986; Burgoon & Le Poire, 1993; Burgoon, Manusov, Mineo, & Hale, 1985; Burgoon, Newton, Walther, & Baesler, 1989; Burgoon, Stacks, & Burch, 1982; Burgoon, Stacks, & Woodall, 1979; Burgoon & Walther, 1990; Burgoon, Walther, & Baesler, 1992; see also Storrs & Kleinke, 1990) has produced the following conclusions, cast here in impression management strategy terms:

1. Positive-valence communicators can enhance their credibility and attractiveness by engaging in far or close distance violations and by using some forms of affiliative touch. Negative-valence communicators reduce credibility and attraction by engaging in violations. The touch findings may be qualified by gender.

2. Both positive-valence and negative-valence communicators can enhance their credibility and attractiveness by engaging in high degrees of gaze, immediacy, and conversational involvement. These all qualify as positive expectancy violations. Negative violations, in the form of gaze aversion, nonimmediacy, and noninvolvement, reduce credibility and attraction. Some forms of touch may also be used by negative-valence communicators but are riskier, especially if initiated by males.

Other relevant research on appropriateness or acceptability indirectly speaks to the likelihood of success of specific nonverbal tactics (see, e.g., Baglan & Nelson, 1982; Burgoon & Walther, 1990; von Raffler-Engel, 1983; Street & Brady, 1982; and the popularized literature on successful dress). In keeping with Goffman's (1959) claims about successful self-presentation, much of this research leads to the conclusion that doing what is appropriate is successful. However, the expectancy violations work is challenging the assumption that the route to success is always conformity to expectations. The conditions under which violations are the more efficacious choice for impression management continue to be a prime area for further investigation.

Relational Communication and Relationship Management

This bipartite function of nonverbal communication addresses how nonverbal behavior defines interpersonal relationships and, in so doing, influences relationship trajectories toward greater or lesser intimacy, commitment, and satisfaction.

Relational Communication

Nonverbal signals may express how interactants feel about each other, about the relationship itself, or about themselves within the context of the relationship. It has been said that every communication has a "content" or "report" aspect and a "relational" or "command" aspect. Nonverbal relational communication can be seen to serve this latter metacommunicative function in that it tells one how to interpret other, copresent messages within the context of the relational definition that exists. But it can also be seen as the "content" of messages about the relationship itself. That is, it should not be viewed as merely augmenting other messages but as making meaningful statements in its own right. Relational messages are not exclusively nonverbal, but a division of labor exists between the verbal and nonverbal channels such that the nonverbal channels do a disproportionate share of the relational "work."

Relational communication bears a close resemblance to identity and impression management, particularly at the level of the specific nonverbal cues used to signal evaluations and self-images. However, relational communication is distinct in at least four respects. First, impression management typically entails an observer perspective, whereas relational communication entails a participant perspective. Those taking an "observer" perspective on another's nonverbal performance tend to attribute that person's behavior to internal traits and dispositions, whereas participants in an interaction, who are themselves "observed," tend to see performances as reactions and feedback to themselves (Ellsworth & Ludwig, 1972). Second, identity and impression management techniques are directed toward a generalized audience, whereas relational communication is directed toward a particular target. Third, unlike identity and impression management research, which exclusively uses individuals (encoders or decoders) as the unit of analysis, relational communication may use the dyad as the unit of analysis. Finally, research on identity and impression management often takes a cause-effect approach (e.g., what nonverbal behaviors create impressions of honesty or cause relational satisfaction), whereas relational communication research often takes a structural approach, focusing on the meanings attributed to nonverbal behavior.

Traditional approaches to relational communication have identified only two or three dimensions (e.g., dominance, affection, inclusion) along which messages may be exchanged. Such perspectives underestimate the variety and richness of message themes that are present in interpersonal encounters. Based on a review of ethological, anthropological, sociological, psychological, and communication literature, Burgoon and Hale (1984) proposed 12 orthogonal but distinctive topoi of relational messages: intimacy, which comprises the subthemes of affection-hostility, intensity of involvement, inclusion-exclusion, trust, and depth-superficiality; emotional arousal (activation); composure; dominance-submission (control); similarity; formality; and task-social orientation. Empirical investigations in interpersonal contexts (Burgoon & Hale, 1987) revealed that these dimensions could be combined into fewer, interrelated message clusters. These clusters offer an organizing scheme for identifying prevalent patterns of nonverbal relational communication. What follows is a summary of the major findings (for details, see Burgoon, 1982, 1991; Burgoon, Buller, Hale, & deTurck, 1984; Burgoon, Kelley, Newton, & Keeley-Dyreson, 1989; Burgoon & Newton, 1991; Cappella, 1983; Coker & Burgoon, 1987; Exline & Fehr, 1978; Hendrick & Hendrick, 1992; Henley, 1977; Heslin & Alper, 1983; Jones & Yarbrough, 1985; Kramer, Alloway, & Pliner, 1975; Le Poire & Burgoon, 1991; Mehrabian, 1972, 1981; Palmer, 1989; Patterson, 1973, 1983; Scheflen, 1974; Siegman, 1978; Thayer, 1986).

Messages of intimacy. A recent phenomenological study of intimacy (Register & Henley, 1992) revealed that, for many, intimacy is defined largely by nonverbal behavior—physical closeness, touches, lingering gazes, prolonged time spent together. Some of the experience of intimacy can be understood as a function of one major ingredient, nonverbal involvement, which itself comprises at least five dimensions: (a) *immediacy* (proximity, direct body orientation, forward lean, postural openness, gaze, and touch that signal approach and inclusion), (b) *expressiveness* (facial, gestural, postural, and vocal displays of animation and activity), (c) *alter-centrism* (kinesic and auditory cues that one is attentive to and oriented toward the other rather than self), (d) *conversational management* (self-synchrony, fluency, coordinated movement, interactional synchrony, and short response latencies that create a well-paced, nonawkward interaction), and (e) *social composure* (e.g., postural and vocal cues of relaxation or anxiety, random movement, adaptor behaviors) (Coker & Burgoon, 1987).

Involvement per se neither implies nor includes positivity. But when it is accompanied by *positive affect* (smiling, nodding, vocal pleasantness, relaxed laughter), which is often the case, it connotes greater attraction, liking, trust, affiliation, depth, similarity, and rapport. Other cues contributing to intimacy messages include touch to more "intimate" body regions, softer voices, postural openness, motor mimicry and mirroring (exhibiting the same behavior as another), wearing similar apparel and "identification symbols" (tie-signs), punctuality, monochronic use of time, and sharing territories and possessions. Involvement may also, however, combine with negative affect, in which case it may create an intense message of hostility. Noninvolvement and nonimmediacy cues signal detachment and privacy. It is important to note that many of the individual behaviors, if viewed singly, might be ambiguous in meaning because they have multiple relational interpretations. But when combined with other cues into a pattern, the appropriate interpretation becomes clear.

Arousal and composure. Emotional arousal and lack of composure are conveyed by a host of vocalic, kinesic, and proxemic cues, some of which are discussed under "Emotion Expression and Management" below. Research has substantiated that composure and relaxation are communicated by such behaviors as asymmetrical limb positions, less body tonus and tension, close proximity, and smiling. Greater kinesic expressiveness and faster tempo also connote composure. While it is likely that people intentionally manipulate these cues to send relational messages of poise and composure, the converse may not be true. Noncomposure may merely reflect a person's current emotive state irrespective of the relationship. This aspect of relational communication needs further exploration.

Dominance. Dominance appears to be expressed by all the behaviors cited under "Impression Management" above as cues of power, status, and prestige as well as by the expressiveness facet of involvement. Submissiveness is expressed by the opposites of these, along with some specific gestures such as the head tilt and open palms that convey vulnerability and some involvement and affiliative cues. One useful way to better understand the innumerable cues that express dominance is to group them according to the principles that underlie them. The following represents a partial list of such principles:

1. Threat. Indicators of superior size and impending physical threat convey dominance. Any actions that emphasize or enlarge one's physical size (e.g., large territories, use of gatekeepers, deeper pitch, erect posture, a "firm" stance) or imply danger (threat stares, threatening gestures) function to outstress the other individual.

2. Elevation. Higher is more dominant. Apart from their symbolic hierarchical function, such cues give the dominant individual a surveillance and protection advantage.

3. Initiation and precedence. Initiating conversation, spacing, touch, or interaction rhythms and changing topics convey dominance. Entering a space first, walking ahead of others, being given a first turn, and so on can be seen as variants on this theme.

4. Expectancy violations. Dominant individuals have the prerogative to violate nonverbal expectations and are more likely to do so. Far and close conversational distances, for instance, convey more dominance than do normative ones.

5. Privileged access. Having access to valued or scarce resources conveys dominance. Spatial intrusions or imposition on another's time, as well as possession of status symbols, fit this principle.

6. Activity. Dynamic, expressive, and fast-paced actions send messages of confidence and authority. A rapid speaking rate, for example, makes a speaker appear sure of herself.

7. Relaxation. Moderate postural and vocal relaxation connote dominance. Dominant people are freer to "drop their guard," to deviate from norms for "proper" behavior.

8. Task performance cues. Individuals expecting to influence group task performance exhibit more cues indicative of status and task-related ability, which enhance their prestige, power, and actual influence. Dominance or power in group situations is therefore partly a function of one's likely ability to contribute to task performance. This is known as an expectation advantage in *expectation states theory* (see Berger, Rosenholtz, & Zelditch, 1980; Ridgeway, Berger, & Smith, 1985).

Formality and task versus social orientation. These last dimensions are interrelated in that part of being task oriented is being more formal, and formality often connotes more of a task than a social orientation. Formality is conveyed by decreased vocal expressiveness, increased resonance and precise articulation, postural tension or erectness, and greater distance. The task cues identified in expectation states theory serve as indicators of a group member's inferred task competence and confidence. They include response latency, gaze, loudness, fluency, posture, gestures, and seating position (Ridgeway et al., 1985). For example, a person expecting to exercise leadership typically sits at the head of a table, and individuals seated at the head of a table become more participative and influential.

Relationship Management

The features unifying research on nonverbal behavior in interpersonal relationships show a macroscopic perspective—looking at entire relationships rather than single encounters—and a consequent concern with longitudinal factors. One strand of research and theorizing examines how nonverbal cues function in the development, maintenance, and dissolution of interpersonal relationships. Work on relationship development has long recognized that nonverbal behaviors signify the state of the relationship and can promote or obstruct the development of intimacy (see, e.g., Altman & Taylor's, 1967, social penetration theory and Knapp's, 1983, 1984a, dimensions of communication in relationship development). The other strand of research examines the connection between nonverbal behavior and such measures of relationship state as intimacy, commitment, and satisfaction.

Several exemplars illustrate the directions of this growing trend in research. Work on initial attraction has shown that kinesic and vocal behaviors mediate attitudinal similarity effects (Cappella & Palmer, 1990). Research on courtship stages and rituals has identified different nonverbal cues associated with each stage and differentiated courtship cues from quasi-courtship ones (see, e.g., Givens, 1978, 1983; Scheflen, 1965; Simpson et al., 1992). Research on relationship stages and types has found significant differences across various relationships (e.g., acquaintance, friend, romantic, superior-subordinate, parent-child, doctor-patient) in nonverbal intimacy, play, privacy, and emotional expressivity (Baxter, 1992; Burgoon, Parrott, et al., 1989; Guerrero & Andersen, 1991; Planalp & Benson, 1992; Wagner & Smith, 1991). Similarly, research on romantic touch has shown that increasingly intimate touch signifies increasing levels of relational commitment (Johnson & Edwards, 1991). Other research on relational escalation, maintenance, or deescalation has developed typologies of combined verbal and nonverbal strategies and tactics relational partners employ (e.g., Cupach & Metts, 1986; Shea & Pearson, 1986; Tolhuizen, 1989) and estimated their frequency of use. Marital conflict research has uncovered nonverbal profiles accompanying different conflict strategies, shown that conflicts often take the form of reciprocal escalating spirals of nonverbal hostility, and confirmed that nonverbal expressions of affect are a deciding factor in whether conflicts are resolved or not (e.g., Alberts, 1989; Alfred, Harper, Wadham, & Woolley, 1981; Gottman, Markman, & Notarius, 1977; Harris, Gergen, & Lannamann, 1986; Huston & Vangelisti, 1991; Julien, Markman, & Lindahl, 1989; Markman & Floyd, 1980; Markman, Notarius, Stephen, & Smith, 1981; Newton & Burgoon, 1990). Research on relational satisfaction has identified which relational message themes and conflict resolution patterns promote satisfaction in physician-patient and marital relationships (e.g., Burgoon, Pfau, Parrott, et al., 1987; Kelley & Burgoon, 1991; Rusbult, Verett, Whitney, Slovik, & Lipkus, 1991). And various programs of research comparing participant and trained observer perspectives have shown that observers and participants share some commonalities in perceptions but also some notable discrepancies (e.g., Burgoon & Newton, 1991; Floyd & Markman, 1983; Rusbult et al., 1991; Street, Mulac, & Wiemann, 1988). Among the important conclusions to be drawn from these lines of work are that nonverbal cues are important barometers of, and influences on, attraction and intimacy; relationship type or stage does indeed mediate forms of nonverbal expression; and nonverbal patterns significantly influence relational trajectories and outcomes.

Areas likely to attract increasing research attention are nonverbal turning points (events that alter the direction of a relationship's development), rare events, and expected but omitted nonverbal cues as relational statements. The absence of a hug at bedtime, for instance, may be more telling to a spouse about the intimacy of the marriage than any other present cue. Rarely performed or intermittent behaviors may be the most significant signals of intimacy, yet they are unlikely to be noted by observers or captured in highly controlled research contexts. Thus research may increasingly incorporate diary and account methods. Also important to assess, from a descriptive standpoint, are the frequency and duration of specific relational cues, their sequences and cycles over time, the interrelatedness among cues, and changes in relational meaning depending on their placement in the relational trajectory. The previous overemphasis on single cue and static analyses will doubtless give way to analyzing the interplay among multiple cues, longitudinal patterns, and the impact of those patterns on relational outcomes such as commitment and satisfaction.

Deception

This function, which bridges several communication functions, concerns the ways in which people send messages designed to foster beliefs contrary to what the actor believes is the true state of affairs. Deception may take many forms—falsehoods, white lies, equivocations, evasions, hyperbole, omissions. An impressive body of literature has been amassed in this area, but scant research has examined nonverbal deception in truly interactive contexts. What follows is a brief overview of the primary theories and lines of deception research most relevant to interpersonal communication.

Previous Theories and Interpersonal Deception Theory

Perhaps the most pervasive "theory" guiding previous deception work has been Ekman and Friesen's (1969a) *leakage hypothesis*, which states that deceivers attempt to censor and control facial expressions more than body and limb movements because they expect others to watch their faces. Therefore, the least controllable or controlled channels and cues should be the best indicators of deceit. This general premise has been extended to produce a leakage hierarchy. Although there has been dispute as to whether the body and limbs or voice are leakiest (DePaulo, Stone, & Lassiter, 1985; DePaulo, Zuckerman, & Rosenthal, 1980; Hocking & Leathers, 1980), the face has generally been considered the least likely to leak information (with some exceptions) and the verbal channel to be the most informative in detecting deception. Expanding upon this hypothesis, Zuckerman, De Paulo, and Rosenthal (1981, 1986) advanced a *four-factor theory*, positing that changes in deceivers' behavior are the result of four psychological processes: *physiological arousal* (due to detection apprehension), *emotional reactions* (arising from guilt), *cognitive complexity* (required to formulate deceptive messages), and *motivation to control behavior* (to create a truthful demeanor). Thus cues exhibited during deception should arise from these factors. In a similar vein, Hocking and Leathers (1980) theorized that people would attempt to control those cues stereotypically associated with deception.

While these theoretical formulations have brought considerable coherence to the deception literature and prompted much research, they overlook the deliberate nature of most deceptions, underestimate the agency of the receiver as a communication participant, and ignore the dynamic changes in deception that are likely to occur when people are allowed to interact and both deceiver and receiver bring their own strategic agendas to the interaction. They also focus on observer and stranger judgments, to the neglect of participant perspectives and interactions among acquainted individuals.

In an attempt to remedy these shortcomings and to shift from a psychological paradigm to a communication one, Buller and Burgoon (1994; Buller, Strzyzewski, & Comstock, 1991; Buller, Strzyzewski, & Hunsaker, 1991; Burgoon, 1989; Burgoon, Buller, Ebesu, & Rockwell, in press; Burgoon et al., 1993) have proposed and begun testing *interpersonal deception theory* (IDT). IDT begins with the premise that deception is a communication event that invokes all the previously cited communication functions of identity management, self-presentation, relational communication, emotion management, conversation management, and social influence, many of which are not relevant to observers. In the process of engaging in deceit, deceivers are usually motivated to protect their image and self-identity while also successfully influencing the other. To do so, they need to manage their communication performance so as to avoid negative relational messages that spoil their identity or relationship while sending positive relational messages that promote trust. They also need to manage their emotions so as to minimize clues to arousal or anxiety prompted by the deceit. And they need to maintain their conversational responsibilities so that the interaction proceeds smoothly. In the process, they may simultaneously engage in strategic (deliberate) and nonstrategic (leakage) behaviors. Three general strategies that encompass numerous nonverbal and verbal tactics are (a) *information management* (increased uncertainty and vagueness, reticence, and nonimmediacy that decrease detectability, disassociate the source from the message, and convey insincerity), (b) *behavior management* (suppression and restraint of behaviors that might leak true intent), and (c) *defensive maneuvers* (designed to preempt more engagement and inquiry by the other interactant). Nonstrategic categories include (a) *arousal and nervousness* (cues betraying one's heightened state of arousal), (b) *negative and dampened affect* (verbal and nonverbal expressions that leak unpleasant feelings possibly associated with guilt and embarrassment or flat affect that falls short of normal expressivity), and (c) *reduced conversational involvement* (nonverbal and verbal nonimmediacy, inattentiveness, poor conversational management, and incompetent communication performances).

Following are several key propositions advanced by the theory:

1. Interactive deception differs fundamentally from noninteractive deception. The interactive process makes new considerations salient, and the requirements of conversation place demands on people that alter the ways in which people act, process information, and interpret another's behavior.

2. Credibility is a central message feature to which both participants are attuned. This proposition articulates a basic maxim of all communication: that participants expect one another to be truthful. Communicators therefore attempt to craft presentations that appear truthful, and receivers are attentive to any clues that "the truth, the whole truth, and nothing but the truth" is not being presented.

3. Deception is manifested through a combination of strategic and nonstrategic behaviors. As noted above, deception is not merely indicated by involuntary actions but also by strategic efforts to maintain one's credibility.

4. Suspicion is manifested through a combination of strategic and nonstrategic behaviors. Receivers also engage in strategic behavior. Like deceivers, when receivers' suspicions have been piqued, they engage in various strategies to ascertain whether deception is occurring and to uncover the truth. Similarly, arousal (in this case engendered by uncertainty), emotional reactions (engendered by negative reactions to being deceived as well as distress over how to proceed), and task complexity (engendered by the need to detect without alerting the deceiver) all may produce "leakage."

5. Receivers recognize deceit and senders recognize suspicion when present. Because deceit alters a sender's behavior and suspicion alters a receiver's behavior, their cointeractants should recognize those deviations, which serve as a form of feedback. Although participants may be aware that something is amiss, they may be reluctant actually to attribute deceit or suspicion to their partner without further observation and verification.

6. Suspicion alters targets' behaviors. The natural consequence of recognizing suspicion is that senders will modify their subsequent communication to create a more credible presentation. This should be true of truthtellers and deceivers alike.

7. Relational familiarity moderates behaviors, perceptions, and interpretations. The interpersonal literature is replete with evidence that, once people become acquainted, a host of new considerations emerge, such as prior familiarity with the person's behavior, anticipated future interactions, relational schemas and expectations, and desire for continued pleasant, honest interactions. These should produce qualitatively different interactions and attributions than interactions between strangers. As a result, much of the previous knowledge about deception may not generalize to interpersonal interactions.

8. Behaviors during deceptive encounters change over time. Consistent with the premise that interactions are dynamic events entailing feedback loops between the two participants and that deception evinces strategic moves and countermoves, deceptive interchanges should show longitudinal changes.

9. Preinteractional and interactional communication factors determine deception and detection success. Specific factors posited to improve deception success are communication skill, the ability to create a favorable image, and the ability to maintain a normal (expected) interaction style. Factors affecting the ability to detect deception include training, behavioral familiarity, and communication skill.

The theory has implications for what patterns of behavior deceivers, truthtellers, and receivers will exhibit during interpersonal exchanges as well as the circumstances under which truth and deception will be detected accurately. Many of the extant research findings summarized below are pertinent to these propositions.

Actual and Perceived Cues to Deception

Perhaps no area of deception research has attracted more attention than the quest for valid nonverbal indicators of deceit. Consistent with the third IDT proposition, research has uncovered numerous nonverbal correlates of actual deception, but the validity of many of them has been challenged. Several meta-analyses, reviews, and recent experiments have attempted to sort out this issue (e.g., DePaulo et al., 1985; deTurck & Miller, 1985; Ekman, O'Sullivan, Friesen, & Scherer, 1991; Kalbfleisch, 1992; Knapp et al., 1987; Miller & Burgoon, 1982; Zuckerman & Driver, 1985; Zuckerman, Driver, & Koestner, 1982; Zuckerman et al., 1981), but whether the consistently emerging cues are present during actual interpersonal interaction needs to be determined.

On the perceptual side, research has consistently shown that the cues receivers stereotypically associate with lying do not match closely the actual correlates of deception (DePaulo et al., 1985; Kraut, 1980; Miller & Burgoon, 1982). The lack of correspondence between the cues and channels that receivers use to make judgments and the ones they should use partly accounts for the generally poor success rate in detecting deception. Channel comparison work addressing the relative controllability or leakage associated with facial versus body versus audio channels (e.g., Bauchner, Kaplan, & Miller, 1980; Miller et al., 1981; Zuckerman, Spiegel, DePaulo, & Rosenthal, 1982) has shown that receivers tend to focus on the face (typically the least leaky channel) and to ignore more revealing vocal information.

Also confounding the ability to arrive at a concise profile of deception cues is the complexity of factors influencing them. Among the confirmed factors altering actual and interpreted cues are communicator characteristics such as gender, dominance, age, social skill, Machiavellianism, self-monitoring ability, relational familiarity, amount of planning and rehearsal, and type of message content (emotional, factual, attitudinal) (e.g., Cody & O'Hair, 1983; deTurck & Miller, 1990; Knapp & Comadena, 1979; O'Hair, Cody, & McLaughlin, 1981; Riggio & Friedman, 1983).

Effects of Suspicion

Evidence to date confirms that the introduction of suspicion can alter both the suspecter's behavior and that of the target of suspicion (Buller, Strzyzewski, & Comstock, 1991; Burgoon, Buller, Dillman, & Walther, 1993; Toris & DePaulo, 1985). Fortunately for deceivers, most people tend to hold a *truth bias*, an assumption that others' messages are honest. This is especially true among acquainted individuals (McCornack & Levine, 1990; McCornack & Parks, 1986). As a consequence, suspicion may not be that prevalent. Nevertheless, when it arises, it causes subtle changes in the suspecter's behavior, but these changes may depend upon the level of suspicion. Suspecters who are moderately suspicious may be unpleasant, nonimmediate, and aroused but fairly fluent, while those who are highly suspicious may be highly immediate, assertive, and poised but not as fluent. Targets of suspicion need not be overtly aware of these specific behavioral changes, but they do sense suspicion when it is present; that is, something in the suspecter's demeanor telegraphs the suspicions to the target. These suspicions, in turn, alter the suspect's behavior. Some individuals may use this feedback to their advantage, adjusting their demeanor to create a more honest-appearing presentation. However, the majority of suspected senders suffer decrements in their own performance. This is true for truthtellers as well as liars. Thus being subjected to suspicion can cause a self-fulfilling prophecy, leading truthtellers to look dishonest and confirming the suspecter's suspicions.

Detection Strategies and Detection Accuracy

The combination of truth biases and reliance on the wrong cues makes untrained observers relatively inaccurate in detecting discrepant and deceptive messages (deTurck & Miller, 1990). Although greater familiarity with deception—whether through exposure to previous samples of behavior (behavioral) or training (knowledge)—can improve detection success, there is growing evidence that too much experience with deception can lead to a lie bias and concomitant reduction in deception success (Burgoon et al., in press). This may explain why law enforcement and military professionals charged with detecting deceit often are no more accurate than lay people (Ekman & O'Sullivan, 1991). Apart from familiarity, influences on success in lie detection include number and choice of channels available for making judgments (for example, transcripts versus video-only versus audio-only information), deceiver's and receiver's motivation to deceive or detect deception, and deceiver's and receiver's social skills and nonverbal sensitivity (DePaulo et al., 1985; Miller et al., 1981).

Emotion Expression and Management

It used to be fashionable to equate nonverbal signals with the expressive function of communication. Though this simplistic view has given way to recognizing that nonverbal signals have multiple social functions, the converse is likely to be true in interpersonal interaction, namely, that nonverbal codes are primary vehicles for expressing emotions as well as for managing one's emotional experiences. Because an entire chapter of this *Handbook* is devoted to this topic, my focus here will be on the twin issues of how nonverbal behaviors are employed in the communication of affective states and how nonverbal resources are marshaled to control or alter those states.

Before beginning, a few definitional distinctions are in order. First is differentiating emotional experience from emotional expression. Much of the prolific writing on emotions has centered on the nature of emotional *experiences* and factors instigating them. Of primary interest here is emotional *expression*, that is, the external manifestations of those emotional states and people's abilities to detect and interpret them. Second, in the nonverbal literature, the terms *emotion, affect,* and *arousal* are often used synonymously. While I will use *emotion* and *affect* interchangeably, the former entails both an arousal dimension and a valence dimension, whereas the latter typically refers to valence alone (specifically, subjective experiences that are hedonically toned). Thus one may use the concept of affect in the context of describing attitudes toward some object (i.e., having positive or negative affect toward it) without implying any particular level of intensity toward it. In turn, *arousal*—which refers to physiological, cognitive, and/or behavioral activation—itself may entail both an intensity dimension and a valence dimension (see Burgoon, Kelley, Newton, & Keeley-Dyreson, 1989) but can refer to states such as watchful readiness or boredom that are not thought of as emotions. In what follows, I will treat emotions and arousal separately.

Theories of Emotion Expression

More theorizing surrounds the expressive function of nonverbal communication than any other. Buck (1981, 1984), Davitz (1969), Dittmann (1972a), Izard (1971),

Plutchik (1962, 1984), Schachter and Singer (1962), and Tomkins (1962, 1984), among others, have addressed such issues as the relationship between internal states and their external manifestations, the dimensionality of emotions, and the manner in which meaning is assigned to the overt behaviors. But the majority of theoretical debate has focused on the acquisition of emotional expressions. Nowhere is the nature-nurture controversy more central than here.

Ekman and Friesen (1969b) articulated three alternative possibilities on the origins of emotional expressions: (a) They arise from inborn neurological programs that are part of our evolutionary development; (b) they are manifestations of experiences common to all humans (such as the need to ward off dangers or to withdraw from pain); or (c) they are shaped strictly by environmental and social factors. The first two positions reflect a *universalist perspective*—that at least certain primary affect displays are produced and understood in the same way by all members of the species (Eibl-Eibesfeldt, 1970, 1972). The latter position underpins the *cultural relativist perspective*—that any cross-cultural similarities are only superficial and that actual use and interpretation are strictly a function of cultural and environmental influences (Birdwhistell, 1970; LaBarre, 1947).

Evidence to support these various alternatives comes from several sources. One is comparative studies of nonhuman primates. As noted earlier, many human behaviors show a striking similarity to those of other primates. This kind of evidence implies evolutionary continuity and innate origins based on survival value. A second source of evidence is child development literature. The extent to which infants and toddlers follow the same stages of emotional development and exhibit the same expressions indirectly supports a biological explanation. More definitive evidence within this body of literature comes from studies of blind, deaf, and limbless children, who, lacking the ability to learn emotional displays through sensory experience, still exhibit universally recognized expressions. A third source of evidence comes from studies examining the configurations associated with emotional expressions (e.g., diagonal lines, angularity, roundness), which have shown that the same configural properties convey meanings of threat, anger, warmth, happiness, and so on (Aronoff, Barclay, & Stevenson, 1988; Aronoff, Woike, & Hyman, 1992). This implies universal properties underlying the expressions themselves. Finally, cross-cultural comparisons on encoding, decoding, and patterns of use supply evidence both of commonalities and of differences across cultural and subcultural groups (see Ekman, 1973; Knapp & Hall, 1992, for excellent reviews of this literature).

As a compromise between the two extremes, Ekman and Friesen advanced *neurocultural theory* (Ekman, 1973, 1978; Ekman & Friesen, 1975; Ekman et al., 1971; Ekman et al., 1972), which holds that neuromuscular programs are biologically inherited but that social factors not only filter what stimuli will elicit different emotions but also dictate when, how, with what meaning, and with what consequences emotional displays will occur. The earlier-introduced concept of display rules applies to this culture-specific management of displays in social settings. Based on his extensive research program and review of emotions literature, Ekman (1984) proposed several principles that provide a useful framework for organizing the emotion expression literature most relevant to interpersonal communication.

1. There is a distinctive pan-cultural signal for each emotion. Although researchers have proposed various labels and estimates for the number of distinctive affects that exist, the cross-cultural work of Ekman and his associates offers definitive support for these six: happiness, sadness, fear, anger, disgust, and surprise. Other affect displays are proposed to be blends of these basic ones. To the extent that these expressions are part of our genetic heritage as humans, they form an elemental universal language that can supplant or augment more ambiguous messages and can cross cultural barriers.

Notwithstanding, significant differences exist in the form and intensity of these displays across cultures and social groups. For example, Matsumoto (1991) hypothesizes that collective cultures display more emotions that promote group cohesion and harmony than do individualistic cultures, while cultures with significant power differences display more of those emotions that preserve such differences.

2. Emotional expressions involve multiple signals. Within the kinesic code, the body is responsible for signaling the intensity of affect, whereas the face signals the specific evaluative state, with various regions of the face differentially salient to sending and interpreting feeling states (Boucher & Ekman, 1975; Cuceloglu, 1972; Ekman & Friesen, 1975). Within the vocal code, acoustic features such as amplitude, fundamental frequency (pitch), tempo, breathing, intonation pattern, and stress contours differentiate emotions (Scherer & Oshinsky, 1977; Williams & Stevens, 1972). Neither haptics, which intuitively seems relevant, nor the other codes have been analyzed systematically for their contributions to coordinated, multichannel emotional displays.

3. There are limits on the duration of an emotion. "Real" emotions typically last from ½ to 4 seconds; expressions of shorter or longer durations than this range are usually false or mock expressions. This is probably one basis for "intuitively" regarding some expressions as insincere or suspicious.

4. The timing and intensity of an emotional expression reflect the specifics of a particular emotional experience. That is, the latency and duration of the manifest expression correlate with the strength and positivity or negativity of the experience.

5. Emotional expression can be controlled, simulated, or inhibited. Just as people can intensify or deintensify emotions, they can also completely conceal or fabricate them and do so convincingly (although false emotions are detectable by the muscle groups that are enlisted as well as by their duration; Ekman et al., 1988).

The last principle is especially relevant to interpersonal interactions, because people may regulate their expressive behaviors during face-to-face encounters as part of self-presentation and are capable, with varying levels of success, of becoming more or less expressive (DePaulo, 1991; DePaulo, Blank, Swaim, & Hairfield, 1992). Although some theorizing proposes that social factors inhibit certain emotional expressions, especially spontaneous ones (e.g., Ekman & Friesen, 1969a, 1969b; Friedman & Miller-Herringer, 1991), an alternative position is that the presence of others facilitates and potentiates some emotional expressivity (Chovil, 1991). No doubt, both processes are operative (Buck, 1991), pointing to the important social and communicative nature of emotional expression. DePaulo (1991) identifies a host of factors governing the degree to which spontaneous and posed emotions are presented during interpersonal interaction.

Although the argument for the universality of emotional expression might imply that emotions are easily recognized by all members of the human species, such is not the case. This leads to a final principle not articulated by Ekman.

6. Decoding accuracy is highly variable. Extensive research examining how accurately various emotions can be detected has revealed that people have difficulty accurately decoding many primary facial affects and most vocal emotions (e.g., Cuceloglu, 1972; Davitz & Davitz, 1959; Zuckerman, Lipets, Koivumaki, & Rosenthal, 1975). Especially relevant to interpersonal communication is Motley and Camden's (1988) finding that spontaneously expressed emotions in interpersonal interactions are much more ambiguous and difficult to decode than the posed expressions so often studied in the emotions literature.

Coupled with the greater frequency of affect blends in normal interaction and the likelihood that people may attempt to manage many emotional expressions to foster favorable impressions, these findings lead to the inescapable conclusion that a major stumbling block in many interpersonal encounters is deciphering one another's true emotional states. Fortunately, there is some evidence that people are more facially expressive with friends than strangers, making their emotional states easier to identify (Wagner & Smith, 1991).

With the exception of the program of research on expressions of positive and negative affect in marital interaction (e.g., Gottman, 1979; Huston & Vangelisti, 1991) and a series of interview studies conducted by Ekman (1965) over two decades ago, little investigation has addressed the dynamics of emotional expressions in ongoing interactions, how conversational context alters the form and interpretation of displays, how presentations are altered over time (for example, abbreviated or exaggerated), how the various channels are integrated to produce displays, how lengthier presentations affect accuracy of interpretation, how nonverbal emotional expressions relate to concurrent verbal and nonverbal messages that have different functions, and how emotional expressions and expressivity relate to such interpersonal outcomes as satisfaction. Inasmuch as interpersonal encounters are prime occasions for emotional and attitudinal expression, it is time that nonverbal expressive behavior be incorporated into analyses of interpersonal processes and that nonverbal research address the processual nature of interpersonal expressive behavior.

Arousal Expression

Several theories to be discussed under "Conversation Structuring and Management" below invoke arousal as a primary mediator or moderator of communication behavior. Of interest here is the degree to which arousal is manifested overtly and nonverbally. Two different forms of arousal may be evident: an orientation or alertness response, which entails cognitive activation but limited physical activation, and a defensive response, which entails strong physiological reactivity (Le Poire, 1991). Both may range from pleasant to aversive. Burgoon, Kelley, Newton, and Keeley-Dyreson (1989) proposed a bidimensional theory of arousal expression to distinguish between nonverbal cues associated with the intensity of arousal and cues associated with its valence. The key propositions of their theory are these:

1. *As arousal intensity increases, speech performance is increasingly impaired, and immediacy, kinesic activation, and kinesic attentiveness follow an inverted-U pattern* (highest arousal change is associated with moderation in the nonverbal cues).

2. *As negatively valenced arousal increases, immediacy, activity, and attentiveness decrease; expressiveness decreases; tension increases; communication performances become more awkward; and negative affect increases.*

Their initial research and subsequent studies (e.g., Burgoon, Le Poire, Beutler, Bergan, & Engle, 1992) have generally supported the hypothesized relationships. Presumably, interpersonal interactants rely on these cues to infer the arousal level of their partners. Such cues may serve as useful diagnostics in assessing when other aspects of interactions such as intimacy escalation, expectancy violations, or alterations in power and status relations create intense positive or negative arousal (see Kemper, 1984; Matsumoto, 1991).

Affect Management

A lesser recognized function of nonverbal communication is to regulate one's experience of strong affect. By voluntarily controlling nonverbal immediacy and expressive behaviors, people can intensify or diminish a felt emotion. Patterson (1987) calls this function "affect management"; Cappella (1991) treats it under the rubric of "stimulation regulation" and "emotional responsiveness patterns"; and DePaulo (1991) considers it a "self-presentational and identity-construction activity." Regardless of the label applied, the principle is an important one. People use their overt nonverbal behavior to regulate their internal emotional experiences. *Integrating emotions* and immediacy behaviors bind people together, while *differentiating emotions* and nonimmediacy behaviors distance them (Kemper, 1984). When facing threats or crises, people may engage in approach behaviors or display distress, which should prompt reciprocal closeness and comforting from others, thereby alleviating their fears and anxieties. When elated, they may express happiness and seek greater involvement to intensify the experience. When embarrassed or ashamed, they may eschew involvement and exhibit embarrassed smiles to elicit sympathy and lessen the aversive emotional state. Thus basic needs such as security, affiliation, and social comparison may be fulfilled by regulating nonverbal involvement and emotional experience (Patterson, 1991).

Conversation Structuring and Management

Because Cappella's chapter in this *Handbook* is devoted to this function, I will only discuss it briefly here. A sizable share of the literature on nonverbal communication has tackled the issue of how nonverbal behaviors influence the progression and patterning of conversation. Five main interest areas are evident in the literature.

The first is the role of contextual nonverbal features in initially defining the situation and defining role relationships. At the outset of an interaction, architectural features, spatial arrangements, physical appearance cues of status, the nature of artifacts in the environment, and other static features identify for the participants the kind of communication that is expected (for example, formal or informal, social or task oriented, public or private) and any constraints dictated by task requirements and the physical setting itself (Altman, 1975; Goffman, 1963). Other dynamic features, such as kinesic and vocalic demeanor, clarify role relationships among participants, for example, who are in high status positions. Together, these features define the nature of the social situation. By clarifying the purposes of an interpersonal encounter and the programs of behavior that are to be invoked in it, they assist in regulating the interaction that follows. Goffman (1974) describes this process as *framing*—creating a perspective through which to understand the social interaction that occurs. For example, a male physician's white lab coat, the medical paraphernalia in an examining room, and the presence of a nurse all serve to frame a gynecological exam as an impersonal, professional medical procedure rather than a sexual encounter. In the absence of the nonverbal framing cues, the physician's behaviors could take on very different connotations.

Second, many of the static or stable proxemic, artifactual, and physical appearance signals play a role in regulating the amount, frequency, and nature of conversation. For example, sheer propinquity and physical attractiveness increase the probability that contact will occur; small volumes of space and horizontal linear perspectives in an environment promote casual conversation; and group seating arrangements govern who speaks to whom, how often, and how cooperatively (see Burgoon, Buller, & Woodall, 1989; Kendon, Harris, & Key, 1975; Knapp & Hall, 1992; Patterson, 1978, 1983, for summaries).

Third, nonverbal signals form the core of greeting and termination rituals. The behaviors and sequences by which people initiate and end conversations, and the cultural variability in those patterns, have been catalogued by several researchers (Kellermann, Reynolds, & Chen, 1991; Kendon, 1990; Knapp, Hart, Friedrich, & Schulman, 1973; Krivonos & Knapp, 1975; Morris, 1977; O'Leary & Gallois, 1985; Pittinger, Hockett, & Darehy, 1960). Although specific rituals vary significantly by culture, the greeting and termination patterns share in common the degree to which they signal accessibility and reinforce the intimacy level of the relationship.

Fourth, literature abounds on turn-taking and the dynamic regulation of episodes. Nonverbal cues are the lubricant that keeps the conversational machine well oiled. Research has identified that speaker and listener behaviors determine whose turn it is to speak, auditor feedback cues that control speaker behavior, behaviors that mark changes in the tone and topic of interaction, the influence of interruptions and other dynamic cues on floor-holding and the flow of conversation, the role of distance and silence in maintaining engagement, and factors influencing the smoothness of interaction (e.g., Drummond, 1989; Duncan, 1974, 1975; Erickson, 1975; Feldstein & Welkowitz, 1978; Gurevitch, 1989; Hodgins & Zuckerman, 1990; Jaffe, 1978; Kendon, 1990; Rosenfeld, 1978; Sharkey & Stafford, 1990; Wiemann & Knapp, 1975). Three theoretical approaches have been advanced to explain how people manage to accomplish smooth turn-taking: a *signaling approach*, in which sender nonverbal cues operate in a fairly deterministic way to determine turns at talk; a *sequential production model*, which relies more heavily on verbal indicators of appropriate junctures for turn switching; and a *resource model*, which combines the other two and views turn-taking signals as conversational resources to be used as needed, especially to gain interpersonal control (see Duncan & Fiske, 1977; Wiemann, 1985).

Finally, much research has centered on dyadic interaction patterns themselves, that is, the manner in which two (or more) individuals match, synchronize, or offset each other's interaction style. Among the various forms of coordinated action that have been distinguished from one another are *matching, motor mimicry, mirroring, reciprocity, convergence, synchrony, divergence, complementarity*, and *compensation* (see Bernieri & Rosenthal, 1991; Burgoon, Dillman, & Stern, 1993; Condon, 1980; Gatewood & Rosenwein, 1981; Ross, Cheyne, & Lollis, 1988). These processes have been studied for both adult-adult and adult-infant interactions (for exemplars, see Beebe, Stern, & Jaffe, 1979; Cappella, 1981; Cappella & Planalp, 1981; Condon, 1980; Condon & Ogston, 1967; Condon & Sander, 1974; Erickson & Shultz, 1982; Kempton, 1980; Kendon, 1990). A premise underlying much of this work is that interpersonal coordination of behavior is a fundamental, automatic, and possibly biologically rooted feature of social organization (Chapple, 1970;

Warner, Malloy, Schneider, Knoth, & Wilder, 1987). Cappella (1991) asserts that, "in combination with evidence from neonatal and infant development, physiological structures, and ethological parallels, the arguments for adaptive selection and genetic endowment . . . produce a highly suggestive, if not airtight, case" (p. 12). Moderate levels of patterning appear to be beneficial to comprehension, smooth interaction, bonding, interpersonal attraction, and stress reduction, while extreme degrees of patterning may reflect rigidity and produce negative affect and dysfunction (Condon, 1980; Warner et al., 1987).

Among the theories that have been advanced to predict and explain intimacy and involvement patterns specifically are Argyle and Dean's (1965; Argyle & Cook, 1976) *equilibrium theory, the norm of reciprocity* (Gouldner, 1960), the *arousal-labeling model* and subsequent *sequential functional model* (Patterson, 1976, 1983), *expectancy violations theory* (Burgoon, Le Poire, & Rosenthal, 1992; Burgoon, Olney, & Coker, 1988; Hale & Burgoon, 1984), *discrepancy arousal theory* (Cappella & Greene, 1982, 1984), *cognitive valence theory* (Andersen, 1985), and *communication accommodation theory* (cited previously). In addition to the Cappella chapter in this *Handbook,* detailed comparisons of these models and the extent of empirical support for each of them can be found in Andersen and Andersen (1984), Burgoon, Stern, and Dillman (in press), Cappella (1983), Hale and Burgoon (1984), and Le Poire (1991). Although the research evidence is quite mixed and has yielded evidence of both matching/reciprocity and compensation within the same experiment, it appears that reciprocity and matching may be the rule to which there are exceptions (Burgoon, Dillman, Stern, & Kelley, 1993; Cappella, 1991).

Social Influence

This function will be discussed only briefly because other chapters cover it in depth. In terms of nonverbal communication, interest in this area has centered on the pragmatics of nonverbal behavior, specifically on how such behavior alters attitudes and overt behaviors of message recipients. The types of dependent variables that have been studied run the gamut from expressed changes in attitude, petition-signing behavior, and task performance to helping behavior (for example, making change for someone), aggression (for example, shocking someone), compliance with orders, and manifestations of increased anxiety and arousal.

The literature related to this function comes from highly diverse disciplines and is not easily synthesized, but it appears that much of it can be subsumed under the following types of strategies, all of which have been found to achieve influence: (a) *dominance, power, status, and authority* (behaviors employing status symbols, dominance cues, threat, or expertise indicators), (b) *credibility* (behaviors emphasizing a communicator's character, composure, sociability, and dynamism), (c) *affiliation and intimacy* (indications of liking, attraction, and immediacy, efforts to establish an intimate relationship), (d) *attractiveness and pleasantness* (enhancement of one's physical and social attractiveness, use of pleasant vocal and facial expressions to create a more enjoyable interaction, manipulation of environmental features such as noise, density, or color that create aversive or pleasant physiological stimulation), (e) *attention, distraction, and reinforcement* (use of nonverbal behaviors such as loudness, fluency, or crowding that heighten attention toward desired message features, distract attention from messages that are likely to be resisted, and/or reinforce learning), (f) *modeling and reciprocity* (use of nonverbal cues to make a model's behavior salient, to reinforce imitation of a model's behavior, or to elicit reciprocal responses), (g) *expectancy signaling* (use of non-verbal cues to signal expectations and elicit behavior conforming to those expectations), and (h) *violations of expectations* (use of unexpected, nonnormative behaviors such as extremes in conversational distance, gaze, or clothing style). (See Burgoon, Buller, & Woodall, 1989; Edinger & Patterson, 1983; Exline & Fehr, 1978; Harris & Rosenthal, 1985; Heslin & Alper, 1983: Knapp & Hall, 1992; Patterson, 1991; Rosenthal, 1985; Wiemann, 1985, for summaries of early research confirming these strategies.)

Some of the more important conclusions emanating from recent investigations that have particular implications for interpersonal communication are as follows:

1. *Contrary to the view that nonverbal cues play only a secondary and weak influence role, nonverbal cues are proving to have direct impact on persuasion, compliance, helping, and hiring decisions,* in addition to having indirect impact through enhanced credibility and attraction. Among the strategies documented recently as promoting interpersonal influence are dominance/power/status appeals (tempo, gestural activity, facial expressivity, mature facial appearance, touch), affiliation and attractiveness/pleasantness appeals (immediacy, smiling, fluency, vocal pleasantness, touch, speech rate similarity, physical attractiveness), and relaxation (vocal, postural) (e.g., Brownlow, 1992; Buller & Aune, 1988, 1992; Buller, Le Poire, Aune, & Eloy, 1992; Burgoon, Birk, & Pfau, 1990). Dominance and power strategies may be more advisable when the speaker does not benefit from compliance; attractiveness strategies are more advisable when the speaker is the main beneficiary of compliance. Although verbal messages are obviously a central component in persuading others and gaining compliance, the nonverbal findings signal that to neglect their role is to do so at one's own peril.

2. *Positive and negative interpersonal expectancies, which are signaled through nonverbal cues, are often signaled within 30 seconds and are capable of producing strong self-fulfilling prophecies in a variety of contexts* (e.g., DePaulo & Coleman, 1987; Vrugt, 1990). People's willingness to comply with others' expectations for them is striking. Nonverbal cues may be a potent "invisible" force accounting for many of people's interpersonal actions by telegraphing what is wanted of them.

3. *Positive expectancy violations (e.g., close or far conversational distance, touch, high degree of gaze) produce more persuasion, compliance, and endorsements for hiring than does conformity to expectations, while negative violations (e.g., gaze aversion) undermine influence.* Sometimes, communicator reward valence moderates these effects, but often both well-regarded and poorly regarded communicators profit from engaging in violations (e.g., Buller, 1987; Burgoon, Coker, & Coker, 1986; Burgoon, Manusov, Mineo, & Hale, 1985; Patterson, Powell, & Lenihan, 1986). Thus the popular advice to conform to norms and expectations may be poor advice when the objective is to gain influence.

Summary

Nonverbal signals are essential ingredients in the interpersonal communication mix. Research substantiates that, rather than being mere auxiliaries to the verbal stream, they carry a significant, and often dominant, portion of the social meaning in face-to-face interchanges.

In analyzing the role of nonverbal signals in interpersonal communication, emphasis here has been on those behaviors that form a socially shared coding system. According to this message orientation, codes of greatest interest are kinesics, vocalics, haptics, proxemics, chronemics, and manipulable features of physical appearance and artifacts. These codes and their constituent cues are coordinated with one another and with the verbal stream to achieve particular functions or purposes, several of which may be operative simultaneously. This leads to the frequent but mistaken claim that nonverbal behaviors are inherently ambiguous or unpredictable in meaning; when the behaviors are viewed as part of a collective, regular and meaningful patterns become apparent.

Social functions for which such patterns have been identified include message production and processing, identification and identity management, impression formation and management, relational communication and relationship management, emotion expression and management, deception, conversation structuring and management, and social influence. The research is impressive in documenting how much responsibility is shouldered by the nonverbal codes in accomplishing these fundamental communication objectives.

Although a substantial amount of research has addressed these social functions, it has often failed to look at the nonverbal behaviors as an integrated system; to study their occurrence in natural, diverse, and cross-cultural interpersonal contexts; to examine them dyadically; or to consider how patterns might differ when interactions occur among familiar others rather than strangers. Our knowledge of interpersonal nonverbal communication will advance slowly until a truly interpersonal perspective is incorporated in the research. Finally, just as the interpersonal communication area in general needs more theorizing and research on processual features of interchange, so must nonverbal researchers be enjoined to devote more future effort to the sequential and longitudinal aspects of nonverbal communication. As cycles, developmental patterns, and temporal adjustments receive greater scrutiny, nonverbal behavior may take on added significance in interpersonal communication.

References

Abele, A. (1986). Functions of gaze in social interaction: Communication and monitoring. *Journal of Nonverbal Behavior, 10,* 83-101.

Alberts, J. K. (1989). A descriptive taxonomy of couples' complaint interactions. *Southern Communication Journal, 54,* 125-143.

Alfred, G. H., Harper, J. M., Wadham, R. A., & Woolley, B. H. (1981). Expanding the frontiers of interaction research. In E. E. Filsinger & R. A. Lewis (Eds.), *Assessing marriage* (pp. 160-170). Beverly Hills, CA: Sage.

Altman, I. (1975). *The environment and social behavior.* Monterey, CA: Brooks/Cole.

Altman, I., & Taylor, D. A. (1973). *Social penetration: The development of interpersonal relationships.* New York: Holt, Rinehart & Winston.

Ambady, N., & Rosenthal, R. (in press). Half a minute: Predicting teacher effectiveness from thin slices of nonverbal behavior and physical attractiveness. *Journal of Personality and Social Psychology.*

Andersen, P. A. (1985). Nonverbal immediacy in interpersonal communication. In A. W. Siegman & S. Feldstein (Eds.), *Multichannel integrations of nonverbal behavior* (pp. 1-36). Hillsdale, NJ: Lawrence Erlbaum.

Andersen, P. A. (1991). When one cannot not communicate: A challenge to Motley's traditional communication postulates. *Communication Studies, 42,* 309-325.

Andersen, P. A., & Andersen, J. F. (1984). The exchange of nonverbal intimacy: A critical review of dyadic models. *Journal of Nonverbal Behavior, 8*, 327-349.

Andersen, P. A., & Sull, K. K. (1985). Out of touch, out of reach: Tactile predispositions as predictors of interpersonal distance. *Western Journal of Speech Communication, 49*, 57-72.

Archer, D., & Costanzo, M. (1988). *The interpersonal perception task (IPT)*. Berkeley: University of California, Media Extension Center.

Argyle, M. (1972). Non-verbal communication in human social interaction. In R. A. Hinde (Ed.), *Non-verbal communication* (pp. 243-269). Cambridge: Cambridge University Press.

Argyle, M. (1974). *Bodily communication*. London: Methuen.

Argyle, M., Alkema, F., & Gilmour, R. (1971). The communication of friendly and hostile attitudes by verbal and non-verbal signals. *European Journal of Social Psychology, 1*, 385-402.

Argyle, M., & Cook, M. (1976). *Gaze and mutual gaze*. Cambridge: Cambridge University Press.

Argyle, M., & Dean, J. (1965). Eye contact, distance and affiliation. *Sociometry, 28*, 289-304.

Argyle, M., Salter, V., Nicholson, H., Williams, M., & Burgess, P. (1970). The communication of interior and superior attitudes by verbal and nonverbal signals. *British Journal of Social and Clinical Psychology, 9*, 221-231.

Aronoff, J., Barclay, A. M., & Stevenson, L. A. (1988). The recognition of threatening facial stimuli. *Journal of Personality and Social Psychology, 54*, 647-655.

Aronoff, J., Woike, B. A., & Hyman, L. M. (1992). Which are the stimuli in facial displays of anger and happiness? Configurational bases of emotion recognition. *Journal of Personality and Social Psychology, 62*, 1050-1066.

Ayres, J. (1989). The impact of communication apprehension and interaction structure on initial interactions. *Communication Monographs, 56*, 75-88.

Baglan, T., & Nelson, D. J. (1982). A comparison of the effects of sex and status on the perceived appropriateness of nonverbal behaviors. *Women's Studies in Communication, 5*, 29-38.

Barge, J. K., Schlueter, D. W., & Pritchard, A. (1989). The effects of nonverbal communication and gender on impression formation in opening statements. *Southern Communication Journal, 54*, 330-349.

Barroso, F., & Feld, J. K. (1986). Self-touching and attentional processes: The role of task difficulty, selection stage, and sex differences. *Journal of Nonverbal Behavior, 10*, 51-64.

Bauchner, J. E., Kaplan, E. P., & Miller, G. R. (1980). Detecting deception: The relationship between available information to judgmental accuracy in initial encounters. *Human Communication Research, 6*, 251-264.

Baumeister, R. F. (1982). A self-presentational view of social phenomena. *Psychological Bulletin, 91*, 3-26.

Bavelas, J. B. (1990). Behaving and communicating: A reply to Motley. *Western Journal of Speech Communication, 54*, 593-602.

Bavelas, J. B., Black, A., Chovil, N., Lemery, C. R., & Mullett, J. (1988). Form and function in motor mimicry: Topographic evidence that the primary function is communicative. *Human Communication Research, 14*, 275-300.

Bavelas, J. B., Black, A., Lemery, C. R., & Mullett, J. (1986). "I show how you feel": Motor mimicry as a communicative act. *Journal of Personality and Social Psychology, 50*, 322-329.

Baxter, L. A. (1992). Forms and functions of intimate play in personal relationships. *Human Communication Research, 18*, 336-363.

Beebe, B., Stern, D., & Jaffe, J. (1979). The kinesic rhythm of mother-infant interactions. In A. W. Siegman & S. Feldstein (Eds.), *Of speech and time: Temporal patterns in interpersonal contexts* (pp. 23-34). Hillsdale, NJ: Lawrence Erlbaum.

Bem, S. L. (1981). Gender schema theory: A cognitive account of sex typing. *Psychological Review, 88*, 354-364.

Berger, C. R., & Calabrese, R. J. (1975). Some explorations in initial interaction and beyond: Toward a developmental theory of interpersonal communication. *Human Communication Research, 1*, 99-112.

Berger, J., Rosenholtz, S. J., & Zelditch, M., Jr. (1980). States organizing processes. *Annual Review of Sociology, 6*, 479-508.

Bernieri, F. J., & Rosenthal, R. (1991). Interpersonal coordination: Behavior matching and interactional synchrony. In R. S. Feldman & B. Rimé (Eds.), *Fundamentals of nonverbal behavior* (pp. 401-432). Cambridge: Cambridge University Press.

Berry, D. S. (1990). Vocal attractiveness and vocal babyishness: Effects on stranger, self, and friend impressions. *Journal of Nonverbal Behavior, 14*, 141-154.

Berry, D. S. (1991). Accuracy in social perception: Contributions of facial and vocal information. *Journal of Personality and Social Psychology, 61*, 298-307.

Berry, D. S. (1992). Vocal types and stereotypes: Joint effects of vocal attractiveness and vocal maturity on person perception. *Journal of Nonverbal Behavior, 16*, 41-54.

Birdwhistell, R. L. (1955). Background to kinesics. *Etc., 13*, 10-18.

Birdwhistell, R. L. (1970). *Kinesics and context: Essays on body motion communication.* Philadelphia: University of Pennsylvania Press.

Boomer, D. S. (1965). Hesitation and grammatical coding. *Language and Speech, 8*, 148-158.

Boomer, D. S. (1978). The phonemic clause: Speech unit in human communication. In A. W. Siegman & S. Feldstein (Eds.), *Nonverbal behavior and communication* (pp. 245-262). Hillsdale, NJ: Lawrence Erlbaum.

Boucher, J. D., & Ekman, P. (1975). Facial areas of emotional information. *Journal of Communication, 25*, 21-29.

Brewer, M. B. (1978). A dual process model of impression formation. In T. K. Srull & R. S. Wyer, Jr. (Eds.), *Advances in social cognition* (Vol. 1, pp. 1-36). Hillsdale, NJ: Lawrence Erlbaum.

Brownlow, S. (1992). Seeing is believing: Facial appearance, credibility, and attitude change. *Journal of Nonverbal Behavior, 16*, 101-115.

Buck, R. (1979). Individual differences in nonverbal sending accuracy and electrodermal responding: The externalizing-internalizing dimension. In R. Rosenthal (Ed.), *Skill in nonverbal communication: Individual differences* (pp. 140-170). Cambridge, MA: Oelgeschlager, Gunn & Hain.

Buck, R. (1981). The evolution and development of emotion expression and communication. In S. S. Brehm, S. M. Kassin, & F. X. Gibbons (Eds.), *Developmental social psychology* (pp. 127-151). New York: Oxford University Press.

Buck, R. (1984). *The communication of emotion.* New York: Guilford.

Buck, R. (1988). Nonverbal communication: Spontaneous and symbolic aspects. *American Behavioral Scientist, 31*, 341-354.

Buck, R. (1991). Social factors in facial display and communication: A reply to Chovil and others. *Journal of Nonverbal Behavior, 15*, 155-161.

Bull, P., & Connelly, G. (1985). Body movement and emphasis in speech. *Journal of Nonverbal Behavior, 9*, 169-187.

Buller, D. B. (1986). Distraction during persuasive communication: A meta-analytic review. *Communication Monographs, 53*, 91-114.

Buller, D. B. (1987). Communication apprehension and reactions to proxemic violations. *Journal of Nonverbal Behavior, 11*, 13-25.

Buller, D. B., & Aune, K. (1988). The effects of vocalics and nonverbal sensitivity on compliance: A speech accommodation theory explanation. *Human Communication Research, 14*, 301-332.

Buller, D. B., & Aune, K. (1992). The effects of speech rate similarity on compliance: Application of communication accommodation theory. *Western Journal of Communication, 56*, 37-53.

Buller, D. B., & Burgoon, J. K. (1994). Deception. In J. A. Daly & J. M. Wiemann (Eds.), *Communicating strategically: Strategies in interpersonal communication* (pp. 191-223). Hillsdale, NJ: Lawrence Erlbaum.

Buller, D. B., Le Poire, B. A., Aune, R. K., & Eloy, S. V. (1992). Social perceptions as mediators of the effect of speech rate similarity on compliance. *Human Communication Research, 19*, 286-311.

Buller, D. B., Strzyzewski, K. D., & Comstock, J. (1991). Interpersonal deception: I. Deceivers' reactions to receivers' suspicions and probing. *Communication Monographs, 58*, 1-24.

Buller, D. B., Strzyzewski, K. D., & Hunsaker, F. G. (1991). Interpersonal deception: II. The inferiority of conversational participants as deception detectors. *Communication Monographs, 58*, 25-40.

Burggraf, C. S., & Sillars, A. L. (1987). A critical examination of sex differences in marital communication. *Communication Monographs, 54*, 276-294.

Burgoon, J. K. (1974). Effects of anomia and personal space invasion on anxiety, nonperson orientation and source credibility. *Central States Speech Journal, 25*, 19-27.

Burgoon, J. K. (1978). A communication model of personal space violations: Explication and an initial test. *Human Communication Research, 4*, 129-142.

Burgoon, J. K. (1980). Nonverbal communication in the 1970s: An overview. In D. Nimmo (Ed.), *Communication yearbook 4* (pp. 179-197). New Brunswick, NJ: Transaction.

Burgoon, J. K. (1982). Privacy and communication. In M. Burgoon (Ed.), *Communication yearbook 6* (pp. 206-249). Beverly Hills, CA: Sage.

Burgoon, J. K. (1983). Nonverbal violations of expectations. In J. M. Wiemann & R. P. Harrison (Eds.), *Nonverbal interaction* (pp. 77-111). Beverly Hills, CA: Sage.

Burgoon, J. K. (1985a). Nonverbal signals. In M. L. Knapp & G. R. Miller (Eds.), *Handbook of interpersonal communication* (1st ed., pp. 344-390). Beverly Hills, CA: Sage.

Burgoon, J. K. (1985b). The relationship of verbal and nonverbal codes. In B. Dervin & M. J. Voight (Eds.), *Progress in communication sciences* (Vol. 6, pp. 263-298). Norwood, NJ: Ablex.

Burgoon, J. K. (1989, May). *Toward a processual view of interpersonal deception.* Paper presented to the annual meeting of the International Communication Association, San Francisco.

Burgoon, J. K. (1991). Relational message interpretations of touch, conversational distance, and posture. *Journal of Nonverbal Behavior, 15,* 233-259.

Burgoon, J. K. (1992). Applying a comparative approach to nonverbal expectancy violations theory. In J. Blumler, K. E. Rosengren, & J. M. McLeod (Eds.), *Comparatively speaking: Communication and culture across space and time* (pp. 53-69). Newbury Park, CA: Sage.

Burgoon, J. K., Birk, T., & Pfau, M. (1990). Nonverbal behaviors, persuasion, and credibility. *Human Communication Research, 17,* 140-169.

Burgoon, J. K., Buller, D. B., Dillman, L., & Walther, J. B. (1993). *Interpersonal deception: IV. Effects of suspicion on perceived communication and nonverbal behavior dynamics.* Manuscript submitted for publication.

Burgoon, J. K., Buller, D. B., Ebesu, A., & Rockwell, P. (in press). Interpersonal deception: V. Accuracy in deception detection. *Communication Monographs.*

Burgoon, J. K., Buller, D. B., Hale, J. L., & deTurck, M. A. (1984). Relational messages associated with nonverbal behaviors. *Human Communication Research, 10,* 351-378.

Burgoon, J. K., Buller, D. B., & Woodall, W. G. (1989). *Nonverbal communication: The unspoken dialogue.* New York: HarperCollins.

Burgoon, J. K., Coker, D. A., & Coker, R. A. (1986). Communicative effects of gaze behavior: A test of two contrasting explanations. *Human Communication Research, 12,* 495-524.

Burgoon, J. K., Dillman, L., & Stern, L. A. (1993). Adaptation in dyadic interaction: Defining and operationalizing patterns of reciprocity and compensation. *Communication Theory, 3,* 196-215.

Burgoon, J. K., Dillman, L., Stern, L. A., & Kelley, D. L. (1993). *Reciprocity and compensation patterns in dyadic interaction: Statistical analysis.* Manuscript submitted for publication.

Burgoon, J. K., & Hale, J. L. (1984). The fundamental topoi of relational communication. *Communication Monographs, 51,* 193-214.

Burgoon, J. K., & Hale, J. L. (1987). Validation and measurement of the fundamental themes of relational communication. *Communication Monographs, 54,* 19-41.

Burgoon, J. K., & Hale, J. L. (1988). Nonverbal expectancy violations: Model elaboration and application to immediacy behaviors. *Communication Monographs, 55,* 58-79.

Burgoon, J. K., & Jones, S. B. (1976). Toward a theory of personal space expectations and their violations. *Human Communication Research, 2,* 131-146.

Burgoon, J. K., Kelley, D. L., Newton, D. A., & Keeley-Dyreson, M. P. (1989). The nature of arousal and nonverbal indices. *Human Communication Research, 16,* 217-255.

Burgoon, J. K., & Koper, R. (1984). Nonverbal and relational communication associated with reticence. *Human Communication Research, 10,* 601-626.

Burgoon, J. K., & Le Poire, B. A. (1993). Effects of communication expectancies, actual communication, and expectancy disconfirmation on evaluations of communicators and their communication behavior. *Human Communication Research, 20,* 75-107.

Burgoon, J. K., Le Poire, B. A., Beutler, L. E., Bergan, J., & Engle, D. (1992). Nonverbal behaviors as indices of arousal: Extension to the psychotherapy context. *Journal of Nonverbal Behavior, 16,* 159-178.

Burgoon, J. K., Le Poire, B. A., & Rosenthal, R. (1992). *Impact of expectancies, target communication, and expectancy disconfirmation on nonverbal interaction patterns.* Manuscript submitted for publication.

Burgoon, J. K., Manusov, V., Mineo, P. J., & Hale, J. L. (1985). Effects of eye gaze on hiring, credibility, attraction and relational messages interpretation. *Journal of Nonverbal Behavior, 9,* 133-146.

Burgoon, J. K., & Newton, D. A. (1991). Applying a social meaning model to relational messages of conversational involvement: Comparing participant and observer perspectives. *Southern Communication Journal, 56,* 96-113.

Burgoon, J. K., Newton, D. A., Walther, J. B., & Baesler, E. J. (1989). Nonverbal expectancy violations and conversational involvement. *Journal of Nonverbal Behavior, 13,* 97-120.

Burgoon, J. K., Olney, C. A., & Coker, R. (1988). The effects of communicator characteristics on patterns of reciprocity and compensation. *Journal of Nonverbal Behavior, 11,* 146-165.

Burgoon, J. K., Parrott, R., Le Poire, B., Kelley, D., Walther, J., & Perry, D. (1989). Privacy and communication: Maintaining and restoring privacy through communication. *Journal of Personal and Social Relationships, 6,* 131-158.

Burgoon, J. K., Pfau, M., Birk, T., & Manusov, V. (1987). Nonverbal communication performance and perceptions associated with reticence: Replications and classroom implications. *Communication Education, 36,* 119-130.

Burgoon, J. K., Pfau, M., Parrott, R., Birk, T., Coker, R., & Burgoon, M. (1987). Relational communication, satisfaction, compliance-gaining strategies and compliance in communication between physicians and patients. *Communication Monographs, 54,* 307-234.

Burgoon, J. K., & Saine, T. (1978). *The unspoken dialogue: An introduction to nonverbal communication.* Boston: Houghton-Mifflin.

Burgoon, J. K., Stacks, D. W., & Burch, S. A. (1982). The role of nonverbal violations of expectations in interpersonal influence. *Communication, 11,* 114-128.

Burgoon, J. K., Stacks, D. W., & Woodall, W. G. (1979). A communicative model of violations of distancing expectations. *Western Journal of Speech Communication, 43,* 153-167.

Burgoon, J. K., Stern, L. A., & Dillman, L. (in press). *Interpersonal adaptation: Dyadic interaction patterns.* New York: Cambridge University Press.

Burgoon, J. K., & Walther, J. B. (1990). Nonverbal expectancies and the consequences of violations. *Human Communication Research, 17,* 232-265.

Burgoon, J. K., Walther, J. B., & Baesler, E. J. (1992). Interpretations and consequences of interpersonal touch. *Human Communication Research, 19,* 237-263.

Camden, C. T., & Kennedy, C. W. (1986). Manager communication style and nurse morale. *Human Communication Research, 12,* 551-563.

Cappella, J. N. (1981). Mutual influence in expressive behavior: Adult-adult and infant-adult interaction. *Psychological Bulletin, 89,* 101-132.

Cappella, J. N. (1983). Conversational involvement: Approaching and avoiding others. In J. M. Wiemann & R. P. Harrison (Eds.), *Nonverbal interaction* (pp. 113-148). Beverly Hills, CA: Sage.

Cappella, J. N. (1984). The relevance of microstructure of interaction to relationship change. *Journal of Social and Personal Relationships, 1,* 239-264.

Cappella, J. N. (1991). The biological origins of automated patterns of human interaction. *Communication Theory, 1,* 4-35.

Cappella, J. N., & Greene, J. O. (1982). A discrepancy-arousal explanation of mutual influence in expressive behavior in adult- and infant-adult interaction. *Communication Monographs, 49,* 89-114.

Cappella, J. N., & Greene, J. O. (1984). The effects of distance and individual differences in arousability on nonverbal involvement: A test of discrepancy-arousal theory. *Journal of Nonverbal Behavior, 8,* 259-286.

Cappella, J. N., & Palmer, M. T. (1990). Attitude similarity, relational history, and attraction: The mediating effects of kinesic and vocal behaviors. *Communication Monographs, 57,* 161-183.

Cappella, J. N., & Planalp, S. (1981). Talk and silence sequences in informal conversations III: Interspeaker influence. *Human Communication Research, 7,* 117-132.

Chapple, E. D. (1970). *Cultural and biological man: Exploration in behavioral anthropology.* New York: Holt, Rinehart & Winston.

Chovil, N. (1991). Social determinants of facial displays. *Journal of Nonverbal Behavior, 15,* 141-154.

Clark, R. A., & Delia, J. G. (1979). Topoi and rhetorical competence. *Quarterly Journal of Speech, 65,* 187-206.

Clevenger, T., Jr. (1991). Can one not communicate? A conflict of models. *Communication Studies, 42,* 340-353.

Cody, M. J., & O'Hair, H. D. (1983). Nonverbal communication and deception: Differences in deception cues due to gender and communicator dominance. *Communication Monographs, 50,* 175-192.

Cohen, A. A. (1977). The communicative functions of hand illustrators. *Journal of Communication, 27,* 54-63.

Cohen, A. A., & Harrison, R. P. (1973). Intentionality in the use of hand illustrators in face-to-face communication situations. *Journal of Personality and Social Psychology, 28,* 276-279.

Coker, D. A., & Burgoon, J. K. (1987). The nature of conversational involvement and nonverbal encoding patterns. *Human Communication Research, 13,* 463-494.

Condon, W. S. (1980). The relation of interactional synchrony to cognitive and emotional processes. In M. R. Key (Ed.), *The relationship of verbal and nonverbal communication* (pp. 49-65). The Hague, the Netherlands: Mouton.

Condon, W. S., & Ogston, W. D. (1967). A segmentation of behavior. *Journal of Psychiatric Research, 5,* 221-235.

Condon, W. S., & Sander, L. W. (1974). Neonate movement is synchronized with adult speech: Interactional participation and language acquisition. *Science, 183,* 99-101.

Costanzo, M., & Archer, D. (1989). Interpreting the expressive behavior of others: The Interpersonal Perception Task (IPT). *Journal of Nonverbal Behavior, 13,* 225-245.

Courtright, J. A., Millar, F. E., Rogers, E., & Bagarozzi, D. (1990). Interaction dynamics of relational negotiation: Reconciliation versus termination of distressed relationships. *Western Journal of Speech Communication, 54,* 429-453.

Cronkhite, G. (1986). On the focus, scope, and coherence of the study of human symbolic activity. *Quarterly Journal of Speech, 72,* 231-246.

Cuceloglu, D. (1972). Facial code in affective communication. In D. C. Speer (Ed.), *Nonverbal communication* (pp. 19-32). Beverly Hills, CA: Sage.

Cupach, W. R., & Metts, S. (1986). Accounts of relational dissolution. *Communication Monographs, 53,* 311-334.

Darwin, C. (1965). *The expression of the emotions in man and animals.* Chicago: University of Chicago Press. (Original work published 1872)

Davitz, J. R. (1969). *The language of emotion.* New York: Academic Press.

Davitz, J. R., & Davitz, L. J. (1959). The communication of feelings by content-free speech. *Journal of Communication, 9,* 6-13.

DePaulo, B. M. (1991). Nonverbal behavior and self-presentation: A developmental perspective. In R. S. Feldman & B. Rimé (Eds.), *Fundamentals of nonverbal behavior* (pp. 351-397). Cambridge: Cambridge University Press.

DePaulo, B. M. (1992). Nonverbal behavior and self-presentation. *Psychological Bulletin, 111,* 203-243.

DePaulo, B. M., Blank, A. L., Swaim, G. W., & Hairfield, J. G. (1992). Expressiveness and expressive control. *Personality and Social Psychology Bulletin, 18,* 276-285.

DePaulo, B. M., & Coleman, L. M. (1987). Verbal and nonverbal communication of warmth to children, foreigners and retarded adults. *Journal of Nonverbal Behavior, 11,* 75-88.

DePaulo, B. M., & Rosenthal, R. (1979). Ambivalence, discrepancy, and deception in nonverbal communication. In R. Rosenthal (Ed.), *Skill in nonverbal communication: Individual differences* (pp. 204-248). Cambridge, MA: Oelgeschlager, Gunn & Hain.

DePaulo, B. M., Stone, J. I., & Lassiter, G. D. (1985). Deceiving and detecting deceit. In B. R. Schlenker (Ed.), *The self and social life* (pp. 323-370). New York: McGraw-Hill.

DePaulo, B. M., Zuckerman, M., & Rosenthal, R. (1980). Detecting deception: Modality effects. In L. Wheeler (Ed.), *Review of personality and social psychology* (pp. 125-162). Beverly Hills, CA: Sage.

deTurck, M. A., & Miller, G. R. (1985). Deception and arousal: Isolating the behavioral correlates of deception. *Human Communication Research, 12,* 181-201.

deTurck, M. A., & Miller, G. R. (1990). Training observers to detect deception effects of self-monitoring and rehearsal. *Human Communication Research, 16,* 603-620.

Dindia, K. (1982). Reciprocity of self-disclosure: A sequential analysis. In M. Burgoon (Ed.), *Communication yearbook 6* (pp. 506-528). Beverly Hills, CA: Sage.

Dittmann, A. T. (1972a). *Interpersonal messages of emotion.* New York: Springer.

Dittmann, A. T. (1972b). The body movement-speech rhythm relationship as a cue to speech encoding. In A. W. Siegman & B. Pope (Eds.), *Studies in dyadic communication* (pp. 135-151). New York: Pergamon.

Donohue, W. A. (1981). Analyzing negotiation tactics: Development of a negotiation interact system. *Human Communication Research, 7,* 273-287.

Dovidio, J. F., & Ellyson, S. L. (1985). Patterns of visual dominance behavior in humans. In S. L. Ellyson & J. F. Dovidio (Eds.), *Power, dominance, and nonverbal behavior* (pp. 129-149). New York: Springer-Verlag.

Drummond, K. (1989). A backward glance at interruptions. *Western Journal of Speech Communication, 53,* 150-166.

Duncan, S., Jr. (1974). On signaling that it's your turn to speak. *Journal of Personality and Social Psychology, 10,* 234-247.

Duncan, S., Jr. (1975). Interaction units during speaking turns in dyadic, face-to-face conversations. In A. Kendon, R. M. Harris, & M. R. Key (Eds.), *Organization of behavior in face-to-face interaction* (pp. 199-213). The Hague, the Netherlands: Mouton.

Duncan, S., Jr., & Fiske, D. W. (1977). *Face-to-face interaction: Research, methods, and theory.* Hillsdale, NJ: Lawrence Erlbaum.

Eagly, A. H. (1987). *Sex differences in social behavior: A social-role interpretation.* Hillsdale, NJ: Lawrence Erlbaum.

Eagly, A. H., & Karau, S. J. (1991). Gender and the emergence of leaders: A meta-analysis. *Journal of Personality and Social Psychology, 60,* 685-710.

Edinger, J. A., & Patterson, M. L. (1983). Nonverbal involvement and social control. *Psychological Bulletin, 93,* 30-56.

Eibl-Eibesfeldt, I. (1970). *Ethology: The biology of human behavior.* New York: Holt, Rinehart & Winston.

Eibl-Eibesfeldt, I. (1972). Similarities and differences between cultures in expressive movements. In R. A. Hinde (Ed.), *Non-verbal communication* (pp. 297-314). Cambridge: Cambridge University Press.

Ekman, P. (1965). Communication through nonverbal behavior: A source of information about an interpersonal relationship. In S. S. Tomkins & C. E. Izard (Eds.), *Affect, cognition, and personality* (pp. 390-442). New York: Springer.

Ekman, P. (1973). Cross-cultural studies of facial expression. In P. Ekman (Ed.), *Darwin and facial expression: A century of research in review* (pp. 169-222). New York: Academic Press.

Ekman, P. (1976). Movements with precise meanings. *Journal of Communication, 26,* 14-20.

Ekman, P. (1978). Facial expression. In A. W. Siegman & S. Feldstein (Eds.), *Nonverbal behavior and communication* (pp. 97-116). Hillsdale, NJ: Lawrence Erlbaum.

Ekman, P. (1984). Expression and the nature of emotion. In K. R. Scherer & P. Ekman (Eds.), *Approaches to emotion* (pp. 319-343). Hillsdale, NJ: Lawrence Erlbaum.

Ekman, P., & Friesen, W. V. (1969a). Nonverbal leakage and clues to deception. *Psychiatry, 32,* 88-105.

Ekman, P., & Friesen, W. V. (1969b). The repertoire of nonverbal behavior: Categories, origins, usage, and coding. *Semiotica, 1,* 49-98.

Ekman, P., & Friesen, W. V. (1975). *Unmasking the face.* Englewood Cliffs, NJ: Prentice-Hall.

Ekman, P., Friesen, W. V., & Ellsworth, P. (1972). *Emotion in the human face: Guidelines for research and an integration of findings.* New York: Pergamon.

Ekman, P., Friesen, W. V., & O'Sullivan, M. (1988). Smiles when lying. *Journal of Personality and Social Psychology, 54,* 414-420.

Ekman, P., Friesen, W. V., & Tomkins, S. (1971). Facial affect scoring technique (FAST): A first validity study. *Semiotica, 3,* 37-58.

Ekman, P., & O'Sullivan, M. (1991). Who can catch a liar? *American Psychologist, 46,* 913-920.

Ekman, P., O'Sullivan, M., Friesen, W. V., & Scherer, K. R. (1991). Face, voice, and body in detecting deceit. *Journal of Nonverbal Behavior, 15,* 125-135.

Ellsworth, P. C., & Ludwig, L. M. (1972). Visual behavior in social interaction. *Journal of Communication, 22,* 375-401.

Erickson, F. (1975). One function of proxemic shifts in face to face interaction. In A. Kendon, R. M. Harris, & M. R. Key (Eds.), *Organization of behavior in face-to-face interaction* (pp. 175-187). The Hague, the Netherlands: Mouton.

Erickson, F., & Shultz, J. (1982). *The counselor as gatekeeper: Social interaction in interviews.* New York: Academic Press.

Exline, R. V., & Fehr, B. J. (1978). Applications of semiosis to the study of visual interaction. In A. W. Siegman & S. Feldstein (Eds.), *Nonverbal behavior and communication* (pp. 117-157). Hillsdale, NJ: Lawrence Erlbaum.

Feldstein, S., & Welkowitz, J. (1978). A chronography of conversation: In defense of an objective approach. In A. W. Siegman & S. Feldstein (Eds.), *Nonverbal communication and behavior* (pp. 329-378). Hillsdale, NJ: Lawrence Erlbaum.

Firestone, I. J. (1977). Reconciling verbal and nonverbal models of dyadic communication. *Environmental Psychology and Nonverbal Behavior, 2,* 30-44.

Fiske, S. T., & Neuberg, S. L. (1990). A continuum of impression formation from category-based to individuating processes: Influences of information and motivation on attention and interpretation. In M. P. Zanna (Ed.), *Advances in experimental social psychology* (Vol. 23, pp. 1-74). New York: Academic Press.

Fiske, S. T., & Taylor, S. E. (1991). *Social cognition.* New York: McGraw-Hill.

Floyd, F. J., & Markman, H. J. (1983). Observational biases in spouse observation: Toward a cognitive/behavioral model of marriage. *Journal of Consulting and Clinical Psychology, 51,* 450-457.

Folger, J. P., & Woodall, W. G. (1982). Nonverbal cues as linguistic context: An information-processing view. In M. Burgoon (Ed.), *Communication yearbook 6* (pp. 63-91). Beverly Hills, CA: Sage.

Forsdale, L. (1981). *Perspectives on communication.* Reading, MA: Addison-Wesley.

Freud, S. (1963). Introductory lectures on psychoanalysis. In J. Strachey (Ed. and Trans.), *The standard edition of the complete psychological works of Sigmund Freud* (Vols. 15, 16). London: Hogarth. (Original work published 1915-1917)

Fridlund, A. J., Sabini, J. P., Hedlund, L. E., Schaut, J. A., Shenker, J. I., & Knauer, M. J. (1990). Audience effects on solitary faces during imagery: Displaying to the people in your head. *Journal of Nonverbal Behavior, 14,* 113-137.

Friedman, H. S. (1979). The concept of skill in nonverbal communication: Implications for understanding social interaction. In R. Rosenthal (Ed.), *Skill in nonverbal communication: Individual differences* (pp. 2-27). Cambridge, MA: Oelgeschlager, Gunn & Hain.

Friedman, H. S., & Miller-Herringer, T. (1991). Nonverbal display of emotion in public and in private: Self-monitoring, personality, and expressive cues. *Journal of Personality and Social Psychology, 61,* 766-775.

Friedman, H. S., Prince, L., Riggio, R. E., & DiMatteo, M. R. (1980). Understanding and assessing nonverbal expressiveness: The Affective Communication Test. *Journal of Personality and Social Psychology, 39*, 333-351.

Frye, J. K. (1980). *FIND: Frye's index to nonverbal data.* Duluth: University of Minnesota Computer Center.

Funder, D. C., & Colvin, C. R. (1991). Explorations in behavioral consistency: Properties of persons, situations, and behaviors. *Journal of Personality and Social Psychology, 60*, 773-794.

Gallaher, P. E. (1992). Individual differences in nonverbal behavior: Dimensions of style. *Journal of Personality and Social Psychology, 63*, 133-145.

Gatewood, J. B., & Rosenwein, R. (1981). Interactional synchrony: Genuine or spurious? A critique of recent research. *Journal of Nonverbal Behavior, 6,* 12-29.

Gifford, R. (1991). Mapping nonverbal behavior on the interpersonal circle. *Journal of Personality and Social Psychology, 61*, 279-288.

Giles, H., Coupland, J., & Coupland, N. (Eds.). (1991). *Contexts of accommodation.* New York: Cambridge University Press.

Giles, H., Mulac, A., Bradac, J. J., & Johnson, P. (1987). Accommodation theory: The last decade and beyond. In M. L. McLaughlin (Ed.), *Communication yearbook 10* (pp. 13-48). Newbury Park, CA: Sage.

Giles, H., & Smith, P. M. (1979). Accommodation theory: Optimal levels of convergence. In H. Giles & R. N. St. Clair (Eds.), *Language and social psychology* (pp. 45-65). Baltimore: University Park Press.

Giles, H., Taylor, D. M., & Bourhis, R. Y. (1973). Towards a theory of interpersonal accommodation through language: Some Canadian data. *Language in Society, 2*, 177-192.

Givens, D. B. (1978). The nonverbal basis of attraction: Flirtation, courtship, and seduction. *Psychiatry, 41*, 346-359.

Givens, D. B. (1983). *Love signals.* New York: Crown.

Goffman, E. (1959). *Presentation of self in everyday life.* Garden City, NY: Doubleday/Anchor.

Goffman, E. (1961). *Encounters: Two studies in the sociology of interaction.* Indianapolis: Bobbs-Merrill.

Goffman, E. (1963). *Behavior in public places.* New York: Free Press.

Goffman, E. (1967). *Interaction ritual.* Garden City, NY: Doubleday.

Goffman, E. (1969). *Strategic interaction.* Philadelphia: University of Pennsylvania Press.

Goffman, E. (1971). *Relations in public.* New York: Basic Books.

Goffman, E. (1974). *Frame analysis.* Cambridge, MA: Harvard University Press.

Goldman-Eisler, F. (1968). *Psycholinguistics: Experiments in spontaneous speech.* New York: Academic Press.

Gottman, J. M. (1979). *Marital interaction: Experimental investigations.* New York: Academic Press.

Gottman, J., Markman, H., & Notarius, C. (1977). The topography of marital conflict: A sequential analysis of verbal and nonverbal behavior. *Journal of Marriage and the Family, 39*, 461-477.

Gouldner, A. W. (1960). The norm of reciprocity: A preliminary statement. *American Sociological Review, 25,* 161-178.

Gudykunst, W. B., & Ting-Toomey, S. (1988). *Culture and interpersonal communication.* Newbury Park, CA: Sage.

Guerrero, L. K., & Andersen, P. A. (1991). The waxing and waning of relational intimacy: Touch as a function of relational stage, gender, and touch avoidance. *Journal of Social and Personal Relationships, 8,* 147-165.

Gurevitch, Z. D. (1989). Distance and conversation. *Symbolic Interaction, 12,* 251-263.

Halberstadt, A. G., & Saitta, M. B. (1987). Gender, nonverbal behavior, and perceived dominance: A test of the theory. *Journal of Personality and Social Psychology, 53,* 257-272.

Hale, J. L., & Burgoon, J. K. (1984). Models of reactions to changes in nonverbal immediacy. *Journal of Nonverbal Behavior, 8,* 287-314.

Hall, E. T. (1969). *The hidden dimension.* Garden City, NY: Anchor/Doubleday.

Hall, E. T. (1973). *The silent language.* Garden City, NY: Anchor/Doubleday.

Hall, E. T. (1977). *Beyond culture.* Garden City, NY: Anchor.

Hall, J. A. (1979). Gender, gender roles, and nonverbal communication skills. In R. Rosenthal (Ed.), *Skill in nonverbal communication: Individual differences* (pp. 32-67). Cambridge, MA: Oelgeschlager, Gunn & Hain.

Hall, J. A. (1984). *Nonverbal sex differences: Communication accuracy and expressive style.* Baltimore: Johns Hopkins University Press.

Hall, J. A., & Halberstadt, A. G. (1986). Smiling and gazing. In J. S. Hyde & M. Linn (Eds.), *The psychology of gender: Advances through meta-analysis* (pp. 136-158). Baltimore: Johns Hopkins University Press.

Harper, R. G. (1985). Power, dominance, and nonverbal behavior: An overview. In S. L. Ellyson & J. F. Dovidio (Eds.), *Power, dominance, and nonverbal behavior* (pp. 29-48). New York: Springer-Verlag.

Harper, R. G., Wiens, A. N., & Matarazzo, J. D. (1978). *Nonverbal communication: The state of the art.* New York: Wiley.

Harrigan, J. A., Kues, J. R., Steffen, J. J., & Rosenthal, R. (1987). Self-touching and impressions of others. *Personality and Social Psychology Bulletin, 13,* 497-512.

Harris, L. M., Gergen, K. J., & Lannamann, J. W. (1986). Aggression rituals. *Communication Monographs, 53,* 252-265.

Harris, M. J., & Rosenthal, R. (1985). Mediation of interpersonal expectancy effects: 31 meta-analyses. *Psychological Bulletin, 97,* 363-386.

Hatfield, E. E., & Sprecher, S. (1986). *Mirror, mirror . . . the importance of looks in everyday life.* Albany: State University of New York Press.

Haviland, J. J., & Malatesta, C. Z. (1981). The development of sex differences in nonverbal signals: Fallacies, facts, and fantasies. In C. Mayo & N. M. Henley (Eds.), *Gender and nonverbal behavior* (pp. 183-208). New York: Springer-Verlag.

Hegstrom, T. G. (1979). Message impact: What percentage is nonverbal? *Western Journal of Speech Communication, 43,* 134-142.

Hendrick, S., & Hendrick, C. (1992). *Liking, loving, & relating* (2nd ed.). Pacific Grove, CA: Brooks/Cole.

Henley, N. M. (1977). *Body politics: Power, sex and nonverbal communication.* Englewood Cliffs, NJ: Prentice-Hall.

Heslin, R., & Alper, T. (1983). Touch: A bonding gesture. In J. M. Wiemann & R. P. Harrison (Eds.), *Nonverbal interaction* (pp. 47-75). Beverly Hills, CA: Sage.

Hocking, J. E., & Leathers, D. G. (1980). Nonverbal indicators of deception: A new theoretical perspective. *Communication Monographs, 47,* 119-131.

Hodgins, H. S., & Zuckerman, M. (1990). The effect of nonverbal sensitivity on social interaction. *Journal of Nonverbal Behavior, 14,* 155-170.

Huston, T. L., & Vangelisti, A. L. (1991). Socioemotional behavior and satisfaction in marital relationships: A longitudinal study. *Journal of Personality and Social Psychology, 61,* 721-733.

Izard, C. E. (1971). *The face of emotion.* Englewood Cliffs, NJ: Prentice-Hall.

Jaffe, J. (1978). Parliamentary procedure and the brain. In A. W. Siegman & S. Feldstein (Eds.), *Nonverbal behavior and communication* (pp. 55-66). Hillsdale, NJ: Lawrence Erlbaum.

Johnson, K. L., & Edwards, R. (1991). The effects of gender and type of romantic touch on perceptions of relational commitment. *Journal of Nonverbal Behavior, 15,* 43-55.

Jones, E. E. (1964). *Ingratiation: A social psychological analysis.* New York: Wiley.

Jones, E. E., & Pittman, T. S. (1982). Toward a general theory of strategic self-presentation. In J. Suls (Ed.), *Psychological perspectives on the self* (Vol. 1, pp. 231-262). Hillsdale, NJ: Lawrence Erlbaum.

Jones, S. E. (1986). Sex differences in touch communication. *Western Journal of Speech Communication, 50,* 227-241.

Jones, S. E., & Yarbrough, A. E. (1985). A naturalistic study of the meanings of touch. *Communication Monographs, 52,* 19-56.

Julien, D., Markman, H. J., & Lindahl, K. M. (1989). A comparison of a global and a microanalytic coding system: Implications for future trends in studying interactions. *Behavioral Assessment, 11,* 81-100.

Kalbfleisch, P. J. (1992). Deceit, distrust, and the social milieu: Application of deception research in a troubled world. *Journal of Applied Communication, 20,* 308-334.

Keeley-Dyreson, M. P., Burgoon, J. K., & Bailey, W. (1991). The effect of stress on decoding kinesic and vocalic communication. *Human Communication Research, 17,* 584-605.

Kellermann, K. (1992). Communication: Inherently strategic and primarily automatic. *Communication Monographs, 59,* 288-300.

Kellermann, K., Reynolds, R., & Chen, J. B. (1991). Strategies of conversational retreat: When parting is not sweet sorrow. *Communication Monographs, 58,* 362-383.

Kelley, D. L., & Burgoon, J. K. (1991). Understanding marital satisfaction and couple type as functions of relational expectations. *Human Communication Research, 18,* 40-69.

Kelley, H. H. (1986). Personal relationships: Their nature and significance. In R. Gilmour & S. Duck (Eds.), *The emerging field of personal relationships* (pp. 3-22). Hillsdale, NJ: Lawrence Erlbaum.

Kemper, T. D. (1984). Power, status, and emotions: A sociological contribution to a psychophysiological domain. In K. R. Scherer & P. Ekman (Eds.), *Approaches to emotion* (pp. 369-383). Hillsdale, NJ: Lawrence Erlbaum.

Kempton, W. (1980). The rhythmic basis of interactional micro-synchrony. In M. R. Key (Ed.), *The relationship of verbal and nonverbal communication* (pp. 67-75). The Hague, the Netherlands: Mouton.

Kendon, A. (1980). Gesticulation and speech: Two aspects of the process of utterance. In M. R. Key (Ed.), *The relationship of verbal and nonverbal communication* (pp. 207-227). The Hague, the Netherlands: Mouton.

Kendon, A. (1983). Gesture and speech: How they interact. In J. M. Wiemann & R. P. Harrison (Eds.), *Nonverbal interaction* (pp. 13-45). Beverly Hills, CA: Sage.

Kendon, A. (1990). *Conducting interaction: Patterns of behavior in focused encounters.* Cambridge: Cambridge University Press.

Kendon, A., Harris, R. M., & Key, M. R. (Eds.). (1975). *Organization of behavior in face-to-face interaction.* The Hague, the Netherlands: Mouton.

Kenny, D. A. (1991). A general model of consensus and accuracy in interpersonal perception. *Psychological Review, 98,* 155-163.

Kenny, D. A., Horner, C., Kashy, D. A., & Chu, L. (1992). Consensus at zero acquaintance: Replication, behavioral cues, and stability. *Journal of Personality and Social Psychology, 62,* 88-97.

Kimble, C. E., & Seidel, S. D. (1991). Vocal signs of confidence. *Journal of Nonverbal Behavior, 15,* 99-106.

Kirouac, G., & Dore, F. Y. (1985). Accuracy of the judgment of facial expression of emotions as a function of sex and level of education. *Journal of Nonverbal Behavior, 9,* 3-7.

Kleinke, C. L. (1975). *First impressions.* Englewood Cliffs, NJ: Prentice-Hall.

Knapp, M. L. (1983). Dyadic relationship development. In J. M. Wiemann & R. P. Harrison (Eds.), *Nonverbal interaction* (pp. 179-207). Beverly Hills, CA: Sage.

Knapp, M. L. (1984a). *Interpersonal communication and human relationships.* Boston: Allyn & Bacon.

Knapp, M. L. (1984b). The study of nonverbal behavior vis-à-vis human communication theory. In A. Wolfgang (Ed.), *Nonverbal behavior: Perspectives, applications, and intercultural insights* (pp. 15-40). Toronto, Canada: Hogrefe.

Knapp, M. L. (1985). The study of physical appearance and cosmetics in Western culture. In J. A. Graham & A. M. Kligman (Eds.), *The psychology of cosmetic treatments* (pp. 45-76). New York: Praeger.

Knapp, M. L., Cody, M. J., & Reardon, K. K. (1987). Nonverbal signals. In C. R. Berger & S. H. Chaffee (Eds.), *Handbook of communication science* (pp. 385-418). Newbury Park, CA: Sage.

Knapp, M. L., & Comadena, M. E. (1979). Telling it like it isn't: A review of theory and research on deceptive communications. *Human Communication Research, 5,* 270-285.

Knapp, M. L., & Hall, J. A. (1992). *Nonverbal communication in human interaction* (3rd ed.). Ft. Worth, TX: Holt, Rinehart & Winston.

Knapp, M. L., Hart, R. P., Friedrich, G. W., & Schulman, G. M. (1973). The rhetoric of goodbye: Verbal and nonverbal correlates of human leave-taking. *Speech Monographs, 40,* 182-198.

Kramer, E. (1963). Judgment of personal characteristics and emotions from nonverbal properties of speech. *Psychological Bulletin, 60,* 408-420.

Kramer, I., Alloway, T., & Pliner, P. (Eds.). (1975). *Nonverbal communication of aggression.* New York: Plenum.

Krauss, R., Morrel-Samuels, P., & Colasante, C. (1991). Do conversational hand gestures communicate? *Journal of Personality and Social Psychology, 61,* 743-754.

Kraut, R. E. (1980). Humans as lie-detectors: Some second thoughts. *Journal of Communication, 30,* 209-216.

Krivonos, P. D., & Knapp, M. L. (1975). Initiating communication: What do you say when you say hello? *Central States Speech Journal, 26,* 115-125.

LaBarre, W. (1947). The cultural basis of emotions and gestures. *Journal of Personality, 16,* 49-68.

Leach, E. (1972). The influence of cultural context on non-verbal communication in man. In R. A. Hinde (Ed.), *Non-verbal communication* (pp. 315-347). Cambridge, MA: Cambridge University Press.

Le Poire, B. A. (1991). Orientation and defensive reactions as alternatives to arousal in theories of nonverbal reactions to change in immediacy. *Southern Communication Journal, 56,* 138-146.

Le Poire, B. A., & Burgoon, J. K. (1991, November). *I KNEW that you liked me: Nonverbal predictors of relational message perceptions.* Paper presented to the annual meeting of the Speech Communication Association, Atlanta.

Lieberman, D. A., Rigo, T. G., & Campain, R. F. (1988). Age-related differences in nonverbal decoding ability. *Communication Quarterly, 36,* 290-297.

Liska, J. (1986). Symbols: The missing link? In J. G. Else & P. Lee (Eds.), *Proceedings of the Tenth Annual Congress on the International Primatological Society: Vol. 3. Primate ontology, cognition, and social behavior.* Cambridge: Cambridge University Press.

Mahl, G. F. (1987). *Explorations in nonverbal and vocal behavior.* Hillsdale, NJ: Lawrence Erlbaum.

Manstead, A. S. R., Wagner, H. L., & MacDonald, C. J. (1986). Deceptive and nondeceptive communications: Sending experience, modality, and individual abilities. *Journal of Nonverbal Behavior, 10,* 147-167.

Manusov, V. (1990). An application of attribution principles to nonverbal behavior in romantic dyads. *Communication Monographs, 57,* 104-118.

Manusov, V. (1991). Perceiving nonverbal messages: Effects of immediacy and encoded intent on receiver judgments. *Western Journal of Speech Communication, 55,* 235-253.

Manusov, V. (1992a, November). *Intentionality attributions for naturally occurring nonverbal behaviors in romantic dyads.* Paper presented to the annual meeting of the Speech Communication Association, Chicago.

Manusov, V. (1992b). Mimicry or synchrony: The effects of intentionality attributions for nonverbal mirroring behavior. *Communication Quarterly, 40,* 69-83.

Manusov, V., & Rodriguez, J. S. (1991). Intentionality behind nonverbal messages: A perceiver's perspective. *Journal of Nonverbal Behavior, 13,* 15-24.

Marche, T. A., & Peterson, C. (1993). The development and sex-related use of interruption behavior. *Human Communication Research, 19,* 388-408.

Markman, H. J. (1988). Where's the communication in interpersonal communication? *Contemporary Psychology, 33,* 307-309.

Markman, H. J., & Floyd, F. (1980). Possibilities for the prevention of marital discord: A behavioral perspective. *American Journal of Family Therapy, 8,* 29-48.

Markman, H. J., Notarius, C. I., Stephen, T., & Smith, R. J. (1981). Behavioral observation systems for couples: The current status. In E. E. Filsinger & R. A. Lewis (Eds.), *Assessing marriage* (pp. 197-216). Beverly Hills, CA: Sage.

Marwell, G., & Schmitt, D. (1967). Dimensions of compliance-gaining behavior: An empirical analysis. *Sociometry, 30,* 350-364.

Matsumoto, D. (1991). Cultural influences on facial expressions of emotion. *Southern Communication Journal, 56,* 128-137.

Mayo, C., & Henley, N. M. (Eds.). (1981). *Gender and nonverbal behavior.* New York: Springer-Verlag.

McCall, G. J. (1987). The self-concept and interpersonal communication. In M. E. Roloff & G. R. Miller (Eds.), *Interpersonal processes: New directions in communication research* (pp. 63-76). Newbury Park, CA: Sage.

McCornack, S. A., & Levine, T. T. (1990). When lovers become leery: The relationship between suspicion and accuracy in detecting deception. *Communication Monographs, 57,* 218-230.

McCornack, S. A., & Parks, M. R. (1986). Deception detection and relationship development: The other side of trust. In M. L. McLaughlin (Ed.), *Communication yearbook 9* (pp. 337-389). Beverly Hills, CA: Sage.

McCroskey, J. C., & McCain, T. A. (1974). The measurement of interpersonal attraction. *Speech Monographs, 41,* 261-266.

McCroskey, J. C., & Young, T. J. (1981). Ethos and credibility: The construct and its measurement after three decades. *Central States Speech Journal, 32,* 24-34.

McLuhan, M., & Fiore, Q. (1967). *The medium is the massage: An inventory of effects.* New York: Bantam.

McNeill, D. (1985). So you think gestures are nonverbal? *Psychological Review, 92,* 350-371.

McNeill, D. (1992). *Hand and mind: What gestures reveal about thought.* Chicago: University Chicago Press.

McNeill, D., & Levy, E. (1982). Conceptual representations in language activity and gesture. In R. J. Jarvella & W. Klein (Eds.), *Speech, place, and action: Studies in deixis and related topics* (pp. 271-295). Chichester, England: Wiley.

Mehrabian, A. (1972). *Nonverbal communication.* Chicago: Aldine-Atherton.

Mehrabian, A. (1981). *Silent messages.* Belmont, CA: Wadsworth.

Mehrabian, A., & Wiener, M. (1967). Decoding of inconsistent communications. *Journal of Personality and Social Psychology, 6,* 109-114.

Miller, G. R., Bauchner, J. E., Hocking, J. E., Fontes, N. E., Kaminski, E. P., & Brandt, D. R. (1981). "And nothing but the truth": How well can observers detect deceptive testimony? In B. D. Sales (Ed.), *Perspectives in law and psychology* (pp. 169-194). New York: Plenum.

Miller, G. R., & Burgoon, J. K. (1982). Factors affecting assessments of witness credibility. In N. L. Kerr & R. M. Bray (Eds.), *The psychology of the courtroom* (pp. 145-179). New York: Academic Press.

Miller, J. B. (1989). Memories of peer relations and styles of conflict management. *Journal of Social and Personal Relationships, 6,* 487-504.

Morris, D. (1977). *Manwatching: A field guide to human behavior*. New York: Abrams.

Morris, D., Collett, P., Marsh, P., & O'Shaughnessy, M. (1979). *Gestures*. New York: Stein & Day.

Morrow, P. C., & McElroy, J. C. (1984). The impact of physical attractiveness in evaluative contexts. *Basic and Applied Social Psychology, 5,* 171-182.

Motley, M. T. (1990a). Communication as interaction: A reply to Beach and Bavelas. *Western Journal of Speech Communication, 54,* 613-623.

Motley, M. T. (1990b). On whether one can(not) communicate: An examination via traditional communication postulates. *Western Journal of Speech Communication, 54,* 1-20.

Motley, M. T. (1991). How one may not communicate: A reply to Andersen. *Communication Studies, 42,* 326-339.

Motley, M. T., & Camden, C. T. (1988). Facial expression of emotion: A comparison of posed expressions versus spontaneous expressions in an interpersonal setting. *Western Journal of Speech Communication, 52,* 1-22.

Mueser, K. T., Grau, B. W., Sussman, S., & Rosen, A. J. (1984). You're only as pretty as you feel: Facial expression as a determinant of physical attractiveness. *Journal of Personality and Social Psychology, 46,* 469-478.

Mulac, A., Studley, L. B., Wiemann, J. M., & Bradac, J. J. (1987). Male/female gaze in same-sex and mixed-sex dyads. *Human Communication Research, 13,* 323-343.

Newton, D. A., & Burgoon, J. K. (1990). Nonverbal conflict behaviors: Functions, strategies, and tactics. In D. D. Cahn (Ed.), *Intimates in conflict* (pp. 77-104). Hillsdale, NJ: Lawrence Erlbaum.

Noller, P. (1985). Video primacy: Another look. *Journal of Nonverbal Behavior, 9,* 28-47.

Norton, R. (1983). *Communicator style: Theory, applications, and measures*. Beverly Hills, CA: Sage.

O'Hair, H. D., Cody, M. J., & McLaughlin, M. L. (1981). Prepared lies, spontaneous lies, Machiavellianism, and nonverbal communication. *Human Communication Research, 7,* 325-339.

O'Leary, M. J., & Gallois, C. (1985). The last ten turns: Behavior and sequencing in friends' and strangers' conversational findings. *Journal of Nonverbal Behavior, 9,* 8-27.

Palmer, M. T. (1989). Controlling conversation: Turns, topics and interpersonal control. *Communication Monographs, 56,* 1-18.

Patterson, M. L. (1973). Compensation in nonverbal immediacy behaviors: A review. *Sociometry, 36,* 237-257.

Patterson, M. L. (1976). An arousal model of interpersonal intimacy. *Psychological Review, 83,* 235-245.

Patterson, M. L. (1978). The role of space in social interaction. In A. W. Siegman & S. Feldstein (Eds.), *Nonverbal communication and behavior* (pp. 265-290). Hillsdale, NJ: Lawrence Erlbaum.

Patterson, M. L. (1983). *Nonverbal behavior: A functional perspective*. New York: Springer-Verlag.

Patterson, M. L. (1987). Presentational and affect-management functions of nonverbal involvement. *Journal of Nonverbal Behavior, 11,* 110-122.

Patterson, M. L. (1991). A functional approach to nonverbal exchange. In R. S. Feldman & B. Rimé (Eds.), *Fundamentals of nonverbal behavior* (pp. 458-495). Cambridge: Cambridge University Press.

Patterson, M. L., Powell, J. L., & Lenihan, M. G. (1986). Touch, compliance, and interpersonal affect. *Journal of Nonverbal Behavior, 10,* 41-50.

Philpott, J. S. (1983). *The relative contribution to meaning of verbal and nonverbal channels of communication: A meta-analysis*. Unpublished master's thesis, University of Nebraska.

Pittinger, R., Hockett, C., & Darehy, J. (1960). *The first five minutes*. Ithaca, NY: Martineau.

Planalp, S., & Benson, A. (1992). Friends' and acquaintances' conversations I: Perceived differences. *Journal of Social and Personal Relationships, 9,* 483-506.

Plutchik, R. (1962). *The emotions: Facts, theories and a new model*. New York: Random House.

Plutchik, R. (1984). Emotions: A general psychoevolutionary theory. In K. R. Scherer & P. Ekman (Eds.), *Approaches to emotion* (pp. 197-219). Hillsdale, NJ: Lawrence Erlbaum.

Postman, N. (1985). *Amusing ourselves to death: Public discourse in the age of show business*. New York: Penguin.

Poyatos, F. (1983). *New perspectives in nonverbal communication*. Oxford: Pergamon.

Poyatos, F. (1992). Audible-visual approach to speech. In F. Poyatos (Ed.), *Advances in nonverbal communication* (pp. 41-57). Amsterdam: Benjamins.

Putnam, L. L., & Wilson, C. E. (1982). Communication strategies in organizational conflicts: Reliability and validity of a measurement scale. In M. Burgoon (Ed.), *Communication yearbook 6* (pp. 549-595). Beverly Hills, CA: Sage.

Raffler-Engel, W. von. (1983). *The perception of nonverbal behavior in the career interview*. Amsterdam: Benjamins.

Raines, R. S., Hechtman, S. B., & Rosenthal, R. (1990). Nonverbal behavior and gender as determinants of physical attractiveness. *Journal of Nonverbal Behavior, 14*, 253-267.

Ray, G. B. (1986). Vocally cued personality prototypes: An implicit personality theory approach. *Communication Monographs, 53*, 266-276.

Register, L. M., & Henley, T. B. (1992). The phenomenology of intimacy. *Journal of Social and Personal Relationships, 9*, 467-481.

Reis, H. T., Wilson, I. M., Monestere, C., Bernstein, S., Clark, K., Seidl, E., Franco, M., Gioioso, E., Freeman, L., & Radoane, K. (1990). What is smiling is beautiful and good. *European Journal of Social Psychology, 20*, 259-267.

Remland, M. S., & Jones, T. S. (1989). The effects of nonverbal involvement and communication apprehension on state anxiety, interpersonal attraction, and speech duration. *Communication Quarterly, 37*, 170-183.

Ricci Bitti, P. E., & Poggi, I. (1991). Symbolic nonverbal behavior: Talking through gestures. In R. S. Feldman & B. Rimé (Eds.), *Fundamentals of nonverbal behavior* (pp. 433-457). Cambridge: Cambridge University Press.

Ridgeway, C. L., Berger, J., & Smith, L. (1985). Nonverbal cues and status: An expectation states approach. *American Journal of Sociology, 90*, 955-978.

Riggio, R. E. (1986). Assessment of basic social skills. *Journal of Personality and Social Psychology, 51*, 649-660.

Riggio, R. E., & Friedman, H. S. (1983). Individual differences and cues to deception. *Journal of Personality and Social Psychology, 45*, 899-915.

Riggio, R. E., Widaman, K. F., & Friedman, H. S. (1985). Actual and perceived emotional sending and personality correlates. *Journal of Nonverbal Behavior, 9*, 69-83.

Rimé, B., & Schiaratura, L. (1991). Gesture and speech. In R. S. Feldman & B. Rimé (Eds.), *Fundamentals of nonverbal behavior* (pp. 239-281). Cambridge: Cambridge University Press.

Riseborough, M. G. (1981). Physiographic gestures as decoding facilitators: Three experiments exploring a neglected facet of communication. *Journal of Nonverbal Behavior, 5*, 172-183.

Rogers, L. E., & Farace, R. V. (1975). Relational communication analysis: New measurement procedures. *Human Communication Research, 1*, 222-239.

Rosenfeld, H. M. (1978). Conversational control functions of nonverbal behavior. In A. W. Siegman & S. Feldstein (Eds.), *Nonverbal behavior and communication* (pp. 291-328). Hillsdale, NJ: Lawrence Erlbaum.

Rosenthal, R. (1985). Nonverbal cues in the mediation of interpersonal expectancy effects. In A. W. Siegman & S. Feldstein (Eds.), *Multichannel integrations of nonverbal behavior* (pp. 105-128). Hillsdale, NJ: Lawrence Erlbaum.

Rosenthal, R., & DePaulo, B. M. (1979). Sex differences in accommodation in nonverbal communication. In R. Rosenthal (Ed.), *Skill in nonverbal communication: Individual differences* (pp. 68-103). Cambridge, MA: Oelgeschlager, Gunn & Hain.

Rosenthal, R., Hall, J. A., DiMatteo, M. R., Rogers, P. L., & Archer, D. (1979). *Sensitivity in nonverbal communication: The PONS Test.* Baltimore: Johns Hopkins University Press.

Ross, H. S., Cheyne, J. A., & Lollis, S. P. (1988). Defining and studying reciprocity in young children. In S. W. Duck (Ed.), *Handbook of personal relationships* (pp. 143-160). New York: Wiley.

Rubin, R. B. (1982). Assessing speaking and listening competence at the college level: The Communication Competency Assessment Instrument. *Communication Education, 31*, 19-32.

Rusbult, C. E., Verett, J., Whitney, G. A., Slovik, L. F., & Lipkus, I. (1991). Accommodation processes in close relationships: Theory and preliminary empirical evidence. *Journal of Personality and Social Psychology, 60*, 53-78.

Sabatelli, R. M., & Rubin, M. (1986). Nonverbal expressiveness and physical attractiveness as mediators of interpersonal perceptions. *Journal of Nonverbal Behavior, 10*, 120-133.

Sadalla, E. K., Kenrick, D. T., & Vershure, B. (1987). Dominance and heterosexual attraction. *Journal of Personality and Social Psychology, 52*, 730-738.

Samter, W., & Burleson, B. R. (1990). Evaluations of communication skills as predictors of peer acceptance in a group living situation. *Communication Studies, 41*, 311-326.

Sapir, E. (1949). The unconscious patterning of behavior in society. In D. Mandelbaum (Ed.), *Selected writings of Edward Sapir in language, culture and personality* (pp. 544-559). Berkeley: University of California Press.

Schachter, S., & Singer, S. (1962). Cognitive, social and physiological determinants of emotional state. *Psychological Review, 69*, 379-399.

Scheflen, A. E. (1965). Quasi-courtship behavior in psychotherapy. *Psychiatry, 28*, 245-257.

Scheflen, A. E. (1974). *How behavior means.* Garden City, NY: Doubleday.

Scherer, K. R. (1980). The functions of nonverbal signs in conversation. In R. N. St. Clair & H. Giles (Eds.), *The social and psychological contexts of language* (pp. 225-244). Hillsdale, NJ: Lawrence Erlbaum.

Scherer, K. R., & Oshinsky, J. S. (1977). Cue utilization in emotion attribution from auditory stimuli. *Motivation and Emotion, 1,* 331-346.

Schlenker, B. R. (1980). *Impression management.* Belmont, CA: Wadsworth.

Schlenker, B. R. (1985). Identity and self-identification. In B. R. Schlenker (Ed.), *The self and social life* (pp. 65-99). New York: McGraw-Hill.

Sharkey, W. F., & Stafford, L. (1990). Turn-taking resources employed by congenitally blind conversers. *Communication Studies, 41,* 161-182.

Shea, B. C., & Pearson, J. C. (1986). The effects of relationship type, partner intent, and gender on the selection of relationship maintenance strategies. *Communication Monographs, 53,* 352-364.

Siegel, S. M., Friedlander, M. L., & Heatherington, L. (1992). Nonverbal relational control in family communication. *Journal of Nonverbal Behavior, 16,* 117-139.

Siegman, A. W. (1978). The telltale voice: Nonverbal messages of verbal communication. In A. W. Siegman & S. Feldstein (Eds.), *Nonverbal behavior and communication* (pp. 183-243). Hillsdale, NJ: Lawrence Erlbaum.

Simpson, J. A., Gangestad, S. W., & Biek, M. (1992). *Personality and nonverbal social behavior: An ethological perspective of relationship initiation.* Manuscript submitted for publication.

Smith, H. J., Archer, D., & Costanzo, M. (1991). "Just a hunch": Accuracy and awareness in person perception. *Journal of Nonverbal Behavior, 15,* 3-18.

Snodgrass, S. E. (1992). Further effects of role versus gender on interpersonal sensitivity. *Journal of Personality and Social Psychology, 62,* 154-158.

Snodgrass, S. E., & Rosenthal, R. (1985). Interpersonal sensitivity and skills in decoding nonverbal channels: The value of face value. *Basic and Applied Social Psychology, 6,* 243-255.

Stacks, D. W., & Burgoon, J. K. (1981). The role of nonverbal behaviors as distractors in resistance to persuasion in interpersonal contexts. *Central States Speech Journal, 32,* 61-73.

Staley, C. C., & Cohen, J. L. (1988). Communicator style and social style: Similarities and differences between the sexes. *Communication Quarterly, 36,* 192-202.

Stamp, G. H., & Knapp, M. L. (1990). The construct of intent in interpersonal communication. *Quarterly Journal of Speech, 76,* 282-299.

Stern, L. A. (1990). *The effect of assertive and unassertive content and assertive and unassertive communication style on perceptions of relational messages, attractiveness, and communication satisfaction.* Unpublished master's thesis, University of Arizona.

Stewart, L. P., Cooper, P. J., & Friedley, S. A. (1986). *Communication between the sexes: Sex differences and sex-role stereotypes.* Scottsdale, AZ: Gorsuch Scarisbrick.

Stier, D. S., & Hall, J. A. (1984). Gender differences in touch: An empirical and theoretical review. *Journal of Personality and Social Psychology, 47,* 440-459.

Storrs, D., & Kleinke, C. L. (1990). Evaluation of high and equal status male and female touchers. *Journal of Nonverbal Behavior, 14,* 87-95.

Street, R. L., Jr., & Brady, R. M. (1982). Speech rate acceptance as a function of evaluative domain, listener speech rate, and communication intent. *Communication Monographs, 49,* 290-308.

Street, R. L., Jr., Mulac, A., & Wiemann, J. M. (1988). Speech evaluation differences as a function of perspective (participant versus observer) and presentational medium. *Human Communication Research, 14,* 333-363.

Street, R. L., Jr., & Murphy, T. L. (1987). Interpersonal orientation and speech behavior. *Communication Monographs, 54,* 42-62.

Sullins, E. S. (1989). Perceptual salience as a function of nonverbal expressiveness. *Personality and Social Psychology Bulletin, 15,* 584-595.

Sunnafrank, M. (1992). On debunking the attitude similarity myth. *Communication Monographs, 59,* 164-179.

Swann, W. B. (1987). Identity negotiation: Where two roads meet. *Journal of Personality and Social Psychology, 53,* 1038-1051.

Swap, W. C., & Rubin, J. Z. (1983). Measurement of interpersonal orientation. *Journal of Personality and Social Psychology, 44,* 208-219.

Tajfel, H. (1981). *Human groups and social categories: Studies in social psychology.* Cambridge: Cambridge University Press.

Tedeschi, J. (Ed.). (1982). *Impression management theory and social psychological research.* New York: Academic Press.

Thayer, S. (Ed.). (1986). The psychology of touch [Special issue]. *Journal of Nonverbal Behavior, 10,* 7-80.

Tolhuizen, J. H. (1989). Communication strategies for intensifying dating relationships: Identification, use and structure. *Journal of Social and Personal Relationships, 6,* 413-434.

Tomkins, S. S. (1962). *Affect, imagery, consciousness.* New York: Springer.

Tomkins, S. S. (1984). Affect theory. In K. R. Scherer & P. Ekman (Eds.), *Approaches to emotion* (pp. 163-195). Hillsdale, NJ: Lawrence Erlbaum.

Toris, D., & DePaulo, B. M. (1985). Effects of actual deception and suspiciousness of deception on interpersonal deception. *Journal of Personality and Social Psychology, 47,* 1063-1073.

Triandis, H. C. (1989). The self and social behavior in differing cultural contexts. *Journal of Personality and Social Psychology, 96,* 506-520.

Vrugt, A. (1990). Negative attitudes, nonverbal behavior and self-fulfilling prophecy in simulated therapy interviews. *Journal of Nonverbal Behavior, 14,* 77-86.

Wagner, H. L., & Smith, J. (1991). Facial expression in the presence of friends and strangers. *Journal of Nonverbal Behavior, 15,* 201-214.

Warner, R. M., Malloy, D., Schneider, K., Knoth, R., & Wilder, B. (1987). Rhythmic organization of social interaction and observer ratings of positive affect and involvement. *Journal of Nonverbal Behavior, 11,* 57-74.

Watzlawick, P., Beavin, J. H., & Jackson, D. D. (1967). *Pragmatics of human communication: A study of interactional patterns, pathologies, and paradoxes.* New York: Norton.

Wiemann, J. M. (1985). Interpersonal control and regulation in conversation. In R. L. Street & J. N. Cappella (Eds.), *Sequence and pattern in communicative behaviour* (pp. 85-102). London: Edward Arnold.

Wiemann, J. M., & Knapp, M. L. (1975). Turn-taking in conversation. *Journal of Communication, 25,* 75-92.

Wiener, M., Devoe, S., Rubinow, S., & Geller, J. (1972). Nonverbal behavior and nonverbal communication. *Psychological Review, 79,* 185-214.

Williams, C. E., & Stevens, K. N. (1972). Emotions and speech: Some acoustical correlates. *Journal of the Acoustical Society of America, 52,* 1238-1250.

Willis, F. N., Jr., & Briggs, L. F. (1992). Relationship and touch in public settings. *Journal of Nonverbal Behavior, 16,* 55-63.

Woodall, W. G., & Burgoon, J. K. (1981). The effects of nonverbal synchrony on message comprehension and persuasiveness. *Journal of Nonverbal Behavior, 5,* 207-223.

Woodall, W. G., & Folger, J. P. (1981). Encoding specificity and nonverbal cue context: An expansion of episodic memory research. *Communication Monographs, 49,* 39-53.

Woodall, W. G., & Folger, J. P. (1985). Nonverbal cue context and episodic memory: On the availability and endurance of nonverbal behaviors as retrieval cues. *Communication Monographs, 52,* 319-333.

Zebrowitz, L. A. (1990). *Social perception.* Pacific Grove, CA: Brooks/Cole.

Zuckerman, M., DePaulo, B. M., & Rosenthal, R. (1981). Verbal and nonverbal communication of deception. In L. Berkowitz (Ed.), *Advances in experimental social psychology* (Vol. 14, pp. 2-59). New York: Academic Press.

Zuckerman, M., DePaulo, B. M., & Rosenthal, R. (1986). Humans as deceivers and lie-detectors. In P. D. Blanck, R. Buck, & R. Rosenthal (Eds.), *Nonverbal communication in the clinical context* (pp. 13-35). University Park: Pennsylvania State University Press.

Zuckerman, M., & Driver, R. E. (1985). Telling lies: Verbal and nonverbal correlates of deception. In A. W. Siegman & S. Feldstein (Eds.), *Multichannel integrations of nonverbal behavior* (pp. 129-148). Hillsdale, NJ: Lawrence Erlbaum.

Zuckerman, M., & Driver, R. E. (1989). What sounds beautiful is good: The vocal attractiveness stereotype. *Journal of Nonverbal Behavior, 13,* 67-82.

Zuckerman, M., Driver, R., & Koestner, R. (1982). Discrepancy as a cue to actual and perceived deception. *Journal of Nonverbal Behavior, 7,* 95-100.

Zuckerman, M., Hodgins, H., & Miyake, K. (1990). The vocal attractiveness stereotype: Replication and elaboration. *Journal of Nonverbal Behavior, 14,* 97-112.

Zuckerman, M., Lipets, M. S., Koivumaki, J. H., & Rosenthal, R. (1975). Encoding and decoding nonverbal cues of emotion. *Journal of Personality and Social Psychology, 32,* 1068-1076.

Zuckerman, M., Miyake, K., & Hodgins, H. S. (1991). Cross-channel effects of vocal and physical attractiveness and their implications for interpersonal perception. *Journal of Personality and Social Psychology, 60,* 545-554.

Zuckerman, M., Spiegel, N. H., DePaulo, B. M., & Rosenthal, R. (1982). Nonverbal strategies for decoding deception. *Journal of Nonverbal Behavior, 6,* 171-186.

8

Culture, Meaning, and Interpersonal Communication

Jürgen Streeck

What Is Culture?

WHAT IS CULTURE? E. B. Tylor, one of the founders of modern anthropology, defined it as "that complex whole which includes knowledge, belief, art, law, morals, custom, and any other capabilities and habits acquired by man as a member of society" (Tylor, 1871, p. 1), and *Webster's College Dictionary* as "the sum total of ways of living built up by a group of human beings and transmitted from one generation to another." Both definitions are useful, assuming that "capabilities and habits" or "ways of living" include those phenomena that communication scholars are interested in, notably, symbols, actions, and interaction patterns. And yet, something about these definitions is remarkable and should be highlighted. This is the easy association of *culture* and *group,* the assumption—which is certainly shared by almost everyone, scholar and lay person alike—that culture always "belongs" to groups and occupies pieces of land with them: an island, a valley, a state, or perhaps just a city block. At the boundary of the territory, the reasoning goes, another culture begins. We can call this a "territorial" view of culture. It appears that the contemporary discourse on cultures—vernacular and academic alike—is still mediated by a cognitive map on which "cultures" appear like nation-states: bounded, distinct, and in different colors. This we regard as the natural order of things, the kind of world where we have all acquired our identities, knowledge, interpretive frames, and customs. But so much is obscured, reified, and distorted by such a map. It makes us forget that humanity has always been in motion; that cultural boundaries are porous and shifting; that cultural forms and bodies of knowledge have spread, mingled, influenced, and changed one another; that cultural boundaries are always the result of the politics of interaction (Anderson, 1991; Barth, 1969; McDermott & Gospodinoff, 1979).

Witness Bosnia-Herzegovina. Until very recently this was a province where people weakly identified with three religions (Islam, Catholicism, Orthodoxy) and, optionally, with two ethnic groups (Croats or Serbs). The Muslims had no ethnic identity other than "Bosnian"—which was at the same time the pan-ethnic category for all the people inhabiting this piece of land. Intermarriage was common. Such a place escapes the territorial view of culture, and its population does not easily lend itself to ethnic and cultural classification. Today, however, the genocidal politics of "ethnic cleansing" accomplish just that: to make reality fit the conventional map. Suddenly, *culture* appears as a fighting word of the Serbian fascists (who refer to the Muslim population as "the Turks"). We must realize that racism does not need a "genetic" interpretation and that "culture" can be given racist interpretations. We have not even begun to consider the consequences.

Reflecting on the ambiguities and contradictory implications of culture is especially important because there is a direct historical link between the nationalisms and tribalisms that we currently observe in Europe and the former Soviet Union and the philosophical traditions from which we in the social sciences and humanities take our concept of culture. The connection is particularly clear in the case of the Baltic states, as Nobel laureate Milosz (1993)—himself a Polish-speaking Lithuanian—has recently pointed out. These states are linguistically anything but homogeneous: Lithuanian and Latvian are Indo-European languages, but Estonian is a Finno-Ugric language. Latvia and Estonia, on the other hand, have for a long time been under German rule, and the aristocracies of these states spoke German. The Lithuanian aristocracy, in contrast, adopted Polish as its language of choice. And today, Latvia and Estonia have very large Russian minorities. Ethnic and linguistic nationalism is obviously a very mixed blessing under these circumstances. This ideology, though, was first brought to the area by G. W. Herder (1744-1803), the German philosopher whose romantic philosophy of language and study of language origin (Herder, 1772/1966) influenced W. von Humboldt (Humboldt, 1836/1988), who influenced Boas (Boas, 1940) and Sapir (Sapir, 1921), who were the forebears of the philosophy of linguistic and cultural relativism that provides the framework for today's scientific interest in culture. Herder lived as a pastor in Lithuania, and his interest in Lithuanian folk songs marked the birth of the idea of a Lithuanian nation. We cannot deny that the identification of "identity" with "culture" and "language" that is so much part of our intellectual convictions has frequently resulted in social fragmentation and ethnic war. This must be kept in mind, notwithstanding the unquestionable legitimacy of the concept "culture" in the struggle for cultural equality of the ethnic minorities in multicultural societies such as that of the United States.

An Anthropological View of Culture

We will therefore uncouple *culture* from *ethnicity, identity, and group* and use the term in two senses, both of them lucidly synthesized by Bruner in his book *Acts of Meaning* (Bruner, 1990). First of all, culture is what distinguishes the human species from other species (or most other species—some animals such as apes and whales have been shown to have limited bodies of tradition) and enables it to survive in a world for which it is biologically maladapted. Humanity was condemned to develop culture because it was not naturally designed to survive; it lacked a biosphere. This is a theme that various philosophical and biological anthropologists, beginning during the Age of Enlightenment, have expounded (Herder, 1772/1966; Kant, 1798/1977, and, more recently, Donald, 1991; Gehlen, 1958, and Plessner, 1964/1980, among others). Culture includes humanity's material creations—symbols, shelter, technology, and so on—but also its mental abilities to operate them; it is both external and internal. Culture, then, is "a set of prosthetic devices by which human beings can exceed or even redefine the 'natural limits' of human functioning" (Bruner, 1990, p. 21). Of chief importance among these prosthetic devices are *symbolic* or *representation systems*, systems "used in constructing meaning" (p. 11). While the modern world consists in a multitude of overlapping, moving, shifting local meaning systems, at its roots culture is a human universal, acquired by the species in the process of evolution. Contemporary representation systems, languages, and systems of social interaction are built upon and contain structures developed at previous evolutionary stages.

> The modern mind has evolved from the primate mind through a series of major
> adaptations, each of which led to the emergence of a new representation system.
> Each . . . new . . . system has remained intact within our current mental architecture, so
> that the modern mind is a mosaic structure of cognitive vestiges from earlier stages of
> human emergence. (Donald, 1991, p. 3)

Each cultural form—symbol, behavior, artifact—can therefore be "read" in its contemporary, local, "cultural" web of meanings or as a reflection and instantiation of older, more global human achievements. Different languages have different morphologies to inflect verbs and nouns (some have no inflection whatsoever), but some versions of the verb-noun (or process-thing) dichotomy is found in all of them. Similarly, politeness is marked by many different devices, but in all speech communities, there are ways to be polite (Brown & Levinson, 1978/1987).

There is another reason for looking at cultural meaning systems from the point of view of their dual nature as partly universal, partly diverse: Independent findings from several disciplines, in particular population genetics and linguistic typology (Cavalli-Sforza, 1991; Greenberg & Ruhlen, 1992), suggest that human language— and thus culture—originated in only one place ("monogenesis") in Africa and spread from there around the globe with humanity's migrations. In the process, they diversified and developed various independent lineages. All languages, in other words, are at one level "dialects" of one another: However diverse they might be, they are of common origin. This invites us to see cultural phenomena as if through a telescope; depending on the age we focus upon, we can variously see them as local and diverse or as global and unified. In so doing, we can gain a sense of their ongoing evolution.

The most important feature of representation systems is that they enable, structure, represent, and communicate *meaning*. Only by using representation systems within which we can represent something *as* something (Goodman, 1968/1976) are we able to make common sense of experience. For example, we can communicate emotional experience by casting it within the metaphorical webs of our common language, which likens it to phenomena that are overt, public, tangible: "I felt *shattered*."

> By virtue of participation in culture, meaning is rendered public and shared.
> Our . . . way of life depends upon shared meanings and shared concepts and depends
> as well upon shared modes of discourse for negotiating differences in meaning and
> interpretation. (Bruner, 1990, p. 11)

In other words, by calling something a "cultural phenomenon" (this is the second aspect of our working definition of culture), we make a commitment to describing it as a *meaningful* thing. We commit ourselves to *meaning analysis* as our preferred type of research practice, and we subscribe to a particular type of *description*: "Culture is not a power, something to which social events, behaviors, institutions, or processes can be causally attributed; it is a context, something within which they can be intelligibly . . . described" (Geertz, 1973, p. 14). It is important to note, though, that culture involves more than meaning in the representational or cognitive sense. Rather,

> meanings in general, and cultural meaning systems in particular, do at least four different things. Meanings represent the world, create cultural entities, direct one to do certain things, and evoke certain feelings. These four functions of meaning—the *representational,* the *constructive,* the *directive,* and the *evocative*—are differently elaborated in particular cultural meaning systems but are always present to some degree in any system. . . . Analytically, cultural meaning systems can be treated as a very large diversified pool of knowledge, or partially shared clusters of norms, or as intersubjectively shared, symbolically created realities. (D'Andrade, 1984, pp. 96, 116)

Precursors to Symbolic Approaches to Culture and Communication

Keeping our definition of culture in the back of our minds for a moment, we will now take a brief look at the history of the Western intellectuals' interest in other cultures.

The first descriptions of other peoples' interpersonal behaviors and customs can be found in the travelogues of Herodotus (445 B.C./1949) and Xenophon (401 B.C./1962) and in Tacitus' "ethnography" *Germania* (98/1970). These reports, along with the later ones by the European explorers (Columbus, 1492-1493/1966; see Hewes, 1974, for an overview) astonish the reader with their detailed accounts of first encounters and different customs but also because they report the facility with which the explorers communicated with the Indians. It was gesture that served as a lingua franca for intercultural exchange. And when the explorers, motivated by the spirit of enlightenment that had taken hold of their own societies, began to make more systematic attempts to record native culture, communication by gesture even enabled them to engage in detailed ethnographic and linguistic fieldwork (Forster, 1777). At this time, the study of distant cultures was regarded as an important avenue toward an understanding of humanity's essence. Again and again in these travelogues, we find the writers wondering whether the emotional lives of the islanders resembled their own, whether there was psychic unity to humankind. Rousseau, "the founder of the sciences of man" (Lévi-Strauss, 1976), suggested: When one wants to study men, one must look around oneself; but to study man, one must first learn to look into the distance; one must first see differences in order to discover characteristics (Rousseau, 1967, chap. 8).

In the eighteenth century, an evolutionary account of the diversity of cultures began to emerge. Montesquieu (1901) had introduced a three-stage development of human communities from "primitive" to "savage" to "civilized." This model survived even into the beginnings of modern anthropology (Mallery, 1880/1978; Tylor, 1856) until it was finally replaced by cultural relativism (which makes any reference to degrees of development or civilization obsolete). The idea of evolution was thus already popular before Darwin began his studies. Especially Locke (1690/1959) and Condillac (1746) conceived of human knowledge as a product of the evolution of *material* sign-systems (languages) that register, store, and enable the manipulation of "information," that is, thought (see also Aarsleff, 1974; Lane, 1976). Sign-systems, according to Condillac, evolve in the communication among groups of people; he recognized the nexus of communication, cognition, and language. However, while he and some of the other philosophers during the Enlightenment were keenly aware of the relationship between knowledge and language, *communication* did not become a topic of scientific attention until much later, approximately the 1930s and 1940s. One reason for this is that, whereas a technology for recording spoken language had existed for more than 2,000 years— alphabetic writing—a technology for recording visual communication—photography and cinematography—only emerged in the nineteenth and twentieth centuries (Edwards, 1992). The existence of such a technology is arguably a precondition for the appearance of organized and systematic scientific inquiry.

In the aftermath of the "romantic" period in the European arts and literature, however, the "soft," subjective domains of human life—interpersonal relations, communication, the emotions—became the dominating theme of a flourishing body of literature, particularly in France, for example, in the works of Balzac, Flaubert, and later Proust. For most of the nineteenth century, there existed thus a division of labor between the increasingly empirical, observational sciences of man and the increasingly introspective literary accounts of human experience. When Freud finally suspended this division and made subjective, psychic experience the subject of rigorous analysis, this was perceived as a revolution (Freud, 1949). Freud's discoveries would eventually lead to an altogether new way of thinking about human relationships. The patterns of relationship and interaction that the adult person engages in are seen as "transferences" from primary childhood relationships and interaction patterns. The transference is mediated by our complex psychic organization, in particular its unconscious part, the "id" and the "primary processes" governing it.

Of great interest to the student of communication is the symbol theory inherent in Freud's view of the unconscious. In his analysis of symbolic productions such as dreams (Freud, 1955) and jokes (Freud, 1960), Freud not only discovered universal processes of symbolization, such as displacement and condensation, but also described their role in psychic organization and the structuring of experience (Jones, 1913). Its symbolic organization makes the human psyche a cultural phenomenon that is structured not unlike a language (Lacan, 1977). In contrast to some contemporary "symbols and meanings" approaches to culture, Freud never lost sight of the *repressive* character of all culture: There will always be an essential and unsurmountable difference between the desires of the human psyche and the social forms of human action and relationship that culture dictates or allows. Acquiring culture does not happen without pain and frustration (Freud, 1958; see Marcuse, 1955, for a critique).

The other great breakthrough of the nineteenth century—in addition to Freud's discovery of the unconscious—was of course Darwin's discovery of the evolution of species (Darwin, 1859/1964). With this discovery, the stage was set for the understanding of the *continuities* between human structures and abilities and their precursors on the evolutionary ladder. In this regard, Darwin's own study of the evolution of *facial expression* is of paradigmatic importance (Darwin, 1872/1955). Here, Darwin demonstrated how a genuinely *communicative* type of behavior—

along with the anatomical and physiological structures that enable it—has developed from more fundamental, purely instrumental behaviors and structures. The instrumental substructure explains the particular shape of the later, specialized communicative adaptation: The shape of a threat display is derived from direct, noncommunicative attack behavior. There is thus a continuity between forms of interaction that are developed prior to the emergence of specialized communicative displays and the shape that these displays eventually take. Communication behavior reflects its precommunicative origins. Darwin's study, in many ways still uncontested (see Ekman, 1973; Izard, 1971), was a very powerful demonstration that the human organism has evolved to its present shape partly in response to the need to communicate and maintain viable social groups (see also Ingold, 1986; Smith, 1977). Culture, however, was rather a nuisance to Darwin. In his eyes, it only obscured the true nature of man, and this he saw as its wicked purpose: to conceal our true emotions from others. Thus, while Darwin took great care to obtain information on facial displays in as many as 20 different cultures—he used reports by and corresponded with missionaries and travelers—in his interpretation of these data, he aimed exclusively at laying bare the natural order of things underneath the veil of normative cultural rules. In contemporary adaptations of Darwin's theory, however, his thesis of the continuity between human and earlier life forms has been extended so that culture and symbol systems as well as the cognitive architecture that they produce can be seen as products of the same evolutionary dynamics that have produced the human body (Donald, 1991; Maturana & Varela, 1987/1992).

The nineteenth and early twentieth centuries were the era of the emergence of the empirical sciences—and their often arbitrary disciplinary boundaries. In Germany, W. Wundt established psychology as an experimental science by postulating the parallel organization of physiological and psychological processes. In France, Durkheim secured a place for sociology by proposing that there is a realm of *social facts* that cannot be reduced to any other order of phenomena. Saussure (1964) used similar arguments to claim the independent status of *langue*—the system of rules and contrasts underlying actual speech performance—and thus linguistics. And in England and later the United States, Tylor, Frazer, Malinoswski, and Boas created two separate versions of the "science of customs" (R. Benedict), which is (social and cultural) anthropology. All of these disciplinary frameworks contributed to our present understanding of communication; but their separation made it—and continues to make it—difficult to integrate this knowledge into a unified science. Today, the split between individual-psychological approaches in the tradition of Wundt, sociological approaches in the tradition of Durkheim, and symbol-theoretic approaches in the tradition of linguistics and cultural anthropology can be felt as clearly as ever.

Wundt's *Völkerpsychologie* (1911/1975) was a monumental attempt to explain language, myth, and customs (i.e., culture) by reference to what he considered universal psychological laws of affect and expression. But despite Wundt's fame during his lifetime (his Institute of Experimental Psychology in Leipzig, the first in the world, attracted such luminaries as the anthropologist Malinowski and the sociologist G. H. Mead), today his work is largely forgotten. Despite the psychological bias of much work on communication and culture, it is all too obvious that cultural organization cannot be explained solely in terms of psychic organization. After Wundt, psychologists other than those of psychoanalytic orientation have generally refrained from any *cultural* analysis of psychic phenomena; the emergence of "cultural psychology" is a recent development (Stigler, Shweder, & Herdt, 1990).

At the same time in France, É. Durkheim developed an explanatory framework of interpersonal relations and communications as *social facts*, to be described in macrosocial categories of status, class, power, and so on. From a Durkheimian perspective, patterns of communication appear as phenomena that are shaped by, and derive their meaning from, the particular place they inhabit within the *totality* of social phenomena (Durkheim, 1895/1982). Action—particularly communicative action—is intelligible only by virtue of its determination by shared norms. In Durkheim's framework, there is a direct link between a society's moral consensus and the single actions that a society's daily life ultimately consists of. Action is a direct manifestation of a society's norms. In other words, there is no place in this framework for the individual actor who has internalized these norms and faces the constant need to reconcile them with his individual goals and motives. It was the American sociologist T. Parsons who later bridged this gap by combining the Durkheimian view of social macrostructure with a "model of the actor" (Parsons, 1937; Parsons et al., 1951). Durkheim's and Parsons's normative sociology became the dominating paradigm for sociologists in the twentieth century, until it was subjected to a penetrating methodological critique by ethnomethodologists (Cicourel, 1964; Garfinkel, 1967; see also Heritage, 1984), who argued that reference to normative rules is always a situated, interpretive, and open-ended process, not a mindless operation that automatically produces socially accepted behavior. Actors appeal to normative rules to *demonstrate* the rationality and rule-guided character of their everyday actions. Norms should therefore be studied as *cognitive* phenomena, that is, as components of members' social knowledge and practical sociological reasoning.

Durkheim also made important contributions to ethnology (it is a general characteristic of the "French school" that sociology and ethnology are not fully separated; see Bourdieu, 1977). Of great interest to the student of culture and communication, although currently not widely read, is the work of Durkheim's nephew M. Mauss (Durkheim & Mauss, 1903/1963). Mauss subjected information provided by a broad range of ethnographic literature, especially by American cultural anthropologists (see below), to a comparative analysis of elementary social forms: self- and personhood (Mauss, 1938/1979), gift exchange (Mauss, 1950/1966), and "techniques of the body" (Mauss, 1935/1973). His work demonstrated how total and pervasive the influence of culture and society on human behavior is:

> I think I can . . . recognize a girl who has been raised in a convent. In general she will walk with her fists closed. And I can still remember my third-form teacher shouting at me: Idiot! why do you walk around the whole time with your hands flapping wide open? Thus there exists education in walking. (Mauss, 1935/1973, p. 72)

Every bit of human behavior is subject to normative social control and thus becomes an element in a *code*. It is this normative structuration that gives human behavior its communicative power.

Interpersonal relations, conceived as social forms, figure prominently in the work of the German contemporary of Durkheim, G. Simmel (Simmel, 1950). To Simmel, society was "merely the name for a number of individuals connected by interaction" (p. 10); accordingly, "the description of the forms of interaction is the science of society in its strictest and most essential sense" (pp. 20-21). In some of Simmel's large, scattered, complex, and little-known oeuvre (as a Jew in Germany, Simmel had considerable difficulty gaining professional recognition), he addresses phenomena at the boundary of individual and society—"skin phenomena," one might say—in which individual and social determinations intersect, for example, shame (a social emotion, typically felt in public) and secrecy (a form of individuation, the withholding of knowledge from "the public domain"). Simmel has written a large number of studies of just the kinds of entities contemporary ethnographers of communication and practitioners of "cultural studies" are fond of: meals, arguing, jewelry, gratitude, letters, female culture, and the "sociology of the senses" (Simmel, 1924). Some of his articles have appeared in the *American Journal of Sociology* (Simmel, 1902, 1903-1904, 1905-1906).

The last intellectual movement originating around the turn of the century that should be mentioned here before we turn to the symbols and meanings approaches is *social anthropology* (Stocking, 1968, 1987). (Conventional wisdom labels British anthropology "social" and American anthropology "cultural." The terminology is not without merits, because it reflects the intellectual roots of the British school in Durkheimian and Marxian sociology—where ideational phenomena are considered "superstructure": reflections of "material," economic, and power relations; and the roots of cultural anthropology in eighteenth- and nineteenth-century philosophical idealism [Kant, von Humboldt].) Social anthropology is "sociological" in that it interprets cultural phenomena as social forms-cum-symbolic representations. Elementary relationships in a society (e.g., kin relations) constitute social forms that are defined by mutual rights and obligations, and they are symbolically represented in rituals, forms of address, kinship terms, and so on. Representations, however, are not simple reflections of the social world; they are themselves subject to social determinations. For example, how rigidly the rules of address for kinfolk must be followed is a function of the degree of "ritualism" of a society at a given point in time—which is itself a sociological state of affairs (Douglas, 1970; Evans-Pritchard, 1964).

The classic ethnographies by Malinowski (1922, 1965), as well as his statement of functionalism in anthropology (1944), are among the better known examples of early work in social anthropology. An important contribution to the study of communication is Radcliffe-Browne's (1965) analysis of the *joking relationship*.

Radcliffe-Browne suggests that, in many relationships that involve contradictory social obligations (e.g., social proximity and avoidance as in the son-in-law/ mother-in-law relationship), humor and joking serve as an institutionalized conflict resolution mechanism; they allow the concurrent enactment of ambivalent sentiments. Among more recent contributions to social anthropology, Leach (1976) and Douglas (1970) have further explored the relationships between economic transactions and acts of communication (Leach) as well as the social-structural shaping of symbolic universes (Douglas).

Culture, Language, and Relativity

While there is much affinity between British social anthropology and the "French school," American cultural and linguistic anthropology has roots in the German idealist and romantic philosophy of the eighteenth and nineteenth centuries (Kant, Herder, von Humboldt). The person who is generally considered as the founder of these disciplines in America, Franz Boas, as well as the linguist E. Sapir, were German-born Jews who brought this tradition with them when they emigrated to America. Boas and Sapir developed the ideas of W. von Humboldt into an empirical science and transformed the linguistic study of "mentality" into an analysis of "culture"; what is common to both versions of the program is the analysis of categories of grammar as categories of experience.

Boas gathered his first linguistic "fieldwork" experience by studying the language of three Bella Coola Indians who were exhibited in Berlin during the 1886 World's Fair. Motivated by this initial work, he subsequently traveled to the American Pacific Northwest and eventually launched one of the major projects of linguistic research, the *Handbook of American Indian Languages* (Boas, 1911/1966a). This project secured invaluable linguistic and ethnological information about the Native Americans at a time when some speakers of most of the languages were still alive. At the same time, these languages proved to be so fundamentally different from the Indo-European languages that the nineteenth-century linguists in Germany had so successfully reconstructed that the conventional grammatical categories that were previously used in linguistic description—most of them had been taken from Latin grammars—turned out to be of little use in organizing the American materials. For hundreds of years, missionaries had confidently misrepresented "exotic" languages in these terms. But now it became clear that new categories were needed to describe languages such as Kwakiutl or Bella Coola. Moreover, the categories that would properly organize the data would first have to be *discovered* in the process of analysis. Not even concepts as fundamental and seemingly universal as "word" and "sentence" could be taken for granted any longer: There are languages in North America (e.g., Apache and Inuit) that can express entire propositions in single, compound words. Or take the noun-category *case* (nominative, accusative, and so on): Some languages have other case sets than Latin (e.g., ergative, absolutive); others have no nominal case marking at all (e.g., English). Similarly, there are languages without the category *gender*, and others with different gender sets (animate-inanimate, rather than masculine-feminine, or animate moving, animate at rest, inanimate long, inanimate round, inanimate high, and inanimate collective, as is the case in Sioux). Importantly, languages not only differ in what they *allow* one—readily—to say, but also in what they *require* one to say, that is, in the distinctions that are *obligatory* in the language. Finally, these categories are not just empty forms but categories of *experience*, that is, *meanings*. "Languages differ not only in the character of their constituent phonetic elements and sound-clusters, but also in the groups of ideas that find expression in fixed phonetic groups" (Boas, 1911/1966a, p. 20; see also Malinowski, 1923).

The study of "exotic" languages thus is the single most important paradigm for the study of "other cultures." It provides a method for understanding different categories of experience—without imposing one's own categories in the process of description. Linguistic analysis thus shows one way out of ethnocentrism; it enables the researcher to study "other mentalities" using methodical procedures with agreed-upon standards of adequacy and validity. The promise is that, by organizing our linguistic data properly so that they can "speak for themselves," we will be enabled to grasp the other's worldview and thus come to understand, if only to a limited extent, the other mind. The condition is that we relinquish our own preconceived cultural categories, such as "noun/verb," "masculine/feminine," or even "we/you." In other words, understanding other cultures, in this view, is not at all a mystical experience, nor does it have much to do with empathy. It means being able to explicate conceptual distinctions and categories of experience that are encoded in a language.

This view of "linguistic relativity," while already implicit in Boas's approach to culture, was fully articulated not by Boas but by E. Sapir (1921) and B. L. Whorf (1956). Sapir (1921) wrote:

The relation between language and experience is often misunderstood. Language is not merely a more or less systematic inventory of the various items of experience which seem relevant to the individual, . . . but is also a self-contained, creative symbolic organization, which not only refers to experience largely acquired without its help but actually defines experience for us (p. 221)

The "Sapir-Whorf hypothesis" has been and continues to be of considerable influence in linguistics and linguistic anthropology (for recent contributions, see Lucy, 1992a, 1992b; Silverstein, 1976; for overviews, Hill & Mannheim, 1992; Rosch, 1987). Research by a growing number of researchers, however, who refer to their work as "prototype theory" (see Taylor, 1989) or "cognitive linguistics" (Langacker, 1987; Rudzka-Ostyn, 1988), shows that relativism can live in a happy marriage with universalism: While linguistic structures at all levels (vocabulary, syntax, and so on) show a great deal of variation, they also reveal a considerable amount of cross-linguistic similarity, in particular in central or basic constructions. For example, research on color terms has shown that these must have evolved according to a universal sequence: The first distinction is black-white (or dark-light), then red is added, then blue/green, and so on (Berlin & Kay, 1969). In all languages, the most basic sentence pattern centers on an animate subject—typically human—that acts upon an inanimate object; active sentences are universally less complex than passive ones; animate nouns are more easily made the head of a relative sentence than inanimate ones, and so on (Comrie, 1981). These linguistic facts indicate that there are indeed universal, basic human experiences—bodily experiences such as gravity, erect posture, movement, agency, manipulation, as well as sensory perception—and that these figure prominently in language structure (Johnson, 1987; Lakoff, 1987). Roughly, the type of event that is most easily encoded in any language is a human event: one brought about and experienced subjectively by a human being. Cultural diversity is always an elaboration of these universal foundations. This is in line with what appears to be the historical record: namely, that humanity and its various cultures developed during thousands and thousands of years of migration away from a common birthplace in Africa.

Is linguistic relativity of interest to students of culture and interpersonal communication? Yes, in several respects. First of all, of course, most communication involves language, and whenever that is the case, cultural comparison raises the issue of *translation* across language systems. One-to-one translations of terms will not do, because we have to take into account the value that the terms have within the "system" of the language: A simple kinship term such as *brother* can have a different value, for example, when members of the same age-grade (or initiation cohort) are also considered brothers. The framework of analysis that Boas established allows us to systematically account for these differences. Second, interpersonal communication and relations are themselves *conceptualized* in different ways in different cultures, and the concepts involved are in need of the same kind of unbiased cultural explication. Whenever human conduct is subjected to interpretive analysis, linguistic relativity becomes an issue.

But Boas's work far transcended the study of culture as language. Another program of research that he helped initiate has been "culture and personality." It was actually E. Sapir who first suggested that language should be seen as only one among various cultural communication systems, and he also suggested that "personality" be made an object of cultural analysis (Sapir, 1927/1991, 1934). Before we turn to the "culture and personality" school, we must ascertain the *nature* of the contribution that Boas has made. The most important aspect of his work is the demonstration that anything that can properly be called "cultural" is *learned*—and not hereditary (Boas, 1940). There is thus no *genetic* basis to differences in human traits, customs, or mentality; even physical traits can in part be environmentally induced (Boas, 1912). The only important process involved in the survival of cultures is therefore *transmission*, and the interaction between the generations—the "knowing" and the "novices"—is thus of particular interest. Culture is dependent on communication; only what can be communicated has a chance to survive in the realm of culture (see D'Andrade, 1981). There is no merit at all to the notion of "racial character" or to the claim, propagated especially by Nazi "anthropologists," that "racial descent is the determining cause for the character of a people" (Boas, 1932). Much of Boas's scientific energy was spent on clarifying this. The scientific study of culture thus emerged from the intellectual fight against the racial ideology of the Nazis and of the "eugenic" movement in the United States. What Boas could neither anticipate nor prevent was that, over time, the term *culture* would be put to ideological uses not unlike those of "race." "Ethnic cleansing" is machinery for cultural purification. Boas himself was very aware that there is no more cultural "purity" than there is "purity" of race. In 1928 he wrote: "We should remember that people of pure descent or of a pure racial type are not found in any part of Europe" (p. 85). Every human being alive is a "racial" and cultural hybrid.

Culture and Personality

The study of "culture and personality," of the acquisition of "national character" by individual members of societies, was initiated by a small circle of intimately related anthropologists with the energetic Margaret Mead at its center and including E. Sapir, R. Benedict, R. Fortune, and G. Bateson (see also Kluckhohn et al., 1948). We describe this school of thought by reviewing three representative studies: Benedict's extremely popular book *Patterns of Culture* (Benedict, 1934) and two far less popular, but nevertheless highly influential studies by G. Bateson, *Naven* (Bateson, 1936/1958) and the "photographic analysis" of *Balinese Character* that he produced with M. Mead (Bateson & Mead, 1942). All of these works—and the "culture and personality" school as a whole—sought to analyze cultures as *integrated wholes* that manifest themselves equally in symbols, customs, and patterns of thought, feeling, and behavior.

Benedict used the term *configuration* to refer to patterns of cultural integration, a term she adopted from Gestalt psychology. Human communities, she suggested, select their cultural institutions from a "great arc" of possibilities (Benedict, 1934, p. 24). It is the particular configuration of choices from this common matrix that makes for the "pattern" of a culture. A "pattern of culture" is thus analogous to the sound pattern of a language—its selection from among possible human sounds and sound sequences that makes up its phonological structure. Patterning is needed in both cases to bring about *intelligibility*.

> A culture that capitalized even a considerable proportion of these [possibilities] would be as unintelligible as a language that used all the clicks, all the glottal stops, all the labials, dentals, sibilants, and gutturals from voiceless to voiced and from oral to nasal. Its identity as a culture depends upon the selection of some segments of this arc. (p. 24)

But, of course, the "great arc" of possibilities contains much more than possible language sounds. It embraces all the possible human ways of dealing with life's circumstances and crises—coming of age, marriage, child rearing, death—all possible ways of dealing with emotion, frustration, and sexual desire; all possible cultural definitions of "normality" and deviance (p. 258); all cultural institutions—initiation, marriage, kinship, government—and, finally, all possible ways of conducting oneself and interacting with others. The selections that a culture makes from these sets form consistent clusters; only certain selections "go together."

> Cultures . . . are more than the sum of their parts. . . . A culture, like an individual, is a more or less consistent pattern of thought and action. . . . This integration of cultures is not in the least mystical. It is the same process by which a style in art comes into being and exists. (pp. 46-47)

Benedict's comparison with style in art points to one of the sources of her work, the analysis of "Weltanschauungen" by the philosopher W. Dilthey, the founder of "hermeneutics" (Dilthey, 1977). Dilthey's studies of worldviews in both philosophical and everyday thinking were framed as cultural history and modeled after art history.

Geertz has pointed out that, to Benedict, "culture" really means "personality writ large" (Geertz, 1988). The best way to characterize a cultural configuration therefore is to describe the prevailing personality type, the prevailing way of the culture's members of carrying themselves, of feeling, and of relating to one another. Benedict drew upon a simple two-way typology that Nietzsche had devised in his study of the ancient Greeks (Nietzsche, 1927) to mark the poles of the arc of possible cultural personality types: the "Appollonian" versus the "Dionysian." The Appollonian is a quintessential middle-of-the-roader, bound by tradition, striving for measure and balance, distrustful of individualism and of any form of ecstatic experience. The Dionysian seeks to find the value of existence in experiences that transcend the mundane order of things—trance, ecstasy, visionary experiences, and so on. Most cultures range somewhere between these poles, taking elements from both.

In *Patterns of Culture* (Benedict, 1934), Benedict reinterprets three ethnographic accounts in light of this typology: R. Bunzel's study of the Zuñi (Bunzel, 1932/1992), a Pueblo people of the American Southwest; R. Fortune's description of the Dobu islanders off the Southern coast of New Guinea (Fortune, 1932); and Boas's work on the Kwakiutl of the Pacific Northwest (Boas, 1966b). We will briefly review her account of the first two groups to flesh out her view of cultural "configurations." The measured Zuñi of the American Southwest are an Appollonian people in the largely Dionysian world that was native North America. While the Dionysian Dakota, for example, may show their grief over the death of a child by "coming naked into the camp, wailing" (p. 112), the Zuñi

> do not . . . convert mourning for a near relative into an ambitious display or a terror situation. They treat it as loss, and as important loss. But they provide detailed techniques for getting past it as quickly and with as little violence as possible. The emphasis is upon making the mourner forget. (p. 109)

Among the Zuñi, the cultural emphasis thus is upon *containing* the emotions so that the individual can continue to participate in the moderate, unemotional ways of the community. The Zuñi attribute intrinsic value to these communal practices; in their "Hellenic" view (p. 79), communal life per se is civilizing. Among the Zuñi the "internal" life of the person is subsumed to the survival needs of the community. The "folk psychology" of the people and the values they place upon felt emotions and their external expression are centered on the requirements of harmonious social life; a premium is placed on social accommodation.

On the island of Dobu, the relationship between individual and society is conceptualized almost in opposite terms, and this has much to do with the structure of the society. While Zuñi society is highly integrated, Dobu society is fragmented, and social life is potentially explosive. Accordingly, folk psychology and philosophy place the individual—that is, one's own needs—in the center of attention, and others are primarily seen as potential dangers to one's well-being. The Dobu islanders count as the savages in the otherwise Appollonian archipelago off southern New Guinea, where they live. "They are lawless and treacherous. . . . The social forms which obtain in Dobu put a premium upon ill-will and treachery and make of them the recognized virtues of their society" (p. 131). The hostile tendencies in Dobuan communicative and community life are maximized by a bizarre lineage and residence pattern. The Dobu are matrilineal; the *susu* (mother's milk), the matrilineal group, is the most stable social unit, and most of Dobu social life takes place inside its boundaries. But the groups are so small that exogamy is required; one's spouse is therefore always from a hostile group. The spouse that marries into the unit is met with all the hostility that an intruder should expect. He or she is subjected to constant humiliation. But this ordeal befalls both spouses in alternating years, for this is how the Dobuans, curiously, resolve the problem of locality and lineage: The couple lives in her village in one year, in his in the next. Add to this the fact that adultery is "a favorite pastime" (p. 138), and one has all the ingredients for a regime of terror and suspicion even in the most intimate of human relationships. "The person with whom one shares the bed is the person to charge with one's fatal illness" (p. 160). The Dobuans live in a world of constant terror, fear, and insecurity.

> Behind a show of friendship, behind the evidences of co-operation, in every field of life, the Dobuan believes that he has only treachery to expect. Everyone else's best endeavours . . . are directed toward bringing his own plans to confusion and ruin.
> (p. 171)

Morality is a kind of zero-sum game: "Any man's gain is another's loss" (p. 146). And the formula equivalent to our saying "thank you" when we receive a gift, is this: "If you now poison me, how should I repay you?" (p. 166).

Lineage and residence rules thus create a context that produces and admits only certain types of emotions; every experience is mediated by a pervasive feeling of fear and paranoia. The configuration necessitates internal and external safeguards to enable social interaction at all: a world of manoeuvering, strong-arming, deceit where "sincerity" and "authenticity" would be impossible moral standards.

The comparison of Zuñi and Dobu society shows the interdependence of social structure and organization on the one hand and prevailing personality type on the other. The two are mediated by forms of interaction that are, in any society, shaped by societal norms and that have pervasive influence on individual psychology. However, all of these forms are possibilities that encompass human nature: Each culture represents a selection.

Dionysian behaviour is stressed in the institutions of certain cultures because it is a permanent possibility in individual psychology, but it is stressed in certain cultures and not in others because of historical events that have in one place fostered its development and in others have ruled it out. (p. 233)

Cultural patterns are local phenomena: The Zuñi are local exceptions to the Dionysian principles that otherwise characterize aboriginal North America, and the Dobuans are savages among their neighbors. There is, in other words, no connection between culture and place (or climate) or between culture and genetic relationships between peoples. Cultural patterns develop and change via *diffusion.*

For Benedict, the analysis of cultural patterns of other societies was also a way of critically reflecting upon the patterns of one's own. Anthropology, to her, is *cultural critique* (Marcus & Fischer, 1986). Geertz (1988) has said about her work that "the culturally at hand is made odd and arbitrary, the culturally distant, logical and straightforward. Our own forms of life become strange customs of a strange people" (p. 106). Benedict (1934) herself described the critical intentions of her work in these words:

There is no royal road to Utopia. There is, however, one difficult exercise to which we may accustom ourselves as we become increasingly culture conscious. We may train ourselves to pass judgment upon the dominant traits of our own civilization. (p. 249)

The Concept "Ethos"

In his book *Naven* (Bateson, 1936/1958), Gregory Bateson suggested a conceptual subdivision of Benedict's concept "configuration." He distinguished the *eidos* from the *ethos* of a culture. "The eidos of a culture is an expression of the standardized cognitive aspects of the individuals, while the ethos is the corresponding expression of their standardized affective aspects" (p. 33). But he also points out that these are only "alternative ways of arranging the data" (p. 296). Bateson has always been very conscious of the fact that explanations of the data are first of all *abstractions.* To say that a behavior is culturally motivated means to subject it to a *class* of descriptions; it is not a reference to a cause: "If 'ethos,' 'social structure,' 'economics,' etc. are words in that language which describes how scientists arrange data, then these words cannot be used to 'explain' phenomena" (p. 281).

In his study of the Iatmul in New Guinea, Bateson addressed their ethos, the ways "in which [their] emotional life . . . is organized in culturally standardized forms" (Bateson & Mead, 1942, p. xi). *Organization,* however, in Bateson's view refers to a *process*; the term is more than just another name for "structure." It means the *process* of shaping personality in contexts of interaction. Among Bateson's many contributions to the study of culture, communication, and personality, his conceptualizations of phenomena in processual terms are perhaps the most important ones. In *Naven,* he interprets a ritual (*Naven* is its name) in terms of its adaptive functions within the ongoing structuration of Iatmul society. The ritual is based upon transvestitism. Men and women exchange not only clothes but also roles. The function of the ritual thus is that of a self-corrective mechanism that counteracts "schismogenetic" forces operating within Iatmul society and interaction. The Iatmul have a divided ethos: Men strive to present themselves in spectacular acts of performance;

women, in contrast, are resigned to an ethos of admiration and spectatorship. The two patterns of behavior thus stand in complementary relation to one another. And, each interaction between men and women that follows this pattern will further reinforce the differences and thus narrow the range of possibilities of action for both. Bateson (1936/1958) calls this process of cumulative interaction *complementary schismogenesis*. Schismogenesis is

> a process of differentiation in the norms of individual behavior resulting from cumulative interaction between individuals. (p. 175)
> . . . Many systems of relationship, either between individuals or groups of individuals, contain a tendency towards progressive change. . . . A must necessarily become more and more assertive, while B will become more and more submissive. . . . Progressive changes of this sort we may describe as complementary schismogenesis. (p. 176)

The more Iatmul men interact with Iatmul women, the more exaggerated and spectacular their actions will become and the more passive and admiring will be the behavior of the women. However, wherever such schismogenetic, cumulative interactions become habitual and binding, personality distortions result.

> The distortion is a progressive specialization in certain directions and results in a corresponding under-development of other sides of the personality. Thus the members of each group see the stunted parts of their own affective life fully developed—indeed overdeveloped—in the members of the other group. It is in such situations that mutual envy arises. (p. 188)

The very structure of Iatmul interaction, then, bears the seed of destruction of Iatmul society. The *Naven* ceremony, with its exchange of roles and identities, suspends and counteracts this schismogenetic process: It provides both groups with contrasting experiences, in effect allowing each party to "see" itself from within the identity of the other—and thus the "latent," unexpressed, complementary part of the self.

Bateson has presented in *Naven* the fundamentals of a theory of character formation. Personality is formed by the cumulative patterning of interaction—which is itself an adaptation to overarching needs of group integration.

> The individual in a symmetrical relationship with another will tend, perhaps unconsciously, to form the habit of acting as if he expected symmetry in further encounters with all other individuals. The ground is thus laid for progressive change. As a given individual learns patterns of symmetrical behavior he not only comes to expect this type of behavior in others, but also acts in such a way that others will experience those contexts in which they in turn will learn symmetrical behavior. . . . They will act back upon the initial individual to produce further change in him in the same direction. (p. 286)

"Personality" is thus a "sedimentation" of the patterning of interactional contexts. It is one manifestation of a larger system that relevantly includes all the other "personalities" that someone regularly interacts with, especially the other members of his or her primary group or family. Bateson later applied this framework of analysis that he first developed in the study of the Naven ritual, to the study of personality disorders, in particular schizophrenia, which he interpreted as an adaptation to persistent, inescapable paradoxes in a person's primary relationships (Bateson, 1972).

The viability and value of Bateson's "formal" method of analyzing communication and culture already became apparent in *Balinese Character* (Bateson & Mead, 1942). In this study, Bateson and Mead used *photographs* as their main body of data. It thus presents a study based upon completely innovative ways of gathering and analysis of data on human interaction and cultural life,

> a new method of stating the intangible relationships among different types of culturally standardized behavior by placing side by side mutually relevant photographs. Pieces of behavior—a trance dancer being carried in procession, a man looking up at an aeroplane, a servant greeting his master in a play, the painting of a dream—may all be relevant to a single discussion: the same emotional thread may run through them. (p. xii)

The account of Balinese culture is the product of *visual abstraction.* By selecting 700 from among 25,000 photographs, and by juxtaposing photographs taken in different contexts and representing different domains of social life, as well as simply by focusing on the often neglected *visual* aspects of human behavior, Bateson and Mead showed how "the Balinese—[through] the way in which they, as living persons, moving, standing, eating, sleeping, dancing, and going into trance, embody that abstraction which (after we have abstracted it) we technically call culture" (p. xii).

Among the features of the Balinese ethos that are revealed by the photographs (and their arrangement) are the preference for crowds and the resulting limited possibilities for withdrawal and individuation. The Balinese prefer being in crowds to being alone. But while they are in a crowd, they might withdraw. They fall into a trancelike state of "awayness." The "social organization of attention" (Chance & Larsen, 1976) in Balinese society explains an important feature of mother-child interaction, which in turn has important adaptive functions for the survival of Balinese culture. In contrast to the Iatmul culture that Bateson had previously studied, Balinese culture is free of schismogenetic processes. In contrast, Balinese culture—behavior, music, feeling—is "anticlimactic." The Balinese *avoid* cumulative processes altogether. The patterning of mother-child interaction is the paradigmatic experience in which the Balinese acquire this disposition. A characteristic sequence involves the mother's physical and emotional stimulation of her infant to the point that the child is becoming excited; at that moment, the mother will withdraw her attention from the child. She in effect invalidates the child's experience. While children initially react with frustration and bewilderment to this pattern, they later internalize it and adapt to it via "unresponsiveness," that is, an avoidance of overly stimulating moments. This disposition, according to the authors, is an essential foundation of Balinese society.

Balinese Character has suffered from the "logocentric" bias of Western science. It is only recently that visual research begins to play a notable role in the study of communication and culture (Collier & Collier, 1986).

Symbolic Anthropology

We will now make a big leap and review a very different approach to the study of culture and communication, the "symbolic anthropology" of C. Geertz (1973,

1984). Like the earlier, "configurational" approaches to anthropology, Geertz aims at accounts of cultures as integrated wholes. His approach concentrates on the *symbolic* aspects of culture. In contrast to other contemporary versions of the "symbols and meanings" approach to culture (e.g., cognitive anthropology), Geertz insists that "culture," "meaning," and "mind" (i.e., culture as "ideation") are *overt, public* phenomena. Culture is public because meaning is (Geertz, 1973, p. 12). "Thinking is a matter of trafficking in the symbolic forms available in one or another community. . . . The community is the shop where thoughts get constructed or deconstructed" (Geertz, 1983, p. 153). Meaning and intention are available to us in the symbols that the natives use: in the language they speak, the art they appreciate, the names they give one another. What we in effect do when we study conduct in its cultural context is to "sort out [its] structures of signification" (Geertz, 1973, p. 9) and to "freeze" its communicated sense into an enduring text.

> Ethnographic description . . . is interpretive; what it is interpretive of is the flow of social discourse; and the interpreting involved consists in trying to rescue the "said" of such discourse from its perishing occasions and fix it in perusable terms. . . . [Another] characteristic of such description [is] . . .: it is microscopic. (Geertz, 1973, p. 20)

Studying human behavior in its cultural context is therefore in some respects like interpreting a poem.

> The anthropologist has to . . . tack between . . . two sorts of descriptions—between increasingly fine-comb observations (of how Javanese distinguish feelings, Balinese name children, Moroccans refer to acquaintances) and increasingly synoptic characterizations ("quietism," "dramatism," "contextualism")—in such a way that, held in the mind together, they present a credible, fleshed out picture of a human form of life. . . . A conception which . . . brings it rather closer to what a critic does to illumine a poem than what an astronomer does to account for a star. (Geertz, 1983, p. 10)

One of the things we must know about to properly understand how the natives conduct their communicative dealings with one another is what, to them, is "personhood." What we call "the self" is not the same thing everywhere, and people's varying conceptions of what it means to be a human person affect the way they relate to and communicate with one another. Interaction styles, in other words, have "folk-philosophical" and "folk-psychological" (Bruner, 1990) underpinnings. For example, the Javanese conception of the person is predicated upon two pairs of conceptual opposites: "inside" and "outside," and "refined" and "vulgar." In contrast to Western conceptions, which regard the outside as a symptom or expression of processes going on "inside" the person, in Java the two realms are seen as independent. Each is subject to its own laws and rules, but neither is in any way indicative of what Westerners perceive as "individuality." "Subjective feeling . . . is considered to be . . . identical across all individuals, and the external actions, movements, postures, speech . . . [are also] conceived as in its essence invariant from one individual to the next" (Geertz, 1984, p. 127).

> The goal is to be *alus* (pure, refined, polished, civilized) in both the separated realms of the self. . . . Through meditation, the civilized man thins out his emotional life to a kind of constant hum; through etiquette, he both shields that life from external disruptions and regularizes his outer behavior in such a way that it appears to others as

a predictable, undisturbing, elegant, and rather vacant set of choreographed motions and settled forms of speech. (p. 128)

What appears as "cultural style," then, is intimately interwoven with metapsychological and metasocial beliefs of a people. Cultural analysis must go beyond mere description and capture the underlying meaning systems that motivate the style.

Java stands in sharp contrast to the small island of Bali just off of its eastern shore—which has retained and developed its flamboyant Hindu traditions. "What is philosophy in Java is theater in Bali" (Geertz, 1984, p. 128). But the Balinese symbolic universe, too, can be understood by focusing on the concept of the self (or its local equivalent). Among the symbolic phenomena pertaining to it are *naming practices*, which constitute "symbolic orders of person-definition" (p. 368). In Bali, they are depersonalizing: the Balinese bear birth-order names (they are called "the third," or "the second"); titles; and—once they become parents—tecnonyms ("the mother of . . ."). Nothing in their names leads the Balinese to believe that they are "someone special." Rather, each time someone calls them by their name, they are reminded that they are "perishing" (p. 390), mere moments in the passage of time, "dramatis personae" in an eternal, spiritual play.

> There is in Bali a persistent and systematic attempt to stylize all aspects of personal expression to the point where anything idiosyncratic, anything characteristic of the individual . . . is muted in favor of his assigned place in the continuing . . . pageant that is Balinese life. (Geertz, 1984, p. 128)

This cultural configuration—"theater of status" as he calls it—is complemented by appropriate kinds of emotion. The Balinese, according to Geertz, are haunted by stage fright, *lek,* the fear that they might botch their acts, "that . . . an aesthetic illusion will not be maintained, that the actor will show through his part and the part thus dissolve into the actor."

> When this occurs . . ., the immediacy of the moment is felt with an excruciating intensity, and men become unwilling consociates locked in mutual embarrassment, as though they had inadvertently intruded upon one another's privacy. *Lek* is the fear of *faux pas.* (Geertz, 1973, p. 402)

Balinese social intercourse is "studied game and drama" (p. 400), but it is drama without climax and overt passion. Passion and violence (very much part of the Balinese psyche, as the 1965 massacres have shown) are enacted in a segregated, symbolic domain, the cockfight. Like the transvestitism of the *Naven* ceremonies, the Balinese cockfight "brings to imaginative realization a dimension of Balinese experience normally well-obscured from view" (p. 444), namely, the violent emotional underpinnings of the rigid status hierarchy. The function of the cockfight is to interpret this hidden dimension. "It provides a metasocial commentary. . . . It is a Balinese reading of Balinese experience, a story they tell themselves about themselves" (p. 448).

Ritual, ceremony, gambling, and cockfights are all constitutive parts of the overall symbolic configuration that is Balinese culture. The existence of the dramatic realm "gambling" relinquishes the expressive requirements made upon other sectors of social intercourse. This is to say that, unless we analyze a culture's self-representation in all of its rituals and theatrical performances, we may be reading only half the story. For, everyday life always represses certain aspects of social and psychic organization and obscures them from our view. These find their way to the surface in circumscribed domains of theatrical action.

The Person Behind the Smile

Geertz presents us with a highly integrated account of Bali, and, not unlike Benedict, he makes the "others" appear exotic: Balinese selves, values, and forms of life are entirely different than ours. The Balinese not only live in a different culture, they are different *persons*. Our only chance to make sense of them is not empathy but the explication of the structures of signification in their symbolic productions.

However, yet another account of Balinese culture challenges Geertz's "theatrical" image. The Norwegian anthropologist U. Wikan has taken a very different approach and written a book about one Balinese woman, Suriati, in an attempt to explain one single public expression on Suriati's part: in line with what her culture demanded of her, Suriati smiled when she told Wikan that her fiancé had died the night before (Wikan, 1990). How did Suriati manage? And what does this management of emotion and expression imply for the conduct of interpersonal communication in Bali?

Wikan's analysis exhibits a pervasive dilemma of Balinese interpersonal life. The dilemma is that, according to the assumptions of their own culture, the Balinese are "inscrutable to one another." The culture puts a premium on keeping a *bright face*. There are many reasons for this. One is that the Balinese have a strong fear of black magic—and believe that anger causes it. Accordingly, they must constantly reassure one another that they are not angry—which they do by maintaining a bright face. But they also realize that, in this fashion, they *hide* their feelings from one another. There is a paradoxical logic to the Balinese rules of emotional expression.

> Balinese are perpetually preoccupied to decipher each other's hidden hearts. So frightful are the consequences that anger or offense may work, it is necessary to be deeply preoccupied. So the "bright" face and composure, while pleasing to humans and gods, also, paradoxically, encapsulate people's fears. For the will to do magic is set in motion by feeling-thoughts that may never be expressed. This sobering realization, that the true feelings of others are inscrutably hidden behind their bright faces and polite demeanors, presents Balinese with an everyday existential problem. (p. 43)

Such paradoxes of expression are not unique to Balinese society but occur in all societies that conceptualize and organize expression as public performance.

These three accounts of Bali that we have reviewed all concentrate on similar situations and experiences in daily life: What does a Balinese experience in a crowd? What is involved in the attitude that Bateson and Mead call "away"? What is the meaning of smiling in public and private situations? What is the Balinese inner experience in this context, and what is the nature of the social forces that shape Balinese subjective experience? What, in sum, is the nature of the relationship between affect, social interaction, expression, and public life?

The titles of the texts are evocative of the different ways in which their authors seek to capture these subtle interfaces of culture, affect, and interpersonal relations.

Balinese Character: A Photographic Analysis represents an effort to capture personality as visible style, as an *aesthetic* phenomenon. The "character" emerges in the data during the process of creating visual records. This is an *aesthetic* analysis, based upon a notion of culture as style. Geertz's study is called "Person, Time, and Conduct" and thus refers to very general experiential categories that are then synthesized into a comparative "philosophical" account of the entire cultural configuration. Geertz uncovers these categories through the analysis of symbolic systems: naming, calendars, rituals, and so on. The nexus that makes the culture what it is appears in each and every cultural domain. Wikan, finally, has given her book a title that is a verb marked for ongoing action and thus indexes an ongoing practical concern: *Managing Turbulent Hearts.* Her book shows the individual member of the culture in the *process* of the ongoing struggle that is her life in the culture, a process in which she is asked to manage her emotions so that she can genuinely show a "bright face." In her account, culture reveals its repressive nature as the flip side of the bright face. There is nothing glamorous to the theatricality of Balinese life as seen from Suriati's perspective. Nor is Suriati such a stranger to us: While we do not share her experiences, we can "picture" them and we can identify with the pain that she feels while she smiles and hides her sadness.

How distant and strange another culture, its members, and their actions appear to us is thus to a great extent dependent upon the perspective and the "unit of analysis" that we choose. *People* can easily be made seem familiar to us; ceremonies, beliefs, customs are easily made to appear strange. The title of Wikan's book also suggests that the human concern that it expresses is not restricted to a particular culture. It is a play on A. Hochschild's book *The Managed Heart* (Hochschild, 1983), a study of American airline stewardesses. Airline companies sell the flight attendant's smile as a commodity, and her feelings become commercialized: The company subsumes the stewardess's emotions and makes them components of the process of service delivery. The boundary separating self and social world is driven deeper inside the person; the self is no longer private. As a result, the regulative interpersonal concept "authenticity" loses its meaning. The logic of interpersonal relations changes when this happens. In Hochschild's view, we lose our natural ability to feel and to learn "how we are doing" in interpersonal relations. The commercialization of feeling alters the selves that participate in interaction and destroys human sensibilities acquired in the process of evolution. The social context—Bali versus Delta Airlines—differs, but the processes involved and the alienation caused by them are similar; human expression is modified and expropriated under the influence of repressive sociocultural demands.

To Hochschild and other critical researchers of human communication, the professionalization of communication involves a process of *alienation* of self and body, self and expression, and self and other. Others scholars, however, notably N. Elias (1978, 1983), have interpreted the historical development of normative rules of expression and conduct as a "civilizing process" in which we acquire techniques of *autonomous* expressive and affective control. Elias's work—sometimes referred to as "configurational sociology"—can be compared with Benedict's analysis of cultural configurations: Whereas Benedict places societies and the prevailing social forms of conduct, feeling, and communication in a cross-culturally comparative perspective, Elias shows the historical variation of human behavior as it unfolds along with changing modes of production, power, and social control. Elias is particularly interested in the representational aspects of interpersonal behavior, that is, in the question of how social formations of interaction are used to display social structure. An enlightening example is his analysis of the *levée*, the daily ceremony enacted when the French king Louis XIV got up in the morning; every movement in this ceremony was used as a codified symbolic resource to express the current status hierarchy at the court. Court societies are of particular interest to those who are interested in the historical origins of manners and rules of interpersonal conduct, because they often have been the birthplace from which these norms subsequently trickled down into the society at large; note the term *courtesy*.

In contrast to the current interest in cultural variations in human conduct and communication, only few scholars currently devote their interest to historical development; an important explanatory dimension is thereby lost. One other name that deserves to be mentioned here is that of R. Sennett (1977, 1990). Sennett has provided a penetrating analysis of the changing character of the public self and its interactions in the large European cities during the eighteenth and nineteenth centuries. The cities were agglomerations of strangers, and this created problems of credibility for the people: The meanings of their respective expressions and actions were no longer embedded in and guaranteed by intimate mutual knowledge. Codes of public behavior therefore had to generate their own criteria of credibility, and these are dramatically different than those that we rely upon today. Today, we associate authenticity with spontaneity; an expression is the more authentic the less it is premeditated. We expect to be *overcome* by emotion; otherwise the emotion is perceived as shallow if not "fake." In contrast, in the eighteenth century in France, for example, it was common for people, men and women alike, to break out in tears and weep loudly during theater performances. When the actors managed to elicit particularly strong emotions, the audience often interrupted the play to have the scene performed again—often several times, each time with the same overwhelming emotional effects. The authenticity of the audience's emotional response, "unnatural" though it may seem to us, was never in question.

The Anthropology of Emotion

Emotions are at the center of various contemporary research programs in the social sciences, and the cultural variability of emotions and emotional expression is one of the main themes of this research. One program—which in some ways continues the tradition of the "culture and personality" framework—is the *anthropology of emotions* (Lutz & White, 1986). Within this program, emphasis is placed upon the *cognitive* and *conceptual* aspects of emotions. When we communicate, we do not transmit "brute," "natural" feelings. Rather, we communicate emotions that we have interpreted in light of the categories that our culture provides, and the expressed emotions are interpreted by the audience by reference to these same schemata. Emotions have names. Every culture theorizes them. They are conceptually linked to kinds of interpersonal circumstances and invoked to justify or criticize actions. In a word, emotions are "unnatural" (Lutz, 1988). They are cultural institutions.

Rosaldo (1980, 1984) describes emotions as *embodied thoughts*:

> What differentiates thought and affect, differentiating a "cold" cognition from a "hot," is fundamentally a sense of the engagement of the actor's self. Emotions are thoughts somehow "felt" in flushes, pulses, "movements" of our livers, minds, hearts, stomachs,

skin. They are *embodied* thoughts, thoughts seeped with the apprehension that "I am involved." (Rosaldo, 1984, p. 143)

Emotions thus tell us "how we are doing" in a social situation: They give us information about our well-being in the context of interaction with others. They are social cognitions. Lutz (1988; Lutz & White, 1986) emphasizes the *conceptual* structure of emotions. "Emotions may be construed as ideas"; they are "judgements" (Lutz & White, 1986, p. 407). She proposes to view "emotions as a form of discourse" (Lutz, 1988, p. 7); "emotion can be viewed as a cultural and interpersonal process of naming, justifying, and persuading by people in relationship to each other" (p. 5). This implies that the categorical distinction between thought and emotion is not a given but a cultural construct, characteristic of Western rationalism in the aftermath of Descartes.

Emotions are conceptually tied to social scenarios (scripts) that involve actors, others, and prototypical interaction problems: frustration of expectations, social incompetence, awareness of the possibility of social failure, danger to oneself or one's significant others, loss of significant relationships (Lutz & White, 1986, p. 427). Through their connection to typified social scenarios, emotions are embedded in the moral order of the community; they link somatic experience with action, rules, and interpersonal as well as intrapsychic coping strategies. We have seen above that the Balinese emotion *lek* (stage fright) can only exist in a world where social life is experienced as a theatrical performance and where people's main preoccupation is not to botch their parts. Lutz (1988) describes the Ifaluk (Micronesian) emotion *song*—"justifiable anger"—which is tied to a scenario that involves offense, moral condemnation, fear/anxiety, and a standardized process of counseling. The emotion—the way it is felt and conceptualized—thus has all the features of an institutionalized, embodied conflict-regulating procedure.

The imagined, metaphorical seat of the emotions varies as well. While we locate love in the heart, the Philippine Ilongot feel *liget* (anger) in the liver (Rosaldo, 1980). Americans imagine anger according to a "hydraulic" model; it is like a hot liquid in a closed container, building up pressure under increasing heat, coming closer and closer to the point of explosion unless its cause—the energy source—is removed (Lakoff & Kövecses, 1987).

The anthropology of emotion suggests that it is not sufficient to ask how a set of presumably basic, universal emotions are *expressed* differently in different cultures. We should not assume that the others "feel the same way," because we cannot presuppose that our respective conceptual schemata are commensurable and that emotions and emotion terms mean the same things across cultures. We need to subject emotions to the scrutiny of conceptual analysis (Gerber, 1985, p. 366) and explicate how experiential, expressive, cognitive, and regulative aspects are integrated in the various emotions that a culture recognizes.

Emotions provide a nexus between various components of interaction processes. They are cognitions about interactive events. They tell us how we experience the interaction; they provide us with information about ourselves in the company of others. But they also regulate interaction because they get expressed, displayed, or performed and thus enable mutual awareness about how everyone subjectively experiences the interaction. Emotional communication in interaction is a subtle, multidimensional process, and we are still very much in the infancy of research into it.

Independent of the question of whether there are, as Ekman (1992) has argued, universal basic emotions, one might object that the anthropology of emotions, with its emphasis on cross-cultural diversity, loses sight of the functions that emotions serve in all societies. Certainly, emotions are components of overall cultural configurations and they are subject to conceptual structuring. But everywhere, emotions serve important functions in the regulation of interpersonal conduct and inform us whether we feel treated fairly or not or are treating others fairly—whether we experience our failure as guilt or as shame is of secondary importance. In other words, emotions might be an expression of a universal human "passion for justice" (Solomon, 1990).

Empirical Studies of Communication in Its Cultural Context

So far in this chapter, we have dealt with culture and communication at abstract levels and in the broadest possible terms. In particular, we have paid little attention to research practice and methodology. This neglect has been deliberate; our goal was to review in very general terms a number of schools of thought that can easily escape the attention of today's communication scholar partly because they are dated, partly because they have been developed in other academic disciplines. We nevertheless believe that they are of paradigmatic interest to students of culture and interpersonal communication, in particular because they make reference, in one way or another, to the person that communicates and to the cultural construction of personhood.

The approaches reviewed thus point up a dimension of interpersonal communication that is difficult to operationalize and not necessarily accessible to direct observation: We can only perceive emotion in its effects or through its expression, and we can only become aware of the cultural constitution of self when we analyze the language that is spoken in a culture. All of these themes thus transcend to a higher or lesser degree the legitimate limitations of existing observational and descriptive methods in the analysis of communication. It is not yet clear whether and how we will eventually be able to subject the affective or expressive dimension of communication to the same rigorous scrutiny with which we currently describe its referential aspects.

Among the existing empirical approaches to interpersonal communication, three in particular are in line with the "symbols and meanings" view of culture that we have adopted in this chapter. These are the *ethnography of communication, microethnography* (or *context analysis*), and *conversation analysis.* There are no agreed-upon boundaries between these methods, because ethnography does not entail a commitment to a school of thought—only to descriptive methods—and "conversation analysis" is certainly an ethnographic method (M. H. Goodwin, 1990; Hopper, 1990-1991; Moerman, 1988). "Microethnography" is but a reference to the order of phenomena described and "context analysis" indexes the conviction, held by practitioners of all these approaches, that symbols and behaviors have meaning only within contexts (Scheflen, 1974). There are certainly differences between these methods, but their complementarity has been demonstrated many times (Auer & diLuzio, 1992). Attempts to link the cultural analysis of interaction to the cultural analysis of language are fewer (Streeck, 1990-1991). Excellent accounts of all of these methods are available: Duranti (1988) and Saville-Troike (1989) for the ethnography of communication; Kendon (1990, chap. 2) for context analysis; and Heritage (1984) and Levinson (1983) for conversation analysis. Our review can therefore be brief.

The *ethnography of communication* began as a belated implementation of Sapir's call that language be studied within the entire ensemble of symbol systems that are in use in a society. Speech is a form of human behavior that is embedded in other forms, an activity among activities, and itself is made up of a multitude of different acts. The research program, when it was finally launched (Bauman & Sherzer, 1989; Gumperz & Hymes, 1972), reflected the history of methods of analysis that had developed since Sapir's initial call (in 1927); structural analysis and taxonomic description were its initial tools. The ethnography of communication began as an application of methods developed in the study of grammatical forms to phenomena of language use and social interaction (Hymes, 1972a). It was as a structural description of social practices and situations. The descriptions have since become less taxonomic and more dynamic, and researchers have moved from the classification of units of behavior to the description of their unfolding over time.

Various kinds of units of communication behavior have been studied: speech communities, speech events, speech acts, and speech genres, among others. Each level of social integration poses its own set of questions and points up phenomena of different kinds. The study of *speech communities* (Carbaugh, 1988; Phillipsen, 1990; Sherzer, 1983) deals with internal variation and linguistic differentiation, with the maintenance and symbolization of a community's integrity and with issues of social and cultural identity among its members, but also with the "cycle of situational frames" (Hall, 1977) that these travel through in their daily lives and with the shifting demands each situation makes on the participants' communicative repertoire. This program of studies yielded a far richer and more differentiated model of linguistic competence than the predominant Chomskyan one, which assumes an idealized homogeneous community of language; the ethnographic account of competence accommodated the real variability of linguistic behavior (Hymes, 1972a, 1972b). The description of *speech events* (Bauman, 1986; Katriel, 1990; Phillips, 1982, 1989)—the ethnography of situated linguistic action—focuses on the impact that variable social factors such as status and rank, situated role, and gender have upon, and the ways in which they are symbolized by, speech behavior (see the contributions in Bauman, 1989; Gumperz, 1972). *Event* is the "basic level" unit in many of these studies (Rosch, 1987); a culture's members can typically identify and label events quite easily. Events provide coherence, integration, and functional meaning-in-context for lower level units such as speech acts as well as for stylistic choices (Agar, 1974; Frake, 1977). Goffman's sociology of "situations and their men" has been a strong influence in this line of research (Goffman, 1961, 1963, 1974, 1981; see also Drew & Wootton, 1988; Levinson, 1988). The ethnography of *speech acts,* or "culturally contexted" speech act analysis (see Moerman, 1988), includes the study of culturally specific kinds of speech acts (Abrahams, 1989), the procedural rules for performing them (Frake, 1964, 1975), and the underlying metalinguistic and philosophical folk conceptions of speech such as truth, sincerity, and the like (Albert, 1972; Duranti, 1984; Goody, 1978; Rosaldo, 1990). The study of *speech genres,* finally, explores the constitutive features of kinds of discourse across individual events, settings, and so on (Atkinson & Drew, 1979; Conley & O'Barr, 1990). Recently, the importance of Bakhtin's theory of oral intertextuality (Bakhtin, 1952-1953/1986) for understanding the nature of genre has been recognized (Briggs & Bauman, 1992). New visions of language are beginning to emerge from the practice of ethnography, as a result of the recognition of the primordially discursive existence of all linguistic and cultural forms. "Langue" (Saussure, 1964) is thus "repositioned" (Urban, 1991); it is no longer seen as the real reality behind the fleeting appearances of "parole," but as an ongoing production, produced by the discursive practices of face-to-face communication (and other discourse genres).

The ethnography of communication typically studies *labeled* acts and events. But not all unit acts of social interaction in a culture are labeled. As soon as we begin to explore the structures of the smaller unit acts—say, the utterance of a sentence or the assembly of a complex gesture—we enter a realm without much linguistic codification. Yet, units at this level are essential components of social interaction and communication—its "ultimate behavioral materials" (Goffman). Micro-units of behavior—tone groups, hand movements, and so on—have no names, but they make up things that have names: cheers, greetings, and other such acts.

This is the realm of *microethnography.* What changes when we enter the microcosm of the single utterance, sequence, or visual act is not just the size of the phenomena under study. Inevitably, our perspective upon the phenomena also changes, from form to process, from *Communicational Structure* (Scheflen, 1973) to *Behaving and Making Sense* (Bremme & Erickson, 1977); what comes into view are the processes in which communicative acts are assembled. In practical terms, microethnographers study small segments of audio- or videotape (often in the context of observational studies of macrophenomena), and they review these segments again and again *as they are unfolding over time.* These research experiences reposition the structural categories that have previously been used for the description of communication. Traditional descriptive categories (e.g., sentence, posture configuration) identify phenomena with *hindsight* (Good, in press); they identify structures that *have already been assembled.* In the study of language, this orientation to "langue" and its units as atemporal objects is a result of, and partly justified by, the material abstraction of language from its unfolding in time in writing. But in the study of body behavior, no such abstraction is possible: A gesture, for example, *only* exists as an object-in-time.

The move into the realm of the microethnographic thus naturally leads to a revolution in the conceptualization of communication. Communication and interaction begin to take on the appearance of *living processes,* and the concepts used to describe them are necessarily becoming more reflective of communication's unfolding over time.

Microethnography can thus be described as the study of the ways in which acts and events are assembled over time in the interaction of mutually copresent people (McDermott & Roth, 1978). Its premise is contextualism (Erickson & Shultz, 1977): Meaning is seen as a "relation between an act and the context in which it regularly occurs" (Scheflen, 1974, p. 14). All of the units involved—acts, their components, contexts—are *cultural units,* elements from a repertoire shared by the members and enabling them to configure the larger units of social integration. Microethnographers have provided very detailed descriptions of interaction processes in social institutions, for example, schools, and exposed the subtle misarticulations that occur when participants bring different cultural repertoires and interpretive methods to the situation (Erickson, 1979; Erickson & Mohatt, 1982; Phillips, 1982; Streeck, 1984).

In this world of microscopic appearances, the customary distinctions between disciplines and approaches disappear. Whether a study is "ethnographic," targeting just one culture, or "basic research," dealing with generic or universal practices, is a question that only the phenomena themselves can answer. We can never know in advance how widely distributed a communication phenomenon is. The most comprehensive oeuvre in context analysis—the work of A. Kendon (1990)—includes strictly local cultural phenomena such as the ritual sign language of an Australian aboriginal society (Kendon, 1988) or codified South Italian gestures (Kendon, 1992) but also presumably universal mechanisms such as self- and interactional synchrony (Kendon, 1990).

Microethnography intersects with another, small research tradition that goes back to the work of Boas. We refer to it as the study of *expressive culture*. One of the projects that Boas launched in his fight against racist theories of human behavior was a study of gestures in New York City, which compared the conversational gestures of Southern Italian and Jewish immigrants of Eastern European descent (Efron, 1942). The immediate aim of this study was to show that patterns of embodied behavior—such as the moving of the hands in gesticulation—are not innate. In a painstaking comparison of Jewish and Italian gestures of first- and second-generation immigrants, Efron demonstrated the slow "hybridization" of the gestural style as people move into the American mainstream. Like all other cultural forms of expression, gestures are learned.

Efron's study could have laid the groundwork for a field devoting itself to empirical study of expressive "behavior in public places" (Goffman, 1963) had it not for a long time remained an isolated attempt; the focus of most research on human expression was almost exclusively psychological. Gesture has alternatively been thought of as a window into *cognitive* or *affective processes* "inside" the person, only rarely as a mode of public behavior. While there are many interesting studies of the *representation* of expressive behavior in the fine arts (Barash, 1987; Baxandall, 1977; Bremmer & Roodenburg, 1991), only few researchers have subjected expressive behavior to microanalytic *cultural* scrutiny (Calbris, 1990; Creider, 1986).

Whatever units and structures there are in communication behavior, they are units and structures *in time*. They do not appear "at once," but "step by step," in the presence and within reach of other participants who can invite, discourage, or preempt them. That these units unfold over time thus implies that they unfold in a *process of interaction* in which every move made or not made by the interlocutor can influence the further shape of the unit (C. Goodwin, 1979). "Real time" is "shared time," and it is nonlinear. Rather, utterances and other communicative acts are produced and received with a *prospective-retrospective* orientation (Cicourel, 1973).

Conversation analysts (Atkinson & Heritage, 1984) describe the procedures by which conversationalists produce their own behavior and understand and deal with the behavior of others (Heritage, 1984, p. 1). Among these procedures are those that enable conversational participants to take turns and produce a "linear" series of conversational utterances with a minimum of overlap, so that mutual hearing and understanding can be secured (Sacks, Schegloff, & Jefferson, 1974); procedures for the sequencing of conversational actions (Schegloff & Sacks, 1979); and procedures for the "repair" of interactional and conversational "trouble" (correcting mishaps in speaking, addressing problems in hearing and understanding, and so on; Schegloff, 1979). Conversation analysis can be regarded as an account of the highly adaptive, systematic organization that allows society's members to sustain social order and relationships in a routine fashion. This organization is designed to let the participants *progress* in their interaction with one another. It is a set of *enabling, forward-looking* rules—not a set of restrictions. Some of these rules or practices have important social-organizational implications that go beyond the realm of conversation. For example, so-called *preference organizations* (Drew, 1984; Pomerantz, 1978, 1984) reveal a "systematic 'bias' in favour of conflict avoidance" (Heritage, 1984, p. 280). Prosocial solution types to problems of interactional and social coordination have become parts of the interactional "langue," of the "prosthetic devices" that we routinely employ in our dealings with one another.

Conversation analysts have reported their findings in culture-free terms and defined conversational organization as a set of "generic," "context-free" practices for the production of "particular," "contextual" scenes (Schegloff, 1972). Charges have therefore been brought that they are oblivious to the cultural variation of these practices. But this debate is ill-framed. Conceiving the issue in terms of the traditional "nature-nurture" dichotomy ("learned" or "cultural" versus "innate" or "universal") obscures the fact that interaction patterns, languages, and other symbol systems have evolved over time, some being vestiges of rather ancient times—but nevertheless part of our *tradition,* not "hard-wired" into our genes. Only when we understand the human repertoires of interaction and communication abilities and resources as products of a *continuing* process of evolution and history, as layered sets of imprints and vestiges from various developmental stages, some very old, some more recent, can we begin to think about their relative order of appearance and ask questions such as these: "How does the structure of natural language reflect the needs of face-to-face interaction?" or "Which features of conversational organization are universal, which ones show cultural variation?" For example, humanity has very likely accumulated experiences in turn-taking long before it invented language, for example, in the context of food sharing. To the extent that humanity developed viable, routine solutions to recurrent social-organization problems of this kind, these became "entrenched" in the culture and subsequently available for the management of more advanced systems or tasks, for example, turn-taking during vocal communication (which requires the sharing of a "channel"). The solution patterns likely became part of the human tradition—*culture*—long before any separation of languages and *cultures.* Not everything that is universal has to be innate.

Conclusion: Where Is Culture?

We have thus returned to our initial reflections on the definition of *culture*: It is a "prosthetic device." At one level, "culture" is just a way of organizing our data, a framing of experience (Goffman, 1974). But we can frame the phenomena of culture and communication in many ways and interpret the very same set of phenomena at various levels of generality or local specificity. For example, we can discover in an elaborate, status-symbolizing ceremony that involves a differential distribution of speaking turns an example of the local culture with its peculiar emphasis on decorum and rank, but we can also see it as a local variant of a very old, vestigial human achievement, namely, to exploit a management system for scarce resources (e.g., the speech channel) for secondary social-organizational resources, such as the negotiation and symbolic representation of differential rank. The phenomena of interpersonal communication—language, embodied behavior, interactional organization—as well as any other cultural achievement are always "local" and "generic," "specific" and "universal" at the same time—the difference is one of research focus. If by some crazy twist of history the study of conversation had first begun in the Amazon basin—or maybe Bosnia-Herzegovina—the local variety of conversational organization would have served equally well to make the point: that talking requires the exchange of turns. This does not mean, of course, that it is all the same—that all languages resemble English (like the Chomskyans used to pretend) or that there is not a tremendous amount of variation; but it is always variation around a universal core—or, rather, away from an older, common core. For this is how humanity evolved.

An altogether different level of cultural organization and symbolic representation has remained almost completely overlooked by students of human communication, the realm of cultural artifacts—of the things we act with, that we build, rebuild, write with and upon, and so on. Cultural meanings do not only reside in symbols, and the human mind and its cultural manifestations are not only located in brains. We are accustomed to making a categorical distinction between person and environment and to attributing everything that is mental or "ideational"—meaning, knowledge, symbols—to the "mind," which we locate inside the brain. But this is a very partial view, motivated perhaps by the antimaterialist, individualistic conception of mind and soul that is so much part of our tradition. But cultural meanings are distributed across many locations, both internal and external, and they are quite obviously embodied in part in *material culture* (Norman, 1988, 1993; Resnick, Levine, & Behrend, 1990). Culture is a vast information pool, transmitted from generation to generation, and increasing constantly in size for the past 50,000 years. Yet this pool is transmitted not only by symbols (language, graphic signs, and so on) but by the entire "culturally constituted reality" including things such as "buildings, roads, vehicles, lawns, furniture, appliances, etc." (D'Andrade, 1981, p. 180). When we use these things, the meanings that we have stored in our minds articulate with the meanings embodied in them, which are themselves inscriptions of years and years of intelligent human action. It is only recently that psychologists and communication researchers have begun to recognize and investigate the distribution of meaning and mind (or "cognition") across different locations and to study the processes of communication within such "systems of distributed cognition" (Hutchins & Klausen, 1990). These systems include human actors, material representation systems, built spaces, and so on—but importantly also "other actors." Human competence typically relies upon the presence of other actors who have partly similar, partly complementary competencies: Couples share memory through a distribution of labor; families develop differential communication roles; and of course workers and learners everywhere depend upon experts.

We rely on our material environment to serve as a stock of ready-made symbolic structures that we can manipulate to externalize cognitive functions (Lave, Murtaugh, & de la Rocha, 1984) and to represent, in an enduring kind of way, interactively assembled conceptual structures: Pens, cups, pieces of paper, and lines in the sand can represent the features of an agreement; doodles stand for action plans. Increasingly, machines and sophisticated symbol-processing technology are becoming routine settings of human communication (C. Goodwin, 1993; Suchman, 1987). The distribution of meaning and mind across various locations, however, is very old. Rain forest dwellers, for example, have for a long time been using the sounds of their environments—the calls of birds and the noise of waterfalls—as external symbolic structures within which to embed their songs and thus their communal knowledge (Feld, 1982). Culture, meaning, and mind cannot be kept within territories or containers. But they can be endangered, destroyed, and extinguished.

References

Aarsleff, H. (1974). The tradition of Condillac: The problem of the origin of language in the eighteenth century and the debate in the Berlin Academy before Herder. In D. Hymes (Ed.), *Studies in the history of linguistics* (pp. 93-156). Bloomington: Indiana University Press.

Abrahams, R. D. (1989). Black talking on the streets. In R. Bauman & J. Sherzer (Eds.), *Explorations in the ethnography of speaking* (pp. 240-262). Cambridge: Cambridge University Press.

Agar, M. (1974). Talking about doing: Lexicon and event. *Language in Society, 3,* 83-89.

Albert, E. (1972). Cultural patterning of speech behavior in Burundi. In J. J. Gumperz & D. Hymes (Eds.), *Directions in sociolinguistics: The ethnography of communication* (pp. 106-129). New York: Holt, Rinehart & Winston.

Anderson, B. (1991). *Imagined communities: Reflections on the origin and spread of nationalism.* New York: Verso.

Atkinson, J., & Heritage, J. (Eds.). (1984). *Structures of social action.* Cambridge: Cambridge University Press.

Atkinson, M., & Drew, P. (1979). *Order in court.* London: Macmillan.

Auer, P., & diLuzio, A. (Eds.). (1992). *The contextualization of language.* Amsterdam: Benjamins.

Bakhtin, M. M. (1986). The problem of speech genres. In C. Emerson & M. Holquist (Eds.), *Speech genres and other late essays.* Austin: University of Texas Press. (Original work published 1952-1953)

Barash, M. (1987). *Giotto and the language of gesture.* Cambridge: Cambridge University Press.

Barth, F. (1969). *Ethnic groups and boundaries: The social organization of culture difference.* Boston: Little, Brown.

Bateson, G. (1958). *Naven* (2nd ed.). Stanford, CA: Stanford University Press. (Original work published 1936)

Bateson, G. (1972). *Steps to an ecology of mind.* New York: Ballantine.

Bateson, G., & Mead, M. (1942). *Balinese character: A photographic analysis.* New York: New York Academy of Sciences.

Bauman, R. (1986). *Story, performance, and event: Contextual studies of oral narrative.* Cambridge: Cambridge University Press.

Bauman, R., & Sherzer, J. (Eds.). (1989). *Explorations in the ethnography of speaking* (2nd ed.). Cambridge: Cambridge University Press.

Baxandall, M. (1977). *Painting and experience in fifteenth century Italy.* Oxford: Clarendon.

Benedict, R. (1934). *Patterns of culture.* Boston: Houghton Mifflin.

Berlin, B., & Kay, P. (1969). *Basic color terms.* Berkeley: University of California Press.

Boas, F. (1912). Changes in the bodily form of descendants of immigrants. In *Race, language and culture* (pp. 6-75). New York: Free Press.

Boas, F. (1928). *Anthropology and modern life.* New York: Dover.

Boas, F. (1932). Rasse und Charakter. *Anthropologischer Anzeiger, 8,* 280-284.

Boas, F. (1940). *Race, language and culture.* New York: Free Press.

Boas, F. (1966a). Introduction. In F. Boas & J. W. Powell (Eds.), *Handbook of American Indian languages.* Lincoln: University of Nebraska Press. (Original work published 1911)

Boas, F. (1966b). *Kwakiutl ethnography.* Chicago: University of Chicago Press.

Bourdieu, P. (1977). *Outline of a theory of practice.* Cambridge: Cambridge University Press.

Bremme, D. W., & Erickson, F. (1977). Behaving and making sense. *Theory into Practice, 16,* 153-160.

Bremmer, J., & Roodenburg, H. (Eds.). (1991). *A cultural history of gesture.* Ithaca, NY: Cornell University Press.

Briggs, C. L., & Bauman, R. (1992). Genre, intertextuality, and social power. *Journal of Linguistic Anthropology, 2*(2), 131-172.

Brown, P., & Levinson, S. C. (1987). *Politeness: Some universals in language usage.* Cambridge: Cambridge University Press. (Original work published 1978)

Bruner, J. (1990). *Acts of meaning.* Cambridge, MA: Harvard University Press.

Bunzel, R. (1992). *Zuñi ceremonialism.* Albuquerque: University of New Mexico Press. (Original work published 1932)

Calbris, G. (1990). *The semiotics of French gestures.* Bloomington: Indiana University Press.

Carbaugh, D. (1988). *Talking American: Cultural discourses on Donahue.* Norwood, NJ: Ablex.

Cavalli-Sforza, L. L. (1991). Genes, peoples and languages. *Scientific American, 263*(5), 104-111.

Chance, M. R. A., & Larsen, R. R. (Eds.). (1976). *The social structure of attention.* New York: Wiley.

Cicourel, A. V. (1964). *Method and measurement in sociology.* New York: Free Press.

Cicourel, A. V. (1973). *Cognitive sociology.* Harmondsworth, England: Penguin.

Collier, J. J., & Collier, M. (1986). *Visual anthropology.* Albuquerque: University of New Mexico Press.

Columbus, C. (1966). *Across the ocean sea: A journal of Columbus' voyage.* New York: Harper & Row. (Original work written 1492-1493)

Comrie, B. (1981). *Language universals and linguistic typology.* Chicago: University of Chicago Press.

Condillac, E. (1746). *An essay on the origin of human knowledge, being a supplement to Mr. Locke's essay on the human understanding.* London: J. Noursse.

Conley, J., & O'Barr, W. (1990). *Rules versus relationships: The ethnography of legal discourse.* Chicago: University of Chicago Press.

Creider, C. (1986). Inter-language comparisons in the study of the interactional use of gesture. *Semiotica, 62*(1-2), 147-164.

D'Andrade, R. (1981). The cultural part of cognition. *Cognitive Science, 5,* 179-195.

D'Andrade, R. G. (1984). Cultural meaning systems. In R. A. Shweder & R. A. LeVine (Eds.), *Culture theory: Essays on mind, self, and emotion* (pp. 88-121). Cambridge: Cambridge University Press.

Darwin, C. (1955). *The expression of emotions in animals and man.* New York: Philosophical Society. (Original work published 1872)

Darwin, C. (1964). *On the origin of species.* Cambridge, MA: Harvard University Press. (Original work published 1859)

Dilthey, W. (1977). *Descriptive psychology and historical understanding.* The Hague, the Netherlands: Martinus Nijhoff.

Donald, M. (1991). *Origins of the modern mind.* Cambridge, MA: Harvard University Press.

Douglas, M. (1970). *Natural symbols: Explorations in cosmology.* London: Barrie & Jenkins.

Drew, P. (1984). Speakers' reportings in invitation sequences. In M. Atkinson & J. Heritage (Eds.), *Structures of social action.* Cambridge: Cambridge University Press.

Drew, P., & Wootton, A. (Eds.). (1988). *Erving Goffman: Studying the interaction order.* Oxford: Polity.

Duranti, A. (1984). *Intentions, self, and local theories of meaning: Words and social action in a Samoan context* (CHIP No. 122). San Diego: University of California, Center for Human Information Processing.

Duranti, A. (1988). Ethnography of speaking: Toward a linguistics of the praxis. In F. J. Newmeyer (Ed.), *Linguistics: The Cambridge Survey* (pp. 210-228). Cambridge: Cambridge University Press.

Durkheim, É. (1982). *The rules of sociological method.* London: Macmillan. (Original work published 1895)

Durkheim, É., & Mauss, M. (1963). *Primitive classification.* Chicago: University of Chicago Press. (Original work published 1903)

Edwards, E. (Ed.). (1992). *Anthropology and photography 1860-1920.* New Haven, CT: Yale University Press.

Efron, D. (1942). *Gesture, race and culture.* The Hague, the Netherlands: Mouton.

Ekman, P. (Ed.). (1973). *Darwin and facial expression.* New York: Academic Press.

Ekman, P. (1992). Are there basic emotions? *Psychological Review, 99*(3), 550-554.

Elias, N. (1978). *The civilizing process: The history of manners.* New York: Urizen.

Elias, N. (1983). *The court society.* Oxford: Basil Blackwell.

Erickson, F. (1979). Talking down: Some cultural sources of miscommunication in interracial interviews. In A. Wolfgang (Ed.), *Nonverbal behavior* (pp. 99-126). New York: Academic Press.

Erickson, F., & Mohatt, G. (1982). Cultural organization of participation structures in two classrooms with Indian students. In G. Spindler (Ed.), *Doing the ethnography of schooling* (pp. 132-175). New York: Holt, Rinehart & Winston.

Erickson, F., & Shultz, J. (1977). When is a context? Some issues in the analysis of social competence. *The Quarterly Newsletter of the Institute for Comparative Human Development, 1*(2), 5-10.

Evans-Pritchard, E. (1964). Nuer modes of address. In D. Hymes (Ed.), *Language in culture and society* (pp. 221-225). New York: Harper & Row.

Feld, S. (1982). *Sound and sentiment.* Philadelphia: University of Pennsylvania Press.

Forster, G. (1777). *A voyage round the world.* London.

Fortune, R. (1932). *Sorcerers of Dobu.* London: Routledge.

Frake, C. (1964). How to ask for a drink in Subanun. *American Anthropologist, 66,* 127-132.

Frake, C. (1975). How to enter a Yakan house. In M. Sanchez & B. Blount (Eds.), *Sociocultural dimensions of language use* (pp. 25-40). New York: Academic Press.

Frake, C. (1977). Plying frames can be dangerous: An assessment of methodology in cognitive anthropology. *The Quarterly Newsletter of the Institute for Comparative Human Development, 1*(3), 1-7.

Freud, S. (1949). *An outline of psychoanalysis.* New York: Norton.

Freud, S. (1955). *The interpretation of dreams.* New York: Basic Books.

Freud, S. (1958). *Civilization and its discontents.* Garden City, NY: Doubleday.

Freud, S. (1960). *Jokes and their relation to the unconscious.* New York: Norton.

Garfinkel, H. (1967). *Studies in ethnomethodology.* Englewood Cliffs, NJ: Prentice-Hall.

Geertz, C. (1973). *The interpretation of cultures.* New York: Basic Books.

Geertz, C. (1983). *Local knowledge.* New York: Basic Books.

Geertz, C. (1984). "From the native's point of view": On the nature of anthropological understanding. In R. A. Shweder & R. A. LeVine (Eds.), *Culture theory: Essays on mind, self, and emotion* (pp. 123-136). Cambridge: Cambridge University Press.

Geertz, C. (1988). *Works and lives.* Stanford, CA: Stanford University Press.

Gehlen, A. (1958). *Der Mensch: Seine Natur und seine Stellung in der Welt.* Frankfurt: V. Klostermann.

Gerber, E. R. (1985). Rage and obligation: Samoan emotion in conflict. In G. M. White (Ed.), *Kirkpatrick, J.* (pp. 35-79). Berkeley: University of California Press.

Goffman, E. (1961). *Encounters.* Indianapolis: Bobbs-Merrill.

Goffman, E. (1963). *Behavior in public places.* New York: Free Press.

Goffman, E. (1974). *Frame analysis.* New York: Harper & Row.

Goffman, E. (1981). *Forms of talk.* Oxford: Basil Blackwell.

Good, D. (in press). Where does foresight end and hindsight begin. In E. Goody (Ed.), *Interaction and intelligence.* Cambridge: Cambridge University Press.

Goodman, N. (1976). *Languages of art* (2nd ed.). Indianapolis: Hackett. (Original work published 1968)

Goodwin, C. (1979). The interactive construction of a sentence in natural conversation. In G. Psathas (Ed.), *Everyday language* (pp. 97-122). New York: Irvington.

Goodwin, C. (1993). *Perception, technology and interaction on a scientific research vessel.* Unpublished manuscript.

Goodwin, M. H. (1990). *He-said-she-said: Talk as social organization among black children.* Bloomington: Indiana University Press.

Goody, E. (Ed.). (1978). *Questions and politeness.* Cambridge: Cambridge University Press.

Greenberg, J. H., & Ruhlen, M. (1992). Linguistic origins of Native Americans. *Scientific American, 267*(5), 94-99.

Gumperz, J., & Hymes, D. (Ed.). (1972). *Directions in sociolinguistics: The ethnography of communication.* New York: Holt, Rinehart & Winston.

Hall, E. T. (1977). *Beyond culture.* Garden City, NY: Anchor/Doubleday.

Herder, J. G. (1966). *Abhandlung über den Ursprung der Sprache.* Stuttgart: Reclam. (Original work published 1772)

Heritage, J. (1984). *Garfinkel and ethnomethodology.* Cambridge, MA: Polity.

Herodotus. (1949). *Herodotus.* Oxford: Clarendon.

Hewes, G. (1974). Gesture language in culture contact. *Sign Language Studies, 4,* 1-34.

Hill, J. H., & Mannheim, B. (1992). Language and world view. *Annual Review of Anthropology, 21,* 381-406.

Hochschild, A. (1983). *The managed heart.* Berkeley: University of California Press.

Hopper, R. (1990-1991). Ethnography and conversation analysis after *Talking culture* [Special issue]. *Research on Language and Social Interaction, 24.*

Humboldt, W. von. (1988). *On language.* Cambridge: Cambridge University Press. (Original work published 1836)

Hutchins, E., & Klausen, T. (1990). *Distributed cognition in an airline cockpit.* San Diego: University of California, Department of Cognitive Science.

Hymes, D. (1962). The ethnography of speaking. In T. Gladwin & W. Sturtevant (Eds.), *Anthropology and human behavior* (pp. 13-53). Washington, DC: Anthropological Society of Washington.

Hymes, D. (1972a). Models of the interaction of language and social life. In J. Gumperz & D. Hymes (Eds.), *Directions in sociolinguistics: The ethnography of communication* (pp. 35-71). New York: Holt, Rinehart & Winston.

Hymes, D. (1972b). *Towards communicative competence.* Philadelphia: University of Pennsylvania Press.

Ingold, T. (1986). *Evolution and social life.* Cambridge: Cambridge University Press.

Izard, C. (1971). *The face of emotion.* New York: Appleton.

Johnson, M. (1987). *The body in the mind.* Chicago: University of Chicago Press.

Jones, E. (1913). *Papers on psycho-analysis.* New York: Wood.

Kant, I. (1977). *Anthropologie in pragmatischer Absicht.* Frankfurt/M.: Suhrkamp. (Original work published 1798)

Katriel, T. (1990). "Griping" as a verbal ritual in some Israeli discourse. In D. Carbaugh (Ed.), *Cultural communication and intercultural contact* (pp. 99-114). Hillsdale, NJ: Lawrence Erlbaum.

Kendon, A. (1988). *Sign languages of Aboriginal Australia.* Cambridge: Cambridge University Press.

Kendon, A. (1990). *Conducting interaction.* Cambridge: Cambridge University Press.

Kendon, A. (1992). Some recent work from Italy on quotable gestures (emblems). *Journal of Linguistic Anthropology, 2*(1), 92-108.

Kluckhohn, C., et al. (Eds.). (1948). *Personality in nature, society, and culture.* New York: Knopf.

Lacan, J. (1977). *Ecrits: A selection.* New York: Norton.

Lakoff, G. (1987). *Women, fire, and dangerous things: What categories reveal about the mind.* Chicago: University of Chicago Press.

Lakoff, G., & Kövecses, Z. (1987). The cognitive model of anger inherent in American English. In D. Holland & N. Quinn (Eds.), *Cultural models in language and thought.* Cambridge: Cambridge University Press.

Lane, H. (1976). *The wild boy of Aveyron.* Cambridge, MA: Harvard University Press.

Langacker, R. W. (1987). *Foundations of cognitive grammar: Vol. 1. Theoretical prerequisites.* Stanford, CA: Stanford University Press.

Lave, J., Murtaugh, M., & de la Rocha, O. (1984). The dialectic of arithmetic in grocery shopping. In B. Rogoff & J. Lave (Eds.), *Everyday cognition: Its development in social context* (pp. 67-94). Cambridge, MA: Harvard University Press.

Leach, E. (1976). *Culture and communication: The logic by which symbols are connected.* Cambridge: Cambridge University Press.

Levinson, S. (1983). *Pragmatics.* Cambridge: Cambridge University Press.

Levinson, S. F. (1988). Putting linguistics on a proper footing. In P. Drew & A. Wootton (Eds.), *Erving Goffman: Studying the interaction order.* Oxford: Polity.

Lévi-Strauss, C. (1976). *Structural anthropology* (Vol. II). Chicago: University of Chicago Press.

Locke, J. (1959). *An essay concerning human understanding.* New York: Dover. (Original work published 1690)

Lucy, J. (1992a). *Grammatical categories and cognition.* Cambridge: Cambridge University Press.

Lucy, J. (1992b). *Language diversity and thought.* Cambridge: Cambridge University Press.

Lutz, C., & White, G. M. (1986). The anthropology of emotions. *Annual Review of Anthropology, 15,* 405-436.

Lutz, C. A. (1988). *Unnatural emotions: Everyday sentiments on a Micronesian atoll and their challenge to Western theory.* Chicago: University of Chicago Press.

Malinowski, B. (1922). *Argonauts of the Western Pacific.* London: Routledge.

Malinowski, B. (1923). The problem of meaning in primitive languages. In C. K. Ogden & I. A. Richards, *The meaning of meaning: A study of the influence of language upon thought and of the science of symbolism; with supplementary essays by B. Malinowski and F. G. Crookshank.* New York: Harcourt, Brace.

Malinowski, B. (1944). *A scientific theory of culture.* Chapel Hill: University of North Carolina Press.

Malinowski, B. (1965). *Coral Gardens and their magic.* Bloomington: Indiana University Press.

Mallery, G. (1978). Introduction to the study of sign language among the North American Indians as illustrating the gesture speech of mankind. In D. J. Umiker-Sebeok & T. A. Sebeok (Eds.), *Aboriginal sign languages of the Americas and Australia* (pp. 291-310). New York: Plenum. (Original work published 1880)

Marcus, G. F., & Fischer, M. M. J. (1986). *Anthropology as cultural critique.* Chicago: University of Chicago Press.

Marcuse, H. (1955). *Eros and civilization.* New York: Vintage.

Maturana, H. R., & Varela, F. J. (1992). *The tree of knowledge: The biological roots of human understanding.* Boston: Shambala. (Original work published 1987)

Mauss, M. (1966). *The gift.* London: Cohen & West. (Original work published 1950)

Mauss, M. (1973). The techniques of the body. *Economy and Society, 2*(1), 70-88. (Original work published 1935)

Mauss, M. (1979). A category of the human mind: The notion of person; the notion of self. In *Sociology and anthropology.* London: Routledge & Kegan Paul. (Original work published 1938)

McDermott, R. P., & Gospodinoff, K. (1979). Social contexts for ethnic borders and school failure. In A. Wolfgang (Ed.), *Nonverbal behavior* (pp. 175-195). New York: Academic Press.

McDermott, R. P., & Roth, D. (1978). Social organization of behavior: Interactional approaches. *Annual Review of Anthropology, 7,* 321-345.

Milosz, C. (1993, November 4). Swing-shift in the Baltics. *The New York Review of Books, 40,* 12-16.

Moerman, M. (1988). *Talking culture: Ethnography and conversation analysis.* Philadelphia: University of Pennsylvania Press.

Montesquieu, C. (1901). *The citizen of the world.* Washington: M. Walter Dunne.

Nietzsche, F. (1927). *The birth of tragedy.* New York: Modern Library.

Norman, D. (1988). *The design of everyday things.* New York: Doubleday.

Norman, D. (1993). *Things that make us smart.* Reading, MA: Addison-Wesley.

Parsons, T. (1937). *The structure of social action.* New York: McGraw-Hill.

Parsons, T., et al. (1951). *Towards a general theory of action.* Cambridge, MA: Harvard University Press.

Phillips, S. (1982). *The invisible culture: Communication in classroom and community on the Warm Springs Indian reservation.* New York: Longman.

Phillips, S. (1989). Warm Springs "Indian time": How the regulation of participation affects the progress of events. In R. Bauman & J. Sherzer (Eds.), *Explorations in the ethnography of speaking* (pp. 92-109). Cambridge: Cambridge University Press.

Phillipsen, G. (1990). Speaking "like a man" in Teamsterville: Culture patterns of role enactment in an urban neighborhood. In D. Carbaugh (Eds.), *Cultural communication and intercultural contact* (pp. 11-20). Hillsdale, NJ: Lawrence Erlbaum.

Plessner, H. (1980). *Conditio humana.* Frankfurt/M.: Fischer. (Original work published 1964)

Pomerantz, A. (1978). Compliment responses: Notes on the cooperation of multiple constraints. In J. Schenkein (Ed.), *Studies in the organization of conversational interaction* (pp. 79-112). New York: Academic Press.

Pomerantz, A. (1984). Agreeing and disagreeing with assessments: Some features of preferred/dis-preferred turn shapes. In M. Atkinson & J. Heritage (Eds.), *Structures of social action* (pp. 57-100). Cambridge: Cambridge University Press.

Radcliffe-Brown, A. R. (1965). *Structure and function in primitive society.* New York: Free Press.

Resnick, L., Levine, J., & Behrend, S. (1990). *Socially shared cognition.* New York: American Psychological Association.

Rosaldo, M. (1980). *Knowledge and passion: Ilongot notions of self and social life.* Cambridge: Cambridge University Press.

Rosaldo, M. (1990). The things we do with words: Ilongot speech acts and speech act theory in philosophy. In D. Carbaugh (Ed.), *Cultural communication and intercultural contact* (pp. 373-408). Hillsdale, NJ: Lawrence Erlbaum.

Rosaldo, M. Z. (1984). Toward an anthropology of self and feeling. In R. A. Shweder & R. A. LeVine (Eds.), *Culture theory: Essays on mind, self, and emotion* (pp. 137-157). Cambridge: Cambridge University Press.

Rosch, E. (1987). Linguistic relativity. *Etc., 44,* 254-279.

Rousseau, J. (1967). *Discourse on the origin of inequality.* New York: Pocket Books.

Rudzka-Ostyn, B. (1988). *Topics in cognitive linguistics.* Amsterdam: Benjamins.

Sacks, H., Schegloff, E., & Jefferson, G. (1974). A simplest systematics for the organization of turn-taking for conversation. *Language, 50,* 696-735.

Sapir, E. (1921). *Language.* New York: Harcourt, Brace.

Sapir, E. (1934). The emergence of the concept of personality in a study of cultures. In D. Mandelbaum (Ed.), *Selected writings of Edward Sapir.* Berkeley: University of California Press.

Sapir, E. (1991). The unconscious patterning of behavior in society. In D. Mandelbaum (Ed.), *Selected writings of Edward Sapir.* Berkeley: University of California Press. (Original work published 1927)

Saussure, F. de. (1964). *Cours de Linguistique Générale.* Paris: Payot.

Saville-Troike, M. (1989). *The ethnography of communication: An introduction* (2nd ed.). Oxford: Basil Blackwell.

Scheflen, A. (1973). *Communicational structure.* Bloomington: Indiana University Press.

Scheflen, A. (1974). *How behavior means.* Garden City, NY: Anchor.

Schegloff, E. A. (1972). Notes on a conversational practice: Formulating place. In D. Sudnow (Ed.), *Studies in social interaction.* New York: Free Press.

Schegloff, E. A. (1979). On the relevance of repair to syntax-for-conversation. In T. Givon (Ed.), *Discourse and syntax* (pp. 261-288). New York: Academic Press.

Schegloff, E. A., & Sacks, H. (1979). Opening up closings. *Semiotica, 7*(4), 289-327.

Sennett, R. (1977). *The fall of public man.* New York: Knopf.

Sennett, R. (1990). *The conscience of the eye: The design and social life of cities.* New York: Knopf.

Sherzer, J. (1983). *Kuna ways of speaking: An ethnographic perspective.* Austin: University of Texas Press.

Silverstein, M. (1976). Shifters, linguistic categories and cultural description. In K. Basso & H. Selby (Eds.), *Meaning in anthropology.* Albuquerque: University of New Mexico Press.

Simmel, G. (1902). The number of members as determining the sociological form of the group. *American Journal of Sociology, 8,* 1-46, 158-196.

Simmel, G. (1903-1904). The sociology of conflict. *American Journal of Sociology, 9,* 490-525, 672-698, 798-811.

Simmel, G. (1905-1906). The sociology of secrecy and of the secret societies. *American Journal of Sociology, 11,* 441-498.

Simmel, G. (1924). The sociology of the senses: Visual interaction. In R. E. Park & E. W. Burgess (Eds.), *An introduction to the science of sociology* (pp. 356-361). Chicago: University of Chicago Press.

Simmel, G. (1950). *The sociology of Georg Simmel* (K. H. Wolff, Ed.). New York: Free Press.

Smith, W. J. (1977). *The behavior of communicating: An ethological approach.* Cambridge, MA: Harvard University Press.

Solomon, R. C. (1990). *A passion for justice.* Reading, MA: Addison-Wesley.

Stigler, J. W., Shweder, R. A., & Herdt, G. (Eds.). (1990). *Cultural psychology.* Cambridge: Cambridge University Press.

Stocking, G. W. (1968). *Race, culture, and evolution: Essays in the history of anthropology.* New York: Free Press.

Stocking, G. W. (1987). *Victorian anthropology.* New York: Free Press.

Streeck, J. (1984). Embodied contexts, transcontextuals, and the timing of speech acts. *Journal of Pragmatics, 8*(1), 113-137.

Streeck, J. (1990-1991). Tao/Sao: Talking culture with Rousseau [Special issue: Ethnography and conversation analysis after *Talking culture*; R. Hopper, Ed.]. *Research on Language and Social Interaction, 24,* 241-261.

Suchman, L. (1987). *Plans and situated action.* Cambridge: Cambridge University Press.

Tacitus, C. (1970). *Germania.* London: Heinemann.

Taylor, J. R. (1989). *Linguistic categorization: Prototypes in linguistic theory.* Oxford: Clarendon.

Tylor, E. (1856). *Researches into the early history of mankind.* Chicago: University of Chicago Press.

Tylor, E. B. (1871). *Primitive culture.* London: J. Murray.

Urban, G. (1991). *A discourse-centered approach to culture.* Austin: University of Texas Press.

Whorf, B. L. (1956). *Language, thought, and reality.* Cambridge: MIT Press.

Wikan, U. (1990). *Managing turbulent hearts: A Balinese formula for living.* Chicago: University of Chicago Press.

Wundt, W. (1975). *Völkerpsychologie: Eine Untersuchung der Entwicklungsgesetze von Sprache, Mythus und Sitte.* Aalen, Germany: Scientia Verlag. (Original work published 1911)

Xenophon. (1962). *Anabasis.* Norman: University of Oklahoma Press.

PART III

Processes and Functions

9

Temporal Qualities of Relationships: Organismic, Transactional, and Dialectical Views

Carol M. Werner

Leslie A. Baxter

TIMING—ACCORDING TO COMEDIANS—is everything. Fortunately, in relationships, it is not necessary to have the exquisite timing of legendary comics as long as one's timing is reasonably good. Knowing when it is appropriate to self-disclose and how intimate to be, anticipating the consequences of arriving early or late for an engagement, providing the right kind of social support at the right time, participating in the appropriate amount of reminiscing about the past, privately projecting the relationship into the future, talking about current relationship concerns, and balancing regular relationship routines with an appropriate amount of novelty all involve temporal processes that are essential aspects of relationships. This chapter has two broad purposes. The first is to review a variety of temporal qualities such as those implied in the above examples, and the second is to examine how those qualities play out in three philosophical orientations underlying relationships research: organismic, transactional, and dialectical approaches. By weaving together temporal and philosophical approaches, we hope to achieve a better understanding of temporal qualities, a richer vocabulary for describing relationship dynamics, and a better understanding of how these contribute to relationship viability.

Research and conceptual analyses attest to the importance of time in relationships. For example, Duck and Sants (1983) thought it was unrealistic for researchers to assume that relationships change only between phases and not within a phase. Warner (1991) reviewed research suggesting that the ability to coordinate

AUTHORS' NOTE: We thank Irwin Altman and Barbara B. Brown for their very helpful comments on previous versions of this chapter.

cycles and sequences of interaction contributes to relationship viability. Levinger (1983) considered an array of models of how relationships develop and rejected several as implausible in part because of restrictive assumptions about such temporal qualities as the sequencing of events and their pace. Duck (1987) and Duck and Montgomery (1991) implicitly used a number of temporal issues to highlight assumptions underlying relationships research. Brand and Hirsch (1990) described how temporal realities can support or constrain relationship opportunities; workday schedules are coordinated with evening entertainment (restaurants, theater and musical performances, and so on), which provides most people with common times to socialize but effectively excludes shift workers. So time and temporal qualities are emerging as important aspects of relationship viability and essential elements of research.

All research is guided by theories and assumptions whether these are acknowledged or implicit (see, for example, Duck & Montgomery, 1991; Steier, 1989). Our position is that it is better for researchers to own up to their assumptions so that decisions about what aspects of relationships to study and how to study them are clear from the outset. At the same time, theoretical and philosophical blind spots can prevent researchers from fully exploring their phenomena. So whereas the traditional concern is that research can be biased by the authors' expectations, it is also the case the research is restricted when authors are unaware of alternative assumptions or ways of thinking about phenomena. By articulating and examining the assumptions underlying several philosophical orientations, we bring them to the fore so that researchers can decide which assumptions are—and ultimately which philosophy is—most appropriate for the particular phenomena under consideration. Thus these underlying philosophical assumptions can be used to pose research questions and define how temporal phenomena will be conceived and studied.

We define *relationship viability* as *the extent to which the individual or group can function effectively to stay alive psychologically and socially, to flourish, to grow and change, and to achieve short- and long-term goals* (see also Werner, Altman, & Brown, 1992, p. 303). Relationship viability encompasses both processes by which viability is achieved and outcome measures by which it is monitored or assessed. The core questions in most relationships research have to some extent involved viability, indexed by diverse questions such as how effectively partners function under stressful conditions, how effectively they manage competing roles and identities, and how successfully they draw on various social networks in coping with short- and long-term stressors. Questions about viability also focus on the consequences of effective functioning, such as how satisfied partners are with their relationship, how much they like and are committed to the partner and the relationship, and/or what they expect to be the future of the relationship. The thesis that we explore here is that temporal and dynamic qualities contribute to our understanding of relationship viability.

Similar to Clark and Reis (1988) and Duck and Sants (1983), we view relationships as ongoing, dynamic *processes*, not steady states. By *dynamic*, we refer to an array of psychological processes and communicative behaviors that people do separately or together that are related to relationship functioning. This includes but is not limited to how relationships form, grow, change, and deteriorate. Dynamic qualities also refer to how relationships are *maintained*, that is, the ways partners manage competing needs and obligations, how they organize and coordinate their activities, the ways in which they introduce novelty and pleasure into their relationship, and how they build a place in which to nurture the relationship. Thus relationships are never entirely stable, they constantly change, and even when a relationship appears to be in a predominantly stable mode, maintaining a viable relationship requires active management and participation by partners. Temporality is central to dynamic processes, and thus this chapter considers the implications of an emphasis on relationship dynamics, such as research on sequences, rhythms, and cycles in speech instead of studies in which data are collapsed into means and variances (Warner, 1988, 1991) or studying variability in interaction instead of averages (Kelley, 1983). Also, we are not interested in temporality or dynamic processes per se but in how they contribute to relationship viability.

Werner and Haggard (1985) laid out a framework of temporal qualities to show the variety of ways in which those qualities could be seen and studied in relationships. In the present chapter, the focus shifts so that, while we consider these temporal qualities, we do so within broader questions: (a) How do temporal qualities contribute to relationship viability? (b) What makes relationships and relationship research dynamic? And (c) how do temporal qualities fit with three philosophical orientations that guide relationships research: organismic, transactional, and dialectic? This is not to say that timing and temporal qualities are more important than other aspects of relationship functioning but that these have been neglected and should be explored. In the next section, we use this framework as a guideline for posing research questions.

Temporal Qualities

We next explore a number of temporal qualities and how they have been shown to function in relationships. These qualities are intended to serve as a guide to theory and research. We believe that they should help researchers to articulate underlying assumptions about how relationships operate; they help to pose important and often unasked questions about relationships; they force decisions about what relationships are like or—if not actual decisions—at least consideration of alternative views. For clarity, we focus primarily on examples of temporal experiences and temporal issues from intimate dyadic relationships, but similar examples and questions can be raised about individuals, nonintimate dyads, families, and other kinds of relationships.

The five major temporal qualities that we consider are *amplitude, salience* (sometimes called "orientation"), *scale, sequencing,* and *pace* or *rhythm.* Except for rhythm, which is exclusively cyclical, each of these can be viewed as operating in *linear or cyclical/spiraling time,* and the first question the researcher needs to pose is whether his or her emphasis is on linearity or cyclicity or both, and what form this temporal quality takes. In a linear view, relationships are viewed as continually changing and moving forward, although continuity may also be assumed; a cyclical view emphasizes repetition, recurrence, and circularity of events, although change in the events and in the relationships may also be expected. Decisions about the relative emphasis on continuity and change and the relative emphasis on recurrent or unique events set the stage for a temporal analysis; these decisions can be influenced by one's assumptions about the five temporal qualities (as indicated by questions such as this one: "Is there a regular or irregular rhythm?"). Table 9.1 lists critical questions that distinguish the temporal qualities.

Table 9.1 Questions Asked by Each Temporal Quality

Temporal Quality	Overarching Dimensions	
	Linear	*Cyclical/Spiraling*
Amplitude	How intense is the phenomenon?	How intense is the recurrent phenomenon?
Salience	Is the focus on past, present, and/or future?	Is the focus on past, present, and/or future recurrent events?
Scale	What is the duration of the phenomenon?	What are durations of and intervals between recurrent phenomena?
Sequence	Is there an order to events?	Is there an order to recurrent events?
Pace/Rhythm	*Pace*: How rapidly do events unfold? (or What is the number of events per unit of time?)	*Rhythm*: How long is the interval between recurrences and what are the pace, order, and amplitude of recurrent events?

NOTE: Naturally, events contain multiple temporal qualities; each is defined separately for clarity.

Linearity and Cyclicity

There is a variety of views on linearity that differ in emphasis on continuity or change and with respect to what may change or remain stable—the couple, its context, or both couple and context. A common view is that relationships change a great deal initially, but once established, get into a relatively stable mode. Those who emphasize change tend to focus on developing relationships and examine how they move forward, continually changing; partners learn more information about each other, engage in a broader range of activities, experience a broader array of emotions together, and become increasingly intimate and interdependent. Relationships can be marked by significant events or turning points, such as engagement, marriage, and minor and major anniversaries, that bespeak a qualitative change in the relationship. In a linear view, once these events occur, the relationship is permanently changed, and there is no return to the previous state. This does not mean that relationships are constantly changing in dramatic ways; a linear view allows continuity and accumulation as illustrated by the ideas that memories are assumed to become part of the present or allow couples or individuals to project relationships into the future. Continuity is also evident in these models when certain experiences are assumed to be required before the relationship can proceed to a deeper level of commitment or intimacy. But there is an emphasis on how relationships and the individuals in them change, especially in early growth stages but also (at least in some views) across the life span. Relationship growth can be stopped or shift to a deterioration trajectory by significant scars such as infidelity, betrayal, and dishonesty.

Theorists who emphasize change differ with respect to whether individuals are relatively stable entities that engage in interactions that produce changed relationships (that is, like marbles that bounce against one another, their shifting locations representing relationship changes) or whether the individuals are themselves changed during interaction. For example, Duck (1987) noted that some researchers focus on the dyad as the unit of analysis and examine how the relationship changes. He considered the "horticultural analogy," describing relationships as growing and blooming like flower seeds (a single entity, not two entities intertwined). In contrast to these views, Aron and Aron (1986) proposed that individuals introduce novelty into relationships in part to experience personal growth and expansion. Baxter (1992b) identified a model of relationship development in which both individuals and their relationship are expected to change; partners come together as separate entities and are changed in the process of building and developing their relationship. And Montgomery (1992) emphasized the interconnectedness of stability and change in both individuals and their dyad. So there are various ways of conceptualizing relationship change, and these vary with respect to the degree of stability or change and emphases on the individual or dyad.

An alternative view of relationships' linear qualities is in theories and research that emphasize stability, especially once a relationship has been established and the couple is engaged, married, or partners describe themselves as committed. For example, linearity might translate into the view that the greatest relationship satisfaction occurs when relationships and their contexts are essentially stable and predictable; experiences and behaviors at time 1 will be similar to those at time 2. Duck and Montgomery (1991) noted that some researchers assume that successful relationships are stable with respect to affect and relationship patterns but move through an ever-changing landscape that engages and challenges the couple without producing any real, long-term change in the relationship (this is similar to the traditional view of personality as a stable guide to action in a changing environment). Some analyses of relationship maintenance and repair emphasize this view, examining what couples do to achieve relationship stability on an ongoing basis or in response to unique, disruptive events (see Dindia & Canary, 1993, for an overview).

Cyclical or spiraling temporality, in contrast, emphasizes recurrence. In cyclical conceptions of relationships, questions about regularity and recurrence of events are central, whereas those are not considered in linear conceptions. Strictly speaking, cyclicity assumes that phenomena recur in identical form in a regular pattern, much like a sine wave or the regular rhythms of music. Some researchers, such as Warner (1988), emphasize this view although Warner notes that no interaction cycles are perfectly regular, which introduces some errors into data analyses that assume regularity. We prefer the term *spiraling* because it is assumed that events, feelings, and behaviors never recur in identical form and do not recur in a temporally regular pattern. So, spiraling time assumes recurrence and routine but also assumes development, change, and the possibility of irregular patterns. Just as the linear qualities of continuity and change can be examined in multiple aspects of relationships (behaviors, feelings, settings, and so on), recurrence can also be seen as pervasive across many aspects of relationships and as contributing in fundamental ways to relationship viability.

We described linear and cyclical qualities as mutually exclusive in order to emphasize their distinct qualities. In fact, however, experiences in people's lives can be either linear (single, often critical events; continual growth and change) or cyclical/spiraling, and what was a single event—and therefore fits a linear view—can become a regular occurrence. It is unrealistic to expect relationships to contain only linear or only cyclical qualities, and both should be explored in theorizing and research. The two overarching dimensions of linear and cyclical/spiraling temporality play out somewhat differently with respect to the subordinate dimensions of amplitude, scale, sequencing, salience, and pace/rhythm.

Linear Qualities

Linear amplitude. "Amplitude" refers to the degree or intensity of partners' subjective experiences and objective behaviors, including such phenomena as the intensity of affect (affection, hostility, sadness, enthusiasm, and so on), the degree of felt intimacy or openness (Derlega, 1984), or the amount of some activity or productivity (Kelley, 1983), and so on. Although it is not naturally thought of as a temporal quality, amplitude is an integral part of cyclical temporal qualities and is a useful construct in linearity as well. The amplitude of events can be thought of as independent of the other temporal qualities, though it is somewhat constrained by them. For example, it is difficult to maintain a high level of affect for a long period of time (scale constraints); there is some question of how quickly affective intensity can increase and decrease (pace constraints) or whether and how rapidly affect can actually reverse direction or change from positive to negative (sequencing and pace considerations); and degree of original affect can be distorted by memories and intervening events (salience effects).

Linear salience. "Linear salience" refers to the extent to which one's thoughts and actions are past, present, or future oriented. Werner and Haggard (1985) noted two major ways in which salience contributed to relationships. First was in the meanings of possessions and in gifts exchanged and displayed (Baxter, 1987; Csikszentmihalyi & Rochberg-Halton, 1981). Possessions often symbolize significant events in the relationship's history (such as the honeymoon, the anniversary trip, family memories), and to the extent that they keep salient more positive aspects of the relationship or how the relationship effectively coped with internal and external problems, objects and memories contribute to relationship viability. A second contribution of salience was illustrated in exchange theories that described how past and present experiences were translated into expectations for the future growth or deterioration of the relationship. Partners accumulate memories, and the extent to which these compare favorably to personal expectations or the extent to which they serve as barriers to leaving a relationship (Levinger & Huesmann, 1980; Rusbult, 1980, 1983), the relationship is expected to continue. In discussing commitment and relationship stability, Kelley (1983) combined temporal scale with salience and said that people don't monitor their relationship costs and benefits on an ongoing basis or at a micro level of scale, but decisions about overall satisfaction are aggregated across time with some people using a longer time frame than others. So viability—in this case commitment to a relationship—can be influenced by recent, short-term experiences, longer scale remembrances, and/or older memories, whatever is salient.

Linear scale. "Linear scale" refers to duration, or how long something lasts. At a micro level, temporal scale can refer to time as a commodity, and Werner and Haggard (1985) and Warner (1991) noted that spending a lot of time on something often connoted greater significance of the activity or event. At a more macro level, linear scale is typically used to describe relationship events or stages in relationships and the experiences that define those stages. Rusbult (1980) conceived of time spent in a relationship as a psychological investment to it and a barrier to leaving it; so, a longer relationship may be more viable because people are more tolerant of, put more effort into getting over, or are better at ignoring rough periods. Werner and Haggard focused on relationship stages as examples of the interconnectedness of time duration and psychological meaning, noting that relationships were expected to move forward within certain normative time frames; a couple describing themselves as "casual daters" after 10 weeks is viewed differently than one casually dating for 10 years. Behaviors and stages are mutually defining, and intimate behaviors that are expected in established relationships are inappropriate between acquaintances. This does not mean that stages are always clearly demarcated or that actions and feelings within a stage are uniform (Duck & Sants, 1983) but that there is a correspondence between how couples define their relationship and what actions are appropriate.

Linear sequencing. "Linear sequencing" refers to the order in which events unfold and the extent to which they are coordinated with others' behaviors. Werner and Haggard (1985) reviewed a range of research indicating that linear sequences give order, meaning, and predictability to interaction. Self-disclosure among acquainting individuals, leave-taking in ordinary encounters, gradual withdrawal from a friendship network as couples approached marriage, and relationship dissolution and divorce have all been found to be most successful if they follow an orderly and expected sequence. Werner and Haggard also pointed to behavioral contingencies as an example of linear sequencing, citing Argyle's (1978) analyses of effective interaction as verbal and nonverbal behaviors fitting together in predictable and comprehensible patterns; they also described other research on interpersonal responsivity or contingency between interacting partners as examples of the importance of effective sequencing in viable relationships. McClintock (1983) and Levinger (1983) described a number of studies in which behavioral sequences were used to get a better understanding of effective relationship functioning, information that is lost when behaviors are aggregated into simple frequency counts. For example, these reviews indicated that, in distressed couples, partners tend to match each other's hostility but respond unpredictably to positive behaviors whereas, in nondistressed couples, partners match positive but not negative behaviors. The research suggests that it is not the actual frequency but the *pattern* of events that contributes to effective or ineffective functioning.

Linear pace. "Linear pace" refers to how quickly events pass per unit of time. Some research examines pace per se, whereas other work examines individuals' perceptions of time's passage. Typically, subjective experiences are opposite to objective events. Long periods of low activity are remembered as having been briefer, whereas periods of intense activity are remembered as having consumed longer periods of time; time "stands still" when partners are so focused on each other that they don't notice changing background events. Werner and Haggard (1985) also reported some theorizing and research that similarity of pace (such as in preferred activities, in speech style) and the appropriateness of the pace with which relationship intimacy progresses were related to more stable relationships.

Multiple temporal qualities. Although these linear temporal qualities have been listed and defined separately, this is done for convenience; we do not mean to imply that they occur in isolation from one another. Behaviors contain multiple layers of temporal qualities, all of which contribute to relationship viability. As an example, consider Warner's (1991) idea that the allocation of time (temporal scale) is an important resource that partners can evaluate and exchange, such as doing a favor or chore that frees up the partner's time; time can also be a potential source of conflict in relationships if a partner was dissatisfied with how time was being spent by the other (such as spending too much time away from home). There are numerous ways that temporal qualities can serve to guide research questions about favors and contact time, that is, the exchange and sharing of time. For example, the concept of "linear amplitude" suggests questions about the physical difficulty of behaviors or how emotionally draining they may be; one is also directed to ask whether intensity is constant, variable, or predictable. "Linear scale" leads to questions about how much time is allocated to couple activities, how much time is exchanged, and what leads to perceptions of equity in time exchange. Questions about "sequencing" in joint activities lead to a focus on coordination and timing, and the realization that these are essential if any act is to be considered a favor. A father taking the children to the zoo when the mother wanted to take them to visit her parents is not a favor and may contribute to conflict. "Linear salience" leads to questions about how partners perceive how time is spent and whether joint time has increased, decreased, or remained steady over the course of the relationship; whether they remember that the other has allocated time toward the relationship; and whether they can expect to count on shared time in the future. And an interest in "linear pace" would lead to explorations of how frequently favors are given or requested, the conditions of these favors (for example, whether these favors are a mechanism for adding variety to daily routines or are necessitated by other factors such as chronic job demands), the relationship between favor frequency and each partner's satisfaction with the relationship, among other things. It is also useful to consider questions that *link* the temporal qualities, such as examining whether past events are salient because of their novel sequencing or unusual amplitude, and so on.

Cyclical/Spiraling Qualities

Cyclical amplitude. Cyclical events are often portrayed as regular sine waves that curve up and down around a horizontal center line. The amplitude is the height of those curves and represents the intensity or degree of change in affect, behavior, or biological variables. Biological functions fill this description nicely, such as the components of circadian rhythms (indexed as body temperature, arousal levels, hormonal changes, and so on); conversation cycles can also be described by their increasing and decreasing degrees of affective intensity. As with linear intensity, amplitude is viewed as both independent of and somewhat constrained by other temporal qualities.

Cyclical salience. "Cyclical salience" refers to whether the time orientation of a recurrent activity emphasizes the relationship's past, present, or future or some combination of these. Werner and Haggard (1985) suggested that recurrent activities should be an important component of partners' assessments of the relationship and asked whether recurrent events might be more significant because of their regularity (for example, their implied stability and continuity, their ability to invoke past experiences). They also noted that holidays and other special celebrations such as birthdays often serve a bonding function by bringing people together for the particular purpose of highlighting an individual or relationship. Wedding anniversaries can be particularly important in this regard because they contain multiple layers of salience; they highlight the couple's history, mark this event in the course of the relationship, and often look toward the future.

Cyclical scale. In a cyclical or spiraling perspective, it is assumed that events recur, so "scale" refers to the duration of the interval between events and the duration of events themselves. For example, spouses who live apart during the week but together on weekends are in a moderate interval, short duration pattern; if they spend time together once a month, they're in a long interval, short duration pattern; and so on. Regular or somewhat regularly occurring interaction patterns having a positive tone can be conducive to relationship stability by providing predictability and regular opportunities for relationship maintenance. Needed novelty can be introduced into relationships by varying the interval or duration of events, or by changing the content of interaction (selecting a different restaurant for a regular date; skiing instead of working) (Altman, Vinsel, & Brown, 1981; Baxter, 1988, 1990).

Cyclical scale has received increasing attention in research. For example, in commenting on the social support literature, Leatham and Duck (1990) urged researchers to pay more attention to routine, mundane, underresearched interactions of normal daily life (namely, short interval, short duration, low amplitude talk) rather than looking only at how support is sought in response to a crisis (typically longer and irregular interval, longer duration, but high amplitude talk). Although Leatham and Duck appeared to assume that routine interaction occurs on a regular basis (approximately equal interval and equal duration), others argue that there is a natural ebbing and flowing of contact with irregular intervals, durations, and amplitudes, and this irregularity is a necessary part of relationships (Altman et al., 1981).

Cyclical sequence. "Cyclical sequencing" refers to repetitions of the same or similar series of behaviors; these can occur in any pattern of cyclical scale and amplitude. Any linear sequence can, through repetition, become a cyclical sequence; examples are regular morning routines or the set of activities that come to define how couples celebrate birthdays and anniversaries. As with linear sequencing, an important aspect of cyclical sequencing is coordination between the couple, such as with effective turn-taking in conversations (Chapple, 1970), or in automatic routines that develop over time and allow a couple to optimize positive interactions (Kelley et al., 1983; Thibaut & Kelley, 1959) or effectively express anger and dissatisfaction. Other researchers have focused on the coordination of daily activities. For example, Brand and Hirsch (1990) discussed the difficulty that shift workers have coordinating their daily routines with their spouses' and children's activities; some women even go so far as to change their sleep cycle on their days off to be a part of their family's routine. These families can sometimes benefit from the lack of partner synchrony, such as not having to pay for or worry about child care because each parent works a different shift and one is always able to be in synchrony with the children.

Warner (1991) noted that analytic strategies distinguish between researchers who adopt a linear or cyclical perspective on sequences. She pointed out that Gottman and his colleagues remove cyclical components prior to analyzing whether behaviors occurred in predictable patterns, whereas Chapple (1970) focused on rhythmic, cyclical patterns. Both approaches allow prediction of behaviors over time, and both showed that coordination of sequences was associated with more positive evaluations of the interaction or the relationship.

Cyclical pace and rhythm. "Cyclical pace" can refer to the pace of any recurrent activities and whether their pace varies or remains fairly constant. Partners can have hectic mornings during the week but more slow-paced weekend mornings, or a morning can build in pace as it progresses. Partners can engage in fast- or slow-paced activities such as rapid-fire tennis matches or slow and deliberate chess games, or they can vary the pace, alternating between slow and rapid activities. At a more macro level, pace can refer to how frequently events recur, which is determined by the scale of the interval between recurrences.

"Rhythm" is defined by the amplitude, scale, sequence, and pace of events. Rhythmic events are often described as being quite regular with respect to these parameters, in which case they can be portrayed as smooth sine waves with a regular amplitude (height of the curve), period (time between onset and offset of activity), and cycle lengths in which the scales of intervals and events are the same. A number of biologically based approaches consider intrapersonal and interpersonal rhythms to be fundamental organizers of human systems. They argue that the extent to which individual rhythms can be coordinated or coupled determines the success of individual couples and larger communities (see Warner, 1988, 1991, for reviews).

Descriptions of rhythmic activities are variable. Chapple (1970) chose to characterize rhythmic conversation patterns as a series of even rectangles indicating a simple on/off, talk/no talk cycle. Warner (1988) was particularly interested in behaviors that fit smooth sine waves, although she noted that curves come in varied shapes, even the spiked form of heart beats. While acknowledging that ongoing cyclical activities are quite variable in both event and interval scale and in amplitude, she argued that the only way to know whether cycles were regular was with statistical analyses, and these are only available for smooth curves.

In contrast to this view, Altman et al. (1981) argued for irregular rhythms in relationships. They focused on the social penetration processes of openness/closedness that are manifested in varying degrees of being together or apart and engaging in intimate or nonintimate conversation and behaviors. Altman et al. suggested that individuals vary in their openness or closedness on a moment-to-moment or day-to-day basis; that cycles of openness and closedness can vary in duration, interval, and amplitude; and that micro-level variations can be embedded in larger openness/closedness cycles. Cyclical patterns vary from individual to individual and couple to couple; some couples shift rapidly from openness to closedness, whereas others change more slowly. They also suggested that couples can change their ways of interacting over the course of the relationship so that particular levels and scales of openness may be effective early in the relationship but may resolve to different levels, frequencies, and cycling pattern over time. So, in contrast to Warner's emphasis on smooth sine waves, Altman et al. would portray these interaction cycles in multiple ways, varying along the dimensions of interval scale, event scale, and amplitude: long intervals between short, narrow peaks; long intervals between high, wide peaks; short, irregular intervals with peaks of irregular heights and widths; and so on. Altman et al. did not believe that any particular pattern was inherently better than another (although they did say that extremes of change and stability would be associated with less viable relationships), were not interested in comparing different kinds of cycles, and were not interested in evaluating whether effectively and ineffectively functioning couples had different kinds of patterns, so statistical analyses were less of a concern to them.

Questions of whether rhythms are regular or irregular are more than semantic ones, because they raise the criterion question: What degree of regularity is necessary for activities to be considered rhythmic? At what interval width are regularly occurring behaviors so spread out temporally that they do not constitute a rhythm? Equally important is the significance question: Are rhythmic events psychologically different than regularly occurring but nonrhythmic events? Cohn and Tronick (1988) distinguished between periodic (regular) and stochastic (cyclic but irregular) cycles, saying that both are possible and both compose cycles as long as the sequences are ordered so that behaviors are predictable over time.

"Entrainment," or "synchrony," refers to the willingness and ability of two partners to effectively coordinate their individual cycles into an overall rhythm. Altman et al. (1981) used the concepts of "matched" and "unmatched" cycles and "timing" and "mistiming" to describe couples with similar or dissimilar openness/closedness patterns. Many researchers argue that effective entrainment can be essential to relationship viability. Chapple (1970) began with the idea that each individual has biological rhythms that influence activity patterns and speech style. People prefer to engage in activities that match their internal physiological rhythm, so they prefer to interact with others whose natural rhythms are similar to their own. As people interact, they slowly coordinate their interactions with their partners; the ease with which this "mutual entrainment" is achieved is predictive of satisfaction with the interaction and relationship (given that other known predictors of attraction are the same). Research indicates that partners are more satisfied by coordinated interactions, but outside observers rate moderately coordinated conversations more favorably than either uncoordinated or too rigidly cyclical ones. Warner (1988) cautions that effective coordination may be most important early in relationships and that established couples can handle and even prefer some arrhythmia in their interactions. Entrainment involves the entire array of temporal qualities, although, to date, most research focuses on whether people coordinate the scales and sequences of events and turn-take effectively. Chapple (1970) did argue that couples who matched activity pace would be most compatible, and it would be interesting to see how people mutually entrain the pace of their interactions, especially how they coordinate across a series of variably paced events.

The research reviewed above on affective sequencing suggests that it is also important to study how couples coordinate their affective amplitude. That work indicated that, in a general way, dysfunctional couples tend to match negative statements and functional couples tend to match positive ones. The work also indicated that, in effective couples, partners coordinated negative with positive statements, so that one partner's complaints were validated or acknowledged by the other, leading to an overall satisfying interaction. (Warner, 1991, described this pattern as distressed couples "cross-complaining" and nondistressed couples as "cross-validating.") It is also likely that, when effective couples do have a negative interaction, they are able to modulate that into and close the interaction with a series of positive exchanges.

Multiple temporal qualities. As noted above, any consideration of the rhythms of activities includes multiple temporal qualities, and we are led to ask whether events unfold in a regular or irregular rhythm and to ask questions about sequences, amplitude, pace, the durations of events, the interval between them, and the extent to which partners can coordinate their rhythms. As with our previous example of layers of linear qualities, using these concepts in combination can serve as a guide for questions about how couples share or exchange time. For the most part, questions about cyclicity parallel those posed earlier about linear exchanges: What is the amplitude and pace of events? How frequently and for how long do exchanges occur? And how are exchanges sequenced and coordinated? The very fact that these are recurrent events changes their nature. For example, whereas in a linear approach, giving time was described as a favor, from a cyclical perspective, there may be a subjective shift in connotation. That is, at what point in a recurrent pattern does a husband who "helps out by cooking dinner" actually become the "husband who cooks dinner" or "husband and wife who share responsibility for cooking dinner"? And at what point is a recurrent event an obligation or drudgery? How do couples achieve a desired level of coordination and regularity in how their time is spent without overburdening one or the other and without losing opportunities for variety and spontaneity?

Summary of Temporal Qualities

In this overview, we have defined and given examples of five temporal qualities within linear and cyclical views of time. In all cases, we endeavored to choose research examples that illustrate how temporal qualities refer to dynamic aspects of relationships and how they are important aspects of relationship viability. We now turn to an examination of philosophical orientations and how these temporal qualities can contribute to a better understanding of relationship processes within each orientation.

Philosophical Orientations

The past decade has seen numerous calls for and actual progress toward research about dynamic qualities of relationships, and there has been considerable success at conducting dynamic and process-oriented analyses. Three philosophical orientations have been particularly instrumental in this regard: organismic, transactional, and dialectical perspectives. Before discussing these orientations, however, we set the stage by introducing Altman and Rogoff's (1987) descriptions of trait and interactional approaches, which have long guided social scientific research. Dynamic qualities are generally not salient in trait and interactional perspectives, and thus these approaches function as counterpoint to the three philosophical orientations developed later in this section, affording a backdrop against which more dynamically oriented perspectives stand in bold relief. Altman and Rogoff's descriptions of organismic and transactional approaches serve as the foundation for our treatment of philosophical orientations using the same labels.

Before we begin, a few caveats are in order. Throughout this section, philosophical orientations are described in only the broadest of strokes to illuminate similarities and differences among them. While each perspective has clearly identifiable characteristics, there are differences of opinion regarding the nature and form of these characteristics and disagreements about which characteristics form the core features of each perspective, so it may be more accurate to think of these descriptions as "fuzzy sets" of characteristics rather than rigidly defining criteria. Furthermore, individual lines of research rarely can be pigeonholed neatly into one or another perspective; guiding assumptions can come from any one of them. In addition, most researchers do not identify their assumptions; others identify some but not all assumptions; and others use different conceptions of the perspectives. So, although we illustrate various constructs with research examples, the authors may disagree with the use we make of their work, and we apologize at the outset for any mis- or overinterpretations. Another point we wish to emphasize is that we are not promoting any particular perspective; each has its advantages and its strong proponents.

Altman and Rogoff (1987) identified trait, interactionist, organismic, and transactional perspectives as four worldviews that have guided behavioral research since the turn of the century. Their analysis is based on the writings of Dewey and Bentley (1949) and Pepper (1942, 1967); other descriptions of the transactional worldview or comparisons among the worldviews also draw on either or both of these early authors, so, although there is not total agreement in some details, there is consensus about the general qualities of each worldview (for example, see Campbell & Gibbs, 1986; Fisher, 1982; Lazarus & Folkman, 1984; Riegel & Meacham, 1978). The four worldviews or philosophical approaches can be distinguished along the dimensions of (a) unit of analysis, such as a focus on individuals, dyads, groups; (b) time and change, such as assumptions about stability and change, homeostatic mechanisms, and teleological goals; and (c) their philosophy of science, including assumptions about determinism and prediction, objectivity of observation, and assumptions about the generalizability of research findings. Research and theorizing about interpersonal relationships fit all four of these orientations, but because they are more explicitly dynamic, our discussion focuses primarily on the organismic and transactional approaches. We begin with brief descriptions of trait and interactional views to provide a contrast or counterpoint to more dynamically oriented perspectives.

Counterpoint: Trait and Interactional Approaches

According to Altman and Rogoff's (1987) analysis, researchers who adopt a trait perspective focus on individuals and their psychological processes as the unit of analysis, view people as largely independent of their context, may assume development and change during formative years but expect stability once personal characteristics are developed, and some though not all assume that there is an ideal end state toward which the individual or personality type is growing. Trait views tend to adopt Aristotle's "material cause" as their form of determinism or the idea that the impetus for behavior resides within the individual (Rychlak, 1977, 1988). Reliable and objective measures of traits are required, and it is expected that studying traits allows the identification of universal principles of behavior.

Although Altman and Rogoff found trait views to be relatively rare in current psychological research, this style is still quite popular in relationships research. Because of their emphasis on stable characteristics, trait studies are usually not thought of as addressing dynamic qualities, and specific temporal qualities have not been a salient concern. A typical trait approach is to define what personal qualities are and how they develop and then to relate these qualities to individual relationship choices or outcomes (we emphasize "individual" choices/outcomes to distinguish this from the couple-level outcomes of interactional work, which follows). Examples of this approach are Carnelley and Janoff-Bulman (1992) on love optimism, Hazan and Shaver (1987) on attachment style, Snyder and Smith (1986) on self-monitoring and friendship choice, and Hendrick and Hendrick (1992) on love styles. Other trait research is more dynamic and behaviorally oriented and addresses questions about time more specifically. For example, Miller and Berg (1984) discussed the behavioral processes by which "openers" (people with the ability to engage others in intimate conversation) build effective close relationships and by which others may fail to do so. This and related work indicates that temporal qualities, such as the pace and amplitude of intimate disclosures, contribute to perceived appropriateness and the viability of the relationship. A great deal of research on traits takes a more interactional approach by examining how partners' traits combine to predict relational outcomes, an approach to which we now turn.

Interactionist perspectives assume that behavior is determined both by aspects of individuals and by aspects of the social and physical environment. This approach is exemplified by the ANOVA strategy in which person and situation are treated as separate factors that may jointly influence behavior but are themselves not changed in the process; the unit of analysis therefore is how combinations of independent factors influence the individual's psychological states and behaviors (cases in which the couple is the unit of analysis are more organismic). Altman and Rogoff drew on Dewey and Bentley's (1949) original billiard ball analogy to describe the interactionist approach; the balls bounce against each other and influence location (environmental factors influence processes and behaviors), but the balls themselves are not changed. Time is considered to be outside of phenomena, and the focus is not on how events unfold in a holistic way but on how changes in the situation effect changes in functioning. Teleological goals or ideal end states are rarely a part of this perspective. Phenomena are not "pulled" toward an ideal outcome; change occurs because of changing circumstances, some of which interact with or "engage" the individual and others of which do not. So, although underlying mechanisms such as homeostasis and drive reduction are familiar features of these approaches, they do not operate in the service of an ultimate state.

With respect to philosophy of science, the emphasis is on Aristotle's "efficient cause" or linear antecedent-consequent relationships, that is, the familiar "cause-effect" issue (Rychlak, 1977, 1988). In complex forms, interactionist approaches specify long series of cause-effect sequences, but these generally deemphasize or ignore reciprocal cause. Indeed, this expectation of linear causal sequences is a primary distinction between interactionist and organismic approaches in which reciprocal or circular cause is a dominant assumption. In addition, it is assumed that the scientist researcher can conduct objective observations from outside of the phenomenon, that observations are precise and replicable, and that a central goal of science is the development of general laws and principles, though an emerging contextual view emphasizes that even general laws are specific to particular kinds of contexts. Altman and Rogoff described this as the dominant approach in psychological research, and our reading of the relationships literature suggests that it is a common approach there, as well.

Similar to trait-oriented research, temporal and dynamic qualities are generally not salient in interactional research. Behaviors are often inferred rather than measured, and although relationships are expected to change and longitudinal research is common, there is little attention paid to mutual influences, especially those that result in enduring changes in partners. A common interactional approach is to explore how two individuals' personalities or attitudes interact or "fit" together to predict relational outcomes. For example, some researchers study matches or mismatches in partners' personalities (consider early work on similarity and complementarity); see, for example, Davis and Latty-Mann (1987) on matches in love styles and satisfaction, Senchak and Leonard (1992) on similarity of attachment style and marital adjustment, and Crohan (1992) and Eidelson and Epstein (1982) on shared dysfunctional beliefs and relationship quality. In these lines of work, a useful dynamic element is added by examining *how* these personal styles and beliefs are manifested in particular day-to-day effective and dysfunctional behaviors to shape relationship outcomes, such as Senchak and Leonard's exploration of conflict behaviors; temporal qualities could be included to consider the roles of sequencing and timing and duration of effective and ineffective behaviors. Other researchers have examined changes in attitudes or affect as a relationship or marriage progresses (Acker & Davis, 1992; Kurdek, 1991, 1992; Sternberg, 1987), and a useful next step in these areas would be examinations of interpersonal styles, ongoing behaviors, and the timing and temporal qualities of behaviors that contribute to change.

Analyses of relationship stages are also studied from an interactional perspective; however, instead of examination of the roles of individual differences, the focus is on perceptions, attributions, and behaviors that contribute to relationship growth and maintenance (Clark & Reis, 1988; Perlman & Fehr, 1986). For example, Berg and Clark (1986) and Berg and McQuinn (1986) examined the pace of relationship development and found that couples differentiated themselves early on as committed or not, and these early commitments were reliable predictors of later relationship stability and success. Stafford and Canary (1991) examined how couples maintain their relationships; they found that different maintenance behaviors supported different qualities of relationships (for example, reassuring the partner predicted commitment and attraction but not interpersonal control) and suggested that an important aspect of relationship viability was the ability to use the appropriate maintenance strategy for different relationship concerns. Implicit was the idea that appropriate behaviors *at the appropriate time* were optimum.

As Werner and Haggard (1985) noted, relationship stage research raises questions about whether time is best viewed as inside of or outside of phenomena: What are the implications of measuring relationship stage qualitatively and self-descriptively or measuring stage quantitatively, as amount of time the couple has known each other? Studies of whether stages differ qualitatively or quantitatively are quite common and raise questions such as these: Do "committed" couples differ from "casually dating" couples simply in the amplitude of their affect (for example, are they more committed, more passionate, more intimate), or are there qualitative differences such as in the kinds of behaviors or kinds of commitment that partners exhibit, or the kinds of interventions needed to restore relationship quality (Duck, 1984; Duck & Sants, 1983)? Leatham and Duck (1990) suggested that it was much more worthwhile to ask people about the processes in their relationship than to ask them to label their relationship stage or point in the marital cycle. Acker and Davis (1992) argued both for more specificity about time course in stage theories and for more empirical research on qualitative versus quantitative indicators of stage. They found that quantitative and qualitative measures provided different—but equally valid and useful—information about relationships. In contrast, in their research on maintenance strategies, Stafford and Canary (1991) examined several strategies (being positive toward the partner, reassuring the partner of one's commitment, sharing tasks, and so on) and found few differences among couples at different relationship stages, suggesting commonality across relationship development.

In summary, there is a wealth of research based in trait and interactionist perspectives, with increasing attention paid to behaviors rather than static descriptions. There is some attention to temporal qualities, especially with respect to the pace of relationship development and the lengths (scale) and subjective meanings of relationship stages. We now turn to a discussion of three philosophical orientations in which temporal qualities are more central.

Organismic Approaches

Unit of Analysis

"Organismic approaches" are defined as *"the study of dynamic and holistic . . . systems in which person and environment components exhibit complex, reciprocal relationships and influences"* (Altman & Rogoff, 1987, p. 19, italics in original). Here, the unit of analysis is the total system; individual units are not—and in fact cannot be—studied apart from the whole: "System components are related to one another in complex ways and . . . it is the overall pattern of relationships between elements that is crucial, not the characteristics of the elements considered in isolation or in specific relationships with other elements" (p. 23). At the same time—and this feature is one distinction between organismic and transactional approaches—the individual elements in the system can be defined and studied independently of each other. So, although the system is the unit of analysis and individual elements are subordinated to it, the system is made up of separately identifiable components. Altman and Rogoff borrowed Laszlo's (1972, cited in Altman & Rogoff, 1987) analogy to illustrate the relationship between a system and its parts. They noted that atoms are made up of neutrons, protons, electrons, and so on, which are arranged in particular ways in becoming an atom. If the parts are reconfigured in different ways, the outcomes are different; this would not be an atom as we know it (to use a well-worn phrase, the whole is more than the sum of its parts). Both the nature of the parts and their particular configurations create the whole, and the nature of the parts can be understood from their contribution to the system.

Although the physical environment is a common feature in biological systems models and in systems analyses of human development (Riegel & Meacham, 1976), it is typically ignored in relationships research. Relationships researchers may include human or social factors of the system such as kin and friendship networks and social resources (employment, crime, schools, shopping areas, transportation), but factors such as physical incivilities (abandoned buildings and automobiles, graffiti, trash), the aesthetic and functional quality of the home or apartment, and the presence of green spaces are typically ignored. If the physical environment is included, it, too, is conceived of as a separately identifiable component—albeit mutually influencing and interdependent. This contrasts with the transactional approach described subsequently in which (a) both the social and the physical environments are integral and inseparable parts of phenomena and are therefore (b) requisite aspects of any analysis.

Time, Change, and Philosophy of Science

Systems are often thought of as living organisms, so change and growth are natural internal processes; changes in individual elements as well as in the system as a whole are of interest, as are changes introduced from outside the system. Many theorists adopt a teleological, homeostatic view, so that internal changes in system functioning are oriented toward moving the system toward an ideal end state, and the system uses maintenance processes such as deviation-countering mechanisms and negative feedback processes to keep functioning in an optimum way. Sometimes a new level of functioning is achieved and other times the system is restored to its previous state. Familiar homeostatic concepts are balance, consistency, need reduction, and predetermined and orderly growth stages. The hierarchical organization of systems—such as power structures in families—contributes to homeostasis; therapeutic interventions based on family systems theory often aim to replace dysfunctional power hierarchies with more adaptive ones, thereby introducing change in order to achieve a new form of stability (Haley, 1976). Thus organicist views are naturally dynamic and consider behaviors that contribute to both change and stability. Change is expected, but time and temporal qualities are usually assumed to be outside of the system; events can be timed by an external clock and the state of system growth relative to some ideal end state can be located on an external time line. Altman and Rogoff devised the term *organismic* specifically to refer to teleologically driven, homeostatic systems in which individual elements remain identifiable and can be separately understood from their functioning in the system.

The idea of systems moving or being pulled toward some perfect end state leads to acceptance of Aristotle's "final cause" (Rychlak, 1977, 1988) as a form of determinism. Organicist researchers may also accept efficient cause as another form of determinism, although it is a complex and circular form. Any point in the system can be an antecedent or consequence (or in some cases an external reinforcer; Bandura, 1978), and mutual, reciprocal cause is typically assumed. Furthermore, changes in one part of the system can reverberate and cause changes in other, even distantly located, parts. So, organicist researchers aim to understand mutual, reciprocal, and reverberating influences over time. Whereas some believe that it is possible to examine and evaluate the extent of influence by studying multiple causal sequences over time (see, for example, Cohn & Tronick, 1988; Phillips & Orton, 1983), others think of this as an "idle exercise" because what is identified as cause or effect depends on the arbitrary point in time when behavior is measured (Bandura, 1978, p. 347).

According to Altman and Rogoff (1987), organicist systems are thought to be governed by a limited number of organizing principles, although these can differ from one system to another; often, the goal of organicist research is to determine the general, underlying organizing principles for different classes of phenomena. Smaller systems can be embedded in larger systems, in which case the rules governing the smaller system become subordinate to those that govern the larger one. Familiar organizing principles are rules and norms that govern social and family interaction. As noted above, system functioning cannot be predicted from knowledge of separate elements; understanding a system requires understanding systemwide principles of organization and functioning. Thus contextual approaches that ground phenomena in their social, physical, or temporal setting do not automatically mean that an approach is organismic; interdependence, mutual influence, and holistic functioning are essential defining qualities.

In other features of their philosophy of science, organicist theories are similar to interactionist approaches; there is a belief in the objectivity of observers and the replicability of observations (see Lazarus & Folkman, 1984, p. 300).

Dynamic and Temporal Features of Organismic Research

There is a wealth of relationships research derived from an organismic orientation. Typical characteristics are holistic models, with psychological and behavioral interdependence, mutual and reverberating influence among the elements, and clear expectations of change and flow over time. Temporal analyses tend to be cyclical, and it is assumed that systems contain recurrent and regular patterns of activity. Good examples of a systems approach come from analyses of social interaction, and most current analyses view interactants as members of a system, although as Gottman (1982) and Cappella (1981) noted, early on and even into the 1970s, the field was dominated by trait and individual orientations. Analyses of interaction and conversational rhythms, mutual adaptation, and reciprocal influence all assume that partners are interconnected and interdependent and that they function at least somewhat differently with this partner (that is, in this system) than with others (Cappella, 1988, 1991; Chapple, 1970; Gottman, 1979; Warner, 1988, 1991). An array of theoretical assumptions, temporal qualities, and related analytic techniques have been brought to bear on conversations, some of them focusing on sequences and the ability to predict current behavior from previous aspects of the interaction (such as with Markov chains and lag sequential analyses; e.g., Ting-Toomey, 1983), others examining mutual entrainment and rhythms through spectral analysis (Chapple, 1970; Warner, 1991), and others examining uni- versus bidirectionality in conversation flow and change (see Cappella, 1988, for discussion). A common theme is that interaction patterns (effective sequencing of content or affect, mutual entrainment, limits to entrainment) are related to the success of the interaction or the relationship as a whole, such as reflected in Gottman's work with distressed and nondistressed couples (Gottman, 1979; Gottman & Levenson, 1992) and Chapple's (1970) and Warner's (1988, 1991) analyses of rhythms and entrainment. However, the relationships between interaction style and success or satisfaction are not simple; as Warner (1991) suggested, the most successful interaction style probably varies with the nature of the conversation and the stage of the relationship.

Temporal and causal issues are interdependent in these lines of work. For example, Chapple (1970) combines linear and reciprocal cause in his explanation of mutual entrainment; that is, the individual's physiological rhythm is given precedence as the reason for conversational rhythms (as opposed to social customs of turn-taking), but he is also interested in the give-and-take between partners (mutual cause) as they adjust their conversational flow. Gottman and his colleagues also use both linear and circular cause in their temporal analyses; they examine whether the partner's or individual's previous behavior is the better predictor of current behavior (a predominantly linear view). And they also examine the "moment to moment adjustment that partners make in response to changes in each other's behavior" (Warner, 1991, p. 93). Cohn and Tronick (1988) compared rhythmic versus bidirectional influence in mother-infant interaction and concluded that bidirectional influence alone could account for changes in behavior. Emerging work in "dynamic systems" reviewed subsequently in this chapter takes the argument one step further and suggests that analyses of bidirectional cause in systems are moot, and it is more fruitful to examine rhythms and mutual coordination as holistic processes.

Kelley et al.'s (1983) analysis of close relationships also adopted an organismic approach in which couples are viewed as complex, emergent systems involving both partners and the social and physical environments. They considered as integral parts of the whole the preexisting qualities of partners, how they "dovetail" or fit together, and qualities that emerge in the process of building a relationship. Their model addresses both the dynamic flow of events and the circular, causal sequences by which relationships grow, develop, and are maintained. The very concept of "interdependence" implies treating the couple as a unit, although often researchers measure partner dependence rather than couple-level interdependence. Kelley's

(1983) analysis of commitment illustrates this organismic approach. He explored commitment as a process rather than static state and showed that multiple contextual, intra-, and interpersonal factors intertwine to support a couple's continued involvement. Public expressions of commitment lead to internal pressures for consistency; they also invoke group support for the couple and reduce the availability of alternative partners (for example, friends no longer offer to "fix up" members of an established couple). Relatively stable interaction sequences and other causal conditions contribute to relationship stability; positive and negative feedback systems keep the relationship on an even keel, such as when one partner provides the other with more rewards when the other seems dissatisfied or when individuals review their perceived and actual costs for leaving the relationship. So multiple, interdependent factors contribute to commitment. The relationship is defined by both partner characteristics and emergent processes, and although change is ongoing, feedback loops maintain stability as the relationship progresses. This analysis is rich with temporal qualities, including discussions of linear and spiraling processes as relationships grow, are maintained, change, or deteriorate; an appreciation of how relationships involve recurrent events with varying intervals; how memories accumulate and change; and incorporation of both micro and macro levels of behavior (such as microanalyses of conversations as well as longer scale events).

Another research domain with strong organismic qualities is research on the embeddedness of close relationships in complex kin and social networks (see, for example, Duck & Silver, 1990; Milardo & Wellman, 1992). Work on how networks provide social support emphasizes the dynamic interdependence among individuals and their networks, and temporal qualities are integral to these analyses. First, individuals and dyads are embedded in multiple networks. Each partner is considered to be part of the other's network (although Leatham & Duck, 1990, caution against assuming that being in a relationship automatically provides support); each partner has his or her own friend and kin networks; and the couple has joint networks of friends and family. Second, support is an integral part of dynamic relationship processes. The nature of the relationships is not fixed but varies as social support is asked for and received; effective provision of support may strengthen the relationship (and ineffective or delayed support may weaken it) (see, for example, chapters by Barbee, Burelson, and Leatham & Duck in Duck & Silver, 1990). Third, social support is a dynamic, temporally complex process. First, a sense of support takes a long time to develop (that is, the scale is long); recurrent or cyclical/spiraling patterns of effective help seeking and giving provide the psychological sense of support (Cutrona, Suhr, & MacFarlane, 1990). Furthermore, the timing of support is an essential ingredient of its impact. The frequency and amplitude of support given and received changes the relationship between interactants, and the timing or relevance of the particular support provided for the particular presenting circumstances plays a major role in its effectiveness and its contribution to the relationship (Eckenrode & Wethington, 1990).

Recent research on how couples cope with daily stressors (daily hassles, work overload, usual and unusual family demands, financial problems, and so on) indicates considerable emphasis on efficient cause in order to understand how one aspect of the system influences others and is reciprocally influenced. For example, common questions about multiple role stress are whether stress in one domain is carried into and influences performance in other domains ("spillover" from work to home, or vice versa) and whether one spouse's stress at work can be brought home and cause stress in the partner ("crossover" from one partner to the other).

Until recently, research on these issues was primarily correlational and was based on retrospective data that necessarily aggregated across spans of time and varieties of stressors. However, Bolger and his colleagues have applied to these questions a daily diary method that allows precise analyses of complex causal relationships (Bolger, DeLongis, Kessler, & Schilling, 1989; Bolger, DeLongis, Kessler, & Wethington, 1989a, 1989b; Caspi, Bolger, & Eckenrode, 1987; Coyne & Bolger, 1990). These studies contain a wealth of temporal qualities, although most are linear rather than cyclical in emphasis. For example, temporal scale is reflected in questions about the durations of stressful episodes; temporal sequencing, in questions of whether stressors change in nature across a stressful episode, whether the emotional effects of stressors change as the stressor persists across days, and whether people rebound after the end of a stressful episode; temporal pace is evident in the concept of work overload as a stressor; and rhythm is implicated in discussions of the disruptions in daily shared routines. Bolger et al. (1989a) suggested that even finer grained analyses could be done to identify both linear and reciprocal causal processes within a single day. Future research might address questions more specific to system functioning as well as other questions suggested by our temporal framework. For example, an organismic approach would provide information about the couple's (the system) rather than individuals' coping mechanisms and whether the couple rebounds after a stressful episode. Awareness of the concept of temporal salience leads to questions about the consequences of memories of stressful experiences or worries about the possibilities of stressors in the future; an awareness of cyclical time and mutual influence suggests questions about how current events lead us to change or reconstruct memories of the past. An interest in temporal rhythms would lead to questions about the intervals, durations, and amplitudes of stressors; whether these are regular or irregular in form; and whether these parameters are related to moods (or one could choose to study the rhythmic patterns of moods). In addition, one could use a "pattern analysis" (Keiser & Altman, 1976; Werner & Haggard, 1992) rather than correlational techniques to understand sequences of behaviors.

So, organismic research examines ongoing processes, interdependence and mutual cause among elements, and general principles of system functioning. This approach is similar but distinctly different than transactional views, which we describe next.

Transactional Approaches

Unit of Analysis

Altman and Rogoff (1987) defined "transactional approaches" as "*the study of the changing relations among psychological and environmental aspects of holistic unities*" (p. 24, italics in original). The term *aspects* was deliberately chosen to convey the idea that the whole cannot be broken up into and is not made up of separate parts; the aspects are mutually defining and inseparable and together contribute to the definition and meaning of events. An implication of this is that all aspects are equally influential; there is no dominant or dominating mechanism that controls functioning; all aspects are equally important, mutually constraining, and events unfold in a coordinated, holistic way (Dewey & Bentley, 1949; Keller, 1985). Transactional approaches explicitly include the social and physical environments and temporal qualities as integral aspects of events. As Campbell (1986) argued:

> The problem is that [people and place] cannot be conveniently pulled apart for the purposes of analysis, however much our social-science instinct tells us to partition the variance. People and situations are not logically independent of one another in the real world. For example, a young male and a given street do not come together by happenstance. He is there because he lives there or because his friends do. His neighborhood and his streets have been part of the socialization process that has contributed to his personality. . . . The street is not separable from its inhabitants. . . . Nor does time conveniently freeze itself in the real world. A social setting can change over time. (p. 116)

Lazarus and his colleagues (Lazarus & Folkman, 1984; Lazarus & Launier, 1978) effectively distinguished between transactional and interactional views in terms of the unity of aspects (although in other ways, their model is organismic; Lazarus & Folkman, 1984, pp. 293-294):

> [A feature that] gives the term *transaction* a quality missing in the concept of interaction, is that transaction implies a newly created level of abstraction in which the separate person and environmental elements are joined together to form a new relational meaning. In interaction . . . [the] variables retain their separate identities. From a transactional perspective, the characteristics of the separate variables are subsumed. . . . An appraisal [evaluation of harm, threat and challenge] does not refer to the environment or to the person alone, but to the integration of both in a given transaction . . . [separate person and environment characteristics] are no longer distinct in the new higher-order variable "threat." (p. 294)

Fisher (1982) distinguished between the terms *dyad* and *marriage,* categorizing the former as interactional because the independent elements were clearly identified and separable, and categorizing the latter as transactional because it immediately implies a higher-order unity—husband and wife are mutually defining and insepa-rable. In his analysis of family transactions, Fisher found that many researchers failed to use relational-level data to define their families. A research approach that answers Fisher's challenge is Johnson, Huston, Gaines, and Levinger's (1992) study of marital "types." They discussed the importance of using relation-level constructs for defining different kinds of marriages and used a variety of couple-level rather than individual characteristics to do so (such as gender asymmetry in the labor force rather than separate scores; degree of shared or separate leisure time and household work as opposed to separate analyses).

Time and Change

Time and change are integral aspects of transactional unities. As the basic definition indicates, focus is on "changing relations," not steady states, fixed properties, or causal chains. Ongoing change may result in emergent and new configurations that cannot be predicted from a knowledge of the separate elements. This quality is unique to transactional approaches; trait and interactional views assume that behavior is determined by and can be predicted from knowledge of separate elements; organicist approaches assume that behavior is caused by mutual and reverberating influence or can be predicted from the rules of system functioning.

Furthermore, unlike the previous philosophical approaches in which time was an outside marker of events, time is an integral part of them; for example, transactional researchers want to understand the natural temporal patterning of events (Werner, Haggard, Altman, & Oxley, 1988) or how events change and flow (Werner, Altman, & Oxley, 1985) and avoid imposing a researcher-determined calendar from the outside.

Philosophy of Science

Transactional views also hold a unique philosophy of science. First, and perhaps most significant, transactional approaches adopt Aristotle's "formal cause," which Rychlak (1988) defined as "a pattern, shape, outline, or recognizable organization in the flow of events or in the ways that objects are constituted . . . behavioral sequences are clearly patterned outlines, recognizable styles of . . . significance to the viewer" (pp. 5-6). Thus formal cause focuses on the flow and organization of behavior and on coherent patterns of behavior. So, unlike organicist and interactional views, which emphasize antecedent-consequent relationships, transactional views examine how the aspects of phenomena fit together in coherent patterns, how events flow and unfold over and in time, and how the patterns shift and change with changing circumstances. Interest is not in whether one aspect causes another but in how the aspects fit together in meaningful ways:

> [One tries] . . . to identify relationships among component parts and processes—but none of the components is "caused" by the prior occurrence of another component; and even more important, none of the components "causes" the action or act of which they are components. (Ginsburg, 1980, p. 307)

Lazarus and Launier (1978) also distinguished between interaction and transaction on causal grounds, saying that "attention to causal variables leads us rapidly away from transaction and description to the more familiar and comfortable [concepts of causality and interaction]" (p. 289).

Typical examples of formal cause are behavioral routines—sequences or patterns of events across time—and how partners coordinate them. A morning routine is usually composed of a variety of regular behaviors done in a more or less regular order: getting up, walking the dog, grooming, eating breakfast, car-pooling, and so on. No separate element causes the next—eating breakfast does not compel one to car-pool, but the morning routine is orderly and coherent, oriented toward the goal of preparing for the day. Examining these routines and how couples synchronize them is a legitimate purpose of scientific inquiry and a question raised almost exclusively by formal cause.

The focus on patterns and configurations does not preclude hypothesis testing, but it does guide the choice of hypotheses. As Fisher (1982) noted: "The problems of specifying hypotheses are exacerbated in transactional research because of the necessity of articulating a theory that by definition does not have independent elements" (p. 317). In describing how to apply a transactional approach to families, it is possible to distinguish between how family interaction patterns shift and change (formal cause) and outside events that might influence those patterns (efficient cause). Fisher proposed

> the necessity of specifying transactional hypotheses as sequences of actions or configurations of behaviors within a specified setting. . . . A transactional hypothesis

might call for the increased occurrence of certain *patterns* of family behaviors in certain kinds of families rather than in others. . . . Or, alternatively, a transactional hypothesis might call for a given sequence of family behavior under certain conditions. (pp. 317-318)

Thus transactional approaches can involve hypotheses about profiles of variables, as well as hypotheses about differences between groups or changes in profiles over time, without ever invoking the concept of efficient cause, although efficient cause might (though not necessarily) provide a useful perspective when considering outside events that result in sudden and dramatic changes (see Dell, 1982a, and Riegel & Meacham, 1978, for further discussion).

In addition to this focus on formal cause, transactional views have two other distinctive philosophical assumptions. First, in contrast to the previous views that sought general and universal principles, transactional approaches assume that phenomena may contain both unique and universal principles; the mechanisms underlying phenomena may or may not recur, and phenomena need to be appreciated both for their uniqueness and for their generality. Second, observers are integral to events; their observations are not objective, replicable, or the same as observations made from other locations in the events. Observations depend on the observer's subjective assumptions as well as their perspective and location in the phenomenon. Werner, Altman, Oxley, and Haggard (1987) suggested several methodological implications of these philosophical assumptions: (a) Researchers should assume that phenomena will change; (b) relationships can be studied from several vantage points within the social structure (dyad, family, network, and so on) and each contributes to understanding; (c) research should draw on the perspectives of multiple observers for a more comprehensive understanding; (d) because of the changing and unique character of phenomena, different aspects and different measures of those aspects may be needed at different times.

Transactional Systems Views

Some family systems approaches use organicist terminology but are fundamentally transactional in their assumptions. Many family researchers/therapists treat the family system as the unit of analysis; they regard families as integrally interconnected and inseparable, with smaller systems nested in larger ones, and many include the therapist as part of the system rather than an outside observer (Bochner & Eisenberg, 1987; Keeney & Sprenkle, 1982; Rosenbaum, 1982; Selvini, 1988). Although change is assumed, change does not operate because of efficient or formal causal mechanisms but because of ongoing and emergent processes. As Bochner and Eisenberg (1987) noted, family systems theorists originally adopted homeostatic assumptions explicitly to get away from efficient causal mechanisms: "The homeostatic paradigm represented an epistemological turn away from thinking of 'forces' or 'causes' and toward thinking of 'relationships' and 'contexts' " (p. 542). Selvini-Palazzoli and her colleagues (Selvini-Palazzoli, Boscolo, Cecchin, & Prata, 1975/1990) rejected efficient cause; they described family members as clearly influencing each other's behaviors but said that it would be epistemologically incorrect to try to identify specific cause-effect sequences. The decision of where to enter the flow of events would be arbitrary and would ignore the prior history and prospective future of mutual constraint and influence. Instead, causality resides in the rules that govern family functioning (see Werner, Altman, & Oxley, 1985, on the rules and social relations that bind transactional unities). So whereas these authors do not explicitly embrace formal cause, they reject even complex forms of efficient cause.

Homeostasis, a fundamental assumption in organismic approaches, is rejected for a variety reasons, including the reality of spontaneous change in families and the absurdity of assuming homeostasis when the goal of family therapy is to help families change (see Bochner & Eisenberg, 1987, for a review). Dell (1982a) proposed redefining homeostasis so that it excluded "resistance to change," in part to allow large, unpredictable fluctuations in a system as had been observed in physics and in family therapy (Dell, 1982b, p. 410). He retained the idea that systems are "organized" but proposed abandoning the term *homeostasis* and substituting instead *coherence*, which "simply implies a congruent interdependence in functioning whereby all aspects of a system fit together" (Dell, 1982a, p. 32). Other organismic relational mechanisms are "behavioral constraint," "influence," and "functional demands" that "organize" how families interact, such as family rules and sets of learned expectations of how family members will act and interact. These are not conceived as causal mechanisms but as organizing principles that guide interaction. These relational mechanisms and the concept of coherence are remarkably similar to the transactional view's formal cause.

Recent analyses of systems as "self-organizing" or "dynamic" indicate that these views are also similar to transactional approaches. As their name implies, these models do not assume that there is a single dominant mechanism or "executive center" that controls or causes system functioning but that the parts are mutually constraining (not mutually causative). So patterns of behavior or coordinated actions emerge and flow rather than being organized and planned from the outset. In a dynamic systems view, the focus is on coordinated patterns of multiple factors, just as in the transactional approach the focus is on coherent and meaningful patterns involving multiple aspects. Thus dynamic systems are distinct from organismic systems models in that they deemphasize separate and sequential cause-effect relationships, opting instead for multiple and mutual influences among the aspects of a system. Although not explicitly claimed, the focus appears to be on formal cause or the processes by which systems are organized and the patterns of organization rather than efficient cause-effect relationships. Similar to a transactional view, there is interdependence and mutual definition between individual and environment; individual capacities are fit to the demands of the task and the physical context in which action occurs; no aspect is more important than any other in influencing how actions unfolds; and actions are coordinated rather than being "caused" in an efficient causal way (Fogel et al., 1992; Thelen, 1992).

Dynamic and Temporal Features of Transactional Research

We draw on two lines of work to illustrate transactional approaches: Selvini-Palazzoli and colleagues' work on family therapy (Selvini, 1988; Selvini-Palazzoli et al., 1975/1990) and Altman, Werner, and Brown's analyses of relationships integral to their physical environments.

Selvini-Palazzoli and her colleagues are best known for their use of paradoxes to treat anorexia and schizophrenia. The work treats anorexics and schizophrenics as integral parts of holistic families. The families are grounded in their physical and social environments; therapy is a dynamic process, and different subsystems of the family may be involved and different individuals may be targeted at different stages of the therapy. Although paradoxes provide a generic approach to intervention, the particular paradox is unique to each family and to the particular issues raised during each therapy session; the interventions are not seen as a cause of change but as an attempt to change the rules of interaction. The therapists are accepted as integral parts of the family, not separate objective observers.

For example, with respect to the physical environment, the therapists note where family members choose to sit at the beginning of each therapy session and how members present themselves through clothing, grooming, and hairstyle. They ask how family members use their dwellings throughout the day to ascertain patterns of interaction; sometimes these patterns are interpreted as representing social custom, such as working-class males who typically frequent men's social clubs at night, and, at other times, these patterns are suggestive of underlying dysfunction with family members avoiding one another. Therapists ask where kin and other family members live and how frequently members of the presenting family visit with them, using changes in visiting patterns as cues to family dynamics.

Another essential part of paradox interventions is that they are never targeted at only one individual but at the system as a whole. So, for example, in one intervention, each member of the family was given a note to read to the anorexic daughter that explicitly stated how her anorexia was serving each member and their interrelationships with other family members. The paradox—reaffirming their need for her anorexia when they had come in for a cure—was designed to force the family to confront the issue openly. Only by including the entire family and their interdependence could the family rules be modified so that the anorexic daughter could be allowed to change. Selvini-Palazzoli and her colleagues' approach to therapy is rich and complex and illustrates in many ways a transactional approach to family therapy.

Transactional research on relationships has been conducted by Altman, Werner, Brown, and their colleagues; however, very little of that work has specifically examined transactional processes within dyads, so there is not a rich pool of information or approaches from varied laboratories by which to evaluate the contribution of transactional perspectives to dyadic functioning. Still, those studies are illustrative, and we describe them briefly.

Werner, Altman, and Oxley (1985) first reviewed research and theory that indicated that homes are not just physical settings but can be viewed as transactional unities comprising simultaneously people, interpersonal processes, temporal qualities, and the physical environment. They showed that dynamic processes including appropriation of place, social rules and relationships, and cognitive/perceptual processes all serve to connect people and place in mutually defining relationships. Using similar temporal qualities to those outlined in this chapter (scale, pace, rhythm, and so on), they then examined how the linking mechanisms and temporal qualities contributed to family experiences. For example, "place attachment" is not only a positive affective tie by an individual to a place; instead, it is psychological bond that involves memories of people, relationships, and activities, plans for immediate and long-term future events, and specific objects and places in the home. They argued that, to understand interpersonal relationships, one needs to understand when and where relationship events occur. Drawing on Korosec-Serfaty's interviews with French farming families, they showed how attachment to home and family involved seasonal rhythms of particular activities in particular parts of the home and farm (attic, cellar, fields), with particular combinations of family members and particular temporal features. Thus the analysis

was holistic and included the total home and family, the temporal qualities underlying events, and the psychological processes that linked people and place together
in time.

In their comparison of Christmas Street with Zuñi Shalako, Werner, Haggard,
Altman, and Oxley (1988) also took a holistic approach, but highlighted temporal
processes instead of the bonding of people with the physical environment. Taking a
yearlong perspective, they reviewed activities and underlying temporal qualities in two
annual celebrations, showing how the salience of different aspects of the celebration
varied across the year (for example, memories of previous enactments were more
salient at some times than others; plans for the upcoming celebration became increasingly salient over time), how the pace and rhythm of events varied across the year, and
how these also contributed to the form and meaning of activities.

Oxley, Haggard, Werner, and Altman (1986) and Werner, Altman, Oxley, and
Haggard (1987) incorporated the entire range of transactional characteristics in
their analysis of Christmas Street. Of particular illustrative value to the present
chapter is their use of formal cause to understand changing interrelationships
among personal, social, and physical variables (that is, the aspects of a transactional
unity). They examined how neighborhood attachment, neighboring behaviors, and
presentation of the physical environment changed between summer and Christmas,
a time when traditional seasonal activities transformed the street into a wonderland
of lights and decorations. In the summer, there were distinct social networks, each
with somewhat different attitudes toward the neighborhood, and social interaction
was limited primarily to those neighbors. In the winter, the networks and attitudes
tended to merge into large, rather coherent groups of residents who expressed
enthusiastic attitudes about the tradition of neighborhood decorating for the Christmas season and who participated in neighborhood parties and activities. Furthermore, in summer, network membership and attitudes were unrelated to decorating
and upkeep of the physical environment, whereas at Christmas, environmental
presentation was an integral aspect of the holiday experience. Thus the profiles of
the neighborhood on these characteristics (namely, the pattern of interrelationship
among friendship choice, group activities, environmental decorating, and so on,
that is of interest in formal cause) were different at the two different times of year.

These descriptions illustrate transactional approaches to therapy and research.
Emerging integrations of transactionalism with dialectical approaches are described subsequently as a part of dialectics.

Dialectical Approaches

Scholars differ with respect to whether dialectical approaches constitute a unique
philosophical orientation. Altman and Rogoff (1987), for example, discussed the
dialectical approach of Altman and his colleagues (1981) as an example of a
transactional approach. More recently, Altman, Brown, Staples, and Werner (1992)
and Werner, Altman, Brown, and Ginat (1993) have discussed a transactional/dia-
lectical perspective, which implies that transactionalism and dialectics are different
but compatible. Our position is that dialectics is similar to transactionalism but
sufficiently distinctive and complex to warrant discussion in its own right. Because
we perceive that the term *dialectics* is frequently misunderstood, we will organize
this section somewhat differently than the discussions of organismic and transactional approaches. In particular, we will open this section by discussing common
misconceptions about dialectics. Similarities and differences between dialectics

and the other two dynamically oriented perspectives with respect to unit of analysis, assumptions about time and change, and philosophy of science will be clarified as we proceed. Then we will turn to a discussion of dynamic and temporal features of dialectical research.

What a Dialectical Perspective Is and Is Not

Dialectics Is Not a Unitary Approach

Dialectics is not a single, unified perspective but a family of distinct perspectives that share in common a commitment to the core concepts of contradiction, change, and totality, each of which will be discussed in the following pages. When most people think of dialectics, they typically, and erroneously, equate it with political economy and the dialectical materialism of Marx, Lenin, and Mao (e.g., Cornforth, 1968). However, a number of distinct dialectical perspectives have emerged throughout the scholarly community, including such fields as developmental psychology (e.g., Riegel & Rosenwald, 1975; Rychlak, 1976), organizational dynamics (e.g., Benson, 1977; Zeitz, 1980), political theory (e.g., Warren, 1984), social psychology (e.g., Billig, 1987, 1991; Billig et al., 1988; Buss, 1979; Georgoudi, 1983; Israel, 1979), and social theory (e.g., Ball, 1979; Mirkovic, 1980; Murphy, 1980). Given this chapter's focus on communication in personal relationships, differences among these several dialectical perspectives will not be discussed except in the broadest of terms.

In the domain of interpersonal communication and personal relationships, at least eight research programs with a dialectical component can be identified: the trans-actional/dialectical approach of Altman, Brown, Werner, and their associates in the study of couples, families, and communities (e.g., Altman, in press; Altman & Gauvain, 1981; Altman et al., 1981; Altman et al., 1992; Brown, Altman, & Werner, 1992; Werner, Brown, Altman, & Staples, 1992; Werner et al., 1993); the dialogic approach of Baxter and her associates applied to friendships, romantic relation-ships, and marital relationships (e.g., Baxter, 1988, 1990, 1992b, 1993, 1994, in press; Baxter & Simon, 1993; Baxter & Widenmann, 1993; Bridge & Baxter, 1992); the family dialectics approach advanced by Bochner and his associates (e.g., Bochner, 1984; Bochner & Eisenberg, 1987; Cissna, Cox, & Bochner, 1990); Conville's (1983, 1988, 1991) work on second-order relational transitions; Masheter's work in the dialectics of "ex's" (Masheter, 1991, 1994; Masheter & Harris, 1986); the social contextual dialectics advanced by Montgomery (1992); the work in cultural communication that explores the individual-communal tension in interac-tion (e.g., Carbaugh, 1988a, 1988b; Katriel & Philipsen, 1981; Philipsen, 1987); and the dialectics of friendship advanced by Rawlins and his associates (e.g., Rawlins, 1983a, 1983b, 1989, 1992; Rawlins & Holl, 1987, 1988). Apart from obvious differences related to the particular relationship type under study, many of these dialectically oriented approaches can be differentiated on other features that will become apparent later in discussing the emergent themes that characterize existing dialectical research on personal relationships.

Dialectics Is Distinct from Dualism

As Giddens (1979) has noted, dualistic thinking is often mistaken for dialectical thinking. In contrast to the static view of opposites evident in dualistic thinking, time and change are integral to dialectical opposition. However, before elaborating on the distinction between dualism and dialectics, some discussion is merited on the more general concept of opposition. Both dualistic and dialectical perspectives are interested in studying the bipolar oppositions that constitute a given system, including individual, dyadic, family, group, network, and societal systems.

Types of oppositions. In general terms, two tendencies or features of a phenomenon occupy a relation of opposition if they are incompatible and mutually negate one another. However, not all oppositions are alike. A distinction is often made between oppositions that are mutually exclusive and exhaustive and oppositions that are mutually exclusive but not exhaustive (Adler, 1927, 1952; Altman et al., 1981; Georgoudi, 1983; Israel, 1979). Mutually exclusive and exhaustive oppositions are usually conceived negatively, that is, opposition is conceived as the absence of some feature or tendency. For example, "independence" and "nonindependence" are mutually exclusive in that they negate one another, and they are exhaustive in that no third possibility exists. In denouncing one tendency, we can only affirm the other and nothing else. By contrast, nonexhaustive, mutually exclusive oppositions tend to be positively defined features rather than one feature whose meaning is the mere absence of the opposing tendency. For example, "independence" and "dependence" illustrate oppositions that are mutually exclusive but not exhaustive. In negating "independence," for example, we could be affirming either of the non-equivalent conditions, "dependence" or "interdependence." As becomes evident later, most of the oppositions that have been studied in the context of personal relationships involve nonexhaustive, mutually exclusive tendencies. The practical import of this observation is the recognition that many oppositions, not just one, may exist in relation to a given bipolar feature (Bakhtin, 1981, 1984). Thus, for example, the researcher interested in examining the feature of "certainty" from a dialectical perspective might identify several dialectical oppositions all contained within the broad opposition of "noncertainty": certainty-randomness, certainty-excitement, certainty-mystery, and so forth. These oppositional pairs probably bear a family resemblance to one another at some level, but they may differ in subtle ways as well. Further, because a given feature is defined through the opposing feature with which it is united, the concept of "certainty" is likely to mean slightly different things depending on the particular contradiction of which it is a part (Baxter, 1994). Scholars need to pay close attention to such subtle complexities before concluding that a complete dialectical understanding of such concepts as "certainty" has been achieved.

The dialectical concept of contradiction is what differentiates dualistic opposition from dialectical opposition (Baxter, 1994). Stated in general terms, a "contradiction" refers to the dynamic tension between unified opposites in a system. Opposition is a necessary but not sufficient element in contradiction; the additional underscored elements of unity between opposites and dynamic tension between opposites are requisite as well. Oppositional tendencies are unified or interdependent in two ways (Altman et al., 1981). First, each tendency presupposes the existence of the other for its very meaning. Second, contradictory tendencies are unified in being part of a larger whole. For example, in the context of personal relationships, individual autonomy and relational connection are regarded as opposites (Baxter, 1988); the total autonomy of parties precludes their relational connection, just as total connection between parties precludes their individual autonomy. However, individual autonomy and relational connection form an inter-dependent unity as well. Connection with others is necessary in the construction of a person's identity as an autonomous individual (e.g., Askham, 1976; Mead, 1934; Zicklin, 1969), just as relational connection is predicated on the existence of the parties' unique identities (e.g., Askham, 1976; Karpel, 1976; Kernberg, 1974; L'Abate & L'Abate, 1979; Ryder & Bartle, 1991). Thus, similar to transactional-ism, dialectics rejects the organismic assumption that individual elements, in this instance oppositions, can be defined separately from one another. Like transaction-alism, dialectical perspectives assume that system elements, that is, oppositions, mutually define one another and are inseparable. This issue will be explored further in our discussion of dialectical totality.

Time and change in dynamic tension. The concept of "contradiction" includes the dynamic tension between opposing tendencies. *Dialectical tension* is not a negative force according to a dialectical perspective; instead, the term simply refers to the ongoing dynamic interaction between oppositions. In fact, it is the interaction or interplay of opposing tendencies that serves as the driving force or catalyst of ongoing change in relationships. By contrast, dualistic approaches emphasize the structural existence of bipolar opposites but ignore their dynamic interaction. The personal relationships literature is replete with the identification of a variety of dualisms or binary oppositions (for a review, see McAdams, 1988). Although substantial research is devoted separately to the bipolar components of a given duality, the bipolarities are conceptualized as relatively static and independent concepts that coexist in parallel but whose dynamic interplay is typically ignored. In contrast to much of the existing research and theory on personal relationships, a dialectical perspective presupposes that effective personal relationships are predicated on the simultaneous need for both opposing tendencies of a contradiction. That is, relationship viability is predicated on the dynamic unity of opposites. Thus, for example, dialectical intimacy necessitates both autonomy for the partners and interdependence between the partners, in contrast to a nondialectical view in which partner autonomy is regarded as evidence of a less satisfying bond. A similar point could be made with respect to other basic contradic-tions, for example, openness-closedness and predictability-novelty. That is, a satisfy-ing, close relationship necessitates both partner openness and partner closedness, both relationship certainty and relationship novelty. This "both/and" feature of a dialectical perspective leads to fundamentally different conceptions of relationship development, closeness, and intimacy than those found in current research and theory (Baxter, 1992b).

Efficient and formal cause. Dialectics is not unitary on the question of determinism, with dialectical researchers likely to vary in the emphasis they place on efficient cause as opposed to formal cause. Because contradictions serve as the drivers of change in relational systems, they could be thought of as efficient causes that function as organismic determinism. That is, contradictory oppositions could be conceived as mutually and reciprocally causal through time. However, the unity of opposites and the fluidity that characterizes their dynamic interplay involves a level of complexity that is probably more amenable to formal-cause analysis. Like transactionalism, dialectics encourages a focus on how contradictions flow and unfold over and in time and in the patterns of ever-changing contradictions that constitute a system's temporal movement.

Dialectical Change Can Be Both Linear and Cyclical/Spiraling

The process of dialectical change is characterized by a struggle or tension between the opposing tendencies of a contradiction, and such struggle can take linear and/or cyclical/spiraling form (Altman et al., 1981; Bakhtin, 1981; Cornforth, 1968). At a given point in time, one tendency typically is more dominant than the other, creating the exigency for efforts to enhance the negated opposing tendency. Consider the long-distance couple for whom geographic separation makes individual autonomy, which they define as physical separation, the dominant condition over connection, which they define as time spent together. To achieve a more satisfying relationship, the couple is likely to undertake efforts designed to enhance the negated tendency of connection. For example, the pair might decide to increase the number of weekends they spend together, that is, change the scale or interval length between joint weekends, and thus change the rhythm of time apart and time together. Such a change would be cyclical or spiraling in nature. If this change is modest in scope, the exigence of negated connection will continue, and the parties will take additional redressive actions until they favor connection at the expense of autonomy, which would create a counterexigency for cyclic or spiraling redressive actions in the opposite direction. Instead of, or in addition to, cycling/spiraling back and forth between time spent together and time apart, the couple might qualitatively transform their understanding of autonomy and connection, ceasing to define the oppositional tendencies in terms of time spent together or apart and redefining them along other semantic dimensions. "Transformative change" refers to such qualitative reframings in which the original opposition is fundamentally changed in character or meaning, and such change is linear in nature because of its one-time, nonrepeating nature. Transformations are not mere changes in amplitude or intensity of an opposition but instead involve fundamental changes in the metric by which intensity or amount is gauged. However, transformational changes may result from cumulative changes in amplitude, that is, the proverbial straw that breaks the camel's back. The pair might continue to experience a dialectical tension in terms of their altered understandings of autonomy and connection, or the transformation could transcend the opposition between tendencies and resolve the initial contradiction. In such a transcendence, the relationship parties would cease to view autonomy and connection as incompatible oppositions, perhaps coming to regard them as mutually enhancing.

Dialectical theorists are not of one mind with respect to the transcendence of dialectical contradictions and the role of teleological forces (Rychlak, 1976). Some dialectical theorists endorse a conception of dialectical change as a process of transcendent development, with the dominance of one dialectical tendency (the thesis) followed by a qualitative change in which the opposing tendency (the antithesis) becomes dominant, followed by a transformative change in which the original opposition of tendencies is somehow transcended (the synthesis). From the perspective of transcendence, relationship change is teleological in nature, with the relational system evolving toward the ideal state of synthesis. Transcendent change emphasizes the temporal quality of sequencing in the thesis-antithesis-synthesis pattern. Other dialectical theorists reject the teleological goal of transcendent change, endorsing instead a dialectical model of indeterminacy in which two opposing tensions may simply continue their ongoing struggle of negation in some cyclic/spiraling and/or linear fashion. From the perspective of indeterminacy, relationship change is characterized by a variety of linear and/or cyclical/spiraling changes over time, including small incremental shifts or sharp jumps in the relation between opposing tendencies, cyclic/spiraling patterns in the back-and-forth struggle of oppositions, and transformations that require an entirely new metric. As Altman et al. (1981) have noted, such change is likely to be irregular and unpredictable in nature. That is, indeterminate change is likely to be characterized by substantial variability through time in scale, amplitude, and pacing features of temporality. Further, indeterminate change is not homeostatic in nature, although a relationship could be at a point of balance on a momentary basis. A dialectical system does not sustain equilibrium or a state of balance between contradictory oppositions but instead experiences ongoing change as a result of dialectical interplay. In short, dialectics is not unitary with respect to the matter of teleological goals, with disagreement among dialectical researchers with respect to transcendent synthesis as opposed to ongoing indeterminacy.

Dialectics Is Not the Equivalent of Interpersonal Conflict

As Giddens (1979) has noted, conflict is often mistaken for dialectical contradiction. Put simply, some but not all dialectical contradictions involve interpersonal conflict. Dialectical contradictions that involve interpersonal conflict are referred to by dialectical theorists as "antagonistic contradictions," in contrast to nonantagonistic contradictions, which do not involve interpersonal conflict between parties (Cornforth, 1968; Giddens, 1979; Mao, 1965). The distinction between antagonistic and nonantagonistic enactments is similar to the concept of substantive synchrony or "matching" discussed by Altman et al. (1981), and invokes the temporality feature of sequencing with respect to coordination (or lack thereof) between relationship partners. If two parties align their respective interests and goals with different poles of a given contradiction, they are "mismatched" in their respective cyclic/spiraling rhythms and the dialectical struggle is antagonistic, that is, likely to involve interpersonal conflict. By contrast, relationship parties who are matched in their cyclic/spiraling rhythms are not likely to engage in interpersonal conflict, because the source of the tension does not reside in partners' blocking one another's goals. Nonantagonistic contradictions are intrapersonal in nature; the individual experiences internally the dialectical pull between contradictory oppositions. We return to antagonistic and nonantagonistic manifestations of contradictions in the next section on emergent themes in the dialectical research. Overall, however, the majority of work has been done with nonantagonistic manifestations.

Dialectical Totality Is Not the Equivalent of Holism

"Dialectical totality" refers to the assumption that phenomena can be understood only in relation to other phenomena (Benson, 1977; Israel, 1979; Mirkovic, 1980). On its face, dialectical totality appears to be the same as any number of other theoretical orientations that emphasize such holistic notions as contextuality and relatedness, for example, organismic theories or transactionalism. However, dialectical totality and other holistic theoretical orientations are not equivalent. Put simply, dialectics is one form of holism, but not all holistic theories are dialectic simply because they examine relations among phenomena and embed phenomena in their contexts. The criterion that distinguishes dialectical holism from other holistic orientations is whether contradictions are the focus of analysis.

Dialectical totality entails four corollaries, all of which implicate the notion of contradiction in some way. The first two corollaries have already been discussed in defining a contradiction. The first corollary, the unity of opposites, involves the notion that a single oppositional tendency cannot be understood without considering its dynamic interdependence with its contradictory opposite. The second corollary is that no single contradiction can be fully understood at a single point in time; a contradiction is not a static phenomenon but a fluid process that changes over time and in time. Thus time and change are integral to dialectical contradictions (Georgoudi, 1983).

The third corollary of dialectical totality is that no single contradiction can be considered in isolation of other contradictions. As Cornforth (1968) has indicated, "A process usually contains not one but many contradictions. It is a knot of contradictions. And so to understand the course of a process we must take into account all its contradictions and understand their interrelationship" (p. 111). In analytically disentangling this dialectical "knot," dialectical theorists have made a number of distinctions in basic types of contradictions. First, *primary contradictions* and *secondary contradictions* have been differentiated (Cornforth, 1968; Israel, 1979; Mao, 1965). *Secondary contradictions,* as the term suggests, are those whose character and effects are conditioned by more significant or central primary contradictions. Philipsen (1987), for example, has argued that the primary contradiction faced by all social systems is the dialectical tension between the individual and the communal. Of course, a contradiction that may perform a key or principal role at one point in time may be secondary at another point in time; thus substantial fluidity characterizes the determination of which contradictions are primary and which are secondary. We return to the issue of primary contradictions below in discussing the contradictions that researchers of personal relationships have repeatedly identified.

A second distinction drawn by dialectical theorists is that between *internal contradictions* and *external contradictions* (Ball, 1979; Cornforth, 1968; Israel, 1979; Mao, 1965; Riegel, 1976). As the terms suggest, internal contradictions are those constituted within the boundaries of the social unit under study, whereas external contradictions are constituted between the social unit and the larger social systems in which it is embedded. Thus, similar to the transactional perspective, dialectics embeds relationships in their multiple social contexts. When the personal relationship is the social unit under study, "internal contradictions" refer to those situated within the dyad, whereas "external contradictions" refer to those situated at the nexus of the dyad and its friendship and kinship networks and the broader society at large (Brown et al., 1992; Montgomery, 1992). Internal contradictions and external contradictions affect one another and thus cannot be understood in isolation of one another. For example, relationship parties face the internal contradiction between individual autonomy and dyadic connection and the external contradiction between autonomy as a couple and integration with others as a couple. These two contradictions can interact in any number of ways. For instance, a couple's efforts to establish connection in their relationship may jeopardize their ability to connect as a couple with friends and family; conversely, their obligations to connect with family and friends may compete with their desire to become an autonomous couple. The distinction between internal and external contradictions is returned to below in the discussion of emergent trends in the dialectical research.

The fourth, and final, corollary of dialectical totality is that contradictions are not reified abstractions but concrete, lived experiences (Bakhtin, 1981, 1984;

Georgoudi, 1983; Israel, 1979). The particular contradictory patterns of a given relationship are likely to display both unique and general principles. Further, this fourth corollary does not commit dialectics to either materialism (objectivity) or idealism (subjectivity) but necessitates a commitment to both in its emphasis on the multifaceted nature of the contradicting process and its complexity—affective, behavioral, cognitive, physical, social, and temporal. The practical import of recognizing the contradicting process as lived experience is that multiple methods are appropriate and relevant to the dialectical enterprise so long as they are targeted toward the understanding of contradictions.

Taken together, these four totality corollaries bear close resemblance to transactionalism. Dialectical opposites are mutually defining and inseparable; they are inherently dynamic so that change is ongoing and continuous; contradictions cannot be understood in isolation but are embedded in a total knot of interrelated contradictions; relationships are embedded in larger social systems; and relationship contradictions may display both unique and general principles. However, dialectics has largely ignored the physical environment, a central tenet of transactionalism; and in its emphasis on contradictions, dialectical totality is more narrowly cast than transactionalism (although recent transactional analyses have embraced dialectics as an essential "motor").

Next, we turn to dynamic and social contextual themes in the dialectical research on communication in personal relationships. Although all dialectical researchers subscribe to the core concepts of contradiction, dialectical change, and dialectical totality, differences of emphasis and direction are evident among the various strands of dialectical work.

Emergent Dynamic and Contextual Themes in Existing Dialectical Research

Baxter's Typology: Internal and External Manifestations of Dialectical Contradictions

Giddens (1984) refers to contradictions as "fault lines," and this metaphor is useful in reminding us that the tension between oppositions is inherently a dynamic, fluid process rather than a static phenomenon. The metaphor is apt, as well, in reflecting the myriad contradictions that have been identified to date by dialectical researchers. In an attempt to summarize common dialectical themes, Baxter (1993, in press) has organized the "fault lines" that have been identified in extant research into six basic clusters or families that can be differentiated according to the dialectical theme that is emphasized. The typology also distinguishes between internal and external foci of contradictions, thereby emphasizing that dyads are integrally related to their larger social contexts. Contradictions associated with any of these family memberships can be manifested in either antagonistic or nonantagonistic form. First, Baxter has identified three basic thematic families of contradictions. The first family of contradictions, the dialectic of *Integration-Separation*, refers to the basic tension between social integration and social division. This dialectical theme revolves around issues of interdependence and independence and appears similar to the dialectical theme of individual-communal identified by several cultural theorists (e.g., Carbaugh, 1988a, 1988b; Katriel & Philipsen, 1981; Philipsen, 1987) and the dialectical theme of person-society articulated by the transactional/dialectical perspective (e.g., Altman et al., 1992; Werner et al., 1993).

The second family of contradictions, the dialectic of *Expression-Nonexpression*, references a basic oppositional tension between informational openness and closedness. This dialectical theme has been identified, as well, in the transactional/dialectical perspective as the regulation of privacy; it is not independent of but serves the person-society dialectic (e.g., Werner et al., 1993). Baxter's separation of independence-interdependence and expressive openness-closedness presumes that these two dialectical themes are conceptually distinct, even though they may be related empirically. Rawlins (1989, 1992) similarly separates these two themes at a conceptual level. The third family of contradictions, the dialectic of *Stability-Change*, refers to the fundamental opposition between continuity and discontinuity. This basic theme has also been identified by scholars aligned with the transactional/dialectical perspective (e.g., Altman et al., 1981). Stability-Change is likely to be interdependent with both Integration-Separation and Expression-Nonexpression at the empirical level; however, it refers conceptually to a distinct dialectical tension. Second, Baxter found that each of these three basic dialectical families of contradictions was manifested internally as well as externally. The distinction between internal and external contradictions is parallel to Rawlins's (1989, 1992) conceptual distinction between interactional and contextual dialectics, respectively. The internal-external distinction is also evident in the transactional/dialectical distinction between within-dyad dialectics and dialectics between the dyad and other social units (e.g., friendship networks, kinship networks) (Altman et al., 1992; Brown et al., 1992).

Dialectical totality argues for the need to study the holistic patterning of these dialectical "families" through time. These contradictions may vary in intensity, scale, and pacing across a relationship's history, and any two contradictions may vary in their degree of synchrony according to their respective linear changes and cyclic ebbs and flows. To date, only limited research attention has been given to how fundamental contradictions are patterned together through time. Rawlins's (1992) work with friendship across the life span suggests that contradictions vary in their intensity and take different shapes depending on the life stage of the relationship parties. Baxter's (1990) study of romantic relationships suggests that each of the internal manifestations of the three fundamental dialectics proceeds at its own cyclic pacing and intensity. With the caveat that these fundamental contradictions function as a fluid whole, they will be discussed separately to emphasize their conceptual differences.

The Integration-Separation cluster. The *internal Integration-Separation contradiction* is a family of related contradictions, all of which appear to bear a "family resemblance" in implicating needs both for partner independence and autonomy and for partner connection or interdependence in relationships. This dialectical family has the largest membership of any of the six family clusters identified by Baxter and includes the following oppositions: openness and closedness or contact regulation (Altman et al., 1981); stability versus self-identity (Askham, 1976); closeness and separateness (L'Abate & L'Abate, 1979); connection versus autonomy (Baxter, 1988, 1990; Baxter & Simon, 1993; Bridge & Baxter, 1992; Goldsmith, 1990; Masheter, 1994); interdependence versus independence (Bochner, 1984); integration versus differentiation (Bochner & Eisenberg, 1987); intimacy versus autonomy (Conville, 1991); intimacy versus identity (La Gaipa, 1981); the communal versus the individual or the personal (Carbaugh, 1988a, 1988b; Katriel & Philipsen, 1981); intimacy versus detachment (Masheter & Harris, 1986); involved versus uninvolved (Miller & Knapp, 1986); the freedom to be dependent versus the freedom to be independent (Rawlins, 1983a, 1989, 1992); and intimacy versus freedom (Wiseman, 1986). Baxter (1988) has argued that the internal Integration-Separation contradiction is so central to relationships that it constitutes the primary contradiction to which all other contradictions cohere. The nonantagonistic manifestation of Connection-Autonomy is exemplified in Rawlins's (1983a, 1992) work on friendship, which has examined across the life cycle the tension between an individual's desire to be free and independent and his or her desire to depend on the partner. Baxter's (1990) study similarly examined the individual's felt pull between desire for autonomy and desire for connection in romantic relationships, finding that this intrapersonal tension was omnipresent in people's experience of their romantic relationships. Masheter and Harris's (1986) case study of a divorcing couple, Nicky and Steve, illustrated an antagonistic version of the Connection-Autonomy contradiction. Nicky wanted greater interdependence in the marriage, while her husband Steve wanted to sustain his autonomy, leading to interpersonal conflict between the partners and ultimately divorce.

As noted earlier, existing nondialectical scholarship has presumed that autonomy negates intimacy. Dialectical intimacy is predicated on the dynamic interdependence of autonomy and connection. Researchers need to turn their attention to the ways in which intimate relationship parties sustain one another's unique identities without undermining their pair unity. From a dialectical perspective, the most intimate and viable relationships may be those in which partner autonomy and pair unity are both celebrated.

The *external Integration-Separation contradiction* involves a couple's management of time and space in coping with the contradictory demands to withdraw from others and to interact with others (Montgomery, 1992). McCall (1970) and Lewis (1972) each have argued that the formation of a pair identity requires effective boundary establishment, that is, selective seclusion from others. A couple needs time alone and privacy from others to establish their own dyadic culture. However, identity as a pair also requires integration with others to gain social recognition and legitimation of the relationship unit (Lewis, 1973; Parks & Eggert, 1991). Several dialectical contradictions that appear in extant research involve the tension between pair integration and separation and thus warrant family membership in the external Integration-Separation cluster: individual-communal identity (Altman & Gauvain, 1981; Werner et al., 1993); inclusion-seclusion (Baxter, 1993, in press); dyad-kin dialectics (Brown et al., 1992); autonomy-connection (Montgomery, 1992); and public-private (Rawlins, 1989, 1992). A nonantagonistic manifestation of this contradiction is illustrated in Rawlins and Holl's (1987) study of adolescent friendship predicaments. On the one hand, adolescents demonstrate their popularity by being seen in public with their friends; on the other hand, public activities in a peer group are likely to undermine opportunities to establish and sustain intimacy with given friends. Riessman's (1990) study of divorce illustrated an antagonistic manifestation of the inclusion-seclusion contradiction along gendered lines. In particular, Riessman observed that husbands tended to complain about their wives' efforts to plan and execute activities and events with family and friends, regarding such efforts as intrusive on the pair's time alone. By contrast, females perceived that they were working on behalf of the couple's well-being by taking actions to integrate with family and friends. Interpersonal conflict was likely between husbands and wives as each partner aligned with a different pole of the inclusion-seclusion contradiction.

Existing nondialectical research has privileged pair seclusion in the attention given to a pair's tendency to withdraw from outside interaction as their relationship develops, that is, the so-called dyadic withdrawal hypothesis (e.g., Johnson & Leslie, 1982; Milardo, Johnson, & Huston, 1983; Surra, 1988; Surra & Milardo, 1991). A dialectical view obligates a more complex view of a couple's boundary establishment, emphasizing the contradictory needs for both integration with and seclusion from outsiders for a viable relationship.

The Expression-Nonexpression cluster. The *internal Expression-Nonexpression* dialectic captures the dilemma of candor and discretion by the relationship parties in their interactions with one another. On the one hand, intimacy is built on a scaffold of open and honest disclosure between two relationship parties. On the other hand, intimacy involves the right to individual privacy (e.g., Altman et al., 1981; Petronio, 1991) and the obligation to protect one's partner from the hurt that may result from excessive honesty (e.g., Rawlins, 1983b). Contradictions from extant research that involve the candor-discretion tension include openness and closedness or intimacy regulation (Altman et al., 1981; Baxter, 1988, 1990, 1993, in press; Baxter & Simon, 1993; Bochner, 1984; Bridge & Baxter, 1992; Masheter, 1994); hide and reveal (Miller & Knapp, 1986); and expressiveness-protectiveness and acceptance-judgment (Rawlins, 1983b, 1989, 1992). Both Rawlins (1983b, 1992) and Baxter (1990) have examined the nonantagonistic form of this contradiction in examining the intrapersonal tension felt by friends and romantic partners, respectively, to reveal and not reveal to the other. Of course, this contradiction could just as well take antagonistic form, with one party desiring more privacy than the other party finds acceptable. Masheter (1994) has captured this dynamic in describing how some divorcing partners appear to specialize in opening up difficult topics while their partners develop a complementary capacity to close down those topics.

Despite long-standing critiques to the contrary (e.g., Bochner, 1982; Parks, 1982), relationships researchers still privilege openness over closedness. Open disclosure is still taken as evidence of intimacy, whereas selective openness is taken as evidence of lessened intimacy. Dialectical intimacy is predicated on the simultaneous need for both candor and discretion in viable relationships, with the obligation for researchers to construct conceptualizations and operationalizations of intimacy that are sensitive to both openness and closedness demands.

The *external Expression-Nonexpression* contradiction revolves around whether or not the parties reveal relational information to third parties. On the one hand, the bond of intimacy necessitates a norm of confidentiality between two relationship parties (e.g., Krain, 1977). On the other hand, relationships must be known to others if they are to provide the support and legitimation so necessary to the pair's well-being. This dialectical theme is evident in the following contradictions identified in extant research: accessibility and inaccessibility (Altman & Gauvain, 1981), revelation and concealment (Baxter, 1993, in press; Baxter & Widenmann, 1993), and seeking and not seeking social support (Goldsmith & Parks, 1990). Several published studies have examined the nonantagonistic version of this contradiction, finding that relationship parties are torn between their desire to tell others about their relationship and their desire to withhold information from others (Baxter & Widenmann, in press; Goldsmith & Parks, 1990). A variety of contradictory motives are implicated in this tension, including a desire to gain others' emotional or material support offset by a fear of others' rejection and nonsupport, a desire to tell others out of the sheer joy of expression or catharsis offset by a fear of losing control over information once it becomes currency in the gossip network, a desire to tell someone to fulfill the expectations of the relationship with the recipient of the disclosure offset by a desire to conceal information for fear that revelation would be inappropriate to the relationship with the recipient, and a desire to reveal information to make the personal relationship public offset by a fear that the partner's expectation of confidentiality will be violated in revelation (Baxter & Widenmann, 1993). Rawlins and Holl's (1987) study of adolescent friendship provided evidence of the antagonistic form of this contradiction. Adolescent friendships are frequently jeopardized when one friend thinks that the other has engaged in "two-faced talking behind the back" in which confidences have been revealed.

In emphasizing the boundary of confidentiality that characterizes an intimate dyad, existing research in personal relationships has emphasized nonrevelation over revelation. The "dyadic withdrawal hypothesis" mentioned above implicates not only withdrawal from others on dimensions of time and space but informational withdrawal, as well. By contrast, a dialectical approach recognizes the simultaneous need for both the revelation and the nonrevelation of relational information to third party outsiders. How relationship pairs effectively negotiate these contradictory demands merits the attention of future researchers.

The Stability-Change cluster. The *internal Stability-Change contradiction* refers to a family of contradictions that revolve around the basic opposition between a relationship party's need for predictability, certainty, and routinization, on the one hand, and his or her simultaneous need for novelty, stimulation, and spontaneity, on the other hand. Contradictions from extant research that implicate this contradiction include stability and change (Altman et al., 1981; Bochner, 1984; Bochner & Eisenberg, 1987; Masheter & Harris, 1986), stability and self-identity (Askham, 1976), predictability and novelty (Baxter, 1988, 1990, 1993, in press; Baxter & Simon, 1993; Masheter, 1994), and continuity and discontinuity (Sigman, 1991). Substantial research under the rubric of uncertainty reduction theory (e.g., Berger & Bradac, 1982; Berger & Calabrese, 1975; Berger & Gudykunst, 1991) has documented that intimacy is facilitated when the parties have certainty and predictability about one another, their interactions together, and the state of their relationship. However, research also documents that parties need the stimulation of spontaneity and novelty to prevent an emotional deadening of affections (e.g., Byrne & Murnen, 1988; Livingston, 1980). In fact, several studies have suggested that boredom, the result of insufficient novelty or excitement, is a frequent cause of breakups among romantic pairs (e.g., Baxter, 1986; Cody, 1982; Hill, Rubin, & Peplau, 1976). In addition, even if relationship parties desired only stability, they would be forced to cope with the instability inherent in the dialectical change process. The nonantagonistic version of the predictability-novelty contradiction is illustrated by Baxter's (1990) study in which informants were interviewed about the times in which they felt an internal pull between their desires for predictability and unpredictability. However, this contradiction could just as easily be experienced antagonistically, if one party were attracted to certainty and routine while the other party were attracted to the excitement of spontaneity and the unknown. Masheter (1994) has provided a vivid example of antagonistic Stability-Change in describing two ex-spouses, one of whom was unwilling to let go of their negative interaction patterns of the past and the other of whom was willing to let go of the past and frame their postdivorce relationship along more positive lines.

Existing research, guided by uncertainty reduction theory, has focused on the role of certainty in relationship development while viewing uncertainty as a negative factor in intimacy. By contrast, a dialectical approach to intimacy presumes that uncertainty reduction is only half of the picture. Dialectical intimacy necessitates uncertainty as well as uncertainty reduction, and the research agenda should turn to examination of the complex interplay between these opposing tendencies and how their effective management contributes to relationship viability.

The *internal Stability-Change* dialectic is particularly relevant to temporal issues of salience. How relationship parties establish temporal continuities between the past, the present, and the future is important to a couple's sense of their underlying stability and adaptiveness. Roberts (1988), among others, has argued that dyadic and family rituals are particularly useful in managing multiple layers of salience simultaneously, and we will return to the communicative form of the ritual in a later section.

The *external Stability-Change contradiction* revolves around the relationship pair's contradictory demands to conform to society's conventionalized ways of relating and to construct a unique pair identity. From a macroperspective, the society reproduces itself to the extent that each relationship adopts conventional forms and practices of relating, yet conventionality dampens exploration of alternative ways of relating that could prove adaptive for the society in the long run (Montgomery, 1992). From the microperspective of a given relationship pair, acceptance of society's conventions of relating provides the partners with "prepackaged" schemata of relating that provide a source of predictability in interacting as a couple with others, thereby increasing the likelihood of the couple gaining acceptance. However, acceptance of such conventions could jeopardize spontaneity and excitement for the couple in their efforts to construct their own unique dyadic culture (Baxter, 1987; McCall, 1970; Owen, 1984). The issues implicated in this contradiction have been addressed in treatments of the following contradictions: conventionality and uniqueness (Baxter, 1993, in press), idealization-realization (Bochner, 1984; Rawlins, 1989, 1992), autonomy and connection (Montgomery, 1992), and public and private (Rawlins, 1989, 1992; Rawlins & Holl, 1987). Obviously, this contradiction could be experienced either antagonistically or nonantagonistically in a given relationship. Fitzpatrick's (1988) Traditional-Independent couple, for example, is likely to manifest the contradiction in antagonistic form, as the Traditional spouse endorses society's gendered conventions for husband and wife roles while the Independent spouse rejects such normative expectations. Bridge and Baxter's (1992) study of friendship in the workplace provided an example of a nonantagonistic version of this contradiction, with coworker friends experiencing intrapersonally a tension between their desire to conform to the workplace norm of impartiality and their desire to treat their friend uniquely.

Existing relationship research has approached the two poles of the internal Stability-Change contradiction dualistically. We can point to research that emphasizes conventions of relating, for example, mass media portrayals of relating (e.g., Alberts, 1986; Brown, 1982; Hubbard, 1987; Kidd, 1975) or people's cognitive structures for typical trajectories of relational escalation and decay (e.g., Honeycutt, Cantrill, & Allen, 1992; Honeycutt, Cantrill, & Greene, 1989). We can point to research that emphasizes relationship parties' idiosyncratic and spontaneous expression of relationship uniqueness (e.g., Baxter, 1992a; Bell & Healey, 1992). We are less successful in pointing to research that examines the simultaneous interplay between societal conventionality and relational uniqueness. Researchers need to devote attention to how parties effectively navigate the contradictory demands embedded in the opposing tendencies of conventionality and uniqueness.

Caveats. Four caveats are in order before leaving this summary of contradictions that have garnered research attention. *First*, it is not Baxter's intent, nor ours, to suggest that these six family clusters of contradictions exhaust the domain of contradictions experienced in personal relationships. Certainly, other contradictions are likely to organize situated interaction between relationship parties. For example, dialectical oppositions that revolve around dominance/submission (Bridge & Baxter, 1992) or love/hate are not readily apparent in Baxter's six family clusters. Conville's (1991) case study, structural approach to relationship processes and the episode analysis method employed by Masheter (1994; Masheter & Harris, 1986) seem particularly well suited to the identification of idiosyncratically emergent contradictions for each relationship that is studied. *Second*, the six basic contradictions identified by Baxter may take different shape depending on the particular relationship that is under study. Cissna et al.'s (1990) study of stepfamily dynamics, for example, illustrates a particular version of the external Integration-Separation contradiction that is unique to remarried pairs in which at least one of the spouses has children. The identity of the remarried couple is implicated in their ability to enact parenting functions in the larger social unit of the stepfamily, yet stepfamily children may undermine such parenting authority as a way to challenge the integrity of the remarriage. Similarly, as Miller and Knapp (1986) have documented, the internal Integration-Separation and internal Expression-Nonexpression contradictions assume a particular ethos in the context of a relationship with someone who is dying. *Third*, we would emphasize that a given contradiction is likely to change shape over the course of a relationship's history. For example, Goldsmith (1990) has usefully demonstrated that the internal tension between integration and separation is likely to be experienced differently at different developmental moments in a relationship's history. In particular, five qualitatively different senses of "autonomy" and "connection" emerged in informant narrative accounts of the development of their relationships from the initial decision to get involved through the decision to make a long-term commitment. Similarly, Stamp and Banski (1992) have recently described the qualitative transformations in spouses' conceptions of "autonomy" and "connection" that accompany the birth of a first child. *Fourth*, and last, we note that contradictions do not function in isolation of one another but constitute dynamic systems of dialectical tensions (Baxter, 1988). Dialectical research from the transactional/dialectical perspective is particularly valuable in demonstrating the complex pattern of interdependence between and among various contradictions (e.g., Altman et al., 1992; Werner et al., 1993).

In short, in this section, we have pointed at a high level of abstraction to some of the basic contradictions that are likely to characterize change in relationships. However, dialectically oriented research needs to examine contradictions as they are instantiated in the emergent interaction dynamics of relationship pairs. In the next section, we turn to research that addresses the dialectical change processes of personal relationships.

Processes of Dialectical Change

Much of the dialectically oriented research to date has been devoted to the preliminary task of documenting that contradictions exist, and much less attention has been devoted to the next step of examining how these contradictions change in personal relationships. Nonetheless, three complementary yet distinct approaches to change can be identified in existing dialectical research: the cyclic/spiraling model advanced by Altman et al. (1981), the dialectical coping model articulated by Baxter (1988, 1990; Baxter & Simon, 1993; Bridge & Baxter, 1992), and the model of second order change advanced by Conville (1983, 1988, 1991).

The Cyclic/Spiraling model. As noted in the first section of this chapter, Altman and his colleagues (1981) have presented a cyclic or spiraling model of dialectical change in relationships. Using the openness-closedness contradiction as their point of reference, Altman et al. posited that relationship parties cycle or spiral back and forth through time between openness and closedness poles (i.e., contact/avoidance and intimacy/superficiality). In particular, they hypothesized that relationship development and deterioration are characterized by systematic differences in the amplitude or intensity of openness/closedness cycles and in the scale or interval length between cyclic swings. The cycling/spiraling model articulated by Altman and his colleagues is applicable to any of the six substantive contradictions discussed earlier or to other contradictions. To our knowledge, no published research has examined dialectical cycling or spiraling as envisioned by the Altman et al. model. A number of researchers have employed a method that is amenable to the assessment of dialectical cycling/spiraling, that is, the RIT procedure in which relationship parties are asked retrospectively to plot fluctuations across their relationship's history (for a description of the RIT procedure, see Huston, Surra, Fitzgerald, & Cate, 1981). In the RIT method, fluctuations revolve around "turning points," that is, points in time when the parties noted a distinct change in their relationship. From a dialectical perspective, "turning points" are likely to be moments of cyclical or spiraling change for relationship parties. However, existing applications of the RIT procedure gauge fluctuations in what are fundamentally nondialectical phenomena such as "probability of marriage from 0% to 100%" (e.g., Cate, Huston, & Nesselroade, 1986; Lloyd & Cate, 1985; Surra, 1985, 1987) or "commitment level from 0% to 100%" (e.g., Baxter & Bullis, 1986; Bullis, Clark, & Sline, 1993). If the two poles of a given contradiction served as the anchor points in the Y axis of an RIT graph, the method could prove very fruitful in assessing cyclical/spiraling change in relationships. Alternatively, researchers could use diary records kept through time by relationship parties (Duck, 1991) as a source of data by which to derive plots of dialectical cycling or spiraling patterns. In other words, methods are available to derive the kinds of graphic plots of cyclic/spiraling patterns that Altman et al. have posited. Only with these kinds of data in hand will researchers be able to determine with any precision fluctuations in the intensity, pacing, and rhythm of cyclic changes associated with the various contradictions of relating.

The dialectical coping model. Baxter (1988) has identified six fundamental coping responses with which relationship parties can seek to manage effectively the dialectical exigencies of their relationship. Through these responses, relationship parties produce either linear or cyclical spiraling changes in their relationship, thereby setting in motion what will constitute future dialectical exigencies for the relationship parties. This focus on relationship parties as both actors and objects of their own actions is what Rawlins (1989, 1992) refers to as the "praxis" dimension of a dialectical perspective. In general, the coping responses represent a variety of ways by which partners shift or reconfigure their emphases from one pole to another or attempt to achieve both poles simultaneously within a given contradiction. These shifting configurations and the flow of events that they represent illustrate formal cause as an aspect of dialectics.

For ease of presentation, Baxter's six responses can be grouped into four more basic types. *First*, relationship parties can attempt to reduce a contradiction by minimizing or devaluing one of the dialectical poles, a response that Baxter labels *Selection*. For example, parties could decide that they don't want any individual autonomy and elect to spend all of their time together. If in fact contradictions are inherent in relating, Selection is a nonviable response, and pressure ought to build in the relationship to fulfill the neglected opposing feature. In fact, Selection does not appear to be a prevalent coping response by relationship parties (Baxter, 1990). *Second*, relationship parties can respond to contradictory demands by seeking to fulfill each demand separately. Parties can accomplish this through either *Cyclic Alternation* or *Segmentation* responses, both of which involve cyclic or spiraling changes through time. In Cyclic Alternation, the relationship parties cycle or spiral between the two poles of a contradiction, separating them temporally with each contradictory demand gaining fulfillment during its temporal cycle. Alternatively, relationship parties can separate the two dialectical poles substantively, targeting some topic, event, or activity domains for fulfillment of one dialectical pole while the opposing pole is fulfilled through other topics, events, or activities. For example, relationship parties appear to fulfill their needs for both revelation and nonrevelation of their relationship to third parties by segmenting both topics and recipients; that is, some topics can be revealed to others while other topics are confidential, and some people can be talked to while others cannot (Baxter & Widenmann, 1993). On the reasonable assumption that parties find it difficult to occupy two domains at a single point in time, the Segmentation response generally involves a cycling or spiraling between domains. Existing research suggests that Cyclic Alternation and Segmentation are the dominant responses enacted by relationship parties as they manage the dialectical exigencies of their relationship (Baxter, 1988; Baxter & Simon, 1993; Baxter & Widenmann, 1993; Bridge & Baxter, 1992). *Third*, relationship parties can respond to both dialectical demands at once. For example, the response of *Moderation* involves compromise efforts by the relationship parties in which each dialectical pole is fulfilled in part. The response of *Disqualification* also addresses both dialectical demands at once, relying on ambiguity and indirectness to sustain the impression that both dialectical demands are being met. Moderation and Disqualification responses have not been identified with much frequency in existing research, but this may well reflect method limitations in the research. In our discussion below of rituals, we return to the question of how relationship parties can simultaneously respond to both dialectical demands. *Fourth*, relationship parties can respond by *Reframing* a contradiction, a response that corresponds to transformational change. For example, the internal Integration-Separation contradiction may be transformed by the parties recognizing how their relationship is enriched by individual autonomy; in this transformation, connection and autonomy no longer are viewed in a zero-sum manner but are reframed as complementary features. The Reframing response appears to be accomplished with limited frequency in ongoing romantic relationships and emerges late in development when it does emerge (Baxter, 1990). However, the Reframing response appears with greater frequency among ex-spouses who are reconstructing a viable relationship along nonintimate lines (Masheter, 1994; Masheter & Harris, 1986).

Although it is useful to know that these four types of coping responses exist and are used with varying frequencies, researchers need to study the enactment of these responses across time. For example, the coping response of Cyclic Alternation implies a clean break point where one cycle ends and another begins. Some cyclic changes may be this dramatic and sudden, but we suspect that other cyclic changes may come about more gradually with cumulative incremental changes of amplitude. Temporal data are also necessary to shed insight into matters of scale and pacing; some contradictions may be managed in cycles of fairly short duration, whereas other contradictions may be calibrated in longer time intervals. For example, issues of openness and closedness may fluctuate on a topic-by-topic basis and thus display moment-to-moment changes of scale. By contrast, issues of stability and change in the underlying definition of the relationship may be characterized by longer cyclic intervals, particularly in well-established relationships. In short, future research needs to examine these coping responses as they function through time.

The Second-Order Change Model. Conville (1983, 1988, 1991) has developed a helical model of second order relational change that emphasizes both linear, transformational change and cyclical/spiraling change. He has distinguished first order from second order change, arguing that "first-order change in a relationship would be change within the context of the given grounds for interaction," whereas "second-order change would be change that itself creates new grounds for interaction" (Conville, 1991, p. 73). Presenting his model through the visual metaphor of a helix, Conville argues that relationships move from periods of relative security and stability, through unstable periods of disintegration and alienation prompted by oppositional tensions, to a transformed state of qualitatively different security or resynthesis. Relational turning points typically mark transitions between these periods. Relationship parties continue to cycle or spiral through security-disintegration-alienation-resynthesis over the course of their relationship's history, qualitatively transforming the definition of their relationship with each full circle cycle or spiral. Conville's model of relational change underscores the functionality of relational crisis, for such crises signify the disintegration of the old relational state and the parties' alienation from it and thereby provide the catalyst for resynthesis. Conville has applied his model of second order change toward an understanding of a variety of relationship case studies, ranging from the friendship of Helen Keller and Anne Sullivan to the romantic relationships of ordinary persons. However, like the other two approaches discussed in this section, future research with the model of second order change needs to gather longitudinal data that shed insight on the temporal qualities of amplitude, scale, and pacing.

Summary. These three models of dialectical change are fully complementary at the conceptual level. However, none of the models has been adequately tested at the empirical level with longitudinal data from relationships. Further, the models tend to deal with one contradiction at a time. Because contradictions are interdependent, an important issue for future researchers is to determine how change that is centered in one contradiction reverberates throughout a system of interdependent contradictions, that is, issues related to temporal sequencing. Attention to this issue is critical if primary and secondary contradictions are to be differentiated empirically.

Bakhtin (1981) has argued that opposing tendencies intersect in every dialogue that occurs between relating parties. In this sense, then, all communication practices occupy a central place in a dialectical perspective. The last section examines selected communication functions and forms that are particularly important from a dialectical perspective.

Effective Management of Dialectical Contradictions

Communication functions. Baxter's (1988) typology of responses to contradictions basically suggests that ongoing contradictions are managed by efforts either to regulate the poles, thereby allowing the parties to attempt to fulfill each opposing need separately at two different points in time or to cope with both poles simultaneously at one point in time. Research in interpersonal communication needs to pursue both of these possible paths of temporal sequencing. With respect to the separation or uncoupling of poles, existing research equips us at best to examine only half of the dialectical poles identified in the six family clusters discussed earlier. Existing scholarship in interpersonal communication emphasizes communication that is used to accomplish integration, neglecting the communicative accomplishment of separation. Greater attention is given to the reduction of uncertainty through communication (e.g., Kellermann & Reynolds, 1990) than to the creation or maintenance of uncertainty (e.g., Bavelas, Black, Chovil, & Mullett, 1990; Eisenberg, 1984). Although research in privacy (e.g., Petronio, 1991) and deception (e.g., Metts, 1989) can be identified, open expression still occupies the position of privilege in the research community. To the extent that relationship parties manage dialectical contradictions by responding separately to each pole, that is, use of cyclic alternation or segmentation, it is important to understand how all six bipolar functions are accomplished communicatively and what their temporal characteristics are.

Overwhelmingly, the contradictions examined in this chapter have been positive contradictions, that is, contradictions in which both poles are positive entities. Thus separation cannot be understood as merely the absence of integration but must be studied in its own right, as must the other neglected dialectical poles. Of course, the dialectical study of poles "in their own right" is framed within the broader agenda of understanding the dynamic interplay in the unity of opposites.

Physical environment. Recent analyses indicate that the physical environment is an integral part of effective relationship management. Altman et al. (1992) used a transactional/dialectical approach to analyze courtship, wedding, and place-making practices around the globe. They showed that where events take place, what objects are involved, which particular friends and family members are invited, and when events occur and in what particular sequence all converged to define the nature of the couple's developing relationship and to project the couple's future degree of integration and separation with kin and friends. This analysis indicated that societies differ in the extent to which young couples are expected to be autonomous versus subordinate to the family (i.e., which pole of the Integration-Separation dialectic is strongest). Further, Altman and his colleagues suggested that an important task of many young couples is to develop a dyadic relationship while simultaneously maintaining and building their familial ties, and that effective use of the physical environment—whether the newlyweds live with the family or separate from it, the location of a home vis-à-vis relatives, use of separate spaces in the home, and so on—contributes to couple viability.

In a related analysis, Altman and Gauvain (1981) examined the rich symbolism of integration and separation conveyed in people's homes, including their physical layouts, the arrangement and choice of furnishings and decorations, the use of individual and group areas for family members, and how the home controls access between residents and outsiders. Gauvain, Altman, and Fahim (1983) extended this view by showing that, when home and community designs do not support the culture's traditional integration-separation practices, there can be serious disruptions in social and psychological functioning. They also showed that people attempt to cope with these disruptions by modifying their homes to achieve previous levels of integration and separation among family members and between the family and outsiders. Although the research by Altman and his colleagues is useful in examining from a transactional/dialectical perspective the roles of physical space in the management of contradictions, future work in this tradition could usefully examine possible temporal changes in how the physical environment is used. For example, it would be interesting to determine the pacing parameters with respect to how many times a couple can move and change residences without experiencing discontinuities of salience between the past, the present, and the future.

Rituals. Researchers need to examine the ways in which relationship parties manage simultaneously both poles of a given contradiction and the ways in which multiple contradictions are simultaneously managed. A number of theorists, representing a wide range of disciplinary interests, have identified the ritual as one of the most important communicative forms in the simultaneous management of dialectical oppositions (Altman et al., 1992; C. Bell, 1992; Bochner, 1984; Philipsen, 1987; Roberts, 1988; Turner, 1969; Werner et al., 1993). As Roberts (1988) has observed, "Ritual can hold both sides of a contradiction at the same time. We all live with the ultimate paradoxes of life/death, connection/distance, ideal/real, good/evil. Ritual can incorporate both sides of contradictions so that they can be managed simultaneously" (p. 16). As discussed earlier, rituals are also key means by which temporal continuity is achieved between the past, the present, and the future. In short, the ritual appears to be a communicative form whose functional specialties are temporal sequencing and temporal salience.

Definitions of "ritual" vary somewhat from theorist to theorist, but we find utility in Philipsen's (1987) conception of a ritual as a communication form in which there is a structured sequence of symbolic acts, the correct performance of which pays homage to something that is sacred in either a religious or a secular sense. Wolin and Bennett (1984) have identified three basic types of rituals in families that we believe to hold wider relevance to personal relationships in general: (a) celebrations, (b) traditions, and (c) patterned interactions. Celebrations are holidays or other occasions that are widely recognized and practiced throughout the culture and that are special to relational partners. Wolin and Bennett include rites of passage (e.g., weddings, baptisms, bar mitzvahs, funerals), annual religious celebrations (e.g., Christmas, Easter, the Passover seder), and secular holidays (e.g., New Year's, the Fourth of July) as typical celebrations that are recognized and enacted by relational partners. Traditions, as Wolin and Bennett conceive them, tend to be more idiosyncratic than cultural in nature, for example, observances of birthdays, anniversaries, family reunions, annual summer vacations, and so forth. Whereas celebrations are calibrated to the society's calendar, traditions are calibrated by the relationship's dyadic calendar (McCall, 1988). Patterned interactions are repeated routines that hold functional significance for relationship parties, for example, eating dinner together, inquiring about one another's day, weekly leisure activities enacted together, and so forth; such routines typically are calibrated to the relationship pair's daily or weekly temporal calendar. Whereas Wolin and Bennett (1984) conceived of each type of ritual as contributing to different levels of identity (celebrations support cultural identities, traditions support family identity, and patterned interactions support individual uniqueness), Werner et al. (1993) adopted a dialectical view and argued that rituals serve multiple identities and, in fact, enable people to manage their often competing identities as individuals, dyadic members, and members of networks, families, and other social groups. In general, much of the existing research on interpersonal rituals examines families as opposed to dyadic relationships (e.g., Altman et al., 1992; Fiese, 1992; Troll, 1988; Werner et al., 1993; Wolin & Bennett, 1984) and much of it has a clinical focus (e.g., Imber-Black, Roberts, & Whiting, 1988). Nonetheless, extant work clearly points to the ritual as a communication form of substantial theoretical significance to the dialectical study of personal relationships.

The use of celebrations and traditions to manage dialectical contradictions has been the focus of attention among transactional/dialectical researchers. Celebrations and traditions involve physical objects and locations (e.g., special dinnerware, holiday decorations, favorite places in the home) that can simultaneously invoke individual, dyadic, and familial identities, thereby highlighting the integration and separation dialectic. Furthermore, celebrations and traditions are recurrent events with varied temporal qualities, and they can make salient aspects of the relationship's history and prospective future. For example, Altman and Ginat's (Altman, 1993; Werner et al., 1993) study of fundamentalist Mormon polygynist families has documented how such traditions as birthdays and family get-togethers are enacted in ways that pay homage simultaneously to members' unique and collective identities. Wives' birthdays, for instance, are usually celebrated by the husband and wife in ways that highlight her uniqueness and the uniqueness of the couple (e.g., the dyad spends the evening away from the family home in a special setting, without the children or other wives), although their other identities as members of the composite family may also be evident. In contrast, the husband's birthday is typically celebrated by the entire family, emphasizing their identity as a collective polygynous family; still, the unique identity of individual family units can be evident in special birthday gifts from each wife and her children. So, celebrations and traditions are holistic, transactional unities that help these families manage the many competing identities implicated in the Integration-Separation dialectic. The recurring cycle of birthdays and reunions also contributes predictability for these families in their management of the Stability-Change dialectic.

Although relationships researchers have examined a variety of patterned interaction rituals (e.g., Baxter, 1987, 1992a; Bell, Buerkel-Rothfuss, & Gore, 1987; Bell & Healey, 1992; Bendix, 1987; Hopper, Knapp, & Scott, 1981; Oring, 1984), very little of this research has been explicitly grounded in a dialectical perspective. Katriel and Philipsen (1981) have provided a dialectically oriented analysis of what they have described as the "communication ritual" enacted among some middle-class Americans. This ritual involves deep sharing of self with another in the context of coping with a personal problem that faces either the ritual's initiator or both parties jointly. In "really communicating," the parties manage the internal Integration-Separation dialectic, simultaneously paying homage to the integrity of the individual self at the same time that relating with others is celebrated.

Ritualized play is a form of patterned interaction that is particularly significant from a dialectical perspective. Bakhtin (1968, 1984) has argued that the *carnivalesque,* that is, the carnival and all playful rituals, allow parties to suspend temporarily their everyday, normal practices and personas in order to deal simultaneously with underlying oppositional tendencies from the relatively safe vantage point of their playful interaction. A number of researchers have similarly noted the potential of ritualized play to manage deep-seated sources of tension in relationships (e.g., Alberts, 1990; Baxter, 1992a; Betcher, 1981; Mechling, 1988; Oring, 1984), but no work to date has been generated explicitly from a dialectical perspective.

The particular symbols contained in a given ritual indicate which specific dialectical themes are addressed. Rites of passage, for example, symbolically link the past with the future and thereby manage the dialectic of Stability-Change in their emphasis on temporal salience. In a more general sense, however, the mere act of performing a ritual of any kind serves to manage the dialectical tension between stability and change. Continuity and stability are served by a ritual's repetition from one time to the next and by the predictability that comes from the internal structure of the ritual's enactment. However, as Roberts (1988) has indicated, rituals are living events that display flexible adaptation to circumstances of the moment, thereby allowing relationship parties simultaneously to embrace sources of discontinuity and change at the same time that continuity and predictability are celebrated.

We do not wish to argue that ritual is the only communicative form in which both oppositions of a contradiction are simultaneously managed. As mentioned earlier, compromises and use of equivocation and ambiguity also allow both dialectical poles of a contradiction to be responded to simultaneously. Additional communicative forms doubtless afford simultaneous responsiveness as well. In general, we would expect that the most successful enactments, that is, those best able to fulfill both dialectical demands, would be characterized by the greatest symbolic complexity or multivocality (Bakhtin, 1981).

Summary

In its emphasis on the ongoing interplay between contradictory oppositions, dialectics joins organismic and transactional perspectives as a third dynamically oriented approach to the study of relationship viability. Contradictions serve as the "motor" of change in personal relationships, and the research agenda for dialectical researchers is that of capturing the pattern of ever-changing relations between the poles of a given contradiction and among interdependent contradictions (both internal and external, antagonistic and nonantagonistic). Dialectics is not a unitary perspective, and differences are apparent among dialectical thinkers with respect to two underlying issues: (a) the relative weighting given to efficient cause as opposed to formal cause and (b) whether the contradicting process is fundamentally indeterminate or teleological. However, in general terms, dialectics appears to be more compatible with transactionalism than with organismic approaches, especially with respect to the dialectical principle of totality.

Conclusion

An ear attentive to the naturally occurring talk of people about their relationships cannot escape the significance of temporality evident in utterances such as these: "We just decided that the time was right to get married." "We're stuck in a rut and don't seem to be moving forward in our relationship." "I thought last night would never end—it seemed an eternity." "We rehash the same argument over and over again." "We just felt in sync." Despite the pervasiveness of temporal themes in people's lived experiences, scholarly attention to relationship temporality has been more limited. Trait and interactionist research, for instance, is dominated by static conceptions of people and relationships, and issues of temporality are relatively absent, although there are many opportunities to include them and our review indicates that these qualities can contribute in important ways to relationship viability. In this chapter, we identified five basic qualities of linear and cyclical/spiraling time in an effort to provide a common vocabulary with which to organize and encourage scholarly dialogue with respect to temporality. However, a common vocabulary does not guarantee that temporality is valued the same way at the level of philosophical assumptions. Organismic, transactional, and dialectical perspectives position temporality in different ways, and we reviewed each approach at some length in an effort to tease out these differences as well as similarities.

In marked contrast to trait and interactional perspectives, all three of the dynamically oriented perspectives share a commitment to relationship maintenance and change (whether those processes are measured in linear or cyclical metrics of amplitude, salience, scale, sequence, and/or pace and rhythm). But organismic, transactional, and dialectical change are not equivalent. We summarized these differences around six basic issues—two issues around the question of unit of analysis: (a) whether elements are analytically separable and (b) whether time is conceived as an outside marker of change or an integral aspect of phenomena; two issues related to assumptions about the nature of change: (c) the source of the change (efficient cause versus formal cause) and (d) whether the change is teleologically driven; and two issues related to philosophy of science: (e) whether dynamic and temporal qualities are objective and replicable (that is, the issue of researcher stance) and (f) whether conclusions about dynamic and temporal qualities are generalizable. Table 9.2 summarizes these differences. As this table makes evident, transactional and dialectical perspectives are closer to one another than either is to the organismic perspective. What this table cannot show—but what we attempted to illustrate in our literature review—is the ongoing change in how relationships are conceived and studied; there have been growing numbers of organismic and transactional analyses, and dramatic increases in attention to the dialectics of relationships. Even trait approaches are becoming more organismic and transactional (Campbell & Gibbs, 1986; Smith & Rhodewalt, 1986; Snyder & Ickes, 1985).

Stark comparisons such as those shown in Table 9.2 are useful for highlighting differences among the three approaches, but reality is much more complex than this. It is not the case that all organismic, transactional, or dialectical theorists adopt all of their perspectives' defining assumptions, and often researchers adopt some of each or some aspects of each. It may be more accurate to say that each of these *characteristic assumptions* resides on a continuum, and research assumptions and goals can be located separately on each continuum. So, research is rarely a "pure" form of any approach, and we are not insisting that it should be. Instead, we argue that each of these continua poses a research question that can guide thinking about phenomena.

Consider, for example, the observer's perspective. Steier (1989) argued strongly that how researchers view families—the inferences made about the meanings of various behaviors, where to break the flow of behavior into meaningful units—is completely subjective and depends on the researcher's cultural values and prior experiences. Cappella (1991), citing the frame-of-reference construct in physics,

Table 9.2 Comparison of Organismic, Transactional, and Dialectical Perspectives

Issue	Organismic	Transactional	Dialectical
Separable elements/ inseparable aspects	Analytically separable system elements but functionally interdependent	Inseparable mutually defining aspects (people, place, and time)	Inseparable contradictory poles and inseparable internal and external contradictions
Conception of time	Outside marker of events	Integral part of events	Integral part of contradictions
Source of change	Reciprocal causation among system elements (mutual efficient cause)	Source of change replaced with a focus on the pattern of changing relations (formal cause)	Either focus on contra-dictions as drivers of change (mutual efficient cause) or focus on pattern of changing relations among contra-dictions (formal cause)
Teleological goal	Homeostasis or steady state	No necessary teleological goal; short- and long-term goals	Either focus on teleological goal in the form of thesis-antithesis-synthesis or focus on indeterminacy
Researcher stance	Researcher as outsider whose observations are objective and replicable	Events have both inside and outside observers whose stances vary according to their contextual/temporal location	Both insider and outsider observations are necessary in capturing fully the contradicting process
Generalizability	Generalizable systems principles	Both unique and universal principles	Both unique and universal dialectical principles

proposed that multiple ways of studying and measuring social interaction would all contribute valid information. Surra and Ridley (1991) acknowledged that one's perspective influenced one's view of events, but assumed that researchers could accurately define and objectively measure the different perspectives. Masheter (1994) blends insider and outsider perspectives by collaborating with interviewees in dialectical analyses of conversations. Arriving at these methodological/conceptual decisions does not automatically categorize Steier or Cappella as transactional, Masheter as dialectical/transactional, and Surra and Ridley as nontransactional, but simply indicates where they place themselves on the objective-subjective continuum.

As additional examples, Kelley et al.'s (1993) model incorporates all of the organismic features, except that these authors endorse the importance of unique characteristics of individuals and relationships (as opposed to the traditional systems assumption of general and generalizable properties). Riegel and Meacham (1978) articulated all of the features of transactionalism except for formal cause, and dialectically oriented researchers are often vague about the form of cause they endorse. The fact of the matter is that there are often subtle distinctions between mutual efficient cause and formal cause, and authors may slip back and forth between the two; it is often not easy to judge where they fall on this or the other dimensions.

On the other hand, once some assumptions are accepted, others are clearly precluded, and the researcher is thus forced closer to one philosophical approach than another. For example, once it is assumed that aspects of a system are mutually defining and inseparable, formal cause is the only viable form of determinism within that system (although efficient cause could introduce changes from without).

On the other hand, one could use formal cause to guide research without embracing other features of transactional approaches. What to call these "mixes" of assumptions is another matter; which dimensions are the critical ones for identifying one's philosophical orientation? For example, many researchers describe themselves as studying "transactions." Closer examination of the work indicates that by "transactions" they mean that they are studying how people are changed over time through interacting with others or through being embedded in a holistic system, such as Pervin and Lewis's (1978) discussion of "reciprocal action-transaction" (p. 15; see also Cutrona et al., 1990; Lazarus & Launier, 1978; Leatham & Duck, 1990). Other "transactional" researchers are often interested in tracing the specific causal paths that lead to specific changes, so they assume efficient cause (see, for example, Lazarus & Folkman, 1984; Oerter, 1992). By focusing on efficient cause (albeit complex and circular) and therefore conceiving of elements as independent, by focusing on people and relationships out of context, by studying homeostasis without considering contradictions and opposition, and by treating time as outside of the system, we would argue that such approaches locate themselves closer to the organismic than the transactional or dialectical orientations. Self-labels of dialecticians are not so ambiguous, but there are distinct types of dialectical approaches, some closer to organismic and others closer to transactional views. And these distinctions result in great differences in how relationships are viewed and studied, so greater specificity regarding underlying assumptions would benefit all of these philosophical approaches.

This has been a wide-ranging chapter, with consideration of temporal qualities, relationship viability, and philosophical assumptions across many content areas of relationships research. We aimed to show that attention to temporal qualities and philosophical assumptions could expand the research horizon by articulating additional research questions, increasing awareness of distinct philosophical assumptions, and improving our understanding of relationship viability.

References

Acker, M., & Davis, M. H. (1992). Intimacy, passion and commitment in adult romantic relationships: A test of the Triangular Theory of Love. *Journal of Social and Personal Relationships, 9,* 21-50.

Adler, M. J. (1927). *Dialectic.* New York: Harcourt.

Adler, M. J. (Ed.). (1952). *The great ideas: A syntopicon of great books of the Western world.* Chicago: Encyclopaedia Britannica.

Alberts, J. K. (1986). The role of couples' conversations in relational development: A content analysis of courtship talk in Harlequin romance novels. *Communication Quarterly, 34,* 127-142.

Alberts, J. K. (1990). The use of humor in managing couples' conflict interactions. In D. D. Cahn (Ed.), *Intimates in conflict: A communication perspective* (pp. 105-120). Hillsdale, NJ: Lawrence Erlbaum.

Altman, I. (1993). Challenges and opportunities of a transactional world view: Case study of Mormon polygynous families. *American Journal of Community Psychology, 21,* 135-163.

Altman, I. (in press). Dialectics, physical environments, and personal relationships. *Communication Monographs.*

Altman, I., Brown, B. B., Staples, B., & Werner, C. M. (1992). A transactional approach to close relationships: Courtship, weddings and placemaking. In B. Walsh, K. Craik, & R. Price (Eds.), *Person-environment psychology* (pp. 193-241). Hillsdale, NJ: Lawrence Erlbaum.

Altman, I., & Gauvain, M. (1981). A cross-cultural and dialectic analysis of homes. In L. Liben, A. Patterson, & N. Newcombe (Eds.), *Spatial representation and behavior across the life span* (pp. 283-320). New York: Academic Press.

Altman, I., & Rogoff, B. (1987). World views in psychology: Trait, interactional, organismic, and transactional perspectives. In D. Stokols & I. Altman (Eds.), *Handbook of environmental psychology* (Vol. 1, pp. 7-40). New York: Wiley.

Altman, I., Vinsel, A., & Brown, B. (1981). Dialectic conceptions in social psychology: An application to social penetration and privacy regulation. In L. Berkowitz (Ed.), *Advances in experimental social psychology* (Vol. 14, pp. 107-160). New York: Academic Press.

Argyle, M. (1978). *The psychology of interpersonal behaviour.* Middlesex, England: Penguin.

Aron, A., & Aron, E. N. (1986). *Love and the expansion of self: Understanding attraction and satisfaction.* Washington, DC: Hemisphere.

Askham, J. (1976). Identity and stability within the marriage relationship. *Journal of Marriage and the Family, 38,* 535-547.

Bakhtin, M. M. (1968). *Rabelais and his world* (H. Iswolsky, Trans.). Bloomington: Indiana University Press. (Original work published 1965)

Bakhtin, M. M. (1981). *The dialogic imagination: Four essays by M. M. Bakhtin* (M. Holquist, Ed.; C. Emerson & M. Holquist, Trans.). Austin: University of Texas Press.

Bakhtin, M. M. (1984). *Problems of Dostoevsky's poetics* (C. Emerson, Ed. and Trans.). Minneapolis: University of Minnesota Press. (Original work published 1929)

Ball, R. (1979). The dialectical method: Its application to social theory. *Social Forces, 57,* 785-798.

Bandura, A. (1978). The self system in reciprocal determinism. *American Psychologist, 33,* 344-358.

Barbee, A. P. (1990). Interactive coping: The cheering-up process in close relationships. In S. Duck with R. Silver (Eds.), *Personal relationships and social support* (pp. 46-65). London: Sage.

Bavelas, J. B., Black, A., Chovil, N., & Mullett, J. (1990). *Equivocal communication.* Newbury Park, CA: Sage.

Baxter, L. A. (1986). Gender differences in the heterosexual relationship rules embedded in break-up accounts. *Journal of Social and Personal Relationships, 3,* 289-306.

Baxter, L. A. (1987). Symbols of relationship identity in relationship cultures. *Journal of Social and Personal Relationships, 4,* 261-280.

Baxter, L. A. (1988). A dialectical perspective on communication strategies in relationship development. In S. Duck (Ed.), *Handbook of personal relationships* (pp. 257-273). New York: Wiley.

Baxter, L. A. (1990). Dialectical contradictions in relationship development. *Journal of Social and Personal Relationships, 7,* 69-88.

Baxter, L. A. (1992a). Forms and functions of intimate play in personal relationships. *Human Communication Research, 18,* 336-363.

Baxter, L. A. (1992b). Interpersonal communication as dialogue: A response to the "Social Approaches" Forum. *Communication Theory, 2,* 330-337.

Baxter, L. A. (1993). The social side of personal relationships: A dialectical perspective. In S. Duck (Ed.), *Social context and relationships: Understanding relationship processes* (Vol. 3, pp. 139-169). Newbury Park, CA: Sage.

Baxter, L. A. (1994). Thinking dialogically about communication in personal relationships. In R. Conville (Ed.), *Uses of "structure" in communication studies* (pp. 23-38). New York: Praeger.

Baxter, L. A. (in press). A dialogic approach to relationship maintenance. In D. Canary & L. Stafford (Eds.), *Communication and relational maintenance.* New York: Academic Press.

Baxter, L. A., & Bullis, C. (1986). Turning points in developing romantic relationships. *Human Communication Research, 12,* 469-493.

Baxter, L. A., & Simon, E. P. (1993). Relationship maintenance strategies and dialectical contradiction in personal relationships. *Journal of Social and Personal Relationships, 10,* 225-292.

Baxter, L. A., & Widenmann, S. (1993). Revealing and not revealing the status of romantic relationships to social networks. *Journal of Social and Personal Relationships, 10,* 321-338.

Bell, C. (1992). *Ritual theory, ritual practice.* New York: Oxford University Press.

Bell, R. A., Buerkel-Rothfuss, N. L., & Gore, K. E. (1987). "Did you bring the yarmulke for the cabbage patch kid?" The idiomatic communication of young lovers. *Human Communication Research, 14,* 47-67.

Bell, R. A., & Healey, J. G. (1992). Idiomatic communication and interpersonal solidarity in friends' relational cultures. *Human Communication Research, 18,* 307-335.

Bendix, R. (1987). Marmot, Memet, and Marmoset: Further research on the folklore of dyads. *Western Folklore, 46,* 171-191.

Benson, J. K. (1977). Organizations: A dialectical view. *Administrative Science Quarterly, 22,* 1-21.

Berg, J. H., & Clark, M. S. (1986). Differences in social exchange between intimate and other relationships: Gradually evolving or quickly apparent? In V. J. Derlega & B. A. Winstead (Eds.), *Friendship and social interaction* (pp. 101-128). New York: Springer-Verlag.

Berg, J. H., & McQuinn, R. D. (1986). Attraction and exchange in continuing and noncontinuing dating relationships. *Journal of Personality and Social Psychology, 50*, 942-952.

Berger, C. R., & Bradac, J. J. (1982). *Language and social knowledge: Uncertainty in interpersonal relations*. London: Edward Arnold.

Berger, C. R., & Calabrese, R. (1975). Some explorations in initial interaction and beyond: Toward a developmental theory of interpersonal communication. *Human Communication Research, 1*, 99-112.

Berger, C. R., & Gudykunst, W. (1991). Uncertainty and communication. In B. Dervin & M. Voigt (Eds.), *Progress in communication sciences* (Vol. 10, pp. 21-66). Norwood, NJ: Ablex.

Betcher, R. W. (1981). Intimate play and marital adaptation. *Psychiatry, 44*, 13-33.

Billig, M. (1987). *Arguing and thinking: A rhetorical approach to social psychology*. New York: Cambridge University Press.

Billig, M. (1991). *Ideology and opinions: Studies in rhetorical psychology*. Newbury Park, CA: Sage.

Billig, M., Condor, S., Edwards, D., Gane, M., Middleton, D., & Radley, A. (1988). *Ideological dilemmas: A social psychology of everyday thinking*. Newbury Park, CA: Sage.

Bochner, A. P. (1982). On the efficacy of openness in close relationships. *Communication Yearbook, 5*, 109-124.

Bochner, A. P. (1984). The functions of human communication in interpersonal bonding. In C. C. Arnold & J. W. Bowers (Eds.), *Handbook of rhetorical and communication theory* (pp. 544-621). Boston: Allyn & Bacon.

Bolger, N., DeLongis, A., Kessler, R. C., & Schilling, E. A. (1989). Effects of daily stress on negative mood. *Journal of Personality and Social Psychology, 57*, 808-818.

Bolger, N., DeLongis, A., Kessler, R. C., & Wethington, E. (1989a). The contagion of stress across multiple roles. *Journal of Marriage and the Family, 51*, 175-183.

Bolger, N., DeLongis, A., Kessler, R. C., & Wethington, E. (1989b). The microstructure of daily role-related stress in married couples. In J. Eckenrode & S. Gore (Eds.), *Stress between work and family* (pp. 95-115). New York: Plenum.

Bochner, A. P., & Eisenberg, E. M. (1987). Family process: System perspectives. In C. R. Berger & S. H. Chaffee (Eds.), *Handbook of communication science* (pp. 540-563). Newbury Park, CA: Sage.

Brand, S., & Hirsch, B. J. (1990). The contribution of social networks, work-shift schedules, and family life cycle to women's well-being. In S. Duck with R. Silver (Eds.), *Personal relationships and social support* (pp. 159-172). London: Sage.

Bridge, K., & Baxter, L. A. (1992). Blended friendships: Friends as work associates. *Western Journal of Communication, 56*, 200-225.

Brown, B. (1982). Family intimacy in magazine advertising, 1920-1977. *Journal of Communication, 32*, 173-183.

Brown, B. B., Altman, I., & Werner, C. M. (1992). Close relationships in the physical and social world: Dialectical and transactional analyses. *Communication Yearbook, 15*, 508-521.

Bullis, C., Clark, C., & Sline, R. (1993). From passion to commitment: Turning points in romantic relationships. In P. J. Kalbfleisch (Ed.), *Interpersonal communication: Evolving interpersonal relationships* (pp. 213-236). Hillsdale, NJ: Lawrence Erlbaum.

Burleson, B. R. (1990). Comforting as social support: Relational consequences of supportive behaviors. In S. Duck with R. Silver (Eds.), *Personal relationships and social support* (pp. 66-82). London: Sage.

Buss, A. R. (1979). *A dialectical psychology*. New York: Irvington.

Byrne, D., & Murnen, S. (1988). Maintaining love relationships. In R. Sternberg & M. Barnes (Eds.), *The psychology of love* (pp. 293-310). New Haven, CT: Yale University Press.

Campbell, A. (1986). The streets and violence. In A. Campbell & J. J. Gibbs (Eds.), *Violent transactions: The limits of personality* (pp. 115-131). New York: Basil Blackwell.

Campbell, A., & Gibbs, J. J. (Eds.). (1986). *Violent transactions: The limits of personality*. New York: Basil Blackwell.

Cappella, J. N. (1981). Mutual influence in expressive behavior: Adult-adult and infant-adult dyadic interaction. *Psychological Bulletin, 89*, 101-132.

Cappella, J. N. (1988). Personal relationships, social relationships and patterns of interaction. In S. Duck (Ed.), *Handbook of personal relationships* (pp. 325-342). New York: Wiley.

Cappella, J. N. (1991). Mutual adaptation and relativity of measurement. In B. M. Montgomery & S. Duck (Eds.), *Studying interpersonal interaction* (pp. 103-117). New York: Guilford.

Carbaugh, D. (1988a). Cultural terms and tensions in the speech at a television station. *Western Journal of Speech Communication, 52*, 216-237.

Carbaugh, D. (1988b). *Talking American: Cultural discourse on Donahue*. Norwood, NJ: Ablex.

Carnelley, K. B., & Janoff-Bulman, R. (1992). Optimism in love relationships: General vs. specific lessons from one's personal experiences. *Journal of Social and Personal Relationships, 9*, 5-20.

Caspi, A., Bolger, N., & Eckenrode, J. (1987). Linking person and context in the daily stress process. *Journal of Personality and Social Psychology, 52*, 184-195.

Cate, R. M., Huston, T. L., & Nesselroade, J. R. (1986). Premarital relationships: Toward the identification of alternative pathways to marriage. *Journal of Social and Clinical Psychology, 4*, 3-22.

Chapple, E. D. (1970). *Culture and biological man: Explorations in behavioral anthropology.* New York: Holt, Rinehart & Winston.

Cissna, K. N., Cox, D. E., & Bochner, A. P. (1990). The dialectic of marital and parental relationships within the stepfamily. *Communication Monographs, 57*, 44-61.

Clark, M. S., & Reis, H. T. (1988). Interpersonal processes in close relationships. In M. R. Rosenzweig & L. W. Porter (Eds.), *Annual review of psychology* (Vol. 39, pp. 609-672). Palo Alto, CA: Annual Reviews.

Cody, M. (1982). A typology of disengagement strategies and an examination of the role intimacy, reactions to inequity and relational problems play in strategy selection. *Communication Monographs, 49*, 148-170.

Cohn, J. F., & Tronick, E. Z. (1988). Mother-infant face-to-face interaction: Influence is bidirectional and unrelated to periodic cycles in either partner's behavior. *Developmental Psychology, 24*, 386-392.

Conville, R. L. (1983). Second-order development in interpersonal communication. *Human Communication Research, 9*, 195-207.

Conville, R. L. (1988). Relational transitions: An inquiry into their structure and function. *Journal of Social and Personal Relationships, 5*, 423-437.

Conville, R. L. (1991). *Relational transitions: The evolution of personal relationships.* New York: Praeger.

Cornforth, M. (1968). *Materialism and the dialectical method.* New York: International Publishers.

Coyne, J. C., & Bolger, N. (1990). Doing without social support as an explanatory concept. *Journal of Social and Clinical Psychology, 9*, 148-158.

Crohan, S. E. (1992). Marital happiness and spousal consensus on beliefs about marital conflict: A longitudinal investigation. *Journal of Social and Personal Relationships, 9*, 89-102.

Csikszentmihalyi, M., & Rochberg-Halton, E. (1981). *The meaning of things: Domestic symbols and the self.* Cambridge, MA: Cambridge University Press.

Cutrona, C. E., Suhr, J. A., & MacFarlane, R. (1990). Interpersonal transactions and the psychological sense of support. In S. Duck with R. Silver (Eds.), *Personal relationships and social support* (pp. 30-45). London: Sage.

Davis, K. E., & Latty-Mann, H. (1987). Love styles and relationship quality: A contribution to validation. *Journal of Social and Personal Relationships, 4*, 409-428.

Dell, P. F. (1982a). Beyond homeostasis: Toward a concept of coherence. *Family Process, 21*, 21-41.

Dell, P. F. (1982b). In search of truth: On the way to clinical epistemology. *Family Process, 21*, 407-414.

Derlega, V. J. (1984). Self-disclosure and intimate relationships. In V. J. Derlega (Ed.), *Communication, intimacy, and close relationships* (pp. 1-9). New York: Academic Press.

Dewey, J., & Bentley, A. F. (1949). *Knowing and the known.* Boston: Beacon.

Dindia, K., & Canary, D. J. (1993). Definitions and theoretical perspectives on maintaining relationships. *Journal of Social and Personal Relationships, 10*, 163-173.

Duck, S. (1984). Perspective on the repair of personal relationships: Repair of what, when? In S. Duck (Ed.), *Personal relationships: Vol. 5. Repairing personal relationships* (pp. 163-184). Orlando, FL: Academic Press.

Duck, S. (1987). Adding apples and oranges: Investigators' implicit theories about personal relationships. In R. Burnett, P. McGhee, & D. Clarke (Eds.), *Accounting for relationships: Explanation representation and knowledge* (pp. 215-224). London: Methuen.

Duck, S. (1991). Diaries and logs. In B. Montgomery & S. Duck (Eds.), *Studying interpersonal interaction* (pp. 141-161). New York: Guilford.

Duck, S., & Montgomery, B. M. (1991). The interdependence among interaction substance, theory, and methods. In B. M. Montgomery & S. Duck (Eds.), *Studying interpersonal interaction* (pp. 3-15). New York: Guilford.

Duck, S., & Sants, H. (1983). On the origin of the specious: Are personal relationships really interpersonal states? *Journal of Social and Clinical Psychology, 1*, 27-41.

Duck, S., with Silver, R. (Eds.). (1990). *Personal relationships and social support.* London: Sage.

Eckenrode, J., & Wethington, E. (1990). The process and outcome of mobilizing social support. In S. Duck with R. Silver (Eds.), *Personal relationships and social support* (pp. 83-103). London: Sage.

Eidelson, R. J., & Epstein, N. (1982). Cognition and relationship maladjustment: Development of a measure of dysfunctional relationship beliefs. *Journal of Consulting and Clinical Psychology, 50*, 715-720.

Eisenberg, E. M. (1984). Ambiguity as strategy in organizational communication. *Communication Monographs, 51*, 227-239.

Fiese, B. H. (1992). Dimensions of family rituals across two generations: Relation to adolescent identity. *Family Process, 31*, 151-162.

Fisher, L. (1982). Transactional theories but individual assessment: A frequent discrepancy in family research. *Family Process, 21*, 313-320.

Fitzpatrick, M. A. (1988). *Between husbands and wives: Communication in marriage.* Newbury Park, CA: Sage.

Fogel, A., Nwokah, E., Dedo, J. Y., Messinger, D., Dickson, K. L., Matusov, E., & Holt, S. A. (1992). Social process theory of emotion: A dynamic systems approach. *Social Development, 1*, 122-142.

Gauvain, M., Altman, I., & Fahim, H. (1983). Homes and social change: A cross-cultural analysis. In N. R. Feimer & E. S. Geller (Eds.), *Environmental psychology: Directions and perspectives* (pp. 180-218). New York: Praeger.

Georgoudi, M. (1983). Modern dialectics in social psychology: A reappraisal. *European Journal of Social Psychology, 13*, 77-93.

Giddens, A. (1979). *Central problems in social theory: Action, structure and contradiction in social analysis.* Berkeley: University of California Press.

Giddens, A. (1984). *The constitution of society.* Berkeley: University of California Press.

Ginsburg, G. P. (1980). Situated action: An emerging paradigm. In L. Wheeler (Ed.), *Review of personality and social psychology* (Vol. 1, pp. 295-325). Beverly Hills, CA: Sage.

Goldsmith, D. (1990). A dialectical perspective on the expression of autonomy and connection in romantic relationships. *Western Journal of Speech Communication, 54*, 537-556.

Goldsmith, D., & Parks, M. R. (1990). Communicative strategies for managing the risks of seeking social support. In S. Duck with R. Silver (Eds.), *Personal relationships and social support* (pp. 104-121). London: Sage.

Gottman, J. M. (1979). *Marital interaction: Experimental investigations.* New York: Academic Press.

Gottman, J. M. (1982). Temporal form: Toward a new language for describing relationships. *Journal of Marriage and the Family, 44*, 943-962.

Gottman, J. M., & Levenson, R. W. (1992). Marital processes predictive of later dissolution: Behavior, physiology, and health. *Journal of Personality and Social Psychology, 63*, 221-233.

Haley, J. (1976). *Problem-solving therapy: New strategies for effective family therapy.* San Francisco: Jossey-Bass.

Hazan, C., & Shaver, P. (1987). Romantic love conceptualized as an attachment process. *Journal of Personality and Social Psychology, 52*, 511-524.

Hendrick, S. S., & Hendrick, C. (1992). *Romantic love.* Newbury Park, CA: Sage.

Hill, C., Rubin, Z., & Peplau, L. (1976). Breakups before marriage: The end of 103 affairs. *Journal of Social Issues, 32*, 147-168.

Honeycutt, J. M., Cantrill, J. G., & Allen, T. (1992). Memory structures for relational decay: A cognitive test of sequencing of de-escalating actions and stages. *Human Communication Research, 18*, 528-562.

Honeycutt, J., Cantrill, J., & Greene, R. (1989). Memory structures for relational escalation: A cognitive test of the sequencing of relational actions and stages. *Human Communication Research, 16*, 62-90.

Hopper, R., Knapp, M. L., & Scott, L. (1981). Couples' personal idioms: Exploring intimate talk. *Journal of Communication, 31*, 23-33.

Hubbard, R. (1987). Relationship styles in popular romance novels, 1950 to 1983. *Communication Quarterly, 33*, 113-125.

Huston, T. L., Surra, C., Fitzgerald, N., & Cate, R. (1981). From courtship to marriage: Mate selection as an interpersonal process. In S. Duck & R. Gilmour (Eds.), *Personal relationships: Vol. 2. Developing personal relationships* (pp. 53-88). New York: Academic Press.

Imber-Black, E., Roberts, J., & Whiting, R. A. (Eds.). (1988). *Rituals in families and family therapy.* New York: Norton.

Israel, J. (1979). *The language of dialectics and the dialectics of language.* Copenhagen: Munksgaard.

Johnson, M. P., Huston, T. L., Gaines, S. O., & Levinger, G. (1992). Patterns of married life among young couples. *Journal of Social and Personal Relationships, 9*, 343-364.

Johnson, M. P., & Leslie, L. (1982). Couple involvement and network structure: A test of the dyadic withdrawal hypothesis. *Social Psychology Quarterly, 45*, 34-43.

Karpel, M. (1976). Individuation: From fusion to dialogue. *Family Process, 15*, 65-82.

Katriel, T., & Philipsen, G. (1981). "What we need is communication": "Communication" as a cultural category in some American speech. *Communication Monographs, 48*, 301-317.

Keeney, B. P., & Sprenkle, D. H. (1982). Ecosystemic epistemology: Critical implications for the aesthetics and pragmatics of family therapy. *Family Process, 21*, 1-19.

Keiser, G., & Altman, I. (1976). Relationship of nonverbal behavior to the social penetration process. *Human Communication Research, 2*, 147-161.

Keller, E. F. (1985). *Reflections on gender and science.* New Haven, CT: Yale University Press.

Kellermann, K., & Reynolds, R. (1990). When ignorance is bliss: The role of motivation to reduce uncertainty in uncertainty reduction theory. *Human Communication Research, 17*, 5-75.

Kelley, H. H. (1983). Love and commitment. In H. H. Kelley, E. Berscheid, A. Christensen, J. H. Harvey, T. L. Huston, G. Levinger, E. McClintock, L. A. Peplau, & D. R. Peterson (Eds.), *Close relationships* (pp. 265-314). New York: Freeman.

Kelley, H. H., Berscheid, E., Christensen, A., Harvey, J. H., Huston, T. L., Levinger, G., McClintock, E., Peplau, L. A., & Peterson, D. R. (Eds.). (1983). *Close relationships.* New York: Freeman.

Kernberg, O. F. (1974). Mature love: Prerequisites and characteristics. *Journal of the American Psychoanalytic Association, 22*, 743-768.

Kidd, V. (1975). Happily ever after and other relationship styles: Advice on interpersonal relations in popular magazines, 1951-1972. *Quarterly Journal of Speech, 61*, 31-39.

Krain, M. (1977). A definition of dyadic boundaries and an empirical study of boundary establishment in courtship. *International Journal of Sociology of the Family, 7*, 107-123.

Kurdek, L. A. (1991). The dissolution of gay and lesbian couples. *Journal of Social and Personal Relationships, 8*, 265-278.

Kurdek, L. A. (1992). Relationship stability and relationship satisfaction in cohabiting gay and lesbian couples: A prospective longitudinal test of the contextual and interdependence models. *Journal of Social and Personal Relationships, 9*, 125-142.

L'Abate, K., & L'Abate, B. (1979). The paradoxes of intimacy. *Family Therapy, 6*, 175-184.

La Gaipa, J. (1981). A systems approach to personal relationships. In S. Duck & R. Gilmour (Eds.), *Personal relationships: Vol. 1. Studying personal relationships* (pp. 67-90). New York: Academic Press.

Lazarus, R. S., & Folkman, S. (1984). *Stress, appraisal, and coping.* New York: Springer.

Lazarus, R. S., & Launier, R. (1978). Stress-related transactions between person and environment. In L. A. Pervin & M. Lewis (Eds.), *Perspectives in interactional psychology* (pp. 287-327). New York: Plenum.

Leatham, G., & Duck, S. (1990). Conversations with friends and the dynamics of social support. In S. Duck with R. Silver (Eds.), *Personal relationships and social support* (pp. 1-29). London: Sage.

Levinger, G. (1983). Development and change. In H. H. Kelley, E. Berscheid, A. Christensen, J. H. Harvey, T. L. Huston, G. Levinger, E. McClintock, L. A. Peplau, & D. R. Peterson (Eds.), *Close relationships* (pp. 315-359). New York: Freeman.

Levinger, G., & Huesmann, L. R. (1980). An "incremental exchange" perspective on the pair: Interpersonal reward and level of involvement. In K. J. Gergen, M. S. Greenberg, & R. J. Willis (Eds.), *Social exchange: Advances in theory and research* (pp. 165-188). New York: Plenum.

Lewis, R. A. (1972). A developmental framework for the analysis of premarital dyadic formation. *Family Process, 11*, 17-48.

Lewis, R. A. (1973). Social reaction and the formation of dyads: An interactionist approach to mate selection. *Sociometry, 36*, 409-418.

Livingston, K. (1980). Love as a process of reducing uncertainty-cognitive theory. In K. Pope et al. (Eds.), *On love and loving* (pp. 133-151). San Francisco: Jossey-Bass.

Lloyd, S. A., & Cate, R. M. (1985). Attributions associated with significant turning points in premarital relationship development and dissolution. *Journal of Social and Personal Relationships, 2*, 419-436.

Mao, T. (1965). *On contradiction.* Beijing: Foreign Languages Press.

Masheter, C. (1991). Postdivorce relationships between ex-spouses: The roles of attachment and interpersonal conflict. *Journal of Marriage and the Family, 53*, 103-110.

Masheter, C. (1994). Dialogues between ex-spouses: Evidence of dialectic relationship development. In R. Conville (Ed.), *Uses of "structure" in communication studies* (pp. 83-101). New York: Praeger.

Masheter, C., & Harris, L. (1986). From divorce to friendship: A study of dialectic relationship development. *Journal of Social and Personal Relationships, 3*, 177-190.

McAdams, D. P. (1988). Personal needs and personal relationships. In S. Duck (Ed.), *Handbook of personal relationships* (pp. 7-22). New York: Wiley.

McCall, G. (1988). The organizational life cycle of relationships. In S. Duck (Ed.), *Handbook of personal relationships* (pp. 467-486). New York: Wiley.

McCall, M. M. (1970). Boundary rules in relationships and encounters. In G. McCall, M. McCall, N. Denzin, S. Suttles, & S. Kurth (Eds.), *Social relationships* (pp. 35-61). New York: Aldine.

McClintock, E. (1983). Interaction. In H. H. Kelley, E. Berscheid, A. Christensen, J. H. Harvey, T. L. Huston, G. Levinger, E. McClintock, L. A. Peplau, & D. R. Peterson (Eds.), *Close relationships* (pp. 68-109). New York: Freeman.

Mead, G. M. (1934). *Mind, self, & society*. Chicago: University of Chicago Press.

Mechling, J. (1988). Play and madness in Joseph Heller's *Catch-22*. *Play & Culture, 1*, 226-238.

Metts, S. (1989). An exploratory investigation of deception in close relationships. *Journal of Social and Personal Relationships, 6*, 159-180.

Milardo, R. M., Johnson, M. P., & Huston, T. L. (1983). Developing close relationships: Changing patterns of interaction between pair members and social networks. *Journal of Personality and Social Psychology, 44*, 964-976.

Milardo, R. M., & Wellman, B. (Eds.). (1992). Social networks [Special issue]. *Journal of Social and Personal Relationships, 9*(3).

Miller, L. C., & Berg, J. H. (1984). Selectivity and urgency in interpersonal exchange. In V. J. Derlega (Ed.), *Communication, intimacy and close relationships* (pp. 161-205). New York: Academic Press.

Miller, V., & Knapp, M. (1986). Communication paradoxes and the maintenance of living relationships with the dying. *Journal of Family Issues, 7*, 255-275.

Mirkovic, D. (1980). *Dialectic and sociological thought*. St. Catherines, Ontario, Canada: Diliton.

Montgomery, B. (1992). Communication as the interface between couples and culture. *Communication Yearbook, 15*, 475-507.

Murphy, R. (1980). *The dialectics of social life*. New York: Columbia University Press.

Oerter, R. (1992, July). *Transactionalism*. Paper presented at the conference, "The City as a Frame for Development," Herten, Germany.

Oring, E. (1984). Dyadic traditions. *Journal of Folklore Research, 21*, 19-28.

Owen, W. (1984). Interpretive themes in relational communication. *Quarterly Journal of Speech, 70*, 274-287.

Oxley, D., Haggard, L. M., Werner, C. M., & Altman, I. (1986). Transactional qualities of neighborhood social networks: A case study of "Christmas Street." *Environment and Behavior, 18*, 640-677.

Parks, M. R. (1982). Ideology in interpersonal communication: Off the couch and into the world. *Communication Yearbook, 5*, 79-108.

Parks, M. R., & Eggert, L. L. (1991). The role of social context in the dynamics of personal relationships. In W. H. Jones & D. Perlman (Eds.), *Advances in personal relationships* (Vol. 2, pp. 1-34). London: Jessica Kingsley.

Pepper, S. C. (1942). *World hypotheses: A study in evidence*. Berkeley: University of California Press.

Pepper, S. C. (1967). *Concept and quality: A world hypothesis*. La Salle, IL: Open Court.

Perlman, D., & Fehr, B. (1986). Theories of friendship: The analysis of interpersonal attraction. In V. J. Derlega & B. A. Winstead (Eds.), *Friendship and social interaction* (pp. 9-40). New York: Springer-Verlag.

Pervin, L. A., & Lewis, M. (1978). Overview of the internal-external issue. In L. A. Pervin & M. Lewis (Eds.), *Perspectives in interactional psychology* (pp. 1-22). New York: Plenum.

Petronio, S. (1991). Communication boundary management: A theoretical model of managing disclosure of private information between married couples. *Communication Theory, 1*, 311-335.

Philipsen, G. (1987). The prospect for cultural communication. In D. L. Kincaid (Ed.), *Communication theory: Eastern and Western perspectives* (pp. 245-254). New York: Academic Press.

Phillips, D. C., & Orton, R. (1983). The new causal principle of cognitive learning theory: Perspectives on Bandura's "Reciprocal Determinism." *Psychological Review, 90*, 158-165.

Rawlins, W. K. (1983a). Negotiating close friendship: The dialectic of conjunctive freedoms. *Human Communication Research, 9*, 255-266.

Rawlins, W. K. (1983b). Openness as problematic in ongoing friendships: Two conversational dilemmas. *Communication Monographs, 50*, 1-13.

Rawlins, W. K. (1989). A dialectical analysis of the tensions, functions, and strategic challenges of communication in young adult friendships. *Communication Yearbook, 12*, 157-189.

Rawlins, W. K. (1992). *Friendship matters: Communication, dialectics, and the life course*. New York: Aldine de Gruyter.

Rawlins, W. K., & Holl, M. (1987). The communicative achievement of friendship during adolescence: Predicaments of trust and violation. *Western Journal of Speech Communication, 51*, 345-363.

Rawlins, W. K., & Holl, M. (1988). Adolescents' interactions with parents and friends: Dialectics of temporal perspective and evaluation. *Journal of Social and Personal Relationships, 5*, 27-46.

Riegel, K. F. (1976). The dialectics of human development. *American Psychologist, 31*, 689-700.

Riegel, K. F., & Meacham, J. A. (1976). *The developing individual in a changing world: Social and environmental issues* (Vol. 2). Chicago: Mouton.

Riegel, K. F., & Meacham, J. A. (1978). Dialectics, transaction, and Piaget's theory. In L. A. Pervin & M. Lewis (Eds.), *Perspectives in interactional psychology* (pp. 23-47). New York: Plenum.

Riegel, K. F., & Rosenwald, G. C. (1975). *Structure and transformation: Developmental and historical aspects*. New York: Wiley.

Riessman, C. K. (1990). *Divorce talk: Women and men make sense of personal relationships*. New Brunswick, NJ: Rutgers University Press.

Roberts, J. (1988). Setting the frame: Definition, functions, and typology of rituals. In E. Imber-Black, J. Roberts, & R. A. Whiting (Eds.), *Rituals in families and family therapy* (pp. 3-46). New York: Norton.

Rosenbaum, R. L. (1982). Paradox as epistemological jump. *Family Process, 21*, 85-90.

Rusbult, C. E. (1980). Commitment and satisfaction in romantic associations: A test of the investment model. *Journal of Experimental Social Psychology, 16*, 172-186.

Rusbult, C. E. (1983). A longitudinal test of the investment model: The development (and deterioration) of satisfaction and commitment in heterosexual involvements. *Journal of Personality and Social Psychology, 45*, 101-117.

Rychlak, J. F. (Ed.). (1976). *Dialectic: Humanistic rationale for behavior and development*. New York: S. Karger.

Rychlak, J. F. (1977). *The psychology of rigorous humanism*. New York: Wiley.

Rychlak, J. F. (1988). *The psychology of rigorous humanism* (2nd ed.). New York: New York University Press.

Ryder, R. G., & Bartle, S. (1991). Boundaries as distance regulators in personal relationships. *Family Process, 30*, 393-406.

Selvini, M. (Ed.). (1988). *The work of Mara Selvini Palazzoli*. Northvale, NJ: Jason Aronson.

Selvini-Palazzoli, M., Boscolo, L., Cecchin, G., & Prata, G. (1990). *Paradoxes and counterparadoxes* (E. V. Burt, Trans.). New York: Jason Aronson. (Original work published 1975)

Senchak, M., & Leonard, K. E. (1992). Attachment styles and marital adjustment among newlywed couples. *Journal of Social and Personal Relationships, 9*, 51-64.

Sigman, S. J. (1991). Handling the discontinuous aspects of continuous social relationships: Toward research on the persistence of social forms. *Communication Theory, 1*, 106-127.

Smith, T. W., & Rhodewalt, F. (1986). On states, traits, and processes: A transactional alternative to the individual difference assumptions in Type A behavior and physiological reactivity. *Journal of Research in Personality, 20*, 229-251.

Snyder, M., & Ickes, W. (1985). Personality and social behavior. In G. Lindzey & E. Aronson (Eds.), *Handbook of social psychology* (3rd ed., Vol. 2, pp. 883-947). New York: Random House.

Snyder, M., & Smith, D. (1986). Personality and friendship: The friendship worlds of self-monitoring. In V. J. Derlega & B. A. Winstead (Eds.), *Friendship and social interaction* (pp. 63-80). New York: Springer-Verlag.

Stafford, L., & Canary, D. J. (1991). Maintenance strategies and romantic relationship type, gender and relational characteristics. *Journal of Social and Personal Relationships, 8*, 217-242.

Stamp, G. H., & Banski, M. A. (1992). The communicative management of constrained autonomy during the transition to parenthood. *Western Journal of Communication, 56*, 281-300.

Steier, F. (1989). Toward a radical and ecological constructivist approach to family communication. *Journal of Applied Communication Research, 17*, 1-26.

Sternberg, R. J. (1987). Explorations of love. In W. H. Jones & D. Perlman (Eds.), *Advances in personal relationships* (Vol. 1, pp. 171-196). New York: JAI.

Surra, C. A. (1985). Courtship types: Variations in interdependence between partners and social networks. *Journal of Personality and Social Psychology, 56*, 357-375.

Surra, C. A. (1987). Reasons for changes in commitment: Variations by courtship style. *Journal of Social and Personal Relationships, 4*, 17-33.

Surra, C. A. (1988). The influence of the interactive network on developing relationships. In R. M. Milardo (Ed.), *Families and social networks* (pp. 48-81). Newbury Park, CA: Sage.

Surra, C. A., & Milardo, R. M. (1991). The social psychological context of developing relationships: Interactive and psychological networks. In W. H. Jones & D. Perlman (Eds.), *Advances in personal relationships* (Vol. 3, pp. 1-36). London: Jessica Kingsley.

Surra, C. A., & Ridley, C. A. (1991). Multiple perspectives on interaction: Participants, peers, and observers. In B. M. Montgomery & S. Duck (Eds.), *Studying interpersonal interaction* (pp. 35-55). New York: Guilford.

Thelen, E. (1992). Development as a dynamic system. *Current Directions in Psychological Science, 1*, 189-193.

Thibaut, J. W., & Kelley, H. H. (1959). *The social psychology of groups.* New York: Wiley.

Ting-Toomey, S. (1983). An analysis of verbal communication patterns in high and low marital adjustment groups. *Human Communication Research, 9,* 306-319.

Troll, L. E. (1988). Rituals and reunions. *American Behavioral Scientist, 31,* 621-631.

Turner, V. (1969). *The ritual process: Structure and anti-structure.* Ithaca, NY: Cornell University Press.

Warner, R. M. (1988). Rhythm in social interaction. In J. E. McGrath (Ed.), *The social psychology of time: New perspectives* (pp. 63-88). Newbury Park, CA: Sage.

Warner, R. M. (1991). Incorporating time. In B. M. Montgomery & S. Duck (Eds.), *Studying interpersonal interaction* (pp. 82-102). New York: Guilford.

Warren, S. (1984). *The emergence of dialectical theory: Philosophy and political inquiry.* Chicago: University of Chicago Press.

Werner, C. M., Altman, I., & Brown, B. B. (1992). A transactional approach to interpersonal relations: Physical environment, social context and temporal qualities. *Journal of Social and Personal Relationships, 9,* 297-324.

Werner, C. M., Altman, I., Brown, B. B., & Ginat, J. (1993). Celebrations in personal relationships: A transactional/dialectical perspective. In S. Duck (Ed.), *Social context and relationships: Understanding relationship processes* (Vol. 3, pp. 109-138). Newbury Park, CA: Sage.

Werner, C. M., Altman, I., & Oxley, D. (1985). Temporal aspects of homes: A transactional perspective. In I. Altman & C. M. Werner (Eds.), *Home environments: Human behavior and the environment* (Vol. 8, pp. 1-32). New York: Plenum.

Werner, C. M., Altman, I., Oxley, D., & Haggard, L. M. (1987). People, place, and time: A transactional analysis of neighborhoods. In W. H. Jones & D. Perlman (Eds.), *Advances in personal relationships* (Vol. 1, pp. 243-275). Greenwich, CT: JAI.

Werner, C. M., Brown, B. B., Altman, I., & Staples, B. (1992). Close relationships in their physical and social contexts: A transactional perspective. *Journal of Social and Personal Relationships, 9,* 411-431.

Werner, C. M., & Haggard, L. M. (1985). Temporal qualities of interpersonal relationships. In M. L. Knapp & G. R. Miller (Eds.), *Handbook of interpersonal communication* (pp. 59-99). Beverly Hills, CA: Sage.

Werner, C. M., & Haggard, L. M. (1992). Avoiding intrusions at the office: Privacy regulation on typical and high-solitude days. *Basic and Applied Social Psychology, 13,* 181-193.

Werner, C. M., Haggard, L. M., Altman, I., & Oxley, D. (1988). Temporal qualities of rituals and celebrations. In J. E. McGrath (Ed.), *The social psychology of time: New perspectives* (pp. 203-232). Newbury Park, CA: Sage.

Wiseman, J. (1986). Friendship: Bonds and binds in a voluntary relationship. *Journal of Social and Personal Relationships, 3,* 191-212.

Wolin, S. J., & Bennett, L. A. (1984). Family rituals. *Family Process, 23,* 401-420.

Zeitz, G. (1980). Interorganizational dialectics. *Administrative Science Quarterly, 25,* 72-89.

Zicklin, G. (1969, August). A conversation concerning face to face interaction. *Psychiatry,* pp. 236-249.

10

The Management of Conversational Interaction in Adults and Infants

Joseph N. Cappella

THIS CHAPTER FOCUSES on how people manage conversations. Who has not come away from some conversation wishing that she had avoided saying a particularly hurtful thing, or that he had commented when he was silent? Who has not felt buoyed by the animation of an outgoing and animated partner or depressed by the emotional flatness of a unresponsive friend? Some conversations have a special feel about them; the partners sense this and want more. Others grind and move in fits and starts; the partners withdraw with a sense of dissatisfaction. The fit is not right. These common thoughts and feelings are the motivating questions of this chapter.

There are two important senses in which conversations can be managed. The more typical connotation of the word *manage* implies that a person intentionally seeks to alter the content, tenor, or events of a conversation toward some preordained end. For example, an overworked spouse might try to move the topic of conversation toward the stresses of the workplace or home to let the other know about his or her experienced difficulties. Management of this type exhibits "control" in the sense that actions are undertaken to achieve what one perceives to be an important need or purpose. Such conversational behaviors are sometimes called "deliberate" (Cappella, 1991).

The second sense assumes that management is more automatic, less cognitively weighed. The research that will be reviewed will show that this automatic sense of management involves control over the more microscopic events during interaction. For example, increases in speech rate by one party tend to produce increases in the partner's speech rate (Cappella & Planalp, 1981). People are, in general, quite unaware that such influences exist and, under most circumstances, do not employ such responses intentionally.[1]

The ability to control conversations, intentionally or unintentionally, depends upon the existence of certain regularities that can be exploited by one or the other conversational partner, and this exploitation depends upon knowledge. For example, to encourage discussion of a topic of interest to me, I try to get a version of that topic onto the floor. I do so because I know that "staying on the topic" is a norm frequently adhered to in discussion. I must know this norm and how to use it in order to achieve the end that I desire. The only difference between the regularities that people consciously employ to control conversations (for example, topic continuity) and those that they do not (for example, speech rate) is that conversationalists are not generally aware of many of the regularities that do govern conversational events. Once made aware of such regularities, people could use them to manage the content and style of their conversations.

Attention to the process of management cannot ignore what it is that people manage in their conversations. In terms of raw stimuli, conversations are a complex mixture of auditory, visual, olfactory, and tactile events that are simultaneous and sequential in time. But such a description of the uninterpreted events of communicative interchanges is more pertinent to the study of psychophysics than to the study of interpersonal relations. If the management of conversations is to be relevant to the study of interpersonal relations, then the events that are managed in those conversations must have an empirically strong and conceptually significant relationship to interpersonal judgments and perceptions.

Consider the example of face-directed gaze. As a raw stimulus, such a behavior is nothing more than gaze fixed at the general facial region of another person. Folklore, literature, and controlled research have shown that this stimulus has a number of possible interpretations. From the point of view of the sender, the gaze may have been directed to gather more information about the other person or, more purposefully, to signal to the other an interest that decorum requires be more indirect than words allow. In either case, the gaze means something other than the mere act of gazing and is a sign of some internal state of the sender.

The second internal state that could have been signaled (namely, interest on the part of the sender) has more immediate and direct relational implications than does the first internal state, information gathering. The recipient of the gaze may not notice it at all or may interpret it as impolite staring, or worse. Although either reaction by the recipient has impact, the latter interpretation has more immediate and severe relational implications than does the former. In either case, the first steps of this hypothetical interaction are headed for trouble because the possible intentions of the sender and the possible interpretations by the receiver are at odds. The relational value of the act is not shared.

This example illustrates a number of principles that will undergird this review of conversational management. First, the uninterpreted value of conversational events can be sharply distinguished from the interpretations that those events receive. Second, the interpretations that can be given to conversational events are multiple, with some having more powerful relational implications than others. Third, the interpreted values of conversational events can be located in at least three places: the motivational states of the sender, the perceptions of the receiver, or in the shared meanings of senders and receivers. This review assumes that conversational management is concerned with interpreted rather than raw conversational events, with interpersonally significant events, and with events whose meaning is broadly shared by the body of conversationalists within a culture.

At least some of the verbal, nonverbal, and vocal events that occur within conversations have the potential to initiate, reinforce, and change the status of relationships between partners. The management of conversations, whether deliberate or unintentional, is in part the management of these meaningful events and is, in this indirect way, the management of relationships. Of course, I would be naive to claim that relationships and interactions are equivalent. Relationships exist in abstracted form in the memory of partners. That abstraction certainly influences the content, structure, and management of conversations, and in turn is influenced by them, but that is not to say that a given conversation is a replica of the relationship in which it takes place. Rather, a given conversation is an indicator of the relationship in which it functions in much the same way that the monthly indicators of the nation's economic welfare are related to the nation's actual economic condition: They are certainly related to the economic condition but are more informative when compared with the trends that the economy has been displaying over time rather than treated as absolutes. The indicators are certainly not the economy itself.

The diversity and kind of stimuli being generated during a conversation are extremely broad. How can anyone hope to study, let alone understand, the various verbal, vocal, and kinesic activities that people carry out while speaking and listening? What is worse, these auditory, visual, tactile, and olfactory stimuli are information dense per unit of time. This means that they are changing rapidly over time (at least the so-called dynamic features are; Kendon, 1967).

Conversationalists have developed strategies for ignoring, combining, and substituting information generated by their partners. Part of the task that researchers have is to understand the organizational shortcuts that conversationalists take so that this route to the simplification of conversational structure can be profitably employed in research.

The most obvious description of the behavioral activities of conversations would be organized along two dimensions: a dimension representing time and a dimension representing a particular type of behavior. Conversational events occur sequentially and this temporal characteristic is one feature of conversational structure.

At any moment in time, numerous behaviors can occur, filling the range from the microscopic and automatic, such as pauses prior to word choices, to the macroscopic and deliberate, such as justifications following accusations. The second dimension of conversational organization concerns these categories. Are these behavior streams sufficiently independent to be treated as distinct or are they interrelated in ways that would allow researchers, and conversational partners, to treat them as functionally equivalent?

Space limitations will not permit us to answer these questions in detail here (but see Cappella & Street, 1985). Research on the temporal organization of conversation has almost always taken an encoding approach, validating the basic time units in terms of criteria generated by the actor. The fundamental units chosen have included the speaking turn (variously defined; see Duncan & Fiske, 1977; Jaffe & Feldstein, 1970; Matarazzo & Wiens, 1972); the phonemic clause (Dittmann, 1972); and units larger than the phonemic clause, often identified as "idea" groupings (Butterworth & Goldman-Eisler, 1979). Even when the researcher does not wish to enter the controversy over which fundamental unit of time will be employed and, consequently, employs a clock time unit, a discrete unit for observation must still be chosen. This choice will often be ad hoc.

The second concerns the possible functional groupings of the various verbal, vocal, and kinesic behaviors. Two approaches to establishing such functional groupings have been advocated in the literature: interpersonal motivations (Patterson, 1982a, 1982b) and interpersonal perceptions (Cappella, 1985a; Cappella &

Street, 1985). Both approaches maintain that the meaning or significance of behaviors will be found in the relationship between the behaviors and some internal state. Patterson argued that the location of meaning is the intentions and motivations of the actor, whereas I have argued that the meaning is located in the effects that the behavior produces in perceivers. Both views are meritorious and deserving of further inquiry. The empirical plausibility of such a venture is discussed by Cappella and Street (1985) and has been pursued in research by Palmer and Lack (in press), Burgoon (1991; Burgoon, Buller, Hale, & de Turck, 1984), and Cappella and Palmer (1989, 1990a).

Managing Conversational Behaviors

According to Ashby (1963), two systems are said to be in communication when the output from each system serves as the input for the other system. For Ashby, a signal could not be considered an input unless it changed the state of the system for which it was an input. Because Ashby was a strict behaviorist when considering the behavior of systems, the state change initiated by the input of another system must be observable. Thus, in Ashby's view, communication involves two systems generating output that serves as input for the other system and eventuates in observable state changes by each.

This view is a good starting point for conversational management. In simple terms, I take conversational management to be the use of one's own verbal, vocal, and kinesic actions to alter behaviors in another. Although it is certainly true that one can alter another's conversational behavior by manipulating the situation, the relationship, the expectations, the affective tone, and perhaps even the other's personality, attitudes, motives, and values, these are more remote and less controllable than are conversational actions. Similarly, no assumption is made that individuals are deliberately controlling their actions in order to influence the flow and direction of the other's actions. Rather, conversational management is concerned with the ways in which overt verbal, vocal, and kinesic behavior influences the same classes of behavior in another in conversation and in service of conversational and interpersonal ends.

A Methodological and Definitional Excursion

Before turning our full attention to the research literature on conversational management, some words should be devoted to methodological and statistical matters specific to the study of conversational management.

Let us formalize the definition of conversational management given above. Consider a conversation between two persons, A and B. Let the behavioral repertoire of person A be denoted by the set $X = (X1, X2, \ldots, XN)$, where the values X are the N discrete behaviors that can be enacted by person A at discrete intervals of time. No real loss of generality is entailed by assuming that the behaviors are discrete rather than continuous or measured on a clock base rather than event time. Analogous definitions can be created for event time and for continuous measures. Let the behavioral repertoire of person B be denoted by the set (Y) identical to the set X for A. Conversational management is defined by two features of the contingent probability between the set of behaviors (X) and the set (Y):

[1] $P[Xi(t + 1) \mid Yi(t)] > 0$

[2] $P[Xi(t + 1) \mid Yj(t)] >$ or $< P[Xj(t + 1)]$

for at least some combination of the behaviors I and J. In words, equations 1 and 2 mean that B's behavior (the Jth one, in fact) must influence the probability of A's behavior (the Ith behavior) at some significant level and, more important, that the size of the probability must be greater than the probability that A will emit the behavior in the absence of B's prior behavior (2). These two features ensure that A's response level in the presence of B's behavior is above A's normal baseline behavior. A similar pair of equations can be written for A's influence on B. Together they constitute the necessary and sufficient conditions for mutual influence.

Other implications should be mentioned. Incorporating the time factor, t, assumes that the behavior of persons A and B is interleaved in time. No such assumption is necessary as, with larger time units, A and B might exhibit mutual influence within a time period. The behaviors I and J do not necessarily need to be different. When they are the same so that the mutual influence concerns the identical behavior, then mutual influence is called matching and mismatching. For example, when dialect choice by person A influences the dialect employed by B (Giles & Powesland, 1975), then a process of matching is observed. Matching and mismatching is clearly a special case of mutual influence. When I is not equal to J but I and J contribute to the same behavioral function, then we are concerned with reciprocity and compensation (Patterson, 1976). For example, when increases in proximity by A produce less facial gaze by B, then compensation has occurred. Compensation and reciprocity represent another special case of mutual influence.

Mutual influence also concerns situations in which the behaviors for each person are neither identical nor functionally similar. In this case, one of the behaviors becomes a focal behavior because of its special status or character in the conversation or in the relationship. For example, attempts to take the floor are an important criterion in the study of conversational regulation, but the behaviors that predict it are neither turn attempts themselves nor functionally equivalent to turn attempts (Duncan & Fiske, 1977). The definition of mutual influence given above can comfortably accommodate these examples.

The only additional requirement is that the definition of equations 1 and 2 applies to groups of partners and not only to a particular pair of partners. Common experience recognizes that some partners develop over a period of time specialized sequences of interaction that allow them certain efficiencies and access to privileged communication while in public. But these idiosyncratic patterns cannot be generalized to other interactions or used to manage other conversations. My assumption is that the types of mutual influence to be reviewed here are regular rather than idiographic.

The operational techniques available to study conversational management are extensive, ranging from conversation analytic descriptions of paired sequences (Hopper, 1992) through experimental manipulations to bivariate time series (Cappella, 1993a). Each of these approaches answers the question: "Does A's behavior affect B's response?" but, beyond that superficial similarity, they ask questions that are quite different and may yield answers that appear to be at odds with one another conceptually.

A few admonitions may be useful, however, before leaving this topic. First, one must be cautious of the approach of "proof by example" championed by conversation analysts. I have argued elsewhere (Cappella, 1990) that conversation analytic approaches ignore baseline probabilities and chance co-occurrences. Single examples may demonstrate the diversity and nuance of real conversations but may also reveal little more than the idiosyncracy of a particular pair of partners.

Second, the considerable variation in individual levels of certain behaviors suggests that individual baselines are important for assessing change in response to some experimental manipulation. In this area of research, within-subjects designs with baseline and postmanipulation measurements of behavioral response are to be preferred to between-subjects designs (see, for example, Coker & Burgoon, 1987).

Finally, studying the dynamic relationship between partners' behaviors can give information unavailable from studies using confederates or from studies using only the mean levels of partners' behavior. Such studies answer questions about microscopic adjustments. Do persons only adjust slowly to their partner's behavior, resulting in changes in mean levels, or are the adjustments visible in the rapid moment-to-moment fluctuations of verbal, vocal, and kinesic actions? Only studying the dynamic changes in partners' responses to one another can answer this question.

The Management of Conversational Turns

The study of how conversations can occur at all without the participants constantly "bumping into one another" verbally has attracted the attention of researchers using a variety of approaches (Beattie, 1978, 1979a, 1979b; Duncan & Fiske, 1977; Goodwin, 1981; Sacks, Schegloff, & Jefferson, 1974; Schenkein, 1978). For the most part, these investigators have been concerned with the how, and a little with the why, of conversational turn-taking but not at all with the "so what" of this feature of conversation.

Being able to get control of the floor, keep that control when necessary, and give it up when finished is a crucial interpersonal skill related to perceptions of power, perceptions of affiliation, and general social competence (Cappella, 1985a). The evidence is overwhelming in its support of the relationship between holding the floor and observers' ratings of control and power (leadership, dominance, and so forth) and ratings of associativity (attraction, social evaluation, and so forth; see Cappella, 1985a). Zimbardo's (1977) studies of shyness suggest that most people identify reluctance to talk as the primary cue of their shyness. Shyness and its associated failed participation can also lead to embarrassment, self-consciousness, and decreased self-esteem (Zimbardo, 1977).

More politically motivated writers (Steinem, 1981) have portrayed some of the covert discrimination that women experience in groups in terms of failure to participate. Women must bear the false reputation of being the talkative ones while at the same time suffering the powerlessness of being the least participative with mostly male colleagues in decision making and social groups. When job and advancement depend upon a positive social image, the inability to participate can be an overwhelming barrier to personal and professional development (at least in Western models of social competence).

An equally pernicious outcome from low participation rates is the perception of shyness created by the reticent person. When others perceive that a person has a certain quality or trait, they often treat the person accordingly, leading him or her to act out the role dictated by the others' perceptions (Farina, Allen, & Saul, 1968;

Farina, Gliha, Boudreau, Allen, & Sherman, 1971). The perception of shyness, whether deserved or not, can lead to behavior that will only increase the shy reaction.

The point is a simple but powerful one. The study of conversational turn-taking and its management has implications far beyond the how and why of the rule of "one speaker at a time." Those who have little trouble with managing the turn-taking in their conversations open themselves to the rewards of positive perception and social competence and all that that entails. Those who cannot manage their conversational participation lose access to the domain in which power is exercised and restrict their potential social rewards.

Although many researchers have been concerned with the structure, regulation, and organization of conversation, only Duncan and his associates (Duncan, 1972, 1973, 1974; Duncan, Bruner, & Fiske, 1979; Duncan & Fiske, 1977; Duncan & Niederehe, 1974) have been concerned specifically with the verbal, vocal, and kinesic behaviors that cue speaker and listener roles. They have also employed the methodologies necessary for the audience to evaluate the reliability of their conclusions.

Turn-taking signals. To isolate the cues that are associated with the taking and the relinquishing of conversational turns, a turn must be defined. Duncan (1972) defines turns on the basis of the intent of the speaker and defines back-channel behaviors on the part of the listener as actions that do not attempt to wrest the floor away from the speaker. Despite the conceptual and operational difficulty that these terms introduce, the evidence indicates that coders can reliably assess both *turns* and *back channels.*

Based upon a small study and a larger replication, Duncan and Fiske (1977) report that six cues are associated with smooth turn-taking:

(a)   a certain pattern of intonation at the end of phonemic clauses (Trager, 1958);

(b)   a sociocentric sequence (Bernstein, 1962) such as "you know";

(c)   the completion of a syntactic clause;

(d)   a paralinguistic drawl (Trager, 1958) on the final syllable or the stressed syllable of a phonemic clause;

(e)   termination of a hand gesticulation or relaxation of a tensed hand position, such as a fist; and

(f)   decrease of paralinguistic pitch or loudness on a sociocentric sequence (Duncan, 1983, p. 151).

One or more of these cues is present in 261 of the 263 smooth turn transitions observed by Duncan and Fiske (1977). Gesturing by the speaker when one or more of the above cues is present seems to have a veto effect. When the speaker gestures while exhibiting one or more of the above cues, the probability that the listener takes the floor is reduced. Duncan and Fiske also report that the sheer number of cues is the best predictor of the probability of smooth transitions. No single cue seems to be more important than any other; no special combination of cues markedly improves the correlation with the probability of a smooth transition; and the relationship between the number of cues and the probability of transition is linear and is not a step function.

The most significant point of controversy for the cues associated with smooth transitions concerns eye gaze. Research by Wiemann and Knapp (1975) and by Kendon (1967) found that gaze by the speaker at the auditor increases toward the end of speakers' turns, thus acting as a signal that the speaker is ready to yield the floor. Duncan and Fiske (1977) found no evidence that this cue functions to mark turn-yielding. However, they did find that auditors tend to shift their heads away from speakers when the auditor begins vocalizing, especially when that vocalization is identified as a turn attempt rather than just a back channel. Thus Duncan and Fiske's evidence does identify head shifting as an important cue in turn-taking but not as a turn-yielding cue.

Within-turn interaction and simultaneous speech. If conversations can be divided into turns and back channels, then partners must be able to negotiate their way through back channels as well as turns. Similarly, not all turn-taking is smooth, with occasional simultaneous claims to the floor made by listener and hearer. Research by Duncan and Fiske (1977), Meltzer, Morris, and Hayes (1971), and others shows that the same set of cues involved in turn-taking are also implicated in within-turn and simultaneous turns (with relative loudness playing an important role in the latter).

Verbal behaviors and turn-taking. Length of turn is not dependent just on vocal and kinesic cues. Much research has shown that turns are cued in various verbal ways as well. For example, "Wh-" questions identify to whom and when the next turn is allocated. Story lines that begin by identifying when a story begins also leave control of the turn to the storyteller until the story is completed (Ryave, 1978). McLaughlin (1984) has reviewed much of this (and other) research related to the more verbal aspects of turn-taking (and conversational structure more broadly).

Explaining turn management and participation. Of the great variety of behaviors initially studied in turn management, five groups remain as important to conversational participation: verbal cues associated with the termination of a speech unit, eye gaze (head shifting), gesticulation, pauses, and vocal amplitude. Turn-yielding is cued by six different behaviors, but five of these are located at or help to designate a verbal unit (deviation from a certain pitch contour, sociocentric sequences, completion of a grammatical clause, drawl, decreased pitch, and/or loudness on a sociocentric sequence). The sixth is termination of gesturing.

Participation in conversation is facilitated when an actor uses these cues appropriately to obtain and to yield the floor. Implicit knowledge of the cues and of the rules must reside in competent conversationalists. The verbal cues that partition the speech into units (phonemic, linguistic, and so forth) are important in that they mark the most likely location of back channels and turn attempts. They are the locations of turn-yielding and turn-taking. Speakers and listeners must be able to recognize these important locations.

However, the other four classes of cues are, I believe, much more important because they indicate what actions are intended at the pause and boundary locations. For example, as the frequency and average duration of pauses decreases then so does the opportunity for the auditor to take the speaking role. If the reticent speaker pauses a great deal, then that speaker will have greater difficulty in maintaining the floor simply because the opportunities for the auditor to take the floor will be far greater. If one of the partners were to exhibit excessive gaze aversion, then gaze aversion would lose its informativeness as a speaker state cue. If a person were to employ a high number of body-focused gestures, then the number of possible object-focused gestures would be fewer and the gesticulation signal would be less available to the apparently fidgety person.

Research on socially insecure individuals has shown them to employ greater gaze aversion, to use more body-focused gestures, and to pause and hesitate more in speech (Cappella, 1985b). Thus the behavior patterns of socially insecure persons involve just those behaviors crucial to the turn-taking process.

The Management of Vocal Behaviors

In the next sections, two conventions are employed. All of the studies reviewed are behavioral in that subjects actually interact with one another or with a confederate rather than reacting to hypothetical encounters using self-reported behaviors. Second, the data are organized on the basis of the independent or manipulated variable.

By "vocal behavior," I mean characteristics of the spoken word independent of the verbal or meaning component. Included in this set would be vocalization duration, pause duration, switching pauses, utterance length, latency to respond, pitch (or fundamental frequency), and intensity or amplitude. These variables have been carefully defined by Jaffe and Feldstein (1970) and by Matarazzo and Wiens (1972).

The evidence on mutual influence in vocal aspects of conversations has been reviewed in detail elsewhere (Cappella, 1981, 1983). The overwhelming conclusion is that matching and reciprocity are the predominant forms of mutual influence. The evidence for matching in speech rate (Webb, 1969, 1972), latency and switching pauses (Cappella & Planalp, 1981; Jaffe & Feldstein, 1970; Matarazzo & Wiens, 1967), pausing (Dabbs, 1980; Jaffe & Feldstein, 1970; Welkowitz, Cariffe, & Feldstein, 1976), fundamental frequency (Buder, 1991), and amplitude (Black, 1949; Meltzer et al., 1971; Natale, 1975) is quite strong and remarkably consistent across samples, operational definitions, and laboratories.

The evidence for matching on utterance duration and vocalization is not as clear cut, but it does appear that matching is the rule in controlled laboratory studies. Less conclusive findings are obtained in more naturally occurring conditions (see Matarazzo, Weitman, Saslow, & Wiens, 1963, versus Welkowitz & Feldstein, 1969). Part of these differences may be attributable to the operational differences between utterance duration and vocalization duration. Utterance duration probably includes both vocalization duration and pauses. Because pause matching is a common finding but vocalization matching is not, matching in utterance duration may be due in part to the matching of pauses only.

Despite these rather strong findings, certain methodologies have uncovered contrary tendencies toward mismatching and compensation. Cappella and Planalp (1981) applied time-series methodologies to the vocal behaviors of individual dyads, with each turn being an observation unit. It was found that certain dyads were compensatory on vocalization and pause behaviors, although the pattern across the 12 dyads was in favor of matching. Matarazzo, Wiens, Matarazzo, and Saslow (1968) found similar compensatory results on utterance duration between individual clients and their therapists. The chief difference between the above two studies and the vast majority of others is the individual versus group level of analysis. When methods are used that permit scrutiny of individual dyads rather than group-level results alone, some dyads exhibit the mismatching that commonsense observation would lead us to expect. Certainly it is not difficult to imagine the reticent person giving over vocal responsibility to the more verbose partner or the very active, high tempo partner driving the less expressive partner toward even greater withdrawal. The individual level of statistical analysis is necessary to uncover these tendencies toward compensation in vocalization and turn duration.

The Management of Kinesic Behaviors

The set of possible kinesic behaviors operative in conversation and interpersonally functional is very extensive. However, two kinesic behaviors have received more attention as independent or manipulated variables than the rest: proximity and eye gaze. Numerous variables in addition to these have been measured as responses to increases and decreases in these two kinesic features.

Proximity. Interpersonal distance has produced the strongest and most consistent set of results on mutual influence of any of the behaviors discussed here. In approximately 40 studies reviewed in Cappella (1981, 1983), all produced at least some results supportive of the compensatory effects of increases in proximity. As proximity (or nearness) increases, one can expect (a) partners to increase their own distance (Becker & Mayo, 1971; Efran & Cheyne, 1973); (b) the time it takes to leave the situation to increase; (c) partner's eye gaze to decrease (Argyle & Dean, 1965; Patterson, 1977; Schulz & Barefoot, 1974); (d) partner's orientation to become less direct (Pellegrini & Empey, 1970; Sawitsky & Watson, 1975); (e) partner's duration of responses to decrease (Baxter & Rozelle, 1975; Johnson & Dabbs, 1976); and (f) partner's affiliative responses to decrease (Cappella, 1986).

Although these findings are consistent, they are also one-sided. Most studies employ a between-subjects design with only two levels of distance, one normal for the situation and one rather close. Thus most findings pertain to half of the compensation process: responses to close distances relative to normal. The question of responses to far distances is still open empirically.

Despite these strong conclusions, there are some empirical hints that the compensation process governing interpersonal distance is limited. Greenbaum and Rosenfeld (1978) found that, for a subgroup of their subjects who were labeled affiliative because they were willing to vocalize, closer proximity was associated with greater eye gaze directed at a stranger at a traffic intersection. For the rest of their subjects who were unwilling to vocalize (and presumably less affiliative), no relationship between proximity and gaze was found. Aiello (1972, 1973, 1977) employed three levels of distance and relatively normal patterns of gaze by his confederates measuring eye gaze and duration of speech in response to subgroups of males and females. The males exhibited compensatory responses on both variables across all levels of confederate distance. The females, however, increased talk and gaze as distance increased from near to moderate, but decreased gaze as distance increased from moderate to far. If one assumes that persons have different upper bounds for desired and tolerated interpersonal involvement, then the results of the above studies become interpretable. More important, the departures from the rule of compensation suggest that mediators of response to nearer distances are important predictors of the kind of reaction that will occur, either increasing approach or increasing avoidance. Both responses are possible under certain conditions, but the compensatory response is the most common.

Eye gaze. The results from a review of the literature on response to eye gaze are similar to those from interpersonal distance, but opposite in direction. People show a marked tendency to reciprocate gaze by another, but this rule is modified significantly by moderators of the response. As gaze increases in a neutral to positive social situation, returned gaze will also increase (Coutts, Schneider, & Montgomery, 1980; Kaplan, Firestone, Klein, & Sodikoff, 1983; R. Noller, 1980), duration of speech will increase (Aiello, 1973; Kleinke, Staneski, & Berger, 1975), and more direct body position may be employed (Sawitsky & Watson, 1975; Sodikoff, Firestone, & Kaplan, 1974). But these response tendencies may be modified by changing elements of the social or personal situation.

In their study of staring at a traffic intersection, Greenbaum and Rosenfeld (1978) observed that greater gaze led to quicker departure by drivers. For females who did not talk to the male confederate, a clear pattern of compensation in returned gaze was exhibited. The most directly supportive study is that of Kaplan et al. (1983). In this case, gaze from a liked confederate was returned during an interview but gaze from a disliked confederate was compensated. Thus the research shows an overall tendency toward reciprocity in gaze in social settings that have a neutral to positive affective tone but a reversal in this trend for settings with a negative affective tone.

Synchrony. Recently, Bernieri (Bernieri & Rosenthal, 1991) has introduced a method of studying interactional structure that asks a set of judges, naive to rules of coding interaction, whether partners in given segments of interaction are in synchrony with one another, are coordinated, behaviorally matched, and so on. To be sure that the judgments distinguish actual synchrony from random coordination, judges are given some segments that are not of real partners but are artificially constructed by juxtaposing segments from different interactions on the same videotape. In a series of studies, Bernieri and his colleagues have been able to show that judges (as a group) are capable of discriminating real from pseudointeractions on synchrony and that these judgments are related to participants' ratings of rapport during the interaction (Bernieri, 1988; Bernieri, Resnick, & Rosenthal, 1988).

This is an important methodological innovation in the study of interactional structure because it seems to bypass the need for detailed coding of behavior. But does judged synchrony have any relationship to behavioral synchrony? A recent, unpublished study done in our laboratory (and replicated by Bernieri in his laboratory) suggests that the two are related. Subjects judged 16 one-minute segments selected so that 8 were low in behavioral synchrony and 8 were high. Mean judgments of synchrony were higher for those segments that were behaviorally synchronous (on a behavioral index of activity) versus those that were low on the index. If it can be shown in later replications that this effect is robust, judgments of synchrony may effectively replace behavioral measures of synchrony where appropriate.

Facial emotion. The face is a region for signaling affect through facial displays of emotion. These displays are mimicked under some conditions. In many interactive contexts, motor mimicry of various sorts occurs (Bavelas, Black, Chovil, Lemery, & Mullett, 1988; Bavelas, Black, Lemery, MacInnis, & Mullett, 1986). This means that, when subjects observe the enactment of a facial behavior in a confederate (resulting from an accident, for example), they mimic the display with their own expression. Cappella and Palmer (1990b) report an intraclass correlation of .492 between partners' smiles across a sample of 40 dyads in unstructured social conversation. Krause, Steimer, Sanger-Alt, and Wagner (1989) cite previously unpublished research in their laboratory indicating that interactions between schizophrenic patients and their healthy partners lead to a depression of facial activity in the healthy partners. Fewer positive emotional displays are generated by the healthy when interacting with the depressed in comparison with facial displays that occur when healthy subjects interact with healthy partners. Cappella (1993b) reports that the timing of smiles and laughter in dyads is mostly congruent, that is, either both smiling or both not smiling, rather than complementary.

Together, the above findings seem to suggest that imitation of facial displays (at least for smiling) is a common characteristic of social interaction. Whether this claim extends to other facial behaviors must await further study.

Other kinesic behaviors. Research on mutual influence with respect to other kinesic behaviors has not been sufficient to warrant definitive conclusions. One area that has received considerable attention is synchrony in body movements. Condon and Ogston (1966, 1967) were first to speculate that an individual's microscopic body movements were synchronized with changes in the person's speech and that body movement changes were synchronized between persons. McDowall (1978a, 1978b) has strongly criticized the previous research for failing to correct for synchronization above chance baselines. Despite counterarguments from Gatewood and Rosenwein (1981) that McDowall's methods were too different than those of Condon and Ogston to warrant a direct comparison, the criticism remains that chance baselines, regardless of the methodology chosen, have never been taken into account in the previous research. Cappella and Palmer (1990b) did report positive intraclass correlation between partners' illustrative gestures across 4 different types of dyads. This is not evidence of temporal synchrony, however, only mean similarity in the amount of gesturing.

Managing Verbal Behaviors

A wide variety of verbal behaviors operate in conversation in service of interpersonal functions. Verbally intimate statements are important in relationship negotiation and development (Altman & Taylor, 1973). Verbally intimate questions are common tools in therapy and counseling. Topic presentation and continuity, in addition to their obvious functions of introducing information and of providing continuity for the purposes of coherence and competence, also are related to issues of confirmation and disconfirmation of the other through acceptance and rejection of the topic presented (Watzlawick, Beavin, & Jackson, 1967). Linguistic choices such as dialect, pronunciation, grammatical and verbal complexity, language choices in bilingual settings, and the like are especially important in judgments of power and status, in seeking and giving approval, and in showing solidarity and separateness (Giles, 1979; Giles & Powesland, 1975). Other features of the verbal stream carry information about dominance and control (Ericson & Rogers, 1965; Rogers & Farace, 1975), about account sequences when some harm has occurred (McLaughlin, Cody, & Rosenstein, 1983), about threat and "face" (Brown & Levinson, 1987), and about conflict strategies (Sillars, 1980). Although not a comprehensive sampling of language features with interpersonal implications, the above list represents several domains in which substantial research effort has been exerted.

Self-Disclosure

Several extensive reviews of the literature on mutual influence in self-disclosure are available (Cappella, 1981; Dindia, 1985). These reviews find overwhelming evidence in support of Jourard's (1959) initial hypothesis of a dyadic effect ("reciprocity" and "matching" in the language adopted here). Correlational studies (Jourard, 1959), controlled interviews (Kaplan et al., 1983), experimental groups (Worthy, Gary, & Kahn, 1969), role-playing studies (Cozby, 1972), naturalistic experiments (Rubin, 1975), controlled sequences of interchanges (Davis, 1976, 1977, 1978), and research on preadolescents (Vondracek & Vondracek, 1971) find that partners tend to match one another's level of self-disclosure.

Although some studies have failed to find reciprocity and matching in self-disclosure (Brewer & Mittleman, 1980; Dindia, 1982; Johnson & Dabbs, 1976), most of these findings can be readily explained in terms of experimental, procedural, or statistical techniques. For example, some studies involve intimate questions without intimate disclosure by the interviewer. They are better included in discussions of intimate questions than of intimacy matching. No studies that directly manipulate intimacy have found compensatory verbal intimacy as a response.

One of the strongest studies in the literature is that of VanLear (1991) with partners interacting over time. Partners met four times for about 30 minutes each time. Their disclosures were carefully coded. In addition to evidence of periodic ebb and flow of disclosure, VanLear showed temporal reciprocity in openness of disclosure at a level of detail unmatched by other research ventures.

Overall, the literature reveals a strong rule, in this case reciprocity, with some suggestion that under certain conditions that rule might be suspended and replaced with a compensatory response (but not a lessening of verbal intimacy) characteristic of withdrawal.

Intimate Questions

The effect of intimate questions on another's response must be sharply separated from the effects due to verbal intimacy on the basis of initial disclosure. Intimate questions tend to produce withdrawal characteristic of compensation rather than the approach response characteristic of reciprocity. For example, Schulz and Barefoot (1974) found that question intimacy increased latency of response, decreased eye gaze, and decreased smiles and laughter. Exline, Gray, and Schuette (1965) obtained similar findings on eye gaze. Johnson and Dabbs (1976) observed decreases in the duration of response to intimate questions. Anderson (1976) obtained curvilinear results with pairs of friends. Gaze increased as question intimacy increased from low to moderate and then decreased as intimacy increased from moderate to high. These results are probably due to the fact that friends have a greater range of expected and tolerable intimacy than do the strangers who populate most other studies.

The research literature has sometimes lumped studies of disclosure and intimate questions together under the topic of verbal intimacy. But common sense suggests and the research shows that intimate questions without the accompanying intimate disclosure by a questioner tend to produce withdrawal by the partner rather than approach.

Linguistic Features

These features of the verbal domain include language choice, dialect, pronunciation, and other aspects of speech independent of content and separate from the vocal features of rate, pauses, loudness, pitch, and other purely auditory characteristics of the speech signal. Typically, linguistic features are concerned with the various representations that the verbal content might take in different linguistic subcultures. The extensive literature on this topic has found evidence that people match, mismatch, and maintain a variety of linguistic features depending upon the social situation. Comprehensive reviews are available in Giles and Powesland (1975), Street (1982), and in this volume and will not be repeated here.

The evidence for linguistic convergence (matching) is abundant. Studies of immigrant groups have shown the strong moves toward linguistic assimilation into the traditions of their new culture (Fishman, 1966). In more narrowed and controlled contexts, individuals show a wide variety of techniques to exhibit convergence toward another's language (Giles, Taylor, & Bourhis, 1973), with pronunciation being a feature commonly imitated (Giles, 1973).

Although convergence and matching are common, Bourhis (1979) points out that individuals will frequently not converge but will employ the language of their particular linguistic subgroup in order to maintain a strong identification with their own group. Under more extreme conditions, individuals will actually diverge from the language chosen by the dominant group in order to accentuate their separation and autonomy (Bourhis, Giles, & Lambert, 1975; Doise, Sinclair, & Bourhis, 1976). For example, Bourhis and Giles (1977) found that native Welsh speakers diverged from the English-speaking instructor who attacked the viability of their native tongue by increasing the accentedness of their Welsh. Of interest, this occurred only for a group that was attending Welsh instruction to enhance their cultural background and not for a second group who was attending the same instruction to enhance their professional opportunities. This latter group actually converged to the English speaker.

The above results parallel in general form the kind of results obtained with other behaviors. Both matching (convergence) and mismatching (divergence) are observed under certain conditions. These conditions are related to whether the situation produces motivations to enhance similarity, attraction, and cohesion between the two speakers and the groups that they and their languages represent or whether the situation produces motivations to maintain difference, autonomy, or even to accentuate separation.

Topic Management

One of the most peculiar and yet fascinating characteristics of conversations is how they manage to cover as many different topics as they do and still seem to remain coherent. Artful conversationalists must be able to achieve their own goals of topical coverage while permitting others to explore theirs, all within the usual social constraint of topical continuity. This is sometimes a difficult chore for conversationalists, to say nothing of researchers who are just beginning to try to understand this process (Clark & Haviland, 1977; Craig & Tracy, 1983; Reichman, 1978).

Tracy (1985) identifies some of the potential self-presentational and relational goals that the management of topics in conversation can achieve. By letting other persons initiate and maintain their own topics, one can show deference to the other, the importance of the other's interests, and friendliness and competence in remaining with the introduced topic. At the same time, one's own needs for autonomy and attention to problems and concerns must be balanced against attention to the other's topical focus. Watzlawick et al. (1967) pointed out the importance of topic shifting and topic continuity in interpersonal relationships by arguing that important topics introduced by persons are statements about themselves or the relationship. When these implicit statements about self and the relationship are ignored or dismissed, for example, through topic shifting, then disconfirmations of the speakers' view of self and view of the relationship are at risk.

Palmer (1989) explored the role of topical continuity and discontinuity on people's judgments of who was conversationally dominant. Transcripts of conversation were rated by one group of judges for the degree to which a comment was a continuation of what had been said in the previous turn. An independent group of judges then rated the degree to which a partner was dominant in the conversation to that point. The two sets of judgments, continuity and dominance, were found to be inversely related so that dominance of person A was predictable from the extent of A's *discontinuity* from B's previous remark. The fact that this relationship held up across the individual turns of the conversation suggests that the microstructure of interaction is the level at which some relational concerns are played out and that control of the topic is crucial to dominance and other relational judgments.

The evidence on how topic changes are conducted is only beginning to accumulate. The problem that this creates is that research on the effectiveness and interpersonal impact of various types of topic changes will remain weak until such descriptive studies are completed. Planalp and Tracy (1980) studied the perceptions of competence that their various types of integrative strategies of topic changing created. They found that the less integrative and more implicit strategies were judged as less competent (less skillful, less involved with the other, and so forth). Tracy (1982) found that continuations on a peripheral comment rather than the theme were judged as less competent than continuations of the theme. This rule held even in the face of topics known by the judges to be important to the topic changer. Even in this case, judged divergences from the theme were not acceptable.

Politeness Behaviors

Brown and Levinson's (1987) theory of politeness in conversation is actually a theory of message production rather than interaction. However, given the theory's power and elegance and its easy extension to the interactional context, it should be briefly considered. The basic features of the position hold that social actors have positive and negative face that they seek to maintain in themselves and others. Positive face is concerned with having a positive, consistent self-image. Negative face is the ability to be free to act and to be free from imposition on one's autonomy.

The theory focuses on what is inevitable in social interaction, namely, threats to the positive and negative face of partners. For example, whenever a person disagrees with another, a threat to positive face occurs; whenever a person makes a request of another for a favor or assistance, a possible threat to negative face occurs. The theory gets interesting, in an interactional sense, when the verbal ways of reducing face threat are discussed (and they are discussed in considerable detail by Brown and Levinson). To mitigate threats to a partner's positive or negative face, the threatener can retreat from a direct (and efficient) disagreement (or request) and become more indirect by employing stylistic variations of positive and negative politeness.

As described so far, the theory is about a person's adjustments in how they frame potential threats verbally, not about how people interact. The move toward interaction involves other aspects of the theory, namely, social distance, power, and ranking. These three factors refer to the perceived social affiliation between the partners, the perceived social power of the speaker by the hearer, and the perceived threateningness of the act within the culture. These three factors are treated as relatively fixed within politeness theory. Because the theory is about individual acts, such an assumption of stability is reasonable. However, affiliation, perceived power, and the content of the interaction (ranking of threat) change over the course of the interaction if for no other reason than the presence of acts that threaten positive and negative face. As the person's positive face is attacked, for example, by disagreement, affiliation may be lowered (distance increased) and the likelihood of politeness strategies increased as well. Similarly, as negative face is threatened, the perceived power of the speaker by the hearer may be increased, and more politeness in response may be expected.

None of these claims has been tested in interactional settings to my knowledge. However, politeness theory is ripe for extension to and empirical testing within interactional contexts. Its detailed attention to features of the interaction that might be used as methods to mitigate the effects of threats, small and large, should not remain unused. If politeness theory is correct, stylistic variations in verbal interaction are not mere window dressing but carry important relationship information.

Multiple Behaviors

All of the research reviewed above typically manipulates one behavior, observing the effect of that manipulation on several possible behavioral outcomes. In naturally occurring conversations, such analytical simplicity is unrepresentative. Only a little research has tried to manipulate more than a single behavior at a time. The manner of the manipulation falls into three categories: confounding of several behaviors, independent manipulation of several behaviors, and indexing of several behaviors.

Behaviors are confounded when two or more behaviors are manipulated to establish a certain condition. For example, Breed (1972) manipulated nonverbal immediacy by manipulating lean, gaze, and orientation at the same time. He found reciprocal response on lean and gaze from his subjects. Other studies that have manipulated immediacy by including physical distance as a part of the confederate's behavior have tended to obtain compensatory reactions (Greenberg & Firestone, 1977; Patterson, Mullens, & Romano, 1971). Proximity seems to be a strong factor that overwhelms the influence of other factors. When eye gaze is confounded with question intimacy, compensatory reactions are produced (Jourard & Friedman, 1970), but when co-occurring with lean, orientation, and interruption, reciprocal reactions are produced (Breed, 1972; Sundstrom, 1975).

Few studies have tried to independently manipulate more than one behavior at the same time. The difficulties of staging such manipulations and training confederates to successfully carry them out are significant barriers. Several studies have tried such manipulations (Aiello, 1973; Greenbaum & Rosenfeld, 1978; Johnson & Dabbs, 1976; Kaplan et al., 1983). Most interactions were nonsignificant, unreported, or uninteresting because each of the factors would be expected to produce compensatory reactions. The Kaplan et al. (1983) study manipulated confederate verbal disclosure, question intimacy, and confederate gaze in an orthogonal design. Question intimacy and disclosure were found to interact with subjects reciprocating the confederate's disclosure intimacy at both levels of question intimacy. Gaze and disclosure also interacted, with intimacy of disclosure being greatest for high gaze, high disclosure by the confederate. The compensatory effects expected from question intimacy were wiped out by the presence of the confederate's verbal disclosure. Gaze and disclosure reinforced one another as expected.

Kaplan et al. carried out one further analysis that merits attention. They tried to create an approach index for the confederate's behavior by adding together all approach behaviors carried out by the confederate, arbitrarily coded one and zero depending on their magnitude. They found a relatively strong linear trend between the index and subjects' disclosure levels, indicative of reciprocity for both *the liked and the disliked interviewer*. On subjects' proportion of eye gaze, they found a positive relationship to confederate approach index for the liked confederate but a negative relationship for the disliked confederate. This is strong evidence for the moderating effects of attraction on gaze behavior but equally strong evidence for the reciprocal nature of self-disclosure.

Burgoon has engaged in an aggressive program of research aimed at understanding the way many different nonverbal behaviors might function in response to changes in a confederate's level of nonverbal involvement. Chief findings have included increased random body movements, more kinesic attentiveness, and more bodily coordination in response to increased involvement by a confederate (Burgoon, Kelley, Newton, & Keeley-Dyreson, 1989).

Overall, it is difficult to draw strong conclusions from the limited research on the relative power of various behaviors to produce reciprocal and compensatory reactions. Interpersonal distance and self-disclosure appear to generate the most consistent findings: compensatory reactions for the former at least at close proximity and reciprocal reactions for the latter. Both have shown the power to overwhelm other behavioral factors but have not yet been pitted against one another in pivotal tests of their relative strengths to induce approach or withdrawal.

Functions of Conversational Interaction: Adults

Studying patterns of social interaction in order to categorize the types of mutual influence, the conditions of its occurrence, and the behaviors upon which it operates is insufficient. It is important to know whether these patterns matter at all to the functioning of interpersonal relationships and the persons in those relationships. Elsewhere, I have called studies of mutual influence "second order" questions and questions about the association between interactional patterns and outcomes "third order" questions (Cappella, 1987).

Third order questions raise significant practical and theoretical issues. Our responsibilities as social scientists are not only to describe social and behavioral realities but to create them. If patterns of interaction are relevant to outcomes, then teaching appropriate interactional styles becomes a socially significant intervention. On the theoretical side, the sociological view of a relationship as a reality somehow different than the sum of the individual perceptions of the relationship is an issue that has received little attention. If a relationship can exist apart from the separate cognitions of the partners, then how can that relationship arise and how can it be treated operationally?

Social Skill

Whether unfounded or not, a belief permeates the interpersonal literature that better relationships exhibit more skilled interaction and that more skilled interaction can lead to more satisfying relationships (Montgomery, 1981; Noller, 1984). Unfortunately, most studies of social competence and social skill are based on conceptions of skill that are barren. Most studies treat communicative skill in terms of the emission of this or that amount of behavior rather than the more complex conception involving appropriateness, timing, and sensitivity to context. Skilled musicianship in no way depends on the frequency and duration of notes of this or that type but on their timing, appropriateness, and sensitivity to context. Similarly, skilled interaction depends upon these same factors. Hence we should expect that interaction patterns would be a more fruitful avenue for studying social skill than would measures of the distribution of the amount of some behavior. Mutual influence emphasizes timing and responsiveness of behavioral action rather than simple amounts and durations; as such, it should be a good candidate for a measure of socially skilled interaction.

Informal Social Interaction

Positive social evaluations have been associated with certain patterns of interaction. Welkowitz and Kuc (1973) found that partners who were rated higher on warmth also exhibited greater similarity on speech latency. Street (1982) constructed audiotapes in which an interviewee's speech rate, latency, and duration converged, partially converged, or diverged with respect to that of an interviewer. The divergent speech was evaluated more negatively. Similar findings on rate, content, and pronunciation were obtained by Giles and Smith (1979). These findings have been replicated in naturalistic contexts as well (Street, 1984).

It is not only vocal features of speech that are related to evaluative social judgments. LaFrance (1979) found a positive association between positional congruence and reported rapport. Davis and Martin (1978) found that the percentage of responsive comments, independent of their frequency, was positively related to attraction. Davis and Perkowitz (1979) observed that the number of pleasurable shocks given depended on how responsive the recipient was and the level of appropriateness of the response. Coordination of gaze during periods of speech and periods of listening clearly differentiated unacquainted pairs from acquainted pairs, with those who liked one another in this group least coordinated (Crown, 1991). Work by Bernieri (1988) found that judges' ratings of movement synchrony between students in a teaching situation were positively associated with the students' self-reports of rapport, a conclusion espoused by Tickle-Degnen and Rosenthal (1987) on the basis of their literature review.

Accumulating evidence is beginning to suggest that deviation from normal mutual adaptation processes may be characteristic of certain at-risk populations. Faraone and Hurtig (1985) studied socially skilled and unskilled males in interaction finding that skillful conversations showed a greater degree of sequential patterning than did the less skillful conversations. Feldstein, Konstantareas, Oxman, and Webster (1982) observed reciprocity in certain speech behaviors for counselors and parents of autistic children but not between the autistic children and their parents. Similar findings have been obtained with adult schizophrenics.

In informal social interaction settings, Street (1982, 1984) has assessed the effects of speech convergence on social attractiveness (as well as other perceptions). Using an unstructured interview context, Street (1984) coded various speech behaviors for the interviewer and interviewee in 1-minute units. He found that speech rate reciprocity by one partner was positively related to judgments of social competence of that partner by others and vice versa. Convergence in latency to respond showed a similar trend for interviewees. In a comprehensive analysis of various vocal behaviors using a variety of measures of mutual influence, Warner (1992) uncovered a relationship between temporal covariation in speech rate and judgments of positive relationship (by participants and by observers). The number of dyads involved and variety of techniques explored suggest a robust finding.

The other side of mutual influence that cannot be ignored is compensation, divergence, and mismatching. Interpersonal and intergroup situations (Bourhis, 1985) can arise in which separation from an obnoxious, intrusive, or aggressive other necessitates verbal, vocal, and kinesic distancing. Similarly, the protection of personal autonomy, personal freedom, in-group identity, or group distinctiveness might require compensatory, diverging, and mismatched responses. Bourhis (1985; see Genesee & Bourhis, 1982) has been investigating this process in the intergroup setting with language choice in Quebec. The evaluation of convergence and divergence in language choice depends upon the role relationship between the interactants and the group affiliation of the judges. Compensatory reactions may be just as socially competent and psychologically necessary as reciprocal responses, the point being that the ability to be responsive is the necessary condition for competence.

The research summarized above suggests that the presence of mutual influence in automatic behaviors is associated with interpersonal outcomes, although these outcomes are not always positive ones.

Established Relationships

Do the associations between interactional pattern and relational outcome for informal social encounters generalize to more established relationships? At the relationship level, Gottman's (1979) widely cited findings are relevant. Although all of his couples tended to show reciprocity in hostile affect in discussions about common problems in their marriages, the less well adjusted couples showed greater hostile affect than the better adjusted couples. These findings have been replicated by Gottman (1979, using the data of Raush, Barry, Hertel, & Swain, 1974) and in other contexts by Margolin and Wampold (1981) and Schaap (1982). Pike and Sillars (1985) also found greater reciprocity in negative vocal affect for dissatisfied as opposed to satisfied married couples. Using face-directed gaze rather than negative affect, Noller's (1984) satisfied couples exhibited greater correlation between partners than did the dissatisfied couples. Overall, partners in satisfying, established relationships appear to differ in the type of mutual influence that their interaction shows relative to those in less satisfied relationships.

Should we conclude from these findings that less well adjusted relationships are ones with reciprocal negative affect? Should we generalize to reciprocity and adjustment? If so, how can we explain the findings on reciprocity and positive relational outcome in informal social relationships? I think that two types of answers can be given. First, it is not reciprocity or compensation per se that matters to persons but the meaning of reciprocity or compensation, which is determined in part by the behaviors upon which reciprocity and compensation are defined. Reciprocal hostility is emotionally a lot more unpleasant than reciprocal involvement (or excitement). Interactional pattern makes a difference to relational outcome because the pattern is defined on behaviors and, together, the behavior's meaning and the pattern help to determine how the interaction feels emotionally to the partners. Second, I suspect that some interactional patterns are valued positively by some spouses and the same patterns are not valued at all by other spouses. Relational patterns in some senses express values and what is important to the partners. If there are significant ideological differences about what to value in relational life, then researchers might expect to find that interactional patterns differ by relational ideology.

Just such a hypothesis was tested by VanLear and Zeitlow (1990). The authors argued that the patterns of social interaction (in this case relational control) that would relate to satisfaction would depend upon the relational ideology of the couples. Simply put, the couples' values determined what types of interactions they found satisfying. The lesson in this study is that researchers cannot preach what types of interaction are desirable or helpful but must first understand what the partners value.

Interactional Management in Infants and Neonates

In reviewing the breadth of findings in adult social interaction, it is tempting to assume that they are the result of social learning and cultural norm. Indeed, perhaps many of the linguistic and verbal patterns are best explained in this way. But the initial tendency to look to culture and socialization for explanation is put into a different light when the interaction patterns of infants and neonates are considered.

Turn-Taking

This feature of interaction would seem to be a likely candidate for slow acquisition by the infant, coming especially after he or she has begun to exercise linguistic skills. However, some evidence suggests that turn-taking develops earlier. Some authors have argued that the timing of action sequences between adults and infants are precise and regular enough to warrant the claim that such action sequences are the precursors to adult turn-taking (Bateson, 1975; Street, 1983). Bateson (1975) in fact has termed such sequential actions "proto-conversations." Research by Stern, Jaffe, Beebe, and Bennett (1975), Beebe, Stern, and Jaffe (1979), and Beebe and Gerstman (1982) indicates that both infant and mother are timing the location of their actions in response to and in coaction with the other in a very precise fashion, necessarily picking up on the movement cues of the other to establish regular patterns of action. Coupled with the finding that the likelihood of coaction decreases with increasing age while turn-taking increases, we have the suggestion that the elements of successfully negotiated turn-taking are present from a very early age.

Rutter and Durkin (1987) studied the turn-taking activity of two groups of children ranging in age from 9 to 36 months. Overlapping of speech segments began to drop by the second year and gaze at the end of one's turn segments (an adult cue) developed by 18 months. Mayer and Tronick (1985) studied whether adult turn-taking cues produced responses (such as vocalizations and smiles) in infants. They found that the usual set of turn-taking cues, namely, intonation, drawl, hand movements, and head movements, regularly predicted infants' responses.

This evidence certainly suggests that infants develop adult cues rather early, are sensitive to adult cues even earlier, and from birth seem attuned to the need for interleaved action. One of the fundamental aspects of human conversation, the alternation of turns, occurs early in the social life of infants and may in some naive form be present even from birth.

Kinesic and Vocal Behaviors

Infants and their primary caretakers also regulate their social interactions with respect to the duration and the timing of vocalizations, movement, and eye gaze, especially as a means of regulating stimulation. Matching appears to be the typical means of vocalization regulation. In both experimental (Bloom, 1975; Gewirtz & Boyd, 1977) and home environments (Lewis & Lee-Painter, 1974) with 3-month-old infants (Anderson, Vietze, & Dokecki, 1977) and 2-year-olds (Schaffer, Collis, & Parsons, 1977), twin offspring (Stern et al., 1975), blacks and whites, and high and low socioeconomic groups (Lewis, 1972), vocalization matching is the rule. Similarly, research has shown infants to match the pitch of voices that they encounter (Webster, Steinhardt, & Santer, 1972).

Beebe, Jaffe, Feldstein, Mays, and Alson (1985) found strong contemporaneous correlations between mothers and their infants (age 3 as well as 4 to 5 months) in latency to respond to the other's vocalization. Rosenthal (1982) found that, at 3-4 days old, infants' vocalizations were affected by the presence or absence of the mother's vocalizations. Even newborns seem to match vocalizations to those of the mother. Field, Guy, and Umbel (1985) analyzed vocalization and smile patterns of 3½-month-olds. When infants imitated the pitch form and contour of the mother's vocalizations, the infants followed up their imitations more with smiling and vocalizations than when they did not imitate. Jasnow and Feldstein (1987) found matching in speech latencies for mothers and their 9-month-old infants (although latencies from infant to mother were negative).

Evidence for movement coordination between infants and adults is growing (Beebe et al., 1979). Beebe and Gerstman (1980) observed that rhythmic hand activities between mothers and their infants co-occurred with changes in other signs of the infant's involvement. Changes in rhythms seemed to be the key to changes in the infant's involvement. Several studies have shown that children of various ages have the ability to imitate their mother's gestures (Abranavel & Sigafoos, 1984; Masur & Ritz, 1984; Meltzoff & Moore, 1977). In a remarkable study, Berghout-Austin and Peery (1983) conducted a statistically reliable test of movement synchrony between neonates and an experimenter. The experimenter simply talked to the neonate at a facial distance of 19 centimeters. Movement synchrony was present in all five infants who were only 30 to 56 hours old!

Together the above studies of infants indicate that adaptation to the adult caretaker, particularly with regard to speech and vocal behaviors, gestural behaviors, and pitch, is a robust observation in normal populations.

Infants also use their gaze to regulate social stimulation probably because it is the sole means for escaping excessive stimulation or encouraging more stimulation (Als, Tronick, & Brazelton, 1979; Stern, 1971, 1977). Evidence for stimulation regulation through gaze is quite extensive (DeBoer & Boxer, 1979; Field, 1977; Fogel, 1977). For example, Fogel (1977) made extensive observations of a single dyad. Significant associations between the infant's gaze at the mother and the mother's use of vocalization and exaggerated facial displays were observed. The role of gaze aversion as a regulator was clearest when the infant was looking away, returning visual attention to the mother only after her facial displays and head nodding ceased, even though these were the actions that had maintained the infant's gaze earlier.

Other evidence of synchrony in involvement levels has been obtained by Als et al. (1979) and Thomas and Martin (1976). These studies have shown that dyads go through periods of high and low involvement that are correlated between the partners over time. When adults are prodded to act unresponsively, infants characteristically intensify their own actions to obtain a response (Brazelton, Tronick, Adamson, Als, & Wise, 1975; Tronick, Als, Adamson, & Wise, 1978). Berneri et al. (1988) had judges rate segments of mothers and infants (age 14-18 months) during play on synchrony. He found that ratings of segments of mothers with their infants were more synchronous than those of mothers with a different infant. Stern, Hofer, Haft, and Dore (1985) studied matching in intensity, timing, and shape of activity between mothers and their 11-month-olds, finding matching across modalities (e.g., gestural rhythm by infant matched by vocal rhythm of mother). Even infants in their first weeks of life exhibit early signs of the synchrony of behavior that is characteristic of and a necessity for well-regulated interaction (Chappell & Sander, 1979; Karger, 1979).

The significance of these periods of play and the infant's sensitivity to the mother's activity levels are demonstrated clearly when disruptions occur. Murray and Trevarthen (1985) had mothers adopt a blank facial expression at one point in interacting with their infants who were 6 to 12 weeks of age. The result of this blank expression in comparison with a normal play period was striking, with the infants exhibiting more signs of distress, less smiling and relaxation, and less gaze toward the mother. In a different study, these same authors played back to the infant a videotape of the mother playing in a previous session with her infant. The mother is behaving normally on the tape but her behavior is "out of sync" with that of her infant. The infant responded to the "out of sync" mother in a manner parallel to the "blank faced mother" suggesting that synchrony rather than affect is the regulative force.

Emotional Displays

Infants are disposed toward facial mimicry as well. Haviland and Lelwicka (1987) studied six boys and six girls who were 10 weeks old as they interacted with their mothers. The mothers randomly produced facial and vocal expressions of anger, sadness, or happiness. The infants showed some matching of their mother's facial responses, specifically the happy and angry faces but not the sad faces. Meltzoff and Moore (1977) conducted two carefully controlled experiments of infants 12 to 21 days old interacting with an experimenter who displayed specific facial and finger configurations. These infants imitated both facial and digital movements even when other, nonimitative behaviors were taken into account. Field, Woodson, Cohen, Garcia, and Greenberg (1982) had a female model pose happy, sad, or surprised expressions to a group of preterm neonates (35 gestational weeks) and a group of full-term normals. They observed few differences between the mouth expressions of the pre- and full-term infants finding basically that the happy faces elicited more widened lips, the sad faces more pouting lips, and the surprised faces more wide open mouths. Field's data suggest an ability *at birth* to imitate features of the facial expressions.

Taken together, I find the evidence on mutual influence between infants (and children) and their adult partners rather remarkable. It is certainly suggestive of the centrality of mutual influence to the life of the organism. Although it is always dangerous to consider the question of nature and nurture in the development of social skills, the very early occurrence of interaction patterns analogous to mutual influence in adults leads to the difficult but exciting question of whether such processes are wired into the organism.

Functions of Interactional Patterns in Infants

As in the adult domain, the simple existence of mutual influence is interesting but not necessarily significant. Does the existence of patterned interaction in the form of mutual adjustment indicate anything about the organism or its relationship to the primary caretaker?

Normal Versus Delayed Development

Typical patterns of mutual influence may not be operating in some situations. Are there consequences to such interactional disruptions? At-risk, preterm infants seem to be easily overstimulated. A study by Lester, Hoffman, and Brazelton (1985) of infants at 3 and 5 months of age showed that interactions with the mother were less synchronous for preterm infants than for the full-term infants. The at-risk infants also typically gaze away more, vocalize less, and have more elevated heart rate than infants less at risk (Field, 1977, 1982). These findings suggest not only a behavioral synchrony but also a physiological synchrony early in the social interactions of infants and their mothers.

Mothers, too, can be the source of interactional problems for their infants. When mothers are asked to "look depressed" (e.g., adopt blank affect) when they are not, their infants exhibit greater facial distress, higher activity and heart rate, and attempts to engage the mother in normal interaction (Cohn & Tronick, 1983). Field et al. (1988) have also shown that the interactional patterns of 3- to 6-month-old infants with depressed mothers are maintained when the infant interacts with a stranger who is not herself depressed.

Gianino and Tronick (1988) have speculated that because periods of asynchronous interaction are common in normal infant-mother interactions, these periods provide the infant with an opportunity to learn coping skills by reinstating the desired level of stimulation, reducing excessive stimulation, or developing an effective means for dealing with an unresponsive partner. The crucial, unanswered question is this: What effects result from continued failures by the infant to regulate the social stimulation that he or she requires?

Perhaps the most chilling outcome for interactional asynchrony has been proposed by Ira Chasnoff (cited in Revkin, 1989). Chasnoff has observed that infants born to mothers who were cocaine users during pregnancy appear to be hypersensitive to social stimulation for periods from 8 weeks up to 4 months. They tend to find intimate contact excessively stimulating and to withdraw from it. He speculates that this condition, presumably cocaine induced, may result in failed attachment and an increased likelihood of child abuse.

Autistic children are often less interested in engaging in conversation and display more self-centered behaviors in social interactions than do normally developing children (Cantwell, Baker, & Rutter, 1978; Feldstein et al., 1982; Mundy, Sigman, Ungerer, & Sherman, 1986). Although autistic children may not differ from normal children regarding levels of certain expressive behaviors such as gaze, distance, and vocalizations (Sigman, Mundy, Sherman, & Ungerer, 1986), they appear less communicatively adaptive (Crown, Feldstein, Jasnow, Beebe, & Jaffe, 1985). Consistent with this claim, Feldstein et al. (1982) reported that, when conversing with a parent or the experimenter, articulate and highly verbal autistic teenagers are less able to match the adult's internal pause and switching pause durations.

Mutual Influence and Attachment

Common sense would suggest that the patterns of interaction between mother and infant would be important to the immediate and future well-being of the infant. In this section, these commonsense ideas are tied to a base of research.

Long-term effects of mother-infant interaction have been posited for language acquisition and learning basic concepts such as contingency. The turn-taking associated with vocalization and movement patterns in early infancy may establish the necessary "proto-conversations" prerequisite to the learning of language. For example, Coates and Lewis (1984) studied interactions between mothers and infants at 3 months and followed up the infants' cognitive and linguistic abilities 6 years later. They found some positive relationships between certain of the cognitive and linguistic measures at 6 years and mother-infant responsiveness at 3 months. The concept of contingency so central to all types of social and physical action is also embodied in the very definition of interaction: My action will affect yours and yours mine. Without the development of back-and-forth turn-taking, infants may have trouble in the teaching and learning settings required for language acquisition (Bateson, 1975; Bruner, 1977).

Perhaps the most important effect associated with mutual influence is its association with the development of a positive affective bond between infant and mother. Secure attachment by the infant is central to exploration, cognitive growth, the development of later interactional ties, and the functioning of all primate species (Ainsworth, 1978; Bowlby, 1969). Ainsworth (1978) found that securely attached infants at 12 months had more sensitive interactions with their mothers at 3 months. These findings were replicated in Germany as well (Grossman, Grossman, Spangler, Suess, & Unzer, 1985).

Isabella, Belsky, and van Eye (1989) provided a more direct test of the synchrony-attachment hypothesis. Mothers and their infants were observed interacting at 1, 3, and 9 months of age and categorized as primarily synchronous or asynchronous during the observed interactional period. These pairs were categorized as secure, avoidant, or resistant at 1 year old according to criteria of Ainsworth's Strange Situation. Pairs that were synchronous at ages 1 and 3 months were categorized as securely attached at 1 year. Isabella and Belsky (1991) have replicated these findings, adding to the robustness of the link between the interactional sensitivity of the mother and her infant and the quality of their attachment.

Caveat Emptor

One must be cautious not to overinterpret the findings presented in this section and the earlier one on adults. Even the results that show that interactional synchrony at an earlier stage affects attachment at a later stage should not be read as necessarily causal findings. It could be that some spurious, unmeasured causal factor exists early in the relationship between mother and her infant that accounts both for early interactional synchrony and for later secure attachment. The crucial experiment (which would manipulate the types of interactional synchrony in matched samples) cannot be done for ethical reasons.

The strongest conclusion that can be reached at this time is that interactional asynchrony is a potential indicator of cognitive, physiological, or behavioral difficulties in the organism and is an associate of insecure attachment.

Theories of Conversational Management

Comprehensive theories of social interaction, even as circumscribed in this review, are currently out of the reach of theorists. A theory broad enough to encompass adult and infant automatic behavior and adult deliberate behavior that will also explain the conditions under which positive and negative relational outcomes will result would have to be a very powerful theory indeed. No such theory exists, although theories of narrower breadth are available. In this section, I will discuss briefly causal theories of conversational management, evolutionary or psychobiological approaches, and some recent theoretical speculations that bridge adult, infant, and biological domains.

Causal Theories

Early interactional theories had been content to offer explanations of very small domains of social interaction and mutual influence. For example, Argyle and Dean (1965) initially sought to explain why distance and eye gaze have a negative or compensatory association. This explanation was applied to other affiliative behaviors with varying success. Theorists are now recognizing that mutual influence in social interaction occurs for a wide variety of behaviors, occurs very early in the social development of children, and for these reasons requires a broad-ranging account. A number of competing accounts have been put forward: drive explanations (Argyle & Dean, 1965; Firestone, 1977), arousal mediated explanations (Andersen, 1985; Burgoon, 1978; Burgoon & Hale, 1988; Burgoon & Jones, 1976; Cappella & Greene, 1982; Hale & Burgoon, 1984; Patterson, 1976, 1982a), and cognitive explanations (Giles, Mulac, Bradac, & Johnson, 1987; Giles & Powesland, 1975; Street & Giles, 1982). All of these explanations have omitted from their focus the nature of turn-taking. Duncan and Fiske (1977) have offered an explanation of turn-taking in terms of social norms and Cappella (1985a) has countered with an account that gives preeminence to cognitive load factors. These latter two will not be discussed here because of their specificity.

In evaluating explanations of mutual influence, several factors must be kept in mind. First, the phenomenon is very general, encompassing a wide variety of behavior and a broad spectrum of developmental stages. A successful theory will be one that is encompassing without being vacuous in its generality. After all, the definition of mutual influence (if one ignores the behaviors to which the *mutuality* refers) encompasses every form of social interaction. Second, a successful account will be capable of explaining the consistent findings of reciprocity and compensation, matching and mismatching in mutual influence. That is, most reviews of individual behaviors find that, even when there is a strong rule for a given response pattern (for example, compensation to increases in proximity), some conditions exist that attenuate and even reverse that rule. A successful theory will incorporate such conditions in such a way as to predict the conditions under which reversal will occur. Explanations cannot offer one account for reciprocity and another account for compensation. Third, explanations must participate in accepted and extant theories of behavior. Mutual influence is not some new or unique domain of behavioral influence but is a fundamental type of behavioral contingency. Explanations of it ought to be just as fundamental and common. Finally, successful explanations must not confuse long-term relational development with the mutual influence decisions that occur on a momentary basis in conversation. For example, Altman and Taylor (1973) indicate that disclosure reciprocity and increased depth of disclosure occur slowly over the course of relational development. That is an important and interesting finding that needs explanation in its own right but should not be inadvertently included as a fact of conversational management.

Drive theories. The three classes of explanations that are capable of explaining both reciprocity and compensation findings are the drive theories, the arousal-based explanations, and the cognitive explanations listed above. I will not attempt to describe the minute differences among each version of each type but will try to describe the generic characteristics of each class of explanation. The drive-based theories are all derived from Argyle and Dean's (1965) approach-avoidance explanation of compensation in verbal and nonverbal affiliative behaviors. Their explanation in turn uses Miller's (1959) approach-avoidance conflict theory developed primarily from the study of maze running by rats under various conditions of hunger and potential shock. Argyle and Dean argue that people simultaneously experience forces driving them toward affiliation with others and avoidance of and autonomy from others, reasoning that, at some points, the drive toward approach would balance the drive to avoid and an equilibrium would be established. Deviations from this equilibrium by the other person would produce reactions to reintroduce the equilibrium by withdrawing whenever approach was too intimate and hence compensation would result.

The variations on this theory have made it more powerful in its range of coverage and more plausible in the application of Miller's initial theory (Argyle & Cook, 1976; Firestone, 1977). All of the modifications rework the basic assumptions of the approach-avoidance gradients.

My objection to all the drive explanations is that they posit a mediating mechanism that is untestable. The only direct evidence that one can obtain about approach and avoidance forces is found in the behaviors that are themselves the objects of explanation for the theory. For example, lean, touch, proximity, and latency to respond are all possible indices of approach and avoidance. But these same behaviors are the affiliative behaviors that the theory is designed to explain. Although the drive theories are plausible, they may be tautological.

Cognitive theories. The cognitively based theories of Giles and his colleagues (Giles & Powesland, 1975; Giles et al., 1987; Street & Giles, 1982) were developed to account for research on speech and linguistic convergence and divergence, and not the broader array of nonverbal behaviors. The situations that this theory, speech accommodation theory, sought to explain were cases of language choice, dialect and pronunciation shifts, and the slowing and speeding up of speech rate. Early versions had conversationalists making rather deliberate choices in their speech styles in order to appear more similar or more different than their partners, thereby increasing attraction, cohesion, and communication efficiency, on the one hand, or maintaining group identity and group autonomy at the cost of communication efficiency, on the other hand. In a recent update of the theory, Street and Giles (1982) maintain that people will:

converge towards the speech patterns believed to be characteristic of their recipients when they (a) desire their social approval and the perceived costs of so acting are proportionally lower than the rewards anticipated; and/or (b) desire a high level of communicational efficiency, and (c) social norms are not perceived to dictate alternative speech strategies. People diverge from those believed characteristics of their recipients when they (a) define the encounter in intergroup terms and desire a positive ingroup identity or (b) wish to bring another's speech behaviors to a personally acceptable level. (pp. 213-214)

Despite the very deliberate language of speech accommodation theory, Street and Giles (1982) claim that the procedures of convergence and divergence are quite automatic, calling the necessary procedural information from memory with the proper cues. My evaluation of this theory is based upon two observations. First, the theory does a good job of explaining the linguistic convergence and divergence for which it was initially intended but not, for example, the findings of speech rate and latency convergence in children or adults for which the theory also seems relevant. In short, it works well in situations in which individuals are making relatively deliberate choices but not so well in situations in which individuals are making relatively automatic reactions. Second, even if Street and Giles are correct in stating that individual responses are automatic, being based upon procedural knowledge, the mere invocation of automatic procedures does not explain how the procedures got into memory, why they have one procedural content rather than another (for example, reciprocating for efficiency), or how procedural knowledge translates into action.

Arousal mediation. The third class of theories is arousal mediation (Burgoon, 1978; Burgoon & Hale, 1988; Burgoon & Jones, 1976; Cappella & Greene, 1982; Patterson, 1976, 1982a). These theories have much in common. All of them assume that behavior that violates expectations or at least is a deviation from an established baseline (Patterson, 1976) can produce arousal. The evidence for this claim is quite strong (Cappella, 1983; Patterson, 1976). The nature of the arousal is assumed to be some kind of cognitive activation (Duffy, 1962) that can result in physiological arousal (heart rate, blood pressure, electroencephalogram, galvanic skin response, and so forth). At this point, the models part company.

Patterson's earlier model and Burgoon's model both assume that the arousal engendered by a deviation from expected behaviors will be reacted to differently depending on how the arousal is labeled (Patterson, 1976) or on the reward characteristics of the actor (Burgoon, 1978). When labeling is positive, the reaction is expected to be reciprocal and, when negative, the reaction is expected to be compensatory. The reward value of the actor and the degree of immediacy (above and below expectations) are assumed to interact such that for punishing actors an inverted U relationship is expected, whereas for a rewarding actor a U-shaped relationship is expected. For both models, a mediating characteristic of the situation, the person, or the relationship affects how the nonverbal or verbal behavior will be responded to (Burgoon & Hale, 1988).

Patterson's (1982a) newer version invites us to consider a much more comprehensive approach to mutual influence processes. As before, unusual levels of behavior attract attention, possible arousal, and meaning analysis. Reactions to the deviant behavior and the instability it creates can take the form of a reassessment of the goals of the interaction, a cognitive-affective reassessment of the actor, and/or a behavioral readjustment along the lines of a compensatory or reciprocal response. This account is more equivocal than the earlier arousal-labeling model and is designed as a comprehensive paradigm from which a wide variety of behavioral, cognitive, and affective adjustments in conversational settings can be studied.

Cappella and Greene (1982) assume that the degree of arousal change determines the nature of the response to deviation from expectation. Under moderate to small amounts of arousal change, reciprocal reactions are expected, whereas under large amounts of arousal change, compensatory reactions are expected. The role of factors such as labeling, reward value of actors, and relationship factors is loaded into the setting of expectation levels and into the size of acceptance regions that mark how much arousal change is too much. The same kinds of relational and situational factors are included as potential mediators of interaction but they are placed in a causally prior position to arousal change, which does all of the work in the model.

The arousal change explanations offer one distinct advantage over competitors such as the drive explanations: The mediating mechanism that they pose is testable independent of the behaviors that are being explained. The technology for measuring levels of arousal exists and can offer clear-cut tests of the proposed mediating mechanisms. Other theories may be equally capable of explaining the empirical facts of mutual influence processes, but I do not see how social scientists will be able to evaluate the psychological reality of those explanations. The reader may argue that my objections are based upon a view of theory that is excessively realist, but when one faces eight competing explanations, each seemingly successful at accounting for the facts, realism appears preferable to instrumentalism.

The theories above are too new. No unequivocal comparative test of these competing explanations, or any subset of them, has yet been conducted. Authors have been content to interpret existing data in the framework of their own explanatory paradigms. Most such ventures have been successful because each of the successful explanations recognizes that there must be a flexible means of accounting for reciprocity and compensation under a variety of situational conditions. In the drive theories, this flexibility is achieved by the relative steepness of approach and avoidance forces under different conditions. In the cognitive theories, situational factors and reward factors are presumed to intervene. In the labeling and reward theories, the nature of the labeling and the quality of the reward permit a variety of situations to switch the direction of effects. In discrepancy-arousal theory, the relative size of the acceptance regions and the location of the expectation levels can be altered with changing situational, personal, and dispositional factors.

Whichever explanatory system is ultimately successful in accounting for mutual influence processes in conversation, I believe that it will have certain characteristics that can be identified now. Context effects cannot be ignored. The verbal, nonverbal, and vocal behaviors that we have been discussing are noticed and attended to when they are unusual relative to some expected baseline (Cappella, 1983). That expectation level must be built into any successful theory. The evidence that certain verbal, vocal, and kinesic behaviors produce various forms of arousal is too great not to ensure some place for arousal in a theory of mutual influence. Its place may not be as important as that hypothesized by discrepancy-arousal theory (Cappella & Greene, 1982), but arousal reactions as mediators cannot be ignored.

Interpersonal Facial Feedback Hypothesis

None of the causal theories currently in the literature specifically accounts for the association between interactional patterns and relational outcomes, either in adults or in children. The question is this: Why should differences in interactional synchrony, reciprocity, compensation, and so on yield differences in attraction, rapport, and satisfaction? One speculative, but intriguing, possibility is what I have called elsewhere the "interpersonal facial feedback hypothesis" (IFFH).

The facial feedback hypothesis holds that facial displays of emotion can affect the displayer's subjective experience of emotion by initiating an emotional reaction consistent with the displayed emotion or modifying the intensity (but probably not the quality) of an existing emotion (Adelman & Zajonc, 1989). In reviewing both the infant and adult literature in this chapter, we have seen that imitation of facial emotional displays is common.

If facial feedback affects emotion states within persons and if people are prone to imitate the facial displays of their partners, then the IFFH follows: The hedonic tone of facial displays of persons to their partners during interaction should predict the person's own affective reaction to the partner. The hypothesis focuses on the correspondence *within the person* between the affective tone of facial display and subjective affect, with the presumption that facial efference is one mechanism through which subjective affect can be changed. Certainly, change in a person's subjective affect can lead to change in facial displays, but the IFFH proposes that the causal arrow can run in the opposite direction as well, with more positive facial expressions bringing about more positive subjective reactions.

A study by Kleinke and Walton (1982) used techniques of reinforcement to alter the frequency of smiles emitted by subjects. Those who emitted more smiles gave the interview and the interviewer higher ratings than those who emitted fewer smiles even though they were not able to ascertain that they were being reinforced to smile.

If the facial feedback hypothesis can be extended to other behaviors such as vocal feedback as was initially suggested by James (1890), then these intrapersonal feedback mechanisms will be viable candidates for explaining interpersonal rapport.

Evolutionary Theories

Causal theories are concerned with explaining how mutual influence comes about through proximate causal mechanisms, cognitive, physiological, or social. But the presence of mutual influence processes in infants' interactions with their primary caretakers suggests that these patterns may be more fundamental, perhaps evolving to become part of the genetic endowment of the species.

I have offered just such an argument elsewhere (Cappella, 1991). The gist of the position is that the inclusive fitness of an individual member of the species is enhanced by trying to ensure the survival of its own gene pool. Because human infants are altricial and therefore in need of lengthy periods of caretaking by the parents to ensure survival, certain goals are predominant early in life. These are attachment and a basic communication system (at least signaling distress and pleasure). Attachment allows the parents to have a strong emotional bond to the infant (and vice versa). This bond is almost certainly necessary to help ensure that caretaking will continue over the duration of time that is required with human infants. Communication allows the infant to signal the parent, and the parent, the infant, even though language is still many months away. Such a basic signaling system permits the infant to tell the caretaker when there is a need to be fulfilled and when not. Similarly, if the infant has the ability to recognize the basic emotions of the caretaker, whether fear, anger, or joy, then the parent can signal the infant vocally or visually when danger is present.

The link between the goals of attachment and emotional communication and patterns of mutual influence are straightforward. The regulation of behavioral intensity (movement, vocalization, gaze, and so on) is hypothesized to be the mechanism through which attachment is established and maintained. Facial and vocal imitation is hypothesized to be the mechanism through which emotional signaling is carried out. The reasoning that leads to these hypothesized mechanisms is both subtle and circumstantial and will not be reproduced here (but see Cappella, 1991).

The implications of this evolutionary argument are, I believe, both important and practical. Social interaction, in part because of its complexity, seems infinitely variable and therefore more likely to be the result of variety in individuals, situations, and social contexts. If the evolutionary roots of adult patterns of mutual influence can be sustained, our sense-making stories about social interaction will have to be adjusted to include our biological heritage and our animal natures, as a part of the account. At least part of the description of patterns of social interaction will have to emphasize their commonalities across peoples, cultures, and contexts. As a practical matter, if one takes evolutionary arguments seriously, then one would also hypothesize that genetic commonality will be more likely to yield interactional synchrony than genetic difference with obvious implications for studies of siblings, fraternal and identical twins, adopted children, and stepchildren.

Conclusion

Mutual influence in interaction is arguably the essential characteristic of interpersonal interaction.

Mutual influence is the defining characteristic of interpersonal communication. Although personal relationships have an existence apart from the interactions that mold, maintain, and destroy them, interpersonal communication is fundamentally coordination of behavior. If person A's behaviors do not affect those of B uniquely and mutually (Cappella, 1987), then one partner cannot be said to be sensitive to alterations in the other's actions in any observable way. Without such contingent responsiveness, it would be difficult to distinguish interleaved action from interaction.

Mutual influence occurs in a wide variety of interpersonal tie-signs. The behaviors for which mutual influence is observed are incredibly diverse, varying from the microscopic and automatic gestures that accompany speech in adults, to the precursors to illustrative gestures in infants, to the deliberate hostile actions of spouses during conflict. The behaviors are not merely visual and aural stimuli, though they are the signs and symbols of interpersonal relatedness.

Mutual influence covaries with important relational and individual conditions. Mutual influence patterns are not simply some interactional anomaly without function. Rather, mutual influence seems to play an important role in adult and infant attachment patterns. The exact nature of this role remains unclear at this time, whether simply associational or causal. Researchers should be cautious about issues of causality here and furthermore cautious about assuming that general patterns of mutual influence (e.g., reciprocity) are a relational "good." Such assumptions are naive and fly in the face of existing data.

Despite the volume of work, future research on mutual influence processes is wide open. Studies need to focus more on the verbal component of interaction with coding systems that are well established and of utility to a broad cross section of researchers. Researchers must be willing to invest the time and energy to code a variety of dependent measures so that failures with a particular behavior are not due to constraints of the situation or to individual predilections away from a particular behavioral outlet. Finally, we must all be sensitive to the social needs of our subject populations. The study of mutual influence is interesting in its own right, but unless these processes can be tied to utilitarian outcomes such as improvements in the social competence of troubled or even impaired persons, our efforts will be seen rightly or wrongly as without social benefit.

Note

1. The claim that people do not use microscopic behaviors intentionally only means that the behaviors are not the object of purposive deliberation, not that the behaviors are not in the service of some broader purpose. The argument follows that of Brand (1984), who distinguishes action complexes that are goal directed from acts within the complex that are means to the goals.

References

Abravanel, E., & Sigafoos, A. D. (1984). Exploring the presence of imitation during early infancy. *Child Development, 55*, 381-392.

Adelman, P. K., & Zajonc, R. B. (1989). Facial efference and the experience of emotion. *Annual Review of Psychology, 40*, 249-280.

Aiello, J. R. (1972). A test of equilibrium theory: Visual interaction in relation to orientation, distance, and sex of the interactants. *Psychonomic Science, 27*, 335-336.

Aiello, J. R. (1973). Male and female behavior as a function of distance and duration of an interviewer's directed gaze: Equilibrium theory revisited (Doctoral dissertation, Michigan State University). *Dissertation Abstracts International, 33*, 4482B-4483B.

Aiello, J. R. (1977). A further look at equilibrium theory: Visual interaction as a function of interpersonal distance. *Environmental Psychology and Nonverbal Behavior, 1*, 122-139.

Ainsworth, M. D. (1978). *Patterns of attachment: A psychological study of the strange situation.* Hillsdale, NJ: Lawrence Erlbaum.

Als, H., Tronick, E., & Brazelton, T. B. (1979). Analysis of face-to-face interaction in infant-adult dyads. In M. E. Lamb, S. J. Suomi, & G. R. Stephenson (Eds.), *Social interaction analysis* (pp. 33-76). Madison: University of Wisconsin Press.

Altman, I., & Taylor, D. A. (1973). *Social penetration.* New York: Holt, Rinehart & Winston.

Andersen, P. A. (1985). Nonverbal immediacy in interpersonal communication. In A. W. Siegman & S. Feldstein (Eds.), *Multichannel integrations of nonverbal behavior* (pp. 1-36). Hillsdale, NJ: Lawrence Erlbaum.

Anderson, B. J., Vietze, P., & Dokecki, P. R. (1977). Reciprocity in vocal interaction of mothers and infants. *Child Development, 48*, 1676-1681.

Anderson, D. R. (1976). Eye contact, topic intimacy, and equilibrium theory. *Journal of Social Psychology, 100*, 313-314.

Argyle, M., & Cook, M. (1976). *Gaze and mutual gaze.* London: Cambridge University Press.

Argyle, M., & Dean, J. (1965). Eye contact, distance and affiliation. *Sociometry, 28*, 289-304.

Ashby, W. R. (1963). *An introduction to cybernetics*. New York: Science Editions.

Bateson, M. C. (1975). Mother-infant exchanges: The epigenesis of conversational interaction. *Annals of the New York Academy of Sciences, 5,* 238-250.

Bavelas, J. B., Black, A., Chovil, N., Lemery, C. R., & Mullett, J. (1988). Form and function in motor mimicry: Topographic evidence that the primary function is communicative. *Human Communication Research, 14,* 275-299.

Bavelas, J. B., Black, A., Lemery, C. R., MacInnis, S., & Mullett, J. (1986). "I show you how I feel": Motor mimicry as a communicative act. *Journal of Personality and Social Psychology, 50,* 322-329.

Baxter, J. C., & Rozelle, R. M. (1975). Nonverbal expressiveness as a function of crowding during a simulated police-citizen encounter. *Journal of Personality and Social Psychology, 32,* 40-54.

Beattie, G. W. (1978). Floor apportionment and gaze in conversational dyads. *British Journal of Social and Clinical Psychology, 17,* 7-15.

Beattie, G. W. (1979a). Contextual constraints on the floor-apportionment function of gaze in dyadic conversation. *British Journal of Social and Clinical Psychology, 17,* 7-15.

Beattie, G. W. (1979b). Sequential temporal patterns of speech and gaze in dialogue. *Semiotica, 23,* 29-57.

Becker, F. D., & Mayo, C. (1971). Delineating personal distance and territoriality. *Environment and Behavior, 3,* 375-381.

Beebe, B., Jaffe, J., Feldstein, S., Mays, K., & Alson, D. (1985). Interpersonal timing: The application of an adult dialogue model to mother-infant vocal and kinesic interactions. In T. M. Field & N. A. Fox (Eds.), *Social perception in infants* (pp. 217-248). Norwood, NJ: Ablex.

Beebe, B., & Gerstman, L. (1980). The "packaging" of maternal stimulation in relation to infant facial-visual engagement. *Merrill-Palmer Quarterly, 26,* 321-329.

Beebe, B., & Gerstman, L. (1982). *Significance of infant-stranger mutual influence*. Paper presented at the meeting of the Society for Research in Child Development, Austin, TX.

Beebe, B., Stern, D., & Jaffe, J. (1979). The kinesic rhythm of mother-infant interactions. In A. W. Siegman & S. Feldstein (Eds.), *Of speech and time* (pp. 23-34). Hillsdale, NJ: Lawrence Erlbaum.

Berghout-Austin, A. M., & Peery, J. C. (1983). Analysis of adult-neonate synchrony during speech and nonspeech. *Perceptual and Motor Skills, 57,* 455-459.

Bernieri, F. J. (1988). Coordinated movement and rapport in teacher-student interactions. *Journal of Nonverbal Behavior, 12,* 120-138.

Bernieri, F. J., Resnick, J. S., & Rosenthal, R. (1988). Synchrony, pseudosynchrony, and dissynchrony: Measuring the entrainment process in mother-infant interactions. *Journal of Personality and Social Psychology, 54,* 243-253.

Bernieri, F. J., & Rosenthal, R. (1991). Interpersonal coordination: Behavior matching and interactional synchrony. In R. S. Feldman & B. Rimé (Eds.), *Fundamentals of nonverbal behavior* (pp. 401-432). Cambridge: Cambridge University Press.

Bernstein, B. (1962). Social class, linguistic codes, and grammatical elements. *Language and Speech, 5,* 221-240.

Black, J. W. (1949a). The intensity of oral responses to stimulus words. *Journal of Speech and Hearing Disorders, 14,* 16-22.

Black, J. W. (1949b). Loudness of speaking: The effect of heard stimuli on spoken responses. *Journal of Experimental Psychology, 39,* 311-315.

Bloom, K. (1975). Social elicitation of infant vocal behavior. *Journal of Experimental Child Psychology, 20,* 51-58.

Bourhis, R. Y. (1979). Language in ethnic interaction: A social psychological approach. In H. Giles & B. St. Jacques (Eds.), *Language and ethnic relations* (pp. 119-136). Oxford: Pergamon.

Bourhis, R. Y. (1985). The sequential nature of language choice in cross-cultural communication. In R. L. Street & J. N. Cappella (Eds.), *Sequence and pattern in communicative behavior* (pp. 120-141). London: Edward Arnold.

Bourhis, R. Y., & Giles, H. (1977). The language of intergroup distinctiveness. In H. Giles (Ed.), *Language, ethnicity, and intergroup relations* (pp. 119-136). London: Academic Press.

Bourhis, R. Y., Giles, H., & Lambert, W. E. (1975). Social consequences of accommodating one's style of speech: A cross-national investigation. *International Journal of the Sociology of Language, 6,* 53-71.

Bowlby, J. (1969). *Attachment and loss: Vol. 1. Attachment*. New York: Basic Books.

Brand, M. (1984). *Intending and acting*. Cambridge: MIT Press.

Brazelton, T. B., Tronick, E., Adamson, L., Als, H., & Wise, S. (1975). Early mother-infant reciprocity. In *Parent-infant interaction: Ciba foundation symposium 33* (pp. 137-148). Amsterdam: Association of Scientific Publishers.

Breed, G. (1972). The effect of intimacy: Reciprocity or retreat? *British Journal of Social and Clinical Psychology, 11,* 135-142.

Brewer, M. B., & Mittleman, J. (1980). Effects of normative control of self-disclosure on reciprocity. *Journal of Personality, 48,* 89-102.

Brown, P., & Levinson, S. (1987). *Politeness: Some universals in language use.* Cambridge: Cambridge University Press.

Bruner, L. J. (1977). Early social interaction and language acquisition. In H. R. Schaffer (Ed.), *Mother-infant interaction.* New York: Academic Press.

Buder, E. (1991). *Vocal synchrony in conversations: Spectral analysis of fundamental voice frequency.* Unpublished doctoral dissertation, University of Wisconsin, Madison, Department of Communication Arts.

Burgoon, J. K. (1978). A communication model of interpersonal space violations: Explication and initial test. *Human Communication Research, 4,* 129-142.

Burgoon, J. K. (1991). Relational message interpretations of touch, conversational distance, and posture. *Journal of Nonverbal Behavior, 15,* 233-260.

Burgoon, J. K., Buller, D. B., Hale, J. L., & de Turck, M. A. (1984). Relational messages associated with nonverbal behaviors. *Human Communication Research, 13,* 463-494.

Burgoon, J. K., & Hale, J. L. (1988). Nonverbal expectancy violations: Model elaboration and application to immediacy behaviors. *Communication Monographs, 55,* 58-79.

Burgoon, J. K., & Jones, S. B. (1976). Toward a theory of personal space expectations and their violations. *Human Communication Research, 2,* 131-146.

Burgoon, J. K., Kelley, D. G., Newton, D. A., & Keeley-Dyreson, M. P. (1989). The nature of arousal and nonverbal indices. *Human Communication Research, 16,* 217-255.

Butterworth, B., & Goldman-Eisler, F. (1979). Recent studies on cognitive rhythm. In A. W. Siegman & S. Feldstein (Eds.), *Of speech and time* (pp. 211-224). Hillsdale, NJ: Lawrence Erlbaum.

Cantwell, D., Baker, L., & Rutter, M. (1978). A comparative study of infantile autism and specific developmental receptive language disorder IV: Analysis of syntax and language function. *Journal of Child Psychology and Psychiatry, 19,* 351-362.

Cappella, J. N. (1981). Mutual influence in expressive behavior: Adult-adult and infant-adult dyadic interaction. *Psychological Bulletin, 89,* 101-132.

Cappella, J. N. (1983). Conversational involvement: Approaching and avoiding others. In J. M. Wiemann & R. P. Harrison (Eds.), *Nonverbal interaction* (pp. 113-152). Beverly Hills, CA: Sage.

Cappella, J. N. (1985a). Controlling the floor in conversation. In A. W. Siegman & S. Feldstein (Eds.), *Nonverbal communication* (pp. 9-103). Hillsdale, NJ: Lawrence Erlbaum.

Cappella, J. N. (1985b). Production principles for turn-taking rules in social interaction: Socially anxious vs. socially secure persons. *Journal of Language and Social Psychology, 4,* 193-212.

Cappella, J. N. (1986). Reciprocal and compensatory reactions to violations of distance norms for high and low self-monitors. In M. L. McLaughlin (Ed.), *Communication yearbook 9* (pp. 359-376). Beverly Hills, CA: Sage.

Cappella, J. N. (1987). Interpersonal communication: Fundamental questions and issues. In C. R. Berger & S. Chaffee (Eds.), *The handbook of communication science* (pp. 184-238). Newbury Park, CA: Sage.

Cappella, J. N. (1990). The method of proof by example in interaction analysis. *Communication Monographs, 57,* 236-242.

Cappella, J. N. (1991). The biological origins of automated patterns of human interaction. *Communication Theory, 1,* 4-35.

Cappella, J. N. (1993a). *Vocal and kinesic coordination in dyadic interaction: Indices of dynamics and their relation to outcome.* Unpublished paper, University of Pennsylvania, Philadelphia, Annenberg School for Communication.

Cappella, J. N. (1993b). The facial feedback hypothesis in human interaction: Review and speculations. *Journal of Language and Social Psychology, 12,* 13-29.

Cappella, J. N., & Greene, J. O. (1982). A discrepancy-arousal explanation of mutual influence in expressive behavior for adult-adult and infant-adult interaction. *Communication Monographs, 49,* 89-114.

Cappella, J. N., & Palmer, M. L. (1989). The structure and organization of verbal and nonverbal behavior: Data for models of reception. *Journal of Language and Social Psychology, 8,* 167-192.

Cappella, J. N., & Palmer, M. L. (1990a). Attitude similarity, relational history, and attraction: The mediating effects of kinesic and vocal behaviors. *Communication Monographs, 57,* 161-183.

Cappella, J. N., & Palmer, M. L. (1990b). The structure and organization of verbal and non-verbal behavior: Data for models of production. In H. Giles & W. P. Robinson (Eds.), *Handbook of language and social psychology* (pp. 141-161). Chichester, England: Wiley.

Cappella, J. N., & Planalp, S. (1981). Talk and silence sequences in informal conversations. Ill: Interspeaker influence. *Human Communication Research, 7,* 117-132.

Cappella, J. N., & Street, R. L. (1985). A functional approach to the structure of communicative behavior. In R. L. Street & J. N. Cappella (Eds.), *Sequence and pattern in communicative behavior* (pp. 1-29). London: Edward Arnold.

Carr, S. J., & Dabbs, J. M. (1974). The effect of lighting, distance, and intimacy of topic on verbal and visual behavior. *Sociometry, 37,* 592-600.

Chappell, P. F., & Sander, L. W. (1979). Mutual regulation of the neonatal-maternal interactive process: Context for the origins of communication. In M. Bulowa (Ed.), *Before speech* (pp. 89-110). London: Cambridge University Press.

Clark, H. H., & Haviland, S. E. (1977). Comprehension and the given-new contract. In R. O. Freedle (Ed.), *Discourse production and comprehension* (pp. 1-40). Norwood, NJ: Ablex.

Coates, D. L., & Lewis, M. (1984). Early mother-infant interaction and infant cognitive status as predictors of school performance and cognitive behavior in six-year-olds. *Child Development, 55,* 1219-1230.

Cohn, J. F., & Tronick, E. Z. (1983). Three-month-old infants' reaction to simulated maternal depression. *Child Development, 54,* 185-193.

Coker, D. A., & Burgoon, J. K. (1987). The nature of conversational involvement and nonverbal encoding patterns. *Human Communication Research, 13,* 463-495.

Condon, W. S., & Ogston, W. D. (1966). Sound film analysis of normal and pathological behavior patterns. *Journal of Nervous and Mental Disease, 28,* 305-315.

Condon, W. S., & Ogston, W. D. (1967). A segmentation of behavior. *Journal of Psychiatric Research, 5,* 221-235.

Condon, W. S., & Sander, L. W. (1974). Synchrony demonstrated between movement of the neonate and adult speech. *Child Development, 45,* 456-552.

Coutts, L. M., Schneider, F. W., & Montgomery, S. (1980). An investigation of the arousal model of interpersonal intimacy. *Journal of Experimental Social Psychology, 16,* 545-561.

Cozby, P. C. (1972). Self-disclosure, reciprocity and liking. *Sociometry, 35,* 151-160.

Craig, R. T., & Tracy, K. (Eds.). (1983). *Conversational coherence.* Beverly Hills, CA: Sage.

Crown, C. L. (1991). Coordinated interpersonal timing of vision and voice as a function of interpersonal attraction. *Journal of Language and Social Psychology, 10,* 29-46.

Crown, C. L., Feldstein, S., Jasnow, M., Beebe, B., & Jaffe, J. (1985). A strategy for investigating autism as a prelinguistic disorder of social development. *Australian Journal of Human Communication Disorders, 13,* 61-76.

Dabbs, J. M. (1980). Temporal patterning of speech and gaze in social and intellectual conversations. In H. Giles (Ed.), *Language: Social psychological perspectives* (pp. 307-310). Oxford: Pergamon.

Davis, J. D. (1976). Self-disclosure in an acquaintance exercise: Responsibility for level of intimacy. *Journal of Personality and Social Psychology, 33,* 787-792.

Davis, J. D. (1977). Effects of communication about interpersonal process on the evolution of self-disclosure in dyads. *Journal of Personality and Social Psychology, 35,* 31-37.

Davis, J. D. (1978). When boy meets girl: Sex roles and the negotiation of intimacy in an acquaintance exercise. *Journal of Personality and Social Psychology, 36,* 684-692.

Davis, D., & Martin, H. J. (1978). When pleasure begets pleasure: Recipient responsiveness as a determinant of physical pleasuring between heterosexual dating couples and strangers. *Journal of Personality and Social Psychology, 36,* 767-777.

Davis, D., & Perkowitz, W. T. (1979). Consequences of responsiveness in dyadic interaction: Effects of probability of response and proportion of content related responses on interpersonal attraction. *Journal of Personality and Social Psychology, 37,* 534-550.

DeBoer, M. M., & Boxer, A. M. (1979). Signal functions of infant facial expression and gaze direction during mother-infant face-to-face play. *Child Development, 50,* 1215-1218.

Dindia, K. (1982). Reciprocity of self-disclosure: A sequential analysis. In M. Burgoon (Ed.), *Communication yearbook 6* (pp. 506-530). New Brunswick, NJ: Transaction.

Dindia, K. (1985). A functional approach to self-disclosure. In R. L. Street & J. N. Cappella (Eds.), *Sequence and pattern in communicative behavior* (pp. 142-160). London: Edward Arnold.

Dittmann, A. T. (1972). The body movement speech rhythm relationship as a cue to speech encoding. In A. W. Siegman & B. Pope (Eds.), *Studies in dyadic communication* (pp. 135-152). New York: Pergamon.

Doise, W., Sinclair, A., & Bourhis, R. Y. (1976). Evaluation of accent convergence and divergence in cooperative and competitive intergroup situations. *British Journal of Social and Clinical Psychology, 14,* 247-252.

Duffy, E. (1962). *Activation and behavior.* New York: Wiley.

Duncan, S. (1972). Some signals and rules for taking turns in conversations. *Journal of Personality and Social Psychology, 23,* 283-292.

Duncan, S. (1973). Toward a grammar for dyadic conversations. *Semiotica, 9,* 29-46.

Duncan, S. (1974). On the structure of speaker-auditor interaction during speaking turns. *Language in Society, 2,* 161-180.

Duncan, S. (1983). Speaking turns: Studies of structures and individual differences. In J. Wiemann & R. P. Harrison (Eds.), *Nonverbal interaction* (pp. 149-178). Beverly Hills, CA: Sage.

Duncan, S., Bruner, L. J., & Fiske, D. W. (1979). Strategy signals in face-to-face interaction. *Journal of Personality and Social Psychology, 37,* 301-313.

Duncan, S., & Fiske, D. W. (1977). *Face-to-face interaction.* Hillsdale, NJ: Lawrence Erlbaum.

Duncan, S., & Niederehe, G. (1974). On signalling that it's your turn to speak. *Journal of Experimental and Social Psychology, 10,* 234-247.

Efran, M. G., & Cheyne, J. A. (1974). Affective concomitants of the invasion of shared space: Behavioral, physiological, and verbal indicators. *Journal of Personality and Social Psychology, 29,* 219-226.

Ericson, P., & Rogers, L. E. (1965). New procedures for analyzing relational communication. *Family Process, 12,* 245-267.

Exline, R. V., Gray, D., & Schuette, D. (1965). Visual behavior in a dyad as affected by interview content and sex of respondent. *Journal of Personality and Social Psychology, 1,* 201-209.

Faraone, S. V., & Hurtig, R. R. (1985). An examination of social skill, verbal productivity, and Gottman's model of interaction using observational methods and sequential analysis. *Behavioral Assessment, 7,* 349-366.

Farina, A., Allen, J. G., & Saul, B. B. (1968). The role of stigmatized social relationships. *Journal of Personality, 36,* 169-182.

Farina, A., Gliha, D., Boudreau, L. A., Allen, J. G., & Sherman, M. (1971). Mental illness and the impact of believing others know about it. *Journal of Abnormal Psychology, 77,* 1-5.

Feldstein, S., Konstantareas, M., Oxman, J., & Webster, C. D. (1982). The chronography of interaction with autistic speakers: An initial report. *Journal of Communicative Disorders, 15,* 451-460.

Field, T. (1982). Affective displays of high risk infants during early interactions. In T. Field & A. Fogel (Eds.), *Emotion and early interaction* (pp. 101-125). Hillsdale, NJ: Lawrence Erlbaum.

Field, T. (1984). Early interactions between infants and their postpartum depressed mothers. *Infant Behavior and Development, 7,* 527-532.

Field, T., Healy, B., Goldstein, S., Perry, S., Bendel, D., Schanberg, S., Zimmerman, E. A., & Kuhn, C. (1988). Infants of depressed mothers show "depressed" behavior even with nondepressed adults. *Child Development, 59,* 1569-1579.

Field, T., Woodson, R., Cohen, D., Garcia, R., & Greenberg, R. (1982). Discrimination and imitation of facial expressions by term and preterm neonates. *Infant and Behavior Development, 6,* 485-490.

Field, T. M. (1977). Effects of early separation, interactive deficits, and experimental manipulations of infant-mother face-to-face interaction. *Child Development, 48,* 763-771.

Field, T. M., Guy, L., & Umbel, V. (1985). Infants' responses to mothers' imitative behaviors. *Infant Mental Health Journal, 6,* 40-44.

Firestone, I. (1977). Reconciling verbal and nonverbal models of dyadic communication. *Environmental Psychology and Nonverbal Behavior, 2,* 30-44.

Fishman, J. A. (1966). *Language loyalty in the United States.* The Hague, the Netherlands: Mouton.

Fogel, A. (1977). Temporal organization in mother-infant face-to-face interaction. In H. R. Schaffer (Ed.), *Studies in mother-infant interaction* (pp. 119-152). New York: Academic Press.

Gatewood, J. B., & Rosenwein, R. (1981). Interactional synchrony: Genuine or spurious? A critique of recent research. *Journal of Nonverbal Behavior, 6,* 12-29.

Genesee, R., & Bourhis, R. Y. (1982). The social psychological significance of code-switching in cross-cultural communication. *Journal of Language and Social Psychology, 1,* 1-27.

Gewirtz, J. L., & Boyd, E. F. (1977). Experiments on mother-infant interaction underlying mutual attachment acquisition: The infant conditions the mother. In T. Alloway, L. Krames, & P. Pliner (Eds.), *Attachment behavior: Advances in the study of communication and affect* (Vol. 3, pp. 109-144). New York: Plenum.

Gianino, A., & Tronick, E. Z. (1988). The mutual regulation model: The infants' self and interactive regulation and coping and defense capacities. In T. M. Field, P. M. McCabe, & N. Schneiderman (Eds.), *Stress and coping across development* (pp. 47-68). Hillsdale, NJ: Lawrence Erlbaum.

Giles, H. (1973). Accent mobility: A model and some data. *Anthropological Linguistics, 15,* 87-105.

Giles, H. (1979). Ethnicity markers in speech. In K. R. Scherer & H. Giles (Eds.), *Social markers in speech* (pp. 251-290). Cambridge: Cambridge University Press.

Giles, H. (1980). Accommodation theory: Some new directions. In S. de Silva (Ed.), *Aspects of linguistic behavior* (pp. 105-136). York: University of York Press.

Giles, H., Mulac, A., Bradac, J., & Johnson, P. (1987). Speech accommodation theory: The first decade and beyond. In M. L. McLaughlin (Ed.), *Communication yearbook 10* (pp. 13-48). Newbury Park, CA: Sage.

Giles, H., & Powesland, P. F. (1975). *Speech style and social evaluation.* London: Academic Press.

Giles, H., & Smith, P. M. (1979). Accommodation theory: Optimal levels of convergence. In H. Giles & R. N. St. Clair (Eds.), *Language and social psychology* (pp. 45-65). Oxford: Basil Blackwell.

Giles, H., Taylor, D. M., & Bourhis, R. Y. (1973). Towards a theory of interpersonal accommodation through language: Some Canadian data. *Language in Society, 2,* 177-192.

Goodwin, C. (1981). *Conversational organization.* New York: Academic Press.

Gottman, J. M. (1979a). Detecting cyclicity in social interaction. *Psychological Bulletin, 86,* 338-348.

Gottman, J. M. (1979b). *Marital interaction.* New York: Academic Press.

Greenbaum, P., & Rosenfeld, H. M. (1978). Patterns of avoidance in response to interpersonal staring and proximity: Effects of bystanders on drivers at a traffic intersection. *Journal of Personality and Social Psychology, 36,* 575-587.

Greenberg, C. I., & Firestone, I. J. (1977). Compensatory responses to crowding: Effects of personal space intrusion and privacy reduction. *Journal of Personality and Social Psychology, 35,* 637-644.

Grossman, K. E., Grossman, K., Spangler, G., Suess, G., & Unzer, L. (1985). Maternal sensitivity and newborn orientation responses as related to the quality of attachment in N. Germany [I. Bretherton & E. Waters (Eds.), Growing points of attachment theory and research]. *Monographs of the Society for Research in Child Development, 50* (1-2, Serial No. 209), 233-256.

Hale, J. L., & Burgoon, J. K. (1984). Models of reactions to changes in nonverbal immediacy. *Journal of Nonverbal Behavior, 8,* 287-314.

Haviland, J. M., & Lelwicka, M. (1987). The induced affect response: 10-week-old infants' responses to three emotional expressions. *Developmental Psychology, 23,* 97-104.

Hopper, R. (1992). *Telephone conversation.* Bloomington: Indiana University Press.

Isabella, R. A., & Belsky, J. (1991). Interactional synchrony and the origins of infant-mother attachment: A replication study. *Child Development, 62,* 373-384.

Isabella, R. A., Belsky, J., & van Eye, A. (1989). Origins of mother-infant attachment: An examination of interactional synchrony during the infant's first year. *Developmental Psychology, 25,* 12-21.

Jaffe, J., & Feldstein, S. (1970). *Rhythms of dialogue.* New York: Academic Press.

James, W. (1890). *The principles of psychology.* New York: Holt.

Jasnow, M., & Feldstein, S. (1987). Adult-like temporal characteristics of mother-infant vocal interactions. *Child Development, 57,* 754-761.

Johnson, C. F., & Dabbs, J. M. (1976). Self-disclosure in dyads as a function of distance and subject-experimenter relationship. *Sociometry, 39,* 257-263.

Jourard, S. M. (1959). Self-disclosure and other cathexis. *Journal of Abnormal and Social Psychology, 59,* 428-431.

Jourard, S. M., & Friedman, R. (1970). Experimenter-subject "distance" and self-disclosure. *Journal of Personality and Social Psychology, 15,* 278-282.

Jourard, S. M., & Resnick, J. L. (1970). The effect of high revealing subjects on self-disclosure of low revealing subjects. *Journal of Humanistic Psychology, 10,* 84-93.

Kaplan, K. J., Firestone, I. J., Klein, K. W., & Sodikoff, C. (1983). Distancing in dyads: A comparison of four models. *Social Psychology Quarterly, 46,* 108-115.

Karger, R. H. (1979). Synchrony in mother-infant interactions. *Child Development, 50,* 882-885.

Kendon, A. (1967). Some functions of gaze direction in social interaction. *Acta Psychologica, 26,* 100-125.

Kleinke, C. L., Staneski, R. A., & Berger, D. E. (1975). Evaluation of an interviewer as a function of interviewer gaze, reinforcement of subject gaze, and interviewer attractiveness. *Journal of Personality and Social Psychology, 31,* 115-122.

Kleinke, C. L., & Walton, J. H. (1982). Influence of reinforced smiling on affective responses in an interview. *Journal of Personality and Social Psychology, 42,* 557-565.

Krause, R., Steimer, E., Sanger-Alt, C., & Wagner, G. (1989). Facial expression of schizophrenic patients and their interaction partners. *Psychiatry, 52,* 1-12.

LaFrance, M. (1979). Nonverbal synchrony and rapport: Analysis by the cross-lag panel technique. *Social Psychology Quarterly, 42,* 66-70.

Lester, B. M., Hoffman, J., & Brazelton, T. B. (1985). The rhythmic structure of mother-infant interaction in term and pre-term infants. *Child Development, 56,* 15-27.

Lewis, M. (1972). State as an infant-environment interaction: An evaluation of infant-mother interaction as a function of sex. *Merrill-Palmer Quarterly, 18,* 95-121.

Lewis, M., & Lee-Painter, S. (1974). An interactional approach to the mother-infant dyad. In M. Lewis & L. A. Rosenbaum (Eds.), *The effect of the infant on its caregiver* (pp. 21-48). New York: Wiley.

Margolin, G., & Wampold, B. E. (1981). Sequential analysis of conflict and accord in distressed and nondistressed marital partners. *Journal of Consulting and Clinical Psychology, 49,* 554-567.

Masur, E. F., & Ritz, E. G. (1984). Patterns of gestural, vocal, and verbal imitation performance in infancy. *Merrill-Palmer Quarterly, 30,* 369-392.

Matarazzo, J. D., Weitman, M., Saslow, G., & Wiens, A. N. (1963). Interviewer influence on durations of interviewee speech. *Journal of Verbal Learning and Verbal Behavior, 1,* 451-458.

Matarazzo, J. D., & Wiens, A. N. (1967). Interviewer influence on durations of interviewee silence. *Journal of Experimental Research in Personality, 2,* 56-69.

Matarazzo, J. D., & Wiens, A. N. (1972). *The interview: Research on its anatomy and structure.* Chicago: Aldine.

Matarazzo, J. D., Wiens, A. N., Matarazzo, R. G., & Saslow, G. (1968). Speech and silence behavior in clinical psychotherapy and its laboratory correlates. In J. Schlien, H. Hunt, J. D. Matarazzo, & C. Savage (Eds.), *Research in psychotherapy* (Vol. 3, pp. 347-394). Washington, DC: American Psychological Association.

Mayer, N. K., & Tronick, E. Z. (1985). Mother's turn-taking signals and infant turn-taking in mother-infant interaction. In T. M. Field & N. A. Fox (Eds.), *Social perception in infants* (pp. 199-216). Norwood, NJ: Ablex.

McDowall, J. J. (1978a). Interactional synchrony: A reappraisal. *Journal of Personality and Social Psychology, 36,* 963-975.

McDowall, J. J. (1978b). Microanalysis of filmed movement: The reliability of boundary detection by observers. *Environmental Psychology and Nonverbal Behavior, 3,* 77-88.

McLaughlin, M. L. (1984). *Conversation: How talk is organized.* Beverly Hills, CA: Sage.

McLaughlin, M. L., Cody, M. J., & Rosenstein, N. E. (1983). Account sequences in conversations between strangers. *Communication Monographs, 50,* 102-125.

Meltzoff, A. N., & Moore, M. K. (1977). Imitation of facial and manual gestures by human neonates. *Science, 198,* 75-78.

Meltzer, L., Morris, W., & Hayes, D. (1971). Interruption outcomes and vocal amplitude: Explorations in social psychophysics. *Journal of Personality and Social Psychology, 18,* 392-402.

Miller, N. (1959). Lateralization of basic S-R concepts: Extensions to conflict behavior, motivation, and social learning. In S. Koch (Ed.), *Psychology: A study of a science* (Vol. 2, pp. 196-292). New York: McGraw-Hill.

Montgomery, B. M. (1981). The form and function of quality communication in marriage. *Family Relations, 30,* 21-30.

Mundy, P., Sigman, M., Ungerer, J., & Sherman, T. (1986). Defining the social deficits of autism: The contribution of nonverbal communication measure. *Journal of Child Psychology and Psychiatry, 27,* 647-656.

Murray, L., & Trevarthen, C. (1985). Emotional regulation of interactions between two-month-olds and their mothers. In T. M. Field & N. A. Fox (Eds.), *Social perception in infants* (pp. 177-198). Norwood, NJ: Ablex.

Natale, M. (1975). Convergence of mean vocal intensity in dyadic communication as a function of social desirability. *Journal of Personality and Social Psychology, 32,* 790-804.

Noller, P. (1980). Gaze in married couples. *Journal of Nonverbal Behavior, 5,* 115-129.

Noller, P. (1984). *Nonverbal communication and marital interaction.* Oxford: Pergamon.

Palmer, M. T. (1989). Controlling conversations: Turns, topics, and interpersonal control. *Communication Monographs, 56,* 1-18.

Palmer, M. T., & Lack, A. L. (in press). Topics, turns, and interpersonal control: Using serial judgement methods. *Communication Studies.*

Patterson, M. L. (1976). An arousal model of interpersonal intimacy. *Psychological Review, 83,* 235-245.

Patterson, M. L. (1977). Interpersonal distance, affect, and equilibrium theory. *Journal of Social Psychology, 101,* 205-214.

Patterson, M. L. (1982a). A sequential functional model of nonverbal exchange. *Psychological Review, 89,* 231-249.

Patterson, M. L. (1982b). Personality and nonverbal involvement: A functional analysis. In W. Ickes & E. S. Knowles (Eds.), *Personality, roles, and social behavior* (pp. 141-164). New York: Springer-Verlag.

Patterson, M. L., Mullens, S., & Romano, J. (1971). Compensatory responses to spatial intrusion. *Sociometry, 34,* 114-121.

Pellegrini, R. J., & Empey, J. (1970). Interpersonal spatial orientation in dyads. *Journal of Psychology, 76*, 67-70.

Pike, G. R., & Sillars, A. L. (1985). Reciprocity and marital communication. *Journal of Personal and Social Relationships, 2*, 303-324.

Planalp, S., & Tracy, K. (1980). Not to change the topic but . . .: A cognitive approach to the management of conversation. In D. Nimmo (Ed.), *Communication yearbook 4* (pp. 237-258). New Brunswick, NJ: Transaction.

Raush, H. L., Barry, W. A., Hertel, R. K., & Swain, M. A. (1974). *Communication, conflict, and marriage*. San Francisco: Jossey-Bass.

Reichman, R. (1978). Conversational coherency. *Cognitive Science, 2*, 283-327.

Revkin, A. C. (1989). Crack in the cradle. *Discover, 10*, 63-69.

Rogers, L. E., & Farace, R. V. (1975). Analysis of relational communication in dyads: New measurement procedures. *Human Communication Research, 1*, 222-239.

Rosenthal, M. K. (1982). Vocal dialogues in the neonatal period. *Developmental Psychology, 18*, 17-21.

Rubin, Z. (1975). Disclosing oneself to a stranger: Reciprocity and its limits. *Journal of Experimental Social Psychology, 11*, 233-260.

Rutter, D. R., & Durkin, K. (1987). Turn-taking in mother-infant interaction: An examination of vocalizations and gaze. *Developmental Psychology, 23*, 54-61.

Ryave, A. L. (1978). On the achievement of a series of stories. In J. Schenkein (Ed.), *Studies in the organization of conversational interaction*. New York: Academic Press.

Sacks, H., Schegloff, E. A., & Jefferson, G. (1974). A simplest systematics for the organization of turn-taking for conversation. *Language, 50*, 696-735.

Sawitsky, J. C., & Watson, M. J. (1975). Patterns of proxemic behavior among preschool children. *Representative Research in Social Psychology, 6*, 109-113.

Schaap, C. (1982). *Communication and adjustment*. Lisse, Netherlands: Swets & Zeitlinger.

Schaffer, H. R., Collis, G. M., & Parsons, G. (1977). Verbal interchange and visual regard in verbal and preverbal children. In H. R. Schaffer (Ed.), *Studies in mother-infant interaction* (pp. 291-324). New York: Academic Press.

Schenkein, J. (Ed.). (1978). *Studies in the organization of conversational interaction*. New York: Academic Press.

Schulz, R., & Barefoot, J. (1974). Nonverbal responsiveness and affiliative conflict theory. *British Journal of Social and Clinical Psychology, 13*, 237-243.

Sigman, M., Mundy, P., Sherman, T., & Ungerer, J. (1986). Social interactions of autistic, mentally retarded, and normal children and their caregivers. *Journal of Child Psychology and Psychiatry, 27*, 647-656.

Sillars, A. L. (1980). The sequential and distributional structure of conflict interaction as a function of attributions concerning the locus of responsibility and stability of conflicts. In D. Nimmo (Ed.), *Communication yearbook 4* (pp. 217-236). New Brunswick, NJ: Transaction.

Sodikoff, C. L., Firestone, L. J., & Kaplan, K. (1974). Subject self-disclosure and attitude change as a function of interviewer self-disclosure and eye-contact. *Personality and Social Psychology Bulletin, 1*, 243-246.

Steinem, G. (1981). The politics of talking in groups. *Ms., 9*, 43 ff.

Stern, D. N. (1971). A micro analysis of mother-infant interaction. *Journal of the American Academy of Child Psychiatry, 10*, 501-517.

Stern, D. N. (1974). Mother and infant at play: The dyadic interaction involving facial, vocal, and gaze behavior. In M. Lewis & L. A. Rosenblum (Eds.), *The effect of the infant on its caregiver* (pp. 187-214). New York: Wiley.

Stern, D. N. (1977). *A first relationship: Mother and infant*. Cambridge, MA: Harvard University Press.

Stern, D. N., Hofer, L., Haft, W., & Dore, J. (1985). Affect attunement: The sharing of feeling states between mother and infant by means of intermodal fluency. In T. M. Field & N. A. Fox (Eds.), *Social perception in infants* (pp. 249-268). Norwood, NJ: Ablex.

Stern, D. N., Jaffe, J., Beebe, B., & Bennett, S. L. (1975). Vocalizing in unison and in alteration: Two modes of communication within the mother-infant dyad. *Annals of the New York Academy of Sciences, 263*, 89-100.

Street, R. L., Jr. (1982). Evaluation of noncontent speech accommodation. *Language and Communication, 2*, 13-31.

Street, R. L., Jr. (1983). Noncontent speech convergence in adult-child interactions. In R. N. Bostrom (Ed.), *Communication yearbook 7* (pp. 369-395). Beverly Hills, CA: Sage.

Street, R. L., Jr. (1984). Speech convergence and speech evaluation in fact-finding interviews. *Human Communication Research, 11*, 139-169.

Street, R. L., Jr., & Giles, H. (1982). Speech accommodation theory: A social cognitive approach to language and speech behavior. In M. Roloff & C. Berger (Eds.), *Social cognition and communication* (pp. 193-226). Beverly Hills, CA: Sage.

Sundstrom, E. (1975). An experimental study of crowding: Effects of room size, intrusion, and goal blocking on nonverbal behavior, self-disclosure, and self-reported stress. *Journal of Personality and Social Psychology, 32,* 645-654.

Thomas, E. A. C., & Martin, J. A. (1976). An analysis of parent-infant interaction. *Psychological Review, 83,* 141-156.

Tickle-Degnen, L., & Rosenthal, R. (1987). Group rapport and nonverbal behavior. *Review of Personality and Social Psychology, 9,* 113-136.

Tracy, K. (1982). On getting the point: Distinguishing "issues" from "events": An aspect of conversational coherence. In M. Burgoon (Ed.), *Communication yearbook 5* (pp. 279-302). New Brunswick, NJ: Transaction.

Tracy, K. (1985). Conversational coherence: A cognitively grounded rules approach. In R. L. Street & J. N. Cappella (Eds.), *Sequence and pattern in communication behavior* (pp. 30-49). London: Edward Arnold.

Trager, G. L. (1958). Paralanguage: A first approximation. *Studies in Linguistics, 13,* 1-12.

Tronick, E., Als, H., Adamson, L., & Wise, S. (1978). The infant's response to entrapment between contradictory messages in face-to-face interaction. *Journal of the American Academy of Child Psychiatry, 17,* 1-13.

VanLear, C. A. (1991). Testing a cyclical model of communicative openness in relationship development: Two longitudinal studies. *Communication Monographs, 58,* 337-361.

VanLear, C. A., & Zeitlow, P. H. (1990). Toward a contingency approach to marital interaction: An empirical integration of three approaches. *Communication Monographs, 57,* 202-218.

Vondracek, S. I., & Vondracek, F. W. (1971). The manipulation and measurement of self-disclosure in preadolescents. *Merrill-Palmer Quarterly, 17,* 51-58.

Warner, R. M. (1992). Speaker, partner, and observer evaluations of affect during social interaction as a function of interaction tempo. *Journal of Language and Social Psychology, 11,* 253-266.

Watzlawick, P., Beavin, J., & Jackson, D. D. (1967). *Pragmatics of human communication.* New York: Norton.

Webb, J. T. (1969). Subject speech rates as a function of interviewer behavior. *Language and Speech, 12,* 54-67.

Webb, J. T. (1972). Interview synchrony: An investigation of two speech rate measures. In A. W. Siegman & B. Pope (Eds.), *Studies in dyadic communication* (pp. 115-133). New York: Pergamon.

Webster, R. L., Steinhardt, M. H., & Santer, M. G. (1972). Change in infants' vocalization as a function of differential acoustical stimulation. *Developmental Psychology, 7,* 39-43.

Welkowitz, J., Cariffe, G., & Feldstein, S. (1976). Conversational congruence as a criterion of socialization in children. *Child Development, 47,* 269-272.

Welkowitz, J., & Feldstein, S. (1969). Dyadic interaction and induced differences in perceived similarity. *Proceedings of the 77th Annual Convention of the American Psychological Association, 4,* 343-344.

Welkowitz, J., & Kuc, M. (1973). Interrelationships among warmth, genuineness, empathy, and temporal speech patterns in interpersonal interaction. *Journal of Consulting and Clinical Psychology, 41,* 472-473.

Wiemann, J. M., & Knapp, M. L. (1975). Turn-taking in conversation. *Journal of Communication, 25,* 75-92.

Worthy, M. G., Gary, A. L., & Kahn, M. (1969). Self-disclosure as an exchange process. *Journal of Personality and Social Psychology, 13,* 59-63.

Zimbardo, P. (1977). *Shyness.* Reading, MA: Addison-Wesley.

11

Supportive Communication

Terrance L. Albrecht

Brant R. Burleson

Daena Goldsmith

SOCIAL SUPPORT IS a fundamental form of human communication, transacted between people within structures of their ordinary and extraordinary relationships and life events. Importantly, supportive relationships between intimates, acquaintances, employers, subordinates, coworkers, friends, relatives, and, at times, strangers, affect multiple forms of emotional and physical well-being. Supportive interactions can result in such outcomes as lessened sorrow or distress, improved recovery from trauma and illness, and resolutions to conflict. For example, though operating in complex ways (Schwarzer & Leppin, 1991), social support can improve resistance to infection and disease, extend life, enhance psychological adjustment and perceptions of self-efficacy, and reduce mortality (Albrecht & Adelman, 1987; Jemmott & Magloire, 1988; Kurdek, 1988; Litwak & Messeri, 1989; Major et al., 1990). And supportive communication is a primary means by which interpersonal relationships are created and sustained (Burleson, 1990; Burleson, Albrecht, & Goldsmith, 1993; Leatham & Duck, 1990). Indeed, a life without any supportive relationships is virtually unthinkable (Albrecht & Adelman, 1987; Brownell & Shumaker, 1984).

Most studies of supportive behaviors across the social and health sciences have addressed the physiological, cognitive, and emotional outcomes of such behaviors rather than the nature of the mutual influence and communication processes through which those behaviors are expressed. Researchers in disciplines (such as social psychology) have examined aspects of support giving and support seeking (e.g., Hill, 1991), but with minimal theoretical or empirical attention given to the analysis of support as a communication phenomenon. Until recently, the focus has been largely on the effects of social relationships on health and well-being as opposed to an emphasis on the dynamics of the interactions in those relationships producing such effects (Albrecht & Adelman, 1984, 1987).

Our goals in the present chapter are twofold: (a) to selectively review the history of this extensive corpus of research and (b) to situate the study of social support as an important area for research within interpersonal communication. We begin by reviewing definitions, justifications, and major approaches to the study of support. We then describe a central controversy in the support literature on models of the effects of support. After evaluating how these effects are created, we present an analysis of the mechanisms through which support is conveyed. Our discussion then turns to the counterside of support, specifically, the dilemmas and negative consequences of supportive interactions in social contexts. We conclude the chapter with a detailed analysis of properties of supportive messages, features of support interactions, and the characteristics of interpersonal networks in which support most commonly occurs.

It should be noted at the outset that ours is a culture-bound treatment of social support—one primarily based on support processes within American society. There is almost certain variation across cultural groups in how social support is mobilized, how it is conceptualized, and the function served by perceptions and actions related to support in relationships. We acknowledge that there have been few empirical, cross-cultural comparisons of the support process (for two rare examples, see Garrison, 1978, on the support networks of Puerto Rican migrant women, and Katriel, 1993, on supportive discourse among Israelis) or even an analysis of support as a cultural category within modern American society (with the exception of Katriel & Philipsen, 1981).

Definitions, Rationale, and Approaches to the Study of Support

The serious study of social support was initially launched in epidemiological studies (e.g., Cassel, 1976) attempting to document whether links existed between the presence of social ties and health (B. Sarason, Sarason, & Pierce, 1990). The well-known (though later controversial) 9-year Alameda County, California, study (Berkman & Syme, 1979) included a significant effort toward establishing an empirical link between social network patterns and mortality rates. The findings from such studies provided an impetus for further exploration of what appeared at the time to be promising health-related outcomes of personal relationships (the most significant factors relating to disease etiology and deterrence of psychological disorders). Since the late 1970s, research on support networks, relationships, and perceptions has burgeoned across fields as researchers have variously defined and measured social support and have attempted to aggregate and integrate the extensive accretion of findings.

Definitions

Most early definitions of support were rooted in the individual's perception of acceptance and caring. For example, Moss (1973) referred to support as "the subjective feeling of belonging, of being accepted or being loved, of being needed all for oneself and for what one can do" (p. 237). Cobb (1976) defined support as the individual's perception of being esteemed and valued, of belonging "to a network of communication and mutual obligation" (p. 300). Tolsdorf (1976) and

Eyres and MacElveen-Hoehn (1983) viewed support as an action or behavior that facilitates coping, mastery, or control. As the area of social support gained increased research interest, conceptual development broadened beyond individual-level perceptions to include processes of exchange between people. For example, Bharadwaj and Wilkening (1980), Caplan (1976), House (1981), Kahn and Antonucci (1980), and Schaefer, Coyne, and Lazarus (1981) were among the first to frame the notion of support in interpersonal terms that included notions of feedback, expressive ties, communication, and interpersonal transactions of affirmation and aid.

Building on this previous groundwork, researchers are currently casting support as an interactional process of helping, comforting, caring for, and aiding others (Albrecht & Adelman, 1987; Albrecht, Burleson, & Sarason, 1992; Burleson, Albrecht, Goldsmith, & Sarason, in press; Cutrona, Suhr, & MacFarlane, 1990; Duck with Silver, 1990; Goldsmith & Parks, 1990; B. Sarason, Sarason, & Pierce, 1990). Hence conceptualizations of supportive communication are thus informed by an understanding of the nature of the process of message transaction: the development, maintenance, and dissolution processes associated with personal relationships and the structures, properties, and functions (e.g., uncertainty reduction and personal control enhancement) of social ties and configurations of social structures. A working understanding of *communication* assumes it is a transactional, symbolic process of mutual influence embedded within relationships and social networks (e.g., Burgoon & Ruffner, 1978; Cappella, 1981). *Supportive communication* is thus verbal and nonverbal behavior that influences how providers and recipients view themselves, their situations, the other, and their relationship (Albrecht & Adelman, 1987) and is the principal process through which individuals coordinate their actions in support-seeking and support-giving encounters (Burleson et al., 1993).

It is somewhat surprising that the interest in social support by scholars in interpersonal communication is relatively recent. There are at least a few possible reasons worth noting for the relative lack of previous empirical attention. The act of "being supportive" is often an intentional, strategic, and planned act of mutual influence. While communication was examined as strategic behavior in earlier studies of interpersonal interaction, it was generally conceived more narrowly as compliance-gaining, persuasion, and control-oriented behavior (e.g., Burgoon, Burgoon, Miller, & Sunnafrank, 1981; Miller, Boster, Roloff, & Seibold, 1977; Miller & Steinberg, 1975), not directly as a means for caring about others in ways that produced emotional, physical, and relational benefit. Further, the deliberate, obligatory, and, at times, admittedly manipulative nature of support (characterizing the process as including a motive of self-interest) may have lacked the requisite self-disclosure, altruism, and openness typically cast by humanists in the 1960s and 1970s as idealistic features of interpersonal communication. Indeed, this less gratuitous, though realistic, way of conceiving of supportive behavior thus ran counter to the "ideology of intimacy" that pervaded interpersonal communication texts during those years (see critiques by Bochner, 1982; Parks, 1982).

Rationale for the Study of Support as Communication

Given the broadening and development of the field of interpersonal communication, we see at least three compelling reasons that the study of social support should be a major issue for the current research agenda (see Burleson, Albrecht, Goldsmith,

& Sarason, in press). First, there are practical reasons that form the basis for a *pragmatic imperative* for the study of interpersonal support processes. As noted above, a massive body of research findings has accumulated over the past two decades demonstrating direct and indirect links between supportive behaviors and emotional and physical health. Several recent reviews of this literature (e.g., Cohen & Wills, 1985; Hobfoll & Stephens, 1990; Schwarzer & Leppin, 1991) are useful for integrating and organizing the plethora of findings. More specifically, researchers have found causal and correlational relationships between aspects of support and (a) disease etiology, life expectancy, and immune system functioning (Jemmott & Magloire, 1988; Kasl, Evans, & Neiderman, 1979; Kennedy, Kiecolt-Glaser, & Glaser, 1990; Wortman, 1984); (b) recovery from illness and the ability to adjust and cope with extreme stress and loss (e.g., Hobfoll & Stephens, 1990; Major et al., 1990; Miller, Wikoff, McMahon, Garrett, & Ringel, 1985); (c) effective role and life transition (Hirsch, 1980); (d) job performance, work innovation, and trust levels between persons in mixed status relationships (Albrecht & Hall, 1991; Albrecht & Halsey, 1992); and (e) reduction in anxiety over impending evaluation (Goldsmith & Albrecht, 1993). Yet, the negative effects of supportive encounters are also a reality and thus in need of continued investigation (see the section on negative effects and dilemmas of support later in this chapter). Briefly, support can create dependencies that delay recovery (e.g., from strokes; McLeroy, DeVellis, DeVellis, Kaplan, & Toole, 1984), exacerbate health problems (Kaplan & Toshima, 1990), reinforce negative self-images (Swann & Brown, 1990), and intensify uncertainty (Goldsmith, 1992; Peters-Golden, 1982); and some supportive interactions can drain providers of important personal resources (Belle, 1982; Hobfoll & Stephens, 1990).

Second, there are scientific reasons that lead to a theoretical imperative for the study of social support as communication. Mutual help giving is central to the formation and development of interpersonal relationships (Burleson, 1990). Adequately comprehending the nature and functions of interpersonal relationships thus requires explication of the character of supportive interactions and how these contribute to a variety of relationship processes. While previous empirical work has focused on relationships as *sources* of support to improve health, current studies are examining how relationships, especially important personal linkages, are the outcomes of ongoing supportive interactions (e.g., among family, Eggert, 1987; friends, Adelman, Parks, & Albrecht, 1987b; Barnes & Duck, in press; Goldsmith & Parks, 1990; and coworkers, Albrecht & Halsey, 1992; Zimmerman & Applegate, 1992).

Finally, there are ethical reasons that promote a *moral imperative* for vigorous research. Supportive actions that flow from altruistic motives (Barbee, 1990) clearly have a moral foundation. Much of supportive behavior (i.e., charity, helping, caring, rescuing, kindness, love) transcends self-interest (Elster, 1990) to the point of serving the interests of the other. A moral imperative for the study of support means the goal for research is one of furthering our understanding of the character of moral action to develop the notion of prosocial and principled conduct and to broaden basic knowledge of what it means to sustain a community in an age of global technology and information.

Approaches to the Study of Social Support

There have been almost as many approaches to the study of support over the past 20 years as there have been reasons for its study. We have identified three general frames that have informed much of the empirical work, including social network approaches, perceptual approaches, and interaction approaches.

Social network approaches. Early research on social support and physical and emotional health focused on the existence of communication networks, or patterns of ties that correlated with various emotional and physical outcomes (e.g., Garrison, 1978; Hirsch, 1980; House, Robbins, & Metzner, 1982). Networks have been typically measured as self-reports of ties to various others by focal individuals (House & Kahn, 1985) and then analyzed according to structural indices including network role designation, size, density/integration, multiplexity, reciprocity, and homogeneity/heterogeneity (e.g., Albrecht, Irey, & Mundy, 1982; Hammer, 1983; Salzinger, Kaplan, & Artemyeff, 1983). (For a review of major structural properties and definitions for all levels of analysis of social support networks, see Albrecht & Adelman, 1987, pp. 60-63.)

The results of this body of work have grown increasingly complex and voluminous in the past decade. Results tend to demonstrate health promoting and health deterring outcomes of the presence and configuration of social ties in people's lives. Whether social network patterns have positive or deleterious effects, the findings to date point to a need for continued study (see, for example, the end of this chapter on communication networks and community). Perhaps the most significant criticism of the early social network studies was the lack of focus on the perceived quality and meaning of social relationships, to supplement and expand data on the quantity and structure of links (Antonucci & Israel, 1986; Wethington & Kessler, 1986).

Perceptual approaches. Researchers studying social support thus moved from early work that established *whether* social ties related to well-being, to research that began to deepen the understanding of *how* supportive ties affect people's lives. Several studies have shown that the individual's perceptions of the adequacy and availability (in short, the somewhat elusive *quality*) of support is a relatively consistent predictor of health (B. Sarason, Pierce, & Sarason, 1990; Wethington & Kessler, 1986). Such findings reinforced perceptual or psychological approaches to the study of support, based on an assessment of the individual's subjective sense of being supported by others as well as the appraisal of the adequacy and motivation of that support (Cohen, McGowan, Fooskas, & Rose, 1984). More recently, having a "sense of support" has been viewed as a relatively stable personality characteristic (Lakey & Cassady, 1990), developed early in life through bonding and attachment experiences (B. Sarason, Pierce, & Sarason, 1990) and serving as an important buffer against stress and health disorders (Pierce, Sarason, & Sarason, 1990; I. Sarason, Sarason, & Pierce, in press).

A number of well-known, though unrelated measures of perceived support exist, such as the Inventory of Socially Supportive Behaviors (ISSB, a global assessment of received support; Barrera, Sandler, & Ramsey, 1981), the Social Support Questionnaire (SSQ, a measure of the perceived availability of support if needed; I. Sarason, Levine, Basham, & Sarason, 1983), the Perceived Support Network Inventory (PSNI, a measure that taps the perceived availability, satisfaction, and conflict dimensions of support as well as perceptions of the types and sources of support; Oritt, Paul, & Behrman, 1985), and the Interpersonal Support Evaluation List (ISEL, a general measure of the perceived adequacy of available support; Cohen & Hoberman, 1983). B. Sarason, Sarason, and Pierce (1990), in their critique of psychological assessment methods of support, conclude that the plethora of measures generally lack relevant validity and reliability information (for representative exceptions, see evaluative results of the ISEL in Lakey & Cassady, 1990, and the ISSB in Sandler & Barrera, 1984). The varying nature of the psychometric properties of these different measures no doubt accounts for some of the conflicting and confusing findings on the stress-strain-support relationship published in the literature (B. Sarason, Sarason, & Pierce, 1990).

Most important, however, these authors call for a shift in the overall theoretical approach for untangling and clarifying the unwieldy corpus of data and findings. Clearly, the psychological perspective has contributed to our understanding of support. Perhaps most noteworthy are the findings such as those by B. Sarason et al. (1991) that perceived support is a "cognitive adaption that individuals make given the constraints and opportunities, both real and imagined, that are placed upon them by a history of experiences that result in working models of self and others" (p. 285). But limits to this approach remain. As Gottlieb (1985) argues, an exclusively psychological perspective does not "gauge actual or experienced support that is expressed in ongoing social interactions"; instead, it measures the "cognitive representation of the phenomenon whose correspondence with social reality is uncertain" (p. 356). Hobfoll and Stokes (1988) suggested that research is needed that attends to the development of supportive relationships, the mobilization and elicitation of aid, the behavioral, cognitive, and emotional responses to help giving, and the thoughts, emotions, and behaviors that interact with such reactions.

Interaction approaches. Hence researchers are addressing the communicative and interactional processes through which support is solicited and enacted, occurring within the context of relatively enduring strong and weak ties (Albrecht & Adelman, 1987; Burleson, Albrecht, & Sarason, in press; Duck with Silver, 1990; Sarason, Pierce, & Sarason, 1990). A central interest, for example, is to understand how and why "a 'provider' attempts to proffer support and a 'recipient' may be helped or benefitted by the attempt" (Dunkel-Schetter & Skokan, 1990, p. 437).

In addition, calls for studying support as communication have been prompted by the way in which interactional processes undergird the structural and perceptual aspects of the supportive experience. Network structures and perceptions of support are both inputs and outputs to supportive communication. One's perceptions of the availability of support can influence the willingness to seek support (an input variable), whereas one's perceptions about the quality of support could be an outcome of supportive transactions. Similarly, the size or density of one's network affects the type and availability of supportive interactions (structure as input); yet the presence and quality of supportive transactions is also a factor in building and maintaining relationships and networks (structure as output). Thus we believe the communication of support is the central phenomenon linking structures, perceptions, as well as the functions/effects of support.

Models of the Effects of Support

As researchers began to empirically investigate the links between social ties and stressors/strain/health, a controversy developed regarding the form of the causal relationship. The nature of the effects were explicated in conceptual and statistical terms. What follows is a description of the key issues and an analysis of the implications for current research efforts.

Two competing models for describing how support affected health outcomes were tested and reported in the literature. Advocates for the "buffering" model argued that support primarily benefited individuals undergoing stressful life events (e.g., Dean & Lin, 1977; House, LaRocco, & French, 1982; LaRocco, 1983; LaRocco, House, & French, 1980; see also Lepore, Evans, & Schneider, 1991). Also termed the *coping* model, it was posited that support protected individuals from fully experiencing the onslaught of stressor conditions. Evidence for this hypothesis was empirically demonstrated by the finding of a significant interaction effect (Stress × Support), where increased stress was found to be moderated by increased levels of support. In contrast, proponents of the alternative "direct" or "main effects" model argued that social support had positive outcomes regardless of the presence or absence of stressors in individuals' lives (Schaefer, 1982; Thoits, 1982, 1983). Evidence for the model was demonstrated by a statistical main effect (e.g., Aneshensel & Stone, 1982; Frydman, 1981) showing positive effects of social ties on psychological or physical health irrespective of circumstances.

Inconsistent empirical evidence for settling the main effects versus buffering/protective effects question has created an ongoing need for conceptual and empirical clarification. A longitudinal study by Lepore et al. (1991) found that buffering effects exist but are short-lived under conditions of chronic stress that curtail the helpful effects of social support. House et al. (1982) suggested that the presence of supportive ties differentially buffers different forms of stress/strain; thus theories should focus on identifying the types of sources and types of support that buffer specific stressors under specific conditions. Schaefer (1982) asserted the need to know more about the processes that occur when people use their relationships during stressful events, the processes that prompt people to respond supportively, and how such processes affect health and well-being. A related view was the proposition that peripheral providers of support may "compensate" for the deficits of support existing within the principal areas of one's network of relationships (as in situations where neighbors may offset the lack of family assistance; Syrotuik & D'Arcy, 1984). Turner (1981) reported both main effects and buffering effects in the same study with the differences explained by social class. He found that support had significant main effects on psychological well-being for adults in middle and upper socioeconomic strata; yet among lower-class respondents, support was strongly related to depressive symptoms only for those experiencing high stress conditions.

It is not surprising therefore that Cohen and Wills (1985) concluded in their exhaustive review of the literature that both models were correct. The evidence they accumulated across studies showed that buffering effects tend to occur when individuals perceive that the support available to them is adequate to meet needs arising specifically from the presence of stressor/strain conditions. Support has main effects on well-being when the measure of support used in the study taps the person's degree of structural integration in a large social network. In short, their review showed that each model represents a unique conceptualization of support. Correspondingly different measures of support thus clearly yield different patterns for describing how support determines outcomes.

A related reason for the inconsistent patterns of effects is that both *social support* and *health* are mulitidimensional constructs that do not refer to singular, specifiable entities. Rather, they are general terms that encompass broad arrays of loosely related phenomena. There is only limited correspondence between measures of enacted support (behaviors) and perceived support (see Dunkel-Schetter & Bennett, 1990) and limited correlation among different measures of enacted support (Tardy, 1988). Similarly, a highly diverse collection of measures have been used to assess health-related outcomes, including longevity, mortality, resistance to infectious disease, incidence of stress-related conditions (ulcers, hypertension), maintenance of health under chronic conditions such as diabetes, rate of decline for progressive disease, heart attack recovery, depression, loneliness, addictive disorders, sexual dysfunction, social maladjustment, and so on. In a real sense, the terms *social support* and *health* are overly general. Yet they facilitate discussion of entities that, at a high level of abstraction, have some similar features and have organizational and heuristic utility. But they cannot and should not be expected to generate precise predictions of the form of the effects generated. Because neither social support nor health are internally coherent constructs, students of this literature should be vigilant in asking which specific types of support are related to which specific aspects of health.

Mechanisms of Supportive Communication

The excessive attention to whether support in general has main or buffering effects has tended to obscure more important questions about how different kinds of social transactions between people influence certain health (as well as relational) outcomes. Research is needed that helps to explain the specific mechanisms through which certain social experiences lead to a feeling of "being supported," and how such feelings, in turn, enhance (under specified conditions) particular aspects of health and well-being.

Mechanisms Connecting Communication, the Sense of Support, and Health

How is it that individuals come to experience a sense of support from others? How is it that communication provides social support? First, some communicative acts are unequivocal acts of support in that the clear intent of the provider is simply to provide needed information. In such instances, communicative acts do not "convey" support; rather, they are acts of support. Consequently, no mechanisms linking communication and support can be described in such cases. That is, in "informational support," *communication* and *social support* are synonymous.

There are, however, several ways in which communication may be said to convey support by creating a sense of support. For example, certain characteristic patterns of communication may help instill within each individual a relatively stable expectation of the general availability of support. Communication may also be supportive when people produce messages aimed at helping others cope with emotionally challenging and stressful situations. In these latter two cases, several mechanisms linking communication and social support can be identified.

Mechanisms linking communication with the management of acute emotional distress. Life is full of emotional disruptions and upsets, even for those who enjoy a strong sense of support. Somehow, these acute hurts and upsets must be managed. One of the chief ways in which people attempt to help those experiencing acute distress is by talking about the problem and trying to improve or change how the distressed person feels. What are the mechanisms through which specific, situated, communicative encounters help an individual deal with the hurts, upsets, anxieties, and disappointments that arise from a variety of life events? The specific emotions considered here include sadness or grief, anxiety and fear, anger and shame or embarrassment. Although the mechanisms discussed in this section are grounded in the extensive literature on human emotion (e.g., Lazarus, 1991), few empirical efforts have directly examined whether these mechanisms adequately describe how certain forms of message behavior moderate emotional distress. Thus the mechanisms described below should be viewed as very general and preliminary hypotheses about how messages might work to reduce emotional distress.

Our general approach to the emotions and their management through supportive communication is heavily informed by appraisal theory (Lazarus, 1991), where emotional states are viewed as resulting from the individual's interpretation of an event—the cognitive process of categorizing an event with respect to its significance for well-being (see Smith & Pope, 1992). Viewing emotions as responses to cognitively based appraisals suggests a very general mechanism for altering or modifying an emotional reaction: prompting a reappraisal of key aspects of the situation and its consequences. We propose, then, that most forms of supportive communication directed at improving the affective state of a distressed individual can be viewed as suggesting or attempting to stimulate some form of reappraisal of the stressful situation.

One of the most common negative emotions support givers confront is sadness, which usually arises from the sense that there has been an irrevocable loss of something good or desired (Lazarus, 1991). The sense of irrevocability is important: If a loss is not irrevocable or is merely anticipated, then other emotions (e.g., anger, fear) will be felt. Because the loss associated with sadness is irrevocable, there is nothing to do but accept this loss and locate it in the larger context of ongoing life events. Supportive messages therefore can assist another move through sadness by helping the other accept the loss by legitimizing the feeling of loss, discussing the magnitude of the loss and worthiness of the lost object, acknowledging the irrevocability of the loss, and encouraging moves by the other to accept the loss. Lazarus suggests that, once the loss has been accepted, "the associated emotional distress is ultimately attenuated" and tends to disappear (Lazarus, 1991, p. 248). At that point, messages from others can help the distressed other place the loss in context by, for example, encouraging the other to focus not just on what has been lost but also on what remains.

Another emotion facing support givers is anxiety or fear (Albrecht & Adelman, 1987), resulting when persons perceive some threat to their well-being (Roseman, 1985). Anxiety and fear are particularly likely when people perceive a situation as ambiguous, uncertain, and potentially uncontrollable. Fear or fright occurs in the face of an imminent harm to well-being; uncertainty is also characteristic of fear because the harm is threatened rather than actual (Lazarus, 1991). The major mechanisms through which supportive messages can diminish fear and anxiety involve reducing the individual's uncertainty about the situation, enhancing the individual's sense of efficacy or control, modifying judgments about the harmfulness of a perceived threat, or identifying ways to escape from the threat. Messages can reduce uncertainty and bolster a sense of control by helping an anxious other to specify the nature and severity of the situation, develop alternatives, identify potential consequences, formulate plans, be willing to take risks, and anticipate the successful completion of projected actions. Depending on the character of the threat, information about its potential harms and effects, along with ways it could be escaped or endured, may also help reduce fear and anxiety.

Perhaps one of the most difficult negative emotions to manage is anger. Anger arises from interference with or blockage of a desired goal, especially when such blockages are viewed as undeserved or unfair (Ellsworth & Smith, 1985; Roseman, 1985). Anger is the common emotional response to "a demeaning offense against me and mine" (Lazarus, 1991, p. 222). Because of its unpleasant nature, those confronted with another's anger may seek to quash it directly ("Calm down!"). Yet, because anger often is a response to what is perceived as an undeserved affront or outcome, such quashing imperatives may be experienced as unjust attacks on the legitimacy of the other's feelings, thereby further fueling the emotional fire. A preferable method of managing another's anger communicatively focuses on working through the emotion (as with sadness), such as acknowledging the legitimacy of the other's feelings, expressing solidarity with the other, decrying injustices, identifying ways of overcoming frustrating impediments to goal achievement, and diminishing the desirability of goals judged to be unattainable (Albrecht & Adelman, 1987).

Shame and embarrassment are emotions that are also often difficult for supporters to manage. Both involve a loss of face associated with an inadequate, inept, or inappropriate role performance (see also Scheff, 1990). In shame, an individual is disgraced or humiliated in his or her own eyes by the failure to live up to an ego ideal (Lazarus, 1991). In embarrassment, the individual suffers public humiliation and loss of face by failing to comport him- or herself in a manner consistent with a publicly claimed social identity (Gross & Stone, 1964). Diverse strategies are available for the management of these related emotions (e.g., Edelman, 1985; Metts & Cupach, 1989). Because both shame and embarrassment stem from an invalidated self-image, these emotions are generally managed by messages expressing reassurance, affirmation, and acceptance (Albrecht & Adelman, 1987).

A problem support givers may encounter when attempting to manage any unpleasant emotion is the intensity with which these emotions are sometimes felt. Regardless of its nature or causes, the negative effects of emotional distress are exacerbated if individuals become captured by the emotion. When caught in the throes of intense, negative emotion, people are less able to reason, reflect, reinterpret, or engage in constructive thoughts and behaviors. Individuals experiencing intense emotional distress "often experience repetitive, unelaborated, ruminative thoughts, as well as narrowing of their focus of attention" and are less able to engage in "problem solving and interpretive processes that would be useful for adjustment" (Clark, 1993, p. 2). We consider here mechanisms associated with two communicative approaches to moderating the intensity of negative emotional states: venting and externalization.

First, emotional energy sometimes seems trapped inside the individual, building pressures that must be released before any constructive process can proceed. Having distressed individuals vent their emotions is one way of managing this problem (Silver & Wortman, 1980). The expression of felt emotions—sometimes repeatedly and forcefully—appears to dissipate the emotion and moderate its intensity (Coates & Winston, 1983; Stiles, 1987). Albrecht and Adelman (1987) maintain that venting is not only a "way to relieve internalized pressures" but it also "creates through talk imagery that crystallizes somewhat unknown cognitions into known and shared entities" (p. 33). However, the venting of negative emotion is often inhibited by social norms that condemn any display of such emotion or limit such displays to private settings. Consequently, support givers may encourage venting by legitimizing the display of emotion, encouraging the expression of feelings, and expressing acceptance of both the distressed other and his or her feelings.

A second method of managing "impacted" negative emotions involves getting distressed others to distance themselves from their emotions and make those feelings an object of cognitive contemplation (externalization). Whereas venting simply aims at getting a distressed other to "blow off steam," externalization has the goal of getting distressed individuals to render their emotional states into objects that can be inspected, reflected upon, and understood. Considerable research documents multiple positive psychological and physical outcomes of externalization (see Clark, 1993; Pennebaker, 1989), which seems to occur by inducing the other to talk about feelings. Clark (1993) suggests that, once talking, the internal logic and cognitive demands of conversation make it very likely that distressed persons will begin getting some understanding of and perspective on their emotions. Initially, this can be achieved simply by asking the other to describe his or her feelings. Subsequently, the other can be encouraged to elaborate on and explore those feelings. Occasional paraphrases and extensions of the other's comments appear to foster the description and exploration of feelings (Carkhuff & Berenson, 1977).

Obviously, we have been able here to consider only a small number of emotions and mechanisms for their modification. Further, the types of positive emotions and the mechanisms through which these may be reinforced and amplified by the supportive communication of others still need to be addressed in future work: Truly supporting another entails validating victories and celebrating successes just as much as healing hurts.

Mechanisms linking communication and an enduring sense of support. B. Sarason, Pierce, and Sarason (1990; see also Pierce et al., 1990; I. Sarason et al., in press) contend that an individual's perception of support is the form of support most strongly related to health outcomes. Although persons may have fluctuating impressions regarding support availability or quality that are tied to particular situations (a *state* sense of support), the Sarasons and their colleagues have been interested in a relatively stable, transcontextual "characteristic related to perceptions of support availability and a propensity to interpret behaviors as supportive" (B. Sarason, Pierce, & Sarason, 1990, p. 99) (a *trait* sense of support). Thus the Sarasons suggest that the sense of support is best viewed as a personality or individual difference variable. Some individuals can be expected to enjoy a rather strong sense of support while others should characteristically view the social milieu as less forthcoming and supportive. These researchers further suggest that "it would be appropriate to define this type of perceived social support as the *sense of acceptance*" (B. Sarason, Pierce, & Sarason, 1990, p. 109, italics in original).

Drawing from the work of Bowlby (e.g., 1988), the Sarasons suggest that attachment experiences in infancy and childhood are the source of an individual's sense of support. Children become securely attached to a primary caretaker when that person (usually a parent) is readily available, responsive to the child's needs, and exhibits loving acceptance. If these conditions are consistently unmet, the child will exhibit either an anxious attachment style or an avoidant/ambivalent attachment style. Echoing Bowlby, the Sarasons suggest that attachment styles represent tacit working models of the role, functions, provisions, and dependability of personal relationships. These working models are the basis of individuals' expectations about availability of others in times of need, the willingness of others to provide support, and the likely efficacy of supportive behaviors. Although working models of social relationships begin early in childhood, they continue to develop over the life course.

Clearly, there are many powerful ways in which communicative experiences create and shape the development and elaboration of attachment styles, working models of relationships, and a sense of support availability (see Bowlby, 1969, 1973, 1980; B. Sarason, Pierce, & Sarason, 1990). In the space available here, we can only briefly consider one communicative mechanism that may influence the initial development of the child's attachment style and one communicative mechanism that later in life may help maintain and elaborate an individual's working model of relationships.

The communicative practices of parents play the central role in the child's development of an attachment style and working models of social relationships. All forms of parental communication are important, but none is more significant than how the parent seeks to nurture (e.g., comfort) and control (e.g., discipline) the child (see Bowlby, 1988). During infancy, most of parents' nurturance and control efforts will, of course, use nonverbal channels of communication. Later in childhood, parental nurturance and control become increasingly verbal in character.

Although there is an extensive literature on the characteristics and effects of the verbal strategies parents use to nurture and control children (see, for example, the review by Applegate, Burke, Burleson, Delia, & Kline, 1985), little of this work has been integrated with attachment theory. An integration of these literatures would help to explicate how the working models of social relationships implicit in parents' nurturance and control efforts are transmitted to their children and shape their developing attachment styles. For example, parental use of reflection-enhancing forms of communication has been found to be associated with the child's development of (a) complex and abstract cognitive schemas for representing other persons and interpreting social conduct, (b) "person-centered" communication skills that enable the child to relate to others in adapted and individuated ways, and (c) more positive interpersonal relationships with peers (see Burleson, Delia, & Applegate, 1992; Hart, Ladd, & Burleson, 1990). These developments are consistent with the unfolding of a secure attachment style and a working model of interpersonal relationships that depicts them as enjoyable, nurturant, and reliable sources of support.

Working models of relationships (and attendant beliefs about the general availability of social support) must somehow be sustained over the life course (Kobak & Sceery, 1988), but thus far few suggestions have been made about how such models are developed during adolescence and the adult years. We hypothesize that the character of everyday, routine interactions with intimates such as family and friends is a particularly important communicative mechanism for the maintenance and elaboration of working models of relationships and beliefs about the social world. In several recent papers, Duck and his associates (Barnes & Duck, in press; Duck, 1988; Leatham & Duck, 1990) have emphasized the significant role that mundane, routine interactions play in the maintenance of close relationships. Duck (1988) stresses that it is the routines and rituals of interaction that implicitly convey vital messages about acceptance, liking, commitment, involvement, and so on. Indeed, it has been specifically proposed that "such routine transactions . . . are the source of feelings of 'perceived support' " (Leatham & Duck, 1990, p. 2).

People tend to seek out relationship patterns later in life with which they are familiar (Rutter, 1984; Sroufe & Fleeson, 1986). This means there is some tendency for the securely attached to form relationships with other securely attached individuals while, sadly, the insecurely attached tend to form relationships with others similar to themselves. It is likely, then, that the character of the mundane interactions occurring within a relationship will reflect and sustain the attachment styles of the participants. The routine conversational interactions among, for example, friends who are each securely attached should be characterized by behaviors that convey warmth, acceptance, and positive regard. Such interactions should help perpetuate a working model of relationships as sources of security, reinforcement, and noncontingent support.

In contrast, routine interactions among pairs of insecurely attached individuals may be characterized by contingency, evaluation, rejection, and disconfirmation. Although it may seem implausible that individuals willingly remain in such mutually abusive relationships, there is some indication that people do stay in such relationships, perhaps because they confirm established working models of the self (Swann & Brown, 1990) and social life (Epstein, 1980). Routine interactions among the insecurely attached should sustain working models of relationships as unreliable sources of support. Happily, there is some indication that attachment styles can be altered later in life (e.g., Main, Kaplan, & Cassidy, 1985); it is possible that routine interactions with a securely attached individual may facilitate the development of more desirable working models by the insecurely attached.

Unfortunately, little research has been undertaken examining routine interactions as a function of attachment styles. Such research is needed and should help illumine the operation of communicative mechanisms that help maintain an individual's dispositional sense of support. For example, by using measures of adult attachment style and Duck, Rutt, Hurst, and Strejc's (1991) Iowa Communication Record, it should be possible to determine whether individuals tend to form intimate relationships with those having similar attachment styles and whether the content and character of routine interactions vary as a function of a dyad's shared attachment style.

Explications of the mechanisms through which messages help moderate emotional distress are vital to advancing our understanding of how communication provides social support. Such explication necessarily draws from more general theories of emotion but can also contribute to these theories. Thus analyses of how supportive messages modify feelings hold the promise of telling us much about our cognitive, emotional, and social lives.

Negative Effects and Dilemmas of Support

We have described a number of ways in which support networks, perceptions of support, and supportive interactions can bring about positive outcomes. However, the effects of support are not always positive. Four kinds of research explore this dark side of support: research on negative effects of enacted and structural support, research on unhelpful support attempts, research on risks and costs of support, and research on support dilemmas.

Negative Effects of Support?

One indication that support might not be an unqualified good comes from studies examining the relationship between measures of enacted support and measures of outcomes. Some studies report the counterintuitive finding that individuals who receive more enacted support report higher levels of stress (Aneshensel & Frerichs, 1982; Barrera, 1981; Cohen & Hoberman, 1983; Sandler & Barrera, 1984) and higher levels of distress (Barrera, 1981; Cohen & Hoberman, 1983; Coyne, Aldwin, & Lazarus, 1981; Fiore, Becker, & Coppel, 1983; Husaini, Neff, Newbrough, & Moore, 1982; Kauffman & Beehr, 1986). These findings may show that support can actually exacerbate problems (e.g., Cohen & Wills, 1985; Kessler & McLeod, 1985). Barrera (1986), however, has suggested three alternative explanations: (a) Individuals experiencing the highest levels of stress seek and receive the most support; (b) individuals exhibiting the greatest distress seek and receive more support; and (c) the negative relationship between support and distress could be a spurious correlation due to the influence of stress on both support and distress. Similarly, Cutrona (1986) found individuals are most likely to seek support when their stress is most acute. Clearly, longitudinal research and more sophisticated causal modeling are needed to explain the correlational findings.

Studies using social network measures of support have shown how personal relationships can be unsupportive sources of stress, conflict, and criticism (Davis, Brickman, & Baker, 1991; Finch, Okun, Barrera, Zautra, & Reich, 1989; Fiore et al., 1983; Manne & Zautra, 1989; Pagel, Erdly, & Becker, 1987; Porritt, 1979; Rook, 1984; Sandler & Barrera, 1984; Schuster, Kessler, & Aseltine, 1990). The importance of these findings is underscored by studies indicating the effect of negative interactions has a greater impact than the effect of positive interactions (Fiore et al., 1983; Pagel et al., 1987; Rook, 1984).

Unhelpful Support Attempts

Even if the negative outcomes associated with enacted support occur because the needy seek more support, it is probably also true that some attempts at support do more harm than good. And even when members of our network are trying to be helpful rather than critical or disagreeable, their support attempts may be unwelcome or inappropriate. Indeed, there is a growing body of qualitative data on the kinds of support-intended acts that are perceived by recipients as helpful and unhelpful, covering a range of populations experiencing specific kinds of stresses, including cancer patients (Dakof & Taylor, 1990; Dunkel-Schetter, 1984; Taylor, Falke, Mazel, & Hilsberg, 1988), students receiving counseling (Elliott, 1985), bereaved spouses and parents (Lehman, Ellard, & Wortman, 1986), individuals with multiple sclerosis (Lehman & Hemphill, 1990), Israeli war widows (Malkinson, 1987), spouses experiencing work stress (Pearlin & McCall, 1990), unemployed women (Ratcliff & Bogdan, 1988), and mentally retarded mothers (Tucker & Johnson, 1989).

However, the proliferation of taxonomies of helpful and unhelpful acts based on these data is both a strength and a limitation of this kind of research. There have been few attempts to discover general categories, dimensions, or theoretical explanations that would cut across specific taxonomies based on specific populations. In addition, the acts in these taxonomies are highly abstract (e.g., "express concern" or "encouragement") and do not show the characteristics of the acts or messages that resulted in the recipients' evaluation. So, for example, "expressing concern" is helpful, while being "overly concerned" or "showing too little concern" or offering "unwanted assistance" are unhelpful. The basis for distinguishing how much concern is appropriate or what kinds of assistance are unwanted remains unclear.

Goldsmith (1992, in press) has suggested many of the behaviors in these taxonomies that are perceived as helpful show regard for "positive face" (a recipient's desire to be viewed as liked and accepted) and "negative face" (a recipient's desire for autonomy and privacy) while unhelpful behaviors threaten positive and negative face. Similarly, Burleson and Samter's research on person-centered comforting (Burleson & Samter, 1985a, 1985b; Samter, Burleson, & Basden-Murphy, 1987) might provide a basis for discriminating among helpful and unhelpful acts. Attempts at building taxonomies of behaviors should include these or other theoretical explanations as a basis for discriminating helpful from unhelpful behaviors both for specific populations and in general.

Risks and Costs of Support

Asking for and/or receiving help from others can create myriad problems for the recipient and the provider that detract from whatever positive outcomes might result. These potential disadvantages can appear as risks that prevent individuals from even seeking or offering aid, and as costs that undermine or detract from the positive effects of aid when it is provided.

The risks and costs for support recipients include *impression management problems* (when asking for help makes them appear weak or less competent; Abdel-Halim, 1982; Wills, 1983), because undesirable information is disclosed in asking for help (DePaulo, 1982; Goldsmith, 1988) or the problem for which help is needed results in stigmatization (Chesler & Barbarin, 1984; Wortman & Dunkel-Schetter, 1979). Recipients may suffer from *negative self-evaluations* because they feel less competent or unable to reciprocate assistance (Abdel-Halim, 1982; DePaulo, 1982; DePaulo & Fisher, 1980; Tripathi, Caplan, & Naidu, 1986; Wills, 1983). Support may in fact lead to *overdependence* on others and may prevent individuals from developing control and competence (Gross, Wallston, & Piliavin, 1979; McLeroy et al., 1984). *Feelings of obligation* and the *inability to reciprocate* can also pose obstacles to seeking support (Greenberg & Shapiro, 1971) or undermine the utility of support that is received (DePaulo, 1982; DiMatteo & Hays, 1981; Tripathi et al., 1986). *"Overinvolvement"* by well-meaning supporters can increase stress and worsen physical and psychological problems (Coyne & DeLongis, 1986). Receiving support may come at the *expense of privacy* (Chapman & Pancoast, 1985; Chesler & Barbarin, 1984; Goldsmith, 1988). Asking for help may *require effort* and may *engender uncertainty and anxiety,* leading some individuals to adopt an "armor of loneliness" rather than risk possible failure or rejection (Kessel, 1964; see also Adelman & Albrecht, 1984).

Providers also face risks and costs. They can suffer a *drainage of resources,* particularly when the need for support is great or extends over a long period of time (Abel, 1989; Chesler & Barbarin, 1984; Cicirelli, 1983). Involvement in the problems of others may make providers *more vulnerable* to stresses in their own lives (Kessler & McLeod, 1985). They may feel a *sense of obligation, frustration, or responsibility* when progress is slow or outcomes are negative (Coyne, Wortman, & Lehman, 1988) and may experience *negative evaluations* by self and others if they are unable to provide effective assistance (Notarius & Herrick, 1988). Providers may suffer *"social contagion"* effects when being with troubled others depresses their own emotional or psychological well-being (Coyne, 1976). Finally, supportive interactions may require *considerable effort* and may produce *anxiety* for the provider (Abel, 1989; Lehman et al., 1986).

If the recipient of support feels threatened by needing help, he or she may react defensively and attribute negative motives to the support provider (Fisher, Goff, Nadler, & Chinsky, 1988; Searcy & Eisenberg, 1992), thus threatening the stability of the relationship. Support providers whose offers are rejected may react with negative evaluations of the would-be recipient and negative attributions about the reasons for rejection (Jung, 1989; Rosen, Mickler, & Collins, 1987). When support is provided, inequities in reciprocity could create relational conflict (Hatfield, Utne, & Traupmann, 1979; Pattison & Pattison, 1981). One individual's need for support can produce uncertainty and conflict for relationship partners as relationship roles and expectations are redefined (Abel, 1989). Support providers may have difficulty managing the demands of multiple relationships (Abel, 1989). Strong, dense network ties may provide necessary tangible support but may constrain individuals from the identity and informational support available from "weak" ties or new relationships (Henderson, 1980; Leslie & Grady, 1988). Social networks may suffer systemic contagion as the stress and distress of some members influence and tax interdependent others (Adelman, 1986; Albrecht et al., 1982).

Dilemmas of support. We use this term to refer to a particularly difficult situation in which providers and/or recipients not only suffer costs in transacting support but are placed in a bind from which it is difficult to escape. One dilemma of support results from the risks of stigmatization and contagion: The individuals who are in the greatest need of help are those who may experience the greatest difficulty in seeking and receiving it. Coyne (1976) describes a destructive cycle of responses that may occur when would-be supporters interact with people who are depressed: The symptoms exhibited by depressed people are aversive to potential supporters and yet arouse strong feelings of guilt that inhibit the open expression of annoyance and hostility. In response to these conflicting and unpleasant feelings, would-be supporters are likely to give insincere reassurances while trying to reject and withdraw from the depressed persons. These reactions confirm the depressed person's sense that he or she is not accepted and that future interaction is uncertain; in response, the depressed person may display more symptoms and convey more distress in an attempt to control the behavior and elicit the sympathy of the other. (See Wortman & Dunkel-Schetter, 1979, who describe a similar "catch-22" experienced by many cancer patients.)

A second dilemma arises from impression management and self-esteem risks of seeking support: Frequently, the individual with the information or power to alleviate distress most effectively is simultaneously the individual who is riskiest to approach for assistance. In the workplace, subordinates may be most reluctant to seek support from supervisors (even though they usually have the information and power to best ease job stress or uncertainty) because risks of impression management and imposition are the greatest in this relationship (Albrecht & Halsey, 1992).

A third dilemma can occur when receivers and providers of support are interdependent and affected by the same stressors. The kind of support one member of the relationship needs to receive may be harmful for the other member of the relationship to provide. Gottlieb and Wagner (1991) studied parents of children with cystic fibrosis or diabetes and found that husbands did not voice their apprehensions about their child's future and that their communication patterns exerted pressure on their wives to act more "maturely," for example, to avoid anxiety-provoking communication, engage in less self-pity and overdramatizing, and concentrate on the child's needs. In contrast, wives expressed their apprehensions frequently and with intense affect; their communication patterns pressured their husbands to express greater emotionality and assume a larger share of responsibility for the child's care. The authors concluded that each spouse saw the other as over- or underinvolved and thus tried to redirect their partner's behavior so that it posed less threat to their own preferred style of coping.

Implications

The dangers and pitfalls of support demonstrate that improvements are needed in the way we conceptualize and study social support. First, more sophisticated methods and models of the support process are needed to examine whether support increases distress or whether increased stress leads to the mobilization of support.

Second, given that much of the research on the negative side of support is atheoretical, there is a need for general taxonomies showing what dimensions of supportive acts differentiate helpful from unhelpful behaviors and explaining why they are important. Just as we need to specify the causal mechanisms that bring about positive effects, we need to specify the mechanisms responsible for negative effects.

Third, we need to collect data on the perceived costs and risks of support in the same studies that collect data on the actual negative effects. The qualitative studies documenting the particular risks and costs seldom measure the actual psychological or physiological impact. The studies that measure impacts often do not measure why the impact was negative and simply speculate as to the risks or costs responsible.

Finally, communication researchers should be especially interested in the features of situations, messages, interactions, relationships, and networks that can alleviate or reduce dilemmas. Some multigoal messages may more successfully address difficulties than single-goal messages (Goldsmith, 1992, in press; Goldsmith & Parks, 1990). Some communication network structures may minimize costs and maximize benefits (Albrecht & Adelman, 1984). Rather than conceptualizing support in terms of positive versus negative effects or in terms of intractable dilemmas, a study of communication processes and effects may theoretically and empirically demonstrate ways in which providers and receivers can minimize negative effects and maximize positive effects in some situations, relationships, and interactions.

Components of a Model of Supportive Communication

Features of Supportive Messages

Goldsmith (1992) suggests a framework for distinguishing the various factors that contribute to a supportive message. It is important to differentiate between a supportive message and an effective supportive message. If we are to avoid the tautological assumption that supportive messages are those that have the effect of being supportive, we need a means of identifying supportive messages that are conceptually independent of the message effects in which we are interested. One possibility is to define supportive acts as "a category of speech acts and events that are culturally recognized as intending to convey various kinds of assistance"

(Goldsmith, 1992, p. 276). The use of measures such as the ISSB assumes researchers and respondents share ideas about what kinds of acts are intended to be supportive and about what those acts look like. Additional research could further illuminate the implicit shared cultural knowledge on which recognition and differentiation of supportive acts is based.

Having defined certain kinds of messages as supportive in intent, we can then focus on the message features that contribute to successful outcomes. At a minimum, we should consider the type of act that is selected and its appropriateness in the situation. In addition, we should examine how the act is conveyed—the degree to which it exhibits dimensions and stylistic features that contribute to perceived helpfulness. Finally, a maximally effective act should address multiple goals in addition to the goal of providing a particular kind of assistance.

Act types and situational differences. Several lines of research suggest ways in which different types of supportive messages are effective in different types of situations. Cutrona and Russell (1990) suggest an "optimal matching" model in which the desirability, controllability, and life domain of stress influences what kind of support (emotional support, social integration, esteem support, tangible aid, informational support) is most useful. They found controllability and domain of stress were the most successful predictors of what type of support was helpful. When stress is uncontrollable, emotional support that comforts and expresses love and acceptance is most helpful. When stress is controllable, instrumental and esteem support help individuals to cope.

Characteristics of the support provider also influence the appropriateness of different kinds of support. Dakof and Taylor (1990) found cancer patients valued esteem and emotional support more frequently than informational aid from nurses and from friends, family, and spouses. In contrast, informational support was more often valued than esteem and emotional support from other cancer patients and physicians. Other research suggests that "source credibility" may also influence the perceived helpfulness of a supportive message. Goldsmith and Parks (1990) found that students discussing a romantic relationship problem with a third party considered how trustworthy the other person would be as well as their "expertise" in relationship problems. Cutrona and Suhr (1992) found that advice from one's spouse was helpful if the spouse was perceived as having expertise or control over the problem discussed but advice was not helpful if the spouse lacked such credibility.

When the stresses for which support is offered extend over a period of time, different kinds of support may be more or less helpful in different phases of coping. Jacobsen (1986) suggests that, during a "crisis" period, emotional support is useful to reassure the recipient and help restore balance. During transition periods, cognitive support is important for helping a recipient reinterpret and restructure his or her life. In "deficit" states of chronic and excessive demands, tangible support may be most important in meeting concrete needs. If a recipient experiences a stressor that unfolds in crisis, transition, and deficit stages, different kinds of support may be needed at different times. If different kinds of stressful situations occur simultaneously, support may need to be tailored not only to the particular stress but also to the particular experience of stress a recipient is undergoing at a particular time.

Comforting. Burleson and Samter (1985a, 1985b; see also Samter et al., 1989) provide convincing evidence that "person-centeredness" is a critical feature of effective comforting messages. Messages that acknowledge, elaborate, and grant legitimacy to the feelings of a distressed other are perceived to be more sensitive and effective. Person-centered messages are evaluatively neutral, feeling centered, accepting of the other, involved with the other, and cognitively oriented to the explanation of feelings. Burleson (in press) has recently proposed that person-centered messages are not only perceived to be more helpful but might bring about positive individual and relational outcomes in both the short and the long term.

Multiple goal messages. Communication situations often include multiple goals and supportive interactions. In addition to meeting the objective of providing support, effective supportive messages must also attend to identity and relational goals. Goldsmith (1992, in press) suggests politeness theory as a framework for describing and explaining multiple goals and message strategies. Supportive messages such as advice, offers of assistance, and even expressions of concern can simultaneously convey implicit criticism of the receiver and can impose on the receiver. Consequently, "facework" strategies that convey acceptance and respect and mitigate criticism and imposition are also important features of supportive messages.

Features of Supportive Interactions

Help-seeking messages. The directness with which support is sought and offered appears to be a key dimension of support-seeking messages. Wills (1983) suggests that indirect ways of expressing a need for assistance may alleviate fears of negative evaluation. Rosen (1983) reports requests for help are more likely if the requests can be made indirectly through third parties or through "camouflaged" strategies such as hints or experience swapping. The potential utility of indirect support seeking is also shown in research where the same "objective" amount of assistance was perceived as less helpful when the receiver explicitly asked for help, compared with conditions where the provider "spontaneously" offered assistance (Cutrona, Cohen, & Igram, 1990; Dovidio & Gaertner, 1983). Hence indirect ways of making known one's need for help are probably important in enabling support providers to "spontaneously" offer help.

The utility of direct help-seeking strategies may vary with the closeness of the relationship between seeker and would-be provider. In more intimate relationships, potential helpers are perceived to have a greater obligation to grant requests and offer resources; consequently, help-seekers make less elaborated requests and offer fewer explanations and inducements (Roloff, Janiszewski, McGrath, Burns, & Manrai, 1988).

A related dimension of help-seeking messages concerns self-presentation strategies a support recipient might employ. (We noted above the dilemmas faced by many help-seekers.) Silver, Wortman, and Crofton (1990) have examined "self-presentational" strategies for dealing with this dilemma that vary in the kind and amount of information a help-seeker provides about his or her distress and individual coping. Providing no information about one's distress or presenting oneself as coping well may make it difficult for others to be aware of one's needs and may actually arouse suspicion when it is evident that an individual is undergoing stress. Presenting oneself as coping poorly may result in rejection. Silver and her colleagues found would-be providers exhibited greater attraction and less avoidance when help-seekers employed a "balanced" coping self-presentation strategy in which the help-seeker realistically discussed her distress and difficulties but simultaneously indicated that she was taking action to cope.

Research on both direct/indirect help-seeking and self-presentation strategies points to the relevance of multiple goals in help-seeking interactions. Goldsmith and Parks (1990) categorize help-seeking strategies according to the ways in which they reconcile potentially conflicting goals of obtaining support and simultaneously protecting identities and relationships. They found four distinct patterns of strategies for seeking help with a problem in a romantic relationship. One group of help-seekers simply disclosed their problem as openly as they could. A second group reported "temporal separation": alternating back and forth between disclosing relational problems and keeping the problems to themselves. A third group added "behavioral separation" to temporal separation, so that, when they disclosed a problem, they admitted the problem verbally but downplayed its seriousness nonverbally. Finally, a fourth group was distinctive in adding to their help-seeking repertoire indirect help-seeking strategies, "moderation" strategies (holding some things back while telling others), and "integrative reframing" (finding a way to discuss a problem without negative identity or relationship repercussions). In general, individuals who had more concerns about disclosing tended to use more strategies and tended to fall in the third and fourth patterns; however, these individuals were not more satisfied with the outcome of their disclosure than respondents who used fewer and simpler strategies. The method in this study limits causal interpretations, and message strategies were reported by respondents at a fairly high level of abstraction. However, this study does integrate help-seeking strategies in a way that is responsive both to the findings on support dilemmas and to calls in communication research to consider how messages adapt to more than one goal at a time.

Interactive dynamics. Examination of the actions of support-seekers takes in a wider view of supportive communication than simply focusing on supportive messages alone, but it is still a snapshot approach to understanding supportive communication processes. Support-seeking and support-giving acts occur in interactions and, as such, are influenced by conversational rules and structures and by interactional dynamics. These issues have been considered even less by social support researchers than those pertaining to supportive acts. Still, three lines of research serve to illustrate interaction-level processes of supportive communication.

Ethnographic research has examined two speech events in mainstream American culture that appear relevant to supportive communication. Katriel and Philipsen (1981) discuss the meaning and cultural significance of the event "really communicating," in which participants talk about problems of self and identity with intimate others in order to experience personal growth. Their analysis suggests a recognizable sequence and set of rules that enable participants to recognize, enact, and evaluate instances of "really communicating." Goldsmith and Baxter (1993) found that college students distinguished a second kind of supportive communication event labeled "concern conversations." Their respondents indicated "really communicating" is a more collaborative, two-way discussion and exchange of information and opinions; in contrast, "concern conversations" involve one party "unloading" while the other tries to help by offering advice, reassurance, assistance, and/or sympathy. These findings suggest support providers and receivers may share cultural expectations about the proper enactment and meaning of supportive communication events. This implicit cultural knowledge may assist communicators in cuing a need for support, enacting coordinated and meaningful exchanges, and evaluating the success of interactions.

Research from a conversation analysis perspective has examined how communicators introduce "troubles talk" into a conversation and how laughter and other "breaks" from talk about serious troubles are negotiated. Jefferson (1984a) demonstrates several ways in which communicators can coordinate transitions from talk about troubles to conversational closing. In another study, Jefferson (1984b) explores the occurrence of laughter in talk about serious troubles, detailing a speaker's prerogative to initiate laughter in telling his or her own troubles and the way in which both parties to the conversation coordinate an appropriate intensity of laughter and return to troubles talk or to lighter topics. This line of research points to the potential difficulties of coordinating a supportive conversation: Even if provider and receiver employ appropriate strategies, they must still coordinate their roles and negotiate the handling of sensitive topics.

A third line of research reveals how responses by young people to an elderly person's "painful self-disclosure" may set in motion an interactive dynamic that undermines the supportiveness of the conversation and contributes to negative stereotypes of the elderly. In a study of conversations among the young and the elderly, Coupland and his colleagues (Coupland, Coupland, & Giles, 1991) reported that younger women often elicited painful self-disclosures from the elderly by asking questions they would not ordinarily ask of a peer (e.g., "Is your husband still alive?" "Do you have trouble sleeping at night?"). When elderly women responded with a disclosure, the younger women faced a dilemma in how to react. Discouraging the disclosure makes the younger woman appear insensitive and threatens rejection of her elderly conversation partner. However, giving an encouraging response may continue the cycle of painful self-disclosure, which may impose on both the younger and the elderly communicators. In contrast, when two elderly women conversed, they frequently responded to a painful self-disclosure with a painful self-disclosure and were able to engage in an appeal to the shared experience of aging. Coupland's discourse analysis reveals how younger speakers may come to hold a stereotype of elderly speakers as poor listeners who talk only about their own problems. These findings have clear implications for research on support and the elderly; they also draw our attention to the fact that any supportive conversation may have interdependent, conversational dynamics that go beyond the individual acts in the conversation.

Features of Supportive Networks and Communities

The components of the model of supportive communication described above may manifest in network patterns that reflect a sense of community among participants. An important direction for current research is to explore how patterns of overlapping relationships (i.e., networks) shape, sustain, and value supportive behaviors of individuals and, in turn, how supportive interactions represent, enact, and reinforce the values and structures of the larger network and community (Albrecht, in press).

Individuals engaged in supportive relationships do not exist in a vacuum. Rather, they are tied through overlapping linkages into a larger social order that weaves the community together in loose and tight patterns. Network structures are outcomes of micro-level "structuring" or the interactive behaviors occurring in dyadic ties (Albrecht, in press; Mehan, 1978). Community networks are essentially iconic representations of micro, relatively repetitive interactions occurring among kin, friends, neighbors, coworkers, acquaintances, and strangers.

Supportive networks form the foundation for the support communities in which individuals are embedded. Networks can be characterized by several structural properties, including size, density, and homogeneity/heterogeneity. Size is usually determined by a straightforward count of the number of direct (one-to-one) links and indirect (second order relationships—the links one has that are mediated by others). *Density* refers to the relative degree of integration or interconnection among a set of ties (computed as the ratio of the number of actual relationships to the number of theoretically possible $[n(n-1)/2]$ relationships in the system under study). The level of network density (or, in other terms, the level of integration of the individual in the network or web of ties) connects individuals in relational circles that can have helpful but also problematic effects (Albrecht & Adelman, 1987; Evans, Palsane, Lepore, & Martin, 1989; Garrison, 1978; Mitchell & Hodson, 1983). *Homogeneity/heterogeneity* refers to the similarity or dissimilarity of persons (usually determined by demographic factors) or the overall composition of types of relationships in the network, such as the proportion of strong/primary ties directly connecting kin, friends) relative to proportions of "weak" ties such as acquaintances, strangers, or indirect links to second order contacts (see Adelman et al., 1987a; Granovetter, 1972).

The data from studies of support networks over the past 15 years have demonstrated the varied positive and negative impacts of high and low interconnection among strong and weak ties. A basic generalization from findings is that individuals in low density, heterogeneous network structures generally fare better overall than those who are not. For example, larger, relatively heterogeneous, low density networks tend to be associated with prosocial outcomes for participants. Such outcomes include greater facilitation of role transition, increased sources of new information, visibility in the workplace, greater perceived personal control, and increased opportunities for access to health care and other professional services in the community (e.g., Hammer, 1983; Hirsch, 1980; Horowitz, 1977; McKinlay, 1973; McLanahan, Wedemyer, & Adelberg, 1981). In contrast, overly dense, restricted, and homogeneous ties can be stifling and heighten the potential for abusive behavior, dysfunctional group pressure, and entrapment (e.g., Crandall, 1988; Garrison, 1978; Pattison & Pattison, 1981; Salzinger et al., 1983). Strained married couples, for example, have been found to have support networks that are conjunctive (husbands' and wives' overlapping confidants) and of limited size, availability, and composition (Veiel, Crisand, Stroszeck-Somschor, & Herrle, 1991). Yet, it is important to recognize that integrated friendship ties can offset anomic reactions (Parks, 1977), foster psychological adjustment under posttraumatic conditions (Kadushin, 1982), and facilitate stress coping (Albrecht et al., 1982; Ray, 1987).

Our understanding of the dynamic, processual, and interactive functioning occurring within social support networks is less well developed. Fruitful directions for the study of the role of communication in support networks include empirical tracking of the ways in which support networks develop over time, the nature of the quality and meaning of one's array of social ties, and the ways in which supportive activity in differing network regions complement or impede interactions in other regions.

Concluding Note

Our review of the social support literature has delineated classes of variables that ought to be included in models of supportive communication and its effects. We have not gone so far as to specify precisely which of the causal mechanisms we have discussed earlier might link particular message features, interaction processes, and relational network characteristics to the outcomes of supportive interactions. We have attempted to offer a menu of important components in understanding supportive communication; clearly, there is much theoretical work to be done in explaining whether, when, and how supportive communication will have short- and long-term consequences. Should we expect that a single message will have a positive effect? Under what circumstances could we expect this to be the case and how would this effect come about? Here again, theories of communication processes have an important contribution to make to the social support literature (e.g., uncertainty reduction theory, Albrecht & Adelman, 1987; cognitive complexity, Burleson, in press).

Our review of the interactional dynamics of supportive communication should also make clear that traditional social scientific methods can be supplemented with cultural and discursive techniques that illumine the process. These methods and findings do not always yield clear results about causal relationships and outcomes; these approaches typically describe what happens when it happens and account for how an interaction comes to have meaning and order. However, such descriptive information is useful in its own right and, to the extent that meaning and order contribute to effectiveness, may suggest contextual and processual features that affect outcomes.

Supportive communication is a central process of interpersonal behavior. We look to a future where research efforts illumine the message, interactional, and structural aspects of social support that are unquestionably a cornerstone for the quality of human life.

References

Abdel-Halim, A. A. (1982). Social support and managerial affective responses to job stress. *Journal of Occupational Behavior, 3,* 281-295.

Abel, E. K. (1989). The ambiguities of social support: Adult daughters caring for frail elderly parents. *Journal of Aging Studies, 3,* 211-230.

Adelman, M. (1986). *The contagion effect: A study on stress and the provision of support.* Unpublished doctoral dissertation, University of Washington, Seattle.

Adelman, M. B., Parks, M. R., & Albrecht, T. L. (1987a). Beyond close relationships: Support in weak ties. In T. L. Albrecht, M. B. Adelman, et al., *Communicating social support* (pp. 126-147). Newbury Park, CA: Sage.

Adelman, M. B., Parks, M. R., & Albrecht, T. L. (1987b). Supporting friends in need. In T. L. Albrecht, M. B. Adelman, et al., *Communicating social support* (pp. 105-125). Newbury Park, CA: Sage.

Albrecht, T. L. (in press). Patterns of sociation and cognitive structure. In G. P. Philipsen & T. L. Albrecht (Eds.), *Contemporary communication theory.* Albany: SUNY Press.

Albrecht, T. L., & Adelman, M. B. (1984). Social support and life stress: New directions for communication research. *Human Communication Research, 11,* 3-32.

Albrecht, T. L., & Adelman, M. B. (1987). *Communicating social support.* Newbury Park, CA: Sage.

Albrecht, T. L., Burleson, B. R., & Sarason, I. G. (1992). Meaning and method in the study of communication and support: An introduction. *Communication Research, 19,* 149-153.

Albrecht, T. L., & Hall, B. J. (1991). The role of personal relationships in organizational innovation. *Communication Monographs, 58,* 273-288.

Albrecht, T. L., & Halsey, J. (1992). Mutual support in mixed status relationships. *Journal of Social and Personal Relationships, 9,* 237-252.

Albrecht, T. L., Irey, K. V., & Mundy, A. K. (1982). Integration in a communication network as a mediator of stress. *Social Work, 27,* 229-234.

Aneshensel, C. S., & Frerichs, R. R. (1982). Stress, support, and depression: A longitudinal causal model. *American Journal of Community Psychology, 10,* 363-376.

Aneshensel, C. S., & Stone, J. D. (1982). Stress and depression: A test of the buffering model of social support. *Archives of General Psychiatry, 39,* 1392-1396.

Antonucci, T. C., & Israel, B. A. (1986). Veridicality of social support: A comparison of principal and network members' responses. *Journal of Consulting and Clinical Psychology, 54,* 432-437.

Applegate, J. L., Burke, J. A., Burleson, B. R., Delia, J. G., & Kline, S. L. (1985). Reflection-enhancing parental communication. In I. E. Sigel (Ed.), *Parental belief systems: The psychological consequences for children* (pp. 107-142). Hillsdale, NJ: Lawrence Erlbaum.

Barbee, A. P. (1990). Interactive coping: The cheering-up process in close relationships. In S. Duck with R. Silver (Eds.), *Personal relationships and social support* (pp. 46-65). London: Sage.

Barnes, M., & Duck, S. (in press). Everyday communicative contexts for social support. In B. R. Burleson, T. L. Albrecht, & I. G. Sarason (Eds.), *The communication of social support: Messages, interactions, relationships and community.* Newbury Park, CA: Sage.

Barrera, M. (1981). Social support in the adjustment of pregnant adolescents: Assessment issues. In B. H. Gottlieb (Ed.), *Social networks and social support* (pp. 69-96). Beverly Hills, CA: Sage.

Barrera, M. (1986). Distinctions between social support concepts, measures, and models. *American Journal of Community Psychology, 14,* 413-445.

Barrera, M., Sandler, I. N., & Ramsey, T. B. (1981). Preliminary development of a scale of social support: Studies on college students. *American Journal of Community Psychology, 9,* 435-447.

Belle, D. E. (1982). The impact of poverty on social networks and supports. *Marriage and Family Review, 5,* 89-103.

Berkman, L. F., & Syme, S. L. (1979). Social networks, host resistance, and mortality: A nine-year follow-up study of Alameda County residents. *American Journal of Epidemiology, 109,* 186-204.

Bharadwaj, L. K., & Wilkening, E. A. (1980). Life domains satisfaction and personal social integration. *Social Indicators Research, 7,* 337-351.

Bochner, A. P. (1982). On the efficacy of openness in close relationships. In M. Burgoon (Ed.), *Communication yearbook 5* (pp. 109-124). New Brunswick, NJ: Transaction.

Bowlby, J. (1969). *Attachment and loss: Vol. 1. Attachment.* New York: Basic Books.

Bowlby, J. (1973). *Attachment and loss: Vol. 2. Separation: Anxiety and anger.* New York: Basic Books.

Bowlby, J. (1980). *Attachment and loss: Vol. 3. Loss: Sadness and depression.* New York: Basic Books.

Bowlby, J. (1988). Developmental psychiatry comes of age. *American Journal of Psychiatry, 145,* 1-10.

Brownell, A., & Shumaker, S. A. (1984). Social support: An introduction to a complex phenomenon. *Journal of Social Issues, 40,* 111-121.

Burgoon, J., Burgoon, M., Miller, G. R., & Sunnafrank, M. (1981). Learning theory approaches to persuasion. *Human Communication Research, 7,* 161-179.

Burgoon, M., & Ruffner, M. (1978). *Human communication.* New York: Holt, Rinehart & Winston.

Burleson, B. R. (1990). Comforting as social support: Relational consequences of supportive messages. In S. Duck with R. Silver (Eds.), *Personal relationships and social support* (pp. 66-82). London: Sage.

Burleson, B. R. (in press). Comforting messages: Features, functions, and outcomes. In J. A. Daly & J. M. Wiemann (Eds.), *Communicating strategically: Strategies in interpersonal communication.* Hillsdale, NJ: Lawrence Erlbaum.

Burleson, B. R., Albrecht, T. L., & Goldsmith, D. (1993). Social support and communication: New directions for theory, research, and practice. *ISSPR Bulletin, 9,* 5-9.

Burleson, B. R., Albrecht, T. L., Goldsmith, D., & Sarason, I. G. (in press). An introduction to the messages, interactions, relationships and community levels of social support. In B. R. Burleson, T. L. Albrecht, & I. G. Sarason (Eds.), *The communication of social support: Messages, interactions, relationships and community.* Newbury Park, CA: Sage.

Burleson, B. R., Albrecht, T. L., & Sarason, I. G. (Eds.). (in press). *The communication of social support: Messages, interactions, relationships and community.* Newbury Park, CA: Sage.

Burleson, B. R., Delia, J. G., & Applegate, J. L. (1992). Effects of maternal communication and children's social-cognitive and communication skills on children's acceptance by the peer group. *Family Relations, 41,* 264-272.

Burleson, B. R., & Samter, W. (1985a). Inconsistencies in theoretical and naive evaluations of comforting messages. *Communication Monographs, 52,* 103-123.

Burleson, B. R., & Samter, W. (1985b). Individual differences in the perception of comforting messages: An exploratory investigation. *Central States Speech Journal, 36,* 39-50.

Caplan, G. (1976). The family as a support system. In G. Caplan & M. Killilea (Eds.), *Support systems and mutual help* (pp. 19-36). New York: Grune & Stratton.

Cappella, J. N. (1981). Mutual influence in expressive behavior: A review of adult and infant-adult dyadic interaction. *Psychological Bulletin, 89,* 101-132.

Carkhuff, R. R., & Berenson, B. G. (1977). *Beyond counseling and therapy* (2nd ed.). New York: Holt, Rinehart & Winston.

Cassel, J. (1976). The contribution of the environment to host resistance. *American Journal of Epidemiology, 104,* 107-123.

Chapman, N. J., & Pancoast, D. L. (1985). Working with the informal helping networks of the elderly: The experiences of three programs. *Journal of Social Issues, 41,* 47-63.

Chesler, M. A., & Barbarin, O. A. (1984). Difficulties of providing help in a crisis: Relationships between parents of children with cancer and their friends. *Journal of Social Issues, 40,* 113-134.

Cicirelli, V. G. (1983). Personal strains and negative feelings in adult children's relationships with elderly parents. *Journal of Academic Psychology Bulletin, 5,* 31-36.

Clark, L. F. (1993, March). *Stress and the cognitive conversational benefits of social interaction.* Unpublished manuscript, Purdue University, Department of Psychology, West Lafayette, IN.

Coates, D., & Winston, T. (1983). Counteracting the deviance of depression: Peer support groups for victims. *Journal of Social Issues, 39,* 169-194.

Cobb, S. (1976). Social support as a moderator of life stress. *Psychosomatic Medicine, 38,* 300-314.

Cohen, L. H., McGowan, J., Fooskas, S., & Rose (1984). Positive life events and social support and the relationship between life stress and psychological disorder. *American Journal of Community Psychology, 12,* 564-587.

Cohen, S., & Hoberman, H. M. (1983). Positive events and social supports as buffers of life change stress. *Journal of Applied Social Psychology, 13,* 99-125.

Cohen, S., & Wills, T. A. (1985). Stress, social support, and buffering hypothesis. *Psychological Bulletin, 98,* 310-357.

Coupland, N., Coupland, J., & Giles, H. (1991). *Language, society, and the elderly: Discourse, identity, and ageing.* Oxford: Basil Blackwell.

Coyne, J. C. (1976). Depression and the response of others. *Journal of Abnormal Psychology, 85,* 186-193.

Coyne, J. C., Aldwin, C., & Lazarus, R. S. (1981). Depression and coping in stressful episodes. *Journal of Abnormal Psychology, 90,* 439-447.

Coyne, J. C., & DeLongis, A. (1986). Going beyond social support: The role of social relationships in adaptation. *Journal of Consulting and Clinical Psychology, 54,* 454-460.

Coyne, J. C., Wortman, C. B., & Lehman, D. R. (1988). The other side of support: Emotional overinvolvement and miscarried helping. In B. H. Gottlieb (Ed.), *Marshalling social support* (pp. 305-330). Newbury Park, CA: Sage.

Crandall, C. S. (1988). Social contagion and binge eating. *Journal of Personality and Social Psychology, 55,* 588-598.

Cutrona, C., Cohen, B. B., & Igram, S. (1990). Contextual determinants of the perceived supportiveness of helping behaviors. *Journal of Social and Personal Relationships, 7,* 553-562.

Cutrona, C. E. (1986). Behavioral manifestations of social support: A microanalytic investigation. *Journal of Personality and Social Psychology, 51,* 201-208.

Cutrona, C. E., & Russell, D. W. (1990). Type of social support and specific stress: Toward a theory of optimal matching. In B. Sarason, I. Sarason, & G. Pierce (Eds.), *Social support: An interactional view* (pp. 319-366). New York: Wiley.

Cutrona, C. E., & Suhr, J. A. (1992). Controllability of stressful events and satisfaction with spouse support behaviors. *Communication Research, 19,* 154-174.

Cutrona, C., Suhr, J., & MacFarlane, R. (1990). Interpersonal transactions and the psychological sense of support. In S. Duck with R. Silver (Eds.), *Personal relationships and social support* (pp. 30-45). London: Sage.

Dakof, G. A., & Taylor, S. E. (1990). Victims' perceptions of social support: What is helpful from whom? *Journal of Personality and Social Psychology, 58,* 80-89.

Davis, R. C., Brickman, E., & Baker, T. (1991). Supportive and unsupportive responses of others to rape victims: Effects on concurrent victim adjustment. *American Journal of Community Psychology, 19,* 443-451.

Dean, A., & Lin, N. (1977). The stress buffering role of social support: Problems and prospects for systematic investigation. *Journal of Nervous and Mental Disease, 165,* 403-417.

DePaulo, B. M. (1982). Social psychological processes in informal help-seeking. In T. A. Wills (Ed.), *Basic processes in helping relationships* (pp. 255-279). New York: Academic Press.

DePaulo, B. M., & Fisher, J. D. (1980). The costs of asking for help. *Basic and Applied Social Psychology, 1,* 23-35.

DiMatteo, M. R., & Hays, R. (1981). Social support and serious illness. In B. H. Gottlieb (Ed.), *Social networks and social support* (pp. 117-148). Beverly Hills, CA: Sage.

Dovidio, J. F., & Gaertner, S. L. (1983). Race, normative structure, and help-seeking. In B. M. DePaulo, A. Nadler, & J. D. Fisher (Eds.), *New directions in helping: Vol. 2. Help-seeking* (pp. 285-302). New York: Academic Press.

Duck, S. (1988). *Relating to others.* Chicago: Dorsey.

Duck, S., Rutt, D. J., Hurst, M. H., & Strejc, H. (1991). Some evident truths about conversations in everyday relationships: All communications are not created equal. *Human Communication Research, 18,* 228-267.

Duck, S., with Silver, R. C. (Eds.). (1990). *Personal relationships and social support.* London: Sage.

Dunkel-Schetter, C. (1984). Social support and cancer: Findings based on patient interviews and implications. *Journal of Social Issues, 40,* 77-98.

Dunkel-Schetter, C., & Bennett, T. L. (1990). Differentiating the cognitive and behavioral aspects of social support. In B. R. Sarason, I. G. Sarason, & G. R. Pierce (Eds.), *Social support: An interactional view* (pp. 267-296). New York: Wiley.

Dunkel-Schetter, C., & Skokan, L. A. (1990). Determinants of social support in personal relationships. *Journal of Social and Personal Relationships, 7,* 437-450.

Edelman, R. J. (1985). Social embarrassment: An analysis of the process. *Journal of Social and Personal Relationships, 2,* 195-213.

Eggert, L. L. (1987). Support in family ties: Stress, coping, and adaptation. In T. L. Albrecht, M. B. Adelman, et al., *Communicating social support* (pp. 80-104). Newbury Park, CA: Sage.

Elliott, R. (1985). Helpful and nonhelpful events in brief counseling interviews: An empirical taxonomy. *Journal of Counseling Psychology, 32,* 307-322.

Ellsworth, P. C., & Smith, C. A. (1985). Patterns of cognitive appraisal in emotion. *Journal of Personality and Social Psychology, 48,* 813-838.

Elster, J. (1990). Selfishness and altruism. In J. Mansbridge (Ed.), *Beyond self interest* (pp. 44-53). Chicago: University of Chicago Press.

Epstein, S. (1980). The self-concept: A review and the proposal of an integrated theory of personality. In E. Staub (Ed.), *Personality: Basic aspects and current research* (pp. 477-505). Englewood Cliffs, NJ: Prentice-Hall.

Evans, G. W., Palsane, M. N., Lepore, S. J., & Martin, J. (1989). Residential density and psychological health: The mediating effects of social support. *Journal of Personality and Social Psychology, 57,* 994-999.

Eyres, S. J., & MacElveen-Hoehn, P. (1983, April). *Theoretical issues in the study of social support.* Paper presented at the conference, "Social Support: What Is It?" University of Washington, Seattle.

Finch, J. F., Okun, M. A., Barrera, M., Jr., Zautra, A. J., & Reich, J. W. (1989). Positive and negative social ties among older adults: Measurement models and the prediction of psychological distress and well-being. *American Journal of Community Psychology, 17,* 585-605.

Fiore, J., Becker, J., & Coppel, D. B. (1983). Social network interactions: A buffer or a stress. *American Journal of Community Psychology, 11,* 423-439.

Fisher, J. D., Goff, B. A., Nadler, A., & Chinsky, J. M. (1988). Social psychological influences on help seeking and support from peers. In B. H. Gottlieb (Ed.), *Marshalling social support* (pp. 267-304). Newbury Park, CA: Sage.

Frydman, M. I. (1981). Social support, life events and psychiatric symptoms: A study of direct, conditional and interaction effects. *Social Psychiatry, 16,* 69-78.

Garrison, V. (1978). Support systems of schizophrenic and nonschizophrenic Puerto Rican migrant women in New York City. *Schizophrenia Bulletin, 4,* 561-596.

Goldsmith, D. (1988). *To talk or not to talk: The flow of information between romantic dyads and members of their communication networks.* Unpublished master's thesis, University of Washington, Seattle.

Goldsmith, D. (1992). Managing conflicting goals in supportive interaction: An integrative theoretical framework. *Communication Research, 19,* 264-286.

Goldsmith, D. (in press). The role of facework in supportive communication. In B. Burleson, T. L. Albrecht, & I. Sarason (Eds.), *The communication of social support: Messages, interactions, relationships, and community.* Newbury Park, CA: Sage.

Goldsmith, D., & Albrecht, T. L. (1993). The impact of supportive communication networks on test anxiety and performance. *Communication Education, 42,* 142-158.

Goldsmith, D., & Baxter, L. A. (1993, November). *A taxonomy of speech events in personal relationships.* Paper presented at the annual meeting of the Speech Communication Association, Miami, FL.

Goldsmith, D., & Parks, M. (1990). Communicative strategies for managing the risks of seeking social support. In S. Duck with R. Silver (Eds.), *Personal relationships and social support* (pp. 104-121). London: Sage.

Gottlieb, B. H. (1985). Social support and the study of personal relationships. *Journal of Social and Personal Relationships, 2,* 351-375.

Gottlieb, B. H., & Wagner, F. (1991). Stress and support processes in close relationships. In J. Eckenrode (Ed.), *The social context of coping* (pp. 165-188). New York: Plenum.

Granovetter, M. (1972). The strength of weak ties. *American Journal of Sociology, 78,* 1360-1380.

Greenberg, M. S., & Shapiro, S. P. (1971). Indebtedness: An adverse aspect of asking for and receiving help. *Sociometry, 34,* 290-301.

Gross, A., Wallston, B. S., & Piliavin, I. M. (1979). Reactance, attribution, equity, and the help recipient. *Journal of Applied Social Psychology, 9,* 297-313.

Gross, E., & Stone, G. P. (1964). Embarrassment and analysis of role requirements. *American Journal of Sociology, 70,* 1-15.

Hammer, M. (1983). "Core" and "extended" social networks in relation to health and illness. *Social Science and Medicine, 17,* 405-414.

Hart, C. H., Ladd, G. W., & Burleson, B. R. (1990). Children's expectations of the outcomes of social strategies: Relationships with sociometric status and maternal disciplinary styles. *Child Development, 61,* 127-137.

Hatfield, E., Utne, M. K., & Traupmann, J. (1979). Equity theory and intimate relationships. In R. L. Burgess & T. L. Huston (Eds.), *Social exchange in developing relationships* (pp. 99-133). New York: Academic Press.

Henderson, S. (1980). Personal networks and the schizophrenias. *Australian & New Zealand Journal of Psychiatry, 14,* 255-259.

Hill, C. A. (1991). Seeking emotional support: The influence of affiliative need and partner warmth. *Journal of Personality and Social Psychology, 60,* 112-121.

Hirsch, B. J. (1980). Natural support systems and coping with major life changes. *American Journal of Community Psychology, 8,* 159-172.

Hobfoll, S. E., & Stephens, M. A. P. (1990). Social support during extreme stress: Consequences and interventions. In B. R. Sarason, I. G. Sarason, & G. R. Pierce (Eds.), *Social support: An interactional view* (pp. 454-481). New York: Wiley.

Hobfoll, S. E., & Stokes, J. P. (1988). The process and mechanics of social support. In S. Duck, D. F. Hay, S. E. Hobfoll, W. Ickes, & B. M. Montgomery (Eds.), *Handbook of personal relationships: Theory, research, and interventions* (pp. 497-517). London: Wiley.

Horowitz, A. (1977). Social networks and pathways to psychiatric treatment. *Social Forces, 56,* 86-105.

House, J. S. (1981). *Work stress and social support.* Reading, MA: Addison-Wesley.

House, J. S., & Kahn, R. L. (1985). Measures and concepts of social support. In S. Cohen & S. L. Syme (Eds.), *Social support and health* (pp. 83-108). Orlando, FL: Academic Press.

House, J. S., LaRocco, J. M., & French, J. R. P., Jr. (1982). Response to Schaefer. *Journal of Social and Health Behavior, 23,* 98-101.

House, J. S., Robbins, C., & Metzer, H. C. (1982). The association of social relationships and activities with mortality: Prospective evidence from the Tecumseh community health study. *American Journal of Epidemiology, 116,* 123-140.

Husaini, B. A., Neff, J. A., Newbrough, J. R., & Moore, M. C. (1982). The stress-buffering role of social support and personal competence among the rural married. *American Journal of Community Psychology, 10,* 409-426.

Jacobsen, D. E. (1986). Types and timing of social support. *Journal of Health and Social Behavior, 27,* 250-264.

Jefferson, G. (1984a). On stepwise transition from talk about a trouble to inappropriately next-positioned matters. In M. Atkinson & J. Heritage (Eds.), *Structures of social action: Studies in conversation analysis* (pp. 191-222). Cambridge: Cambridge University Press.

Jefferson, G. (1984b). On the organization of laughter in talk about troubles. In M. Atkinson & J. Heritage (Eds.), *Structures of social action: Studies in conversation analysis* (pp. 346-369). Cambridge: Cambridge University Press.

Jemmott, J. B., III, & Magloire, K. (1988). Academic stress, social support, and secretory immunoglobulin A. *Journal of Personality and Social Psychology, 55,* 803-810.

Jung, J. (1989). Social support rejection and reappraisal by providers and recipients. *Journal of Applied Social Psychology, 19,* 159-173.

Kadushin, C. (1982). Social density and mental health. In P. V. Marsden & N. Lin (Eds.), *Social structure and network analysis* (pp. 147-158). Beverly Hills, CA: Sage.

Kahn, R. L., & Antonucci, T. C. (1980). Convoys over the life course: Attachment, roles, and social support. In P. B. Baltes & O. G. Brim (Eds.), *Life span development and behavior* (pp. 253-286). New York: Academic Press.

Kaplan, R. M., & Toshima, M. T. (1990). The functional effects of social relationships on chronic illnesses and disability. In B. R. Sarason, I. G. Sarason, & G. R. Pierce (Eds.), *Social support: An interactional view* (pp. 427-453). New York: Wiley.

Kasl, S. V., Evans, A. S., & Neiderman, J. C. (1979). Psychosocial risk factors in the development of infectious mononucleosis. *Psychosomatic Medicine, 41,* 445-466.

Katriel, T. (1993). Lefargen: A study in Israeli semantics of social relations. *Research on Language and Social Interaction, 26,* 31-53.

Katriel, T., & Philipsen, G. (1981). "What we need is communication": "Communication" as a cultural category in some American speech. *Communication Monographs, 48,* 301-317.

Kauffman, G. M., & Beehr, T. A. (1986). Interactions between job stressors and social support: Some counter-intuitive results. *Journal of Applied Psychology, 71,* 522-526.

Kennedy, S., Kiecolt-Glaser, J. K., & Glaser, R. (1990). Social support, stress, and the immune system. In B. R. Sarason, I. G. Sarason, & G. R. Pierce (Eds.), *Social support: An interactional view* (pp. 253-266). New York: Wiley.

Kessel, N. (1964). The armour of loneliness. *20th Century, 1023,* 134-140.

Kessler, R. C., & McLeod, J. D. (1985). Social support and mental health in community samples. In S. Cohen & S. L. Syme (Eds.), *Social support and health* (pp. 219-240). Orlando, FL: Academic Press.

Kobak, R. R., & Sceery, A. (1988). Attachment in late adolescence: Working models, affect regulation, and representations of self and others. *Child Development, 59,* 135-146.

Kurdek, L. A. (1988). Perceived social support in gays and lesbians in cohabiting relationships. *Journal of Personality and Social Psychology, 54,* 504-509.

Lakey, B., & Cassady, P. B. (1990). Cognitive processes in perceived social support. *Journal of Personality and Social Psychology, 59,* 337-343.

LaRocco, J. M. (1983). Theoretical distinctions between causal and interaction effects of social support. *Journal of Health and Social Behavior, 24,* 91-92.

LaRocco, J. M., House, J. S., & French, J. R. P., Jr. (1980). Social support, occupational health, and stress. *Journal of Health and Social Behavior, 21,* 202-218.

Lazarus, R. S. (1991). *Emotion and adaptation.* New York: Oxford University Press.

Leatham, G., & Duck, S. (1990). Conversations with friends and the dynamics of social support. In S. Duck with R. Silver (Eds.), *Personal relationships and social support* (pp. 1-29). London: Sage.

Lehman, D. R., Ellard, J. H., & Wortman, C. B. (1986). Social support for the bereaved: Recipients' and providers' perspectives on what is helpful. *Journal of Consulting and Clinical Psychology, 54,* 438-446.

Lehman, D. R., & Hemphill, K. J. (1990). Recipients' perceptions of support attempts and attributions for support attempts that fail. *Journal of Social and Personal Relationships, 7,* 563-574.

Lepore, S. J., Evans, G. W., & Schneider, M. L. (1991). Dynamic role of social support in the link between chronic stress and psychological distress. *Journal of Personality and Social Psychology, 61,* 899-909.

Leslie, L. A., & Grady, K. (1988). Social support for divorcing mothers: What seems to help? *Journal of Divorce, 11,* 147-165.

Litwak, E., & Messeri, P. (1989). Organizational theory, social supports, and mortality rates: A theoretical convergence. *American Sociological Review, 54,* 49-66.

Main, M., Kaplan, N., & Cassidy, J. (1985). Security in infancy, childhood, and adulthood: A move to the level of representation [pp. 66-106; in I. Bretherton & E. Waters (Eds.), Growing points of attachment theory and research]. *Monographs of the Society for Research in Child Development, 50*(1-2, Serial No. 209).

Major, B., Cozzarelli, C., Sciaccitano, A. M., Cooper, M. L., Testa, M., & Mueller, P. M. (1990). Perceived social support, self-efficacy, and adjustment to abortion. *Journal of Personality and Social Psychology, 59,* 452-463.

Malkinson, R. (1987). Helping and being helped: The support paradox. *Death Studies, 11,* 205-219.

Manne, S. L., & Zautra, A. J. (1989). Spouse criticism and support: Their association with coping and psychological adjustment among women with rheumatoid arthritis. *Journal of Personality and Social Psychology, 56,* 608-617.

McKinlay, J. B. (1973). Social networks, lay consultation and help seeking behavior. *Social Forces, 51,* 275-292.

McLanahan, S. S., Wedemyer, N. V., & Adelberg, T. (1981). Network structure, social support, and psychological well being in the single parent family. *Journal of Marriage and the Family, 43*, 601-612.

McLeroy, K. R., DeVellis, R., DeVellis, B., Kaplan, B., & Toole, J. (1984). Social support and physical recovery in a stroke population. *Journal of Social and Personal Relationships, 1*, 395-413.

Mehan, H. (1978). Structuring school structure. *Harvard Educational Review, 48*, 32-64.

Metts, S., & Cupach, W. R. (1989). Situational influences on the use of remedial strategies in embarrassing predicaments. *Communication Monographs, 56*, 151-162.

Miller, G. R., Boster, F. J., Roloff, M., & Seibold, D. R. (1977). Compliance-gaining message strategies: A typology and some findings concerning effects of situational differences. *Communication Monographs, 44*, 37-54.

Miller, G. R., & Steinberg, M. (1975). *Between people: A new analysis of interpersonal communication.* Chicago: Science Research Associates.

Miller, P., Wikoff, R. L., McMahon, M., Garrett, M. J., & Ringel, K. (1985). Indicators of medical regimen adherences for myocardial infarction patients. *Nursing Research, 34*, 268-272.

Mitchell, R. E., & Hodson, C. A. (1983). Coping with domestic violence: Social support and psychological health among battered women. *American Journal of Community Psychology, 11*, 629-654.

Moss, G. E. (1973). *Illness, immunity, and social interaction.* New York: Wiley.

Notarius, C. I., & Herrick, L. R. (1988). Listener response strategies to a distressed other. *Journal of Social and Personal Relationships, 5*, 97-108.

Oritt, E. J., Paul, S. C., & Behrman, J. A. (1985). The perceived support network inventory. *American Journal of Community Psychology, 13*, 565-582.

Pagel, M. D., Erdly, W. W., & Becker, J. (1987). Social networks: We get by with (and in spite of) a little help from our friends. *Journal of Personality and Social Psychology, 53*, 793-804.

Parks, M. R. (1977). Anomia and close friendship communication networks. *Human Communication Research, 4*, 48-57.

Parks, M. R. (1982). Ideology in interpersonal communication: Off the couch and into the world. In M. Burgoon (Ed.), *Communication yearbook 5* (pp. 79-107). New Brunswick, NJ: Transaction.

Pattison, E. M., & Pattison, M. L. (1981). Analysis of a schizophrenic psychosocial network. *Schizophrenia Bulletin, 7*, 135-143.

Pearlin, L. I., & McCall, M. E. (1990). Occupational stress and marital support: A description of microprocesses. In J. Eckenrode & S. Gore (Eds.), *Stress between work and family* (pp. 39-60). New York: Plenum.

Pennebaker, J. W. (1989). Confession, inhibition, and disease. In L. Berkowitz (Ed.), *Advances in experimental social psychology* (Vol. 22, pp. 211-243). New York: Academic Press.

Peters-Golden, H. (1982). Breast cancer: Varied perceptions of social support in the illness experience. *Social Science and Medicine, 16*, 483-491.

Pierce, G. R., Sarason, I. G., & Sarason, B. R. (1990). Integrating social support perspectives: Working models, personal relationships, and situational factors. In S. Duck with R. Silver (Eds.), *Personal relationships and social support* (pp. 173-189). London: Sage.

Porritt, D. (1979). Social support in crisis: Quantity or quality? *Social Science & Medicine, 13A*, 715-721.

Ratcliff, K. S., & Bogdan, J. (1988). Unemployed women: When "social support" is not supportive. *Social Problems, 35*, 54-63.

Ray, E. B. (1987). Supportive relationships and occupational stress in the workplace. In T. L. Albrecht, M. B. Adelman, et al., *Communicating social support* (pp. 172-191). Newbury Park, CA: Sage.

Roloff, M. E., Janiszewski, C. A., McGrath, M. A., Burns, C. S., & Manrai, L. A. (1988). Acquiring resources from intimates: When obligation substitutes for persuasion. *Human Communication Research, 14*, 364-396.

Rook, K. S. (1984). The negative side of social interaction: Impact on psychological well-being. *Journal of Personality and Social Psychology, 46*, 1097-1108.

Roseman, J. (1985). Cognitive determinants of emotion. In P. Shaver (Ed.), *Review of personality and social psychology* (Vol. 6, pp. 1-36). Beverly Hills, CA: Sage.

Rosen, S. (1983). Perceived inadequacy and help-seeking. In B. M. DePaulo, A. Nadler, & J. D. Fisher (Eds.), *New directions in helping: Vol. 2. Help-seeking* (pp. 73-107). New York: Academic Press.

Rosen, S., Mickler, S. E., & Collins, J. E. (1987). Reactions of would be helpers whose offer of help is spurned. *Journal of Personality and Social Psychology, 53*, 288-297.

Rutter, M. (1984). Psychopathology and development, II: Childhood experiences and personality development. *Australia-New Zealand Journal of Psychiatry, 18*, 314-327.

Salzinger, S., Kaplan, S., & Artemyeff, C. (1983). Mothers' personal social networks and child maltreatment. *Journal of Abnormal Psychology, 92*, 68-76.

Samter, W., Burleson, B., & Basden-Murphy, L. B. (1987). Comforting conversations: The effects of strategy type on evaluations of messages and message producers. *Southern Speech Communication Journal, 52,* 263-284.

Sandler, I. N., & Barrera, M., Jr. (1984). Toward a multimethod approach to assessing the effects of social support. *American Journal of Community Psychology, 12,* 37-52.

Sarason, B. R., Pierce, G. R., & Sarason, I. G. (1990). Social support: The sense of acceptance and the role of relationships. In B. R. Sarason, I. G. Sarason, & G. R. Pierce (Eds.), *Social support: An interactional view* (pp. 97-128). New York: Wiley.

Sarason, B. R., Pierce, G. R., Shearin, E. N., Sarason, I. G., Waltz, J. A., & Poppe, L. (1991). Perceived social support and working models of self and actual others. *Journal of Personality and Social Psychology, 60,* 273-287.

Sarason, B. R., Sarason, I. G., & Pierce, G. R. (1990). Traditional views of social support and their impact on assessment. In B. R. Sarason, I. G. Sarason, & G. R. Pierce (Eds.), *Social support: An interactional view* (pp. 9-25). New York: Wiley.

Sarason, I. G., Levine, H. M., Basham, R. B., & Sarason, B. R. (1983). Assessing social support: The social support questionnaire. *Journal of Personality and Social Psychology, 44,* 127-139.

Sarason, I. G., Sarason, B. R., & Pierce, G. R. (in press). Relationship specific social support: Toward a model for the analysis of supportive interactions. In B. R. Burleson, T. L. Albrecht, & I. G. Sarason (Eds.), *The communication of social support: Messages, interactions, relationships, and community.* Newbury Park, CA: Sage.

Schaefer, C. (1982). Shoring up the "buffer" of social support. *Journal of Health and Social Behavior, 23,* 96-98.

Schaefer, C., Coyne, J. D., & Lazarus, R. S. (1981). The health-related functions of social support. *Journal of Behavioral Medicine, 4,* 381-406.

Scheff, T. J. (1990). *Microsociology: Discourse, emotion, and social structure.* Chicago: University of Chicago Pres.

Schuster, T. L., Kessler, R. C., & Aseltine, R. H. (1990). Supportive interactions, negative interactions, and depressed mood. *American Journal of Community Psychology, 18,* 423-438.

Schwarzer, R., & Leppin, A. (1991). Social support and health: A theoretical and empirical overview. *Journal of Social and Personal Relationships, 8,* 99-128.

Searcy, E., & Eisenberg, N. (1992). Defensiveness in response to aid from a sibling. *Journal of Personality and Social Psychology, 62,* 422-433.

Silver, R. C., & Wortman, C. B. (1980). Coping with undesirable life events. In J. Garber & M. Seligman (Eds.), *Human helplessness: Theory and applications* (pp. 279-340). New York: Academic Press.

Silver, R. C., Wortman, C. B., & Crofton, C. (1990). The role of coping in support provision: The self-presentational dilemma of victims of life crisis. In B. R. Sarason, I. G. Sarason, & G. R. Pierce (Eds.), *Social support: An interactional view* (pp. 397-426). New York: Wiley.

Smith, C. A., & Pope, L. K. (1992). Appraisal and emotion: The interactional contribution of dispositional and situational factors. In M. S. Clark (Ed.), *Emotion and social behavior* (pp. 32-62). Newbury Park, CA: Sage.

Sroufe, L. A., & Fleeson, J. (1986). Attachment and the construction of relationships. In W. W. Hartup & Z. Rubin (Eds.), *Relationships and development* (pp. 51-71). Hillsdale, NJ: Lawrence Erlbaum.

Stiles, W. B. (1987). "I have to talk to somebody": A fever model of self disclosure. In V. J. Derlega & J. H. Berg (Eds.), *Self-disclosure: Theory, research, and therapy* (pp. 257-282). New York: Plenum.

Swann, W. B., & Brown, J. D. (1990). From self to health: Self-verification and identity disruption. In B. R. Sarason, I. G. Sarason, & G. R. Pierce (Eds.), *Social support: An interactional view* (pp. 150-172). New York: Wiley.

Syrotuik, J., & D'Arcy, C. (1984). Social support and mental health: Direct, protective and compensatory effects. *Social Science and Medicine, 18,* 229-236.

Tardy, C. H. (1988). Social support: Conceptual clarification and measurement options. In C. H. Tardy (Ed.), *A handbook for the study of human communication: Methods and instruments for observing, measuring, and assessing communication processes* (pp. 347-364). Norwood, NJ: Ablex.

Taylor, S. E., Falke, R. L., Mazel, R. M., & Hilsberg, B. L. (1988). Sources of satisfaction and dissatisfaction among members of cancer support groups. In B. H. Gottlieb (Ed.), *Marshalling social support* (pp. 187-208). Newbury Park, CA: Sage.

Thoits, P. A. (1982). Conceptual, methodological, and theoretical problems in studying social support as a buffer against life stress. *Journal of Health and Social Behavior, 23,* 145-159.

Thoits, P. A. (1983). Main and interactive effects of social support: Response to LaRocco. *Journal of Health and Social Behavior, 24,* 92-95.

Tolsdorf, C. C. (1976). Social networks, support, and coping: Exploratory study. *Family Process, 15,* 407-417.

Tripathi, R. C., Caplan, R. D., & Naidu, R. K. (1986). Accepting advice: A modifier of social support's effect on well-being. *Journal of Social and Personal Relationships, 3,* 213-228.

Tucker, M. B., & Johnson, O. (1989). Competence-promoting versus competence inhibiting social support for mentally retarded mothers. *Human Organization, 48,* 95-107.

Turner, R. J. (1981). Social support as a contingency in psychological well-being. *Journal of Health and Social Behavior, 22,* 357-367.

Veiel, H. O. F., Crisand, M., Stroszeck-Somschor, H., & Herrle, J. (1991). Social support networks of chronically strained couples: Similarity and overlap. *Journal of Social and Personal Relationships, 8,* 279-292.

Wethington, E., & Kessler, R. C. (1986). Perceived support, received support, and adjustment to stressful life events. *Journal of Health and Social Behavior, 27,* 78-89.

Wills, T. A. (1983). Social comparison in coping and help-seeking. In B. M. DePaulo, A. Nadler, & J. D. Fisher (Eds.), *New directions in helping: Vol. 2. Help-seeking* (pp. 109-141). New York: Academic Press.

Wortman, C. B. (1984). Social support and the cancer patient: Conceptual and methodological issues. *Cancer, 53,* 2339-2360.

Wortman, C. B., & Dunkel-Schetter, C. (1979). Interpersonal relationships and cancer. *Journal of Social Issues, 35,* 120-155.

Zimmerman, S., & Applegate, J. (1992). Person-centered comforting in the hospice interdisciplinary team. *Communication Research, 19,* 240-263.

12

Power, Dominance, and Social Interaction

Charles R. Berger

POWER, SOCIAL INFLUENCE, persuasion, coercion, dominance, leadership, authority, control, compliance-gaining, and related constructs have enjoyed considerable currency among social scientists in general and among communication scientists in particular. Russell (1938) argued that "the fundamental concept in social science is Power, in the same sense in which Energy is the fundamental concept in physics" (p. 10). Power and dominance frequently have occupied center stage in theories developed to explain interpersonal behavior (Bales, 1970; Blau, 1964; Blood & Wolfe, 1960; R. Brown, 1965; Carson, 1969; Cartwright, 1959; Haley, 1959; Kelley & Thibaut, 1978; Leary, 1957; Schutz, 1958; Thibaut & Kelley, 1959). In addition to these theories, numerous studies have demonstrated that judgmental dimensions related to power and dominance serve as continua along which relationships are ordered (Forgas, 1979; Rosenberg & Sedlak, 1972; Triandis, Vassiliou, & Nassiakou, 1968; Wish, Deutsch, & Kaplan, 1976).

Communication researchers have also accorded power and related constructs a central role in their explanations of verbal and nonverbal interaction. Blakar (1979) observed that language is not only an obvious resource for exerting power, but language can structure individuals' experiences when they engage in informal social interactions not directly concerned with social influence, suggesting that there are more subtle relationships between language and power. Patterson (1983) asserted that the exercise of power is a key function served by nonverbal communication. Burgoon and Hale (1984) theorized that dominance is one of several fundamental *topoi* of relational communication, and they have adduced evidence to support their claim (Burgoon & Hale, 1987). Consistent with these findings, Wish, D'Andrade, and Goodnow (1980) found a factor they labeled "forceful" versus "forceless" to underlie judgments of speech acts. Research on the communicator style concept revealed that dominance is a key dimension along which such style judgments are made (Norton, 1983). Similarly, factor-analytic studies of evaluations of spoken language employing the semantic differential technique have consistently recovered a factor some have labeled *dynamism,* which includes such scales as strong-weak and active-passive (Mulac, 1975, 1976; Zahn & Hopper, 1985). The composition of this factor is not unlike the *potency* factor recovered in earlier factor-analytic studies employing semantic differential scales (Mehrabian, 1972; Osgood, Suci, & Tannenbaum, 1957). This body of evidence demonstrates that dimensions related to power and dominance are crucial to our understanding of the dynamics of social relationships and the communication that both takes place within them and acts to define them.

Although power and related constructs have frequently been invoked to explain social change at a number of different levels of analysis (dyads, groups, institutions, and societies), there is considerable ambiguity surrounding the meanings of these constructs and their relationships to each other. These definitional issues will not be addressed in detail in this chapter; however, a number of different perspectives from which to view power will be considered. A useful overview of these definitional issues has been presented by Ng (1980). This chapter will focus on the relationships between power and interpersonal communication. That relationship is reciprocal; that is, persons can actualize power through their communicative conduct, as Blaker (1979) suggested, and, just as important, verbal and nonverbal behavior may serve as a basis for making inferences about individuals' abilities to exercise power. Communication, then, is at once both an antecedent and a consequence of power.

The focus of attention will be upon the power construct rather than similar constructs because power has been viewed frequently as more abstract. Weber (1947), for instance, defined power (Macht) to be inclusive of both imperative control (Herrschaft) and authority (Legitime Herrschaft). Sites (1973) viewed control as the actualization of social power, whereas Burr, Ahern, and Knowles (1977) defined power as the potential or ability to exert influence and control as the actual behavioral attempt to induce change. This is not to say that all power theorists necessarily view the power construct to be prepotent over the others; however, for purposes of the present chapter, social power will be viewed as the regnant construct of the set.

The first section of this chapter will consider a number of conceptual and measurement issues related to the power construct. The second section will explore the relationships between social power and social interaction. The role of power in the production of communicative conduct as well as the relationships between perceptions of communicative action and attributions of power will be examined. In addition, research related to compliance-gaining and request strategies will be considered.

Conceptual and Measurement Issues

In the first part of this section, definitional issues related to social power will be considered. Then, two general approaches to the study of power will be contrasted, the individual and the interactional. Finally, some alternative ways of measuring social power will be discussed.

On Defining Social Power

Given the popularity of the concept of social power in the literature of the social sciences, it is not surprising that a considerable number of alternative definitions for the construct have been advanced by various theorists. The following sample of these definitions gives some idea of the commonalities they share as well as the differences among them. Russell (1938) defined power as "the production of intended effects" (p. 35). Lasswell and Kaplan (1950) argued, "Power is a special case of the exercise of influence: it is the process of affecting the policies of others with the help of (actual or threatened) severe deprivations for nonconformity with the policies intended" (p. 76). Simon (1957) proposed the following view of power: "For the assertion, 'A has power over B,' we can substitute the assertion, 'A's behavior causes B's behavior' " (p. 5). Dahl (1957) opined, "My intuitive idea of power, then, is something like this: A has power over B to the extent that he can get B to do something that B would not otherwise do" (pp. 202-203). Winter (1973) asserted that Dahl's definition is too restrictive because "getting someone else to believe that he really wants to do what you want him to do is surely a very sophisticated technique for getting power" (p. 5). In Winter's view, "Social power is the ability or capacity of O to produce (consciously or unconsciously) intended effects on the behavior or emotions of another person P" (p. 5).

Both Cartwright (1959) and Schopler (1965) noted the considerable amount of variation in definitions of power and the tendency for various researchers to use such terms as *power, influence,* and *authority* as if they have the same meaning. Cartwright (1959) offered the following general definition of power:

> Power refers to the induction of (psychological) forces by one entity b upon another a
> and to the resistance to this induction set up by a. Because the behavior of a is
> determined by the totality of forces operating upon him at any given time, the power of
> b over a is concerned only with those influences on a's behavior originating with b.
> (p. 188)

Thibaut and Kelley (1959) argued, "Generally, we can say that the power of A over B increases with A's ability to affect the quality of outcomes attained by B" (p. 101). They further distinguished between two types of power: (a) fate control and (b) behavior control. A has fate control over B when A can determine B's outcomes regardless of the behaviors that B enacts. Behavior control is achieved by A when variations in his or her behavior "make it desirable for B to vary his behavior too" (p. 103). Thibaut and Kelley also differentiated between power that is usable from power that is unusable. They argued that, if person B can exercise counterpower over A, then A may refrain from attempting to influence B because B can influence A's outcomes. In their view, the extent to which one person in the relationship is dependent on the other for his or her outcomes determines the degree to which the partner has power over the dependent individual. Emerson (1962) made a similar point when he observed, "The power of A over B is equal to, and based upon, the dependence of B upon A" (p. 33). Finally, in discussing the nature of power, Blau (1964) stated:

> It is the ability of persons or groups to impose their wills on others despite resistance
> through deterrence either in the form of withholding regularly supplied rewards or in
> the form of punishment, inasmuch as the former as well as the latter constitute, in
> effect, a negative sanction. (p. 117)

In Blau's view, power is asymmetrical; thus, when persons are interdependent and can influence each other to an equal degree, each individual lacks power. By contrast, Thibaut and Kelley (1959) argued that, when persons are highly dependent on each other, they have high power over each other.

Although the above definitions of social power have been advanced by researchers representing a variety of theoretical perspectives, they share two principal commonalities. First, these definitions point to the ability of power wielders to produce changes in the behavior and/or affect of their relational partners. People who have power can produce effects in others. Second, a number of the definitions point to the fact that the abilities of targets to resist influence or to affect the outcomes of the individuals making influence attempts are related to the ability of influence agents to exercise power over targets. Many of the definitions imply that power is an attribute of a relationship between people rather than an attribute of a single individual (Cartwright, 1959; Emerson, 1962; Winter, 1973).

The definitions also vary with respect to their approach to the issue of intentionality. Some of the definitions stress that power is achieved only when intended effects are produced, whereas others do not directly address this issue. In the definitions proposed by Dahl (1957) and Thibaut and Kelley (1959), for example, individuals might exercise considerable influence over others without intending to do so but still be credited with possessing power over the others in question. By contrast, Russell (1938) and Winter (1973) explicitly restricted their definitions to intended effects; however, Winter (1973) left open the possibility of producing intended effects unconsciously. While the intentionality issue cannot be treated in detail here, some clarity might be introduced into the discussion by distinguishing between influence *goals,* on the one hand, and the *plans* that individuals use to achieve their goals, on the other (Berger, 1987, 1988, in press; Berger & diBattista, 1992; Berger & Jordan, 1992; Berger, Karol, & Jordan, 1989). Given this distinction, an influence agent could have an explicit intention to reach a particular influence goal but have no specific, well-thought-out plan for so doing. In this situation, individuals might successfully reach influence goals but be unable to articulate how they were able to accomplish the task. While the distinction between goal and plan intentions may serve a useful purpose, some theorists have argued that plans themselves imply commitments to action and are sets of intentions (Bratman, 1987, 1990), while others have viewed plans as cognitive structures that guide action (Brand, 1984; De Lisi, 1987; G. A. Miller, Galanter, & Pribram, 1960). These definitional disputes notwithstanding, it seems reasonable to insist that power be defined in terms of the production of intended effects if intentionality refers to goal achievement; however, it does not seem reasonable to argue that plan intentionality be included in a definition of social power.

Another way in which these definitions differ is with respect to the issue of the asymmetry of power relations. As noted previously, Blau (1964) viewed power as an inherently asymmetrical relationship, whereas Thibaut and Kelley (1959) allowed for the possibility that two persons could simultaneously exercise power over each other. Emerson's (1962) analysis leads to a conclusion similar to Thibaut and Kelley's (1959). If power is a relationship attribute rather than an individual attribute, it seems reasonable to suggest that persons can exert mutual power over each other. Certainly, it is possible for two persons to influence each other with respect to different issues; person A influences B with respect to issue X, while person B influences A with respect to issue Y. Both individuals show evidence of power over each other but in different domains of influence. Wolfe (1959) argued that husbands and wives in conjugal dyads with an autonomic authority structure exercise influence in this manner.

A number of theorists have identified several different types of power. Perhaps the most widely cited analysis of this kind was presented by French and Raven (1959) and was subsequently modified by Collins and Raven (1969) and Raven (1965). In this typology, *informational power* is attitude or behavior change produced by the content of the influence attempt itself. *Coercive power* is based upon the ability of the influence agent to mediate punishments for the person being influenced. By contrast, *reward power* refers to the ability of the influence agent to mediate rewards for the influence. *Legitimate power* stems from the belief on the part of those being influenced that the agent of influence has the right to influence them. *Referent power* arises when individuals use groups as frames of reference for making judgments about the appropriateness of their attitudes and/or behavior. *Expert power* is based upon the influencee's belief that the source of influence has knowledge relevant to the domain of influence.

In another widely cited typology of social influence processes, Kelman (1958, 1961) distinguished among three processes of social influence: (a) compliance, (b) identification, and (c) internalization. Compliance occurs when a person accepts influence from a source to gain rewards, avoid punishments, or both. Identification happens when individuals accept influence "because this behavior is associated with a satisfying self-defining relationship to this person or group" (Kelman, 1961, p. 63). Internalization is the acceptance of the induced behavior because it is consistent with the individual's value system. Clearly, compliance is similar to coercive and reward power, whereas identification is similar to referent power. Internalization seems to include elements of both informational and expert power.

Wheeless, Barraclough, and Stewart (1983) attempted to subsume the typologies of French and Raven (1959) and Kelman (1958, 1961), as well as those of Etzioni (1961) and Parsons (1963), into three categories of power types: (a) preview expectations/consequences, (b) invoke relationships/identification, and (c) summon values/obligations. Types of power in the first category include reward and coercive. Expert and referent power as well as identification are included in the second category, and legitimate power and internalization are placed in the third category. These authors employed the three categories as a potential way in which to organize the diffuse literature related to the study of compliance-gaining strategies. Although the French and Raven (1959) and Kelman (1958, 1961) typologies, as well as others, have been frequently cited in the literature, they have not stimulated a great deal of research. In part, this lack of heuristic power can be explained by the fact that, although taxonomies may aid in understanding the complexities of the power construct itself, they do not constitute explanatory theories of social power. Consequently, they are not capable of generating numerous hypotheses for empirical research. This observation should not be construed as an indictment of taxonomies, but it is meant to indicate that theoretical elaboration beyond the taxonomy is necessary before such presentations can become significant generative mechanisms for programmatic research.

Individual Approaches to Social Power

Because it already has been observed that social power is an attribute of a relationship rather than an individual, it may seem paradoxical to have a section of this chapter dealing with "individual approaches to social power." It should be noted, however, that not only is there a substantial tradition of social power research that focuses upon the individual, but some researchers in this individually oriented tradition explicitly acknowledge that social power is a characteristic of a relationship and not an individual (Winter, 1973). Moreover, it is probably safe to say that most researchers considered here view individual power strivings as at least partially the product of social forces; that is, power strivings are acquired through interactions with significant others. Thus, although the focus of these efforts is on the individual, the importance of social interaction in the acquisition and performance of power-related behaviors is not lost. Minton (1967) has discussed a number of issues concerning the relationships between power and personality.

Freudian and neo-Freudian approaches. Adler (1927, 1930, 1966) distinguished between healthy and neurotic strivings for power. Healthy striving for superiority is balanced against social interest, whereas neurotic power strivings may be the product of an early inferiority complex. Horney (1937) also stressed the difference between the desire for power that comes from a sense of strength and that which stems from feelings of weakness and insecurity. Horney argued that persons with a neurotic need for power try to avoid situations in which they are relatively helpless; moreover, such persons have a need to dominate others and have strong inhibitions against domineering behavior. Freud (1924) contended that ego strength and narcissism are positively related and that power strivings are part of narcissism. Horney's (1937) notion that persons with neurotic needs for power wish to dominate others but have strong inhibitions against domineering behavior is similar to Haley's (1959, 1962) argument, based upon the thinking of Bateson, Jackson, Haley, and Weakland (1956), that families that contain schizophrenic members tend to avoid direct attempts to influence each other even when they wish to exert control. In these families, influence is exerted indirectly. Some evidence supporting this position is reported by Mishler and Waxler (1968).

The distinction between power strivings arising from a sense of mastery and competence, and power strivings produced by a sense of inferiority and weakness, is one that has not received much attention in the power literature. Winter (1973) is one of the few exceptions to this generalization because he distinguished between hope for power and fear of power. It is reasonable to suppose that power strivings emanating from these two different bases should produce quite different types of communication aimed at producing social influence. Moreover, given this distinction, considerable variation in the modes of resistance to influence would be expected. For example, persons whose power strivings stem from feelings of inferiority might be more prone to reject opposing positions out of hand and to refuse to be accommodative. Stylistic differences in modes of attempted influence and modes of resistance that are rooted in different bases for power striving are deserving of research attention.

Motivational approaches. Theorists who have examined power as a motive have generally worked from the perspective presented by Murray (1938). Murray's theory of personality contained a number of different needs that include need for dominance (*n* Dominance). Murray (1938) noted that *n* Dominance might, at times, fuse with needs for aggression or achievement. Veroff (1957, 1958) presented a conceptualization of need for power (*n* Power) and developed a projective technique for measuring the construct. Veroff and Veroff (1972) reviewed several studies that employed the Veroff measure. Veroff's general concern was to measure the desire for power. On the basis of several studies, Veroff and Veroff (1972) asserted that the power incentive should not be looked upon as a positive goal in which one derives joy from influencing others but as a negative goal in which one avoids feelings of powerlessness.

In attempting to improve Veroff's measure of *n* Power, Uleman (1972) found evidence for a construct he labeled need for influence (*n* Influence). Persons with high levels of *n* Influence are those who enjoy influencing others for the sake of seeing themselves being influential (positive incentive). Winter (1973) also developed an alternative way to measure *n* Power that explicitly differentiated between hope for power (positive incentive) and fear of power (negative incentive). Hope for power involves the active attempt to influence others, whereas fear of power is concerned with the avoidance of others' influence. Winter (1973) presented evidence indicating that the measures of *n* Power developed by Veroff, Uleman, and Winter showed low to moderate correlations with each other. These data suggest that *n* Power is a multidimensional construct in need of further explication.

The authoritarian personality. As part of their study of the relationship between political ideology and personality functioning, Adorno, Frenkel-Brunswick, Levinson, and Sanford (1950) found that persons with high levels of authoritarianism not only showed greater concern for power in their relationships with others, they also tended to admire uncritically persons who were in positions of power. Moreover, high authoritarians expected persons with lower power to accept without question influence from persons with higher power levels. Adorno et al. (1950) reported additional relationships between authoritarianism and such variables as ethnocentrism, political-economic conservatism, and prejudice; however, a methodological critique of the research by Christie and Jahoda (1954) called into question a number of the findings reported in *The Authoritarian Personality.* In Rokeach's (1960) work on general authoritarianism or dogmatism, he suggested that persons with closed systems of thinking and believing are likely to feel alone and helpless. As a consequence, they may develop feelings of self-inadequacy and self-hate. These feelings might be overcome by being excessively concerned with power and status. One of the subcomponents of his dogmatism scale is purported to measure these concerns.

Alienation is a concept related to feelings of inadequacy. Although this concept was developed within the context of sociological inquiry and not as part of the research on authoritarianism and dogmatism, it does seem to be related to these constructs. Seeman (1959) argued that felt powerlessness is a subcomponent of alienation, and Nettler (1957) and Srole (1956) developed measures of alienation. If powerlessness is a component of alienation, then one would expect persons with high levels of alienation to be closed-minded and highly authoritarian.

Locus of control. In his discussion of phenomenal causality, Heider (1958) distinguished between internal and external causality. As we observe ourselves and others, we may infer that particular events are caused by factors that reside within the individual, such as ability or motivation, or factors that reside outside of the individual, such as task difficulty or luck. Ability and task difficulty are relatively stable factors, whereas motivation and luck are less stable. Rotter (1966) made a distinction similar to Heider's in his discussion of locus of control. To Rotter, locus of control is a set of generalized expectations for internal or external control of reinforcement. He distinguished between the two as follows:

> When a reinforcement is perceived by the subject as following some action of his own but not being entirely contingent upon his action, then, in our culture, it is typically perceived

as the result of luck, chance, fate, as under the control of powerful others, or as unpredictable because of the great complexity of forces surrounding him. When the event is interpreted in this way, we have labeled this a belief in external control. If the person perceives that the event is contingent upon his own behavior or his own relatively permanent characteristics, we have termed this a belief in internal control. (Rotter, 1966, p. 1)

deCharms (1968, 1972) differentiated between "origins" and "pawns." In discussing the construct of personal causation, he argued:

When a person initiates intentional behavior, he experiences himself as having originated the intention and the behavior. He is the locus of causality of the behavior and he is said to be intrinsically motivated. Since he himself is the originator, we refer to the person as an origin. When something external to the person impels him to behavior, he experiences himself as the instrument of the outside source, and the outside source is the locus of causality. He is said to be extrinsically motivated. Since the person is impelled from without we refer to him as a pawn. We sometimes talk of people as primarily pawns implying that they more characteristically see themselves pushed around by outside forces. Conversely, we refer to people as primarily origins implying that they characteristically see themselves as originating their own behavior. (deCharms, 1972, pp. 66-67)

In an overview of the locus of control research, Lefcourt (1976) pointed out that, although Rotter (1966) and deCharms (1968, 1972) made dichotomous distinctions, both theorists conceived of locus of control as a continuous variable. Collins (1974) found that Rotter's (1966) locus of control construct involved four distinct beliefs. Individuals might be external because they believe that the world is (a) difficult, (b) unjust, (c) governed by luck, or (d) politically unresponsive.

Although power per se is not mentioned in the definitions advanced by Rotter (1966) and deCharms (1972), it is obvious that persons with high levels of internal locus of control or origins are those who believe that they are responsible for effecting change in their environments, whereas their externally controlled or pawn counterparts feel that they are controlled by their environments. Because several of the definitions of social power reviewed earlier emphasized the notion that persons with power are able to effect changes in the behavior or attitudes of others, these locus of control measures may represent attitudes or beliefs individuals have about their abilities to exercise influence.

Machiavellianism. Drawing upon the writings of Machiavelli, whose insights into the wielding of power are still studied some 450 years after their origination, Christie and Geis (1970) developed a scale designed to measure the construct of Machiavellianism. A majority of the items on the scale were taken from Machiavelli's *The Prince* and the *Discourses*. Christie and Geis (1970) argued that, to be an effective manipulator, a person must possess the following four characteristics:

(a) a relative lack of emotions in interpersonal relationships,

(b) a lack of concern for conventional morality,

(c) a lack of gross psychopathology, and

(d) low ideological commitment.

Persons who become emotionally involved in relationships are likely to distort their perceptions of their relationship partners to such a degree that they are unable to understand how they might be able to wield influence over them. The lack of concern for conventional morality enables the manipulator to use any means to achieve the goal of influence. Lacking gross psychopathology is critical for the accurate social perception necessary to understand how one might influence another. Finally, low ideological commitment enables individuals to be flexible in the stand they take on issues. People not committed to a particular ideology can change their positions when it is to their advantage for achieving their goals. Those who are highly committed lack such flexibility. Both Christie and Geis (1970) and Guterman (1970) reported evidence that provides partial support for this conceptualization of the high Machiavellian.

Summary. Several of the constructs discussed here are directly related to individual strivings for power, whereas others are obviously related to power but the term itself is not employed in their definition. Machiavellianism, *n* Power, and *n* Influence are constructs that centrally concern the exercise of power. The differences among them appear to be stylistic. For example, Uleman (1972) suggested that persons with high levels of *n* Influence are likely to exercise influence in relatively subtle ways. By contrast, persons with high levels of *n* Power are likely to assert their power in a group by being loud, cantankerous, and obnoxious. Uleman (1972) observed that *n* Power may arise out of feelings of inferiority, whereas *n* Influence may be based on feelings of mastery and effectance (White, 1959). It seems possible that both *n* Power and *n* Influence might differ sharply from Machiavellianism. Evidence supporting this possibility is presented by both Uleman (1972) and Winter (1973). Uleman found no relationship between Veroff's (1957) measure of *n* Power and Machiavellianism. Winter (1973) also found no relationship between his *n* Power measure and Machiavellianism. However, Uleman (1972) found a negative relationship (r = −.31) between *n* Influence and Machiavellianism; high *n* Influence individuals tended to be low in Machiavellianism. These findings suggest that, although persons may have a general concern for exerting influence, there are subtle differences in the constraints they will place upon their influence behaviors and considerable variation in the styles with which they will exercise influence. Given these findings, it seems likely that Norton's (1983) dominant communicator style dimension might actually consist of a number of stylistic subtypes.

Although not dealing directly with power-related issues, such constructs as authoritarianism, dogmatism, and locus of control are related to the exercise of power. Here, too, there is the possibility that some of these constructs—for example, authoritarianism and dogmatism—may be concerned with issues of influence style, whereas locus of control is more concerned with beliefs in one's ability to exercise control over one's environment. A detailed analysis of the possible stylistic differences that might be displayed between high authoritarians and persons with high levels of *n* Power, *n* Influence, and Machiavellianism cannot be presented here. However, it would be fruitful to assess the discriminant validity of these constructs.

Interaction Approaches to Power

Theorists who focus upon social relationships between individuals rather than upon individuals themselves will be considered in this section. As a consequence of this relational focus, these theorists view power as the product of interactions between people and not the result of individuals' desires to wield influence over others. It should be pointed out, however, that, in spite of their interactional approach, some of these theorists explicitly recognize that people may vary in their individual desires to influence others (Thibaut & Kelley, 1959). Although these individual needs for power may exist, they tend to be ignored in the theories themselves, however.

Social exchange theories. In general, this genre of theory seeks to explain the development, maintenance, and decay of social relationships in terms of the balance between the rewards that persons obtain and the costs that they incur by selecting themselves into various social relationships. There are a number of such theories (Adams, 1965; Blau, 1964; Foa & Foa, 1974; Homans, 1961; Kelley & Thibaut, 1978; Thibaut & Kelley, 1959; Walster, Walster, & Berscheid, 1978) that differ somewhat from each other. These relatively subtle differences cannot be dealt with in detail here; however, Roloff (1981) discussed several of these theories in detail, pointing out the differences among them. Because both Blau (1964) and Thibaut and Kelley (1959) presented extended discussions of power, their theories will be examined here.

Thibaut and Kelley (1959) argued that when two persons are involved in a relationship they both can choose to enact various behaviors that when considered jointly may produce various configurations of outcomes (rewards and costs) for each party in the relationship. They further asserted that each individual in the relationship evaluates his or her outcomes against two standards: (a) comparison level (CL) and (b) comparison level for alternatives (CL_{alt}). CL involves the comparison between the individuals' internal standards and the particular relationships in which they are involved. By contrast, CL_{alt} is the comparison between the particular relationship and all other alternative relationships that are available to the individual, plus the alternative of remaining alone. Thibaut and Kelley's explicit reason for postulating these two comparison levels was to explain why persons remain in what appear to be extremely undesirable relationships with others. Individuals might evaluate relationships in which they are involved quite negatively, but the available alternatives, including being alone, might be so much more aversive that the individuals choose to remain in their current relationships. Relationships will survive to the extent that those involved in them experience outcomes that are above CL_{alt}. CL is critical in determining one's *attraction* to a relationship, whereas CL_{alt} is an important determinant of an individual's *dependency* on the relationship.

Thibaut and Kelley (1959) argued that, as outcomes become more favorable, that is, as people receive more rewards at less cost, and these outcomes begin to exceed CL_{alt}, the individual becomes more dependent upon the relationship. The level of dependency on the relationship for satisfaction is directly related to the amount of power the individual has in the relationship. Greater dependency on the relationship lessens one's power in the relationship. Conversely, the less one is dependent upon the relationship for favorable outcomes, the more power one has within the relationship. This hypothesis is similar to one advanced by Waller and Hill (1951), which they labeled the "Principle of Least Interest." This principle asserts that, in romantic relationships, the least interested party is more powerful. This is so because the people who are more dependent upon their relationships for rewards are at the mercy of the less interested parties.

As was pointed out earlier, Thibaut and Kelley (1959) differentiated between fate control and behavior control. In the fate control situation, the behavioral alternatives chosen by one person in the relationship completely determine the outcomes of the other person, no matter what behaviors the other person chooses. This situation is much like that of pawns or people who are externally controlled. No matter what they do, their environment, in this case their interaction partner, determines their outcomes. In the case of behavior control, the ability of more powerful people to exercise influence over their partner's outcomes is considerably less profound. Variations in the more powerful individuals' behaviors produce variations in the behaviors of the less powerful. Of course, it is possible for less powerful people to choose to enact behaviors that will reduce the outcomes of the individuals with greater power; however, Thibaut and Kelley (1959) observed that individuals with higher levels of fate control and behavior control can be more directive in interactions with their less powerful counterparts and can use their abilities to deliver large amounts of rewards to enhance their power. As a consequence, there is a tendency for the powerful to become more powerful in relationships; although, if power is overused, those who are subjected to it may choose to leave the relationship and obviate the ability of more powerful people to wield their power.

Consistent with Thibaut and Kelley's (1959) analysis of dependence and power is Blau's (1964) assertion that "regular rewards make recipients dependent on the supplier and subject to his power, since they engender expectations that make their discontinuation a punishment" (p. 116); hence the person who can supply services that others demand can exercise power over them. Blau outlined four conditions that give rise to social independence and thus reduce the likelihood that one will be subjected to another's power. First, if individuals possess strategic resources, they are likely to be more independent. Second, the more alternative sources of supply people have, the more likely they are to be socially independent. This condition is similar to Thibaut and Kelley's (1959) concept of CL_{alt}. Third, if coercive force can be used to compel suppliers to render services, then dependency will be reduced. Included in this condition is the possibility of forming coalitions to force dispensing of needed services. Fourth, people can reduce their needs for various services, thus reducing their dependence upon suppliers.

The four conditions that promote social independence can be employed to delineate four strategies that can be used to acquire and maintain power. First, power wielders who dispense valuable services to others must remain indifferent to the services others might be able to provide them. Obviously, if power holders were to become dependent upon services offered by others, they would become subject to their power. Second, the powerful must ensure that those who are dependent upon them do not have access to alternative sources of supply for their needs and wants. Such alternative sources weaken dependence and thus reduce power. Third, people in powerful positions must be certain that those who are in the subordinate position cannot employ coercive force to obtain their supplies. As a result, powerful individuals might take steps to discourage the formation of coalitions among those who are dependent upon them. Finally, power wielders must ensure that those who are dependent upon them for their supplies do not change their needs so that the value of their supplies diminishes; thus powerful individuals may have a vested interest in maintaining the status quo in order to ensure the continued dependency of their subordinates.

Blau (1964) argued that sheer dependence upon a person for benefits gives that individual potential power; it is only when the person delivers these benefits that his or her power is actualized. He contended that, as individuals' power increases, those who are subject to their power are more eager to do the powerful individuals' bidding; furthermore, increased power enables power holders to risk some power to gain even more power. Like Thibaut and Kelley (1959), Blau (1964) suggested that the powerful tend to become more powerful; however, power tends to be expended by its use. Consequently, if powerful persons overuse their power, those who are dependent upon them may resort to one or more of the four strategies for social independence outlined previously.

The views of power advanced by Blau (1964) and Thibaut and Kelley (1959) share a considerable number of commonalities. Perhaps the most important of these is the idea that, in social relationships, power is not simply determined by the actions of one individual but by the joint actions of relationship partners. Because of this fact, people who are subject to others' influence can enact behavioral alternatives that may reduce others' power. Moreover, these theories suggest that powerful people are never completely secure in their superior positions. Needs and wants may change, thus redefining what is rewarding and costly to subordinates. Radical changes in these domains might completely eliminate dependence and reduce power to almost nil. One of the most consistent demonstrations of this kind of shift involves the relationship between parents and their children. Parents have considerable power over children when children are dependent upon them for various resources; however, as children become capable of obtaining their resources from alternative sources, their dependence upon parents diminishes, thus reducing the power of parents to influence them. Blood and Wolfe (1960) have made a similar argument in the domain of marital relationships. Their resource theory asserts that the spouse who brings the largest number of resources to the relationship, relative to those provided by the other spouse, exerts the greatest amount of power in the relationship. There is a considerable literature (Berger, 1980) demonstrating that spouses who have greater incomes, educational levels, and social participation tend to be seen as exerting more power in the marital relationship.

Relational control. The central assumption underlying the relational control perspective is that, when persons interact with each other, the messages that they exchange communicate at two different levels simultaneously. The content level is concerned with the literal meaning of the message, while the relationship level is concerned with what the message implies about the relationship between the persons involved in the interaction (Watzlawick, Beavin, & Jackson, 1967). The distinction between content and relationship communication levels is similar to Ruesch and Bateson's (1951) notions of the report and command functions of messages. Relationship-level communication indicates how the literal content of the message should be taken and is thus metacommunicative. The two imperative statements, "Shut the door," and "If it isn't too much trouble, could you please close the door," are quite similar on the content level, in that they both request that the auditor shut the door; however, the two statements imply very different kinds of relationships between the speaker and the auditor.

A number of interaction coding systems have been developed to measure relationship-level communication or relational control (Ellis, Fisher, Drecksel, Hoch, & Werber, 1976; Ericson & Rogers, 1973; Folger & Puck, 1976; Mark, 1971; Rogers & Farace, 1975). The one developed by Rogers and Farace (1975) has generated the most subsequent research, although the system developed by Ellis et al. (1976) has also produced several studies (for example, Drecksel & Fisher, 1977;

Ellis, 1979). Because of the heuristic provocativeness of the Rogers and Farace coding system, their position is examined in greater detail.

Following Watzlawick et al. (1967), Rogers and Farace (1975) distinguished among three types of relational control: (a) symmetry, (b) transitory, and (c) complementarity. In contrasting symmetrical and complementary transactions, Rogers and Farace (1975) assert:

> In a symmetrical transaction or relationship, one interactor behaves toward the other as the other behaves toward him. There is an equivalence of conduct between the two individuals: there is a symmetry of relational control. In a complementary transaction, however, the interactors' behaviors are maximally differentiated. The control definition offered by one interactor is accepted by the other. (p. 226)

When there is a movement toward neutralizing control by one or both parties in the interaction, a transitory type of relational control is being exhibited. Using their coding system, individuals' messages can be classified as either one up, one down, or neutralizing, based upon certain grammatical and stylistic attributes. One-up messages represent bids for relational control or dominance, whereas one-down messages indicate acceptance of the other's control or the yielding of control. Neutralizing messages are those that attempt to neutralize control.

Critical to the relational control position is the argument that, to understand fully how relational control is exercised in interaction sequences, pairs of messages exchanged between interactants must be employed as the unit of analysis rather than the messages of each individual in the interaction. For example, if two persons, A and B, are involved in an interaction, they might exchange the following sequence of messages: ABABABABAB. According to the relational control perspective, the most appropriate way to determine who is exerting the most control in the relationship is to classify the first message from A as either one up, one down, or neutralizing and then to classify B's response to that message into one of the same three categories. Then, using B's message as a beginning point, one classifies A's second message as a response to B's, and so on. The important point is that one cannot determine whether or not a particular control move has been "successful" unless one knows the response that was made to the move. The coding of successive pairs of messages provides more information about relational control than does the study of messages sent by individuals.

Rogers and Farace (1975) underscored the importance of a dyadic level of analysis in the study of relational control by asserting:

> A distinctive aspect of relational analysis is that it necessitates at least a dyadic level of analysis, in contrast to the more predominant monadic analyses. Whether the transaction is symmetrical or complementary, both interactors must participate in the definition of the relationship. Thus, the smallest unit of relational analysis is a paired exchange of two messages. (p. 226)

Although this is an important point, it should be noted that the social exchange theories discussed in the previous section make a similar set of assumptions. Recall that, in Thibaut and Kelley's (1959) approach, interaction outcomes are generally jointly determined by the behavioral alternatives enacted by the parties involved in the interaction. Moreover, Blau's (1964) analyses of the conditions of social dependence and social independence both recognized the contingent nature of power relationships. Power holders can lose their abilities to exercise influence if those dependent upon them find alternative sources of supply for their wants or adjust their needs so that they no longer require certain resources. Even though a particular person is able to dispense potentially large numbers of resources and thus acquire considerable power, unless there are people who need those copious resources, the individual's ability to exercise power will be severely limited. Obviously, in this case, both interactors participate in the definition of the power relationship.

One important contribution of the relational control position is its focus upon actual messages that are exchanged between persons. However, Folger and Poole (1982) and Berger (1983) have raised questions concerning the ability of a perspective that focuses solely upon message exchanges, and does not consider the interpretations that social actors have of these messages, to adequately explain control patterns in ongoing interactions. The problem raised by these authors can be illustrated by asking the question of whether or not persons who are involved in interactions interpret one-up, one-down, or neutralizing messages in the same way that the Rogers and Farace (1975) coding system indicates they might. In terms of participants' judgments concerning dominance or control in relationships, it would seem critical to establish whether or not the control moves represented in the Rogers and Farace coding system are actually perceived that way by interactors; for it is these judgments about dominance and control that may be instrumental in producing interpersonal conflict and alterations in the courses of relationships.

Summary. In this section, interactive approaches to the study of power have been examined. These perspectives define power or control as properties of relationships rather than individuals. These positions stand in marked contrast to those that view power as a property of individuals; however, there is no necessary incompatibility between these views. Kipnis (1976) developed a descriptive model of the power act consisting of seven steps: (a) power motivation, (b) request for compliance, (c) resources, (d) region of inhibition, (e) means of influence, (f) response of target, and (g) consequences for power holder. His model begins from an individual orientation (power motivation) and becomes more "interactive" as it progresses. Certainly, individuals approach interactions with differing predispositions for exercising power; however, it is equally true that the local conditions of exchange can alter significantly the manifestations of these predispositions. Consequently, both perspectives are necessary for a complete understanding of how power is exercised in social interactions.

Measuring Social Power

Here, various approaches to the measurement of social power are considered. Research that has compared various measurement approaches is also discussed. The three general classes of measures examined are projective tests, self-report measures, and indices of power derived from interaction behaviors. Frequently, studies employ some combination of these approaches. For example, several studies conducted by family sociologists and clinical psychologists have presented family members with the task of arriving at a consensus decision. Before the discussion begins, individual preferences are assessed through self-reports. The issue is then discussed. At the conclusion of the discussion, a decision is reached and recorded. Given these data, one can compare the pre- and postdiscussion verbal reports to determine the extent to which each group member influenced the final decision, for example, how the family might spend a gift of $1,000. Also, the audio- or video-tapes of the discussion can be analyzed to determine who dominated the discussion. Measures of power based on pre-post comparisons are termed *outcome power measures,* whereas measures of power based upon attributes of the interaction itself are called *measures of process power.* The question of how these two approaches to measuring power relate to each other will be addressed.

Projective measures. Veroff (1957, 1958), Uleman, (1972), and Winter (1973) have all used the Thematic Apperception Test (TAT) as a way of measuring the individual's need to exercise power. This test consists of presenting individuals with ambiguous pictures and having them write stories about the characters in the pictures. The stories are then analyzed using coding schemes that contain various power-related themes. The more of these themes that are present in the story, the more the individual's fantasy life is dominated by power imagery. The use of this approach assumes that the fantasy themes that are included in the stories are indicators of their authors' need states.

The coding schemes are developed by placing people in situations in which their need for power is likely to be aroused. While in the arousal situation, individuals complete the TAT. Their story responses are then compared with those of a group of individuals who have completed the TAT under neutral conditions. Themes that appear in the stories written under aroused conditions that do not appear in stories written under neutral conditions are taken to be indicators of aroused power motivation. Veroff's (1957, 1958) arousal situation was one in which candidates for student government offices were waiting to learn whether or not they had won an election. Uleman (1972) placed individuals in a gambling situation in which they could exercise considerable control as a way of arousing the power motive. Winter (1973) aroused the power motive by having participants watch a film of John F. Kennedy's inaugural speech.

As noted earlier, Winter (1973) reported that the same stories scored by the three systems outlined above do not produce power motivation scores that correlate highly with each other. There are at least two explanations for this lack of convergence. First, as Murray (1938) pointed out, the arousal of n Dominance might also lead to the arousal of such related motives as n Achievement and n Aggression. Situations designed to arouse the power motive and produce power fantasy in TAT stories might also produce imagery related to these other motives, resulting in confounded coding schemes. Second, the arousal situations employed by these three researchers are vastly different. Veroff's election arousal situation seemed to be aimed at producing a concern for achieving status in an organization, while Uleman's (1972) situation involved the exercise of influence in a face-to-face interaction context. Winter's (1973) approach seemed to be directed toward raising concern for the exercise of political power. It could be that n Power is considerably more domain-specific than first thought; that is, there may not be a general need for power but differential desires to exercise power in different social domains. Researchers intending to use this approach to study power should examine these three scoring systems very carefully. There appears to be considerable ambiguity concerning what each one of the three approaches to n Power measures.

Another projective measure of power was reported by Klopper, Tittler, Friedman, and Hughes (1978). These researchers were interested in determining how family members perceived the prominence of others in their family. Rather than asking family members to respond verbally to this question, family members were individually given the task of arranging figures representing family members on a felt board in any way they wished. Prominence was measured by examining figure placement and figure height. Figures placed on the left-hand side of the board and figures placed higher relative to the others were scored as more prominent. The correlation between these two measures was .64. Moreover, based upon observations of family interaction in a decision-making task, measures of individual family members' talk time and communication received correlated moderately well with the two prominence measures, with correlations ranging from .46 to .68. These findings stand in marked contrast to those of Turk and Bell (1972), who found that verbal reports of who is most powerful in the family did not generally correlate well with interaction-based measures of family power.

Self-report measures. There are a number of different approaches to the measurement of power through self-report instruments. First, there are numerous personality inventories—for example, the California Personality Inventory (CPI)—that contain dominance scales. These scales consist of items that ask the respondents for evaluations of their ability to exercise influence. Uleman (1972) reported that his projective measure of *n* Influence correlated .31 (p < .05) with the CPI dominance scale, but Winter (1973) failed to find any relationship between his measure of *n* Power and the same CPI dominance scale. In addition to personality inventories containing dominance scales are specific scales designed to measure the following constructs explicated previously: Machiavellianism (Christie & Geis, 1970), locus of control (Rotter, 1966), authoritarianism (Adorno et al., 1950), and dogmatism (Rokeach, 1960). Other scales have been devised to index various power-related communication attributes. Infante and Rancer (1982) developed an argumentiveness scale that shows virtually no relationship to their verbal aggressiveness scale (Infante & Wigley, 1986). Those with high argumentiveness tend to enjoy debating issues and arguing the relative merits of others' attitudes and beliefs on various issues. By contrast, highly verbally aggressive individuals attack the self-concepts of others by "putting them down" (Infante, 1987).

There are self-report measures that ask respondents to indicate the extent to which they feel power relative to another person or persons. For example, Heer (1958) asked married couples "who *won*" when there was a disagreement between them. Blood and Wolfe (1960) asked wives to indicate the extent to which they or their husbands were responsible for making decisions across eight decision areas. For each decision area, respondents indicated on a five-point scale the extent to which the husband or wife had influence. This technique has become one of the mainstay self-report measures of family sociologists interested in family power and has been employed in numerous studies (Blood, 1967; Burchinal & Bauder, 1965; Buric & Zecevic, 1967; Burr et al., 1977; Centers, Raven, & Rodrigues, 1971; Cromwell & Cromwell, 1978; Kandel & Lesser, 1972; Lamouse, 1969; Lupri, 1969; Michel, 1967; Price-Bonham, 1976; Safilios-Rothschild, 1967; Turk & Bell, 1972). Finally, Turk and Bell (1972) asked family members to answer the question, "Who is the boss in your family?"

Although the Blood and Wolfe (1960) self-report measure of power has been widely used, Heer (1963) and Safilios-Rothschild (1969, 1970) have warned that, because only wives were interviewed in several studies, there is no guarantee that if husbands responded to the same set of items their responses would be similar to those of their wives. In fact, several studies (Burchinal & Bauder, 1965; Buric &

Zecevic, 1967; Douglas & Wind, 1978; Heer, 1962; Larson, 1974; Olson & Rabunsky, 1972; Turk & Bell, 1972) have demonstrated that family members frequently disagree when they are asked to estimate the extent to which each family member has power. Apparently, perceptions of power may indeed be in the eye of the beholder. Researchers employing this kind of self-report procedure to measure power should be sure to obtain estimates from all group members rather than relying upon the estimates of some subset of a group. Furthermore, at the level of the group, the degree of consensus concerning who is the most powerful member of the group might be an important variable worth studying in its own right. One might expect to find significant differences between groups that vary with respect to the degree of consensus they exhibit about who is the most powerful group member. Highly cohesive groups, for example, might show higher levels of consensus.

Considerable interest has been shown by communication researchers in the study of various compliance-gaining and compliance-resisting strategies. Marwell and Schmitt (1967) devised a list of 16 compliance-gaining techniques including, for example, promise and threat. In an apparently independent effort, Falbo (1977) asked persons to indicate how they "get their way." From these responses, she developed a similar list of 16 power strategies. Falbo and Peplau (1980) examined power strategies that are used in intimate relationships. Schenck-Hamlin, Wiseman, and Georgacarakos (1982) discussed properties that can be used to generate 14 compliance-gaining strategies. Fitzpatrick and Winke (1979) derived a list of five strategies for dealing with interpersonal conflict. McLaughlin, Cody, and Robey (1980) studied strategies that persons employ to resist compliance-gaining attempts. In many of the studies that have used these strategy lists, individuals have been asked to imagine themselves or others in a given situation in which they desire to exercise influence. They are then given a list of strategies that might be used to achieve their objective and asked to indicate on a scale the likelihood that each strategy would be used. These measures are not indices of power per se but represent attempts to assess, via self-reports, the kinds of persuasive messages persons are most likely to create under a specified set of conditions.

Finally, there are numerous studies demonstrating that individuals' judgments of others' communicative action can be decomposed into a number of independent continua, one of which is related to power and dominance (Berlo, Lemert, & Mertz, 1969; Mulac, 1975, 1976; Norton, 1983; Wish et al., 1980; Zahn & Hopper, 1985). Factor-analytic studies of information sources (Berlo et al., 1969) as well as semantic differential evaluations of spoken language (Mulac, 1975, 1976; Zahn & Hopper, 1985) have consistently produced a factor that investigators have labeled "dynamism." Apparently, this dimension is used by perceivers to characterize both discourse itself as well as the individuals who produce it.

Interaction measures. Numerous efforts have been made to make inferences concerning the relative power of group members by observing various attributes of their communication behavior. As described previously, individuals are given a task that involves discussion and their conversations are recorded. Various facets of their verbal and nonverbal communication are then scored to provide estimates of the degree of influence they exerted in the interaction. These communication-based estimates of power are frequently correlated with the outcome of the decision to see whether there is any relationship between influence demonstrated through communicative conduct and influence on the final decision of the group.

In early studies using this approach, Strodtbeck (1951, 1954) had family members discuss an issue about which they disagreed, as determined by individually completed attitude questionnaires. The object of the discussion was to reach a consensus on the issue. The outcome of this "revealed differences" procedure was then correlated with the amount of time each person spoke (Strodtbeck, 1951). This study showed that the family member who spoke the most was the most influential in the final group decision; that is, the process measure of power (amount of talk) was positively related to the outcome measure of power (degree of influence in the decision). Although these early findings were encouraging, subsequent studies failed to find consistent relationships between process and outcome measures. For example, in a tour de force comparison of self-report, process, and outcome power measures, Turk and Bell (1972) failed to find any relationship between the following four process measures: (a) units of action initiated, (b) instrumental acts initiated, (c) index of directive control (Bales, 1950), and (d) interruptions and outcome measures of power derived from the revealed differences procedure and a discussion test developed by Kenkel (1957). This latter procedure asks family members to indicate individually how a sum of money given to the family should be spent. The family is then brought together, and a group consensus is reached. Individual influence is measured by the extent to which each family member's preferences are reflected in the group consensus. Turk and Bell (1972) failed to find consistent relationships between self-report and process measures of power.

Hadley and Jacob (1973) employed total talking time and successful interruptions as process measures of power and a coalition game and a modified version of the revealed differences technique as ways of assessing outcome power. Although the two process measures were significantly related to each other, the outcome measures were not. Furthermore, the outcome measures were not found to be related to the process measures. The finding that the two different tasks used to generate discussion in this study did not yield comparable results in terms of the outcome measures is consistent with the findings of a study reported by Cromwell, Klein, and Wieting (1975). These investigators found that the Kenkel (1957) technique produced interaction measures of power that did not correlate well with interaction measures generated when another discussion technique SIMFAM (Strauss & Tallman, 1971) was employed. It appears that the task given to a group may exert considerable impact upon the process measures that are used to index power.

The general hypothesis underlying the above studies is that persons who are more dominant verbally—that is, those who talk more frequently, longer, interrupt more, and so on—should be more influential in the decision-making outcome of the group. It seems reasonable to suppose, however, that under some circumstances it is what and not how much persons say that allows them to acquire power in a group and thus have greater influence in decision-making outcomes. The "quiet expert" in a problem-solving group, who has the solution to the problem, may have to say very little to influence the group decision. Obviously, to be influential in such a situation, the "quiet expert" must say something; although if persons enter group situations in which other group members already recognize their power, they may be able to exert considerable influence by simply raising an eyebrow or displaying a particular facial expression. It is said that the late Mayor Richard M. Daley of Chicago could determine the outcome of various deliberations by simply nodding his head at the critical moment and remaining silent. There may be good reason to expect very little relationship between process and outcome measures of power in certain situations.

Researchers interested in the relationship between family communication and mental illness have also attempted to index power by studying the communicative conduct of family members. Mishler and Waxler (1968) distinguished between power attained through attention control and power gained through control of the other person. Participation rate, who speaks to whom, and statement length were employed as indices of attention control. Interruptions were used to index direct control of the other person, and questions were employed to assess indirect control of the other person. Murrell and Stachowiak (1967) measured power by counting the number of units of interaction sent and received. Persons who sent more and those who received more were scored as more powerful. Leighton, Stollak, and Ferguson (1971) used number of times talked, duration of times talked, total talk time, and interruptions as measures of control in family interactions. Obviously, the interaction indices of power used by these researchers are very similar to those employed by the family sociologists.

Over the past two decades, considerable research attention has focused on gender differences in speech (Eakins & Eakins, 1978; Key, 1975; Kramarae, 1981; Lakoff, 1975; Pearson, 1985; P. M. Smith, 1979, 1985; Tannen, 1990; Thorne & Henley, 1975; Thorne, Kramarae, & Henley, 1983). One of the central hypotheses underlying this line of research is that gender differences in speech both reflect and support male dominance. Lakoff (1975) pointed to a number of lexical and syntactical forms that she felt typically differ between males and females such that male dominance is sustained. For example, females tend to use weaker expletives than males.

(1)   Darn it! I forgot to return the library book.
(2)   Oh Shit! I forgot to return the library book.

In Lakoff's view, females are more likely to utter sentence 1 than 2. In terms of syntactic differences, she claimed that females use more tag questions than do males. Consider the following two sentences:

(3)   That's a beautiful sunset.
(4)   That's a beautiful sunset, isn't it?

The assertion made in sentence 3 is quite clear. The person uttering it is sure that the sunset is beautiful; however, sentence 4 seems to convey considerably more uncertainty and lack of confidence. Lakoff also proposed that women generally use more formal, grammatically correct language than men. In addition, Lakoff argued that females may indicate uncertainty in their answers to questions by raising the vocal intonation while giving the answer. For example,

(5)   (a) Who is the mayor of Chicago?
        (b) Ah . . . Rich Daley . . . ?

The use of a rising intonation in an answer tends to create the impression that the person uttering the statement is not certain of its correctness; in fact, the answer may become a question to the question asker. A potential alternative explanation for females' use of tag questions and rising intonation when providing answers is that, because females are more socially skilled than males, they employ speech forms that invite responses from their cointeractants. Thus tag questions or the use of rising intonations could be viewed as attempts to encourage one's interaction partner to participate in the conversation. This potential alternative function of tag questions and rising vocal intonations certainly deserves serious consideration by those who examine sex differences in speech. Lakoff also contended that females make more complex requests than do males in order to be less offensive. The following options, for example, might be available for requesting a glass of wine:

(6) (a) Get me a glass of wine.
  (b) How about a glass of wine.
  (c) Will you get me a glass of wine?
  (d) If it isn't asking too much, could you please get me a glass of wine?
  (e) If you don't mind, would you get me a glass of wine, please?

In Lakoff's view, females making a request would be more likely to choose options d and e, while males would be more prone to choose alternatives a and b.

Some have argued that the gender differences suggested above are indicative of a more general speech style dimension that they have labeled "powerful" versus "powerless speech" (Erikson, Lind, Johnson, & O'Barr, 1978; Lind & O'Barr, 1979; O'Barr, 1982). Their observations of witness testimony in courtroom trials led them to conclude that the following features of speech differentiated high and low power witnesses: (a) intensifiers ("so," "very"); (b) hedges ("kinda," "I guess"); (c) especially formal grammar; (d) hesitation forms ("uh," "you know"); (e) gestures; (f) questioning forms (rising intonation in declarative situations); and (g) polite forms ("please," "thank you"). Lower power witnesses tended to use more of these forms. Other investigators have extended this work beyond the courtroom setting (Bradac & Mulac, 1984a, 1984b; Gibbons, Busch, & Bradac, 1991).

This line of research suggests a very different set of communicative behaviors that might be used to index power, when compared with those employed by sociologists of the family and researchers in clinical psychology. These researchers tend to employ relatively gross communication measures to assess power, for example, amount of interaction, whereas the communication researchers tend to look more at particular features of speech and nonverbal behavior as indicative of power differentials in interaction (see Bradac, 1992; Ellyson & Dovidio, 1985; Knapp & Hall, 1992; Liska, 1992). There is no incompatibility between these two lines of research, and they might complement each other. At this juncture, what is needed are measurement studies that examine the extent to which these various measures of power correlate with each other. If they correlate highly, then it might be necessary to measure only a few of them to provide an index of power; however, most probably they will not correlate well with each other, which may mean that there are different facets of power that need to be explicated at the conceptual level.

One difficulty with the interaction-oriented approaches to the measurement of power discussed so far is that they are really not "interactive." Recall that relational approaches to the study of power (Rogers & Farace, 1975) argue that one cannot understand how control patterns develop in relationships unless one studies interlocking pairs of messages. Even if individuals dominate discussions by speaking frequently and for long periods of time, one cannot know how successful their influence attempts have been unless the responses of other group members to the influence attempts are assessed. There are remarkably few studies outside of the relational control literature that have taken into account how successful or unsuccessful a given individual's influence attempts have been, although there are a few (for example, Cromwell et al., 1975).

Because considerable discussion already has been devoted to relational control coding schemes, they will not be described again here; however, it is important to recognize that one of the great strengths of these systems is their emphasis on the exchange of messages as a unit of analysis rather than the individual message. Relational measurement schemes seemingly do a better job of actualizing the notion that power is a relationship attribute. This does not mean that interaction indices of power that are individually based are without value. The relative value of these approaches depends upon the research question being asked. Consequently, in making a choice among these alternative measurement approaches to studying power, it is important that researchers have a clear idea of the assumptions about power they are making so that the most appropriate measurement approach is used.

Summary. In this section, several different approaches to the measurement of social power have been examined. There are numerous projective and self-report measures of power-related constructs that locate power within the individual. In addition, there is considerable literature that has indexed power through the study of interaction behavior. However, when only individual communicative conduct is measured, it is being assumed that power is an individual property. It is only when measurement systems capture the give-and-take between interactants that power is being studied as a relationship property. The study of exchanges over time is considerably more difficult than the study of individuals; however, because this measurement approach is more isomorphic to relationship conceptions of power, it is likely to be potentially more productive.

Social Power and Communicative Conduct

In this section, research that has linked social power with communicative behavior will be discussed. There are three principal ways in which this link can be studied. First, persons' desires for power can be measured and their communication behavior observed. A similar strategy is to place persons in high and low power positions in a group and observe how their role assignments influence their communicative behavior. In both instances, power is the independent variable, and communicative conduct, the dependent variable. A second general approach is to observe or manipulate communicative conduct and have observers make inferences or attributions about the power levels of those whose conduct has been varied. Using this approach, communicative action is the independent variable, and power attributions, the dependent variable. A third approach is to study the mutual influences of communicative conduct and power in an exchange-oriented format. Obviously, in ongoing interactions, communication and power rapidly alternate roles as independent and dependent variables; that is, persons make attributions concerning their own and others' power levels and then communicate on the bases of these inferences. Their conduct based upon these attributions may cause their estimates of power to be updated. Most of the research that has linked power and communication falls into the first two categories.

Communicative Conduct of Power-Oriented Individuals

In this section, two types of studies will be considered: those that measure power as a trait and then attempt to see whether the trait is manifested in interaction behavior and studies that place persons in positions of power to see how they behave vis-à-vis their less powerful counterparts. Germane to the first type of study, some observers have expressed skepticism concerning the relationships between personality traits and communicative action, especially nonverbal communication (Bull, 1983); however, careful studies of these relationships have revealed that nonverbal behaviors manifested during conversations appear to discriminate reliably among selected personality dimensions (Gifford, 1991). Consequently, it seems useful to pursue such relationships, keeping in mind that situational factors may interact with personality predispositions to produce differences in both verbal and nonverbal interaction.

Trait-oriented studies. As a part of an effort to validate his measure of *n* Power, Veroff (1957) reported that persons with high *n* Power levels were more likely to be rated by their instructors as trying to convince others of their views and more argumentative. Terhune (1968) found that men with high *n* Power and low levels of *n* Affiliation and *n* Achievement displayed more exploitative behavior in the Prisoner's Dilemma game. In a review of studies using the Veroff measure of *n* Power, Veroff and Veroff (1972) interpreted the findings of a number of studies as indicating that the measure taps a concern for power that stems from feelings of inferiority rather than from feelings of mastery over the environment. Uleman (1972) reported that, although people scoring high on his measure of *n* Influence were rated by peers as being more dominant, he could find no evidence that high *n* Influence individuals are more argumentative. In fact, he interpreted his data as indicating that those with high *n* Influence do not need to feel that they are "right" and thus be contentious; apparently, high *n* Influence individuals enjoy exercising power in more subtle ways.

Following on the work of Haley (1969), who analyzed the power tactics of Jesus Christ, Winter (1973) argued that, to gain power, individuals must (a) attract attention and (b) surround themselves with a cadre of loyal followers who do not threaten their own visibility. Jesus gained attention by attacking the establishment. His "organization" consisted of relatively obscure disciples. Winter (1973) reported evidence that people scoring high on his measure of *n* Power display similar characteristics. In the area of attention-gaining strategies, he found that individuals with high levels of *n* Power (a) wrote more letters to their school newspaper, (b) displayed their names on the doors of their dormitory rooms more frequently, (c) possessed more status symbols, (d) were perceived to be more dominant in group discussions, and (e) selected seating positions in group discussion situations that would make them more prominent. Winter (1973) also found that those with high *n* Power tended to direct negative or critical remarks to high status persons when they were asked the following question: "If you could say one sentence—any sentence—to anyone, anywhere in the world, in person and without fear of reprisal, what would you say, and to whom?" Those with low *n* Power levels responded to the same question by making a positive remark or a negative remark to a low status person. Winter (1973) interpreted this result as indicating that high *n* Power individuals establish their visibility by attacking established authority. In the domain of maintaining an organization, Winter (1973) found that those with high *n* Power tended to designate as friends those persons whom others rated as relatively unpopular; thus it appears that high *n* Power individuals surround themselves with persons who are not likely to threaten their visibility.

Other studies employing Winter's (1973) *n* Power measure have reported findings that lend support to his analysis. High *n* Power persons placed in supervisory roles during an industrial simulation situation rated themselves to be more influential than low n Power individuals placed in the same roles (Fodor & Farrow, 1979). Fodor and Smith (1982) found that those with high n Power who were placed in leadership positions in decision-making groups were rated more influential in the decision outcome than low n Power leaders; however, the quality of decision making, as indexed by the number of facts and proposals considered by the group and the moral dimensions of the decision alternatives, was lower in groups led by high n Power individuals. Furthermore, high n Power leaders appear to experience greater arousal than low n Power leaders when group goals are blocked (Fodor, 1984, 1985). Such power stress may have a number of deleterious effects on physical health (McClelland, 1976, 1982, 1985). Other motivational variables, like n Power, have been linked with communication and leadership in group interaction contexts. Sorrentino and Field (1986) reported that group members with high levels of both n Achievement and n Affiliation participated more and were nominated as group leaders more often than individuals scoring low on these two motives. These effects persisted over several group meetings.

Mason and Blankenship (1987) found that high n Power males are more likely to inflict physical abuse on their intimate partners, whereas no significant relationship between these two variables was observed for females. Consistent with these findings, Winter (1988) reported that males with high n Power demonstrated more profligate impulsive behaviors (drinking, aggression, sexual exploitation) ($r = .67$) when they had been raised in families with no younger siblings than when their families included younger siblings ($r = .00$). The relationship between n Power and profligate behaviors was not significant for females, regardless of their birth-order status. These findings were explained in terms of the idea that the early responsibility training that older siblings may receive in their families may nullify the relationship between n Power and the frequency of profligate behaviors, especially for males. Although not employing a measure of n Power, a study by Infante, Chandler, and Rudd (1989) found that individuals involved in physically violent marriages were significantly more verbally aggressive than their counterparts in nonviolent marriages; however, those involved in nonviolent marriages were more argumentative than those involved in violent marriages. Not only do these findings provide support for the discriminant validity of these two measures, they also suggest that those who are unable to argue are more prone to become physically violent, while those who are verbally aggressive trigger physical violence because of their propensity to employ ad hominem attacks on others.

Considerable literature has examined the relationship between other trait measures related to dominance and verbal and nonverbal communicative behaviors that are indicators of dominance. In an interview situation in which a number of embarrassing questions were asked, interviewees with high levels of abasement broke eye contact with the interviewer by looking left to a significantly greater extent than did low abasement interviewees (Libby & Yaklevich, 1973). Beekman (1975) reported a correlation of $-.34$ between dominance and filled pause rate for males involved in informal social interaction with females. Females showed no relationship between the same two variables. Scherer (1979) correlated a number of paralinguistic variables derived from videotapes of simulated jury deliberations with a trait measure of dominance. He obtained the following correlations between dominance and five paralinguistic features: verbal productivity (.15), interruptions (.50), repetitions (.15), silent pauses ($-.44$), and pitch range (.47). Of the five variables studied by Scherer, productivity, repetitions, and pitch range were found to be the best predictors of perceived influence in the group. With the exception of pitch range, variables that correlated poorly with trait dominance were good predictors of perceived influence. Finally, this study revealed a number of cultural differences between West German and American persons on these indices.

Aries, Gold, and Weigel (1983) correlated scores from the dominance scale of the CPI with a number of verbal and nonverbal indicators of dominance (for example, talk time, verbal acts initiated, interruptions, arms away from body, open legs, and backward lean). In groups consisting of all males, modest but significant correlations were obtained between the dominance scale and the verbal and non-verbal dominance indicators (r = .31). Correlations for all female groups were of similar magnitudes to those found in all male groups, but only one was significant (r = .29). However, the correlations between the communication indicators and personality measures of dominance were virtually nil in mixed-sex groups (r = .05). This pattern of findings was interpreted as indicating that when situational variables are rendered less influential, for example, by having homogenous groups, individual differences will exert considerably more influence upon behavior than when situational variables such as gender differences are salient. Roger and Schumacher (1983) reported that dyads consisting of two highly dominant people, as measured by the dominance scale of the Edwards Personal Preference Schedule (EPPS), showed significantly higher rates of successful interruptions in the later stages of an initial encounter than did dyads consisting of either two low dominance scorers or a high and a low. There were no significant differences between the three groups when compared on rates of unsuccessful interruptions. Kimble and Seidel (1991) found that individuals scoring high on assertiveness tended to speak louder than their low assertiveness counterparts when answering trivia questions.

Although the foregoing studies of trait dominance and communicative behavior tend to show direct relationships between the two variables, there are studies suggesting that these relationships are influenced by situational factors. Exline and Messick (1967) found that, under conditions of low social reinforcement, dependent persons increased their looking at a confederate as the confederate increased the rate of reinforcement given; however, dominant individuals decreased their looking at the confederate as reinforcements were increased. Exline (1972) had subjects interact with a confederate who gazed 50% of the time at the subject when speaking and either 100% or 0% when listening. When listening, dominant individuals' gaze toward the confederate was not influenced by the confederate's behavior. By contrast, people with low dominance levels looked more often at the inattentive confederate (0%). Exline (1972) argued that, in general, "powerful people do not monitor less powerful people" (p. 192). Ellyson (1974) reported that highly dominant people looked less at a confederate while listening than did low dominance individuals, thus adding further support to the argument advanced by Exline (1972). In two subsequent studies (Ellyson, Dovidio, Corson, & Vinicur, 1980; Exline, Ellyson, & Long, 1975), positive relationships were found between expressed control (Schutz, 1958) and patterns of dominance expressed in looking behavior. Both studies revealed that those scoring high on expressed control showed little difference between their rates of looking while speaking and looking while listening. By contrast, those scoring low on dominance were found to look significantly less while speaking than while listening. These findings provide further support for the notion that persons in low power positions monitor those with higher power when the high power person is speaking and show deference by avoiding eye contact when they speak to superiors (see Dovidio & Ellyson, 1985).

Having seen how n Power, n Influence, and dominance are reflected in social interaction behavior, the focus now shifts to research exploring the relationship between authoritarianism, dogmatism, locus of control, and Machiavellianism on the one hand and empirical indicators of dominance as represented in communicative behavior on the other. Relatively little research has been done to link the variables of authoritarianism and dogmatism to specific dominance behaviors in interaction situations. Given the description of authoritarian individuals, one would expect them to be more aggressive and punitive than their equalitarian counterparts; however, in their review of this literature, Cherry and Byrne (1977) asserted that there are a number of situational variables that determine whether this relationship will be obtained. Rubin and Brown (1975) found that, in 16 studies that have examined the link between authoritarianism and various bargaining processes, 7 found no effects for authoritarianism. In those studies that did find effects, high authoritarians tended to bargain less cooperatively than lows. Herb and Elliott (1971) reported that high authoritarians displayed more rigid body postures than lows in situations in which they were either a superior or a subordinate in a group task. When confederates made high authoritarians play a subordinate role, they tended to lean forward more often than the lows. One interpretation of these findings is that high authoritarians nonverbally play leadership roles when their authority is challenged by other group members.

Druckman (1967) found that highly dogmatic individuals were both more resistant to change and less willing to compromise from a given position in a dyadic bargaining situation. They tended to view compromise from a given position as defeat. Zagona and Zurcher (1964, 1965) reported that high dogmatics were more concerned with problems of leader selection and group structure. Frye, Vidulich, Meierhoefer, and Joure (1972) and Talley and Vamos (1972) suggest that high dogmatics show higher levels of concern for the structure and operation of a group when they are placed in an unstructured situation. In the former study, highly dogmatic group members made more negative statements about the situation than did group members with low dogmatism levels. Finally, Roloff and Barnicott (1979) found that highly dogmatic people reported that they were more likely to employ all 16 of Marwell and Schmitt's (1967) compliance-gaining techniques than were low dogmatics.

A number of studies have examined the link between locus of control and behavior related to power and dominance. Phares (1965) found that, when persons were asked to change another person's expressed attitude, internally controlled people were more persuasive than externally controlled individuals. Goodstadt and Hjelle (1973) reported that internally controlled individuals who were given a range of power strategies with which to influence another were less likely to use coercive strategies than those who were externally controlled. This study also revealed the tendency for internals to rely more on informal means of influence rather than the formal means that were associated with their supervisory role. These findings are consistent with other studies demonstrating that power holders who encounter resistance to their influence attempts are more likely to resort to coercive means of influence (Berger & Jordan, 1991; deTurck, 1985; Goodstadt & Kipnis, 1970; Hirokawa, Mickey, & Miura, 1991; Instone, Major, & Bunker, 1983; Kipnis & Consentino, 1969). Externally controlled individuals tend to anticipate that they will be unable to influence others and are, as a result, more prone to employ coercive means of influence. These studies are among the few that have examined the responses of persons whose influence attempts are thwarted.

Additional research has found relationships between locus of control and dominance in interaction settings. Bugental, Henker, and Whalen (1976) reported that internally controlled people were judged to be more persuasive in vocalic communication channels than in the content of their messages; by contrast, externally controlled individuals were judged to be more persuasive in the content of their messages than in the vocal presentation of their messages. This difference was interpreted as indicating that externals have expectations of failing at persuasion that "leak" through their vocalic communication, whereas internals, who are confident of their persuasive powers, show greater persuasiveness in the nonverbal, vocalic channel. Doherty and Ryder (1979) reported that, in a simulated conflict situation involving married couples, internally controlled husbands displayed more assertive behavior than did externally controlled husbands. A similar trend was observed for wives but failed to reach conventional significance levels. Cialdini and Mirels (1976) tested the notion that individuals who were successful at persuading another would make attributions about the target of their influence attempts consistent with their own locus of control orientation. In support of this reasoning, they found that internally controlled persuaders enhanced the perceived intelligence and attractiveness of persons who yielded to them and derogated those who resisted their influence attempts. Externally controlled individuals showed the reverse pattern of attributions. Canary, Cody, and Marston (1987) found that internals claimed greater confidence and persistence when pursuing compliance-gaining goals and chose stronger strategies for exerting influence. By contrast, those who viewed themselves as relatively powerless chose weaker and more emotion-based strategies. In general, the studies reviewed here show very consistent support for the proposition that internally controlled people both are more confident of their abilities to exert influence and are behaviorally more persuasive in social influence situations. Because of their increased confidence, they are more likely to employ prosocial means of influence, whereas their externally controlled counterparts are more likely to use coercion and other antisocial influence strategies.

The final trait-oriented variable to be considered here is Machiavellianism. Given the potential links of this variable to social influence phenomena, it is surprising to find that relatively few studies have examined the relationship between Machiavellianism and behavior in social influence situations. Geis (1970) reported that high Machiavellians (high Machs) were more successful in an interpersonal bargaining situation than were lows. Braginsky (1970) found that high Mach children used more manipulative strategies, were more successful in producing influence, and were judged to be more effective at persuasion in general than their low Mach counterparts. Hacker and Gaitz (1970) reported that high Machs participated more in discussions, asked for more information, and more often provided their own orientation. These behaviors are generally associated with greater dominance. Roloff and Barnicott (1978) observed weak but significant correlations between Machiavellianism and the use of prosocial compliance-gaining techniques ($r = .21$) and a positive relationship between Machiavellianism and the use of psychological force techniques ($r = .34$); however, no significant relationship was found between Machiavellianism and punishing activity techniques. This latter finding is somewhat surprising because Guterman (1970) reported that high Machs tended to score low on need for social approval. The correlations between Machiavellianism and use of various compliance-gaining techniques may be low because high Machs use a greater variety of influence strategies of all kinds than do their low Mach counterparts. This seems quite likely because it is assumed that high Machs have a broader strategy repertoire because of their low need for social approval (Guterman, 1970), lack of commitment to conventional morality, and low level of ideological commitment (Christie & Geis, 1970).

At least three general conclusions can be drawn from this overview of trait measures. First, there seem to be consistent relationships between these measures and communicative behaviors associated with exercise of power. Second, when researchers report correlations between these trait measures and various measures of dominant behavior, they are relatively weak. Part of the explanation for these weak correlations lies in the fact that the reliabilities of the trait measures and the interaction indices may be relatively low. Moreover, because an individual behavior (for example, interruptions or question asking) may serve a number of communicative functions including dominance or control, it is not surprising that any one behavioral index of dominance or power correlates minimally with a trait measure. Several behavioral indices of dominance should do a better job of "predicting" trait dominance given the potential variability in the functions that individual behaviors serve. In support of this reasoning, Aries et al. (1983) found that a combination of nine behavioral indices of dominance produced a multiple correlation of .67 with a trait measure of dominance as a criterion. The average correlation of the same set of predictors with the same criterion was only .31. Substantial proportions of variance in trait dominance can be accounted for when a number of behavioral indices of dominance are employed simultaneously as predictors. Finally, individual differences in the propensity to exercise power may be overridden by situational influences; however, this assertion does not imply that trait measures of power should be abandoned. Instead, efforts should be made to specify a general set of conditions under which trait differences will be manifested directly in communicative conduct and conditions under which such differences are likely to be nullified.

Assumed power differences. In this section, research that has investigated the relationships between power and communicative conduct by comparing the communicative action of groups that are presumed to differ with respect to power (for example, males and females; individuals in different social positions) is summarized. The next section explores research that has placed individuals in roles that differ with respect to power and reports observations of their behavior vis-à-vis each other. These kinds of studies are generally carried out in laboratory situations and use some kind of simulation to enable persons to enact different roles. First, studies that assume power differences are examined.

Lott and Sommer (1967) observed that college upperclassmen sat closer to peers than to freshmen who were not doing well in school. This study also revealed that upperclassmen sat closer to peers than to professors. Dean, Willis, and Hewitt (1975) examined the initial interaction distances of military personnel of different ranks. They found that, when subordinates initiated interaction with superiors, the rank of the superior was related to initial interaction distance. The greater the difference in rank, the greater the interaction distance; however, when a superior initiated interaction, there was no relationship between rank and distance. Apparently, higher status people have the option of controlling initial distance and subordinates must be more rank conscious when they initiate interaction. Brown and Ford (1961) noted that it is the prerogative of higher status individuals to determine when to change from formal forms of address involving title plus last name (Dr. Jones, Mrs. Smith) to the informal use of first names. The distance study demonstrates a similar general principle. Mishler (1975) observed that parents tended to initiate and continue dialogue with their children by asking them questions. He argued that parents use question asking as a way of controlling their children. Compared with their patients, physicians show higher levels of such potentially dominance-related behaviors as longer speaking turns, social touch, and pausing while speaking (Street & Buller, 1987). Moreover, doctors were found to be more domineering when interacting with patients under 30 years of age (Street & Buller, 1988).

Over the past 20 years, considerable research effort has been devoted to the study of gender differences in both verbal and nonverbal communication. As was pointed out earlier, Lakoff (1975) suggested a number of differences between male and female speech that presumably both reflect and reinforce male dominance. She proposed that females are less likely to use strong expletives and more likely to use tag questions, rising intonation when answering questions, more polite forms of requests, and more formal, correct grammar. All of these forms were alleged to indicate weakness and submissiveness. In addition, Henley (1973, 1977) argued that males exercise dominance over females by initiating various forms of touch, while Tannen (1990) contended that male communication generally reflects a concern for power, and female communication, a concern for solidarity. Consistent with the idea that males are preoccupied with power, even at relatively young ages, is evidence suggesting that boys are more likely than girls to model the behavior of opposite-sex adults who have high levels of power (Bussey & Bandura, 1984). Visual depictions of males in magazines and art tend to emphasize the face relative to depictions of females in these media, and increased facial prominence is associated with judgments of greater ambition (Archer, Iritani, Kimes, & Barrios, 1983). Andrews (1987) found that males expressed greater confidence in their ability to express persuasive arguments and were more inclined to attribute their persuasive success to their natural communication ability. As an extensive literature has addressed gender differences in the use of power-related communicative acts, it cannot be exhaustively reviewed here. Useful overviews have been presented by Eakins and Eakins (1978), Kramarae (1981), Pearson (1985), P. M. Smith (1979, 1985), Tannen (1990), and Thorne and Henley (1975).

In general, there is a moderate tendency for men to be designated as overall leaders in task-oriented groups and a weaker tendency for women to be accorded socioemotional leadership roles; although, as the social complexity of the task and the longevity of the group increase, the likelihood that males will emerge as overall leaders decreases. Evidence also suggests that men make more task-relevant contributions during group deliberations, while women tend to make contributions in the service of group harmony (Eagly & Karau, 1991). These sex differences in group behavior have been explained in terms of the gender-role differences (Eagly, 1987). Males are expected to specialize in behaviors that lead to task completion, while females are expected to maintain group harmony. Some evidence suggests that, even when women with high levels of dominance are paired with men with low dominance levels in task-oriented groups, men tend to emerge as leaders (Carbonell, 1984; Megargee, 1969); however, when the gender-relatedness of the task is controlled, this effect seems to be attenuated (Carbonell, 1984), and Fleischer and Chertkoff (1986) failed to replicate the effect. Although these studies of emergent leadership in groups are informative, they do not identify the complex of verbal and nonverbal behaviors that might explain why these differential patterns of leadership designation occur. In many studies, only gross rates of task and socioemotional participation are examined.

A considerable number of investigations have examined sex differences in the use of specific verbal and nonverbal behaviors. Markel, Prebor, and Brandt (1972) found that males showed greater vocal intensity than females. Crosby and Nyquist (1977) found support for a number of the gender differences in speech posited by Lakoff (1975); moreover, other studies reported that males interrupt females more than females interrupt males in mixed-sex interactions (West & Zimmerman, 1983; Zimmerman & West, 1975), lending support to the male dominance hypothesis. Consistent with Lakoff's contention, women tend to use more formal, grammatically correct language than men (Fischer, 1958; Levine & Crockett, 1966; Trudgill, 1972; Wolfram, 1969). Men speak in longer utterances regardless of the sex of their conversational partner, and men talk more than women in mixed-gender dyads (Mulac, 1989). Women employ more tag questions in their speech than do men (Gleason & Weintraub, 1978; Hartman, 1976; McMillan, Clifton, McGrath, & Gale, 1977). Women have been found to use more tentative language (disclaimers, tag questions, and hedges) in mixed-sex than same-sex interactions (Carli, 1990). Women's speech is judged to be more masculine in mixed-sex groups, while men's speech shows less variation as a function of group composition (Hogg, 1985). Female speakers using a tentative style have been found to be more influential with males than female speakers employing an assertive style, while male speakers appear to be equally influential regardless of their speech style (Carli, 1990). Both males and females exhibit higher levels of sex-role-stereotypic interaction behavior in interactions with those of the same sex (Carli, 1989). Consistent with the idea that women may be more tentative than men in social influence contexts, Conrad (1991) reported that, while supervisors generally used progressively more coercive influence strategies in attempting to influence noncompliant subordinates, females changed to coercive strategies more slowly than males.

Several studies investigating the gender-linked language effect have revealed reliable differences in the language of males and females on a variety of variables and that some of these language differences, in turn, produce elevated ratings of the sociointellectual status and aesthetic quality of female language users and higher ratings of dynamism for males, although there are some inconsistencies across these studies (Lawrence, Stucky, & Hopper, 1990; Mulac, 1989; Mulac, Bradac, & Mann, 1985; Mulac, Incontro, & James, 1985; Mulac, Lundell, & Bradac, 1986; Mulac, Wiemann, Widenmann, & Gibson, 1988; Zahn, 1989). Critically, in many of these studies, judges rated transcribed language samples without knowing the gender of the person whose utterances were contained in the transcript. Apparently, then, some male and female differences in language use give rise to differential perceptions of power; however, this research does not indicate whether these differential perceptions are translated into actual influence (Mulac, 1989). Furthermore, Zahn (1989) observed that language effects within each gender were considerably larger than those effects resulting from sex differences, suggesting that variables other than gender might be more influential in producing differential judgments of dominance based on language use.

In contrast to findings supporting sex differences in dominance-related communication behaviors, several studies have found no gender differences. Some studies have reported no significant sex differences in the propensity for individuals to interrupt members of the opposite sex (Dindia, 1987; Kennedy & Camden, 1983). Drass (1986) also found no relationship between biological sex and likelihood of interrupting during discussions; however, gender identity, the set of meanings individuals attribute to themselves as males or females, did predict interruption behavior. The more "malelike" an individual's self-definition, regardless of biological sex, the greater the likelihood that they would interrupt. Robinson and Reis (1989) reported that both males and females who interrupted others were judged to be more assertive and less sociable than those who did not interrupt. Edelsky (1979) found no support for the assertion that females use the rising intonation in answering questions more frequently than do males. Several studies (Baumann, 1976; Martin & Craig, 1983; Mulac & Lundell, 1986) have found no sex differences in the use of tag questions, and one study (Dubois & Crouch, 1975) reported that men used more tag questions than women.

Brouwer, Gerritsen, and De Haan (1979) compared the speech of males and females who asked for train tickets and information at the Central Station of Amsterdam, Holland. The number of words, diminutives, civilities, polite forms, requests for information, hesitations, repetitions, and self-corrections were examined. Women were found to make more information requests and show more hesitations in their speech than men; however, there were no differences on any of the other speech variables. The gender of the ticket seller was considerably more influential in this situation. Both male and female ticket buyers used more words, diminutives, civilities, and hesitations when they were speaking with a male ticket agent. Wood and Karten (1986) found that the gender-role-stereotypic behavior of both males and females in mixed-sex discussion groups disappeared when information regarding the relative competence of group members was made available to each individual in the group. Similarly, Molm (1985) found that gender exerted virtually no independent effects on power use or evaluations of individuals' personalities, competence, or power but did exert effects on other evaluations. In addition, when males and females were placed in equivalent positions of structural power, there were no gender differences in actual power use. Apparently, status can override differential effects of gender in certain circumstances. Howard, Blumstein, and Schwartz (1986) found that sex and sex role orientation generally affected the use of only weak influence tactics in close relationships.

Other studies demonstrate the problems associated with positing a simple relationship between gender and dominance. Kimble, Yoshikawa, and Zehr (1981) compared the assertiveness of males and females in four-person groups consisting of either all males, all females, or two males and two females. Assertiveness was indexed by rating both content and vocalic communication for assertiveness. In addition, loudness, speech rate, and average pause duration between speakers were measured. The hypotheses that males would be more assertive than females and that male assertiveness would be more prevalent in mixed-gender groups were not supported by the data. However, these researchers did find that the woman who spoke second in a mixed-gender group was significantly less assertive than her first speaking sister. In all-male groups, the first speaking male was more verbally assertive than the last speaking one. Miller, Reynolds, and Cambra (1987) found that men of Chinese and Japanese ancestry produced proattitudinal persuasive messages with higher levels of language intensity than women from the same two cultures. No significant differences in language intensity were observed between the persuasive messages generated by Caucasian males and females.

A number of studies of gender differences in the initiation of touch have also produced contradictory evidence regarding the propositions that (a) dominant individuals in interactions have the prerogative of initiating touch with subordinates, and (b) because males tend to dominate interactions with females, males tend to initiate more touch than females in cross-sex interactions. While early studies supported this asymmetry hypothesis (Henley, 1973, 1977; Major, 1981), a review of several studies germane to these propositions revealed inconsistent findings (Stier & Hall, 1984). Subsequent studies have added confusion to this picture. Jones (1986) found more opposite-sex touching categorized as controlling by women and by men in mixed-sex interactions. In their observational study of some 4,500 dyads, Hall and Veccia (1990) found that, among younger people, males tended to initiate more touch than females; however, as age increased, they found a complete reversal of this relationship. By contrast, in their study of 799 instances of touch, Major, Schmidlin, and Williams (1990) reported that adult males initiated more touch than females in mixed-sex interactions; however, among children, this tendency was reversed. Moreover, no significant sex differences in adult touch initiation were observed in greeting and departure situations, whereas gender differences were manifested in public, nonintimate situations. Contrary to Major's (1981) prediction that initiators of touch are judged to be more powerful and dominant, Burgoon, Walther, and Baesler (1992) found no relationship between touching and dominance judgments, and participant and confederate gender failed to interact with these variables. Similarly, Storrs and Kleinke (1990) reported that interviewer touch had no impact on ratings of interviewer status. Although Patterson, Powell, and Lenihan (1986) found that touch increased overall compliance, neither sex of experimenter nor sex of subject interacted with touch to produce differential compliance. Female subjects complied more with a female experimenter, however, producing a significant sex of experimenter by sex of subject interaction.

To highlight a recurring theme, one difficulty with focusing solely on touch or any other single nonverbal behavior as an indicator of dominance is that touch and other individual behaviors can serve multiple functions, depending upon the verbalizations that accompany them and the social context within which the behaviors are enacted. For instance, Jones and Yarbrough (1985) isolated 12 distinct and relatively unambiguous meanings for touch: 5 of which they subsumed under the broad category of *positive affect touches*; 2 of which were included in the category *playful touches*; 3 of which were members of a category they labeled *control touches*; while the remaining 2 types were included in a category called *ritualistic touches*. Note that only 3 of the 12 touch types isolated in this investigation were concerned with control or dominance; moreover, it is difficult to imagine how unobtrusive observers in public situations who simply count the number of touching events could determine, without additional interview data, the type of touch that was meant in a given instance of touching. Touching observed between family members at an airport, for instance, might be relatively unambiguously classified as ritualistic; however, even in this seemingly straightforward case, observers probably could not be certain whether touches they recorded were ritualistic in fact or whether they were expressions of positive affect or attempts to control. In a related study, Burgoon (1991) reported that, although touching was judged to be a potential indicator of dominance, there were significant variations in dominance judgments depending on the type of touch. Those engaging in hand holding and hand shaking were judged to be as dominant as those who were not touching, while those initiating arm, face, or shoulder touches were judged to be more dominant.

Given the findings of these investigations, it seems fair to conclude that studies showing gender asymmetry in the frequency of touch initiation between women and men provide only the flimsiest of bases for making inferences regarding differential dominance between genders. In general, the effects of gender on verbal and nonverbal communication related to the assertion of power and dominance in social interaction, while detectable, appear not to be highly durable. Apparently, other variables such as status and perceived competence can dampen significantly or completely nullify sex differences in the use of dominance behaviors. To add to these complexities regarding gender differences in the performance of dominance behaviors is the finding that males and females have not been found to differ with respect to their overall levels of *n* Power, although their modes of expression of this motive may differ (Winter, 1988).

Erikson et al. (1978), Lind and O'Barr (1979), O'Barr (1982), and O'Barr and Atkins (1980) examined powerful and powerless speech styles exhibited by witnesses giving courtroom testimony. They developed stimulus tapes and transcripts to represent these two communication styles. In general, the powerless speech style is characterized by the use of more hedges, polite forms, tag questions, speaking in italics, empty adjectives, hypercorrect grammar, direct quotations, special lexicon, rising intonation in giving answers, and less humor. Although women tended to demonstrate more speech attributes associated with the powerless style, O'Barr and Atkins (1980) suggested that it might be more productive to focus attention on the variable of powerlessness rather than gender because people in positions of power, regardless of gender, may be more prone to use powerful forms (Wood & Karten, 1986). O'Barr and Atkins (1980) found that, when females spoke with a powerful style, they were rated to be more persuasive than females who used the powerless style of speech. The same pattern of findings was obtained for males. A study reported by Lamb (1981) reached a similar conclusion. Not only have subsequent studies found that people rate sources who use powerful speech forms to be more controlling and dynamic than sources who use powerless forms (Bradac & Mulac, 1984a, 1984b; Gibbons et al., 1991), Bradac and Mulac (1984b) reported that speaker gender exerted no main effect or interaction effect on these judgments. In a study related to the consequences of powerful and powerless speech forms, Sadalla, Kenrick, and Vershure (1987) reported that males demonstrating dominant behavior were judged to be more heterosexually attractive than males who were less dominant. By contrast, variations in females' dominance produced no concomitant variation in judgments of their sexual attractiveness. While concerns over sex differences may continue to motivate research that simply compares the communication behaviors of women and men, these findings suggest that the powerful-powerless distinction may be a more useful variable theoretically than gender because of its greater abstractness and potential explanatory power.

Considerable research attention has been paid to the issue of gender stereotyping of speech. In an early study, Kramer (1977) had males and females rate male and female speakers on 51 speech characteristics. She found that participants listed the following attributes as more characteristic of male speech: demanding voice, deep voice, being boastful, using swear words, dominating speech, speaking loudly, showing anger rather than concealing it, coming straight to the point, using militant speech, using slang, using authoritarian speech, speaking forcefully, lounging and leaning back while talking, using aggressive speech, speaking bluntly, and having a sense of humor in speech. Female speakers were attributed the following characteristics: enunciating clearly, using a high pitch, using hands and face to express ideas, gossiping, showing concern for listener, using gentle speech, speaking quickly, talking about trivial topics, using a wide range in pitch and rate, using friendly speech, talking frequently, using emotional speech, using many details, speaking smoothly, using open and self-revealing speech, speaking enthusiastically, smiling a lot when talking, using good grammar, speaking politely, and using gibberish.

Several studies have shown that female language users are judged to be higher in sociointellectual status than male language users, while male language users typically are judged to be more dynamic, although these differences are not always significant and are sometimes reversed (Lawrence et al., 1990; Mulac, 1989; Mulac, Bradac, & Mann, 1985; Mulac, Incontro, & James, 1985; Mulac et al., 1986; Mulac et al., 1988; Zahn, 1989). In related research conducted in the medical domain, Burgoon, Birk, and Hall (1991) reported that both male and female patients expected male physicians to use more verbally aggressive compliance-gaining strategies than female physicians. In general, the existence of such stereotypes may mean that, even if males and females change their manners of speaking to be discrepant with stereotypes, persons may fail to perceive such changes because of their stereotyped conceptions. These stereotypes may make it difficult for females to exert influence even if they employ a more powerful speech style, although the findings of some studies suggest that stylistic changes by males and females have considerable impacts upon addressees' perceptions of their power (Bradac & Mulac, 1984b; O'Barr & Atkins, 1980). Moreover, actual differences in language use and gender stereotypes exert independent effects on judgments of speakers' relative power (Mulac, Incontro, & James, 1985). Consequently, it should be possible for individuals, regardless of their gender, to nullify others' stereotypic perceptions of their power by varying their speech style along the powerful-powerless speech style continuum.

Finally, it has frequently been observed that in marital conflict situations wives frequently are less supportive of their husbands than their husbands are of them, and wives have been observed to use more coercive influence tactics and to make more negative statements than their husbands (Noller, 1985; Rausch, Barry, Hertel, & Swain, 1974; Rogers-Millar & Millar, 1979; Zietlow & Sillars, 1987). Wives' patterns of communication in such conflicts hardly can be characterized as submissive relative to their husbands'. In their study of marital conflict styles, Burggraf and Sillars (1987) reported that biological sex accounted for no significant variance in style choice, while couple type (Fitzpatrick, 1988), mutual influence processes, and mutually established beliefs and expectations were significant determinants of conflict style. They also concluded that patterns of marital conflict are highly reciprocal and that communication in contemporary marriage does not adhere to a single, sex-linked pattern.

Summary. In this survey of literature in which dominance is assumed to be an independent variable and dominance expressed through communicative conduct a dependent variable, we have seen that there is some consistency across studies. Trait measures of dominance frequently predict dominance in communicative conduct with some degree of accuracy, and in relationships in which power differentials are assumed, there appear to be differences in the communication behavior of high and low power persons. Within the domain of sex differences, where it has frequently been assumed that males assume dominant roles when interacting with females, there are numerous examples of conflicting findings, however. Apparently, power asymmetries in social interaction that stem from sex differences can be nullified by other variables operating in the interaction context. Moreover, even with high levels of consistency in this literature's findings, one could not confidently make causal inferences from such studies. In the case of personality research, there is always the possibility that, when significant relationships are observed between trait measures of dominance and behavioral measures, unmeasured variables correlated with the trait measure are the actual causes of behavior. If, for example, n Power is positively correlated with n Achievement, observed differences between high and low n Power persons may be due to their correlated differences in n Achievement. Unfortunately, in most of the trait-oriented studies considered here, no effort was made to control for this possibility.

A similar problem exists with respect to the studies that assume power differences between people. The fact that females sometimes may display verbal and nonverbal behaviors that are consistent with a powerless style of speech does not necessarily mean that gender per se is the critical causal variable producing such differences. Females may manifest such behavior more frequently because they are generally in lower power positions, for example. In this case, status is the causal variable, not gender. One way to avoid such confounding is to randomly assign individuals to play roles that differ with respect to power and observe their communication to see if there are differences among role incumbents. This experimental paradigm ensures that potential confounding variables are controlled and makes causal inference more certain. The studies that follow have generally employed this approach.

Induced power differences. In an early study of the relationship between position in a status hierarchy and communication, Kelley (1951) found that individuals in low status groups sent more task-irrelevant messages in a problem-solving situation than did members of high status groups. Low status individuals made more conjectures about the job being done by the high status group than did the highs with reference to the lows. Kelley concluded that communication can serve as a substitute for blocked upward mobility in a status hierarchy. Cohen (1958) pointed out that one must distinguish between the effects of status and power on communication. He observed that Kelley (1951) created status differences between groups by informing group members that the task they were performing was more or less important than the one being done by the other group. Although this induction may have introduced status differences, it did not produce power differences, because the groups were not dependent upon each other for their outcomes. In short, status and power may or may not be correlated; for example, a prominent professor may or may not be able to wield influence in his department, and a criminal may be able to exert considerable influence upon others by the use of threats.

In his study, Cohen (1958) not only used Kelley's status manipulation but also made it clear to the low status groups that their success was dependent upon the high status group. In addition, Cohen led some groups to believe that they could move up to the high status group, whereas other low status group members were told that they had no possibility of upward mobility. In contrasting the communication of mobile and nonmobile low status groups, Cohen reported that the mobile groups sent longer messages with less irrelevant content to the high status groups. Groups with mobility possibilities made fewer conjectures about the job being done by the high status group and were less critical of these groups. One general conclusion drawn in this study was that those low power individuals who have the possibility of becoming part of a group with greater power are considerably more circumspect in their communication toward members of the high power group than are those with no mobility possibilities.

In a study related to the Kelley (1951) and Cohen (1958) experiments, Tjosvold (1978) reported that, when low power individuals strongly affirmed the personal effectiveness of those with higher power levels, the high power individuals were more attracted to those with low power; however, this increased liking did not raise the likelihood that the high power individuals would yield to the demands of those with low power. When low power persons ingratiate themselves to high power individuals by affirming their superiority, they are not likely to increase the probability that they will actually influence those with high power, even though the high power individuals increase their liking for them.

Mehrabian and Williams (1969) studied the verbal and nonverbal behavior of people who were asked to persuade others. Individuals given this assignment showed greater eye contact, increased rates of positive head nodding, gesticulation, facial activity, speech rate, speech volume, and intonation. Persuaders' voices were rated as less halting. In a related study, Rosenfeld (1966) found that those who were asked to gain approval from others were more likely to speak more frequently and for longer durations than their approval-avoiding counterparts. Approval seekers also showed more smiles, positive head nods, and gesticulations. Although the Rosenfeld (1966) study did not deal with attempted influence, the approval seekers in his study manifested verbal and nonverbal behaviors similar to those observed by Mehrabian and Williams (1969). It appears that, when individuals are given the objective of persuading another, they are likely to try to ingratiate themselves with their targets by displaying behaviors designed to elicit social approval.

Ellyson et al. (1980) manipulated status differences by leading college students to believe that they were interacting with either a low status other (a high school student who wished to work in a gas station) or a high status other (a chemistry honors student bound for a prestigious medical school). Observations of subjects' looking behavior during the interactions revealed that, when they believed that they were in the high status position vis-à-vis their partner, subjects' rates of looking while speaking were about the same as their rates of looking while listening, a high dominance pattern of visual behavior. However, when they believed that their status relative to their partner was low, their rate of looking while listening was significantly greater than their rate of looking while speaking, a low dominance pattern. In a similar study, individuals who were accorded either expert power or reward power both showed the high dominance pattern of visual behavior while their low power counterparts manifested the low dominance pattern (Dovidio, Ellyson, Keating, Heltman, & Brown, 1988).

Leffler, Gillespie, and Conaty (1982) also examined the nonverbal behavior of individuals interacting under discrepant status conditions. In their study, people were paired into student-teacher dyads in which the teacher was given the task of instructing the student. After an initial session, roles were reversed during a second session. This study revealed that high status individuals (teachers) claimed more direct space with their bodies, talked more, and attempted more interruptions than did their lower status students. Moreover, using both touching and pointing, teachers intruded more on students than did students on teachers. Wood and Karten (1986) found that individuals placed in high status positions in discussion groups engaged in more task-oriented communication and less positive socioemotional behavior than their low status counterparts. As noted previously, the induction of status differences in this study nullified sex differences in these two types of group behavior.

The studies reviewed above consistently show that those placed in high status positions, or in situations in which they are encouraged to wield influence, demonstrate verbal and nonverbal conduct that is more dominant than that manifested by those in low status or low power positions. Moreover, the Leffler et al. (1982) study indicates that individuals can very quickly adjust dominance-related behaviors as they move up or down a status ranking. Although this body of research shows consistent relationships between status, power, and dominant communicative conduct, it does not address the issue of how dominance hierarchies emerge in groups, that is, why certain persons end up talking more, interrupting more, and having more impact upon group decisions than others in the group. Employing expectation states theory or status characteristics theory, Berger, Fisek, Norman, and Zelditch (1977) have argued that, under certain conditions in specific types of groups, high status group members become more powerful because other group members believe that the high status group members are more competent or intelligent. It is through the common belief that high status members are more competent that they are then allowed to become more dominant behaviorally. These investigators have conducted numerous experiments indicating that individuals who are believed to have high status by others exert more influence on decision outcomes than do those believed to have lower status.

Attributing Power from Communicative Conduct

Here the focus will be on studies in which communication behavior is either manipulated or measured and then related to participants' or observers' attributions of power. For example, persons in a small group study might be asked to rank order their fellow group members in terms of their influence in the group. The degree to which each person participated in the group is then correlated with these rankings. In a more controlled setting, an investigator might vary the actions of stimulus persons and then have observers make judgments concerning the power of the stimulus persons. In either case, the hypothesis under test is that the ways in which persons behave influence the extent to which they are judged to be powerful by others. Correlational studies of attributed power are examined first, then experimental studies are considered.

Correlational studies. A large number of studies have investigated the relationship between the rate of verbal participation in small groups and leadership rankings. Stein and Heller (1979) found a mean correlation of .65 between the two variables based upon 77 correlations. Because verbal participation appears to account for about 42% of the variance on the average in leadership rankings, this leaves considerable room for other facets of communicative behavior to account for leadership status variance. Stein (1975) reported that observers were able to approximate the leadership rankings of actual group members when they were given records of the group's meeting that contained only verbal communication, only nonverbal communication, or both verbal and nonverbal communication. Moreover, observers were still accurate (beyond chance) in their rankings when the effects of verbal participation were controlled. It appears that observers at least partially based their judgments of relative leadership on cues other than those associated with verbal participation rate. Although these studies are instructive, they do not tell us what specific communication behaviors, beyond verbal productivity, are important in generating perceptions of power.

Scherer (1979) examined the relationships between a number of paralinguistic variables and perceived influence in simulated jury situations. Across both American and West German samples, verbal productivity was significantly related to the ratings of perceived influence made by jury members (U.S., $r = .42$; W.G., $r = .54$), although Scherer noted that the frequency of verbalization is more important than the duration of verbalizations in determining perceived influence. While the verbal productivity measures showed consistent relationships with perceived influence across the two cultures studied, there were a number of cultural differences found. For example, pitch range and loudness correlated positively with perceived influence for Americans ($r = .49$; $r = .32$, respectively); however, the same two variables failed to correlate with perceived influence in the West German sample. For the U.S. jurors, number of silent pauses correlated $-.44$ with perceived influence, whereas the number of speech disturbances correlated positively ($r = .38$). This latter correlation is somewhat out of line with that which would be expected. American jurors who interrupted more were judged to be more influential ($r = .45$); however, the same relationship was not found for West Germans. Scherer's findings alert us to the fact that correlates of perceived influence show considerable variation across cultures. Brooke and Ng (1986) reported that those rated as highly influential in group discussions took significantly more speaking turns and spoke more words than those rated as less influential. They found no significant differences between the two groups in terms of their use of polite forms, tag questions, and hedges. In contrast to these studies, Burgoon, Birk, and Pfau (1990) found no significant correlations between judgments of the dynamism of individuals presenting public speeches and 16 different nonverbal behaviors, including behaviors subsumed by such categories as vocalic potency cues and kinesic dominance cues; however, 7 of the 16 behaviors showed significant correlations with rated persuasiveness. Dynamism correlated modestly with persuasiveness ($r = .39$).

Experimental studies. Several studies have examined the relationship between speech rate and evaluations of the persuasiveness of a source. Miller, Maruyama, Beaber, and Valone (1976) and Apple, Streeter, and Krauss (1979) both reported that fast-talking persons were judged more persuasive than slow talkers. In addition, Brown, Strong, and Rencher (1974) found that higher rates of speech produced increased ratings of speaker competence. This speaker competence finding was replicated by Street and Brady (1982) and Street, Brady, and Putnam (1983). Ray (1986) also replicated the positive relationship between speech rate and perceived speaker competence; however, this main effect was qualified by a significant interaction with pitch variety. High rate with high pitch variety produced considerably higher competence ratings than the combination of high rate and low pitch variety. By itself, pitch variety was also positively related to perceived competence. In a study that examined the effects of speech rate on both dominance and competence judgments, Buller, LePoire, Aune, and Eloy (1992) reported that both perceived dominance and perceived competence increased with increases in speech rate; however, at very fast speech rates, attributed levels of these qualities decreased. In addition, dominance was positively associated with immediate compliance, while competence was not.

Two studies that manipulated the number of nonfluencies in speech revealed that persons displaying elevated rates of nonfluencies were judged to be less credible than those who showed fewer nonfluencies. Miller and Hewgill (1964) found that increasing rates of repetitions induced a deleterious effect upon ratings of both competence and dynamism. Increased rates of vocalized pauses showed a similar effect upon these credibility ratings but not as consistent as that shown by repetitions. McCroskey and Mehrley (1969) manipulated both message disorganization and rate of nonfluencies. Their study revealed that message disorganization lowered competence ratings of the source but not dynamism ratings; however, nonfluencies had significant negative effects on both of these credibility dimensions. Moreover, the greatest amount of actual attitude change was found in the organized message-fluent condition of the study. The other three conditions examined in the experiment showed no differential attitude change. Apple et al. (1979) found that, for males, increases in voice pitch lowered observers' ratings of their persuasiveness. Brown et al. (1974) also reported that increases in voice pitch tended to lower ratings of competence. Studies that have manipulated interruptions in conversations generally have shown that those who interrupt are judged to be more assertive or dominant but less appropriate and attractive (Hawkins, 1991; Robinson & Reis, 1989).

In the Mehrabian and Williams (1969) study cited earlier, the effects of relaxation, shoulder orientation, distance, and eye contact on perceived persuasiveness were examined. This study revealed that males who were slightly relaxed were judged to be more persuasive than males who were either slightly tense or moderately or very relaxed. By contrast, slightly tense and slightly relaxed females were seen to be more persuasive than moderately or very relaxed females. Males who showed an indirect shoulder orientation were perceived to be more persuasive than males who displayed a direct shoulder orientation, but variations in shoulder orientation produced no differences for females. At close distances, there was no relationship between amount of eye contact and perceived persuasiveness for either gender; however, at a greater distance, males who increased eye contact were judged less persuasive, whereas females who increased eye contact were judged more persuasive. Dovidio and Ellyson (1982) manipulated the relative amount of time persons spent looking while speaking and looking while listening. They found that attributions of power increased as the proportion of looking while speaking increased. Attributions of power decreased as the rate of looking while listening increased. The person who is attentive while another is speaking is more likely to be judged less powerful than the person who is relatively inattentive while others are speaking. Moreover, persons who gaze at their partner while they speak are more likely to be judged to be powerful than those who look less at their conversational partner. Burgoon, Newton, Walther, and Baesler (1989) found that confederates who violated expected levels of interaction involvement by being uninvolved in their conversations were perceived to be less dominant than those who showed normal or above-normal involvement levels.

Lee and Ofshe (1981) designed an experiment in which they pitted social characteristics theory (Berger et al., 1977) against their notion that the demeanors of persons influence perceptions of competence. The social characteristics formulation suggests that status increases perceived competence, which then allows those so perceived to become more dominant. By contrast, Lee and Ofshe (1981) asserted that a dominant demeanor increases perceptions of competence; behavior precedes attributions of competence. In their study, participants viewed specially edited videotapes of jury deliberations in which a target person argued for a particular level of monetary settlement. Target status was varied by flashing a high, moderate, or low status occupational title on the screen when the target person spoke. Demeanor was manipulated by varying the tone of voice, volume of voice, speech rate, number and length of pauses, body posture, facial expressions, hand gestures, gaze direction, number of nervous movements, and dress of the target juror. Using these variables, three demeanor conditions were devised: deference demanding, deferential, and neutral. After viewing the tapes, observers indicated the level of settlement they felt was appropriate, as a measure of the target person's influence. In addition, several attribution measures were completed.

This study revealed that those who viewed the deference-demanding version of the tape showed more persuasion than those who viewed the other two versions of the tape, while the status manipulation showed no significant impact upon the settlement awarded. Although both higher status and deference-demanding versions of the tapes produced higher ratings on scales tapping confidence and assertiveness, only the demeanor variable exerted significant effects upon ratings of the quality of arguments presented and the competence of the target person; that is, persons rated the target in the deference-demanding condition as both more competent and presenting higher quality arguments. Lee and Ofshe (1981) interpreted the findings of this study as a repudiation of social characteristics theory and support for their two-process formulation; however, Berger and Zelditch (1983) argued that Lee and Ofshe's (1981) manipulation of status was so pallid relative to the demeanor manipulation that status exerted relatively little influence on both actual influence and source attributions. Nemeth (1983) concurred with Berger and Zelditch's (1983) observation concerning the manipulation employed in the study; however, she observed that both formulations could be correct. Ofshe and Lee (1983) attempted to defend their manipulation.

Consistent with the status characteristics theory formulation, there is evidence that task cues related to the confidence with which individuals interact in groups are more predictive of interpersonal influence than are dominance cues involving threat and intrusive interaction styles (Ridgeway, 1987; Ridgeway, Berger, & Smith, 1985; Ridgeway & Diekema, 1989). Sev'er (1989) reported that task cues exerted significant effects on both influence and perceptions, while the diffuse status characteristic of race only affected attribution judgments. Although Mohr (1986) found no significant effects for either status or demeanor on measures of influence, he did find that individuals whose actions were consistent with a low dominance demeanor were judged to be significantly more assertive when it was revealed that they had high status. Although not directly related to status characteristics theory, a study by Holtgraves, Srull, and Socall (1989) suggests that conversational recall is influenced by the status of the person whose remarks are being recalled. Specifically, they found that, when recalling remarks made by high status individuals during conversations, individuals were more prone to confuse actual remarks with assertive paraphrases of those remarks than when they recalled remarks made by low status people. Their evidence indicates that these effects are produced when information is encoded into memory rather than when it is retrieved. Apparently, status information significantly affects the way in which remarks made during conversations are characterized.

Summary. The studies reviewed in this section support the conclusion that perceptions of power can be strongly influenced by variations in both verbal and nonverbal behaviors. However, it should be emphasized that, although relationships between behavioral variations and changes in attributed power can be demonstrated relatively consistently, power-relevant attributions may or may not be directly related to actual influence (Buller et al., 1992; Mohr, 1986; Sev'er, 1989). In fact, under certain conditions, some people might increase their resistance to influence as they attribute more dynamism or potency to another. Also considered were two explanations for the achievement of dominant positions in groups. Social characteristics theory argues that status is translated into dominance through a set of beliefs concerning the superior competence of high status persons. Two-process theory argues that observations of behavior are the causes of competence judgments. Dominant behaviors cause attributions, not vice versa. Both of these positions could be correct if one allows for a dynamic conception of social interaction in which initial attributions can be modified by observations of subsequent actions. Alterations in attributions would then produce alterations in action. It is to these more dynamic conceptions that we now turn.

Interactive Approaches to Interpersonal Communication and Power

Now that the roles that variations in power orientations play in producing variations in communicative conduct and the role that communicative conduct plays in making inferences concerning power have been examined, attention now turns to research that attempts to deal with communication and power in a more dynamic, exchange-oriented framework. There are two lines of research relevant here: (a) relational control and (b) accommodation theory.

Relational control. Earlier in this chapter, the assumptions underlying the relational control approach and a coding system (Rogers & Farace, 1975) designed to capture the control dimension of exchanges between persons were examined. Some findings that have emerged from this literature now will be considered. It should be emphasized that this research tradition does not generally deal with perceptions or attributions of power; rather, inferences concerning relative influence are made by studying patterns of message exchanges between persons. In a series of studies (Courtright, Millar, & Rogers-Millar, 1979; Millar, Rogers-Millar, & Courtright, 1979; Rogers-Millar & Millar, 1979), a distinction was drawn between domineeringness and dominance. Domineeringness is indexed by the sheer number of one-up messages sent by one person to another, whereas dominance is indexed by the number of one-up messages that are responded to by one-down messages from the other. Domineeringness is an individual attribute, while dominance is an attribute of the relationship between individuals. In studies investigating these two variables, Courtright et al. (1979) and Rogers-Millar and Millar (1979) failed to find consistently strong correlations between them. This outcome led Rogers-Millar and Millar (1979) to conclude that measures like domineeringness, that focus upon the frequency of individual behaviors, are not measures of power because they fail to capture the response of the other individual and do not correlate well with measures like dominance that do take the response of the other individual into account. The distinction made here is like the one made earlier between potential and actual power. Obviously, one cannot be influential unless one makes influence attempts (domineeringness); however, merely because such attempts are made does not guarantee they will be successful. Even so, the findings reviewed thus far certainly indicate that domineering individuals are more likely to be seen as group leaders and as more influential by others in the group, rendering domineering people potentially more influential.

In relating the above measures to other variables, Millar et al. (1979) reported that, in a sample of married couples, the more one spouse was clearly dominant, the less each spouse was able to predict the other spouse's responses. Greater similarity in dominance was associated with greater understanding. The more domineering messages sent by one spouse to the other, the less likely it was that the other was able to predict the sender's behavior. Rogers-Millar and Millar (1979) found that domineering behavior of wives was associated with lower levels of marital satisfaction and greater role strain, whereas husbands' domineering behavior was related to the frequency of nonsupportive statements and shorter discussion times. Increased dominance was associated with greater marital satisfaction and lowered role strain. Courtright et al. (1979) reported that the more domineering the husband, the less satisfied are both spouses with the marriage and the less able they are to predict each other's responses. In addition, husband dominance was slightly related (r = .22) to the husband's level of marital satisfaction. Most of the correlations reported in these studies were in the .20 to .30 range and rarely exceeded .40. Apparently, satisfaction and understanding are related to both domineeringness and dominance, but these relationships are relatively weak. In another study of married couples, VanLear and Zietlow (1990) found complex relationships between marital satisfaction and patterns of relational control between spouses. These relationships depended upon the type of marriage arrangement in which the couples participated (Fitzpatrick, 1977, 1984, 1988). Using a similar approach to measuring relational control, Fisher and Drecksel (1983) reported that relationships between strangers cycled through periods of competitive symmetrical interaction, while complementary and equivalent symmetrical patterns remained consistent over time.

Rogers, Courtright, and Millar (1980) refined the original Rogers and Farace (1975) coding system by adding an intensity dimension to try to capture degrees of message control. These intensity measures showed significant but generally weak correlations with such variables as dyadic understanding and communication satisfaction. Folger and Poole (1982) have argued that, unless these relational coding schemata are validated with reference to participants' culturally shared meanings of control, these schemata are not likely to yield a great deal in the way of explanatory power. Rogers and Millar (1982) countered that one does not need to be concerned with individuals' interpretations in order to study communication; however, Berger (1983) pointed out that, while it is true that "one can do communication research without considering interpretative processes . . . it is equally true that persons cannot 'do communication' without interpretative processes" (p. 24). In a research program aimed at validating relational control coding systems, systematic relationships have been found between one-up and one-down control moves and discrete nonverbal behaviors (Friedlander & Heatherington, 1989; Siegel, Friedlander, & Heatherington, 1992).

Speech accommodation theory. Although not directly focused upon social power, speech accommodation theory is related to the kinds of adjustments in both verbal and nonverbal communication that persons make during their interactions with others. The theory has been developed and expanded by Giles and Powesland (1975), Giles and Smith (1979), Giles (1980), and Street and Giles (1982). The theory seeks to explain why persons sometimes adjust various attributes of their speech (accent, dialect, and rate) so that they become more similar or converge and why persons sometimes show divergence on such speech attributes. In general, convergence represents an effort to build solidarity, whereas divergence may represent an effort at asserting a unique social identity. A consistent finding in this literature is that speakers who use standard dialects or high prestige varieties of speech tend to be judged more competent and confident than those who use less prestigious varieties (Sebastian & Ryan, 1985).

Bradac and Mulac (1984a) employed the speech accommodation framework to investigate the consequences of reciprocal and nonreciprocal uses of powerful and powerless speech by high and low status persons. These investigators constructed alleged counseling episodes between a therapist and a client in which both persons used the same speech style (powerful or powerless) or one used a powerful style and the other a powerless style. Persons listened to one of the eight versions of the tape and then made a number of ratings of the conversational participants. This study revealed that observers rated both the high power speech style and the counselor as higher in dynamism; however, a triple interaction occurred for the speech style, reciprocity, and gender of observer variables. Females made especially high dynamism ratings when either the counselor or the client displayed nonreciprocal high power; however, males judged the high power version as more dynamic regardless of the reciprocity conditions. Observers' ratings of the attractiveness of the persons on the tapes showed that both the counselor and the client were perceived as more attractive when they used powerful speech. In another speech accommodation study, Hogg (1985) reported that females' speech became more masculine in mixed-sex groups and became more feminine when females interacted in same-sex groups. Similar accommodation effects were not observed for males.

Summary. In this section, the relationship between social power and communicative conduct has been examined. First, power was cast in the role of an independent variable and communicative conduct as a dependent variable. Here, it was found that trait measures such as *n* Power, dominance, control, and locus of control are fairly consistent predictors of such dominance behaviors as interruptions, verbal productivity, and eye gaze. While there are consistencies in these relationships, the correlations between trait measures and behavioral measures of power tend to be modest. Considerable consistency in the relationships between power and communicative conduct was evident when studies that either assumed or manipulated status or power differences between persons were considered; although, in the case of gender differences, a number of inconsistent findings were noted.

Research that casts communication behavior in the role of an independent variable and attributions of power as a dependent variable was then explored. In these cases, a great deal of consistency was found between both measurements or manipulations of various verbal and nonverbal behaviors and inferences made about the degree of influence people have in groups. Those who participate more frequently, talk fast (up to a point), speak with few hesitations, and show a pattern of dominance in eye gaze are likely to be perceived to be more influential. Finally, literature that has considered the study of power from an interactive perspective was examined. This literature suggests that individual measures of power such as verbal participation rate do not index the same constructs as measures that are based on the joint actions of persons. The issue of the role that interpretative processes play in the way power is wielded in social interaction situations was raised.

Compliance-Gaining Strategies

Over the past two decades, communication researchers have devoted considerable energy to studying strategies persons use to wield influence in various social contexts (see Chapter 15). One important tributary to this research torrent was propelled by Marwell and Schmitt's (1967) initial study of compliance-gaining

Table 12.1 Marwell and Schmitt's (1967) 16 Compliance-Gaining Techniques

1. Promise: If you comply, I will reward you.
2. Threat: If you do not comply, I will punish you.
3. Expertise (positive): If you comply, you will be rewarded because of "the nature of things."
4. Expertise (negative): If you do not comply, you will be punished because of "the nature of things."
5. Liking: Actor is friendly and helpful to get target in "good frame of mind" so that he will comply with request.
6. Pregiving: Actor rewards target before requesting compliance.
7. Aversive Stimulation: Actor continuously punishes target, making cessation contingent on compliance.
8. Debt: You owe me compliance because of past favors.
9. Moral Appeal: You are immoral if you do not comply.
10. Self-Feeling (positive): You will feel better about yourself if you comply.
11. Self-Feeling (negative): You will feel worse about yourself if you do not comply.
12. Altercasting (positive): A person with "good" qualities would comply.
13. Altercasting (negative): Only a person with "bad" qualities would not comply.
14. Altruism: I need your compliance very badly, so do it for me.
15. Esteem (positive): People you value will think better of you if you comply.
16. Esteem (negative): People you value will think worse of you if you do not comply.

techniques. A smaller, albeit no less important tributary to this flow emanated from the constructivist research tradition (Applegate, 1982; Clark, 1979; Clark & Delia, 1976; Delia, Kline, & Burleson, 1979; Leichty & Applegate, 1991; O'Keefe & Delia, 1979). It is difficult to be an effective docent in the Museum of Compliance-Gaining Research because its contents are so diffuse, stemming, in part, from their lack of firm theoretical grounding, although attempts have been made to place the study of strategic communication in general and compliance gaining in particular into a coherent theoretical frame (Berger, in press; Dillard, 1990a, 1990b; Greene, 1990; Kellermann, 1988; M. J. Smith, 1984; Wheeless et al., 1983). In addition, several researchers have invoked Brown and Levinson's (1978, 1987) politeness theory as a framework for predicting strategy choice (Baxter, 1984; Craig, Tracy, & Spisak, 1986; Holtgraves & Yang, 1990, 1992; Leichty & Applegate, 1991; Lim & Bowers, 1991).

From the perspective of the present chapter, however, one problem with both the compliance-gaining and constructivist approaches to the study of persuasive strategies concerns the situations that are used to elicit responses for analysis. Several studies in the compliance-gaining tradition (for example, deTurck, 1985; Miller, Boster, Roloff, & Seibold, 1977; Roloff & Barnicott, 1978, 1979) have followed the lead of Marwell and Schmitt (1967) and presented research participants with the list of 16 strategies as presented in Table 12.1, although other researchers have constructed their own strategy lists for particular purposes (Kearney & Plax, 1988). In many studies, people are asked to imagine themselves in a particular situation in which they would like to exercise influence. They then indicate on scales the likelihood that they would use each of the 16 strategies in the imagined situation.

Clark (1979) has questioned the use of this technique, as there may be persuasion strategies that persons use that are not on the list. Furthermore, in their everyday interactions with others, persons do not select strategies from lists. In contrast to the compliance-gaining approach, constructivist researchers generally have asked individuals to imagine themselves in a situation and have them construct a message that they would employ in such a situation.

A problem common to both of these approaches is that they tend to focus exclusively upon the verbal content of messages and exclude the role that nonverbal behavior plays in compliance gaining and persuasion. The literature reviewed in this chapter indicates that such nonverbal behaviors as body orientation, speech rate, pitch, fluency, interaction distance, and patterns of eye gaze both are related to trait measures of power and are strong determinants of attributions of power. In fact, it is plausible to argue that these nonverbal behaviors are more significant in determining the experience of power and dominance than are variables related to verbal content. One conclusion to be drawn is that failure to take into account nonverbal behavior in the study of communication and power relationships is to doom oneself to study the tip of a very large iceberg.

Another problem common to both of these approaches is that neither of them is concerned with decision processes that are activated by the responses that influence targets give to influence attempts; that is, there may be any number of unique strategies that depend on the responses of others for their activation. This same problem also exists in studies that have asked persons to generate strategies they would use to gain or to resist influence in general or in given situations (Cody, McLaughlin, & Jordan, 1980; Falbo, 1977; McLaughlin et al., 1980; McQuillen, 1986). Another problem growing from the fact that noninteractive situations have been so frequently employed to study strategy use concerns iterative mechanisms persons use to select another strategy or strategies when the strategy they have used fails. Those studies that have taken this problem seriously, although not all of them have studied ongoing interactions, have found that, while influence agents usually employ initially positive strategies for gaining compliance (Tracy, Craig, Smith, & Spisak, 1984), progressively more coercive forms of influence are employed by power holders who encounter resistance from influence targets (Berger & Jordan, 1991; deTurck, 1985, 1987; Goodstadt & Kipnis, 1970; Hirokawa et al., 1991; Instone et al., 1983; Kipnis & Consentino, 1969). In the Hirokawa et al. (1991) study, changes to more direct and less polite strategies were most evident when the request for compliance was highly legitimate. A useful model of strategy choice must include an explanation for the changes in strategy implementation that occur as social influence episodes unfold.

Fortunately, there is evidence that those interested in compliance gaining are shifting their priorities to the study of ongoing interactions, as some have recommended (Berger, 1985; G. R. Miller, 1983; Miller, Boster, Roloff, & Seibold, 1987). Witteman and Fitzpatrick (1986) found that, in compliance-gaining interactions between spouses, the kinds of compliance-gaining strategies used depended on the type of relationship in which the couples were involved. Independents employed a wider range of strategies than either Traditionals or Separates. In another study involving observations of married couples' interactions, Newton and Burgoon (1990) reported that both husbands and wives were more likely to use the positive strategy of content validation to deal with disagreements. Husbands were judged to be more persuasive by their wives when they used supportive strategies; by contrast, wives were perceived to be more persuasive when they avoided using accusations. Wives' use of supportive strategies did not influence husbands' judgments of their persuasiveness. Several of the strategies showed reciprocity effects between spouses. Studies such as these tell us considerably more about the dynamics of compliance-gaining strategy deployment in ongoing social interactions than do studies employing hypothetical scenarios and lists of strategies.

Several studies have sought to isolate dimensions of compliance-gaining message choices (Cody & McLaughlin, 1980; Cody et al., 1980; Dillard, 1988; Falbo,

1977; Kaminski, McDermott, & Boster, 1977; Marwell & Schmitt, 1967; Miller et al., 1977; Roloff & Barnicott, 1978, 1979; Schenk-Hamlin et al., 1982; Wiseman & Schenk-Hamlin, 1981). These studies have produced varying numbers of dimensions, even those that have employed the same set of strategies. There is evidence, however, that the multidimensional solutions found in some of these studies (Kaminski et al., 1977; Marwell & Schmitt, 1967; Miller et al., 1977; Roloff & Barnicott, 1978, 1979) are spurious and that a single dimension related to verbal aggressiveness may underlie choices rather than a more complex set of dimensions (Hunter & Boster, 1987). Such a positive-negative dimension was suggested by Berger (1985). In addition to this problem, it appears that message selection data do not exhibit a high degree of correspondence with reported or actual compliance-gaining behavior (Dillard, 1988) and that situational dimensions of compliance gaining (Cody & McLaughlin, 1980; Cody, McLaughlin, & Schneider, 1981; Cody, Woelfel, & Jordan, 1983) generally do not predict strategy choice (Dillard & Burgoon, 1985).

Perhaps because of the problems outlined above, there are signs that the volume of compliance-gaining research is ebbing. This is an unfortunate trend because the idea that most persuasive activity takes place within face-to-face interactions involving small groups of people rather than in mass audience contexts, whether they are mediated or unmediated, is an important theme animating much of the compliance-gaining research. Most of the laboratory research on persuasion conducted during the 1950s and 1960s generally emulated mass audience situations and frequently employed stimulus materials that were alleged to be media messages. This experimental paradigm dovetailed nicely with experimental designs built around the logic of variance analysis. Although this research paradigm made the control of extraneous variables possible, it could not easily accommodate the feedback processes that are involved when individuals engage in face-to-face social influence episodes. Under these conditions, individuals not only can defend their beliefs against attack but they can also engage in counterpersuasion. The compliance-gaining research enterprise generally failed to incorporate these critical features of interpersonal influence episodes into its research designs. Nonetheless, there are signs that research attention may be shifting toward the serious study of reciprocal influence processes.

Conclusion

As the theory and research reviewed in this chapter indicate, over the past two decades there has been a marked increase in the amount of research linking dominance and nonverbal communication. This development serves as a counterweight to the still apparent tendency of some to limit the study of interpersonal influence processes to the domain of verbal communication. What is needed at this juncture, however, is the integration of both verbal and nonverbal channels in the study of communication and social power. In addition, more must be done to devise theories that focus specifically on the relationships between communication and power. Theories of social exchange emphasize the psychological calculations that interactants make concerning the desirability of specific relationships relative to alternatives. These theories do not make detailed predictions about specific attributes of verbal and nonverbal interaction, however. Furthermore, while relational control researchers have devised useful coding schemes for capturing relationship aspects of social power and conducted some provocative studies, these coding schemes exist in a theoretical vacuum. With no theory to guide inquiry, questions arise concerning what it is that the research done in this tradition seeks to explain. This lack of theoretical direction may explain why this line of research appears to be waning. What is needed are theoretical models that explain the dynamics of power and communication in ongoing social interaction and assess these dynamics using measurement tools that capture both interactivity and change.

References

Adams, J. S. (1965). Inequity in social exchange. In L. Berkowitz (Ed.), *Advances in experimental social psychology* (Vol. 2, pp. 267-299). New York: Academic Press.

Adler, A. (1927). *Understanding human nature.* Garden City, NY: Doubleday.

Adler, A. (1930). Individual psychology. In C. Murchison (Ed.), *Psychologies of 1930* (pp. 395-405). Worcester, MA: Clark University Press.

Adler, A. (1966). The psychology of power, 1928. *Journal of Individual Psychology, 22,* 166-172.

Adorno, T. W., Frenkel-Brunswick, E., Levinson, D. J., & Sanford, R. N. (1950). *The authoritarian personality.* New York: Harper & Row.

Andrews, P. H. (1987). Gender differences in persuasive communication and attribution of success and failure. *Human Communication Research, 13,* 372-385.

Apple, W., Streeter, L. A., & Krauss, R. M. (1979). Effects of pitch and speech rate on personal attributions. *Journal of Personality and Social Psychology, 37,* 715-727.

Applegate, J. L. (1982). The impact of construct system development on communication and impression formation in persuasive contexts. *Communication Monographs, 49,* 277-289.

Archer, D., Iritani, B., Kimes, D. D., & Barrios, M. (1983). Face-ism: Five studies of sex differences in facial prominence. *Journal of Personality and Social Psychology, 45,* 725-735.

Aries, E. J., Gold, C., & Weigel, R. H. (1983). Dispositional and situational influences on dominance behavior in small groups. *Journal of Personality and Social Psychology, 44,* 779-786.

Bales, R. F. (1950). *Interaction process analysis.* Reading, MA: Addison-Wesley.

Bales, R. F. (1970). *Personality and interpersonal behavior.* New York: Holt, Rinehart & Winston.

Bateson, G., Jackson, D. D., Haley, J., & Weakland, J. (1956). Toward a theory of schizophrenia. *Behavioral Science, 1,* 251-264.

Bauman, M. (1976). Two features of "women's speech"? In B. L. Dubois & I. Crouch (Eds.), *The sociology of the languages of American women* (pp. 33-40). San Antonio, TX: Trinity University.

Baxter, L. A. (1984). An investigation of compliance-gaining as politeness. *Human Communication Research, 10,* 427-456.

Beekman, S. J. (1975, August). *Sex differences in nonverbal behavior.* Paper presented at the meeting of the American Psychological Association, Chicago.

Berger, C. R. (1980). Power and the family. In M. E. Roloff & G. R. Miller (Eds.), *Persuasion: New directions in theory and research* (pp. 197-224). Beverly Hills, CA: Sage.

Berger, C. R. (1983, November). *Thinking and relating: Social cognition and relational control.* Paper presented at the annual convention of the Speech Communication Association, Washington, DC.

Berger, C. R. (1985). Social power and interpersonal communication. In M. L. Knapp & G. R. Miller (Eds.), *Handbook of interpersonal communication* (pp. 439-499). Beverly Hills, CA: Sage.

Berger, C. R. (1987). Planning and scheming: Strategies for initiating relationships. In R. Burnett, P. McGhee, & D. D. Clarke (Eds.), *Accounting for relationships: Explanation, representation and knowledge* (pp. 158-174). London: Methuen.

Berger, C. R. (1988). Planning, affect and social action generation. In R. L. Donohew, H. Sypher, & E. T. Higgins (Eds.), *Communication, social cognition and affect* (pp. 93-116). Hillsdale, NJ: Lawrence Erlbaum.

Berger, C. R. (in press). A plan-based approach to strategic communication. In D. E. Hewes (Ed.), *Cognitive bases of interpersonal communication.* Hillsdale, NJ: Lawrence Erlbaum.

Berger, C. R., & diBattista, P. (1992). Information seeking and plan elaboration: What do you need to know to know what to do? *Communication Monographs, 59,* 368-387.

Berger, C. R., & Jordan, J. M. (1991, May). *Iterative planning and social action: Repairing failed plans.* Paper presented at the annual convention of the International Communication Association, Chicago.

Berger, C. R., & Jordan, J. M. (1992). Planning sources, planning difficulty, and verbal fluency. *Communication Monographs, 59,* 130-149.

Berger, C. R., Karol, S. H., & Jordan, J. M. (1989). When a lot of knowledge is a dangerous thing: The debilitating effects of plan complexity on verbal fluency. *Human Communication Research, 16,* 91-119.

Berger, J., Fisek, M. H., Norman, R. Z., & Zelditch, M. (1977). *Status characteristics and social interaction.* New York: Elsevier.

Berger, J., & Zelditch, M. (1983). Artifacts and challenges: A comment on Lee and Ofshe. *Social Psychology Quarterly, 46,* 59-62.

Berlo, D. K., Lemert, J. B., & Mertz, R. (1969). Dimensions for judging the acceptability of message sources. *Public Opinion Quarterly, 33,* 563-576.

Blakar, R. M. (1979). Language as a means of social power. In J. L. Mey (Ed.), *Pragmalinguistics: Theory and practice* (pp. 131-169). The Hague, the Netherlands: Mouton.

Blau, P. M. (1964). *Exchange and power in social life.* New York: Wiley.

Blood, R. O. (1967). *Love match and arranged marriage: A Tokyo-Detroit comparison.* New York: Free Press.

Blood, R. O., & Wolfe, D. M. (1960). *Husbands and wives: The dynamics of married living.* New York: Free Press.

Bradac, J. J. (1992). Thoughts about floors not eaten, lungs ripped, and breathless dogs: Issues in language and dominance. In S. A. Deetz (Ed.), *Communication yearbook 15* (pp. 457-468). Newbury Park, CA: Sage.

Bradac, J. J., & Mulac, A. (1984a). Attributional consequences of powerful and powerless speech styles in a crisis-intervention context. *Journal of Language and Social Psychology, 3,* 1-19.

Bradac, J. J., & Mulac, A. (1984b). A molecular view of powerful and powerless speech styles: Attributional consequences of specific language features and communicator intentions. *Communication Monographs, 51,* 307-319.

Braginsky, D. D. (1970). Machiavellianism and manipulative interpersonal behavior in children. *Journal of Experimental Social Psychology, 6,* 77-99.

Brand, M. (1984). *Intending and acting: Toward a naturalized theory of action.* Cambridge: MIT Press.

Bratman, M. E. (1987). *Intention, plans, and practical reason.* Cambridge, MA: Harvard University Press.

Bratman, M. E. (1990). What is intention? In P. R. Cohen, J. Morgan, & M. E. Pollack (Eds.), *Intentions in communication* (pp. 15-31). Cambridge: MIT Press.

Brooke, M. E., & Ng, S. H. (1986). Language and social influence in small conversational groups. *Journal of Language and Social Psychology, 5,* 201-210.

Brouwer, D., Gerritsen, M., & De Haan, D. (1979). Speech differences between women and men: On the wrong track? *Language in Society, 8,* 33-50.

Brown, B. L., Strong, W. J., & Rencher, A. C. (1974). Fifty-four voices from two: The effects of simultaneous manipulations of rate, mean fundamental frequency, and variance of fundamental frequency on ratings of personality from speech. *Journal of the Acoustical Society of America, 55,* 313-318.

Brown, P., & Levinson, S. (1978). Universals in language usage: Politeness phenomena. In E. Goody (Ed.), *Questions and politeness* (pp. 56-289). Cambridge: Cambridge University Press.

Brown, P., & Levinson, S. (1987). *Politeness: Some universals in language usage.* Cambridge: Cambridge University Press.

Brown, R. (1965). *Social psychology.* New York: Free Press.

Brown, R., & Ford, M. (1961). Address in American English. *Journal of Abnormal and Social Psychology, 62,* 375-385.

Bugental, D. B., Henker, B., & Whalen, C. K. (1976). Attributional antecedents of verbal and vocal assertiveness. *Journal of Personality and Social Psychology, 34,* 405-411.

Bull, P. (1983). *Body movement and interpersonal communication.* New York: Wiley.

Buller, D. B., LePoire, B. A., Aune, R. K., & Eloy, S. V. (1992). Social perceptions as mediators of the effect of speech rate similarity on compliance. *Human Communication Research, 19,* 286-311.

Burchinal, L. G., & Bauder, W. W. (1965). Decision-making and role patterns among Iowa farm and non-farm families. *Journal of Marriage and the Family, 27,* 525-530.

Burggraf, C. S., & Sillars, A. L. (1987). A critical examination of sex differences in marital communication. *Communication Monographs, 54,* 276-294.

Burgoon, J. K. (1991). Relational message interpretations of touch, conversational distance, and posture. *Journal of Nonverbal Behavior, 15,* 233-259.

Burgoon, J. K., Birk, T., & Pfau, M. (1990). Nonverbal behaviors, persuasion, and credibility. *Human Communication Research, 17,* 140-169.

Burgoon, J. K., & Hale, J. L. (1984). The fundamental topoi of relational communication. *Communication Monographs, 51,* 193-214.

Burgoon, J. K., & Hale, J. L. (1987). Validation and measurement of the fundamental themes of relational communication. *Communication Monographs, 54,* 19-41.

Burgoon, J. K., Newton, D. A., Walther, J. B., & Baesler, E. J. (1989). Nonverbal expectancy violations and conversational involvement. *Journal of Nonverbal Behavior, 13,* 97-119.

Burgoon, J. K., Walther, J. B., & Baesler, E. J. (1992). Interpretations, evaluations, and consequences of interpersonal touch. *Human Communication Research, 19,* 237-263.

Burgoon, M., Birk, T. S., & Hall, J. R. (1991). Compliance and satisfaction with physician-patient communication: An expectancy theory interpretation of gender differences. *Human Communication Research, 18,* 177-208.

Buric, O., & Zecevic, A. (1967). Family authority, marital satisfaction, and the social network in Yugoslavia. *Journal of Marriage and the Family, 27,* 325-336.

Burr, W. R., Ahern, L., & Knowles, E. M. (1977). An empirical test of Rodman's theory of resources in cultural context. *Journal of Marriage and the Family, 39,* 505-514.

Bussey, K., & Bandura, A. (1984). Influence of gender constancy and social power on sex-linked modeling. *Journal of Personality and Social Psychology, 47,* 1292-1302.

Canary, D. J., Cody, M. J., & Marston, P. J. (1987). Goal types, compliance-gaining and locus of control. *Journal of Language and Social Psychology, 5,* 249-269.

Carbonell, J. L. (1984). Sex roles and leadership revisited. *Journal of Applied Psychology, 53,* 377-382.

Carli, L. L. (1989). Gender differences in interaction style and influence. *Journal of Personality and Social Psychology, 56,* 565-576.

Carli, L. L. (1990). Gender, language, and influence. *Journal of Personality and Social Psychology, 59,* 941-951.

Carson, R. C. (1969). *Interaction concepts of personality.* Chicago: Aldine.

Cartwright, D. (1959). A field theoretical conception of power. In D. Cartwright (Ed.), *Studies in social power* (pp. 183-220). Ann Arbor, MI: Institute for Social Research.

Centers, R., Raven, B. H., & Rodrigues, A. (1971). Conjugal power structure: A re-examination. *American Sociological Review, 36,* 264-278.

Cherry, F., & Byrne, D. (1977). Authoritarianism. In T. Blass (Ed.), *Personality variables in social behavior* (pp. 109-133). Hillsdale, NJ: Lawrence Erlbaum.

Christie, R., & Geis, F. L. (1970). *Studies in Machiavellianism.* New York: Academic Press.

Christie, R., & Jahoda, M. (Eds.). (1954). *Studies in the scope and method of "The Authoritarian Personality."* Glencoe, IL: Free Press.

Cialdini, R. B., & Mirels, H. L. (1976). Sense of personal control and attributions about yielding and resisting persuasion targets. *Journal of Personality and Social Psychology, 33,* 395-402.

Clark, R. A. (1979). The impact of self interest and desire for liking on the selection of communicative strategies. *Communication Monographs, 46,* 257-273.

Clark, R. A., & Delia, J. G. (1976). The development of functional persuasive skills in childhood and early adolescence. *Child Development, 47,* 1008-1014.

Cody, M. J., & McLaughlin, M. L. (1980). Perceptions of compliance-gaining situations: A dimensional analysis. *Communication Monographs, 47,* 132-148.

Cody, M. J., McLaughlin, M. L., & Jordan, W. J. (1980). A multidimensional scaling of three sets of compliance-gaining strategies. *Communication Quarterly, 28,* 34-46.

Cody, M. J., McLaughlin, M. L., & Schneider, M. J. (1981). The impact of relational consequences and intimacy on the selection of interpersonal persuasion tactics: A reanalysis. *Communication Quarterly, 29,* 91-106.

Cody, M. J., Woefel, M. L., & Jordan, W. J. (1983). Dimensions of compliance-gaining situations. *Human Communication Research, 9,* 99-113.

Cohen, A. R. (1958). Upward communication in experimentally created hierarchies. *Human Relations, 11,* 41-53.

Collins, B. E. (1974). Four components of the Rotter internal-external scale: Belief in a difficult world, a just world, a predictable world, and a politically responsive world. *Journal of Personality and Social Psychology, 29,* 381-391.

Collins, B. E., & Raven, B. H. (1969). Group structure: Attraction, coalitions, communication, and power. In G. Lindzey & E. Aronson (Eds.), *Handbook of social psychology* (Vol. 4, pp. 102-204). Reading, MA: Addison-Wesley.

Conrad, C. (1991). Communication in conflict: Style-strategy relationships. *Communication Monographs, 58,* 135-155.

Courtright, J. A., Millar, F. E., & Rogers-Millar, L. E. (1979). Domineeringness and dominance: Replication and expansion. *Communication Monographs, 46,* 179-192.

Craig, R., Tracy, K., & Spisak, F. (1986). The discourse of requests: Assessment of a politeness approach. *Human Communication Research, 12,* 437-468.

Cromwell, R. E., Klein, D. M., & Wieting, S. G. (1975). Family power: A multitrait-multimethod analysis. In R. E. Cromwell & D. H. Olson (Eds.), *Power in families* (pp. 151-181). Beverly Hills, CA: Sage.

Cromwell, V. L., & Cromwell, R. E. (1978). Perceived dominance in decision-making and conflict resolution among Anglo, Black and Chicano couples. *Journal of Marriage and the Family, 40,* 749-759.

Crosby, F., & Nyquist, L. (1977). The female register: An empirical study of Lakoff's hypotheses. *Language in Society, 6,* 313-322.

Dahl, R. A. (1957). The concept of power. *Behavioral Science, 2,* 201-215.

Dean, L. M., Willis, F. N., & Hewitt, J. (1975). Initial interaction distance among individuals equal and unequal in military rank. *Journal of Personality and Social Psychology, 32,* 294-299.

deCharms, R. (1968). *Personal causation: The internal affective determinants of behavior.* New York: Academic Press.

deCharms, R. (1972). Personal causation training in schools. *Journal of Applied Social Psychology, 2,* 95-113.

De Lisi, R. (1987). A cognitive-developmental model of planning. In S. L. Friedman, E. K. Scholnick, & R. R. Cocking (Eds.), *Blueprints for thinking: The role of planning in cognitive development* (pp. 79-109). Cambridge: Cambridge University Press.

deTurck, M. A. (1985). A transactional analysis of compliance-gaining behavior: Effects of noncompliance, relational contexts, and actor's gender. *Human Communication Research, 12,* 54-78.

deTurck, M. A. (1987). When communication fails: Physical aggression as a compliance-gaining strategy. *Communication Monographs, 54,* 106-112.

Delia, J. G., Kline, S. L., & Burleson, B. R. (1979). The development of persuasive communication strategies in kindergartners through twelfth-graders. *Communication Monographs, 46,* 241-256.

Dillard, J. P. (1988). Compliance-gaining message-selection: What is our dependent variable? *Communication Monographs, 55,* 162-183.

Dillard, J. P. (1990a). The nature and substance of goals in tactical communication. In M. J. Cody & M. L. McLaughlin (Eds.), *The psychology of tactical communication* (pp. 70-90). Philadelphia: Multilingual Matters.

Dillard, J. P. (1990b). A goal-driven model of interpersonal influence. In J. P. Dillard (Ed.), *Seeking compliance: The production of interpersonal influence messages* (pp. 41-56). Scottsdale, AZ: Gorsuch Scarisbrick.

Dillard, J. P., & Burgoon, M. (1985). Situational influences on the selection of compliance-gaining messages: Two tests of the predictive utility of the Cody-McLaughlin typology. *Communication Monographs, 52,* 289-304.

Dindia, K. (1987). The effects of sex of subject and sex of partner on interruptions. *Human Communication Research, 13,* 345-371.

Doherty, W. J., & Ryder, R. G. (1979). Locus of control, interpersonal trust, and assertive behavior among newlyweds. *Journal of Personality and Social Psychology, 37,* 2212-2220.

Douglas, S. P., & Wind, Y. (1978). Examining family role and authority patterns: Two methodological issues. *Journal of Marriage and the Family, 40,* 35-47.

Dovidio, J. F., & Ellyson, S. L. (1982). Decoding visual dominance: Attributions of power based on relative percentages of looking while speaking and looking while listening. *Social Psychology Quarterly, 45,* 106-113.

Dovidio, J. F., & Ellyson, S. L. (1985). Patterns of visual dominance behavior in humans. In S. L. Ellyson & J. F. Dovidio (Eds.), *Power, dominance, and nonverbal behavior* (pp. 129-149). New York: Springer-Verlag.

Dovidio, J. F., Ellyson, S. L., Keating, C. F., Heltman, K., & Brown, C. E. (1988). The relationship of social power to visual displays of dominance between men and women. *Journal of Personality and Social Psychology, 54,* 233-242.

Drass, K. A. (1986). The effect of gender identity on conversation. *Social Psychology Quarterly, 49,* 294-301.

Drecksel, G. L., & Fisher, B. A. (1977, February). *Relational interaction characteristics of women's consciousness-raising groups.* Paper presented at the annual convention of the Western Speech Communication Association, Phoenix, AZ.

Druckman, D. (1967). Dogmatism, prenegotiation experience, and simulated group representation as determinants of dyadic behavior in a bargaining situation. *Journal of Personality and Social Psychology, 6,* 279-290.

Dubois, B. L., & Crouch, I. (1975). The question of tag questions in women's speech: They don't really use more of them, do they? *Language in Society, 4,* 289-294.

Eagly, A. H. (1987). *Sex differences in social behavior.* Hillsdale, NJ: Lawrence Erlbaum.

Eagly, A. H., & Karau, S. J. (1991). Gender and the emergence of leaders: A meta-analysis. *Journal of Personality and Social Psychology, 60,* 685-710.

Eakins, B. W., & Eakins, R. G. (1978). *Sex differences in human communication.* Boston: Houghton Mifflin.

Edelsky, C. (1979). Question intonation and sex roles. *Language in Society, 8,* 15-32.

Ellis, D. G. (1979). Relational control in two group systems. *Communication Monographs, 46,* 153-166.

Ellis, D. G., Fisher, R. A., Drecksel, G. L., Hoch, D. D., & Werber, W. S. (1976). *Rel/Com.* Unpublished coding manual, University of Utah.

Ellyson, S. L. (1974). *Visual behavior exhibited by males differing as to interpersonal control orientation in one- and two-way communication systems.* Unpublished doctoral dissertation, University of Delaware.

Ellyson, S. L., & Dovidio, J. F. (Eds.). (1985). *Power, dominance, and nonverbal behavior.* New York: Springer-Verlag.

Ellyson, S. L., Dovidio, J. F., Corson, R. L., & Vinicur, D. L. (1980). Visual dominance behavior in female dyads: Situational and personality factors. *Social Psychology Quarterly, 43,* 328-336.

Emerson, R. M. (1962). Power-dependence relations. *American Sociological Review, 27,* 31-41.

Ericson, P. M., & Rogers, L. E. (1973). New procedures for analyzing relational communication. *Family Process, 12,* 245-267.

Erikson, B., Lind, E. A., Johnson, B. C., & O'Barr, W. M. (1978). Speech style and impression formation in a court setting: The effects of "powerful" and "powerless" speech. *Journal of Experimental Social Psychology, 14,* 266-279.

Etzioni, A. (1961). *A comparative analysis of complex organizations.* New York: Macmillan.

Exline, R. V. (1972). Visual interaction: The glances of power and preference. In J. K. Cole (Ed.), *Nebraska Symposium on Motivation: 1971* (pp. 163-206). Lincoln: University of Nebraska Press.

Exline, R. V., Ellyson, S. L., & Long, B. (1975). Visual behavior as an aspect of power role relationships. In P. Pilner, L. Krames, & T. Alloway (Eds.), *Advances in the study of communication and affect* (Vol. 1, pp. 21-51). New York: Plenum.

Exline, R. V., & Messick, D. (1967). The effects of dependency and social reinforcement upon visual behavior during an interview. *British Journal of Social and Clinical Psychology, 6,* 256-266.

Falbo, T. (1977). Multidimensional scaling of power strategies. *Journal of Personality and Social Psychology, 35,* 537-547.

Falbo, T., & Peplau, L. A. (1980). Power strategies in intimate relationships. *Journal of Personality and Social Psychology, 38,* 618-628.

Fisher, B. A., & Drecksel, G. L. (1983). A cyclical model of developing relationships: A study of relational control interaction. *Communication Monographs, 50,* 66-78.

Fitzpatrick, M. A. (1977). A typological approach to communication in relationships. In B. Ruben (Ed.), *Communication yearbook 1* (pp. 263-274). Rutgers, NJ: Transaction.

Fitzpatrick, M. A. (1984). A typological approach to marital interaction: Recent theory and research. In L. Berkowitz (Ed.), *Advances in experimental social psychology* (Vol. 8, pp. 2-47). New York: Academic Press.

Fitzpatrick, M. A. (1988). *Between husbands and wives: Communication in marriage.* Newbury Park, CA: Sage.

Fitzpatrick, M. A., & Winke, J. (1979). You always hurt the one you love: Strategies and tactics in interpersonal conflict. *Communication Quarterly, 27,* 3-11.

Fischer, J. L. (1958). Social influences on the choice of a linguistic variant. *Word, 14,* 47-56.

Fleischer, R. A., & Chertkoff, J. M. (1986). Effects of dominance and sex on leader selection in dyadic work groups. *Journal of Personality and Social Psychology, 50,* 94-99.

Foa, E., & Foa, U. (1974). *Societal structures of the mind.* Springfield, IL: Charles C Thomas.

Fodor, E. M. (1984). The power motive and reactivity to power stress. *Journal of Personality and Social Psychology, 47,* 853-859.

Fodor, E. M. (1985). The power motive, group conflict, and physiological arousal. *Journal of Personality and Social Psychology, 49,* 1408-1415.

Fodor, E. M., & Farrow, D. L. (1979). The power motive as an influence on use of power. *Journal of Personality and Social Psychology, 37,* 2091-2097.

Fodor, E. M., & Smith, T. (1982). The power motive as an influence on group decision making. *Journal of Personality and Social Psychology, 42,* 178-185.

Folger, J. P., & Poole, M. S. (1982). Relational coding schemes: The question of validity. In M. Burgoon (Ed.), *Communication yearbook 5* (pp. 235-257). New Brunswick, NJ: Transaction.

Folger, J. P., & Puck, S. (1976, April). *Coding relational communication: A question approach.* Paper presented at the annual convention of the International Communication Association, Portland, OR.

Forgas, J. P. (1979). *Social episodes: The study of interaction routines.* London: Academic Press.

French, J. R. P., & Raven, B. (1959). The bases of social power. In D. Cartwright (Ed.), *Studies in social power* (pp. 150-167). Ann Arbor, MI: Institute for Social Research.

Freud, S. (1924). On narcissism: An introduction. 1914. In *Collected papers* (Vol. 4, pp. 30-60). London: Hogarth.

Friedlander, M. L., & Heatherington, L. (1989). Analyzing relational control interaction in family therapy interviews. *Journal of Counseling Psychology, 36,* 139-148.

Frye, R. L., Vidulich, R. N., Meierhoefer, B., & Joure, S. (1972). Differential T-group behaviors of high and low dogmatic participants. *Journal of Psychology, 81,* 301-309.

Geis, F. (1970). The con game. In R. Christie & F. L. Geis (Eds.), *Studies in Machiavellianism* (pp. 106-129). New York: Academic Press.

Gibbons, P., Busch, J., & Bradac, J. J. (1991). Powerful versus powerless language: Consequences for persuasion, impression formation, and cognitive response. *Journal of Language and Social Psychology, 10,* 115-133.

Gifford, R. (1991). Mapping nonverbal behavior on the interpersonal circle. *Journal of Personality and Social Psychology, 61,* 279-288.

Giles, H. (1980). Accommodation theory: Some new directions. In S. deSilva (Ed.), *Aspects of linguistic behavior* (pp. 105-136). York: University of York Press.

Giles, H., & Powesland, P. (1975). *Speech style and social evaluation.* London: Academic Press.

Giles, H., & Smith, P. (1979). Accommodation theory: Optimal levels of convergence. In H. Giles & R. St. Clair (Eds.), *Language and social psychology* (pp. 45-65). Oxford: Basil Blackwell.

Gleason, J. B., & Weintraub, S. (1978). Input language and the acquisition of communicative competence. In K. E. Nelson (Ed.), *Children's language* (Vol. 1, pp. 171-222). New York: Gardner.

Goodstadt, B. E., & Hjelle, L. A. (1973). Power to the powerless: Locus of control and the use of power. *Journal of Personality and Social Psychology, 27,* 190-202.

Goodstadt, B. E., & Kipnis, D. (1970). Situational influences in the use of power. *Journal of Applied Psychology, 54,* 201-207.

Greene, J. O. (1990). Tactical social action: Towards some strategies for theory. In M. J. Cody & M. L. McLaughlin (Eds.), *The psychology of tactical communication* (pp. 41-56). Philadelphia: Multilingual Matters.

Guterman, S. S. (1970). *The Machiavellians.* Lincoln: University of Nebraska Press.

Hacker, S., & Gaitz, C. M. (1970). Interaction and performance correlates of Machiavellianism. *Sociological Quarterly, 2,* 94-102.

Hadley, T., & Jacob, T. (1973). Relationship among measures of family power. *Journal of Personality and Social Psychology, 27,* 6-12.

Haley, J. (1959). The family of the schizophrenic: A model system. *Journal of Nervous and Mental Disease, 129,* 357-374.

Haley, J. (1962). Family experiments: A new type of experimentation. *Family Process, 1,* 265-293.

Haley, J. (1969). *The power tactics of Jesus Christ and other essays.* New York: Grossman.

Hall, J. A., & Veccia, E. M. (1990). More "touching" observations: New insights on men, women, and interpersonal touch. *Journal of Personality and Social Psychology, 59,* 1155-1162.

Hartman, M. (1976). A descriptive study of language of men and women in Maine around 1900 as it reflects the Lakoff hypotheses in "Language and woman's place." In B. L. Dubois & I. Crouch (Eds.), *The sociology of languages of American women* (pp. 81-90). San Antonio, TX: Trinity University.

Hawkins, K. (1991). Some consequences of deep interruption in task-oriented communication. *Journal of Language and Social Psychology, 10,* 185-203.

Heer, D. M. (1958). Dominance and the working wife. *Social Forces, 36,* 341-347.

Heer, D. M. (1962). Husband and wife perceptions of family power structure. *Marriage and Family Living, 24,* 65-67.

Heer, D. M. (1963). The measurement and bases of family power: An overview. *Marriage and Family Living, 25,* 133-139.

Heider, F. (1958). *The psychology of interpersonal relations.* New York: Wiley.

Henley, N. M. (1973). Status and sex: Some touching observations. *Bulletin of the Psychonomic Society, 2,* 91-93.

Henley, N. M. (1977). *Body politics: Power, sex, and nonverbal communication.* Englewood Cliffs, NJ: Prentice-Hall.

Herb, T. R., & Elliott, R. F. (1971). Authoritarianism in the conversation of gestures. *Kansas Journal of Sociology, 7,* 93-101.

Hirokawa, R. Y., Mickey, J., & Miura, S. (1991). Effects of request legitimacy on the compliance-gaining tactics of male and female managers. *Communication Monographs, 58,* 421-436.

Hogg, M. A. (1985). Masculine and feminine speech in dyads and groups: A study of speech style and gender salience. *Journal of Language and Social Psychology, 4,* 99-112.

Holtgraves, T., Srull, T. K., & Socall, D. (1989). Conversation memory: The effects of speaker status on memory for the assertiveness of conversation remarks. *Journal of Personality and Social Psychology, 56,* 149-160.

Holtgraves, T., & Yang, J. (1990). Politeness as universal: Cross-cultural perceptions of request strategies and inferences based on their use. *Journal of Personality and Social Psychology, 59,* 719-729.

Holtgraves, T., & Yang, J. (1992). Interpersonal underpinnings of request strategies: General principles and differences due to culture and gender. *Journal of Personality and Social Psychology, 62,* 246-256.

Homans, G. C. (1961). *Social behavior: Its elementary forms.* New York: Harcourt Brace Jovanovich.

Horney, K. (1937). *The neurotic personality of our time.* New York: Norton.

Howard, J. A., Blumstein, P., & Schwartz, P. (1986). Sex, power, and influence tactics in intimate relationships. *Journal of Personality and Social Psychology, 51,* 102-109.

Hunter, J. E., & Boster, F. J. (1987). A model of compliance-gaining message selection. *Communication Monographs, 54,* 63-84.

Infante, D. A. (1987). Aggressiveness. In J. C. McCroskey & J. A. Daly (Eds.), *Personality and interpersonal communication* (pp. 157-192). Newbury Park, CA: Sage.

Infante, D. A., Chandler, T. A., & Rudd, J. E. (1989). Test of an argumentative skill deficiency model of interspousal violence. *Communication Monographs, 56,* 163-177.

Infante, D. A., & Rancer, A. S. (1982). A conceptualization and measure of argumentativeness. *Journal of Personality Assessment, 46,* 72-80.

Infante, D. A., & Wigley, C. J. (1986). Verbal aggressiveness: An interpersonal model and measure. *Communication Monographs, 53,* 61-69.

Instone, D., Major, B., & Bunker, B. B. (1983). Gender, self-confidence, and social influence strategies: An organizational simulation. *Journal of Personality and Social Psychology, 44,* 322-333.

Jones, S. E. (1986). Sex differences in touch communication. *Western Journal of Speech Communication, 50,* 227-241.

Jones, S. E., & Yarbrough, E. (1985). A naturalistic study of the meanings of touch. *Communication Monographs, 52,* 19-56.

Kaminski, E. P., McDermott, S. T., & Boster, F. J. (1977, April). *The use of compliance-gaining strategies as a function of Machiavellianism and situation.* Paper presented at the annual convention of the Central States Speech Association, Southfield, MI.

Kandel, D. B., & Lesser, G. S. (1972). Marital decision-making in American and Danish urban families: A research note. *Journal of Marriage and the Family, 34,* 134-138.

Kearney, P., & Plax, T. G. (1988). Situational and individual determinants of teachers' reported use of behavior alteration techniques. *Human Communication Research, 14,* 145-166.

Kellermann, K. (1988, March). *Understanding tactical action: Metagoals in conversation.* Paper presented at the Temple University conference on goals and discourse, Philadelphia.

Kelley, H. H. (1951). Communication in experimentally created hierarchies. *Human Relations, 4,* 39-56.

Kelley, H. H., & Thibaut, J. W. (1978). *Interpersonal relations: A theory of interdependence.* New York: Wiley.

Kelman, H. C. (1958). Compliance, identification, and internalization: Three processes of attitude change. *Journal of Conflict Resolution, 2,* 51-60.

Kelman, H. C. (1961). Processes of opinion change. *Public Opinion Quarterly, 25,* 57-78.

Kenkel, W. F. (1957). Influence differentiation in family decision making. *Sociology and Social Research, 42,* 18-25.

Kennedy, C. W., & Camden, C. T. (1983). A new look at interruptions. *Western Journal of Speech Communication, 47,* 45-48.

Key, M. R. (1975). *Male/female language.* Metuchen, NJ: Scarecrow.

Kimble, C. E., & Seidel, S. D. (1991). Vocal signs of confidence. *Journal of Nonverbal Behavior, 15,* 99-105.

Kimble, C. E., Yoshikawa, J. C., & Zehr, H. D. (1981). Vocal and verbal assertiveness in same-sex and mixed-sex groups. *Journal of Personality and Social Psychology, 40,* 1047-1054.

Kipnis, D. (1976). *The powerholders.* Chicago: University of Chicago Press.

Kipnis, D., & Consentino, J. (1969). Use of leadership powers in industry. *Journal of Applied Psychology, 53,* 460-466.

Klopper, E. J., Tittler, B., Friedman, S., & Hughes, S. J. (1978). A multi-method investigation of two family constructs. *Family Process, 17,* 83-93.

Knapp, M. L., & Hall, J. A. (1992). *Nonverbal communication in human interaction* (3rd ed.). Fort Worth, TX: Holt, Rinehart & Winston.

Kramer, C. (1977). Perceptions of female and male speech. *Language and Speech, 20,* 151-161.

Kramarae, C. (1981). *Women and men speaking.* Rowley, MA: Newbury House.

Lakoff, R. (1975). *Language and the woman's place.* New York: Harper & Row.

Lamb, T. A. (1981). Nonverbal and paraverbal control in dyads and triads: Sex or power differences? *Social Psychology Quarterly, 44,* 49-53.

Lamouse, A. (1969). Family roles of women: A German example. *Journal of Marriage and the Family, 31,* 145-152.

Larson, L. E. (1974). System and sub-system perception of family roles. *Journal of Marriage and the Family, 36,* 123-138.

Lasswell, H., & Kaplan, A. (1950). *Power and society.* New Haven, CT: Yale University Press.

Lawrence, S. G., Stucky, N. P., & Hopper, R. (1990). The effects of sex dialects and sex stereotypes on speech evaluations. *Journal of Language and Social Psychology, 9,* 209-224.

Leary, T. (1957). *Interpersonal diagnosis of personality.* New York: Ronald.

Lee, M. T., & Ofshe, R. (1981). The impact of behavioral style and status characteristics on social influence: A test of two competing theories. *Social Psychology Quarterly, 44,* 73-82.

Lefcourt, H. M. (1976). *Locus of control: Current trends in theory and research.* Hillsdale, NJ: Lawrence Erlbaum.

Leffler, A., Gillespie, D. L., & Conaty, J. C. (1982). The effects of status differentiation on nonverbal behavior. *Social Psychology Quarterly, 45,* 153-161.

Leichty, G., & Applegate, J. L. (1991). Social-cognitive and situational influences on the use of face-saving persuasive strategies. *Human Communication Research, 17,* 451-484.

Leighton, L., Stollak, G., & Ferguson, L. (1971). Patterns of communication in normal and clinic families. *Journal of Consulting and Clinical Psychology, 36,* 252-256.

Levine, L., & Crockett, H. J. (1966). Speech variation in a Piedmont community: Post-vocalic r. In S. Lieberson (Ed.), *Explorations in sociolinguistics* (pp. 76-98). The Hague, the Netherlands: Mouton.

Libby, W. L., & Yaklevich, D. (1973). Personality determinants of eye contact and direction of gaze aversion. *Journal of Personality and Social Psychology, 27,* 197-206.

Lim, T., & Bowers, J. W. (1991). Facework: Solidarity, approbation, and tact. *Human Communication Research, 17,* 415-450.

Lind, E. A., & O'Barr, W. M. (1979). The social significance of speech in the courtroom. In H. Giles & R. St. Clair (Eds.), *Language and social psychology* (pp. 66-87). Oxford: Basil Blackwell.

Liska, J. (1992). Dominance-seeking language strategies: Please eat the floor, dogbreath, or I'll rip your lungs out, OK? In S. A. Deetz (Ed.), *Communication yearbook 15* (pp. 427-456). Newbury Park, CA: Sage.

Lott, D. F., & Sommer, R. (1967). Seating arrangements and status. *Journal of Personality and Social Psychology, 7,* 90-95.

Lupri, E. (1969). Contemporary authority patterns in the Western German family: A study in cross-national validation. *Journal of Marriage and the Family, 31,* 134-144.

Major, B. (1981). Gender patterns in touching behavior. In C. Mayo & N. M. Henley (Eds.), *Gender and nonverbal behavior* (pp. 15-37). New York: Springer-Verlag.

Major, B., Schmidlin, A. M., & Williams, L. (1990). Gender patterns in social touch: The impact of setting and age. *Journal of Personality and Social Psychology, 58,* 634-643.

Mark, R. A. (1971). Coding communication at the relationship level. *Journal of Communication, 21,* 221-232.

Markel, N. N., Prebor, L. D., & Brandt, J. F. (1972). Biosocial factors in dyadic communication: Sex and speaking intensity. *Journal of Personality and Social Psychology, 23,* 11-13.

Martin, J. N., & Craig, R. T. (1983). Selected linguistic sex differences during initial social interactions of same-sex and mixed-sex student dyads. *Western Journal of Speech Communication, 47,* 16-28.

Marwell, G., & Schmitt, D. R. (1967). Dimensions of compliance-gaining behavior: An empirical analysis. *Sociometry, 30,* 350-364.

Mason, A., & Blankenship, V. (1987). Power and affiliation motivation, stress, and abuse in intimate relationships. *Journal of Personality and Social Psychology, 52,* 203-210.

McClelland, D. C. (1976). Sources of stress in the drive for power. In G. Serban (Ed.), *Psychopathology of human adaptation* (pp. 247-270). New York: Plenum.

McClelland, D. C. (1982). The need for power, sympathetic activation and illness. *Motivation and Emotion, 6,* 31-41.

McClelland, D. C. (1985). *Human motivation.* Glenview, IL: Scott, Foresman.

McCroskey, J. C., & Mehrley, R. S. (1969). The effects of disorganization and nonfluency on attitude change and source credibility. *Speech Monographs, 36,* 13-21.

McLaughlin, M. L., Cody, M. J., & Robey, C. S. (1980). Situational influences on the selection of strategies to resist compliance-gaining attempts. *Human Communication Research, 7,* 14-36.

McMillan, J. R., Clifton, A. K., McGrath, C., & Gale, W. S. (1977). Women's language: Uncertainty or interpersonal sensitivity and emotionality? *Sex Roles, 3,* 545-559.

McQuillen, J. S. (1986). The development of listener-adapted compliance-resisting strategies. *Human Communication Research, 12,* 359-375.

Megargee, E. I. (1969). Influence of sex roles on the manifestation of leadership. *Journal of Applied Psychology, 53,* 377-382.

Mehrabian, A. (1972). *Nonverbal communication.* Chicago: Aldine.

Mehrabian, A., & Williams, M. (1969). Nonverbal concomitants of perceived and intended persuasiveness. *Journal of Personality and Social Psychology, 13,* 37-58.

Michel, A. (1967). Comparative data concerning the interaction in French and American families. *Journal of Marriage and the Family, 29,* 337-344.

Millar, F. E., Rogers-Millar, L. E., & Courtright, J. A. (1979). Relational control and dyadic understanding. In D. Nimmo (Ed.), *Communication yearbook 3* (pp. 213-224). New Brunswick, NJ: Transaction.

Miller, G. A., Galanter, E., & Pribram, K. H. (1960). *Plans and the structure of behavior.* New York: Holt, Rinehart & Winston.

Miller, G. R. (1983). On various ways of skinning symbolic cats: Recent research on persuasive message strategies. *Journal of Language and Social Psychology, 2,* 123-140.

Miller, G. R., Boster, F., Roloff, M., & Seibold, D. (1977). Compliance-gaining message strategies: A topology and some findings concerning effects of situational differences. *Communication Monographs, 44,* 37-51.

Miller, G. R., Boster, F., Roloff, M. E., & Seibold, D. (1987). MBRS rekindled: Some thoughts on compliance gaining in interpersonal settings. In M. E. Roloff & G. R. Miller (Eds.), *Interpersonal processes: New directions in communication research* (pp. 89-116). Newbury Park, CA: Sage.

Miller, G. R., & Hewgill, M. A. (1964). The effect of variations in nonfluency on audience ratings of source credibility. *Quarterly Journal of Speech, 50,* 36-44.

Miller, M. D., Reynolds, R. A., & Cambra, R. E. (1987). The influence of gender and culture on language intensity. *Communication Monographs, 54,* 101-112.

Miller, N., Maruyama, G., Beaber, R. J., & Valone, K. (1976). Speed of speech and persuasion. *Journal of Personality and Social Psychology, 34,* 615-624.

Minton, H. L. (1967). Power as a personality construct. In B. A. Maher (Ed.), *Progress in experimental personality research* (Vol. 4, pp. 229-267). New York: Academic Press.

Mishler, E. G. (1975). Studies in dialogue and discourse: II. Types of discourse initiated by and sustained through questioning. *Journal of Psycholinguistic Research, 4,* 99-121.

Mishler, E. G., & Waxler, N. E. (1968). *Interaction in families: An experimental study of family processes in schizophrenia.* New York: Wiley.

Mohr, P. B. (1986). Demeanor, status cue or performance? *Social Psychology Quarterly, 49,* 228-236.

Molm, L. D. (1985). Gender and power use: An experimental analysis of behavior and perceptions. *Social Psychology Quarterly, 48,* 285-300.

Mulac, A. (1975). Evaluation of the speech dialect attitudinal scale. *Speech Monographs, 42,* 184-189.

Mulac, A. (1976). Assessment and application of the revised speech dialect attitudinal scale. *Communication Monographs, 43,* 238-245.

Mulac, A. (1989). Men's and women's talk in same-gender and mixed-gender dyads: Power or polemic? *Journal of Language and Social Psychology, 8,* 249-270.

Mulac, A., Bradac, J. J., & Mann, S. K. (1985). Male/female language differences and attributional consequences in children's television. *Human Communication Research, 11,* 481-506.

Mulac, A., Incontro, C. R., & James, M. R. (1985). Comparison of gender-linked language effect and sex role stereotypes. *Journal of Personality and Social Psychology, 49,* 1098-1109.

Mulac, A., & Lundell, T. L. (1986). Linguistic contributions to the gender-linked language effect. *Journal of Language and Social Psychology, 5,* 81-102.

Mulac, A., Lundell, T. L., & Bradac, J. J. (1986). Male/female language differences and the attributional consequences in a public speaking situation: Toward an explanation of the gender-linked language effect. *Communication Monographs, 53,* 115-129.

Mulac, A., Wiemann, J. M., Widenmann, S. J., & Gibson, T. W. (1988). Male/female language differences and effects in same-sex and mixed-sex dyads: The gender-linked language effect. *Communication Monographs, 55,* 315-335.

Murray, H. A. (1938). *Explorations in personality.* New York: Oxford University Press.

Murrell, S., & Stachowiak, J. (1967). Consistency, rigidity and power in the interaction patterns of clinic and nonclinic families. *Journal of Abnormal Psychology, 72,* 265-272.

Nemeth, C. J. (1983). Reflections on the dialogue between status and style: Influence processes of social control and social change. *Social Psychology Quarterly, 46,* 70-74.

Nettler, G. (1957). A measure of alienation. *American Sociological Review, 22,* 670-677.

Newton, D. A., & Burgoon, J. K. (1990). The use and consequences of verbal influence strategies during interpersonal disagreements. *Human Communication Research, 16,* 477-518.

Ng, S. H. (1980). *The social psychology of power.* London: Academic Press.

Noller, P. (1985). Negative communications in marriage. *Journal of Social and Personal Relationships, 2,* 289-301.

Norton, R. (1983). *Communicator style: Theory, applications, and measures.* Beverly Hills, CA: Sage.

O'Barr, W. M. (1982). *Linguistic evidence: Language, power, and strategy in the courtroom.* New York: Academic Press.

O'Barr, W. M., & Atkins, B. K. (1980). "Women's language" or "powerless language." In S. McConnell-Ginet, R. Borker, & N. Furman (Eds.), *Women and language in literature and society* (pp. 93-110). New York: Praeger.

Ofshe, R., & Lee, M. T. (1983). "What are we to make of all this?" Reply to Berger and Zelditch. *Social Psychology Quarterly, 46,* 63-65.

O'Keefe, B. J., & Delia, J. B. (1979). Construct comprehensiveness and cognitive complexity as predictors of the number and strategic adaptation of arguments and appeals in a persuasive message. *Communication Monographs, 46,* 231-240.

Olson, D. H., & Rabunsky, C. (1972). Validity of four measures of family power. *Journal of Marriage and the Family, 34,* 224-234.

Osgood, C. E., Suci, G. J., & Tannenbaum, P. H. (1957). *The measurement of meaning.* Urbana: University of Illinois Press.

Parsons, T. (1963). On the concept of influence. *Public Opinion Quarterly, 27,* 37-62.

Patterson, M. L. (1983). *Nonverbal behavior: A functional perspective.* New York: Springer-Verlag.

Patterson, M. L., Powell, J. L., & Lenihan, M. G. (1986). Touch, compliance, and interpersonal affect. *Journal of Nonverbal Behavior, 10,* 41-50.

Pearson, J. (1985). *Gender and communication.* Dubuque, IA: William C. Brown.

Phares, E. J. (1965). Internal-external control as a determinant of amount of social influence exerted. *Journal of Personality and Social Psychology, 2,* 642-647.

Price-Bonham, S. (1976). A comparison of weighted and unweighted decision-making scores. *Journal of Marriage and the Family, 38,* 629-640.

Rausch, H. L., Barry, W. A., Hertel, R. K., & Swain, M. A. (1974). *Communication and conflict in marriage.* San Francisco: Jossey-Bass.

Raven, B. H. (1965). Social influence and power. In I. D. Steiner & M. Fishbein (Eds.), *Current studies in social psychology* (pp. 371-382). New York: Holt, Rinehart & Winston.

Ray, G. B. (1986). Vocally cued personality prototypes: An implicit personality theory approach. *Communication Monographs, 53,* 266-276.

Ridgeway, C. L. (1987). Nonverbal behavior, dominance, and the basis of status in task groups. *American Sociological Review, 52,* 683-694.

Ridgeway, C. L., Berger, J., & Smith, L. (1985). Nonverbal cues and status: An expectations states approach. *American Journal of Sociology, 90,* 955-978.

Ridgeway, C. L., & Diekema, D. (1989). Dominance and collective hierarchy formation in male and female task groups. *American Sociological Review, 54,* 79-93.

Robinson, L. F., & Reis, H. T. (1989). The effects of interruption, gender, and status on interpersonal perceptions. *Journal of Nonverbal Behavior, 13,* 141-153.

Roger, D. B., & Schumacher, A. (1983). Effects of individual differences on dyadic conversational strategies. *Journal of Personality and Social Psychology, 45,* 700-705.

Rogers, L. E., Courtright, J. A., & Millar, F. E. (1980). Message control intensity: Rationale and preliminary findings. *Communication Monographs, 47,* 201-219.

Rogers, L. E., & Farace, R. B. (1975). Relational communication analysis: New measurement procedures. *Human Communication Research, 1,* 222-239.

Rogers, L. E., & Millar, F. E. (1982). The question of validity: A pragmatic response. In M. Burgoon (Ed.), *Communication yearbook 5* (pp. 249-257). New Brunswick, NJ: Transaction.

Rogers-Millar, L. E., & Millar, F. E. (1979). Domineeringness and dominance: A transactional view. *Human Communication Research, 5,* 238-246.

Rokeach, M. (1960). *The open and closed mind.* New York: Basic Books.

Roloff, M. E. (1981). *Interpersonal communication: The social exchange approach.* Beverly Hills, CA: Sage.

Roloff, M. E., & Barnicott, E. F. (1978). The situational use of pro- and anti-social compliance gaining strategies by high and low Machiavellians. In B. Ruben (Ed.), *Communication yearbook 2* (pp. 193-208). New Brunswick, NJ: Transaction.

Roloff, M. E., & Barnicott, E. F. (1979). The influence of dogmatism on the situational use of pro-and anti-social compliance gaining strategies. *Southern Speech Communication Journal, 45,* 37-54.

Rosenberg, S., & Sedlak, A. (1972). Structural representations of implicit personality theory. In L. Berkowitz (Ed.), *Advances in experimental social psychology* (Vol. 6, pp. 235-297). New York: Academic Press.

Rosenfeld, H. M. (1966). Instrumental affiliative functions of facial and gestural expressions. *Journal of Personality and Social Psychology, 4,* 65-72.

Rotter, J. B. (1966). Generalized expectancies for internal versus external control of reinforcement. *Psychological Monographs, 80* (1, Whole No. 609).

Rubin, J. Z., & Brown, B. R. (1975). *The social psychology of bargaining and negotiation.* New York: Academic Press.

Ruesch, J., & Bateson, G. (1951). *Communication: The social matrix of society.* New York: Norton.

Russell, B. (1938). *Power: A new social analysis.* London: George Allen & Unwin.

Sadalla, E. K., Kenrick, D. T., & Vershure, B. (1987). Dominance and heterosexual attraction. *Journal of Personality and Social Psychology, 52,* 730-738.

Safilios-Rothschild, C. (1967). A comparison of power structure and marital satisfaction in urban Greek and French families. *Journal of Marriage and the Family, 29,* 345-352.

Safilios-Rothschild, C. (1969). Family sociology or wives' family sociology? A cross-cultural examination of decision-making. *Journal of Marriage and the Family, 31,* 290-301.

Safilios-Rothschild, C. (1970). The study of family power structure: A review 1960-1969. *Journal of Marriage and the Family, 32,* 539-552.

Schenck-Hamlin, W. J., Wiseman, R. L., & Georgacarakos, G. N. (1982). A model of properties of compliance-gaining strategies. *Communication Quarterly, 30,* 92-99.

Scherer, K. R. (1979). Voice and speech correlates of perceived social influence in simulated juries. In H. Giles & R. St. Clair (Eds.), *Language and social psychology* (pp. 88-120). Oxford: Basil Blackwell.

Schopler, J. (1965). Social power. In L. Berkowitz (Ed.), *Advances in experimental social psychology* (Vol. 2, pp. 177-218). New York: Academic Press.

Schutz, W. C. (1958). *Firo: A three-dimensional theory of interpersonal behavior.* New York: Holt, Rinehart & Winston.

Sebastian, R. J., & Ryan, E. B. (1985). Speech cues and social evaluation: Markers of ethnicity, social class and age. In H. Giles & R. St. Clair (Eds.), *Recent advances in language, communication and social psychology* (pp. 112-143). London: Lawrence Erlbaum.

Seeman, M. (1959). On the meaning of alienation. *American Sociological Review, 24,* 783-791.

Sev'er, A. (1989). Simultaneous effects of status and task cues: Combining, eliminating, or buffering? *Social Psychology Quarterly, 52,* 327-335.

Siegel, S. M., Friedlander, M. L., & Heatherington, L. (1992). Nonverbal relational control in family communication. *Journal of Nonverbal Behavior, 16,* 117-139.

Simon, H. A. (1957). *Models of man.* New York: Wiley.

Sites, P. (1973). *Control: The basis of social order.* New York: Dunellen.

Smith, M. J. (1984). Contingency rules theory, context, and compliance behaviors. *Human Communication Research, 10,* 489-512.

Smith, P. M. (1979). Sex markers in speech. In K. R. Scherer & H. Giles (Eds.), *Social markers in speech* (pp. 109-146). New York: Cambridge University Press.

Smith, P. M. (1985). *Language, the sexes and society.* Oxford: Basil Blackwell.

Sorrentino, R. M., & Field, N. (1986). Emergent leadership over time: The functional value of positive motivation. *Journal of Personality and Social Psychology, 50,* 1091-1099.

Srole, J. (1956). Social integration and certain corollaries: An exploratory study. *American Sociological Review, 21,* 709-716.

Stein, T. R. (1975). Identifying emergent leaders from verbal and nonverbal communications. *Journal of Personality and Social Psychology, 32,* 125-135.

Stein, T. R., & Heller, T. (1979). An empirical analysis of the correlations between leadership status and participation rates reported in the literature. *Journal of Personality and Social Psychology, 37,* 1993-2002.

Stier, D. S., & Hall, J. A. (1984). Gender differences in touch: An empirical and theoretical review. *Journal of Personality and Social Psychology, 47,* 440-459.

Storrs, D., & Kleinke, C. L. (1990). Evaluation of high and equal status male and female touchers. *Journal of Nonverbal Behavior, 14,* 87-95.

Strauss, M. A., & Tallman, I. (1971). SIMFAM: A technique for observational measurement and experimental study of families. In J. Aldous, T. Condon, R. Hill, M. Strauss, & I. Tallman (Eds.), *Family problem solving* (pp. 381-438). Hinsdale, IL: Dryden.

Street, R. L., & Brady, R. M. (1982). Speech rate acceptance ranges as a function of evaluative domain, listener speech rate, and communication context. *Communication Monographs, 49,* 290-308.

Street, R. L., Brady, R. M., & Putnam, W. B. (1983). The influence of speech rate stereotypes and rate similarity on listeners' evaluations of speakers. *Journal of Language and Social Psychology, 2,* 37-56.

Street, R. L., & Buller, D. B. (1987). Nonverbal response patterns in physician-patient interactions: A functional analysis. *Journal of Nonverbal Behavior, 11,* 234-253.

Street, R. L., & Buller, D. B. (1988). Patients' characteristics affecting physician-patient nonverbal communication. *Human Communication Research, 15,* 60-90.

Street, R. L., & Giles, H. (1982). Speech accommodation theory: A social cognitive approach to language and speech behavior. In M. Roloff & C. Berger (Eds.), *Social cognition and communication* (pp. 193-226). Beverly Hills, CA: Sage.

Strodtbeck, F. L. (1951). Husband-wife interaction over revealed differences. *American Sociological Review, 16,* 468-473.

Strodtbeck, F. L. (1954). The family as a three person group. *American Sociological Review, 19,* 23-29.

Talley, W. M., & Vamos, O. (1972). An exploratory study of dogmatism and its relation to group response. *Canadian Counsellor, 6,* 278-282.

Tannen, D. (1990). *You just don't understand.* New York: William Morrow.

Terhune, K. W. (1968). Motives, situation, and interpersonal conflict within prisoner's dilemma. *Journal of Personality and Social Psychology, 8* (Monograph Suppl. 3, Pt. 2), 1-24.

Thibaut, J. W., & Kelley, H. H. (1959). *The social psychology of groups.* New York: Wiley.

Thorne, B., & Henley, N. (Eds.). (1975). *Language and sex: Difference and dominance.* Rowley, MA: Newbury House.

Thorne, B., Kramarae, C., & Henley, N. (Eds.). (1983). *Language, gender and society.* Rowley, MA: Newbury House.

Tjosvold, D. (1978). Affirmation of the high-power person and his position: Ingratiation in conflict. *Journal of Applied Social Psychology, 8,* 230-243.

Tracy, K., Craig, R. T., Smith, M., & Spisak, F. (1984). The discourse of requests: Assessment of a compliance-gaining approach. *Human Communication Research, 10,* 513-538.

Triandis, H. C., Vassiliou, V., & Nassiakou, M. (1968). Three cross-cultural studies of subjective culture. *Journal of Personality and Social Psychology, 8* (Monograph Suppl. 4, Pt. 2), 1-42.

Trudgill, P. (1972). Sex, covert prestige, and linguistic change in the urban British English of Norwich. *Language in Society, 1,* 179-195.

Turk, J. L., & Bell, N. W. (1972). Measuring power in families. *Journal of Marriage and the Family, 34,* 215-222.

Uleman, J. S. (1972). The need for influence: Development and validation of a measure, and comparison with need for power. *Genetic Psychology Monographs, 85,* 157-214.

VanLear, C. A., & Zietlow, P. H. (1990). Toward a contingency approach to marital interaction: An empirical integration of three approaches. *Communication Monographs, 57,* 202-218.

Veroff, J. (1957). Development and validation of a projective measure of power motivation. *Journal of Abnormal and Social Psychology, 54,* 1-9.

Veroff, J. (1958). A scoring manual for the power motive. In J. W. Atkinson (Ed.), *Motives in fantasy, action and society* (pp. 219-233). Princeton, NJ: Van Nostrand.

Veroff, J., & Veroff, J. B. (1972). Reconsideration of a measure of power motivation. *Psychological Bulletin, 78,* 279-291.

Waller, W., & Hill, R. (1951). *The family: A dynamic interpretation.* New York: Dryden.

Walster, E., Walster, G., & Berscheid, E. (1978). *Equity: Theory and research.* Boston: Allyn & Bacon.

Watzlawick, P., Beavin, J. H., & Jackson, D. D. (1967). *Pragmatics of human communication.* New York: Norton.

Weber, M. (1947). *The theory of social and economic organization.* New York: Oxford University Press.

West, C., & Zimmerman, D. H. (1983). Small insults: A study of interruptions in cross-sex conversations between unacquainted persons. In B. Thorne, C. Kramarae, & N. Henley (Eds.), *Language, gender and society* (pp. 102-117). Rowley, MA: Newbury House.

Wheeless, L. R., Barraclough, R., & Stewart, R. (1983). Compliance-gaining and power in persuasion. In R. N. Bostrom (Ed.), *Communication yearbook 7* (pp. 105-145). Beverly Hills, CA: Sage.

White, R. W. (1959). Motivation reconsidered: The concept of competence. *Psychological Review, 66,* 297-333.

Winter, D. G. (1973). *The power motive.* New York: Free Press.

Winter, D. G. (1988). The power motive in women and men. *Journal of Personality and Social Psychology, 54,* 510-519.

Wiseman, R. L., & Schenk-Hamlin, W. (1981). A multidimensional scaling validation of an inductively-derived set of compliance-gaining strategies. *Communication Monographs, 48,* 251-270.

Wish, M., D'Andrade, R. G., & Goodnow, J. E. (1980). Dimensions of interpersonal communication: Corresponding between structures for speech acts and bipolar scales. *Journal of Personality and Social Psychology, 39,* 848-860.

Wish, M., Deutsch, M., & Kaplan, S. J. (1976). Perceived dimensions of interpersonal relations. *Journal of Personality and Social Psychology, 33,* 409-420.

Witteman, H., & Fitzpatrick, M. A. (1986). Compliance-gaining in marital interaction: Power bases, processes, and outcomes. *Communication Monographs, 53,* 130-143.

Wolfe, D. M. (1959). Power and authority in the family. In D. Cartwright (Ed.), *Studies in social power* (pp. 99-117). Ann Arbor, MI: Institute for Social Research.

Wolfram, W. A. (1969). *A sociolinguistic description of Detroit Negro speech.* Washington, DC: Center for Applied Linguistics.

Wood, W., & Karten, S. J. (1986). Sex differences in interaction style as a product of perceived sex differences in competence. *Journal of Personality and Social Psychology, 50,* 341-347.

Zagona, S. V., & Zurcher, L. A. (1964). Participation, interaction, and role behavior in groups selected from the extremes of the open-closed cognitive continuum. *Journal of Psychology, 58,* 255-264.

Zagona, S. V., & Zurcher, L. A. (1965). Notes on the reliability and validity of the dogmatism scale. *Psychological Reports, 16,* 1234-1236.

Zahn, C. J. (1989). The bases for differing evaluations of male and female speech: Evidence from ratings of transcribed conversation. *Communication Monographs, 56,* 59-74.

Zahn, C. J., & Hopper, R. (1985). Measuring language attitudes: The speech evaluation instrument. *Journal of Language and Social Psychology, 4,* 113-123.

Zietlow, P. H., & Sillars, A. L. (1987, February). *Life stage differences in marital communication and conflict.* Paper presented at the Western Speech Communication Association convention, Salt Lake City, UT.

Zimmerman, D. H., & West, C. (1975). Sex roles, interruptions and silences in conversation. In B. Thorne & N. Henley (Eds.), *Language and sex: Difference and dominance* (pp. 105-129). Rowley, MA: Newbury House.

13

Emotion in Interpersonal Communication

Sandra Metts

John Waite Bowers

EMOTION IS A fundamental, potent, and ubiquitous aspect of social life. Affective arousal forms a subtext underlying all interaction, giving it direction, intensity, and velocity as well as shaping communicative choices. Emotion is also one of the most consequential outcomes of interaction, framing the interpretation of messages, one's view of self and other, and one's understanding of the relationship that gave rise to the feeling. It is virtually impossible to encounter a day that is free of emotion: People are to some degree stressed, depressed, excited, happy, lonely, in love, and in hate in rather continuous, connected streams of affective movement. Moreover, some people seem characteristically to be happy (sad, lonely) persons, emotional (unemotional) persons, or to be easily hurt (angered) and so forth.

The powerful role played by emotion in human behavior and cognition has led some scholars to propose that a comprehensive theory of emotion and emotion knowledge might well be the organizing principle that would integrate currently unrelated constructs in social psychology. Schwartz and Shaver (1987), for example, state:

> The dance of social interaction is a dance designed to encourage, elicit, avoid, mask, and feign certain feelings; the topics with which social psychologists are familiar—attitudes, altruism, aggression, self-presentation, conformity, obedience, and so on—are all tied to this dance of feelings. It seems unlikely that we will achieve a systematic, integrated understanding of such phenomena without a clear and comprehensive conception of emotion. (p. 237)

As we noted in an earlier version of this chapter (Bowers, Metts, & Duncanson, 1985), however, mainstream research in communication is rarely focused in the affective concerns that motivate and channelize most communication processes.

The purpose of this present chapter is to provide a broad overview of emotion theories and to profile empirical research that offers promising directions for building models of emotion in interpersonal communication. The organization of the chapter reflects these two foci. The first section reviews and extends the several prominent approaches to theorizing about emotions presented in the 1985 edition of this chapter (Bowers et al., 1985). The second section details and integrates research on emotion at three levels: individual, social, and dyadic. Specifically, we discuss individual differences in emotion processing and responding, interaction constraints imposed by the social imperative to display positive emotions, and the manifestation of these influences on the conversational patterns of intimate couples.

Theories of Emotion

Theories of emotion are remarkably disparate, both within and across the disciplines of psychology, social psychology, physiology, and sociology. Several key issues remain unresolved. Among the most problematic and recurrent are those concerning (a) the nature of emotional experience (that is, the relative importance of physiological activation and cognitive, interpretive processes); (b) the function of emotional experience (to ensure survival of the species or to give meaning to social organization and interaction); (c) the origin of emotional experience and expression (innate, phylogenic patterns or acquired patterns); (d) the domain of legitimate inquiry (a set of 5 to 15 basic or primary emotional states or a potentially infinite array of unique, subjective experiences). Moreover, no single one of these issues, or even combination of issues, clearly separates the major theories of emotion into exhaustive and mutually exclusive camps.

For these reasons, the representative theories of emotion reviewed here are organized loosely into four groups. The theories in the first group share a common analytic orientation toward classifying emotional states according to similarities and differences along underlying dimensions. The common assumption is that emotional states are relatively coherent and uniform experiential structures with inherent features that ordinary social actors can articulate. These approaches share a methodological preference for respondent ratings of attributes associated with emotion terms provided by researcher or self-report descriptions of experienced or typical emotional states (e.g., anger, sadness). Factor analysis or multidimensional scaling techniques are used to identify emotion families or the underlying structures of specific emotions.

The second group of theories focuses attention on the reciprocal effect of social consciousness on emotional experience and emotional experience on social meaning. The common thread within this group is a transactional metaphor, one in which the experience of emotion is a combination of biological, psychological, and behavioral impulses that cohere meaningfully because they are rooted in social norms, rules, and expectations.

The third group of theories concern themselves more or less directly with the ongoing and complicated controversy regarding the nature of the relationship between physiological activation and cognitive processes in emotional experience. Although the more subtle points in the debate are beyond the scope of our review, we identify three positions within this group of theories: (a) Physiological activation constitutes specific primary emotions independent of cognitive appraisal; (b) physiological arousal is felt as undifferentiated sensation and requires cognitive mediation ("labeling") to be recognized as a particular emotion; (c) activation and cognitive processes are both essential in the experiencing of emotional states.

The final portion of the review of theories is a brief account of Leventhal's "perceptual motor theory." We treat this theory separately because its developmental orientation provides an integrative framework for many of the points raised by theorists in the preceding sections.

The classification of emotion theories we use here is intended to provide an organizing framework for reviewing a large number of perspectives; it is not intended to minimize the several points of contact, at various levels, among theories in different groups. As the second portion of this chapter indicates, empirical research draws productively from these points of contact as well as from individual theories.

Language Analytic Approaches

Emotion Prototypes

The goal of prototype analysis is to explain the organization of emotion knowledge in much the same way that other kinds of knowledge are categorized in human information processing, that is, in hierarchical levels along a vertical dimension and in more finely differentiated sets across a horizontal dimension. The vertical dimension typically indicates three levels of specificity: the superordinate (vehicle), the basic (car), and the subordinate level (Toyota Corolla). For most ordinary purposes, the basic level is preferred; it is sufficiently specific to distinguish an object or event without being more detailed than necessary. The horizontal dimension segments categories that occur at the same level on the vertical dimension. The distinctions between these categories are somewhat fuzzy but can be clarified through comparison to a prototype, "a list of weighted features, an abstract image, or a highly characteristic exemplar representing the core meaning of the category" (Shaver, Wu, & Schwartz, 1992, p. 186). Members of the same category vary in the degree to which they approach or differ from the prototype.

The research agenda of Schwartz and Shaver (1987; Shaver, Schwartz, Kirson, & O'Connor, 1987; Shaver et al., 1992) exemplifies this approach. In one study, respondents were asked to compare 135 emotion terms on similarity (Shaver et al., 1987). Hierarchical cluster analysis yielded a hierarchy with six major nodes at the basic level of categorization: love, joy, anger, sadness, fear, and possibly surprise. Other emotions formed variants and blends of these six emotions (Figure 13.1).

Respondent descriptions of the six prototypical emotions revealed clear and consistent distinctions in their macro- or episodic structures, each having a characteristic beginning with motivational and cognitive antecedents, a characteristic range of responses (subjective, physiological, and behavioral), and techniques of self-control in the case of most negative emotions. For example, antecedents of the fear prototype included an interpretation of events as potentially threatening (e.g., anticipation of physical harm, rejection, or failure) and a set of situational factors that increase the perceived vulnerability to such threats (e.g., being alone or unable to escape the situation). Characteristic responses were arousal of the autonomic nervous system in preparation for flight (e.g., trembling), some type of verbalization (e.g., screaming or yelling), and attempted escape from the situation (e.g., running or walking quickly). Coping attempts included hiding from the threat,

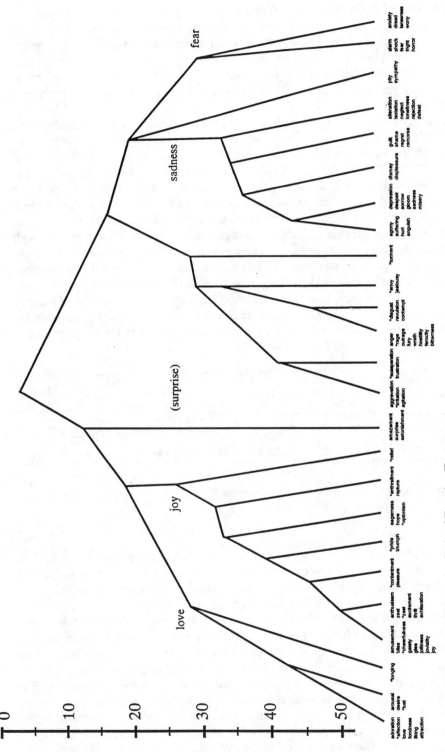

Figure 13.1. Hierarchical Cluster Analysis of Emotion Terms
SOURCE: Adapted from Schwartz and Shaver (1987, pp. 204-205).

freezing and being quiet, or a pair of internal reactions such as becoming disoriented or cognitively impaired by visualizations of the danger. Finally, two self-control mechanisms are comforting oneself or acting unafraid.

Respondent descriptions also revealed a pronounced tendency for antecedent conditions to be interpersonal contexts. For example, the joy episode is often motivated by receiving praise from another person and the anger episode by receiving an insult. Summary data taken from the descriptions indicated that all of the love episodes, 91% of the anger episodes, 90% of the sadness episodes, 47% of the fear episodes, and 40% of the joy episodes originated in the context of a relationship.

Plutchik's "psychoevolutionary theory" also casts emotional experience at the level of prototypical, coherent sequences but is more directly premised on the belief that emotion sequences function to assure survival of an organism (Plutchik, 1962, 1970, 1980a, 1980b, 1980c, 1984). From ethology he takes the observation that certain behaviors (such as hitting, biting, vomiting, running away) are evidence that may be used to infer the presence of emotional states in humans and other animals. From Darwinism he takes the view that emotions are "appropriate reactions to emergencies" that increase an organism's chances for survival through adaptation. Accordingly, he sees an emotion as a complex and probabilistic sequence of events in response to a stimulus that culminates in one of eight universal categories of adaptive behavior. This chain consists of a stimulus event, an inferred cognition, a feeling, a behavior, and an effect that serves a survival function. Variation is possible at each stage of the sequence, but prototypical patterns are evident. Three examples of prototypical sequences leading to the development of an emotion are presented in Figure 13.2.

Stimulus Event	Inferred Cognition	Feeling	Behavior	Effect
threat	"danger"	fear	running away	protection
potential mate	"possess"	joy	courting/mating	reproduction
gruesome	"poison"	disgust	pushing away	rejection

Figure 13.2. Three Prototypical Survival Sequences
SOURCE: Adapted from Plutchik (1984, p. 208).

Because there are eight basic functions (destruction, reproduction, incorporation, orientation, protection, reintegration, rejection, and exploration), it would follow that there would be eight primary emotions. Moreover, because the functions are polar opposites (e.g., incorporation is opposed to rejection), the primary emotions would be expected to be polar opposites as well. Plutchik confirmed these expectations based on judges' ratings of *intensity, similarity,* and *polarity* for 150 emotion terms. A factor analysis revealed that four pairs of emotion terms form eight peripheral points (polar opposites) in a circumplex arrangement: anger and fear, joy and sadness, acceptance and disgust, and surprise and anticipation. The more "abstract" emotions tend to be blends of the basic emotions in a manner analogous to describing secondary colors as blends of the primary colors on a color wheel (e.g., love = joy + acceptance; submission = fear + acceptance; and awe = fear + surprise). These derivative emotions can then be located relative to the basic

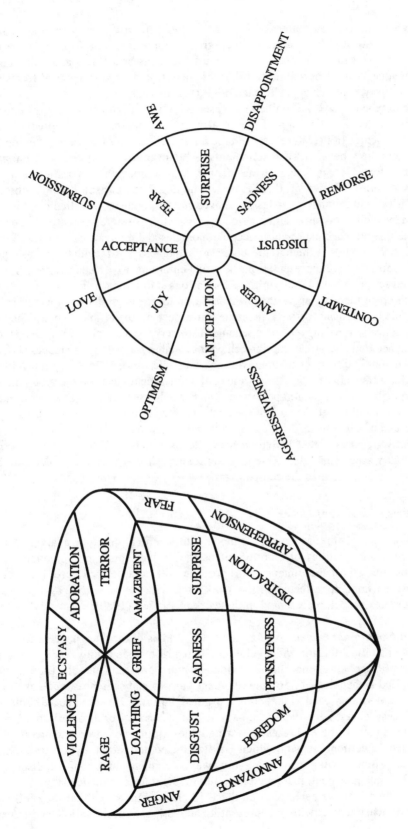

Figure 13.3. A Multidimensional Model of the Emotions and Primary Dyads Formed by the Combination of Adjacent Pairs of Basic Emotions
SOURCE: Adapted from Plutchik (1984, pp. 203, 205).

513

emotions in various patterns of intensity and similarity. For example, a more intense form of sadness appears to be grief and a less intense form appears to be pensiveness; a more intense form of disgust appears to be loathing and a less intense form appears to be boredom. Similarity is manifested by placement of terms next to, far away from, or opposite each other (Figure 13.3).

Prototype analysis has gained increased attention in critical reviews of emotion theory. It has intuitive appeal. Cultural, and even international, appreciation for certain themes in literature, art, and media as well as the fine-grained distinctions listeners draw between such statements as "I am in love with George" compared with "I love George" suggest that people do recognize characteristic features of basic emotions. However, there is to date no direct comparison between observed qualities of emotional episodes/sequences and respondents' recalled descriptions. Humans tend to organize all experience in narrative form, retrospectively defining socially legitimated cause-and-effect chronologies and motivations (Harvey, Weber, & Orbuch, 1990). Whether the coherent sequences abstracted from consensual self-report data are representations of actual emotional experience or are culturally shared scripts invoked as definitions for various emotion terms is an open question.

Prototype theorists argue that, whether a prototype is grounded in experience or grounded in semantics, it is an important aspect of social knowledge. They are, pragmatically speaking, episodic schema. They serve as a template for understanding and generating one's own emotion behavior as well as for making inferences about the motivations and feelings of others during social interactions. Operating much like an implicit personality theory, observations of a few salient pieces of the prototype may be enough to invoke the full prototype, which is then used to fill in (infer) information that was not observed. We might speculate, for example, whether people who experience and/or observe in their partner several of the behavioral, physiological, and cognitive features of the "love prototype" (detailed by Fehr, 1988) take it for granted that other aspects are also present. Determining whether they are or not may be a fundamental purpose of the courtship process.

Dimensional Approaches

Dimensional approaches are not incompatible with a prototype analysis, but the search is for qualities of emotion states rather than episodic components. Two representatives of the dimensional approach will be described here: the multidimensional model, reflected in the work of Davitz (1964, 1969, 1970), and the circumplex model, represented in the work of Russell (1980).

Multidimensional models. Among the many studies of the "language of emotion," as Davitz terms it, is the widely cited multistage dimension study. Using the verbal descriptions of emotional states provided by more than 1,200 people, Davitz (1969) compiled a checklist of 556 nonredundant phrases and sentences, such as "I have a sense of vitality" and "I feel empty, drained, hollow." He asked naive subjects to rate these phrases for their adequacy in characterizing each of 50 emotions. A cluster analysis of the phrases appearing in descriptions of three or more emotions yielded 12 content clusters, which Davitz labeled activation, hypoactivation, hyperactivation, moving toward, moving away, moving against, comfort, discomfort, tension, enhancement, incompetence, dissatisfactions, and inadequacy.

A factor analysis performed on these 12 clusters indicated that they fell along four dimensions: *activation* (representing activation, hypoactivation, and hyperactivation); *relatedness* (representing moving toward, moving away, and moving against); *hedonic tone* (representing comfort, discomfort, and tension); and *competence* (representing enhancement, incompetence, dissatisfaction, and inadequacy).

Davitz does not claim to have discovered new dimensions in the structure of emotional meaning and acknowledges the similarity of his findings to other dimensional systems (for example, Osgood and Tannenbaum's activity, potency, and evaluation). He does assert, however, that research and clinical practices have failed to address the implications of these findings. When we label an experience an emotion, we do so on the basis of the configuration of the cluster elements and the relative emphasis of the dimensions. Thus "change in either an aspect of the experience represented by a particular cluster or in the pattern of emphasis among the various aspects of experience involves change in the emotional state and the label of that state" (Davitz, 1969, p. 143). If this is true, laboratory manipulations of aversive stimuli (such as electrical shocks) to induce anxiety may actually be inducing various other emotional states in subjects. Empirical studies of the relation between perceived ability to control and the effects of aversive stimuli suggest that this may indeed be the case (for example, see Thompson, 1981).

Criticism has been voiced against the dimensional approach because the choice of rating scales selected by the researcher necessarily constrains the dimensions that are possible to discover for any set of emotion terms. However, Smith and Ellsworth (1985) contend that this limitation need not force investigators to abandon an otherwise useful analytic tool (e.g., a priori scales help interpretation of factor loadings), so long as the scales are theoretically derived. With this in mind, Smith and Ellsworth (1985) had subjects rate emotional experiences on eight dimensions of cognitive appraisal gleaned from a review of previous studies. These dimensions included pleasantness, attentional activity (consideration and attention), control (over situation, self, and others), certainty (understand the situation, uncertain, and could predict outcomes/processes), goal-path obstacles, legitimacy (fair, cheated), responsibility (self is responsible or other is responsible), and anticipated effort. The resulting factor structure indicated that six of these eight dimensions were used by respondents to distinguish emotional experience: pleasantness, effort, certainty, attentional activity, self-other responsibility/control, and situational control.

Circumplex models. A circumplex is a two-dimensional, circular structure used to demonstrate relative similarity and difference among a set of elements in a particular domain—in this case, emotions. Placement on the circumference of the circle indicates degree of similarity, with emotions close to each other correlating highly, emotions one quarter of the radius of the circle apart (90-degree angle) having almost no correlation, and emotions directly across from each other having an inverse correlation. In practice, the correlation between any two categories equals the cosine of the angle between them.

One of the clearest examples of a circumplex model is Russell's (1980, 1989) depiction. It derives from multidimensional scaling of subject ratings of similarity items for all possible pairs of 28 emotion terms. These terms are arrayed in patterned clusters around the circumference of a circle created from two orthogonal dimensions: activation or arousal (high to low) and pleasure/displeasure. Although Russell provides labels for these underlying dimensions post hoc, he argues that labels are not essential. It is the arrangement of emotion terms around the circumference that is important. Near emotions are similar and distant emotions are

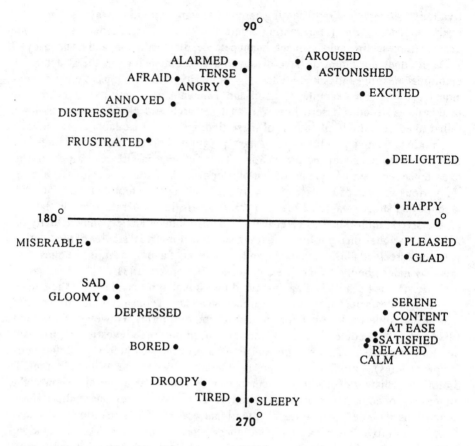

Figure 13.4. Circumplex Model of Emotion-Related Categories
SOURCE: Russell (1989, pp. 86).

dissimilar (see Figure 13.4). Vectors moving outward from the center of the circle represent intensity. The separation of intensity from the arousal dimension is useful for characterizing such states as extreme serenity, which is not active or arousing but is very intense.

Application of a circumplex model to emotions has been criticized on several grounds. Primary among the criticisms is the limitation of the two-dimensional space inherent in the model. Larsen and Diener (1992) find it unrealistic to think that the complex array of human emotions can be described using only two dimensions. They illustrate by noting that anger and fear may fall quite close together on the circumference of the model (i.e., in the active/unpleasant octant). However, beyond the level of arousal and negative tone, these two emotions are quite different. Moreover, a two-dimensional model fails to account for finer discriminations among emotions based on autonomic features such as facial response.

Frijda (1986) is even more broadly critical of the two-dimensional model because it fails to account for the totality of emotional experience. It ignores the situations that give rise to emotions, their manifestation and/or expression, their physiological correlates, and the actions that precede and follow from emotion, all of which, according to Frijda, are essential aspects of discrete emotional experiences.

A common methodological criticism is that the initial set of emotion terms for respondents to rate tends to be based on investigator preference rather than on systematic or theoretical principles. Words like *droopy, zest,* and *aroused,* for example, are not common in most speakers' emotional lexicon. In addition, procedures for how to represent equal proportions of active/passive, positive/negative terms have not to date been standardized. After failing to replicate Russell's (1980) model, Gehm and Scherer (1988, p. 106) suggested that he may have oversampled from "active" or "intense" emotions, yielding a biased structure.

Commentary

As noted previously, investigators searching for emotion prototypes and for underlying dimensions of emotion knowledge place considerable faith in self-report data and the validity of researcher provided rating scales. Although these methods are suitable for the goals of the research, several concerns have been raised.

First, implicit in this approach is the view of emotions as coherent states that emerge from and recede into social environments with little change in level of intensity, valence, and definition from the beginning of the event to the end. This perspective does not reflect the complex, dynamic, and processual nature of emotional experience. Confused, confounded, and theoretically incompatible emotions can be felt in rapid succession and simultaneously, such as love and hate, embarrassment and gratitude, and anger and shame. Berscheid (1986) points out, in her review of Denzin's (1984) book, that current methods that rely on retrospective accounts (e.g., Describe the last time you felt "fear," "anger," "joy") may fail to recognize that

> the last time the respondent experienced anger may also have been the last time fear, sadness, contempt, and a host of other emotions were experienced in tentative vague and confusing succession (and, thus, that anger may simply be the most recent characterization of the episode, a characterization that now colors the entire account). (p. 516)

Second, emotion states are not recalled with equal clarity or vividness. In particular, intense emotional experiences, particularly when negatively valenced, are "sharpened" in memory compared with less intense and positive emotions. Thomas and Diener (1990) examined the recall biases associated with the intensity dimension by assessing how accurately subjects could estimate the intensity and relative frequency of positive affect (happy, joyful, pleased, and enjoyment/fun) and negative affect (depressed/blue, unhappy, frustrated, angry/hostile, and worried/anxious) in their daily lives. They also assessed the extent to which intensity might bias recall of frequency and vice versa. In one study, subjects completed momentary mood reports four times a day for 3 weeks and, in a second study, subjects completed mood reports at the end of each day for 6 weeks. In both studies, preestimate ratings were taken 1 week before the mood-reporting period and retrospective estimates were taken 1 week after the mood-reporting period.

Results indicated that subjects overestimated the intensities for both positive and negative emotions, confirming the commonsense notion that the very intense emotional events in people's lives provide more vivid recollections than the less intense and more neutral occasions. Subjects also underestimated the frequency of positive affect compared with negative; that is, negative emotions were more memorable.

A study conducted by Morgan and Heise (1988) helps explain these findings. In a multidimensional scaling of semantic differential ratings of 30 emotion terms, Morgan and Heise (1988) found a three-factor solution. Examination of the factor structure indicated that positive emotions were relatively simple in structure, differentiated almost entirely by level of activation. Because all involved a sense of powerfulness, potency did not help to differentiate the positive emotions further. Negative emotions, on the other hand, were differentiated by hedonic tone, activation, and potency. Thus the more vivid recollection of negative emotions compared with positive emotions may derive largely from the greater intensity and distinctiveness of the experience. These findings also prompt concern over whether the dimensions of hedonic valence, intensity, potency, activity, and perhaps others used in dimensional analyses to categorize emotions tap different experiential domains when applied to positive versus negative emotions. This issue is implied again in the third concern discussed here.

The third general criticism of prototype/dimensional approaches regards the lack of specificity in measures of the intensity dimension. Frijda, Ortony, Sonnemans, and Clore (1992) argue that intensity is not a simple construct. They list a number of "parameters" for the subjective experience of intensity, parameters that are typically used interchangeably. Ten of these are presented here (with illustrative questions) to show the diversity in measurement options:

1. A global rating of overall felt intensity (How intense was your emotional reaction to situation X?)
2. A peak amplitude of felt intensity (How intense was the most intense moment of your emotion?)
3. Average felt intensity (How intense was your emotional experience over its entire course?)
4. Felt duration (How long did your emotional experience last?)
5. Peak latency (How long after situation X did your emotional reaction reach its peak?)
6. Degree of recurrence of the emotion (To what degree did the emotion in response to situation X recur?)
7. Degree of preoccupation with situation-relevant thoughts (To what extent were you preoccupied with thoughts relevant to situation X?)
8. Drasticness of the actual emotion-induced actions (How drastic were the consequences of what you actually did?)
9. Amplitude of felt physiological change (How intense were the bodily symptoms of your emotion?)
10. Duration of felt physiological response (For how long did you feel bodily symptoms of your emotion?)

In an examination of how these measures interact, Frijda et al. (1992) found that about 40% of the variance in overall felt intensity and felt average intensity could be explained by a combination of (a) recurrence of thoughts about the emotional event, (b) bodily arousal, (c) duration of the emotion, and (d) action drasticness. Regressions were performed for each of four emotions (sadness, fear, anger, and joy) with peak intensity and overall intensity as dependent variables and all other items as predictors. No strong predictors emerged for sadness and joy. Felt bodily arousal predicted felt overall intensity for fear and anger, and relative duration and action drasticness contributed to the intensity of anger but not to that of fear. These findings suggest that not only are positive and negative emotions qualitatively different but specific emotions within each domain differ on several parameters of intensity as well.

Psychosocial Theories

Theorists who might be associated with the label "psychosocial" focus their attention primarily on emotional experience as a social phenomenon. Emotions are conceived of as emergent and multifaceted interactions between the self and the environment or, more accurately, the individual's construal of the environment. These theories view emotions as "social constructions," or emerging transactions between an individual and the social environment. Independent of physiological arousal, social knowledge and subjective appraisal channelize interpretations of experience as emotion. This perspective is represented here by the work of Joseph de Rivera, James Averill, and Richard Lazarus.

de Rivera's work (1977, 1984; de Rivera & Grinkis, 1986) provides what he considers to be an alternative to the view of emotions as mental prototypes or dimensional composites. Instead, he considers them to be "social relationships" in the sense that the texture of emotional feelings are based on four interpersonal "choices" that people make—choices that lead ultimately to transformation of a person's perception of the situation, transformation of the body, and transformation of the stance a person takes vis-à-vis another. The four interpersonal choices include (a) the "it-me" choice (directing an emotion toward another or toward self), (b) the "positive-negative" choice (attraction toward or repulsion from), (c) the "extension-contraction" choice (giving to the other or wanting to get from the other), and (d) the choice of "psychological space" (i.e., *belonging* to another, social *recognition* and comparison, and *being*, which is composed of the material, social, and spiritual self). These four choices are treated by de Rivera as orthogonal dimensions that combine to give emotions their characteristic structure. For example, admiration is "being attracted to an other whom one wants to be like" (de Rivera & Grinkis, 1986, p. 353). It is an *it* emotion, formed from *attraction*, wanting to *get from the other* who has *social recognition/comparison*. Pride might be considered a corresponding *me* emotion.

de Rivera argues that all *it* emotions have correlate *me* emotions and the determination depends upon the individual's transaction with the social environment. Contempt, for example, is an *it* emotion and when experienced (or anticipated) from another person elicits shame, its comparable *me* emotion. Of course, excessive public contempt from another person could also elicit anger, another *it* emotion.

Wicker, Payne, and Morgan (1983) found evidence of "transformations" consistent with de Rivera's perspective in a comparison of guilt and shame. The authors asked subjects to describe guilt and shame experiences, and to rate these experiences on theoretically derived dimensions. Results indicated that shame was the more incapacitating or overpowering emotion; subjects who had experienced shame felt "more submissive, inferior, inhibited and lacking in status, power and self confidence" (p. 36). They also reported greater alienation from others and greater desire to punish others, compete with them, or hide from them. By comparison, subjects who had experienced guilt felt more active and in greater control. Thus shame is more other oriented than guilt and entails greater self-consciousness and feelings of exposure to the evaluation of others.

Averill's (1973, 1980a, 1980b, 1992) "constructivist theory" also situates the experience and enactment of emotions within a social framework, arguing that individuals construct, evaluate, and understand emotional episodes through their knowledge of social rules and norms, not through any inherent link between physiological arousal and behavior. Emotions are sequences of appraisal and response that constitute a "syndrome" of features that Averill terms a "transitory social role." Like other transitory social roles, emotions are given intra- and interpersonal coherence through shared social rules.

A transitory social role is "entered" when an individual appraises a *situation* and his or her *behavioral reactions* as "emotional." The appraisal of a situation is an evaluation of it as desirable or undesirable according to personal values important to the individual (not an evaluation of its truth or falsity). The appraisal does not precede and then activate the emotional role; it is literally part of the role itself. As Averill (1980a) explains:

> I may be angry at John for insulting me, when in actuality John was only trying to be helpful by correctly pointing out a mistake I had made. John's insult is based on my appraisal of the situation; it is as much a part of my anger as is my feeling of hurt. (p. 310)

Averill's position on the simultaneous assessment of situation and affective response would prove useful to the prototype theorists. It would neutralize the dilemma evident in sequences such as Plutchik (1984) offers in which, for example, a threatening event triggers the cognition "dangerous." It is difficult to imagine how an event can be considered threatening before the awareness of danger has been registered. Perceptions of danger and threat would seem to be mutually interdependent.

Averill also contends that behavioral responses are appraised. Based on implicit knowledge of social norms and rules, individuals evaluate their responses in a given situation to determine whether they should be interpreted as "actions" or "passions." Actions are behaviors that are under conscious control, rational, and voluntary. Passions, on the other hand, are passive, irrational, and involuntary. When individuals appraise their responses to a situation as passions, they ascribe to themselves a transitory emotional role and the norms of feeling and behavior commensurate with that role (emotion).

In sum, emotions are "transitory social roles (socially constituted syndromes) that are based on an individual's appraisal of the situation and interpreted as passions rather than actions" (Averill, 1980a, p. 13). Three characteristics distinguish these roles: First, they are socially determined sets of responses, each set governed by norms, rules, and expectancies. Like the forms and rules of language, these roles are culturally shared, implicit, and understood on an intuitive (rather than intellectual) level. Second, social roles are transitory in that appraisal (that is, the imposition of meaning on experience) is continual, and when appraisals change so also do social roles. Third, a social role is like a syndrome because it includes diverse but systematically related elements (a set of responses that covary in a systematic fashion). Some of these elements may be biological, some psychological, and some sociological, but no single element is essential for the syndrome to exist. Finally, emotions are distinguished from other types of syndromes (e.g., organic/disease syndromes) and from generalized social roles by the fact that emotions have objects; that is, we are proud *of* something or angry *at* someone.

Unlike theorists who view physiological arousal and labeling as essential to emotion experience, Averill sees labeling as one possible part of the process of entering a transitory social role. If a particular emotion label is assigned to a situation, it serves merely as a convenient symbol for the meaning of the entire episode.

Lazarus shares many of the same assumptions influencing Averill but is somewhat more psychological in his emphasis on the appraisal process in emotional experience. Lazarus and colleagues (Lazarus, 1984; Lazarus, Averill, & Opton, 1970; Lazarus, Coyne, & Folkman, 1984; Lazarus, Kanner, & Folkman, 1980; Lazarus & Smith, 1988) have advanced a sophisticated theory of cognition and arousal grounded in the fact that human beings are by nature sense-making creatures. They continuously evaluate their relationship with the environment (i.e., immediate and potential encounters) to determine its significance to their well-being, that is, the personal significance of the "demands and constraints" in ongoing transactions and "options for meeting them" (Lazarus et al., 1984, p. 222). The initial determination of personal benefit or harm in a situation is called "primary appraisal." The assessment of personal resources for dealing with the situation (coping activities) is called "secondary appraisal." These two types of assessments yield the quality and intensity of the emotional state, experienced as a "patterned somatic reaction." In addition, "reappraisal" evaluates the success or failure of coping efforts in light of initial appraisals and thereby perpetuates the process.

Lazarus contends that his view of appraisal is not analogous to current notions of "information processing," despite the fact that the comparison is often drawn in criticisms of his work. He argues that information processing is derived from the computer metaphor, and treats social information as though it were received serially, registered, encoded and stored, and then retrieved and re-stored when necessary. The process is linear, and the sequence rather "fixed." But Lazarus rejects this image: "We do not always have to await revelation from information processing to unravel the environmental code. Personal factors such as beliefs, expectations, and motives or commitments influence attention and appraisal at the very outset of any encounter" (Lazarus, 1984, p. 250). Evaluations are often holistic and simultaneous rather than built sequentially from observed elements. Thus the process need not be deliberate, rational, or within conscious awareness. This is not to say, however, that it is not cognitive or that it is a process independent of appraisal.

Commentary

Most theorists associated with what we have called the "psychosocial perspective" assign only minimal direct influence to physiological arousal. They reject explicitly any inherent antecedent causal relationship between arousal and emotional experience or between a stimulus event and an emotional state. In contrast to the linear model predicting that arousal stimulates a need to know why, which then motivates a cognitive appraisal of the environment (Schachter & Singer, 1962), the psychosocial model posits a continuous appraisal process. Definitions of emotion reflect this dynamic and processual orientation: transformations, transactions, social constructions, and transitory social roles. A host of psychological and social elements influence and are influenced by the appraisal process, becoming intrinsic parts of what an individual experiences as an emotional state.

The theories presented here have been criticized for privileging cognition in the emotional experience (e.g., Bornstein, 1992; Zajonc, 1980, 1984a, 1984b). Further, although appraisal models draw from a foundation of laboratory research, this research has been criticized for relying on unrealistically controlled stimuli (e.g., film manipulations) divorced from the complexities of social life (Parkinson & Manstead, 1992). And, in fact, assessing the relative contribution of social knowledge, cognitive appraisal, and spontaneous arousal/feeling to the experience of emotion is a challenge that has not yet been undertaken. A similar challenge underlies the collection of theories in the next section.

Psychophysiological Theories

Most current theories that address the relation between physical activation and cognitive processes in emotion align with one of three views: (a) favoring physiological determinism, (b) favoring cognitive determinism, (c) favoring an integration of the two.

The origins of the controversy are usually traced to the early work of James (1890/1950), who proposed that the production of emotion begins with a person's awareness of an "exciting fact" in the environment. The biological systems of the body respond to this awareness, and the individual's perception of these bodily changes as they occur constitutes the emotion. More specifically, James placed the locus of arousal in the viscera, or internal organs of the body, and argued that a particular pattern of visceral change signaled the particular emotion that was felt.

The Jamesian explanation of emotional arousal held considerable influence until Cannon's critique in 1927. Following a series of experiments on laboratory animals, Cannon concluded that the viscera are not a defensible locus of emotional arousal for several reasons. First, visceral reactions are not differentiated enough to account for the variety of emotions commonly experienced. Second, the viscera are too slow in reacting and too insensitive to give rise to emotions. The viscera can be separated surgically from the central nervous system without affecting emotional expressiveness. And, finally, visceral changes can be induced artificially (for instance, adrenaline injections) without giving rise to a corresponding change in emotional state. Cannon concluded that the viscera function to maintain the body's internal homeostasis but do not function in the perception of emotional experience. He proposed an alternative locus of arousal in the central neural pathway, particularly the thalamic center.

While relatively few contemporary theorists believe that every emotion has a corresponding pattern of physiological arousal, most are convinced that biological feedback systems do play a critical role in the experiencing of emotional states. The question that separates members of this group, however, is whether arousal per se is both the necessary and the sufficient determinant of emotional experience or whether arousal is necessary but insufficient without cognitive mediation.

Tomkins (1980, 1984) and Tomkins and McCarter (1964) represent the first position. They identify nine primary, innate affects: three positive and six negative. These affects are activated by neural firing, and variations in the density of neural firing account for the quality of emotional response. According to Tomkins (1980):

> If internal or external sources of neural firing suddenly increase, [a person] will startle or become afraid, or become interested, depending on the suddenness of the increase in stimulation. If internal or external sources of neural firing reach and maintain a high, constant level of stimulation, which deviates in excess of an optimal level of neural firing, he will respond with anger or distress, depending on the level of stimulation. If internal or

external sources of neural firing suddenly decrease, he will laugh or smile with enjoyment, depending on the suddenness of the decrease in stimulation. (pp. 143-144)

These patterns of variation in neural firing presumably activate the skin and the musculature of the face, causing the flushing and facial expressions characteristic of each of the nine primary affects. Afferent feedback to the autonomic system from the face (and the secondary involvement of the skeletal and visceral systems) then constitutes a particular primary emotional experience. Tomkins argues that whether we are aware of this feedback or not, and quite independently of cognitive appraisal, this feedback is inherently positive or negative, acceptable or unacceptable. "Certainly the infant who emits his birth cry upon exit from the birth canal has not 'appraised' the new environment as vale of tears before he cries" (Tomkins, 1980, p. 145). The child will eventually learn to avoid situations activating unacceptable responses and seek situations activating acceptable responses, but the responses themselves are involuntary and independent of cognitive evaluation.

Ekman and his colleagues provide evidence that autonomic activity can distinguish between positive and negative emotions and among some negative emotions as well. For example, Ekman, Levenson, and Friesen (1983) instructed professional actors and scientists in two conditions. The first involved moving certain muscles of the face in patterns characteristic of six basic emotions (anger, fear, sadness, happiness, surprise, disgust) without being told what emotion was being represented. The second condition required subjects to "relive" the experiencing of each of the six emotions. Four physiological measures, including heart rate, hand temperature, skin resistance, and forearm flexor muscle tension, were taken continuously throughout both conditions. Various patterns of these autonomic responses were found to distinguish anger, fear, and sadness from happiness, disgust, and surprise and to further distinguish anger from fear and sadness.

In addition, Ekman, Davidson, and Friesen (1990) found that the Duchenne smile (a smile in which both eye and lip muscles are active) is a basic expression of pleasure that can be distinguished from other types of smiling and occurs when no other persons are present. Specifically, the Duchenne smile occurred more often among subjects who were watching pleasant (versus unpleasant) films and revealed a stronger relationship to measures of cerebral symmetry and subjects' self-reports of positive affect than did other patterns of smiling.

Despite this evidence, however, not all scholars consider the face to be the primary source of feedback to the cortical system (see Izard, 1990). In a review of studies testing the "facial feedback hypothesis," Buck (1980) asserts that

at present there is insufficient evidence to conclude that facial feedback is either necessary or sufficient for the occurrence of emotion, and the evidence for *any* contribution of facial feedback to emotional experience is less convincing than the evidence for visceral feedback. (p. 822)

Buck argues further that facial displays are a highly visible means for communicating affective processes, but because social organization has encouraged control of affect displays, the result has been more complex facial feedback to the experiencer. This additional feedback, however, "seems to have been secondary to their readout functions" (Buck, 1980, p. 122). The viscera, on the other hand, are beyond voluntary control, which prompts Buck, like James, to attribute causal significance to their activation.

A model of emotional experience quite different than the biological model guiding the work of Tomkins and Ekman is Schachter and Singer's (1962) cognitive labeling model. They view physiological arousal as undifferentiated and generalized sensation. Because the meaning of arousal is unclear, it gives rise to a search for some explanation. Cognitive appraisal of the immediate environment provides an explanation (usually a causal antecedent), which is then used to identify the emotion to be felt. "It is the cognition which determines whether the state of physiological arousal will be labeled as 'anger,' 'joy,' 'fear,' or whatever" (Schachter & Singer, 1962, p. 380).

In the Schachter and Singer (1962) classic study of drug-induced arousal, subjects were injected with epinephrine or a placebo and then exposed to a confederate acting in a euphoric or angry manner. Epinephrine subjects who were fully informed about the injection and its effects were not significantly affected by the manipulation. Uninformed epinephrine subjects were significantly responsive to the manipulation, although the impact of the confederate's mood was greater on subjects' overt behavior than on self-reports of affective state. Presumably, unexplained arousal motivated the search for a causal explanation and the social context provided that information. Placebo subjects who received saline injections were similar to the informed epinephrine subjects in their response patterns.

Although Schachter and Singer's work is frequently cited as evidence for cognitive determinance and emotional plasticity, attempts to replicate the 1962 study cast some doubt on the findings. Maslach (1979) performed a modified replication of the original study using posthypnotically triggered arousal. She found that the confederate's mood (happy or angry) had a significant effect on subjects' overt behaviors but not on reports of emotional states. In fact, posthypnosis subjects whose arousal had been triggered by seeing a cue word reported significantly greater negative affect, regardless of the confederate's mood, than did posthypnosis subjects who were not given the cue word or control subjects who had not been hypnotized. Maslach draws two important conclusions from her findings: First, the confederate's mood seems to represent normative information for an uninformed subject to use in modeling behavior so as to be socially appropriate. However, this kind of normative information does not indicate the *cause* for the feeling that presumably motivates the search for the emotional label. Second, the fact that unexplained arousal was correlated with self-reports of negative affect even in the happy condition suggests that "strong unexplained arousal per se is typically perceived as a negative state by adults and not as an undifferentiated, affectively neutral state, as the Schachter-Singer model proposes" (Maslach, 1979, p. 969).

Similar conclusions were reached by Marshall and Zimbardo (1979), who compared epinephrine-induced arousal subjects to placebo subjects in a euphoric condition. They found that uninformed aroused subjects reported negative affect despite the confederate's positive mood, and that increased levels of arousal (larger dosages of epinephrine) produced only increased negative affect. These results are consistent with Maslach's negative bias hypothesis: In instances of strong unexplained arousal, the search for an emotion label will be biased in the direction of negatively toned emotions irrespective of environmental conditions.

A summary of the "cognition-arousal" literature presented to this point indicates evidence to support two different notions of emotional experience. The first holds that emotions *are* the felt sensations of physiological arousal. The primary emotions, at least, are programmed responses to feedback from the somatic muscles and skin of the face, from the viscera, from the autonomic nervous system, or from some combination of these sources. The second holds that emotions are plastic sensations. They consist of an undifferentiated, affectively neutral level of arousal that is defined or identified by a cognitive appraisal of the immediate environment. While staunch advocates of either position might resist compromise theories, other scholars have taken a more integrative position. Carroll Izard, George Mandler, and Theodore Kemper represent these perspectives.

Integrative Models

Izard (1971, 1975, 1977, 1990) acknowledges his debt to the work of Tomkins and shares with him the position that certain basic emotional responses are highly informative to human beings independent of interpretive cognitions. He posits the existence of a set of fundamental, transcultural emotions differing only slightly from Tomkins's nine primary affects. These *fundamental* emotions include interest, joy, surprise, sadness, anger, disgust, contempt, fear, shame, shyness, and guilt (Izard & Buechler, 1980).

Izard extends these premises, however, and incorporates them into the larger framework of the human personality using six subsystems, only one of which is emotion. Because the subsystems are interrelated and interactive, emotional experiences are not generally limited to the fundamental emotions. Although in childhood, and on occasion in adult life, the emotion subsystem does operate independently, more typically it is involved with the other subsystems in complex ways. For example, a basic drive from the drive subsystem may combine with a fundamental emotion to produce an "affect." A fundamental emotion may also combine with one or more other fundamental emotions, whether simultaneously or in sequence, to produce "patterns" of dispositional or mood states. For example, depression occurs when sadness is accompanied by anger, disgust, contempt, or fear. Finally, the cognitive and perceptual subsystems can interact with fundamental emotions, affects, or patterned emotional states to regulate, sustain, and attenuate them.

Stable personality traits are formed, according to Izard (1977), when stabilized patterns of interaction develop among subsystems. That is, when a particular affect or pattern of affects interacts frequently with recurring cognitions, a stable "affective-cognitive structure" is formed. Configurations of these structures become "affective-cognitive orientations" or personality traits such as passivity or skepticism.

Mandler (1975, 1980) also believes that both physiological arousal and cognitive processes are integral to the experiencing of an emotional state. However, he does not envision a set of primary emotions. Rather, he proposes unique emotional experiences based on the subjective evaluation of a "discrepancy-generated arousal." According to Mandler (1980), autonomic arousal occurs when "well-developed, well-organized habitual, and previously adaptive actions fail, cannot be completed, or in some way are inhibited" (p. 228). This interruption stimulates the autonomic nervous system, which is then recognized and registered in consciousness as the "intensity dimension" of emotional experience. However, arousal leads to subjectively experienced emotions only when the current situation is evaluated as "affective." Evaluation of arousal is the analysis of its meaning in relation to each person's unique combination of past experiences, perceptions, expectations, belief systems, and so forth. Because no two meanings will be identical, no two emotional experiences will be identical. The appearance of commonality across emotional experience is, according to Mandler, an artifact of linguistic constraints that reduce complex experience to communicable labels.

In a test of the discrepancy-evaluation model, MacDowell and Mandler (1989) employed a tailor-made version of Rogue, a computerized role-playing game in which a player moves a symbol called the "rogue" through a succession of dungeon levels. Subjects played Rogue for three 1-hour sessions during which physiological intensity (heart rate and skin resistance) was continuously monitored. Interruptions were operationalized as two discrepant events with outcomes better than the typical sequence would predict and two discrepant events with outcomes worse than the typical sequence would predict (i.e., finding less/more gold than expected and eliminating a previously difficult opponent—a monster—or being eliminated by previously innocuous opponents). Subjective intensity was measured by subjects' ratings of their mood intensity as events occurred in the game. Results indicated that interruptions in expected chains of events caused physiological arousal and indicated that arousal associated with outcomes better than expected were interpreted positively and outcomes less than expected were interpreted negatively.

One notable extension of Mandler to the relationships area is found in the theorizing of Berscheid (1983). Beginning with the premise that a close relationship is one in which a couple's interdependence patterns are "characterized by high frequency and strength, covering a diverse range of activities, for a relatively long duration of time" (p. 143), Berscheid postulated that the greater the number of interconnections a couple has, the greater will be their "emotional investment" in the relationship and the greater will be the chance for interruption to evoke emotion. When sequences are smoothly enmeshed, there will be little emotional arousal. When coordination results in activities being completed earlier than expected or when obstacles to goals are suddenly removed, hot positive emotions will result. When lack of coordination leads to delays or obstacles suddenly thwarting goal attainment, hot negative emotions will result.

The final integrative model to be reviewed here is one proposed by Kemper (1978, 1984). He builds his model from the unlikely union of pure physiology and pure sociology. The sociological structure he erects is built on the social conditions most likely to induce emotions—social relations. He defines emotions as responses to "real, anticipated, imagined, or recollected outcomes of social relationships" (Kemper, 1978, p. 32). For Kemper, the biological property of emotions entails not merely the survival of organisms but the preservation of patterns of social organization, or sometimes the change of patterns to a more useful form. Thus emotions are not inherently positive or negative but are useful in various ways for maintaining social structure: "Integrating" emotions (loyalty, pride, respect, love) bind groups together whereas "differentiating" emotions (fear, anger, contempt, envy) maintain the differences between the groups. Kemper argues that, at the interpersonal level, emotions operate the same way because the same fundamental properties of social structure are present: power, status, and resources.

The novelty of Kemper's model is in the way he links physiological arousal to the dimensions of power and status. He notes first that the central nervous system has two subsystems: the parasympathetic nervous system and the sympathetic nervous system. These two systems release different types of neurochemicals (hormones) that offset each other and keep the body in homeostasis, controlling both excessive overarousal and excessive underarousal (lethargy).

The positive emotions are accounted for as the sense of contentment and well-being associated with a neurochemical called acetylcholine released by the parasympathetic system. Release of acetylcholine would indicate, in Kemper's model, that power and status are felt to be in equilibrium. However, when power and/or status do not meet satisfactory levels, the parasympathetic nervous system is activated "with norepinephrine as the organismic correlate of status loss (anger) and epinephrine as the organismic correlate of power insufficiency (fear)" (pp. 37-38).

A Developmental Perspective

Leventhal's (1979, 1980, 1984) "perceptual motor theory" is included here as a separate theory because it contains elements of arousal, primary emotions, mental schemata, and elaborate cognitive structures, all of which appear in previous sections. In addition, Leventhal offers his model as an account of the *mechanisms* that function in the construction of emotional experience, not the emotions per se. Emotion is, after all, according to Leventhal, a composite, highly differentiated experience that can never be observed or studied.

According to Leventhal (1980, 1984), emotion processing occurs at three levels or systems: the sensory-motor, the schematic, and the conceptual. The sensory-motor system is the innate, biologically determined receptivity to emotion cues observable in infants. These responses are much like reflexes in that their elicitation does not depend on situated learning; however, they are more complex than reflexes because they depend on rather elaborate patterns of stimulation and involve reactions of several muscle groups. These are, then, expressive reactions that constitute the "primary affective palette."

The schematic level consists of prototypical schemata formed over time from nonverbal, perceptual, and motor memory structures. Initial memories contained detailed impressions of emotional experience: the specific situation that aroused strong emotion, the emotional feeling itself (i.e., motor memory of expressive and autonomic reactions), and instrumental or coping reactions. Through repeated elicitation (e.g., repeated angry episodes), these detailed and specific memories are eventually blended into a prototype episode. They can be elicited by stimuli that have features of specific eliciting episodes and/or by stimuli that have features of the prototype.

Conceptual processing has two components, both of which store propositional (as opposed to episodic or schematic) information. One component stores information *about* past emotional episodes, which can be used to talk about emotional experiences, and one stores information that can be used for the performance of emotional acts. Both processes are under more voluntary control and are more effortful than the sensory-motor or schemata systems. They allow individuals to reflect on their emotional experiences and to practice expressive control of emotional reactions.

According to Leventhal, all three mechanisms operate simultaneously and only the product, or synthesis, of their interaction (not the emotion itself) can be observed.

Summary

Although this review indicates important differences, contradictions, and incompatibilities in the theory and research of emotion, it also indicates important areas of convergence and commonality. By stepping back from the specifics of any particular approach, we are able to suggest several conclusions derived from this review.

(1) Emotions can be viewed as two approaches to the environment: First, as "reaction/responses" to an objective environment, and, second, as "interpretive subjective states" that actively construe an environment in ways consistent with that state. In common experience, both views are probably operative.

(2) Physiological involvement and cognitive interpretation are concomitant aspects of emotional states, though the relative influence of each kind of information is variable. Some emotional states are predominantly physiological reactions, and others are complex, abstract, and predominantly cognitive constructions. Most common emotions fall along a continuum between these extremes.

(3) Very intense and negatively toned emotions tend to be more memorable and finely discriminated than less intense and positive-toned emotions. When arousal is unexplained, it tends to be evaluated negatively.

(4) Some emotional states are perceived to be more intense than other emotional states or than the same emotional state in other instances of its occurrence. This is due to a high level of physical responsiveness, a high level of personal involvement in some element of the appraisal process, or both.

(5) Arousal is subjectively experienced, but for most emotions it is stimulated by social/relational linkages: expressed evaluations (e.g., insults or praise), interruptions in goal attainment, or resources (acquired, desired, or lost) relative to other people.

(6) Although a few environmental events bear a rather direct relationship to an emotional state (for example, a sudden loud noise), most stimulus events are perceptually defined, often retrospectively.

(7) Appraisal is an ongoing process raised to consciousness, and sometimes focused by, an array of factors. These might include recognition of one's felt arousal (autonomic, visceral, facial), interpreting one's behavior as explainable by emotional attributions (e.g., as passions), realizing that others' behaviors could be meaningful only if one were experiencing an emotion (e.g., expressions of sympathy).

(8) Although the range of emotional experience is potentially infinite, in actual practice, emotion experiences reflect commonalities within and across individuals. This is due, in part, to the stabilization of processing and response patterns within individuals during maturation. It is also due to the standardization of norms and rules for feeling and expressing emotions for individuals in the same society. The limitations of language and the limitations of vocal/nonverbal affect display restrict and channelize emotional experience and expression. We cannot talk to ourselves or others about feelings and we cannot enact those feelings without a common code.

These conclusions point to the complex nature of emotions. They are as much a sociological phenomenon as they are a private experience. The following section of this chapter will review the research conducted by scholars who have explored the psychological, sociological, and dyadic aspects of emotions.

The Pragmatics of Emotion

This section concerns itself more directly with the link between emotion and interpersonal communication. We take as our starting point the premise that emotion is information. Whether the emotion is rooted in strong or weak arousal, is positively or negatively valenced, is linked directly or indirectly to environmental stimuli, the sensations that people recognize in themselves and others are information. It is interpreted and potentially communicated. When it is communicated, verbally and nonverbally, it is subject to the constraints and pragmatic limitations of any message. Persons are responsible for the clarity, appropriateness, and consequences of the message. Receivers are prone to give wide latitude to emotion messages, but they are not without their parameters.

This perspective allows us to focus on three research areas that have much to offer scholars interested in emotion and interpersonal communication. First, we can turn our attention on individual differences in how individuals respond to and use this information. Second, we can consider how social convention favors the positive emotions over the negative, and thus the constraints society places on social actors (i.e., how and what emotional information they should feel and express). And, finally, considering emotions as information allows us to examine the effect of its expression on intimate relationships.

The association among these areas is complex. Individual differences and social convention are both important contributors to the dynamics of interpersonal relationships. The impact of individual differences is at its most pronounced as interactions move further from social scripts and routines. In intimate relationships, the need to negotiate interdependent goals, resources, and outcomes leads to complicated and novel episodes for which social scripts are not readily available. Routines emerge over time, but these tend to be reflections of a couple's individual communication preferences rather than standardized social scripts. In addition, the imperative to exhibit positive emotions is relaxed in close relationships, allowing greater openness of negative information; however, negative emotions are likely to be read as indicating failing relational health. Thus interactions require a delicate balance in the frequency and intensity of negative versus positive emotions. The interactions of satisfied couples seem to maintain this balance whereas the interactions of dissatisfied couples seem not to do so.

We turn now to a more detailed review of these three areas of research.

Individual Differences in Emotion Experience

The social environment is not inert, nor is it organized. It is an undifferentiated collection of stimuli that must be interpreted to be used. As Buss (1987) notes, individuals actively *select* situations that they enter or avoid; they foreground (*evoke*) elements in situations that they will attend to; and they *manipulate* elements in the situation in ways that will advance their goals.

Research indicates that individuals differ systematically in how they sort, store, and retrieve emotional information taken from their social environment. They also differ in patterns of appraisal, frequency of emotional arousal, and intensity of response, even when the environment might seem to have prototypical episode cues (Smith & Pope, 1992).

Emotion Cues and Response Styles

Intensity and frequency. Individuals differ in both the degree of felt arousal (or intensity) and the frequency of experiencing emotions. In a series of studies on intensity of emotional reactions (recorded as momentary and daily mood reports), Diener, Larsen, Levine, and Emmons (1985) found a high correlation between positive and negative affect intensities, and a high correlation within subjects for intensity and frequency of specific types of emotions (i.e., joyful, depressed, and angry).

Of interest, when the effect of intensity was controlled, the relationship between positive and negative affect showed a significant inverse correlation. This suggests that intensity and frequency are independent dimensions. Diener, Sandvik, and Pavot (1989) offer support for this argument in a study comparing frequency of experiencing positive feelings (e.g., being in a "good mood") to intensity of experiencing positive moods as predictors of individuals' view of themselves as "happy people." Results indicated that frequency was the better predictor.

Thus dispositional "emotional response styles" might be categorized in quadrants formed from the orthogonal dimensions of frequency and intensity. Profiles might include frequent negative emotions strongly felt, infrequent negative emotions strongly felt, frequent negative emotions weakly felt, frequent positive emotions strongly felt, and so forth.

Moreover, people develop characteristic patterns in the *type of emotion* they are likely to experience in the presence of ambiguous cues. According to Shasti and Feldman (1986), certain portions of the mental, affective network are more regularly accessed and therefore more readily activated in subsequent information processing. Thus some people are more likely than others to construe internal and external stimuli as affect cues, to make more consistently negative or positive attributions for these cues, and to organize them into certain patterns of emotional states in novel or ambiguous situations.

Evidence of this tendency is particularly compelling in studies of two similar emotions: shame and guilt. As Tangney (1992a) and others have noted, the interpretive shadings between guilt and shame depend critically on perceived differences between constitutive elements such as transgression and mistake, between loss of face and loss of trust. According to Tangney (1992b), the "*objective structure* of the eliciting situation is less important than the manner in which the situation is *construed* in determining whether one feels shame or guilt (sex per se vs. infidelity)" (p. 206).

Studies of individual differences in proneness to guilt and shame (Tangney, 1990) reveal characteristic patterns in response to ambiguous negative situations (affect-stimulating scenarios). Control subjects exhibit significantly greater emotional variability in their response styles than do subjects high in shame or guilt proneness (as measured by the Self-Conscious Affect and Attribution Inventory). Moreover, proneness to shame and proneness to guilt are independent constructs. Persons high in shame proneness are more likely than other persons to feel anger, suspiciousness, resentment, irritability, indirect hostility, and to blame others, whereas persons high in guilt proneness are less likely than other persons to externalize blame, feel anger, hostility, and resentment.

Independent confirmation of differences in proneness to feel guilt was obtained in a study of recollected conversations by Vangelisti, Daly, and Rudnick (1991). They found that guilt was reportedly more easily induced in some individuals than others. As might be expected, susceptibility to guilt induction during interaction was correlated with dispositional guilt.

Importance. Responses to emotion cues also include characteristic attitudes about the legitimacy of emotions in making decisions and building arguments. Individual differences are evident in a family of research efforts directed toward understanding differences in the salience of emotion information relative to "objective" information. Isen (1987), for example, distinguishes affective and logic-based information processing, noting that some people rely more regularly on affective categories in memory and more directly (immediately) tap these categories when constructing plans and making decisions.

M. Booth-Butterfield and S. Booth-Butterfield (1990) take much the same perspective, suggesting that some people are more likely than others to use their own emotions as information for guiding communicative decisions. To assess the validity of this perspective, they created the Affect Orientation Scale, a scale that evidenced reliability and construct validity across four studies.

Shasti and Feldman (1986) place the origin of individual differences in preference for emotional information in an individual's past experience. When emotion has proved to be a useful criterion in a person's life, and affect-based decisions have been effective, affect cues become a highly "weighted" (important) type of evidence in a person's mental representation of how social events can be understood and controlled. Affective information then is relatively more immediate, "sensible" (tied to the senses), and informative (meaningful) for some people than others. Thus some people are seen as "intuitive" and some people as "analytic or logical" thinkers.

Moderating Factors

Although certain types of personality dispositions and processing styles are associated rather directly with the processing of emotional information, for many constructs, the association is less direct. For example, associations between dispositional empathy and social behavior (Davis, 1983; Hatfield, Cacioppo, & Rapson, 1992) appear to be weaker for individuals (college students) who also score high on heterosexual anxiety (Davis & Outhout, 1992). The emotions literature is, in fact, quite rich with potential moderating variables. We have selected two general types of features, mood states and beliefs, to serve as illustration of this point.

Moods and chronic mood states. Moods (and chronic mood states such as depression and loneliness) have been shown to influence an individual's social behavior. Cunningham (1988), for example, induced three moods among subjects: elation, depression, and a neutral state. Elation increased subjects' interest in engaging in active social behavior (i.e., talking about job or school). Depression was more strongly associated with reduced interest in passive social behavior (i.e., being with friends) than were elation or neutral moods. Mood also influenced both the perception of positive outcomes to be gained from social and nonsocial activity and the self-perception of energy.

Forgas and colleagues have demonstrated in a variety of studies the important role of mood in the attribution process (see Forgas, 1991). In a study of how mood biases evaluations of one's own and one's interactional partner's social skills, Forgas, Bower, and Krantz (1984) induced subjects to feel happy or sad using a hypnotic mood induction technique. Subjects then viewed the videotape of an interaction they engaged in on the previous day with instructions to "identify and score" positive skilled behaviors and negative unskilled behaviors. Happy subjects tended to identify far more positive skilled behaviors than negative unskilled behaviors, both in themselves and in their partners, than did sad subjects. The one exception to this bias was that sad subjects identified more unskilled negative behaviors in their own communication than in that of the partners.

Forgas et al. (1984) attribute the comparatively more negative view of self compared with partner as related to the social norm mandating against negative evaluation of "superficially known others." However, this negative self-evaluation finding is also consistent with the literature on chronic mood states, particularly loneliness (e.g., Jones, Freeman, & Goswick, 1981; Spitzberg & Canary, 1985) and depression (e.g., Coyne, 1976; Ottaviani & Beck, 1988), indicating that chronic negative affect is associated with negative ratings of performance. In a description of this trend and its consequences for chronically lonely individuals, Spitzberg and Canary (1985) describe a self-fulfilling prophecy model of loneliness maintenance. Accordingly, chronically lonely people do not see themselves as competent, are perceived by others as incompetent, begin to internalize cues of low self-esteem, to devalue the potential rewards of interaction, and become increasingly less adept at social intercourse and further isolated from social support networks that might help break the cycle.

Finally, a study with clear implications for response patterns in the chronically depressed is a study of reactions to successful and unsuccessful interpersonal influence attempts by Segrin and Dillard (1991). Segrin and Dillard found that depression influenced the intensity of negative affect following a failed attempt at interpersonal influence but was significantly less influential in determining affective response under conditions of successful attempts.

Subjects were assigned to experimental conditions where they met with success, failure, or ambiguity when attempting to influence a confederate to serve as a volunteer. Both nondepressed and depressed subjects felt less positive emotion (e.g., happy, pleased, relaxed) as their compliance-gaining efforts moved from success to ambiguity to failure. However, depressed subjects felt more negative affect in all outcome conditions compared with the nondepressed and felt significantly greater negative affect in the unsuccessful attempt compared with the nondepressed. Segrin and Dillard conclude that depressed persons experience positive emotion in much the same way as nondepressed but react with a great deal more intense negative feeling (e.g., anger, guilt, negative affect) to failure when compared with the nondepressed.

Beliefs. Among the several types of stable beliefs that influence emotional response is an implicit assumption that life has pattern and meaning. Antonovsky and Sagy (1986) coined the phrase *sense of coherence* to refer to the belief that one's life is "comprehensible, orderly, and predictable." They reasoned that people who have a high sense of coherence will be adaptable and flexible in dealing with problems and therefore will feel less stress in negative situations. Their predictions were supported in a variety of studies indicating that high scores on the coherence measure were associated with lower levels of anxiety both before and after a distressing event.

This sense of coherence may be related at some level to a generalized predisposition toward "trust" as well. Trusting individuals tend to assess events in their social environments over extended periods of time. Thus momentary disturbances and anomalies are smoothed and lend an overall impression of coherence and stability (Holmes & Rempel, 1989). Appraisal theorists would be advised to consider the effects of both trust and sense of coherence on the appraisal process.

A second belief that seems to moderate emotional reactions to distressing events is response "efficacy." Catanzaro and Mearns (1990) describe it as a person's assumption that she or he can regulate the scope and intensity of response to negative situations. Based on the results of three studies using the Negative Mood Regulation Scale (NMR), Catanzaro and Mearns conclude that individuals with high expectancies for mood regulation become less depressed immediately after a distressing event and are more likely to engage in active coping attempts compared with individuals with low expectancies. Self-perceived efficacy as rendered in this line of research appears to be a variable that would enrich Lazarus's appraisal model, particularly as it contributes to variation in second-level appraisal.

Finally, a construct that has explanatory power for a number of phenomena is the belief that one's happiness is dependent on the attainment of certain goals. McIntosh and Martin (1992) refer to this belief as "linking." "Linking means believing that goals are *necessary* for happiness. It means believing that happiness can be achieved *only if* certain things fall into place. In effect, linking entails placing situational contingencies on one's happiness" (p. 229). Furthermore, the more that people believe goals are linked to their happiness, the more they ruminate (i.e., have repetitive, intrusive, aversive thoughts) about goals they want but do not have. Rumination tends to continue until the desired goal is attained or abandoned. In either case, the rumination has made the process decidedly negative.

Linking and rumination may explain a number of individual differences in interpersonal relationships. For example, to the extent that a person feels his or her romantic partner is the only possible source of happiness, any perceived threat to the relationship may lead to rumination and eventually to excessive or dispositional jealousy.

Cultural Preference for the Positive: "Put on a Happy Face"

Positive and negative affect are not isomorphic domains and, for ordinary people, negative affect is more "informative" than positive; it is noticed, it is debilitating, and it is remembered. Among the several "feeling" and "display" rules that Hochschild (1979, 1983) discusses is a cultural injunction against feeling negative emotions (particularly petty and violent emotions) unless obviously related to protection, and a bias toward feeling positive emotions (particularly in response to the positive affect of others). Social harmony/cohesion mandates positive and affiliative emotions and sanctions negative and conflictual emotions. In fact, Scheff (1984) argues that the "coarse" emotions (anger, shame, guilt, and fear) are "taboo" in this culture and that people work actively to suppress or redefine (relabel) them when experienced.

Empirical verification of a preference for the positive and criticism of the negative is found more or less explicitly in a number of emotion studies. For example, negative emotions are more quickly noticed and more likely to be judged as indicative of stable personality traits compared with positive emotions (see Weiner, 1986). Elliott and MacNair (1991) exposed subjects to videotapes of depressed/nondepressed persons who also displayed a physical disability, were described as alcoholic, or appeared in a neutral condition. Results indicated that depressed targets elicited more attributional activity than nondepressed and were held accountable for their depressed behavior *regardless of their circumstances*.

Similarly, Liu, Karasawa, and Weiner (1992) found across three scenario studies that dispositional inferences were more likely to be made when other people displayed negative emotions than when they displayed positive emotions, *even when the presence of an aversive event was known*. Liu et al. argue that persons who display negative emotions are "nonnormative" and potentially threatening. Dispositional attributions may enable observers to better predict and thereby avoid aversive situations that might be expected from negative emotions. Liu et al. note also that the tendency to make dispositional attributions despite knowledge of cause may be operating in the tendency to blame persons for their negative affective states (e.g., depression) and therefore to withhold social support.

Person perception research also indicates direct evidence of an evaluative bias toward positive emotions. In a series of four studies, Sommers (1984) investigated perceptions of hypothetical others among college students. He found that respondents believed positive emotions to be more typically experienced than negative emotions. In addition, ratings of popularity, sociableness, and likableness for hypothetical students who described their typical and atypical affective experiences revealed the most favorable ratings for those whose affective experiences were entirely positive or typically positive. "Entirely negative" and "typically negative" descriptions were negatively evaluated across scenarios, but hypothetical females whose emotional profiles were "typically negative" were viewed even more negatively than males.

Other evidence confirms the differential impact of the preference for the positive on women. Women, more so than men, are expected not only to feel positive emotion but to display it as an appropriate response while interacting with others. This is true in response to another person's success (Graham, Gentry, & Green, 1981) but not in response to her own success (Johnson & Shulman, 1988; Stoppard & Gruchy, 1993).

Helgeson and Gollob (1991) found in a scenario study that, although men and women were both expected to behave in ways that would make the actor and recipient in the scenario feel better, the likelihood of men engaging in a behavior was better predicted by the subjects' judgments of how the actor felt, whereas the likelihood of women engaging in a behavior was better predicted by the subjects' judgments of how the recipient felt. These findings confirm the cultural expectation that women should do emotional work that will facilitate the "good feelings" of others, an expectation that holds with less force for men (Hochschild, 1983).

Adhering to a generalized positive affective orientation is problematic. Situated appraisals sometimes indicate that positive emotions are not appropriate. If women have internalized both the mandate to be positive and the mandate to be situationally appropriate, they should feel ambivalence in some situations. In a series of studies concerned with creating and validating the Ambivalence over Emotional Expressiveness Questionnaire (AEQ), King and Emmons (1990) found that women reported themselves as more expressive of positive emotion and intimacy than men, and more ambivalent over expression of positive emotion than negative emotion. King and Emmons conclude that women are put in nurturant roles that prescribe positive emotion even when it is in conflict with situational demands for neutrality or emotional detachment.

In sum, negative emotions are socially disruptive and positive emotions are socially normative. Particularly for women, the imperative to be affectively positive in response to the communication of others is strong. The fact that this imperative is suspended in intimate contexts contributes to the sense of emotional negotiation evident in intimate dialogue.

Intimate Communication

When individuals form close relationships, they bring with them fairly stable affective processing and response styles. These are not immutable properties, but they do influence "front-line" processing and tendencies to produce particular types of messages. The picture is further complicated by the fact that current moods, chronic states, and dispositional patterns in one's partner moderate, exacerbate, neutralize, or enhance these properties.

The coordination and mutual accommodation of individual differences is framed by the paradox of intimacy. Intimacy is, by definition, a state of openness and familiarity. It is the domain in which the prescription for positive emotion is suspended. In theory, a sign of intimacy is that individuals can feel and express negative emotion without incurring dispositional attributions. Unfortunately, the highly "informative" quality of negative emotions, their greater intensity, and their tendency to activate a surveillance reaction in partner makes their relationship to intimacy very complex.

Research on marital couples indicates that some couples manage these dilemmas well. They are able to move from the relatively scripted and impression-managed stages of dating into a positive emotional cycle in marriage. Clark (1987) reports the results of a study of transitions through nine emotional states as described by 9 men and 11 women who had moved from dating into marriage. Two transitions characterized satisfied couples (p. 13): (a) the transition from romantic attachment to state K (e.g., being close, loved, caring for the other, love and affection) and (b) the transition from romance to state T (e.g., warm, happy, liking, loyal, trusting, able to communicate, sympathetic, considerate).

Other couples, however, do not manage the change from the polite formality of dating into the more openly expressive state of marriage. Clark (1987) also found three transitions for dissatisfied couples: P (e.g., bored, unsympathetic, insecure, unfulfilled, tense, lonely, distant, suspicious, afraid, bitter), G (e.g., passive, anxious, tied down), and A (e.g., selfish, restless, angry, quarrelsome, indebted, jealous). These three negative subgroups were "maximally connected" such that "once a couple gets into any of them they are likely to move around in that sub-system for quite a while, finding it difficult to escape" (p. 14).

Obviously, such characterizations of a relationship's affective quality resides principally in, and subsequently shapes, a couple's communication practices. There is abundant evidence that couples develop self-perpetuating interaction cycles that are as difficult to escape as the do-loops identified by Clark (1987).

In a study of the sequencing of married couples' responses during discussions of important relational issues, Notarius and Johnson (1982) found that wives reciprocated their husbands' positive and negative speaking turns through verbal and nonverbal affect displays, and husbands tended to respond to their wives' positive and negative turns with neutral turns. Yet on polygraph measures of skin potential responses, husbands showed increased physiological reactivity after wives' negative turns even though they displayed neutral behaviors. By contrast, wives' physiological arousal was apparently "discharged" through overt expressions of negative affect. Notarius and Johnson (1982, p. 488) extrapolate from these findings and other research a "positive feedback loop" for marital interactions in which wives perceive and reciprocate in kind their husbands' emotional messages, but husbands restrain emotional expression and do not reciprocate their wives' expression. Wives then respond with greater expression, which in turn pushes their husbands into an even more controlled expressive stance.

This cycle has the potential to escalate to an explosive final stage where one or the other partner, in total frustration, loses control or withdraws from the interaction (or, perhaps, from the relationship). In light of this potential, Gottman (1982) argues that the ability to *deescalate negative affect* is a more important factor than reciprocal positive affect in distinguishing satisfied from dissatisfied married couples.

Longitudinal data, in fact, confirms this prediction. Levenson and Gottman (1983) videotaped 30 couples in three situations: as they waited together quietly, as they discussed the day's events (15 minutes) and as they attempted to solve a marital problem (5 minutes). In a follow-up study conducted 3 years later, Levenson and Gottman (1985) assessed the satisfaction of 19 of the original 30 couples. Results indicated that negative affect reciprocity (measured as heart rate, skin conductance, sweating, and general somatic activity) during the problem-solving discussion at time 1 was strongly predictive of change in marital satisfaction at time 2. Specifically, satisfaction was negatively associated with greater reciprocity of the husband's negative affect by the wife, and less reciprocity of the wife's negative affect by the husband. Thus the cycle for distressed couples' interactions consists of increasing amounts of negative emotion from the wife while the husband withdraws emotionally.

Finally, examination of specific emotional states evidences similar patterns. Observer codings of the negative emotions of sadness, anger, disgust/contempt, fear, and whining, and the positive emotions of affection, humor, interest, anticipation, excitement/joy (Specific Affect Coding System), indicates a strong anger-contempt theme in the negative emotions for husbands during conflict (Gottman & Levenson, 1986). These two emotions accounted for 77% of the husband's negative affect and only 6.7% of the wife's negative affect. The bulk of the wife's negative emotions consisted of whining, sadness, and fear (93.2%).

In addition, longitudinal research (Gottman & Krokoff, 1989) reveals that these emotions are related to satisfaction in different ways for husbands and wives. A wife's expression of contempt and anger correlated negatively with her current marital satisfaction, and her fear predicted a decline in her satisfaction over time. For husbands, whining predicted a decline in his satisfaction. Of interest, wife's sadness predicted a decline in satisfaction for both partners.

This research highlights the critical role of negative affect in interaction cycles among married couples. Not only is generalized negative affect problematic, but the presence of particular emotions—all of which are negative—and the absence of other more positive emotions characterize dissatisfied couples. Future research should explore the extent to which individual differences in responding to and using emotional information moderate the effect of gender role expectations on these interaction cycles.

Conclusion

There is no doubt that emotions are mutable, transient, elusive, and confusing. Despite decades of research, we are still grappling with the question of what an emotion is and how it works. Even the most adroit emotion scholar must inevitably face the fact that a state of brief momentary surprise or anger shares little with the lasting state of affect called love, yet they reside under the same general rubric in emotion study. And even the most dedicated scholar of interpersonal communication must face the fact that emotions are sometimes felt but not expressed, expressed but not felt, intensified, attenuated, and sent both strategically and unintentionally. In short, emotions pose a challenge for those who study them and for those who study their role in interpersonal communication. Fortunately, meeting this challenge will advance our understanding of the broader domain of social behavior. We hope this chapter contributes to that endeavor.

References

Antonovsky, H., & Sagy, S. (1986). The development of a sense of coherence and its impact on responses to stress situations. *Journal of Social Psychology, 126,* 213-225.

Averill, J. R. (1973). Personal control over aversive stimuli and its relationship to stress. *Psychological Bulletin, 86,* 286-333.

Averill, J. R. (1980a). A constructivist view of emotion. In R. Plutchik & H. Kellerman (Eds.), *Emotion: Theory, research, and experience* (pp. 305-339). New York: Academic Press.

Averill, J. R. (1980b). On the paucity of positive emotions. In K. R. Blankstein, P. Pliner, & J. Polivy (Eds.), *Assessment and modification of emotional behavior* (pp. 7-45). New York: Plenum.

Averill, J. R. (1992). The structural bases of emotional behavior: A metatheoretical analysis. In M. S. Clark (Ed.), *Emotion* (pp. 1-24). Newbury Park, CA: Sage.

Berscheid, E. (1983). Emotion. In H. H. Kelley, E. Berscheid, A. Christensen, J. H. Harvey, T. L. Huston, G. Levinger, E. McClintock, L. A. Peplau, & D. R. Petersen (Eds.), *Close relationships* (pp. 110-168). New York: Freeman.

Berscheid, E. (1986). [Book review]. *Journal of Social and Personal Relationships, 3,* 515-517.

Booth-Butterfield, M., & Booth-Butterfield, S. (1990). Conceptualizing affect as information in communication production. *Human Communication Research, 16,* 451-476.

Bornstein, R. F. (1992). Inhibitory effects of awareness on affective responding: Implications for the affect-cognition relationship. In M. S. Clark (Ed.), *Emotion* (pp. 235-255). Newbury Park, CA: Sage.

Bowers, J. W., Metts, S. M., & Duncanson, W. T. (1985). Emotion and interpersonal communication. In M. L. Knapp & G. R. Miller (Eds.), *Handbook of interpersonal communication* (pp. 500-550). Beverly Hills, CA: Sage.

Buck, R. (1980). Nonverbal behavior and the theory of emotion: The facial feedback hypothesis. *Journal of Personality and Social Psychology, 38,* 811-824.

Buss, D. M. (1987). Selection, evocation, and manipulation. *Journal of Personality and Social Psychology, 53,* 1214-1221.

Cannon, W. B. (1927). The James-Lange theory of emotions: A critical examination and an alternative theory. *American Journal of Psychology, 39,* 106-124.

Catanzaro, S. J., & Mearns, J. (1990). Measuring generalized expectancies for negative mood regulation: Initial scale development and implications. *Journal of Personality Assessment, 54,* 546-563.

Clark, D. D. (1987). Emotion, decision and the long-term course of relationships. In R. Burnett, P. McGhee, & D. Clarke (Eds.), *Accounting for relationships: Explanation, representation and knowledge* (pp. 3-21). London: Methuen.

Coyne, J. C. (1976). Depression and the response of others. *Journal of Abnormal Psychology, 85,* 186-193.

Cunningham, M. R. (1988). What do you do when you're happy or blue? Mood, expectancies, and behavioral interest. *Motivation and Emotion, 12,* 309-331.

Davis, M. H. (1983). Measuring individual differences in empathy: Evidence for a multidimensional approach. *Journal of Personality and Social Psychology, 44,* 113-126.

Davis, M. H., & Outhout, H. A. (1992). The effect of dispositional empathy on romantic relationship behaviors: Heterosocial anxiety as a moderating influence. *Personality and Social Psychology Bulletin, 18,* 76-83.

Davitz, J. R. (1964). *The communication of emotional meaning.* New York: McGraw-Hill.

Davitz, J. R. (1969). *The language of emotion.* New York: Academic Press.

Davitz, J. R. (1970). A dictionary and grammar of emotion. In M. B. Arnold (Ed.), *Feelings and emotions: The Loyola Symposium* (pp. 251-258). New York: Academic Press.

de Rivera, J. (1977). *A structural theory of the emotions.* New York: International Universities Press.

de Rivera, J. (1984). Development and the full range of emotional experience. In C. Z. Malatesta & C. E. Izard (Eds.), *Emotion in adult development* (pp. 45-63). Beverly Hills, CA: Sage.

de Rivera, J., & Grinkis, C. (1986). Emotions as social relationships. *Motivation and Emotion, 10,* 351-369.

Diener, E., Larsen, R. J., Levine, S., & Emmons, R. A. (1985). Intensity and frequency: Dimensions underlying positive and negative affect. *Journal of Personality and Social Psychology, 48,* 1253-1265.

Diener, W., Sandvik, W., & Pavot, W. (1989). Happiness is the frequency not intensity, of positive versus negative affect. In F. Stack, M. Argyle, & N. Schwarz (Eds.), *The social psychology of subjective well-being* (pp. 2-20). New York: Pergamon.

Ekman, P., Davidson, R. J., & Friesen, W. V. (1990). The Duchenne smile: Emotional expression and brain physiology II. *Journal of Personality and Social Psychology, 58*, 342-353.

Ekman, P., Levenson, R. W., & Friesen, W. V. (1983). Autonomic nervous system activity distinguishes among emotions. *Science, 221*, 1208-1210.

Elliott, T. R., & MacNair, R. R. (1991). Attributional processes in response to social displays of depressive behavior. *Journal of Social and Personal Relationships, 8*, 129-132.

Fehr, B. (1988). Prototype analysis of the concepts of love and commitment. *Journal of Personality and Social Psychology, 55*, 557-579.

Fitness, J., & Strongman, K. (1991). Affect in close relationships. In G. O. Fletcher & F. D. Fincham (Eds.), *Cognition in close relationships* (pp. 175-202). Hillsdale, NJ: Lawrence Erlbaum.

Forgas, J. P. (1991). Affect and cognition in close relationships. In G. O. Fletcher & F. D. Fincham (Eds.), *Cognition in close relationships* (pp. 151-174). Hillsdale, NJ: Lawrence Erlbaum.

Forgas, J. P., Bower, G. H., & Krantz, S. (1984). The influence of mood on perceptions of social interactions. *Journal of Experimental Social Psychology, 20*, 497-513.

Frijda, N. H. (1986). *The emotions.* Cambridge: Cambridge University Press.

Frijda, N. H., Ortony, A., Sonnemans, J., & Clore, G. L. (1992). The complexity of intensity: Issues concerning the structure of emotion intensity. In M. S. Clark (Ed.), *Emotion* (pp. 60-89). Newbury Park, CA: Sage.

Gehm, T. L., & Scherer, K. R. (1988). Factors determining the dimensions of subjective emotional space. In K. R. Scherer (Ed.), *Facets of emotion: Recent research* (pp. 94-114). Hillsdale, NJ: Lawrence Erlbaum.

Gottman, J. M. (1982). Emotional responsiveness in marital conversations. *Journal of Communication, 32*, 108-120.

Gottman, J. M., & Krokoff, L. J. (1989). Marital interaction and marital satisfaction: A longitudinal view. *Journal of Consulting and Clinical Psychology, 57*, 47-52.

Gottman, J. M., & Levenson, R. W. (1986). Assessing the role of emotion in marriage. *Behavioral Assessment, 8*, 31-48.

Graham, J. W., Gentry, K. W., & Green, J. (1981). The self-presentational nature of emotional expression: Some evidence. *Personality and Social Psychology Bulletin, 7*, 467-474.

Harvey, J. H., Weber, A. L., & Orbuch, T. L. (1990). *Interpersonal accounts: A social psychological perspective.* Cambridge, MA: Basil Blackwell.

Hatfield, E., Cacioppo, J. T., & Rapson, R. L. (1992). Primitive emotional contagion. In M. S. Clark (Ed.), *Emotion and social behavior* (pp. 151-177). Newbury Park, CA: Sage.

Helgeson, V. S., & Gollob, H. F. (1991). Judgments of men's and women's feelings during hypothetical social interactions. *Sex Roles, 25*, 537-553.

Hochschild, A. (1979). Emotion work, feeling rules and social structure. *American Journal of Sociology, 75*, 551-575.

Hochschild, A. R. (1983). *The managed heart.* Berkeley: University of California Press.

Holmes, J. G., & Rempel, J. K. (1989). Trust in close relationships. In C. Hendrick (Ed.), *Close relationships* (pp. 187-220). Newbury Park, CA: Sage.

Isen, A. (1987). Positive affect, cognitive processes, and social behavior. In L. Berkowitz (Ed.), *Advances in experimental social psychology* (Vol. 2, pp. 203-255). New York: Academic Press.

Izard, C. E. (1971). *The face of emotion.* New York: Appleton-Century-Crofts.

Izard, C. E. (1975). Patterns of emotions and emotion communication in hostility and aggression. In P. Pliner, L. Krames, & T. Alloway (Eds.), *Nonverbal communication of aggression: Advances in the study of communication and affect* (Vol. 2, pp. 77-101). New York: Plenum.

Izard, C. E. (1977). *Human emotions.* New York: Plenum.

Izard, C. E. (1990). Facial expressions and the regulation of emotions. *Journal of Personality and Social Psychology, 58*, 87-498.

Izard, C. E., & Buechler, S. (1980). Aspects of consciousness and personality in terms of differential emotions theory. In R. Plutchik & H. Kellerman (Eds.), *Emotion: Theory, research, and experience* (pp. 165-187). New York: Academic Press.

James, W. (1950). *The principles of psychology.* New York: Dover. (Original work published 1890)

Johnson, J. T., & Shulman, G. A. (1988). More alike than meets the eye: Perceived gender differences in subjective experience and display. *Sex Roles, 19*, 67-79.

Jones, W. H., Freeman, J. E., & Goswick, R. A. (1981). The persistence of loneliness: Self and other determinants. *Journal of Personality, 49*, 27-48.

Kemper, T. D. (1978). Toward a sociology of emotions: Some problems and some solutions. *American Sociologist, 13*, 30-40.

Kemper, T. D. (1984). Power, status, and emotions: A sociological contribution to a psychophysiological domain. In K. R. Scherer & P. Ekman (Eds.), *Approaches to emotion* (pp. 369-384). Hillsdale, NJ: Lawrence Erlbaum.

King, L. A., & Emmons, R. A. (1990). Conflict over emotional expression: Psychological and physical correlates. *Journal of Personality and Social Psychology, 58*, 864-877.

Larsen, R. J., & Diener, E. (1992). Promises and problems with the circumplex model of emotion. In M. S. Clark (Ed.), *Emotion* (pp. 25-59). Newbury Park, CA: Sage.

Lazarus, R. S. (1984). Thoughts on the relations between emotion and cognition. In K. R. Scherer & P. Ekman (Eds.), *Approaches to emotion* (pp. 247-258). Hillsdale, NJ: Lawrence Erlbaum.

Lazarus, R. S., Averill, J. R., & Opton, E. M., Jr. (1970). Towards a cognitive theory of emotion. In M. B. Arnold (Ed.), *Feelings and emotions: The Loyola Symposium* (pp. 207-232). New York: Academic Press.

Lazarus, R. S., Coyne, J. C., & Folkman, S. (1984). Cognition, emotion and motivation: The doctoring of Humpty-Dumpty. In K. R. Scherer & P. Ekman (Eds.), *Approaches to emotion* (pp. 221-238). Hillsdale, NJ: Lawrence Erlbaum.

Lazarus, R. S., Kanner, A. D., & Folkman, S. (1980). Emotions: A cognitive-phenomenological analysis. In R. Plutchik & H. Kellerman (Eds.), *Emotion: Theory, research, and experience* (pp. 189-217). New York: Academic Press.

Lazarus, R. S., & Smith, C. A. (1988). Knowledge and appraisal in the cognition-emotion relationship. *Cognition and Emotion, 2*, 281-300.

Levenson, R. W., & Gottman, J. M. (1983). Marital interaction: Physiological linkage and affective exchange. *Journal of Personality and Social Psychology, 45*, 587-597.

Levenson, R. W., & Gottman, J. M. (1985). Six physiological and affective predictors of change in relationship satisfaction. *Journal of Personality and Social Psychology, 49*, 85-94.

Leventhal, H. (1979). A perceptual-motor processing model of emotion. In P. Pliner, K. R. Blankstein, & I. M. Spigel (Eds.), *Perception of emotion in self and others: Advances in the study of communication and affect* (Vol. 5, pp. 1-46). New York: Plenum.

Leventhal, H. (1980). Toward a comprehensive theory of emotion. In L. Berkowitz (Ed.), *Advances in experimental social psychology* (Vol. 13, pp. 139-207). New York: Academic Press.

Leventhal, H. (1984). A perceptual-motor theory of emotion. In K. R. Scherer & P. Ekman (Eds.), *Approaches to emotion* (pp. 271-292). Hillsdale, NJ: Lawrence Erlbaum.

Liu, J. H., Karasawa, K., & Weiner, B. (1992). Inferences about the causes of positive and negative emotions. *Personality and Social Psychology Bulletin, 18*, 603-615.

MacDowell, K. A., & Mandler, G. (1989). Constructions of emotion: Discrepancy, arousal, and mood. *Motivation and Emotion, 13*, 105-124.

Malatesta, C. Z., & Izard, C. E. (Eds.). (1984). *Emotion in adult development.* Beverly Hills, CA: Sage.

Mandler, G. (1975). *Mind and emotion.* New York: Wiley.

Mandler, G. (1980). The generation of emotion: A psychological theory. In R. Plutchik & H. Kellerman (Eds.), *Emotion: Theory, research, and experience* (pp. 219-243). New York: Academic Press.

Marshall, G. D., & Zimbardo, P. G. (1979). Affective consequences of inadequately explained physiological arousal. *Journal of Personality and Social Psychology, 37*, 970-988.

Maslach, C. (1979). Negative emotional biasing of unexplained arousal. *Journal of Personality and Social Psychology, 37*, 953-969.

McIntosh, W. D., & Martin, L. L. (1992). The cybernetics of happiness: The relation of goal attainment, rumination, and affect. In M. S. Clark (Ed.), *Emotion and social behavior* (pp. 222-246). Newbury Park, CA: Sage.

Morgan, R. L., & Heise, D. (1988). Structure of emotions. *Social Psychology Quarterly, 51*, 19-31.

Notarius, C. I., & Johnson, J. S. (1982). Emotional expression in husbands and wives. *Journal of Marriage and the Family, 44*, 483-490.

Ottaviani, R., & Beck, A. T. (1988). Recent trends in cognitive theories of depression. In K. Fiedler & J. P. Forgas (Eds.), *Affect, cognition and social behaviour* (pp. 209-218). Toronto: Hogrefe.

Parkinson, B., & Manstead, A. S. R. (1992). Appraisal as a cause of emotion. In M. S. Clark (Ed.), *Emotion* (pp. 122-149). Newbury Park, CA: Sage.

Plutchik, R. (1962). *The emotions: Facts, theories and a new model.* New York: Random House.

Plutchik, R. (1970). Emotions, evolution and adaptive processes. In M. Arnold (Ed.), *Feelings and emotions: The Loyola Symposium* (pp. 3-24). New York: Academic Press.

Plutchik, R. (1980a). A general psychoevolutionary theory of emotion. In R. Plutchik & H. Kellerman (Eds.), *Emotion: Theory, research, and experience* (pp. 3-33). New York: Academic Press.

Plutchik, R. (1980b). *Emotion: A psychoevolutionary synthesis.* New York: Harper & Row.

Plutchik, R. (1980c). A language for the emotions. *Psychology Today, 13*(9), 68-79.

Plutchik, R. (1984). Emotions: A general psychoevolutionary theory. In K. R. Scherer & P. Ekman (Eds.), *Approaches to emotion* (pp. 197-219). Hillsdale, NJ: Lawrence Erlbaum.

Russell, J. A. (1980). A circumplex model of affect. *Journal of Personality and Social Psychology, 39,* 345-356.

Russell, J. A. (1989). Measures of emotion. In R. Plutchik & H. Kellerman (Eds.), *Emotion: Theory, research, and experience* (pp. 83-111). New York: Academic Press.

Schachter, S., & Singer, J. E. (1962). Cognitive, social, and physiological determinants of emotional state. *Psychological Review, 69,* 379-399.

Scheff, T. J. (1984). The taboo on coarse emotions. In P. Shaver (Ed.), *Review of personality and social psychology* (Vol. 5, pp. 146-169). Beverly Hills, CA: Sage.

Schwartz, J. C., & Shaver, P. (1987). Emotions and emotion knowledge in interpersonal relations. In W. Jones & D. Perlman (Eds.), *Advances in personal relationships* (Vol. 1, pp. 197-241). Greenwich, CT: JAI.

Segrin, C., & Dillard, J. P. (1991). (Non)depressed persons' cognitive and affective reactions to (un)successful interpersonal influence. *Communication Monographs, 58,* 115-134.

Shasti, L., & Feldman, J. (1986). Neural nets, routines, and semantic networks. In N. Sharkey (Ed.), *Advances in cognitive science* (pp. 158-203). New York: Wiley.

Shaver, P. R., Schwartz, J. C., Kirson, D., & O'Connor, C. (1987). Emotion knowledge: Further explorations of a prototype approach. *Journal of Personality and Social Psychology, 52,* 1061-1086.

Shaver, P. R., Wu, S., & Schwartz, J. C. (1992). Cross-cultural similarities and differences in emotion and its representation: A prototype approach. In M. S. Clark (Ed.), *Emotion* (pp. 175-212). Newbury Park, CA: Sage.

Smith, C. A., & Ellsworth, P. C. (1985). Patterns of cognitive appraisal in emotion. *Journal of Personality and Social Psychology, 48,* 813-838.

Smith, C. A., & Pope, L. K. (1992). Appraisal and emotion: The interactional contributions of dispositional and situational factors. In M. S. Clark (Ed.), *Emotion and social behavior* (pp. 32-62). Newbury Park, CA: Sage.

Smith, T. W., Sanders, J. D., & Alexander, J. F. (1990). What does the Cook and Medley Hostility Scale measure? Affect, behavior, and attributions in the marital context. *Journal of Personality and Social Psychology, 58,* 699-708.

Sommers, S. (1984). Reported emotions and conventions of emotionality among college students. *Journal of Personality and Social Psychology, 74,* 385-393.

Spitzberg, B. H., & Canary, D. J. (1985). Loneliness and relationally competent communication. *Journal of Social and Personal Relationships, 2,* 387-402.

Stoppard, J. M., & Gruchy, C. D. G. (1993). Gender, context, and expression of positive emotion. *Personality and Social Psychology Bulletin, 19,* 143-150.

Tangney, J. P. (1990). Assessing individual differences in proneness to shame and guilt: Development of the self-conscious affect and attribution inventory. *Journal of Personality and Social Psychology, 59,* 102-111.

Tangney, J. P. (1992a). Shamed into anger: The relation of shame and guilt to anger and self-reported aggression. *Journal of Personality and Social Psychology, 62,* 669-675.

Tangney, J. P. (1992b). Situtational determinants of shame and guilt in young adulthood. *Journal of Personality and Social Psychology, 18,* 199-206.

Thomas, D. L., & Diener, E. (1990). Memory accuracy in the recall of emotions. *Journal of Personality and Social Psychology, 59,* 291-297.

Thompson, S. C. (1981). Will it hurt less if I can control it? A complex answer to a simple question. *Psychological Bulletin, 90,* 89-101.

Tomkins, S. S. (1980). Affect as amplification: Some modifications in theory. *Perceptual and Motor Skills, 18,* 119-158.

Tomkins, S. S. (1984). Affect theory. In K. R. Scherer & P. Ekman (Eds.), *Approaches to emotion* (pp. 163-196). Hillsdale, NJ: Lawrence Erlbaum.

Tomkins, S. S., & McCarter, R. (1964). What and where are the primary affects? Some evidence for a theory. *Perceptual and Motor Skills, 18,* 119-158.

Vangelisti, A. L., Daly, J. A., & Rudnick, J. R. (1991). Making people feel guilty in conversations: Techniques and correlates. *Human Communication Research, 18,* 3-39.

Weiner, B. (1986). *An attributional theory of motivation and emotion.* New York: Springer-Verlag.

Wicker, F. W., Payne, G. C., & Morgan, R. D. (1983). Participant descriptions of guilt and shame. *Motivation and Emotion, 7,* 25-39.

Wilson, T. D., & Klaaren, K. J. (1992). "Expectation whirls me round": The role of affective expectations in affective experience. In M. S. Clark (Ed.), *Emotion and social behavior* (pp. 1-31). Newbury Park, CA: Sage.

Zajonc, R. B. (1980). Feeling and thinking: Preferences need no inferences. *American Psychologist, 35*, 151-175.

Zajonc, R. B. (1984a). The interaction of affect and cognition. In K. R. Scherer & P. Ekman (Eds.), *Approaches to emotion* (pp. 239-246). Hillsdale, NJ: Lawrence Erlbaum.

Zajonc, R. B. (1984b). On the primacy of affect. In K. R. Scherer & P. Ekman (Eds.), *Approaches to emotion* (pp. 239-246). Hillsdale, NJ: Lawrence Erlbaum.

14

Communication and Interpersonal Influence

David R. Seibold

James G. Cantrill

Renee A. Meyers

IT IS NOT UNWONTED to view interpersonal communication, at least partly and under specifiable conditions, as persons' symbolic interactions strategically controlled in the pursuit of personal objectives (Goffman, 1969; Grimshaw, 1981; Kellermann, in press-a). Granted, interactants may not be consciously aware of all the goal-oriented objectives embedded in their communication routines (Brown & Levinson, 1978; Langer, Blank, & Chanowitz, 1978); and much of mutual influence in interpersonal communication is the manifestation of tacitly accepted conventions rather than instrumental goals (Bochner, 1984; Bochner, Cissna, & Garko, 1991; Duncan, 1981; Jacobs & Jackson, 1982, 1983; Lewis, 1969). But reflection and research reveal that actors use talk strategically to manage their own identities (Schlenker, 1980) and those of others (Weinstein & Deutschberger, 1963), to negotiate meaning in a variety of interpersonal settings (Schenkein, 1978), to accomplish personal and interpersonal tasks (Clark & Delia, 1979; Grimshaw, 1980), and to pursue multiple goals in talk simultaneously (Craig, 1986, 1990; O'Keefe & Delia, 1982; Tracy & Coupland, 1990).

For example, findings underscore that people participate each day in a variety of goal-oriented interpersonal situations requiring assessment of obstacles to sought-after personal ends and identification of symbolic means for securing influence and compliance from others (Cody & McLaughlin, 1980; Dillard, 1989, 1990a; Forgas, 1976, 1979). That persons are differentially competent at communicative influence in these situations (Applegate & Delia, 1980; O'Keefe, Murphy, Meyers, & Babrow, 1989; Weinstein, 1966, 1969) and that they variously select symbolic strategies and message tactics including ingratiation (Stires & Jones, 1969), suggestions (Johnson & Masotti, 1990), humor (O'Quin & Aronoff, 1981; Stephenson, 1951), sarcasm (Ball, 1965), personal insult (Abelson & Miller, 1967; Dollard, 1939), apology (Kaufer & Neuwirth, 1982; Schlenker & Darby, 1981), compromising (Clark, O'Dell, & Willihnganz, 1986), embarrassment (Gross & Stone, 1966), praise (Kanouse, Gumpert, & Canavan-Gumpert, 1981), refusals (Kline & Floyd, 1990), attributions (Gottlieb & Ickes, 1978; Seibold & Spitzberg, 1982), promises (Gahagan & Tedeschi, 1968; Tedeschi, 1970), threats (Friedland, 1976; Schlenker, Bonoma, & Tedeschi, 1970), irony (Brown, 1980), requests (Craig, Tracy, & Spisak, 1986), honesty (Monteverde, Paschke, & Tedeschi, 1974), deception (Knapp & Comadena, 1979; Neuliep & Mattson, 1990), questions (Bennett, 1982; Churchill, 1978; Goody, 1978a, 1978b), requests (Eisenthal, Koopman, & Stoeckle, 1990; Francik & Clark, 1985; Houlihan & Jones, 1990; Leedon, Persaud, & Shovein, 1986; Tracy, Craig, Smith, & Spisak, 1984), comforting (Burleson, 1983, 1984a, 1984b), name-calling (Steele, 1975), hinting (Falbo, 1977), degradation (Garfinkel, 1956), manipulativeness (Buss, Gomes, Higgins, & Lauterbach, 1987; Singer, 1964), argument (Cronkhite, 1983; Hample & Dallinger, 1990; Krause, 1972; Trapp, 1983), benevolence (Fung, Kipnis, & Rosnow, 1987), indebtedness (Greenberg & Shapiro, 1971), explanation (Duffy et al., 1986), disclosure (Baxter, 1979; Gilbert, 1976), accounts (McLaughlin, Cody, & O'Hair, 1983; McLaughlin, Cody, & Rosenstein, 1983; Shields, 1979), and politeness (Baxter, 1984; Ervin-Tripp, Gui, & Lampert, 1990), among a multitude of others, perhaps justifies this separate chapter on the influence-oriented character of interpersonal communication.

Communicative Influence

Most of the research we review in this chapter focuses on situations in which actors' communication is strategically directed toward achieving instrumental objectives (Clark, 1984; Clark & Delia, 1979), especially inducing or persuading another to behaviorally comply with a specific recommendation or request. Britton (1971) has characterized the function of language in such situations as "conative": "The speaker's intention to change his listener's behavior, opinions or attitudes [is] deliberate and recognizable—recognizable, that is to an observer even where it is so disguised as to deceive a victim to whom it is addressed" (p. 212). To limit our review to the space allotted, we shall be concerned only with research indicating ways in which (adult) actors' strategies for managing identities and relationships in influence contexts facilitate the achievement of more prominent instrumental goals. Therefore we will not survey literature revealing the specific tactics individuals use to display self-concepts and the many ways in which they negotiate personal identities (see Baumeister, 1982; Cialdini & Richardson, 1980; Gardner & Martinko, 1988; Goffman, 1955, 1959; Gove, Hughes, & Geerken, 1980; Leichty & Applegate, 1991; O'Keefe & Shepherd, 1989; Schlenker, 1980; Swann & Hill, 1982; Tedeschi & Reiss, 1981; Thompson & Seibold, 1978; Weary & Arkin, 1981; Weber & Vangelisti, 1991). Also, we will give only passing attention to research on primarily interpersonal objectives, such as investigations of relationship initiation, maintenance, and disengagement strategies (Ayres, 1983; Baxter, 1979, 1982; Belk et al., 1988; Bell & Daly, 1984; Burleson, 1983; Cody, 1982; Falbo & Peplau, 1980; Knapp, 1978). And when we do treat these matters, it will be instances in which persons are concerned with identity and interpersonal objectives in order to accomplish some instrumental objective. We shall tentatively assume that these strategic considerations are more likely to modify selection of regulative and persuasive strategies than to obviate or completely determine them (Clark, 1984).

Our use of the term *strategies* invites clarification. *Strategies* are actors' intended lines of action and general choices in transforming plans into practice so as to accomplish particular goals. *Communication* strategies are anticipated and actual discourse patterns performed in the service of a personal or interpersonal agenda, and they subsume specific (often multiple) message tactics appropriate to the actor's goal(s) and line(s) of action. Communication strategies reflect the mental processes (for example, inference patterns, schemas, and formulations of general presentational lines) and behavioral routines involved in actors' choices of situationally responsive, socioculturally appropriate, and linguistically competent messages to influence the outcomes of interactions in ways that satisfy identity and interpersonal or instrumental goals. In view of the multiple levels and multiple intentions of actors involved in coordinated symbolic interaction, it is possible to think of nearly all communication as strategic as communicators concomitantly seek to manage textual coherence, interactional efficiency, and face presentation and protection (O'Keefe & Delia, 1982; Weinstein, 1966). However, our review will be restricted to research on the regulative and persuasive strategies people purposely select or enact in interpersonal contexts characterized by obstacles to instrumental objectives.

In our chapter in the first edition of this volume (Seibold, Cantrill, & Meyers, 1985), it was apparent from our treatment of investigations of compliance-gaining message selection and message strategy sequences (for example, foot-in-the-door and door-in-the-face) that researchers in these areas promoted a static, fixed, and overly rational conception of communicative strategies. They tacitly implied or methodologically required that actors engaged in instrumental influence attempts in interpersonal contexts—which usually were partly cooperative and partly competitive (Beisecker, 1970)—have

(a) conscious awareness of the influence "situation," including all embedded role relationships, salient sociocultural characteristics of the setting, and a clearly identifiable instrumental/interpersonal task;

(b) sufficient time to rationally assess the situation and consider options;

(c) the intention to formulate a plan designed to accomplish a well-defined outcome;

(d) a diverse, complex, and differentiated repertoire of strategies and tactics to draw upon;

(e) sufficient awareness and individual perspective-taking ability to weigh the consequences of enacting each strategic alternative; and

(f) an ability to choose some strategies and forgo others (that is, all strategies considered acceptable are personally accessible and can be competently enacted, and some strategies—perhaps judged by the actors to be unacceptable or inappropriate under the circumstances—can be eschewed even when they may be habitual modes of response for that actor).

These conditions and choices were unspoken tenets of what we termed—ex post facto—a source-oriented "Strategic Choice Model." We suggested that this hypothetical model implicitly undergirded much of the research conducted before 1985 on persons' selection, construction, and/or enactment of the most optimal among communication strategies considered appropriate for achieving instrumental objectives. Although some of these are characteristic of routine influence attempts, it was apparent that this conception obscured and oversimplified the interactional, adaptive, and partially nonreflective character of communicative influence strategies. Furthermore, research conducted in whole or in part within the Strategic Choice Model paradigm of the 1970s and early 1980s ignored the relationship between message strategies and the multiple goals motivating them and providing coherence. Consequently, we were quick to critique the limitations of early influence research by recourse to the weaknesses of the Strategic Choice Model (see Seibold et al., 1985, pp. 575-577, 595-597). Fortunately, important message influence research conducted since 1985 reflects a progression away from the limiting tenets of a Strategic Choice Model orientation and toward what we hypothetically term a *Goal Limitation Model* orientation. Much of our review in this version of the chapter will examine message influence research in terms of assumptions that appear to us to signal a shift toward an emergent cognition-based, goal-driven metaperspective.

Strategic, goal-oriented behavior requires consideration of the *outcome* (or *outcomes*) of the strategy enacted and evaluation of the extent to which the goal sought was achieved. Although some of the most central research on compliance-gaining strategies reports no message effects at all (Miller & Burgoon, 1978; Wheeless, Barraclough, & Stewart, 1983), the range of message tactic-outcome linkages reported in the literature on communicative influence is extremely broad. In addition to diverse behavioral compliance measures (Cialdini, Cacioppo, Bassett, & Miller, 1978; Debevec, Madden, & Kernan, 1986; DeVries, Burnette, & Redmon, 1991; Foss & Dempsey, 1979; Levine, Moss, Ramsey, & Fleishman, 1978), research in this domain has reported such disparate communicative influence outcomes as reduced aggressiveness (Paul & Thelen, 1983), altered level of performance (Kanouse et al., 1981), liking (McAllister & Bregman, 1983), stigma acceptance (Thompson & Seibold, 1978), oppositional behavior (Heilman, 1976), reciprocity (Hill & Stull, 1982; Jefferson, 1979), bargaining (Hornstein, 1965), interpersonal judgments (Becker, Kimmel, & Bevill, 1989), attributed influence (Layton & Moehle, 1980), negative persuasion (Abelson & Miller, 1967), communication satisfaction (Cupach, 1982), attitude change (Eagly, 1974; LaLumia & Baglan, 1981), intimacy (Berg & Archer, 1982), various forms of responsiveness (Davis, 1982), and helping (Enzle & Harvey, 1982; Grace, Bell, & Sugar, 1988). This range of influence findings is so broad as to make reliable summary claims about tactic-outcome linkages implausible without a framework for interpreting interpersonal influence (and without a coherent perspective on the "situations" generating these communication-influence linkages, as Miller, Cody, & McLaughlin, this volume, point out). Our focus on investigations of compliance-gaining "strategies" and more general studies of communicative "influence" in a variety of applied contexts enjoins us to consider a variety of such outcomes.

Scope of Review

This version of the chapter is divided into five sections, including the preceding comments. Having already established the importance and pervasiveness of interpersonal influence research, and dealt with a number of conceptual and definitional problems related to the study of communicative influence, the next section will examine strategic-tactical messages. Focusing primarily on compliance-gaining strategies research, we forgo the historical perspective of Seibold et al. (1985) as well as the focus in that version of the chapter on individual differences and situational dimensions predicting strategy choices. Instead, we examine the taxonomic focus of much of the research on compliance-gaining strategies since 1985 and its limitations; passing attention is paid to the continuing debate on method-ologies used for studying message choices. This review and critique of compliance-gaining studies serves as the backdrop for a third section on the cognitive, goal-based processes underlying strategic message choices. We introduce the Goal Limitation Model as a metatheoretical perspective whose tenets signal a shift (a) away from the static, overly rational, and reflective character of past communica-tive influence research (whose assumptions we combined and indicted, in the 1985 version of the chapter, as the Strategic Choice Model) and (b) toward a more processual, cognitive, habituated-or-adaptive orientation toward strategic message choices. Within that emerging paradigm, we treat several specific lines of research as well as two broad-based and theoretical programs of research on the goal-plan-ning-message production process. In the fourth section, we examine research on interpersonal influence in applied settings. In particular, we update research in two areas treated in the 1985 chapter—sequential request strategies and managerial communicative influence—noting researchers' similar move toward more proces-sual perspectives on these processes. The chapter concludes with a summary examination of continuing challenges facing the area and the potential for theoreti-cal linkages to other domains of influence research.

Strategic-Tactical Message Choices

People use talk to pursue myriad interpersonal goals (Kraut & Higgins, 1984): dyadic negotiation (Wilson & Putnam, 1990), managing conflicts (Sillars, 1980b; Witteman, 1992) and disagreements (Newton & Burgoon, 1990), seeking informa-tion (Bell & Buerkel-Rothfuss, 1990), remediating embarrassment (Metts & Cupach, 1989), and disengaging from relationships (Wilmot, Carbaugh, & Baxter, 1985), among others. In turn, researchers have documented numerous strategies used in pursuit of these goals, including message repertoires associated with information seeking (Berger & Kellermann, 1983) and avoidance (Berger & Kellermann, 1989), relationship "tests" (Baxter & Wilmot, 1984), affinity seeking (Richmond, McCroskey, & Davis, 1986), account giving (Weiner, Figueroa-Munoz, & Kakihara, 1991), conversational complaining (Alberts, 1988), offering criticism (Seibold & Chan, 1993), and handling conflict (Canary & Spitzberg, 1989).

While all of these goals and attendant message strategies are influence related, arguably most central to the study of interpersonal influence is an understanding of *compliance-gaining*. Broadly stated, the goal of compliance-gaining attempts is "to communicatively induce change in the target so that his or her actions are different from what they would have been without the influence attempt and are consistent with the source's regulative wishes" (Seibold et al., 1985, p. 559). More specifically, Kellermann's (in press-a) review of empirical research on the exist-ence of compliance-gaining goals revealed a core group of eight distinct goals: giving advice, gaining assistance, sharing activities, changing opinions, changing the status of a relationship, obtaining permission, enforcing an obligation, and protecting a right/changing a habit. And, as with other research on interpersonal goals, studies of compliance-gaining have necessarily included classification of compliance-gaining messages. Indeed, so much attention has been given to taxo-nomic development since the publication of the previous edition of the *Handbook of Interpersonal Communication* that Kellermann and Cole (in press) characterize "the study of interpersonal influence in the 1980s as the study of the categorization and classification of messages for gaining compliance" (p. 1). We first turn to research studies that formed the basis for that characterization.

Compliance-Gaining Strategies Research

In our chapter (Seibold et al., 1985) in the first edition of the *Handbook,* we assayed studies of compliance-gaining message strategies and tactics as "perhaps the most visible line of research on communicative influence in interpersonal contexts" (p. 560) based on our review of the 40 published studies and conference papers in the area since the seminal work in communication by Miller, Boster, Roloff, and Seibold (1977). By 1990 Boster (1990) estimated 100 papers on compliance gaining had been printed or presented, the bulk of these appearing in the 1980s. We have found an additional 24 studies reported since Boster's tally, so there is good reason to believe that compliance-gaining continues to be a central focus of communication research on interpersonal influence.

Seibold et al. (1985, pp. 560-562) offered a detailed treatment of the Marwell and Schmitt (1967a, 1967b) and the Miller et al. (1977) investigations as a historical, methodological, and theoretical backdrop for reviewing research trends to 1985. They then proceeded to review findings and limitations (pp. 562-572) associated with the four streams of investigations composing compliance-gaining research to that time:

> (1) studies of agents' perceptions of compliance-gaining *situation dimensions* and their
> relationship to strategic choices, (2) investigations of the effects of *individual*
> *differences* on compliance-gaining strategy use, (3) efforts to develop and to test or
> apply systems for *classifying* compliance-gaining strategies and tactics, and (4)
> research on the utility of various *methods* employed to study compliance-gaining
> message choices. (Seibold et al., 1985, p. 560, italics added)

That four-part delineation of developments in compliance-gaining research through 1985 served well for the time and served as the basis for subsequent reviews (e.g., Garko, 1990). Furthermore, compliance-gaining research since 1985 could readily be parceled into the same four subareas today, although there have been relatively few individual difference studies (see 2 above). For notable exceptions, see Boster (1985), Boster and Levine (1988), Boster, Levine, and Kazoleas (1989), Boster and Lofthouse (1986), DeTurck (1985), Hunter and Boster (1987), Koper and Boster (1988), Neuliep (1986), Sprowl (1986), and Sprowl and Senk (1986) (also see related studies by Applegate & Woods, 1991; Buller & Burgoon, 1986; Burleson, 1989; Kline, 1991; O'Keefe et al., 1989). However, the same four subareas will not be used as a template for our review in this second edition of the *Handbook,* for several reasons. First, space limitations in the present edition preclude the same comprehensive review. For the same reason, none of the compliance-gaining review provided in Seibold et al. (1985, pp. 560-572) is included in this version. Readers interested in compliance-gaining literature before 1985 are referred to the earlier chapter (including nearly 40 references on compliance gaining and more than 100 other influence citations that have been removed from the text references in this chapter). Second, developments in at least one of the areas—situational effects on compliance-gaining message choices (1 above)—are more fully treated elsewhere in the *Handbook* (see Miller et al., this volume; also see DeTurck, 1987;

Dillard & Burgoon, 1985; Hazelton, Cupach, & Canary, 1987; Lamude & Lichtenstein, 1985; Levine & Wheeless, 1990; Williams & Untermeyer, 1988). Third,
because the most important developments (and limitations) within these four areas
have been those associated with taxonomic classification of compliance-gaining
messages (3 above), the greatest attention and space will be given to what these
message scheme studies have contributed to our understanding of compliance-
gaining. Some attention also will be given to the continuing controversy surrounding methodologies for studying compliance-gaining message choices (4 above).
Fourth, and most important, what we view as a significant shift toward examining
actors' goals in compliance-gaining situations and their goal-related choices mini-
mizes the importance of developments in the four subareas of our original review
and hence the need to treat them in the same detail as we did in Seibold et al. (1985).
The limitations of taxonomic studies will make clear one reason for the shift toward
goal research. We will try to highlight how tenets of what we term the *emergent
Goal Limitation Model* are replacing the assumptions of the Strategic Choice Model
implicit in compliance-gaining research through the 1980s. We also will use this
hypothetical construction as a platform for the next section, in which we review
important theoretical advances in both compliance-gaining goal research and goal-
related message production. We term that section "Processes Underlying Strategic-
Tactical Choices."

Compliance-gaining taxonomy studies. Reviews by Wheeless et al. (1983) and by
Seibold et al. (1985) identified a variety of compliance-gaining taxonomic schemes
in a multitude of social science research areas. Most recently, Kellermann and Cole
(in press) located 71 schemes for classifying compliance-gaining messages in the
same and other literatures on interpersonal and organizational communication,
marketing and consumer behavior, education, clinical/child/social psychology, and
the like (e.g., Arch, 1979; Dillard, 1990d; Kearney, Plax, Richmond, & McCroskey,
1985).

Within interpersonal communication research, Kellermann and Cole (in press)
found seven schemes to be employed most frequently by researchers: (a) the list
of 16 compliance-gaining techniques proposed by Marwell and Schmitt (1967b)
and introduced into communication by Miller et al. (1977); (b) the response to it
by Wiseman and Schenck-Hamlin (1981) and Schenck-Hamlin, Wiseman, and
Georgacarakos (1982); (c) Clark's (1979) multigoal perspective on specific tactics;
(d) the "persuade package" taxonomy proposed by Schank and Abelson (1977) and
advanced by Rule and Bisanz (1987); (e) Falbo's power strategies (Falbo, 1977;
Falbo & Peplau, 1980), especially as applied to interpersonal relationships (Cowan,
Drinkard, & MacGavin, 1984) and organizational relationships (Offermann &
Schrier, 1985), other schemes of strategies germane to interpersonal relationships
in organizational contexts including (f) Kipnis's (1984; Kipnis & Schmidt, 1988;
Kipnis, Schmidt, Swaffin-Smith, & Wilkinson, 1984) and (g) the power perspective
of Riccillo and Trenholm (1983).

The development of these taxonomies was, in part, a result of researchers' need
to classify compliance-gaining behaviors in order to pursue empirical questions of
interest concerning determinants and effects of compliance-gaining message use.
Unfortunately, the proliferation of taxonomies has resulted in a confusing array of
lists with different strategies or similarly named strategies that are defined and/or
operationalized differently. Indeed, Kellermann and Cole's survey of 71 compliance-gaining taxonomies (1991, cited in Kellermann & Cole, in press) resulted in

an initial list of 820 strategies and 1,460 strategy examples. Their own exacting efforts at synthesizing these strategies led to the extraction of 64 conceptually distinct strategies. Furthermore, the process led them to pose a variety of indictments of both specific taxonomies and taxonomic research in general. Their analysis in the latter area warrants review here because it raises important questions about the validity of much compliance-gaining research and offers direction for alternative efforts in the area.

In brief, Kellermann and Cole (in press) identify three problems concerning the classification of compliance-gaining messages. First, existing taxonomies are not exhaustive. Both the number and the diversity of strategies in each list suggest that any one is insufficient with regard to the range of strategies available to those who would attempt to induce compliance. Indeed, Kellermann and Cole review a number of findings indicating that many strategies remain unclassified in compliance-gaining message analysis research. This lack of exhaustiveness is a function of lack of integration of extant schemes, which itself is a consequence of researchers' tendencies (a) to select strategies for study that are most relevant to the domain of behaviors they study (e.g., consumer behavior versus classroom behavior), (b) to define general strategies in terms of specific situations they study (e.g., "selling cameras" versus "student control" problems), (c) to use preferred or idiosyncratic labels for what are essentially the same strategies (resulting in labels for the same strategy that vary across taxonomies), and (d) to use similar labels for what are really different strategies. Kellermann and Cole (in press) summarily demonstrate the last two problems with strategy labels by testing their 64 derived strategies against strategies in each of the 71 influence taxonomies they located in social science literature:

> The vast majority of the 64 . . . strategies we found suffer from these terminological problems. The "positive affect" strategy is referred to by 17 different labels and is itself used 21 times to refer to over 10 conceptually different strategies. The "value appeal" strategy has 5 names . . . while also being used to refer to 5 other methods of gaining compliance. "Debt" is referred to in 6 different ways and is used to refer to 2 other separate strategies. The "negative affect" strategy can be found under 10 different names and is used for at least 4 other distinctly different strategies. The "threat" strategy has gone by 13 different names and has been used to refer to 8 conceptually different strategies. The "assertion" strategy is referred to in 10 different ways and is used to refer to 7 other distinctly different strategies. *We found that each of 64 conceptually distinct strategies was, on average, referred to by more than 7 different names while simultaneously referring to 4 other strategies.* (p. 10, italics added)

In addition to the inexhaustiveness/lack of integration problem, Kellermann and Cole (in press) identify a second difficulty with current typologies of compliance-gaining strategies. They note that distinct and clear conceptual definitions of strategies within specific taxonomies often are not to be found. Even when examples of strategies are provided, inferring the meaning of the strategy from them is difficult, thus making claims based upon the strategy open to alternative interpretation. In general, across taxonomies used commonly by interpersonal communication researchers, Kellermann and Cole find three problems with how the strategies in each are defined: (a) insufficiency (definitions are incomplete), (b) incomprehensibility (the definitions are not readily understandable), and (c) irrelevancy (the definitions are inapplicable or immaterial). Because the strategies in these taxonomies, taken together, "overlap" one another, compliance-gaining taxonomies tend to be atheoretical collections of strategies that do not vary systematically with regard to specific characteristics. The consequence, Kellermann and Cole (in press) argue, is that "knowledge about compliance gaining behavior cannot be generalized beyond the level of individual strategies because the features that relate and differentiate the strategies from each other are unknown" (p. 15). Absent theory-based strategy definitions, researchers cannot rely upon these typologies to make the comparative or individual distinctions necessary for empirical analysis of compliance-gaining messages and their use.

Third, Kellermann and Cole (in press) found both conceptual and empirical problems with the examples used by researchers to represent each strategy in the compliance-gaining taxonomies. Based on their own analysis of 42% of the 1,460 examples evident in the 71 taxonomies studied, Kellermann and Cole observed that (a) the examples are often poor representatives of their intended strategies; (b) the examples also often represent features of other, unintended strategies; (c) sometimes the strategy features represented in the examples provided to subjects as stimuli are not representative of the context in which they are said to occur; (d) many of these difficulties are compounded when only single examples of each strategy are presented to subjects. In addition to these conceptual problems with the validity of examples used to represent strategies in compliance-gaining taxonomies, Kellermann and Cole (in press) note that the operational validity of compliance-gaining examples is suspect: "Most examples are never assessed for their validity . . . [and] even when checks are conducted, the validation procedures are of questionable value" (p. 34). In their own analysis, more than 50% of the 605 examples tested failed to represent their intended strategies (and the failure rate was as high as 70%-80% for the "altruism" and "direct request" strategy examples).

Kellermann and Cole's (in press) analytical and empirical findings concerning compliance-gaining taxonomies are sobering. Readers of compliance-gaining findings reported in terms of specific strategy names tacitly assume that the names are meaningful and the strategies are appropriately operationalized: "Neither of these presumptions should be made; strategy names are often not meaningful and operationalizations are often not valid. Research findings dependent on such presumptions must necessarily be questioned" (p. 36). More sobering with regard to compliance-gaining message behavior, Kellermann and Cole (in press) conclude that "the status of our knowledge, at best, is unclear. It is difficult and sometimes impossible to know whether a knowledge claim has actually been tested and/or replicated. *Put simply, our knowledge of compliance gaining message behavior is no better than our classification schemes and our classification schemes are in disarray*" (p. 42, italics added). Characterizing even their own 64-strategy list as an "atheoretical hodge-podge," they propose that only theoretically derived classification systems, rather than lists that are intuitively based, will result in valid findings regarding compliance-gaining message use. "Unfortunately," they lament, "more than a decade of work on compliance gaining taxonomies has still not produced a method that adequately classifies compliance gaining messages" (Kellermann & Cole, in press, p. 43). Before turning to recent efforts at theoretically based strategy investigation, we briefly note other methodological issues confronting readers of the compliance-gaining research literature.

Compliance-gaining methodology studies. Since our last review (Seibold et al., 1985), compliance-gaining researchers have attended somewhat more to observable compliance-gaining behaviors (e.g., Baglan, LaLumia, & Bayless, 1986; Baxter, 1990; Dillard, 1988; Neuliep, 1986). The area has been confronted with the same methodological matters of single message examples and repeated measures confronting interpersonal communication researchers in general (see Poole & McPhee, this volume, for a review).

However, the most central methodological issue of concern to compliance-gaining message researchers continues to be one we also treated in the first edition of the *Handbook:* the validity of "selection" versus "construction" methods of strategy elicitation. (See Seibold et al., 1985, for a description of each method and the research designs in which each is typically employed.) Fueled by a seven-study and pointed report by Burleson et al. (1988) and buttressed by Burke's (1989) study, these defenses of the superiority of the construction method and attacks on the selection method were debated in analytical responses by Boster (1988), Hunter (1988), and Seibold (1988)—to which Burleson and Wilson (1988) replied. An exceptionally clear summary of the particular issues in that exchange is available in Plax, Kearney, and Sorensen (1990) and will not be revisited here. Instead, it is worth noting that these researchers offer empirical evidence germane to the debate. For example, Sorensen, Plax, and Kearney (1989) compared coded teachers' message constructions with results obtained from the Behavior Alteration Technique (BAT) strategy selection checklist. They found no evidence of the superiority of the construction method in the classroom situation. For the most part, results using both methods were "comparable," and the researchers argued for "functional equivalence" of the procedures. Plax et al. (1990) offered a more rigorous test and concluded that "at best . . . the construction procedure will provide data 'similar' to those obtained with strategy checklists" (p. 139). Moreover, Plax et al. (1990) report:

> Our results do not reflect the allegations leveled against the selection method. Alternatively, these data suggest that when compared to findings obtained with the selectionist procedure, the construction approach is less sensitive to real world differences that should exist; provides similar results for other known predictions; and is just as likely to elicit socially desirable prosocial messages. (p. 128)

We hope these results will shift the debate and empirical research away from direct comparison of the methods (in hopes of establishing the superiority of either) and toward studies of the validity of each. Once obtained, this would enable multimethod studies of compliance-gaining messages. Even then, however, results' generalizability would depend on the theoretical coherence of the strategies described, as Kellermann and Cole (in press) note. We return to this issue in the next section.

Processes Underlying Strategic-Tactical Choices

Our review thus far suggests that, for all we know about the structure, endorsement, and production of various compliance-gaining requests, researchers in this area continue to face a number of significant barriers to understanding the nature of interpersonal influence. Some of these obstacles are lodged in the shortcomings of our taxonomies for compliance-gaining behaviors. Kellermann and Cole (in press) convincingly argue that the fragmented, atheoretical basis for previous approaches to cataloging influence strategies and tactics has resulted in an underidentified and often obscure picture of instrumental communication. Alternatively, fundamental differences in methodological choices have often produced incommensurate research findings or can be challenged in terms of faulty operationalizations. And, as we initially observed, the inherent limitations of the Strategic Choice Model may have fomented an overly rationalistic perspective of strategic language use. On the other hand, the greatest value in the tradition of compliance-gaining studies may, in fact, be in the promotion of such self-criticism and the ensuing motivation to search for more general understandings of interpersonal influence.

Another conclusion to be drawn from this survey is that researchers have largely focused on identifying the range of strategic and tactical possibilities in the pursuit of influence and have generally eschewed an analysis of how actors choose among those competing options. With the notable exceptions of early constructivist studies and those associated with the sequential request paradigm, the psychological bases for endorsing one tactic over another or complying with a request because it instantiates an appropriate strategy have generally been ignored. Indeed, Berger, Karol, and Jordan (1989) indicted compliance-gaining research for not considering how our cognitive representations of influence situations translate into observable action sequences. Cody and McLauglin's (1990) analysis, however, suggested that some researchers have begun to center on cognitive *accounts* of strategic-tactical communication, realizing that the study of actor and target "goals" offers a more parsimonious approach to understanding why interpersonal influence operates as it does. Others (Canary, Cody, & Marston, 1986; Cody, Canary, & Smith, in press) point out that interaction goals may be the salient feature actors use in distinguishing between compliance-gaining situations.

Taken as a whole, the contemporary shift toward understanding compliance-gaining behavior in light of influence *goals* begins to redress many of the drawbacks found in previous lines of research. Although these approaches are relatively few in number and ambitious in their designs, such goal-cognition studies place greater emphasis on theory building and testing, resulting in more consistency and corroboration between research findings. Additionally, scholars exploring the link between goals and compliance behavior may be starting to tacitly embrace a set of commitments counter to the Strategic Choice Model. What we shall term the *Goal Limitation Model* undergirding this research views actors' choices as being the result of interactional goals and objectives that (a) marshal the generally nonconscious use of influence schema by which we represent compliance-gaining situations, (b) orient our evaluation of how effective a particular tactic might be in that situation, and (c) can be governed by either habituated or adapted responses to influence contingencies. As an emergent metaperspective concerning the study of interpersonal influence, the Goal Limitation Model is implicit in research identifying actors' compliance goals as well as the study of how those cognitions affect message construction or endorsement.

Identifying Influence Goals

Since the first edition of this *Handbook* was published, a number of studies have focused on identifying the range of influence goals actors may pursue in compliance-gaining situations (Bisanz & Rule, 1989, 1990; Canary, Cunningham, & Cody, 1988; Canary et al., 1986; Cody et al., in press; Dillard, 1989, 1990a; Dillard,

Segrin, & Harden, 1989; Rule & Bisanz, 1987; Rule, Bisanz, & Kohn, 1985). Although Kellermann and Kim's (1991) comparison of 95 analyses in the compliance-gaining tradition yielded 49 distinct interaction goals, individual researchers have adopted restrictive conceptualizations (i.e., discriminating between compliance goals and other social goals or subsidiary objectives) and have identified a relatively limited set of "desired end states" (Roloff & Jordan, 1992) germane to compliance-gaining. Reviews (for example, Kellermann, in press-a) of such goal-oriented studies reveal that the typical range of influence goals consists of no more than a dozen or so categories, and Kellermann (in press-a) contends "there seems to be a core group of 8 distinct compliance gaining goals (perhaps requiring further differentiation)" (p. 3).

Dillard's (1989, 1990a; Dillard et al., 1989) research program presents one especially compact approach that distinguishes between primary and secondary influence goals. "The primary goal provides the initial push which activates the cognitive calculus that incorporates all of the secondary goals. Secondary goals then function to shape, and typically constrain, the behaviors whose overriding purpose is to alter the behavior of the target" (Dillard et al., 1989, p. 21). Any one of the four basic types of secondary goals—concerns for promoting the self-concept (identity goals), producing socially appropriate self-presentations (interaction goals), increasing or maintaining valued assets (resource goals), or maintaining a preferred composure (arousal management goals)—may temporarily become more salient in compliance-gaining situation, thus assuming the status of a primary influence goal (see Clark & Delia, 1979). In turn, the desire for more specific end states such as to protect a right (Cody et al., in press), initiate a relationship (Canary et al., 1986), acquire an object, or stop an annoying habit (Rule et al., 1985) can serve as the raison d'être for instigating a bid for influence.

Regardless of whether one adopts a more limited or inclusive approach to influence goals, goal-oriented approaches to compliance-gaining seem to hold a number of basic assumptions regarding their origin and function. In particular, (a) individuals hold influence goals that guide compliance-gaining behaviors; (b) the pursuit of a specific goal guides the selection or production of different compliance-gaining behaviors; (c) agents and targets may have multiple goals in any compliance-gaining scenario; and (d) persons may be only dimly aware of their interaction goals, let alone the way those goals affect personal choices. Furthermore, Meyer's (1990) analysis of the cognitive processes underlying message production highlights the fact that (e) the way in which actors use such goals is the product of the interface between experience-bound compliance-gaining rules and the opportunities for influence represented by situational features (see Berger et al., 1989; Cody & McLaughlin, 1990; Roloff & Jordan, 1992; Rule & Bisanz, 1987). It is these assumptions that form the basis of a *Goal Limitation Model* implicit in compliance-gaining research in the 1990s. And although it is a metatheoretical construction—one that could not be expected to exist in an absolute sense or be accepted en toto by any individual researcher—this hypothetical archetype makes clear (a) how compliance-gaining research is no longer characterized by the static, nonprocessual tenets of the Strategic Choice Model so characteristic of the 1980s' compliance-gaining research, and (b) the basic foci of continuing research in the area. The task for researchers, then, has been one of discovering the manner in which these processes mediate the link between situated goals, subsequent planning, and actual production of influence messages.

Goals, Plans, and Actions

Two approaches typify complementary research lines investigating the goal-planning-action process in compliance-gaining situations. Although both perspectives consider the use of influence goals based on different premises, taken together they implicate a number of limitations and possibilities for compliance-gaining behavior. Both approaches model the implicit decision-making schemes persons employ in constructing messages. The first examines features of actors' beliefs concerning the fit between goals, situations, and effective compliance-gaining behaviors. The second focuses on impression formation processes that direct actors' perceptions of compliance-bound situations and tasks. In tandem, these approaches to compliance-gaining representation and processing better enable us to anticipate various strategic and tactical choices to be made in pursuing interpersonal influence.

Efficiency and appropriateness. That actors wish to be effective in seeking influence is one of the most taken-for-granted assumptions about the link between goals and behaviors. However, the desire to achieve instrumental aims, alone, cannot account for the choice of a specific strategy or tactic; as capable social beings prone to seeking a multitude of goals, actors' considerations of precisely *what* it means to be effective in various situations must differ. A number of studies explore this distinction. Reardon (1981) noted that social appropriateness and the desire to appear consistent modify perceptions of how effective a compliance-gaining behavior might be. Cody et al. (1986) pointed to the use of inherent situational constraints in evaluating effectiveness. Canary et al. (1986) factored in personality variables such as locus of control, along with concerns for appropriateness, in measuring perceptions of strategies. Hample and Dallinger (1987) suggested that other editing criteria in the construction of influence messages include personal principles and perceived standards for discourse competence. And others (Hertzog & Bradac, 1984; Roloff & Janiszewski, 1989) have argued that agents focus on the amount of resistance they anticipate in an influence situation and design requests to overcome those obstacles. Thus, in general, researchers have embraced a reasonably complex view of what grounds perceptions of effectiveness in compliance-gaining situations.

Canary and Spitzberg's (1987, 1989) direct examination of how actors perceive the effectiveness and appropriateness of influence behaviors in conflict situations is a fine illustration of the general trends in some research. Arguing that the dual concerns of meeting goals and upholding situational or relational rules define what it means to be communicatively competent, the researchers discovered that, while effectiveness and appropriateness are significantly correlated, the perceived *general* appropriateness of a compliance-gaining behavior only accounts for roughly 4% of the variance in message choice. Alternatively, actors' perceptions of the specific appropriateness seemed most sensitive to distinguishing between effective and ineffective selections. In short, Canary and Spitzberg's work suggests that persons' behaviors depend on social as well as situational conventions linked to specific opportunities for influence. Their research, however, does not fully address why different situations result in stronger perceptions of the association between perceived effectiveness and situated appropriateness for some behaviors rather than others.

A comprehensive program of study aimed at exploring perceptions of request effectiveness has been pursued by Kellermann and her associates (Berger &

Kellermann, 1983; Cole, 1993; Kellermann, in press-a, in press-b; Kellermann & Cole, 1991, in press; Kellermann & Kim, 1991; Kellermann, Reynolds, & Chen, 1991). Instead of assuming that request effectiveness and appropriateness are *separate* dimensions of compliance-gaining situations, these researchers demonstrate that perceptions of effectiveness *depend on* the relationship between beliefs concerning the appropriateness and efficiency of various behaviors. That is, the most face-threatening messages need not be the least efficient choices while a more appropriate or more polite approach is not necessarily the one that induces prompt compliance; nonetheless, persons evaluate message effectiveness in terms of how efficient and appropriate the discourse appears. To the extent instrumental goals implicate both task and social concerns, perceptions of request appropriateness and efficiency are contingent upon how pressing the task becomes. Furthermore, perceptions of the goals sought in specific situations, rather than the situations themselves, mediate estimates of appropriateness and efficiency, which, in effect, constrain tactical choices. As a theory of metagoals, Kellermann's reasoning follows an assumption implicit in other studies (for example, Rule et al., 1985) of compliance-gaining in which influence situations are represented in consciousness via distinct sets of goals.

Kellermann (in press-a) argued that, in lieu of focusing attention on identifying the absolute number of distinct goals actors use to distinguish situations, there is more profit to be had in identifying what distinguishes goals from one another. Instead of looking to generalized differences like amount of directness inherent in a request (Dillard, 1989), she attended to the more interpersonal concern of maintaining one's own or the target's public image to differentiate types of goals. With this more restricted focus, she observed that seemingly competitive wishes (to be approved of, yet be autonomous from others) structured goal orientations into becoming more or less face threatening.

Predicting an inverse relationship between the face threat of various influence goals and the perceived appropriateness and efficiency of 56 compliance-gaining behaviors, Kellermann and Kim (1991) found that none of the 49 different social goals they employed resulted in a unique or distinct pairing with a particular set of tactics. Some behaviors were seen as universally dysfunctional and some were considered functional for each goal; none of the goals permitted the use of all influence tactics. Additionally, threats to the target's public self interacted with the pressing, task-oriented nature of a goal affecting the perceived and relative appropriateness or efficiency of a goal (see Kellermann, in press-a). In this research, tactical choices (identified via vernacular performance verbs embedded in speech acts) resulted from concerns for appropriateness and efficiency that were highlighted by the end state being sought. Unfortunately, because the social goals employed in the research design were "conversational" in nature, that could apply across a range of compliance-gaining situations, and because their subjects were given no latitude in the choice of situated goals, we do not know the extent to which these relationships codetermine the choice among potentially competing goals in any given influence situation.

Message design logics. Additional clues to the relationship among choices, goals, and compliance-gaining proclivities may be extracted from another family of studies dealing with influence impression formation. In this line of research, analysis centers on the extent to which actors are more or less cognitively complex in thinking about compliance-gaining situations and the targets of influence. For example, Bingham and Burleson (1989) found that individuals who made finer discriminations among interpersonal and situational features were more likely to employ goals and message strategies that better preserved desired identities and relationships. Due to their experience, such cognitively complex persons possess both the cognitive capability and the impetus to employ advanced message constructions because, unlike less adept actors, they believe these approaches are more effective (see Fiske & Taylor, 1991). Alternatively, Wilson, Cruz, and Kang's (1992) research suggested that these strategic choices, in fact, may not be all that much more effective. They found that cognitively complex individuals were more responsive to specific features of interactions, which led to a variety of different attributions. In turn, these attributions were used to formulate a wider variety of influence messages, some of which were well adapted to the situation and some of which were not altogether effective. In accord with the implicit Goal Limitation Model we outlined earlier, these researchers might conclude that perceptions of appropriateness and efficiency are not as pivotal in the construction or endorsement of compliance-gaining messages as is the extent to which an agent is cognitively complex in her or his perception of the influence opportunity.

Growing out of the constructivist approach to interpersonal influence studies (see the extensive review in our chapter in the first edition of this *Handbook*), O'Keefe's research program is central to studies that explore the connection between actors' perceptions and the calculus they use to construct messages (O'Keefe, 1988, 1990; O'Keefe & Delia, 1982, 1988; O'Keefe & McCornack, 1987; O'Keefe & Shepherd, 1987). Not only does her work serve as a foundation for most other influence studies that focus on cognitive complexity, it also provides systematic and exemplary research in the emerging Goal Limitation Model tradition. Fundamental to her perspective is the distinction between *goal structures* and *message design logics*. As with other researchers, O'Keefe suggests that a wide variety of goals may exist that become the instrumental ends to which a compliance-gaining attempt is directed. The extent to which an actor represents multiple goals in an influence situation determines the goal structure she or he employs. Minimal goal structures are not oriented toward a clear goal or set of goals; unifunctional goal structures are devoted to accomplishing a single task- or face-oriented goal; multifunctional goal structures simultaneously consider both task and face goals. Different goal structures evolve with interpersonal development, and cognitive complexity mediates message production by altering the kind and number of goals a person thinks relevant to a situation. In this sense, O'Keefe's approach resembles the work of others. However, the greatest value in her perspective is found in the argument that goals, alone, do not provide enough guidance in constructing messages. Actors must have a set of implicit "rules" to draw upon in linking goals with strategic and tactical choices.

Message design logics are independent of goal structures and provide just the sort of cognitive guidance lacking in many perspectives on compliance-gaining. These alternative sets of premises and beliefs can be thought of as implicit communication theories persons use to reason through influence scenarios and select possible behaviors. O'Keefe's studies verify the existence of at least three common message design logics. The most basic is what she terms an "expressive" logic reflected in an actor's simple statement of a request without an adaptation to situational or interpersonal constraints. A "conventional" logic relies upon the existence of various predetermined rules for message behavior that are the product of socialization. Finally, a "rhetorical" logic prompts the actor to redefine the influence situation by creating uniquely adapted compliance-gaining messages. As with goal structures, a person's repertoire of message design logics increases with experience and, as she or he comes to think about influence messages in more complex ways, the behavior becomes more strategic. This is not to claim that influence behavior will always appear to be more complex in its enactment; "when simply making one's ideas or wants known to others is sufficient for the purposes at hand, all three message-design systems will generate similar looking messages" (O'Keefe, 1988, p. 91).

A pair of studies (i.e., O'Keefe & McCornack, 1987; O'Keefe & Shepherd, 1987) indicate that the message design logic perspective provides a coherent account for the association among goals, strategic choices, and social actors. Regardless of how cognitively complex persons are, the predominant message design system they employ influences their perceptions of others' interpersonal competence, social appropriateness, and overall effectiveness in compliance-gaining situations. Presumably, such attributions also influence the actual production of influence messages as well. Alternatively, actors' goal structures are reflected in their ability to address multiple goals. Those who differentiate more between compliance-gaining situations and targets are better able to redress the need to meet secondary goals such as face wants and thus present more effective requests. In short, cognitive complexity mediates the use of situational features in forming impressions of influence options as well as employing goals to direct instrumental behaviors.

Future Directions and Continuing Limitations in Compliance-Goal Studies

Mirroring general trends in communication research, a number of teams have recently begun to examine cognitive processes leading up to the choice of one or another compliance-gaining behavior. Cast at a molar level of analysis, this research has started to explicate the goal-oriented mechanisms implied in a variety of prior influence studies. For example, some previous researchers (Canary et al., 1986; Cody et al., 1986; Roloff & Janiszewski, 1989) have speculated that goal-oriented, situational, strategic, and tactical features get loaded into memory in the form of schema that may be used in an almost mindless fashion in compliance-gaining scenarios. But, given that these scholars have focused on exploring other issues (such as the trade-off between efficiency and appropriateness), their analysis of such cognitive mechanisms has been largely missing. Alternatively, other researchers (Meyer, 1990; Schank & Abelson, 1977) have been much more pointed in their study of the cognitive underpinnings yet have failed to test fully the elaborated frameworks. However, a rather limited number of other scholars have developed and tested cognitive accounts of interpersonal influence; this body of research may be seminal to future studies of compliance gaining in that it clearly demonstrates how interaction goals fundamentally affect the steps people take in thinking about influence options.

One attempt to map cognitive structures linking goals and behaviors was represented in Wilson's (1990) "Cognitive Rules Model." Wilson's approach assumes that persons' knowledge concerning the pursuit of goals is stored in memory, and assumptions as to how one should act in light of goals are linked to rules that unify situational features with desired outcomes. In essence, various combinations of these nonconscious cognitive rules become activated in interpersonal situations, which results in the formation of an interaction goal or set of goals that direct the choice among strategic and tactical options. Different rules trigger different goals resulting in different behaviors. Because situations may implicate multiple rules, the presence in memory of larger rule repertoires may result in actors being aware of and pursuing multiple goals. A particular set of rules gets activated depending on how distinct the rule-to-situation fit appears, how frequently that set of rules has been used, and the recency with which the set has been employed. While behavior appears goal directed, the mental process of structuring compliance gaining is rule governed.

In an experiment testing assumptions of the model, Wilson (1990) found that, in unambiguous situations, the accessibility of cognitive rules largely determined the likelihood of forming and pursuing a primary influence goal. If the situation is relatively ambiguous, the sequence of goal formation and subsequent behavior is mediated more by the frequency that a set of rules has been activated in the past, and the recency thereof, rather than by an adapted search for more informative situational features. This effect seems generally independent of cognitive complexity and the hypothesized warrant for seeking multiple goals in more face-threatening scenarios. However, because Wilson only varied the clarity of situational features in four compliance-gaining contexts, other situational stimuli might result in a different configuration of rule usage. Nonetheless, Wilson's model provides a testable, cognitive framework that potentially explains how actors make the choices they do in compliance-gaining encounters.

A more general program that models the cognitive foundations for compliance-gaining has been outlined by Greene and his colleagues (Greene, 1984, 1990; Greene & Lindsey, 1989; Greene, Smith, & Lindsey, 1990). A central aim of this research is to describe how types of communication, including interpersonal influence opportunities, are represented in memory and processed in the production of messages. Separate compliance-gaining elements such as the actor-target relationship are mentally represented in procedural records dealing with specific actions and their consequences. Various procedures get "assembled" to produce compliance-gaining behaviors if and when situational features match experience-based action-outcome contingencies. As with other cognitive accounts, Greene assumes that frequency and recency of use can mediate the matching process. Additionally, a variety of cognitive heuristics lend a degree of efficiency to the assembly process (see Cialdini, 1987). The assembled strategic plan may be very general or very specific, includes everything from provisions for primary and secondary goals to how a specific utterance is to be articulated, and may be imperfectly represented by how an actor behaves in seeking compliance. Finally, those action assemblies that repeatedly reinforce anticipated act-outcome associations may come to be stored as a unit; consequently, some general behaviors may become habitual and it is only when the novelty of a situation passes a critical threshold that an actor must turn to the taxing process of tailoring a more adapted assembly.

Two tests of Greene's general model provide indirect support for a number of assumptions pertinent to compliance-gaining. Both studies presume that patterns of syntactic and representational features, revealed in vocal hesitations during message production or memories of influence attempts after a delay, are indicative of underlying cognitive processes. Greene and Lindsey (1989) found that, when presented with the need to address multiple social goals instead of a single objective, actors exhibited delays and hesitancies as would be predicted if they had to exert additional cognitive effort in assembling more complex messages. If subjects were allowed time to plan their communication in advance, less cognitive loading was evident. Yet, insofar as the task subjects faced was only marginally related to a compliance-gaining scenario, we can only extrapolate the findings to the realm of interpersonal influence. Alternatively, Greene et al. (1990) directly examined persons' memories for various features of compliance-gaining messages. In a series of five studies, these researchers discovered that subjects display substantially greater recall for specific compliance-gaining acts than they do for strategic sequences of behaviors. That is, subjects were able to distinguish what was said better than they could reconstruct it when various parts of an influence attempt were initiated. This would be expected if separate procedures for compliance are more readily accessible in memory than prepackaged sequences of action-outcome contingencies. Greene et al. specifically avoided providing their subjects with scenarios containing behaviors that were likely to be routinized given common experiences. However, because this study did not focus on the production of messages in light of goals, the conclusions can only offer a tentative link to goal-planning-behavior research.

Taken together, current studies of compliance-gaining goals, the association between those goals and situation-specific perceptions of request efficiency and appropriateness, and the processes by which various elements are combined to create messages point to a number of conclusions regarding the cognitive underpinnings of compliance behavior. In very fundamental ways, interpersonal influence can be seen as the product of actors (a) comparing their goals against implied social constraints in light of their experiences in similar contexts, (b) drawing upon similarly experience-bound decision rules and accompanying procedures, (c) tacitly selecting those strategies that best fit the cognitive calculus being manipulated, and (d) engaging tactics of language use that they believe are called for at that time and place. Research indicates that this process is generally nonconscious in origin, sometimes mindless in application, and prone to habitual patterns and shortcomings of human cognition. Notably, studies of the processes underlying strategic-tactical choices, in both design and cumulative effect, more closely resemble tenets of the Goal Limitation Model than they do the traditional Strategic Choice Model. This body of research also brings us closer to understanding the range and quality of actors' compliance-gaining abilities and predispositions.

As provocative and illuminating as current research is, however, the study of the goal-oriented nature of interpersonal influence still has its shortcomings. In particular, two significant reservations become apparent from reviewing work in the area. First, perhaps because there have been so few direct examinations of actors' compliance-gaining goals, existing goal typologies may be an artifact of the influence scenarios used to examine their effects on behavior. This lack of trans-situational applicability is noted by only some of those interested in the link between goals and actions (e.g., O'Keefe & Shepherd, 1987); other researchers either fail to mention the limitation or seemingly assume that "a goal, is a goal, is a goal." On the other hand, more comprehensive approaches (e.g., Kellermann, in press-a) are based on the collapsing of goals drawn from a variety of different studies. Insofar as goal-related indeterminacy seems an inherent problem in this approach, it may be more productive to follow Wilson's (1990) lead and henceforth focus on the identification of rules that give rise to goal orientations (see Greene, 1990). And, in doing so, researchers might also address Dillard et al's. (1989) concerns regarding the extent to which rules qua goals change over the course of an interaction.

A second problematic issue facing goal theorists and researchers pivots on the determination of what is salient to actors in the pursuit of influence. If Kellermann (in press-a) is correct in claiming that actors' immediate concerns are what distinguish types of goals, researchers must begin to focus on more than the typical reliance on face needs as mediators of request efficiency and appropriateness. A number of reasons warrant this expansion of foci. In many situations, alternative goals, such as meeting deadlines or conserving personal resources, may be far more salient. Furthermore, studies (Bingham & Burleson, 1989) reveal that only those who are relatively complex in their perceptions focus on identity of relationship dimensions in casting influence. And the problem is complicated by the fact that the association between cognitive representations of goals and ensuing behaviors is indeterminate (Greene et al., 1990; Tedeschi, 1990) and that a person's beliefs that the simple exposition of ideas will suffice in a compliance-gaining scenario will oftentimes mask what particular goal is being sought (O'Keefe, 1990). As Kellermann and Kim (1991) suggest that researchers should investigate what makes a goal more or less task oriented, future studies should examine what prompts the hierarchy of salient concerns actors face in confronting targets and venues of influence. Clearly, most of these concerns will be the product of sociocultural factors, which indicates, as Eagly (1987) concluded, that there is more to the goal-planning-action sequence than can be captured by purely cognitive accounts of interpersonal influence.

Influence in Applied Settings

An understated assumption concerning interpersonal influence research is that such studies are inherently bound to the *praxis* of social interaction. Indeed, Cialdini's (1980) call for "full-cycle social psychology" explicitly recognized that laboratory studies of compliance, which began as empirical testaments to anecdotal evidence, were slowly returning to the field to verify that corpus of research in more ecologically valid and applied settings. In this section, we examine two particularly instructive applied research domains—the sequential request and managerial influence traditions—to illustrate ongoing attempts to ground influence scholarship in practical conduct.

Sequential Techniques

Interpersonal influence in applied settings often proceeds in stages, each of which establishes the foundation for further changes in beliefs or behavior. Individuals slowly come to embrace new opinions, and actors often induce others to gradually comply with target requests. Although they acknowledge that influence can occur quite dramatically, Miller and Burgoon's (1978) "expanded view" of persuasion suggested that interpersonal influence is generally a slow process. This seems to be an appropriate conceptualization, from our perspective, that mirrors what actually occurs in society. Agents have long recognized the value of "setting up" the targets of compliance-gaining attempts and this fact has not been lost even on those wed to the Strategic Choice Model and the legacy of Marwell and Schmidt. For example, Chmielewski's (1982) research suggested that individuals will strategically retreat from the use of preferred message tactics when presented with sequential opportunities to further attempt to influence others in a conflict situation. With a focus upon the factors that mediate the selection of compliance-gaining strategies, Chmielewski demonstrated that the sources of influence attempts will devalue the perceived worth of tactics found to be ineffective even though associated cognitions (for example, social normative beliefs regarding the appropriateness of particular tactics) remain relatively stable across time. Research such as this speaks to the psychological reality of persons' naive assumptions about the sometimes sequential nature of interpersonal influence.

Independent of the compliance-gaining strategies tradition we have previously reviewed, other researchers have established the utility of sequentially manipulating single-message tactics in both marketplace encounters as well as controlled social scientific settings. A fine example of research concerning sequential compliance gaining was conducted by Cialdini et al. (1978). These researchers examined the common sales practice of inducing customers to make a decision to purchase an item and subsequently informing them that the lower price could not be offered for a variety of reasons. Called "low-balling," the technique is assumed to be more effective than simply offering a commodity at a higher price without a previous setup. In each of three experiments, Cialdini and his associates demonstrated that a preliminary decision to take an action persevered, even when the cost associated with compliance was increased. Low-balled subjects complied at a significantly higher rate than those who had only been informed of the full cost of the target behavior at the outset (also see Burger & Petty, 1981). Alternatively, other investigators have focused on processes of sequentially "luring" targets (Joule, Gouilloux, & Weber, 1989), producing the "That's not all!" effect so prevalent in late-night television advertising (Burger, 1986), or increasing monetary contributions by legitimizing even paltry sums after issuing the target request (Reeves, Macolini, & Martin, 1987). As with the low-ball tactic, these sequential approaches demonstrate increased compliance in a range of situations.

The foot-in-the-door/door-in-the-face research tradition. Although the aforementioned techniques seem effective means of social influence, most research concerning sequential request strategies has focused on the *foot-in-the-door* (FID) and the *door-in-the-face* (DIF) techniques. Their strategic forms essentially mirror one another, and effectiveness is always gauged against nonsequential, similar critical requests. In seminal FID research, Freedman and Fraser (1966) reasoned that, if one could get a target to comply with a minimal request (that is, get a foot in the door), further compliance with a larger request would be more likely to occur. The FID subjects were first asked to answer a few questions concerning household products they had in their homes. Subjects were contacted 3 days later and asked to permit a team of researchers to visit their homes and classify all household products that the subjects had accumulated. When compared with a control condition, the FID subjects exhibited the predicted behavior—those who had complied with the smaller request were more likely to comply with the critical request than those who had not received the initial request. Alternatively, Cialdini et al. (1975) first proposed the "rejection-then-moderation," or DIF, technique for gaining compliance. Basing their analysis upon the notion of a reciprocity norm (Gouldner, 1960), Cialdini et al. assumed that, by getting subjects to reject a request to donate 2 hours of volunteer service per week for at least 2 years, the same individuals would be more likely to comply with a subsequent request to donate a single afternoon of voluntary action. The researchers again observed the sequential effect in comparison with control subjects' compliance rates.

In the past 20 years, numerous research groups have examined the FID and DIF techniques and, though the number of FID studies roughly doubles those for DIF, a sizable body of empirical data have been generated. Recent meta-analyses of the research lines (Beaman, Cole, Preston, Klentz, & Steblay, 1983; Dillard, Hunter, & Burgoon, 1984; Fern, Monroe, & Avila, 1986) suggest that both effects are reliable given appropriate conditions, even though only a small mean effect size (rarely greater than .20) can be demonstrated across studies. The fact that both the FID and the DIF techniques are associated with such small effects may partially account for why noninteractional variables such as source credibility (Tybout, 1978) and monetary incentives (Furse, Stewart, & Rados, 1981) have exerted a greater influence upon compliance rates than sequential organization in some studies. Nonetheless, because some researchers (Cantrill & Seibold, 1986; Scott, 1977) have reported that the FID and DIF techniques are associated with as much as a 50% increase in compliance compared with control subjects' behavior, it seems important to more closely examine their utility for communicative influence attempts.

The general pattern of research findings in the sequential request paradigm suggests there are a number of limiting conditions that constrain the effectiveness of the FID and DIF techniques. The optimal magnitude of the initial and critical requests associated with both methods of gaining compliance has garnered the most attention. FID and DIF techniques require requests that are neither too small nor too large. Although some FID studies (Baron, 1973; Miller & Suls, 1977; Snyder & Cunningham, 1975) demonstrate that sequential influence occurs only when the initial request requires paltry levels of compliance, research conducted by Seligman, Bush, and Kirsch (1976) suggests that a basement threshold exists beyond which the technique is not operative. That is, it is only when the initial request for compliance induces "sufficient commitment" on the part of the target that critical request rates are significantly different than single-message requests (see Carducci, Deuser, Bauer, Large, & Ramaekers, 1989). In the DIF case, there is a ceiling for optimal initial request size, sometimes governed by established behavioral customs (for example, Schwarzwald, Raz, & Zvibel, 1979). The initial DIF request must be large enough to guarantee rejection by the target of an influence attempt (Cialdini & Ascani, 1976; Cialdini et al., 1975) but, as Even-Chen, Yinon, and Bizman (1978) showed, large initial requests that induce incredulity in targets result in critical request compliance rates lower than those observed for control subjects. Furthermore, Dillard and Burgoon (1985) argued that the FID and DIF thresholds are likely to vary depending upon the specific target behavior that is being requested, a conclusion that is reinforced in Dillard's (1991) review of sequential request meta-analyses and Cantrill's (1991) multivariate exploration of FID and DIF request perception.

A second conditional factor is the length of delay between the first and second requests. Insofar as few studies (Cann, Sherman, & Elkes, 1975; Shanab & Isonio, 1982) have unambiguously measured effect differences between immediately presenting the critical requests versus delaying its presentation for up to 10 days, Dillard (1991) considers the effects of timing to be far from conclusive. Whereas the existence of a delay between the first and second requests does not seem to alter the effectiveness of the FID technique, DIF influence may be contingent upon the critical request immediately following the first (see Beaman, Steblay, Preston, & Klentz, 1988). But, as DeJong (1979) noted, the *strongest* effects in the FID research line are associated with those studies in which there is little or no delay between the two requests. Furthermore, "the length of the delay itself may be less important than whether the occasion of the second request somehow reminds people of their earlier behavior" (p. 2223). This was probably the case in the Cann et al. (1975) and Seligman, Bush, and Kirsch (1976) studies.

The similarities between the actors and the tasks associated with initial and critical requests have also been manipulated. In general, it appears to matter little if FID requestors differ between the first and second requests in either a direct request situation (Freedman & Fraser, 1966) or in circumstances that only imply a larger request for help (Miller & Suls, 1977; Wagener & Laird, 1980). On the other hand, relevant meta-analyses suggested that the same actors must advance both the initial and the critical requests for the DIF technique to be effective. Also, DIF studies (Cialdini et al., 1975) as well as FID research (Goldman, Seever, & Seever, 1982; Miller & Suls, 1977) demonstrate that the two requests need not concern the same subject matter for sequential effects to occur (DeJong, 1981, Study 1; Seligman, Miller, et al., 1976). However, such results have generally been observed only in studies that employed prosocial topics in the critical requests (see Patch, 1986), and attempts to modify consumer behavior have generally failed (Furse et al., 1981).

A number of variations have been made in the FID and DIF research lines that further specify the range of effectiveness associated with these sequential message techniques. For example, Goldman and his associates (Goldman & Creason, 1981; Goldman, Creason, & McCall, 1981; Goldman, Gier, & Smith, 1981) reported that, by adding an intermediary request to either the FID or the DIF sequence, compliance rates can be further increased through the use of a "two-feet-in-the-door" or a "two-doors-in-the-face" technique. Also, Reingen (1978) increased FID and DIF compliance rates by including a statement legitimizing even trivial compliance levels to the critical request (see, as well, Cialdini & Schroeder, 1976; Fraser, Hite, & Sauer, 1988). Alternatively, research conducted by Scott (1977) and Zuckerman, Lazzaro, and Waldgeir (1979) revealed a sequential FID effect only if no incentive was offered for initial request compliance (DeJong & Funder, 1977). Hence a wide variety of manipulations have been included in FID and DIF studies, allowing researchers the opportunity to specify more precisely the conditions under which successful outcomes result from use of these sequential message techniques.

Future directions. Dillard (1991) has observed that, because most research in the sequential request tradition has focused on variables that mediate compliance, relatively little effort has been expended in trying to identify underlying influence mechanics. Generally, theoretical accounts for why the FID and DIF techniques work have been applied a posteriori and research designs typically do not reflect concern for theory testing. Furthermore, the predictions of theories enlisted to account for FID effectiveness are often vitiated by those associated with DIF compliance even though the mirrorlike nature of the request sequences suggests that a *single* theoretical account would be expected. Thus future research should focus on theory testing and building in identifying frameworks to champion the underlying mechanism of compliance associated with each sequential technique.

The main explanatory construct in the FID paradigm has been Bem's (1972) self-perception theory. Some researchers (Freedman & Fraser, 1966) assert that, by complying with an initial request, targets attribute to themselves a "doer" self-perception that governs critical request compliance. A number of FID studies and meta-analyses argue against this explanation, however (see Dillard, 1991). For example, Scott (1977) included a variety of cognitive measures including situational and self-attributions, behavioral intentions, and attitudes toward the act of compliance. Although she elicited an FID effect in her experimental subjects, none of the cognitive variables approached statistical significance. Other studies suggest that subjects pay more attention to situational perceptions (Rittle, 1981), social norms (Kilbourne, 1988, 1989), self-inferences (Dillard, 1990b), social reinforcements (Crano & Sivacek, 1982), or social labels (Sharkin, Mahalik, & Claiborn, 1989) than to self-attributions in deciding whether to comply with critical requests. Hence Beaman et al. (1988) are warranted in concluding that a "self-perception explanation, despite its intuitive appeal, lacks solid experimental support" (p. 242).

The picture is no less obscure when one considers the various theoretical bases for DIF compliance. Although a reciprocal concessions account has been favored by many in the DIF tradition (for example, Cialdini et al., 1975; Mowen & Cialdini, 1980; Patch, 1986), direct tests of the explanatory construct have failed to reveal that targets perceive an urge to reciprocate when presented with the critical request (Goldman, McVeigh, & Richterkessing, 1984). Consequently, scholars have turned to alternative frameworks. Pendelton and Batson (1979) discovered that targets are likely to comply with critical requests in an attempt to manage their self-presentations rather than act in accord with an altered self-perception, and Goldman et al. (1984) essentially replicated the effect. A variety of other research groups (for example, Fraser et al., 1988; Goldman & Creason, 1981; Miller, Seligman, Clark, & Bush, 1976; Shanab & Isonio, 1980; Shanab & O'Neill, 1979) contest that DIF subjects perceptually contrast the first and second requests and therefore judge the critical request more leniently than control subjects. However, the only study to directly measure perceived contrasts between initial and critical requests (Cantrill & Seibold, 1986) did not detect significant differences between treatment and control respondents' perceptions despite incurring significant compliance rates through the use of either DIF or FID.

Clearly, a number of issues remain problematic in our understanding of the FID and DIF techniques. The fact that most existing theoretical explanations are fragmented or lead to conflicting predictions of whether or not compliance occurs suggests that more studies that simultaneously examine both techniques are mandated. Recently, Dillard (1991) has argued that the major questions to be answered in the examination of FID and DIF are cognitive in nature, and we would heartily agree. In fact, one of the more promising contemporary approaches to understanding sequential compliance suggests that targets draw upon the most available information in deciding to acquiesce to initial and critical requests. Similar to what Howard (1990) focused on in examining the "foot-in-the-mouth" effect, Tybout, Sternthal, and Calder (1983) have manipulated the specific cognitive sets available to targets when processing critical requests. Those who had been induced to consider that their obligation to the requestor has yet to be fulfilled were more willing to comply with critical requests in either the FID or the DIF sequence. Continued research into the cognitive origins of compliance should prove fruitful as researchers further probe for the generative mechanisms underlying sequential influence strategy effects.

Managerial Influence

Writing in 1988, Case, Dosier, Murkison, and Keys stated that "in recent years, the subjects of power and influence have become topics of great interest within the management field" (p. 25). Deluga (1988) noted that "effective leadership implies an understanding of how managers and employees influence one another" (p. 456). Most recently, Yukl and Falbe (1990) suggested that "one of the most important determinants of managerial effectiveness is success in influencing subordinates, peers, and superiors" (p. 132).

While the subject of managerial influence continues to attract attention from researchers in multiple disciplines (especially communication, management, marketing, psychology, social psychology), investigators today are more sophisticated both in conception and in design than a decade ago. When we published the first edition of this chapter in 1985, we critiqued current research on managerial influence as being too focused on a unidirectional, rational, strategic model. Since that critique, researchers in this domain have broadened their view of managerial influence considerably. Although studies of superior-subordinate, downward influence are still prominent, scholars have begun to view managerial influence as more complex and varied. The review of the literature that we present next illustrates this new outlook in at least four ways: (a) an increased interest in discovering the *mediating factors* that shape the influence process, (b) an expanded view of influence *relationships* that includes associations at all levels of the organization, (c) an appreciation for alternative, indirect *forms* of influence strategies, and (d) a small but important move toward delineating the *effects* of managerial influence. These advances will be apparent in the following review of relevant literature, critique of current research, and suggestions for avenues of investigation for the coming decade.

Factors That Mediate the Influence Process

In recent years, researchers have abandoned a view of managerial influence as direct, planned, and unidirectional and instead have begun to conceive of it as mediated interaction. In the next section, we review research concerned with illuminating some of these individual and situational mediators.

Gender as a mediating variable. Consonant with a move toward more diversity in the organizational workplace, gender as a mediating factor has received increased research attention. As Hirokawa, Kodama, and Harper (1990) state:

> The percentage of women in managerial positions in the United States has been
> growing steadily over the last two decades. . . . This rapid growth of women in
> management positions, supported by the continuing impact of women's movements
> and affirmative actions policies, has naturally led to an expanding body of literature
> attempting to describe and evaluate female management styles and performance as
> well as to compare and contrast female to male managers on a variety of psychological
> and behavioral dimensions. (pp. 30-31)

In a programmatic set of investigations, Hirokawa and colleagues have investigated the gender-influence relationship, focusing on the question of whether male and female managers differ in their use of persuasive tactics due to gender differences alone or whether situational variables affect that relationship. To date, they have investigated the effects of three situational variables—type of request, source of power, and legitimacy of the request—on the gender-influence relationship.

In an initial study, Harper and Hirokawa (1988) sought to determine whether male and female managers' persuasive tactics differed across obligatory and nonobligatory requests. Their results indicated that both men and women used power-based strategies (reward or punishment) in an obligatory request situation and were less direct (used more altruistic or rationale-based strategies) in a nonobligatory request situation. Harper and Hirokawa (1988) concluded that differences that did exist between male and female managers were due to the mediating factor of request type (obligatory versus nonobligatory) and not to the managers' gender per se. In a second study, Hirokawa et al. (1990) investigated managers' power as a mediating factor in the influence process. Their results indicated that "observed differences between the anticipated persuasive communication strategies and tactics of male and female managers are largely the result of power differences" (p. 47). In a third investigation of the gender-influence relationship, Hirokawa, Mickey, and Miura (1991) studied the effects of request legitimacy on the compliance-gaining tactics of male and female managers. Their results corroborated previous investigations. They concluded that "the data from this study continue to support the notion that the sex of the manager, per se, does not exert substantial influence on the tactic used to gain compliance. That is, any differences to be observed between the compliance-gaining tactics of men and women in this study were better accounted for by the degree of request legitimacy possessed by those individuals" (p. 434).

In a similar vein, Schleuter, Barge, and Blankenship (1990) investigated the effect of request type (obligatory versus nonobligatory) on the influence strategies used by lower-level and upper-level male and female managers. Contrasting the theories of socialization and structuralism, they found that, in general, differences in influence were connected to the hierarchical level of the influencer (more strongly favoring a structuralist position). They state that, while "support was found for both perspectives tested in this study, the structuralist perspective does provide a more coherent explanation for the differences observed in influence choices between upper and lower level male and female managers" (p. 63). Similar conclusions were drawn in a study that examined gender and *perceived* power in manager-subordinate relations. In an investigation of subordinate perceptions, Ragins and Sundstrom (1990) found that subordinates perceived no overall differences in power between male and female managers who had similar positions in the organization.

Contradicting this set of findings, however, Offerman and Kearney (1988) found strong support "for the prediction that one's own sex affects what type of social influence strategies women and men consider themselves likely to use, with strategy choice being consistent with general sex-role expectations" (p. 365). The difference found in this final investigation, however, may be due to the fact that Offerman and Kearney (1988) used college students in their sample, while the other four investigations tapped impressions of actual organizational members.

Additional mediating variables. Other mediating factors that have been examined include such individual characteristics and situational variables as (a) the impact of a manager's expertise versus his or her formal authority (Wilson & Kenny, 1985), (b) Theory X and Theory Y management styles (Neuliep, 1987), (c) employee preferences for forms of social influence (Monroe, Borzi, & DiSalvo, 1989; Vecchio & Sussmann, 1989), (d) the target's communication style (Garko, 1992), (e) the role of culture in Brazilian and American managers' influence attempts (Rossi & Todd-Mancillas, 1987), and (f) the importance of accountability and ambiguity (Fandt & Ferris, 1990). Results showed that (a) managerial expertise was consistently rated as a primary power factor, (b) Theory X and Theory Y managers select influence strategies consistent with those orientations, (c) congruity between employee preferences and superior's influence attempts may help account for variance in employee response to such attempts, (d) managers are more likely to employ strong forms of influence (assertiveness, higher authority) with a subordinate who communicates in an unattractive rather than an attractive style, (e) American managers are somewhat more flexible in their choice of influence strategies than Brazilian managers, who respond more rigidly and authoritatively, and (f) when accountability is high and ambiguity low, employees use positive information to defend their behavior and create a positive image.

The results of these investigations corroborate a view of managerial influence as a complex, mediated process. To date, researchers have only begun to explore the variety and importance of these mediators. Continued programmatic research in this area is vital if we are to ever fully understand the extent of this complexity. In the next section, we explore how researchers have begun to alter their view of influence *relationships*.

Alternate Influence Relationships

Upward influence. Recently, researchers have begun to investigate influence relationships beyond the superior-subordinate downward interaction. The subject of upward influence has especially attracted research attention. Some of this research had looked specifically at the types of influence strategies subordinates select. Fairholm (1985), using a list of 22 power tactics (including such strategies as "using ambiguity," "controlling the agenda," "forming coalitions," "using a proactive strategy," and "using charisma"), found that subordinates most often selected subtle influence strategies such as "using a proactive strategy" or "using outside experts" or "displaying charisma" when trying to influence their superiors. Case et al. (1988) found that subordinates often used a *combination* of several tactics when attempting to persuade superiors. In several of the interviews they conducted with employees, participants reported using three or four carefully integrated influence tactics, designed to break down resistance to an idea or plan. The following is an example:

> One accountant reported a sequence of steps in which the manager first convinced his subordinates of the merits of a plan and encouraged them to mention their support to the boss; he then presented a logical rational presentation to the superior, after which follow-up and persistent reminders were used until the influence attempt was successful. (Case et al., 1988, p. 30)

Other research on upward influence has investigated how relationship and organizational factors affect subordinates' influence attempts. Schilit (1987) found that middle-level managers exerted more influence in less risky strategic decision situations, were more influential if they had a long working relationship with the superior, and were employed in a smaller organization. Such findings are also reflected in a recent investigation conducted by Krone (1992). She found that the leader-member relationship, along with the centralization of authority in an organization, and the subordinate's organizational membership all affected upward influence tactic choices. In-group members, those who worked in organizations with decentralized decision-making practices, and members who were more effectively socialized into an organization, all tended to participate in the influence process more often and select more open upward influence strategies (overt influence attempts with desired outcomes fully disclosed) over strategic influence tactics (partially open/obvious attempts). Similarly, Scandura, Graen, and Novak (1986) found that subordinates having high quality leader-member relationships "reported high levels of decision influence, regardless of their superior's ratings of their expertise" (p. 583). Finally, Fairhurst, Rogers, and Sarr (1987), in an ambitious investigation that involved coding 11,825 individual messages, found that the leader-member relationship affected the subordinate's ability to execute upward influence. Managers high in comparative dominance had less understanding of their subordinates, perceived them to be less motivated to participate in decision making, and tended to give them lower performance ratings. On the other hand, managers who perceived their subordinates to be motivated to participate in decision making were more likely to treat their employees in a more equal and considerate manner.

Still other researchers have investigated how upward influence is affected by the locus of control of the influencer (Kapoor, Ansari, & Shukla, 1986; Lamude, Daniels, & White, 1987). Typically, results show that externally and internally controlled subordinates differ in their use of tactics, although these differences can be mediated by situational variables such as the managerial style of the boss (Ansari & Kapoor, 1987; Kapoor et al., 1986) or the type of influence request (Lamude et al., 1987).

Multilevel influence relationships. Beyond the topic of upward influence, some researchers have conceived of influence as multilevel, occurring between individuals at every level of the organization. Perhaps fueled by current organizational trends toward greater employee participation, empowerment, and teamwork, researchers have begun to investigate influence as a pervasive and participatory process. Although much of this work is still *theoretical* in nature (Barnes & Kriger, 1987; Cohen & Bradford, 1989; Conger & Kanungo, 1988), writers suggest that managers (a) view the person to be influenced as an ally rather than an adversary, (b) seek to understand the needs and goals of the influence, (c) seek win-win outcomes, (d) strive to create bases of trust across formal and informal boundaries, (e) express confidence in subordinates accompanied by high performance expectations, (f) foster opportunities for subordinates to participate in decision making, (g) provide autonomy from bureaucratic control, and (h) use power in a positive manner. As Conger and Kanungo (1988) state: "Words of encouragement, verbal feedback, and other forms of social persuasion often are used by leaders, managers, and group members to empower subordinates and co-workers" (p. 479).

Other researchers have sought to *operationalize* this view of influence and test its impact in the organizational setting. Yukl and Falbe (1990) investigated influence tactics and objectives in upward, downward, and lateral influence attempts. Using the Kipnis, Schmidt, and Wilkinson (1980) list of influence tactics as a starting point, they added two categories—inspirational appeals and consultation tactics—to the original scale. Inspirational appeals were defined as emotional requests or proposals designed to increase confidence and appeal to values and ideals. Consultation tactics were conceived as strategies that seek participation in decision making or in planning how to implement a proposed policy, strategy, or change. Results revealed that these two tactics were among the strategies respondents reported using most frequently in their influence attempts.

Yet another way participative influence has been operationalized is via network analysis. In a set of studies, Brass (1984, 1985) investigated networks of a large newspaper publishing business and found that power and influence were multilevel concepts. He discovered that contact beyond the proximal work group, being in a critical path in work flow interactions, having access to and control of communication in relation to the dominant coalition, and maintaining a position of centrality or betweenness in the organizational network proved to be the best predictors of individual influence. Finally, using still a different operationalization of influence as a participative process, Tjosvold (1985, 1989) created a model of goal interdependence, which states that "employees use the organizations' structure and values to conclude that their goals are cooperative, competitive, or independent and that these conclusions very much affect the dynamics and outcomes of interaction" (p. 49). In an investigation of 46 hospital managers and employees, Tjosvold (1989) found that, from the perspective of both managers and employees, those with cooperative goals influenced collaboratively, exchanged needed resources, worked productively, and developed positive feelings. Tjosvold (1989) concluded that "the nature of the interdependence between managers and employees appears to be a powerful antecedent to the type of influence used and its success. . . . This study suggests that leaders who develop strong cooperative relationships with employees facilitate productivity and efficiency, strengthen work relationships, and improve the attitudes of employees" (p. 59).

This research on alternate influence relationships again reinforces a view of influence as a complex process. No longer can one conceive of organizational influence as unidirectional and downward. It is instead a multilevel, participative process that occurs at all levels of organization. In the next section, we overview research that reconceptualizes the forms of influence strategies available to individuals. Specifically, this literature introduces indirect, political strategies rather than the direct, rational strategies examined in the past.

Alternate Forms of Influence Tactics

Research on alternate *forms* of influence tactics is still in its infancy and is often more theoretical than empirical in nature. Still, it provides food for thought and points out some important avenues for further study. Krone (1992) delineated three types of influence tactics: (a) *open upward influence* strategies, which are overt and include fully disclosed desired outcomes; (b) *strategic upward influence*, which includes tactics that are less explicit and direct; and (c) *political upward influence* strategies, which are more deceptive and may include such tactics as distorting information, managing one's self-presentation, and using ingratiation behaviors. The strategies of impression management and ingratiation have especially attracted scholars' attention.

Impression management and ingratiation. Liden and Mitchell (1988) developed a model of ingratiatory behaviors in organizational settings that includes causes of ingratiatory behavior, reasons for an individual's choice of an ingratiatory strategy, types of ingratiatory behaviors, and the outcomes or reaction to such attempts. They concluded their article by calling for additional empirical work to test their model as well as to investigate the prevalence and impact of ingratiation in organizational work life. In a combined laboratory and field study, Wayne and Ferris (1990) examined impression management strategies and their impact on supervisor liking of the subordinate. Both in the laboratory (where impression management strategies were manipulated) and in the field (where supervisors and subordinates were asked to answer questions regarding impression management tactics), "supervisor-focused impression management tactics were positively related to supervisor liking for the subordinate" (p. 495). The investigators suggested that it may be advantageous for the subordinate to attempt to manage the quality of exchange that occurs between him- or herself and the superior by using various impression management strategies. In an investigation of counselor-trainee self-presentation strategies on supervisors' evaluation of progress, Ward, Friedlander, Schoen, and Klein (1985) found that, when trainees used counterdefensive interaction (attributing improvement to the client or accepting personal responsibility for the client's deterioration), they were judged more socially skilled than trainees who employed defensive communication (taking credit for the client's improvement or blaming the client for deterioration). The findings suggested that the supervisors perceived the counterdefensive trainee as sincerely interested in understanding her mistakes and her effectiveness as a counselor.

Additional forms of influence strategies. In other investigations of alternate forms of influence, Sutton and Louis (1987) speculated that the socialization process is as important for influencing "insiders" in several ways, including affecting their commitment to the organization, their interpretation of the environment, and their view of what values and goals the organization favors. Finally, in an article about everyday rituals in management control, Golding (1991) illustrates how organizational rituals are used to achieve and maintain managerial influence. He states: "Alternative meanings and understandings abound, but there are, when required, certain preferred definitions of situations which are reinforced periodically. Some individuals, because of hierarchical position, have more ability to ensure that their definitions are enforced in preference to other possible alternatives" (p. 570). Golding suggests that management is an "artful" practice involving both positive and negative rituals. These rituals include (a) rituals of secrecy whereby only higher level members of the organization are privy to certain types of information or where no open record of various documents exists (e.g., appraisal schemes), (b) rituals of distinctiveness in which various members of the organization receive certain privileges (eating in the board room, taking longer lunch hours, eating in separate dining rooms, and so on), and (c) rituals of oppression (intimidation or status degradation). These rituals serve as indirect reminders of the influence hierarchy and reinforce its continued existence.

Although research on alternate forms of influence is scarce in comparison with investigations of more direct tactics, this avenue of inquiry is vitally important because it again points up the complex nature of the influence process. Individuals use a variety of strategies to pursue their goals, only some of which are open, direct, and overt. Becoming aware of the "hidden" side of influence promises to broaden our understanding of influence practices in organizations and make us more cognizant of its many faces. In the next section, we turn to research on influence *effects* in organizations, highlighting how these investigations have begun to draw links between the influence process and individual and organizational outcomes.

Effects of Influence

Writing in 1985, we stated that "the study of communicative influence effects must receive more attention" (p. 583). Although our call for action has not produced a groundswell of research on this topic, it is heartening to note that some examination of influence effects is being conducted. Two effects variables have been especially prominent in the literature—subordinate satisfaction and subordinate commitment.

Subordinate satisfaction and commitment. Infante and Gordon (1991) found that supervisors who were perceived as argumentative and affirming, rather than overtly aggressive in their communication style, had more satisfied subordinates. Hinkin and Schriesheim (1988) found that a supervisor's use of personal assertiveness had a strong negative correlation with both employee satisfaction and commitment, and that supervisor use of rational explanation had a strong positive correlation with employee satisfaction and commitment. Scheer and Stern (1992) found similar results, concluding that supervisor use of positively framed contingent reward influence resulted in greater employee satisfaction and trust. Likewise, in an investigation of expected use of influence strategies by male and female supervisors, Eman-Wheeless, Hudson, and Wheeless (1987) found that employees were more satisfied when their supervisor used a more direct, logical style that included support for requests and written detailed directives. Finally, Richmond et al. (1986) discovered that supervisors who use positive affinity-seeking strategies rather than power-based strategies create more satisfied employees.

Additional effects variables. In investigations of other types of effects variables, Johnson (1992) found that superiors who used a prosocial compliance-gaining strategy (as opposed to an antisocial strategy) were seen by subordinates as more competent and as people with whom they would feel comfortable working (task attraction). Dobos, Bahniuk, and Hill (1991) looked at the relationship of power-gaining communication strategies and career success. They found that connection power (relationships with mentors, peers, and supervisors) and information adequacy power (extent to which an employee perceives she or he has received and sent adequate information) were important indicators of career success. They concluded that "communication relations with work colleagues as well as having a mentor who takes a personal interest in their career seemed to help managers to achieve an interrelated set of outcomes, from higher rank to becoming more confident and developing perceptions of self as more successful and influential, and with more perceived fast-track visibility in the organization" (p. 45). Finally, Smith, Carson, and Alexander (1984), in an unusual investigation of leadership and influence in churches, found that some pastors were more influential than others in producing such effects as greater membership growth, greater giving, and more property development. They discovered that "the group of superior performers demonstrated their impact, not only on a single criterion measure and within a single organizational unit, but also on multiple criterion measures and across several organizational units" (p. 774).

Certainly literature on the influence-outcome relationship is still in its infancy. Only a few effects variables have been investigated, and in only a few studies. Continued research in this vein is critically important for understanding the impact of communicative influence in the organization and for making recommendations to practitioners about the relationship between choice of influence strategy and effect upon the influence. Both theoretical and practical implications would accrue from increased attention to this area of research.

Critique

Since we completed the first edition of this chapter in 1985, investigations of managerial influence have grown both in number and in sophistication. Researchers are examining important mediating factors, alternate types of influence relationships, various forms of influence strategies, and some effects variables. Still, this body of literature is not without flaws. Two of the most serious problems that remain include (a) a lack of theoretical development and integration and (b) little examination of actual communication in the influence transaction. On the first count, few investigations of managerial influence are firmly grounded in relevant theoretical perspectives. Save for a few studies reviewed here (Brass, 1984, 1985; Fairhurst et al., 1987; Schleuter et al., 1990), much research is still variable-analytic in design. While such research provides important information about different influence strategies, processes, and outcomes, it does not cohere in a cumulative fashion or lend insight into why influence occurs as it does. Communication-based theories are essential frameworks if we are to fully understand how influence-as-interaction shapes, and is shaped by, the individuals, structures, and practices of the organization in which it occurs.

On the second count, managerial influence researchers continue to use hypothetical scenarios, questionnaires that tap superiors' or subordinates' perceptions, or self-reports as methodological tools (an exception is the research conducted by Fairhurst et al., which used audiotaped conversations). While it is indeed true that (a) such measures provide important information about the types of strategies individuals "say" they would use, and (b) collecting "actual" influence transactions in the organization is extremely difficult, it is also equally true that, until we begin to investigate actual interaction, we will never really know if what people "say" they would do and what they really do are congruent activities. Using realistic hypothetical scenarios, as many current researchers have opted to do, is certainly a step closer to that goal. Creating influence strategies that more accurately reflect the forms of influence that occur in an organization is also a move in the right direction. And as almost all research overviewed for this section demonstrated, using actual organizational employees (rather than student subjects) now seems to be a taken-for-granted practice. But it is imperative, if we as communication specialists want to make theoretical advances in this area, want to better understand the complexity of the influence process, or want to make concrete suggestions to the hundreds of practitioners who practice influencing every day, that we begin to study *actual* interactions as they occur in *actual* organizations. Certainly we are not suggesting that is an easy task, only a necessary one.

In sum, there is much to be heartened about in overviewing the literature on managerial influence. It is a vital area of research; it is exploring important and interesting questions; it has begun to recognize the complex nature of influence interaction; it is making important methodological advances. Such vitality and progress bode well for the next decade of investigations.

Conclusion

As in the 1985 version of this chapter (Seibold et al., 1985), we have reviewed interpersonal influence research in the areas of compliance-gaining message strategies, sequential request strategies, and managerial influence strategies. We have found research in each of these areas to be distinguished from earlier work in terms of theoretical, methodological, and practical advances. In each area, more over, studies have moved from a simple, static, source-oriented conception of communicative influence to more complex interactional understandings. In particular, research on compliance-gaining strategies is progressively moving from the restrictive tenets of the Strategic Choice Model we introduced in the 1985 review as an interpretive metaperspective to a focus on goal-message relationships within a tacit rubric we herein have termed the *Goal Limitation Model.* In general, the shift toward more cognitive and more interactional conceptionalizations and empirical studies noted in the review is consistent with other reviews of influence research (see Burgoon, 1990; Burgoon & Miller, 1990; Hewes, Roloff, Planalp, & Seibold, 1988; Miller, 1987; Miller, Boster, Roloff, & Seibold, 1987).

In this review we have emphasized important theoretical advances in understanding communicative interpersonal influence, emphasizing promising theoretical research programs over individual research studies. However, as in the "Conclusion" to Seibold et al. (1985, pp. 596-597) and consistent with others' concerns (Kellermann, in press-a; Kellermann & Cole, in press), we return to the theme that most research on influence message strategies continues to be atheoretical. While the works by Dillard, by Canary, by Green, and especially that of O'Keefe and of Kellermann, reviewed above, represent important advances, they are too few in number and in impact at this time. This is also true of more restricted efforts to introduce accommodation theory (Buller & Aune, 1988, 1992) and rhetorical (Garko & Cissna, 1988) perspectives to the area as well as efforts to integrate theory on language and power (Bradac, 1992) and negotiation (Chatman, Putnam, & Sondak, 1991). For although we have gained an increased understanding of the goal-oriented and strategic message character of instrumental communication, not until *theoretical* advances like those reviewed in the chapter and those noted above are further developed can we hope to link present insights into strategic messages to other domains of interpersonal influence. Only with stronger theoretical perspectives can we hope to integrate these findings with relevant research on physician-patient compliance (Burgoon, Birk, & Hall, 1991; Burgoon & Burgoon, 1989; Burgoon et al., 1987; Burgoon et al., 1990; Frankel & Beckman, 1989; Garrity & Lawson, 1989; Gerber, 1986; Hanson, 1986); influence tactics of parents and other authority figures (Applegate, Coyle, Seibert, & Church, 1989; Smith, 1983); conflict (Conrad, 1991) and grievance tactics (Martin & Cusella, 1986); message strategies in therapy (Cooke & Kipnis, 1986) and in managing harassment (Bingham, 1991); compliance tactics in business relationships (Kale, 1989; Keith, Jackson, & Crosby, 1990), in politics (Raven, 1990), and in personal relationships (Dillard & Fitzpatrick, 1985; Edgar & Fitzpatrick, 1988; Fitzpatrick, 1989; Howard, Blumstein, & Schwartz, 1986; Witteman & Fitzpatrick, 1986); communicative influence in bargaining (Esser, 1989; Galinat & Muller, 1988); strategies related to alcoholic behavior (Seibold & Thomas, in press; Thomas & Seibold, in press) and sexual behavior (Craig, Kalichman, & Follingstad, 1989; Lang & Frenzel, 1988); media portrayal of compliance tactics (Haefner & Comstock, 1990) and training (Berlew, 1985); interviewing tactics (McGaughey & Stiles, 1983; Ragan & Hopper, 1981) and game tactics (Chmielewski, 1982; Seibold & Steinfatt, 1979); gender and influence (Becker, 1986; Carli, 1989; Eagly, 1983; Indvik & Fitzpatrick, 1983); interpersonal strategies for organizational empowerment (Conger & Kanungo, 1988) and compliance (Garko, 1992; Hellweg, Geist, Jorgensen, & White-Mills, 1990; Krone, 1992); strategies of interaction in intercultural contexts (Irvine, 1974; Kilbourne, 1989; Neuliep & Hazelton, 1985) and with special populations (Bliss, 1985; Rueda & Smith, 1983; Weiss & Weinstein, 1968); children's strategic communication (Haslett, 1983a, 1983b; O'Keefe & Benoit, 1983; Renshaw & Asher, 1983; Weiss & Sachs, 1991) and teachers' classroom strategies (Jordon, McGreal, & Wheeless, 1990; Kearney & Plax, 1987; Kearney, Plax, Smith, &

Sorensen, 1988; Kearney, Plax, Sorensen, & Smith, 1988; Plax, Kearney, & Down, 1986; Plax, Kearney, Down, & Stewart, 1986; Plax, Kearney, McCroskey, & Richmond, 1986; Plax, Kearney, & Tucker, 1986; Plax et al., 1990; Richmond, McCroskey, Kearney, & Plax, 1987; Roach, 1991; Sorensen, Plax, & Kearney, 1989; Wheeless, Stewert, Kearney, & Plax, 1987), among many areas investigating persuasive and regulative message strategies.

References

Abelson, R. P., & Miller, J. C. (1967). Negative persuasion via personal insult. *Journal of Experimental Social Psychology, 3,* 321-333.

Alberts, J. K. (1988). An analysis of couples' conversational complaints. *Communication Monographs, 55,* 184-197.

Ansari, M. A., & Kapoor, A. (1987). Organizational context and upward influence tactics. *Organizational Behavior and Human Decision Processes, 40,* 39-49.

Applegate, J., Coyle, K., Seibert, J., & Church, S. (1989). Interpersonal constructs and communicative ability in a police environment: A preliminary investigation. *International Journal of Personal Construct Psychology, 2,* 385-399.

Applegate, J. L., & Delia, J. G. (1980). Person-centered speech, psychological development, and the contexts of language usage. In R. St. Clair & H. Giles (Eds.), *The social and psychological contexts of language* (pp. 245-282). Hillsdale, NJ: Lawrence Erlbaum.

Applegate, J., & Woods, E. (1991). Construct system development and attention to face wants in persuasive situations. *The Southern Communication Journal, 56,* 194-204.

Arch, D. C. (1979). The development of influence strategy scales in buyer-seller interactions. In N. Beckwith, M. Houston, R. Mittelstaedt, K. B. Monroe, & S. Ward (Eds.), *1979 educators' conference proceedings* (pp. 440-444). Chicago: American Marketing Association.

Ayres, J. (1983). Strategies to maintain relationships: Their identification and perceived usage. *Communication Quarterly, 31,* 62-67.

Baglan, T., LaLumia, J., & Bayless, O. L. (1986). Utilization of compliance-gaining strategies: A research note. *Communication Monographs, 53,* 289-293.

Ball, D. W. (1965). Sarcasm as sociation: The rhetoric of interaction. *Canadian Review of Sociology and Anthropology, 2,* 190-198.

Barnes, L. B., & Kriger, M. P. (1987). The hidden side of organizational leadership. *Sloan Management Review, 28,* 15-25.

Baron, R. A. (1973). The "foot-in-the-door" phenomenon: Mediating effects of size of first request and sex of requester. *Bulletin of Psychonomic Sociology, 2,* 113-114.

Baumeister, R. F. (1982). A self-presentational view of social phenomena. *Psychological Bulletin, 91,* 3-26.

Baxter, L. A. (1979). Self-disclosure as a relationship disengagement strategy: An exploratory investigation. *Human Communication Research, 5,* 216-222.

Baxter, L. A. (1982). Strategies for ending relationships: Two studies. *Western Journal of Speech Communication, 46,* 223-241.

Baxter, L. A. (1984). An investigation of compliance-gaining as politeness. *Human Communication Research, 10,* 427-456.

Baxter, L. A. (1990). Dialectical contradictions in relationship development. *Journal of Social and Personal Relationships, 7,* 69-88.

Baxter, L. A., & Wilmot, W. W. (1984). "Secret tests": Social strategies for acquiring information about the state of the relationship. *Human Communication Research, 11,* 171-201.

Beaman, A. L., Cole, C. M., Preston, M., Klentz, B., & Steblay, N. M. (1983). Fifteen years of foot-in-the-door research. *Personality and Social Psychology Bulletin, 9,* 181-196.

Beaman, A. L., Steblay, N., Preston, M., & Klentz, B. (1988). Compliance as a function of elapsed time between first and second requests. *Journal of Social Psychology, 128,* 233-243.

Becker, B. (1986). Influence again: An examination of reviews and studies of gender differences in social influence. In J. S. Hyde & M. C. Linn (Eds.), *The psychology of gender: Advances through meta-analysis* (pp. 178-209). Baltimore: Johns Hopkins University Press.

Becker, J. A., Kimmel, H. D., & Bevill, M. J. (1989). The interactive effects of request form and speaker status on judgments of requests. *Journal of Psycholinguistic Research, 18,* 521-531.

Beisecker, T. (1970). Verbal persuasive strategies in mixed-motive interactions. *Quarterly Journal of Speech, 66,* 149-159.

Belk, S., Snell, W., Garcia-Falconi, R., Hernandez-Sanchez, J., Hargrove, L., & Holtzman, W. (1988). Power strategy use in the intimate relationships of women and men from Mexico and the United States. *Personality and Social Psychology Bulletin, 14,* 439-447.

Bell, R. A., & Buerkel-Rothfuss, N. L. (1990). S(he) loves me, s(he) loves me not: Predictors of relational information-seeking in courtship and beyond. *Communication Quarterly, 38,* 64-82.

Bell, R. A., & Daly, J. A. (1984). The affinity-seeking function of communication. *Communication Monographs, 51,* 91-115.

Bem, D. J. (1972). Self-perception theory. In L. Berkowitz (Ed.), *Advances in experimental social psychology* (Vol. 6, pp. 2-62). New York: Academic Press.

Bennett, A. (1982). Strategies and counterstrategies in the use of yes-no questions in discourse. In J. J. Gumperz (Ed.), *Language and social identity* (pp. 95-107). Cambridge: Cambridge University Press.

Berg, J. H., & Archer, R. L. (1982). Responses to self-disclosure and interaction goals. *Journal of Experimental Social Psychology, 18,* 501-512.

Berger, C. R., Karol, S. H., & Jordan, J. M. (1989). When a lot of knowledge is a dangerous thing: The debilitating effects of plan complexity on verbal fluency. *Human Communication Research, 16,* 91-119.

Berger, C. R., & Kellermann, K. (1983). To ask or not to ask: Is that a question? In R. Bostrom (Ed.), *Communication yearbook 7* (pp. 342-368). Beverly Hills, CA: Sage.

Berger, C. R., & Kellermann, K. (1989). Personal opacity and social information gathering: Explorations in strategic communication. *Communication Research, 16,* 314-351.

Berlew, D. (1985). How to increase your influence. *Training and Development Journal, 39,* 60-63.

Bingham, S. G. (1991). Communication strategies for managing sexual harassment in organizations: Understanding message options and their effects. *Journal of Applied Communication Research, 19,* 88-115.

Bingham, S. G., & Burleson, B. R. (1989). Multiple effects of messages with multiple goals: Some perceived outcomes of responses to sexual harassment. *Human Communication Research, 16,* 184-216.

Bisanz, G. L., & Rule, B. G. (1989). Gender and the persuasion schema: A search for cognitive invariants. *Personality and Social Psychology Bulletin, 15,* 4-18.

Bisanz, G. L., & Rule, B. (1990). Children's and adult's comprehension of narratives about persuasion. In M. Cody & M. McLaughlin (Eds.), *The psychology of tactical communication* (pp. 48-69). Clevedon, England: Multilingual Matters.

Bliss, L. (1985). The development of persuasive strategies by mentally retarded children. *Applied Research in Mental Retardation, 6,* 437-447.

Bochner, A. P. (1984). The functions of human communication in interpersonal bonding. In C. C. Arnold & J. W. Bowers (Eds.), *Handbook of rhetorical and communication theory* (pp. 544-621). Boston: Allyn & Bacon.

Bochner, A., Cissna, K., & Garko, M. (1991). Optional metaphors for studying interaction. In B. Montgomery & S. Duck (Eds.), *Studying interpersonal interaction* (pp. 16-34). New York: Guilford.

Boster, F. J. (1985). Argumentation, interpersonal communication, persuasion, and the process(es) of compliance-gaining message use. In J. R. Cox, M. O. Sillars, & G. B. Walker (Eds.), *Argument and social practice: Proceedings of the Fourth SCA/AFA Conference on Argumentation* (pp. 578-591). Annandale, VA: Speech Communication Association.

Boster, F. J. (1988). Comments on the utility of compliance-gaining message selection tasks. *Human Communication Research, 15,* 169-177.

Boster, F. J. (1990). An examination of the state of compliance-gaining message behavior research. In J. Dillard (Ed.), *Seeking compliance* (pp. 7-17). Scottsdale, AZ: Gorsuch Scarisbrick.

Boster, F. J., & Levine, T. (1988). Individual differences and compliance-gaining message selection: The effects of verbal aggressiveness, argumentativeness, dogmatism, and negativism. *Communication Research Reports, 5,* 114-119.

Boster, F. J., Levine, T., & Kazoleas, D. (1989, November). *The impact of argumentativeness and verbal aggressiveness on strategic diversity and persistence in compliance-gaining behavior.* Paper presented at the annual meeting of the Speech Communication Association, San Francisco.

Boster, F. J., & Lofthouse, L. J. (1986, May). *Situational and individual difference determinants of the persistence and content of compliance gaining behavior: A test of the generalizability of some compliance gain message choice findings.* Paper presented at the annual meeting of the International Communication Association, Chicago.

Bradac, J. (1992). Thoughts about floors not eaten, lungs ripped, and breathless dogs: Issues in language and dominance. In S. Deetz (Ed.), *Communication yearbook 15* (pp. 457-468). Newbury Park, CA: Sage.

Brass, D. J. (1984). Being in the right place: A structural analysis of individual influence in an organization. *Administrative Science Quarterly, 29,* 518-539.

Brass, D. J. (1985). Men's and women's networks: A study of interaction patterns and influence in an organization. *Academy of Management Journal, 28,* 327-343.

Britton, J. (1971). What's the use? *Educational Review, 23,* 205-219.

Brown, P., & Levinson, S. (1978). Universals in language usage: Politeness phenomena. In E. N. Goody (Ed.), *Questions and politeness: Strategies in social interaction* (pp. 56-289). New York: Cambridge University Press.

Brown, R. L., Jr. (1980). The pragmatics of verbal irony. In R. W. Shuy & A. Shnukal (Eds.), *Language use and the uses of language* (pp. 111-127). Washington, DC: Georgetown University Press.

Buller, D., & Aune, K. (1988). The effects of vocalics and nonverbal sensitivity on compliance: A speech accommodation theory explanation. *Human Communication Research, 14,* 331-332.

Buller, D., & Aune, R. (1992). The effects of speech rate similarity on compliance: Application of communication accommodation theory. *Western Journal of Communication, 56,* 37-53.

Buller, D., & Burgoon, J. (1986). The effects of vocalics and nonverbal sensitivity on compliance: A replication and extension. *Human Communication Research, 13,* 126-144.

Burger, J. (1986). Increasing compliance by improving the deal: The that's-not-all technique. *Journal of Personality and Social Psychology, 51,* 277-283.

Burger, J. M., & Petty, R. E. (1981). The low-ball compliance technique: Task or person commitment? *Journal of Personality and Social Psychology, 40,* 492-500.

Burgoon, J. K., Pfau, M., Parrott, R., Birk, T., Coker, R., & Burgoon, M. (1987). Relational communication, satisfaction, compliance-gaining strategies, and compliance in communication between physicians and patients. *Communication Monographs, 54,* 307-324.

Burgoon, M. (1990). Social influence. In H. Giles & P. Robinson (Eds.), *Handbook of language and social psychology* (pp. 51-72). London: Wiley.

Burgoon, M., Birk, T., & Hall, J. R. (1991). Compliance and satisfaction with physician-patient communication: An expectancy theory interpretation of gender differences. *Human Communication Research, 18,* 177-208.

Burgoon, M., & Burgoon, J. K. (1989). Compliance-gaining and health care. In J. P. Dillard (Ed.), *Seeking compliance* (pp. 161-188). Scottsdale, AZ: Gorsuch Scarisbrick.

Burgoon, M., & Miller, G. R. (1990). Paths. *Communication Monographs, 57,* 152-160.

Burgoon, M., Parrott, R., Burgoon, J. K., Coker, R., Pfau, M., & Birk, T. (1990). Primary care physicians' selection of verbal compliance-gaining strategies. *Health Communication, 2,* 13-28.

Burke, J. A. (1989). A comparison of methods for eliciting persuasive strategies: Strategy selection versus message construction. *Communication Reports, 2,* 72-82.

Burleson, B. R. (1983). Social cognition, empathic motivation, and adults' comforting strategies. *Human Communication Research, 10,* 295-304.

Burleson, B. R. (1984a). Age, social-cognitive development, and the use of comforting strategies. *Communication Monographs, 51,* 140-153.

Burleson, B. R. (1984b). Comforting communication. In H. E. Sypher & J. L. Applegate (Eds.), *Communication by children and adults: Social cognitive and strategic processes* (pp. 63-104). Beverly Hills, CA: Sage.

Burleson, B. R. (1989). The constructivist approach to person-centered communication: Analysis of a research exemplar. In B. Dervin, L. Grossberg, B. O'Keefe, & E. Wartella (Eds.), *Rethinking communication: Vol. 2. Paradigm exemplars* (pp. 29-46). Newbury Park, CA: Sage.

Burleson, B. R., & Wilson, S. (1988). On the continued undesirability of item desirability: A reply to Boster, Hunter, and Seibold. *Human Communication Research, 15,* 178-191.

Burleson, B. R., Wilson, S. R., Waltman, M. S., Goering, E. M., Ely, T. K., & Whaley, B. B. (1988). Item desirability effects in compliance-gaining research: Seven studies documenting artifacts in strategy selection procedure. *Human Communication Research, 14,* 429-486.

Buss, M. D., Gomes, M., Higgins, D. S., & Lauterbach, K. (1987). Tactics of manipulation. *Journal of Personality and Social Psychology, 52,* 1219-1229.

Canary, D. J., Cody, M. J., & Marston, P. J. (1986). Goal types, compliance-gaining and locus of control in managing interpersonal conflict. *Journal of Language and Social Psychology, 5,* 249-269.

Canary, D. J., Cunningham, E. M., & Cody, M. J. (1988). Goal types, gender, and locus of control in managing interpersonal conflict. *Communication Research, 15,* 426-446.

Canary, D. J., & Spitzberg, B. H. (1987). Appropriateness and effectiveness perceptions of conflict strategies. *Human Communication Research, 14,* 93-118.

Canary, D. J., & Spitzberg, B. H. (1989). A model of the perceived competence of conflict strategies. *Communication Research, 15,* 630-649.

Cann, A., Sherman, S. J., & Elkes, R. (1975). Effects of initial request size and timing of a second request on compliance: The foot in the door and the door in the face. *Journal of Personality and Social Psychology, 32,* 774-782.

Cantrill, J. G. (1991). Inducing health care voluntarism through sequential requests: Perceptions of effort and novelty. *Health Communication, 3,* 59-74.

Cantrill, J. G., & Seibold, D. R. (1986). The perceptual contrast explanation of sequential request strategy effectiveness. *Human Communication Research, 13,* 253-267.

Carducci, B., Deuser, P., Bauer, A., Large, M., & Ramaekers, M. (1989). An application of the foot in the door technique to organ donation. *Journal of Business Psychology, 4,* 245-249.

Carli, L. (1989). Gender differences in interaction style and influence. *Journal of Personality and Social Psychology, 56,* 565-576.

Case, T., Dosier, L., Murkison, G., & Keys, B. (1988). How managers influence superiors: A study of upward influence tactics. *Leadership and Organization Development Journal, 9,* 25-31.

Chatman, J. A., Putnam, L., & Sondak, H. (1991). Integrating communication and negotiation research. In M. H. Bazerman, R. J. Lewicki, & B. H. Sheppard (Eds.), *Research on negotiation in organizations: Handbook of negotiation research* (Vol. 3, pp. 139-164). Greenwich, CT: JAI.

Chmielewski, T. J. (1982). A test of a model for predicting strategy choice. *Central States Speech Journal, 33,* 505-518.

Churchill, L. (1978). *Questioning strategies in sociolinguistics.* Rowley, MA: Newbury House.

Cialdini, R. B. (1980). Full-cycle social psychology. In L. Bickman (Ed.), *Applied social psychology annual* (Vol. 1, pp. 21-48). Beverly Hills, CA: Sage.

Cialdini, R. B. (1987). Compliance principles of compliance professionals: Psychologists of necessity. In M. P. Zanna, J. M. Olson, & C. P. Herman (Eds.), *Social influence: The Ontario Symposium* (Vol. 5, pp. 165-184). Hillsdale, NJ: Lawrence Erlbaum.

Cialdini, R. B., & Ascani, K. (1976). Test of a concession procedure for inducing verbal, behavioral, and further compliance with a request to give blood. *Journal of Applied Psychology, 61,* 295-300.

Cialdini, R. B., Cacioppo, J. T., Bassett, R., & Miller, J. A. (1978). Low-ball procedure for producing compliance: Commitment then cost. *Journal of Personality and Social Psychology, 36,* 463-476.

Cialdini, R. B., & Richardson, K. D. (1980). Two indirect tactics of image management: Basking and blasting. *Journal of Personality and Social Psychology, 39,* 406-415.

Cialdini, R. B., & Schroeder, D. A. (1976). Increasing compliance by legitimizing paltry contributions: When even a penny helps. *Journal of Personality and Social Psychology, 34,* 599-604.

Cialdini, R. B., Vincent, J. E., Lewis, S. K., Catalan, J., Wheeler, D., & Darby, B. L. (1975). Reciprocal concessions procedure for inducing compliance: The door-in-the-face technique. *Journal of Personality and Social Psychology, 31,* 206-215.

Clark, R. A. (1979). The impact of self-interest and desired liking on selection of persuasive strategies. *Communication Monographs, 46,* 257-273.

Clark, R. A. (1984). *Persuasive messages.* New York: Harper & Row.

Clark, R. A., & Delia, J. G. (1979). Topoi and rhetorical competence. *Quarterly Journal of Speech, 65,* 187-206.

Clark, R. A., O'Dell, L., & Willihnganz, S. (1986). The development of compromising as an alternative to persuasion. *Central States Speech Journal, 37,* 220-224.

Cody, M. J. (1982). A typology of disengagement strategies and an examination of the role intimacy, reactions to inequity and relational problems play in strategy selection. *Communication Monographs, 49,* 148-170.

Cody, M. J., Canary, D. J., & Smith, S. W. (in press). Compliance-gaining goals: An inductive analysis of actors' goal types, strategies, and successes. In J. Daly & J. Weimann (Eds.), *Communicating strategically.* Hillsdale, NJ: Lawrence Erlbaum.

Cody, M. J., Greene, J. O., Marston, P. J., O'Hair, H. D., Baaske, K. T., & Schneider, M. J. (1986). Situation perception and strategy selection. In M. L. McLaughlin (Ed.), *Communication yearbook 9* (pp. 391-420). Beverly Hills, CA: Sage.

Cody, M. J., & McLaughlin, M. L. (1980). Perceptions of compliance-gaining situations: A dimensional analysis. *Communication Monographs, 47,* 132-148.

Cody, M. J., & McLaughlin, M. L. (1990). Introduction. In M. J. Cody & M. L. McLaughlin (Eds.), *The psychology of tactical communication* (pp. 1-30). Clevedon, England: Multilingual Matters.

Cohen, A. R., & Bradford, D. L. (1989). Influence without authority: The use of alliances, reciprocity, and exchange to accomplish work. *Organizational Dynamics, 17,* 4-17.

Cole, T. D. (1993). *Strategic dimensions of compliance gaining strategies.* Unpublished master's thesis, University of California at Santa Barbara, Department of Communication.

Conger, J. A., & Kanungo, R. N. (1988). The empowerment process: Integrating theory and practice. *Academy of Management Review, 13,* 471-482.

Conrad, C. (1991). Communication in conflict: Style-strategy relationships. *Communication Mono-graphs, 58,* 135-155.

Cooke, M., & Kipnis, D. (1986). Influence tactics in psychotherapy. *Journal of Consulting and Clinical Psychology, 54,* 22-26.

Cowan, G., Drinkard, J., & MacGavin, L. (1984). The effects of target, age and gender on the use of power strategies. *Journal of Personality and Social Psychology, 47,* 1391-1398.

Craig, M. E., Kalichman, S. C., & Follingstad, D. R. (1989). Verbal coercive sexual behavior among college students. *Archives of Sexual Behavior, 18,* 421-434.

Craig, R. T. (1986). Goals in discourse. In D. G. Ellis & W. A. Donohue (Eds.), *Contemporary issues in language and discourse processes* (pp. 257-273). Hillsdale, NJ: Lawrence Erlbaum.

Craig, R. T. (1990). Multiple goals in discourse: An epilogue. *Journal of Language and Social Psychology, 9,* 163-170.

Craig, R. T., Tracy, K., & Spisak, F. (1986). The discourse of requests: Assessment of a politeness approach. *Human Communication Research, 12,* 437-468.

Crano, W. D., & Sivacek, J. (1982). Social reinforcement, self-attribution, and the foot-in-the-door phenomenon. *Social Cognition, 1,* 110-125.

Cronkhite, G. (1983). Conventional postulates of interpersonal argument. In D. Zarefsky, M. Sillars, & J. Rhodes (Eds.), *Argument in transition: Proceedings of the Third Summer Conference In Argumentation* (pp. 697-706). Annandale, VA: Speech Communication Association.

Cupach, W. R. (1982, May). *Communication satisfaction and interpersonal solidarity as outcomes of conflict message strategy use.* Paper presented at the annual meeting of the International Communication Association, Boston.

Davis, D. (1982). Determinants of responsiveness in dyadic interaction. In W. Ickes & E. S. Knowles (Eds.), *Personality, roles and social behavior* (pp. 85-140). New York: Springer-Verlag.

Debevec, K., Madden, T., & Kernan, J. (1986). Physical attractiveness, message evaluation, and compliance: A structural examination. *Psychological Reports, 58,* 503-508.

DeJong, W. (1979). An examination of self-perception mediation of the foot-in-the-door effect. *Journal of Personality and Social Psychology, 37,* 2221-2239.

DeJong, W. (1981). Consensus information and the foot-in-the-door effect. *Personality and Social Psychology Bulletin, 7,* 423-430.

DeJong, W., & Funder, D. (1977). Effect of payment for initial compliance: Unanswered questions about the foot-in-the-door phenomenon. *Personality and Social Psychology Bulletin, 3,* 662-665.

Deluga, R. J. (1988). Relationship of transformational and transactional leadership with employee influencing strategies. *Group and Organization Studies, 13,* 456-467.

DeTurck, M. (1985). A transactional analysis of compliance-gaining behavior: Effects of noncompliance, relational contexts, and actors' gender. *Human Communication Research, 12,* 54-78.

DeTurck, M. (1987). When communication fails: Physical aggression as a compliance-gaining strategy. *Communication Monographs, 54,* 106-112.

DeVries, J., Burnette, M., & Redmon, W. (1991). AIDS prevention: Improving nurses' compliance with glove wearing through performance feedback. *Journal of Applied Behavior Analysis, 24,* 705-712.

Dillard, J. P. (1988). Compliance-gaining message-selection: What is our dependent variable. *Communication Monographs, 55,* 162-183.

Dillard, J. P. (1989). Types of influence goals in personal relationships. *Journal of Social and Personal Relationships, 6,* 293-308.

Dillard, J. P. (1990a). A goal-driven model of interpersonal influence. In J. P. Dillard (Ed.), *Seeking compliance: The production of interpersonal influence messages* (pp. 41-56). Scottsdale, AZ: Gorsuch Scarisbrick.

Dillard, J. P. (1990b). Self-inference and the foot-in-the-door technique: Quantity of behavior and attitudinal mediation. *Human Communication Research, 16,* 422-447.

Dillard, J. P. (1990c). The nature and substance of goals in tactical communication. In M. J. Cody & M. L. McLaughlin (Eds.), *The psychology of tactical communication* (pp. 70-90). Philadelphia: Multilingual Matters.

Dillard, J. P. (Ed.). (1990d). *Seeking compliance.* Scottsdale, AZ: Gorsuch Scarisbrick.

Dillard, J. P. (1991). The current status of research on sequential-request compliance techniques. *Personality and Social Psychology Bulletin, 17,* 283-289.

Dillard, J. P., & Burgoon, M. (1985). Situational influences on the selection of compliance-gaining messages: Two tests of the predictive utility of the Cody-McLaughlin typology. *Communication Monographs, 52,* 289-304.

Dillard, J. P., & Fitzpatrick, M. A. (1985). Compliance-gaining in marital interaction. *Personality and Social Psychology Bulletin, 11,* 419-433.

Dillard, J. P., Hunter, J. E., & Burgoon, M. (1984). Sequential-request persuasive strategies: Meta-analysis of foot-in-the-door and door-in-the-face. *Human Communication Research, 10,* 461-488.

Dillard, J. P., Segrin, C., & Harden, J. M. (1989). Primary and secondary goals in the production of interpersonal influence messages. *Communication Monographs, 56,* 19-38.

Dobos, J., Bahniuk, M. H., & Hill, S. E. K. (1991). Power-gaining communication strategies and career success. *The Southern Communication Journal, 57,* 35-48.

Dollard, J. (1939). The dozens: Dialectic of insult. *American Imago, 1,* 3-25.

Duffy, G., Roehler, L., Meloth, M., Vavrus, L., Book, C., Putnam, J., & Wesselman, R. (1986). The relationship between explicit verbal explanations during reading skill instruction and student awareness and achievement: A study of reading teacher effects. *Reading Research Quarterly, 21,* 237-252.

Duncan, J., Jr. (1981). Conversational strategies. In T. A. Sebeok & R. Rosenthal (Eds.), *The Clever Hans phenomenon: Communication with horses, whales, apes, and people* (pp. 144-157). New York: New York Academy of Sciences.

Eagly, A. H. (1974). Comprehensibility of persuasive arguments as a determinant of opinion change. *Journal of Personality and Social Psychology, 29,* 758-773.

Eagly, A. H. (1983). Gender and social influence. *American Psychologist, 38,* 971-981.

Eagly, A. H. (1987). Social influence research: New approaches to enduring issues. In M. P. Zanna, J. M. Olson, & C. P. Herman (Eds.), *Social influence: The Ontario Symposium* (Vol. 5, pp. 271-285). Hillsdale, NJ: Lawrence Erlbaum.

Edgar, T., & Fitzpatrick, M. A. (1988). Compliance-gaining in relational interaction: When your life depends on it. *The Southern Speech Communication Journal, 53,* 385-405.

Eisenthal, S., Koopman, C., & Stoeckle, J. (1990). The nature of patients' requests for physicians' help. *Academic Medicine, 65,* 401-405.

Eman-Wheeless, V., Hudson, D. C., & Wheeless, L. R. (1987). A test of the expected use of influence strategies by male and female supervisors as related to job satisfaction and trust in supervisor. *Women's Studies in Communication, 10,* 25-36.

Enzle, M. E., & Harvey, M. D. (1982). Rhetorical requests for help. *Social Psychology Quarterly, 45,* 172-176.

Ervin-Tripp, S., Gui, J., & Lampert, M. (1990). Politeness and persuasion in children's control acts. *Journal of Pragmatics, 14,* 307-331.

Esser, J. (1989). Agreement pressure and opponent strategies in oligopoly bargaining. *Personality and Social Psychology Bulletin, 15,* 596-603.

Even-Chen, M., Yinon, Y., & Bizman, A. (1978). The door in the face technique: Effects of the size of the initial request. *European Journal of Social Psychology, 8,* 135-140.

Fairholm, G. W. (1985). Power tactics on the job. *Personnel, 62,* 45-50.

Fairhurst, G. T., Rogers, L. E., & Sarr, R. A. (1987). Manager-subordinate control patterns and judgments about the relationship. In M. L. McLaughlin (Ed.), *Communication yearbook 10* (pp. 395-415). Newbury Park, CA: Sage.

Falbo, T. (1977). Multidimensional scaling of power strategies. *Journal of Personality and Social Psychology, 35,* 537-547.

Falbo, T., & Peplau, L. A. (1980). Power strategies in intimate relationships. *Journal of Personality and Social Psychology, 38,* 618-628.

Fandt, P. M., & Ferris, G. R. (1990). The management of information and impressions: When employees behave opportunistically. *Organizational Behavior and Human Decision Processes, 45,* 140-158.

Fern, E., Monroe, K., & Avila, R. (1986). Effectiveness of multiple request strategies: A synthesis of research results. *Journal of Marketing Research, 23,* 144-152.

Fiske, S. T., & Taylor, S. E. (1991). *Social cognition* (2nd ed.). Reading, MA: Addison-Wesley.

Fitzpatrick, M. A. (1989). After the decision: Compliance-gaining in marital interaction. In D. Brinberg & J. Jaccard (Eds.), *Dyadic decision-making* (pp. 216-248). New York: Springer-Verlag.

Forgas, J. P. (1976). The perception of social episodes: Categorical and dimensional representations in two different social milieus. *Journal of Personality and Social Psychology, 34,* 199-209.

Forgas, J. P. (1979). *Social episodes: The study of interaction routines.* London: Academic Press.

Foss, R. D., & Dempsey, C. B. (1979). Blood donation and the foot-in-the-door technique: A limiting case. *Journal of Personality and Social Psychology, 37,* 580-590.

Francik, E., & Clark, H. (1985). How to make requests that overcome obstacles to compliance. *Journal of Memory and Language, 24,* 560-568.

Frankel, R., & Beckman, H. (1989). Conversation and compliance with treatment recommendations: An application of microinteractional analysis in medicine. In B. Dervin, L. Grossberg, B. O'Keefe, & E. Wartella (Eds.), *Rethinking communication: Vol. 2. Paradigm exemplars* (pp. 60-74). Newbury Park, CA: Sage.

Fraser, C., Hite, R., & Sauer, P. (1988). Increasing contributions in solicitation campaigns: The use of large and small anchorpoints. *Journal of Consumer Research, 15,* 284-287.

Freedman, J. L., & Fraser, S. (1966). Compliance without pressure: The foot-in-the-door technique. *Journal of Personality and Social Psychology, 4,* 195-202.

Friedland, N. (1976). Social influence via threats. *Journal of Experimental Social Psychology, 12,* 552-563.

Fung, S., Kipnis, D., & Rosnow, R. (1987). Synthetic benevolence and malevolence as strategies of relational compliance-gaining. *Journal of Social and Personal Relationships, 4,* 129-141.

Furse, D. H., Stewart, D. W., & Rados, D. L. (1981). Effects of foot-in-the-door, cash incentives, and followups on survey response. *Journal of Marketing Research, 18,* 473-478.

Gahagan, J. P., & Tedeschi, J. T. (1968). Strategy and the credibility of promises in the prisoner's dilemma game. *Journal of Conflict Resolution, 12,* 224-234.

Galinat, W., & Muller, G. (1988). Verbal responses to different bargaining strategies: A content analysis of real-life, buyer-seller interaction. *Journal of Applied Social Psychology, 18,* 160-178.

Gardner, W. L., & Martinko, M. J. (1988). Impression management in organizations. *Journal of Management, 14,* 231-338.

Garfinkel, H. (1956). Conditions of successful degradation ceremonies. *American Journal of Sociology, 61,* 420-424.

Garko, M. (1990). Perspectives on and conceptualizations of compliance and compliance-gaining. *Communication Quarterly, 38,* 138-157.

Garko, M. G. (1992). Persuading subordinates who communicate in attractive and unattractive styles. *Management Communication Quarterly, 5,* 289-315.

Garko, M. G., & Cissna, K. N. (1988). An axiological reinterpretation of I. A. Richard's theory of communication and its application to the study of compliance-gaining. *The Southern Speech Communication Journal, 53,* 121-139.

Garrity, T., & Lawson, E. (1989). Patient-physician communication as a determinant of medication misuse in older, minority women. *Journal of Drug Issues, 19,* 245-260.

Gerber, K. (1986). Compliance in the chronically ill: An introduction to the problem. In K. E. Gerber & A. M. Nehemkis (Eds.), *Compliance: The dilemma of the chronically ill* (pp. 13-23). New York: Springer.

Gilbert, S. J. (1976). Empirical and theoretical extensions of self-disclosure. In G. R. Miller (Ed.), *Explorations in interpersonal communication* (pp. 197-215). Beverly Hills, CA: Sage.

Goffman, E. (1955). On face-work: An analysis of ritual elements in social interaction. *Psychiatry, 18,* 213-231.

Goffman, E. (1959). *The presentation of self in everyday life.* Garden City, NY: Doubleday.

Goffman, E. (1969). *Strategic interaction.* Philadelphia: University of Pennsylvania Press.

Golding, D. (1991). Some everyday rituals in management control. *Journal of Management Studies, 28,* 569-583.

Goldman, M., & Creason, C. R. (1981). Inducing compliance by a two-door-in-the-face procedure and a self-determination request. *Journal of Social Psychology, 114,* 229-235.

Goldman, M., Creason, C. R., & McCall, C. G. (1981). Compliance employing a two-feet-in-the-door procedure. *Journal of Social Psychology, 114,* 259-265.

Goldman, M., Gier, J. A., & Smith, D. E. (1981). Compliance as affected by task difficulty and order of tasks. *Journal of Social Psychology, 114,* 75-83.

Goldman, M., McVeigh, J. F., & Richterkessing, J. L. (1984). Door-in-the-face procedure: Reciprocal concession, perceptual contrast, or worthy person? *Journal of Social Psychology, 123,* 245-251.

Goldman, M., Seever, M., & Seever, M. (1982). Social labeling and the foot-in-the-door effect. *Journal of Social Psychology, 117,* 19-23.

Goody, E. N. (1978a). Introduction. In E. N. Goody (Ed.), *Questions and politeness: Strategies in social interaction* (pp. 1-16). New York: Cambridge University Press.

Goody, E. N. (1978b). Towards a theory of questions. In E. N. Goody (Ed.), *Questions and politeness: Strategies in social interaction* (pp. 17-43). New York: Cambridge University Press.

Gottlieb, A., & Ickes, W. (1978). Attributional strategies of social influence. In J. H. Harvey, W. Ickes, & R. F. Kidd (Eds.), *New directions in attribution research* (Vol. 2, pp. 261-296). Hillsdale, NJ: Lawrence Erlbaum.

Gouldner, A. W. (1960). The norm of reciprocity: A preliminary statement. *American Sociological Review, 25,* 161-178.

Gove, W. R., Hughes, M., & Geerken, M. R. (1980). Playing dumb: A form of impression management with undesirable side effects. *Social Psychology Quarterly, 43,* 89-102.

Grace, C., Bell, P., & Sugar, J. (1988). Effects of compliance techniques on spontaneous and asked-for helping. *Journal of Social Psychology, 128,* 525-532.

Greenberg, M. S., & Shapiro, S. P. (1971). Indebtedness: An adverse aspect of asking for and receiving help. *Sociometry, 34,* 290-301.

Greene, J. O. (1984). A cognitive approach to human communication: An action assembly theory. *Communication Monographs, 51,* 289-306.

Greene, J. O. (1990). Tactical social action: Towards some strategies for theory. In M. J. Cody & M. L. McLaughlin (Eds.), *The psychology of tactical communication* (pp. 31-47). Clevedon, England: Multilingual Matters.

Greene, J. O., & Lindsey, A. E. (1989). Encoding messages in the production of multiple-goal messages. *Human Communication Research, 16,* 120-140.

Greene, J. O., Smith, S. W., & Lindsey, A. E. (1990). Memory representations of compliance-gaining strategies and tactics. *Human Communication Research, 17,* 195-231.

Grimshaw, A. D. (1980). Selection and labeling of instrumentalities of verbal manipulation. *Discourse Processes, 3,* 203-229.

Grimshaw, A. D. (1981). Talk and social control. In M. Rosenberg & R. H. Turner (Eds.), *Social psychology: Sociological perspectives* (pp. 200-232). New York: Basic Books.

Gross, E., & Stone, G. P. (1966). Embarrassment and the analysis of role requirements. In C. W. Backman & P. F. Secord (Eds.), *Problems in social psychology: Selected readings* (pp. 383-394). New York: McGraw-Hill.

Haefner, M., & Comstock, J. (1990). Compliance gaining on prime time family programs. *The Southern Communication Journal, 55,* 402-420.

Hample, D., & Dallinger, J. (1987). Individual differences in cognitive editing standards. *Human Communication Research, 14,* 123-144.

Hample, D., & Dallinger, J. (1990). Arguers as editors. *Argumentation, 4,* 153-170.

Hanson, R. W. (1986). Physician-patient communication and compliance. In K. E. Gerber & A. M. Nehemkis (Eds.), *Compliance: The dilemma of the chronically ill* (pp. 183-212). New York: Springer.

Harper, N. L., & Hirokawa, R. Y. (1988). A comparison of persuasive strategies used by female and male managers I: An examination of downward influence. *Communication Quarterly, 36,* 157-168.

Haslett, B. J. (1983a). Preschoolers' communicative strategies in gaining compliance from peers: A developmental study. *Quarterly Journal of Speech, 69,* 84-99.

Haslett, B. J. (1983b). Communicative functions and strategies in children's conversations. *Human Communication Research, 9,* 114-129.

Hazelton, V., Cupach, W., & Canary, D. (1987). Situation perception: Interactions between competence and messages. *Journal of Language and Social Psychology, 6,* 57-63.

Heilman, M. E. (1976). Oppositional behavior as a function of influence attempt intensity and retaliation threat. *Journal of Personality and Social Psychology, 33,* 574-578.

Hellweg, S. A., Geist, P., Jorgensen, P., & White-Mills, K. (1990). An analysis of compliance-gaining instrumentation in the organizational communication literature. *Management Communication Quarterly, 4,* 244-271.

Hertzog, R. L., & Bradac, J. J. (1984). Perceptions of compliance-gaining situations. *Communication Research, 11,* 363-391.

Hewes, D., Roloff, M., Planalp, S., & Seibold, D. (1988). Interpersonal communication research: What should we know? In G. M. Phillips & J. T. Wood (Eds.), *Speech Communication Association 75th anniversary volume* (pp. 130-180). Carbondale: Southern Illinois University Press.

Hill, C. T., & Stull, D. E. (1982). Disclosure reciprocity: Conceptual and measurement issues. *Social Psychology Quarterly, 45,* 238-244.

Hinkin, T. R., & Schriesheim, C. A. (1988). Power and influence: The view from below. *Personnel, 65,* 47-50.

Hirokawa, R. Y., Kodama, R. A., & Harper, N. L. (1990). Impact of managerial power on persuasive strategy selection by female and male managers. *Management Communication Quarterly, 1,* 30-50.

Hirokawa, R. Y., Mickey, J., & Miura, S. (1991). Effects of request legitimacy on the compliance-gaining tactics of male and female managers. *Communication Monographs, 58,* 421-436.

Hornstein, H. A. (1965). The effects of different magnitudes of threat upon interpersonal bargaining. *Journal of Experimental Social Psychology, 1,* 282-293.

Houlihan, D., & Jones, R. (1990). Exploring the reinforcement of compliance with "do" and "don't" requests and the side effects: A partial replication and extension. *Psychological Reports, 67,* 439-449.

Howard, D. (1990). The influence of verbal responses to common greetings of compliance behavior: The foot-in-the-mouth effect. *Journal of Applied Social Psychology, 20,* 1185-1196.

Howard, J. A., Blumstein, P., & Schwartz, S. (1986). Sex, power, and influence tactics in intimate relationships. *Journal of Personality and Social Psychology, 51,* 102-109.

Hunter, J. E. (1988). Failure of the social desirability response set hypothesis. *Human Communication Research, 15*, 162-168.

Hunter, J. E., & Boster, F. (1987). A model of compliance-gaining message selection. *Communication Monographs, 54*, 63-84.

Indvik, J., & Fitzpatrick, M. A. (1983). A review of communication research on psychological gender: Actors, behaviors and contexts. *Communication, 12*, 55-76.

Infante, D. A., & Gordon, W. I. (1991). How employees see the boss: Test of an argumentative and affirming model of supervisors' communicative behavior. *Western Journal of Speech Communication, 55*, 294-304.

Irvine, J. T. (1974). Strategies of status manipulation in the Wolof greeting. In R. Baumann & J. Sherzer (Eds.), *Explanations in the ethnography of speaking* (pp. 167-191). London: Cambridge University Press.

Jacobs, S., & Jackson, S. (1982). Conversational argument: A discourse analytic approach. In R. Cox & C. A. Willard (Eds.), *Advances in argumentation theory and research* (pp. 205-237). Carbondale: Southern Illinois University Press.

Jacobs, S., & Jackson, S. (1983). Strategy and structure in conversational influence attempts. *Communication Monographs, 50*, 285-304.

Jefferson, G. (1979). A technique for inviting laughter and its subsequent acceptance declination. In G. Psathas (Ed.), *Everyday language: Studies in ethnomethodology* (pp. 79-96). New York: Irvington.

Johnson, C. M., & Masotti, R. M. (1990). Suggestive selling by waitstaff in family-style restaurants: An experiment and multisetting observations. *Journal of Organizational Behavior Management, 11*, 35-54.

Johnson, G. M. (1992). Subordinate perceptions of superior's communication competence and task attraction related to superior's use of compliance-gaining tactics. *Western Journal of Communication, 56*, 54-67.

Jordon, F., McGreal, E., & Wheeless, V. (1990). Student perceptions of teacher sex-role orientation and use of power strategies and teacher sex as determinants of student attitudes toward learning. *Communication Quarterly, 38*, 43-53.

Joule, R., Gouilloux, F., & Weber, F. (1989). The lure: A new compliance procedure. *Journal of Social Psychology, 129*, 741-749.

Kale, S. (1989). Dealer dependence and influence strategies in a manufacturer-dealer dyad. *Journal of Applied Psychology, 74*, 379-384.

Kanouse, D. E., Gumpert, P., & Canavan-Gumpert, D. (1981). The semantics of praise. In J. H. Harvey, W. Ickes, & R. F. Kidd (Eds.), *New directions in attribution research* (Vol. 3, pp. 97-115). Hillsdale, NJ: Lawrence Erlbaum.

Kapoor, A., Ansari, M. A., & Shukla, R. (1986). Upward influence tactics as a function of locus of control and organizational context. *Psychological Studies, 31*, 190-199.

Kaufer, D. S., & Neuwirth, C. M. (1982). Foregrounding norms and ironic communication. *Quarterly Journal of Speech, 68*, 28-36.

Kearney, P., & Plax, T. (1987). Situational and individual determinants of teachers' reported use of behavior alteration techniques. *Human Communication Research, 14*, 145-166.

Kearney, P., Plax, T., Richmond, V. P., & McCroskey, J. C. (1985). Power in the classroom III: Teacher communication techniques and messages. *Communication Education, 34*, 19-28.

Kearney, P., Plax, T., Smith, V., & Sorensen, G. (1988). Effects of teacher immediacy and strategy type on college student resistance to on-task demands. *Communication Education, 37*, 54-67.

Kearney, P., Plax, T., Sorensen, G., & Smith, V. (1988). Experienced and prospective teachers' selections of compliance-gaining messages for "common" student misbehaviors. *Communication Education, 37*, 150-164.

Keith, J., Jackson, D., & Crosby, L. (1990). Effects of alternative types of influence strategies under different channel dependence structures. *Journal of Marketing, 54*, 30-41.

Kellermann, K. (in press-a). A goal-directed approach to gaining compliance: Differences in behavioral acceptability for different compliance gaining goals. *Communication Monographs.*

Kellermann, K. (in press-b). Understanding tactical choice: Metagoals in conversation. *Human Communication Research.*

Kellermann, K., & Cole, T. (1991). *Compliance gaining strategies in the research literature: A cross taxonomy integration.* Unpublished manuscript, University of California at Santa Barbara, Department of Communication.

Kellermann, K., & Cole, T. (in press). Classifying compliance gaining messages: Do you know what taxonomies your strategies are in? *Communication Theory.*

Kellermann, K., & Kim, M. (1991, May). *Working within constraints: Tactical choices in the pursuit of social goals.* Paper presented at the International Communication Association Annual Convention, Chicago.

Kellermann, K., Reynolds, R., & Chen, J. B. (1991). Strategies of conversational retreat: When parting is not so sweet sorrow. *Communication Monographs, 58,* 364-383.

Kilbourne, B. (1988). A new application of the foot-in-the-door technique: Friend or stranger? *Psychological Reports, 62,* 31-36.

Kilbourne, B. (1989). A cross-cultural investigation of the foot-in-the-door compliance inductions procedure. *Journal of Cross Cultural Psychology, 20,* 3-38.

Kipnis, D. (1984). The use of power in interpersonal setting. In S. Oskamp (Ed.), *Applied social psychology annual: Vol. 5. Applications in organizational setting* (pp. 179-210). Beverly Hills, CA: Sage.

Kipnis, D., & Schmidt, S. M. (1988). Upward-influence styles: Relationship with performance evaluations, salary and stress. *Administrative Science Quarterly, 33,* 528-542.

Kipnis, D., Schmidt, S. M., Swaffin-Smith, C., & Wilkinson, I. (1984). Patterns of managerial influence: Shotgun managers, tacticians, and bystanders. *Organizational Dynamics, 12,* 58-67.

Kipnis, D., Schmidt, S. M., & Wilkinson, I. (1980). Intraorganizational influence tactics: Explorations in getting one's way. *Journal of Applied Psychology, 65,* 440-452.

Kline, S. L. (1991). Construct differentiation and person-centered regulative messages. *Journal of Language and Social Psychology, 10,* 1-27.

Kline, S. L., & Floyd, C. (1990). On the art of saying no: The influence of social cognitive development of messages on refusals. *Western Journal of Communication, 54,* 454-472.

Knapp, M. L. (1978). *Social intercourse: From greeting to goodbye.* Boston: Allyn & Bacon.

Knapp, M. L., & Comadena, M. F. (1979). Telling it like it isn't: A review of theory and research on deceptive communications. *Human Communication Research, 5,* 270-285.

Koper, R. J., & Boster, F. J. (1988). Factors affecting verbal aggressiveness and compliance gaining effectiveness: The relationship between communication rewards, communication approach/avoidance, and compliance gaining messages. In D. O'Hair & B. R. Patterson (Eds.), *Advances in interpersonal communication research* (pp. 129-146). Las Cruces, NM: CRC.

Krause, M. S. (1972). Strategies in argument. *Journal of Psychology, 81,* 269-279.

Kraut, R. E., & Higgins, E. T. (1984). Communication and social cognition. In R. S. Wyer & T. K. Srull (Eds.), *Handbook of social cognition* (Vol. 3, pp. 87-127). Hillsdale, NJ: Lawrence Erlbaum.

Krone, K. J. (1992). A comparison of organizational, structural, and relationship effects on subordinates' upward influence choices. *Communication Quarterly, 40,* 1-15.

LaLumia, J., & Baglan, T. (1981). Choice of strategies for attitude change: An exploratory analysis. *Psychological Reports, 48,* 793-794.

Lamude, K. G., Daniels, T. D., & White, K. D. (1987). Managing the boss: Locus of control and subordinates' selection of compliance-gaining strategies in upward communication. *Management Communication Quarterly, 1,* 232-259.

Lamude, K. G., & Lichtenstein, A. (1985). The effects of motivational needs and rights situational dimension on compliance gaining strategies. *Communicative Research Reports, 2,* 164-171.

Lang, R., & Frenzel, R. (1988). How sex offenders lure children. *Annals of Sex Research, 1,* 303-317.

Langer, E. J., Blank, A., & Chanowitz, B. (1978). The mindlessness of ostensibly thoughtful action: The role of "placebic" information in interpersonal interaction. *Journal of Personality and Social Psychology, 36,* 635-642.

Layton, B. D., & Moehle, D. (1980). Attributed influence: The importance of observing change. *Journal of Experimental Social Psychology, 16,* 243-252.

Leedon, C., Persaud, D., & Shovein, J. (1986). The effect on smoking behavior of an assertive request to refrain from smoking. *International Journal of the Addictions, 21,* 1113-1117.

Leichty, G., & Applegate, J. (1991). Social-cognitive and situational influences on the use of face-saving persuasive strategies. *Human Communication Research, 17,* 451-484.

Levine, B. A., Moss, K. C., Ramsey, P. H., & Fleishman, J. A. (1978). Patient compliance with advice as a function of communicator expertise. *Journal of Social Psychology, 104,* 309-310.

Levine, T. R., & Wheeless, L. R. (1990). Cross-situational consistency and use/nonuse tendencies in compliance-gaining tactic selection. *The Southern Communication Journal, 56,* 1-11.

Lewis, D. K. (1969). *Convention: A philosophical study.* Cambridge, MA: Harvard University Press.

Liden, R. C., & Mitchell, T. R. (1988). Ingratiatory behaviors in organizational settings. *Academy of Management Review, 13,* 572-587.

Martin, E., & Cusella, L. (1986). Persuading the adjudicator: Conflict tactics in the grievance procedure. In M. McLaughlin (Ed.), *Communication yearbook 9* (pp. 533-554). Newbury Park, CA: Sage.

Marwell, G., & Schmitt, D. R. (1967a). Compliance-gaining behavior: A synthesis and model. *Sociological Quarterly, 8,* 317-328.

Marwell, G., & Schmitt, D. R. (1967b). Dimensions of compliance-gaining behavior: An empirical analysis. *Sociometry, 30,* 350-364.

McAllister, H. A., & Bregman, N. J. (1983). Self-disclosure and liking: An integration theory approach. *Journal of Personality, 51,* 202-212.

McGaughey, K. J., & Stiles, W. B. (1983). Courtroom interrogation of rape victims: Verbal response mode use by attorneys and witnesses during direct examination vs. cross-examination. *Journal of Applied Social Psychology, 13,* 78-87.

McLaughlin, M. L., Cody, M. J., & O'Hair, H. D. (1983). The management of failure events: Some contextual determinants of accounting behavior. *Human Communication Research, 9,* 108-224.

McLaughlin, M. L., Cody, M. J., & Rosenstein, N. E. (1983). Account sequences in conversations between strangers. *Communication Monographs, 50,* 102-125.

Metts, S., & Cupach, W. (1989). Situational influence on the use of remedial strategies in embarrassing predicaments. *Communication Monographs, 56,* 151-162.

Meyer, J. M. (1990). Cognitive processes underlying the retrieval of compliance-gaining strategies: An implicit rules model. In J. P. Dillard (Ed.), *Seeking compliance: The production of interpersonal influence messages* (pp. 57-74). Scottsdale, AZ: Gorsuch Scarisbrick.

Miller, G. R. (1987). Persuasion. In C. Berger & S. Chaffee (Eds.), *Handbook of communication science* (pp. 446-483). Newbury Park, CA: Sage.

Miller, G. R., Boster, F., Roloff, M., & Seibold, D. (1977). Compliance-gaining message strategies: A typology and some findings concerning effects of situational differences. *Communication Monographs, 44,* 37-51.

Miller, G. R., Boster, F. J., Roloff, M. E., & Seibold, D. R. (1987). MBRS rekindled: Some thoughts on compliance gaining in interpersonal settings. In M. E. Roloff & G. R. Miller (Eds.), *Interpersonal processes: New directions in communication research* (Vol. 14, pp. 89-117). Newbury Park, CA: Sage.

Miller, G. R., & Burgoon, M. (1978). Persuasion research: Review and commentary. In B. Rubin (Ed.), *Communication yearbook 2* (pp. 29-47). New Brunswick, NJ: Transaction.

Miller, R. L., Seligman, C., Clark, N. T., & Bush, M. (1976). Perceptual contrast versus reciprocal concession as mediators of induced compliance. *Canadian Journal of Behavioral Science, 8,* 401-409.

Miller, R. L., & Suls, J. (1977). Helping, self-attribution, and the size of an initial request. *Journal of Social Psychology, 103,* 203-207.

Mitchell-Kernan, C. (1972a). Signifying, loud-talking and marking. In T. Kochman (Ed.), *Rappin' and stylin' out* (pp. 315-335). Urbana: University of Illinois Press.

Monroe, C., Borzi, M., & DiSalvo, V. (1989). Conflict behaviors of different subordinates. *Southern Communication Journal, 54,* 311-329.

Monteverde, R. J., Paschke, R., & Tedeschi, J. T. (1974). The effectiveness of honesty and deceit as influence tactics. *Sociometry, 37,* 583-591.

Mowen, J. C., & Cialdini, R. B. (1980). On implementing the door-in-the-face compliance technique in a business context. *Journal of Marketing Research, 22,* 253-258.

Neuliep, J. (1986). Self-report vs. actual use of persuasive messages by high and low dogmatics. *Journal of Social Behavior and Personality, 1,* 213-222.

Neuliep, J. W. (1987). The influence of Theory X and Theory Y management styles on the selection of compliance-gaining strategies. *Communication Research Reports, 4,* 14-19.

Neuliep, J. W., & Hazelton, V. (1985). A cross cultural comparison of Japanese and American persuasive strategy selection. *International Journal of Intercultural Relations, 9,* 389-404.

Neuliep, J. W., & Mattson, M. (1990). The use of deception as a compliance-gaining strategy. *Human Communication Research, 16,* 409-421.

Newton, D. A., & Burgoon, J. K. (1990). The use and consequences of verbal influence strategies during interpersonal disagreements. *Human Communication Research, 16,* 477-518.

Offerman, L. R., & Kearney, C. T. (1988). Supervisor sex and subordinate influence strategies. *Personality and Social Psychology Bulletin, 14,* 360-367.

Offerman, L. R., & Schrier, P. E. (1985). Social influence strategies: The impact of sex, role, and attitudes toward power. *Personality and Social Psychology Bulletin, 11,* 286-300.

O'Keefe, B. J. (1988). The logic of message design: Individual differences in reasoning about communication. *Communication Monographs, 55,* 80-103.

O'Keefe, B. J. (1990). The logic of regulative communication: Understanding the rationality of message designs. In J. P. Dillard (Ed.), *Seeking compliance: The production of interpersonal influence messages* (pp. 87-105). Scottsdale, AZ: Gorsuch Scarisbrick.

O'Keefe, B. J., & Benoit, P. J. (1983). Children's arguments. In R. Cox & C. A. Willard (Eds.), *Advances in argumentation theory* (pp. 154-183). Carbondale: Southern Illinois University Press.

O'Keefe, B. J., & Delia, J. G. (1982). Impression formation and message production. In M. E. Roloff & C. R. Berger (Eds.), *Social cognition and communication* (pp. 33-72). Beverly Hills, CA: Sage.

O'Keefe, B. J., & Delia, J. G. (1988). Communicative tasks and communicative practices: The development of audience-centered message production. In B. Raforth & D. Rubin (Eds.), *The social construction of written communication* (pp. 70-98). Norwood, NJ: Ablex.

O'Keefe, B. J., & McCornack, S. A. (1987). Message logic and message goal structure: Effects on perceptions of message quality in regulative communication situations. *Human Communication Research, 14,* 68-92.

O'Keefe, B. J., Murphy, M., Meyers, R. A., & Babrow, A. (1989). The development of persuasive communication skills: The influence of developments in interpersonal construct on the ability to generate communication-relevant beliefs and on level of persuasive strategy. *Communication Studies, 40,* 29-40.

O'Keefe, B. J., & Shepherd, G. (1987). The pursuit of multiple objectives in face-to-face persuasive interactions: Effects of construct differentiation on message organization. *Communication Monographs, 54,* 398-419.

O'Keefe, B. J., & Shepherd, G. (1989). The communication of identity during face-to-face persuasive interactions: Effects of perceiver's construct differentiation and target's message strategies. *Communication Monographs, 16,* 375-404.

O'Quin, K., & Aronoff, J. (1981). Humor as a technique of social influence. *Social Psychology Quarterly, 44,* 349-357.

Patch, M. (1986). The role of source legitimacy in sequential request strategies of influence. *Personality and Social Psychology Bulletin, 12,* 199-205.

Paul, S. C., & Thelen, M. H. (1983). The use of strategies and messages to alter aggressive interactions. *Aggressive Behavior, 9,* 183-193.

Pendelton, M. G., & Batson, C. D. (1979). Self-presentation and the door-in-the-face technique for inducing compliance. *Personality and Social Psychology Bulletin, 5,* 77-81.

Plax, T., Kearney, P., & Down, T. (1986). Communicating control in the classroom and satisfaction with teaching students. *Communication Education, 35,* 379-388.

Plax, T., Kearney, P., Down, T., & Stewart, R. (1986). College student resistance toward teachers' use of selective control strategies. *Communication Research Reports, 3,* 20-27.

Plax, T., Kearney, P., McCroskey, J., & Richmond, V. (1986). Power in the classroom VI: Verbal control strategies, nonverbal immediacy and affective learning. *Communication Education, 35,* 43-55.

Plax, T., Kearney, P., & Sorensen, G. (1990). The strategy selection-construction controversy II: Comparing pre- and experienced teachers' compliance-gaining message constructions. *Communication Education, 39,* 128-141.

Plax, T., Kearney, P., & Tucker, L. (1986). Prospective teachers' use of behavior alteration techniques on common student misbehaviors. *Communication Education, 35,* 32-42.

Ragan, S. L., & Hopper, R. (1981). Alignment talk in the job interview. *Journal of Applied Communication Research, 9,* 85-103.

Ragins, B. R., & Sundstrom, E. (1990). Gender and perceived power in manager-subordinate relations. *Journal of Occupational Psychology, 63,* 273-287.

Raven, B. H. (1990). Political applications of the psychology of interpersonal influence and social power. *Political Psychology, 11,* 493-520.

Reardon, K. K. (1981). *Persuasion: Theory and context.* Beverly Hills, CA: Sage.

Reeves, R., Macolini, R., & Martin, R. (1987). Legitimizing paltry contributions: On-the-spot vs. mail-in requests. *Journal of Applied Social Psychology, 17,* 731-738.

Reingen, P. H. (1978). On inducing compliance with requests. *Journal of Consumer Research, 5,* 96-102.

Renshaw, P. D., & Asher, S. R. (1983). Children's goals and strategies for social interaction. *Merrill-Palmer Quarterly, 29,* 353-374.

Riccillo, S. C., & Trenholm, S. (1983). Predicting managers' choice of influence mode: The effects of interpersonal trust and worker attributions on managerial tactics in a simulated organizational setting. *The Western Journal of Speech Communication, 47,* 323-339.

Richmond, V. P., McCroskey, J. C., & Davis, L. M. (1986). The relationship of supervisor use of power and affinity-seeking strategies with subordinate satisfaction. *Communication Quarterly, 34,* 178-193.

Richmond, V. P., McCroskey, J. C., Kearney, P., & Plax, T. (1987). Power in the classroom VII: Linking behavior alteration techniques to cognitive learning. *Communication Education, 36,* 1-12.

Rittle, R. H. (1981). Changes in helping behavior: Self versus situational perceptions as mediators of the foot-in-the-door effect. *Personality and Social Psychology Bulletin, 7,* 431-457.

Roach, D. (1991). Graduate teaching assistants' use of behavior alteration techniques in the university classroom. *Communication Quarterly, 39,* 178-188.

Roloff, M. E., & Janiszewski, C. (1989). Overcoming obstacles to interpersonal compliance: A principle of message construction. *Human Communication Research, 16,* 33-61.

Roloff, M. E., & Jordan, M. (1992). Achieving negotiation goals: The "fruits and foibles" of planning ahead. In L. Putnam & M. E. Roloff (Eds.), *Communication and negotiation* (pp. 21-45). Newbury Park, CA: Sage.

Rossi, A. M., & Todd-Mancillas, W. R. (1987). Machismo as a factor affecting the use of power and communication in the managing of personnel disputes: Brazilian versus American male managers. *Journal of Social Behavior and Personality, 2,* 93-104.

Rueda, R., & Smith, D. C. (1983). Interpersonal tactics and communicative strategies of Anglo-American and Mexican-American mildly mentally retarded and non-retarded students. *Applied Research in Mental Retardation, 4,* 153-161.

Rule, B. G., & Bisanz, G. L. (1987). Goals and strategies of persuasion: A cognitive schema for understanding social events. In M. P. Zanna, J. M. Olson, & C. P. Herman (Eds.), *Social influence: The Ontario Symposium* (Vol. 5, pp. 185-206). Hillsdale, NJ: Lawrence Erlbaum.

Rule, B. G., Bisanz, G. L., & Kohn, M. (1985). Anatomy of a persuasion schema: Targets, goals, and strategies. *Journal of Personality and Social Psychology, 48,* 1127-1140.

Scandura, T. A., Graen, G. B., & Novak, M. A. (1986). When managers decide not to decide autocratically: An investigation of leader-member exchange and decision influence. *Journal of Applied Psychology, 71,* 579-584.

Schank, R. C., & Abelson, R. P. (1977). *Scripts, plans, goals and understanding: An inquiry into human knowledge structures.* Hillsdale, NJ: Lawrence Erlbaum.

Scheer, L. K., & Stern, L. W. (1992). The effect of influence type and performance outcomes on attitude toward the influencer. *Journal of Marketing Research, 24,* 128-142.

Schenck-Hamlin, W. J., Wiseman, R. L., & Georgacarakos, G. N. (1982). A model of properties of compliance-gaining strategies. *Communication Quarterly, 30,* 92-100.

Schenkein, J. (1978). Identity negotiations in conversation. In J. Schenkein (Ed.), *Studies in the organization of conversational interaction* (pp. 57-78). New York: Academic Press.

Schilit, W. K. (1987). Upward influence activity in strategic decision making: An examination of organizational differences. *Group and Organization Studies, 12,* 343-368.

Schlenker, B. R. (1980). *Impression management: The self-concept, social identity, and interpersonal relations.* Belmont, CA: Wadsworth.

Schlenker, B. R., Bonoma, T., & Tedeschi, J. T. (1970). Compliance to threats as a function of the wording of the threat and the exploitativeness of the threatener. *Sociometry, 33,* 394-408.

Schlenker, B. R., & Darby, B. W. (1981). The use of apologies in social predicaments. *Social Psychology Quarterly, 44,* 271-278.

Schleuter, D. W., Barge, J. K., & Blankenship, D. (1990). A comparative analysis of influence strategies used by upper and lower-level male and female managers. *Western Journal of Speech Communication, 54,* 42-65.

Schwarzwald, J., Raz, M., & Zvibel, M. (1979). The applicability of the door-in-the-face technique where established behavioral customs exist. *Journal of Applied Social Psychology, 9,* 576-586.

Scott, C. A. (1977). Modifying socially conscious behavior: The foot-in-the-door technique. *Journal of Consumer Research, 4,* 156-164.

Seibold, D. R. (1988). A response to "item desirability in compliance-gaining research." *Human Communication Research, 15,* 152-161.

Seibold, D. R., Cantrill, J. G., & Meyers, R. A. (1985). Communication and interpersonal influence. In M. L. Knapp & G. R. Miller (Eds.), *Handbook of interpersonal communication* (1st ed., pp. 551-611). Beverly Hills, CA: Sage.

Seibold, D. R., & Chan, M. (1993). *Work colleagues' strategies for communicating criticism.* Unpublished manuscript, University of California at Santa Barbara, Department of Communication.

Seibold, D. R., & Spitzberg, B. H. (1982). Attribution theory and research: Review and implications for communication. In B. Dervin & M. J. Voigt (Eds.), *Progress in communication sciences* (Vol. 3, pp. 85-125). Norwood, NJ: Ablex.

Seibold, D. R., & Steinfatt, T. M. (1979). The creative alternative game: Exploring interpersonal influence processes. *Simulation & Games, 10,* 429-457.

Seibold, D. R., & Thomas, R. W. (in press). College students' interpersonal influence processes in alcohol intervention situations: A critical review and reconceptualization. *Journal of Applied Communication Research.*

Seligman, C., Bush, M., & Kirsch, K. (1976). Relationship between compliance in the foot-in-the-door paradigm and size of first request. *Journal of Personality and Social Psychology, 33,* 517-520.

Seligman, C., Miller, R., Goldberg, G., Gelberd, L., Clark, N., & Bush, M. (1976). Compliance in the foot-in-the-door technique as a function of issue similarity and persuasion. *Social Behavior and Personality, 4,* 267-271.

Shanab, M. E., & Isonio, S. A. (1980). The effects of delay upon compliance with socially undesirable requests in the door-in-the-face paradigm. *Bulletin of the Psychonomic Society, 15*, 76-78.

Shanab, M. E., & Isonio, S. A. (1982). The effects of contrast upon compliance with socially undesirable requests in the foot-in-the-door paradigm. *Bulletin of the Psychonomic Society, 20*, 180-182.

Shanab, M. E., & O'Neill, P. (1979). The effects of contrast upon compliance with socially undesirable requests in the door-in-the-face paradigm. *Canadian Journal of Behavioral Science, 11*, 236-244.

Sharkin, B., Mahalik, J., & Claiborn, C. (1989). Application of the foot-in-the-door effect to counseling. *Journal of Counseling Psychology, 36*, 248-251.

Shields, N. M. (1979). Accounts and other interpersonal strategies in a credibility detracting context. *Pacific Sociological Review, 22*, 255-272.

Sillars, A. L. (1980a). The stranger and the spouse as target persons for compliance-gaining strategies: A subjective utility model. *Human Communication Research, 6*, 265-279.

Sillars, A. L. (1980b). Attributions and communication in roommate conflicts. *Communication Monographs, 47*, 180-200.

Singer, J. E. (1964). The use of manipulative strategies: Machiavellianism and attractiveness. *Sociometry, 27*, 128-150.

Smith, J. E., Carson, K. P., & Alexander, R. A. (1984). Leadership: It can make a difference. *Academy of Management Journal, 27*, 765-776.

Smith, T. E. (1983). Parental influence: A review of the evidence of influence and a theoretical model of the parental influence process. *Research in Sociology of Education and Socialization, 4*, 13-45.

Snyder, M., & Cunningham, M. R. (1975). To comply or not comply: Testing the self-perception explanation of the "foot-in-the-door" phenomenon. *Journal of Personality and Social Psychology, 31*, 64-67.

Sorensen, G., Plax, T., & Kearney, P. (1989). The strategy selection-construction controversy: A coding scheme for analyzing teacher compliance-gaining message constructions. *Communication Education, 38*, 102-118.

Sprowl, J. (1986). Sales communication: An analysis of sex differences in compliance-gaining strategy use. *Communication Research Reports, 3*, 90-93.

Sprowl, J., & Senk, M. (1986). Sales communication: Compliance-gaining strategy choice and sales success. *Communication Research Reports, 3*, 64-68.

Steele, C. M. (1975). Name-calling and compliance. *Journal of Personality and Social Psychology, 31*, 361-369.

Stephenson, R. M. (1951). Conflict and control functions of humor. *American Journal of Sociology, 56*, 569-574.

Stires, L. K., & Jones, E. E. (1969). Modesty versus self-enhancement as alternative forms of ingratiation. *Journal of Experimental Social Psychology, 5*, 79-82.

Sutton, R. I., & Louis, M. R. (1987). How selecting and socializing newcomers influences insiders. *Human Resource Management, 26*, 347-361.

Swann, W. B., & Hill, C. A. (1982). When our identities are mistaken: Reaffirming self-conceptions through social interaction. *Journal of Personality and Social Psychology, 43*, 59-66.

Tedeschi, J. T. (1970). Threats and promises. In P. Swingle (Ed.), *The structure of conflict* (pp. 155-191). New York: Academic Press.

Tedeschi, J. T. (1990). Self-presentation and social influence: An interactionist perspective. In M. J. Cody & M. L. McLaughlin (Eds.), *The psychology of tactical communication* (pp. 301-323). Clevedon, England: Multilingual Matters.

Tedeschi, J. T., & Reiss, M. (1981). Verbal strategies in impression management. In C. Antaki (Ed.), *The psychology of ordinary explanations of social behavior* (pp. 271-309). New York: Academic Press.

Thomas, R. W., & Seibold, D. R. (in press). Interpersonal influence processes in the "home treatment method" of alcoholism intervention. *Journal of Alcohol and Drug Education.*

Thompson, T. L., & Seibold, D. R. (1978). Stigma management in normal-stigmatized interactions: Test of the disclosure hypothesis and a model of stigma acceptance. *Human Communication Research, 4*, 231-242.

Tjosvold, D. (1985). The effects of attribution and social context on superiors' influence and interaction with low performing subordinates. *Personnel Psychology, 38*, 361-375.

Tjosvold, D. (1989). Interdependence and power between managers and employees: A study of the leader relationship. *Journal of Management, 15*, 49-62.

Tracy, K., & Coupland, N. (1990). Multiple goals in discourse: An overview of issues. *Journal of Language and Social Psychology, 9*, 1-13.

Tracy, K., Craig, R. T., Smith, M., & Spisak, F. (1984). The discourse of requests: Assessment of a compliance-gaining approach. *Human Communication Research, 10*, 513-538.

Trapp, R. (1983). Generic characteristics of argument in everyday discourse. In D. Zarefsky, M. O. Sillars, & J. Rhodes (Eds.), *Argument in transition: Proceedings of the Third Summer Conference on Argumentation* (pp. 516-530). Annandale, VA: Speech Communication Association.

Tybout, A. M. (1978). Relative effectiveness of three behavioral influence strategies as supplements to persuasion in a marketing context. *Journal of Marketing Research, 15,* 229-242.

Tybout, A. M., Sternthal, B., & Calder, B. J. (1983). Information availability as a determinant of multiple request effectiveness. *Journal of Marketing Research, 20,* 280-290.

Vecchio, R. P., & Sussmann, M. (1989). Preferences for forms of supervisory social influence. *Journal of Organizational Behavior, 10,* 135-143.

Wagener, J. J., & Laird, J. D. (1980). The experimenter's foot-in-the-door: Self-perception, body weight, and volunteering. *Personality and Social Psychology Bulletin, 6,* 441-446.

Ward, L. G., Friedlander, M. L., Schoen, L. G., & Klein, J. G. (1985). Strategic self-presentation in supervision. *Journal of Counseling Psychology, 32,* 111-118.

Wayne, S. J., & Ferris, G. R. (1990). Influence tactics, affect, and exchange quality in supervisor-subordinate interactions: A laboratory experiment and field study. *Journal of Applied Psychology, 75,* 487-499.

Weary, G., & Arkin, R. M. (1981). Attributional self-presentation. In J. H. Harvey, W. Ickes, & R. F. Kidd (Eds.), *New directions in attribution research* (Vol. 3, pp. 223-246). Hillsdale, NJ: Lawrence Erlbaum.

Weber, D., & Vangelisti, A. (1991). "Because I love you . . .": The tactical use of attributional expressions in conversations. *Human Communication Research, 17,* 606-624.

Weiner, B., Figueroa-Munoz, A., & Kakihara, C. (1991). The goals of excuses and communication strategies related to causal perceptions. *Personality and Social Psychology Bulletin, 17,* 4-13.

Weinstein, E. A. (1966). Toward a theory of interpersonal tactics. In C. W. Backman & P. F. Secord (Eds.), *Problems in social psychology* (pp. 394-398). New York: McGraw-Hill.

Weinstein, E. A. (1969). The development of interpersonal competence. In D. A. Goslin (Ed.), *Handbook of socialization theory and research* (pp. 753-775). Chicago: Rand McNally.

Weinstein, E. A., & Deutschberger, P. (1963). Some dimensions of altercasting. *Sociometry, 26,* 454-466.

Weiss, D., & Sachs, J. (1991). Persuasive strategies used by preschool children. *Discourse Processes, 14,* 55-72.

Weiss, D., & Weinstein, E. A. (1968). Interpersonal tactics among mental retardates. *American Journal of Mental Deficiency, 72,* 653-661.

Wheeless, L. R., Barraclough, R., & Stewart, R. (1983). Compliance-gaining and power in persuasion. In R. Bostrom (Ed.), *Communication yearbook 7* (pp. 105-145). Beverly Hills, CA: Sage.

Wheeless, L. R., Stewart, R. A., Kearney, P., & Plax, T. (1987). Locus of control and personal constructs in students' reactions to teacher compliance attempts: A reassessment. *Communication Education, 36,* 250-258.

Williams, L., & Untermeyer, N. (1988). Compliance-gaining strategies and communicator role: An analysis of strategy choices and persuasive efficacy. *Communication Research Reports, 5,* 10-18.

Wilmot, W. W., Carbaugh, D. A., & Baxter, L. (1985). Communicative strategies used to terminate romantic relationships. *Western Journal of Speech Communication, 49,* 204-216.

Wilson, D. C., & Kenny, G. K. (1985). Managerially perceived influence over interdepartmental decisions. *Journal of Management Studies, 22,* 155-174.

Wilson, S. R. (1990). Development and test of a cognitive rules model of interaction goals. *Communication Monographs, 57,* 81-103.

Wilson, S. R., Cruz, M. G., & Kang, K. H. (1992). Is it always a matter of perspective? Construct differentiation and variability in attributions about compliance gaining. *Communication Monographs, 59,* 350-367.

Wilson, S. R., & Putnam, L. L. (1990). Interaction goals in negotiation. In J. A. Anderson (Ed.), *Communication yearbook 13* (pp. 374-406). Newbury Park, CA: Sage.

Wiseman, R. L., & Schenck-Hamlin, W. (1981). A multidimensional scaling validation of an inductively-derived set of compliance-gaining strategies. *Communication Monographs, 48,* 251-270.

Witteman, H. (1992). Analyzing interpersonal conflict: Nature of awareness, type of initiating event, situational perceptions, and management styles. *Western Journal of Communication, 56,* 248-280.

Witteman, H., & Fitzpatrick, M. A. (1986). Compliance-gaining in marital interaction: Power bases, processes, and outcomes. *Communication Monographs, 53,* 130-143.

Yukl, G., & Falbe, C. M. (1990). Influence tactics and objectives in upward, downward, and lateral influence attempts. *Journal of Applied Psychology, 75,* 132-140.

Zuckerman, M., Lazzaro, M. M., & Waldgeir, D. (1979). Undermining effects of the foot-in-the-door technique with extrinsic rewards. *Journal of Applied Social Psychology, 9,* 292-296.

15

Communicative Competence
and Interpersonal Control

Malcolm R. Parks

WE ARE SO SURROUNDED by the little triumphs of everyday life that we often do not recognize them for what they are. Even our most routine social successes are the product of a sophisticated set of communicative competencies: whether the favor asked and received from a friend, the rationale presented to and accepted by an employer, the criticism tactfully given and thoughtfully heard, or the emotion expressed and addressed. This chapter is about these everyday competencies, about the processes by which we communicate to satisfy our needs and desires.

Picturing communicative competence requires very broad strokes on a very large canvas. Indeed, the very breadth of the concept has contributed to its rather muddled theoretical status. There are numerous controversies regarding how communicative competence ought to be conceptualized. But there is also a great deal of consensus, and in the first two sections of this chapter, I will identify these common themes. Some pieces of the conceptual canvas are better covered than others. So, in the third section, I will integrate literature from several different perspectives to identify the more specific behavioral and cognitive processes by which communicative competence occurs.

Judgments of competence and incompetence are evaluative by their very nature. And while there are many relevant perspectives and many unknowns regarding competence, there is also a remarkable level of consensus about what constitutes incompetence. We can agree that it is a mark of incompetence when communication fails to accomplish even simple social tasks, when self-esteem is damaged, and when physical health is threatened. We can also agree that socially inappropriate and violent behavior is usually undesirable. In the fourth section of the chapter, I will show how these undesirable consequences often flow from inadequacies in the individual's conception and enactment of interpersonal control. And in the final section of the chapter, I will explore the often uneasy relationship between conceptions of interpersonal control and conceptions of socially appropriate behavior.

The Many Worlds of Communicative Competence

The concept of competence means so many things to so many people that a series of basic ontological issues must be addressed before any sort of coherent conceptualization can be offered. Chief among these issues are questions regarding whether competence is to be judged from an actor's or an observer's perspective, whether competence is a cognition or a behavior, and whether people are competent in some generalized sense or only in terms of specific situations or audiences.

Competence as Both an Actor and Observer Variable

Communicative competence can be fairly judged from two quite different, not necessarily compatible, perspectives. One is the actor's own perspective. In this case, competence is usually conceptualized according to the degree to which the actor is satisfied and feels she or he has realized his or her own interactive objectives. But we can also view competence through the eyes of observers. Here we ask others to evaluate the competence of a given communicator. Spitzberg and Cupach (1989) further divide this second perspective into judgments made by fellow participants and judgments made by third party observers.

As one might expect, actor and observer judgments of communicative competence are only minimally related to one another. A series of studies by Spitzberg, for example, have generally shown little or no correlation between actors' self-evaluations of competence and ratings given by their conversational partners (Spitzberg, 1982, 1986; Spitzberg & Hecht, 1984). Similar findings have emerged from studies in more specific areas, such as social skills for dating (Curran, Wallander, & Fischetti, 1980; Kolko & Milan, 1985). Although third party observers and conversational partners tend to rate an actor in somewhat similar ways, there is little correlation between how actors rate their own competence and how third party observers rate the actor's competence (Curran, 1982; Powers & Spitzberg, 1986; Spitzberg & Cupach, 1985).

Differences in actor-observer perceptions of competence probably occur for many of the same reasons that other differences in actor-observer perceptions occur. These include differences in the relative salience of the actor's behavior and differences in the amount of information available to actors and observers (Jones & Nisbett, 1972; Storms, 1973). In addition, as Spitzberg and Cupach (1989) note, how we evaluate others' competence may be confounded by how we rate our own competence, thus producing further differences between the actor's own evaluation and the observer's evaluation.

These differences, however, extend beyond matters of perceptual bias and information availability. Actor and observer conceptualizations of communicative competence are fundamentally different. Each has value, but each is based on a different ontological stance. Actor-based conceptualizations valorize individual empowerment and action, while observer-based conceptualizations subtly or explicitly emphasize harmony with broader social expectations and values.

Elements of both perspectives are found in most conceptualizations of communicative competence, a fact that no doubt contributes to the murkiness of the concept. In this chapter, I will emphasize the actor-based conceptualization when I conceptualize competence in terms of a personal control process. In the final section of the chapter, however, I will return to the observer perspective to argue that opportunities for individual control depend in part on adherence to broader codes of social conduct.

Competence as Both Cognition and Behavior

Many writers view competence only in terms of the inner aspects of action. Discussions of these inner aspects focus almost universally on cognitive rather than affective considerations. From this perspective, *competence* refers to the individual's ability to understand or report knowledge of how goals can be satisfied (Chomsky, 1965; McCroskey, 1982a; Phillips, 1984; Pylyshyn, 1973). Other writers draw a further distinction between possessing knowledge and the ability to report it. They point out that we may use many types of knowledge about interaction but not be able to report what we are doing or the knowledge we are using (Sternberg, 1985). Writers in this tradition use such terms as *performance* or *skill* to describe the process by which actual behavior occurs.

Most communication theorists, however, reject the bifurcation of cognition and behavior by suggesting that competence is a higher-order term having both cognitive and behavioral dimensions (Allen & Brown, 1976; Hymes, 1974; Parks, 1977a, 1985; Spitzberg & Cupach, 1989; Wiemann, 1977; Wiemann & Backlund, 1980). It is wise to remember that the difference between cognition and behavior is literally only skin deep. Although conceptualizing competence in a purely cognitive sense may be useful to a linguist, it is less useful to the communication scholar who is concerned with the world of social action. Action occurs on both sides of the skin. Knowledge and performance, cognition and overt behavior, are merely different aspects of the same larger process. To be competent therefore we must not only "know" and "know how," we must "do" and "know that we did."

Competence as Both Specific and General

A final source of conceptual slippage is the confusion surrounding the generality of communicative competence. It has most often been viewed as a trait, a concept whose qualities display themselves across time and situations (for example, Foote & Cottrell, 1955; McCroskey, 1982a). Certainly most measures of communicative competence have adopted a trait perspective. Indeed, a trait perspective is assumed in nearly all of the 80 or so measures reviewed by Spitzberg and Cupach (1989) in their *Handbook of Interpersonal Competence Research*.

Situationally specific views of competence also abound. A few define the overall concept as something that occurs in a specific context with a particular audience (Parks, 1977a, 1985; Wiemann, 1977). More often, the situational perspective is to be found scattered across the constellations of concepts developed by researchers concerned with some particular problem or setting. So, for example, we have extensive literatures on "heterosocial skills" for romantic relationships (for example, Dodge, Heimberg, Nyman, & O'Brien, 1987) and on the skills that distinguish delinquents and nondelinquent juveniles (for example, Gaffney & McFall, 1981). By the same token, sets of specific competencies and incompetencies have been associated with a host of particular interpersonal and psychological problems.

Lay judgments of competence probably reflect larger actor-observer differences in perception (see Nisbett & Ross, 1980; Sillars, 1985). If so, people should be more likely to judge others' competence from a trait perspective and their own from a situational perspective. Not all situations, however, are created equal. Some situations may be viewed as so critical that one's competence in them is taken as symptomatic of one's overall competence across situations.

Whether competence is general or specific ultimately depends on the type of assessment one wishes to make and on the degree of generality exhibited in an individual's behavior. We may assess one or more specific components of the process by which competency occurs, or we may assess some indicator of the overall process. In either case, it should be clearly understood that competency is not a fixed quality that we "carry" around with us, even though some components may be more "portable" or generalizable than others. Instead, it is a quality of the process by which we interact with others. A person does not "have" a competence trait, although some individuals' behavior may be more "traitlike" because of its consistency across time and situations. Thus the question of whether a given person's competence is generalized or limited to specific situations or audiences is an empirical one.

Conceptualizing Communicative Competence

Communicative competence is not so much a single concept as a broad conceptual vehicle for summarizing a host of more specific concerns and commitments. Beneath this breadth, however, we can discern a relatively small number of fundamental themes. These can be seen in the various definitions of communicative competence presented in Table 15.1. Following Spitzberg and Cupach (1989), three themes that run through nearly all conceptualizations of communicative competence may be identified. These are control, adaptation, and collaboration. Each is explored in more detail below, followed by the presentation of a working definition of communicative competence.

Competence as Control

Communication is inherently strategic and goal directed. We take it as axiomatic that there would be no reason to communicate if we were not dependent upon others for the fulfillment of our wishes and that these wishes or needs are fulfilled by influencing or controlling others' responses to us (Kellermann, 1992). Notions of efficacy and goal-directedness make up the primary motivational constructs in the literature on competence and social skill (Greene & Geddes, 1993). The concern for control also permeates communicators' everyday thoughts. Waldron (1990), for example, found that nearly half of the thoughts people reported having during interactions dealt with their goals and strategies for attaining them.

The control perspective lies either explicitly or implicitly at the heart of nearly every definition of communicative competence (see Table 15.1 for examples). Indeed, it is the common thread uniting a vast array of psychological and sociological concepts. For example, psychological concepts such as optimal stimulation (Hebb & Thompson, 1954; Leuba, 1955) and exploratory behavior (White, 1959; Woodworth, 1958) portray individuals as active participants in environmental events who seek to influence their surroundings in specific ways.

Theories of social exchange and interdependence also reflect the control orientation. Exchange theorists of many stripes share the assumption that individuals are

Table 15.1 Representative Definitions of Communicative Competence

"An individual's ability to adapt effectively to the surrounding environment over time" (Spitzberg & Cupach, 1984, p. 35)

"The ability of an interactant to choose among available communicative behaviors in order that he may successfully accomplish his own interpersonal goals during an encounter while maintaining the face and line of his fellow interactants within the constraints of the situation" (Wiemann, 1977, p. 195)

"The ability of an individual to demonstrate knowledge of the appropriate communicative behavior in a given situation" (Larson, Backlund, Redmond, & Barbour, 1978, p. 21)

"The fitness or ability to carry on those transactions with the environment which result in [an organism] maintaining itself, growing, and flourishing" (Argyris, 1965, p. 59)

"The ability to formulate and achieve objectives, to collaborate effectively with others, to be interdependent; and the ability to adapt appropriately to situational and environmental variation" (Bochner & Kelly, 1974, p. 288)

"An organism's capacity to interact effectively with its environment" (White, 1959, p. 297)

"Interpersonal competence is essentially found in relational contexts in which individuals have sufficient power over their own actions and the actions of others that they may set, pursue, and achieve the interpersonal objectives deemed necessary for a mutually satisfying exchange with their social environment." (Wiemann & Kelly, 1981, p. 292)

"The ability to accomplish interpersonal tasks. . . . interpersonal competence boils down to the ability to manipulate others' responses." (Weinstein, 1969, p. 755)

"A synonym for ability. It means a satisfactory degree of ability for performing certain implied kinds of tasks. . . . our main strategy of definition will be analytical, to name its parts, as manifested in observable behavior. These we take to be: (1) health, (2) intelligence, (3) empathy, (4) autonomy, (5) judgment, and (6) creativity." (Foote & Cottrell, 1955, pp. 36 & 41)

"The ability to attain relevant interactive goals in specified social contexts using socially appropriate means and ways of speaking that result in positive outcomes with significant others" (Stohl, 1983, p. 688; see also Ford, 1985)

goal seekers. Interpersonal behavior is control oriented and manipulative in character (Kelley & Thibaut, 1978; Wood, Weinstein, & Parker, 1967).

The control theme emerges even more explicitly in discussions of power and social influence strategies (see Chapters 13 and 14, this volume). Typologies of power and social influence testify to the richness and variety of interpersonal control strategies (for example, Etzioni, 1961; French & Raven, 1960; Marwell & Schmitt, 1969). And although its tone is quite different, the same theme is foundational for the more dyadically oriented literature on relational control strategies (Parks, 1977b).

Still another view of the control perspective is afforded by the dramaturgical approach of Goffman (1959, 1967) and those who have been influenced by his work. When we view social interaction as theater, with actors playing roles and improvising performances, we should not assume that the "cast" works for nothing. Rather, the performance is orchestrated for the fulfillment of personal goals and needs. Control will be a primary motive for the actor (Goffman, 1959).

The control perspective is implicit in social cognitive approaches to communication (Berger & Bradac, 1982; Delia, O'Keefe, & O'Keefe, 1982; Roloff & Berger, 1982). Although these approaches emphasize cognitive activities, no one presumes that social knowledge is developed merely to add another volume to some cognitive library. We seek social knowledge so as to be more effective at influencing others (Kelley, 1972).

While there are obviously important differences among these perspectives, they converge in a common view of human action. They, along with any number of other perspectives one might identify, all share the assumption that human action is purposive, goal directed, and strategic. Hence a basic function of communication is control over the physical and social environment (Miller & Steinberg, 1975).

Competence as Adaptation

Competence implies a sensitivity to differences in situations and responses. Indeed, an inherent part of a strategic perspective is the belief that behavior is altered on an ongoing basis in order to account for changing situational factors and changing responses from others (Kellermann, 1992). Such flexibility, as Spitzberg and Cupach (1989) point out, requires us to select behaviors from a repertoire in ways that are responsive to variations in the social context, to improvise behavior when existing choices are found wanting, and to alter our behavioral choices so as to respond to problems that may arise as interaction unfolds.

Adaptation is so fundamental that it is often used almost as a synonym for *competence*. Duran (1983, 1992), for example, developed a measure of adaptiveness based on previous definitions of competence and subjects' lists of the abilities and behaviors that they believed characterized competent communicators. This measure, the Communicative Adaptability Scale, operationalizes six factors: (a) social experience, the desire to interact with a variety of individuals and groups; (b) social composure, the ability to manage anxiety; (c) social confirmation, the willingness to acknowledge and affirm others; (d) appropriate disclosure, the ability to use cues from others to regulate the intimacy of one's own behavior; (e) articulation, the ability to use language appropriately; and (f) wit, the ability to manage social tension through humor. These factors are best viewed not as characteristics of adaptability itself but as skills and abilities that allow people to behave in adaptive, flexible ways.

One of the best ways to appreciate the importance of adaptiveness is to consider the fate of rigid interpersonal patterns. There is a long history of associating rigidity with incompetence and dissatisfaction (for example, Scott, 1966). Many negative personality characteristics, like dogmatism (Rokeach, 1960), are typified by a rigid cognitive and behavioral approach to others. People who score lower on Duran's adaptability scale have been shown to be more anxious in interaction, less attentive and responsive, and generally less satisfied with their interactions than those reporting higher levels of adaptiveness (for review, see Duran, 1992). Finally, rigid behavioral patterns have been consistently found to distinguish between distressed and nondistressed families, from Haley's (1967) classic study of talk patterns in disturbed families through the more recent work by Gottman and his associates (for example, Gottman & Levenson, 1984). In short, the ability to creatively and responsively adapt one's behavior is a defining characteristic of communicative competence.

Competence as Collaboration

One cannot be socially competent alone. Many of our goals are inherently social; they cannot be achieved without the aid of others. But even in the most rudimentary cases, social action occurs in interaction with others, an interaction that is itself situated within a broader social context. As Goffman (1967) emphasizes, this means that at least some concern for others, at least some willingness to take into account others' identities and actions, is a precondition for sustained interaction. If nothing else, the individual must sustain the interaction long enough to take from it whatever he or she selfishly desires.

The need to sustain interaction while pursuing individual or mutual goals explains why, quite apart from any moral stance, many conceptualizations and measures of competence include a dual concern for effectiveness and appropriateness (Canary & Spitzberg, 1987). Put another way, communicators are often pursuing multiple goals (Clark & Delia, 1979; Seibold, this volume). The management of these comparatively complex message situations has been the focus of a great deal of research and theory, most notably Brown and Levinson's (1978) work on politeness and the work of O'Keefe and her colleagues on message design logics (O'Keefe, 1988; O'Keefe & McCornack, 1987; O'Keefe & Shepard, 1987). To be competent, communicators must often reconcile potentially incompatible requirements to influence others, to maintain others' identities and their own, and to sustain ongoing relationships (O'Keefe, 1988). In Brown and Levinson's terms, this implies that communication is always "face-threatening" to some degree; it imposes on others, and it implicitly conveys the reality that communicators' approval for one another will be at least partly a function of how their responses match each other's expectations.

A Working Definition

Control, adaptation, and collaboration figure prominently in most definitions of communicative competence. They can also be seen in the following definition, which I will adopt as a working definition for the remainder of this chapter:

> Communicative competence represents the degree to which individuals satisfy and perceive that they have satisfied their goals within the limits of a given social situation without jeopardizing their ability or opportunity to pursue their other subjectively more important goals.

This definition clearly locates communicative competence judgments in the cognitive and behavioral activities associated with personal control. Successful personal control does not necessarily imply that people have to maximize their outcomes. What can be achieved in a given situation is often limited by factors quite beyond our control, and as Simon (1979) points out, we are often satisfied by an outcome that is merely adequate rather than maximal. This is especially true in situations where we are pursuing several goals at the same time and may need to weigh the satisfaction of one against others. In the next section, I will examine the more specific behavioral and cognitive processes by which control is actualized. This definition does not simplistically equate competence with goal satisfaction. There is a difference between competence and good fortune. One must feel responsible for satisfying goals. This implies that the actor's own judgment of competence will be paramount. The way in which individuals make their own competency assessments is previewed at the end of the next section and examined in more detail in the section after that.

This definition also references notions of adaptation and collaboration. Adaptation is treated implicitly. Because this definition is focused on competence in a particular situation, there is no presumption that competence in one situation will translate into competence in other situations. Hence competence across situations will require adaptation to differences in goals, audiences, and task demands. The collaborative theme is more explicitly recognized. Pursuing any one goal by means of socially inappropriate behavior may jeopardize the individual's other goals and would therefore be a mark of incompetence. The complexities of balancing socially appropriate behavior with personal control are addressed later in the chapter.

How Communicative Competence Occurs

Consider the case of Jill, who has just approached her friend Tom. As she comes nearer, her face brightens as she smiles and says, "Tom, it's so good to see you." Tom returns her greeting and asks her how things have been going. Jill sighs and says, "OK, I guess, but I'm having a hard time getting the $30 I need for the concert ticket." Tom responds, "I'd like to help, but I'm nearly broke, too." "That's too bad," Jill says; "Are you OK?" Tom nods affirmatively. Jill says, "I was hoping you'd be able to help, but I don't want to put you in a bad spot." She pauses and then adds in an uncertain voice, "Please don't think I'm pushy, but even $5 would help." Tom pauses for a moment and then agrees to loan her $5. Jill thanks him profusely, and as she prepares to leave, adds, "Remember you can always count on me when things are the other way around."

Even simple encounters like this one reveal the complexity of competence judgments. Think of all the things we might judge. We might evaluate this encounter in terms of the precision with which specific muscle movements produced phonemes or facial expressions. Or we might ask if the speakers' morphemes were appropriate for the participants' speech community. We might look at the use of speech acts, the application of personal constructs or scripts, or the use of particular compliance-gaining strategies. We might look at politeness behavior or equivocation. We could consider the skill with which Jill created messages that sought both compliance and a continued relationship with Tom. A broader analysis might examine the sequential development of the episode or focus on how this episode reflected the unfolding relationship between Tom and Jill.

All of these levels of judgment would be legitimate, yet their variety poses staggering problems for any general theory of communicative competence. What is needed is a description of the control process that explicitly integrates many levels of abstraction. Only when we have a model of how the overall control process occurs can we judge competence and specify specific competencies.

One way to account for this complexity is to conceptualize the control process in terms of a hierarchy of actions ranging from raw sensory input and output to higher-order cognitive processes. That is, elements as different as the muscle movements behind Jill's smile and her calculations of how her request might stress her relationship with Tom can all be related coherently if we see them as different levels in the same larger control process.

One of the most useful road maps to the control process comes from W. T. Powers's (1973) hierarchical control theory, particularly as it has been applied and extended by Carver and Scheier (1982). These investigators conceptualized personal action as a process that occurred across nine levels of abstraction. These levels are (a) intensity control, (b) sensation control, (c) configuration control, (d) transition control, (e) sequence control, (f) relationship control, (g) program control, (h) sequence control, and (i) system concept control. Each of these is discussed in more detail below. Together, they sketch a picture of personal action ranging from raw muscle movements to conceptions of self and other. Moreover, each of the levels is linked to the ones below and above it with a negative feedback loop. That is, each level operates by sensing the condition in the level below it, comparing it with some "reference value" from the level above it, and then acting so as to reduce any discrepancies. So all the levels are cybernetically linked. As a result, widely varying behaviors are marshalled into a coherent performance in which, if we are competent, we are constantly adjusting our muscles to help us say and do the things that serve the goals and understandings that are in our heads.

None of our models of encoding and decoding adequately accounts for the complexities of ongoing conversation, as Bavelas and Coates (1992) have so elegantly demonstrated. There are alternatives to the hierarchical control model, but they tend to focus on a narrower range of processes and are probably too limited to cover the incredible variety of findings associated with communicative competence (for example, Bower & Cirilo, 1985; Clark & Clark, 1977; Greene, 1984; Greene & Geddes, 1993). Thus I believe that the hierarchical control model provides the most coherent way of organizing and integrating the incredibly diverse research on communicative competence. My discussion begins with brief descriptions of competence in the lower stages of the model and then lengthens as we move into the upper stages, where we encounter the bulk of the research associated with communicative competence.

Level 1: Intensity Control

This level occupies the world just inside the skin, the world of "raw" sensory contact, muscle movements, and spinal activities (W. T. Powers, 1973). This level contains only the most rudimentary information about the intensity of sensation or muscle movement. Competence at even this mundane level has direct implications for how we view competence in a larger social sense. Damage to specific muscles or sensory receptors may have far-reaching consequences. Harless and McConnell (1982), for example, found that hearing loss among the elderly was associated with reductions in self-esteem, a variable that is inextricably linked to perceptions of communicative competence. Fortunately, they also found that self-esteem was higher among those who compensated for their hearing loss with hearing aids. Practitioners interested in the treatment of competency problems are urged to begin by assessing the physical aspects of hearing, seeing, and speaking. There is little point in treating higher-order problems like an inability to take the role of the other without first determining if the basic physiological equipment is impaired.

Level 2: Sensation Control

The diverse bits and pieces of the first level are gathered and directed by a higher-order process that W. T. Powers (1973) calls sensation or vector control. Sensory nuclei located in the upper spine and brain stem creatively organize strands of sensory information into packages. These packages might, for example, include all the discrete muscle actions that make up a larger motion such as a smile.

Competence at the lower levels is primarily defined in terms of the accuracy with which we sense incoming sensory information and the fidelity with which our muscles produce the bits and pieces that make up larger verbal and nonverbal messages. While these lower levels have received less attention from competence researchers, it is worth remembering that even the most subtle insight or eloquently expressed idea must pass through them (Pearce, Cronen, & Conklin, 1979).

Level 3: Configuration Control

The still relatively small packages of sensory information and muscle movements at the previous level are themselves organized into somewhat broader configurations at the next higher level. These configurations control things like overall body position, movement of limbs, perception of visual forms, and speech at the phonemic level (W. T. Powers, 1973).

Once we reach the level of bodily movement and speech sounds, the discussion of the control hierarchy will become increasingly familiar to those interested in communicative competence. This familiarity should not mislead us into thinking that activities at these lower levels are directly subject to our conscious thoughts and feelings. Once higher-order understandings or intentions set the parameters, action at the lower levels unfolds rather automatically with little direct awareness (Bargh, 1989).

Level 4: Transition Control

Transition control is what allows us to execute an organized movement such as nodding the head, changing the tone of voice, or pronouncing a word. It is also what allows us to recognize those same actions in others. It is what allows us to discriminate changes in language intensity or the emotional intensity of nonverbal expression. Transition control summarizes and directs the more microscopic changes in lower-order configurations, sensations, and intensities. Errors at this level might, for example, take the form of mispronouncing words or substituting one word for another. Research has consistently shown that these "verbal slips" are not random but are predictable in terms of the speaker's higher-order concerns and interests (Motley, 1986; Motley, Camden, & Baars, 1982).

Level 5: Sequence Control

Competence at the level of sequence control generally consists of the ability to organize perception and action into sequences that serve higher-order goals. This implies a rather highly developed skill at discriminating between the various blocks and sequences making up the behavioral stream (Athay & Darley, 1981). Several more specific communication skills fit here, like the ability to accurately decode nonverbal cues (Gottman & Porterfield, 1981) and to recognize when others' verbal messages are garbled or incomplete (Flavell, Speer, & Green, 1981).

The individual's skill in placing behaviors into the stream of interaction is a major aspect of competency at this level. Others will judge us negatively, for example, if our comment is perceived as an interruption rather than as a "back-channel behavior" (Berger & Bradac, 1982). A number of researchers have shown that the inability to adapt the tempo of one's behavior to the tempo of others' behavior produces stress and disruption in the interaction (see Capella, this volume). Still others have found that, even when women who were socially incompetent in dating situations knew how to convey understanding and rapport, they often failed because they had difficulty synchronizing their comments with the comments of their partners (Peterson, Fischetti, Curran, & Arland, 1981). All of these findings testify as to why interaction management skills are highlighted in most major approaches to communicative competence (see, for example, Spitzberg & Cupach, 1984; Wiemann, 1977).

People must, of course, synchronize with others not only in terms of the timing of their behaviors but also in terms of their content. We might therefore be able to distinguish competent and incompetent communicators in terms of their judgments about what topics are appropriate for conversation. And there is evidence to support this view, if we assume that incompetence and depression are linked. Kuiper and McCabe (1985), for instance, found that depressed people tended to rate negative conversational topics as more acceptable than did nondepressed people. Broader studies of competence have also shown that less competent communicators show less sensitivity to situational incentives for intimacy or influence attempts (for example, Hazleton, Cupach, & Canary, 1987).

Level 6: Relationship Control

The relationship control level is concerned with how the individual judges larger relationships among his or her actions, the actions of others, and events in the environment. These relationships may be of many types: cause-effect, exclusive-inclusive, statistical, chronological, and so on (W. T. Powers, 1973). This level also covers some of the most frequently discussed and important competencies, those dealing with the closely related processes of cognitive complexity, empathy, and social perspective-taking (Spitzberg & Cupach, 1984, 1989).

The work on personal constructs (Kelly, 1955) and cognitive complexity is among the most influential in discussions of communicative competence. The constructivist tradition spawned by Kelly emphasizes that control at the relationship level occurs in terms of a system of personalized constructs that summarize and direct action. This system can be described not only in terms of its contents but also in terms of its organization. Delia and his colleagues and students have repeatedly demonstrated that the degree of complexity and abstraction in subjects' personal construct systems is positively related to the effectiveness and adaptiveness of their persuasive messages (Burleson, 1987; Delia et al., 1982; O'Keefe & Delia, 1982). That is, people create more effective messages when they are able to construe others from a variety of perspectives and when they construe others in abstract rather than surface-level terms. They are also better able to resist the compliance-gaining attempts of others should they choose to do so (McQuillen, 1986). They remember conversations more accurately (Neuliep & Hazleton, 1986). Cognitively complex people are not only able to take the role of the other better—in other words, to empathize—but are also better able to adapt to variations in the information they have about the causes of others' behavior (Hale & Delia, 1976; Wilson, Cruz, & Kang, 1992). One of the broadest demonstrations of the role of cognitive complexity comes from a study of career advancement by Sypher and Zorn (1986). They found that people with higher levels of cognitive complexity, who could generate greater numbers of persuasive arguments to further their position on work issues and who displayed a greater ability to take others' perspectives, rose to higher positions within the company over the 4 years of the study.

It is not only communicators' own complexity that counts but also their ability to create messages that alter the complexity of their receivers' view of the situation. Receivers' complexity has been shown to increase with the complexity of information given to him or her (Samter, Burleson, & Basden-Murphy, 1989). Thus creating messages that increase receiver complexity in line with the source's goals would be a mark of competency. Mischel (1973), for example, found that children were better able to follow an injunction against eating pretzels and marshmallows when they were encouraged to think of them as logs and clouds and not just as food.

A related line of inquiry is the work on message design logics by O'Keefe and her associates (O'Keefe, 1988; O'Keefe & McCornack, 1987; O'Keefe & Shepard, 1987). She suggests that people approach the multiple demands of interaction according to one of three perspectives: expressive, conventional, or rhetorical. Each of these message design logics implies a different view of communicative competence. Competence in the expressive logic would be equated with the openness and accuracy of self-expression. Competence in the conventional logic would be judged according to the degree of match between messages and the rules of the social situation, that is, finding the right key for each particular social door. Competence in the rhetorical logic appears to be judged according to the degree to which actors' messages create a context in which the participants have a consensus regarding goals and identities. O'Keefe (1988) sees the three design logics as forming a natural hierarchy of sophistication and development—from expressive, to conventional, to rhetorical. The research to date supports this view. O'Keefe and McCornack (1987), for example, found that people who operated from "higher" message logics were perceived as more likely to gain compliance, better at motivating others to act in concert with the source's goals, more supportive, and more likeable. On a related note, Bingham and Burleson (1989) found that higher message logics were perceived as more effective and more relation maintaining in situations where a person was responding to sexual harassment.

Thus cognitive complexity and the use of higher message design logics represent important competencies. Even so, it is worth noting that the complexity of one's construct system or the sophistication of one's messages contribute to overall communicative effectiveness only insofar as they are required to satisfy higher-order goals. The real key is to match one's cognitive construal with the complexity of the situation and with the complexity of the goals being sought. Relational satisfaction may depend more on the similarity of the partners' social cognitive skills than on the sheer level of those skills (Burleson & Denton, 1992). In a more specific way, complexity for its own sake may be debilitating because of the deterioration in responsiveness and verbal fluency associated with having more complex mental plans for action (Berger, Karol, & Jordan, 1989; Greene & Lindsey, 1989). Moreover, relationships vary markedly in the complexity of the situations they present. Requesting a favor, for example, may be much more complex in a nonintimate relationship than in an intimate relationship where a history of trust and reciprocation makes direct requests more effective and politeness strategies less necessary (Jordan & Roloff, 1990; Lim, 1990).

Another area of special relevance to the study of communicative competence is the research on errors and bias in the attribution process. The typical person's approach to social judgment seems riddled with shortcomings when judged against rigorous logical standards (Fiske & Taylor, 1984). Among the biases we routinely bring to the attribution process are tendencies to give more weight to information that is vivid, concrete, or readily available; to treat a very small amount of information as if it were highly representative; to search only for information that confirms our preconceptions; to distort or ignore information that violates our expectations; and to overestimate the consistency and constancy of others' behavior. We are also biased by tendencies to rely on preconceived ideas of cause and effect, to prefer simple explanations to complex ones, to underestimate situational influences on others' behavior, and to err in our judgments of how relevant a given piece of information might be.

These findings probably paint an overly dismal picture of our capacities to exert relationship control. Nonetheless, awareness of these biases and the ability to correct for them represent basic competencies. The psychological literature on human inference is rich in ideas for doing so (for example, Nisbett & Ross, 1980). Communication scholars have taken a special interest in the debiasing process by which people compare information they have been given with other information they have indirectly obtained through their social network. Research findings indicate that this "second guessing" is rather common and that people are able to adjust their inferences accurately when they suspect others are presenting biased information (Doelger, Hewes, & Graham, 1986; Hewes, Graham, Doelger, & Pavitt, 1985; Hewes, Graham, Monsour, & Doelger, 1989). Based on these findings, it is apparent that a basic competency is the ability to debias messages by gathering and comparing information about a focal person from others.

Finally, the ability to equivocate and even to lie successfully must be regarded as a basic communicative competency. In the case of equivocation, the source presents a message that is ambiguous with respect to one or more of the following characteristics: its content, the identity of the source, whether it is really directed at the listener, or what the context is. In the case of deception, the source presents a message that is clear but false. Equivocation and deception allow speakers to deal with competing situational and relational demands (Bavelas, Black, Chovil, & Mullett, 1990; Parks, 1982).

Level 7: Program Control

Programs represent comparatively broad and structured sequences of actions. They include acts to be performed and a series of decision rules for determining how to act at any given point, and they may be organized hierarchically (Carver & Scheier, 1982; W. T. Powers, 1973). The ability to organize the welter of constructs and attributions into a coherent framework must count as a fundamental communicative competence. Programs not only direct our behavior but also provide predictions and explanations for others' behavior (Berger & Bradac, 1982).

Programlike structures have been given many names: *cognitive schemata, scripts, regulative rules, procedural records, episodes, unitized assemblies, plans,* and *self-regulatory plans.* These terms are not synonymous, varying in content and level of abstraction, but all share the common theme that people punctuate the stream of interaction into relatively coherent "chunks" that represent general plans for action and evaluation. Programlike structures summarize "action-outcome-in-situation-contingencies" (Greene & Geddes, 1993). They organize and direct lower-order perceptions and behaviors according to some scenario that is itself subordinate to some higher perception of the way the interaction ought to unfold. People probably have thousands of programlike representations by the time they reach adulthood (Abelson, 1976; Schank & Abelson, 1977).

Scholars of communicative competence often assert that one's competence depends upon having a large repertoire of behavioral strategies (for example, Allen & Brown, 1976; Steffen & Redden, 1977; Weinstein, 1969). The more programs one has, the more adaptive and responsive he or she can be. But the sheer size of the repertoire may be less important than its adequacy for the social tasks one routinely faces. Strictly speaking, one's "programming" need only be as extensive as the activities one must pursue.

Writers have also devoted a great deal of attention to the specific content of programs. The collaborative element of competence is reflected in the belief that programs should always contain components that function to maintain and support

Table 15.2   Eight Functional Communicative Skills

Conversational skill
  The ability to initiate, maintain, and end conversations that are enjoyable for all participants

Comforting skill
  The ability to make people feel better when they are down, upset, or depressed

Referential skill
  The ability to convey information to others in a way that can be easily understood

Conflict-management skill
  The ability to reach a solution that is mutually satisfying to the participants in a conflict or dispute

Persuasive skill
  The ability to get people to believe or do things they probably wouldn't otherwise believe or do

Ego-supportive skill
  The ability of one person to make another feel good about him- or herself

Narrative skill
  The ability to entertain people through stories, jokes, and/or gossip

Regulative skill
  The ability to help someone who has broken a commonly held rule or norm understand why his or
  her action was wrong and to discover how to correct the mistake

---

SOURCE: Adapted from Burleson (1990).

the identities of others (Weinstein, 1969; Wiemann, 1977). Educators have devised long lists of ideal speaking and listening skills. Some of the more common entries include abilities to use language in emergency situations, to question others' viewpoints, to organize messages, to use appropriate facial expressions and paralanguage, to distinguish facts from opinions, and to seek or give directions (Allen & Brown, 1976; Backlund, Brown, Gurry, & Jandt, 1982; Rubin, 1982).

One of the most inclusive and useful attempts to specify program contents can be found in the work of Burleson and his colleagues (Burleson, 1990; Burleson, Werking, Samter, & Holloway, 1988). Burleson's approach suggests that our programming must be sufficient to cover eight different functional skill areas. Each of these areas is described in Table 15.2.

Efforts to conceptualize competence in terms of a list of program contents are extremely useful from a practical perspective, but they do not tell the whole story. The various skills and abilities noted above are only useful to the extent that they serve the more general goals of the individual. Moreover, a given behavior may be either an asset or a liability depending on the circumstances. Finally, programs are more than lists of specific behaviors. They are also decision-making mechanisms for sorting out the contingencies of social action (Carver & Scheier, 1982). The criteria by which an individual makes these decisions are at least as important as the content of the decisions themselves.

Even when one possesses the programming to behave competently, it may not be successfully activated and assembled. In perhaps the best available discussion of this problem, Greene and Geddes (1993) describe several factors that might lead to difficulties in implementing programlike structures from memory. These include the failure to see the relevance of the program to the context, the tendency to retrieve more easily plans that have broad rather than narrow application, the inability to override ineffective but habitual behaviors, the loss in effectiveness that occurs when several different programlike structures compete for attention, the inability to reconcile incompatibilities when more than one program is activated, and the tendency to reconcile conflicting programs by using alternative but potentially less effective programs that do not contain conflicting elements.

Our awareness of making the decisions involved with program control probably varies quite widely. It is not so much the degree of conscious awareness of programs that influences communicative competence as the degree to which the level of mindfulness and mindlessness is commensurate to the level of novelty and change in the social and physical context. Chronic mindlessness is no doubt dangerous, however, because it contributes to the belief that one lacks control. Assuming that there is variability in the individual's social environment, chronic mindlessness can cause him or her to become less responsive to changing conditions, thereby impairing behavioral effectivness, reducing self-esteem, and, in extreme instances, damaging her or his health (Rodin & Langer, 1977). On the other hand, there are many routine social situations in which a low level of awareness is acceptable, even desirable (Greene & Geddes, 1993; Langer & Weinman, 1981). These situations lack change and variety, thus making extensive conscious monitoring unnecessary. Although many introductory discussions associate competence with high levels of self-awareness, a more sophisticated view would associate competence with the ability to shift the level of conscious awareness in accordance with situational demands.

Level 8: Principle Control

Communicative competence, of course, requires much more than merely executing the accumulated software of socialization. As we move from program control to still higher levels in the control hierarchy, we encounter a series of general principles that function to decide which programs will be executed, to create new programming, to monitor the degree to which lower-order operations require conscious attention, and to evaluate the successfulness of programs in achieving one's goals (Carver & Scheier, 1982; Newell, Shaw, & Simon, 1963; W. T. Powers, 1973).

Principles are what we often describe as the communicator's goals in a given situation. Communicative competence at this level rests on the ability to select or create programs that are consistent with the goals or principles one wishes to pursue. Maladaptive, unsuccessful behavior often occurs because individuals lack the necessary programming to actualize their principles (Carver & Scheier, 1982). They may, for example, have the goal of being liked by others but have no specific strategies (programs) for achieving that goal. Or they may think they know how to be liked but discover that their behavior fails to elicit the desired result. The fact that programming may be absent or inadequate underscores the importance of the creative aspects of competence. Indeed, the ability to creatively pursue goals under novel circumstances or in the face of disruptions must be ranked among the fundamental competencies. Few of us have difficulty thinking of "regrettable messages," things we wished we had not said (see Knapp, Stafford, & Daly, 1986). Competence is partly in the avoidance of social error but perhaps even more in the ability to engage collaboratively in conversational repairs (see Goffman, 1971; Hall, 1991).

An important source of creativity is the ability to recontextualize memory. Cognitive research shows that we do not so much retrieve memories as re-create them afresh (Kihlstrom, 1981). As memories are re-created, opportunities for recontextualization—that is, to adapt information from different domains and apply it to present problems—occur. Such an ability is closely related to cognitive complexity, and some research supports the belief that cognitively complex individuals should be able to perform more competently in situations where existing programs have been disrupted (Reardon, 1982).

Level 9: System Concept Control

The very highest level of the control hierarchy is usually conceptualized in terms of a system of idealized self-concepts (Carver & Scheier, 1982; Markus & Smith, 1981; W. T. Powers, 1973). These present the most enduring and powerful reference points for our communication (Keenan & Baillet, 1980; Rogers, 1981). More specifically, they function to provide a set of principles or goals, which in turn, as we have already observed, direct and decipher our social encounters. Thus a person whose idealized self-concept contained the system concept "I'm a responsible person" might attempt to realize it by drawing on the principle of "following through on commitments to others" (Carver & Scheier, 1982).

The core competency at the level of system concept control is the ability to translate idealized self-concepts into the more specific principles or goals that direct overt action. People may wish to see themselves as caring and just but behave incompetently because they cannot figure out how to translate those idealized images into concrete interactive objectives.

System concept control also involves our most generalized self-esteem evaluations. Writers from William James (1890) onward have conceptualized self-esteem in terms of our ability to control successfully, that is, to satisfy the goals selected by our idealized self-concepts. Thus the highest level of the control hierarchy contains its own mechanism for evaluating communicative competence. Any measure that taps the individual's assessment of his or her ability to exert control or produce desirable conditions (for example, self-esteem, communication apprehension, perceived control, satisfaction) should also be at least a partial measure of global communicative competence.

Self-concepts and self-esteem do change over time, but only gradually. They are comparatively fixed at any one point, and the individual will act so as to maintain them. The simplest way to do this, of course, is to involve principles, programs, and lower-order operations in ways that reinforce the system concepts. Yet, when failures do occur, we may need to turn to strategies to protect our self-concepts and our perceptions of control (Taylor & Brown, 1988; Thompson, 1981). Reaching out to others for social support in a time of interpersonal crisis accomplishes this. So do a number of more cognitively oriented strategies, such as "self-handicapping" strategies that maintain our perceptions of competence when we expect to fail (Jones & Berglas, 1978).

Competency at this highest level ultimately depends on the ability to select socially tenable self-images. Self-concepts are social in character; they require someone to accept the self we are claiming to be. Some idealized selves are so misaligned with social reality that others cannot reasonably be expected to support them. An extreme example of this might be Goethe's (1774/1990) young Werther, who so obsessively defines himself in terms of his beloved, but unavailable, Lotte that he not only behaves inappropriately and incompetently but, in the end, can find no alternative to suicide. Short of massive delusion, the self that cannot be supported by others cannot ultimately support itself.

Summarizing Competencies in the Control Hierarchy

The control hierarchy offers several advantages over other attempts to organize the literature on communicative competence. First, it is capable of locating and relating extremely diverse activities, everything from idealized self-concepts down to the movements of specific muscles. Second, the control hierarchy easily accommodates both source and receiver perspectives. From a source-oriented or top-driven perspective, communicators attempt to realize their idealized self-conceptions by forming goals that are expressed in programs and that, in turn, create successively more detailed instructions for overt behavior. From a receiver-oriented or bottom-driven perspective, raw sensory input is transformed into progressively larger and more abstract perceptions that allow us to understand successively larger, more complex understandings of interactions and from which we identify our goals and discover both who we are and who we want to be.

Perhaps the most important advantage of the control hierarchy is that it provides a coherent framework for identifying specific communicative competencies. It serves both as a vehicle for summarizing previous research and as a heuristic device for suggesting lines for future research. Thirty of these communicative competencies have been summarized in Table 15.3. Some of these competencies are admittedly more relevant in some settings than others. The competencies in interpersonal settings may overlap with, but also differ from, the competencies required in organizational, media, or other settings.

At the very highest level of the hierarchy, people make their own competency assessments. A person's own global sense of competence is determined by the extent to which he or she feels responsible for satisfying goals and, when the person fails, by the extent to which he or she reacts in ways that promote future success or at least ward off future failure. Because these global competency judgments have such far-reaching consequences for the individual, I will explore them in greater detail in the next section.

Hope and Hopelessness in Global Competency Judgments

I have chosen to orient my discussion of global competency judgments around perceptions of incompetence and failure rather than perceptions of competence and success. This orientation has more implications for training and therapy. It also reflects the harsh fact that failures have more impact than successes. Satisfaction disappears with continued success, but pain does not disappear with continued adversity. Dutch psychologist Nico Frijda (1988) calls this the "iron law of hedonic asymmetry." Accordingly, I begin by relating global competency judgments to the burgeoning literature on helplessness, hopelessness, and depression. I then consider the mechanisms by which perceptions of failure can become generalized across time and situations. Finally, I will address the negative consequences for individuals that generalized judgments of incompetence produce.

Competency, Helplessness, and Hopelessness

Global judgments of incompetence begin with the perception of some failure of control. Incompetence is associated with the belief not only that one's actions have produced undesirable outcomes, but also that one is incapable of altering the

Table 15.3 Specific Communicative Competencies

Level in Control Hierarchy	Competency
9. System Concept	Ability to satisfy personal goals in a given context without jeopardizing more important goals in other contexts
	Ability to translate idealized self-concepts into principles of social interaction
	Ability to draw social support and to use cognitive strategies that preserve the perception of competence when failure occurs
	Ability to select socially viable self-images
8. Principle	Ability to translate principles of action into specific programs of action
	Ability to improvise plans of action when interaction is disrupted
	Ability to collaborate with others in making conversational repairs
	Ability to recontextualize information across situational domains
	Ability to monitor awareness levels and adjust them to the degree of change in the situation
7. Program	Ability to organize diverse constructs and attributions into a coherent plan of action
	Ability to draw on a repertoire of plans for action sufficiently large to address common situational needs
	Ability to match plans of action to situational constraints and to resolve conflicts among relevant alternatives
	Ability to incorporate concerns for others' identities into messages
6. Relationship	Ability to match complexity of messages and interpretations to the complexity of the goals sought and the relationship with others present
	Ability to interpret one's own actions and the actions of others from a variety of perspectives
	Ability to predict and explain others' behavior, to empathize or role-take to the degree required to satisfy personal goals
	Ability to revise interpretations of events and people in accordance with changing goals and situational demands
	Ability to create messages that increase the complexity of others' perspectives on persons and interactions
	Ability to recognize and adjust to common attributional biases
	Ability to reconcile conflicting goals with equivocal or deceptive messages
5. Sequence	Ability to judge the appropriateness of conversational topics
	Ability to manage turn-taking, to synchronize verbal and nonverbal contributions with those of others
	Ability to detect omissions or errors in others' messages
	Ability to decode verbal and nonverbal patterns accurately
	Ability to produce verbal and nonverbal codes in coherent sequences or "chunks"
4. Transition	Ability to organize muscle movements into decodable words and nonverbal cues
3. Configuration	Ability to discriminate degrees of emotional intensity in verbal and nonverbal displays
	Ability to decode verbal and nonverbal cues accurately
2. Sensation	Ability to package specific muscle movements into varying verbal and nonverbal cues
1. Intensity	Ability to code and decode faithfully raw sensory information

negative outcomes. Most of our general measures of communicative competence tap these perceived failures of interpersonal control (for descriptions of these measures, see Spitzberg & Cupach, 1989). The perception of failure can take one of two forms (Bandura, 1977). It may be based on the belief that one lacks the ability or skill to make an effective response, or it may be based on the belief that there is simply no response that could produce positive outcomes.

Failure, however, is not sufficient to produce perceptions of global incompetence. Interpersonal failures may lead either to renewed efforts to achieve positive outcomes or to feelings of incompetence, helplessness, and even hopelessness. The determining factor is the degree of hope or hopelessness that the individual assigns to his or her ability to change negative outcomes (Abramson, Metalsky, & Alloy, 1989). If the individual believes that negative consequences can be altered, then renewed efforts to achieve will follow, and perceptions of competence need not suffer. If, on the other hand, the individual believes that positive outcomes will not occur and that there is nothing she or he can do to avoid negative outcomes, a sense of hopelessness, depression, and incompetence sets in.

Perceptions of hope and hopelessness are heavily influenced by the causal attributions the actor makes for failure. When the failure can be attributed to transitory or controllable causes, feelings of helplessness and hopelessness are reduced and future performance may be unaffected or even improved. However, when failures are attributed to uncontrollable stable, global external causes (for example, discrimination on the part of others) or to stable, global internal characteristics of the self, feelings of helplessness and hopelessness are amplified, and performance suffers (Abramson, Seligman, & Teasdale, 1978; Abramson et al., 1989; Miller & Norman, 1979). A prime example of this occurs when the individual attributes communicative failures to negative characteristics of the self such as character defects or a lack of social skill.

The significance of these attributional patterns is underscored by research relating them to clinical depression. In a meta-analysis of 104 studies involving almost 15,000 subjects, Sweeney, Anderson, and Bailey (1986) found consistent positive associations between depression and the tendency to attribute negative events to internal, stable, and global causes. They also found a positive relationship between depression and the perception that the individual lacked ability. A more recent meta-analysis by Segrin (1990) also confirmed the positive relationship between depression and perceived social skill deficits. In short, sense-making patterns that center on the inability to avoid negative outcomes rob the individual of hope, in turn leading to feelings of incompetence and depression and to impaired interpersonal performance.

People who believe that their social failures are due to uncontrollable causes also experience high levels of anxiety when they are called upon to interact. Hopeless depression and social anxiety frequently occur together (Abramson et al., 1989). In one recent study, anxiety emerged as the single strongest correlate of depression when interactions of depressed and nondepressed persons were compared along 12 self-report and observer-rated measures of social skill (Segrin, 1992).

Many of the communicative anxiety variables familiar to communication scholars can be subsumed under the helplessness/hopelessness framework. These include communication apprehension (McCroskey, 1977, 1982b; Richmond & McCroskey, 1985), reticence (Phillips, 1968, 1991), stage fright (Clevenger, 1959), unwillingness to communicate (Burgoon, 1976), predispositions toward verbal behavior (Mortensen, Arntson, & Lustig, 1977), and shyness (Buss, 1984; Zimbardo, 1977). There are obviously differences among these terms, but they all share molar similarities. All of them focus on the actual or anticipated failure to produce predictable, positive outcomes in communicative settings. Each is a form of incompetence. Each can be conceptualized in terms of the helplessness/hopelessness framework and each should reflect the sense-making patterns that, when generalized, become characteristic of depression.

These considerations underline the value of cognitive restructuring as part of a treatment program for communicative incompetence. Improving discrete communication skills is certainly important. As Phillips (1991) points out, improving behavior alone can lead to positive outcomes, which, in turn, create enhanced self-esteem. The best results, however, are likely to be obtained when behavioral training and cognitive restructuring are used together. Although the data on the treatment of communicative incompetence are far from complete, cognitive therapies do figure prominently in the treatment of depression and are often more effective than therapies involving antidepressive drugs or behavioral skills training alone (see Abramson et al., 1989; Beck, Rush, Shaw, & Emery, 1979).

The Generalization of Competence and Incompetence

A given individual's level of competence or incompetence exists along a continuum of generalization. That is, some people display a great deal more cross-situational consistency in their behavior than others. This fact has long been recognized by communication researchers interested in competence and its conceptual cousins like communication apprehension. There are several approaches to classifying degrees of generalization: traits versus states, situational responses versus dispositions, or traits versus contexts versus audiences versus specific situations (Duran, 1992; McCroskey, 1982b; Spitzberg & Cupach, 1989).

Although previous approaches to communication competence and apprehension are useful for identifying degrees of generalization, they have less to say about its causes. Work on the cognitive elements in helplessness and hopelessness is much more informative in this respect. It suggests that the degree of generalization should depend on the structure of the individual's attributions for success or failure (Abramson et al., 1978; Miller & Norman, 1979; Sweeney et al., 1986). Successes and failures that are attributed to internal, stable, and global causes are more likely to generalize from one situation to another. Suppose, to illustrate, that a manager fails to persuade her superior to make a desired policy change. If she attributes the cause to something like lacking persuasive skill or assertiveness, she will be more likely to generalize the expectation of failure to other situations. A failure caused by something rather general and enduring about oneself is likely to occur again. If, however, she concludes that this failure was the result of the boss being distracted, her lack of preparation, or her inability to use a particular persuasive strategy, then less generalization should occur because causes of failure are seen as transitory and potentially more controllable. The same dynamics apply to successes. Expectations of success are likely to generalize when people attribute them to internal, stable, and global characteristics.

Performance follows these expectations, so that people who expect to fail in more and more situations will actually fail in more and more situations. Once expectations of success or failure begin to generalize, the pace of generalization is likely to accelerate because outcomes that are consistent with expectations are more likely to be attributed to internal causes than outcomes that are inconsistent with expectations (Abramson et al., 1978; Miller & Norman, 1979; Sweeney et al., 1986). In other words, new failures or successes are likely to be attributed to the same internal causes that created the previous failures or successes.

Consequences of Generalized Incompetence

Chronic failures in the communicative control process result in anxiety, in the loss of motivation to perform, in disruptions in actual performance, in cognitive deficits, in negative emotional responses, and ultimately in mental and physical illness. Lines of research from nearly every approach related to the control process converge in support of this point.

The first recourse of the incompetent communicator is simply to avoid those situations in which failure is expected. Avoidance behavior has been documented extensively in the literature on helplessness and shyness (for example, Cheek & Buss, 1981; Diener & Dweck, 1978; Zimbardo, 1977). Reviews of the literature on communicative anxiety also document wide patterns of avoidance (for example, Daly & Stafford, 1984; Richmond & McCroskey, 1985). These include tendencies to avoid seating positions, group roles, employment opportunities, and even housing options that require interaction with others.

If complete avoidance is not possible, chronically incompetent communicators avoid as much of the interaction as possible by minimizing their responsiveness. Research with communication apprehensives, for example, reveals a consistent pattern of reduced eye contact, minimal head and body movement, and a preference for body positions that distance the individual from fellow communicators (Daly & Stafford, 1984). Similar patterns can be observed in the communication of depressed persons. Compared with nondepressed persons, depressed subjects smile less, look at their conversational partners less often, take fewer speaking turns, and are perceived to be generally less responsive (Segrin, 1992).

Task performance suffers under these conditions, further reinforcing and generalizing the individual's sense of incompetence. Performance difficulties have been documented across a wide range of social tasks in the literature on communicative anxiety (Daly & Stafford, 1984; Richmond & McCroskey, 1985), shyness (Zimbardo, 1977), learned helplessness, and depression (Abramson et al., 1989). Communicative competence can also be associated with performance on less social tasks. A number of studies, for example, reveal a positive correlation between academic performance and communicative competence (for example, Rubin & Graham, 1988).

These performance difficulties are exacerbated by a number of cognitive deficits that ultimately impair future performance and reinforce the expectation of failure. These include failures to monitor ongoing performance and to remind oneself to concentrate (Diener & Dweck, 1978). Other cognitive deficits revolve around the way people judge performance. Helpless, depressed persons overestimate the number of failures they have had in the past and do not allow their successes to alter their expectation of future failure (Abramson et al., 1978; Diener & Dweck, 1980).

Negative emotional responses characterize the incompetent individual. Many of these are directed at the self: fatigue, frustration, guilt, self-blame, self-criticism, and reduced self-esteem (Miller & Norman, 1979). However, incompetent persons also direct hostility at others or at society in general. Delinquent behavior among adolescents of both sexes is negatively related to scores on measures of interpersonal problem-solving competence (for example, Freedman, Rosenthal, Donahoe, Schlundt, & McFall, 1978; Gaffney & McFall, 1981). Even when communicatively incompetent persons do not mean to do so, their behavior will often be interpreted as hostile by those who do not know them, as Burgoon and Koper (1984) found when they had strangers view videotapes of shy persons interacting.

Repeated failures in the control process are closely associated with depression, as I have already noted. They are also associated with borderline personality disorders and suicidal behavior (Abramson et al., 1989). The health risks of generalized social incompetence are only now being quantified. Even so, House, Landis, and Umberson (1988) concluded that the data linking disease and mortality to the inability to form adequate social relationships are now stronger than the evidence that first prompted the surgeon general to issue public warnings on the risks of cigarette smoking in 1964.

The dire consequences associated with generalized incompetence occur for relatively few people, though most people probably experience them to some degree when they fail at some communicative task. The intensity of response to a given communicative failure will depend to a great extent on the causal attributions the individual makes for the failure. Negative consequences are more extreme when the individual attributes failures to personal characteristics or to factors that are beyond her or his control. Three other factors appear to influence the intensity of response to interpersonal failures (Abramson et al., 1989; Thompson, 1981). One is the subjective importance of the task. The more important it is to a person, the more intense the feeling of incompetence that results from failure. Another factor is the individual's ability to predict the onset and duration of stressful events. When stressful events occur without warning and have uncertain durations, feelings of incompetence and its associated symptoms should be more intense. Finally, the availability of social support should mediate the experience of failures. Reactions to failure should be more intense when the individual lacks sources of emotional support and aid.

Personal Control in Social Context

In spite of the importance of the interpersonal control process, few writers equate competence with the unbridled pursuit of personal control. A review of the definitions presented earlier in the chapter reveals that most writers argue for limits (see Table 15.1). These include the constraint that competent control activities are confined to what others judge to be socially appropriate, and the related constraints specifying that interaction should be mutually satisfying and should support the identities of all participants. Images of interpersonal collaboration through socially appropriate behavior run across the breadth of the literature dealing with social competence (Spitzberg & Cupach, 1989).

Unfortunately, the relationship between effective personal control and social appropriateness is considerably more complex than is often acknowledged. Codes of appropriateness are not merely constraints on the pursuit of personal control. They are also both a means of achieving personal control and a product of personal control.

Codes of propriety and collaboration contribute to personal control in several ways. For one thing, they remind us of the fact that our outcomes are interrelated over time. Thus the salesperson who makes a sale by treating the customer in socially inappropriate, yet effective ways is comparatively incompetent because such behavior is likely to lead to more complaints, fewer repeat customers, and fewer new customers. Socially appropriate behavior is also prompted by the recognition that we will often have to help others satisfy their goals in order to get them to help satisfy our goals. Competence and the ability to engage in social contracts go hand in hand (Athay & Darley, 1981).

More often than not, communicators will have a vested interest in the success of one another's control efforts. In many cases, personal goals are shared with others and a concern for mutually acceptable behavior is a reflection of mutual goals. But it is also in our interest to help others when their goals differ from ours. People who consistently fail to satisfy their goals are likely to display more anger, to be violent, to be more exploitative, to be less generous, and to be less cooperative (Forsyth & McMillan, 1981; Hokanson, Sacco, Blumberg, & Landrum, 1980; Miller & Norman, 1979; Zimbardo, 1977).

These considerations suggest that perceptions of effectiveness and appropriateness, instead of being antagonistic, should be compatible. This belief is partially supported by the general trend for studies to find positive correlations between measures of effectiveness and appropriateness (Canary & Spitzberg, 1987, 1989; Spitzberg & Canary, 1985). One limitation of these studies, however, is that they usually correlate the subjects' perceptions of their own effectiveness with their perceptions of their conversational partner's appropriateness. In terms of the theoretical tensions between appropriateness and effectiveness, it would be more informative to examine the correlation between the subjects' perceptions of their own effectiveness and their partner's perceptions of the subject's appropriateness.

One final factor complicates the relationship between personal effectiveness and social appropriateness. To advocate that personal control efforts be limited to socially appropriate behavior is to assume that the current social arrangements are just. It is not difficult, however, to think of examples where the rules for conduct are patently unjust, whether in the dysfunctional family or the oppressive government. Thus it is through the pursuit of what others would call inappropriate personal control that we liberate ourselves from unjust social groups and institutions.

Summary

Human interaction is inherently strategic. This view extends from the roots of classical rhetoric to the modern flowering of communication science. Certainly every conception of communicative competence rests on a strategic perspective. And the heart of the strategic perspective is the interpersonal control process. Its essence is found in the way individuals pursue their goals with others. I have built upon previous definitions of competence to suggest:

> Communicative competence represents the degree to which individuals satisfy and perceive that they have satisfied their goals within the limits of a given social situation and without jeopardizing their ability or opportunity to pursue their other subjectively more important goals.

While the concept of control is highlighted in this definition, competent communicators are people who exert control in ways that are both adaptive and collaborative. Doing so requires the further virtues of responsibility and foresight.

The concept of interpersonal control or effectiveness is at the heart of almost all definitions of communicative competence. It is a unifying metatheoretical construct that empowers individual action and allows us to make sense of ourselves and others. Images of interpersonal influence simply imply that people find some consequences of their communication to be more desirable than others and therefore communicate so as to obtain the more desirable ones (Miller & Steinberg,

1975). This does not mean that we are relentless profit maximizers. Because we usually have multiple goals scattered across multiple situations, we usually move on to other tasks as soon as an adequate solution is found. We satisfy rather than maximize (Simon, 1979).

One road map to the often bewildering range of activities associated with communicative competence is control theory (Carver & Scheier, 1982; W. T. Powers, 1973). In this theory, the process of personal control is seen as unfolding across nine hierarchically organized and cybernetically interconnected levels. At each level, from the lowest levels of raw sensory input and muscle motion to the highest levels of idealized self-concepts, I have paused to look at the road map and ask: What constitutes competence at this level of action or interpretation? This leads to the identification of about 30 specific communication competencies (Table 15.3). Control theory provides a convenient way of organizing previous research conducted in many different settings. Most well-recognized competencies are included in the list. Control theory is also heuristic, helping us identify underresearched competencies.

Some might argue that placing interpersonal control at the heart of communication competence represents a uniquely Western cultural perspective. I would disagree. There is obviously wide cultural variation with respect to what goals are appropriate to pursue and what strategies are appropriate for pursuing them. Certainly some cultures privilege communal goals over purely individual goals. Nonetheless, even when one is seeking a communal goal, it is for that person also an individual goal. The communicative competencies I have presented (see Table 15.3) are relevant across many cultures, even as the particulars of goals and strategies change.

The most important judgments of competence and incompetence are the ones individuals make for themselves. Judgments of competence and incompetence have far-reaching impact. If we look across the research on competence, communicative anxiety, helplessness, and depression, we find that feelings of incompetence are associated with avoidance, a loss of motivation to perform, anxiety and withdrawal, decreased social responsiveness, deficits in actual performance, a variety of cognitive and emotional difficulties, negative self-evaluations, and mental and physical illness. Moreover, incompetent communicators are likely to treat others poorly, sometimes reacting with hostility and violence. A sense of interpersonal control therefore not only is essential for the individual's own well-being but also promotes prosocial behavior toward others.

Competence implies not only that goals are satisfied but also that individuals feel responsible for their success. This does not mean that people must take total responsibility, only that they can meaningfully connect their actions to their outcomes. Those who do not feel responsible for their share of the positive consequences are unlikely to feel competent and are less likely to continue behaviors that ensure positive outcomes in the future.

Of course, people do not always accurately judge the relationship between their own efforts and the outcomes they receive. There is what I would call "false competence" and "ignorant competence." False competence occurs when the individual takes responsibility for positive consequences that he or she did not actually produce. Conversely, ignorant competence occurs when the individual fails to take responsibility for positive consequences that he or she did in fact produce. True communicative competence, as I have defined it, requires control and responsibility in both perception and fact.

Finally, competent communicators have the foresight to recognize three essential qualities of social life. First, there are limits to how much any given situation or person can be controlled. Expecting to influence others in unrealistic ways is a mark of incompetence. In popular parlance, it is a mark of "codependence" (Beattie, 1987). Second, competent communicators have the foresight to recognize that their goals are interdependent. The pursuit of any one goal may influence the opportunity to pursue other goals. Success at all costs is a mark of incompetence because it usually results in the frustration of the individual's other goals. Third, competent communicators recognize that they usually have a vested interest in maintaining the rules of social conduct because they recognize, however dimly, that their ability to pursue their own goals often depends on the freedom of others to pursue their goals. Interpersonal control, then, is more often the ally of social appropriateness than its enemy.

References

Abelson, R. P. (1976). Script processing in attitude formation and decision-making. In J. S. Carroll & J. W. Payne (Eds.), *Cognition and social behavior* (pp. 33-45). Hillsdale, NJ: Lawrence Erlbaum.

Abramson, L. Y., Metalsky, G. I., & Alloy, L. B. (1989). Hopelessness depression: A theory-based subtype of depression. *Psychological Review, 96*, 358-372.

Abramson, L. Y., Seligman, M. E. P., & Teasdale, J. D. (1978). Learned helplessness in humans: Critique and reformulation. *Journal of Abnormal Psychology, 87*, 49-74.

Allen, R. R., & Brown, K. L. (Eds.). (1976). *Developing communication competence in children.* Skokie, IL: National Textbook.

Argyris, C. (1965). Explorations in interpersonal competence—I. *Journal of Applied Behavioral Science, 1*, 58-83.

Athay, M., & Darley, J. M. (1981). Toward an interaction-centered theory of personality. In N. Cantor & J. F. Kihlstrom (Eds.), *Personality, cognition, and social interaction* (pp. 281-308). Hillsdale, NJ: Lawrence Erlbaum.

Backlund, P. M., Brown, K. L., Gurry, J., & Jandt, F. (1982). Recommendations for assessing speaking and listening skills. *Communication Education, 31*, 9-17.

Bandura, A. (1977). Self-efficacy: Toward a unifying theory of behavioral change. *Psychological Review, 84*, 191-215.

Bargh, J. A. (1989). Conditional automaticity: Varieties of autonomic influence in social perception and cognition. In J. S. Uleman & J. A. Bargh (Eds.), *Unintended thought* (pp. 3-51). New York: Guilford.

Bavelas, J. B., Black, A., Chovil, N., & Mullett, J. (1990). *Equivocal communication.* Newbury Park, CA: Sage.

Bavelas, J. B., & Coates, L. (1992). How do we account for the mindfulness of face-to-face dialogue? *Communication Monographs, 59*, 301-305.

Beattie, M. (1987). *Codependent no more.* Center City, MN: Hazelden Foundation.

Beck, A. T., Rush, A. J., Shaw, B. F., & Emery, G. (1979). *Cognitive therapy of depression.* New York: Guilford.

Berger, C. R., & Bradac, J. J. (1982). *Language and social knowledge.* London: Edward Arnold.

Berger, C. R., Karol, S. H., & Jordan, J. M. (1989). When a lot of knowledge is a dangerous thing: The debilitating effects of plan complexity on verbal fluency. *Human Communication Research, 16*, 91-119.

Bingham, S. G., & Burleson, B. R. (1989). Multiple effects of messages with multiple goals. *Human Communication Research, 16*, 184-216.

Bochner, A. P., & Kelly, C. W. (1974). Interpersonal competence: Rationale, philosophy, and implementation of a conceptual framework. *Speech Teacher, 23*, 270-301.

Bower, G. H., & Cirilo, R. K. (1985). Cognitive psychology and text processing. In T. A. Van Dijk (Ed.), *Handbook of discourse analysis* (Vol. 1, pp. 71-105). Orlando, FL: Academic.

Brown, P., & Levinson, S. (1978). Universals in language usage: Politeness phenomena. In E. N. Goody (Ed.), *Questions and politeness* (pp. 56-311). Cambridge: Cambridge University Press.

Burgoon, J. K. (1976). The unwillingness-to-communicate scale: Development and validation. *Communication Monographs, 43,* 60-69.

Burgoon, J. K., & Koper, R. J. (1984). Nonverbal and relational communication associated with reticence. *Human Communication Research, 10,* 601-626.

Burleson, B. R. (1987). Cognitive complexity. In J. C. McCroskey & J. A. Daly (Eds.), *Personality and interpersonal communication* (pp. 305-349). Newbury Park, CA: Sage.

Burleson, B. R. (1990). Comforting as social support: Relational consequences of supportive behaviors. In S. Duck with R. Silver (Eds.), *Personal relationships and social support* (pp. 66-82). London: Sage.

Burleson, B. R., & Denton, W. H. (1992). A new look at similarity and attraction in marriage: Similarity in social-cognitive and communication skills as predictors of attraction and satisfaction. *Communication Monographs, 59,* 268-287.

Burleson, B. R., Werking, K. J., Samter, W., & Holloway, R. (1988, May). *Person-centered communication and friendship in young adults: Which skills matter most?* Paper presented at the annual convention of the Speech Communication Association, New Orleans.

Buss, A. H. (1984). A conception of shyness. In J. A. Daly & J. C. McCroskey (Eds.), *Avoiding communication* (pp. 39-50). Beverly Hills, CA: Sage.

Canary, D. J., & Spitzberg, B. H. (1987). Appropriateness and effectiveness perceptions of conflict strategies. *Human Communication Research, 14,* 93-118.

Canary, D. J., & Spitzberg, B. H. (1989). A model of the perceived competence of conflict strategies. *Human Communication Research, 15,* 630-649.

Carver, C. S., & Scheier, M. F. (1982). Control theory: A useful conceptual framework for personality-social, clinical, and health psychology. *Psychological Bulletin, 92,* 111-135.

Cheek, J. M., & Buss, A. H. (1981). Shyness and sociability. *Journal of Personality and Social Psychology, 41,* 330-339.

Chomsky, N. (1965). *Aspects of a theory of syntax.* Cambridge: MIT Press.

Clark, H. H., & Clark, E. V. (1977). *Psychology and language: An introduction to psycholinguistics.* New York: Harcourt Brace Jovanovich.

Clark, R. A., & Delia, J. G. (1979). Topoi and rhetorical competence. *Quarterly Journal of Speech, 65,* 187-206.

Clevenger, T. (1959). A synthesis of experimental research in stage fright. *Quarterly Journal of Speech, 45,* 134-145.

Curran, J. P. (1982). A procedure for the assessment of social skills: The simulated social interaction tests. In J. P. Curran & P. M. Monti (Eds.), *Social skills training* (pp. 348-398). New York: Guilford.

Curran, J. P., Wallander, J. L., & Fischetti, M. (1980). The importance of behavioral and cognitive factors in heterosexual-social anxiety. *Journal of Personality, 48,* 285-292.

Daly, J. A., & Stafford, L. (1984). Correlates and consequences of social-communicative anxiety. In J. A. Daly & J. C. McCroskey (Eds.), *Avoiding communication* (pp. 125-144). Beverly Hills, CA: Sage.

Delia, J. G., O'Keefe, B. J., & O'Keefe, D. J. (1982). The constructivist approach to communication. In F. E. X. Dance (Ed.), *Human communication theory: Comparative essays* (pp. 147-191). New York: Harper & Row.

Diener, C. I., & Dweck, C. S. (1978). An analysis of learned helplessness: Continuous changes in performance, strategy, and achievement cognitions following failure. *Journal of Personality and Social Psychology, 36,* 451-462.

Diener, C. I., & Dweck, C. S. (1980). An analysis of learned helplessness: II. The processing of success. *Journal of Personality and Social Psychology, 39,* 940-952.

Dodge, C. S., Heimberg, R. G., Nyman, D., & O'Brien, G. T. (1987). Daily heterosocial interactions of high and low social anxious college students: A diary study. *Behavior Therapy, 18,* 90-96.

Doelger, J. A., Hewes, D. E., & Graham, M. L. (1986). Knowing when to "second-guess": The mindful analysis of messages. *Human Communication Research, 12,* 301-338.

Duran, R. L. (1983). Communicative adaptability: A measure of social communicative competence. *Communication Quarterly, 31,* 320-326.

Duran, R. L. (1992). Communicative adaptability: A review of conceptualization and measurement. *Communication Quarterly, 40,* 253-268.

Etzioni, A. (1961). *A comparative analysis of complex organizations.* New York: Free Press.

Fiske, S. T., & Taylor, S. E. (1984). *Social cognition.* New York: Random House.

Flavell, J. H., Speer, J. R., & Green, F. L. (1981). The development of comprehension monitoring and knowledge about communication. *Monographs for the Society for Research in Child Development, 46,* 1-65.

Foote, N. N., & Cottrell, L. S. (1955). *Identity and interpersonal competence.* Chicago: University of Chicago Press.

Ford, M. E. (1985). The concept of competence: Themes and variations. In H. A. Marlowe & R. B. Weinberg (Eds.), *Competence development: Theory and practice in special populations* (pp. 3-49). Springfield, IL: Charles C Thomas.

Forsyth, D. R., & McMillan, J. H. (1981). Attributions, affect, and expectations: A test of Weiner's three-dimensional model. *Journal of Educational Psychology, 73,* 393-403.

Freedman, B. J., Rosenthal, L., Donahoe, C. P., Schlundt, D. G., & McFall, R. M. (1978). A social-behavioral analysis of skill deficits in delinquent and nondelinquent adolescent boys. *Journal of Consulting and Clinical Psychology, 46,* 1448-1462.

French, R. P., & Raven, B. (1960). The bases of social power. In D. Cartwright & A. Zander (Eds.), *Group dynamics* (pp. 607-623). Evanston, IL: Row, Peterson.

Frijda, N. H. (1988). The laws of emotion. *American Psychologist, 43,* 349-358.

Gaffney, L. R., & McFall, R. M. (1981). A comparison of social skills in delinquent and nondelinquent adolescent girls using a behavioral role-playing inventory. *Journal of Consulting and Clinical Psychology, 49,* 959-967.

Goethe, W. (1990). *The sorrows of young Werther.* New York: Vintage. (Original work published 1774)

Goffman, E. (1959). *The presentation of self in everyday life.* Garden City, NY: Doubleday/Anchor.

Goffman, E. (1967). *Interaction ritual.* Garden City, NY: Doubleday/Anchor.

Goffman, E. (1971). *Relations in public.* New York: Basic Books.

Gottman, J. M., & Levenson, R. W. (1984). Why marriages fail: Affective and physiological patterns in marital interaction. In J. Masters (Ed.), *Boundary areas in social and developmental psychology* (pp. 67-106). New York: Academic Press.

Gottman, J. M., & Porterfield, A. L. (1981). Communicative competence in the nonverbal behavior of married couples. *Journal of Marriage and the Family, 43,* 817-824.

Greene, J. O. (1984). A cognitive approach to human communication: An action assembly theory. *Communication Monographs, 51,* 289-306.

Greene, J. O., & Geddes, D. (1993). An action assembly perspective on social skill. *Communication Theory, 3,* 26-49.

Greene, J. O., & Lindsey, A. E. (1989). Encoding processes in the production of multiple-goal messages. *Human Communication Research, 16,* 120-140.

Hale, C., & Delia, J. (1976). Cognitive complexity and social perspective-taking. *Communication Monographs, 43,* 195-203.

Haley, J. (1967). Speech sequences of normal and abnormal families with two children present. *Family Process, 6,* 81-97.

Hall, B. J. (1991). An elaboration of the structural possibilities for engaging in alignment episodes. *Communication Monographs, 58,* 79-100.

Harless, E. L., & McConnell, F. (1982). Effects of hearing aid use on a self concept in older persons. *Journal of Speech and Hearing Disorders, 47,* 305-309.

Hazleton, V., Cupach, W. R., & Canary, D. J. (1987). Situation perception: Interactions between competence and messages. *Journal of Language and Social Psychology, 6,* 57-63.

Hebb, D. O., & Thompson, W. R. (1954). The social significance of animal studies. In G. Lindzey (Ed.), *Handbook of social psychology* (Vol. 1, pp. 532-561). Cambridge, MA: Addison-Wesley.

Hewes, D. E., Graham, M. L., Doelger, J., & Pavitt, C. (1985). "Second-guessing": Message interpretation in social networks. *Human Communication Research, 11,* 299-334.

Hewes, D. E., Graham, M. L., Monsour, M., & Doelger, J. A. (1989). Cognition and social information-gathering strategies: Reinterpretation assessment in second-guessing. *Human Communication Research, 16,* 297-321.

Hokanson, J. E., Sacco, W. P., Blumberg, S. R., & Landrum, G. C. (1980). Interpersonal behavior of depressive individuals in a mixed-motive game. *Journal of Abnormal Psychology, 89,* 320-332.

House, J. S., Landis, K. R., & Umberson, D. (1988). Social relationships and health. *Science, 241,* 540-545.

Hymes, D. (1974). *Foundations in sociolinguistics.* Philadelphia: University of Pennsylvania Press.

James, W. (1890). *The principles of psychology.* New York: Holt, Rinehart & Winston.

Jones, E. E., & Berglas, S. (1978). Control of attributions about the self through self handicapping strategies: The appeal of alcohol and the role of underachievement. *Personality and Social Psychology Bulletin, 4,* 200-206.

Jones, E. E., & Nisbett, R. E. (1972). The actor and the observer: Divergent perceptions of the causes of behavior. In E. E. Jones, D. E. Kanouse, H. H. Kelley, R. E. Nisbett, S. Valins, & B. Weiner (Eds.), *Attribution: Perceiving the causes of behavior* (pp. 79-94). Morristown, NJ: General Learning Press.

Jordan, J. M., & Roloff, M. E. (1990). Acquiring assistance from others: The effect of indirect requests and relational intimacy on verbal compliance. *Human Communication Research, 16,* 519-555.

Keenan, J. M., & Baillet, S. D. (1980). Memory for personally and socially significant events. In R. S. Nickerson (Ed.), *Attention and performance* (Vol. 8, pp. 651-669). Hillsdale, NJ: Lawrence Erlbaum.

Kellermann, K. (1992). Communication: Inherently strategic and primarily automatic. *Communication Monographs, 59,* 288-300.

Kelley, H. H. (1972). Attribution theory in social interaction. In E. E. Jones et al. (Eds.), *Attribution: Perceiving the causes of behavior* (pp. 1-26). Morristown, NJ: General Learning Press.

Kelley, H. H., & Thibaut, J. W. (1978). *Interpersonal relations: A theory of interdependence.* New York: Wiley.

Kelly, G. A. (1955). *The psychology of personal constructs* (Vols. 1, 2). New York: Norton.

Kihlstrom, J. F. (1981). On personality and memory. In N. Cantor & J. F. Kihlstrom (Eds.), *Personality, cognition and social interaction* (pp. 123-149). Hillsdale, NJ: Lawrence Erlbaum.

Knapp, M. L., Stafford, L., & Daly, J. A. (1986). Regrettable messages: Things people wish they hadn't said. *Journal of Communication, 36,* 40-58.

Kolko, D. J., & Milan, M. A. (1985). Conceptual and methodological issues in the behavioral assessment of heterosocial skills. In L. L'Abate & M. A. Milan (Eds.), *Handbook of social skills training and research* (pp. 50-73). New York: Wiley.

Kuiper, N. A., & McCabe, S. B. (1985). The appropriateness of social topics: Effects of depression and cognitive vulnerability on self and other judgments. *Cognitive Therapy and Research, 9,* 371-379.

Langer, E. J., & Weinman, C. (1981). When thinking disrupts performance: Mindfulness on an overlearned task. *Personality and Social Psychology Bulletin, 7,* 240-243.

Larson, C., Backlund, P., Redmond, M., & Barbour, A. (1978). *Assessing functional communication.* Falls Church, VA: Speech Communication Association and ERIC.

Leuba, C. (1955). Toward some integration of learning theories: The concept of optimal stimulation. *Psychological Reports, 1,* 27-33.

Lim, T. (1990). Politeness behavior in social influence situations. In J. P. Dillard (Ed.), *Seeking compliance: The production of interpersonal influence messages* (pp. 75-86). Scottsdale, AZ: Gorsuch Scarisbrick.

Markus, H., & Smith, J. (1981). The influence of self-schema on the perception of others. In N. Cantor & J. F. Kihlstrom (Eds.), *Personality, cognition, and social interaction* (pp. 233-262). Hillsdale, NJ: Lawrence Erlbaum.

Marwell, G., & Schmitt, D. (1969). Dimensions of compliance-gaining behavior: An empirical analysis. *Sociometry, 30,* 350-364.

McCroskey, J. C. (1977). Oral communication apprehension: A summary of recent theory and research. *Human Communication Research, 4,* 78-96.

McCroskey, J. C. (1982a). Communication competence and performance: A research and pedagogical perspective. *Communication Education, 31,* 1-7.

McCroskey, J. C. (1982b). Oral communication apprehension: A reconceptualization. In M. Burgoon (Ed.), *Communication yearbook 6* (pp. 136-170). Beverly Hills, CA: Sage.

McQuillen, J. S. (1986). The development of listener-adapted compliance-resisting strategies. *Human Communication Research, 12,* 359-375.

Miller, G. R., & Steinberg, M. (1975). *Between people: A new analysis of interpersonal communication.* Chicago: Science Research Associates.

Miller, I. W., & Norman, W. H. (1979). Learned helplessness in humans: A review and attribution-theory model. *Psychological Bulletin, 86,* 93-118.

Mischel, W. (1973). Toward a cognitive social learning reconceptualization of personality. *Psychological Review, 80,* 252-283.

Mortensen, C. D., Arntson, P. H., & Lustig, M. (1977). The measurement of verbal predispositions: Scale development and application. *Human Communication Research, 3,* 146-158.

Motley, M. T. (1986). The production of verbal slips and double entendres as clues to the efficiency of normal speech production. *Journal of Language and Social Psychology, 4,* 275-293.

Motley, M. T., Camden, C. T., & Baars, B. J. (1982). Experimental verbal slip studies: A review and an editing model of language encoding. *Communication Monographs, 50,* 421-432.

Neuliep, J. W., & Hazleton, V. (1986). Enhanced conversation recall and reduced conversational interference as a function of cognitive complexity. *Human Communication Research, 13,* 211-224.

Newell, A., Shaw, J., & Simon, H. A. (1963). Chess-playing programs and the problem of complexity. In E. Feigenbaum & J. Feldman (Eds.), *Computers and thought* (pp. 39-70). New York: McGraw-Hill.

Nisbett, R., & Ross, L. (1980). *Human inference: Strategies and shortcomings of social judgment.* Englewood Cliffs, NJ: Prentice-Hall.

O'Keefe, B. J. (1988). The logic of message design: Individual differences in reasoning about communication. *Communication Monographs, 55,* 80-103.

O'Keefe, B. J., & Delia, J. G. (1982). Impression formation and message production. In M. E. Roloff & C. R. Berger (Eds.), *Social cognition and communication* (pp. 33-72). Beverly Hills, CA: Sage.

O'Keefe, B. J., & McCornack, S. A. (1987). Message design logic and message goal structure: Effects on perceptions of message quality in regulative communication situations. *Human Communication Research, 14,* 68-92.

O'Keefe, B. J., & Shepard, G. J. (1987). The pursuit of multiple objectives in face-to-face persuasive interactions: Effects of construct differentiation on message organization. *Communication Monographs, 54,* 396-419.

Parks, M. R. (1977a, October). *Issues in the explication of communication competence.* Paper presented at the annual convention of the Western Speech Communication Association, Phoenix, AZ.

Parks, M. R. (1977b). Relational communication: Theory and research. *Human Communication Research, 3,* 372-381.

Parks, M. R. (1982). Ideology in interpersonal communication: Off the couch and into the world. In M. Burgoon (Ed.), *Communication yearbook 5* (pp. 79-107). New Brunswick, NJ: Transaction.

Parks, M. R. (1985). Interpersonal communication and the quest for personal competence. In M. L. Knapp & G. R. Miller (Eds.), *Handbook of interpersonal communication* (pp. 171-201). Beverly Hills, CA: Sage.

Pearce, W. B., Cronen, V. E., & Conklin, F. (1979). On what to look at when analyzing communication: A hierarchical model of actors' meanings. *Communication, 4,* 195-220.

Peterson, J., Fischetti, M., Curran, J. P., & Arland, S. (1981). Sense of timing: A skill deficit in heterosocially anxious women. *Behavior Therapy, 12,* 195-201.

Phillips, G. M. (1968). Reticence: Pathology of the normal speaker. *Speech Monographs, 35,* 39-49.

Phillips, G. M. (1984). A competent view of "competence." *Communication Education, 33,* 24-36.

Phillips, G. M. (1991). *Communication incompetencies: A theory of training oral performance behavior.* Carbondale: Southern Illinois University Press.

Powers, W. G., & Spitzberg, B. H. (1986). Basic communication fidelity and image management. *Communication Research Reports, 3,* 60-63.

Powers, W. T. (1973). *Behavior: The control of perception.* Chicago: Aldine.

Pylyshyn, Z. W. (1973). The role of competence theories in cognitive psychology. *Journal of Psycholinguistic Research, 2,* 21-50.

Reardon, K. K. (1982). Conversational deviance: A structural model. *Human Communication Research, 9,* 59-74.

Richmond, V. P., & McCroskey, J. C. (1985). *Communication: Apprehension, avoidance, and effectiveness.* Scottsdale, AZ: Gorsuch Scarisbrick.

Rodin, J., & Langer, E. J. (1977). Long-term effects of control relevant intervention with the institutionalized aged. *Journal of Personality and Social Psychology, 35,* 897-902.

Rogers, T. B. (1981). A model of the self as an aspect of the human information processing system. In N. Cantor & J. F. Kihlstrom (Eds.), *Personality, cognition, and social interaction* (pp. 193-214). Hillsdale, NJ: Lawrence Erlbaum.

Rokeach, M. (1960). *The open and closed mind.* New York: Basic Books.

Roloff, M. E., & Berger, C. R. (1982). Social cognition and communication: An introduction. In M. E. Roloff & C. R. Berger (Eds.), *Social cognition and communication* (pp. 9-32). Beverly Hills, CA: Sage.

Rubin, R. B. (1982). Assessing speaking and listening competence at the college level: The communication competency assessment instrument. *Communication Education, 31,* 19-32.

Rubin, R. B., & Graham, E. (1988). Communication correlates of college success: An exploratory investigation. *Communication Education, 37,* 14-27.

Samter, W., Burleson, B. R., & Basden-Murphy, L. (1989). Behavioral complexity is in the eye of the beholder: Effects of cognitive complexity and message complexity on impressions of the source of comforting messages. *Human Communication Research, 15,* 612-629.

Schank, R. C., & Abelson, R. P. (1977). *Scripts, plans, goals, and understanding.* Hillsdale, NJ: Lawrence Erlbaum.

Scott, W. A. (1966). Flexibility, rigidity, and adaptation: Toward clarification of concepts. In O. J. Harvey (Ed.), *Experience, structure and adaptability* (pp. 369-400). New York: Springer.

Segrin, C. (1990). A meta-analytic review of social skill deficits in depression. *Communication Monographs, 57,* 292-308.

Segrin, C. (1992). Specifying the nature of social skill deficits associated with depression. *Human Communication Research, 19,* 89-123.

Sillars, A. L. (1985). Interpersonal perception in relations. In W. Ickes (Ed.), *Compatible and incompatible relationships* (pp. 277-305). New York: Springer-Verlag.

Simon, H. A. (1979). *Models of thought.* New Haven, CT: Yale University Press.

Spitzberg, B. H. (1982, May). *Relational competence: An empirical test of a conceptual model.* Paper presented at the annual convention of the International Communication Association, Boston.

Spitzberg, B. H. (1986, November). *Validating a measure of conversational skills.* Paper presented at the annual convention of the Speech Communication Association, Chicago.

Spitzberg, B. H., & Canary, D. J. (1985). Loneliness and relationally competent communication. *Journal of Social and Personal Relationships, 2,* 387-402.

Spitzberg, B. H., & Cupach, W. R. (1984). *Interpersonal communication competence.* Beverly Hills, CA: Sage.

Spitzberg, B. H., & Cupach, W. R. (1985). Conversational skill and locus of perception. *Journal of Psychopathology and Behavioral Assessment, 7,* 207-220.

Spitzberg, B. H., & Cupach, W. R. (1989). *Handbook of interpersonal competence research.* New York: Springer-Verlag.

Spitzberg, B. H., & Hecht, M. L. (1984). A component model of relational competence. *Human Communication Research, 10,* 575-599.

Steffen, J. J., & Redden, J. (1977). Assessment of social competence in an evaluation-interaction analogue. *Human Communication Research, 4,* 31-37.

Sternberg, R. J. (1985). *Beyond IQ: A triarchic theory of human intelligence.* Cambridge: Cambridge University Press.

Stohl, C. (1983). Developing a communicative competence scale. In R. N. Bostrom (Ed.), *Communication yearbook 7* (pp. 685-716). Beverly Hills, CA: Sage.

Storms, M. D. (1973). Videotape and the attribution process: Reversing actors' and observers' points of view. *Journal of Personality and Social Psychology, 27,* 165-175.

Sweeney, P. D., Anderson, K., & Bailey, S. (1986). Attributional style in depression: A meta-analytic review. *Journal of Personality and Social Psychology, 50,* 974-991.

Sypher, B. D., & Zorn, T. E. (1986). Communication-related ability and upward mobility: A longitudinal investigation. *Human Communication Research, 12,* 420-431.

Taylor, S. E., & Brown, J. D. (1988). Illusion and well-being: A social psychological perspective on mental health. *Psychological Bulletin, 103,* 193-210.

Thompson, S. C. (1981). Will it hurt less if I can control it? A complex answer to a simple question. *Psychological Bulletin, 90,* 89-101.

Waldron, V. R. (1990). Constrained rationality situational influences on information acquisition plans and tactics. *Communication Monographs, 57,* 184-201.

Weinstein, E. A. (1969). The development of interpersonal competence. In D. A. Goslin (Ed.), *Handbook of socialization theory and research* (pp. 753-775). Chicago: Rand McNally.

White, R. W. (1959). Motivation considered: The concept of competence. *Psychological Review, 66,* 297-333.

Wiemann, J. M. (1977). Explication and test of a model of communicative competence. *Human Communication Research, 3,* 195-213.

Wiemann, J. M., & Backlund, P. (1980). Current theory and research in communicative competence. *Review of Educational Research, 50,* 185-199.

Wiemann, J. M., & Kelly, C. W. (1981). Pragmatics of interpersonal competence. In C. Wilder-Mott & J. H. Weakland (Eds.), *Rigor and imagination: Essays from the legacy of Gregory Bateson* (pp. 283-297). New York: Praeger.

Wilson, S. R., Cruz, M. G., & Kang, K. H. (1992). Is it always a matter of perspective? Construct differentiation and variability in attributions about compliance gaining. *Communication Monographs, 59,* 350-367.

Wood, R., Weinstein, E. A., & Parker, T. B. (1967). Children's interpersonal tactics. *Sociological Inquiry, 37,* 129-138.

Woodworth, R. S. (1958). *Dynamics of behavior.* New York: Holt, Rinehart & Winston.

Zimbardo, R. S. (1977). *Shyness: What it is, What to do about it.* Reading, MA: Addison-Wesley.

PART IV

Contexts

16

Task/Work Relationships: A Life-Span Perspective

Fredric M. Jablin

Kathleen J. Krone

FROM CHILDHOOD THROUGH retirement, task-oriented relationships are an omnipresent part of our lives. Moreover, whether it is performing one's chores as a member of the family unit, participating in classroom or extracurricular school activities, working in a part- or full-time job, or serving as a volunteer member of a community action group, the effective completion of task-oriented activities usually involves some degree of interpersonal communication. Given the invariable presence of task-oriented activities in our lives, and the correspondingly important role interpersonal communication plays in facilitating the completion of these tasks, it is not surprising to discover that the nature, functions, and constraints associated with interpersonal communication in task settings have received a considerable amount of research attention. In particular, the great majority of studies in this area have focused on exploring the dynamics of interpersonal communication in the *work/organizational setting*. Consistent with this trend, the primary goal of this chapter is to organize, review, and interpret interpersonal communication research that has attempted to examine task relationships in work/organizational settings.

In updating and revising this chapter, we have taken the same strategy to interpreting the literature as in the original version: We consider communication in the work/organizational setting from a developmental, "life-span" perspective (Jablin, 1985a, 1987a). As a consequence, the first section of this chapter examines literature concerned with how people learn about interpersonal communication in work/organizational relationships prior to ever entering into them. Maintaining this developmental perspective, the roles and characteristics of interpersonal communication in the process of becoming assimilated into, and eventually becoming an integral part of, work organizations are then explored. In addition, we briefly consider how individuals disengage from interpersonal relationships in particular work environments as their careers evolve over time.

While a variety of schemes might have been used to organize and review the literature on interpersonal communication in task/organizational relationships, the life-span approach was chosen because it (a) recognizes the developmental nature of interpersonal and organizational relationships/processes, (b) incorporates the notion that interpersonal and organizational communication processes are dynamic versus static in nature, and (c) allows us to explore interpersonal communication in task relationships within work/organizational settings as well as within other task environments.

Anticipation of Interpersonal Communication at Work

Vocational/Occupational Development

Prior to ever entering into work relationships, most of us have developed certain beliefs and expectations about how people communicate and interact in the job setting. As Drucker (1973) observes, "By the time a human being has reached the age of four or five he has been conditioned to work" (p. 184). To a large extent, this conditioning and development of attitudes and stereotypes are by-products of the process of vocational development, which for most people occurs during maturation from childhood to "young adulthood" (Crites, 1969). Vocational development is the process by which a person chooses (deliberately or accidentally) a career direction and develops expectations about what that profession or career will be like. There are at least five basic sources of information that affect our vocational development and perceptions of how people communicate at work: (a) family, (b) educational institutions, (c) the mass media, (d) peers, and (e) part-time jobs (see Jablin, 1987a; Vangelisti, 1988). Although communication with each of these sources or "microsystems" often overlaps and/or is embedded within one another (Bronfenbrenner, 1979, 1986), they are considered here separately to facilitate discussion of their unique characteristics.

Family. Probably the first "significant others" we observe in a set of coordinated task relationships are members of our families, and in particular our parents, who are central figures in the socialization of their children (e.g., Leifer & Lesser, 1976). Research findings suggest that parents are often influential in their children's career choices (e.g., Brown, Brooks, & Associates, 1984; Sebald, 1986; Wilks, 1986) and that parental characteristics and behaviors may be related to the degree to which their children are attracted to various occupations (e.g., Vondracek, Lerner, & Schulenberg, 1986).

Moreover, other studies indicate that by the time most children enter the first grade they are already integrally involved in the performance of routine household chores on a regular basis (Goldstein & Oldham, 1979). Recent research in this area suggests that the types of tasks parents and children perform in the household, the manner in which tasks are assigned and performed, comments about tasks as they are being performed, and the like may be crucial in children's development of work-related schemes. The research of Goodnow and her associates (for example, Goodnow, 1988; Goodnow, Bowes, Dawes, & Taylor, 1988; Goodnow, Bowes, Warton, Dawes, & Taylor, 1991; Goodnow & Delaney, 1989; Goodnow & Warton, 1991) is of particular interest because it views children's learning about work as involving the sending of various kinds of messages from parents to their children. Findings suggest, among other things, that children learn early on (certainly by age 5) how to respond to requests for work (for example, a "no" is less acceptable than a "no" with some justification or account; see Leonard, 1988) and how to justify asking others to perform tasks (for example, reference to the other's competence or efficiency; see Goodnow et al., 1988). Similarly, children learn quickly which jobs they can and cannot ask someone else in the family to do and those they must do themselves (Goodnow & Warton, 1991). Gender marking also appears to occur in the ways parents label and explain task assignments (for example, describing a task as "boys'" or "girls'" work). Relatedly, with respect to how parents guide children in task participation, gender differences also often are evident; for instance, some research has shown fathers to be more likely to tell their children to do something than ask them to do it, whereas mothers rely more on requests and reminders in managing household work (Goodnow et al., 1988).

In addition, two other findings from this research program are of interest. First, it appears that mothers' interactions with children teach a lot about task relationships, including the acceptable limits to an interaction and how one signals "that an expected relationship is being violated" (Goodnow & Delaney, 1989, p. 223). Second, it seems apparent from these studies (e.g., Goodnow & Warton, 1991) that metaphors are key mechanisms by which parents communicate to their children work "principles" (for example, "you're not pulling your weight," "you're not the only star in the sky").

Other evidence also suggests that children are learning about the world of work and task relationships from conversations that parents have between themselves in their children's presence but in which the children are not directly involved (ambient messages; see Jablin, 1987a). For example, Jablin (1993) has found that students report that their parents frequently discuss work during dinner and in after-dinner informal conversations. Topics frequently discussed in these conversations include the general day's events at work and company news but also often involve relationships with coworkers, supervisors, clients, and customers. Typically, most of these conversations convey little information about what parents do in their jobs but offer children information about how people relate with others in the work setting (also see Jablin, 1987a).

Educational institutions. Of the various sources from which we obtain vocational information, educational institutions are one of the most important. This would appear to be true because (a) school, unlike some of the other sources, has the explicit mandate to socialize people (Gecas, 1981); (b) school serves as a transitional institution between family and job (see Dreeben, 1968; Gecas, 1981); (c) "the relationships of authority and control between administrators and teachers, teachers and students, students and students, and students and their work replicate the hierarchical divisions of labor which dominate the workplace" (Bowles & Gintis, 1976, p. 12); and (d) school is probably the first context in which a child experiences and participates in *formal* organizing activity on a daily basis (within the classroom and in extracurricular activities, in which he or she learns about leadership, teamwork, allocating tasks, work relationships, and the like; see Mihalka, 1974).

To date, however, only one study has attempted to explore what students learn as they progress through school about the communication behaviors of persons in work roles and occupations. In this investigation, Jablin (1985b) sought to discover what occupations students (as reported by their teachers) talk and read about in school and the types of interpersonal communicator styles (Norton, 1978) they attribute to persons in these roles. Results of the study indicate that, as students progress from elementary through secondary school, their classroom discussions and texts increasingly depict the communication styles of persons in work relationships as "inactive" and "unresponsive-unreceptive." Though this trend was consistent across all occupations, findings also revealed that students (as reported by their teachers) attributed distinctive styles of communication to persons in different occupations.

It also seems apparent that, once a student has selected a vocation and receives specific education in that field, the manner in which she or he communicates with other members of the field, the public, clients, and so on is somewhat constrained by the interaction norms learned during his or her occupational or professional training (e.g., Bucher & Stelling, 1977; Moore, 1969; Pfeffer, 1981; Van Mannen & Barley, 1984). In particular, specialized occupational and/or professional training teaches students special languages or codes that allow members of the occupation to communicate with one another (Moore, 1969). These codes also affect how members of the occupation or profession view the world and conceptualize and talk about problems, events, activities, and people.

Media. A considerable amount of evidence exists suggesting that the mass media, and in particular television (even network news programs; see Ryan & Sim, 1990), often transmit an inaccurate and/or distorted, frequently sex-role-stereotyped image of occupations (e.g., Beuf, 1974; DeFleur & DeFleur, 1967; Freuh & McGhee, 1975; Glennon & Butsch, 1982; Huston & Alvarez, 1990; Jeffries-Fox & Signorielli, 1979; Morgan, 1980; Noble, 1975; O'Bryant & Corder-Bolz, 1978; Signorielli, 1991; Wober, Reardon, & Fazal, 1987). While in recent years television shows have shown more women in nontraditional roles (e.g., attorney, police officer), men continue to be portrayed in traditional male occupations (Huston & Alvarez, 1990; Williams, Baron, Phillips, Travis, & Jackson, 1986). With respect to communication behavior, there is a tendency to represent successful role occupants as fairly "aggressive" communicators who spend a majority of their time giving orders or advice to others (DeFleur, 1964; Theberge, 1981; Turow, 1974, 1980). Thus it is not surprising that, when DeFleur (1964) interviewed 237 children about the occupational characteristics they most admired, "power" (ability to "boss" others) consistently ranked highest. Content analyses of television representations of "talk" at work have also shown that most conversations have little to do with work; rather, conversations are focused on "social" topics (Katzman, 1972; Turow, 1974).

In addition, a recent content analysis of prime-time television programs by Berg and Trujillo (1989) suggests that television may teach viewers about selected visions of organizational life, including metaphors used to depict organizing processes (organization as family, machine, organism, and political arena), "keys" to success on the job (e.g., work hard, cooperate with others, be creative, and pay attention to detail), and other "lessons" about getting along in organizations (including "rules should be followed and occasionally broken," "things don't always go according to plan," "personal and professional lives are difficult and often impossible to separate," and "honesty is the best organizational policy"). Whether or not individuals actually learn these "lessons" from viewing programs, however, remains to be determined.

Although many television shows contain business themes and frequently show characters in occupations (a recent content analysis indicated 42% of weekend daytime children's programming included business themes and about 33% of the major characters were shown in specific occupations; see Signorielli, 1991), the research evidence concerning the effects of television representations of occupational behavior/communication on children is very difficult to draw causal relationships from. However, several studies have reported findings suggesting that mass media occupational sex typing and portrayals of interpersonal interaction at work may affect children's occupational aspirations and their expectations of the ways in which individuals actually behave on the job (Abel, Fontes, Greenberg, & Atkin, 1980; Bogatz & Ball, 1971; DeFleur & DeFleur, 1967; Dominick, 1974; Morgan, 1987; Siegel, 1958; Wroblewski & Huston, 1987). In particular, the available evidence indicates that this may be especially true for occupations that children do not often come into contact with in their everyday lives (e.g., Noble, 1983; Wroblewski & Huston, 1987).

Peers. Of the five sources that are likely to affect one's vocational development and beliefs about communication at work, the least is probably known about the effects of peers' influences. Yet, with respect to peer influences, research in related areas suggests that friends influence adolescents' career aspirations (Bain & Anderson, 1974) and that it is not unusual for peers to discuss and compare their career aspirations with one another (Duncan, Haller, & Portes, 1968; Simpson, 1962; Woelfel & Haller, 1971). Thus, while little research has explored the specifics of how adolescents' interactions affect their perceptions of communication in occupations and work contexts, it seems clear that "peers function as significant others who confirm or disconfirm the desirability of occupations" (Peterson & Peters, 1983, p. 81).

In addition, evidence suggests that children and adolescents may learn about some dimensions of task-related communication through their interactions with peers and friends that are not readily available from other sources. In particular, peer-related interactions often provide children and adolescents with opportunities to establish relationships with others as "equals" (coworkers). In other words, because peer group task-related activities are usually voluntary in nature (in contrast to task-related activities in school and family settings), communication patterns in these contexts tend to be based on equality, mutual respect, and friendship bonds (Larson, 1983; Smollar & Yountis, 1982; Zarbatany, Hartmann, & Rankin, 1990). However, this does not mean that status hierarchies and conflicts do not develop in peer groups but that "status within peer groups is more fluid than in more structured contexts and depends much more on negotiation" (Gecas, 1981, p. 185). As a consequence, it is likely that childhood and adolescent peer group interactions teach us about ways of managing conflict (e.g., Shantz, 1987) and *negotiating* roles. As Gecas (1981) argues, more opportunities exist for "role making" (versus "role taking") in contexts involving peers and friends than in other contexts in which children and adolescents find themselves.

Part-time jobs. Statistics indicate that over 50% of males and females ages 16 to 19 hold part-time jobs (Rotchford & Roberts, 1982). Several tentative conclusions about the communication characteristics of adolescents' part-time jobs can be drawn from recent reviews (e.g., Charner & Fraser, 1988; Greenberger & Steinberg, 1986) and empirical studies: (a) Workers do not have very close communication relationships with their supervisors or coworkers and rarely talk to their supervisors about personal matters (Greenberger, Steinberg, Vaux, & McAuliffe, 1980). (b) Part-time jobs differ greatly with respect to the opportunities they provide adolescents to communicate with others in the work setting as well as with respect to characteristics of typical interaction episodes (for example, some jobs allow workers more opportunities to influence others, give instructions, and so on than other jobs; e.g., Greenberger, Steinberg, & Ruggiero, 1982; Ruggiero & Steinberg, 1981). (c) Although adolescents usually do not perceive their part-time job experiences as important and relevant to their career plans (Steinberg, Greenberger, Vaux, & Ruggiero, 1981; Wijting, Arnold, & Conrad, 1977), research findings also indicate that these work experiences generally enhance adolescents' knowledge of the world of work, may reinforce positive and/or negative work habits and behaviors (e.g., Steinberg & Dornbusch, 1991), facilitate the development of basic communication skills required in most work settings (Charner & Fraser, 1984; Snedeker, 1982), and teach them a considerable amount about the nature of *relationships* at work (Greenberger et al., 1980; Phillips & Sandstrom, 1990).

Summary. This section has attempted to review research related to the period in one's life when one is learning and developing attitudes about how people in general communicate in work/organizational relationships. Five basic influences on the development of these attitudes were considered: (a) family, (b) educational institutions, (c) the mass media, (d) peers, and (e) part-time jobs. Indicative of the research literature, each of these influences was considered independent of the others. However, it seems evident that people actually experience these influences in combination and that, while these sources may often reinforce one another, they may also frequently provide conflicting information (for example, behaviors parents stress as important in completing tasks in the family setting may not always be productive in the school setting; see Alexander, Entwisle, Cadigan, & Pallas, 1987). In addition, it is important to realize that the "exosystems" (for example, parents' world of work; see Bronfenbrenner, 1979) associated with the various microsystems discussed in the preceding sections may affect the nature of what children and adolescents learn about occupations and task-related behavior/communication within a particular setting. For instance, if a parent loses his or her job or is demoted at work, these events may affect the nature of task-related interaction within the family, the reinforcement of children's career aspirations, and the availability and kinds of models from which children can learn task-related behavior (see Flanagan, 1990; Radin & Harold-Goldsmith, 1989; Vondracek et al., 1986). In brief, the interactive effects of the various microsystems, as well as factors affecting each of them, require greater consideration in future research exploring vocational development and how people learn about communication in work/ organizational relationships.

In closing, probably the two most frequent themes evident in the research reviewed on vocational development are as follows: (a) While in most cases it is not until late in the vocational development process that individuals learn much about the specific communication behaviors/skills required of various organizational positions and occupations, they are learning from a very young age "about the communication styles (ways of communicating, e.g., friendly, relaxed, contentious, dominant, animated) associated with occupations and work relationships" (Jablin, 1987a, p. 685). (b) We learn early in life that "power" is an integral element of interpersonal communication in work and organizational relationships.

Organizational Choice

Once an individual has chosen (consciously or unconsciously) an area to pursue for a career, and received the requisite training to perform tasks associated with that job, he or she typically will seek an organizational position in which to enact the role. For the job seeker, a concomitant of the job search process is the formation of expectations about the jobs and organizations in which he or she has applied for employment. Typically, recruits acquire expectations about specific jobs and organizations from organizational literature (annual reports, advertisements, training brochures, and the like), interpersonal interactions with friends and other social network ties (see Granovetter, 1974; Kilduff, 1990), and/or organizational representatives (e.g., Jablin, 1987a). In particular, one of the most frequent and critical methods of information exchange between organization and applicant is the selection interview (Harris, 1989; Jablin & Miller, 1990).

Selection interview. The importance of the interview as a selection and recruitment device is epitomized by the fairly large number of literature reviews that have been published over the last 30 years summarizing research in this area (for example, see Arvey & Campion, 1982; Eder & Ferris, 1989; Goodall & Goodall, 1982; Harris, 1989; Jablin & McComb, 1984; Jablin & Miller, 1990; Mayfield, 1964; Schmitt, 1976; Street, 1986; Ulrich & Trumbo, 1965; Wright, 1969). It is important to note that communication-related behavior has been a major focus of this research tradition, though the great majority of studies have concentrated solely on exploring the communication perceptions and behaviors of interviewers versus interviewees and generally have failed to examine the two parties in dynamic interaction (see Jablin & McComb, 1984; Jablin & Miller, 1990). Several generalizations about interpersonal communication in the selection interview can be drawn from recent reviews and studies:

(1) Generally, applicants' interview communication expectations (including likelihood of accepting job offers) often appear related to their perceptions of their recruiters as trustworthy, competent, composed, enthusiastic, empathic, and well-organized communicators (see Alderfer & McCord, 1970; Fisher, Ilgen, & Hoyer, 1979; Jablin, Tengler, & Teigen, 1982; Liden & Parsons, 1986; Rynes & Miller, 1983; Schmitt & Coyle, 1976; Taylor & Bergmann, 1987; Teigen, 1983).

(2) Applicants do not particularly like or trust interviewers and appear hesitant to accept job offers if their only sources of information are recruiters (see Downs, 1969; Fisher et al., 1979; Rynes, Bretz, & Gerhart, 1991); however, in interviews conducted by job incumbents versus personnel representatives, applicants perceive interviewers as providing more "realistic" and/or accurate organization/job information (Jablin, Tengler, & Teigen, 1985; Rynes et al., 1991).

(3) An interviewee's satisfaction and/or attraction to an organization in which she or he has applied for employment appears related to the quality and amount of organizational and job information the recruiter provides, the degree to which the recruiter shows interest in the applicant, and the extent to which the recruiter asks the interviewee open-ended questions and allows him or her sufficient "talk time" (see Herriot & Rothwell, 1983; Jablin, Tengler, McClary, & Teigen, 1987; Karol, 1977; Powell, 1991; Tengler, 1982; Turban & Dougherty, 1992).

(4) Most questions applicants ask their interviewers are closed ended, singular in form, typically not phrased in the first person, asked after interviewers ask for applicants' inquiries, and seek job-related information (see Babbitt & Jablin, 1985; Einhorn, 1981).

(5) Applicants' perceptions of their interviewers as empathic listeners appear to be negatively related to the degree to which interviewers interject "interruptive statements" while the interviewees are speaking (McComb & Jablin, 1984).

(6) Interviewees who display "high" versus "low" levels of nonverbal immediacy (operationalized by such variables as eye contact, smiling posture, interpersonal distance, and body orientation), who are "high" in vocal activity, and who engage their interviewers in "response-response" versus primarily "question-response" conversations tend to be favored by interviewers (Anderson & Shackleton, 1990; Byrd, 1979; Einhorn, 1981; Forbes & Jackson, 1980; Imada & Hakel, 1977; Keenan, 1976; Keenan & Wedderburn, 1975; McGovern & Tinsley, 1978; Tengler & Jablin, 1983; Trent, 1978).

(7) Recruiters find interviewees more acceptable if they receive favorable information about them prior to or during their interviews (see Herriot & Rothwell, 1983; Macan & Dipboye, 1990; Phillips & Dipboye, 1989; Tucker & Rowe, 1979); however, recruiters do not necessarily adopt confirmatory question strategies to validate their expectancies (see Binning, Goldstein, Garcia, & Scattaregia, 1988; Constantin, 1976; Lindvall, Culberson, Binning, & Goldstein, 1986; McDonald & Hakel, 1985; Sackett, 1982).

(8) Interviewers tend to employ inverted funnel question sequences (they begin with closed questions and then progress to more open-ended questions), thus limiting applicant "talk time" during the crucial opening "decision-making" minutes of interviews (Tengler & Jablin, 1983). In addition, recruiters tend to "hold the floor" more often after answering questions (Axtmann & Jablin, 1986).

(9) Structured interview question formats (for example, Behavior Description Interviews—see Janz, 1989; Janz, Hellervik, & Gilmore, 1986—Situational Interviews—see Latham, 1989; Latham, Saari, Pursell, & Campion, 1980—and Comprehensive Structured Interviews—see Campion, Pursell, & Brown, 1988; Pursell, Campion, & Gaylord, 1980) appear more valid than unstructured question approaches (Harris, 1989; Jablin & Miller, 1990).

(10) Applicants and recruiters tend to have differential expectations and perceptions of numerous communication behaviors evidenced in interviews such as talkativeness, listening, questioning, and topics of discussion (Cheatham & McLaughlin, 1976; Engler-Parish & Millar, 1989; Harlan, Kerr, & Kerr, 1977; Herriot & Rothwell, 1981, 1983; Posner, 1981; Shaw, 1983; Taylor & Sniezek, 1984).

(11) Recruiters tend to rate more highly applicants who talk more in their interviews (though such talk is not necessarily in response to questions), who elaborate on answers, and whose discussion on topics is close to their interviewers' expectations (see Einhorn, 1981; Herriot & Rothwell, 1983; Tengler & Jablin, 1983; Ugbah & Majors, 1992). Related research also suggests that interviewers may be influenced by applicants who display self-enhancing impression management techniques (for instance, agreeing with the interviewer, emphasizing positive traits, complimenting the interviewer; see Baron, 1989; Gilmore & Ferris, 1989).

(12) Applicant communication competence/ability is often reported by recruiters to be crucial in their decisions about them (see Graves & Karren, 1992; Hollandworth, Kazelskis, Stevens, & Dressel, 1979; Kinicki & Lockwood, 1985; Kinicki, Lockwood, Hom, & Griffeth, 1990; Posner, 1981; Ugbah & Majors, 1992).

Job/organizational expectations. The interview is important not only as an interpersonal communication event but also because of the role it plays in "signaling" (e.g., Rynes et al., 1991) or communicating job/organizational expectations to potential employees. For example, Teigen (1983) discovered that 38% of the "talk" (operationalized by word count) and 18% of the topics discussed in selection interviews are devoted to information exchanges about organizational climate issues (job duties and responsibilities, advancement potential, pay/benefits, supervision, coworker relations). Additionally, he concluded from some of his results that "interviewees who recruiters consider attractive candidates may be provided with certain kinds of climate information not given to less attractive candidates" (Teigen, 1983, p. 188).

At the same time, however, it is essential to observe that research indicates that, regardless of the mode of information exchange between employer and applicant, the "typical outcome of this process is the emergence of inflated expectations by the recruit of what his or her potential job and organization will be like (Wanous, 1977, 1980)" (Jablin, 1982, p. 264). In fact, some evidence suggests that new recruits often have extremely inflated expectations of the communication climates of their jobs and organizations, including the amounts of information they will receive from and send to others, from whom they will receive information, the timeliness of the information they will receive, and the channels that will be used for communication (Jablin, 1984). Obviously, it is probably not very desirable for recruits to possess such inflated expectations of the interpersonal communication environments of their jobs and organizations because these inflated expectations will be very difficult to meet. And, "as a result of large discrepancies between expectations and reality, recruits with inflated communication climate expectations may have a higher probability of job turnover and/or less job satisfaction" (Jablin, 1981, p. 2).

Summary. The preceding discussion has provided an overview of the nature and effects of interpersonal communication exchanges between applicants and organizations during the selection-recruitment process. Particular attention was focused on the communication dynamics of the selection interview, because it is typically the first context in which applicants and organizational representatives meet and interact on a face-to-face basis. Generally speaking, research pertaining to the interview suggests that recruiters prefer applicants who are "active-dynamic" communicators, while applicants prefer interviewers who are credible communicators and who allow applicants ample time to express themselves. At the same time, however, it seems apparent that, regardless of the mode of information exchange between applicants and employers, a by-product of the selection-recruitment process is the emergence within applicants of inflated expectations of the interpersonal communication climates of the organizations in which they are seeking employment.

In conclusion, the study of how and what people learn about interpersonal communication in work relationships prior to entering their chosen occupations and/or job settings is still a relatively new area of communication research. However, it seems evident that individuals *do* anticipate the interpersonal communication environments of work settings they may enter, and that these expectations are likely to affect their communication behaviors and perceptions once on the job (see Jablin, 1987a).

Interpersonal Communication in the Organizational Setting

Upon entry into an organization, a recruit formally begins the organizational assimilation process. "Organizational assimilation refers to the process by which organizational members become a part of, or are absorbed into, the culture of an organization" (Jablin, 1982, p. 256). This process is typically considered to contain two reciprocal components: the organization's planned and unplanned attempts to "socialize" the recruit and the new employee's efforts to "individualize" his or her role. Each of these components of assimilation will be reviewed briefly below, followed by a discussion of the role of interpersonal communication in the organizational assimilation process.

According to Van Mannen (1975), organizational socialization is the "process by which a person learns the values, norms and required behaviors that permit him [or her] to participate as a member of the organization" (p. 67). Or, as Schein (1968) has proposed, it is the "process of 'learning the ropes,' the process of being indoctrinated and trained, the process of being taught what is important in the organization" (p. 2). It also should be noted that, while the organizational socialization process may appear to have its greatest impact during one's initial tenure in the organization, it is a *continuous* process that will "change and evolve as the individual remains longer with the organization" (Porter, Lawler, & Hackman, 1975, p. 161). Moreover, it is essential to keep in mind that, at the same time the organization is trying to socialize the new employee, the recruit is striving to individualize his or her role by modifying the organization so that it can better satisfy his or her needs, values, and ideas (for example, see Schein, 1968).

When viewed concurrently, the employee individualization and organizational socialization processes characterize the fundamental elements of organizational "role taking" (Katz & Kahn, 1966) and "role making" (Graen, 1976; Graen & Scandura, 1987). As has often been noted in the research literature, a role "is at once the building block of social systems and the summation of the requirements with which the system confronts the individual member" (Katz & Kahn, 1966, p. 171). Moreover, roles are learned, have content and stylistic dimensions, possess formal and informal duties, rights, and privileges, and, perhaps most important, can be understood by scrutinizing the role expectations that are communicated to and from an individual by members of his or her "role set" (task-related relevant others). Thus it is as "a result of the communication of expectations by members of the role set that the new employee 'encounters' his or her organizational role and learns the values, behaviors, and patterns of thinking that are considered acceptable to the organizational system" (Jablin, 1982, p. 259). At the same time, however, it is important to realize that new employees are not merely passive receivers of role sendings but can proactively negotiate or "make" their roles by attempting to alter the expectations of members of their role sets (Graen, 1976).

As is evident from the above discussion, communication is essential to the organizational assimilation/role-making process. Generally speaking, there are three primary sources of information available to assist new recruits (as well as existing organizational members) in the role-making process: (a) "official" media-related management sources (such as handbooks, manuals, official house magazines, and newsletters), (b) superiors and subordinates, and (c) members of one's work group (coworkers). Of these sources, interpersonal interactions with superiors/subordinates and other work group members are probably most influential in the assimilation/role-making process. This is due largely to the general inability of media-related (typically written) downward management messages to alter employee behavior. Rather, most research suggests that such types of documents serve to inform employees of desired behaviors but rarely by themselves can cause changes in behavior (Redding, 1972; Weiss, 1969).

In addition, superior-subordinate communication is generally perceived as crucial to an employee's organizational assimilation for the following reasons:

(1) The supervisor frequently interacts with the subordinate and thus may serve as a role model (Weiss, 1977), (2) the supervisor has formal power to reward and punish the employee, (3) the supervisor mediates the formal flow of downward communication to the subordinate (for example, the supervisor serves as an interpreter/filter of management messages), and (4) the supervisor usually has a personal as well as formal role relationship with the recruit. (Jablin, 1982, p. 269)

Also, it is important to observe that an employee's superior is of critical importance to his or her individualization efforts. As Graen (1976) suggests, "Although other members of the new person's role set can enter the negotiation of the definition of the new person's role . . . only the leader is granted the authority to impose formal sanctions to back up his negotiations" (p. 1206).

On the other hand, formal and informal interactions with coworkers in one's task group also appear to perform an important function in the organizational assimilation process. As Feldman (1981, p. 314) notes, "New recruits turn to other members of the work group to get help in interpreting the events they experience, to learn the nuances of seemingly clear-cut rules, and to learn the informal networks" (also see Hudson & Jablin, 1992; Miller & Jablin, 1991). Further, group members can serve as a normative referent for "appropriate" behavior and as a source of emotional support against the organization's socialization attempts (Becker, Geer, Hughes, & Strauss, 1961; Burns, 1955; Feldman, 1977). Additionally, some evidence suggests that, in the uncertain environment of a new job, recruits may model and/or assume the attitudes and behaviors of their coworkers (Crawford, 1974; Katz, 1980; Rakestraw & Weiss, 1981; Weiss, 1977; White & Mitchell, 1979).

In summary, a considerable amount of evidence exists suggesting that new recruits, as well as continuing members of organizations, "make sense of" (Louis, 1980, 1990) and understand their work environments primarily as a result of their interpersonal interactions with (a) supervisors/subordinates and (b) work group members/coworkers. Given the apparent importance of these types of communication relationships to becoming assimilated into organizations, the following two sections of this chapter provide selective reviews of these respective research literatures. Because few studies in either of these areas have used longitudinal or time-series research designs, these literature reviews have been organized topically rather than in a developmental fashion.

Superior-Subordinate Communication

As has often been observed, within work organizations there are always *subordinates* and *superiors* "even though these terms may not be expressly used, and even though there may exist fluid arrangements whereby superior and subordinate roles may be reversible" (Redding, 1972, p. 18). Generally, research concerning superior-subordinate communication has focused "on those exchanges of information and influence between organizational members, at least one of whom has formal (as defined by official organizational sources) authority to direct and evaluate the activities of other organizational members" (Jablin, 1979, p. 1202). With respect to the types of messages exchanged between superiors and subordinates, Katz and Kahn (1966, pp. 239-241) suggest that superior-to-subordinate communication(s) usually focuses on information concerning organizational procedures and practices, indoctrination of goals, job instructions, job rationale, or feedback about performance. Relatedly, subordinates' communication(s) to superiors tends to be concerned with information about the subordinates themselves; their coworkers, and their problems; information about tasks that need to be done; or information about organizational policies and practices (Katz & Kahn, 1966, p. 245).

Since the late 1970s, several extensive multidisciplinary reviews of empirical research exploring the nature and functions of superior-subordinate communication have been published (Dansereau & Markham, 1987; Jablin, 1979, 1985a). The following discussion briefly summarizes the findings of studies related to the 10 topical research categories identified in these reviews as well as the findings of more recent studies in each area.

Interaction patterns and related attitudes. Probably one of the most consistent findings in superior-subordinate communication research is that supervisors spend from one third to two thirds of their time communicating with subordinates. Further, the majority of this communication concerns task-related issues and is conducted in face-to-face meetings (e.g., Luthans & Larsen, 1986; Whitely, 1984, 1985). In addition, superiors and subordinates tend to have differential perceptions about (a) the amount of time they spend communicating with one another (including sending and receiving messages), (b) who initiates these communication contacts, and (c) the importance of their interactions (e.g., Harrison, 1985; Volard & Davies, 1982; Whitely, 1984). Research also suggests that subordinates' perceptions of social support may be related to the frequency with which they interact with their supervisors about job-related matters (Beehr, King, & King, 1990; Kirmeyer & Lin, 1987). Finally, it is important to note that scholars have begun to apply a variety of methodologies to assessing interaction patterns in superior-subordinate communication, including relational coding (e.g., Dugan, 1989; Fairhurst, Rogers, & Sarr, 1987), discourse and language analysis (e.g., Fairhurst & Chandler, 1989; Gioia, Donnellon, & Sims, 1989), as well as schemes based on forms of operant conditioning (e.g., Komaki, 1986; Komaki, Zlotnick, & Jensen, 1986).

Openness in communication. Redding (1972, p. 330) distinguishes two basic dimensions of openness in superior-subordinate communication: openness in message sending ("candid disclosure of feelings of 'bad news,' and important company facts") and openness in message receiving ("encouraging, or at least permitting, the frank expressions of views divergent from one's own"); recent studies suggest this conceptualization of openness is not culture specific (for example, Stewart, Gudykunst, Ting-Toomey, & Nishida, 1986, report it is applicable to superior-subordinate relationships in Japan). In addition, research suggests that in an open communication relationship between a leader and member, "both parties perceive the other interactant as a willing and receptive listener and refrain from responses that might be perceived as providing negative relational or disconfirming feedback" (Jablin, 1979, p. 1204). Most studies also indicate that workers are more satisfied with their jobs when they have "open" versus "closed" communication relationships with their superiors. Further, positive associations have been reported between subordinates' perceptions of openness and the degree to which their supervisors display "warmth" in their nonverbal behavior (Tjosvold, 1984). Finally, from a conceptual perspective, Eisenberg and Witten (1987) and Sussman (1991) have questioned the notion that openness in communication is always rational or desirable and suggest that the strategic, political, and "contingent" character of communication in organizational relationships be more closely scrutinized in future research.

Upward distortion. A long tradition of laboratory and field research has investigated the frequent phenomenon of upward distortion that occurs when persons of lower hierarchical rank in organizations communicate with persons of higher hierarchical rank (who also typically have power over the advancement of the persons of lower rank). Moreover, numerous variables have been found to moderate the occurrence of upward distortion, including subordinates' mobility aspirations, ascendancy and security needs, trust in superiors, gender, and motivation (for example, see Glauser, 1984; Jablin, 1979).

With respect to the types of messages that are most frequently distorted, studies generally have found that subordinates are most reluctant to communicate information to their superiors that is negative or unfavorable. On the other hand, superiors seem to compensate for the positive "halo" often associated with the messages they receive from subordinates by viewing them as less accurate than messages that are unfavorable to subordinates. Relatedly, it seems apparent that supervisors' willingness to believe subordinates' "accounts" (e.g., Scott & Lyman, 1968) of problematic behavior is influenced by the employees' past reputation, the plausibility of the accounts, and evidence corroborating the accounts (Morris & Coursey, 1989). Other research indicates that subordinates' upward communication distortion is related to supervisors' downward communication such that subordinates distort communication to and/or withhold communication from their superiors when they perceive their superiors to actively withhold information (Fulk & Mani, 1986).

Upward influence. Studies of upward influence in superior-subordinate communication have focused on two basic dimensions: (a) the effects a superior's influence in the organizational hierarchy has on his or her relationships with subordinates, and (b) subordinates' use of influence with their superiors (see Jablin, 1979). Regarding the former category of research, studies have concentrated on what is often termed the "Pelz Effect" (Pelz, 1952). Essentially, this effect suggests that subordinate satisfaction with supervision is a by-product not only of an open, supportive relationship between the two parties but also of the supervisor's ability to satisfy his or her subordinates' needs by possessing influence with those higher in the organizational hierarchy.

A considerable number of studies have been directed at exploring the generalizability of the Pelz Effect (e.g., Daniels & Logan, 1983; Jablin, 1980a, 1980b; Trempe, Rigney, & Haccoun, 1985). Results of these investigations have been supportive of the effect and suggest that it holds for a supervisor's *strategic* (personnel and administrative policy decisions) and *work-related* influence, and appears to exist under conditions of high and low leader supportiveness, though it has its greatest impact in situations where subordinates perceive their superiors as supportive leaders (Jablin, 1980a, 1980b). In addition, other studies have shown that a leader's upward influence also may enhance subordinates' feelings of organizational control and sense of cooperation within their work groups and that this may be the case even for subordinates with high job autonomy (Anderson & Tolson, 1991; Anderson, Tolson, Fields, & Thacker, 1990a, 1990b).

The message strategies that subordinates employ to influence their superiors' decisions have also been a focus of much recent research (e.g., Allen & Porter, 1983; Ansari & Kapoor, 1987; Chacko, 1990; Cheng, 1983; DeLuga, 1991a, 1991b; DeLuga & Perry, 1991; Erez, Rim, & Keider, 1986; Kipnis, Schmidt, & Wilkinson, 1980; Krone, 1991, 1992; Offermann & Kearney, 1988; Porter, Allen, & Angle,

1981; Schilit & Locke, 1982; Schriesheim & Hinkin, 1990). Generally, these studies suggest a variety of basic strategies that subordinates employ to influence their superior's decisions, including logical or rational presentation of ideas, informal or non-performance-specific exchanges (for example, ingratiation), formal exchange (exchanging desired work behaviors for rewards), adherence to rules (essentially a form of negative influence), upward appeal (bypassing one's direct superior and appealing to a person of higher authority), threats or sanctions, manipulation (arguing such that the target is not aware of the influence attempt), formal coalitions (power equalization), and persistence or assertiveness ("wearing down" the other party's resistance) (Schilit & Locke, 1982, p. 305).

Results of research exploring the frequencies with which these different types of message strategies are used in influence attempts indicates that subordinates report using rational, information-based tactics most frequently. However, various methodological problems associated with research in this area limit the generalizability of this conclusion (see Krone & Ludlum, 1990). Moreover, it seems apparent that a subordinate's selection and use of a message strategy in an influence attempt may be dependent on a wide variety of personal characteristics (e.g., gender, manifest needs, locus of control, self-confidence) and situational (e.g., likelihood of resistance, norms, goals/reasons for attempting influence, task characteristics), organizational (e.g., level in hierarchy, subunit size, organizational size, type of organization, presence of unions, span of control, centralization), and relationship factors (e.g., power, status, trust, leader-member exchange).

Semantic-information distance. The term *semantic-information distance* was coined by Tompkins (1962) to describe the gap in agreement and/or understanding that often exists between subordinates and superiors on specified issues. Research in this area has clearly demonstrated numerous topics in which large gaps in understanding exist between superiors and subordinates, including subordinates' basic job duties and supervisors' authority. In addition, studies (Gerloff & Quick, 1984; Hatfield & Huseman, 1982; Richmond, Wagner, & McCroskey, 1983; Schnake, Dumler, Cochran, & Barnett, 1990) also indicate that perceptual congruence about various aspects of superior-subordinate communication is to some degree positively associated with subordinates' general job satisfaction and related outcomes. However, it should be recognized that perceptual *in*congruence in the superior-subordinate dyad is, within limits, a natural consequence of role structuration in organizations and thus may be dysfunctional for the relationship only if "it impairs the productivity, stability or adaptability of the dyad" (Sussman, 1975, p. 198).

Studies in this area have also focused on differences in "metaperceptions" (Laing, Phillipson, & Lee, 1966), that is, superiors' and subordinates' views of the other person's views. Results of these investigations suggest that superiors and subordinates not only have different "direct" perspectives on specified issues but also often do not understand one another's metaperspectives (Infante & Gorden, 1979; Lamude, Daniels, & Graham, 1988; Smircich & Chesser, 1981). Moreover, Eisenberg, Monge, and Farace (1984), in a study of communication rules (initiation and termination) that guide superior-subordinate interaction, report that "the accurate perception of a subordinate's view of these rules by a supervisor is positively associated with performance evaluation" (p. 267).

Effective versus ineffective superiors. In his review of the literature, Jablin (1979) suggests that "over the years the identification of effective as compared to ineffective communication behaviors of superiors has received more investigation than any other area of organizational communication" (p. 1208). But he also notes in his analysis that two basic and somewhat contradictory perspectives/conclusions can be drawn from the literature: (a) a common profile of the communication characteristics of "effective" supervisors exists, and (b) the communication qualities of "effective" leaders varies and is contingent on numerous situational factors.

Dansereau and Markham (1987) provide a fairly succinct summary of the communication behaviors most frequently reported in studies suggesting a common communication "style" of effective leaders (also, see Redding, 1972):

> In particular, "good" supervisors" are considered to be: (1) "communication minded" (enjoy communicating), (2) approachable, open, willing, and empathic listeners, (3) oriented toward asking or persuading in contrast to demanding or telling, (4) sensitive to the needs and feelings of subordinates, and (5) open in communicating information to subordinates and willing to explain "why" policies and regulations are being enacted. (Dansereau & Markham, 1987, p. 348)

On the other hand, as noted above, a considerable amount of research also exists suggesting that "effective" leadership behaviors are contingent on a host of situational factors including gender, task type, organizational climate, and work-unit size. Moreover, in recent years the general assumption that leaders manifest one stable supervisory style in their interactions with *all* subordinates has come under attack by Graen and others in their studies of "Vertical Dyad Linkage Theory" (VDL) or "Leader-Member Exchange" (LMX) (e.g., Crouch & Yetton, 1988; Dansereau, Graen, & Haga, 1975; Dienesch & Liden, 1986; Fairhurst & Chandler, 1989; Fairhurst, Rogers, & Sarr, 1987; Graen, Novak, & Sommerkamp, 1982; Graen & Scandura, 1986, 1987; Graen & Schiemann, 1978; Liden & Graen, 1980; Nachman, Dansereau, & Naughton, 1985; Vecchio & Gobdel, 1984; Vecchio, Griffith, & Hom, 1986). According to the VDL model of leadership, because of their competence, trustworthiness, and motivation, certain subordinates are chosen by supervisors to receive "preferential treatment." Such "high level" dyadic structures are characterized by openness and honesty, intimacy, support, liking, respect, and trust between superior and subordinate (see Graen & Scandura, 1987). Curiously, these characteristics are quite similar to those noted above by Dansereau and Markham (1987) as associated with "effective" supervisors. Hence it is likely that extant studies aimed at determining the communication characteristics of "effective" supervisors may have identified the characteristics of supervisors in high-versus low- or mid-level leader-member exchanges.

In sum, the research of Graen and others has brought into question the assumption that supervisors or managers possess an "average" communication style. Rather, these investigations suggest that the dyadic communication exchange patterns (and their related "effectiveness") that exist between superiors and subordinates be viewed as somewhat unique to distinctive kinds of leader-member exchanges.

Personal characteristics. The mediating effects of the personal characteristics of superiors and subordinates on their communication behavior historically have been of interest to researchers. For example, characteristics that have been examined include communication apprehension (e.g., McCroskey, Richmond, & Davis, 1986), communication competence (e.g., Johnson, 1992; Monge, Bachman, Dillard, & Eisenberg, 1982; Smith & DeWine, 1991), locus of control (e.g., Lamude, Daniels,

& White, 1987), and communicator style (e.g., Garko, 1992; Infante & Gorden, 1989; Richmond, McCroskey, & Davis, 1982; Richmond, McCroskey, Davis, & Koontz, 1980), as well as the gender composition of the dyad. With respect to this latter area, studies have focused attention on gender differences in verbal and nonverbal communication between superiors and subordinates (e.g., Baker, 1991; Graham, Unruh, & Jennings, 1991; Steckler & Rosenthal, 1985), perceptions of the communication competence of male and female managers (Penley, Alexander, Jernigan, & Henwood, 1991; Wheeless & Berryman-Fink, 1985), relationships between perceptions of psychological femininity and masculinity and communication-related components of leadership behavior (Baril, Elbert, Mahar-Potter, & Reavy, 1989; Serafini & Pearson, 1984), perceptions of the communication behavior of pregnant managers (Corse, 1990), the persuasive strategies used by female and male managers in their downward influence attempts (Harper & Hirokawa, 1988; Hirokawa, Kodama, & Harper, 1990; Hirokawa, Mickey, & Miura, 1991; Schlueter, Barge, & Blankenship, 1990), and the effectiveness of women managers using stereotypical feminine/masculine communication management styles (Camden & Kennedy, 1986), among other issues.

Recent studies have also examined relationships between characteristics of superiors and subordinates and their impact on subordinates' job satisfaction. Investigations have explored relationships between subordinates' satisfaction with supervision and their supervisors' argumentativeness and verbal aggressiveness (Gorden & Infante, 1987; Gorden, Infante, & Graham, 1988; Infante & Gorden, 1985, 1991), persuasiveness (Johnson, Luthans, & Hennessey, 1984), and use of power and affinity-seeking strategies (Richmond, McCroskey, & Davis, 1986), among other variables. In turn, other studies have found that employees' communication abilities (especially cognitive differentiation) are related to their upward mobility in the organizations in which they work (e.g., Sypher & Zorn, 1986).

Feedback. Over the last 15 years, a voluminous amount of research has explored feedback in superior-subordinate communication (see Cusella, 1987; Dansereau & Markham, 1987). Generally speaking, studies have focused on five major areas, including relationships between feedback and performance, feedback and motivation, feedback and attributional processes, the use of rewards and punishments as feedback, and the feedback-seeking behavior of individuals.

Findings of research exploring feedback in superior-subordinate relationships suggest a variety of conclusions, several of which are summarized below:

(1) Feedback from supervisors high versus low in credibility is judged by subordinates as more accurate and can positively influence subordinates' levels of satisfaction, motivation, and willingness to use suggestions expressed in the feedback (Bannister, 1986; Cusella, 1982; Earley, 1986; O'Reilly & Anderson, 1980).

(2) "Feedback and incentives work to increase motivation or performance only if they change a person's goal and intentions, or build commitment to those they already hold" (Cusella, 1987, p. 643).

(3) "Feedback messages have an impact not only on a subordinate's feelings of competence and self-determination but also on his or her performance success" (Cusella, 1987, p. 651) and self-confidence (McCarty, 1986).

(4) When subordinates perform poorly, superiors tend to attribute this poor performance to factors internal rather than external to the subordinates; as a result,

superiors tend to direct their responses toward the subordinates (for example, in the form of reprimands) rather than attempting to alter the work situation (Green & Mitchell, 1979; Kipnis, Schmidt, Price, & Stitt, 1981; Mitchell & Wood, 1980).

(5) Supervisors tend to give negative feedback sooner to poorly performing subordinates than they give positive feedback to well-performing subordinates (Fisher, 1979; Pavett, 1983).

(6) When required to give unfavorable feedback to subordinates, superiors tend to distort the feedback by altering its content and in particular by positively inflating it (Fisher, 1979; Ilgen & Knowlton, 1980; Larson, 1986).

(7) Supervisors tend to overestimate the value subordinates place on supervisory feedback (Greller, 1980; Ilgen, Peterson, Martin, & Boeschen, 1981).

(8) "While it is clear that a leader's reward/feedback behavior influences the behavior of subordinates, the reverse is also true to the extent that leader feedback behavior and subordinate performance are mutually causal" (Cusella, 1987, p. 658).

(9) Superior and subordinate relational feedback responses are somewhat constrained by the interactants' formal organizational roles and the superior's initial attributions (effort or ability) concerning his or her subordinate's performance (Dugan, 1989; Watson, 1982).

(10) Supervisors' goals (directional or motivational) are important in determining the nature of the feedback they provide subordinates (Kim & Miller, 1990).

(11) Individuals rate specific feedback and feedback including distinctiveness, consistency, and consensus information more positively than feedback low on these dimensions (Liden & Mitchell, 1985).

(12) Managers often confront poor performers by asking attribution-seeking ("why") questions, by enacting aligning actions, and through problem-solving behaviors; if such actions do not improve performance, they quickly adopt punitive approaches to control poor performers (Fairhurst, Green, & Snavely, 1984a, 1984b; Gioia & Sims, 1986; Morris, Gaveras, Baker, & Coursey, 1990).

(13) Individuals in organizations often seek feedback when they fear they are not attaining goals; rather than diminishing others' perceptions of his or her effectiveness, seeking negative feedback can enhance others' perceptions of the feedback seeker's effectiveness (Ashford, 1986; Ashford & Tsui, 1991; Larson, 1989; Morrison & Bies, 1991).

Conflict. The study of the role of communication in superior-subordinate conflict has also received a considerable amount of research attention (see Knapp, Putnam, & Davis, 1988; Putnam, 1988; Putnam & Poole, 1987). Working from earlier conceptualizations of superior-subordinate conflict advanced by Blake, Shepard, and Mouton (1964) and Kilmann and Thomas (1977), a number of investigations have been directed at developing and validating coding schemes and/or scales to measure and analyze conflict strategies (e.g., King & Miles, 1990; Putnam & Wilson, 1982; Riggs, 1983; Ross & DeWine, 1988; Shockley-Zalabak, 1988; Weider-Hatfield, 1988; Wilson & Waltman, 1988; Womack, 1988a, 1988b). Results from these and other studies suggest that supervisors generally use "controlling" or "forcing" strategies when managing conflicts with subordinates.

However, several factors have been discovered to affect a supervisor's choice of conflict management mode, including his or her level of self-confidence, perceptions of skill, management communication style, organizational level, position (line versus support staff), perceptions of the subordinate's personality (for instance, perception of the subordinate as a "difficult" person), and gender and gender combinations in the dyad (Conrad, 1983, 1991; Crouch & Yetton, 1987; Monroe, Borzi, & DiSalvo, 1989; Monroe, DiSalvo, Lewis, & Borzi, 1990; Morley & Schockley-Zalabak, 1986; Putnam & Wilson, 1982; Turner & Henzl, 1987; Wheeless & Reichel, 1990). Relatedly, Richmond et al. (1983) report that subordinates and superiors have difficulty agreeing on how "active" supervisors actually are in managing conflict, while Goering, Rudick, and Faulkner (1986) suggest that the communication strategies superiors and subordinates use to manage conflict are reciprocally related to the behaviors enacted by the other person. In addition, results of a recent study by Conrad (1991) suggest that supervisors' responses to conflict style measures "cannot be assumed to predict communication strategies in conflict situations" (p. 149). Finally, viewing conflict episodes from a somewhat different perspective, Bies, Shapiro, and Cummings (1988) report that a boss may mitigate or prevent conflict with subordinates by providing sincere and adequate causal accounts (as perceived by the subordinates) for his or her refusing subordinates' requests.

Although not specifically focused on conflict per se, researchers have also examined the communication tactics and strategies superiors use in their attempts to obtain subordinate compliance. Most of these studies have employed measures of influence tactics similar to those used in research exploring subordinates' upward influence attempts (see earlier section). Similar to findings of studies of subordinates' upward influence behavior, supervisors report using rational tactics to influence subordinates more than any other means (e.g., Kipnis et al., 1980). However, results of studies also suggest that supervisors' choice of influence tactics is related to other factors including their level in the organizational hierarchy, individual differences (e.g., Machiavellianism), gender, national culture, type of resistance offered by subordinates, organizational formalization, goals, worker status as a volunteer or paid employee, performance attributions, and social context, among other issues (e.g., Adams, Schlueter, & Barge, 1988; Drake & Moberg, 1986; Hirokawa & Miyahara, 1986; Sullivan, Albrecht, & Taylor, 1990; Tjosvold, 1985; Vecchio & Sussman, 1991). In turn, it is interesting to note that subordinates report carrying out their bosses' requests because of their supervisors' legitimate power, expert power, and persuasiveness (e.g., Rahim, 1989; Yukl & Falbe, 1991).

Systemic variables. In his 1979 review, Jablin noted that less empirical, as opposed to theoretical, research had been pursued exploring the effects systemic organizational variables (technology, structure, environment, and so on) have on superior-subordinate communication. Unfortunately, this conclusion still holds true today (see Jablin, 1987b). In fact, the only tentative conclusions Dansereau and Markham (1987) were able to offer in their analysis of the literature were that "(1) organizational size and work group size have not been shown to moderate the quality of communication in superior-subordinate relationships, and (2) the communication behaviors and perceptions of superiors may be somewhat dependent on their hierarchical positions or roles in organizations" (pp. 350-351). Two recent studies, however, suggest several other conclusions. First, findings from Krone's (1992) research indicate that subordinates' perceptions of strategic centralization are related to the message strategies they use to influence their superiors' decision-making behavior. Second, Courtright, Fairhurst, and Rogers (1989) report that the interaction patterns of managers and subordinates may differ in organizations characterized by "mechanistic" versus "organic" systems (Burns & Stalker, 1961). Specifically, they found that in the mechanistic facility they studied "competitive interchanges, interruptions, and statements of nonsupport typified interaction" between superiors and subordinates, while in the organic organization "the use of a variety of question and answer combinations and conversational elaboration, and lack of managerial orders and commands characterized communication" (Courtright et al., 1989, p. 773).

Summary. The preceding section has attempted to provide an overview of selected results of contemporary empirical research exploring the communication dynamics of probably the most common interpersonal task relationship found in organizations: the interaction of superiors/leaders and subordinates/work group members. As noted in extant reviews of this literature (Dansereau & Markham, 1987; Jablin, 1979, 1985a), three items seem to be studied consistently as factors affecting communication between superiors and subordinates—power and status, trust, and semantic-information distance. Moreover, given that investigations of superior-subordinate communication have traditionally focused on power- and status-related issues, it is not surprising to discover that a considerable amount of recent research has concentrated on exploring the message strategies that each member of the dyad uses to influence the behavior and attitudes of the other party (in conflict and nonconflict situations). In addition, it appears evident that the current popularity of research examining the cognitive processes that superiors and subordinates use to interpret messages from one another is largely a result of the endemic presence of semantic-information distance in superior-subordinate communication. Finally, it is important to realize that, because few studies have examined the development and negotiation of superior-subordinate communication relationships, or processes associated with their maintenance or deterioration (with notable exceptions, see Dockery & Steiner, 1990; Graen, Liden, & Hoel, 1982; Jablin, 1984; Lee, 1993; Miller, 1989; Mossholder, Niebuhr, & Norris, 1990; Waldron, 1991; Waldron & Hunt, 1992), it is difficult to draw conclusions about the nature of communication in superior-subordinate relationships over phases of the organizational assimilation process (see Jablin, 1987a, for a discussion of applicable research).

Work Group and Coworker Communication

The previous sections highlighted the well-documented importance of interpersonal communication between leaders and members in organizations. The following discussion focuses on interpersonal communication among coworkers within and between work groups. This emphasis is significant for three reasons. First, interpersonal communication between coworkers and within groups differs from leader-member communication on key dimensions such as relationship rules (e.g., Henderson & Argyle, 1986) and message strategy choices (e.g., Kipnis et al., 1980). Second, the use of groups to accomplish work in organizations is on the rise. Work groups not only complete internal task-related functions; increasingly, they are called upon to coordinate the implementation of complex projects (e.g., health care teams), make decisions, and manage conflicts (Putnam, 1989). Moreover, as the ethnic and gender composition of the workforce changes, groups attempt to meet the above-noted challenges under conditions of increasing cultural and communicative complexity (see Adler, 1991). Third, across the life span, interpersonal relationships with coworkers are important sources of support (Ray, 1987), career development information (Kram & Isabella, 1985), friendship (Bridge & Baxter, 1992; Fine, 1986), and information and influence affecting job satisfaction (see Zalesny & Ford, 1990).

Consistent with the above discussion and the temporal emphasis of a life-span perspective, we assume that group-level socialization and individualization are continuous processes. Group membership is fluid rather than static, and any given individual will make multiple transitions into and out of various types of work groups over the course of his or her working lifetime. In addition, ongoing changes in work group technology or leadership, for example, will catalyze resocialization and individualization among existing employees. We further assume that individuals simultaneously are members of multiple work groups and that these groups are embedded in organizations (Putnam & Stohl, 1990). Thus socialization and individualization processes occur simultaneously at the group and organizational levels. Existing models of small group socialization (Moreland & Levine, 1982, 1989) tend to overlook the inevitability of overlapping group memberships and of intersections between group and organizational processes even though individuals routinely experience both at once. Finally, we assume that the nature and intensity of group socialization and individualization will vary depending on factors such as the group's longevity and/or permanence. Current research in organizational assimilation tends to assume that newcomers enter well-established, stable work groups rather than newly formed or temporary ones. The nature of socialization and individualization processes in newly formed or temporary groups is much less understood (with some exceptions, for example, norm formation; see Bettenhausen & Murnighan, 1985).

When employees enter a preexisting work group, they enter a social environment that includes varying degrees of support and information consisting of "ambient" and "discretionary" messages (Hackman, 1976; Jablin, 1987a). Ambient messages are nonselective, often unintentional, and directed to all members of the work group, while discretionary messages are intentionally and somewhat contingently communicated to specific group members. Research on "social information processing" in organizations (Caldwell & O'Reilly, 1982; O'Reilly & Caldwell, 1979, 1985; White & Mitchell, 1979) exemplifies the effects of ambient communication among coworkers on their job attitudes. The original social information processing framework proposed that a worker's job attitudes are socially constructed and are largely a result of normative and informational cues communicated to the worker by others in the work environment, particularly coworkers (Salancik & Pfeffer, 1978). As applied to organization newcomers, this approach suggested that a recruit's job attitudes arise in part from the elements of the work environment that coworkers make salient through their "everyday" talk.

In assessing the validity of the social information processing approach to job attitudes, it is important to realize that the entire model has yet to be fully tested and that the effects of social cues on work-related attitudes have been more readily observable in laboratory situations than in natural work settings (Zalesny & Ford, 1990). Further, available research has demonstrated that, in addition to social cues, objective features of the task (Griffin, Bateman, Wayne, & Head, 1987), increasing experience with the task (Vance & Biddle, 1985), and even relatively stable, affective dispositions (Staw, Bell, & Clausen, 1986; Staw & Ross, 1985) affect task-related attitudes. Nevertheless, the majority of studies conducted within this framework continue to garner support for the argument that one critical factor in an employee's job satisfaction is working in an environment where coworkers express positive job/work attitudes (e.g., O'Reilly & Caldwell, 1979, 1985; White & Mitchell, 1979). Indeed, available research indicates that the expression of negative task-related attitudes by coworkers undermines the impact of positive task attitudes expressed by a supervisor (Schnake & Dumler, 1987). The effects of social information processing even appear to occur in organizational training groups. Specifically, George and Bettenhausen (1990) have found that the extent to which prosocial behavior is emphasized in new employee training groups is positively related to trainees' subsequent ratings of prosocial customer service behavior once on the job (in this case, in retail stores).

More purposeful in nature, discretionary communication is often directed toward new members in order to educate or socialize them to selective group norms and values as well as to preferred task behaviors (Feldman, 1984). Through the exchange of discretionary messages with recruits, coworkers provide information concerning rewards and costs present in the group and organization, who controls the allocations of rewards, and the behaviors that lead to receiving rewards (Hackman, 1976). In the process, recruits often actively seek information from coworkers about the above type of issues (Feldman & Brett, 1983). More specifically, newcomers appear to use different types of information acquisition strategies depending on the type of information sought from coworkers (see Comer, 1991; Miller, 1989; Miller & Jablin, 1991). In addition, under certain circumstances, newcomers even will call into question and challenge established group practices (Levine & Moreland, 1982), although such change attempts typically are more effective when the individual and the group have grown mutually committed to one another (Moreland & Levine, 1982, 1989).

While the research base is growing, much of what is known about ambient and discretionary communication between newcomers and groups assumes relational uniformity within a work group and appears insensitive to the possibility of variation in individual-group relationships. Factors such as team member exchange quality (Seers, 1989), relational multiplexity in network ties (Albrecht & Hall, 1991a; Bullis & Bach, 1991), stages of relational development (Gabarro, 1987), relationship "blends" (Bridge & Baxter, 1992), and relational closeness (Fine, 1986) might be important features affecting how group members produce and process ambient and discretionary messages.

From a more general perspective, communication among members of organizational work groups can be thought of as serving formal-organizational functions (for example, to generate information, process information, coordinate interdependent organizational tasks, disseminate decisions, or build group consensus) as well as psychological-individual functions (such as to provide members with feedback about their self-concepts and perspectives about social reality, gratify needs for affiliation, or reduce uncertainty and feelings of anxiety and insecurity) (see Jablin & Sussman, 1983; Schein, 1980). Earlier, Jablin (1985a) reviewed and classified into topical areas literature related to the interpersonal communication behavior of workers in organizational task groups. In the following section, we locate these topics within a small group assimilation framework as well as discuss several new areas of research related to small group communication in organizations.

Task characteristics/technology and communication. One of the most consistent conclusions that continues to be drawn from small group research is that task type and task technology need to be incorporated into theories of small group behavior because these factors significantly affect group processes such as workers' interpersonal interaction patterns (Hirokawa, 1990; McGrath, 1986). As Jablin and Sussman (1983) concluded in their review of laboratory and field studies of group communication networks, it is apparent that "groups when given the opportunity generally adapt their communication structures to the nature of the work or task at hand" (p. 34). More recently, research has begun to view the relationship between communication in groups and task/technology as mutually causal. While characteristics of the task/technology do indeed shape and constrain certain features of the communication process, ongoing communication practices also affect how new technologies are implemented (Poole & DeSanctis, 1990). For example, research has shown that communication practices enacted during the implementation of new diagnostic equipment in a hospital differentially structured the operation of that technology (Barley, 1986). In addition, preliminary analyses suggest that the way a group uses a computer-mediated communication technology, such as a group decision support system (GDSS), may affect other aspects of a group's processes and outcomes (Poole, Holmes, & DeSanctis, 1991). Thus newcomers to groups not only will adapt their communication to existing task requirements but also will learn to participate in communication practices that shape and sustain group definitions and uses of task-related technology.

Group problem-solving and decision-making practices. The communication dynamics of problem-solving and decision-making groups have received considerable research attention, but not within a socialization/individualization framework. One established area of problem-solving research with temporal implications involves differences in problem-solving strategy effectiveness within short-term versus long-term groups. For short-lived task groups working on applied fact-finding problems, nominal (individuals initially work alone and later join together to discuss their ideas) and delphi (members complete sets of sequential questionnaires but never meet in face-to-face discussion) strategies appear more effective than conventional interacting groups (Huber & Delbecq, 1972; Van de Ven & Delbecq, 1971, 1974). In contrast, for ongoing, long-term groups, choice of interaction strategy is more complex and contingent on numerous factors, "including group motivation, time limitations, distribution of problem solving information, the nature of the problem, status differences among group members, and socio-emotional variables related to the group's development" (Jablin & Seibold, 1978, pp. 351-152).

While the model needs to be tested in the organizational setting, the results of research on the "functional approach" to group decision making supports the notion that the quality of a group's decisions is affected by the group's ability to perform decisional functions including effectively assessing (a) the decision situation, (b) the requirements of an acceptable choice, and (c) the positive and negative qualities associated with alternative choices (Hirokawa, 1985, 1988). Given future confirmation of these results within organizations, critical decisional functions could be made a part of training programs for new and established employees who might have acquired less effective decision-making habits over time (Gersick & Hackman, 1990).

The increased use of electronic groups in task settings (see Finholt & Sproull, 1990) has spawned a considerable amount of research related to the effectiveness of group problem-solving and decision-making technologies. For example, it has been argued that the effectiveness of face-to-face brainstorming techniques is constrained by "social process losses" (e.g., production blocking, free riding, and evaluation apprehension; see Davis, 1992). Electronic brainstorming claims to overcome some of these losses; related empirical research is still in its early stages, however, and results of studies are somewhat mixed. Connolly, Jessup, and Valacich (1990) found that anonymous four-person electronic groups produced more nonre-dundant ideas, and had higher levels of participation, but were more critical and less satisfied than their counterparts who were members of nonanonymous groups. Gallupe, Bastianutti, and Cooper (1991) discovered that, while electronic nominal and electronic interacting groups generated more ideas than nonelectronic nominal and nonelectronic interacting groups, those in the interacting groups were more satisfied with the idea generation process than those in the nominal groups. In turn, Valacich, Dennis, and Nunamaker (1992) discovered that, regardless of whether they were working in an anonymous or nonanonymous condition, larger electronic groups (nine members) generated significantly more and higher quality ideas than smaller electronic groups (three members). However, members of the smaller groups made fewer critical remarks, were the most satisfied, and rated themselves as the most effective.

Research also has burgeoned related to the use of group decision support systems (GDSS) in small group decision making (see Kiesler & Sproull, 1992). Investigations exploring possible relationships between the use of GDSS and various social processes have produced mixed but interesting results. For instance, some studies have concluded that member participation and influence are more evenly distributed within computer-supported groups than other types of groups (Siegel, Dubrovsky, Kiesler, & McGuire, 1986; Zigurs, Poole, & DeSanctis, 1988). Other investigations, however, report that equality of member participation in group decision making is unaffected by the use of computer support (Watson, DeSanctis, & Poole, 1988). In considering this research, Poole and DeSanctis (1990, 1992) compellingly argue that these types of differences in social process may be due in part to distinctions in how groups draw on available rules and resources in using the technology. In conclusion, to the extent that group problem-solving and decision-making technologies become increasingly available and accessible in organizational settings, their use should prompt resocialization and individualization attempts among group members.

Group development. Small group research appears to be growing increasingly sensitized to the complexities of developmental processes and is illuminating ways in which group development departs from a simple progression of a uniform series of stages. For example, Gersick (1988, 1989) proposes that, in the course of their development, small groups progress in a pattern of "punctuated equilibrium" that includes periods of inertia alternating with periods of behavioral change. Based on her research results, she argues for models of group development that include the extent to which (a) group members pay attention to "timing and pacing" in the course of completing their work, (b) a group is able to make transitions (for instance, from a discussion mode to a structuring or choice-making mode, which often occurs around the midpoint of the group's history), and (c) a group is influenced by its environment. The results of other studies challenge the previously held assumption that all groups follow a single uniform sequence of phases in the development of decisions (Poole, 1981, 1983a, 1983b; Poole & Roth, 1989a, 1989b). Instead, this research proposes and finds evidence for a contingency theory of decision development. Under certain conditions, a group's decision paths conform to a traditional, unitary sequence of activities (e.g., an orientation phase, followed by an evaluation phase, followed by a control phase). However, under other conditions, more complex (unitary and nonunitary cycles) or solution-oriented decision sequences are observed (Poole & Roth, 1989a). Features of a group's structure (i.e., cohesiveness, power concentration, conflict history, and size) and of its task (i.e., difficulty level, coordination requirements) both predict the types of decision paths a group follows, although structural features are stronger predictors of decision sequences than are task variables (Poole & Roth, 1989b). Thus it appears that not all groups follow identical stages of decision development. While the traditional unitary sequence model of decision development is evident under certain conditions (e.g., low intragroup conflict), most groups follow either more complex decision paths or less complex ones (emphasizing solution-centered activity with little problem definition or analysis) depending on the nature of the group's structure and its task (Poole & Roth, 1989a, 1989b).

Future research should explore how stability and change in membership (more typical of actual organizational experience) affect decision development in task groups. In addition, it would seem useful to consider how group development and group socialization processes might affect each other over time (see Moreland & Levine, 1988).

Small group conflict and negotiation. Conflict and conflict management are inevitable features of group life in organizations, yet these processes currently occupy only a peripheral role in conceptual models of small group assimilation. This is an important area for further development given that increased conflict is a possible consequence of individualization attempts in small groups and a likely consequence of increased cultural diversity in group membership (Adler, 1991). Along these lines, available research (though limited) suggests that the constructive management of conflict is key to obtaining more even rates of participation among minority and nonminority members of multicultural task groups (Kirchmeyer & Cohen, 1992).

Small group conflict studies have focused on a variety of areas including how frequency of conflict, perceptions of fairness, and the use of different conflict management strategies affect group decision quality and satisfaction. This research has revealed (a) a curvilinear relationship between the number of conflict episodes experienced by group members and the subsequent quality of their decisions; (b) that individuals in groups characterized by integrative conflict management strategies perceive themselves as making higher quality decisions than persons in groups characterized by distributive strategies; (c) positive relationships between group members' perceptions of inequity and amount of perceived conflict; and (d) less perceived inequity among members of groups characterized by integrative conflict management styles than those in groups characterized by avoidance styles (Wall, Galanes, & Love, 1987; Wall & Nolan, 1987).

Other scholars have begun to conceptualize conflict management in groups as a negotiation process. Group negotiation is characterized as a decision-making process in which three or more individuals represent their own interests and attempt to resolve conflicting preferences (Mannix, Thompson, & Bazerman, 1989; Thompson, Mannix, & Bazerman, 1988). Group negotiation is considered more challenging than dyadic negotiation due to increased information processing demands, the need for social decision rules (e.g., majority versus unanimity rules to reach decisions), and more complex interpersonal processes. Thus far, research has shown that the use of different decision rules and types of agendas affect group outcomes. In particular, higher level group outcomes have been associated with the use of unanimous versus majority decision rules (Thompson et al., 1988) and the use of a package agenda (i.e., a group discusses all of the issues at once) versus a sequential agenda (Mannix et al., 1989).

Also with a focus on intragroup conflict, Robey, Farrow, and Franz (1989) combined the use of qualitative case analysis with quantitative data on communication patterns to examine relationships among participation, influence, conflict, and conflict resolution processes that occurred in group discussions related to the development of an information system in an insurance company. Tracking a series of group meetings over a 22-month time period, their results showed that participation in discussion positively affected decision influence, and influence positively affected both the incidence of conflict (i.e., disagreements among members) and its resolution. Thus results of this study suggest that interpersonal influence processes are central both to the presence of conflict in groups and also to its management.

How group decision-making technology affects group interaction processes and conflict outcomes has been a recent focus of study as well. In particular, research findings indicate that moderate levels of conflict occur in both technologically supported (computerized systems for brainstorming, problem solving, voting, and so on) and manually supported (manual versions of the above decision process methods) groups. However, data suggest that technologically supported groups are characterized by a greater proportion of periods of "open discussion," more analytic remarks and more comments about group process and orientation, and fewer periods of "critical work" (idea-based disagreements in which no opposing sides have been identified) than manually supported groups (Poole et al., 1991).

Using fantasy theme analysis, Putnam, Van Hoeven, and Bullis (1991) studied the rituals and fantasy themes of negotiators and their team members. They observed teachers' bargaining and caucus sessions and conducted interviews with members of an administrative team and a teachers' team from two different school districts. Their results revealed that both teams developed symbolic convergence (Bormann, 1986) on common enemies and past negotiations and that they shared different meanings within their groups for the rite of bargaining. Other recent research acknowledges that groups of constituents can affect a negotiator's communication behavior and has focused on identifying relationships between negotiator-constituent interaction and negotiator communication at the bargaining table (Turner, 1990, 1992). In particular, levels of goal congruence and trust between negotiators and their constituents have been found to affect the types of strategies negotiators use while caucusing with their constituents as well as the types of strategies negotiators use during bargaining (Turner, 1990).

Conflict and conflict management *between* groups also is gaining visibility, with many arguing that managers and group members increasingly will need negotiation and mediation skills to manage intergroup conflict effectively (e.g., Brett & Rognes, 1986). Indeed, one study has demonstrated that low conflict organizations are characterized by more intergroup *strong* ties (individuals have high frequency of contact) than are high conflict organizations (Nelson, 1989).

A final area of research focuses attention on the importance of external communication to a small group's survival in an organization. Using data from project team managers and selected team members, Ancona and Caldwell (1988) identified four sets of communication-related boundary activities (i.e., scout, ambassador, sentry, and guard) that group members use to manage their dependence with external groups. Scout activities involve acquiring various types of information from the environment; ambassador activities involve developing and maintaining relationships with outsiders to keep them informed of the group's activities; sentry activities involve monitoring the extent to which outsiders' requests for information and resources penetrate the group's boundaries; and guard activities involve monitoring the release of information and resources in such a way that the group's survival is ensured. In addition, Ancona (1990) examined team-context interaction in five consulting teams. Teams employed three strategies toward their environments: informing, parading, and probing. Findings showed that probing teams (groups that focused on external processes and required members to interact across group boundaries to become more aware of outsiders' needs and to experiment with solutions to problems) were rated the highest performers among the teams. These results support those of earlier research on quality circles that has shown that contacts with external groups facilitates the adoption of the quality circles' proposals (Stohl, 1986, 1987).

Moderators. A number of additional factors affect the communication behavior of task group members in problem-solving or decision-making situations. For example, trust-destroying communication negatively affects interaction processes and problem-solving effectiveness. Specifically, with the destruction of trust, feedback responses among group members become "tense, inflexible and personal" (Leathers, 1970, p. 186), verbal fluency decreases (Prentice, 1975), communication distortions occur (Zand, 1972), and group performance diminishes (Klimoski & Karol, 1976). Further, the degree of "orientation behavior" that is displayed by group members (messages directed at resolving conflicts, facilitating achievement of group goals, making helpful suggestions, or lessening tension) is associated with the probability that members will reach consensus decisions (Kline, 1970, 1972; Knutson, 1972). Also, research exploring feedback responses in task groups suggests that, when groups receive feedback concerning correctness following *each* decision they make (in this case, employment decisions), they learn to make better decisions (Tindale, 1989). In addition, the impact of feedback on group members is contingent on other variables, including individual differences among group members (for example, achievement motivation), group task structure, the ways in which members process feedback, as well as the nature of the feedback information—evaluative content, task/process focus, aggregation level, and so on (see Cusella, 1987; Nadler, 1979).

Summary. The preceding section has highlighted selected research concerning interpersonal communication among coworkers within and between organizational groups. Results of this analysis suggest that recruits' communication relationships with their coworkers play important information and socioemotional functions in the assimilation of newcomers into organizations. For both new and continuing employees, the "ambient" and "discretionary" messages they exchange with one another often have considerable impact on their work attitudes and behaviors. However, given that employees (especially new recruits) are likely to receive these types of messages from multiple sources (often presenting conflicting perspectives) within their task environments, research exploring the message characteristics that lead workers to attend to and accept certain of these communications and not others still is needed (Weiss & Nowicki, 1981).

Finally, it seems clear that research examining group communication consequences of task and technology, small group problem solving and decision making, developmental processes, and conflict will be enriched by adopting an organizational assimilation framework and by conducting studies in actual organizational settings. Research along these lines will be more likely to confront and incorporate the organizational realities of group embeddedness, simultaneous stability and fluidity in group membership, multiple group memberships in both temporary and ongoing groups, and a range of social and material factors that prompt groups and their members to experience resocialization/individualization activity.

Dynamic Outcomes of Assimilation

As frequently noted in findings from studies reviewed here, employees' communication relationships with their supervisors/employees and coworkers may affect a number of outcomes of the organizational assimilation process. Among the outcomes that have been mentioned in studies considered to this point are workers' levels of job satisfaction, motivation, and work performance. However, from an interpersonal communication perspective, there are at least four other important dynamic outcomes of the organizational assimilation process that merit consideration: (a) the emergence of shared perceptions of organizational communication climates; (b) the degree of employee involvement in emergent communication networks; (c) the development of shared meaning or cultural knowledge; and (d) the refinement of essential and unique communication capacities/competencies.

Communication climate. It is generally assumed that, as an employee is assimilated into an organization, "she/he develops an evolving set of perceptions about what the organization is like as a communication system" (Jablin, 1982, p. 273), that is, the communication climate of the organization. Though numerous factors constitute an individual's perceptions of the communication climate of his or her organization, most conceptualizations of the climate construct place heavy emphasis on perceptions of interpersonal communication with superiors/subordinates and co-workers (Albrecht, 1979; Dennis, 1974; Falcione, Sussman, & Herden, 1987; Goldhaber & Rogers, 1979; Jablin, 1980c; Roberts & O'Reilly, 1974). Thus researchers generally agree that an individual's communication relationships with his or her superiors/subordinates and coworkers play key roles in the development of overall organizational communication climate perceptions. Comparatively little is known concerning the specific ways in which perceptions of dyadic, group, and organizational climates are interrelated (see Falcione et al., 1987, for a discussion of issues concerning dyadic and group communication climates). Moreover, little research has explored how perceptions of dyadic, group, or overall organizational communication climates are jointly constructed over time.

However, one longitudinal investigation provides some exploratory data concerning the development of perceptions of communication climate. Jablin (1984) examined recruits' (newly hired nursing assistants) perceptions of the communication climates of their new jobs and organizations on their first days of work (expectations) and after 6, 12, and 18 weeks of employment. In addition, a sample of recruits completed communication logs/diaries during their third and ninth weeks of employment. Results of the research revealed that after 6 weeks of work recruits' communication climate perceptions (including all scales measuring attributes of superior-subordinate and peer communication) were significantly deflated from their initial expectations, but, rather than increasing or decreasing over the remaining months of the study, remained at the 6-week level. Somewhat similarly, the communication log data indicated that between their third and ninth weeks of work the recruits became less positive toward their interactions with superiors, peers, and patients.

In summary, the communication climate perceptions of the recruits in Jablin's (1984) study were (a) sharply influenced by their initial "encounters" in their organizations and (b) evidenced this "encounter effect" for at least their first 6 months of work. Whether or not this is a typical pattern of development of communication climate perceptions obviously should be a focus of future research. Moreover, inquiries aimed at exploring relationships between communication with superiors/subordinates and coworkers and the development of climate perceptions that evolve as recruits remain in their organizations for longer periods of time need to be conducted.

Communication networks. To a large extent, employee participation in emergent organizational communication networks (a process concurrent to the development of climate perceptions; see Jablin, 1980c; Rentsch, 1990) also is a dynamic outcome of the organizational assimilation process. Specifically, it is likely that, as a result of the regular communication a new organizational member has with his or her superiors/subordinates and coworkers, he or she will become a "link" in a number of overlapping sets of relatively stable interaction patterns or structures. The nature of these links appears to be important in ordering communication processes related to individualization (e.g., organizational innovation) and socialization (e.g., organizational identification). More specifically, communication about new ideas is most likely to occur in relationships that are rooted in both friendship and work-related matters (Albrecht & Hall, 1991b; Albrecht & Ropp, 1984). Similarly, the development of organizational identification is positively related to relational multiplexity (Bullis & Bach, 1991).

Further, as an employee is assimilated into an organization, it is likely not only that he or she will become a link in several networks but that he or she also will assume certain specific network roles, such as "group member" (a participant in a group within a network), "intergroup linker" (liaison, that is, a person who links two or more groups but is not a member of a group him- or herself; bridge, a group member who links his or her group to another group), or an "isolate" (a person who maintains minimal linkages with other network members; see Farace, Monge, & Russell, 1977; Monge, Edwards, & Kirste, 1978; Monge & Eisenberg, 1987). Moreover, it should be noted that the types of network roles an individual performs will probably affect his or her communication attitudes and behaviors (Albrecht, 1979; Monge et al., 1978).

Only a limited amount of research has explored how emergent networks develop in organizations over time (see Monge & Eisenberg, 1987). However, based upon recent research (Danowski, 1980; Eisenberg, Monge, & Miller, 1983; McLaughlin & Cheatham, 1977) that suggests possible relationships between the degrees to which individuals are "connected" or "integrated" into the communication networks of their organizations and their group attitude uniformity, morale, and organizational commitment (under certain conditions), two propositions appear tenable. First, it seems reasonable to hypothesize that organizational members who frequently are "isolates" in communication networks have not been very effectively assimilated into their organizations (though there may be exceptions to this; for instance, Granovetter's, 1973, discussion of "weak ties" in networks; findings from Ray's, 1991, research that suggest that individuals may assume isolate roles to cope with stress in the work setting). Second, and in contrast, it seems likely that recruits who eventually assume intergroup linker or group member roles have been "effectively" (at least relative to isolates) assimilated into their organizations. Third, one would expect that an individual's "zone size" (the extent of linkages an individual has with others in a network; see Barnes, 1969) with respect to the particular networks in which she or he is involved should become of a higher order as the newcomer becomes assimilated into the organization. Higher-order zone size may reflect an individual's "sphere of influence" (Farace et al., 1977) and by implication the ability to build coalitions to support his or her individualization efforts. However, the validity of these propositions should be viewed as tentative until they are tested by future research.

Cultural knowledge and shared meaning. Acquiring and acting upon cultural knowledge and participating in the development and expression of shared meaning are two possible outcomes of assimilation processes if organizations are viewed as cultures (Smircich, 1983; Smircich & Calas, 1987). Cultural knowledge includes an awareness of the scripts and rules that guide thought and action in the organization. Through the assimilation process, organizational members learn and perhaps refine organizational scripts and rules (Gioia, 1986; Reichers, 1987; Smircich & Calas, 1987). These processes then enable them to experience organizational events and activities as coherent and predictable. Based on this perspective on organizational culture, an "effectively" assimilated individual would be one who has acquired knowledge of organizational/communication rules and whose behavior is guided by these rules (see Schall, 1983, for an example).

Participating in the development and expression of shared meaning also can be thought of as assimilation outcomes. An emphasis on these processes reflects an approach to understanding organizations as systems of shared symbols and meanings (Smircich, 1983; Smircich & Calas, 1987). From this perspective on organizational culture, the capacities to develop and share meaning could be thought of as assimilation outcomes. For example, participating in storytelling (Brown, 1985), expressing fantasy themes in group interaction (Putnam, Van Hoeven, & Bullis, 1991), and expressing shared meaning metaphorically (Burrell, Buzzanell, & McMillan, 1992; Smith & Eisenberg, 1987) can be seen as both products of organizational assimilation processes and producers of those processes.

Refinement of communication capacities/competencies. Elsewhere, Jablin and his associates (Jablin, Cude, House, Lee, & Roth, in press) have developed a conceptual model of communication competence in organizations that suggests that due to occupational socialization and organizational selection processes most organizational newcomers meet the basic "threshold" communication competency levels required of their entry-level roles. They have developed the notion of "above-threshold" communication competency to describe the knowledge levels and communication capacities that go beyond the minimal communication competencies required to adequately perform one's job in an organization. For instance, a threshold communication competence might be the ability to interpret a message from a client in terms of only one decoding scheme (for example, the one dictated by precedent), whereas an above-threshold level of competence would be the ability to recognize the equivocality associated with the message and apply multiple decoding schemes to understand the "meanings" of the message. Jablin et al. go on to define organizational communication competence as a set of abilities or resources available to an individual for use in the communication process. While as yet unresearched, these concepts have interesting implications for organizational assimilation processes and outcomes. Through ongoing assimilation processes, organizational members can continue to develop new communication abilities and resources (i.e., above-threshold competencies). An "effectively" assimilated organizational member may be one who has sufficient above-threshold communication competencies necessary to negotiate his or her dyadic and group role relationships. Additional above-threshold communication competencies may enable members to become involved in multiplex network relationships that foster integration into the innovation process of the organization. Acquiring above-threshold competencies also may enable members to use language in ways that capture imagination and help to create and sustain meaning dyadically, in groups, and in the organization.

Summary. The preceding section has suggested four closely interrelated dynamic communication outcomes of the organizational assimilation process: (a) the development of perceptions of organizational communication climate, (b) participation in organizational communication networks, (c) the development and use of cultural knowledge and the expression of shared meanings, and (d) the refinement of interpersonal communication capacities/competencies. Interpersonal communication between managers and employees and between peers is intrinsic to all of these outcomes/processes. At the same time, however, it is evident that to date few empirical studies have been conducted exploring how organizational members' perceptions of communication climate, involvement in networks, acquisition of cultural knowledge and shared meanings, and refinement of interpersonal communication capacities/competencies develop over time. Each of these areas represents fruitful foci for research and beg further investigation.

Conclusion

Within work organizations, numerous types of interpersonal relationships exist. The great majority of these relationships, however, can be categorized as involving interactions with supervisors/employees or with coworkers (and in particular fellow members of one's task group). Based upon the research reviewed in the preceding pages, it also appears evident that these types of communication relationships play instrumental roles in the organizational assimilation process—the *continuous* process by which workers share in and become cognitively and behaviorally a part of their organizations' "realities."

Throughout this discussion of the functions and roles of interpersonal communication in organizational task relationships, research summaries, conclusions, and recommendations for future research have been provided. However, an assessment of the research examined in these sections suggests several additional, more general conclusions. First, it is obvious that the great majority of studies that have explored interpersonal communication relationships in work organizations have failed to consider adequately the (positive and negative) constraints that the *embeddedness* of these relationships within a larger organizational system has upon communication processes. Such systemic factors as organizational structures, organizational (and communication) technologies, and relevant external organizational environments are likely to affect interpersonal communication relationships in organizations and consequently should be considered as potential moderating variables when we are creating research designs (Dansereau & Markham, 1987; Jablin & Sussman, 1983).

Second, and closely related to the above concern, is the tendency of most studies to consider the relationships of people in various organizational roles independent of the other roles they perform, both within the organization and external to it. For example, at a very basic level, an employee within an organization is likely to perform at least three roles: superior, subordinate, and coworker (peer). Yet, when we conduct studies of communication relationships in organizations, we typically focus upon a person in only one of his or her roles. We fail to recognize, for example, that the nature of an individual's superior-subordinate relationship affects the nature of the person's coworker relationships, and vice versa. Along these lines, Sias (1993) has discovered that coworker communication is affected by differential treatment by their superior in his or her relationships with individual members of the work group (subordinates). In fact, her data not only indicate that group members are aware of differential superior-subordinate treatment within the work group but that they also (a) talk about it with one another, (b) make judgments about the fairness and equity of the treatment, and (c) depending on the nature of the differential treatment alter their communication with the target (coworker) of the treatment. In brief, most extant research is remiss in considering how an individual's communicative behavior is affected by his or her numerous role relationships within the organization.

Similarly, most investigations of communication behavior in organizational task relationships ignore the fact that employees often assume task roles in other settings (family, community) and that these other roles may affect their communicative behavior in their organizational relationships (especially, if role conflict exists; see Feldman, 1981; Greenhaus & Beutell, 1985). In essence, it is suggested that we need to show greater concern for the effects intra- and extra-organizational role sets have on communicative behavior and attitudes among organizational members.

Third, as noted repeatedly in this chapter, it is apparent that our knowledge of the dynamics of interpersonal communication in task/organizational relationships is severely constrained by the paucity of longitudinal as well as cross-sectional research conducted in this area. Thus we are in the interesting position of being able to identify and describe various communicative "states" that exist in task/organizational relationships, while knowing little of what causes them to develop in these ways. Moreover, our understanding of the "life cycles" that communication in task relationships follow is extremely limited. In summary, it is recommended that future research exploring communication processes in task/organizational relationships be directed at examining these relationships from a developmental perspective.

Finally, although the present discussion has focused on communication processes in task relationships within work organizations, it is probably fair to conclude that similar processes and characteristics would exist in other types of task-related collectivities. In other words, while recognizing that there always will be variability due to situation-specific factors, it is suggested that the assimilation-communication processes that have been outlined here are inherent to most ongoing relationships that occur within task-related groups/collectivities.

Interpersonal Communication and Disengagement from Work

Probably just as frequently as we enter into new work/organizational relationships, we disengage from other of these types of associations. Essentially, other than disengagement due to "personal" reasons, there are at least four major situations in which people typically disengage from their work relationships: (a) some form of geographic transfer (lateral or upward) within the same organization, (b) entry into a new job and organization, (c) a job layoff due to organizational "downsizing" or restructuring, or (d) retirement from work. Relationships between interpersonal communication and work/task disengagement in each of these contexts are discussed briefly below.

Job Transfer

It is estimated that organizations geographically transfer more than 300,000 workers and their families in the United States annually (Brett & Werbel, 1980). Moreover, these workers are often characterized as "on the 'fast track': They are selected for frequent promotion because of exceptional ability, and they reap the benefits of challenging work that brings personal growth and satisfaction" (Brett, 1982, p. 451).

Until lately few studies had explicitly explored the roles and functions of communication in the job transfer process; rather, research had focused on such issues as transferees' responses to relocation, their personal characteristics, and motives for seeking transfers (e.g., Anderson, Milkovich, & Tsui, 1981; Brett, 1982; Pinder, 1978; Turban, Campion, & Eyring, 1992). Several recent studies by Kramer (1989, 1991, 1993), however, have provided seminal information on the nature of transferees' and stayers' interpersonal communication during the job transfer process. Results of his program of longitudinal research, founded on principles associated with uncertainty reduction theory (Berger & Calabrese, 1975; Deci, 1975) and the organizational assimilation perspective, have revealed that the communication behaviors (for example, feedback seeking/giving, social support, and initiation of topics of conversation) and the communication relationships of transferees, their supervisors, and coworkers change as transferees experience "phases of the job transfer process: A Loosening Phase during which transferees prepare to leave old locations; a Transition Phase during which transferees assume new positions; and a Tightening Phase during which time the work setting becomes routine" (Kramer, 1993, p. 179). In particular, findings from these studies suggest that communication during the job transfer process not only helps the transferee make sense of his or her new work environment but also assists those in the old work location adapt to and make sense of uncertainty created by the transferees' job change.

In sum, although Kramer's research provides support for the importance of communication in the job transfer process, it is important to recognize that his findings are based on self-report data (questionnaires and interviews) collected from transferees over relatively short periods of time (a maximum of 4 months). Future research should be directed at collecting actual communication behavior from transferees and relevant others (for example, spouses and family members, supervisors, and coworkers) over longer periods of time. In addition, studies should explore the effects that the transferring of employees has upon the communication behaviors of members of their "old" work groups, for example, the effects of the transfer of an employee on the various interpersonal networks that exist among members of the group.

Voluntary Organization Change

Generally speaking, it is very rare for an individual to be employed in just one organization during his or her work career (Schein, 1978). Consequently, the phenomenon of a worker quitting his or her job to assume a position in another organization is fairly common in organizations. Yet, it is curious to observe that very little research has explored the role of employees' experiences with and perceptions of interpersonal communication in their work environments on their decisions to leave their organizations.

However, in his preliminary model of communication as an antecedent of voluntary turnover, Jablin (1987a) has identified a number of factors related to interpersonal communication in organizations that appear related to the turnover process. In particular, he notes that the "quality of an employee's communication relationship with his or her superior appears to be consistently and often strongly related to commitment and turnover" (Jablin, 1987a, p. 721). For example, a number of studies have found that employees who perceive they have "leadership" exchanges with their bosses have higher job satisfaction and lower turnover rates than those workers who report "supervision" exchanges with their superiors (Ferris, 1985; Graen, Liden, & Hoel, 1982; Katerberg & Hom, 1981; Liden & Graen, 1980). Employee turnover also has been shown to be negatively associated with the frequency with which workers and their bosses communicate (Dansereau et al., 1975; Graen & Ginsburgh, 1977; Graen, Orris, & Johnson, 1973; Katz & Tushman, 1983; Krackhardt, McKenna, Porter, & Steers, 1981; Louis, Pozner, & Powell, 1983) and the frequency with which supervisors provide feedback to subordinates (Dansereau, Cashman, & Graen, 1973; Parsons, Herold, & Leatherwood, 1985; Wells & Muchinsky, 1985). In addition to superior-subordinate communication, Jablin's (1987a) model suggests several other variables related to interpersonal communication that may be associated with the voluntary turnover process, including employees' integration in organizational communication networks, the quality of coworker communication relationships, and "unmet" communication expectations. Of these factors, research in the latter area has produced the most consistent set of findings. These studies (Jablin, 1984; Wilson, 1983) indicate that newcomers who quit their jobs tend to report higher levels of "unmet" expectations with respect to the communication environments of their jobs than those who remain in their new organizations.

Jablin's (1987a) model is also of interest because it speculates about communication correlates of job/organizational "withdrawal" and the communication consequences of turnover for those who remain in the organization. For example, building upon theory and research in the area of interpersonal leave-taking processes, the model suggests that in the early stages of the withdrawal process the "talk" of workers will "emphasize differences or distinctions between themselves and other organizational members," whereas in later stages of the process, their "talk" will "emphasize a concern for the welfare of remaining members, the passing on of important job/organization knowledge to others, and attempts at recruiting stayers to replace (at least temporarily) the leaver in critical task-related communication networks" (Jablin, 1987a, p. 723). Clearly, hypotheses such as these require empirical study. In addition, research is needed exploring the similarities and differences between the roles and functions of communication in interpersonal leave-taking processes and organizational exit processes (Wilson, 1983).

Job Layoff

In recent years, as many organizations have undergone restructuring to more effectively compete in the global market, job layoffs have become commonplace events (for example, between 1983 and 1986 an estimated 7.6 million workers were involuntarily dismissed from their jobs; see Cappelli, 1992; Leana & Ivancevich, 1987). Unfortunately, most experts predict that large scale job layoffs will likely continue throughout this decade (e.g., Leana & Feldman, 1992). Although job layoffs have become commonplace in our society, few studies have explored interpersonal communication issues associated with the layoff process.

The little communication research that has been conducted in the area suggests several *tentative* conclusions. First, it appears that most management communication with employees prior to layoffs is tightly controlled and restricted and is usually designed only to meet legal requirements (D'Aveni & Macmillian, 1990; Schweiger & Denisi, 1991; Sutton, 1990; Tombaugh & White, 1990). Second, studies suggest that rumors often are rampant in organizations prior to, as well as subsequent to, layoff announcements and can have many detrimental effects (e.g., Jick, 1985; Schweiger & Denisi, 1991; Smeltzer & Zener, 1992; Sutton, 1984, 1990). Third, layoff announcements are frequently communicated to employees via impersonal, written messages versus face-to-face conversations (Greenhalgh, 1984; Jick, 1985; Latack & Dozier, 1986). Finally, studies by Brockner and his colleagues (e.g., Brockner, 1988; Brockner, Grover, Reed, Dewitt, & O'Malley, 1987) suggest that employees within organizations who are "survivors" of layoffs often experience increased levels of stress, guilt, role ambiguity, and job insecurity.

In considering the above research, it is interesting to note that the actual communication practices of organizations regarding layoffs are frequently the opposite of the approaches recommended by experts in the area. For example, researchers exploring stress and "social justice" in organizations strongly recommend that organizations provide detailed social "accounts" to explain layoffs, how they are handling the process, and what they are doing to help those laid off cope with job loss (Bies, 1987; Brockner et al., 1987; Greenhalgh & Rosenblatt, 1984; Jick, 1985). It is believed that such actions not only help those who are laid off manage the layoff process but also can reduce the stress and job insecurity "survivors" usually experience (e.g., Brockner, 1988). In addition, it is odd that although most experts recommend that layoff decisions be communicated to employees by their immediate supervisors, many organizations use impersonal mechanisms to communicate layoff decisions to workers (Latack & Dozier, 1986). In brief, there seem to be many inconsistencies between the worlds of practice and "theory" in terms of the process of communication during and after job layoffs.

Given the prevalence of "downsizing" among contemporary organizations, research exploring interpersonal communication processes associated with job layoffs is sorely needed (especially in light of the discrepancies between organizational practices and "theory" noted above). Moreover, these studies should investigate the interpersonal communication behaviors and perceptions of *both* those who are laid off from work as well as job survivors. In particular, empirical research might examine (a) how "leavers'" and "stayers'" interpersonal communication with others (especially in the form of social support, for example, see Ullah, Banks, & Warr, 1985) can help buffer the high levels of stress and job insecurity associated with layoffs (e.g., Ashford, Lee, & Bobko, 1989; Jick, 1985), and (b) how the communication behaviors of those who are laid off change as they progress through stages of the layoff experience (for discussions of various stage models, see Jones, 1979; Kaufman, 1982; Latack & Dozier, 1986).

Retirement

For most persons, their final disengagement from formal work-related organizational relationships occurs in the form of retirement. However, it should be recognized that many older people, while not necessarily working in full-time jobs, are either employed in paid part-time positions or work as volunteers in community service organizations (e.g., Cliff, 1991; Phillipson & Strang, 1983). At the same time, however, it is important to realize that the retirement transition is usually distinct from the other role transitions discussed in this section in that "it is often preceded by the individuals experiencing physical/health maladies; few structural parameters guide the process; the transition is usually associated with a decline in power, income and status; and there are vast changes with respect to whom, about what, and how one communicates with others in the organization" (Cude & Jablin, 1992, p. 36).

The process of retirement from work is frequently likened to the organizational assimilation process. For example, Atchley (1976) proposes an anticipatory stage, which he terms "preretirement" (composed of two phases) followed by the "retirement" stage (composed of five phases). Similar to the anticipatory socialization phase of the organizational assimilation process, realism of expectations during the "preretirement" stage often is predictive of successful adaptation to subsequent phases. Additionally, during the "preretirement" stage, "people begin to gear themselves for separation from their jobs and the social situations within which they carried out those jobs" (Atchley, 1977, p. 154). In other words, they may experience a form of "reverse socialization" or "decruitment" (Joynt, 1983; Shaw & Grubbs, 1981) from their jobs and organizations, while at the same time preparing for their new retirement roles (assuming they are voluntarily entering into retirement). Cude and Jablin (1992) suggest that reverse socialization processes occurring during this stage should, in part, focus on developing workers' skills in establishing new communication network ties and relationships because these skills are often central to successful adaptation to retirement (e.g., van Tilburg, 1992). The specific nature of the interpersonal communication interactions that occur with the soon-to-be retiree and his or her fellow workers during this disengagement period deserve intensive study. Such investigations might focus on how "talk" during this period functions to prepare the employee for retirement as well as serving as a mechanism for his or her fellow workers to adjust to the employee's impending departure.

Findings from other research suggest that many organizations have already recognized their responsibility in helping to prepare employees for the likely changes that will occur in their interpersonal communication environments upon retirement. Specifically, Avery and Jablin (1988) report that, of the 44 *Fortune* 100 organizations responding to their survey, 77% offered formal retirement preparation programs, and in all cases interpersonal communication problems and adjustments that employees may experience subsequent to retirement were topics of discussion. In addition, their findings revealed that the most frequent communication issues covered in these programs concern the transition from worker to retiree and its effects on the individual's communication relationship with his or her spouse as well as the effects of retirement on the process of meeting new people and making new friends. It is also interesting to observe that, consistent with other studies that have shown that retirees perceive the loss of contact with company colleagues as the aspect of work they miss the most (McDermott, 1980), the respondents to Avery and Jablin's (1988) survey believed that the most difficult change in interpersonal communication that a retiree must adjust to after leaving full-time employment is the loss of communication with peers at work. Obviously, the generalizability of these survey results to non-*Fortune* 100 organizations and the effectiveness of organizational programs designed to prepare employees for changes in their interpersonal communication environments upon retirement require investigation.

Finally, it is recommended that in the future studies should begin to explore the nature and characteristics of the interpersonal communication relationships individuals develop after retirement while they are serving as volunteers in community service groups or holding part-time jobs. Given research that suggests that younger people often have distorted perceptions of the elderly (Clark, 1981), these investigations might focus on interaction patterns that develop in intergenerational task relationships.

Summary

The preceding sections have outlined four situations involving individuals' disengagement from work/organizational relationships: (a) job transfer, (b) voluntary organizational change, (c) job layoff, and (d) retirement. Given the limited amount of research that has explored the roles and functions of interpersonal communication in each of these contexts, it is very difficult to draw any firm conclusions from this literature analysis. Consequently, at this time it is prudent only to suggest that the "realism" of interpersonal communication expectations that individuals hold prior to their disengagement from work/organizational relationships appears to affect their ability to adapt successfully to the new environments they are entering. Further, it also seems evident from the studies reviewed here that researchers have focused most of their attention on "disengagers" and their communication perceptions and behaviors rather than on the effects of individuals' disengagement on the interpersonal communication networks and processes of those who remain in the "old" task environments. Clearly, research is needed that explores how task groups cope and ultimately adapt to the loss of one of the "nodes" in their interpersonal communication networks.

Concluding Statement

This chapter has attempted to examine the roles, functions, and characteristics of interpersonal communication in work/organizational relationships. However, unlike most traditional treatments of this subject, this analysis approached work/organizational relationships and settings from a very broad orientation—from a "life-span" perspective. Consequently, this chapter explored (a) the processes by which people anticipate and learn about interpersonal communication in work/organizational relationships, (b) the roles and characteristics of interpersonal communication in the organizational assimilation process, and (c) the functions of interpersonal communication in disengagement from work/organizational settings.

An analysis of the literature reviewed in this chapter indicates that the majority of our knowledge of interpersonal communication in task relationships is concentrated within the period when individuals are employed in work organizations. In other words, our understanding of how and what people learn about interpersonal communication in work/organizational relationships prior to ever entering into them, as well as processes associated with interpersonal communication and disengagement from work/organizational relationships, is very limited. While numerous reasons can be posited for this bias in our research, it seems evident that until we recognize the *developmental* nature of how people learn to communicate in task settings even our understanding of interpersonal communication in the organizational assimilation process will remain constrained. In closing, it is hoped that the research recommendations provided in the preceding pages can stimulate and provide direction for future investigations of interpersonal communication in task/work relationships from a developmental perspective.

References

Abel, J., Fontes, B., Greenberg, B., & Atkin, C. (1980). *The impact of television on children's occupational role learning.* Unpublished paper, Michigan State University.

Adams, C. H., Schlueter, D. W., & Barge, J. K. (1988). Communication and motivation within the superior-subordinate dyad: Testing the conventional wisdom of volunteer management. *Journal of Applied Communication Research, 16*, 69-81.

Adler, N. J. (1991). *International dimensions of organizational behavior.* Boston: PWS-Kent.

Albrecht, T. L. (1979). The role of communication in perceptions of organizational climate. In D. Nimmo (Ed.), *Communication yearbook 3* (pp. 343-357). New Brunswick, NJ: Transaction.

Albrecht, T. L., & Hall, B. J. (1991a). Facilitating talk about new ideas: The role of personal relationships in organizational innovation. *Communication Monographs, 58*, 273-288.

Albrecht, T. L., & Hall, B. J. (1991b). Relational and content differences between elites and outsiders in innovation networks. *Human Communication Research, 17*, 535-561.

Albrecht, T. L., & Ropp, V. A. (1984). Communicating about innovation in networks of three U.S. organizations. *Journal of Communication, 34*(3), 78-91.

Alderfer, C. P., & McCord, C. G. (1970). Personal and situational factors in the recruitment interview. *Journal of Applied Psychology, 54*, 377-385.

Alexander, K. L., Entwisle, D. R., Cadigan, D., & Pallas, A. (1987). Getting ready for first grade: Standards of deportment in home and school. *Social Forces, 66*, 57-86.

Allen, R. W., & Porter, L. W. (1983). *Organizational influence processes.* Glenview, IL: Scott, Foresman.

Ancona, D. G. (1990). Outward bound: Strategies for team survival in an organization. *Academy of Management Journal, 33*, 334-365.

Ancona, D. G., & Caldwell, D. F. (1988). Beyond task and maintenance: Defining external functions in groups. *Group and Organization Studies, 13*, 468-494.

Anderson, J. C., Milkovich, G. T., & Tsui, A. (1981). A model of intraorganizational mobility. *Academy of Management Review, 6*, 529-538.

Anderson, L. R., & Tolson, J. (1991). Leaders' upward influence in the organization: Replication and extensions of the Pelz Effect to include group support and self-monitoring. *Small Group Research, 22*, 59-75.

Anderson, L. R., Tolson, J., Fields, M. W., & Thacker, J. W. (1990a). Extension of the Pelz Effect: The impact of leaders' upward influence on group members' control within the organization. *Basic and Applied Social Psychology, 11*(1), 19-32.

Anderson, L. R., Tolson, J., Fields, M. W., & Thacker, J. W. (1990b). Job autonomy as a moderator of the Pelz Effect in relation to group members' perceived control within the organization. *Journal of Social Psychology, 130*, 707-708.

Anderson, N., & Shackleton, V. (1990). Decision making in the graduate selection interview: A field study. *Journal of Occupational Psychology, 63*, 63-76.

Ansari, M. A., & Kapoor, A. (1987). Organizational context and upward influence tactics. *Organizational Behavior and Human Decision Processes, 40*, 39-49.

Arvey, R. D., & Campion, J. E. (1982). The employment interview: A summary and review of recent research. *Personnel Psychology, 35*, 281-322.

Ashford, S. J. (1986). Feedback-seeking in individual adaptation: A resource perspective. *Academy of Management Journal, 29*, 465-487.

Ashford, S. J., Lee, C., & Bobko, P. (1989). Content, causes and consequences of job insecurity: A theory-based measure and substantive test. *Academy of Management Journal, 32*, 803-829.

Ashford, S. J., & Tsui, A. S. (1991). Self-regulation for managerial effectiveness: The role of active feedback seeking. *Academy of Management Journal, 34*, 251-280.

Atchley, R. C. (1976). *The sociology of retirement*. Cambridge, MA: Schenkman.

Atchley, R. C. (1977). *The social forces in later life* (2nd ed.). Belmont, CA: Wadsworth.

Avery, C. M., & Jablin, F. M. (1988). Retirement preparation programs and organizational communication. *Communication Education, 37*, 68-80.

Axtmann, L., & Jablin, F. M. (1986, May). *Distributional and sequential interaction structure in the employment screening interview*. Paper presented at the annual meeting of the International Communication Association, Chicago.

Babbitt, L. V., & Jablin, F. M. (1985). Characteristics of applicants' questions and employment screening interview outcomes. *Human Communication Research, 11*, 507-535.

Bain, R. K., & Anderson, J. G. (1974). School context and peer influences on educational plans of adolescents. *Review of Educational Research 44*, 429-445.

Baker, M. A. (1991). Gender and verbal communication in professional settings. *Management Communication Quarterly, 5*, 36-63.

Bannister, B. D. (1986). Performance outcome feedback and attributional feedback: Interactive effects on recipient responses. *Journal of Applied Psychology, 71*, 203-210.

Baril, G. L., Elbert, N., Mahar-Potter, S., & Reavy, G. C. (1989). Are androgynous managers really more effective? *Group & Organization Studies, 14*, 234-249.

Barley, S. R. (1986). Technology as an occasion for structuring: Evidence from observations of CT scanners and the social order of radiology departments. *Administrative Science Quarterly, 31*, 78-108.

Barnes, J. A. (1969). Networks and political process. In J. C. Mitchell (Ed.), *Social networks in urban situations*. Manchester: Manchester University Press.

Baron, R. A. (1989). Impression management by applicants during employment interviews: The "too much of a good thing" effect. In R. W. Eder & G. R. Ferris (Eds.), *The employment interview: Theory, research and practice* (pp. 204-215). Newbury Park, CA: Sage.

Becker, H. S., Geer, B., Hughes, E. C., & Strauss, A. (1961). *Boys in white: Student culture in medical school*. Chicago: University of Chicago Press.

Beehr, T. A., King, L. A., & King, D. W. (1990). Social support and occupational stress: Talking to supervisors. *Journal of Vocational Behavior, 36*, 61-81.

Berg, L. V., & Trujillo, N. (1989). *Organizational life on television*. Norwood, NJ: Ablex.

Berger, C. R., & Calabrese, R. J. (1975). Some explorations in initial interaction and beyond: Toward a developmental theory of interpersonal communication. *Human Communication Research, 1*, 99-112.

Bettenhausen, K., & Murnighan, J. K. (1985). The emergence of norms in competitive decision-making groups. *Administrative Science Quarterly, 30*, 350-372.

Beuf, A. (1974). Doctor, lawyer, household drudge. *Journal of Communication, 24*(2), 142-145.

Bies, R. J. (1987). The predicament of injustice: The management of moral outrage. In B. M. Staw & L. L. Cummings (Eds.), *Research in organizational behavior* (Vol. 9, pp. 289-319). Greenwich, CT: JAI.

Bies, R. J., Shapiro, D. L., & Cummings, L. L. (1988). Causal accounts and managing organizational conflict: Is it enough to say it's not my fault? *Communication Research, 15*, 381-399.

Binning, J. F., Goldstein, M. A., Garcia, M. F., & Scattaregia, J. H. (1988). Effects of pre-interview impressions on questioning strategies in same and opposite-sex employment interviews. *Journal of Applied Psychology, 73*, 30-37.

Blake, R. R., Shepard, H., & Mouton, J. S. (1964). *Managing intergroup conflict in industry*. Houston: Gulf.

Bogatz, G. A., & Ball, S. J. (1971). *The second year of Sesame Street: A continuing evaluation*. Princeton, NJ: Educational Testing Service.

Bormann, E. G. (1986). Symbolic convergence theory and communication in group decision-making. In R. Y. Hirokawa & M. S. Poole (Eds.), *Communication and group decision-making* (pp. 219-236). Beverly Hills, CA: Sage.

Bowles, S., & Gintis, H. (1976). *Schooling in capitalist America: Educational reforms and the contradictions of economic life*. New York: Basic Books.

Brett, J. M. (1982). Job transfer and well being. *Journal of Applied Psychology, 67*, 450-463.

Brett, J. M., & Rognes, J. K. (1986). Intergroup relations in organizations. In P. S. Goodman et al. (Eds.), *Designing effective workgroups* (pp. 362-391). San Francisco: Jossey-Bass.

Brett, J. M., & Werbel, J. D. (1980). *The effect of job transfer on employees and their families*. Washington, DC: Employee Relocation Council.

Bridge, K., & Baxter, L. A. (1992). Blended relationships: Friends as work associates. *Western Journal of Communication, 56*, 200-225.

Brockner, J. (1988). The effects of work layoffs on survivors: Research, theory and practice. In B. M. Staw & L. L. Cummings (Eds.), *Research in organizational behavior* (Vol. 10, pp. 213-255). Greenwich, CT: JAI.

Brockner, J., Grover, S., Reed, T., DeWitt, R., & O'Malley, M. (1987). Survivors' reactions to layoffs: We get by with a little help for our friends. *Administrative Science Quarterly, 32,* 526-541.

Bronfenbrenner, U. (1979). *The ecology of human development: Experiments by nature and design.* Cambridge, MA: Harvard University Press.

Bronfenbrenner, U. (1986). Ecology of the family as a context for human development: Research perspectives. *Developmental Psychology, 22,* 723-742.

Brown, D., Brooks, L., & Associates. (1984). *Career choice and development.* San Francisco: Jossey-Bass.

Brown, M. H. (1985). That reminds me of a story: Speech action in organizational socialization. *Western Journal of Speech Communication, 49,* 27-42.

Bucher, R., & Stelling, J. G. (1977). *Becoming professional.* Beverly Hills, CA: Sage.

Bullis, C., & Bach, B. W. (1991). An explication and test of communication network content and multiplexity as predictors of organizational identification. *Western Journal of Speech Communication, 55,* 180-197.

Burns, T. (1955). The reference of conduct in small groups: Cliques and cabals in occupational milieux. *Human Relations, 8,* 467-486.

Burns, T., & Stalker, G. M. (1961). *The management of innovation.* London: Tavistock.

Burrell, N. A., Buzzanell, P. M., & McMillan, J. J. (1992). Feminine tensions in conflict situations as revealed by metaphoric analyses. *Management Communication Quarterly, 6,* 115-149.

Byrd, M. L. V. (1979). *The effects of vocal activity and race of applicant on the job selection interview decision.* Unpublished doctoral dissertation, University of Missouri, Columbia.

Caldwell, D. F., & O'Reilly, C. A. (1982). Task perceptions and job satisfaction: A question of causality. *Journal of Applied Psychology, 67,* 361-369.

Camden, C. T., & Kennedy, C. W. (1986). Manager communicative style and nurse morale. *Human Communication Research, 12,* 551-563.

Campion, M. A., Pursell, E. D., & Brown, B. K. (1988). Structured interviewing: Raising the psychometric properties of the employment interview. *Personnel Psychology, 41,* 25-42.

Cappelli, P. (1992). Examining managerial displacement. *Academy of Management Journal, 35,* 203-217.

Chacko, H. E. (1990). Methods of upward influence, motivational needs, and administrators' perceptions of their supervisors' leadership styles. *Group & Organization Studies, 15,* 253-265.

Charner, I., & Fraser, B. S. (1984). *Fast food bs.* Washington, DC: National Institute for Work and Learning.

Charner, I., & Fraser, B. S. (1988). *Youth and work: What we know, what we don't know, what we need to know.* Washington, DC: William T. Grant Foundation Commission on Youth and America's Future.

Cheatham, T. R., & McLaughlin, M. L. (1976). A comparison of co-participant perceptions of self and others in placement center interviews. *Communication Quarterly, 24,* 9-13.

Cheng, J. L. C. (1983). Organizational context and upward influence: An experimental study of the use of power tactics. *Group & Organizational Studies, 8,* 337-355.

Clark, M. M. (1981). Unleashing the productive value of long life. In N. G. McCluskey & E. F. Borgatta (Eds.), *Aging and retirement* (pp. 213-222). Beverly Hills, CA: Sage.

Cliff, D. (1991). Negotiating a flexible retirement: Further paid work and quality of life in early retirement. *Aging and Society, 11,* 319-340.

Comer, D. R. (1991). Organizational newcomers' acquisition of information from peers. *Management Communication Quarterly, 5,* 64-89.

Connolly, T., Jessup, L. M., & Valacich, J. S. (1990). Effects of anonymity and evaluative tone on idea generation in computer-mediated groups. *Management Science, 36,* 689-703.

Conrad, C. (1983). Power and performance as correlates of supervisors' choice of modes of managing conflict: A preliminary investigation. *Western Journal of Speech Communication, 47,* 218-228.

Conrad, C. (1991). Communication in conflict: Style-strategy relationships. *Communication Monographs, 58,* 135-155.

Constantin, S. W. (1976). An investigation of information favorability in the employment interview. *Journal of Applied Psychology, 61,* 743-749.

Corse, S. J. (1990). Pregnant managers and their subordinates: The effects of gender expectations on hierarchical relationships. *The Journal of Applied Behavioral Science, 26,* 25-47.

Courtright, J. A., Fairhurst, G. T., & Rogers, L. E. (1989). Interaction patterns in organic and mechanistic systems. *Academy of Management Journal, 32,* 773-802.

Crawford, J. L. (1974). Task uncertainty, decision importance, and group reinforcement as determinants of communication processes in groups. *Journal of Personality and Social Psychology, 29*, 619-627.

Crites, J. O. (1969). *Vocational psychology*. New York: McGraw-Hill.

Crouch, A., & Yetton, P. (1987). Manager behavior, leadership style, and subordinate performance: An empirical extension of the Vroom-Yetton conflict rule. *Organizational Behavior and Human Decision Processes, 39*, 384-396.

Crouch, A., & Yetton, P. (1988). Manager-subordinate dyads: Relationships among task and social contact, manager friendliness and subordinate performance in management groups. *Organizational Behavior and Human Decision Processes, 41*, 65-82.

Cude, R. L., & Jablin, F. M. (1992). Retiring from work: The paradoxical impact of organizational commitment. *Journal of Managerial Issues, 4*, 31-45.

Cusella, L. P. (1982). The effects of source expertise and feedback valence on intrinsic motivation. *Human Communication Research, 9*, 17-32.

Cusella, L. P. (1987). Feedback, motivation, and performance. In F. M. Jablin, L. L. Putnam, K. H. Roberts, & L. W. Porter (Eds.), *Handbook of organizational communication: An interdisciplinary perspective* (pp. 624-678). Newbury Park, CA: Sage.

Daniels, T. D., & Logan, L. L. (1983). Communication in women's career development relationships. In R. N. Bostrom (Ed.), *Communication yearbook 7* (pp. 532-552). Beverly Hills, CA: Sage.

Danowski, J. A. (1980). Group-attitude belief uniformity and connectivity of organizational communication networks for production, innovation, and maintenance content. *Human Communication Research, 6*, 299-308.

Dansereau, F., Cashman, J., & Graen, G. (1973). Instrumentality theory and equity theory as complementary approaches in predicting the relationship of leadership and turnover among managers. *Organizational Behavior and Human Performance, 10*, 184-200.

Dansereau, F., Graen, G., & Haga, W. J. (1975). A vertical dyad linkage approach to leadership within formal organizations. *Organizational Behavior and Human Performance, 13*, 46-78.

Dansereau, F., & Markham, S. E. (1987). Superior-subordinate communication: Multiple levels of analysis. In F. M. Jablin, L. L. Putnam, K. H. Roberts, & L. W. Porter (Eds.), *Handbook of organizational communication: An interdisciplinary perspective* (pp. 343-388). Newbury Park, CA: Sage.

D'Aveni, R. A., & MacMillian, I. C. (1990). Crisis and the content of managerial communication: A study of the focus of top managers in surviving and failing firms. *Administrative Science Quarterly, 35*, 634-657.

Davis, J. H. (1992). Some compelling intuitions about group consensus decisions, theoretical and empirical research, and interpersonal aggregation phenomena: Selected examples, 1950-1990. *Organizational Behavior and Human Decision Processes, 52*, 3-38.

Deci, E. L. (1975). *Intrinsic motivation*. New York: Plenum.

DeFleur, M. L. (1964). Occupational roles as portrayed on television. *Public Opinion Quarterly, 28*, 57-74.

DeFleur, M. L., & DeFleur, L. B. (1967). The relative contribution of television as a learning source for children's occupational knowledge. *American Sociological Review, 32*, 777-789.

DeLuga, R. J. (1991a). The relationship of subordinate upward-influencing behavior, health care manager interpersonal stress, and performance. *Journal of Applied Social Psychology, 21*, 78-88.

DeLuga, R. J. (1991b). The relationship of upward-influencing behavior with subordinate impression management characteristics. *Journal of Applied Social Psychology, 21*, 1145-1160.

DeLuga, R. J., & Perry, J. T. (1991). The relationship of subordinate upward influencing behavior, satisfaction and perceived superior effectiveness with leader-member exchanges. *Journal of Occupational Psychology, 64*, 239-252.

Dennis, H. S. (1974). *A theoretical and empirical study of managerial communication climate in complex organizations*. Unpublished doctoral dissertation, Purdue University.

Dienesch, R. M., & Liden, R. C. (1986). Leader-member exchange model of leadership: A critique and further development. *Academy of Management Review, 11*, 618-634.

Dockery, T. M., & Steiner, D. D. (1990). The role of initial interaction in leader-member exchange. *Group & Organization Studies, 15*, 395-413.

Dominick, J. R. (1974). Children's viewing of crime shows and attitudes of law enforcement. *Journalism Quarterly, 51*, 5-12.

Downs, C. W. (1969). Perceptions of the selection interview. *Personnel Administration, 32*, 8-23.

Drake, B. H., & Moberg, D. J. (1986). Communicating influence attempts in dyads: Linguistic sedatives and palliatives. *Academy of Management Review, 11*, 567-584.

Dreeban, R. (1968). *What is learned in school*. Reading, MA: Addison-Wesley.

Drucker, P. (1973). *Management: Tasks, responsibilities, and practices*. New York: Harper & Row.

Dugan, K. W. (1989). Ability and effort attributions: Do they affect how managers communicate performance feedback information? *Academy of Management Journal, 32,* 87-114.

Duncan, O. D., Haller, A. D., & Portes, A. (1968). Peers influences on aspirations: A reinterpretation. *American Journal of Sociology, 74,* 119-137.

Earley, P. C. (1986). Supervisors and shop stewards as sources of contextual information in goal setting: A comparison of the United States with England. *Journal of Applied Psychology, 71,* 111-117.

Eder, R. W., & Ferris, G. R. (Eds.). (1989). *The employment interview: Theory, research and practice.* Newbury Park, CA: Sage.

Einhorn, L. J. (1981). An inner view of the job interview: An investigation of successful interview behaviors. *Communication Education, 30,* 217-228.

Eisenberg, E. M., Monge, P. R., & Farace, R. V. (1984). Coorientation of communication rules in managerial dyads. *Human Communication Research, 11,* 261-271.

Eisenberg, E. M., Monge, P. R., & Miller, K. I. (1983). Involvement in communication networks as a predictor of organizational commitment. *Human Communication Research, 10,* 179-201.

Eisenberg, E. M., & Witten, M. G. (1987). Reconsidering openness in organizational communication. *Academy of Management Review, 12,* 418-426.

Engler-Parish, P. G., & Millar, F. E. (1989). An exploratory relational control analysis of the employment screening interview. *Western Journal of Speech Communication, 53,* 30-51.

Erez, M., Rim, Y., & Keider, I. (1986). Two sides of the tactics of influence: Agent vs. target. *Journal of Occupational Psychology, 59,* 25-39.

Fairhurst, G. T., & Chandler, T. A. (1989). Social structure in leader-member interaction. *Communication Monographs, 56,* 215-239.

Fairhurst, G. T., Green, S. G., & Snavely, B. K. (1984a). Managerial control and discipline: Whips and chains. In R. N. Bostrom (Ed.), *Communication yearbook 8* (pp. 83-111). Beverly Hills, CA: Sage.

Fairhurst, G. T., Green, S. G., & Snavely, B. K. (1984b). Face support in controlling poor performance. *Human Communication Research, 11,* 272-295.

Fairhurst, G. T., Rogers, L. E., & Sarr, R. A. (1987). Manager-subordinate control patterns and judgments about the relationship. In M. McLaughlin (Ed.), *Communication yearbook 10* (pp. 395-415). Newbury Park, CA: Sage.

Falcione, R. L., Sussman, L., & Herden, R. P. (1987). Communication climate in organizations. In F. M. Jablin, L. L. Putnam, K. H. Roberts, & L. W. Porter (Eds.), *Handbook of organizational communication: An interdisciplinary perspective* (pp. 195-227). Newbury Park, CA: Sage.

Farace, R. V., Monge, P. R., & Russell, H. M. (1977). *Communicating and organizing.* Reading, MA: Addison-Wesley.

Feldman, D. C. (1977). The role of initiation activities in socialization. *Human Relations, 30,* 977-990.

Feldman, D. C. (1981). The multiple socialization of new members. *Academy of Management Review, 6,* 309-318.

Feldman, D. C. (1984). The development and enforcement of group norms. *Academy of Management Review, 9,* 47-53.

Feldman, D. C., & Brett, J. M. (1983). Coping with new jobs: A comparative study of new hires and job changers. *Academy of Management Journal, 26,* 258-272.

Ferris, G. R. (1985). Role of leadership in the employee withdrawal process: A constructive replication. *Journal of Applied Psychology, 70,* 777-781.

Fine, G. A. (1986). Friendships in the work place. In V. J. Derlega & B. A. Winstead (Eds.), *Friendship and social interaction* (pp. 185-206). New York: Springer-Verlag.

Finholt, T., & Sproull, L. S. (1990). Electronic groups at work. *Organization Science, 1,* 41-64.

Fisher, C. D. (1979). Transmission of positive and negative feedback to subordinates: A laboratory investigation. *Journal of Applied Psychology, 64,* 533-540.

Fisher, C. D., Ilgen, D. R., & Hoyer, W. D. (1979). Source credibility, information favorability, and job offer acceptance. *Academy of Management Journal, 22,* 94-103.

Flanagan, C. A. (1990). Change in family work status: Effects on parent-adolescent decision making. *Child Development, 61,* 163-177.

Forbes, R. J., & Jackson, P. R. (1980). Non-verbal behavior and the outcome of selection interviews. *Journal of Occupational Psychology, 53,* 65-72.

Freuh, T., & McGhee, P. (1975). Traditional sex-role development and amount of time spent watching television. *Journal of Applied Developmental Psychology, 11,* 109.

Fulk, J., & Mani, S. (1986). Distortion of communication in hierarchical relationships. In M. L. McLaughlin (Ed.), *Communication yearbook 9* (pp. 483-510). Beverly Hills, CA: Sage.

Gabarro, J. J. (1987). The development of working relationships. In J. W. Lorsch (Ed.), *Handbook of organizational behavior* (pp. 172-189). Englewood Cliffs, NJ: Prentice-Hall.

Gallupe, R. B., Bastianutti, L. M., & Cooper, W. H. (1991). Unblocking brainstorms. *Journal of Applied Psychology, 76,* 137-142.

Garko, M. G. (1992). Persuading subordinates who communicate in attractive and unattractive styles. *Management Communication Quarterly, 5,* 289-315.

Gecas, V. (1981). Contexts of socialization. In R. Rosenberg & R. H. Turner (Eds.), *Social psychology: Sociological perspectives* (pp. 165-199). New York: Basic Books.

George, J. M., & Bettenhausen, K. (1990). Understanding prosocial behavior, sales performance, and turnover: A group-level analysis in a service context. *Journal of Applied Psychology, 75,* 698-709.

Gerloff, E. A., & Quick, J. C. (1984). Task role ambiguity and conflict in supervisor-subordinate relationships. *Journal of Applied Communication Research, 12,* 90-102.

Gersick, C. J. G. (1988). Time and transition in work teams: Toward a new model of group development. *Academy of Management Journal, 31,* 9-41.

Gersick, C. J. G. (1989). Marking time: Predictable transitions in task groups. *Academy of Management Journal, 32,* 274-309.

Gersick, C. J. G., & Hackman, J. R. (1990). Habitual routines in task-performing groups. *Organizational Behavior and Human Decision Processes, 47,* 65-97.

Gilmore, D. C., & Ferris, G. R. (1989). The effects of applicant impression management tactics on interviewer judgments. *Journal of Management, 15,* 557-564.

Gioia, D. A. (1986). Symbols, scripts, and sensemaking: Creating meaning in the organizational experience. In H. P. Sims, Jr., D. A. Gioia, et al. (Eds.), *The thinking organization: Dynamics of organizational social cognition* (pp. 49-74). San Francisco: Jossey-Bass.

Gioia, D. A., Donnellon, A., & Sims, H. P. (1989). Communication and cognition in appraisal: A tale of two paradigms. *Organizational Studies, 10,* 503-530.

Gioia, D. A., & Sims, H. P. (1986). Cognition-behavior connections: Attribution and verbal behavior in leader-subordinate interactions. *Organizational Behavior and Human Decision Processes, 37,* 197-229.

Glauser, M. J. (1984). Upward information flow in organizations: Review and conceptual analysis. *Human Relations, 37,* 613-643.

Glennon, L. M., & Butsch, R. (1982). The family as portrayed on television: 1946-1978. In D. Pearl, L. Bouthilet, & J. Lazar (Eds.), *Television and behavior: Ten years of scientific progress and implications for the eighties* (Vol. 2, pp. 264-271). Washington, DC: Government Printing Office.

Goering, E. M., Rudick, K. L., & Faulkner, M. M. (1986, May). *The validity of a self-reported conflict management scale in measuring conflict management behaviors.* Paper presented at the annual meeting of the International Communication Association, Chicago.

Goldhaber, G. M., & Rogers, D. P. (1979). *Auditing communication systems: The ICA communication audit.* Dubuque, IA: Kendall/Hunt.

Goldstein, B., & Oldham, J. (1979). *Children and work: A study of socialization.* New Brunswick, NJ: Transaction.

Goodall, D. B., & Goodall, H. L. (1982). The employment interview: A selective review of the literature with implications for communication research. *Communication Quarterly, 30,* 116-123.

Goodnow, J. J. (1988). Children's household work: Its nature and functions. *Psychological Bulletin, 103,* 5-26.

Goodnow, J. J., Bowes, J. M., Dawes, L. J., & Taylor, A. J. (1988, August). *The flow of work in families.* Paper presented at the 5th Australian Developmental Conference, Sydney.

Goodnow, J. J., Bowes, J. M., Warton, P. M., Dawes, L. J., & Taylor, A. J. (1991). Would you ask someone else to do this task? Parents' and children's ideas about household work requests. *Developmental Psychology, 27,* 817-828.

Goodnow, J. J., & Delaney, S. (1989). Children's household work: Task differences, styles of assignment, and links to family relationships. *Journal of Applied Developmental Psychology, 10,* 209-226.

Goodnow, J. J., & Warton, P. M. (1991). The social bases of social cognition: Interactions about work and their implications. *Merrill-Palmer Quarterly, 37,* 27-58.

Gorden, W. I., & Infante, D. A. (1987). Employee rights: Content, argumentativeness, verbal aggressiveness, and career satisfaction. In C. A. B. Osigweh (Ed.), *Communicating employee responsibilities and rights: A modern management mandate* (pp. 149-163). Westport, CT: Quorum.

Gorden, W. I., Infante, D. A., & Graham, E. E. (1988). Corporate conditions conducive to employee voice: A subordinate perspective. *Employee Responsibilities and Rights Journal, 1,* 101-111.

Graen, G. (1976). Role-making processes within complex organizations. In M. D. Dunnette (Ed.), *Handbook of industrial and organizational psychology* (pp. 1201-1245). Chicago: Rand McNally.

Graen, G., & Ginsburgh, S. (1977). Job resignation as a function of role orientation and leader acceptance: A longitudinal investigation of organizational assimilation. *Organizational Behavior and Human Performance, 19,* 1-17.

Graen, G., Liden, R., & Hoel, W. (1982). Role of leadership in the employee withdrawal process. *Journal of Applied Psychology, 67*, 868-872.

Graen, G., Novak, M., & Sommerkamp, P. (1982). The effects of leader-member exchange and job design on productivity and satisfaction: Testing a dual attachment model. *Organizational Behavior and Human Performance, 30*, 109-131.

Graen, G. B., Orris, J. B., & Johnson, T. W. (1973). Role assimilation processes in a complex organization. *Journal of Vocational Behavior, 3*, 395-420.

Graen, G. B., & Scandura, T. A. (1986). A theory of dyadic career reality. In K. Rowland & G. Ferris (Eds.), *Research in personnel and human resources management* (Vol. 4, pp. 147-181). Greenwich, CT: JAI.

Graen, G. B., & Scandura, T. A. (1987). Toward a psychology of dyadic organizing. In B. Staw & L. Cummings (Eds.), *Research in organizational behavior* (Vol. 9, pp. 175-208). Greenwich, CT: JAI.

Graen, G., & Schiemann, W. (1978). Leader-member agreement: A vertical dyad linkage approach. *Journal of Applied Psychology, 63*, 206-212.

Graham, G. H., Unruh, J., & Jennings, P. (1991). The impact of nonverbal communication in organizations: A survey of perceptions. *Journal of Business Communication, 28*, 45-62.

Granovetter, M. S. (1973). The strength of weak ties. *American Journal of Sociology, 78*, 1360-1380.

Granovetter, M. S. (1974). *Getting a job: A study of contacts and careers.* Cambridge, MA: Harvard University Press.

Graves, L. M., & Karren, R. J. (1992). Interviewer decision processes and effectiveness: An experimental policy-capturing investigation. *Personnel Psychology, 45*, 313-340.

Green, S. G., & Mitchell, T. R. (1979). Attributional processes of leaders in leader-member interactions. *Organizational Behavior and Human Performance, 23*, 429-458.

Greenberger, E., & Steinberg, L. D. (1986). *When teenagers work: The psychological and social costs of adolescent employment.* New York: Basic Books.

Greenberger, E., Steinberg, L. D., & Ruggiero, M. (1982). A job is a job is a job . . . Or is it? *Work and Occupations, 9*, 79-96.

Greenberger, E., Steinberg, L. D., Vaux, A., & McAuliffe, S. (1980). Adolescents who work: Effects of part-time employment on family and peer relations. *Journal of Youth and Adolescence, 9*, 189-202.

Greenhalgh, L. (1984). Managing the job insecurity crisis. *Human Resource Management, 22*, 431-444.

Greenhalgh, L., & Rosenblatt, Z. (1984). Job insecurity: Toward conceptual clarity. *Academy of Management Review, 9*, 438-448.

Greenhaus, J. H., & Beutell, N. J. (1985). Sources of conflict between work and family roles. *Academy of Management Review, 10*, 76-88.

Greller, M. M. (1980). Evaluation of feedback sources as a function of role and organizational level. *Journal of Applied Psychology, 65*, 16-23.

Griffin, R. W., Bateman, T. S., Wayne, S. J., & Head, T. C. (1987). Objective and social factors as determinants of task perceptions and responses: An integrated perspective and empirical investigation. *Academy of Management Journal, 30*, 501-523.

Hackman, J. R. (1976). Group influences on individuals. In M. D. Dunnette (Ed.), *Handbook of industrial and organizational psychology* (pp. 1455-1525). Chicago: Rand McNally.

Harlan, A., Kerr, J., & Kerr, S. (1977). Preference for motivator and hygiene factors in a hypothetical interview situation: Further findings and some implications for the employment interview. *Personnel Psychology, 30*, 557-566.

Harper, N. L., & Hirokawa, R. Y. (1988). A comparison of persuasive strategies used by female and male managers I: An examination of downward influence. *Communication Quarterly, 36*, 157-168.

Harris, M. M. (1989). Reconsidering the employment interview: A review of recent literature and suggestions for future research. *Personnel Psychology, 42*, 691-726.

Harrison, T. M. (1985). Communication and participative decision making: An exploratory study. *Personnel Psychology, 38*, 93-116.

Hatfield, J. D., & Huseman, R. C. (1982). Perceptual congruence about communication as related to satisfaction: Moderating effects of individual characteristics. *Academy of Management Journal, 25*, 349-358.

Henderson, M., & Argyle, M. (1986). The informal rules of working relationships. *Journal of Organizational Behaviour, 7*, 259-275.

Herriot, P., & Rothwell, C. (1981). Organizational choice and decision theory: Effects of employers' literature and selection interview. *Journal of Occupational Psychology, 54*, 17-31.

Herriot, P., & Rothwell, C. (1983). Expectations and impressions in the graduate selection interview. *Journal of Occupational Psychology, 56*, 303-314.

Hirokawa, R. Y. (1985). Discussion procedures and decision-making performance: A test of a functional perspective. *Human Communication Research, 14*, 203-224.

Hirokawa, R. Y. (1988). Group communication and decision-making performance: A continued test of the functional perspective. *Human Communication Research, 14*, 487-515.

Hirokawa, R. Y. (1990). The role of communication in group decision-making efficacy: A task contingency perspective. *Small Group Research, 21*, 190-204.

Hirokawa, R. Y., Kodama, R. A., & Harper, N. L. (1990). Impact of managerial power on persuasive strategy selection by male and female managers. *Management Communication Quarterly, 4*, 30-50.

Hirokawa, R. Y., Mickey, J., & Miura, S. (1991). Effects of request legitimacy on the compliance-gaining tactics of male and female managers. *Communication Monographs, 58*, 421-436.

Hirokawa, R. Y., & Miyahara, A. (1986). A comparison of influence strategies utilized by managers in American and Japanese organizations. *Communication Quarterly, 34*, 250-265.

Hollandworth, J. G., Kazelskis, R., Stevens, J., & Dressel, M. E. (1979). Relative contributions of verbal, articulative and nonverbal communication to employment interview decisions in the job interview setting. *Personnel Psychology, 32*, 359-367.

Huber, G. P., & Delbecq, A. L. (1972). Guidelines for combining judgments of individual members in decision conferences. *Academy of Management Journal, 15*, 161-174.

Hudson, D. C., & Jablin, F. M. (1992, May). *Newcomer information-giving during organizational entry: Conceptualization and the development of a message categorization scheme.* Paper presented at the annual meeting of the International Communication Association, Miami.

Huston, A. C., & Alvarez, M. M. (1990). The socialization context of gender role development in early adolescence. In R. Montemayer, G. R. Adams, & T. P. Gullotta (Eds.), *From childhood to adolescence: A transitional period?* (pp. 156-179). Newbury Park, CA: Sage.

Ilgen, D. R., & Knowlton, W. A. (1980). Performance attributional effects on feedback from superiors. *Organizational Behavior and Human Performance, 25*, 441-456.

Ilgen, D. R., Peterson, R. B., Martin, B. A., & Boeschen, D. A. (1981). Supervisor and subordinate reactions to performance appraisal sessions. *Organizational Behavior and Human Performance, 28*, 311-330.

Imada, A. S., & Hakel, M. D. (1977). Influence of nonverbal communication and rater proximity on impressions and decisions in simulated employment interviews. *Journal of Applied Psychology, 62*, 295-300.

Infante, D. A., & Gorden, W. I. (1979). Subordinate and superior perceptions of self and one another: Relations, accuracy, and reciprocity of liking. *Western Journal of Speech Communication, 43*, 212-223.

Infante, D. A., & Gorden, W. I. (1985). Superiors' argumentativeness and verbal aggressiveness as predictors of subordinates' satisfaction. *Human Communication Research, 12*, 117-125.

Infante, D. A., & Gorden, W. I. (1987). Superior and subordinate communication profiles: Implications for independent-mindedness and upward effectiveness. *Central States Speech Journal, 38*, 73-80.

Infante, D. A., & Gorden, W. I. (1989). Argumentativeness and affirming communicator style as predictors of satisfaction/dissatisfaction with subordinates. *Communication Quarterly, 37*, 81-90.

Infante, D. A., & Gorden, W. I. (1991). How employees see the boss: Test of an argumentative and affirming model of supervisors' communicative behavior. *Western Journal of Speech Communication, 55*, 294-304.

Jablin, F. M. (1979). Superior-subordinate communication: The state of the art. *Psychological Bulletin, 86*, 1201-1222.

Jablin, F. M. (1980a). Superior's upward influence, satisfaction, and openness in superior-subordinate communication: A re-examination of the "Pelz Effect." *Human Communication Research, 6*, 210-220.

Jablin, F. M. (1980b). Subordinate's sex and superior-subordinate status differentiation as moderators of the Pelz Effect. In D. Nimmo (Ed.), *Communication yearbook 4* (pp. 349-366). New Brunswick, NJ: Transaction.

Jablin, F. M. (1980c). Organizational communication theory and research: An overview of communication climate and network research. In D. Nimmo (Ed.), *Communication yearbook 4* (pp. 327-347). New Brunswick, NJ: Transaction.

Jablin, F. M. (1981, August). *Organizational entry and organizational communication: Job retrospections, expectations, and turnover.* Paper presented at the annual meeting of the Academy of Management, San Diego.

Jablin, F. M. (1982). Organizational communication: An assimilation approach. In M. E. Roloff & C. R. Berger (Eds.), *Social cognition and communication* (pp. 255-286). Beverly Hills, CA: Sage.

Jablin, F. M. (1984). Assimilating new members into organizations. In R. N. Bostrom (Ed.), *Communication yearbook 8* (pp. 594-626). Beverly Hills, CA: Sage.

Jablin, F. M. (1985a). Task/work relationships: A life-span perspective. In M. L. Knapp & G. R. Miller (Eds.), *Handbook of interpersonal communication* (pp. 615-654). Beverly Hills, CA: Sage.

Jablin, F. M. (1985b). An exploratory study of organizational communication socialization. *Southern Speech Communication Journal, 50*, 261-282.

Jablin, F. M. (1987a). Organizational entry, assimilation, and exit. In F. M. Jablin, L. L. Putnam, K. H. Roberts, & L. W. Porter (Eds.), *Handbook of organizational communication: An interdisciplinary perspective* (pp. 679-740). Newbury Park, CA: Sage.

Jablin, F. M. (1987b). Formal organization structure. In F. M. Jablin, L. L. Putnam, K. H. Roberts, & L. W. Porter (Eds.), *Handbook of organizational communication: An interdisciplinary perspective* (pp. 389-419). Newbury Park, CA: Sage.

Jablin, F. M. (1993). *Dinner-time talk: Ambient messages from parents to children about work.* Unpublished manuscript, University of Texas at Austin.

Jablin, F. M., Cude, R. L., House, A., Lee, J., & Roth, N. L. (in press). Communication competence in organizations: Conceptualization and comparison across multiple levels of analysis. In G. Barnett & L. Thayer (Eds.), *Organization communication: Emerging perspectives* (Vol. 4, pp. 114-140). Norwood, NJ: Ablex.

Jablin, F. M., & McComb, K. B. (1984). The employment screening interview: An organizational assimilation and communication perspective. In R. N. Bostrom (Ed.), *Communication yearbook 8* (pp. 137-163). Beverly Hills, CA: Sage.

Jablin, F. M., & Miller, V. D. (1990). Interviewer and applicant questioning behavior in employment interviews. *Management Communication Quarterly, 4*, 51-86.

Jablin, F. M., & Seibold, D. R. (1978). Implications for problem-solving groups of empirical research on "brainstorming": A critical review of the literature. *Southern Speech Communication Journal, 43*, 327-356.

Jablin, F. M., & Sussman, L. (1983). Organizational group communication: A review of the literature and model of the process. In H. H. Greenbaum, R. L. Falcione, & S. A. Hellweg (Eds.), *Organizational communication: Abstracts, analysis and overview* (Vol. 8, pp. 11-50). Beverly Hills, CA: Sage.

Jablin, F. M., Tengler, C. D., McClary, K. B., & Teigen, C. W. (1987, May). *Behavioral and perceptual correlates of applicants' communication satisfaction in employment screening interviews.* Paper presented at the annual meeting of the International Communication Association, Montreal.

Jablin, F. M., Tengler, C. D., & Teigen, C. W. (1982, May). *Interviewee perceptions of employment screening interviews: Relationships among perceptions of communication satisfaction, interviewer credibility and trust, interviewing experience and interview outcomes.* Paper presented at the annual meeting of the International Communication Association, Boston.

Jablin, F. M., Tengler, C. D., & Teigen, C. W. (1985, August). *Applicant perceptions of job incumbents and personnel representatives as communication sources in screening interviews.* Paper presented at the annual meeting of the Academy of Management, San Diego.

Janz, T. (1989). The patterned behavior description interview: The best prophet of the future is the past. In R. W. Eder & G. R. Ferris (Eds.), *The employment interview: Theory, research and practice* (pp. 158-168). Newbury Park, CA: Sage.

Janz, T., Hellervik, L., & Gilmore, D. C. (1986). *Behavior description interviewing.* Boston: Allyn & Bacon.

Jeffries-Fox, S., & Signorielli, N. (1979). Television and children's conception of occupations. In H. S. Dordick (Ed.), *Proceedings of the Sixth Annual Telecommunications Policy Research Conference* (pp. 21-38). Lexington, MA: Lexington.

Jick, T. D. (1985). As the ax falls: Budget cuts and the experience of stress in organizations. In T. A. Beehr & R. S. Bhagat (Eds.), *Human stress and cognition in organizations: An integrated perspective* (pp. 83-114). New York: Wiley.

Johnson, A. L., Luthans, F., & Hennessey, H. W. (1984). The role of locus of control in leader influence behavior. *Personnel Psychology, 37*, 61-75.

Johnson, G. M. (1992). Subordinate perceptions of superior's communication competence and task attraction related to superior's use of compliance-gaining tactics. *Western Journal of Communication, 56*, 54-67.

Jones, W. H. (1979). Grief and involuntary career change: Its implications for counseling. *Vocational Guidance Quarterly, 31*, 196-200.

Joynt, P. (1983). Decruitment: A new personnel function. *International Studies of Management and Organization, 12*, 43-53.

Karol, B. L. (1977). *Relationship of recruiter behavior, perceived similarity, and prior information to applicants' assessments of the campus recruitment interview.* Unpublished doctoral dissertation, Ohio State University.

Katerberg, R., & Hom, R. (1981). Effects of within-group and between-group variation in leadership. *Journal of Applied Psychology, 66*, 218-223.

Katz, D., & Kahn, R. L. (1966). *The social psychology of organizations*. New York: Wiley.

Katz, R. (1980). Time and work: Toward an integrative perspective. In B. M. Staw & L. L. Cummings (Eds.), *Research in organizational behavior* (Vol. 2, pp. 81-127). Greenwich, CT: JAI.

Katz, R., & Tushman, M. L. (1983). A longitudinal study of the effects of boundary spanning supervision on turnover and promotion in research and development. *Academy of Management Journal, 26*, 437-456.

Katzman, N. (1972). Television soap operas: What's been going on anyway. *Public Opinion Quarterly, 36*, 200-212.

Kaufman, H. G. (1982). *Professionals in search of work*. New York: Wiley.

Keenan, A. (1976). Effects of non-verbal behaviour on candidates' performance. *Journal of Occupational Psychology, 49*, 171-176.

Keenan, A., & Wedderburn, A. A. I. (1975). Effects of non-verbal behaviour on candidates' impressions. *Journal of Occupational Psychology, 48*, 129-132.

Kiesler, S., & Sproull, L. (1992). Group decision making and communication technology. *Organizational Behavior and Human Decision Processes, 52*, 96-123.

Kilduff, M. (1990). The interpersonal structure of decision making: A social comparison approach to organizational choice. *Organizational Behavior and Human Decision Processes, 47*, 270-288.

Kilmann, R. H., & Thomas, K. W. (1977). Developing a forced-choice measure of conflict-handling behavior: The MODE instrument. *Educational and Psychological Measurement, 37*, 309-325.

Kim, Y. Y., & Miller, K. I. (1990). The effects of attributions and feedback goals on the generation of supervisory feedback message strategies. *Management Communication Quarterly, 4*, 6-29.

King, W. C., & Miles, E. W. (1990). What we know—and don't know—about measuring conflict: An examination of the ROCI-II and OCCI conflict instruments. *Management Communication Quarterly, 4*, 222-243.

Kinicki, A. J., & Lockwood, C. A. (1985). The interview process: An examination of factors recruiters use in evaluating job applicants. *Journal of Vocational Behavior, 26*, 117-125.

Kinicki, A. J., Lockwood, C. A., Hom, P. W., & Griffeth, R. W. (1990). Interviewer predictions of applicant qualifications and interviewer validity: Aggregate and individual analyses. *Journal of Applied Psychology, 75*, 477-486.

Kipnis, D., Schmidt, S. M., Price, K., & Stitt, C. (1981). Why do I like thee: Is it your performance or my orders? *Journal of Applied Psychology, 65*, 324-328.

Kipnis, D., Schmidt, S. M., & Wilkinson, I. (1980). Intraorganizational influence tactics: Explorations in getting one's way. *Journal of Applied Psychology, 65*, 440-457.

Kirchmeyer, C., & Cohen, A. (1992). Multicultural groups: Their performance and reactions with constructive conflict. *Group and Organization Management, 17*, 153-170.

Kirmeyer, S. L., & Lin, T. (1987). Social support: Its relationship to observed communication with peers and superiors. *Academy of Management Journal, 30*, 138-151.

Klimoski, R. J., & Karol, B. L. (1976). The impact of trust on creative problem solving groups. *Journal of Applied Psychology, 61*, 630-633.

Kline, J. A. (1970). Indices of orienting and opinionated statements in problem-solving discussions. *Speech Monographs, 37*, 282-286.

Kline, J. A. (1972). Orientation and group consensus. *Central States Speech Journal, 23*, 44-47.

Knapp, M. L., Putnam, L. L., & Davis, L. L. (1988). Measuring interpersonal conflict in organizations: Where do we go from here? *Management Communication Quarterly, 1*, 414-429.

Knutson, T. J. (1972). An experimental study of the effects of orientation behavior on small group consensus. *Speech Monographs, 39*, 159-165.

Komaki, J. L. (1986). Toward effective supervision: An operant analysis and comparison of managers at work. *Journal of Applied Psychology, 71*, 270-279.

Komaki, J. L., Zlotnick, S., & Jensen, M. (1986). Development of an operant-based taxonomy and observational index of supervisory behavior. *Journal of Applied Psychology, 71*, 260-269.

Krackhardt, D., McKenna, J., Porter, L. W., & Steers, R. M. (1981). Supervisory behavior and employee turnover: A field experiment. *Academy of Management Journal, 24*, 249-259.

Kram, K. E., & Isabella, L. A. (1985). Mentoring alternatives: The role of peer relationships in career development. *Academy of Management Journal, 28*, 110-132.

Kramer, M. W. (1989). Communication during intraorganizational job transfers. *Management Communication Quarterly, 3*, 213-248.

Kramer, M. W. (1991). *A longitudinal study of the effects of communication on the intraorganizational job transfer*. Unpublished doctoral dissertation, University of Texas at Austin.

Kramer, M. W. (1993). Communication and uncertainty reduction during job transfers: Leaving and joining processes. *Communication Monographs, 60,* 178-198.

Krone, K. J. (1991). The effects of leader-member exchange on subordinates' upward influence attempts. *Communication Research Reports, 8,* 9-18.

Krone, K. J. (1992). A comparison of organizational, structural, and relationship effects on subordinates' upward influence choices. *Communication Quarterly, 40,* 1-15.

Krone, K. J., & Ludlum, J. T. (1990). An organizational perspective on interpersonal influence. In J. P. Dillard (Ed.), *Seeking compliance: The production of interpersonal influence messages* (pp. 123-142). Scottsdale, AZ: Gorsuch Scarisbrick.

Laing, R. D., Phillipson, H., & Lee, A. R. (1966). *Interpersonal perception: A theory and method of research.* New York: Springer.

Lamude, K. G., Daniels, T. D., & Graham, E. E. (1988). The paradoxical influence of sex on communication rules coorientation and communication satisfaction in superior-subordinate relationships. *Western Journal of Speech Communication, 52,* 122-134.

Lamude, K. G., Daniels, T. D., & White, K. D. (1987). Managing the boss: Locus of control and subordinates' selection of compliance-gaining strategies in upward communication. *Management Communication Quarterly, 1,* 232-259.

Larson, J. R. (1986). Supervisors' performance feedback to subordinates: The impact of subordinate performance valence and outcome dependence. *Organizational Behavior and Human Decision Processes, 37,* 391-408.

Larson, J. R. (1989). The dynamic interplay between employees' feedback-seeking strategies and supervisors' delivery of performance feedback. *Academy of Management Review, 14,* 408-422.

Larson, R. W. (1983). Adolescents' daily experience with family and friends: Contrasting opportunity systems. *Journal of Marriage and the Family, 45,* 739-750.

Latack, J. C., & Dozier, J. B. (1986). After the ax falls: Job loss as a career transition. *Academy of Management Review, 11,* 375-392.

Latham, G. P. (1989). The reliability, validity and practicality of the situational interview. In R. W. Eder & G. R. Ferris (Eds.), *The employment interview: Theory, research and practice* (pp. 169-182). Newbury Park, CA: Sage.

Latham, G. P., Saari, L. M., Pursell, E. D., & Campion, M. A. (1980). The situational interview. *Journal of Applied Psychology, 65,* 422-427.

Leana, C. R., & Feldman, D. C. (1992). *Coping with job loss: How individuals and communities respond to layoffs.* New York: Lexington.

Leana, C. R., & Ivancevich, J. M. (1987). Involuntary job loss: Institutional interventions and a research agenda. *Academy of Management Review, 12,* 301-312.

Leathers, D. G. (1970). The process effects of trust-destroying behavior in small groups. *Speech Monographs, 37,* 180-187.

Lee, J. (1993). *Maintenance communication in superior-subordinate work relationships.* Unpublished doctoral dissertation, University of Texas at Austin.

Leifer, A. D., & Lesser, G. S. (1976). *The development of career awareness in young children.* Washington, DC: National Institute of Education.

Leonard, R. (1988, August). *Ways of studying early negotiations between children and parents.* Paper presented at the 5th Australian Developmental Conference, Sydney.

Levine, J. M., & Moreland, R. L. (1982). Innovation and socialization in small groups. In S. Moscovici, G. Mugny, & E. Van Avermaet (Eds.), *Perspectives on minority influence* (pp. 143-169). Cambridge: Cambridge University Press.

Liden, R. C., & Graen, G. (1980). Generalizability of the vertical dyad linkage model of leadership. *Academy of Management Journal, 23,* 451-465.

Liden, R. C., & Mitchell, T. R. (1985). Reactions to feedback: The role of attributions. *Academy of Management Journal, 28,* 291-308.

Liden, R. C., & Parsons, C. K. (1986). A field study of job applicant interview perceptions, alternative opportunities, and demographic characteristics. *Personnel Psychology, 39,* 109-122.

Lindvall, D. C., Culberson, D. K., Binning, J. F., & Goldstein, M. A. (1986, April). *The effects of perceived labor market condition and interviewer sex on hypothesis testing in the employment interview.* Paper presented at the 29th Annual Conference of the Midwest Academy of Management.

Louis, M. R. (1980). Surprise and sense making: What newcomers experience in entering unfamiliar organizational settings. *Administrative Science Quarterly, 25,* 226-251.

Louis, M. R. (1990). Acculturation in the workplace: Newcomers as lay enthnographers. In B. Schneider (Ed.), *Organizational climate and culture* (pp. 85-129). San Francisco: Jossey-Bass.

Louis, M. R., Pozner, B. Z., & Powell, G. N. (1983). The availability and helpfulness of socialization practices. *Personnel Psychology, 36*, 857-866.
Luthans, F., & Larsen, J. K. (1986). How managers really communicate. *Human Relations, 39*, 161-178.
Macan, T. H., & Dipboye, R. L. (1990). The relationship of interviewers' preinterview impressions to selection and recruitment outcomes. *Personnel Psychology, 43*, 745-768.
Mannix, E. A., Thompson, L. L., & Bazerman, M. H. (1989). Negotiation in small groups. *Journal of Applied Psychology, 74*, 508-517.
Mayfield, E. C. (1964). The selection interview: A re-evaluation of published research. *Personnel Psychology, 17*, 239-260.
McCarty, P. A. (1986). Effects of feedback on the self-confidence of men and women. *Academy of Management Journal, 29*, 840-847.
McComb, K. B., & Jablin, F. M. (1984). Verbal correlates of interviewer empathic listening and employment interview outcomes. *Communication Monographs, 51*, 353-371.
McCroskey, J. C., Richmond, V. P., & Davis, L. M. (1986). Apprehension about communicating with supervisors: A test of a theoretical relationship between types of communication apprehension. *Western Journal of Speech Communication, 50*, 171-182.
McDermott, V. (1980). *The role of interpersonal processes in adjusting to retirement.* Paper presented at the annual meeting of the Central States Speech Association, Chicago.
McDonald, T., & Hakel, M. D. (1985). Effects of applicant race, sex, suitability, and answers on interviewer's questioning strategy and rating. *Personnel Psychology, 38*, 321-334.
McGovern, T. V., & Tinsley, H. E. A. (1978). Interviewers evaluations of interviewee nonverbal behavior. *Journal of Vocational Behavior, 13*, 163-171.
McGrath, J. E. (1986). Studying small groups at work: Ten critical needs for theory and practice. In P. S. Goodman et al. (Eds.), *Designing effective work groups* (pp. 362-391). San Francisco: Jossey-Bass.
McLaughlin, M. L., & Cheatham, T. R. (1977). Effects of communication isolation on job satisfaction of bank tellers: A research note. *Human Communication Research, 3*, 171-175.
Mihalka, J. A. (1974). *Youth and work.* Columbus, OH: Charles E. Merrill.
Miller, K. I., & Monge, P. R. (1985). Social information and employee anxiety about change. *Human Communication Research, 11*, 365-386.
Miller, V. D. (1989, May). *A quasi-experimental study of newcomers' information seeking behaviors during organizational entry.* Paper presented at the annual meeting of the International Communication Association, San Francisco.
Miller, V. D., & Jablin, F. M. (1991). Information seeking during organizational entry: Influences, tactics, and a model of the process. *Academy of Management Review, 16*, 92-120.
Mitchell, T. R., & Wood, R. E. (1980). Supervisors' responses to subordinate poor performance: A test of an attributional model. *Organizational Behavior and Human Performance, 25*, 123-138.
Monge, P. R., Bachman, S. G., Dillard, J. P., & Eisenberg, E. M. (1982). Communicator competence in the workplace: Model testing and scale development. In M. Burgoon (Ed.), *Communication yearbook 5* (pp. 505-527). New Brunswick, NJ: Transaction.
Monge, P. R., Edwards, J. A., & Kirste, K. K. (1978). The determinants of communication and communication structure in large organizations: A review of research. In B. Ruben (Ed.), *Communication yearbook 2* (pp. 311-331). New Brunswick, NJ: Transaction.
Monge, P. R., & Eisenberg, E. M. (1987). Emergent communication networks. In F. M. Jablin, L. L. Putnam, K. H. Roberts, & L. W. Porter (Eds.), *Handbook of organizational communication: An interdisciplinary perspective* (pp. 304-342). Newbury Park, CA: Sage.
Monroe, C., Borzi, M. G., & DiSalvo, V. S. (1989). Conflict behaviors of difficult subordinates. *Southern Communication Journal, 54*, 311-329.
Monroe, C., DiSalvo, V. S., Lewis, J. J., & Borzi, M. G. (1990). Conflict behaviors of difficult subordinates: Interactive effects of gender. *Southern Communication Journal, 56*, 12-23.
Moore, W. E. (1969). Occupational socialization. In D. A. Goslin (Ed.), *Handbook of socialization theory and research* (pp. 1075-1086). Chicago: Rand McNally.
Moreland, R. L., & Levine, J. M. (1982). Socialization in small groups: Temporal changes in individual-group relations. In L. Berkowitz (Ed.), *Advances in experimental social psychology* (Vol. 15, pp. 137-192). New York: Academic Press.
Moreland, R. L., & Levine, J. M. (1988). Group dynamics over time: Development and socialization in small groups. In J. E. McGrath (Ed.), *The social psychology of time: New perspectives* (pp. 151-181). Newbury Park, CA: Sage.
Moreland, R. L., & Levine, J. M. (1989). Newcomers and oldtimers in small groups. In P. B. Paulus (Ed.), *Psychology of group influence* (2nd ed., pp. 143-186). Hillsdale, NJ: Lawrence Erlbaum.

Morgan, M. (1980). *Longitudinal patterns of television use and adolescent role socialization.* Unpublished doctoral dissertation, University of Pennsylvania.

Morgan, M. (1987). Television, sex-role attitudes, and sex-role behavior. *Journal of Early Adolescence, 7*, 269-282.

Morley, D. M., & Shockley-Zalabak, P. (1986). Conflict avoiders and compromisers: Toward an understanding of their organizational communication style. *Group and Organizational Behavior, 11*(4), 387-402.

Morris, G. H., & Coursey, M. (1989). Negotiating the meaning of employees' conduct: How managers evaluate employees' accounts. *Southern Communication Journal, 54*, 185-205.

Morris, G. H., Gaveras, S. C., Baker, W. L., & Coursey, M. L. (1990). Aligning actions at work: How managers confront problems of employee performance. *Management Communication Quarterly, 3*, 303-333.

Morrison, E. W., & Bies, R. J. (1991). Impression management in the feedback-seeking process: A literature review and research agenda. *Academy of Management Review, 16*, 522-541.

Mossholder, K. W., Niebuhr, R. E., & Norris, D. R. (1990). Effects of dyadic duration on the relationship between leader behavior perceptions and follower outcomes. *Journal of Organizational Behavior, 11*, 379-388.

Nachman, S., Dansereau, F., & Naughton, T. J. (1985). Levels of analysis and the vertical dyad linkage approach to leadership. *Psychological Reports, 57*, 661-662.

Nadler, D. A. (1979). The effects of feedback on task group behavior: A review of experimental research. *Organizational Behavior and Human Performance, 23*, 309-338.

Nelson, R. E. (1989). The strength of strong ties: Social networks and intergroup conflict in organizations. *Academy of Management Journal, 32*, 377-401.

Noble, G. (1975). *Children in front of the small screen.* Beverly Hills, CA: Sage.

Noble, G. (1983). Social learning from everyday television. In M. J. A. Howe (Ed.), *Learning from television: Psychological and educational research* (pp. 101-124). New York: Academic Press.

Norton, R. W. (1978). Foundations of a communicator style construct. *Human Communication Research, 4*, 99-112.

O'Bryant, S. L., & Corder-Bolz, C. R. (1978). The effects of television on children's stereotyping of women's work roles. *Journal of Vocational Behavior, 12*, 233-244.

Offermann, L. R., & Kearney, C. T. (1988). Supervisor sex and subordinate influence strategies. *Personality and Social Psychology Bulletin, 14*, 360-367.

O'Reilly, C. A., & Anderson, J. C. (1980). Trust and the communication of performance appraisal information: The effect of feedback on performance and job satisfaction. *Human Communication Research, 6*, 290-298.

O'Reilly, C. A., & Caldwell, D. F. (1979). Informational influence as a determinant of task characteristics and job satisfaction. *Journal of Applied Psychology, 64*, 157-165.

O'Reilly, C. A., & Caldwell, D. F. (1985). The impact of normative social influence and cohesiveness on task perceptions and attitudes: A social information processing approach. *Journal of Occupational Psychology, 58*, 193-206.

Parsons, C. K., Herold, D. M., & Leatherwood, M. L. (1985). Turnover during initial employment: A longitudinal study of the role of causal attributions. *Journal of Applied Psychology, 70*, 337-341.

Pavett, C. M. (1983). Evaluation of the impact of feedback on performance and motivation. *Human Relations, 36*, 641-654.

Pelz, D. (1952). Influence: A key to effective leadership in the first line supervisor. *Personnel, 29*, 209-217.

Penley, L. E., Alexander, E. R., Jernigan, I. E., & Henwood, C. I. (1991). Communication abilities of managers: The relationship to performance. *Journal of Management, 17*, 57-76.

Peterson, G. W., & Peters, D. F. (1983). Adolescents' construction of social reality: The impact of television and peers. *Youth and Society, 15*, 67-85.

Pfeffer, J. (1981). Management as symbolic action: The creation and maintenance of organizational paradigms. In L. L. Cummings & B. M. Staw (Eds.), *Research in organizational behavior* (Vol. 3, pp. 1-52). Greenwich, CT: JAI.

Phillips, A. P., & Dipboye, R. L. (1989). Correlational tests of predictions from a process model of the interview. *Journal of Applied Psychology, 74*, 41-52.

Phillips, S., & Sandstrom, K. L. (1990). Parental attitudes toward youth work. *Youth and Society, 22*, 160-183.

Phillipson, C., & Strang, P. (1983). *The impact of pre-retirement education: A longitudinal evaluation.* Keele: University of Keele, Department of Adult Education.

Pinder, C. C. (1978). Corporate transfer policy: Comparative reaction of managers and their spouses. *Industrial Relations, 33*, 654-665.

Poole, M. S. (1981). Decision development in small groups I: A comparison of two models. *Communication Monographs, 48*, 1-24.

Poole, M. S. (1983a). Decision development in small groups II: A study of multiple sequences in decision making. *Communication Monographs, 50*, 206-232.

Poole, M. S. (1983b). Decision development in small groups III: A multiple sequence model of group decision development. *Communication Monographs, 50*, 321-341.

Poole, M. S., & DeSanctis, G. (1990). Understanding the use of group decision support systems: The theory of adaptive structuration. In J. Fulk & C. Steinfeld (Eds.), *Organizations and communication technology* (pp. 173-193). Newbury Park, CA: Sage.

Poole, M. S., & DeSanctis, G. (1992). Microlevel structuration in computer-supported group decision making. *Human Communication Research, 15*, 5-49.

Poole, M. S., Holmes, M., & DeSanctis, G. (1991). Conflict management in a computer-supported meeting environment. *Management Science, 37*, 926-953.

Poole, M. S., & Roth, J. (1989a). Decision development in small groups IV: A typology of group decision paths. *Human Communication Research, 15*, 323-356.

Poole, M. S., & Roth, J. (1989b). Decision development in small groups V: Test of a contingency model. *Human Communication Research, 15*, 549-589.

Porter, L. W., Allen, R. W., & Angle, H. L. (1981). The politics of upward influence in organizations. In L. L. Cummings & B. Staw (Eds.), *Research in organizational behavior* (Vol. 3, pp. 109-149). Greenwich, CT: JAI.

Porter, L. W., Lawler, E. E., & Hackman, H. R. (1975). *Behavior in organizations*. New York: McGraw-Hill.

Posner, B. Z. (1981). Comparing recruiter, student, and faculty perceptions of important applicant job characteristics. *Personnel Psychology, 34*, 329-339.

Powell, G. N. (1991). Applicant reactions to the initial employment interview: Exploring theoretical and methodological issues. *Personnel Psychology, 44*, 67-83.

Prentice, D. S. (1975). The effect of trust-destroying communication on verbal fluency in the small group. *Speech Monographs, 42*, 262-270.

Pursell, E. D., Campion, M. A., & Gaylord, S. R. (1980). Structured interviewing: Avoiding selection problems. *Personnel Journal, 59*, 907-912.

Putnam, L. L. (1988). Communication and interpersonal conflict in organizations. *Management Communication Quarterly, 1*, 293-301.

Putnam, L. L. (1989). Perspectives for research on group embeddedness in organizations. In S. S. King (Ed.), *Human communication as a field of study* (pp. 163-181). New York: SUNY Press.

Putnam, L. L., & Poole, M. S. (1987). Conflict and negotiation. In F. M. Jablin, L. L. Putnam, K. H. Roberts, & L. W. Porter (Eds.), *Handbook of organizational communication: An interdisciplinary perspective* (pp. 549-599). Newbury Park, CA: Sage.

Putnam, L. L., & Stohl, C. (1990). Bona fide groups: A reconceptualization of groups in context. *Communication Studies, 41*, 248-265.

Putnam, L. L., Van Hoeven, S. A., & Bullis, C. A. (1991). The role of rituals and fantasy themes in teachers' bargaining. *Western Journal of Speech Communication, 55*, 85-103.

Putnam, L. L., & Wilson, C. E. (1982). Communication strategies in organizational conflicts: Reliability and validity of a measurement scale. In M. Burgoon (Ed.), *Communication yearbook 6* (pp. 629-652). Beverly Hills, CA: Sage.

Radin, N., & Harold-Goldsmith, R. (1989). The involvement of selected unemployed and employed men with their children. *Child Development, 60*, 454-459.

Rahim, M. A. (1989). Relationships of leader power to compliance and satisfaction with supervision: Evidence from a national sample of managers. *Journal of Management, 15*, 545-556.

Rakestraw, T. L., & Weiss, H. M. (1981). The interaction of social influences and task experience on goals, performance, and performance satisfaction. *Organizational Behavior and Human Performance, 27*, 326-344.

Ray, E. B. (1987). Supportive relationships and occupational stress in the workplace. In T. Albrecht & M. Adelman (Eds.), *Communicating social support* (pp. 172-191). Newbury Park, CA: Sage.

Ray, E. B. (1991). The relationship among communication network roles, job stress, and burnout in educational organizations. *Communication Quarterly, 39*, 91-102.

Redding, W. C. (1972). *Communication within the organization: An interpretive review of theory and research*. New York: Industrial Communication Council.

Reichers, A. E. (1987). An interactionist perspective on newcomer socialization rates. *Academy of Management Review, 12*, 278-287.

Rentsch, J. R. (1990). Climate and culture: Interaction and qualitative differences in organizational meanings. *Journal of Applied Psychology, 75,* 668-681.

Richmond, V. P., McCroskey, J. C., & Davis, L. M. (1982). Individual differences among employees, management communication style, and employee satisfaction: Replication and extension. *Human Communication Research, 8,* 170-188.

Richmond, V. P., McCroskey, J. C., & Davis, L. M. (1986). The relationship of supervisor use of power and affinity-seeking strategies with subordinate satisfaction. *Communication Quarterly, 34,* 178-193.

Richmond, V. P., McCroskey, J. C., Davis, L. M., & Koontz, K. A. (1980). Perceived power as a mediator of management communication style and employee satisfaction: A preliminary investigation. *Communication Quarterly, 28,* 37-46.

Richmond, V. P., Wagner, J. P., & McCroskey, J. C. (1983). The impact of perceptions of leadership style, use of power, and conflict management style on organizational outcomes. *Communication Quarterly, 31,* 27-36.

Riggs, C. J. (1983). Communication dimensions of conflict tactics in organizational settings: A functional analysis. In R. Bostrom (Ed.), *Communication yearbook 7* (pp. 517-531). Beverly Hills, CA: Sage.

Roberts, K. H., & O'Reilly, C. A. (1974). Measuring organizational communication. *Journal of Applied Psychology, 59,* 321-326.

Robey, D., Farrow, D. L., & Franz, C. R. (1989). Group process and conflict in system development. *Management Science, 35,* 1172-1191.

Ross, R. G., & DeWine, S. (1988). Assessing the Ross-DeWine conflict management message style (CMMS). *Management Communication Quarterly, 1,* 389-413.

Rotchford, N. L., & Roberts, K. H. (1982). Part-time workers as missing persons in organizational research. *Academy of Management Review, 7,* 228-234.

Ruggiero, M., & Steinberg, L. D. (1981). The empirical study of teenage work: A behavioral code for the assessment of adolescent job environments. *Journal of Vocational Behavior, 19,* 163-174.

Ryan, J., & Sim, D. A. (1990). When art become news: Portrayals of art and artists on network television news. *Social Forces, 68,* 869-889.

Rynes, S. L., Bretz, R. D., & Gerhart, B. (1991). The importance of recruitment in job choice: A different way of looking. *Personnel Psychology, 44,* 487-521.

Rynes, S. L., & Miller, H. E. (1983). Recruiter and job influences on candidates for employment. *Journal of Applied Psychology, 68,* 147-154.

Sackett, P. R. (1982). The interviewer as hypothesis tester: The effects of impressions of an applicant on interviewer questioning strategy. *Personnel Psychology, 35,* 789-804.

Salancik, G. R., & Pfeffer, J. (1978). A social information processing approach to job attitudes and task design. *Administrative Science Quarterly, 23,* 224-253.

Schall, M. S. (1983). A communication-rules approach to organizational culture. *Administrative Science Quarterly, 28,* 557-581.

Schein, E. H. (1968). Organizational socialization and the profession of management. *Industrial Management Review, 9,* 1-16.

Schein, E. H. (1978). *Career dynamics: Matching individual and organizational needs.* Reading, MA: Addison-Wesley.

Schein, E. H. (1980). *Organizational psychology* (3rd ed.). Englewood Cliffs, NJ: Prentice-Hall.

Schilit, W. K., & Locke, E. A. (1982). A study of upward influence in organizations. *Administrative Science Quarterly, 27,* 314-316.

Schlueter, D. W., Barge, K. J., & Blankenship, D. (1990). A comparative analysis of influence strategies used by upper and low-level male and female managers. *Western Journal of Speech Communication, 54,* 42-65.

Schmitt, N. (1976). Social and situational determinants of interview decisions: Implications for the employment interview. *Personnel Psychology, 29,* 79-101.

Schmitt, N., & Coyle, B. W. (1976). Applicant decisions in the employment interview. *Journal of Applied Psychology, 61,* 184-192.

Schnake, M. E., & Dumler, M. P. (1987). The social information processing model of task design: Conflicting cues and individual differences. *Group and Organization Studies, 12,* 221-240.

Schnake, M. E., Dumler, M. P., Cochran, D. S., & Barnett, T. R. (1990). Effects of differences in superior and subordinate perceptions of superiors' communication practices. *Journal of Business Communication, 27,* 37-50.

Schriesheim, C. A., & Hinkin, T. R. (1990). Influence tactics used by subordinates: A theoretical and empirical analysis of the Kipnis, Schmidt, and Wilkinson subscales. *Journal of Applied Psychology, 75,* 246-257.

Schweiger, D. M., & Denisi, A. S. (1991). Communication with employees following a merger: A longitudinal field experiment. *Academy of Management Journal, 34*, 110-135.

Scott, M., & Lyman, S. (1968). Accounts. *American Sociological Review, 22*, 46-62.

Sebald, H. (1986). Adolescents' shifting orientation toward parents and peers: A curvilinear trend over recent decades. *Journal of Marriage and the Family, 48*, 5-13.

Seers, A. (1989). Team-member exchange quality: A new construct for role-making research. *Organizational Behavior and Human Decision Processes, 43*, 118-135.

Serafini, D. M., & Pearson, J. C. (1984). Leadership behavior and sex role socialization: Two sides of the same coin. *Southern Speech Communication Journal, 49*, 396-405.

Shantz, C. U. (1987). Conflicts between children. *Child Development, 58*, 283-305.

Shaw, J. B., & Grubbs, L. L. (1981). The process of retiring: Organizational entry in reverse. *Academy of Management Review, 6*, 41-47.

Shaw, M. R. (1983). Taken-for-granted assumptions of applicants in simulated selection interviews. *Western Journal of Speech Communication, 47*, 138-156.

Shockley-Zalabak, P. (1988). Assessing the Hall conflict management survey. *Management Communication Quarterly, 1*, 302-320.

Sias, P. (1993). *Communicative consequences of differential superior-subordinate treatment: A fairness perspective.* Unpublished doctoral dissertation, University of Texas at Austin.

Siegel, A. E. (1958). The influence of violence in the mass media upon children's role expectations. *Child Development, 29*, 35-56.

Siegel, J., Dubrovsky, V., Kiesler, S., & McGuire, T. W. (1986). Group processes in computer-mediated communication. *Organizational Behavior and Human Decision Processes, 37*, 157-187.

Signorielli, N. (1991). *A sourcebook on children and television.* Westport, CT: Greenwood.

Simpson, R. L. (1962). Parental influence, anticipatory socialization, and social mobility. *American Sociological Review, 17*, 754-761.

Smeltzer, L. R., & Zener, M. F. (1992). Development of a model for announcing major layoffs. *Group & Organization Management, 17*, 446-472.

Smircich, L. (1983). Concepts of culture and organizational analysis. *Administrative Science Quarterly, 28*, 339-358.

Smircich, L., & Calas, M. B. (1987). Organizational culture: A critical assessment. In F. M. Jablin, L. L. Putnam, K. H. Roberts, & L. W. Porter (Eds.), *Handbook of organizational communication: An interdisciplinary perspective* (pp. 228-263). Newbury Park, CA: Sage.

Smircich, L., & Chesser, R. J. (1981). Superiors' and subordinates' perceptions of performance: Beyond disagreement. *Academy of Management Journal, 24*, 198-205.

Smith, G. L., & DeWine, S. (1991). Perceptions of subordinates and requests for support: Are males and females perceived differently when seeking help? *Group & Organization Studies, 16*, 408-427.

Smith, R. C., & Eisenberg, E. M. (1987). Conflict in Disneyland: A root-metaphor analysis. *Communication Monographs, 54*, 367-380.

Smollar, J., & Yountis, J. (1982). Social development through friendship. In K. H. Rubin & H. S. Ross (Eds.), *Peer relationships and social skills in childhood* (pp. 279-298). New York: Springer-Verlag.

Snedeker, B. (1982). *Hard knocks: Preparing youth for work.* Baltimore: Johns Hopkins University Press.

Staw, B. M., Bell, N. E., & Clausen, J. A. (1986). The dispositional approach to job attitudes: A lifetime longitudinal test. *Administrative Science Quarterly, 31*, 56-77.

Staw, B. M., & Ross, J. (1985). Stability in the midst of change: A dispositional approach to job attitudes. *Journal of Applied Psychology, 70*, 469-480.

Steckler, N. A., & Rosenthal, R. (1985). Sex differences in nonverbal and verbal communication with bosses, peers, and subordinates. *Journal of Applied Psychology, 70*, 157-163.

Steinberg, L., & Dornbusch, S. M. (1991). Negative correlates of part-time employment during adolescence: Replication and elaboration. *Developmental Psychology, 27*, 304-313.

Steinberg, L. D., Greenberger, E., Vaux, A., & Ruggiero, M. (1981). Early work experience: Effects on adolescent occupational socialization. *Youth and Society, 12*, 403-422.

Stewart, L. P., Gudykunst, W. B., Ting-Toomey, S., & Nishida, T. (1986). The effects of decision-making style on openness and satisfaction within Japanese organizations. *Communication Monographs, 53*, 236-251.

Stohl, C. (1986). Quality circles and changing patterns of communication. In M. L. McLaughlin (Ed.), *Communication yearbook 9* (pp. 511-531). Beverly Hills, CA: Sage.

Stohl, C. (1987). Bridging the parallel organization: A study in quality circle effectiveness. In M. L. McLaughlin (Ed.), *Communication yearbook 10* (pp. 416-429). Newbury Park, CA: Sage.

Street, R. L. (1986). Interaction processes and outcomes in interviews. In M. L. McLaughlin (Ed.), *Communication yearbook 9* (pp. 215-250). Beverly Hills, CA: Sage.

Sullivan, J. J., Albrecht, T. L., & Taylor, S. (1990). Process, organizational, relational, and personal determinants of managerial compliance-gaining communication strategies. *Journal of Business Communication, 70*, 331-355.

Sussman, L. (1975). Communication in organizational hierarchies: The fallacy of perceptual congruence. *Western Journal of Speech Communication, 39*, 191-199.

Sussman, L. (1991, January/February). Managers: On the defensive. *Business Horizons*, pp. 81-87.

Sutton, R. I. (1984). Managing organizational death. *Human Resource Management, 22*, 391-412.

Sutton, R. I. (1990). Organizational decline processes: A social psychological perspective. In B. M. Staw & L. L. Cummings (Eds.), *Research in organizational behavior* (Vol. 12, pp. 205-253). Greenwich, CT: JAI.

Sypher, B. D., & Zorn, T. E. (1986). Communication-related abilities and upward mobility: A longitudinal investigation. *Human Communication Research, 12*, 420-431.

Taylor, M. S., & Bergmann, T. J. (1987). Organizational recruitment activities and applicants' reactions at different stages of the recruitment process. *Personnel Psychology, 40*, 261-285.

Taylor, M. S., & Sniezek, J. A. (1984). The college recruitment interview: Topical content and applicant reactions. *Journal of Occupational Psychology, 57*, 157-168.

Teigen, C. W. (1983). *Communication of organizational climate during job screening interviews: A field study of interviewee perceptions, "actual" communication behavior and interview outcomes.* Unpublished doctoral dissertation, University of Texas at Austin.

Tengler, C. D. (1982). *Effects of question type and question orientation on interview outcomes in naturally occurring employment interviews.* Unpublished master's thesis, University of Texas at Austin.

Tengler, C. D., & Jablin, F. M. (1983). Effects of question type, orientation, and sequencing in the employment screening interview. *Communication Monographs, 50*, 245-263.

Theberge, L. (1981). *Crooks, conmen and clowns: Businessmen in T.V. entertainment.* Washington, DC: Media Institute.

Thompson, L. L., Mannix, E. A., & Bazerman, M. H. (1988). Group negotiation: Effects of decision rules, agendas and aspiration. *Journal of Personality and Social Psychology, 54*, 86-95.

Tindale, R. S. (1989). Group vs. individual information processing: The effects of outcome feedback on decision making. *Organizational Behavior and Human Decision Processes, 44*, 454-473.

Tjosvold, D. (1984). Effects of leader warmth and directiveness on subordinate performance on a subsequent task. *Journal of Applied Psychology, 69*, 422-427.

Tjosvold, D. (1985). The effects of attribution and social context on superiors' influence and interaction with low performing subordinates. *Personnel Psychology, 38*, 361-376.

Tombaugh, J. R., & White, L. P. (1990). Downsizing: An empirical assessment of survivors' perceptions in a postlayoff environment. *Organizational Development Journal, 8*(2), 32-43.

Tompkins, P. K. (1962). *An analysis of communication between headquarters and selected units of a national labor union.* Unpublished doctoral dissertation, Purdue University.

Trempe, J., Rigney, A. J., & Haccoun, R. R. (1985). Subordinate satisfaction with male and female managers: Role of perceived supervisory influence. *Journal of Applied Psychology, 70*, 44-47.

Trent, L. W. (1978). *The effects of varying levels of interviewee nonverbal behavior in the employment interview.* Unpublished doctoral dissertation, Southern Illinois University.

Tucker, D. H., & Rowe, P. M. (1979). Relationship between expectancy, causal attributions, and final hiring decisions in the employment interview. *Journal of Applied Psychology, 64*, 27-34.

Turban, D. B., Campion, J. E., & Eyring, A. R. (1992). Factors relating to relocation decisions of research and development employees. *Journal of Vocational Behavior, 41*, 183-199.

Turban, D. B., & Dougherty, T. W. (1992). Influence of campus recruiting on applicant attraction to firms. *Academy of Management Journal, 35*, 739-765.

Turner, D. B. (1990). Intraorganizational bargaining: The effect of goal congruence and trust on negotiator strategy use. *Communication Studies, 41*, 54-75.

Turner, D. B. (1992). Negotiator-constituent relationships. In L. L. Putnam & M. E. Roloff (Eds.), *Communication and negotiation* (pp. 233-249). Newbury Park, CA: Sage.

Turner, L. H., & Henzl, S. A. (1987). Influence attempts in organizational conflict: The effects of biological sex, psychological gender, and power position. *Management Communication Quarterly, 1*, 32-57.

Turow, J. (1974). Advising and ordering in daytime, primetime. *Journal of Communication, 24*, 138-141.

Turow, J. (1980). Occupation and personality in television dramas: An industry view. *Communication Research, 7*, 295-318.

Ugbah, S. D., & Majors, R. E. (1992). Influential communication factors in employment interviews. *Journal of Business Communication, 29*, 145-159.

Ullah, P., Banks, M. H., & Warr, P. B. (1985). Social support, social pressures, and psychological distress during unemployment. *Psychological Medicine, 15*, 283-295.

Ulrich, L., & Trumbo, D. (1965). The selection interview since 1949. *Psychological Bulletin, 63*, 100-116.

Valacich, J. S., Dennis, A. R., & Nunamaker, J. F. (1992). Group size and anonymity effects on computer-mediated idea generation. *Small Group Research, 23*, 49-73.

Vance, R. J., & Biddle, T. F. (1985). Task experience and social cues: Interactive effects on attitudinal reactions. *Organizational Behavior and Human Decision Processes, 35*, 252-265.

Van de Ven, A. H., & Delbecq, A. L. (1971). Nominal versus interacting group processes for committee decision-making effectiveness. *Academy of Management Journal, 14*, 203-212.

Van de Ven, A. H., & Delbecq, A. L. (1974). The effectiveness of nominal, delphi, and interacting group decision-making effectiveness. *Academy of Management Journal, 14*, 203-212.

Vangelisti, A. L. (1988). Adolescent socialization into the workplace: A synthesis and critique of current literature. *Youth and Society, 19*, 460-484.

Van Mannen, J. (1975). Breaking in: Socialization to work. In R. Dubin (Ed.), *Handbook of work, organization and society* (pp. 67-120). Chicago: Rand McNally.

Van Mannen, J., & Barley, S. R. (1984). Occupational communities: Culture and control in organizations. In B. M. Staw & L. L. Cummings (Eds.), *Research in organizational behavior* (Vol. 6, pp. 287-365). Greenwich, CT: JAI.

van Tilburg, T. (1992). Support networks before and after retirement. *Journal of Social and Personal Relationships, 9*, 433-445.

Vecchio, R., & Gobdel, B. (1984). The vertical dyad linkage model of leadership: Problems and prospects. *Organizational Behavior and Performance, 34*, 5-20.

Vecchio, R. P., Griffith, R. W., & Hom, P. W. (1986). The predictive utility of the vertical dyad linkage approach. *The Journal of Social Psychology, 126*(5), 617-625.

Vecchio, R. P., & Sussmann, M. (1991). Choice of influence tactics: Individual and organizational determinants. *Journal of Organizational Behavior, 12*, 73-80.

Volard, S. V., & Davies, M. R. (1982). Communication patterns of managers. *Journal of Business Communication, 19*, 41-53.

Vondracek, F. W., Lerner, R. M., & Schulenberg, J. E. (1986). *Career development: A life-span developmental approach.* Hillsdale, NJ: Lawrence Erlbaum.

Waldron, V. R. (1991). Achieving communication goals in superior-subordinate relationships: The multi-functionality of upward maintenance tactics. *Communication Monographs, 58*, 289-306.

Waldron, V. R., & Hunt, M. D. (1992). Hierarchical level, length, and quality of supervisory relationship as predictors of subordinates' use of maintenance tactics. *Communication Reports, 5*, 82-89.

Wall, V. D., Galanes, G. J., & Love, S. B. (1987). Small, task-oriented groups: Conflict, conflict management, satisfaction, and decision quality. *Small Group Behavior, 18*, 31-55.

Wall, V. D., & Nolan, L. L. (1987). Small group conflict: A look at equity, satisfaction, and styles of conflict management. *Small Group Behavior, 18*, 188-211.

Wanous, J. P. (1977). Organizational entry: Newcomers moving from outside to inside. *Psychological Bulletin, 84*, 601-618.

Wanous, J. P. (1980). *Organizational entry: Recruitment, selection, and socialization of newcomers.* Reading, MA: Addison-Wesley.

Watson, K. M. (1982). An analysis of communication patterns: A method for discriminating leader and subordinate roles. *Academy of Management Journal, 25*, 107-120.

Watson, R. T., DeSanctis, G., & Poole, M. S. (1988). Using a GDSS to facilitate group consensus: Some intended and unintended consequences. *MIS Quarterly, 12*, 463-480.

Weider-Hatfield, D. (1988). Assessing the Rahim organizational conflict inventory-II (ROCHI-II). *Management Communication Quarterly, 1*, 350-366.

Weiss, H. M. (1977). Subordinate imitation of supervisor behavior: The role of modeling in organizational socialization. *Organizational Behavior and Human Performance, 19*, 89-105.

Weiss, H. M., & Nowicki, C. E. (1981). Social influence on task satisfaction: Model competence and observer field dependence. *Organizational Behavior and Human Performance, 27*, 345-366.

Weiss, W. (1969). Effects of the mass media of communication. In G. Lindzey & E. Aronson (Eds.), *Handbook of social psychology* (Vol. 5, pp. 77-195). Reading, MA: Addison-Wesley.

Wells, D. L., & Muchinsky, P. M. (1985). Performance antecedents of voluntary and involuntary managerial turnover. *Journal of Applied Psychology, 70*, 329-336.

Wheeless, L. R., & Reichel, L. S. (1990). A reinforcement model of the relationships of supervisors' general communication styles and conflict management styles to task attraction. *Communication Quarterly, 38*, 372-387.

Wheeless, V. E., & Berryman-Fink, C. (1985). Perceptions of women managers and their communication competencies. *Communication Quarterly, 33*, 137-148.

White, S. E., & Mitchell, T. R. (1979). Job enrichment vs. social cues: A comparison and competitive test. *Journal of Applied Psychology, 64*, 1-9.

Whitely, W. (1984). An exploratory study of managers' reactions to properties of verbal communication. *Personnel Psychology, 37*, 41-59.

Whitely, W. (1985). Managerial work behavior: An integration of results from two major approaches. *Academy of Management Journal, 28*, 344-362.

Wijting, J. P., Arnold, C. R., & Conrad, K. A. (1977). Relationships between work values, socio-educational and work experiences, and vocational aspirations of 6th, 9th, 10th, and 12th graders. *Journal of Vocational Behavior, 11*, 51-65.

Wilks, J. (1986). The relative importance of parents and friends in adolescent decision making. *Journal of Youth and Adolescence, 15*, 323-334.

Williams, T. M., Baron, D., Phillips, S., Travis, L., & Jackson, D. (1986, August). *The portrayal of sex roles on Canadian and U.S. television*. Paper presented at the annual meeting of the International Association for Mass Communication Research, New Delhi, India.

Wilson, C. E. (1983). *Toward understanding the process of organizational leave-taking*. Paper presented at the annual meeting of the Speech Communication Association, Washington, DC.

Wilson, S. R., & Waltman, M. S. (1988). Assessing the Putnam-Wilson organizational communication conflict instrument (OCCI). *Management Communication Quarterly, 1*, 367-388.

Wober, J. M., Reardon, G., & Fazal, S. (1987). *Personality, character aspirations and patterns of viewing among children*. London: IBA Research Paper.

Woelfel, J., & Haller, A. O. (1971). Significant others, the self-reflective act and the attitude formative process. *American Sociological Review, 36*, 74-87.

Womack, D. F. (1988a). Assessing the Thomas-Kilmann conflict mode survey. *Management Communication Quarterly, 1*, 321-349.

Womack, D. F. (1988b). A review of conflict instruments in organizational settings. *Management Communication Quarterly, 1*, 437-445.

Wright, O. R. (1969). Summary of research on the selection interview since 1964. *Personnel Psychology, 22*, 391-413.

Wroblewski, R., & Huston, A. C. (1987). Televised occupational stereotypes and their effects on early adolescents: Are they changing? *Journal of Early Adolescence, 7*, 283-297.

Yukl, G., & Falbe, C. M. (1991). Importance of different power sources in downward and lateral relations. *Journal of Applied Psychology, 76*, 416-423.

Zalesny, M. D., & Ford, J. K. (1990). Extending the social information processing perspective: New links to attitudes, behaviors, and perceptions. *Organizational Behavior and Human Decision Processes, 47*, 205-246.

Zand, D. E. (1972). Trust and managerial problem solving. *Administrative Science Quarterly, 17*, 229-239.

Zarbatany, L., Hartmann, D. P., & Rankin, D. B. (1990). The psychological functions of preadolescent peer activities. *Child Development, 61*, 1067-1080.

Zigurs, I., Poole, M. S., & DeSanctis, G. (1988). A study of influence in computer-mediated group decision making. *MIS Quarterly, 12*, 625-644.

17

Social and Personal Relationships

Steve Duck

Garth Pittman

THE FIRST EDITION of this chapter began with the claim that "people's lives are fabricated in and by their relationships with other people." It went on to argue that communication was a basic component of those relationships. The present edition of the chapter places the emphasis somewhat differently. We argue that people's lives are fabricated in and by their conversations with others, that their psychological processes are embedded in those conversations, and that their relationships are also constituted by the same means.

The central theses of the present chapter are that relationships are not a special part of life, that the everyday conversations of real life are places where construction of experience is "ratified," and hence that relationships are a routine component of the partners' construction of their worlds. In this sense, we follow those social theorists who argue for the role of the practical in the creation of both a community of minds and the sense of individuality through relationships (e.g., Burkitt, 1991). While we develop a general case with these themes, we also explore self-disclosure as an example of a line of research that has taken a different tack and, we believe wrongly, tended to ignore the importance of everyday conversations in the development, construction, and maintenance of social and personal relationships.

We believe that interpersonal communication research has a profound contribution to make to the field of personal relationships by clarifying the means by which presumed social psychological effects (such as commitment or attitude similarity) exert their influence in real life communication. Second, we believe that such a contribution can be extended through consideration of what it is about the everyday conduct of relationships that fosters agreement about what "the relationship" is. We note with interest and curiosity that there is often debate about whose perspective on a relationship is primary (Christensen, Sullaway, & King, 1983) and we often discover that two partners in an exchange happen to define it differently or that the two partners happen to disagree with an outside ("scientific") observer about it (Duck, 1990). A part of our case here is that the differing perspectives on relational activity are all relevant to its characterization at a definitional level and that they form a composite that is "the relationship" that research needs to address. The other part of our case is that the actual conduct of relationships is accomplished through the juxtaposition and resolution of different views of the relationship and the world. Third, we explore the advantages of seeing conceptualizations of relationships as dynamic and continually changing processes rather than as states or static categories and we relate such a view to the nature of the human enterprise in facing up to a constantly changing set of experiences (Duck, 1990, 1991).

Relationships are often described as entities that move through time and around turning points rather than as organisms that are transformed over time (see Surra, 1987). This trajectory metaphor tends to represent relationships as "automatic" consequences of particular states or individual qualities of the relational partners before they ever met or it seems to imply that relationship characteristics can be predicted from elements independent of the busy conduct of relationships through interpersonal communication. For example, it might suggest that relationship satisfaction can be predicted from the individual personality characteristics or exchange orientations of the two partners independently (Rusbult & Buunk, 1993; Walster, Walster, & Berscheid, 1978). Our view, by contrast, emphasizes the importance of the transformative influences of interaction or talk and stresses the important roles of everyday routines and trivial behavior in sustaining relationships or guiding behavior and experience in them (Dainton & Stafford, in press; Duck, in press). Our approach does not view relationships as states, or relational forces as traits, but attends to the variances of everyday lives and the things that people are doing in them.

In line with recent concerns about the *achievement* of relating and the things that are *done* in conversation (e.g., Gergen & Gergen, 1987), we have become interested in the ways in which persons achieve stability in relationships as well as change. For instance, life is experienced as variable and complex yet is represented in subjective descriptions that strip it of both variance and complexity when persons use state labels to describe relationships as "a marriage." Yet, as noted by Billig (1987), much thinking and experiencing actually capitalize on the variability that is a fundamental part of life and this argument may be extended to relationship "states," which are actually not so much states as unfinished business (Duck, 1990). Thinking is the unfinished business of weighing up different aspects of an issue (Billig, 1987), while relationships can be characterized as the weighing up of different aspects of partner and relationship future (Duck, 1990). Hence even "stable" relationships evidence instability of (or, at least, variance in) ratings of the relationship, and our case is that these variances are importantly apparent in daily conversation and conversational patterns.

The most significant emphases in our approach are on the influence of two important effects: (a) the fundamental role of change and "ongoingness" in an unfolding future, so that human adaptation to change becomes a central theoretical issue, and (b) the regular routine work of the relationship participants that provides a background for their conduct of the human experience. We seek to support the recent interest in relationship maintenance and the negotiation of "relationship form" as a continuous activity (Baxter & Simon, 1993; Duck, 1985). Such routines are likely to be examples of the important differences in competence, knowledge, and behavior that are present in different relationship partners (Andersen, 1993). Relationship partners do not have the same competencies, urges, skills, and uniform goals or intentions all the time in every relational encounter.

While *process* has recently become a "buzzword" in the relationship field, it is a mistake to act as if process in relationships occurs only in drama (such as turning points or relationship disengagement) because process is most easily seen in terms of gross change. Yet even stability requires stabilizing governing mechanisms (Baxter & Simon, 1993; Duck, in press; Montgomery, 1993; Rusbult & Buunk, 1993). Equally, there are qualities of relationships (e.g., relationship satisfaction) that are not deducible merely from the individual characteristics of partners but emerge from the partners' continuous interaction. Just as one person cannot "be similar" alone but two can together, so relationships have emergent qualities (like intimacy) that are dependent on continuous styles of action, not on states or the qualities of partners separately. Such qualities and the relationships themselves are evident in conversation. Relational growth is a social and communicative achievement, not something automatically generated by the mixing of two persons' individual characteristics (Duck & Sants, 1983).

On the contrary, the relationship is created from the blending of the two persons' views on a number of things, which are presented to one another in the daily conversations of life. We propose that everyday conversation presents the "rhetorical visions" of one person to another, as much about life as a whole as about the relationship itself (Duck & Pond, 1989). Thus the relationship is partly "made" through conversation about *other* issues and yet is also itself the subject of agreement between the two persons about itself.

It is important to place this claim in context by exploring some of the features of everyday experience that relationship partners confront in their normal lives. We do this because relational experience is a subset of other human experiences and the processes in relationships are also a subset of, and example of, the processes in life as a whole.

Several authors have noted that participants in relationships have views of relational phenomena that differ from the views taken by outsiders. Olson (1977) first raised the question of how such differences should be resolved in scientific study of relationships and later writers have developed the point extensively (Duck, 1990; Duck & Sants, 1983; Surra & Ridley, 1991). While this issue is important in relationships, we wish to emphasize its broader relevance as an instantiation of a fundamental fact of human life, namely, that different persons take different views of phenomena, a situation dignified by Kelly (1969) into the theoretical assumption of "constructive alternativism."

This fact is something with hidden communicative interest in a general sense that is also specifically relevant in relationships. Because such constructive alternativism occurs, one constant feature of life is that a person will continually run into ways of construing the world (or specific events) that are dissonant with, or different than, his or her own ways of doing so. It is possible to understand conversation in relationships as a rhetorical activity in which interlocutors propose and present their own views in the hope of persuading others to adopt them (Duck & Pond, 1989). One does not need to assume that this process occurs only in relation to "big" ideas but that it can refer also to any view of the world that is demonstrated by any of the talk uttered by a person. In this view, the conversations in relationships are persuasive devices and the communicative activities of relationship partners reflect a general human process. In the communications of everyday life, we believe that the trafficking of symbols and the trading of ideas accomplishes for individuals the function of providing test and validation (or test, challenge, and change) of their views of the world at all levels (Duck, 1994). In a sense then we see the differences between people as a fact that preexists their relationship and that initiates the communication between them as well as providing the grist for its mills. Conversation generally accomplishes the trafficking of meaning, the testing of ideas, and the construction of agreements, just as conversation in personal relationships does the same thing (as an example of this occurrence in a wider context) (Duck, 1991).

Mental Creation of Relationships

One view of communication is that it simply expresses and externalizes the mental structures and processes of the individuals doing the communicating. Berger (1993) has noted the prevalence of this view as one that represents communication as a process that transplants the ideas and thoughts of one person into another's mind. In such a view, one would spend most of one's time in relationship research exploring such things as the operation of mental processes, the deduction of inferences about others, and the psychological variables that construct the person's approach to and behavior in relationships. The relationship would exist because the two people are behaviorally and psychologically interdependent and a person's mental representation of it would be a mental representation "of something" almost tangible. The communication between them would reflect that and would not be truly problematic. By contrast, the present chapter argues that it is in fact the communication between the two parties that creates the mental representation of the relationship and indeed in some sense creates the relationship.

Arguing against the above "conduit metaphor," Reddy (1979) shows that such a model presents a misleading view of the ways in which words and messages act. Instead, Reddy proposes a tool-maker metaphor. In this metaphor, communication provides blueprints that are open to different interpretations and the task of communication is to bring variable interpretations into some form of conjunction. In this analogy, a relationship would be a process of construction from the two mental creations imported by the two different viewpoints. Relational communication would be a process of dualistic presentation of different views of the world and the symbolic or direct negotiation of them into a shared system of understanding or "commonly objectivated reality." Indeed, Berger and Kellner (1964) used just that phrase to describe the social construction of reality and—a point often overlooked outside the communication discipline—they spent most of their article discussing the ways in which the constructive process occurred through talk. The emphasis on negotiation does not imply that the only way in which people end up similar is through this constructive, negotiative process. This important but subtle point is a major part of our argument in this chapter. One needs to attend to the different senses in which relationships are mental creations and the different ways in which they are based on similarity. The concerns are these: How do people develop the similarities in outlook (or mental construction of the world) that are apparent fortuitously, on the one hand, and how do they construct others or realign themselves, on the other hand?

The above two ways of looking at relationships appear to be somewhat at odds and yet each has its adherents. In essence, each of the two ways of looking at relationships faces us with a different version of the central question of interpersonal communication and relationships: What makes something social? Max Weber (1967) argued that something is social when it takes account of other people. He claimed that "action is social insofar as, by virtue of the subjective meaning attached to it by the acting individual or individuals, it takes account of the behavior of others and is thereby oriented in its course" (Weber, 1967, pp. 156-157).

This is not the complete answer that it sounds; for example, people can create personal meanings for themselves about social and personal relationships. Although the focus of their attention involves the taking account of other people—and is therefore social in Weber's terms—persons can construct entirely inappropriate views of others' roles, intentions, and behaviors and can act upon such misconstructions in social interaction. As Duck, Pond, and Leatham (1994) have shown, lonely persons construct cognitive schemas for interaction that in some sense misrepresent the realities of interaction as judged at least by other observers. For the lonely person, however, the view of others is constructed into the cognitive schema of relating and the lonely person's mental creation of relationships is reflected in communication with strangers but not with friends (Duck et al., 1994).

The fact that a person's action or communication is "oriented" in its course by taking account of the behavior of others is an important element of the mental construction of relationships at the personal individual level. We need to explore the ways in which such actions are developed and the ways in which they direct or influence social behavior and communication. More than this, however, we need to address the tantalizing remnants of Weber's (1967) position in a way that also addresses Berger and Kellner's (1989) proposals. To do that we make two arguments: (a) that a person's mental creation of relationships, in the sense outlined above, is presented and honed in talk, not just represented in talk but fashioned in talk; (b) that it is the *sharing* of such representations that is important (and here we do not mean any of the several types of similarity that can be meaningfully distinguished and applied to relating, or the symbolic interdependence researched by others; e.g., Stephen, 1986). Rather, we mean the recognition of the fact that the two partners have particular views of the relationship that take account of each other. This is the MIA part of "taking account of others' actions," the social force that is created when one person realizes through talk that the other person takes account of one's actions in similar ways (Duck, 1994).

Talk and the Mental Creation of Relationships

That talk serves many functions simultaneously is hardly news to readers of this *Handbook*. Our position is based on the view that everyday talk is rhetorical and presents the person's visions of almost everything. Within that overall characteristic, talk serves three specific relationship functions: instrumental, indexical, and essential (Duck & Pond, 1989). Instrumental talk achieves relational purposes, such as asking someone out on a date; indexical talk serves to manifest the relationship, such as personal idioms do; and the essential function of talk serves to embody the relationship through its simple occurrence and presentation to the two individuals of their views of the world. In this latter sense, the talk is the relationship, and Duck, Rutt, Hurst, and Strejc (1991) have shown that the mere occurrence of talk is taken by conversants as a sign of the healthy continuance of their relationship. In this latter sense, the casual talk of everyday life presents a rhetorically informative mental creation of the relationship in some of the ways understood by pragmatists and researchers of power, control, and intimacy alike (Giles & Powesland, 1975; Watzlawick, Beavin, & Jackson, 1967). Casual talk also embraces symbolic terminology and celebratory functions of talk, such as the playfulness recently identified by Baxter (1992) as an important element of the talk of relational partners.

Our argument is that, in the daily talk of relating, individuals continually juxtapose their views of numerous sorts and types of events and objects, not just on the occasions when they focus on their relationship or one another. They are continually and unavoidably manifesting to one another not only the specific content of their views of specific subjects but also displaying their global approach to life as a whole. By the processes of analysis and reflective consideration identified by Berger and Bradac (1982) and others, individuals are able to gather, assimilate, accommodate, and also challenge information supplied both deliberately and willy-nilly by others. They do this through communication and not in the abstract senses sometimes implied by psychological work on information processing. The acts of gathering and processing information are essentially communicative and social acts, not just individual ones. They are based upon, reflect back to, and help to shape the individual's personal mental creation of the relationship.

In this sense, then, the act of everyday talk is a relationship implement that fashions and creates the relationship because it affects the meanings of the two individual partners. Thus this part of the process involves shaping of their individual views of one another by taking account of each other. It is a social process in Weber's sense, informative in Berger and Bradac's sense. But it is not the whole process.

The second string of our argument is developed from this first one and focuses on the fact that talk also allows persons to create something together from the two images that they express independently and to recognize that they are doing so. Berger and Kellner (1964) noted the same thing when they pointed out that married partners offer their meaningful experience of the world to one another and conjointly reconstruct a new reality that accommodates the two views. "Reconstruction of the world in marriage occurs principally in the course of conversation," they aver (Berger & Kellner, 1964). They claim also that the act of talking has the result of hardening or stabilizing the reality that is jointly constructed. For instance, it serves to negotiate some role relativities and some behavioral sequences in ways that purely individual impression formation discussed above does not do jointly. We are simply claiming here that such talk can also stabilize views of the relationship.

Having argued that the presentation of views of the world is a constant feature of everyday communication, and communication about relationships, we now argue that one of the important pieces of information that is gleaned from such activity is evidence of sharing. As noted earlier, we do not mean evidence of "similarity." Similarity has been widely researched in the context of relationship development and decline (Byrne, 1971; Duck, 1994), and there are really several sorts of similarity that are different both in themselves and in their psychological effect upon relationships. Whole chapters have been devoted to differentiating them elsewhere and we do not do it again here (but see Duck, 1977,1994). It is clear that there is an important psychological and interpersonal difference between *"real" similarity* (i.e., correspondence between two persons' characteristics, in whichever of many possible ways this is measured), *perceived similarity* (when two persons correctly perceive that they are similar), and *assumed similarity* (when two persons incorrectly assume that they are similar or are more similar than they are "really").

In line with the argument developed above and with the point lying behind Weber's (1967) discussion, we are interested in the social force of these psychological relationships of similarity. We refer to it as "sharing" when two people, as separate individuals, first of all recognize that similarity exists between them and then, second, acknowledge it in their talk. There are thus three elements to sharing and not one: The first is the existence of similarity (which could be manifested in talk), the second is the recognition or realization of similarity by the two individuals (which could be achieved through attention to talk or through reflection on talk and behavior), and the third is the acknowledgment of the recognition, which can occur only in talk, because it is essentially a dyadic and social concept.

Thus the mental creation of relationships has more than one element to it and the role of communication in the whole process is likewise a differentiated one. Through the daily activities of talk, the two partners in a relationship achieve a comprehension of one another's psychology, an understanding of roles and complementarity of behavior that reorganizes the relationship, and a realization of sharing that is itself an important message about the stability, nature, and futurity of the relationship.

While such sharing can be about any topic, its social effects are relational and profound. Ultimately a sequence of interaction becomes "a relationship" when and only when the two partners believe that it is one. This chapter argues this radical view on the basis that the partners create this belief at two different levels. In the constant talk of everyday life, there can occur a meshing of ideas and conceptions that involves the sculpting of jointly fashioned realities. The social power of such a thing comes from the recognition of that fashioning at the same time as the partners are simply chattering away about a whole host of other things. Thus, while the mental representation of relationships is one thing, the mental creation of them is another that is achieved through talk, the very same medium through which they are enacted and embodied.

Everyday Talk and the Management of Relationships

Many readers will recognize the debt that the above orientation owes to Berger and Kellner (1964) and to the growing interest in social constructivist ways of viewing social behavior (e.g., Baxter, 1993; Gergen & Gergen, 1987). However, we do not minimize the effects of psychological processes upon relationships but seek to explain their social force. We conceptualize the influence of individual psychological processes upon social behavior as empowered through conversation. Research has too long used social cognitive structures of relationships (such as attitude similarity, commitment, relationship disengagement, or maintenance of relationships) without attending to operative conversational mechanisms that "work" them. Neither has such work illuminated the social nature of the talk through which individual psychological variables are effected and brought to social reality in everyday life (Barnes & Duck, in press; Dixson & Duck, 1993; Duck & Pond, 1989). Those who focus on language and talk in everyday life see it as "centrally concerned with the ways in which sociopsychological constructs (attitudes, attributions, norms, identities) are constructed and reconstructed for individuals via interaction" (Giles & Coupland, 1991, p. xii). We believe that such a list of interpersonal constructs should be extended to include all the mechanisms involved in the creation, maintenance, and deterioration of personal relationships (Duck, in press). It is important for scholars to ensure that major psychological variables are not represented only as abstracted constructs that do not have a real life conversational form. "Relationships," like other concepts, operate through daily talk, the very real social and interpersonal medium by which they are most often achieved in real life—once this is seen as more than a conduit for ideas. However, the main part of our case is that the construction of relationships is part of a wider human tendency to co-construct meaning with others and to do this through the mechanisms of communication and conversation that relationships themselves entail.

Duck and Pond (1989) suggested that relationships are constructed and enacted through the presentation of rhetorical visions in daily conversation, as are impressions of partners and evaluations of their value as partners. This argument is a rhetorical version of the argument of Berger and Kellner (1964), who suggested that marriage involves the social construction of reality for a couple. Indeed, it is often forgotten in the discussion of Berger and Kellner's article that they contended that such social construction of a "common objectivated reality" occurs in and through everyday talk. We likewise propose that routine daily conversation is a continual process—the unfinished business of improvisation (Duck, 1990)—and that persons there present and enact their comprehension of the world including the relationships in which they are embedded.

In this model, relationships are projected through conversations and behaviors rather more than through abstract states of interdependence. Talk is not just a simple pipeline for emotional expression (Berger, 1993). Instead, it is a transformative mechanism by which people transact their daily business, including achieving their goals, influencing others, presenting rhetorical visions, and "performing" the abstract concepts listed above. In this view, talk, especially everyday conversation between friends and acquaintances, does not simply function to transmit cognition, unreconstructed, from one individual's brain to a waiting world. Instead, it is a complex process that indexes and constructs the relationship (Berger, 1993; Dixson & Duck, 1993; Shotter, 1992). Talk not only serves instrumental and indexical purposes in relationships but also works to "essentialize" them (Duck & Pond, 1989).

Present models of relationships based on uncertainty reduction theory (e.g., Berger, 1993) correctly identify the role of uncertainty reduction and information gathering in relationship "work." Of course, in any model of relating that is based on the assumption of awareness by participants, it makes sense to assume that they know what they are doing and where they are going in a relationship. Indeed, the whole assumption is precisely that they are gathering information for a purpose rather than casually—a purpose that they have clear in their minds and are intent on executing. We do not dispute such purposes but wish to reinforce the recognition of the fact that even everyday trivial talk offers untold possibilities for unplanned and indirect acquisition of information about a partner (Berger, 1988; Berger & Bradac, 1982). Second, we emphasize the real significance for people of the fact that development of relationships is achieved through problematic decision making. To follow Billig's argument as developed by Shotter (1992) and by Duck (1990), individuals may not make once-and-for-all decisions about anything, including relationships, but continually have the opportunity to reprocess and reevaluate any and all aspects of them, even when they do not expect to.

At present, studies of relationships are usually done in a style that precludes testing of such an idea. However, the growing social discourse tradition (e.g., Billig, 1987; Billig et al., 1988; Potter & Wetherell, 1987) and the (unrelated) increased use of diary methods, such as the Rochester Interaction Record (RIR—

Wheeler & Nezlek, 1977) or the Iowa Communication Record (ICR—Duck et al., 1991), would permit such ideas to be tested and added to the body of scientific research on relationships. Such methods have already shown that such uncertainty is endemic to relationships (Duck & Miell, 1984, 1986). Partners in a 20-week longitudinal study characteristically reported uncertainty about their partners' attachment to their relationships. They saw their friends as their friends but did not see themselves as the friends of other people. They were unwilling to presume that their partners' apparent liking for them was certain to last or continue. For most subjects, the relationship was seen as mostly dependent on the actions, feelings, and whims of their partner and only to a lesser extent on their own. More recent studies (e.g., Duck et al., 1991) also confirm the principles of this argument. However, to relate such uncertainty to interpretative transformation of relationships, the day-to-day reports of subjects in relationships need to be matched up with direct behavioral observations of their communicative and intimate behaviors (Sillars, 1991). To such methods could be added interviews to assess their relational concerns at a particular point of study although existing work seems to show that day-to-day reporting of experience is only partly related to such overall global assessments of relationships (Duck et al., 1991). It is becoming clear that the assumption that relationships are steady states that develop steadily may be an unsafe and misleading assumption.

Perhaps an answer to such dilemmas is provided by consideration of the content of interactions and the ways in which it changes in relationship growth (Cappella, 1991). The assumption in many theories is that the behavioral content of interactions (rather than the talk that surrounds it) is a good index of its present state (Rusbult & Buunk, in press). Accordingly, the growth of intimacy and attachment to relationships should appear in the content of interactions (Gottman, 1989). These writers emphasize the need to view the content of interactions as the key variable in describing a relationship but also stress the importance of the temporal context when one comes to interpret that content. Both, in short, stress that relationships occur across time and between people at the behavioral level.

In similar fashion, Hinde (1981) talks of the content of interactions and makes several important points about the manner in which it is conducted. Thus a passionate kiss is different from a dutiful one. Equally, the patterning of content is important to our understanding of the nature of a given relationship: A kiss followed by a slap indicates a different setup from that identified by a slap followed by a kiss.

Although such points are necessary and useful, they are also faintly puzzling. For one thing, to say that we researchers must focus on the content of interaction is both interesting and circular. The content of an interaction is not just the behavior that can be observed in it, even if we can agree on what that would mean. Indeed, to say that an understanding of the content of an interaction would help us to define a relationship exactly begs the question, because to define the bounds and effective meaning of the content, we have to define the relationship first. As Penman (1980) and other communication workers indicate, the punctuation of interactions very largely depends on the observer's view of the nature of the relationship. Indeed, for Penman (1980), the nature of a relationship is "deduced [for an outside observer] from the flow of exchanges between the individuals constituting, and constituted in, the relationship" (p. 2). Insiders may see things differently, and in any case, only they can experience the "magic moment" of sharing (as defined above) when they see a "relationship" as having emerged from what may previously have been thought to be a sequence of uncharmed interactions. Thus *the content* of interaction is not an evaluatively neutral term as it appears to be but depends on the standpoint of the observer, and so constitutes a kind of "theorette" about the phenomena (Duck & Montgomery, 1991). The content for one participant may not correspond with the content for the other participant, and both may fail to correspond with "the content" as perceived by an outside observer.

To make use of Hinde's (1981) example about a passionate kiss, we can see that even this "content" can have different meanings. It could indicate

(a) a passionate relationship,

(b) an intent to form a passionate relationship and to signal this intent to the partner,

(c) a mistaken belief about the partner's wishes,

(d) an uncontrolled desire felt only by the kisser, or

(e) some combination of these separate meanings.

Accordingly, it behooves us to note that to interpret "the content" we need to have a perspective on it and that this will largely depend upon our viewpoint as an observer of the events.

We note also that views of the content of relationships are not only matters of conversational dispute (and so also the subject of conversation between people), but "the contents" of interaction are perceived as the mental representations of the relationship. As such they can also be affected, both for outside observers and for the partners themselves, by beliefs about the likely course of the relationship and other cultural paraphernalia. For instance, as noted above, a passionate kiss can be a signal to both parties that a more intense form of relationship would be appropriate and desirable. The "content" of such interactions serves not only defining effects but also signaling effects that indicate intent as well as views of present state and could lead to talk about the relationship. Thus "content" leads to, and is indicative of, transformations of the relationship that become a subject for talk that could resolve whether an outcome is acceptable to both parties. Progress in relationships is not automatic, however, and depends to a great extent on the partners' discussion of such things in everyday conversation. This in turn "essentializes" their clarity about the future of the relationship, the extent to which they share beliefs about the future, their understanding of the appropriate phases in a trajectory toward the desired end point, and their ability to enact those desires in ways that accomplish their goals. In short, relational development is not automatic but can nevertheless follow trajectories created through conversation in an everyday cultural context.

In all cases the existence and the changing of a relationship are partly due to a process of continual review and rationalization. In spite of, or perhaps because of, the uncertainties noted earlier as features of day-to-day relational reports (Duck & Miell, 1986), partners evolve rational, smooth, and sensible accounts of their relationship's growth. If one compares past retrospections and future projections for a relationship's trajectory, then one invariably finds that subjects smoothe out the reported trajectory in a way that does not reflect what they have been reporting in their day-to-day accounts (Miell, 1987). In short, they produce precisely the trajectories that we would expect—and, indeed, have assumed in most theories of growth—and yet these are inaccurate and much-edited representations of the truth (see Delia, 1980). Here again is not an error or a bias but an important psychological phenomenon, a product of the continual reviewing and reassessing of interactions and their interpretations that is perhaps a necessary activity in order to produce the sense of being in a relationship. It is the sense of smooth continuity that creates a relationship from a set or series of interactions. It also indicates the theoretical risks inherent in believing what subjects tell us about "relationshipping." To paraphrase Duncan (1967), subjects do not relate and then behave or review their interactions; they relate in and through their behavior and reviewing of interactions.

In a study of the behavior characterizing the development of friendship, Hays (1984) found that dyads developing successful close friendships showed different behavioral and attitudinal trends than those who did not. Specifically, the dyads' breadth of interaction and the intimacy level of their interactions were positively related to the intensity of their friendship, beyond the level accounted for by the sheer quantity of interaction. Those persons who were most adept at developing the relationship were also best at developing its breadth, rather than its depth alone. Growth of intimacy seems to depend on the abilities of the partners to develop this nonautomatic aspect of behavior and the communication about the relationship.

This rather obvious, but frequently unmentioned, point was supported by Duck and Miell's (1984) studies, in which partners who had kept private records of their relationship were subsequently interviewed about them, either individually or in pairs. In terms of both successful and unsuccessful relationships, individuals interviewed alone spoke more freely about their private feelings on the relationship. In the presence of their partner, they spoke not of what they knew their partner knew but of what it was legitimate for them to let their partner know was public knowledge about the relationship—what "should" be admitted to third parties, namely, the interviewers.

Such points make it clear that "what a person knows about another person" is not a simple set of absolute pieces of information untainted by social desirabilities, cultural norms, and the realities of social discourse. Indeed, an important aspect of "the store of information" is that it contains many doors. Social knowledge is not absolute; it is not neutral and it is not simple, invariant, closed to subsequent reinterpretation, or always presentable in the same form irrespective of circumstances. Conversation itself, especially the unprompted daily talk that occurs between acquaintances, associates, and friends, constantly presents the partners with the unfinished business of discursive thinking and relating. Thus the building up of new information about another person does not always have precisely determinable effects on the stability or existence of the relationship, even when it shows the other in an unfavorable light (Honeycutt, 1993). That there are points in relationships (and there are relationships) that require that one should exercise tolerance and not act as a strictly "rational" information-processing model might seem to imply that one will do so. Indeed, one of the implicit demands of close relationships is that one's own secrets (usually, presumably, secrets precisely because they are embarrassing or show one up in a bad light) are supposed to be shared with one's partner as an index of the relationship's stability and depth while one also keeps faith with the other about his or her secrets (Kelvin, 1977). So new information, even if it is negative, has less and less total impact on the relationship, unless it violates grander norms about conduct of relationships rather than about persons.

Thus to focus only on the important strategic and planning work that persons do in gathering information during communication is to overlook the important ways in which people are tentative, undecided, discursive, and reflective in encounters, especially everyday conversation, or to underplay the ways in which they use knowledge about the process of information gathering itself. Thus, while strategic intentions and execution of intentions have significant effects upon the behavior of relating persons, researchers should explore also the effects of context on such strategy in the activities of day-to-day living. Practical everyday influences upon such strategies have been a major and serious omission of previous work, which has tended, for example, to use appeals to naive motives like "reciprocity" to account for people's use of self-disclosure in relationships. A more complex picture is needed, one that is framed in a better grasp of the role of meaning construction and identity management in the early stages of relationship development. For instance, Clark and Delia (1979) have argued that every communicative transaction involves the overt and/or tacit negotiation of identities and relationship definition between interactants. Miell (1984) contends that even self-disclosure may be used strategically, whether for purposes of relational control, relational development, or identity management. What Miell (1984) shows is that changes in relationship definition are also signaled by the same means, as transactions contain both a definition and the seeds of the next definition. Changes in self-disclosure are not just automatic responses to the "demands" of reciprocity. In addition, we argue, self-disclosive behavior communicates current relational needs as well as recasting past experiences and foreshadowing future ones. We will now take a closer look at self-disclosure work to (a) reposition it relative to other mechanisms as above and (b) reexplore the way it really works.

Self-Disclosure

In general terms, *self-disclosure* has been defined as "any information exchange that refers to the self, including personal states, dispositions, events in the past, and plans for the future" (Chelune et al., 1979, p. 152). A large amount of work has used this or a similar definition and focused on self-disclosure as a relational development mechanism especially in terms of reciprocity.

Given our perspective, the main issue in self-disclosure research focuses on the reasons why people do it. Jourard, a humanistic psychologist, the founding father of self-disclosure theory and research, felt that the primary goal of self-disclosure was the maintenance of one's mental health. Says Jourard (1971): "Self-disclosure is the act of making yourself manifest, showing yourself so others can perceive you" (p. 19). Essentially this makes self-disclosure a declarative, individually expressive act rather than a socially communicative one. Jourard's contention was that by self-disclosing to another we are able to validate our thoughts and feelings and understand more fully how we conform to the world around us. For Jourard (1959), self-disclosure was a prerequisite for a healthy personality, but in real life, people may not have "reasons" like this or may have other reasons that, embedded in the conversational realities of everyday life, tend to influence self-disclosing behavior.

Jourard's viewpoint was originally focused on determining whether specific personality traits could be attributed to various types and degrees of self-disclosure. Taking the act of self-disclosure out of its everyday-life context, a search for the personality basis of self-disclosure used the Jourard Self-Disclosure Questionnaire (JSDQ), and over several years of extensive research, Jourard and others, who were interested in the personality traits that determine self-disclosure, compiled a laundry list of self-disclosure profiles. Some of their findings indicated that females disclose more than males (Dimond & Munz, 1967; Jourard & Lasakow, 1958), that later-borns disclose more than first-borns (Dimond & Hellkamp, 1969; Dimond & Munz, 1967), that Jewish males disclose more than Baptists, Methodists, and Catholics (Jourard, 1961), and that whites disclose more than blacks (Jourard & Lasakow, 1958).

Although much of the research using the JSDQ has been contradictory, and it has been determined to be a weak indicator for predicting specific acts of self-disclosure (Chelune et al., 1979, p. 4), it remains a strong prototype for researchers measuring individual self-discloser characteristics.

Although the JSDQ-type assessment tools focused on the individual's personality constructs as a determination of self-disclosure, early research was not limited solely to the "self-disclosure as trait" perspective. Altman and Taylor (1973) felt that a pure trait-disclosure relationship was unrealistic and that it was necessary to consider self-disclosure in the context of specific relationships and settings. Social penetration theory (Altman & Taylor, 1973) links self-disclosure to relational interaction by relying on self-disclosure as a primary mechanism for creating varying degrees of intimacy within relationships. Altman and Taylor argued that self-disclosure is particularly important at the initial stages of a relationship, as partners search for similarity and compatibilities. At this stage of the relationship, say Altman and Taylor, the participants need to match breadth and depth of self-disclosure to promote a sense of mutual trustworthiness, necessary for the relationship to progress into more intimate stages. To this end, hundreds of studies over the years have examined the connection between self-disclosure and relational interaction. Researchers have examined the connection between self-disclosure and attraction (Alexander, 1977), self-disclosure and intimacy (Klos & Loomis, 1978), and self-disclosure and trust (Wheeless & Grotz, 1977), to name a few early examples.

At the risk of oversimplifying the major trends in self-disclosure research over the last 30 years, ideas and assumptions about self-disclosure have moved from more static, traitlike perspectives to an understanding that most characteristics of self-disclosure vary across situational contexts. The distinct domains of "trait versus state," discussed above, have given way to a more "interactional" model of self-disclosure, wherein personality characteristics and social situational influences influence each other to determine self-disclosure behavior. Incorporating both of these domains, Cozby (1973) defined self-disclosure as both a personality construct and a process variable that occurs during interpersonal interactions. Although this definition is general, according to Chelune et al. (1979), it allows flexibility, enabling researchers to link self-disclosure to personal characteristics that can be generalized across social-situational contexts; conversely, it allows researchers to define social contexts that presuppose individual differences.

Indeed, much of the research in the field has required the duality of Cozby's definition. For example, Shaffer, Tomarelli, and Smith (1982) examined how individual levels of personal and environmental awareness (personal characteristics) influence individuals' determination of strategies for presenting an image of themselves to others. Franzoi, Davis, and Young (1985) studied the impact of an individual's self-awareness and perspective taking, and how these two personality characteristics are likely to influence the quality of close relationships. Another study, by Shaffer, Ogden, and Wu (1987), examined how self-monitoring characteristics affect the social act of reciprocity.

The link between gender and self-disclosure has been perhaps the variable that has received the most attention in self-disclosure research over the past 35 years. Originally, gender was seen as traitlike, with the idea that particular characteristics of gender would be consistent from situation to situation. Although it is now generally understood that there are mediating factors that require a more complex understanding of the role of gender and self-disclosure, there are several current studies that, for the most part, remain true to traditional traitlike perspectives of self-disclosure.

For instance, Snell, Miller, and Belk (1988) and Snell, Miller, Belk, Garcia-Falconi, and Hernandez-Sanchez (1989) examined the relationship between gender and self-disclosure, using a number of questionnaires similar to the original Jourard Self-Disclosure Questionnaire. Subjects were asked to self-report anticipated levels of self-disclosure for specific disclosure recipients: female friends, male friends, and spouses/lovers (Snell et al., 1988) and mothers, fathers, a female therapist, and a male therapist (Snell et al., 1989). Findings were compatible with earlier studies indicating that females displayed emotional intimacy with both sexes, while males were more inclined to disclose to female recipients than to other males. There is an undeniable weakness in the method of data collection when subjects are asked to self-report on previous events or hypothesize about future ones. It is not surprising that these two studies reflect traditional views of gender and self-disclosure, given the fact that they used traditional measurement techniques that have for decades implicitly assessed self-disclosure as a trait. If you take a fishing rod, you do not catch bears! The "theorette" (Duck & Montgomery, 1991) contained in the measurement technique has its own built-in results. The studies do not focus on the interactive and communicative aspects of self-disclosure so much as on the expressive tendencies of the subjects, which of course may be a traitlike tendency. By focusing on only one person's perspective on self-disclosure and assessing it in probabilistic fashion, the authors could hardly find any other than a traitlike noncommunicative outcome.

Another study, by Papini, Farmer, Clark, Micka, and Barnett (1990), examined self-disclosure as a function of gender and age. Papini et al. used the ESDS developed by Snell to measure levels of self-disclosure by adolescent boys and girls to parents and to friends. The findings indicated that—after a certain age—females exhibit greater emotional self-disclosure to parents and to peers than males. The "age" variable supports earlier findings of Rotenberg and Mann (1986), who ascertained that the norm of reciprocity becomes operational by sixth grade. The "gender" variable was consistent with previous gender research results, but because the methodology was similar to that of Snell et al. (1989), these findings are again not surprising.

By contrast, Spencer (1992) has shown that the patterns of self-disclosure between parents and adolescents follow from elements of the everyday social situation not predictable only from traits. His work has indicated some of the pragmatic achievements of self-disclosure once it is studied as it occurs naturally in conversation rather than through the perspective of one participant. For example, parents occasionally *teach* children or adolescents by self-disclosing about their experiences in childhood or their learning from problematic situations.

Sprecher (1987) focused specifically on a situational ramification of self-disclosure reciprocity. She examined "disclosure given" and "disclosure received," exploring the way in which reciprocity in such behavior correlated with the amounts of love and liking experienced by dating partners. The study compared "perceived other" disclosure with "actual other" disclosure as reported by the discloser. According to Sprecher, the majority of the research on self-disclosure and liking focuses on the discloser and not on the receiver. In her study, she wanted to see what impact receiving disclosure would have on the receiver's feelings of liking and loving. The findings indicated that men felt more satisfaction, more liking and love, when they received self-disclosure as opposed to when they self-disclosed. Of interest, females experienced no significant difference in their feelings of liking for their partner, whether they were the givers or the receivers of disclosure.

One of the conclusions that Sprecher (1987) puts forward is that perhaps self-disclosure is linked to liking because of the perceived reciprocity. Partners may be responding favorably to the "other's disclosure" because in their minds what they are receiving is not disclosure but reciprocity to their disclosures.

Additional situational factors have been explored by Corcorran (1988), who examined the degree to which subjects are likely to disclose when confidentiality of the disclosure to an interviewer was assured. Subjects were asked to respond "yes" or "no" to statements that required them to answer questions in a socially undesirable way and thus Corcorran introduced to the equation the notion of impression management in real communications in everyday-life self-disclosure. The findings indicated that the male subjects disclosed more to the female interviewer than the female subjects. Corcorran cited two possible reasons for this. First, Singer (1978) reported that men are more likely than are women to take risks when being interviewed about personal information. Second, Rosen (1977) suggested that women may value the self-protection of the presentation of a good image more highly than men do. Although this study did not focus on the dynamics of reciprocity per se, the findings are instructive because they point to the fact that differences between men and women may be a result of a number of practical factors in conversation, including the topic and the image management goals of both sexes. These factors are essentially ones that stem from the practice of self-disclosure in a socially compelling context rather than from "pure traits."

In support of such an argument, both Shaffer and Tomarelli (1989) and Miller (1990) have shown that the production of given self-disclosures in the course of conversations is affected by issues of impression management that interact with other goals of the interlocutors and that such issues are affected by the speaker's goals and also by the perception of others' goals. Miller (1990) showed that an understanding of the complex strategies that individuals use to enhance affinity behavior in others must take into account underlying interpersonal and intrapersonal dynamic processes before comprehension of specific production of self-disclosures.

These last two studies are good examples of how research is facilitating the weaving together of the theoretical explanation of self-disclosure in the context of other conversational goals and realities of everyday life. Shaffer et al., Miller, and others are promoting a body of literature that combines trait and state variables to explain self-disclosure behavior. This approach supports an interactional approach to self-disclosure research, wherein self-disclosure can be viewed as "enactments of strategies to achieve a variety of different goals" (Miller, 1990, p. 51).

Changes in self-disclosure are not just automatic responses to the "demands" of reciprocity. Berger and Kellerman (1989), for instance, examined evasive tactics that individuals incorporate and Altman and Taylor (1973) examined a number of interpersonal boundary processes by which a person or group regulates interaction with another. Self-disclosure functions to regulate interpersonal intimacy and influence a relationship's direction by signaling to another a desired level of inclusion and affection. In so doing, an individual is able to project a particular version of self that is comparable with one's view of the appropriateness of the relationship. This "appropriateness" is no doubt bound in cultural practices, but, in addition, we argue, these relational processes are negotiated within the relationship.

Such negotiations are obscured by the focus on self-disclosure out of its everyday context, stripped of many of the processes of mental creation and negotiation of scene-relevant behavior that we identified earlier as major components of everyday conversations. Too much research already relies on information gathered from highly structured, laboratory-type settings, creating an unrealistic depiction of interactional communication. Laboratory-type studies often record self-disclosive behavior as a highly charged, high stakes communication process. Scholars are beginning to ascertain, however, that this is not always the case. Dindia, Fitzpatrick, and Kenny (1989) have found that, in naturally occurring conversations, self-disclosure does not appear with anything like the frequency that is indicated in the laboratory research; Duck and Miell (1986) have suggested that most conversations between friends are mundane and nonintimate (Duck et al., 1991). Eisenberg (1990) goes so far as to say that our deeply held, implicit models of communication prevent us from fully appreciating the value of personally involving, minimally disclosing exchanges. Although many highly regarded studies have used laboratory-type configurations, perhaps it is time for researchers to choose a methodology that taps the more mundane, nonintimate side of our communicative behavior. "Everyday talk" as a whole, not merely its dramatic components (such as "charged" self-disclosures), represents a fundamental core concept that could begin to develop our understanding of how "traits" get out into the world, in the ways argued at the start of the chapter. To the extent that self-disclosure is a trait, it will be articulated in the form of communication that occurs in everyday communication, for instance. Also, to the extent that self-disclosure is itself a complex of different sorts of behavior, this too will be determinable from everyday interaction and will enable researchers to assess whether self-disclosure should be treated as essentially the same sort of communication in all circumstances. For instance, study of daily life patterns of communication have been predicted to show differentiation as a function of the life concerns that afflict the speaker at the time of measurement (Duck, 1987). We should not forget that people have a range of interlocutors available to them, such that the choice of interlocutor is itself a relevant feature of the self-disclosive communications that we might observe in everyday life.

Self-disclosure, like the other forms of communication that we have discussed more generally above, acts to situate the person within particular relationships, but also the act of self-disclosure itself is crafted within the person's own view of the world. It demonstrates the person's willingness to reside within a particular social environment and helps to punctuate a person's preferred communication and relational style, thus defining and "essentializing" it to some extent. It also serves to emphasize that the speaker warrants the partner and defines certain styles of relational expression as important in relationships. Self-disclosure thus serves to regulate the individual, relational, and worldview issues that the individual stresses. It invites the partner into an exclusive relational club where the most important issues of the day reside. Such socially forceful facts are likely missed by research that does not place self-disclosure in its everyday rhetorical and relational context.

Conclusion

Our case has been that everyday communication structures and reflects the worldviews and continual dilemmas of the persons in a relationship as they each attempt to cope with a continually unfolding realm of experience. Partners may have thoughts about the relationship itself and indeed construct it mentally from their experience of the conversations therein, but also use those conversations as a crucible in which to ferment and test their view of the world. For these reasons, the conversations of daily life are likely to reflect the variable concerns and different issues that persons in relationships frequently discuss, rather than the solidified certainties of the stable-sounding and invariant labels that relationships often carry. By contrast, we have suggested that relational experience is varied and complex, not stable and certain. We argue that daily conversations reflect the persons' continual attempts to place themselves and their experience in context.

Such a view challenges researchers of interpersonal communication to place daily conversation in its social and constructive context. To pin down the role of such conversations is somewhat akin to studying AIDS. To date, AIDS researchers have been unable to provide a cure in part because one of the features of the AIDS virus is that the cells regularly shed their molecular identity for another. It is difficult to affix a scientific gaze on a constantly changing entity and so it is with the study of interpersonal communication. If we accept a transformational metaphor, then we also accept the difficulties inherent in trying to categorize and affect the true identity of relationshipping (Duck, 1984).

We can thus see that a communicational perspective on relationships requires us to note the several different social and constructive processes that are components of relationshipping and to contextualize relationship behavior in the wider setting of everyday-life concerns. Information gathering is one large set of processes. The negotiation of a relationship's form is another. The maintenance of a relationship's place in a social network is a third. The processing of information relative to knowledge of relational objectives and norms is a fourth. Finally, an important source of communicative and relational effects is simply the passage of time, which necessitates changes in communication to persons, about relationships, and in connection with surrounding circumstances. It also requires the important business of coping with human errors, moods, and changes in life purposes. All of these constructive efforts are a natural part of the human enterprise of dealing with the passage of time in a relational context.

References

Alexander, B. B. (1977). Disclosure reciprocity and attraction as functions of consistency in self-presentation. *Dissertation Abstracts International, 38,* 2424b.

Altman, I., & Taylor, D. A. (1973). *Social penetration: The development of interpersonal relationships.* New York: Holt, Rinehart & Winston.

Andersen, P. (1993). Cognitive schemata in personal relationships. In S. W. Duck (Ed.), *Understanding relationship processes: Vol. 1. Individuals in relationships* (pp. 1-29). Newbury Park, CA: Sage.

Barnes, M. K., & Duck, S. W. (in press). Everyday communication of social support. In T. Albrecht, B. Burleson, & I. Sarason (Eds.), *Communication and social support.* Newbury Park, CA: Sage.

Baxter, L. A. (1992). Forms and functions of intimate play in personal relationships. *Human Communication Research, 18,* 336-363.

Baxter, L. A. (1993). Thinking dialogically about communication in personal relationships. In R. L. Conville (Ed.), *Structures of interpretation* (pp. 29-47). Norwood, NJ: Ablex.

Baxter, L. A., & Simon, E. (1993). Relationship maintenance strategies and dialectical contradictions in personal relationships. *Journal of Social and Personal Relationships, 10*, 225-242.

Berger, C. R. (1988). Uncertainty and information exchange in developing relationships. In S. W. Duck, D. F. Hay, S. E. Hobfoll, W. Ickes, & B. Montgomery (Eds.), *Handbook of personal relationships* (pp. 239-256). Chichester: Wiley.

Berger, C. R. (1993). Goals, plans and mutual understanding in personal relationships. In S. W. Duck (Ed.), *Understanding relationship processes: Vol. 1. Individuals in relationships* (pp. 30-59). Newbury Park, CA: Sage.

Berger, C. R., & Bradac, J. (1982). *Language and social knowledge*. London: Edward Arnold.

Berger, C., & Kellerman, K. (1989). Personal opacity and social information gathering: Explorations in strategic communication. *Communication Research, 16*, 314-351.

Berger, P., & Kellner, H. (1964). Marriage and the construction of reality: An exercise in the microsociology of knowledge. *Diogenes, 46,* 1-24.

Billig, M. (1987). *Arguing and thinking: A rhetorical approach to social psychology*. Cambridge: Cambridge University Press.

Billig, M., Condor, S., Edwards, D., Gane, M., Middleton, D., & Radley, A. (1988). *Ideological dilemmas: A social psychology of everyday thinking*. London: Sage.

Burkitt, I. (1991). *Social selves: Theories of the social formation of personality*. London: Sage.

Byrne, D. (1971). *The attraction paradigm*. New York: Academic Press.

Cappella, J. N. (1991). Mutual adaptation and relativity of measurement. In B. M. Montgomery & S. W. Duck (Eds.), *Studying interpersonal interaction* (pp. 103-117). Guilford: New York.

Chelune, G. J., & Associates. (1979). *Self-disclosure: Origins, patterns, and implications of openness in interpersonal relationships*. San Francisco: Jossey-Bass.

Christensen, A., Sullaway, M., & King, C. (1983). Systematic error in behavioral reports of dyadic interaction: Egocentric bias and content effects. *Behavioral Assessment 5*, 129-142.

Clark, R. A., & Delia, J. G. (1979). Topoi and rhetorical competence. *Quarterly Journal of Speech, 65*, 187-206.

Corcorran, K. J. (1988). The relationship of interpersonal trust to self-disclosure when confidentiality is assured. *Journal of Psychology, 122*, 193-195.

Cozby, P. C. (1973). Self-disclosure: A literature review. *Psychological Bulletin, 79*(2), 73-91.

Dainton, M., & Stafford, L. (1993). Everyday routines of relationships. *Journal of Social and Personal Relationships, 10*, 255-271.

Delia, J. G. (1980). Some tentative thoughts concerning the study of interpersonal relationships and their development. *Western Journal of Speech Communication, 44*, 97-103.

Dimond, R. E., & Hellkamp, D. T. (1969). Race, sex, ordinal position of birth, and self-disclosure of high school students. *Psychological Reports, 25*, 235-238.

Dimond, R. E., & Munz, D. C. (1967). Ordinal position of birth and self-disclosure of high school students. *Psychological Reports, 21*, 829-833.

Dindia, K. (1988). A comparison of several statistical tests of reciprocity of self-disclosure. *Communication Research, 15*, 726-752.

Dindia, K., Fitzpatrick, M. A., & Kenny, D. A. (1989, May). *Self disclosure in spouse and stranger interaction: A social relations analysis*. Paper presented at the International Communication Association, New Orleans.

Dixson, M., & Duck, S. W. (1993). Understanding relationship processes: Uncovering the human search for meaning. In S. W. Duck (Ed.), *Understanding relationship processes: Vol. 1. Individuals in relationships* (pp. 175-206). Newbury Park, CA: Sage.

Duck, S. W. (1977). *The study of acquaintance*. Farnborough, England: Teakfields/Saxon House.

Duck, S. W. (1984). A rose is a rose (is a tadpole is a freeway is a film), is a rose. *Journal of Social and Personal Relationships, 1,* 507-510.

Duck, S. W. (1985). Social and personal relationships. In M. L. Knapp & G. R. Miller (Eds.), *Handbook of interpersonal communication* (pp. 655-686). Beverly Hills, CA: Sage.

Duck, S. W. (1987). How to lose friends without influencing people. In M. E. Roloff & G. R. Miller (Eds.), *Interpersonal processes: New directions in communication research* (pp. 278-298). Newbury Park, CA: Sage.

Duck, S. W. (1990). Relationships as unfinished business: Out of the frying pan and into the 1990s. *Journal of Social and Personal Relationships, 7*, 5-28.

Duck, S. W. (1991, May). *New lamps for old: A new theory of relationships and a fresh look at some old research*. Paper presented at the Third Conference of the International Network on Personal Relationships, Normal-Bloomington, IL.

Duck, S. W. (1994). *Meaningful relationships: Talking, sense, and relating*. Newbury Park, CA: Sage.

Duck, S. W. (in press). Steady as (s),he goes: Relational maintenance as a shared meaning system. In D. J. Canary & L. Stafford (Eds.), *Communication and relationship maintenance*. New York: Academic Press.

Duck, S. W., & Miell, D. E. (1984). Towards an understanding of relationship development and breakdown. In H. Tajfel, C. Fraser, & J. Jaspars (Eds.), *The social dimension: European perspectives on social psychology*. Cambridge: Cambridge University Press.

Duck, S. W., & Miell, D. E. (1986). Charting the development of personal relationships. In R. Gilmour & S. W. Duck (Eds.), *Emerging field of personal relationships* (pp. 133-144). Hillsdale, NJ: LEA.

Duck, S. W., & Montgomery, B. M. (1991). The interdependence among interaction substance, theory, and methods. In B. M. Montgomery & S. W. Duck (Eds.), *Studying interpersonal interaction* (pp. 3-15). Guilford: New York.

Duck, S. W., & Pond, K. (1989). Friends, romans, countrymen, lend me your retrospections: Rhetoric and reality in personal relationships. In C. Hendrick (Ed.), *Close relationships* (pp. 17-38). Newbury Park, CA: Sage.

Duck, S. W., Pond, K., & Leatham, G. B. (1992). Loneliness and the evaluation of relational events. *Journal of Social and Personal Relationships, 11*, 251-276.

Duck, S. W., Rutt, D. J., Hurst, M. H., & Strejc, H. (1991). Some evident truths about conversation in everyday relationships: All communications are not created equal. *Human Communication Research, 18*, 228-267.

Duck, S. W., & Sants, H. K. A. (1983). On the origin of the specious: Are personal relationships really interpersonal states? *Journal of Social and Clinical Psychology, 1*, 27-41.

Duncan, H. D. (1967). The search for a social theory of communication in American sociology. In F. E. X. Dance (Ed.), *Human communication theory* (pp. 227-241). New York: Holt, Rinehart & Winston.

Eisenberg, E. M. (1990). Jamming: Transcendence through organizing. *Communication Research, 17*(2), 139-164.

Franzoi, S. L., Davis, M. H., & Young, R. D. (1985). The effects of private self-consciousness and perspective taking on satisfaction in close relationships. *Journal of Personality and Social Psychology, 48*, 1584-1594.

Gergen, K. J., & Gergen, M. M. (1987). Narratives of relationship. In R. Burnett, P. McGhee, & D. D. Clarke (Eds.), *Accounting for relationships* (pp. 269-315). London: Methuen.

Giles, H., & Coupland, N. (1991). *Language in social context*. Milton Keynes, England: Open University.

Giles, H., & Powesland, P. F. (1975). *Speech style and social evaluation*. London: Academic Press.

Gottman, J. M. (1989, May). *The future of relationships*. Paper to Second Iowa International Conference on Personal Relationships, Iowa City.

Hays, R. B. (1984). The development and maintenance of friendship. *Journal of Social and Personal Relationships, 1*, 75-98.

Hinde, R. A. (1981). The bases of a science of interpersonal relationships. In S. W. Duck & R. Gilmour (Eds.), *Personal relationships: Vol. 1. Studying personal relationships* (pp. 1-22). London: Academic Press.

Honeycutt, J. M. (1993). Memory structures for the rise and fall of personal relationships. In S. W. Duck (Ed.), *Understanding relationship processes: Vol. 1. Individuals in relationships* (pp. 60-86). Newbury Park, CA: Sage.

Jourard, S. M. (1959). Healthy personality and self-disclosure. *Mental Hygiene, 43*, 499-507.

Jourard, S. M. (1961). Religious denomination and self-disclosure. *Psychological Reports, 8*, 446.

Jourard, S. M. (1971). *The transparent self* (rev. ed.). New York: Van Nostrand Reinhold.

Jourard, S. M., & Lasakow, P. (1958). Some factors in self-disclosure. *Journal of Abnormal and Social Psychology, 56*, 91-98.

Kelly, G. A. (1969). *Clinical psychology and personality* (B. Maher, Ed.). New York: Wiley.

Kelvin, P. (1977). Predictability, power and vulnerability in interpersonal attraction. In S. W. Duck (Ed.), *Theory and practice in interpersonal attraction* (pp. 355-378). London: Academic Press.

Klos, D. S., & Loomis, D. F. (1978). A rating scale of intimate disclosure between late adolescents and their friends. *Psychological Reports, 42*, 815-820.

Miell, D. E. (1984). *Cognitive and communicative strategies in developing relationships: Converging and diverging social environments*. Unpublished doctoral dissertation, University of Lancaster, United Kingdom.

Miell, D. E. (1987). Remembering relationship development: Constructing a context for interactions. In R. Burnett, P. McGhee, & D. Clarke (Eds.), *Accounting for relationships* (pp. 60-73). London: Methuen.

Miller, L. C. (1990). Intimacy and liking: Mutual influence and the role of unique relationships. *Journal of Personality and Social Psychology, 59*, 50-60.

Montgomery, B. M. (1993). Relationship maintenance versus relationship change: A dialectical dilemma. *Journal of Social and Personal Relationships, 10,* 205-223.

Olson, D. H. (1977). Insiders' and outsiders' views of relationships: Research studies. In G. Levinger & H. Raush (Eds.), *Close relationships: Perspectives on the meaning of intimacy* (pp. 115-135). Amherst: University of Massachusetts Press.

Papini, D. R., Farmer, F. F., Clark, S. M., Micka, J. C., & Barnett, J. K. (1990). Early adolescent age and gender differences in patterns of emotional self-disclosure to parents and friends. *Adolescence, 25,* 959-976.

Penman, R. (1980). *Communication processes and relationships.* New York: Academic Press.

Potter, J., & Wetherell, M. (1987). *Discourse and social psychology.* London: Sage.

Reddy, M. J. (1979). The conduit metaphor: A case of frame conflict in our language about language. In A. Ortony (Ed.), *Metaphor and thought* (pp. 284-324). New York: Cambridge University Press.

Rosen, C. E. (1977). Why clients relinquish their rights to privacy under sign-away procedures. *Professional Psychology, 8,* 17-24.

Rotenberg, K. J., & Mann, L. (1986). The development of the norm of the reciprocity of self-disclosure and its function in children's attraction to peers. *Child Development, 57,* 1349-1357.

Rusbult, C. E., & Buunk, B. (1993). Interdependence and relational maintenance. *Journal of Social and Personal Relationships, 10,* 175-204.

Shaffer, D. R., Ogden, J. K., & Wu, C. (1987). Effects of self-monitoring and prospect of future interaction on self-disclosure reciprocity during the acquaintance process. *Journal of Personality, 55*(1), 75-96.

Shaffer, D. R., & Tomarelli, M. M. (1989). When public and private self-foci clash: Self-consciousness and self-disclosure reciprocity during the acquaintance process. *Journal of Personality and Social Psychology, 56,* 765-776.

Shaffer, D. R., Tomarelli, M. M., & Smith, J. E. (1982). Self-monitoring as a determinate of self-disclosure reciprocity during the acquaintance process. *Journal of Personality and Social Psychology, 43,* 163-175.

Shotter, J. (1992). What is a "personal relationship"? A rhetorical-responsive account of "unfinished business." In J. H. Harvey, T. L. Orbuch, & A. L. Weber (Eds.), *Attributions, accounts and close relationships* (pp. 19-39). New York: Springer-Verlag.

Sillars, A. L. (1991). Behavioral observation. In B. M. Montgomery & S. W. Duck (Eds.), *Studying interpersonal interaction* (pp. 197-218). New York: Guilford.

Singer, E. (1978). The effect of informed consent procedures on respondents' reactions to surveys. *Journal of Consumer Research, 5,* 49-57.

Snell, W. E., Miller, R. S., & Belk, S. S. (1988). Development of the emotional self-disclosure scale. *Sex Roles, 18,* 59-73.

Snell, W. E., Miller, R. S., Belk, S. S., Garcia-Falconi, R., & Hernandez-Sanchez, J. E. (1989). Men's and women's emotional disclosures: The impact of disclosure recipient, culture, and the masculine role. *Sex Roles, 21,* 467-486.

Spencer, E. E. (1992). *Self-disclosure in family conversational interaction: Communication between parents and older adolescents.* Unpublished doctoral dissertation, University of Texas at Austin.

Sprecher, S. (1987). The effects of self-disclosure given and received on affection for an intimate partner and stability of the relationship. *Journal of Social and Personal Relationships, 4,* 115-127.

Stephen, T. D. (1986). Communication and interdependence in geographically separated relationships. *Human Communication Research, 13,* 191-210.

Surra, C. A. (1987). Reasons for changes in commitment: Variations by courtship style. *Journal of Social and Personal Relationships, 4,* 17-33.

Surra, C. A., & Ridley, C. (1991). Multiple perspectives on interaction: Participants, peers and observers. In B. M. Montgomery & S. W. Duck (Eds.), *Studying interpersonal interaction* (pp. 35-55). Guilford: New York.

Walster, E., Walster, G. W., & Berscheid, E. (1978). *Equity theory and research.* Boston: Allyn & Bacon.

Watzlawick, P., Beavin, J., & Jackson, D. (1967). *Pragmatics of human communication: A study of interactional patterns, pathologies and paradoxes.* New York: Norton.

Weber, M. (1967). Subjective meaning in the social situation. In G. B. Levitas (Ed.), *Culture and consciousness: Perspectives in the social sciences.* New York: Braziller.

Wheeler, L., & Nezlek, J. (1977). Sex difference in social participation. *Journal of Personality and Social Psychology, 35,* 742-754.

Wheeless, L. R., & Grotz, J. (1977). The measurement of trust and its relationship to self-disclosure. *Human Communication Research, 2,* 338-346.

18

Interpersonal Communication and Health Care

Teresa L. Thompson

RESEARCH ON INTERPERSONAL communication in the health care context has improved markedly in both quantity and quality since Adler (1977) called for a shift to problem-oriented doctor-patient research in the early years of *Human Communication Research*. Several years after Adler's call, T. L. Thompson (1984) criticized the research on health communication as being simplistic in its conceptualization of communication, as not building on past research, and as focusing exclusively on the health care provider rather than the dyad as the unit of analysis. As the following review will indicate, research on health care provider-patient interaction is now much more sophisticated both conceptually and methodologically. The student of interpersonal communication in health care can now find a variety of articles focusing on theoretical issues, descriptive studies, skill assessments, measurement concerns, and outcome measures including compliance, recovery, physiological indices, satisfaction, and malpractice. More specific foci addressed in the literature include such issues as language, control, disconfirmation, openness, gender, and nonverbal communication. All of these issues will be addressed in the present review.

This research has been conducted by social scientists, nurses, and, to a lesser extent, physicians. The present review will focus on research conducted by social scientists more than the other two groups, because it is generally most sophisticated both conceptually and methodologically. Research on communication conducted by those in the medical fields, however, has also improved markedly in recent years. There are some notable exceptions of extraordinarily sophisticated research conducted by physicians and nurses.

Communication research found in the nursing journals tends, for the most part, to be skill oriented or anecdotal. For instance, Garvin and Kennedy's (1990) review of this research includes headings such as "Support," "Self Disclosure," "Empathy," and "Confirmation." The empirical research they review typically focuses on the interpersonal skills that nurses have, need, or should acquire. Many other communication articles in the nursing journals are not data based but are arguments of the "this is what we need to do" variety or are case studies of instances when awareness of nonverbal communication, listening, or other communication variables were especially important (e.g., Ball & Heath, 1989; Douglass, 1989; Hargreaves, 1987; Kay-Herndon, 1989; Reale, 1988; Woy, 1987). This is not to belittle the salience of such pieces, as they can be very important and have quite an impact on care providers (see, for instance, the work of Connolly & Shekleton, 1991, on communicating with ventilator dependent patients). But most of these pieces do not *extend* our understanding of interpersonal communication in health care and will not be discussed herein. Finally, there are some articles that purport to discuss "communication theory," as if it were a unified theoretical perspective. Such pieces tend to argue for the central import of the communication process during nursing care.

Research on communication in the medical journals is much sparser, although less so than it has been in the past. Wyatt's (1991) review found that less than 1% of the medical literature focuses on relationships between physicians and patients, thus further reinforcing the power of the biomedical model of medicine (Mishler, 1981). Wyatt noted that many of these articles attempt to offer "quick fixes" to psychosocial concerns. As was the case with the research in the nursing journals, many of these pieces tend to be anecdotal case studies or "how-to" arguments, citing research but not providing new data (e.g., Bendich, 1988).

Thus the present review will focus on research conducted by social scientists, although it will also include some research by medical care providers. The boon in the amount of research conducted in this area is exemplified by the inauguration in 1989 of the journal *Health Communication,* which, along with such periodicals as *Social Science and Medicine* and *Medical Care,* has published much of the research discussed herein. The review will first provide a brief rationale for this line of research and will then begin with discussion of descriptive studies of interpersonal communication in health care. This will lead into an assessment of interpersonal skills, followed by some of the more specific outcome measures and other variables listed above. The review will conclude with a discussion of measurement concerns and theoretical perspectives.

As is the case with most of the reviews in this *Handbook,* this chapter will attempt to be representative rather than exhaustive. The research that the author identifies as being most important to our understanding of interpersonal communication in the health care context will be reviewed.

Because of space limitations, several topics that are interesting and important but not central to general health communication concerns will not be reviewed. Such issues include communication with specific populations (e.g., AIDS patients, children, the elderly, or the "difficult" patient) or communication with specific types of care providers (e.g., dentists, therapists, or nurses). Finally, organizational issues such as communication in health care teams or between health care providers will not be the focus of specific discussion. Some of these research areas, however, will be discussed in the context of other issues.

Rationale

Although some have criticized the study of communication in specific contexts (e.g., Berger, 1991), others have argued that there is a need for midrange theories in our attempt to understand human behavior (e.g., Merton, 1957). Midrange theoretical perspectives provide insight into limited behaviors or behaviors in specific contexts. Scholars then build upon those theories to increase the extent of our understanding. The study of interpersonal communication in health care provides such an opportunity. Theoretical perspectives generated within this specialized context can then serve as the foundation for future theorizing. However, the study of interpersonal communication within health care is also important in and of itself because of the great need that exists within the area. The dissatisfaction with communication experienced by both physicians and patients is well documented (e.g., Fuller & Quesada, 1973; Haas & Puretz, 1992; Koos, 1955; Korsch & Negrete, 1972). Communication affects numerous variables within health care, including diagnosis, understanding of instructions and subsequent compliance, and openness when communicating about taboo topics such as bodily functions and sexuality that are often a part of health care.

The health care context is, in some ways, a relatively unique one. Few other interpersonal contexts are characterized by the urgency or life-and-death nature that can exist in health care interactions. Health communication is also characterized by frequent interaction among those with pronounced status differences, because physicians are elevated to a rather high status in our culture.

In addition to these unique characteristics and likely impacts of interpersonal communication in health care, evidence indicates a lack of provider concern about communication. While many physicians tend to look at emphasizing communication as a waste of valuable time, some research shows that more time is wasted because physicians did not take time to communicate with patients about issues than would have been required if communication had originally occurred (Korsch & Negrete, 1972). It has also been argued that dissatisfaction with the lack of interpersonal skills of care providers leads patients to rely on medical "quacks" or "hucksters" who do have such skills (Korsch & Negrete, 1972; Simoni & Ball, 1975). There is an indication of a deterioration of communication skills during medical school, evidencing a need for research and training (Ceropski & Kline, 1985; Helfer & Ealy, 1972).

While the concerns expressed above seem to imply that all communication problems are due to the behavior of the care provider, such an assumption would, of course, be simplistic and misleading. Patient behaviors also reflect such problems as a lack of listening, comprehension, or question asking. Some of the current social scientific research reflects a more transactional, dyadic perspective on health care than has been evidenced in the past and attempts to look at the interdependence of provider and patient. We begin with discussion of several such studies.

A Primary Focus on Describing Communication

Although the research to be reviewed in this chapter does not neatly break down into distinct categories, there is a rough distinction that can be drawn between those studies that are more descriptive and those that look at communication as an independent variable that affects numerous outcomes. Very little health research looks at communication as a dependent variable, and most of the work that does is not terribly illuminating. A few notable exceptions will be discussed. We will first look at the research that attempts to describe provider-patient interaction and then move on to the outcome literature. Although some of the studies to be discussed in the "descriptive" sections also look at the outcomes of communication, they do a particularly good job of delineating the interpersonal interaction that occurs in the health care context. In some cases, outcomes will also be reviewed, so that these studies need not be discussed again in the "outcomes" sections.

Content of Communication

Several studies have looked at the types of communication that occur during interactions between health care providers and their patients. One rather unusual study looked at telephone consultations between primary care nurses and patients. It is interesting that little research has focused on this topic, given that receptionist nurses screen calls to almost all physicians and serve to translate much communication from the patient to the physician (Marklund & Bengtsson, 1989). This study recorded these conversations and then used a stimulated recall technique. The results indicated that the nurses focused communication mainly on issues related to medical diagnosis and management strategy and spent little time on patients' concerns, ideas, and expectations (Timpka & Arborelius, 1990).

Although not purely descriptive, another study manipulated three different types of communication (providing explanations, giving irrelevant information, and giving no information) and examined their impacts on patients' reactions to stress. Meyers (1965) found that irrelevant communication caused tension in the patient and that no information at all was preferable to irrelevant information. Providing explanations, however, allowed the patients to cognitively structure their thoughts, understand more, and put things in perspective. This was true even of patients who had been extremely fearful prior to the having information.

Larsson and Starrin (1990) studied 3,200 patient-nurse assistant interactions and found that most communication could be categorized as "facts and practical issues," followed by communication of an "everyday character" and then "personal and emotional" communication. However, increases of communication in the latter two categories and decreased "facts and practical" communication were associated with more positive patient reactions and more cheerful patients.

In another very specific context, Gibb and O'Brien (1990) conducted an ethnographic study of how nurses relate with elderly clients. They found that patterns of speech style varied in relation to the physical procedure being carried out at the time. For instance, they found that mechanical, nurse-directed activities led to social, chatty interaction and were more beneficial to both participants. By contrast, activities that involved more mutual involvement of interactants required that communication focus on this collaboration and thus on the task. This led to less sociable interaction.

Information giving. An interesting line of research has focused on information given by the care provider to the patient. Noting that some patients receive more information from physicians than do others, Street (1991a) examined patients' communicative styles and personal characteristics as determinants of the amount of information received from caregivers. His data indicated that

(a) information regarding diagnosis and health matters was primarily related to the patient's anxiety, education, and question asking;

(b) information regarding treatment was primarily a function of the patient's question asking and expression of concerns; and

(c) patients' assertiveness and expressiveness were strongly influenced by physicians' use of "partnership-building" utterances that solicited the patient's questions, concerns, and opinions (Street, 1991a, p. 541).

Street's data are of special interest to those of us studying communication, because past research had typically focused on demographic characteristics as determinants of the amount of information received by patients (e.g., Arntson & Philipsborn, 1982). Research by Crane (1975) has also gone beyond this, by indicating that physicians respond to critically or terminally ill patients not only in terms of physiological definitions of illness but also in terms of the extent to which the patient is capable of communicating with others.

Other data by Street (1992a) indicate that physician characteristics also determine how much information is communicated. Additionally, this study confirmed the findings reported above and discovered that patients who express more negative affect also receive more information. We will return to Street's research later in this chapter.

The theme of information giving has also surfaced in Simoni and Ball's (1975) work on what we can learn from "medical hucksters." Simoni and Ball noted that, among the poor, hucksters are ranked higher than other care providers on giving important information as well as on credibility, accessibility, and providing explanations. For these reasons, medical hucksters are sought out by many.

Burn unit staff members also emphasize the importance of providing full information to patients (Brack, LaClave, & Campbell, 1987). Brack et al.'s research, however, found possible double-binding communication patterns in burn units, as nurses attempt to behave optimistically even if they are pessimistic about a patient's prognosis.

Summarizing a series of studies on doctor-patient communication, Waitzkin (1984) concluded that "physicians tend to underestimate patients' desire for information and to misperceive the process of information giving" (p. 2441). He cites several other variables that influence the likelihood of information giving, including characteristics of patients, physicians, and the clinical situation.

Time allocation. Some of the studies that have attempted to describe various aspects of encounters between care providers and patients have focused specifically on the length of interactions, the amount of talk time contributed by the care provider versus the patient, and the kinds of statements that constitute the interactions. In a rather comprehensive meta-analytic study of such research, Roter, Hall, and Katz (1988) reported that physician-patient interactions average about 16 minutes in length in the United States (5-6 minutes in Britain). Patients typically contribute about 40% of the dialogue, with physicians providing the other 60%. About half of patient talk is devoted to giving information, 20% to what Roter et al. labeled "positive talk," and 6% to 7% to each of the categories of question asking, social conversation, and negative talk. These findings are consistent with those of Arntson, Droge, and Fassl (1978), who reported that doctors ask twice as many questions and give twice as many commands as patients, and that patients typically do not ask for explanations.

This small amount of time devoted to question asking is interesting, in light of the fact that increased patient question asking is associated with increased understanding of treatment regimens and a better medical outcome (Beisecker, 1990). Fisher (1983) found that changes in treatment decisions occurred as a result of patient questions. Roter et al.'s finding, however, is consistent with that of Korsch, Gozzi, and Francis (1968), who reported that only 24% of the patients participating in their study asked the physician about their *main* concern. It is also consistent with research indicating that physicians discourage question asking (Frankel, 1984;

Mishler, 1984; Svarstad, 1974; Waitzkin, 1984, 1985; Weiss, 1986; West, 1984), even though patients desire information (McIntosh, 1974; Quint, 1965). Several studies have now documented methods of encouraging patient question asking (Feeser & Thompson, 1993; Greenfield, Kaplan, & Ware, 1985; Robinson & Whitfield, 1985; Roter, 1977).

The Roter et al. meta-analysis mentioned above also reported that 38.5% of physician time was spent in information giving, followed by 22.6% of the time in information seeking; 15% of the time was "positive" talk, 10% of the time was spent in partnership building, followed by 6% of the time in social conversation. Partnership building included attempts to facilitate greater patient input and interpret and synthesize patients' talk.

The notion of allocation of time to communicative activities has also been discussed in research that has indicated that "lack of time" is the reason given by many care providers for not communicating with patients more (MacLeod Clark, 1985). However, MacLeod Clark's (1983) earlier research uncovered no relationship between the amount of time available and the quality of communication. Two very early studies also found that, even when care providers are given extra time, they do not use it to interact more frequently with patients (Aydelotte, 1960; New, Nite, & Callahan, 1959).

Other research has determined that "interaction by all grades of staff is not satisfactory in the quantity or quality, and raises the question as to whether nurses have the communication skills that are necessary in order to assess, plan, implement and evaluate the nursing care of a patient" (Crotty, 1985, p. 130). The notion of requisite communication skills for health care providers has been examined in a number of other studies as well.

Communication Skills

Although the field of communication long ago shifted from the notion of "skills" to a conceptualization of competence or competencies, the medical and nursing literature still uses the term *skills*. To provide consistency, then, we will use the term *skills* within this chapter. Overall, the evidence indicates that some care providers are cognizant of the need for communication skills (Eastwood, 1985) and that their estimation of their communication skills is higher than observation of their skills would warrant (Dockrell, 1988). Different studies, however, have focused on different skills to reach this conclusion. In her study of physiotherapy students, Dockrell (1988) examined attendance to such behaviors as eye contact, tone of voice, facial expression, and touch and to behaviors such as listening, responding with interest, and explaining procedures. Dockrell's emphasis on attendance to nonverbals was derived from the evidence indicating that the provider-patient relationship depends to some degree on the provider's ability to understand the patient's nonverbals (Dimatteo & Taranta, 1979).

In a much more specific context, Mallett (1990) conducted an ethnographic study of communication between nurses and postanesthetic patients. She determined that the small sample of nurses she studied were skilled communicators in terms of gaining the patients' attention and adapting to the patients' low level of consciousness but she raised questions about the therapeutic value of the communication. In this study, *therapeutic value* was used to mean "do the patient some good" (pp. 45-46).

B. M. Thompson's (1986) listing of interpersonal skills required by care providers includes (a) obtaining information (listening, asking open questions, and reflecting);

(b) giving information (decreasing complexity, repeating, explicitly categorizing, providing specificity, and using primacy and importance effects); and (c) enhancing rapport (using empathy and communicating warmth with behaviors indicating immediacy). Thompson's work focused on nurses and is reflective of the kind of orientation typically found in such work, as was described earlier. The same is also true of the list developed by Lubbers and Roy (1990), which includes listening, relationship building, instructing, motivating, exchanging routine information, and giving feedback as requisite skills for nurses.

Lubbers and Roy's work built on the earlier research of Morse and Piland (1981) and DiSalvo, Larsen, and Backus (1986). Morse and Piland asked nurses to rate the importance of a number of communication skills in the nurse-patient relationship. From most to least important, they were listening, instruction, management of conflict, routine information exchange, advising, small group communication, persuading, giving orders, and public speaking. The work of Worobey and Cummings (1984) yielded similar conclusions. The list generated by DiSalvo et al. is somewhat more extensive. Again from most to least important were listening, instructing, advising, giving feedback, interviewing, relationship building, persuading, soliciting feedback, motivating, routine information exchange, oral report giving, small group communication, small group leadership, negotiating, conflict resolution, and public speaking. The reader will note that listening is highly ranked in all of the delineations.

Findings by Morrison and Burnard (1989) indicate that nurses see themselves as more authoritative and less facilitative than they should be in their interpersonal relationships. These self-perceptions are confirmed by Wilkinson's (1991) observational research, which found an overall poor level of facilitative communication in nurses' interaction with cancer patients. Facilitative communication was interpreted as communication that allowed nurses to assess how patients feel about and are dealing with their illnesses.

Research on communication skills of health care providers other than nurses frequently takes a much narrower focus. For instance, Guy, Haskell, Hutson, and Schuman's (1977) study of home visits by family practitioners looked only at listening and speaking clearly. They determined that these skills were adequate. Other research on physicians focuses only on interviewing skills. Mace (1971), for example, concluded that only 10% of the physicians studied did a good job even with history taking in the initial interview. Poor interviewing skills in psychiatric residents, who emphasize interpersonal factors much more than do other medical specialties, were also summarized by McCready and Waring (1986). Cassell, Coulehan, and Putnam (1989) provide a more positive frame, as they discuss "making good interview skills better" (p. 145). They describe such skills as showing interest, allowing the patient to explain all of his or her concerns, using open-ended questions, using positive nonverbal behavior, using pauses, repeating/summarizing patient communication, attending to patient body language, expressing feelings and empathy, touching, and reassuring or confirming the patient. We will return to this notion of reassurance or confirmation later in our discussion.

Training. There is evidence that the communication skills cited above can be improved with appropriate training (Evans, Kiellerup, Stanley, Burrows, & Sweet, 1987; Evans, Stanley, & Burrows, 1992; Farsad, Galliguez, Chamberlin, & Roghmann, 1978; French, 1983; Kalisch, 1971; Omololu, 1984; Rubin, Judd, & Conine, 1977). In addition to the training programs described in the piece just mentioned, particularly helpful approaches are described in Sharf, Wood, and Flaherty (1982) and in several articles in Stewart and Roter (1989).

We turn now to another skill/behavior identified in much of the work on communication skills—nonverbal communication.

Nonverbal Communication

Although it is, of course, not possible to separate verbal from nonverbal communication in a truly meaningful way because they are highly interdependent, some research has provided insight into the nonverbal aspects of interpersonal communication between health care providers and patients that can be examined in conjunction with the research that focuses on verbal communication. Attention to nonverbal communication is important for diagnosis by care providers and helps in the assessment of the quality and intensity of symptoms (Friedman, 1979). This is especially true when the patient has difficulty describing the problem.

In an attempt to describe nonverbal patterns in physician-patient interaction, Street and Buller (1987) videotaped encounters between 38 patients and 10 different physicians. Their results indicated more nonverbal dominance by physicians than by patients, as evidenced by the use of more social touch by physicians. They also found reciprocation of some nonverbal behaviors indicating affiliation, such as body orientation, illustrative gestures, and gaze. Physicians who were more affiliative tended to have more satisfied patients.

The relationship between nonverbals and satisfaction has also been investigated by DiMatteo, Taranta, Friedman, and Prince (1980). Although they found no relationship between nonverbal behaviors and patients' ratings of technical care, measures of nonverbal skills did predict patient satisfaction with medical care as an art. Important nonverbal behaviors included sensitivity to body movement and posture cues to emotion in patients and the ability to express emotion nonverbally.

Rapport between physicians and patients is also communicated nonverbally. High rapport doctors face their patients directly, with uncrossed legs and arms in symmetrical, side-by-side positions. They also engage in moderate levels of eye contact with patients (Harrigan, Oxman, & Rosenthal, 1985).

Similar to the perspective described earlier in the research of Street and Buller (1987), other researchers have attempted to identify *patterns* of nonverbal interaction. Using lag sequential analysis (Sackett, 1979) on the coding of behaviors indicating immediacy (touching, forward leans, or direct body orientation) and relaxation (arm asymmetry; sideways lean; leg, hand, or neck relaxation; or a reclining angle), Smith and Larsen (1984) found higher levels of behaviors indicating both immediacy and relaxation from physicians than from patients. Both interactants "assume a certain immediacy and relaxation in an interview and show little deviation" (p. 261). In other words, the interactants did *not* adapt to each other's behavior. This finding is not consistent with some of the research stemming from communication accommodation theory (e.g., Street, 1991b), although it is similar to Street and Buller's (1988) report of a great deal of consistency in the nonverbals of physicians across different patients. Smith and Larsen argued that their method may have missed many of the subtleties of the interaction.

However, Street and Buller (1988) found some evidence of adaptation or reciprocation. They found that physicians typically reciprocated patients' (a) adjustments in response latency, (b) pauses, (c) body orientation, and (d) interruptions. Other evidence of adaptation included compensation by physicians in terms of turn duration and gestural rates. Patient characteristics of age and anxiety influenced physicians' nonverbal adaptation.

704 HANDBOOK OF INTERPERSONAL COMMUNICATION

Patterns of communication have also been examined by focusing on the coordination of verbal and nonverbal behaviors by physicians and patients. Heath (1984) discovered that the gaze direction of the doctor influences the articulation of an utterance by patients. Patients use gestural activity to realign their physician's gaze and to encourage their participation in talk. Verbal and nonverbal communication are also coordinated to signal the end of the medical consultation (Heath, 1985).

Touch. Touch has probably received more attention by health communication researchers than has any other nonverbal variable. Although we will not review all of this literature here, a few findings will be noted. Several factors seem to affect the likelihood of touching. Physicians use less task touch with anxious patients (Street & Buller, 1988). Lack of physical impairment of the recipient, high social status of the initiator, and same sex are all associated with increased touching (Watson, 1975). The gender influence may occur because female nurses interpret female patients as being more receptive to touch and are thus more comfortable touching female than male patients (P. L. Lane, 1989). Some touch research has indicated that training nurses to touch patients more frequently also increases the amount of verbal interaction, rapport, and approach behavior that occurs (Aguilera, 1967).

Language

Moving from a focus on nonverbal to verbal communication directs us to a discussion of language use. Most of the research on language in the health care context bemoans and documents the difficulty patients have understanding their care providers. Care providers report that they try to use everyday rather than medical language with their patients (Bourhis, Roth, & MacQueen, 1989), although empirical observation does not support this (Aasterud, 1965; Samora, Saunders, & Larson, 1961; Scott & Weiner, 1984; Shuy, 1976; Swenson, 1984). Analyses of discourse indicate that physicians are particularly likely to resort to quasi-scientific explanations when emotional issues that they would rather evade are raised (Raimbault, Cachin, Limal, Eliacheff, & Rappaport, 1975). Although some argue that patients now understand more than they did in the past, evidence does not support this (Thompson & Pledger, 1993).

The consequences of misunderstanding due to language use have also been examined. Arguing from a general semantic's perspective, Baziak and Dentan (1960) note that medical language use leads care providers to perceive only certain, less important aspects of their patients. Glaser and Strauss (1965) reported that a "circle of noncommunication" (p. 123) is created between patients and physicians, and the patients' lack of familiarity with technical terms causes a passive attitude and more general deference to the physician, resulting in minimal communication by both of them. This contention is similar to the observation made by Gelman (1980), that esoteric language becomes a double-edged sword that dominates and alienates, making vulnerable patients more vulnerable. In the only experimental study on this topic, Jackson (1992) found that cognitive satisfaction, comprehension, and recall scores were lower when technical language was used.

Control

Implicit in much of the research discussed above (dispersing information, interruption, language that dominates, and so on) is the notion of control over the interaction. Many care providers and researchers have argued that patients should be given more control over the interaction and the course of their health care (Friedman & DiMatteo, 1979). It has long been suggested that the traditional sick role should give way to a more active role (Tryon & Leonard, 1965). Some research has even asked health care providers to generate suggestions regarding how to increase patient involvement in health care (Weiss, 1986), has suggested mutual participation as the key to managing the "difficult patient" (Powers, 1985, p. 445), or has noted that even children need some control (Hunsberger, Love, & Byrne, 1984). However, much physician dissatisfaction stems from a lack of control (Ort, Ford, & Liske, 1964). Fuller and Quesada (1973) describe a "spiralling down" control struggle that occurs between physicians and patients regarding expectations. As one partner's expectations are not met, that person becomes unwilling or unable to hear or meet the needs of the other.

Actual patterns of relational control have been described in several observational studies of provider-patient interaction. In a study of interaction between terminally ill patients and nurses, Pepler and Lynch (1991) noted more instances of the nurse offering the patient control or decision-making opportunities than any other behavior. Patients sent messages of relational control and accepted offers of control.

O'Hair (1989), von Friederichs-Fitzwater, Callahan, Flynn, and Williams (1991), and McNeilis and Thompson (in press) have all applied the Rogers and Farace (1975) relational coding scheme to provider-patient interactions. Studying physician-patient encounters, O'Hair concluded that "although physicians attempted and gained control of the interaction to a large extent, patients demonstrated instances of attempted (and even successful) relational control maneuvers" (p. 97). He also found several transitory dyadic exchanges. Building on O'Hair's work, von Friederichs-Fitzwater et al. (1991) studied physician-patient interchanges in four different contexts, and found frequent examples of neutralized symmetry rather than the complementarity O'Hair had discovered. They also found that physicians changed topics frequently, especially when patients initiated emotional issues. While physicians asked more questions, they did not answer all questions asked by patients. von Friederichs-Fitzwater et al. conclude that there is a tendency toward domineering behavior on the part of the patient and toward control on the part of the doctor.

Studying dentist-patient interactions, McNeilis and Thompson's (in press) results were similar to those of O'Hair. They found dentists making more one-up controlling statements than did patients and that the predominant pattern of interaction was complementary.

Consistent with the findings of provider control reported by O'Hair and McNeilis and Thompson, Coulthard and Ashby (1975) report that the most frequent patterns were doctor-initiated information-seeking exchanges rather than patient-initiated information giving. They found that doctors (a) do not respond to patients' attempts at initiation, (b) interrupt patients who are giving information that the physician does not want, and (c) ask leading questions.

Using Brown and Levinson's (1978) politeness framework, Aronsson and Satterlund-Larsson (1987) determined that physicians sometimes invite patient collaboration with open-ended, "thinking-aloud" messages during the opening phases of interaction. Patients, however, found this indirectness ambiguous. After the physician had extracted the initial information, the patient was seldom encouraged to talk. Patients interrupted more, perhaps because patients were rarely talking and the physicians had little need to interrupt. Physicians presupposed patient agreement and rarely secured it or attempted to elicit patient opinions. The patients avoided challenging the physicians by not voicing disagreement and by "lying" (p. 25) through omission. They found that politeness norms led to vague and ambiguous talk.

S. Fisher (1984) also reported physician control. Looking at the negotiation of whether or not to do Pap smears, she found that each phase of the interaction expressed the physician's control and the patient's trust. Physicians controlled "whether or not patients would be undressed, whether or not prior Pap smear history would be discussed, and whether or not Pap smears would be done (sometimes without discussing the decision with patients). . . . [P]atients neither questioned the lack of information shared with them, nor used interactional strategies to move the decision-making toward a Pap smear" (p. 25).

This research implies a negative evaluation of provider control of the interaction. This theme is continued in Hughes's (1980) discussion of how nurses may turn compulsive caring into manipulation of patients. Turnock (1989) reported few communication problems as long as ICU nurses were able to control interactions. This occurred when patients were rather sick and dependent. As patients improved and were able to participate more, the quality of the communication became poorer.

Summarizing a large body of research on patient power in doctor-patient communication, Beisecker (1990) concluded that noncompliance with physician's orders may be a way for patients to assert their independence and power. Her summary, too, indicates little patient control over interactions or medical decision making. This lack of patient opportunities for control is a potential cause for concern, as is the next issue to be discussed—disconfirmation.

Disconfirmation

Another important communication concept to emerge in some of the provider-patient interaction literature is the notion of disconfirmation (Laing, 1969). Although there are various types of disconfirmation, the most extreme instances involve communicating to someone that they do not exist. Other types of disconfirmation communicate that people's perceptions of themselves are not valid.

Disconfirmation has been studied in three contexts in health care—in regard to communication about pain, during attempts at reassurance, and as a communication skill of nurses. In the first category, Dangott, Thornton, and Page (1978) noted that health providers frequently deny that their patients are experiencing pain, even when cues indicate otherwise. This type of disconfirmation would be labeled "imperviousness" by Laing (1969).

Second, studies of reassurance from care providers have indicated that about a quarter of all calls for reassurance from patients result in disconfirming responses. Thompson, Mowles, and Cusella (1989) found that 27% of the responses they studied communicated to patients that their perceptions were not valid. Such disconfirmation in response to requests for reassurance is of concern, because other data indicate that appropriate reassurance is related to doctor-shopping (Kasteller, Kane, Olsen, & Thetford, 1976), voluntary termination by patients of the relationship with their doctor (Hayes-Bautista, 1976), better treatment outcomes (Friedman & DiMatteo, 1979), less postoperative vomiting (M. M. Fisher, 1984), decreased duration and severity of symptoms and functional impairment (Buchsbaum, 1986), and higher patient satisfaction (Feletti, Firman, & Sanson-Fisher, 1986).

Finally, Garvin and Kennedy (1990) reviewed several studies on confirmation as a nursing skill and concluded that "the nurse's intention to focus on the patient resulted in desired outcomes" (p. 223). Such desired outcomes included appropriate blood pressure levels and heart rate (Fuller & Foster, 1982; Powers & Wooldridge, 1982). However, Garvin and Kennedy note that "investigators of confirming communication have not demonstrated conclusively that this type of communication is more effective than disconfirming communication" (p. 223). The conceptualization of confirmation/disconfirmation in the nursing literature is a bit broader than that originally described by Laing and would lead to such outcomes as the next issue to be discussed—openness.

Openness

Because much provider-patient interaction requires communication about topics that are difficult or awkward to discuss, the concept of openness has been the focus of some research by those in health communication. Little of the research on openness looks at it as a relational concept, however. Instead, most studies look either at openness on the part of the patient or at openness on the part of the care provider.

The importance of this issue is emphasized by findings indicating that a patient's initial communication may not be a very accurate indicator of what he or she is really experiencing or what he or she is really concerned about (D. L. Davis, 1984; Elder, 1963). If this is the case, the accuracy of the diagnosis is likely to be impaired. The data indicate that the patient's openness is likely to be influenced by trust and receptivity in the physician and the patient's level of communication apprehension, at least during interactions between female patients and their gynecologists (Wheeless, 1987). In general practice, Eisenthal, Koopman, and Stoeckle (1990) have noted that the phrasing of the patient's request for help from the physician can provide important information for physicians. They provide a classification system for physicians to help with this interpretation.

The need for a focus on the communicative openness of care providers is made apparent by data evidencing the fact that, even when patients want to talk, care providers may be reluctant to listen (Altschul, 1983). This is particularly likely when emotionally charged topics are being discussed (Altschul, 1983). Most research on the communicative openness of care providers has focused on how willing they are to provide patients with information about their prognosis and treatment options. For instance, a study of end-stage renal disease found that physicians communicate their personal views more easily than they do information about treatment options (McCauley, Johnson, & Copley, 1989). Social and health care environments influence the disclosure practices of nurse-midwives more than do patient characteristics (Trandel-Korenchuk, 1987). Research on Italian breast cancer patients indicates that only a minority are told that they have cancer, although those who have been told report much higher levels of satisfaction than those who have not been told (Mosconi, Meyerowitz, Liberati, & Liberati, 1991). However, this study also found a great deal of disagreement between patients and physicians on what the patient has been told. Satisfaction was highest when perceptions on this converged.

Although there is now a great deal more openness when communicating terminal prognoses than in the past (Seale, 1991), situations of "closed awareness" (p. 943) are still not infrequent. More particularly, Seale noted that patients and their families perceive inadequacy in regard to being told *enough* about what is wrong with the patient, the reasons for treatment decisions, and how to care for the patient.

Within some other cultures, such as Japan, there is much less openness when communicating terminal prognoses than is found in Western cultures (Takahashi, 1990).

Gender Issues

One final factor to be discussed in our review of descriptive studies is gender. Gender differences that affect interpersonal communication in the health care context have been nicely summarized by Weisman and Teitelbaum (1985, 1989; see also Zare, Sorenson, & Heeren, 1984). Generally, they conclude that women receive more health care messages and information than do men, although physicians give shorter and less technical answers to women's questions (Wallen, Waitzkin, & Stoeckle, 1979). Female patients ask more questions than do male patients (Beisecker, 1990). Female physicians spend more time with patients (Weisman & Teitelbaum, 1985) but are also interrupted more frequently (West, 1984).

Outcome Measures

The research discussed up to this point in the chapter has attempted in some way to describe interpersonal communication in health care. Another body of research has examined the *outcomes* of this communication. Numerous types of outcome measures have been used. Summarizing the meeting of a group of researchers at the International Conference on Doctor-Patient Communication, Beckman et al. (1989) have provided a listing of health care outcomes that include process, short-term, intermediate, and long-term measures (see Table 18.1). Some of these measures have already been the subject of research, while others are variables that should be but have not yet been studied much by researchers. It is hoped that this listing will provoke additional research. Many of those outcomes that help us illuminate interpersonal communication in health care will be discussed below.

Patient Satisfaction and Perceptions

Although it is nice if patient satisfaction occurs, and although satisfaction has some affects on other outcomes, patient satisfaction, in and of itself, is not as important as are outcomes such as compliance, physiological/medical indices, and malpractice suits. However, satisfaction is the most frequently studied outcome of provider-patient interaction and is more closely related to provider-patient communication than is any other outcome measure (Roter, 1989), so this research will be briefly reviewed. Even more than the other sections of this chapter, this portion of the review seeks to be representative rather than complete. We will also focus only on communicative determinants of satisfaction.

Interpersonal skills and competence are mentioned as frequently as is technical competence when patients discuss their expectations of care providers (Reader, Pratt, & Mudd, 1957). Before summarizing the research on patient satisfaction, two factors should be mentioned. Some of the research does not distinguish between patient satisfaction with care versus satisfaction with provider communication. The two variables are, however, highly related. They will be included together in our review, as we focus on patient satisfaction with the overall experience. Second, as others have noted (Hulka, Zyzanski, Cassel, & Thompson, 1970; Ware & Snyder,

Table 18.1 Health Care Outcomes Requiring Study

Process Outcomes
   1. Coparticipation/mutuality
   2. Patient assertiveness
   3. Provider empathy/encouragement
   4. Direct evaluation of medication compliance
   5. Agreement on evaluation, treatment options
   6. Solicitation for patients' attribution of concerns
   7. Completed solicitation of patient's concerns
   8. Frequency of interruption
   9. Frequency of open-ended questions

Short-Term Outcomes
   1. Patient satisfaction
   2. Tension release
   3. Health/disease knowledge acquistion
   4. Doctor satisfaction
   5. Intention to comply
   6. Acceptance of recommended services

Intermediate Outcomes
   1. Adherence/compliance
   2. Accuracy of diagnosis
   3. Anxiety reduction
   4. Health/disease knowledge
   5. Completion of recommended service
   6. Increased self-esteem
   7. Increased self-confidence
   8. Altered locus of control

Long-Term Outcomes
   1. Symptom resolution
   2. Physiological status
   3. Behavioral status
   4. Functional status
   5. Anxiety reduction
   6. Quality of life
   7. Global health perception
   8. Costs of care/use
   9. Work loss
   10. Cure rate
   11. Survival

SOURCE: Adapted from Beckman, Kaplan, and Frankel (1989, p. 225).

1975; Woolley, Kane, Hughes, & Wright, 1978), much of this research has used simple measures of satisfaction, which are likely to lead to underreporting of dissatisfaction.

Overall, the research indicates that increased levels of satisfaction are associated with increased levels of the following behaviors from care providers: (a) information giving, partnership building, positive talk, and social talk (Roter, 1989); (b) meeting maternal expectations regarding not interrupting, displaying positive nonverbal affect, not being irritated by questions, and providing information without having it requested (Howell-Koren & Tinsley, 1990); (c) communication leading to increased patient knowledge (Woolley et al., 1978); (d) communicating in a task/informational and personal manner (S. D. Lane, 1983); (e) higher communicative involvement and expressiveness (Street, 1989; Street & Wiemann, 1987);

(f) demonstration of personal concern, providing information about findings, and demonstrating listening skills (Matthews, Sledge, & Lieberman, 1987); (g) clarity and retention of communication and affiliative behavior (Lochman, 1983); (h) attentiveness, setting the patient at ease, and relieving uncertainty (Tymstra, 1986); (i) high emotional expressivity rather than neutrality (DiMatteo, Linn, Chang, & Cope, 1985); (j) communication of awareness of patient concerns (Liptak, Hulka, & Cassel, 1977); (k) restatement of medical information (Kupst, Presser, Schulman, & Paul, 1975); (l) communication leading to provider-patient agreement on perceived patient problems (Molzahn & Northcott, 1989; Roth, Heffron, & Skipper, 1983); (m) information and support (Webb, 1986); (n) clear-cut explanations regarding diagnosis and cause of disease (Gotcher & Edwards, 1990; Korsch et al., 1968), expected duration of the illness, and the treatment (Decastro, 1972); (o) early acknowledgment of problems, a sympathetic approach, and sharing of information and uncertainty (Quine & Pahl, 1986); (p) patient-centered utterances (Street, 1992a); and (q) specificity of instructions, expressions of trust in the patient's caretaking, offers of continued interest, and provider expressions of positive feelings, warmth, and friendliness (Korsch & Negrete, 1972; Korsch et al., 1968). Increased satisfaction is also associated with decreases in the following provider behaviors: (a) question asking (Roter, 1989); (b) communicative dominance (Street, 1989; Street & Wiemann, 1987); (c) control or directives (Lochman, 1983; Street, 1992a); and (d) use of unclear terms and jargon (Korsch et al., 1968; Tymstra, 1986). Patients who ask more questions and who are encouraged to do so are also more satisfied (Feeser & Thompson, 1993; Roter, 1984).

Other perceptual variables. A few other provider or patient perceptions have also been studied in relation to provider-patient communication. Increased information sharing leads to decreased levels of concern in the patient, but concern levels increase with shared responsibility (Arntson, Makoul, Pendleton, & Schofield, 1989). Physician and patient perceptions of physicians' communicative styles are significantly different, and physicians' self-perceptions of their communication are not associated with patients' satisfaction with medical care (Street & Wiemann, 1988). Of particular note is Street's (1992b) recent finding that observational assessments of behaviors occurring during provider-patient interaction are frequently unrelated to patients' perceptions of those same behaviors. For instance, the amount of information provided by physicians was quite different than patients' perceptions of the doctors' informativeness.

Compliance

Of the many outcome measures that can be addressed, the one that appears to elicit the most concern from health care providers is the issue of compliance with health care instructions. Although some (e.g., Friedman & DiMatteo, 1979) have urged that we conceptualize the issue as one of *cooperation* rather than compliance—reminding us that both the provider and the patient should be involved in decision making about treatments—most literature and care providers continue to use the term *compliance*. Indeed, many care providers do not see compliance as a communicative issue. Rather, they blame personality characteristics in the patient for a lack of compliance. Patients are labeled "noncompliant." However, much research has now indicated that the way instructions are communicated helps account for good portions of the variance in compliance rates.

The importance of the issue of compliance is made clear when one examines the research that indicates a low rate of compliance with doctor's orders (Dervin, Harlock, Atwood, & Garzona, 1980). Noncompliance rates frequently average around 50% (Marston, 1970). This lack of compliance creates health hazards and leads to a waste of resources and frustration on the part of the care provider (Stone, 1979). While many noncommunication variables influence compliance, there are also many communication variables that can increase or decrease cooperation rates. These include ambiguity of information (Ley & Spelman, 1967); simplicity and specificity of instructions (Charney, 1972; Korsch & Negrete, 1972); physician expressions of trust in the mother's caretaking and offers of continued interest in the child (Korsch & Negrete, 1972); provision of explanations and demonstrations of warmth (Francis, Korsch, & Morris, 1969); the adequacy of information given to the patient (Pruyn, Ruckman, van Brunschot, & van den Borne, 1985); empathic understanding on the part of the care provider (Squier, 1990); and rapport building (DiMatteo, 1979). One rather extensive study found that compliance with doctors' orders is related to doctors' directiveness, doctors' emotional attitude toward the patient, and patients' partnership status (Heszen-Klemens & Lapkinska, 1984). A lack of compliance is associated with formality, antagonism, and mutual withholding of information (M. S. Davis, 1968). Although there is some disagreement within the literature about this issue (e.g., Arntson et al., 1978; S. D. Lane, 1983), some have concluded that patient satisfaction increases compliance (Becker, Drachman, & Kirscht, 1972; Cassata, 1978; Francis et al., 1969; Korsch & Negrete, 1972).

Several studies have focused on patients' comprehension and recall of instructions as determinants of compliance (Jette, 1982; Schraa & Dirks, 1982). Analyses of videotapes indicate no single communicative strategy for resultant compliance (Mazzuca & Weinberger, 1986), although demonstrating respect, sharing current clinical data, and acknowledging patient statements predict high comprehension in patients (Mazzuca, Weinberger, Kurpius, Froehle, & Heister, 1983). Just providing information, however, does not lead to improved cooperation (Stone, 1979).

Breaking cooperation down into voluntary versus involuntary noncooperation, Jette (1982) notes that ambiguous language use and lack of information are associated with involuntary noncompliance. Voluntary cooperation can be improved by communicating information about the likely effectiveness of the treatment and the likely consequences of lack of cooperation, by simplifying the treatment regimen and instructions, and by communicating acceptance and respect. Summarizing several studies on socioemotional factors and compliance, Jette concludes that care providers need to achieve a delicate balance between friendliness and providing direction.

Care providers attempt a variety of different strategies to gain compliance from their patients. S. D. Lane (1982) found that doctors typically try the following approaches: (a) Give the patient a thorough explanation, (b) tell him or her the benefits of the advice, (c) get tough, and (d) withdraw. If noncompliance still results, physicians (a) overwhelm the patient with knowledge, (b) tell the patient of the dire consequences that will occur if he or she doesn't comply, (c) disclose to patients, or (d) use personal persuasion tactics. More recently, Burgoon, Parrott, Burgoon, Birk, et al. (1990) found that physicians report using expertise strategies most frequently, followed by verbal aggressiveness. Patients, however, claim that physicians use verbally unaggressive messages such as liking and positive expertise most frequently (Burgoon, Parrott, Burgoon, Coker, et al., 1990).

Pediatricians typically use questions to inform parents, using compliance-gaining strategies only to motivate parents who do not comply with usual parenting practices (Parrott, Burgoon, & Ross, 1992). Physicians do not use information they are given about patients' health locus of control in order to adapt their compliance-gaining strategies (Holloway & Rogers, 1992). Perhaps intuitively, however, physicians use more verbally aggressive strategies with patients with an internal health locus of control who have a potentially severe or nonthreatening medical condition and with patients with a moderately severe medical condition who are in the midrange on health locus. These approaches increase compliance (Burgoon, Parrott, Burgoon, Coker, et al., 1990).

Other research has also focused on the effectiveness of various strategies. Building on her earlier research, S. D. Lane (1983) reported that a combination of threatening and personal compliance-gaining tactics led to adherence. No specific relational strategies were found to predict compliance in two other studies (Burgoon et al., 1987; McNeilis & Thompson, in press). Howze, Broyden, and Impara (1992) indicated that informal caregivers such as hair stylists could be used to reach patients about issues like mammography.

Finally, Roter's (1989) meta-analysis of a large number of physician-patient studies indicated that compliance was positively associated with information giving and positive talk and negatively associated with question asking and negative talk. Recall was determined by information giving and decreased question asking.

Physiological/Medical Outcomes

Perhaps the most unique aspect of the study of health communication among areas of study within the field of communication is the ability to study physiological or medical outcomes as dependent upon communicative independent variables. In one of the earliest pieces on communication and health to be published within the field of communication, Dance (1970) argued that "the quality of communication seriously affected the degree of medical success" (p. 30). Other studies have concluded that touch from the care provider reduces pain (Krieger, 1975) and that pain is relieved more quickly, thoroughly, and without the use of pharmaceuticals if patients are given more thorough information and attempts are made to ensure that they understand the information they have been given (Tarasuk, Rhymes, & Leonard, 1965). These independent variables also lead to fewer postoperative complications, such as sepsis, and lower levels of psychological stress indicators, such as 17-hydroxicorticosteroids (Boore, 1978; Hayward, 1975). Doyle and Ware (1977) also concluded that interpersonal competence on the part of the health care provider leads to increased tolerance of pain and discomfort, shorter hospital stays, and less postoperative pain. Dumas, Anderson, and Leonard (1965) reported that adequate preoperative communication with patients, which includes answering patient questions and giving information to alleviate anxiety, leads to reduced postoperative vomiting. Similarly, Egbert, Battit, Welch, and Bartlett (1964) found that encouragement and education by anesthetists reduced pain and enabled patients to leave the hospital earlier. Anesthetists seem to be the health care providers most inclined to study this issue. In other research, data have indicated that "an explanation will do more to assuage the patient's fears than the narcotic pre-medication and will reduce the dosage required" (Lemaitre & Finnegan, 1975, p. 86). Similar research is summarized by Evans and Hind (1987). Maguire (1985) reported that not addressing the patient's anxiety leads to a slower and less complete recovery.

In one of the more thorough studies of the outcomes of doctor-patient interaction, Heszen-Klemens and Lapkinska (1984) noted improvements in patients' health status when the doctor asked more questions or gave more advice, and when the physician and patient engaged in emotional exchange. Overall, they found that increased activity on the part of the physician led to better treatment results.

Kaplan, Greenfield, and Ware (1989) summarize eight studies on the impact of interpersonal communication on medical outcomes and report observed effects in six of them. Specifically, Orth, Stiles, Scherwitz, Hennrikus, and Valbonna (1987) noted effects on blood pressure control, Starfield et al. (1981) on problem resolution, Stewart, McWhinney, and Buck (1979) on perceived recovery, and Bass et al. (1986) on problem resolution. Another study also found effects on problem resolution (Headache Study Group, 1986). More specifically, "improvement in or resolution of the patient's health problem was found to occur more often when there was agreement between doctors and patients about the nature and severity of the patient's health problem" (Kaplan et al., 1989, p. 230). Kaplan et al. (1989) also report three new studies that observed that more patient control, elicitation of information, and show of emotion were related to improvements in blood sugar and blood pressure control and improvements in functional limitations. Increased levels of physician control and decreased physician information giving and show of emotion led to elevated levels of blood glucose and blood pressure and more functional limitations.

Research on children indicates that maintenance of contact and free communication of information by physicians reduces postoperative pain (McGrath & DeVeber, 1986). Even premature infants in neonatal intensive care recover more quickly with increased interaction, particularly tactile interaction, from care providers (Gillotti & Thompson, in press).

King (1991) focused on the role of communication in managing pain related to anxiety. Noting the neuronal and neurophysiological links between psychological states such as anxiety and the perception of pain, he identified communicative strategies that address the anxiety and thus the pain. For instance, Johnston (1973) discovered that descriptive information regarding sensations that are likely to be experienced helps reduce pain more than does procedural information. Providing patients with information about pain coping strategies also helps reduce pain (Bray, 1986; Janis, 1983; Johnson, Rice, Fuller, & Endress, 1978; Rowland, 1978).

Specific physiological responses of patients to care provider behavior have also been noted. Garvin, Kennedy, Baker, and Polivka (1992) reported that provider-patient communication was associated with increased heart rate, although systolic and diastolic blood pressure did not change during interaction. Similar results have been reported by Thomas et al. (1982) and by Smith and Cantrell (1988), especially when personal questions were asked by a nurse to a patient. Hellmann and Grimm (1984) found changes in diastolic blood pressures in hypertensive patients while communicating. Gillotti and Thompson (in press) also reported increased heart rate during interaction between premature infants and care providers.

Some studies, however, have concluded that process and outcome assessments are distinct but complementary (Romm & Hulka, 1979) or that communication affects patient satisfaction but not outcome (Woolley et al., 1978). Differences appear to emerge dependent upon the kind of health problem being studied and the specific communicative behaviors under investigation. As would be expected, the treatment of some illnesses does not appear to respond directly to communication.

Malpractice

Moving to a broader outcome than compliance or physiology and to our final outcome variable, we find that several studies have now linked provider-patient interaction with malpractice suits brought by patients. Davison (1985) argued that "conflicts that develop in the course of medical decision-making are not strictly of an ethical nature, but are due simply to a failure in communication between the parties involved" (p. 3). In an analysis of litigation in cosmetic surgery, Macgregor (1984) noted that many such conflicts have their roots in the quality of interaction between the doctor and the patient, in the ineffectiveness of initial interviews, and in the physician's lack of attention to nonverbal cues. Researchers within the field of nursing also have linked communication problems with lawsuits (Bernzweig, 1980, 1985; Cushing, 1982).

May and Stengel (1990) examined suers versus nonsuers and determined that the perceived concern of the doctor about the personal effect of care was a distinguishing factor. Such perceived concern, of course, is communicated through the doctor's behavior. Contrary to their initial expectations, however, May and Stengel did not find that such variables as informing the patient about his or her care or rushing the patient's visit differentiated the two groups. Earlier, May and DeMarco (1986) had determined that, while communication problems alone are rarely the basis for legal action by dissatisfied patients, those patients who approach a lawyer about a complaint have perceived professional failure in treatment combined with a lack of communication about their diagnosis and insensitivity from their physician.

Measurement Concerns

Roter's (1989) attempt to meta-analyze the literature on physician-patient interaction was hampered because of the wide variety of scales and coding systems that are used in such research. Many studies appear to develop their own measuring systems rather than attempting to use those developed by past researchers. This makes it difficult to generalize research findings across contexts and studies and thus to build our knowledge base. Stiles and Putnam (1989) review a large number of measures used to analyze verbal and nonverbal behavior in provider-patient interaction, and it is hoped that future researchers will look at their work prior to developing new measures.

The present review will mention only a few noteworthy measurement devices or new methodological approaches. Schneider and Tucker (1992) and Cockburn et al. (1991) have offered paper-and-pencil measures to assess patient satisfaction in health care contexts. Schneider and Tucker's focuses particularly on communicative satisfaction.

Malpiede, Leff, Wilson, and Moore (1982) provide a paper-and-pencil assessment of perceptions of interactions between caregivers and patients. Observational coding systems are described in Bain (1976), Callahan and Bertakis (1991), Hawes (1972), Oliver and Redfern (1991), and Powers, Murphy, and Wooldridge (1983). Three different interaction analysis systems were compared by Inui, Carter, Kukull, and Haigh (1982), who provide suggestions about the appropriateness, validity, utility, and pragmatic value of each.

Finally, alternative approaches to the study of provider-patient communication have been discussed by Sharf (1990), Waitzkin (1990), and Daubenmire, Searles, and Ashton (1978). Daubenmire et al. describe an approach based on synchronology, while the approaches of Sharf and Waitzkin are more qualitative. Sharf nicely demonstrates the utility of a narrative application, while Waitzkin advocates a multidimensional method incorporating both qualitative and quantitative measures.

Theoretical Perspectives

Perhaps the most significant development in the research on interpersonal communication in the health care context in the last 10 years is the appearance of several attempts at theoretical offerings in the area. Although we are not anywhere close to a "theory" of health communication, movement has occurred in that direction. Most of this work has been published in communication or nursing journals—little has emanated from the field of medicine or the allied health professions—and has only appeared since 1989. Many of these theories have very specific foci or scopes. These include theories or models from scholars such as (a) Reardon and Buck (1989), who discuss the role of communication, emotion, and cognition in coping with cancer; (b) Ellis, Miller, and Given (1989) on communication and home care givers; (c) Rouse's (1989) delineation of the role of emotional communication in dentistry; (d) Williams, Giles, Coupland, Dalby, and Manasse's (1990) model of elderly social support and health; (e) Ballard-Reisch's (1990) work on participative decision making in the physician-patient relationship; (f) J. M. Morse (1991) on negotiating commitment and involvement; (g) Cowley's (1991) grounded theoretical discussion of the symbolic awareness context; (h) Heslin's (1989) model of supportive nursing care; (i) Squier (1990), who provides a model of empathic understanding as it affects adherence to treatment regimens; and (j) Nievaard's (1987) discussion of communication climate and patient care.

Other theoretical perspectives are a bit broader, such as Kasch's (1986) discussion of nursing action as a process in social interaction (see also Kasch & Dine, 1988; Kasch & Lisnek, 1984; and Flaskerud's, 1986, response to Kasch's work). Kasch focuses on consensus as a process of negotiation, which is determined, in part, by the nurse's interpersonal competence. Pierloot (1983) contrasts four models of the doctor-patient relationship in an attempt to provide insight regarding the appropriateness of each to various contexts and approaches. Perhaps broadest of all and most in line with mainstream perspectives within the field of communication are the views offered by Street (1991b) and Roter (1989; see also Roter & Hall, 1991). Street uses accommodation theory, discussed elsewhere in this volume, to integrate diverse and sometimes contradictory findings from research on provider-patient interaction. The strength of his work stems from the dyadic perspective that looks at the interdependence of provider and patient communication. Similarly, Roter and Hall build on social exchange theory but go well beyond that to look at the reciprocity of behavior in the health care context. Both of these offerings provide promising foundations on which future health communication research and theory should build. They are also examples of how research or theory in a specific setting can help extend our understanding of communication in general.

Summary and Suggested Directions

Several important points can be derived from the research that has been cited in this chapter. Generally, this research indicates a lack of time spent on communication in health care encounters as well as a lack of emphasis on relational factors during this communication. There is frequently a lack of provider interest in communication or communication skills. Health care providers typically maintain control of interactions. Much language use by care providers is unclear to the receivers of the information. Other ambiguity arises due to politeness norms, as physician attempts to invite participation may be difficult for patients to interpret. Communication has important effects on compliance by patients, on recovery and pain, on patient satisfaction, and on the likelihood of patients suing.

Patients report wanting more control but frequently do not ask questions or take an active role in health interactions. There is, however, evidence of adaptation, accommodation, or reciprocity in the communicative behaviors of providers and patients, both verbally and nonverbally.

Conclusion

The primary goal of this chapter has been to provide information on which future researchers may build in their attempts to illuminate our understanding of communication in the health care context in particular and interpersonal communication in general. As this review has indicated, many of the criticisms leveled at this area of research in the past have been largely, although not completely, overcome. However, much of the research cited herein has still focused on the behavior of the health care provider rather than the patient or, more appropriately, the dyad. That research that has looked at the interdependence of the communicative behavior of the interactants in the health care context, albeit most difficult to do, is also most illuminating. Such research is also most likely to move away from the negative evaluation of provider behavior inherent in much of the research conducted to date. For instance, although much of the research on control is implicitly or explicitly critical of the fact that care providers typically maintain control, we have cited other evidence that indicates that patients are not comfortable having too much control themselves. Patients go to health care providers for answers and solutions and do not necessarily respond positively to having control returned to them. While they want some control, they also want care providers to maintain greater control.

In addition to the above criticism, it is apparent that most of the research on interpersonal communication in health care is still atheoretical, although that problem is not as severe as it was in the past (T. L. Thompson, 1984). Using such theoretical perspectives as were described above (accommodation, reciprocity, and so on) not only can help overcome the lack of a dyadic focus but will provide conceptual underpinnings to allow researchers to integrate and build findings.

As research continues, it is hoped that it will begin with more detailed description of interpersonal communication in health care. There are still many facets of such interaction that are yet to be uncovered. For instance, researchers are just beginning to look at triadic health encounters. Beisecker's (1989) work on the role of a companion during interaction between elderly individuals and physicians is such an example. The presence of a third person changes the context and is worthy of more study.

As we relate description of communication in health care with outcomes, it is hoped that future researchers will move beyond satisfaction as a dependent measure and focus on those that are more difficult to study but are more important. As we refer back to Table 18.1, numerous outcomes that are salient and unique to the health care context can be identified. Outcomes such as accuracy of diagnosis and altered health locus of control are important but have received very little research. Outcomes such as adherence/compliance, symptom resolution, and functional status are still in need of a great deal of investigation. Considering the current state of health care, such long-term outcomes as costs and use of scarce resources should also be examined. (See Geist & Hardesty's, 1992, discussion of the impact of DRGs on hospitals for an excellent beginning in this direction.)

As researchers move to more adequately describe the communication that occurs during interactions between providers and patients and uncover the outcomes of that communication, we have the opportunity to extend our understandings of both interpersonal communication and the provision of health care.

References

Aasterud, M. (1965). Explanations to the patient. In J. K. Skipper & R. C. Leonard (Eds.), *Social interaction and patient care* (pp. 82-87). Philadelphia: Lippincott.

Adler, K. (1977). Doctor-patient communication: A shift to problem-oriented research. *Human Communication Research, 3,* 179-190.

Aguilera, D. C. (1967). Relationship between physical contact and verbal interaction between nurses and patients. *Journal of Psychiatric Nursing, 5,* 5-21.

Altschul, A. T. (1983). The consumer's voice: Nursing implications. *Journal of Advanced Nursing, 8,* 175-183.

Arntson, P., Droge, D., & Fassl, H. E. (1978). Pediatrician-patient communication: A final report. In B. Ruben (Ed.), *Communication yearbook 2* (pp. 505-522). New Brunswick, NJ: Transaction.

Arntson, P., Makoul, G., Pendleton, D., & Schofield, T. (1989). Patients' perceptions of medical encounters in Great Britain: Variations with health loci of control and sociodemographic factors. *Health Communication, 2,* 75-96.

Arntson, P. H., & Philipsborn, H. F. (1982). Pediatrician-parent communication in a continuity-of-care setting. *Clinical Pediatrics, 21,* 302-307.

Aronsson, K., & Satterlund-Larsson, U. (1987). Politeness strategies and doctor-patient communication: On the social choreography of collaborative thinking. *Journal of Language and Social Psychology, 6,* 1-27.

Aydelotte, M. K. (1960). *An investigation of the relation between nursing activity and patient welfare.* Iowa City: University of Iowa Press.

Bain, D. J. (1976). Doctor-patient communication in general practice consultations. *Medical Education, 10,* 125-131.

Ball, K., & Heath, J. C. (1989). Special messages: Bob's story and Janet's story. *Nursing, 19,* 60-61.

Ballard-Reisch, D. S. (1990). A model of participative decision making for physician-patient interaction. *Health Communication, 2,* 91-104.

Bass, M. J., Buck, C., Turner, L., Dickie, G., Pratt, G., & Robinson, H. C. (1986). The physician's actions and the outcome of illness in family practice. *Journal of Family Practice, 23,* 43-47.

Baziak, A. T., & Dentan, R. K. (1960). The language of the hospital and its effects on the patient. *ETC: A Review of General Semantics, 17,* 261-268.

Becker, M. H., Drachman, R. H., & Kirscht, J. P. (1972). Motivations as predictors of health behavior. *Health Service Reports, 87,* 852-862.

Beckman, H., Kaplan, S. H., & Frankel, R. (1989). Outcome based research on doctor-patient communication: A review. In M. Stewart & D. Roter (Eds.), *Communicating with medical patients* (pp. 223-227). Newbury Park, CA: Sage.

Beisecker, A. E. (1989). The influence of a companion on the doctor-elderly patient interaction. *Health Communication, 1,* 55-70.

Beisecker, A. E. (1990). Patient power in doctor-patient communication: What do we know? *Health Communication, 1,* 105-122.

Bendich, S. (1988). Appreciating bodily phenomena in verbally oriented psychotherapy sessions. *Issues in Mental Health Nursing, 9,* 1-7.

Berger, C. (1991). Communication theories and other curios. *Communication Monographs, 58,* 101-113.

Bernzweig, E. P. (1980). When in doubt—speak out. *American Journal of Nursing, 80,* 1175-1176.

Bernzweig, E. P. (1985). How a communications breakdown can get you sued. *RN, 48*(12), 47-48.

Boore, J. (1978). *A prescription for recovery.* London: Royal College of Nursing.

Bourhis, R. Y., Roth, S., & MacQueen, G. (1989). Communication in the hospital setting: A survey of medical and everyday language use amongst patients, nurses and doctors. *Social Science & Medicine, 23,* 339-346.

Brack, G., LaClave, L. J., & Campbell, J. L. (1987). A survey of attitudes of burn unit nurses. *The Journal of Burn Care & Rehabilitation, 8,* 299-306.

Bray, C. A. (1986). Postoperative pain: Altering the patient's experience through education. *AORN Journal, 43,* 672-683.

Brown, P., & Levinson, S. (1978). Universals in language use: Politeness phenomena. In E. N. Goody (Ed.), *Questions and politeness*. Cambridge: Cambridge University Press.

Buchsbaum, D. G. (1986). Reassurance reconsidered. *Social Science & Medicine, 23,* 423-427.

Burgoon, M., Parrott, R., Burgoon, J. K., Birk, T., Pfau, M., & Coker, R. (1990). Primary care physicians' selection of verbal compliance-gaining strategies. *Health Communication, 2,* 13-28.

Burgoon, M., Parrott, R., Burgoon, J. K., Coker, R., Pfau, M., & Birk, T. (1990). Patients' severity of illness, noncompliance, and locus of control and physicians' compliance-gaining messages. *Health Communication, 2,* 29-46.

Burgoon, J. K., Pfau, M., Parrott, R., Birk, T., Coker, R., & Burgoon, M. (1987). Relational communication, satisfaction, compliance-gaining strategies, and compliance in communication between physicians and patients. *Communication Monographs, 54,* 307-324.

Callahan, E. J., & Bertakis, K. D. (1991). Development and validation of the Davis observation code. *Family Medicine, 23,* 19-24.

Cassata, D. M. (1978). Health communication theory and research: An overview of the communication-specialist interface. In B. Ruben (Ed.), *Communication yearbook 2* (pp. 495-503). New Brunswick, NJ: Transaction.

Cassell, E. J., Coulehan, J. L., & Putnam, S. M. (1989). Making good interview skills better. *Patient Care, 23,* 145-148, 155-156, 158.

Ceropski, J. M., & Kline, S. L. (1985). Person-centered communication in medical practice. In G. M. Phillips & J. T. Wood (Eds.), *Emergent issues in human decision-making* (pp. 120-141). Carbondale: Southern Illinois University Press.

Charney, E. (1972). Patient-doctor communication: Implications for the clinician. *Pediatrics Clinics of North America, 19,* 263-279.

Cockburn, J., Hill, D., Irwig, L., DeLuise, T., Turnbull, D., & Schofield, P. (1991). Development and validation of an instrument to measure satisfaction of participants at breast screening programmes. *European Journal of Cancer, 27,* 827-831.

Connolly, M. A., & Shekleton, M. E. (1991). Communicating with ventilator dependent patients. *Dimensions of Critical Care Nursing, 10,* 115-122.

Coulthard, M., & Ashby, M. (1975). Talking with the doctor, 1. *Journal of Communication, 25,* 140-147.

Cowley, S. (1991). A symbolic awareness context identified through a ground theory study of health visiting. *Journal of Advanced Nursing, 16,* 648-656.

Crane, D. (1975). The social potential of the patient: An alternative to the sick role. *Journal of Communication, 25,* 131-139.

Crotty, M. (1985). Communication between nurses and their patients. *Nurse Education Today, 5,* 130-134.

Cushing, M. (1982). Failure to communicate. *American Journal of Nursing, 82,* 1597-1598.

Dance, F. E. X. (1970). The communication of health. *The Ohio Speech Journal, 8,* 28-30.

Dangott, L., Thornton, B. C., & Page, P. (1978). Communication and pain. *Journal of Communication, 28,* 30-35.

Daubenmire, M. J., Searles, S. S., & Ashton, C. A. (1978). A methodologic framework to study nurse-patient communication. *Nursing Research, 27,* 303-310.

Davis, D. L. (1984). Medical misinformation: Communication between outport Newfoundland women and their physicians. *Social Science & Medicine, 18,* 273-278.

Davis, M. S. (1968). Variations in patients' compliance with doctors' advice: An empirical analysis of patterns of communication. *A.P.H.A., 58,* 274-288.

Davison, R. (1985). Ethical conflicts in medicine as a consequence of poor communication. In B. F. Sharf & P. Arntson (Eds.), *Proceedings of a summer conference on health communication* (p. 3). Evanston, IL: Northwestern University, School of Speech.

Decastro, F. J. (1972). Doctor-patient communication: Exploring the effectiveness of care in a primary care clinic. *Clinical Pediatrics, 11,* 86-87.

Dervin, B., Harlock, S., Atwood, R., & Garzona, C. (1980). The human side of information: An exploration in a health communication context. In D. Nimmo (Ed.), *Communication yearbook 4* (pp. 591-608). New Brunswick, NJ: Transaction.

DiMatteo, M. R. (1979). A social-psychological analysis of physician-patient rapport: Toward a science of the art of medicine. *Journal of Social Issues, 35,* 12-33.

DiMatteo, M. R., Linn, L. S., Chang, B. L., & Cope, D. W. (1985). Affect and neutrality in physician behavior: A study of patients' values and satisfaction. *Journal of Behavioral Medicine, 8,* 397-409.

DiMatteo, M. R., & Taranta, A. (1979). Nonverbal communication and physician-patient rapport: An empirical study. *Professional Psychology, 10,* 540-547.

DiMatteo, M. R., Taranta, A., Friedman, H. S., & Prince, L. M. (1980). Predicting patient satisfaction from physicians' nonverbal communication skills. *Medical Care, 18,* 376-387.

DiSalvo, V. S., Larsen, J. K., & Backus, D. K. (1986). The health care communicator: An identification of skills and problems. *Communication Education, 35,* 231-242.

Dockrell, S. (1988). An investigation of the use of verbal and nonverbal communication skills by final-year physiotherapy students. *Physiotherapy, 77,* 52-55.

Douglass, T. (1989). A real case for nonverbal communication in nursing practice. *The Washington Nurse, 19*(10), 12-14.

Doyle, B. J., & Ware, J. E., Jr. (1977). Physician conduct and other factors that affect consumer satisfaction with medical care. *Journal of Medical Education, 52,* 793-801.

Dumas, R. G., Anderson, B. J., & Leonard, R. C. (1965). The importance of the expressive function in preoperative preparation. In J. K. Skipper & R. C. Leonard (Eds.), *Social interaction and patient care* (pp. 16-28). Philadelphia: Lippincott.

Eastwood, C. M. (1985). Nurse-patient communication skills in Northern Ireland: The educational problems. *International Journal of Nursing Studies, 22,* 99-104.

Egbert, L. D., Battit, G. E., Welch, C. E., & Bartlett, M. K. (1964). Reduction of post-operative pain by encouragement and instruction of patients. *The New England Journal of Medicine, 270,* 825-827.

Eisenthal, S., Koopman, C., & Stoeckle, J. D. (1990). The nature of patients' requests for physicians' help. *Academic Medicine: Journal of the Association of American Medical Colleges, 65,* 401-405.

Elder, R. G. (1963). What is the patient saying? *Nursing Forum, 2,* 25-37.

Ellis, B. H., Miller, K. I., & Given, C. W. (1989). Caregivers in home health care situations: Measurement and relations among critical concepts. *Health Communication, 1,* 207-226.

Evans, B. J., Kiellerup, F. D., Stanley, R. O., Burrows, G. D., & Sweet, O. (1987). A communication skills programme for increasing patients' satisfaction with general practice consultations. *British Journal of Medical Psychology, 60,* 373-378.

Evans, B. J., Stanley, R. O., & Burrows, G. D. (1992). Communication skills training and patients' satisfaction. *Health Communication, 4,* 155-170.

Evans, K., & Hind, T. (1987). Getting the message across. *Nursing Times, 83,* 40-42.

Farsad, P., Galliguez, P., Chamberlin, R., & Roghmann, K. J. (1978). Teaching interviewing skills to pediatric house officers. *Pediatrics, 61,* 382-388.

Feeser, T., & Thompson, T. L. (1993). A test of a method of increasing patient question asking in physician-patient interactions. *Cosmetic Dermatology, 6*(9), 51-55.

Feletti, G., Firman, D., & Sanson-Fisher, R. (1986). Patient satisfaction with primary-care consultations. *Journal of Behavioral Medicine, 9,* 389-399.

Fisher, M. M. (1984). Reduction of postoperative vomiting in high risk patients. *Anaesthesia, 39,* 279-281.

Fisher, S. (1983). Doctor talk/patient talk: How treatment decisions are negotiated in doctor/patient communication. In S. Fisher & A. Todd (Eds.), *The social organization of doctor-patient communication* (pp. 135-157). Washington, DC: Center for Applied Linguistics.

Fisher, S. (1984). Doctor-patient communication: A social and micropolitical performance. *Sociology of Health and Illness, 6,* 1-29.

Flaskerud, J. H. (1986). On "Toward a theory of nursing action: Skills and competence in nurse-patient interaction." *Nursing Research, 35,* 250-252.

Francis, V., Korsch, B. M., & Morris, M. J. (1969). Gaps in doctor-patient communication: Patients' response to medical advice. *The New England Journal of Medicine, 280,* 535-540.

Frankel, R. M. (1984). From sentence to sequence: Understanding the medical encounter from microinteractional analysis. *Discourse Processes, 7,* 135-170.

French, H. P. (1983). *Social skills for nursing practice.* Beckenham: Croom Helm.

Friedman, H. S. (1979). Nonverbal communication between patients and medical practitioners. *Journal of Social Issues, 35,* 82-99.

Friedman, H. S., & DiMatteo, M. R. (1979). Health care as an interpersonal process. *Journal of Social Issues, 35,* 1-11.

Fuller, B. F., & Foster, G. M. (1982). The effects of family/friend visits vs. staff interaction on stress/arousal of surgical intensive care patients. *Heart & Lung, 11,* 457-463.

Fuller, D. S., & Quesada, G. M. (1973). Communication in medical therapeutics. *Journal of Communication, 23,* 361-370.

Garvin, B., & Kennedy, C. (1990). Interpersonal communication between nurses and patients. *Annual Review of Nursing Research, 8,* 213-234.

Garvin, B. J., Kennedy, C. W., Baker, C. F., & Polivka, B. J. (1992). Cardiovascular responses of CCU patients when communicating with nurses, physicians, and families. *Health Communication, 4,* 291-301.

Geist, P., & Hardesty, M. (1992). *Negotiating the crisis: DRGs and the transformation of hospitals.* Hillsdale, NJ: Lawrence Erlbaum.

Gelman, S. R. (1980). Esoterica: A zero sum game in the helping professions. *Social Casework, 61,* 48-53.

Gibb, H., & O'Brien, B. (1990). Jokes and reassurance are not enough: Ways in which nurses relate through conversation with elderly clients. *Journal of Advanced Nursing, 15,* 1389-1401.

Gillotti, C., & Thompson, T. L. (in press). The impact of verbal and tactile stimulation from care providers on recovery in the NICU. *Neonatal Network.*

Glaser, B. G., & Strauss, A. L. (1965). *Awareness of dying.* Chicago: Aldine.

Gotcher, J. M., & Edwards, R. (1990). Coping strategies of cancer patients: Actual communication and imagined interaction. *Health Communication, 2,* 255-266.

Greenfield, S., Kaplan, S., & Ware, J. E. (1985). Expanding patient involvement in care. *Annals of Internal Medicine, 102,* 520-528.

Guy, L. J., Haskell, E. G., Hutson, A. C., & Schuman, S. H. (1977). Why home visits? Analysis of 142 planned home visits. *Journal of Family Practice, 4,* 337-341.

Haas, A., & Puretz, S. L. (1992). Encouraging partnerships between health care providers and women recommended for gynecological surgery. *Health Communication, 2,* 29-38.

Hargreaves, S. (1987). The relevance of non-verbal skills in physiotherapy. *Physiotherapy, 73,* 685-688.

Harrigan, J. A., Oxman, T. E., & Rosenthal, R. (1985). Rapport expressed through nonverbal behavior. *Journal of Nonverbal Behavior, 9,* 95-110.

Hawes, L. C. (1972). Development and application of an interview coding system. *Central States Speech Journal, 23,* 92-99.

Hayes-Bautista, D. E. (1976). Termination of the patient-practitioner relationship: Divorce, patient style. *Journal of Health and Social Behavior, 17,* 12-21.

Hayward, J. (1975). *Information: A prescription against pain.* London: Royal College of Nursing.

Headache Study Group of the University of Western Ontario. (1986). Predictors of outcome in headache patients presenting to family physicians: A one year prospective study. *Headache Journal, 26,* 285-294.

Heath, C. (1984). Participation in the medical consultation: The coordination of verbal and nonverbal behaviour between the doctor and patient. *Sociology of Health & Illness, 6,* 311-338.

Heath, C. (1985). The consultation's end: The coordination of speech and body movement. *International Journal of the Sociology of Language, 51,* 27-42.

Helfer, R. E., & Ealy, K. F. (1972). Observation of pediatric interviewing skills. *American Journal of Diseases of Children, 123,* 556-560.

Hellmann, R., & Grimm, S. A. (1984). The influence of talking on diastolic blood pressure readings. *Research in Nursing & Health, 7,* 253-256.

Heslin, K. (1989). The supportive role of the staff nurse in the hospital palliative care situation. *Journal of Palliative Care, 5,* 20-26.

Heszen-Klemens, I., & Lapkinska, E. (1984). Doctor-patient interaction, patients' health behavior and effects of treatment. *Social Science and Medicine, 19,* 9-18.

Holloway, R. L., & Rogers, J. C. (1992). Physician adaptation to patients' locus of control and congruence with health recommendations. *Health Communication, 4,* 67-78.

Howell-Koren, P. R., & Tinsley, B. J. (1990). The relationships among maternal health locus of control beliefs and expectations, pediatrician-mother communication, and maternal satisfaction with well-infant care. *Health Communication, 2,* 233-254.

Howze, E. H., Broyden, R. R., & Impara, J. C. (1992). Using informal caregivers to communicate with women about mammography. *Health Communication, 4,* 227-244.

Hughes, J. (1980). Manipulation: A negative element in care. *Journal of Advanced Nursing, 5,* 21-29.

Hulka, B. S., Zyzanski, S. J., Cassel, J. C., & Thompson, S. J. (1970). Scale for measurement of attitudes toward physicians and primary health care. *Medical Care, 8,* 429.

Hunsberger, M., Love, B., & Byrne, C. (1984). A review of current approaches used to help children and parents cope with health care procedures. *Maternal-Child Nursing Journal, 13,* 145-165.

Inui, T. S., Carter, W. B., Kukull, W. A., & Haigh, V. H. (1982). Outcome-based doctor-patient interaction analysis: I. Comparison of techniques. *Medical Care, 20,* 535-549.

Jackson, L. D. (1992). Information complexity and medical communication: The effects of technical language and amount of information in a medical message. *Health Communication, 4,* 197-210.

Janis, I. L. (1983). Stress inoculation in health care: Theory and research. In D. Meichenbaum & M. E. Jeremko (Eds.), *Stress reduction and prevention* (pp. 67-99). New York: Plenum.

Jette, A. M. (1982). Improving patient cooperation with arthritis treatment regimens. *Arthritis and Rheumatism, 25,* 447-453.

Johnson, J., Rice, V., Fuller, S., & Endress, M. (1978). Sensory information, instruction in a coping strategy, and recovery from surgery. *Research in Nursing and Health, 1,* 4-17.

Johnston, J. (1973). Effects of accurate expectations about sensations on the sensory and distress components of pain. *Journal of Personality and Social Psychology, 27,* 261-275.

Kalisch, B. J. (1971). An experiment in the development of empathy in nursing students. *Nursing Research, 20,* 202-211.

Kaplan, S. H., Greenfield, S., & Ware, J. E. (1989). Impact of the doctor-patient relationship on the outcomes of chronic disease. In M. Stewart & D. Roter (Eds.), *Communicating with medical patients* (pp. 228-245). Newbury Park, CA: Sage.

Kasch, C. R. (1986). Toward a theory of nursing action: Skills and competency in nurse-patient interaction. *Nursing Research, 35,* 226-230.

Kasch, C. R., & Dine, J. (1988). Person-centered communication and social perspective taking. *Western Journal of Nursing Research, 10,* 317-326.

Kasch, C. R., & Lisnek, P. M. (1984). Role of strategic communication in nursing theory and research. *Advances in Nursing Science, 7,* 56-71.

Kasteller, J., Kane, R. L., Olsen, D. M., & Thetford, C. (1976). Issues underlying the prevalence of "doctor-shopping" behavior. *Journal of Health & Social Behavior, 17,* 328-339.

Kay-Herndon, P. (1989). The secret in Sally's eyes. *Nursing, 18,* 176.

King, P. E. (1991). Communication, anxiety, and the management of postoperative pain. *Health Communication, 3,* 127-138.

Koos, E. L. (1955). "Metropolis": What city people think of their medical services. *American Journal of Public Health, 45,* 1551-1557.

Korsch, B. M., Gozzi, E. K., & Francis, V. (1968). Gaps in doctor-patient communication: 1. Doctor-patient interaction and patient satisfaction. *Pediatrics, 42,* 855-871.

Korsch, B. M., & Negrete, V. F. (1972). Doctor-patient communication. *Scientific American, 227,* 66-74.

Krieger, D. (1975). Therapeutic touch. *American Journal of Nursing, 75,* 784-787.

Kupst, M. J., Presser, K., Schulman, J. L., & Paul, M. H. (1975). Evaluation of methods to improve communication in the physician-patient relationship. *American Journal of Orthopsychiatry, 45,* 420-429.

Laing, R. D. (1969). *Self and others.* New York: Pantheon.

Lane, P. L. (1989). Nurse-client perceptions: The double standard of touch. *Issues in Mental Health Nursing, 10,* 1-13.

Lane, S. D. (1982, May). *Compliance-gaining strategies used by health care practitioners: A pilot study.* Paper presented at the Annual Convention of the International Communication Association, Boston.

Lane, S. D. (1983). Compliance, satisfaction, and physician-patient communication. In R. N. Bostrom (Ed.), *Communication yearbook 7* (pp. 772-801). Beverly Hills, CA: Sage.

Larsson, G., & Starrin, B. (1990). Patient-nurse interactions: Relationships between person characteristics, empathy, content of communication, and patients' emotional reactions. *Scandinavian Journal of Caring Science, 4,* 129-135.

Lemaitre, G., & Finnegan, J. (1975). *The patient in surgery: A guide for nurses* (3rd ed.). New York: W. B. Saunders.

Ley, P., & Spelman, M. S. (1967). *Communicating with the patient.* London: Trinity.

Liptak, G. S., Hulka, B. S., & Cassel, J. C. (1977). Effectiveness of physician-mother interaction during infancy. *Pediatrics, 60,* 186-192.

Lochman, J. E. (1983). Factors related to patients' satisfaction with their medical care. *Journal of Community Health, 9,* 91-109.

Lubbers, C. A., & Roy, S. J. (1990). Communication skills for continuing education in nursing. *The Journal of Continuing Education in Nursing, 21,* 109-112.

Mace, D. R. (1971). Interviewing, and the physician-patient relationship. In R. H. Coombs & C. E. Vincent (Eds.), *Psychosocial aspects of medical training* (pp. 380-403). Springfield, IL: Charles C Thomas.

Macgregor, F. C. (1984). Cosmetic surgery: A sociological analysis of litigation and a surgical specialty. *Aesthetic Plastic Surgery, 8,* 219-224.

MacLeod Clark, J. (1983). Nurse patient communication in surgical wards. In J. Wilson-Barrett (Ed.), *Nursing research: Ten studies in patient care* (pp. 167-201). Chichester: Wiley.

MacLeod Clark, J. (1985). Communication: Why it can go wrong. *Nursing, 2,* 1119-1120.

Maguire, P. (1985). Consequences of poor communication between nurses and patients. *Nursing, 2,* 1115-1118.

Mallett, J. (1990). Communication between nurses and post-anaesthetic patients. *Intensive Care Nursing, 6,* 45-53.

Malpiede, D. M., Leff, M. G., Wilson, K. M., & Moore, V. M. (1982). Assessing interaction between medical trainees and parents of pediatric patients. *Journal of Medical Education, 57,* 696-700.

Marklund, B., & Bengtsson, C. (1989). Medical advice by telephone at Swedish health centres: Who calls and what are the problems. *Family Practice, 6,* 42-46.

Marston, M. (1970). Compliance with medical regimens. *Nursing Research, 19,* 312-323.

Matthews, D. A., Sledge, W. H., & Lieberman, P. B. (1987). Evaluation of intern performance by medical inpatients. *The American Journal of Medicine, 83,* 938-944.

May, M. L., & DeMarco, L. (1986). *Patients and doctors disputing: Patients' complaints and what they do about them* (Disputes Processing Research Program, Working Papers Series 7). Madison: University of Wisconsin Law School, Institute for Legal Studies.

May, M. L., & Stengel, D. B. (1990). Who sues their doctors? How patients handled medical grievances. *Law & Society, 24,* 105-120.

Mazzuca, S. A., & Weinberger, M. (1986). How clinician communication patterns affect patients' comprehension and satisfaction. *The Diabetes Educator, 12,* 370-373.

Mazzuca, S. A., Weinberger, M., Kurpius, D. J., Froehle, T. C., & Heister, M. (1986). Clinician communication associated with diabetic patients' comprehension of their therapeutic regimen. *Diabetes Care, 6,* 347-350.

McCauley, C. R., Johnson, J. P., & Copley, J. B. (1989). Communication of information about therapeutic alternatives: End-stage renal disease model. *Southern Medical Journal, 82,* 418-422.

McCready, J. R., & Waring, E. M. (1986). Interviewing skills in relation to psychiatric residency. *Canadian Journal of Psychiatry, 31,* 317-322.

McGrath, P. A., & DeVeber, L. L. (1986). Helping children cope with painful procedures. *American Journal of Nursing, 86,* 1278-1279.

McIntosh, J. (1974). Process of communication, information seeking and control associated with cancer: A selected review of the literature. *Social Science and Medicine, 8,* 167-187.

McNeilis, K., & Thompson, T. L. (in press). The impact of relational control on compliance in dentist-patient interactions. In G. Kreps & D. O'Hair (Eds.), *Relational communication and health outcomes.* Cresskill, NJ: Hampton.

Merton, R. K. (1957). *Social theory and social structure.* New York: Free Press.

Meyers, M. E. (1965). The effect of types of communication on patients' reactions to stress. In J. K. Skipper & R. C. Leonard (Eds.), *Social interaction and patient care* (pp. 128-140). Philadelphia: Lippincott.

Mishler, E. G. (1981). Viewpoint: Critical perspectives of the biomedical model. In E. G. Mishler, S. R. Amarasingham, S. D. Osherson, S. T. Hauser, N. E. Waxler, & R. Liem (Eds.), *Social contexts of health, illness, and patient care* (pp. 1-23). Cambridge: Cambridge University Press.

Mishler, E. G. (1984). *The discourse of medicine.*Norwood, NJ: Ablex.

Molzahn, A. E., & Northcott, H. C. (1989). The social bases of discrepancies in health/illness perceptions. *Journal of Advanced Nursing, 14,* 132-140.

Morrison, P., & Burnard, P. (1989). Students' and trained nurses' perceptions of their own interpersonal skills: A report and comparison. *Journal of Advanced Nursing, 14,* 321-329.

Morse, B. W., & Piland, R. N. (1981). An assessment of communication competencies needed by intermediate-level health care providers: A study of nurse-patient, nurse-doctor, nurse-nurse communication relationships. *Journal of Applied Communication Research, 9,* 30-41.

Morse, J. M. (1991). Negotiating commitment and involvement in the nurse-patient relationship. *Journal of Advanced Nursing, 16,* 455-468.

Mosconi, P., Meyerowitz, B. E., Liberati, M. C., & Liberati, A. (1991). Disclosure of breast cancer diagnosis: Patient and physician reports. *Annals of Oncology, 2,* 273-280.

New, P. K., Nite, G., & Callahan, J. M. (1959). *Nursing service and patient care: A staff experiment.* Kansas City, MO: Community Studies, Inc.

Nievaard, A. C. (1987). Communication climate and patient care: Causes and effects of nurses' attitudes to patients. *Social Science & Medicine, 24,* 777-784.

O'Hair, D. (1989). Dimensions of relational communication and control during physician-patient interactions. *Health Communication, 2,* 97-115.

Oliver, S., & Redfern, S. J. (1991). Interpersonal communication between nurses and elderly patients: Refinement of an observation schedule. *Journal of Advanced Nursing, 16,* 30-38.

Omololu, C. B. (1984). Communication behaviours of undergraduate medical students before and after training. *British Journal of Medical Psychology, 57,* 97-100.

Ort, R. S., Ford, A. B., & Liske, R. E. (1964). The doctor-patient relationship as described by physicians and medical students. *Journal of Health and Human Behavior, 5,* 25-33.

Orth, J. E., Stiles, W. B., Scherwitz, L., Hennrikus, B., & Valbonna, C. (1987). Patient exposition and provider explanation in routine interviews and hypertensive patients' blood pressure control. *Health Psychology, 6,* 29-42.

Parrott, R., Burgoon, M., & Ross, C. (1992). Parents and pediatricians talk: Compliance-gaining strategies' use during well-child exams. *Health Communication, 4,* 57-66.

Pepler, C. J., & Lynch, A. (1991). Relational messages of control in nurse-patient interactions with terminally ill patients with AIDS and cancer. *Journal of Palliative Care, 7,* 18-29.

Pierloot, R. A. (1983). Different models in the approach to the doctor-patient relationship. *Psychotherapy and Psychosomatics, 39,* 213-224.

Powers, J. S. (1985). Patient-physician communication and interaction: A unifying approach to the difficult patient. *Southern Medical Journal, 78,* 445-447.

Powers, M. J., Murphy, S. P., & Wooldridge, P. J. (1983). Validation of two experimental nursing approaches using content analysis. *Research in Nursing & Health, 6,* 3-9.

Powers, M. J., & Wooldridge, P. J. (1982). Factors influencing knowledge, attitudes, and compliance of hypertensive patients. *Research in Nursing & Health, 6,* 3-9.

Pruyn, J. F. A., Ruckman, R. M., van Brunschot, C. J. M., & van den Borne, H. W. (1985). Cancer patients' personality characteristics, physician-patient communication and adoption of the Moerman diet. *Social Science & Medicine, 20,* 841-847.

Quine, L., & Pahl, J. (1986). First diagnosis of severe mental handicap: Characteristics of unsatisfactory encounters between doctors and parents. *Social Science & Medicine, 22,* 53-62.

Quint, J. C. (1965). Institutionalized practices of information control. *Psychiatry, 28,* 119-132.

Raimbault, G., Cachin, O., Limal, C., Eliacheff, C., & Rappaport, R. (1975). Aspects of communication between patients and doctors: An analysis of the discourse in medical interviews. *Pediatrics, 55,* 401-405.

Reader, G., Pratt, L., & Mudd, M. (1957). What patients expect from their doctors. *The Modern Hospital, 89,* 88-94.

Reale, C. J. (1988). The wrong label: Nurses had labeled this patient "uncommunicative." *Nursing, 18,* 87-88.

Reardon, K. K., & Buck, R. (1989). Emotion, reason, and communication in coping with cancer. *Health Communication, 1,* 41-54.

Robinson, E. J., & Whitfield, M. J. (1985). Improving the efficiency of patients' comprehension monitoring: A way of increasing patients' participation in general practice consultations. *Social Science & Medicine, 21,* 915-919.

Rogers, L. E., & Farace, R. V. (1975). Analysis of relational communication in dyads: New measurement procedures. *Human Communication Research, 1,* 222-239.

Romm, F. J., & Hulka, B. S. (1979). Care process and patient outcome in diabetes mellitus. *Medical Care, 17,* 748-757.

Roter, D. (1989). Which facets of communication have strong effects on outcome: A meta-analysis. In M. Stewart & D. Roter (Eds.), *Communicating with medical patients* (pp. 183-196). Newbury Park, CA: Sage.

Roter, D. L. (1977). *Patient participation in the patient-provider interaction: The effects of patient question asking on the quality of interaction, satisfaction and compliance.* Unpublished dissertation for doctor of public health, Johns Hopkins University, Baltimore.

Roter, D. L. (1984). Patient question asking in physician-patient interaction. *Health Psychology, 3,* 395-409.

Roter, D. L., & Hall, J. A. (1991). Health education theory: An application to the process of patient-provider communication. *Health Education Research, 6,* 185-194.

Roter, D. L., Hall, J. A., & Katz, N. R. (1988). Patient-physician communication: A descriptive summary of the literature. *Patient Education and Counseling, 12,* 99-119.

Roth, P., Heffron, W., & Skipper, B. (1983). Patient, physician problem lists: A comparative study. *Family Practice Research Journal, 2,* 164-170.

Rouse, R. A. (1989). A paradigm of intervention: Emotional communication in dentistry. *Health Communication, 1,* 239-252.

Rowland, E. J. (1978). Nursing care for patients with pain. *AORN Journal, 27,* 1180-1194.

Rubin, F. L., Judd, M. M., & Conine, T. A. (1977). Empathy: Can it be learned and retained? *Physical Therapy, 57,* 644-647.

Sackett, G. P. (1979). The lag sequential analysis of contingency and cyclicity in behavioral interaction research. In J. D. Osotsky (Ed.), *Handbook of infant development* (pp. 623-649). New York: Wiley.

Samora, J., Saunders, L., & Larson, R. F. (1961). Medical vocabulary knowledge among hospital patients. *Journal of Health and Human Behavior, 2,* 83-92.

Schneider, D. E., & Tucker, R. K. (1992). Measuring communicative satisfaction in doctor-patient relations: The doctor-patient communication inventory. *Health Communication, 4,* 19-28.

Schraa, J. C., & Dirks, J. F. (1982). Improving patient recall and comprehension of the treatment regimen. *Journal of Asthma, 19,* 159-162.

Scott, N., & Weiner, M. F. (1984). "Patientspeak": An exercise in communication. *Journal of Medical Education, 59,* 890-893.

Seale, C. (1991). Communication and awareness about death: A study of a random sample of dying people. *Social Science and Medicine, 32,* 943-952.

Sharf, B. F. (1990). Physician-patient communication as interpersonal rhetoric: A narrative approach. *Health Communication, 31,* 217-232.

Sharf, B. F., Wood, B. S., & Flaherty, J. A. (1982). Two birds with one stone: Training communication specialists while teaching medical students. *Communication Education, 31,* 305-314.

Shuy, R. W. (1976). The medical interview: Problems in communication. *Primary Care, 3,* 365-386.

Simoni, J. J., & Ball, R. A. (1975). Can we learn from medicine hucksters? *Journal of Communication, 25,* 174-181.

Smith, B. J., & Cantrell, P. J. (1988). Distance in nurse-patient encounters. *Journal of Psychosocial Nursing and Mental Health Services, 26*(2), 22-26.

Smith, C. K., & Larsen, K. M. (1984). Sequential nonverbal behavior in the patient-physician interview. *Journal of Family Practice, 18,* 257-261.

Squier, R. W. (1990). A model of empathic understanding and adherence to treatment regimens in practitioner-patient relationships. *Social Science & Medicine, 30,* 325-339.

Starfield, B., Wray, C., Hess, K., Gross, R., Birk, P. S., & D'Lugoff, B. C. (1981). The influence of patient-practitioner agreement on outcome of care. *American Journal of Public Health, 71,* 127-132.

Stewart, M., & Roter, D. (1989). *Communicating with medical patients.* Newbury Park, CA: Sage.

Stewart, M. A., McWhinney, I. R., & Buck, W. C. (1979). The doctor-patient relationship and its effect upon outcome. *Journal of the Royal College of General Practice, 29,* 77-82.

Stiles, W. B., & Putnam, S. M. (1989). Analysis of verbal and nonverbal behavior in doctor-patient encounters. In M. Stewart & D. Roter (Eds.), *Communicating with medical patients* (pp. 211-222). Newbury Park, CA: Sage.

Stone, G. C. (1979). Patient compliance and the role of the expert. *Journal of Social Issues, 35,* 34-59.

Street, R. L. (1989). Patients' satisfaction with dentists' communicative style. *Health Communication, 1,* 137-154.

Street, R. L. (1991a). Information-giving in medical consultations: The influence of patients' communicative styles and personal characteristics. *Social Science and Medicine, 32,* 541-548.

Street, R. L. (1991b). Accommodation in medical consultations. In H. Giles, J. Coupland, & N. Coupland (Eds.), *Contexts of accommodation* (pp. 131-156). Cambridge: Cambridge University Press.

Street, R. L. (1992a). Communicative styles and adaptations in physician-patient consultations. *Social Science and Medicine, 34,* 1155-1163.

Street, R. L. (1992b). Analyzing communication in medical consultations: Do behavioral measures correspond to patients' perceptions? *Medical Care, 30,* 976-988.

Street, R. L., & Buller, D. B. (1987). Nonverbal response patterns in physician-patient interactions: A functional analysis. *Journal of Nonverbal Behavior, 11,* 234-253.

Street, R. L., & Buller, D. B. (1988). Patients' characteristics affecting physician-patient nonverbal communication. *Human Communication Research, 15,* 60-90.

Street, R. L., Jr., & Wiemann, J. M. (1987). Patient satisfaction with physicians' interpersonal involvement, expressiveness, and dominance. In M. McLaughlin (Ed.), *Communication yearbook 10* (pp. 591-612). Newbury Park, CA: Sage.

Street, R. L., Jr., & Wiemann, J. M. (1988). Differences in how physicians and patients perceive physicians' relational communication. *Southern Speech Communication Journal, 53,* 420-440.

Svarstad, B. L. (1974). *The doctor-patient encounter: An observational study of communication and outcome.* Unpublished doctoral dissertation, University of Wisconsin, Madison.

Swenson, P. (1984). Communicating with surgeons is possible when you learn the language. *AORN, 40,* 784.

Takahashi, Y. (1990). Informing a patient of a malignant illness: Commentary from a cross-cultural viewpoint. *Death Studies, 14,* 83-91.

Tarasuk, M. B., Rhymes, J. P., & Leonard, R. C. (1965). An experimental test of the importance of communication skills for effective nursing. In J. K. Skipper & R. C. Leonard (Eds.), *Social interaction and patient care* (pp. 110-120). Philadelphia: Lippincott.

Thomas, S. A., Friedmann, E., Noctor, M., Sappington, E., Gross, H., & Lynch, J. J. (1982). Patients' cardiac responses to nursing interviews in a CCU. *Dimensions of Critical Care, 1,* 198-205.

Thompson, B. M. (1986). Interpersonal skills: Learning the importance of listening. *The Australian Nurses' Journal, 16*(3), 45-47, 61.

Thompson, C. L., & Pledger, L. M. (1993). Doctor/patient communication: Is patient knowledge of medical terminology improving? *Health Communication, 5,* 89-97.

Thompson, T. L. (1984). The invisible helping hand: The role of communication in the health and social service professions. *Communication Quarterly, 32,* 148-163.

Thompson, T. L., Mowles, J., & Cusella, L. P. (1989, November). *The communication of reassurance from health care providers to patients.* Paper presented at the annual convention of the Speech Communication Association, San Francisco.

Timpka, T., & Arborelius, E. (1990). The primary-care nurse's dilemmas: A study of knowledge use and need during telephone consultations. *Journal of Advanced Nursing, 15,* 1457-1465.

Trandel-Korenchuk, D. M. (1987). The effect of social and care environments on the disclosure practices of nurse midwives relative to methods of pain management in childbirth. *Journal of Obstetric, Gynecologic & Neonatal Nursing, 16,* 258-265.

Tryon, P. A., & Leonard, R. C. (1965). Giving the patient an active role. In J. K. Skipper & R. C. Leonard (Eds.), *Social interaction and patient care* (pp. 120-127). Philadelphia: Lippincott.

Turnock, C. (1989). A study into the views of intensive care nurses on the psychological needs of their patients. *Intensive Care Nursing, 5,* 159-166.

Tymstra, T. (1986). False positive results in screening tests: Experiences of parents of children screened for congenital hypothyroidism. *Family Practice, 3,* 92-96.

von Friederichs-Fitzwater, M. M., Callahan, E. J., Flynn, N., & Williams, J. (1991). Relational control in physician-patient encounters. *Health Communication, 1,* 17-36.

Waitzkin, H. (1984). Doctor-patient communication. *Journal of the American Medical Association, 252,* 2441-2446.

Waitzkin, H. (1985). Information giving in medical care. *Journal of Health and Social Behavior, 26,* 81-101.

Waitzkin, H. (1990). On studying the discourse of medical encounters. *Medical Care, 28,* 473-488.

Wallen, J., Waitzkin, H., & Stoeckle, J. D. (1979). Physician stereotypes about female health and illness: A study of patient's sex and the informative process during medical interviews. *Women & Health, 4,* 135-146.

Ware, J. E., Jr., & Snyder, M. K. (1975). Dimensions of patient attitudes regarding doctors and medical care services. *Medical Care, 13,* 669.

Watson, W. H. (1975). The meanings of touch: Geriatric nursing. *Journal of Communication, 25,* 104-112.

Webb, C. (1986). Professional and lay social support for hysterectomy patients. *Journal of Advanced Nursing, 11,* 167-177.

Weisman, C. S., & Teitelbaum, M. A. (1985). Physician gender and the physician-patient relationship: Recent evidence and relevant questions. *Social Science & Medicine, 20,* 1119-1127.

Weisman, C. S., & Teitelbaum, M. A. (1989). Women and health care communication. *Patient Education and Counseling, 13,* 183-199.

Weiss, S. J. (1986). Consensual norms regarding patient involvement. *Social Science and Medicine, 22,* 489-496.

West, C. (1984). *Routine complications.* Bloomington: University of Indiana Press.

Wheeless, V. E. (1987). Female patient and physician communication and discussion of gynecological health care issues. *Southern Speech Communication Journal, 52,* 198-211.

Wilkinson, S. (1991). Factors which influence how nurses communicate with cancer patients. *Journal of Advanced Nursing, 16,* 677-688.

Williams, A., Giles, H., Coupland, N., Dalby, M., & Manasse, H. (1990). The communicative contexts of elderly social support and health: A theoretical model. *Health Communication, 2,* 123-144.

Woolley, F. R., Kane, R. L., Hughes, C. C., & Wright, D. D. (1978). The effects of doctor-patient communication on satisfaction and outcome of care. *Social Science and Medicine, 12,* 123-128.

Worobey, J. L., & Cummings, H. W. (1984). Communication effectiveness of nurses in four relational settings. *Journal of Applied Communication Research, 12,* 128-141.

Woy, D. (1987). In Lynne's eyes. *Nursing, 17,* 152.

Wyatt, N. (1991). Physician-patient relationships: What do doctors say? *Health Communication, 3,* 157-174.

Zare, N., Sorenson, J. R., & Heeren, T. (1984). Sex of provider as a variable in effective genetic counseling. *Social Science & Medicine, 19,* 671-675.

19

All in the Family: Interpersonal Communication in Kin Relationships

Mary Anne Fitzpatrick

Diane M. Badzinski

WE BELIEVE THAT it is important for a handbook on interpersonal communication to include a chapter on family communication. The family is where most of us learn to communicate and, even more important, where most of us learn how to think about communication (Bruner, 1990). The family is a universal *social* form, usually a small kinship-structured group. Although many definitions of kinship suggest a biological reckoning (e.g., Wilson, 1975), it is the social definition of who belongs to whom and who is related to whom that is more critical (Reiss, 1971). To be kin to someone acknowledges a special tie of who stands in what relationship to whom, who owes what to whom, and how individuals of particular kin relationships are expected to pay their social debts. The kin group socializes the newborn to these obligations. And that socialization takes place through communication.

This chapter is about communication in kin relationships. We have organized this review in three major sections. First, we discuss the three major classes of definitions of the family guiding the research enterprise. Second, we demonstrate the importance of communication in any theoretical or conceptual attempt to understand the family. Third, we selectively examine some of the research that has been conducted on family interaction. In the concluding section, we offer some suggestions for future research.

Definitions of the Family

What is a family? In our previous version of this chapter, we left *family* as a primitive, undefined term (Fitzpatrick & Badzinski, 1985). Now we want to consider various definitions of *family* before we settle on the one most useful for research and theory. Definitions of *family* are often thinly viewed political or ideological statements rather than scientifically neutral views. Activists argue that refusing to consider homosexual couples as "family" severely limits their rights and duties to one another. In a recent court action in Minnesota, a homosexual woman had to sue the parents of her partner, who had recently become handicapped, for the right to take care of her partner in a home they had shared.

Following Wamboldt and Reiss (1989), three definitions of the family can be excavated from the extant research on the family: family structure, task orientation, and transactional process.

Family Structure

The first class of definitions is based on family structure. Most of us use the term *family* in at least two ways: (a) when we mean partners and children (family of procreation) and (b) when we mean relatives by blood or marriage such as parents and siblings, grandparents, aunts, uncles, and cousins (family of origin). Many singles and childless couples have families of origin, even when they do not have families of procreation. But they would be unlikely to live with other members of their family. A *family of origin,* then, is the extended family or any group of individuals that has established biological or sociolegal legitimacy by virtue of shared genetics, marriage, or adoption. A *family of procreation,* usually called the "nuclear family," is further restricted to those living in the same house. Family structure definitions presuppose clear criteria for membership in the family and hierarchies within the family based on sex and age.

Social changes like the high divorce rate, new birth technologies, and the rise in feminism are making definitions of the family based solely on structural characteristics less useful. A divorced family including a child who spends one half of the week with one stepparent and parent, and the other half with another parent and stepparent, does not necessarily follow the same criteria for who is, and who is not, a member of the family. New fertility technologies (donor eggs, surrogate mothers, and so forth) are challenging definitions of the family based on shared genetic heritage. The influence of feminism as a challenge to automatic male privilege is shaking the typical hierarchies in the family.

Social changes as reflected in demographic patterns present obvious difficulties for structural definitions of the family. In spite of this obvious problem, the tendency in most family research is to use "the household" as the working definition of the family. Much of the research that examines family interaction uses a family structure approach in that the families involved are sociolegal units and the members reside in the same household. It is much easier to determine who lives with whom than it is to assess the quality of family task performance or the subjective experience of group identity and affection.

Psychosocial Task Definitions

The second set of definitions focuses on whether certain tasks of family life are performed. Here a family is a psychosocial group, consisting of at least one adult member and one or more other persons, that works toward mutual need fulfillment, nurturance, and development. Task definitions are usually concerned with describing the functions of the family.

A good working task definition defines the family as the social unit that accepts responsibility for the socialization and nurturance of children (Lerner & Spanier, 1978). In this definition, although children are the essential ingredient, those adults who take responsibility for caring for the children are also included, whether there is one parent or two, whether the adults are/are not married to one another, and even whether the adults taking primary responsibility are/are not the natural parents of the children. One or more grandparents may even be the primary caretakers of the children. The structure of the family can vary in this definition as its focus is on the fulfillment of the task of raising children.

A definition that focuses exclusively on the task of raising children ignores the variety of pathways through the family. For example, should young couples who have not yet had their children (or intend to remain childless as do about 8%-10%), and older couples who have raised their children, be counted as families, even though there are no children to be socialized and nurtured? In this model, the childless couple is usually considered a natural stage of the nuclear family at both ends of the cycle. What about the couple who is childless throughout life, either through choice or because of infertility? Is it useful to distinguish between couples and families? And what about single households that include young adults, never married men and women, the divorced, and the widowed? Singles do not constitute a family by either of the definitions.

In sum, the basic insight of the psychosocial task definitions is the focus on the goals the family serves for individuals and for society. Communication is viewed as able either to facilitate or to impede goal attainment. The difficulty of definitions based on defining the family as a task-oriented system is that each of the various types and stages of families is faced with very different tasks. And such definitions tend to ignore the fact that "the family" is not a homogeneous unit. This view masks intrafamily conflicts of interest, particularly the interests of women and children. In the next section, we turn to a definition of the family that avoids some of the problems faced by the structural and the task-oriented viewpoints.

Transactional Process Definitions

A final group of definitions of the family gives central importance to transactional processes. A family is defined as a group of intimates who generate a sense of home and group identity, complete with strong ties of loyalty and emotion, and an experience of a history and a future (Wamboldt & Reiss, 1989).

Group of Intimates

To define the family as a group of intimates requires that we understand the meaning of intimacy. Two separate concepts central to the meaning of intimacy are interdependence and commitment.

Intimacy as interdependence. Interdependence involves the extent to which people have an impact on each other and influence one another's feelings, thoughts, or behaviors (Kelley et al., 1983). In an interdependent relationship, one person's behavior has continual effects, either direct or indirect, on the other's behavior or attitudes (Lewin, 1948; see also Levinger & Huston, 1990). High interdependence does not necessarily mean that relationships will be free of problems because conflict may occur over such issues as power, control, or equality. Nor does interdependence mean that relationships will necessarily be warm. Highly interdependent families may be very cold and distant. Interdependence in a family may exist to various degrees and it may be symmetrical (equal) or asymmetrical across various family members and combinations.

Intimacy as commitment. What does it mean when people say they are committed to their relationship? In the ideal, family members are committed to one another's well-being at both the personal and the structural levels (Levinger & Huston, 1990). Personal commitment results from the satisfactions occasioned by being a member of a family. Structural commitments to a family include barriers to dissolving the relationship such as a strong belief in the permanence of marriage, profamily attitudes prevalent in the society as a whole or among family and friends, or wanting to stay together for the sake of the children (Levinger, 1965, 1976). Structural factors may help family members to persevere with relationships even during periods when things may not be going so well and may encourage couples and families to work at overcoming their difficulties (Levinger & Huston, 1990), and even to get professional help.

Rusbult and Buunk (1993) argue that strong commitment to a relationship not only makes individuals more likely to remain with their partners but also promotes a variety of relational maintenance behaviors such as adaptive social comparison and perceived relationship superiority, derogation of attractive and threatening alternatives, effective management of jealousy and extrarelationship involvements, willingness to sacrifice for the good of the relationship, and tendencies to accommodate rather than retaliate when a partner behaves poorly.

Sense of home and group identity. This attribute of a family is captured by a family's identity. Reiss (1981) has called this sense of identity "family paradigms" or the worldviews that families hold affecting how they process information from the surrounding environment. Identity for one family may be tied to its concept of surviving in a complex or hostile world; another family may be religious; yet another intellectual or fun loving. Steinglass and his colleagues (Steinglass, Bennett, Wolin, & Reiss, 1987) argue that some families with an alcoholic member may even come to define themselves as "the alcoholic family" even when the problem drinker no longer drinks.

Family identity is shaped by the social and the cultural context in which the family functions. In other words, the norms and values of a particular society at a particular time impinge on the family (Hinde, 1979). And historical circumstances exert an influence on how the family comes to see itself.

Ties of loyalty and emotion in the family. The ties of emotion and loyalty among family members exert strong influences on the communication that occurs and how it is interpreted. Family communication may be more intense than other forms of human communication. As Sieburg (1985) explains: "Because of the intimate nature of the relationships involved, any miscommunication in the family is likely to be more painful and the consequences more serious than in other human groups" (p. 71).

For many, the prototype (i.e., central features) of love involves sharing, communication, honesty, trust, understanding, and openness (Luby & Aron, 1990). Family communication is not universally positive and loving. High levels of expressed criticism and negativity, for example, occur in many families and may be related to the etiology of schizophrenia (Goldstein, 1987).

The family has a history and a future. The family has a *history* in two senses of that word. First, as Kelley (1986) notes, personal relationships gain their significance from their cumulative effects, with each interaction building on all the previous interactions between the parties. In any relationship, each interaction is influenced by other interactions in that relationship. In addition, because each of the participants in a relationship affects the interaction that occurs, an individual is likely to behave differently depending on his or her interaction partner. Second, experiences and behaviors in one's current family are likely to be affected by previous family experience, particularly in the family of origin (Hinde, 1979). We repeat the behaviors we have experienced in our families. Children abused as children abuse their own children, children of alcoholics become alcoholics, children of divorce are more likely to divorce, and so forth. The intergenerational transmission of negative interpersonal behaviors poses very real problems in families.

Summary

There are three very different definitions of the family. Each definition subtly emphasizes a different aspect of the family to be examined. Family structure definitions include as family members those who have established biological or sociolegal legitimacy by virtue of shared genetics, marriage, or adoption. These definitions specify criteria for membership and particular hierarchies based on age and sex. A variety of societal changes make family structure definitions less viable.

Psychosocial task definitions of the family define the family as a group that works toward mutual need fulfillment as well as the nurturance and development of the members. Although this definition helps us to focus on the goals of family life, each of the various stages and types of families has markedly different goals, making the definition less useful than it might be.

Transactional process approaches define the family as a group of intimates who generate a sense of home and group identity, complete with strong ties of loyalty and emotion, and experience a history and a future. Admittedly, this definition is complex and contains many abstract concepts that themselves need to be defined. Yet the transactional definition has two advantages over the other two approaches. First, the transactional definition of the family also places a very strong emphasis on communication as the major vehicle in establishing levels of interdependence and commitment, forming ties of loyalty and identity, and transmitting a sense of family identity, history, and future. Second, this definition can encompass the many forms of modern family life because this approach allows families to define themselves rather than base the definition of the family on sociolegal or genetic criteria.

A Communication Approach

During the 1960s, the structural-functional, the interactional, and the developmental perspectives were predominant metatheoretical orientations (Nye & Berardo, 1981). During the 1980s, greater emphasis was placed on the conflict (Sprey, 1979), exchange (Nye, 1979), and system theory (Galvin & Brommel, 1992) perspectives. During the late 1980s, feminist (Ferree, 1990) and ethnic theories (Vega, 1990) gained ascendance.

Of these metatheoretical approaches, only the interactionist approach, which defines the family as a "unit of interacting personalities" (Burgess & Locke, 1953), *explicitly* assigns a central role to communication. Bochner (1976) takes up this theoretical framework in an early article on family communication (see also Yerby, Beurkel-Rothfuss, & Bochner, 1994). Recently, a major sociological handbook on family theory argued that communication theory is one of the newest emerging paradigms for studying the family in the 1980s (Fitzpatrick & Ritchie, 1993). In that influential handbook (Boss, Doherty, LaRossa, Schumm, & Steinmetz, 1993), communication theory is grouped with such emerging paradigms as feminist theory, ethnic and racial theories, discourse and ethnomethodological work, and biosocial perspectives on the family (see Cappella, 1991, for an interesting argument about the origins of automatic communication behavior).

Approaches that consider communication to be important only within one metatheoretical perspective, or even those that argue that there is *one* communication theory, are misdirected. Regardless of the metatheoretical orientation to the family, the concept of communication is necessary, albeit not always sufficient, in any attempt to explain, predict, and understand family outcomes.

The linchpin of our rationale for the theoretical importance of communication in kin relationships is our modification of Hill's chart of frequently used factors in all major theoretical approaches to the family (Burr, Hill, Nye, & Reiss, 1979, p. xiii). This taxonomical effort lists the exogenous and endogenous factors of central concern to family theorists. In the following sections, we discuss the major concepts of interest in analyzing the family. In this discussion, the role of communication in understanding the family becomes clear.

Exogenous Variables

Exogenous variables include both the extreme exogenous factors affecting family structures and processes as well as the input variables that are more proximate to internal family processes. Extreme exogenous variables are those that deal with the social, political, and economic environment in which a kin group finds itself. Input variables include value orientations, social class, and access to resources and social networks (see reviews by Menaghan & Parcel, 1990; Voydanoff, 1990). Historians who study both types of exogenous variables have shown us that nostalgia for a lost family tradition that never existed has prejudiced our understanding of the contemporary family (Goode, 1963). Current family forms are considered dysfunctional to the extent that they deviate from such nostalgic views. Without a historical framework, our understanding of current family difficulties such as incest or violence is severely hampered (Gordon, 1988).

The nineteenth-century family has been described by one historian as an emotional iceberg (Shorter, 1975) yet one responsible for the provision of livelihoods and the education and care of its members. In contrast, the twentieth-century family has become an emotional refuge in an increasingly bureaucratic environment (Parsons & Bales, 1955) that has taken over many of the other major functions of the family (for example, the education and socialization of children).

What happens to the family when it starts to lose some of its historical functions? Some theorists argue that the functions performed by families are highly interdependent. When peers, and not parents, socialize adolescents, the emotional relationships between parents and adolescent children are probably significantly altered (Csikszentmihalyi, Rathunde, & Whalen, 1993). If toddlers are placed in nonparental care (Belsky, 1990), emotional bonds between children and their parents may be affected. Limiting the family, once a multifunctional unit of society,

Table 19.1 Seven Family Myths Not Supported by Historical Research on the American Family

1. Great extended families did not exist in preindustrial America.
2. Outsiders, not kin, augmented the household as boarders and lodgers.
3. Chain migration, with members following another to new locations, kept many family ties close during industrialization.
4. Work was still a family's effort, even though the workplace changed to an industrial setting.
5. The glorification of motherhood as a career was a relatively late phenomenon, developing primarily in the middle class in the nineteenth century.
6. The decline in the birthrate was quite evident by the beginning of the twentieth century.
7. Greater stability and uniformity in family life cycle transitions have been achieved in this century in contrast to previous time periods.

SOURCE: Hareven (1980).

to the performance of only an emotional function may damage the ability of the family to handle even that one function (Lasch, 1977).

The previous argument is very controversial. Feminists (e.g., Thorne, 1992) argue that functionalist views privilege the experience of men and fathers in families rather than that of women and mothers. Three themes have especially mystified women's varied experiences of the family: ideologies of motherhood, the notion of the family as a domestic refuge, and an emphasis on love and consensus as the sole basis of family relations. The feminist arguments for alternative conceptions of the family are compelling, although emotional and psychological factors have achieved preeminence in a society's view of the family. Whereas feminist writers are correct in wanting women and mothers to have a voice in defining those emotional and psychological functions, the very demands for a female voice place increasing pressure on family members to communicate. If the major function of the modern family is emotional, greater demands are placed on all participants to engage in expressive communication.

A societal commitment to expressivity is potentially emotionally risky (Moscovici, 1967; Parks, 1982). Such commitments may also be potentially physically dangerous. The open expression of strong negative feelings to individuals with whom one lives in close physical proximity may exacerbate tensions. An individual is more likely to observe, commit, or be a victim of violence within his or her own family than in any other setting (Gelles, 1974). The modern family is a place in which hatred and violence are felt, expressed, and learned as consistently as love.

A consideration of such exogenous variables strengthens our theoretical work on the family. Exogenous factors set the scope conditions for our conceptual efforts by reminding us of the historical and cultural limitations of our empirical generalizations. Additionally, exogenous variables can be directly and productively linked to internal family processes (for a classic example, see Bott, 1957). At the very least, these factors remind us of the range and diversity possible in family systems (van den Berghe, 1978). Environmental diversity dramatically affects the input variables, and through these the meaning and even the frequency of communicative exchanges are altered.

Endogenous Variables

The internal, performance, and output variables are the endogenous factors in theoretical approaches to the family. The specific variables covered by these factors

Table 19.2 Major Endogenous Variables Across All Theories of the Family

(A) Internal	(B) Performance	(C) Output
Family rules	Marrying	Marital satisfaction
Power allocation	Relationship adjusting	Parental satisfaction
Role differentiation	Problem solving	Family solidarity
Affection and support structure	Child socializing	Adequacy of function
Communication structure	Family planning	Status attainment
Information-processing structure	Tension managing	
Coordination of subsystems		

are diagrammed in Table 19.2. As we have argued, the exogenous variables can be used to predict kinship communication patterns.

Communication—save in its most narrow definition of communication structure, that is, who speaks to whom—is overlooked in this taxonomy of major family variables. Although the centrality of communication in a variety of relational processes is one of the *topoi* for communication scholars, communication is assigned a peripheral role in traditional psychological and sociological studies of families and close relationships.

There are at least three senses in which communication can be conceptually related to these endogenous variables. First, communication can be construed as the underlying causal mechanism that translates the set of internal variables into the outcome variables. Second, communication can be seen as the intervening variable linking internal, performance, and output processes. Third, communication can be seen as constitutive in that it produces and reproduces the social structure of marriage and the family (McPhee, personal communication, 1984).[1] One's metatheoretical framework determines which of these three orientations toward communication in kin relationships can be most fruitfully adopted. Without the explication of the nature and function of communication, however, the specification of the relationships between the internal, performance, and output variables is incomplete.

Internal Variables

Internal family variables are frequently operationalized by a variety of verbal and nonverbal messages. The gestures, words, actions, silences, even the presence or absence of a family member, are representative of a number of different internal family concepts (Raush, Grief, & Nugent, 1979). Family rules are often defined through observation of the interaction that takes place among family members (Napier & Whitaker, 1978). Power allocation and role differentiation can be signaled by behaviors such as successful interruptions, talk-overs, and talk time (for example, Folger, 1978; Millar & Rogers, 1976). The affection and support structure of a family are manifested by the occurrence or nonoccurrence of specific nonverbal affect cues (for example, Lamb, 1976b) as well as language characteristics (Berger & Bradac, 1982). The communication structure is defined as who speaks to whom and how often (Farace, Monge, & Russell, 1977; Haley, 1967; Waxler & Mishler, 1970). The information-processing structure is measured by how information is shared in a family (Reiss, 1981). Finally, *coordination* is defined as the meshing of interaction sequences among or between partners (Berscheid, 1983).

A close examination of these internal variables suggests that a more parsimonious structure is possible. Perhaps the basic dimensions internal to the family are affect and power or cohesion and adaptability (Olson, Sprenkle, & Russell, 1979). These are the major dimensions of interpersonal behavior according to a number of different perspectives (Bochner, Kaminski, & Fitzpatrick, 1977). Control subsumes the internal concepts of family rules, power allocations, role differentiation, communication and information-processing structures, and coordination, whereas affect subsumes the affection and support structures (Olson et al., 1983).

The trend toward using verbal and nonverbal communication as operational definitions of internal family variables obscures important characteristics of these variables. Although the direct exchange of verbal and nonverbal messages is central to family processes, communication alone cannot explain all of the variance in family outcomes. We believe that the cognitive and affective perspectives, represented by these internal family variables, would be better operationalized through a consideration of the attitudes, values, and/or relational theories that individuals and families hold concerning family interaction (Fitzpatrick, 1988; Ritchie & Fitzpatrick, 1990). In other words, internal variables are best construed as the factors that account for the observed regularities in the performance variables and not as performance variables per se.

Performance Variables

Performance variables are overt behavioral activities. For communication researchers, these activities are primarily verbal and nonverbal exchanges. The six performance variables isolated in Table 19.2 are behavioral episodes that occur in families. These episodes can be examined at either the molar or the molecular levels. Gottman (1979), who views conflict resolution as the major behavioral episode capable of predicting marital satisfaction, coded the specific molecular cues exchanged between couples during conflict. The interaction sequences between marital partners were the best predictor of a couple's experienced satisfaction with a marriage (Gottman, 1979).

An explicit analytical separation of classes of internal and performance variables may help in the development of concepts and theories at the same level of abstraction, that is, the individual, dyadic, triadic, and so forth. Performance variables can be studied at the individual level of social behavior by focusing on the communication style of a given individual (Norton, 1983). These variables can also be studied at the dyadic level by examining messages in sequence at the interact, double interact, or higher order. Many of the existing dyadic-level concepts are better considered communication concepts (for example, complementarity, reciprocity, dominance, and so forth) because the linking between two individuals occurs behaviorally through the exchange of messages.

Although theories need not restrict themselves to concepts at the same order of abstraction, theories of communication in close relationships must explicitly deal with the issue of how these classes of concepts translate across various levels of analysis. Is it an individual's marital satisfaction that is explained by an interaction pattern between spouses? Or is it some more abstract concept of satisfaction with the relationship for both people (and under what conditions)?

Output Variables

The very idea that central family processes should predict "outcomes" should give the reader pause. Studies of the modern family are based on powerful value assumptions and these become very clear as we consider this set of ultimate dependent variables. We are trying to predict, in our theories and our research, a set of value-laden goals for families. Examine the output column in Table 19.2. For example, although our research is very concerned with happiness for adults (marital and parental satisfaction), little attention is paid to happiness for children.

Here we need to struggle with a consideration of the "normalcy" of a family. Originally, *normality* was defined as the absence of disease in a family, although more detailed models have had to evolve to deal with the complex ethnic, racial, and class differences in this society (Walsh, 1992). Many Marxist and radical critiques of the family maintain that the family is the ultimate dysfunctional and destructive social form.[2] For these critics, the "normal" family is a nightmare. Only the family glues individuals to others based upon a sense of incompleteness, stymies the free formation of one's identity, exerts greater social control than children need, and indoctrinates members with elaborate and unnecessary taboos (Cooper, 1970). The very intensity of such critiques reminds us to scrutinize our values. We are not suggesting that the enterprise of predicting to a set of ultimate dependent variables be abandoned but that these values be clearly stated and examined as we pursue research on family communication.

The first major family outcome variables that we have isolated in Table 19.2 are satisfaction and stability measures. Satisfaction concerns one's subjectively experienced contentment with either a marital or a parent-child relationship. Family solidarity is a stability dimension that objectively examines whether or not a given family is intact. Parents separate or divorce and children run away, and such events can be taken as measures of family instability.

Family functioning is a multidimensional construct, usually defined in one of three major ways. Primarily, the family is measured according to its ability to accomplish major family goals. These goals are usually specified by the theorist and typically include the appropriate socialization of the children and the stabilization of the adult personality. Optimal family functioning may include the development of a specified set of interaction competencies (Farber, 1964).

A second approach to optimal family functioning asks: Does the organization of the family violate societal principles? A family is, for example, organized along age and gender lines. The presence of coalitions across such lines is said to result in dysfunctional outcomes (Lewis, Beavers, Gossett, & Phillips, 1976; Mishler & Waxler, 1968). One way to measure these coalitions is to see if parents are more responsive interactively to one another than either one is to the children.

The third approach to optimal family functioning considers whether the family contains a diseased member. The psychological or even some physical problems (e.g., ulcerative colitis) of a child are defined as prima facie evidence of family dysfunction (for example, Henry, 1965). In recent years, there has been an increased emphasis on examining the relationships between family processes and the physical health of adult members (e.g., Gottman & Levenson, 1992).

Finally, *status attainment* refers to the maintenance or achievement of a particular socioeconomic position for a family. Often, whether a child attains the same or better status level as the parent, particularly the father, is of concern. Status attainment involves measuring the occupational choices made by a child in comparison with the father. Often the exposure to a model and the ability to talk with others about various occupations leads to a child's awareness and eventual choice of specific jobs or careers (Woelfel & Haller, 1971).

The social-time dimension. Although not represented in Table 19.2, Hill (1979, cited in Burr et al., 1979) isolated another class of major factors often treated in theories of the family. These are family development, family learning over time, intergenerational processes, economic life cycles and family performance, and family innovations. Each of these concepts adds the social-time dimension to the model and recognizes the longitudinal nature of the family. Such concepts serve to remind us that families follow a repeated pattern of organization, disorganization, and change. Any comprehensive approach to the family must take into account the repeated continuities and discontinuities in family life.

One of the difficulties in discussing the family in a developmental perspective is that most of the research conducted on the topic has used cross-sectional post hoc designs. Such designs provide a poor basis for detecting developmental trends (Baltes, 1968; Rollins, 1975) because there is potential confusion between cohort effects and actual developmental changes (see also Mares & Fitzpatrick, in press, for a discussion of this point in regard to the aging couple). The scarcity of longitudinal research is not the only problem in studying family development. Most family stage theories, concerned only with intact families, mark family developmental stages according to the age of the oldest child (Duvall, 1971). This approach ignores other family systems, for example, the common one of a single mother rearing two female children (Aldous, 1978). Furthermore, the age of the oldest child may not be a particularly sensitive marker of internal family dynamics.

Despite these difficulties in achieving a reasonable and broadly applicable model of family development, theorists have dealt increasingly with notions of change through time in family systems (see Vangelisti, 1993, for an interesting argument about time and family communication).

Summary

Explicating the role of communication in predicting family outcome variables clarifies the ways different internal variables have led to different outcomes. A traditional orientation to male and female roles, for example, constrains the communication between marital partners, which leads to a high degree of satisfaction for some couples yet not for others (Fitzpatrick, 1983).

In this section, we have delineated the major factors related to family processes and have argued that many family theories have underplayed or ignored the role of communication in predicting family outcomes. To rectify this omission, we have offered three ways to examine communication as the link among the internal, performance, and output variables. We have also proposed that a complete theory of family communication must take into account exogenous factors as they impinge on internal family processes. In the next section, we consider the empirical research on communication in the family.

Overview of Research on Communication in Family Relationships

Four organizational principles guide this review. We adopt a system theory metaphor (Galvin & Brommel, 1992). Thus we have split off the subsystems in the family that can be (and have been) examined apart from one another. In other words, we focus on dyads, triads, and so forth in organizing these sections. You will notice, however, that most of the empirical research has concentrated on the dyad rather than the larger subsystem units.[3]

Our second principle of organization considers the levels of analysis issue. The study of marital and family interaction cuts across many disciplinary boundaries. Each discipline approaches the study of the family in a somewhat unique fashion. Part of this uniqueness comes from the different weights each discipline places on the various levels of analysis from which an examination of the family can proceed. The endogenous and exogenous variables we previously discussed in Table 19.2, for example, would be of differential interest to workers in various academic disciplines.

One can conceptualize these levels of analysis as the study of processes within individuals; interactions between individuals; properties of the component relationships, themselves; the family group, as a whole; and the influences of the broader community on the family (Fitzpatrick & Wamboldt, 1990). Given the enormous body of research on the family, this review selectively concentrates on studies concerned with the first two levels: that is, processes within individuals and interactions between family members. We include these two levels because, at a minimum, a theory of communication must include how individual-level processes (e.g., cognitions, emotions) affect the encoding, exchanging, and decoding of messages.

Our third organizational principle limits discussion to those research endeavors dedicated to predicting at least one of the output variables in Table 19.2. We have tried to give the reader a sense of the type and kind of empirical research that has been conducted on communication in kinship relations without any attempt to be comprehensive.

Our fourth organizational principle takes the transactional definition seriously and incorporates different types of families such as homosexual partners and cohabiting couples.

Family Dyads

In this section, we consider communication in the marital (i.e., courting, established, and divorcing), homosexual, cohabiting, sibling, and mother-child dyads. Space limitations preclude a discussion of other family dyads (e.g., grandmother-grandchild and so forth). Noller and Fitzpatrick (1993) offer a more comprehensive review.

The Marital Pair: Courting

The voluminous research on initial attraction has been little help in explaining or predicting courtship progress or early marital processes (Huston & Levinger, 1978). One major explanation for this fact may be the overidentification of the concept of attraction with the concept of attitude (Berscheid, 1982). In ongoing relationships, individuals do not have the clear, bipolar unambivalent responses to one another implied by the attitude construct. Commitment to *attraction as attitude* skews research and theory on relationships into both a stability framework and an exclusively cognitive one at that (Berscheid, 1983; Graziano & Musser, 1982).

Processes within individuals. The theoretical approaches concerned with the processes through which partners select mates are stage or filter theories (Duck, 1976; Kerckhoff & Davis, 1962; Lewis, 1973; Murstein, 1967). Each implies that individuals progress toward long-term commitments by filtering various pieces of information concerning cognitive compatibility. The successful completion or passing through of a particular stage is accomplished through the (mutual) discovery of similarities and value consensus. In some approaches, relational partners are viewed as rational buyers in the marriage marketplace, moving from a state of surface contact to a state of deep mutual involvement through an incremental exchange of rewards (Huesmann & Levinger, 1976; Levinger & Huesmann, 1980).

In her excellent textbook, Brehm (1985) argues that stage theories are too cognitive and individualistic. An excellent critique of stage approaches that brings out a conflict framework can be found in Bochner (1983). An even more interesting perspective on stage theories is that of Conville (1991), who grants priority to *how* partners move through transformations and representations of relationships rather than to questions of *what* stages are.

Vangelisti and Daly (1990) have begun to explore the role of expectations in close relationships. In a series of studies, these researchers uncovered a number of long-term and short-term expectations for romantic relationships. The most strongly held expectations were those centering on commitment, relaxation, openness, frankness, and reliability. Women and people with high self-esteem had stronger expectations for their romantic relationships than did males or people with low self-esteem. Importantly, perceived marital quality was strongly inversely related to the degree to which people's expectations have been violated.

Interpersonal processes. Huston and his associates (Huston, Surra, Fitzgerald, & Cate, 1981) developed a typology of courtship styles based on the time and rate trajectory of couples' reports of relational progress and commitment to the relationship (see Cate & Lloyd, 1992). These styles were further discriminated by the frequency and character of the interaction within the couples as well as between the couples and others. Although we cannot fully describe the courtship styles, one style is particularly striking. A couple type emerges marked by less positive affect and less companionship than other couples. Intriguingly, these couples resemble a type of married couple, called the "separates," identified in another theoretical perspective (Fitzpatrick, 1984). It appears that some couples begin marriage relatively disaffiliated and noncompanionate yet holding traditional sex role ideologies (Huston et al., 1981).

Interaction in courtship has significant impact on early marriage outcomes. Dissatisfaction with the relationship after 1 year of marriage, $2\frac{1}{2}$ years of marriage, and 5 years of marriage seems to be related to communication problems present before marriage (Markman, 1979, 1981, 1984). Initially, all couples were satisfied with their relationship, but the more positively the partners rated their communication during a laboratory negotiation session before marriage, the more satisfied they were with their relationship at the later times. Negative communication seemed to precede the development of relationship dissatisfaction. In particular, couples who were less satisfied with their marriages after a year tended to make less use of mutual strategies (mutual discussion, mutual negotiation) and more use of coercive and destructive strategies than more satisfied couples (Noller & Callan, 1989).

A longitudinal study (Kelly, Huston, & Cate, 1985) assessed four dimensions: love for the partner, conflict and negativity, ambivalence about whether to continue the relationship, and maintenance (self-disclosure, problem solving, behavior change). Newlyweds answered questions retrospectively about their courtship and answered the same questions 2 years later. The more conflict there was in courtship, the less in love the wife was 2 years later and the less satisfied she was with her marriage. Conflict before marriage was not related to feelings of positivity about the partner at the time of marriage but was related to feelings about the partner later on. Wives who had husbands who worked at relationship problems during courtship by self-disclosing, confronting problems, and trying to solve them tended to love their husbands more later in the marriage.

The Marital Pair: Established

The key output variable motivating much of the research on the marital pair is marital satisfaction. Satisfaction and related concepts such as happiness, adjustment, marital quality, lack of distress, or integration reference subjectively experienced contentment with the marital relationship (Hicks & Platt, 1970; Lewis & Spanier, 1979). Marital satisfaction is important because it predicts the stability of a relationship.

Processes within individuals. Happy couples report more satisfaction with the social and emotional aspects of their relationships and more intimacy such as showing understanding, asking each other for advice, looking at one another, and laughing a lot together. In contrast, distressed couples report more destructive communication behaviors such as not listening, becoming angry as the result of a disagreement, accusing the spouse, and avoiding conflict. Happy and distressed couples reported conflicts about the same topics, although distressed couples had more frequent conflict and spent more time in conflict. The areas of higher conflict for the distressed were communication, sexuality, and dispositional characteristics (enduring traits) of the partner (Schaap, Buunk, & Kerkstra, 1988).

A number of negative communication behaviors, such as criticizing, complaining, and sarcasm, are typical of distressed spouses (Revenstorf, Vogel, Wegener, Hahlweg, & Schindler, 1980; Ting-Toomey, 1983). The ratio of agreement to disagreement is a very strong predictor of marital adjustment, with happy couples displaying the higher ratios of agreement to disagreement (Schaap et al., 1988). Couples also use a variety of strategies to maintain their marriages (Baxter & Dindia, 1990; Dindia & Baxter, 1987). Three underlying dimensions organized the perceptual space of husbands and wives when rating these strategies. In other words, husbands and wives saw strategies as ranging on continua from constructive to destructive communication styles, from ambivalence-based to satiation-based conditional use, and from proactive to passive.

Interpersonal processes. Happy and distressed couples report differences in the sequence and patterning of their conflicts (Christensen, 1988). The pattern of wife demand-husband withdraw was related to marital dissatisfaction whereas the pattern of husband demand-wife withdraw was not (Noller & White, 1990). Husbands are more likely to withdraw in response to wife demands when the issue being discussed is more important to their wives than it is to them (Christensen & Heavey, 1990). The Structural Model of Marital Interaction (Gottman, 1979) hypothesizes more patterning and structure in the interaction of dissatisfied than satisfied couples. Furthermore, satisfied couples are expected to exhibit more positivity and to be less likely to reciprocate negative behaviors. All the concepts in the model are tested in terms of affect. Even dominance, a type of patterning, is measured by the asymmetry in predictability of emotional responsiveness between husbands and wives. Based on this model, both the frequencies of the individual behaviors that couples exhibit in the presence of one another and their interaction patterns are examined.

Although all couples are equally likely to reciprocate positive affect, unhappy couples are more likely to reciprocate negative communication behaviors than are happy couples (Gottman, Markman, & Notarius, 1977; Rubin, 1977). The interaction of an unhappy pair shows more asymmetry in predictability than does the interaction of a happy one. In an unhappy marriage, one spouse is more emotionally dominant than another. Such extreme patterning seems to occur even at the physiological level (Levenson & Gottman, 1983). As they communicate with one another even on the topic, "How was your day?" the unhappily married showed a high degree of predictable physiological responses to one another's comments. Such physiological chaining of responses suggests one reason that couples report feelings of being trapped in a marriage.

Recently, Gottman (1993a; Gottman & Levenson, 1992) has proposed a *Cascade Model of Marital Dissolution.* Gottman clearly demonstrates the importance of examining patterns of communication across time to predict marital decay. There is a trajectory or cascade toward divorce with couples who eventually divorce remaining unhappily married for some time, seriously considering dissolution, then actually separating and divorcing. This cascade is predicted by a balance between positivity and negativity in the interaction. A causal mechanism in this theory is "flooding." Respondents say that a partner's negative behavior toward them is unprovoked, intense, overwhelming, and so disorganizing that they want to run away. Flooding sets off a process of distance and isolation in the marriage.

Indeed, in this theory, Gottman isolates three stable types of marriages: volatile couples (highest in emotional expressivity), validating couples (middle in emotional expressivity), and conflict avoiding couples (lowest in emotional expressivity). Gottman (1993, p. 66) acknowledges that these types are very similar to those isolated by Fitzpatrick (see discussion below).

In contrast to the Gottman (1979, 1993b) model based on affect is the Rogers and Farace (1975) model, which is based on power. Coding schemes and theories define couples according to their usual patterns of control in conversations (Ericson & Rogers, 1973; Mark, 1971; Sluzki & Beavin, 1965). Three types of couples can be defined by the message exchange patterns: symmetrical, complementary, and parallel (Lederer & Jackson, 1968; Watzlawick, Beavin, & Jackson, 1967).

Symmetrical couples have higher levels of role discrepancy; the couples who manifest lower proportions of competitive symmetry have higher levels of satisfaction in their marriages (Rogers, 1972). Symmetrical exchanges are more common among upper class couples (Mark, 1971), although these results are not replicated (Ericson, 1972).

Complementary couples, in which the husband is dominant, report higher levels of satisfaction and less role discrepancy (Courtright, Millar, & Rogers-Millar, 1979; Millar & Rogers, 1976). Parallel couples use a balance of these patterns across topics or situations. Because the research has been limited both on topics discussed and on interaction duration, it has been difficult to define parallel couples (see Noller & Fitzpatrick, 1993, pp. 136-140).

A major approach that links affect and power is that of Fitzpatrick and her colleagues (Fitzpatrick, 1988; Noller & Fitzpatrick, 1993, chap. 10). This polythetic classification scheme (Fitzpatrick, 1976, 1983, 1984; Fitzpatrick & Indvik, 1982) is based on three conceptual dimensions: interdependence, communication, and ideology. Interdependence and communication are affect dimensions, measured through the self-reports of individuals. Control has been measured by the gender role orientations, and the ideological beliefs and standards that couples hold on a variety of family issues have been salient in distinguishing among couples.

Based on these dimensions, individuals can be categorized in terms of one of three relationships definitions, which are traditional, independent, and separate. Traditionals (validating couples) are very interdependent in their marriages, have conventional ideological values about marriage and family life, and report an expressive communication style with their spouses. Independents (volatile couples) are moderately interdependent in their marriages, have nonconventional views about marriage and family life, and report a very expressive communication style with their mates. Separates (conflict avoiding couples) are not very interdependent in their marriage, are ambivalent about their views on marriage and family life, and report very little expressivity in their marital communication. An active program of research (e.g., Fitzpatrick, 1988; Fitzpatrick, Fey, Segrin, & Schiff, 1993; Fitzpatrick & Ritchie, 1994; Fitzpatrick, Vangelisti, & Firman, in press; Segrin & Fitzpatrick, 1992) has shown that the couple types can be discriminated on a number of self-report and behavioral dimensions.

An alternative typology focused on marital structure examined husbands' and wives' day-to-day lives together (Johnson, Huston, Gaines, & Levinger, 1992). The main classification principles centered on extent of participation in the labor force and in household activities. The four types of couples isolated did not differ in level of marital satisfaction. It remains to be seen if such an approach can predict patterns of communication in the marriage or the family.

The Marital Pair: Divorcing

Although it may seem curious to list separation and divorce as stages in the marital career, estimates on the divorce rate suggest between 30% to 40% of all marriages experience this stage (Thorton & Freedman, 1983). Even larger percentages of couples separate at some point in their marriages. Separation and divorce can be viewed as stages in a marital career not only because they occur frequently but also because they are viewed by individuals as serious crises involving major developmental changes. Most people marry, and marrying is associated with significant changes in the way we view ourselves, our partners, and our worlds. Consequently, the breakup (or potential breakup) of this relationship is a serious crisis (Bloom, White, & Asher, 1979). In most scales of stress and illness, the death of a spouse, divorce, and marital separation receive the highest stress scores (Holmes & Rahe, 1976).

Processes within individuals. Prior to 1960, most scholars were concerned with the identification of a broad range of demographic and personality correlates of marital happiness and stability (Burgess & Wallin, 1953; Terman, 1938). Longitudinal studies of the personality characteristics correlated with marital distress show that high levels of neuroticism in wives and low impulse control in husbands predict marital dissatisfaction and divorce (Kelly & Conley, 1987).

In an interesting study, Kurdek (1991) examined the demographic and personality variables that differentiated marriages breaking up after 1 year in contrast to those that remained stable as well as marriages differing in marital quality after 1 year. Those who separated/divorced during the first year had fewer years of education, lower incomes, knew each other fewer months, and had more (step)children. Three personality variables were particularly involved in marital distress and separation: Instrumental and external motives, in contrast to intrinsic motives, for being in the relationship, low social support, and severity of psychological distress are related to marital distress and instability.

Interpersonal processes. Divorce is not a single event but a series of legal, psychological, sexual, economic, and social events strung out over a period of time (Bohannan, 1970; Wallerstein & Kelly, 1980). One of the difficulties of studying divorce is that the legal fact is a poor marker for an interpersonal process. This legal step can occur at any number of places along a psychological continuum of relational dissolution. The separation that proceeds a divorce involves repeated distancing, partial reconciliation, new withdrawal, and eventual equilibrium for many couples (Weiss, 1975). This approach-avoidance conflict occurs because love erodes before attachment fades (Weiss, 1975). Attachment is a bonding process that gives rise to a feeling of ease when the partner is accessible (Bowlby, 1972). Attachment explains why many couples who are separating experience extreme distress even if both desired to separate.

Like the revisionist views of courtship (Bolton, 1961), disengagement is now conceptualized as a dialectical process that does not follow the same trajectory for all couples. The research on what individuals actually say during relational disintegration is nonexistent, although Miller and Parks (1982) have developed a taxonomy of disengagement strategies. Disengagement processes are difficult to examine as they occur. The procedures developed for retrospective accounts of courtship progress may be profitably adapted in this area (Huston et al., 1981).

What couples say to others is critical in the dissolution process. Six months after separation, women rehash and ruminate on the causes of the relationship disintegration (Harvey, Weber, Yarkin, & Stewart, 1982). Women relate dissolution to interpersonal problems rather than to the structural factors that men mention (Hill, Rubin, & Peplau, 1976). Called "grave dressing" (Duck, 1982) or "accounts" (Harvey et al., 1982; Weiss, 1975), these statements are histories of a relationship that structure events in a narrative sequence to allocate blame for relationship failures. Such accounts bring the social context into the study of relationships. Theorists in other areas of family processes would be wise to follow this lead and consider social context.

In considering marital dissolution, not only the stages through which a relationship passes but also patterned differences among individuals or couples (Kressel, Jaffee, Tuchman, Watson, & Deutsch, 1980) demand consideration. Kressel and his associates (1980) isolated types of divorcing couples. Each couple type approached the divorce in a different manner. Especially when children are involved, divorced couples continue in relationships with one another. A description of the form of this relationship appears in Ahrons and Rodgers (1987). These styles range from "Perfect Pals" to "Fiery Foes."

The Cohabiting Couple

Cohabitation is seen as a way to achieve closeness without sacrificing autonomy and independence (Newcomb, 1987). Most couples see cohabitation not as an alternative to marriage but as a prelude, because most plan to marry (Risman, Hill, Rubin, & Peplau, 1981). Cohabitation does, however, delay marriage (Newcomb

& Bentler, 1980). Between 20% and 30% of cohabiting couples marry one another (Newcomb, 1987).

Processes within individuals. In comparing cohabiting and married couples, few differences are found (Macklin, 1980). One large Australian study (Sarantakos, 1984) found no differences between the married and cohabiting couples on expressiveness, sex practices, empathy, organization (planning, rules, and responsibilities), sex roles, the involvement of women in careers, or cultural activities. Married couples did see their relationships as more stable and believed that they were more committed and helpful to their partners than were cohabiting couples. Finally, there was more conflict, even violent conflict, in cohabiting than in married couples.

Interpersonal processes. Does cohabiting help or hinder a subsequent marriage? Getting to know the foibles and idiosyncrasies of one's future partner potentially should prepare one for marriage. Of course, if a marriage contract is added to a cohabiting relationship that is failing, it is more likely to lead to shattered expectations and unhappiness (Newcomb, 1987). Lower levels of satisfaction and less satisfactory communication occur in marriages preceded by cohabitation (DeMaris & Leslie, 1984; Watson, 1983).

The Homosexual Couple

Homosexual males, in particular, are stereotyped as promiscuous and not interested in establishing lasting relationships (Blumstein & Schwartz, 1983). Yet, even without the social support given to married couples (e.g., recognized marriages, joint income tax), significant numbers of homosexual men and women have established healthy, functioning relationships. A number of different research strategies have been employed to examine these relationships. One strategy is to compare homosexual and heterosexual couples (e.g., Kurdek & Schmitt, 1986a, 1986b). Another is to explore these relationships in depth and to develop typologies of couples (e.g., McWhirter & Mattison, 1984). A third is to import an idea from an established line of inquiry on heterosexual couples and use it with a homosexual sample (Fitzpatrick, Jandt, Myrick, & Edgar, 1993).

Kurdek (1989) argues that at least three factors make it important to study homosexual couples separately from heterosexual couples. First, homosexual couples exist without supportive legal, social, and economic institutions. Second, partners in homosexual relationships cannot follow socially proscribed norms regarding partner roles. Third, because homosexual partners without children cannot assume roles associated with biological parenthood, their relationships are not affected by the complexities involved in negotiating spouse, worker, and parent roles. Kurdek (1989) further maintains that a close examination of homosexual couples can shed light on the role that gender-linked socialization plays in relational functioning.

Processes within individuals. The most popular means of classifying homosexual couples has been through sexual exclusivity. Researchers have used sexual fidelity as a means of classifying homosexuals. Bell and Weinberg (1978) used this open-closed dichotomy to explain a number of individual differences. For instance, gay males in closed relationships reported a higher degree of self-acceptance whereas those in open relationships were significantly more tense and depressed.

Blasband and Peplau (1985) found no differences between open and closed couples in their level of satisfaction with, and commitment to, the relationship. Openness in the relationship does not mean that couples are not committed.

Interpersonal processes. In a longitudinal study of relationship quality in homosexual couples, greater relationship quality was reported by lesbian, compared with homosexual male, couples and by couples living together for more than 11 years (Kurdek, 1989). Reciprocal expressiveness and equality of power seem to be important themes in lesbian relationships (Kurdek & Schmitt, 1986a; Peplau & Cochran, 1981). For male partners, relational quality after 1 year was best predicted by satisfaction with social support, high levels of expressiveness, and few beliefs that conflict was destructive.

Using the Relational Dimensions Instrument, a sample of lesbian and male homosexual couples were characterized as Traditional, Separate, Independent, and Mixed couples. Compared with the major random sample of heterosexual couples (Fitzpatrick & Indvik, 1982), there were significantly more male Separate couples, about the same proportion of Traditionals and fewer Independents. For lesbian couples, there were significantly more Traditionals yet fewer Separates and Independents. The sampling strategy may account for these results. The sample was drawn from Couples National Network, an organization formed to provide education and outreach to individuals involved in homosexual relationships. Indeed, Harry and Lovely (1979) found that individuals who were most integrated into the homosexual community were in relationships that were more "marriagelike." That is, they tended to live with their lovers, had monogamous arrangements, and had more emotional intimacy. And their social lives were more likely to include relationships with other homosexual couples. In typology terms, such individuals are more likely to have traditional orientations toward relationships. Some of these individuals pair a traditional orientation with a close interdependent bond (i.e., Traditionals) and others will pair that ideology with a less connected bond (i.e., Separates).

The Sibling Relationship

Eighty percent of the population live the first third of their lives in families with siblings. The interactions that children have with their siblings have a profound influence on the personal happiness that they experience in the family growing up (Bowerman & Dobash, 1974). And early affective relationships between siblings appear to predict interaction between them in adulthood (Bank & Kahn, 1982a, 1982b).

Influenced by Freud (1949), much of the early literature on family interaction discussed the sibling relationship in terms of negative affect (Bossard & Boll, 1950). Children show signs of hostility, anxiety, and competition at the birth of a younger sibling (Cameron, 1963). Siblings tend to compete in the family for the love, attention, and favor of one or both of the parents (Levy, 1937). Sibling rivalry purportedly is much stronger when the age interval between children is 4 years or less (Koch, 1956). Some recent observational work in families finds no empirical support for this age interval hypothesis in the observed aggressive, imitative, or prosocial behaviors of children toward their close or far interval siblings (Abramovitch, Corter, & Lando, 1979; Abramovitch, Corter, & Peplar, 1980; Dunn & Kendrick, 1981). During the beginning of the school years, however, increased positive behavior and decreased aggression to a widely spaced (much younger) sibling may appear (Minnett, Vandell, & Santrock, 1983). Whatever the degree of hostility between siblings, it may be resolved by consistent parental affection, the development of an attachment bond between siblings, and the socialization of aggression (Tsukada, 1979).

Other more positive aspects of the interaction between siblings have been given less attention. The possession of a sibling may make early socialization complete because siblings provide peer role models and training in cooperation, conflict management, and accommodation. They also offer to one another companionship, security, and love (Duberman, 1973). Indeed, siblings may create for one another very different environments within the family.

Processes within individuals. The most extensive work that has been undertaken on sibling relationships examines the effects of birth order on personality development and achievement (Falbo, 1981; Toman, 1961). Characteristic personality traits for each birth order are described. Even the eventual marital adjustment of an individual is linked to position in the family of origin (Toman, 1961). It is entirely plausible that individual differences in tactics, aggression, sex role preferences, and interests in later-born children can be attributed to the processes of identification and modeling of older siblings. The conforming, achievement, and affiliative behaviors of only and first-born children may be attributed to the children's special relationship to the parents (Sutton-Smith & Rosenberg, 1970).

Very few studies of the interaction between parents and children or between siblings have been conducted to test these ideas. Much of this research has been motivated by curiosity rather than theory. Arguing that a structural subposition in a family unit leads to given personality outcomes for an individual leaves the question of "why" unanswered. Some appreciation of the psychological or communication conditions that occur when an individual occupies a particular birth-order position (Schvaneveldt & Ihinger, 1979) is necessary to understand why a specific birth position in a family leads to given outcomes for a family member. Furthermore, serious methodological flaws must be corrected in these studies (Schooler, 1972). Sampling error, as well as failure to control for socioeconomic status, cohort effects, or the stage in family development, leave most of the empirical findings on this topic in confusion. Finally, behavioral genetics researchers argue that only about 1% to 2% of the variance in behavior for siblings is due to birth-order position (Dunn & Plomin, 1990).

Interpersonal processes. Sibling status variables of age, birth order, birth interval, and sex do not account adequately for sibling differences (Scarr & Grajek, 1982). Dunn (1983) argues that these constructs may be inadequate to account for sibling behavior because they reference complementary behaviors (A is older than B) in an attempt to predict reciprocal behaviors (A and B are mutually aggressive). Conceptual discriminations between peer, sibling, and parent-child interaction in terms of reciprocity and complementarity would help. Although recent theoretical interest in the development and maintenance of peer relationships in children may not be directly applicable to the study of siblings (for example, Hartup, 1978; La Gaipa, 1981), valuable lines of research could examine the nature of differences in peer and sibling interactions.

Peer interactions are reciprocal interactions in that each can understand the reasoning and perspective of the other. Sibling relationships include the direct reciprocity of peers because of their intensity, familiarity, intimacy, and the recognition and sharing of interests. The frequent imitation by siblings of the actions of one another, the demonstration of joy and excitement in coaction sequences, and the willingness of each to engage in prosocial and comforting actions are examples of reciprocity of interaction between sibling pairs.

Parent-child interactions are complementary interactions in that the behavior of each differs from but fits that of the other. Given the age differences between siblings, these relationships also have aspects of the parent-child relationship (Dunn, 1983, pp. 788-789). Caregiving, teaching, attachment, and language are aspects of inherent complementarity in sibling relationships. Unfortunately, however, few studies (see Dunn, 1983) actually mathematically examine the reciprocal or complementary structure of the interaction. Sibling studies report rates and/or frequencies; these are inadequate for summarizing social interaction over time.

Four-year-olds are capable of making speech adjustments to two-year-olds (Shatz & Gelman, 1977) and can adjust their communication to dolls representing others (Sachs & Devin, 1976). All the 2- and 3-year-olds studied (Dunn & Kendrick, 1982) made systematic adjustments in speaking to their 14-month-old siblings. Older siblings tend to clarify their speech for their conversational partner, but only those older siblings who had particularly warm relationships with the infants used expressive linguistic features. Conversational turns in these sibling interactions were shorter than those of the mother with the infant and were not responded to as strongly by the infant. Both mother and infant attempted to maintain the attention of the other, whereas sibling-infant turns were primarily nonverbal sequences such as alternate imitations of one another over a shorter span of time.

Comparisons of the interactions of 4- to 8-year-old children with parents and with siblings indicated that the interaction behavior of a target child was remarkably different with parents versus siblings (Baskett & Johnson, 1982). Interactions with the parent were more numerous and varied than were those with a sibling. Children talked, laughed, and touched the parents more and were more compliant with their wishes. Undesirable behaviors directed to parents seemed designed primarily to draw attention (for example, whining, demands for attention, and so forth). Only one prosocial behavior occurred more frequently in sibling interactions than in parent-child interactions: Siblings did tend to play or work with one another more. In general, brothers and sisters used more physical aggression, yelling, hitting, and negative commands with one another than they did with parents. Regardless of the state of the relationships between the siblings, the siblings preferred interacting with a parent to interacting with their sibling.

Preschool-age children both offer their toys and talk to their 18-month-old siblings. The toddlers watch and imitate the older children and take over the toys the older child abandoned (Lamb, 1978). Both same- and mixed-sex sibling dyads of close and far spacing interact a great deal. A sib initiates or responds to the other member of the dyad once a minute. Regardless of the sex or age differences among the dyads, older children in each pair initiate more (84%) of the antagonistic acts and most of the prosocial acts as well. In both same- and mixed sex dyads, younger children initiate most of the imitative behaviors. In same-sex dyads, older boys are more physically aggressive than older girls. Girls tend to initiate more prosocial acts and respond positively to the prosocial acts of a sister (Abramovitch et al., 1979; Abramovitch et al., 1980).

Eighteen months later, a subset of the same-sibling pairs (mixed and same sex) was observed. Their ages ranged from 3 years to 7 years and as before they were categorized according to small age spacing (1 to 2 years) or large age spacing (2½ to 4 years). The interaction patterns among the children were approximately the same. Older children engaged in more cooperation, help, and praise. Although older children initiated interaction more often, the younger child maintained the interaction by reciprocating prosocial behavior, submitting to aggressive behavior, and imitating his or her siblings. As children got older, they tended to increase the number of prosocial acts in their sibling contacts. Yet there also was an increase in mixed-sex antagonism and a decrease in mixed-sex imitation. The occurrence of these sex differences in the interactive behaviors of siblings may indicate the beginning of sex typing (Peplar, Abramovitch, & Corter, 1981).

Children as young as 4 years old serve as attachment figures for siblings. In one sample of young children, over 52% were effective in caring for their younger siblings who were distressed when the mother left the room. Infants seem to use the sibling as an attachment figure and a secure base from which to explore (Stewart, 1983).

Recently there has been an increased interest in studying sibling relationships in middle childhood. Sibling relationships become more egalitarian during middle childhood, although there is some disagreement as to whether this represents a decrease in dominance attempts by both siblings (Buhrmester, 1992) or an increase in the power exerted by young children on their older siblings (Vandell, Minnett, & Santrock, 1987).

For preadolescents, Furman and Buhrmester (1985) found that affection, hostility, and rivalry are relatively independent dimensions of children's relationships with siblings. One recent study examined preadolescents' perceptions of their sibling relationships and the links between sibling relationships and parent-child relationships in 103 families. Sibling ratings of affection were highly correlated but ratings of hostility and rivalry were not related. Children who spent the most time interacting with their fathers and who rated their relationship with the father as a warm one had the most positive and the least negative sibling relationships (Stocker & McHale, 1992).

Little work has been done on the interaction patterns of older sibling pairs. The majority of adolescents say they are close to their siblings. Adolescent females report more affect toward their siblings than do males; same-sex siblings are preferred; and younger children have stronger affect toward older siblings than vice versa. In addition, affect decreases with age and is stronger in families with two children (Bowerman & Dobash, 1974). The sibling relationship with the greatest contrast in feeling, and hence the most risk for conflict, is the older brother-younger sister relationship. The least contrast in feeling, with less risk for conflict, is the older sister-younger brother relationship. Although Raffaelli (1992) does not find support for these gender differences in conflict among siblings in early adolescence, she does find that sibling conflict in this period does not appear to be motivated by rivalry. Instead, sibling conflict appears to create a context where age-appropriate issues of individuation and differentiation are played out.

According to Dunn (1992), three new themes in sibling research have emerged. The first is an examination of the links between sibling relationships and parent-child relationships. We need to know how extensive these links are and what processes mediate such associations. One important question is whether the security of children's attachment to parents is linked to the quality of their later sibling relationships. Attachment theory would predict that children who are insecurely attached to their parents would be more hostile to their siblings (Teti & Ablard, 1989).

A second important theme in this research concerns differential parental treat-ment. Boer and his colleagues (Boer, Goedhart, & Treffers, 1992) argue that there is a consensus in the research that differential maternal treatment is linked to more conflicted and hostile sibling relationships. Indeed, there may be some interactive effects of attachment security and differential treatment. Differential treatment may be particularly problematic for children who are insecurely attached (Volling & Belsky, 1991).

A final theme centers on the effect of parental intervention in sibling conflict. Correlational evidence exists that parental intervention is related to increases in sibling conflict (Brody & Stoneman, 1987) but it is not clear that parental interven-tion leads to increased conflict between siblings.

Importantly, siblings influence one another at every stage in the development of their personal identities. Such influence may be accomplished through social comparison processes, which specifically occur in sibling but not necessarily in peer interactions (Tesser, 1980). Siblings tend to compare themselves with one another on a number of dimensions such as attractiveness, intelligence, accomplish-ments, and so forth.

More than peers or even other family members, siblings are accessible to one another during the entire length of the developmentally formative years. They share time, space, and personal history to a degree unlikely in peer relationships (Bank & Kahn, 1982a, 1982b). We may turn to our siblings later in life in times of family crises, such as divorce (Ambrose, Harper, & Pemberton, 1983). Indeed, at the end of our lives, our living companions and our best friends will often turn out to be our siblings (Bedford & Gold, 1989).

The Parent-Child Relationship

Early work on the relationship between parents and children assumed that influence processes were unidirectional in a family. The assumption underlying these *social mold* approaches viewed the child as a passive partner in socialization, awaiting the molding of its parents (Hartup, 1978). With the realization that a child contributes to the marriage and the family, more child-centered theories emerged (Bell, 1968). Peterson and Rollins (1987) call these *mirror reverse* orientations because they stipulate that children's behavior may change or influence parents. Not only when they reach adolescence or adulthood but also as an infant, a neonate, or even in utero, children can influence a broad variety of family processes (Lerner & Spanier, 1978). The behavior of even the youngest child can stimulate, elicit, motivate, and reward the actions of parents.

Currently, both the social mold and the mirror reverse orientations have been supplanted by a perspective that views parents and children as simultaneously and mutually influencing one another. These mutual influence approaches (e.g., Cappella, 1987) see each family member serving as the stimuli for the other's behavior. Most of the research on processes within individuals operates on a social mold frame-work, although we do see some development of the mirror reverse and mutual influence perspectives in studies of interpersonal processes.

Processes within individuals. Research on individual social behaviors generally focuses on how parental message selection influences the development of a variety of characteristics in the child (Hess, 1981). Parental messages can be broadly characterized as support and control messages (Rollins & Thomas, 1979; Steinmetz, 1979). Behaviors that make a child feel comfortable in the presence of a parent are support messages. These include praising, approving, encouraging, physical displays of affection, giving help, and cooperating with a child.

Behaviors designed to gain compliance with the wishes of the parent are called control messages. Control messages include coercion, induction, and love withdrawal. Coercive messages focus on external reasons the child should comply with the parent. These messages involve physical punishment, the direct application of force, the deprivation of material objects or privileges, or the threat of these. Controlling strategies have been negatively associated with children's self-esteem, academic achievement, and creativity (Peterson & Rollins, 1987).

Vangelisti (1992) identified problems in the relationships of parents and adolescent children as stemming from the negotiation of control. The majority of adolescents' past communication problems with parents focused on parents' attempts to control their behavior. Those adolescents who blame their parents for past communication problems are likely to be significantly less satisfied with their relationship than were those adolescents who blamed other factors. In highly salient situations, Comstock and Buller (1991) found that older adolescents willingly used competitive strategies with parents but it was the parent's initial strategy that set the tone of the response.

Induction messages focus on the internal reasons the child should comply with the parent. Induction involves explanations and reasons for compliance. A parent might, for example, point out the consequences of an act for the child or for others. A major program of research that examines inductive messages used by parents with children is that of the constructivists (e.g., Applegate, Burleson, & Delia, 1992). These theorists are particularly concerned with reflection-enhancing communication or messages that encourage children to see how actions grow out of and create psychological states. Individual differences in parental message style are related to the development of communication competence in children.

Love withdrawal uses a combination of internal and external forces for compliance. These techniques indicate disapproval of the child's behavior with the implication that love will not be restored until the child does what the parent wishes. Love withdrawal is manifested by ignoring the child, isolating the child, explicit statements of rejection, or nonverbal behaviors signaling coldness or disappointment (Rollins & Thomas, 1979).

Stafford and Bayer (1993) have written a comprehensive review of the effects of supportive and controlling parental messages on self-control, self-esteem, and communication competence. These authors, for example, note that the empirical research on love withdrawal has had mixed results but it may be because the concept has been poorly operationalized. The interested reader should consult Stafford and Bayer (1993).

In examining the effects of parental messages on children, both sex composition of the dyad (e.g., father-daughter) and developmental level of the child must be considered. We need to consider not parents and children but fathers and mothers, sons and daughters. The use of message techniques should vary in subtlety as the child develops cognitively (Applegate, Burke, Burleson, Delia, & Kline, 1983). Indeed, the ability of a mother or father to adjust his or her messages based on the developmental level of the child is paramount in all styles.

Beyond considering the sex composition of the dyad and the developmental level of the child, it may be of great theoretical utility to link the input and performance variables that we have been discussing to the output variables in Table 19.2. Certain compliance-gaining procedures may work equally well in socializing a child to the wishes of a parent yet have remarkably different effects on family solidarity. And as Stafford and Bayer (1993) point out, certain message styles may only be effective in the short term in gaining compliance.

(1) Multiple messages. Our discussion of parent-child communication has proceeded as if communication existed on only one level. Of course, communication occurs across many levels (Bateson, 1975). Messages that contradict one another across the various levels of communication are taken to be related to a variety of dysfunctional outcomes for families. One type of inconsistent message that has been examined extensively is the *double bind*. Messages from different channels (verbal, prosodic, kinesic, facial, and so forth) may create a paradox by the simultaneous assertion of contradictory meanings. (a) If this situation occurs many times, (b) in an intense relationship (c) in which partners cannot comment on the paradox (d) or escape the situation, (e) this constitutes a double bind (Abeles, 1976).

Despite the importance of this construct in the interactional view, there is little empirical support that double binds actually lead to dysfunctional family outcomes (Olson, 1972). Double binds are, however, very difficult to examine. Given all the previously named conditions (a through e), it may be impossible to create double binds in a laboratory experiment.

The most obvious pathology associated with the double bind—namely, schizophrenia—is now believed to have a neurochemical basis (Garmezy, 1974). There are, however, communication difficulties in families of schizophrenics. Indeed, the onset of schizophrenia seems to require both a genetic predisposition and a disturbed family environment. Parents of schizophrenics are unable to share a focus of attention, to take the perspective of one another, and to communicate meaning clearly and accurately (Goldstein & Strachan, 1987). Thus parents of schizophrenics do show communication deficits. And these families are marked by high levels of criticism and negativity (Goldstein, 1985, 1987).

Despite the disappointing laboratory tests on the double bind, studies on the consistency of verbal and nonverbal channels of communication continue to be viewed as valuable enterprises. There appear to be significant differences in the communication consistency of mothers of disturbed versus normal children (Bugental & Love, 1975). Specifically, mothers of disturbed children sent more inconsistent messages than mothers of normal children (mean age 9; see Bugental, Love, Kaswan, & April, 1971). Mothers may have "perfidious female faces" in that, in both normal and disturbed families, mothers smiled regardless of the content of the messages they sent to their children (Bugental, 1974; Bugental, Love, & Gianetto, 1971). Although intriguing, these results have not been replicated in five other studies (Jacob & Lessin, 1982).

Although the examination of inconsistency in family communication continues to be a topic of importance for all interested in family processes, more attention should be paid to theoretical models of the relationships among channels of communication. Communication channels carry differential levels of information for receivers. This area may be especially important in studying individuals who have interaction histories with one another such as family members. The psychological reality of channel inconsistency is a major point that must be considered in studies of family communication (Folger & Poole, 1980). Inconsistencies in channel usage probably reach a particular level before they are perceived by communicators (Atkinson & Allen, 1983). Functional approaches to the study of nonverbal communication that examine multiple cues may give the study of inconsistent family communication a needed theoretical transfusion (for example, Patterson, 1983).

(2) Interpersonal processes. Much of the research on interpersonal processes has focused on the mother-child dyad. As young as 7 weeks, infants and their mothers have been observed in "proto-conversations" or interactive sequences characterized by eye gazing, face-to-face orientation, patterns of turn-taking, variations in vocal intonation, and obvious mutual pleasure (Bateson, 1975; Stern, 1977). Researchers in mother-infant interaction have developed elaborate and powerful models of dyadic interaction to explain these processes. In these models, communication, in its most basic form, involves mutuality, intersubjectivity, and reciprocity (Ryan, 1974).

Infants are predisposed to the development of primitive communication skills. From early on, the behavior of an infant forms patterned, functional units that are easy to recognize. The first communication from a baby is a cry. As infants selectively attend to the world around them, they indicate a preference for human faces over other shapes and look at faces and try to talk to them rather than to bottles or breasts (R. Q. Bell, 1974). Infants also have preferences for the human voice, and by the end of the first month can be quieted by soft, high-pitched talking (Kaplan & Kaplan, 1971).

Caregivers recognize these patterned units and assume that at least some of them provide indications of what is happening inside the infant (Richards, 1974). They respond to the differential cries of an infant and identify three types of cries: hunger, pain, or anger. Objectively, these cries differ in terms of pitch, pattern, and intonation (Wasz-Hockert, Lind, Vuorenkoski, Partenen, & Valarne, 1968; Wolff, 1971). The caregiver helps the infant not only to achieve appropriate levels of tension and arousal but also to organize the behavior to which the caregiver contingently responds (Sroufe, 1979). A baby's smiles, burps, and coos are responded to by an adult as turns in conversation. Caregivers use tag questions and other postcompleters to pass the conversational turn to a baby (Snow, 1972). Indeed, the greater the use of questions by the mother, the greater the mother's desire to interact reciprocally with her infant (Snow, 1977). Effective caregivers even fill in a turn for an inactive baby (Spieker, 1982) by acting as if the baby had responded in the appropriate sequence.

Caregivers adjust their speech when speaking to infants and children at early stages of language acquisition. Mothers adjust their speech to young infants to keep the conversation going and to engage the attention of the infant (Kaye, 1980; Snow, 1977). With infants of 6 months or older, the mother adjusts her speech by using syntactically simpler utterances to make herself understood by the child. Many theorists believe that this adjustment helps both the child's understanding and the child's general linguistic capacity (Bellinger, 1980; but see Stafford & Bayer, 1993, pp. 81-84).

"Baby talk" differs from other talk in prosody, in redundancy, and in grammatical complexity (Wells & Robinson, 1982). The various features of baby talk serve different and orthogonal functions. The clarification function is served by the "comm register," which includes the attention-getting devices noted in "motherese" (Snow, 1977) and in the simplification of speech and its prosodic characteristics. The expressive function is served by the "aff register," which is primarily verbal and includes the use of pet names, the playful repetition of names, and the use of diminutives and endearments. Because babies are both linguistically incompetent and typically inspire affection, baby talk occurs in both comm and aff registers.

Clarification and expressive functions may be extended to adult conversations. In families or close relationships, those who are perceived as incompetent may periodically be addressed in the comm register and those who inspire affection may be addressed at certain times in the aff register. Research on caregiver-elderly interaction suggests that the elderly, during caretaking interactions in nursing homes, are addressed in the comm register (Giles, 1984; Giles, Coupland, & Wiemann, 1990) and that spouses and lovers tend to be addressed in the aff register (Hopper, Knapp, & Scott, 1981).

These early interactions facilitate the learning of language. Reciprocity (sensitivity to the partner) and intersubjectivity (experience of two persons with shared knowledge of the world) set the stage for the onset of intentional communication. Babies begin to look at a desired object, gesture and vocalize toward it, and alternate glances between the desired object and the caregiver. The emergence at 9 months of this intentional signaling is a major stage in language development (Bates, 1979; Bates, Camaioni, & Volterra, 1975). By developing a stable group of conventional gestures, babies are making the discovery that the objects they desire have names (Spieker, 1982). The similar focus on objects by the caregiver and the infant helps the infant to learn words. Primitive communication, followed by attachment between infants and caregivers, sets the stage not only for language learning but for most other facets of a child's development.

(3) The attachment bond. The interaction we have been describing takes place during the first 6 months of an infant's life. These interaction patterns set the stage for the development of the attachment bond. Attachment is a tie that one person forms to another specific person, which binds them together in space and endures over time. An infant appears to become attached to the figure or figures with whom he or she has the most interaction (Ainsworth, 1973; Ainsworth & Bell, 1969). Attachment is indicated by behaviors that promote proximity such as signaling behavior like crying, smiling, and vocalizing; orienting behavior such as looking, moving toward, or following the other; and active physical contact such as clinging or embracing.

Attachment theory claims that during the first year of life children develop fairly stable attitudes about themselves and the world around them on the basis of the responsiveness of their caregivers (Bowlby, 1980; but see Dunn, 1988). Children whose caregivers are responsive come to see themselves as worthy of love and others as trustworthy and dependable. Infants may be secure, avoidant, or anxious-ambivalent (Ainsworth, Blehar, Waters, & Wall, 1978). Secures are generally comfortable with closeness or intimacy and are not concerned about being abandoned; avoidants are generally uncomfortable with closeness; anxious-ambivalents crave closeness but tend to be afraid of abandonment.

The attachment bond between a mother and an infant predisposes the infant to comply, at a later date, with the wishes of the mother. The willingness to be obedient rather than any understanding of the content of the mother's message emerges from the development of a secure attachment bond in the dyad. Infants categorized as securely or anxiously attached to their mothers at 18 months of age were followed at 24 months. Infants who could employ their caregivers as a secure base from which to explore and who positively greeted their mothers following a stressful separation experience (or were comforted by her presence) displayed more skill in problem solving and were more cooperative than were the less securely attached toddlers (Matas, Arend, & Sroufe, 1982). Infants appear initially inclined to be social and, somewhat later, ready to comply with the wishes of those persons who are most significant in their environment (Stayton, Hogan, & Ainsworth, 1982). Compliance from the young occurs only when affect has been established in the relationships.

Previous work on attachment placed primary emphasis on emotion. Recent explanations have, however, assigned a central role to cognitive factors. The appearance of separation anxiety between 8 and 12 months is considered the behavioral manifestation of attachment. Separation distress at the temporary (permanent) loss of the caregiver occurs at this stage in cognitive development because the infant can retrieve a schema for an event that is not in the immediate visual field. The infant's ability to recall stored information, to retrieve a past schema, and to compare that schema with the present information is now thought to lead to the emotional distress (Kagan, 1979).

In our discussion, we have shifted between the terms *caregiver* and *mother*. Most theories assume the primacy of the mother-infant bond (Bowlby, 1972; Freud, 1949; Winnicott, 1964). In these theories, the mother is uniquely important in the child's life because she spends the most time with the child and has the most interaction. The amount of actual mother-infant interaction is, however, highly overestimated, and simple time spent together is a poor predictor of the quality of an infant's relationships with anyone (Lamb, 1976b). A few hours of pleasurable interaction appear to be more conducive to the development of a bond between the infant and an adult than do more extensive hours with a less stimulating caregiver (Birnbaum, 1971; Lamb, 1976b).

The ability of an infant to form attachments to more than one primary figure has clear survival value (Mead, 1942). Infants form attachments to both fathers and mothers, although the nature of the interaction between infant and each parent may differ. Fathers engage in more play and mothers in more caregiving activities with an infant. Infants prefer the physical, nonintellectual, rough-and-tumble play initiated by fathers (Lamb, 1976a; Parke & O'Leary, 1976). American fathers do not seem to mind child socializing yet they still reject child care (Slocum & Nye, 1976). Even cross-culturally, taking a child to the park is now an appropriate role for both fathers and mothers, yet changing a diaper is still women's work.

In a careful review of the existing literature, Belsky (1990) has recently argued that inconsistent, unresponsive, and unsupportive care for children, particularly when it is tinged with negative affect, eventually fosters uncooperative and problematic behavior. Belsky (1990) argues that more than 20 hours a week of nonmaternal care for a child under 1 year of age may be a risk factor leading to less secure attachments between mothers and children. There has been a firestorm of controversy on this issue (Belsky, 1990, p. 895) especially because 51% of mothers with children under the age of 1 are employed outside the home (O'Connell & Bachu, 1987). And there is recent evidence for continuity of attachment style from infancy and into school years (Main, Kaplan, & Cassidy, 1985). The attachment approach has been extended to the study of adult romantic relationships and marriage (Feeney, Noller, & Callan, in press; Fitzpatrick et al., 1993).

Family Triads and Beyond

Riskin and Faunce's (1972) observation that the least studied family unit was the family itself still holds today. As we have seen, much of the research on the family involves studying husband-wife or mother-child dyads. Although some research does consider triads or even a four-person family group, relatively little research effort is directed at the whole family. The research that is conducted, however, is increasingly sophisticated.

Processes within individuals. One of the marked changes since this last review was written (Fitzpatrick & Badzinski, 1985) has been in the growth and development of the field of personal and social relationships. This growth had a marked impact on studies of family communication. In many journals traditionally dedicated to the study of social processes (e.g., *Journal of Personality and Social Psychology*), the object of the study or the target of the research will be some close relationship partner or family member rather than the ubiquitous college sophomore. In the space allotted, we could not possibly do justice to this research but we do alert the reader to be aware of this trend.

Family structure (e.g., intact nuclear family) is a social category that is potentially a cue for the formation of stereotypes. A stereotype is a special form of cognitive schema that oversimplifies and overgeneralizes. In exploring the degree to which family structure was stereotyped, Ganong, Coleman, and Mapes (1990) found that the nuclear family is the standard by which all other family forms are evaluated. Individuals believed to be from nuclear families are evaluated more positively than individuals in any other family form. Married adults are perceived more favorably than are adults with other statuses; and children whose parents are married are perceived more favorably than are children whose parents are not married to each other. Despite the increase in family diversity, cultural stereotypes related to family structure have not changed in recent years. What are the implications of these stereotypes? Stereotypes may affect perceptions such that what is perceived is consistent with already held beliefs. Beliefs about a group may also affect interactions with members of the group. Finally, such stereotypes may affect how members of different family forms perceive and value themselves.

People have clear expectations about how family members should communicate (Vangelisti, 1991). These expectations include mind reading, positive affect, conflict, honesty, personal boundaries, and support. Individuals who had high expectations about the display of positive affect in the family were likely to describe their own family as open, able to speak about a broad variety of topics, and physically affectionate.

Interpersonal processes. An extremely good introduction to designing studies of family interaction is that of Howe and Reiss (1993). In this chapter, they discuss the strengths and weaknesses of two related observational methods for examining family process: simulation and experimentation. They provide an overview of many classic studies of family interaction and the decision processes through which researchers proceed in order to amplify, isolate, or contrast aspects of family process.

Studying the family group is a complicated enterprise. Consider the triad with the parents as P1 and P2. There are at least nine different direct and indirect ways that the interaction in any triad can be modified (Parke, 1979). A researcher could examine the impact of:

(a) P1's modification of P2's behavior on the child,

(b) P2's modification of P1's behavior on the child,

(c) P1-child relationship on P2-child interaction,

(d) P2-child relationship on P1-child interaction,

(e) P1's modification of child's behavior on P2-child interaction,

(f) P2's modification of child's behavior on P1-child interaction,

(g) P1-child relationship on P1-P2 relationship,

(h) P2-child relationship on P1-P2 relationship, and

(i) P1-P2 relationship on the child.

Each of the nine listed influence pathways in triadic interaction can be studied in a triad (and generalizations beyond to the four- and five-person family). Each may be an important piece of the puzzle of family process. Recent research is exploring many of these pathways as well as extensions to other potential triads. Since the early 1980s, for example, Belsky and his colleagues in the Pennsylvania Infant and Family Development project have been trying to examine direct and indirect effects in family process. In one study that explored the ninth (i) pathway, Belsky, Youngblade, Rovine, and Volling (1991) argued that the quality of the marital relationship influences parent-child relationships. They found that husbands who are less in love with their wives and less maritally satisfied behave toward their children in a more negative and intrusive manner than did the happily married husbands. Mothers seem less affected in their relationships with their children by the level of marital distress. Relationship linkages are being systematically examined (Hinde & Stevenson-Hinde, 1988; Patterson, 1992).

In mother-infant-toddler triads, the interaction between a mother and a first-born child changed in negative direction when the mother was feeding or caring for the newborn (Kendrick & Dunn, 1980). The intervention of a mother in sibling quarrels has been linked to differences in the frequency of hostile behavior between siblings 3 months later (Kendrick & Dunn, 1982). Parent-infant interaction may be affected by the presence of the other parent. Mothers interact with and smile more at their infants alone than they do in the presence of the fathers; in contrast, fathers engage in those activities with the infant only when the mother is present (Parke & O'Leary, 1976). The overall quality of mother-infant interaction may be decreased by the presence of the father (Clarke-Stewart, 1982; Parke & O'Leary, 1976). Yet it appears that the quality of the father-infant interaction is higher when the mother is present.

If these findings generalize, we may be able to argue for a radical shift in the quality of interaction with the addition of another person to the mother-child dyad. This shift has intriguing implications for models of family communication. It may be that there is an inherent limitation in the amount and quantity of affect that can be expressed in these family triads.

As the research on family interaction expands to consider the variety of effects listed above (as well as many others), the relationships among relationships need to be considered. That is, we need to consider how the mutual influence process might operate across family subgroups. That is, relationships across various family members may be *congruous*, in that members interact in similar, albeit developmentally appropriate, ways with one another. Relationships may be *complementary*, in that members interact in different, albeit developmentally appropriate, ways. And we need to take seriously the idea that various relationships may be *independent* of one another. The research on family interaction is increasing in methodological sophistication. Unfortunately, much of the research does not allow us to make particular theoretical claims about which processes or mechanisms underlie these interactional differences. In studies that find unhappily married fathers are more negative to their children as well as their wives, a number of mechanisms might be offered to explain these findings. Personality explanations, for example, might argue that the father has a set of negative traits that cause him to be unpleasant to his wife and his children. Alternately, personality explanations might argue that the mother and child share a set of negative personality traits that "draw" negative behavior from the husband. Attachment theory would propose that the husband's negative interpersonal behavior to his wife stems from his insecure attachment to her, derived from his early experiences. This insecure attachment leads him also to be negative in his interpersonal behavior to his children—and so forth. Experiments need to be designed to rule out potential competing theoretical explanations for interactional behaviors (see Howe & Reiss, 1993).

(1) Family interaction and deviance. The major paradigm guiding research on the family as a unit was that which linked disturbed family communication processes to psychological and social deviance outcomes for offspring. Such a perspective dates to at least the 1950s. Bateson's group at Palo Alto, Bowen and Wynne at NIMH, Lidz and his associates at Yale, and Ackerman's research group at the Family Mental Health Clinic in New York were independently arriving at the conclusion that observable, ongoing family interaction patterns could be directly linked to negative outcomes for children (Raush et al., 1979).

The purpose of the research is usually to discriminate functional from dysfunctional families on the basis of their interaction patterns. Whereas work in the early 1960s concentrated on the differences between normal and schizophrenic families (see the review by Jacob, 1975), research in the 1970s branched out to include abusive and neglectful families (for example, Burgess & Conger, 1978), families with an abnormally aggressive (for example, Patterson, 1976) or delinquent child (for example, Alexander, 1973), or an alcoholic (for example, Steinglass et al., 1987) or depressed parent (Coyne, Kahn, & Gottlib, 1987).

Overall, researchers have found that clinic-referred children and adolescents are likely to come from families in which positive, nurturant, and supportive behaviors occur at depressed rates whereas noxious, aversive, or negative interactions are relatively frequent (Conger, 1981, 1983). Although some research was conducted to see how normal families of various levels of functioning interacted (for example, Lewis et al., 1976; Loeb, 1975), most family research explores the interaction differences between healthy and unhealthy families. The differences between these two types are expected to outweigh the differences within these types.

The key question in this type of research is this: What is the role of the family in the etiology, course, treatment, and prevention of psychopathological disorders (Jacob, 1987)? Although the mapping of interaction differences in disturbed and nondisturbed families continues (for example, Coyne et al., 1987), two new directions are evident in family interaction studies. First, concern is now shown for describing normal family processes in a range of different temporal, structural, and sociocultural contexts (Walsh, 1992). The basic research strategy should be to maximize the variance between groups and minimize the variance within groups. Unfortunately, often the variance within groups (i.e., within either the troubled or the normal family) is far too high. In a systematic review of the literature up until that time, Jacob (1975) found that, within the schizophrenic family category, the research might include families with very young adolescents who suffered from the disorder and families with 40-year-old children who suffered form the disorder. Similarly, grouping families into a normal group simply because they share a set of sociodemographic similarities with one another may be obscuring important process differences within various family types.

The second major trend is a rather subtle move away from pathology to the study of health. The question becomes: How is it that some children are so resilient to negative family environments (e.g., Rutter, 1985)? Rather than focus on dysfunction, the emphasis in this tradition is on why and how some families are able to adjust and adapt to stress, distress, and crises.

(2) Baby makes three. One extensively studied family process is the birth of the first child. From one dyad (husband-wife), the family now contains three (husband-wife, father-child, mother-child). The birth of a child represents a 200% increase in the number of dyads in the family as well as the possibility of a triad (mother-father-child). Change from an existing pattern may induce stress, crisis, and even dysfunction, yet change is often a necessary condition for developmental growth.

For many couples, the arrival of a child has a negative impact on their marital quality, especially for wives (LaRossa, 1977; LeMasters, 1957). The birth of the first child has even been called a "crisis" (LeMasters, 1957). Considering the birth of a baby to be a crisis is an overstatement, although the event necessitates a rather complex shift in identity, role behavior, and communication (Cowan & Cowan, 1988). The arrival of a child may shift equalitarian role patterns in a marriage into more traditional ones. One national probability sample indicated that, after the birth of a first child, wives lose not only decision-making power in their relationships but also help from husbands with housework. Not only did such self-reported behaviors change, but the ideological beliefs of couples also took a turn toward traditionalism (Hoffman & Manis, 1978).

In spite of the traditionally gloomy forecast for marital partners during the transition to parenthood, three changes have occurred in the literature over time that have moderated the negative picture (Fitzpatrick, Vangelisti, & Firman, under review). First, as noted by a number of scholars (e.g., MacDermid, Huston, & McHale, 1990), retrospective and cross-sectional studies have been supplemented by longitudinal studies. Although numerous cross-sectional studies have found a negative association between marital satisfaction and the presence of children (Glenn & McLanahan, 1982), MacDermid and his associates (1990) suggest that most of these studies fail to account for the fact that declines in marital satisfaction are typical during the early years of marriage (Huston, McHale, & Crouter, 1986; White & Booth, 1985)—regardless of spouses' parental status. Longitudinal data reveal little if any difference (MacDermid et al., 1990; White & Booth, 1985).

Second, the literature has moved beyond the point of considering differences between parents and nonparents. Scholars have begun to examine variability among those who become parents. More specifically, when spouses' expectations about the changes they will experience as parents are positive yet unrealistic, their reports about marital satisfaction tend to decline over time (Belsky, Lang, & Huston, 1986).

A third important modification in the literature is that it has begun to emphasize the impact of a couple's perception of their interaction patterns on their adjustment to pregnancy and parenthood. A couple's communication patterns are clearly linked to marital success. Given the dramatic changes associated with pregnancy and childbirth, couples are likely to experience changes in their interaction patterns. For instance, Stamp and Banski (1992) found that the anticipated increase in responsibility associated with having a child may encourage some couples to demand more autonomy in their relationships. Such demands may result in conflict. In contrast, those who experience anxiety and self-doubt in their new role as parents may need more reassurance and comforting from their partners (Brown, 1986; Richardson, 1983).

(3) Family paradigms. A program of research comparing normal and disturbed families that stands out for its theoretical and methodological sophistication is that of Reiss and his colleagues (Oliveri & Reiss, 1981a, 1981b; D. Reiss, 1981). Believing that theories of the family built around impulse, affect, or power have fared badly in explaining or predicting family behavior, D. Reiss (1981) has developed a model emphasizing the families' construction of reality or family paradigms. Families are said to differ along three dimensions: (a) their experience of the world as ordered; (b) their belief in the world as open, accessible, or accommodating; and (c) their experience of novelty in the world.

This program of research is of special importance to communication researchers for three reasons. First, a family's construction of social reality is represented in the interaction of family members with one another. The social construction of reality is indicated by the lexical speech, the nonlexical speech, and the nonverbal behavior of family members as it is organized into recurring patterns. Second, the model offers a rigorous communication explanation for how parental problems lead to deficiencies in offspring. Third, Fitzpatrick and her colleagues (Fitzpatrick, 1990; Fitzpatrick & Ritchie, 1993, 1994) see many similarities in the family types elaborated by Reiss to those of Fitzpatrick and those of McLeod and Chaffee (1972). For Fitzpatrick (1990), the measurement associated with each type allows us to tap into family schemata, or information-processing structures, driving family communication. Empirical research is ongoing to test these ideas (Fey, in progress; Fitzpatrick, Krcmar, & Leutwiler, 1993).

Summary

In this section, we have seen that the interaction between any two family members can be affected in a variety of direct and indirect ways by the presence and behavior of a third person (Hinde, 1987). Although this point is often acknowledged by theorists, very little systematic research has addressed this question. The research that we have reviewed points to major interaction differences when the dyad becomes a triad. Interactional research is very strong on descriptive charm. One of the greatest weaknesses in this research (apart from its scarcity) is how rarely these interactional differences are connected to major family outcomes (but see Grych & Fincham, 1990) and, more important, how rarely direct mechanisms are proposed to explain the interactional differences. One exciting new exception to the preceding generalization, in proposing a mechanism for interactional differences, is the new work on "nonshared environment" (Reiss, Plomin, & Hetherington, 1991).

The proper domain of communication research is the study of messages. But these messages must be connected to the theoretically relevant internal and output family process concepts.

Conclusion

We had three goals in this chapter. First, we alerted the reader to a number of issues surrounding definitions of the family. We settled on a transaction definition because it allows us to study a broad range of families.

Second, we offered a taxonomy of variables that need to be considered when studying family communication. A fundamental question for the study of communication in kin groups is this: In each of the subsystems of the family, how do the input variables (Table 19.2) affect performance and consequently lead to particular outputs? Throughout the review, we have seen that scholars in various traditions have approached pieces of this question. Some have been concerned only with the performance variables, rarely linking these to major family outcomes. As Cappella (1991) has argued, extensive analyses of interaction sequences, although not without their descriptive charm, do not yield much information about potential connections among important concepts. When a link is made, it is usually between a performance and an output variable with little consideration of internal variables. Researchers, for example, typically relate interaction patterns to levels of marital satisfaction (Ting-Toomey, 1983).

Third, we reviewed the literature on various family dyads and triads in reference to both individual and interpersonal processes. In contrast to the manner in which we built this review of the literature, newer programs of research are being built on *developmental family systems* perspectives. Here, we do not see the disconnected dyads in the family. Rather, theorists consider changes in life experiences, family processes, and individual adjustment. And multiple methods and multiple informants are used rather than relying on the perspective of one family member exclusively. Hetherington and her associates (1992), for example, conducted a longitudinal study to examine transformations in marital, parent-child, and sibling relationships and the effects these changes have on the adjustment of early adolescent children following the remarriage of a divorced mother.

Thirty years ago, Haley (1963) argued that our theories of family process were stymied by a lack of dyadic-level constructs. This is no longer true, for a variety of such concepts appear in the kinship literature. Naturally, the names of what are actually the same concepts often differ, or, perversely, different concepts often have the same name. Take, for example, the concept of complementarity. In the sibling literature, this concept has a decidedly cognitive flavor, for it is defined as not sharing the same point of view (Dunn, 1983). In the marital literature, complementarity has a decidedly behavioristic tinge, for it is the exchange of maximally different control messages (Millar & Rogers, 1976). Or consider that the Consensual family of McLeod and Chaffee (1972) is not the Consensus-Sensitive family of D. Reiss (1981). Because many dyadic-level (and above) constructs are communication constructs (reciprocity, symmetry, dominance, attachment, control, and so forth), such explications will help in theory-building efforts in interpersonal communication.

Our review of the kinship literature suggests directions for new research and theory. Few studies consider more than one family dyad at a time, and most of the research energy is spent on husbands and wives. In addition to an expansion of the family dyads and triads that are studied, greater care will be paid to sampling not only actors (family dyads or units) but also behaviors and contexts. The need for well-designed laboratory studies of family interaction is apparent.

Measurement of these important constructs must move beyond observations of behavior in the presence of target others to an examination of pattern and sequence in family interaction. Complex interactional models of family processes need to be tested. The results of these models should include frequency data, simultaneous behaviors, tests of interactional structure through time, and sequential analysis. Reporting findings in this manner (for example, Gottman, 1979; Sillars, 1980; Williamson, 1983) allows numerous connections to be built with other programs of research. This type of methodological reporting will also prove useful in examining the psychological reality of communication for family members. It is possible that family members themselves count frequencies of behavior and not complex interactional sequences when assessing their relationships. Individuals in ongoing relationships may not be able to see the patterns in which they are enmeshed even though these patterns actually predict certain classes of outcomes in family life.

Models of interaction are incomplete without some consideration of cognitive or interpretative processes (Fitzpatrick & Ritchie, 1993). Indeed, it would be of major conceptual importance for theorists to link the interactional and cognitive perspectives. To accomplish this link for family systems, two points must be taken into account. First, major cognitive developmental differences separate not only parents and children but also siblings only a few years apart in age. Second, the study of interaction and the study of cognition are radically different in levels of abstraction. Thus the rules of correspondence between these levels must be specified. Third, to code the interaction that occurs among family members without concern for the meaning that these individuals are assigning to these messages may lead us in the wrong direction.

Innumerable pronouncements have been made about the modern family and its alleged demise. Despite changes in traditional family patterns, Americans consistently report that a happy marriage and a good family are the most important aspects of life (Thorton & Freedman, 1983). The study of communication in kin relationships will become a major part of interpersonal communication theory and research in the next decade not only because the family is important to the society at large but also because it presents an interesting context in which to pursue important questions about human communication.

Notes

1. This chart is essentially an analytical device isolating the central factors employed in the theoretical approaches to the study of kin relationships. Theories that employ a constitutive approach would tend to see less of a conceptual differentiation between internal and performance factors (Poole, McPhee, & Seibold, 1982). For example, role differentiation would not exist separate and apart from its instantiation in the ongoing conflict or problem-solving activities of a couple or a family.

2. All these output measures are clearly value laden. The concept of family functioning and normalcy is a different order of value orientation because it is hidden in the conceptual arguments of the theorist. Our point here is only to consider the nature of the assumptions of the theorists studying adequacy of family functioning.

3. The system analogy reminds us of the fundamental law of family interaction (Bossard, 1956, p. 293). That is, the number of reciprocal relationships or dyads (X) in a family with a given number of members (Y) is as follows: $X = Y(Y - 1)/2$. Consequently, a family with 7 children has 36 possible dyadic combinations. Even the proverbial two-child family has 6 dyadic links. This equation deals only with dyads. All subsystems should be considered. Adding or subtracting even one family member has implications for the structure of family interactions (Broderick & Smith, 1979).

References

Abeles, G. (1976). Researching the unsearchable: Experimentation on the double bind. In C. E. Sluzki & D. C. Ransom (Eds.), *Double bind: The foundation of the communication approach to the family* (pp. 113-150). New York: Grune & Stratton.

Abramovitch, R., Corter, C., & Lando, B. (1979). Sibling interaction in the home. *Child Development, 50*, 997-1003.

Abramovitch, R., Corter, C., & Peplar, D. J. (1980). Observations of mixed-sex sibling dyads. *Child Development, 51*, 1268-1271.

Ahrons, C. R., & Rodgers, R. H. (1987). *Divorced families: A multidisciplinary developmental view.* New York: Norton.

Ainsworth, M. D. S. (1973). The development of infant-mother attachment. In B. M. Caldwell & H. N. Riccinti (Eds.), *Review of child development research* (Vol. 3, pp. 1-94). Chicago: University of Chicago Press.

Ainsworth, M. D. S., & Bell, S. M. V. (1969). Some contemporary patterns of mother-infant interaction in the feeding situation. In J. A. Ambrose (Ed.), *Stimulation in early infancy* (pp. 133-163). London: Academic Press.

Ainsworth, M. D. S., Blehar, M. C., Waters, E., & Wall, S. (1978). *Patterns of attachment: A psychological study of strange situation.* Hillsdale, NJ: Lawrence Erlbaum.

Aldous, J. (1978). *Family careers.* New York: John Wiley.

Alexander, J. F. (1973). Defensive and supportive communication in normal and deviant families. *Journal of Consulting and Clinical Psychology, 40,* 223-231.

Ambrose, P., Harper, J., & Pemberton, R. (1983). *Surviving divorce: Men beyond marriage.* London, UK: Harvester.

Applegate, J. L., Burke, J. A., Burleson, B. R., Delia, J. G., & Kline, S. L. (1983, November). *Reflection-enhancing parental communication.* Paper presented at the annual meeting of the Speech Communication Association, Washington, DC.

Applegate, J. L., Burleson, B. R., & Delia, J. G. (1992). Reflection-enhancing parenting as an antecedent to children's social-cognitive and communication development. In I. E. Sigel, A. V. McGillicuddy-DeLisi, & J. J. Goodnow (Eds.), *Parental belief systems: The psychological consequences for children* (Vol. 2., pp. 3-39). Hillsdale, NJ: Lawrence Erlbaum.

Atkinson, M. L., & Allen, V. L. (1983). Perceived structure of nonverbal behavior. *Journal of Personality and Social Psychology, 45,* 458-463.

Baltes, P. B. (1968). Longitudinal and cross-sectional sequences in the study of age and generational effects. *Human Development, 11,* 145-171.

Bank, S. P., & Kahn, M. D. (1982a). *The sibling bond.* New York: Basic Books.

Bank, S. P., & Kahn, M. D. (1982b). Intense sibling loyalty. In M. E. Lamb & B. Sutton-Smith (Eds.), *Sibling relationships: Their nature and significance across the life span* (pp. 251-266). Hillsdale, NJ: Lawrence Erlbaum.

Baskett, L. M., & Johnson, S. M. (1982). The young child's interaction with parents versus sibling: A behavioral analysis. *Child Development, 53,* 643-650.

Bates, E. (1979). *The emergence of symbols.* New York: Academic Press.

Bates, E., Camaioni, L., & Volterra, V. (1975). The acquisition of performatives prior to speech. *Merrill-Palmer Quarterly, 21,* 205-226.

Bateson, M. C. (1975). Mother-infant exchanges: The epigenesis of conversational interaction. In D. Aaronson & R. Rieber (Eds.), *Developmental psycholinguistics and communication disorders* (Vol. 263, pp. 101-113). New York: Annals of New York Academy of Science.

Baxter, L., & Dindia, K. (1990). Marital partners' perceptions of marital maintenance strategies. *Journal of Social and Personal Relationships, 7,* 187-208.

Bedford, V. H., & Gold, D. T. (1989). Siblings in later life: A neglected family relationship [Special Issue]. *American Behavioral Scientist, 33,* 3-126.

Bell, A. P., & Weinberg, M. (1978). *Homosexualities: A study of diversity among men and women.* New York: Simon & Schuster.

Bell, R. Q. (1968). A reinterpretation of the direction of effect in studies of socialization. *Psychological Review, 75,* 81-95.

Bell, R. Q. (1974). Contributions of human infants to caregivers and social interaction. In M. Lewis & L. A. Rosenblum (Eds.), *The effect of the infants on its caregivers* (pp. 1-20). New York: Wiley.

Bellinger, D. (1980). Consistency in the pattern of change in mother's speech: Some discriminant analyses. *Journal of Child Language, 7,* 464-487.

Belsky, J. (1990). Parental and nonparental child care and children's socioemotional development: A decade in review. *Journal of Marriage and the Family, 52,* 885-903.

Belsky, J., Lang, M., & Huston, T. L. (1986). Sex typing and division of labor as determinants of marital change across the transition to parenthood. *Journal of Personality and Social Psychology, 50,* 517-522.

Belsky, J., Youngblade, L., Rovine, M., & Volling, B. (1991). Patterns of marital change and parent-child interaction. *Journal of Marriage and the Family, 53,* 885-899.

Berger, C. R., & Bradac, J. J. (1982). *Language and social knowledge*. London: Edward Arnold.

Berscheid, E. (1982). Attraction and emotion in interpersonal relationships. In M. S. Clark & S. T. Fiske (Eds.), *Affect and cognition* (pp. 37-120). Hillsdale, NJ: Lawrence Erlbaum.

Berscheid, E. (1983). Emotions. In *Close relationships* (pp. 110-168). New York: Freeman.

Birnbaum, J. A. (1971). *Life patterns, personality style and self-esteem in gifted family oriented and career committed women*. Unpublished doctoral dissertation, University of Michigan.

Blasband, D., & Peplau, L. A. (1985). Sexual exclusivity versus openness in gay male couples. *Archives of Sexual Behavior, 14,* 395-412.

Bloom, B. L., White, S. W., & Asher, S. J. (1979). Marital disruption as a stressful event. In G. Levinger & O. C. Moles (Eds.), *Divorce and separation* (pp. 184-210). New York: Basic Books.

Blumstein, P., & Schwartz, P. (1983). *American couples*. New York: William Morrow.

Bochner, A. P. (1976). Conceptual frontiers in the study of families: An introduction to the literature. *Human Communication Research, 2,* 381-397.

Bochner, A. P. (1983). Functions of communication in interpersonal bonding. In C. Arnold & J. W. Bowers (Eds.), *Handbook of rhetorical and communication theory* (pp. 544-621). Boston: Allyn & Bacon.

Bochner, A. P., Kaminski, E. P., & Fitzpatrick, M. A. (1977). The conceptual domain of interpersonal communication behavior: A factor-analytic study. *Human Communication Research, 3,* 291-302.

Boer, F., Goedhart, A. W., & Treffers, P. D. A. (1992). Siblings and their parents. In F. Boer & J. Dunn (Eds.), *Children's sibling relationships: Developmental and clinical issues* (pp. 41-54). Hillsdale, NJ: Lawrence Erlbaum.

Bohannan, P. (1970). The six stations of divorce. In P. Bohannan (Ed.), *Divorce and after* (pp. 29-55). New York: Doubleday.

Bolton, C. D. (1961). Mate selection as the development of a relationship. *Marriage and Family Living, 22,* 234-240.

Boss, P., Doherty, W., LaRossa, R., Schumm, W., & Steinmetz, S. (Eds.). (1993). *Sourcebook of family theories and methods: A contextual approach*. New York: Plenum.

Bossard, J. H. S. (1956). *The large family system: An original study in the sociology of the family*. Philadelphia: University of Pennsylvania Press.

Bossard, J. H. S., & Boll, E. S. (1950). *Ritual in family living*. Philadelphia: University of Pennsylvania Press.

Bott, E. (1957). *Family and social network*. London: Tavistock.

Bowerman, C. E., & Dobash, R. M. (1974). Structural variations in intersibling affect. *Journal of Marriage and the Family, 36,* 48-54.

Bowlby, J. (1972). *Attachment and loss* (Vol. 1). London: Hogarth.

Bowlby, J. (1980). *Attachment and loss* (Vol. 3). London: Hogarth.

Brehm, S. (1985). *Intimate relationships*. New York: Random House.

Broderick, C., & Smith, J. (1979). The general systems approach to the family. In W. R. Burr, R. Hill, F. I. Nye, & I. L. Reiss (Eds.), *Contemporary theories about the family* (Vol. 2, pp. 112-129). New York: Free Press.

Brody, G. H., & Stoneman, Z. (1987). Sibling conflict: Contributions of the siblings themselves, the parent-sibling relationship, and the broader family system. *Journal of Children in Contemporary Society, 19,* 39-53.

Brown, M. A. (1986). Marital support during pregnancy. *Journal of Obstetric, Gynecologic, and Neonatal Nursing, 15,* 475-483.

Bruner, J. (1990). *Acts of meaning*. Cambridge, MA: Harvard University Press.

Bryant, B., & Crockenberg, S. (1980). Correlates and discussion of prosocial behavior: A study of female siblings with their mothers. *Child Development, 51,* 529-544.

Bugental, D. E. (1974). Interpretations of naturally occurring discrepancies between words and intonations: Modes of inconsistency resolution. *Journal of Personality and Social Psychology, 30,* 125-133.

Bugental, D. E., & Love, L. (1975). Nonassertive expression of parental approval and disapproval, and its relationship to child disturbance. *Child Development, 46,* 747-752.

Bugental, D. E., Love, L., & Gianetto, R. (1971). Perfidious feminine faces. *Journal of Personality and Social Psychology, 17,* 314-318.

Bugental, D. E., Love, L., Kaswan, J., & April, C. (1971). Verbal-nonverbal conflict in parental messages to normal and disturbed children. *Journal of Abnormal Psychology, 77,* 6-10.

Buhrmester, D. (1992). The developmental courses of sibling and peer relationships. In F. Boer & J. Dunn (Eds.), *Children's sibling relationships: Developmental and clinical issues* (pp. 19-40). Hillsdale, NJ: Lawrence Erlbaum.

Burgess, E. W., & Locke, H. (1953). *The family*. New York: American Book.

Burgess, E. W., & Wallin, P. (1953). *Engagement and marriage*. Philadelphia: Lippincott.

Burgess, R. L., & Conger, R. D. (1978). Family interaction in abusive, neglectful, and normal families. *Child Development, 49*, 1163-1173.

Burr, W. R., Hill, R., Nye, F. I., & Reiss, I. L. (Eds.). (1979). *Contemporary theories about the family* (Vols. 1, 2). New York: Free Press.

Cameron, N. (1963). *Personality development and psychopathology: A dynamic approach*. Boston: Houghton Mifflin.

Cappella, J. A. (1984). The relevance of the microstructure of interaction to relationship change. *Journal of Personality and Social Relationships, 1*, 239-264.

Cappella, J. N. (1987). Interpersonal communication: Fundamental questions and issues. In C. R. Berger & S. H. Chaffee (Eds.), *Handbook of communication science* (pp. 184-238). Newbury Park, CA: Sage.

Cappella, J. N. (1991). The biological origins of automated patterns of human interaction. *Communication Theory, 1*, 4-35.

Cate, R., & Lloyd, S. (1992). *Courtship*. Newbury Park, CA: Sage.

Christensen, A. (1988). Dysfunctional interaction patterns in couples. In P. Noller & M. A. Fitzpatrick (Eds.), *Perspectives on marital interaction*. Clevedon, England: Multilingual Matters.

Christensen, A., & Heavey, C. L. (1990). Gender, power and marital conflict. *Journal of Personality and Social Psychology, 59*, 73-85.

Clarke-Stewart, K. A. (1982). And daddy makes three. In J. Belsky (Ed.), *In the beginning: Readings on infancy* (pp. 204-215). New York: Columbia University Press.

Comstock, J., & Buller, D. B. (1991). Conflict strategies adolescents use with their parents: Testing the cognitive communicator characteristics model. *Journal of Language and Social Psychology, 10*, 47-65.

Conger, J. J. (1981). Freedom and commitment: Families, youth and social change. *American Psychologist, 36*, 1475-1484.

Conger, R. D. (1983). Behavioral assessment for practitioners: Some reasons and recommendations. In E. E. Filsinger (Ed.), *Marriage and family assessment* (pp. 137-151). Beverly Hills, CA: Sage.

Conville, R. (1991). *Relational transitions: The evolution of personal relationships*. New York: Praeger.

Cooper, D. (1970). *The death of a family*. New York: Pantheon.

Courtright, J. A., Millar, F. E., & Rogers-Millar, L. E. (1979). Domineeringness and dominance: Replication and extension. *Communication Monographs, 46*, 179-192.

Cowan, C., & Cowan, P. A. (1988). *When partners become parents*. New York: Brasin.

Coyne, J. C., Kahn, J., & Gottlib, I. H. (1987). Depression. In T. Jacob (Ed.), *Psychopathology and the family* (pp. 509-533). New York: Plenum.

Csikszentmihalyi, M., Rathunde, K., & Whalen, S. (1993). *Talented teenagers: The roots of success and failure*. Cambridge: Cambridge University Press.

DeMaris, A., & Leslie, G. R. (1984). Cohabitation with the future spouse: Its influence upon marital satisfaction and communication. *Journal of Marriage and the Family, 46*, 77-84.

Dindia, K., & Baxter, L. (1987). Strategies for maintaining and repairing marital relationships. *Journal of Social and Personal Relationships, 4*, 143-158.

Duberman, L. (1973). Step-kin relationships. *Journal of Marriage and the Family, 35*, 283-292.

Duck, S. (1982). A topography of relationship disengagement and dissolution. In S. Duck (Ed.), *Personal relationships: Vol. 4. Dissolving personal relationships* (pp. 1-30). New York: Academic Press.

Duck, S. W. (1976). Interpersonal communication in developing acquaintance. In G. R. Miller (Ed.), *Explorations in interpersonal communication* (pp. 127-148). Beverly Hills, CA: Sage.

Dunn, J. (1983). Sibling relationships in early childhood. *Child Development, 54*, 787-811.

Dunn, J. (1988). *The beginnings of social understanding*. Cambridge, MA: Harvard University Press.

Dunn, J. (1992). Sisters and brothers: Current research on developmental issue. In F. Boer & J. Dunn (Eds.), *Children's sibling relationships: Developmental and clinical issues* (pp. 1-28). Hillsdale, NJ: Lawrence Erlbaum.

Dunn, J., & Kendrick, C. (1981). Social behavior of young siblings in the family context: Differences between same-sex and different-sex dyads. *Child Development, 52*, 49-56.

Dunn, J., & Kendrick, C. (1982). The speech of two- and three-year-olds to infant siblings: "Baby talk" and the context of communication. *Journal of Child Language, 9*, 579-595.

Dunn, J., & Plomin, R. (1990). *Separate lives: Why siblings are so different*. New York: Basic Books.

Duvall, E. (1971). *Family development*. Philadelphia: Lippincott.

Ericson, P. M. (1972). *Relational communication: Complementarity and symmetry and their relation to dominance-submission*. Unpublished doctoral dissertation, Michigan State University.

Ericson, P. M., & Rogers, L. E. (1973). New procedures for analyzing relational communication. *Family Process, 12,* 245-257.

Falbo, T. (1981). Relationship between birth category, achievement, and interpersonal orientation. *Journal of Personality and Social Psychology, 41,* 121-131.

Farace, R. V., Monge, P. R., & Russell, H. M. (1977). *Communicating and organizing.* Reading, MA: Addison-Wesley.

Farber, B. (1964). *Family: Organization and interaction.* San Francisco: Chandler.

Feeney, J. A., Noller, P., & Callan, V. J. (in press). Attachment style, satisfaction and communication in marriage. *Advances in Personal Relationships, 5.*

Ferree, M. M. (1990). Beyond separate spheres: Feminism and family research. *Journal of Marriage and the Family, 52,* 866-884.

Fey, J. (in progress). *Personality and family interaction.* Doctoral dissertation, University of Wisconsin.

Fitzpatrick, M. A. (1976). *A typological approach to communication in relationships.* Unpublished doctoral dissertation, Temple University.

Fitzpatrick, M. A. (1983). Predicting couples' communication from couples' self reports. In R. Bostrom (Ed.), *Communication yearbook 7* (pp. 49-82). Beverly Hills, CA: Sage.

Fitzpatrick, M. A. (1984). A typological approach to marital interaction: Recent theory and research. In L. Berkowitz (Ed.), *Advances in experimental social psychology* (Vol. 18, pp. 1-47). New York: Academic Press.

Fitzpatrick, M. A. (1988). *Between husbands and wives: Communication in marriage.* Newbury Park, CA: Sage.

Fitzpatrick, M. A. (1990). Aging, health and family communication. In H. Giles, N. Coupland, & J. Wiemann (Eds.), *Communication, health and aging* (pp. 213-228). Manchester: Manchester University Press.

Fitzpatrick, M. A., & Badzinski, D. M. (1985). All in the family: Communication in kinship relations. In M. L. Knapp & G. R. Miller (Eds.), *Handbook of interpersonal communication* (pp. 687-736). Beverly Hills, CA: Sage.

Fitzpatrick, M. A., Fey, J., Segrin, C., & Schiff, J. (1993). Internal working models of relationships. *Journal of Language and Social Psychology, 12,* 103-131.

Fitzpatrick, M. A., & Indvik, J. (1982). The instrumental and expressive domains of marital communications. *Human Communication Research, 8,* 195-213.

Fitzpatrick, M. A., Jandt, F., Myrick, F. I., & Edgar, T. (1993). In R. J. Ringer (Ed.), *Queer words queer images: Communication and the (RE) construction of homosexuality.* New York: New York University Press.

Fitzpatrick, M. A., Krcmar, M., & Leutwiler, T. (1993, May). *Children's recognition of family communication environments and their social behavior with peers.* Paper presented at the annual meetings of the International Communication Association, Washington, DC.

Fitzpatrick, M. A., & Ritchie, L. D. (1993). Communication theory and the family. In P. Boss, W. Doherty, R. LaRossa, W. Schumm, & S. Steinmetz (Eds.), *Sourcebook of family theories and methods: A contextual approach* (pp. 565-585). New York: Plenum.

Fitzpatrick, M. A., & Ritchie, L. D. (1994). Communication schemata within the family: Multiple perspectives on family interaction. *Human Communication Research, 20,* 275-301.

Fitzpatrick, M. A., Vangelisti, A., & Firman, S. (in press). Marital interaction and change during pregnancy: A typological approach. *Personal Relationship.*

Fitzpatrick, F., & Wamboldt, F. (1990). Where is all said and done: Towards an integration of intrapersonal and interpersonal models of marital and family communication. *Communication Research, 17,* 421-431.

Folger, J. (1978). *The communicative indicants of power, dominance and submission.* Unpublished doctoral dissertation, University of Wisconsin—Madison.

Folger, J. P., & Poole, M. S. (1980). Relational coding schemes and the question of validity. In M. Burgoon (Ed.), *Communication yearbook 5* (pp. 235-248). New Brunswick, NJ: Transaction.

Freud, S. (1949). *An outline of psychoanalysis.* New York: Norton.

Furman, W., & Buhrmester, D. (1985). Children's perceptions of the qualities of sibling relationships. *Child Development, 56,* 448-461.

Galvin, K. M., & Brommel, B. J. (1992). *Family communication.* Glenview, IL: Scott, Foresman.

Ganong, L. H., Coleman, M., & Mapes, D. (1990). A meta-analytic review of family structure stereotypes. *Journal of Marriage and the Family,* 287-297.

Garmezy, N. (1974). Children at risk: The search for antecedents of schizophrenia. *Schizophrenia Bulletin, 1,* 14-90.

Gelles, R. J. (1974). *The violent home: A study of physical aggression between husbands and wives.* Beverly Hills, CA: Sage.

Giles, H. (1984). *Communication and the aged.* Unpublished manuscript, University of California, Santa Barbara.

Giles, H., Coupland, N., & Wiemann, J. (Eds.). (1990). *Communication, health and aging.* Manchester: Manchester University Press.

Glenn, N., & McLanahan, S. (1982). Children and marital happiness. *Journal of Marriage and the Family, 44,* 63-72.

Goldstein, M. J. (1985). Family factors that antedate the onset of schizophrenia and related disorders: The results of a fifteen year prospective longitudinal study. *Acta Psychiatrica Scandinavica, 71,* 7-18.

Goldstein, M. J. (1987). Family interaction patterns that antedate the onset of schizophrenia and related disorders. In K. Hahlweg & M. J. Goldstein (Eds.), *Understanding major mental disorder: The contribution of family interaction research* (pp. 11-32). New York: Family Process Press.

Goldstein, M. J., & Strachan, A. M. (1987). The family and schizophrenia. In T. Jacob (Ed.), *Family interaction and psychopathology.* New York: Plenum.

Goode, W. J. (1963). *World revolution and family patterns.* New York: Free Press.

Gordon, L. (1988). *Heroes of their own lives: The politics and history of family violence.* New York: Viking.

Gottman, J. M. (1979). *Marital interaction: Experimental investigations.* New York: Academic Press.

Gottman, J. M. (1993a). A theory of marital dissolution and stability. *Journal of Family Psychology, 7,* 57-75.

Gottman, J. M. (1993b). *What predicts divorce.* Hillsdale, NJ: Lawrence Erlbaum.

Gottman, J. M., & Levenson, R. W. (1992). Marital processes predictive of later dissolution: Behavior, physiology, and health. *Journal of Personality and Social Psychology, 63,* 221-233.

Gottman, J. M., Markman, H., & Notarius, C. (1977). The topography of marital conflict: Sequential analysis of verbal and nonverbal behavior. *Journal of Marriage and the Family, 39,* 461-477.

Graziano, W. G., & Musser, L. M. (1982). The joining and the parting of the ways. In S. Duck (Ed.), *Personal relationships: Vol. 4. Dissolving personal relationships* (pp. 75-106). New York: Academic Press.

Grych, J. H., & Fincham, F. D. (1990). Marital conflict and children's adjustment: A cognitive-contextual framework. *Psychological Bulletin, 108,* 267-290.

Haley, J. (1963). *Strategies of psychotherapy.* New York: Grune & Stratton.

Haley, J. (1967). Speech sequences of normal and abnormal families with two children present. *Family Process, 6,* 81-97.

Hareven, T. (1980, April). *American families in transition: Historical perspectives in change.* Washington, DC: Research Forum on Family Issues, White House Conference on Families.

Harry, J., & Lovely, R. (1979). Gay marriages and communities of sexual orientation. *Alternative Lifestyles, 2,* 177-200.

Hartup, W. W. (1978). Perspectives on child and family interaction: Past, present and future. In R. M. Lerner & G. B. Spanier (Eds.), *Child influences on marital and family interaction: A life-span perspective* (pp. 23-46). New York: Academic Press.

Harvey, J. H., Weber, A. L., Yarkin, K. L., & Stewart, B. E. (1982). An attributional approach to relationship breakdown and dissolution. In S. Duck (Ed.), *Personal relationships: Vol. 4. Dissolving personal relationships* (pp. 107-126). New York: Academic Press.

Henry, J. (1965). *Pathways to madness.* New York: Vintage.

Hess, R. D. (1981). Approaches to the measurement and interpretation of parent-child interaction. In R. W. Henderson (Ed.), *Parent-child interaction: Theory, research, and prospects* (pp. 207-234). New York: Academic Press.

Hetherington, M., Clingempeel, W. G., Anderson, E. R., Deal, J., Hagan, M., Hollier, E., & Lindner, M. (1992). Coping with marital transitions: A family systems perspective. *Monographs of the Society for Research in Child Development, 57*(2-3, Serial No. 227).

Hicks, M. W., & Platt, M. (1970). Marital happiness and stability: Review of research in the sixties. *Journal of Marriage and the Family, 32,* 553-574.

Hill, C. T., Rubin, Z., & Peplau, L. A. (1976). Breakups before marriage: The end of 103 affairs. *Journal of Social Issues, 32,* 147-168.

Hinde, R. A. (1979). *Towards understanding relationships.* New York: Academic Press.

Hinde, R. A. (1987). *Individuals, relationships and culture.* Cambridge: Cambridge University Press.

Hinde, R. A., & Stevenson-Hinde, J. (Eds.). (1988). *Relationships within families: Mutual influences.* Oxford: Clarendon.

Hoffman, L. W., & Manis, J. D. (1978). Influences of children on marital interaction and parental satisfactions and dissatisfactions. In R. M. Lerner & G. B. Spanier (Eds.), *Child influences on marital and family interaction: A life-span perspective* (pp. 165-214). New York: Academic Press.

Holmes, T. H., & Rahe, R. H. (1976). The social readjustment rating scale. *Journal of Psychosomatic Research, 11,* 213-218.

Hopper, R., Knapp, M. L., & Scott, L. (1981). Couples' personal idioms: Exploring intimate talk. *Journal of Communication, 31*, 23-33.

Howe, G., & Reiss, D. (1993). Simulation and experimentation in family research. In P. Boxx, W. Doherty, R. LaRossa, W. Schumm, & S. Steinmetz (Eds.), *Sourcebook of family theory and methods: A contextual approach* (pp. 303-324). New York: Plenum.

Huesmann, L. R., & Levinger, G. (1976). Incremental exchange theory: A formal model for progression in dyadic social interaction. In L. Berkowitz & E. Walster (Eds.), *Advances in experimental social psychology* (Vol. 9, pp. 192-229). New York: Academic Press.

Huston, T. L., & Levinger, G. (1978). Interpersonal attraction and relationships. (M. R. Rosenweig & L. W. Porten, Eds.) *Annual Review of Psychology, 29*, 115-156.

Huston, T. L., McHale, S., & Crouter, A. (1986). When the honeymoon's over: Changes in the marriage relationship over the first year. In R. Gilmour & S. Duck (Eds.), *The emerging field of personal relationships* (pp. 109-132). Hillsdale, NJ: Lawrence Erlbaum.

Huston, T. L., Surra, C. A., Fitzgerald, N. M., & Cate, R. M. (1981). From courtship to marriage: Mate selection as an interpersonal process. (S. Duck & R. Gilmour, Eds.) *Personal Relationships 2: Developmental Psychology, 20*, 772-736.

Jacob, T. (1975). Family interaction in disturbed and normal families: A methodological and substantive review. *Psychological Bulletin, 82*, 33-65.

Jacob, T. (1987). *Family interaction and psychopathology.* New York: Plenum.

Jacob, T., & Lessin, S. (1982). Inconsistent communication in family interaction. *Clinical Psychology Review, 2*, 295-309.

Johnson, M. P., Huston, T. L., Gaines, S. O., & Levinger, G. (1992). Patterns of married life among young couples. *Journal of Social and Personal Relationships, 9*, 343-364.

Kagan, J. (1979). Overview: Perspective on human infancy. In J. D. Osofsky (Ed.), *Handbook of infant development* (pp. 1-28). New York: Wiley.

Kaplan, E., & Kaplan, G. (1971). The pre-linguistic child. In J. Elliot (Ed.), *Human development and cognitive processes* (pp. 358-380). New York: Holt, Rinehart & Winston.

Kaye, K. (1980). Why we don't talk "baby talk" to babies. *Journal of Child Language, 7*, 489-508.

Kelley, H. H. (1983). Love and commitment. In H. H. Kelley (Ed.), *Close relationships* (pp. 265-314). New York: Freeman.

Kelley, H. H. (1986). Personal relationships: Their nature and significance. In R. Gilmour & S. Duck (Eds.), *The emerging field of personal relationships* (pp. 3-19). Hillsdale, NJ: Lawrence Erlbaum.

Kelly, C., Huston, T., & Cate, R. M. (1983). Premarital relationships correlates of the erosion of satisfaction in marriage. *Journal of Social and Personal Relationships.*

Kelly, L. E., & Conley, J. J. (1987). Personality and compatibility: A prospective analysis of marital stability and marital satisfaction. *Journal of Personality and Social Psychology, 52*, 27-40.

Kendrick, C., & Dunn, J. (1980). Caring for a second child: Effects on the interaction between mother and first-born. *Developmental Psychology, 16*, 303-311.

Kendrick, C., & Dunn, J. (1982). Protest or pleasure? The response of first-born children to interaction between their mothers and infant siblings. *Journal of Child Psychology and Psychiatry and Allied Disciplines, 23*, 117-129.

Kerckhoff, A. C., & Davis, K. E. (1962). Value consensus and need complementarity in mate selection. *American Sociological Review, 27*, 295-303.

Koch, H. L. (1956). Some emotional attitudes of the young child in relation to characteristics of the sibling. *Child Development, 27*, 393-426.

Kressel, K., Jaffee, N., Tuchman, B., Watson, C., & Deutsch, M. (1980). A typology of divorcing couples: Implications for mediation and the divorce process. *Family Process, 19*, 101-116.

Kurdek, L. (1989). Relationship quality of newly married husbands and wives: Marital history, stepchildren and individual difference predictors. *Journal of Marriage and the Family, 51*, 1053-1064.

Kurdek, L. (1991). Marital stability and changes in marital quality in newlywed couples: A test of the contextual model. *Journal of Social and Personal Relationships, 8*, 27-48.

Kurdek, L., & Schmitt, P. J. (1986a). Relationship quality of gay men in closed or open relationships. *Journal of Homosexuality, 12*, 85-99.

Kurdek, L., & Schmitt, P. J. (1986b). Relationship quality of partners in heterosexual married, heterosexual cohabiting, gay and lesbian relationships. *Journal of Personality and Social Psychology, 51*, 711-720.

La Gaipa, J. J. (1981). Children's friendships. In S. Duck & R. Gilmour (Eds.), *Personal relationships: Vol. 2. Developing personal relationships* (pp. 67-70). New York: Academic Press.

Lamb, M. E. (Ed.). (1976a). *The role of the father in child development.* New York: Wiley.

Lamb, M. E. (1976b). Proximity seeking attachment behaviors: A critical review of the literature. *Genetic Psychology Monographs, 93*, 63-89.

Lamb, M. E. (1978). The development of sibling relationships in infancy: A short-term longitudinal study. *Child Development, 49,* 1189-1196.

LaRossa, R. (1977). *Conflict and power in marriage: Expecting the first child.* Beverly Hills, CA: Sage.

Lasch, C. (1977). *Haven in a heartless world.* New York: Basic Books.

Lederer, W. J., & Jackson, D. D. (1968). *The mirages of marriage.* New York: Norton.

LeMasters, E. E. (1957). Parenthood as crisis. *Marriage and Family Living, 19,* 352-355.

Lerner, R. M., & Spanier, G. B. (Eds.). (1978). *Child influences on marital interaction: A life-span perspective.* New York: Academic Press.

Levenson, R. W., & Gottman, J. M. (1983). Marital interaction: Physiological linkage and affective exchange. *Journal of Personality and Social Psychology, 45,* 587-597.

Levinger, G. (1965). Marital cohesiveness and dissolution: An integrative review. *Journal of Marriage and the Family, 27,* 19-28.

Levinger, G. (1976). A social psychological perspective on marital dissolution. *Journal of Social Issues, 32*(1), 21-47.

Levinger, G., & Huesmann, L. R. (1980). An incremental exchange perspective on the pair relationships: Interpersonal reward and level of involvement. In K. J. Gergen, M. S. Greenberg, & R. H. Willis (Eds.), *Social exchange: Advances in theory and research* (pp. 165-196). New York: Wiley.

Levinger. G., & Huston, T. (1990). The social psychology of marriage. In F. D. Fincham & T. N. Bradbury (Eds.), *The psychology of marriage* (pp. 19-58). New York: Guilford.

Levy, D. M. (1937). Studies in sibling rivalry. *American Orthopsychiatric Association Research Monographs, 2.*

Lewin, K. (1948). The background of conflict in marriage. In G. Lewin (Ed.), *Resolving social conflicts* (pp. 84-102). New York: Harper & Row.

Lewis, J. M., Beavers, W. R., Gossett, J. T., & Phillips, V. A. (1976). *No single thread: Psychological health in family systems.* New York: Brunner/Mazel.

Lewis, R. A. (1973). A longitudinal test of a developmental framework for premarital dyadic formation. *Journal of Marriage and the Family, 35,* 16-25.

Lewis, R. A., & Spanier, G. (1979). Theorizing about the quality and the stability of marriage. In W. Burr, R. Hill, F. I. Nye, & I. R. Reiss (Eds.), *Contemporary theories about the family* (Vol. 1, pp. 268-294). New York: Free Press.

Loeb, R. C. (1975). Concomitants of boys' locus of control in parent-child interactions. *Developmental Psychology, 11,* 353-358.

Luby, V., & Aron, A. (1990). Prototype analysis of the constructs of like, love and in love. In *Proceedings of 5th International Conference on Personal Relationships,* Oxford.

MacDermid, S. M., Huston, T. L., & McHale, S. M. (1990). Changes in marriage associated with the transition to parenthood: Individual differences as a function of sex-role attitudes and changes in the division of household labor. *Journal of Marriage and the Family, 52,* 475-486.

Macklin, E. D. (1980). Nontraditional family forms: A decade of research. *Journal of Marriage and the Family, 42,* 905-922.

Main, M., Kaplan, N., & Cassidy, J. (1985). Security in infancy, childhood, and adulthood: A move to the level of representation. *Monographs of the Society for Research in Child Development, 1-2*(Serial No. 209).

Mares, L., & Fitzpatrick, M. A. (in press). Communication and the aging couple. In J. Nussbaum & N. Coupland (Eds.), *Handbook on communication and aging.*

Mark, R. A. (1971). Coding communication at the relationship level. *Journal of Communication, 21,* 221-232.

Markman, H. J. (1979). Application of a behavioral model of marriage in predicting relationship satisfaction of couples planning marriage. *Journal of Consulting and Clinical Psychology, 47,* 747-750.

Markman, H. J. (1981). Prediction of marital distress: A five year follow-up. *Journal of Consulting and Clinical Psychology, 49,* 760-762.

Markman, H. J. (1984). The longitudinal study of couples; interactions: Implications for understanding and predicting the development of marital distress. In K. Hahlweg & N. Jacobson (Eds.), *Marital interaction: Analysis and modification* (pp. 253-281). New York: Guilford.

Matas, L., Arend, R. A., & Sroufe, A. (1982). Continuity of adaptation in the second year. In J. Belsky (Ed.), *In the beginning: Readings on infancy* (pp. 144-156). New York: Columbia University Press.

McLeod, J., & Chaffee, S. (1972). The construction of social reality. In J. Tedeschi (Ed.), *The social influence process* (pp. 50-99). Chicago: Aldine-Atherton.

McWhirter, D., & Mattison, A. M. (1984). *The male couple: How relationships develop.* Englewood Cliffs, NJ: Prentice-Hall.

Mead, M. (1942). *And keep your powder dry: An anthropologist looks at America*. New York: William Morrow.

Menaghan, E. G., & Parcel, T. L. (1990). Parental employment and family life: Research in the 1980s. *Journal of Marriage and the Family, 52*, 1079-1098.

Millar, F. E., & Rogers, E. (1976). A relational approach to interpersonal communication. In G. R. Miller (Ed.), *Explorations in interpersonal communication* (pp. 87-104). Beverly Hills, CA: Sage.

Miller, G. R., & Parks, M. R. (1982). Communication in dissolving relationships. In S. Duck (Ed.), *Personal relationships: Vol. 4. Dissolving personal relationships* (pp. 127-154). New York: Academic Press.

Minnett, A. M., Vandell, D. L., & Santrock, J. W. (1983). The effects of sibling status on sibling interaction: Influence of birth order, age spacing, sex of child, and sex of sibling. *Child Development, 54*, 1064-1072.

Mishler, E. G., & Waxler, N. E. (1968). *Interaction in families: An experimental study of family processes and schizophrenia*. New York: Wiley.

Moscovici, S. (1967). Communication processes and the properties of language. In L. Berkowitz (Ed.), *Advances in experimental social psychology* (Vol. 3, pp. 225-270). New York: Academic Press.

Murstein, B. I. (1967). Empirical tests of role, complementary needs and homogamy theories of mate choice. *Journal of Marriage and the Family, 29*, 689-696.

Napier, A., & Whitaker, C. (1978). *The family crucible*. New York: Harper & Row.

Newcomb, M. D. (1987). Cohabitation and marriage: A quest for independence and relatedness. In S. Oskamp (Ed.), *Family processes and problems: Social psychological aspects* (pp. 128-156). Newbury Park, CA: Sage.

Newcomb, M. D., & Bentler, P. M. (1980). Cohabitation before marriage: A comparison of couples who did and did not cohabit before marriage. *Alternative Lifestyles, 3*, 65-85.

Noller, P., & Callan, V. J. (1989, November). Communication in the first year of marriage. *Proceedings of Australian Family Research Conference*, Ballarat, VIC.

Noller, P., & Fitzpatrick, M. A. (1993). *Communication in family relationships*. Englewood Cliffs, NJ: Prentice-Hall.

Noller, P., & White, A. (1990). The validity of the Patterson Communication Questionnaire. *Psychological Assessment: A Journal of Consulting and Clinical Psychology, 2*, 478-482.

Norton, R. (1983). *Communication style: Theory, applications, and measures*. Beverly Hills, CA: Sage.

Nye, F. I. (1979). Choice, exchange, and the family. In W. R. Burr, R. Hill, F. I. Nye, & I. L. Reiss (Eds.), *Contemporary theories about the family* (Vol. 2, pp. 1-41). New York: Free Press.

Nye, F. I., & Berardo, F. M. (1981). Introduction. In F. I. Nye & F. M. Berardo (Eds.), *Emerging conceptual frameworks in family analysis* (pp. 1-9). New York: Praeger.

O'Connell, M., & Bachu, A. (1987). *Fertility of American women: June 1986* (Current Population Reports, Series P-20, No. 421). Washington, DC: Government Printing Office.

Oliveri, M. E., & Reiss, D. (1981a). The structure of families' ties to their kin: The shaping role of social constructions. *Journal of Marriage and the Family, 43*, 391-407.

Oliveri, M. E., & Reiss, D. (1981b). A theory-based empirical classification of family problem-solving behavior. *Family Process, 20*, 409-418.

Olson, D. H. L. (1972). Empirical unbinding of the double bind: Review of research and conceptual reformulations. *Family Process, 11*, 69-94.

Olson, D. H. L., McCubbin, H. I., Barnes, H., Larsen, A., Muxen, M., & Wilson, M. (1983). *Families: What makes them work*. Beverly Hills, CA: Sage.

Olson, D. H. L., Sprenkle, D. H., & Russell, C. S. (1979). Circumplex model of marital and family system: Cohesion and adaptability dimensions, family types, and clinical applications. *Family Process, 18*, 3-28.

Parke, R. D. (1979). Perspectives on father-infant interaction. In J. D. Osofsky (Ed.), *Handbook of infant development* (pp. 549-590). New York: Wiley.

Parke, R. D., & O'Leary, S. (1976). Family interaction in the newborn period: Some findings, some observations, and some unresolved issues. In K. Riegel & J. Meacham (Eds.), *The developing individual in a changing world* (Vol. 2, pp. 653-663). The Hague, the Netherlands: Mouton.

Parks, M. (1982). Ideology in interpersonal communication: Off the couch and into the world. In M. Burgoon (Ed.), *Communication yearbook 5* (pp. 79-108). New Brunswick, NJ: Transaction.

Parsons, T., & Bales, R. F. (1955). *Family socialization and interaction process*. New York: Free Press.

Patterson, G. (Ed.). (1992). *Depression and aggression in family interaction*. Hillsdale, NJ: Lawrence Erlbaum.

Patterson, G. R. (1976). The aggressive child: Victim and architect of a coercive system. In E. J. Marsh, L. A. Hammerlynck, & L. C. Handy (Eds.), *Behavior modification and families* (pp. 267-316). New York: Brunner/Mazel.

Patterson, M. L. (1983). *Nonverbal behavior: A functional perspective*. New York: Springer-Verlag.

Peplar, D., Abramovitch, R., & Corter, C. (1981). Sibling interaction in the home: A longitudinal study. *Child Development, 52*, 1344-1347.

Peplau, L. A., & Cochran, S. D. (1981). Value orientations in the intimate relationships of gay men. *Journal of Homosexuality, 6*, 1-9.

Peterson, G. W., & Rollins, B. C. (1987). Parent-child socialization. In M. B. Sussman & S. K. Steinmetz (Eds.), *Handbook of marriage and the family* (pp. 471-506). New York: Plenum.

Poole, M. S., McPhee, R. D., & Seibold, D. R. (1982). A comparison of normative and interactional explanations of group decision-making: Social decision schemes versus valence distributions. *Communication Monographs, 49*, 1-19.

Raffaelli, M. (1992). Sibling conflict in early adolescence. *Journal of Marriage and the Family, 54*, 652-663.

Raush, H. L., Grief, A. C., & Nugent, J. (1979). Communication in couples and families. In W. Burr, R. Hill, F. I. Nye, & I. L. Reiss (Eds.), *Contemporary theories about the family* (Vol. 1, pp. 468-492). New York: Free Press.

Reiss, D. (1981). *The family's construction of reality*. Cambridge, MA: Harvard University Press.

Reiss, D., Plomin, R., & Hetherington, M. (1991). Genetics and psychiatry: An unheralded window on the environment. *American Journal of Psychiatry, 148*(3), 283-291.

Reiss, I. L. (1971). *The family system in America*. New York: Holt, Rinehart & Winston.

Revenstorf, D., Vogel, B., Wegener, C., Hahlweg, K., & Schindler, L. (1980). Escalation phenomena in interaction sequences: An empirical comparison of distressed and nondistressed couples. *Behavior Analysis and Modification, 2*, 97-116.

Richards, M. P. M. (1974). The development of psychological communication in the first year of life. In K. J. Connally & J. S. Bruner (Eds.), *The growth of competence* (pp. 119-134). New York: Academic Press.

Richardson, P. (1983). Women's perceptions of change in relationships shared with their husbands during pregnancy. *Maternal Child Nursing Journal, 12*, 1-19.

Riskin, J., & Faunce, E. E. (1972). An evaluation review of family interaction research. *Family Process, 11*, 365-455.

Risman, B. J., Hill, C. T., Rubin, Z., & Peplau, L. A. (1981). Living together in college: Implications for courtship. *Journal of Marriage and the Family, 34*, 77-83.

Ritchie, L. D., & Fitzpatrick, M. A. (1990). Family communication patterns: Measuring intrapersonal perceptions of interpersonal relationships. *Communication Research, 17*(4), 523-544.

Rogers, L. E. (1972). *Dyadic systems and transactional communication in a family context*. Unpublished doctoral dissertation, Michigan State University.

Rogers, L. E., & Farace, V. (1975). Analysis of relational communication in dyads. *Human Communication Research, 1*, 229-239.

Rollins, B. C. (1975). Response to Miller about cross-sectional family life cycle research. *Journal of Marriage and the Family, 37*, 259-260.

Rollins, B. C., & Thomas, D. L. (1979). Parental support, power, and control techniques in the socialization of children. In W. R. Burr, R. Hill, F. I. Nye, & I. L. Reiss (Eds.), *Contemporary theories about the family* (Vol. 1, pp. 317-364). New York: Free Press.

Rubin, M. E. Y. (1977). *Differences between distressed and nondistressed couples in verbal and nonverbal communication codes*. Unpublished doctoral dissertation, Indiana University.

Rusbult, C. E., & Buunk, B. P. (1993). Commitment processes in close relationships: An interdependence analysis. *Journal of Social and Personal Relationships, 10*, 175-204.

Rutter, M. (1985). Resilence in the face of adversity: Protective factors and resistance to psychiatric disorder. *British Journal of Psychiatry, 147*, 598-611.

Ryan, J. (1974). Early language development. Towards a communicational analysis. In M. P. M. Richards (Ed.), *The integration of a child into a social world* (pp. 185-214). New York: Cambridge University Press.

Sachs, J. S., & Devin, J. (1976). Young children's use of age-appropriate speech styles in social interaction and role-playing. *Journal of Child Language, 3*, 81-98.

Sarantakos, S. (1984). *Living together in Australia*. Melbourne: Longman Cheshire.

Scarr, S., & Grajek, S. (1982). Similarities and differences among siblings. In M. E. Lamb & B. Sutton-Smith (Eds.), *Sibling relationships: Their nature and significance across the lifespan* (pp. 357-382). Hillsdale, NJ: Lawrence Erlbaum.

Schaap, C., Buunk, B., & Kerkstra, A. (1988). Marital conflict resolution. In P. Noller & M. A. Fitzpatrick (Eds.), *Perspectives on marital interaction*. Clevedon, England: Multilingual Matters.

Schooler, C. (1972). Birth order effects: Not here, not now. *Psychological Bulletin, 78*, 161-175.

Schvaneveldt, J. D., & Ihinger, M. (1979). Sibling relationships in the family. In W. R. Burr, R. Hill, F. I. Nye, & I. L. Reiss (Eds.), *Contemporary theories about the family* (Vol. 1, pp. 453-467). New York: Free Press.

Segrin, C., & Fitzpatrick, M. A. (1992). Depression and verbal aggression in various types of marriages. *Communication Studies, 43,* 79-91.

Shatz, H., & Gelman, R. (1977). Beyond syntax: The influence of conversational constraints on speech modifications. In C. E. Snow & C. A. Ferguson (Eds.), *Talking to children* (pp. 189-198). Cambridge: Cambridge University Press.

Shorter, E. (1975). *The making of the modern family.* New York: Basic Books.

Sieburg, E. (1985). *Family communication: An integrated systems approach.* New York: Gardner.

Sillars, A. (1980). *Communication and attributions in interpersonal conflict.* Unpublished doctoral dissertation, University of Wisconsin, Madison.

Slocum, W. L., & Nye, F. I. (1976). Provider and housekeeper roles. In F. I. Nye (Ed.), *Role structure and analysis of the family* (pp. 81-100). Beverly Hills, CA: Sage.

Sluzki, C. E., & Beavin, J. (1965). Simetra y complementaridad: Una definicion operacional y una tipologia de parejas. *Acta Psiquiatrica y Psicologica de America Latina, 11,* 321-330.

Snow, C. E. (1972). Mothers' speech to children learning language. *Child Development, 43,* 549-565.

Snow, C. E. (1977). Mother's speech research: From input to interaction. In S. C. Snow & C. Ferguson (Eds.), *Talking to children: Language input and acquisition* (pp. 31-50). Cambridge: Cambridge University Press.

Spieker, S. (1982). Early communication and language development. In J. Belsky (Ed.), *In the beginning: Readings on infancy* (pp. 121-132). New York: Columbia University Press.

Sprey, J. (1979). Conflict theory and the study of marriage and the family. In W. R. Burr, R. Hill, F. I. Nye, & I. L. Reiss (Eds.), *Contemporary theories about the family* (Vol. 2, pp. 130-159). New York: Free Press.

Sroufe, L. A. (1979). Socioemotional development. In J. D. Osofsky (Ed.), *Handbook of infant development* (pp. 462-516). New York: Wiley.

Stafford, L., & Bayer, C. (1993). *Parent-child communication.* Newbury Park, CA: Sage.

Stamp, G. H., & Banski, M. A. (1992). The communicative management of constrained autonomy during the transition to parenthood. *Western Journal of Communication, 56,* 281-300.

Stayton, D., Hogan, R., & Ainsworth, M. D. S. (1982). Infant obedience and maternal behavior. In J. Belsky (Ed.), *In the beginning: Readings on infancy* (pp. 194-203). New York: Columbia University Press.

Steinglass, P., Bennett, L. A., Wolin, S. J., & Reiss, D. (1987). *The alcoholic family.* New York: Basic Books.

Steinmetz, S. K. (1979). Disciplinary techniques and their relationship to aggressiveness, dependency, and conscience. In W. R. Burr, R. Hill, F. I. Nye, & I. L. Reiss (Eds.), *Contemporary theories about the family* (Vol. 2, pp. 405-438). New York: Free Press.

Stern, D. (1977). *The first relationship: Infant and mother.* London: Fontana.

Stewart, R. B. (1983). Sibling attachment relationships: Child-infant interactions in the strange situation. *Developmental Psychology, 19,* 192-199.

Stocker, C. M., & McHale, S. M. (1992). The nature and family correlates of preadolescents' perceptions of their sibling relationships. *Journal of Social and Personal Relationships, 9,* 179-195.

Sutton-Smith, B., & Rosenberg, B. G. (1970). *The sibling.* New York: Holt, Rinehart & Winston.

Terman, L. M. (1938). *Psychological factors in marital happiness.* New York: McGraw-Hill.

Tesser, A. (1980). Self-esteem maintenance in family dynamics. *Journal of Personality and Social Psychology, 39,* 77-91.

Teti, D. M., & Ablard, K. E. (1989). Security of attachment and infant-sibling relationships: A laboratory study. *Child Development, 60,* 1519-1528.

Thorne, B. (1992). Feminism and the family: Two decades of thought. In B. Thorne & M. Yalom (Eds.), *Rethinking the family: Some feminist questions.* Boston: Northeastern University Press.

Thorton, A., & Freedman, D. (1983). The changing American family. *Population Bulletin, 38,* 1-44.

Ting-Toomey, S. (1983). An analysis of verbal communication patterns in high and low marital adjustment groups. *Human Communication Research, 9,* 306-319.

Toman, W. (1961). *Family constellation.* New York: Springer.

Tsukada, G. K. (1979). Sibling interaction: A review of the literature. *Smith College Studies in Social Work, 3,* 229-247.

Vandell, D. L., Minnett, A. M., & Santrock, J. W. (1987). Age differences in sibling relationships during middle childhood. *Journal of Applied Developmental Psychology, 8,* 247-257.

van den Berghe, P. L. (1978). *Human family systems: An evolutionary view.* New York: Elsevier.

Vangelisti, A., & Daly, J. (1990, November). *Expectations in close relationships*. Paper presented at the annual meetings of the International Communication Association, Dublin, Ireland.

Vangelisti, A. L. (1991). *Expectations in the family: Perceptions of communication and family satisfaction*. Unpublished manuscript, University of Texas.

Vangelisti, A. L. (1992). Messages that hurt. In W. R. Cupach & B. H. Spitzberg (Eds.), *The dark side of interpersonal communication*. Hillsdale, NJ: Lawrence Erlbaum.

Vangelisti, A. L. (1993). Communication in the family: The influence of time, relational prototypes and irrationality. *Communication Monographs, 60*, 42-54.

Vega, W. A. (1990). Hispanic families in the 1980s: A decade of research. *Journal of Marriage and the Family, 52*, 1015-1024.

Volling, B., & Belsky, J. (1991). *The contributions of mother-child and father-child relationships to the quality of sibling interaction: A longitudinal study*. Manuscript submitted for publication.

Voydanoff, P. (1990). Economic distress and family relations: A review of the eighties. *Journal of Marriage and the Family, 52*, 1099-1116.

Wallerstein, J. S., & Kelly, J. B. (1980). *Surviving the breakup*. New York: Basic Books.

Walsh, F. (Ed.). (1992). *Normal family processes*. New York: Guilford.

Wamboldt, F., & Reiss, D. (1989). Task performance and the social construction of meaning: Juxtaposing normality with contemporary family research. In D. Offer & M. Sabshin (Eds.), *Normality: Context and theory* (pp. 2-40). New York: Basic Books.

Wasz-Hockert, O., Lind, J., Vuorenkoski, J., Partenen, J., & Valarne, E. (1968). The infant cry. In *Clinics in developmental medicine* (No. 29). London: S.M.I.P.

Watson, R. E. L. (1983). Premarital cohabitation vs. traditional courtship: Their effects on subsequent marital adjustment. *Family Relations, 32*, 139-147.

Watzlawick, P., Beavin, J. H., & Jackson, D. D. (1967). *Pragmatics of human communication*. New York: Norton.

Waxler, N. E., & Mishler, E. G. (1970). Sequential patterning in family interaction: A methodological note. *Family Process, 9*, 211-220.

Weiss, R. S. (1975). *Marital separation*. New York: Basic Books.

Wells, C. G., & Robinson, W. P. (1982). The role of adult speech in language development. In C. Fraser & K. R. Scherer (Eds.), *Advances in the social psychology of language* (pp. 11-77). Cambridge, MA: Cambridge University Press.

White, L. K., & Booth, A. (1985). The transition to parenthood and marital quality. *Journal of Family Issues, 6*, 435-449.

Williamson, R. (1983). *Relational control and communication in marital types*. Unpublished doctoral dissertation, University of Wisconsin, Madison.

Wilson, E. O. (1975). *Sociobiology: The new synthesis*. Cambridge, MA: Harvard University Press.

Winnicott, D. W. (1964). *The child, the family and the outside world*. London: Penguin.

Woelfel, J., & Haller, A. O. (1971). Significant others, the self reflective act and the attitude formation process. *American Sociological Review, 36*, 74-87.

Wolff, P. H. (1971). Mother-infant relations at birth. In J. G. Howels (Ed.), *Modern perspectives in international child psychiatry* (pp. 80-97). New York: Brunner/Mazel.

Yerby, J., Beurkel-Rothfuss, N., & Bochner, A. (1994). *Understanding family communication*. Scottsdale, AZ: Gorsuch.

Author Index

Subject Index

About the Authors

Terrance L. Albrecht (Ph.D., Michigan State University) is Professor and Chair of the Department of Communication and Professor of Management at the University of South Florida. Her interest areas include the study of social support processes in organizational innovation and mixed status organizational relationships and the role of social support in cancer survivorship. She was the lead author of *Communicating Social Support* (Sage) and is coeditor (with Brant Burleson and Irwin Sarason) of *Communication of Social Support: Messages, Interactions, Relationships and Community* (Sage).

Diane M. Badzinski (Ph.D., University of Wisconsin—Madison, 1988) is Assistant Professor of Communication Studies at the University of Nebraska at Lincoln. Her research focuses on the relationship between message behaviors and comprehension and the role of affect and cognition in interpersonal relationships.

Leslie A. Baxter is Professor in the Communication Studies Department at the University of Iowa. Her research interests focus on the contradictory dilemmas of relating in friendship, romantic, and marital relationships.

Charles R. Berger (Ph.D., Michigan State University, 1968) is Professor of Rhetoric and Communication at the University of California, Davis. He is a former editor of *Human Communication Research* and is currently coeditor of *Communication Research*. He is a Fellow of the International Communication Association. His current research interests include the relationships between cognitive plans and communicative performance and the verbal and nonverbal adaptations individuals make in response to communication failure.

Arthur P. Bochner (Ph.D., Bowling Green State University, 1971) is Professor of Communication, University of South Florida, and Co-Director of the Institute for Interpretive Human Studies. His recent publications focus on broadening the scope of research on interpersonal communication to include local narratives that display how people construct meaning through conversations.

John Waite Bowers (Ph.D., Iowa, 1962) is Professor Emeritus of Communication at the University of Colorado, Boulder. He currently lives contentedly in Boulder, where he volunteers for the Boulder Public Library.

Judee K. Burgoon is Professor of Communication at the University of Arizona. She holds a doctorate in communication and educational psychology from West Virginia University. Her current research interests include all facets of nonverbal and relational communication, dyadic interaction patterns, conflict, and interpersonal deception. A Fellow of the International Communication Association and recent editor of *Communication Monographs,* she has written seven books and more than 120 articles and chapters in communication, psychology, and journalism.

Brant R. Burleson (Ph.D., University of Illinois at Urbana-Champaign, 1982) is Professor in the Department of Communication, Purdue University, West Lafayette, Indiana. His research interests center on functional communication skills, especially prosocial communication skills such as comforting, and ways in which these skills facilitate interpersonal relationships. His recent research has focused on how interpersonal skills contribute to the initiation and maintenance of intimate relationships, especially how similarities in people's communication skills affect interpersonal attraction and relationship development. Along with Terrance L. Albrecht and Irwin G. Sarason, he recently cowrote a book, *The Communication of Social Support* (Sage). Currently, he is editor for *Communication Yearbook,* a Sage publication sponsored by the International Communication Association.

James G. Cantrill (Ph.D., University of Illinois, 1985) is Associate Professor of Communication and Performance Studies at Northern Michigan University. His current research interests focus on the cognitive foundations for effective environmental advocacy campaigns and the role culture plays in grassroots environmentalism. He hosted the 1993 Conference on Communication and Our Environment, provides ongoing consulting for the U.S. Forest Service, and has recently published articles in the *Journal of Applied Communication Research* and the *Journal of Environmental Education.*

Joseph N. Cappella (Ph.D., Michigan State University, 1974) is Professor, Annenberg School for Communication, University of Pennsylvania. Current research interests include social interaction in adult and child-adult pairs; mathematical and statistical representations; and biological, evolutionary, and cognitive explanations of conversational regularities.

Michael J. Cody (Ph.D., Michigan State University, 1978) is Professor of Communication Arts and Sciences at the University of Southern California. His research interests are in the areas of persuasion, nonverbal communication, and interpersonal communication. He is coauthor of *Persuasive Communication* (Holt, Rinehart & Winston, 1994), and *Interpersonal Communication: A Goals-Based Approach* (St. Martin's Press, 1994).

Steve Duck is currently Daniel and Amy Starch Research Professor of Psychology and Communication Studies at the University of Iowa and editor of the *Journal of Social and Personal Relationships.* He also founded, and currently coordinates, the professional organization for relationship scholars (INPR—International Network on Personal Relationships), which recently swelled to 1,000 members after being founded from 75 charter members in 1989. He has published 30 books and over 200 chapters and articles on relationships, television effects, and personal construct theory. He is looking forward with interest to the second half of his career.

Mary Anne Fitzpatrick (Ph.D., Temple University, 1976) is currently Professor and Chair of the Department of Communication Arts, University of Wisconsin— Madison. Her most recent book, *Communication in Family Relationships* (Prentice-Hall), was cowritten with Patricia Noller. She is past president of the International Communication Association and a Fellow of that association.

Kelly Fudge is a doctoral student in the Speech Communication Department at the University of Texas at Austin. Her research interests include the functions of television content in interpersonal relationships as well as the influence of new media in interpersonal communication.

Howard Giles (Ph.D., University of Bristol, 1971) is Professor and Chair of the Department of Communication, University of California at Santa Barbara. His current research interests are in the social factors affecting the maintenance and loss of minority languages as well as in cross-cultural issues of aging, communication, and identity. In addition, he has long-standing interests in language effects, accommodation theory, and miscommunication.

Daena Goldsmith (Ph.D., University of Washington, 1990) is Assistant Professor of Speech Communication at the University of Illinois at Urbana-Champaign. Her research examines facework in supportive interactions as well as the broader role of culture in interpersonal communication.

Fredric M. Jablin (Ph.D., Purdue University) is Professor of Speech Communication and Management (in the Graduate School of Business) at the University of Texas at Austin. His research has been published in a wide variety of communication, psychology, personnel, and management journals and he is one of the editors of the *Handbook of Organizational Communication: An Interdisciplinary Perspective* (1987). He is also coeditor of the forthcoming *New Handbook of Organizational Communication* (Sage). His research has examined various facets of superior-subordinate communication, group problem solving, interaction in the employment interview, and communication processes associated with organizational entry, assimilation, and exit.

Scott Jacobs (Ph.D., University of Illinois, 1982) is Associate Professor of Communication at the University of Arizona. His research interests include conversational organization, argumentation, and language use in applied settings. He has recently cowritten *Reconstructing Argumentative Discourse* (University of Alabama Press).

Mark L. Knapp is Chair of the Department of Speech Communication and Jesse H. Jones Centennial Professor in Communication at the University of Texas at Austin. His publications include *Nonverbal Communication in Human Interaction* and *Interpersonal Communication and Human Relationships*. He is past President of the International Communication Association and the Speech Communication Association. He is a Fellow of the International Communication Association. He edited *Human Communication Research* and developed and edited the Sage Series on Interpersonal Communication.

Kathleen J. Krone (Ph.D., University of Texas at Austin) is Assistant Professor in the Department of Communication Studies at the University of Nebraska—Lincoln. Her research interests are in the area of organizational communication and include interpersonal influence, leader-member relationships, and emotional expression.

Margaret L. McLaughlin (Ph.D., University of Illinois at Urbana-Champaign, 1972) is Professor of Communication Arts and Sciences at the University of Southern California. She is coeditor (with Lynn C. Miller) of the forthcoming *Intimate Decisions: Accounting for Risk-Taking in Sexual Behavior and Courtship* (Sage). Her current research interests include discourse analysis, small group interaction, and computer-mediated communication.

Robert D. McPhee is Associate Professor at the University of Wisconsin—Milwaukee. His current research interests are communication theory and social theory, organizational communication, and research methodology. He is currently chair of the SCA's organizational Communication Division and associate editor of organizational communication and related manuscripts for *Human Communication Research.*

Sandra Metts (Ph.D., University of Iowa, 1983) is Professor in the Department of Communication at Illinois State University. Her research interests focus on the management of problematic social and relational episodes. Recent books include *Self-Disclosure* (with Val Derlega, Sandra Petronio, and Stephen Margulis) and *Facework* (with William Cupach). Her work also appears in a variety of journals such as *Communication Monographs, Human Communication Research,* and *Journal of Social and Personal Relationships* as well as in edited volumes such as *Communication Yearbook 13, Studying Interpersonal Interaction, Human Sexuality: The Societal and Interpersonal Contexts, Theoretical Perspectives on Relationship Loss,* and *AIDS: A Communication Perspective.*

Renee A. Meyers (Ph.D., University of Illinois, 1987) is Associate Professor in the Department of Communication at the University of Wisconsin—Milwaukee. Her primary research interests include the study of argumentation in small groups and organizations as well as the consumer-organization interface. Her research has appeared in such publications as *Communication Monographs, Human Communication Research,* and *Communication Yearbook.* She serves on the editorial boards of *Communication Monographs, Communication Studies,* and *Communication Quarterly,* among other journals. She is a past recipient of the SCA Distinguished Dissertation award.

Gerald R. Miller was Chair of the Department of Communication and University Distinguished Professor of Communication at Michigan State University. He was the author of nearly 150 articles on interpersonal communication and related areas. He was a past President of the International Communication Association and the founding editor of *Human Communication Research.* He was a Fellow of the International Communication Association and the American Psychological Association as well as a Distinguished Scholar of the Speech Communication Association. He succumbed to cancer in 1993.

Lynn Carol Miller (Ph.D., University of Texas at Austin) is Associate Professor of Communication Arts and Sciences and Psychology at the University of Southern California. She is a member of the editorial board of the *Annual Review of Personality and Social Psychology,* is consulting editor for the *Journal of Personality and Social Psychology,* and is a recipient of the Gerald R. Miller Early Career Award. Her current research interests include interpersonal dynamics, the coherence of mental models, negotiating safer sex, and applications of computer simulations to communication processes.

Malcolm R. Parks (Ph.D., Communication, Michigan State University, 1976) is Associate Professor of Speech Communication at the University of Washington.

His research interests include the development of personal relationships and networks, communicative competence, and deceptive communication.

Garth Pittman is a doctoral student in the Communication Studies Department at the University of Iowa. His current research interests are in the area of interpersonal and small group communication, with a specific focus on the interactional dynamics of self-identity.

Marshall Scott Poole is Professor of Speech-Communication at the University of Minnesota. He received his Ph.D. from the University of Wisconsin—Madison. His research interests include group and organizational communication, communication technologies, conflict management, communication theory, and research methods.

David R. Seibold (Ph.D., Michigan State University) is Professor of Communication at the University of California at Santa Barbara. His research interests include interpersonal influence, group decision making, and organizational change processes. Published widely, he serves on the editorial boards of several communication publications and is former Chairperson of the Interpersonal Communication Division of the International Communication Association.

Jürgen Streeck (Dr. phil, Freie Universität Berlin, 1981) is Assistant Professor and teaches language and culture in the Department of Speech Communication at the University of Texas at Austin. His research focuses on cultural, conceptual, and interactional features of language and visual symbols in face-to-face communication. He has done field research among African American children, in Germany, and in the Philippines and has published numerous articles and three books on substantive and methodological issues in language and communication research.

Richard L. Street, Jr. is Professor of Speech Communication and Internal Medicine at Texas A&M University. His research and teaching interests include the study of communicative processes and outcomes in health care settings. He has published numerous articles in international journals, *Human Communication Research, Medical Care, Social Science and Medicine, Journal of Language and Social Psychology,* and *Communication Monographs* as well as several book chapters. He is also coeditor, along with Joseph N. Cappella, of *Sequence and Pattern in Communicative Behavior* (London: Edward Arnold, 1985).

Teresa L. Thompson (Ph.D., Temple University, 1980) is Professor of Communication at the University of Dayton. She is founding editor of the journal *Health Communication* and author of *Communication for Health Professionals: A Relational Perspective.* Her research focuses on various aspects of health care provider-patient interaction, with particular emphasis on compliance with treatment regimens and medical recovery as outcome variables.

Carol M. Werner is Professor of Psychology at the University of Utah. Her research, which spans social and environmental psychologies, has examined personal and social aspects of privacy regulation and relationship management. Recent publications include "Celebrations in Personal Relationships: A Transactional/ Dialectical Perspective" (with Altman, Brown, and Ginat) in S. Duck (editor), *Understanding Personal Relationships* (Volume 3; Sage, 1993).